Sociology

Sociology

FOURTH EDITION

ALEX THIO

OHIO UNIVERSITY

HarperCollinsCollegePublishers

Acquisitions Editor: Alan McClare
Developmental Editor: Philip Herbst
Project Coordination and Text Design: Thompson Steele Production Services
Cover Design: Linda Wade
Cover Photo: Melba Levick
Photo Researcher: Karen Koblik
Author Photo: Fred C. Tom
Art Production: Interactive Composition Corporation
Electronic Production Manager: Eric Jorgensen
Electronic Page Makeup: Thompson Steele Production Services
Manufacturing Manager: Hilda Koparanian
Printer and Binder: RR Donnelley & Sons Company
Cover Printer: New England Book Components, Inc.

Sociology, Fourth Edition

Library of Congress Cataloging-in-Publication Data

Thio, Alex
    Sociology / Alex Thio. — 4th edition
          p.   cm.
    Includes bibliographical references and indexes.
    ISBN 0–673–99135–0 (student edition). ISBN 0–673–99787–1 (instructor edition)
    1. Sociology.   I. Title.
    HM51.T53   1996
    301—dc20   95–24107

96 97 98 9 8 7 6 5 4 3 2

Brief Contents

PART ONE
The Nature of Sociology   1

PART TWO
Individual and Society   51

PART THREE
Social Inequalities   217

PART FOUR
Social Institutions   335

PART FIVE
Moving into the Future   483

Detailed Contents

Readings

Preface

We live in a period of rapid social change, and it is an exciting time to be studying sociology. We will explore these changes in this new edition of *Sociology*. It is a major revision packed with current information and new ideas from sociological research. Students will learn to think analytically and critically about the daily life they think they know. Moreover, the simple, fast-paced writing style of *Sociology*, its frequent examples, and illustrations from current events make it easier for students to learn sociology.

It has been a pleasure to write and revise this book, and I hope that students will have fun reading it. When they finish it, they will look at the familiar world around them with a fresh eye and enhanced understanding.

NEW TO THIS EDITION
A great number of substantive changes have been made as follows:

◆ There are two new chapters, one on social interaction in everyday life and the other on global stratification and inequality.
◆ A global analysis is provided in virtually all chapters.
◆ The three major sociological perspectives—functionalism, the conflict perspective, and symbolic interactionism—are presented in *every* chapter.
◆ All the boxed readings are new, intended to reinforce the text as well as demonstrate the relevance of sociology in diverse aspects of today's life.
◆ A new unique feature is the list of myths and realities about society and social behavior in every chapter.
◆ The number of tables and figures has been increased, with some U.S. and global maps added, to strengthen the points made in the text.
◆ Many new topics have been introduced throughout the text, as indicated below.

Chapter 1   Thinking Sociologically
New sections on:
◆ The importance of studying social diversity, or the American mosaic
◆ The significance of analyzing the global diversity of today

◆ The nature of sports as seen through the functionalist, conflict, and symbolic interactionist perspectives
◆ How sociology can enrich our lives

Chapter 2   Doing Sociology
New sections on:
◆ The deductive approach in research
◆ The inductive approach in research
◆ The three sociological perspectives on social research
◆ The feminist approach to research

Chapter 3   Culture
New sections on:
◆ How the U.S. pop culture reflects our society's status quo and patriarchal values while exerting its influence on peoples around the world
◆ Multiculturalism in the United States
◆ Culture clash around the globe
◆ The three sociological perspectives on culture
◆ A global analysis of culture

Chapter 4   Society
New sections on:
◆ Groups
◆ Institutions
◆ Postindustrial societies
◆ The conflict perspective on society
◆ A global analysis of society

Chapter 5   Groups and Organizations
New sections on:
◆ How to classify organizational theories
◆ The nature of organizations as seen through the three sociological perspectives
◆ The feminist model of organizations
◆ A global analysis of organizations

Chapter 6   Social Interaction in Everyday Life
This is a new chapter. Some of the subjects covered are unique to this text:
◆ The functionalist perspective on interaction
◆ The conflict perspective on interaction
◆ A global analysis of communication
◆ U.S. diversity in communication

- How women and men tend to speak different "genderlects"
- How men and women play the gendered game of proxemics
- The art of managing impressions
- Humorology: subverting reality with humor

Chapter 7   Socialization
New sections on:
- The feminist theory of gender development
- The functionalist perspective on socialization
- The conflict perspective on socialization
- A global analysis of socialization

Chapter 8   Deviance
New sections on:
- Drug abuse
- Pornography
- Shaming theory
- Feminist theory
- Power theory
- Phenomenological theory
- Classifying deviance theories into functionalist, conflict, and symbolic interactionist perspectives
- An analysis of deviance around the world

Chapter 9   Sexual Behavior
New sections on:
- U.S. diversity in sexual activities
- A global analysis of sexual practices
- Myths about homosexuality
- Incidence and characteristics of coercive sex
- Commercial sex as seen through the three sociological perspectives

Chapter 10   Stratification and Class
New sections on:
- A global view of stratification, comparing the egalitarian, master-slave, feudal, caste, and class systems
- Feminization of poverty
- Popular beliefs about welfare
- Reforming welfare programs
- The symbolic interactionist perspective on stratification and class
- How social equality can be achieved

Chapter 11   Rich and Poor Nations
This is a new chapter. Some of the subjects covered are unique:
- Social classes in global society
- Upward mobility in global society
- Downward mobility in global society
- How three theories (modernization, dependency, and cultural theories) explain global inequality, and how they are related to the three major sociological perspectives

Chapter 12   Race and Ethnicity
New sections on:
- Northern and Western European Americans
- Using the three sociological perspectives to analyze race and ethnicity
- A global analysis of racial and ethnic relations

Chapter 13   Women and Men
New sections on:
- Sexual harassment
- The three sociological perspectives on gender inequality
- The future of gender
- A global analysis of gender inequality.

Chapter 14   Age and Aging
New sections on:
- A global analysis of aging
- Aging and mental disorders
- The three sociological perspectives on age and aging

Chapter 15   Family
New sections on:
- A global analysis of the family
- The symbolic interactionist perspective on the family
- Gay and lesbian marriages
- Native American families
- African American families
- Hispanic American families
- Asian American families

Chapter 16   Education
New sections on:
- The conflict theory about education as inequality reinforcer and cultural imperialism
- The symbolic interactionist perspective on education
- Schools in Belgium
- Schools in Finland
- Schools in France
- Schools in Japan
- Schools in Portugal

Chapter 17   Religion
New sections on:
- The three sociological perspectives on the nature of religion
- How religion in some ways engages in confrontation with the secular world while in other ways makes compromises with the sameworld.
- New trends in U.S. religion

Chapter 18   Politics

New sections on:
◆ A global analysis of political violence
◆ Government responses to international terrorism
◆ Causes of war and achievement of peace
◆ The three sociological perspectives on war

Chapter 19   Economy

New sections on:
◆ The nature of capitalism as seen through the three sociological perspectives
◆ The economies of Canada, Latin America, Western Europe, Eastern Europe, Russia, China, and Southeast Asia

Chapter 20   Science and Medicine

New sections on:
◆ A global analysis of health
◆ Sexism in medical research.

Chapter 21   Population and Environment

New sections on:
◆ A global analysis of population characteristics
◆ An analysis of population and environment from each of the three sociological perspectives.

Chapter 22   Urbanization and City Life

New sections on:
◆ The megacities of the world
◆ The three sociological perspectives on urbanization.

Chapter 23   Collective Behavior, Social Movements, and Social Change

New sections on:
◆ A global analysis of social change
◆ How the theories of social change are related to the three sociological perspectives

DISTINGUISHING FEATURES

A unique blend of style and substance makes this text stand out from the rest. This distinguishing feature and others make it easier for faculty and students to teach and learn sociology.

Solid Scholarship

There is a great deal of substance to the text. All analyses are based on empirical studies or data-informed theories or both. In addition, no attempt has been made to gloss over or water down complex sociological issues, such as the phenomenological theory of deviance or the causes of upward and downward mobility in global society. Such issues are confronted head-on but explained in a clear and interesting fashion.

Current Research

Special care has been taken to present the most recent findings from the sociological literature. Sociology is a fast-growing field, reflecting the significant changes that have recently taken place all over the world. Thus the publication of many studies cited in this text is as recent as the mid-1990s. Many current events reported in the nation's first-rate newspapers and newsmagazines are also discussed to demonstrate the relevancy of sociology to today's world.

Social Diversity

The diversity of U.S. society, including various racial and ethnic groups as well as women and men of various social classes, is presented in a balanced way. The achievements of women and members of various ethnic groups are presented as in Chapter 15 (Family), where Native American, African American, Hispanic American, and Asian American families are discussed.

Global Analyses

In virtually all chapters there are analyses of how peoples around the world live or how their lives affect ours in the United States. Such global analyses enhance and deepen our understanding of other cultures. The analyses also help us gain special insight into our own society by looking at it more objectively—from an outsider's point of view.

Critical Thinking

To promote truly critical thinking, a number of myths and realities about social behavior are discussed in each chapter. Many students tend to assume that sociology is only common sense—that there is nothing new in sociology or that whatever is there they have known all along. In this text students will find some of their firmest assumptions challenged and start to look at the familiar world around them with a critical, fresh eye.

Boxed Readings

All boxed readings are new to this edition. They are extremely current, reflecting various aspects of today's fast-changing world as well as the relevancy of sociology to students' lives. These boxes are divided into four types: Global Village, featuring a wealth of information on other societies; American Mosaic, highlighting social diversity; Cutting Edge, emphasizing current issues and crucial changes in our society; and Enriching Our Lives, focusing on how sociology serves us. Students will broaden and deepen their understanding of the world in which they live as well as learn to use sociological knowledge to improve their lives.

Lively Writing

The writing style is second to none. It is simple, direct, and vibrant, making sociology come alive. Many professors have described the writing as clear and engaging. Numerous students have been known to enjoy reading the book.

Theoretically Illuminating

The three major sociological perspectives are introduced in the first chapter and then consistently applied in *all* the other chapters, which is unique to this text. The application of these theoretical approaches to a specific subject in each chapter is balanced, substantive, and interesting. We can learn more about society from the three perspectives than from one or two only. Together the three illuminate different facets of society, providing a broader and more realistic view of the subject. In addition, other theoretical views, especially feminist theory, are presented in various chapters.

LEARNING AIDS

An effective system of learning aids is incorporated into the text to motivate students and facilitate learning. Students are encouraged to think about the materials by themselves or by discussing important issues in class. It is frequently through such active involvement, as opposed to passive acceptance of what one reads, that students really begin to sharpen their thinking skills. Then the understanding and absorption of ideas presented in the text will come easily.

Chapter-Opening Vignettes

Along with a chapter outline and a myths and realities box, each chapter opens with a new thought-provoking story. This will stimulate students' interest as well as fix their attention on the main themes of the chapter.

Stimulating Graphics

There are colorful figures, tables, maps, and beautiful photos throughout. They are designed not only to spark student interest but, more importantly, to reinforce comprehension and retention of the points made in the text.

Discussion-and-Review Questions

In every chapter there are questions at the end of each main section. Instructors can use them as a springboard for lively discussion in class. Students can use them to review the main ideas that have just been discussed, before moving on to the next topic. However the questions are used, students will learn more as active thinkers than as passive recipients of ideas and facts.

Chapter Summaries

Each chapter ends with a full summary in a question-and-answer format. The standard form of summary in an introductory text tends to turn students into passive consumers of knowledge. In contrast, the question-and-answer format encourages students to become actively involved, by inviting them to join the author in thinking about important issues. Students who have actively thought about what they have read will more easily understand and remember it later.

Key Terms

The most important words are boldfaced and defined when introduced. They are listed and defined again at the end of each chapter, with a page cross-reference to facilitate study. All key terms with their definitions are also presented in the glossary at the end of the book.

Suggested Readings

In line with the currency of the material in the text, the most up-to-date books for further reading are listed at the end of each chapter. These sources enable students to seek additional knowledge about the subject matter of each chapter. Most books are readily available in school libraries.

SUPERB SUPPLEMENTS

Accompanying this text is a highly useful support package for instructors and students.

◆ *Instructor's Resource Manual* includes learning objectives, chapter summaries, lecture topics, ideas for demonstrations, projects and applications, a list of films and videotapes appropriate for each chapter, key terms and classroom discussion questions.

◆ *The Test Bank,* prepared by Peter Morrill of Bronx Community College, includes approximately 65 multiple choice, 10 true/false, 15 short answer, and 10 essay questions for each chapter. All questions are page referenced to the text.

◆ *TestMaster* software provides the complete test bank in both DOS and Macintosh formats.

◆ *The Supershell Tutorial,* by Peter Morrill includes chapter outlines, sample test questions, and key term exercises.

◆ *The Student Study Guide and Practice Tests,* by Peter Morrill, includes learning objectives; "strengthening what you know" (a series of questions and exercises designed to guide the student through the learning objectives); and practice tests including multiple choice and short answer questions.

ACKNOWLEDGMENTS

I am extremely grateful to the numerous instructors all over the country who have adopted the past editions of this text. I am equally thankful for the invaluable help from many colleagues at various universities and colleges in reviewing the manuscript for the current edition. Unsolicited responses from adopters and insightful criticisms and suggestions from reviewers have helped me produce the best introductory sociology text today. The reviewers for this edition include:

Edward G. Armstrong, University of Wisconsin–Stout

Karen Conner, Drake University

Lynda F. Dickson, University of Colorado, Colorado Springs

Linda Evans, Central Connecticut State University

Doris W. Ewing, Southwest Missouri State University

Jan Fiola, Moorehead State University

Cecilia Garza, Texas A&M International

Earlene O'Dell, Northeast State Technical Community College

Anthony M. Orum, University of Illinois at Chicago

Timothy J. Owens, Indiana University at Indianapolis

Edgar Patterson, Southern Illinois University

Charles Tolbert, Louisiana State University

I am also thankful to Professor Peter Morrill. His tireless pursuit of appropriate articles for the boxes has significantly strengthened the text. His *Instructor's Resource Manual, Test Bank, Student Study Guide and Practice Tests,* and *SuperShell* have contributed immensely to the text's support package.

I owe a special debt to Alan McClare, sociology editor at HarperCollins, for making it easy and fun to work on this project. A lot of thanks also goes to Philip Herbst, the developmental editor, for greatly enhancing the quality of this revision. I am grateful, too, to Andrea Fincke, the project editor, for efficiently guiding the production of the book.

Finally, I am grateful to my wife and children for their understanding and patience. They have made it possible for me to take a great deal of pleasure, without much guilt, in writing this book.

—Alex Thio

About the Author

Alex Thio is Professor of Sociology at Ohio University. Born of Chinese parentage in Penang, Malaysia, he grew up in a multicultural environment. He acquired fluency in Mandarin (modern standard Chinese), two Chinese dialects (Fukienese and Hakka), Malay, and Indonesian. He also picked up a smattering of English and Dutch.

Professor Thio attended primary school in Malaysia and high school in Indonesia. He then came to the United States and worked his way through Central Methodist College in Missouri, where he majored in social sciences and took many literature and writing courses. Later he studied sociology as a graduate student at the State University of New York at Buffalo, and completed his doctorate while working as a research and teaching assistant.

Dr. Thio regularly teaches courses on introductory sociology, deviance, social problems, and criminology. In addition to teaching, he enjoys writing. He has written many articles, as well as the popular texts *Deviant Behavior* and *Sociology: A Brief Introduction*, both of which are published by HarperCollins. The author is very grateful for the feedback he often receives from faculty and students, which he believes improves significantly the quality of his books. If you have any questions, comments, or suggestions, please write him at the Department of Sociology, Ohio University, Athens, OH 45701 (Internet: athio@ohiou.edu).

He lives with his wife Jane and daughters Diane and Julie in Athens, Ohio. His hobbies include reading, moviegoing, and traveling.

A Visual Guide To:

Sociology

Fourth Edition

Alex Thio
Ohio University

ISBN 0-673-99135-0

Written in a clear, concise, and lively style, *Sociology's* unique blend of readability and scholarship presents substantive sociological concepts with a wealth of cross-cultural and global examples. This fourth edition features two new chapters—one on social interaction and one on global inequality—as well as an increased focus on the major sociological perspectives in every chapter; expanded treatment of global and multicultural issues; all new, engaging boxed readings; and a new "Myths and Realities" section at the beginning of every chapter, which invites students to challenge common assumptions. *Sociology, 4/e* is full of up-to-date research and data, timely news reports from popular sources, real-life vignettes, and case studies all meant to invite and engage students in the pursuit of understanding the social world.

Found in virtually every chapter, new global analysis sections examine how people around the world live and how their lives affect ours in the United States. This material enhances and deepens students' understanding of other cultures as well as their own.

A GLOBAL ANALYSIS

All over the world, socialization appears largely the same in some ways and different in other ways. Researchers rarely study socialization with a global approach, but the existing findings reveal some interesting similarities and differences.

In a study of three significantly different cultures (U.S., French, and Japanese), researchers found some similarities in how mothers respond to their five-month-olds. When infants cry, mothers respond with nurturance. If the babies simply vocalize, showing no distress, mothers will respond with imitation. Mothers generally respond more to infants' vocalizing than to infants' looking (Bornstein et al., 1991). Such uniformities across different societies suggest the influence of biological factors on socialization. Thus more research can be expected to find other ways in which uniformities exist.

But most of the studies that have been conducted suggest the powerful influence of culture on socialization. This is most vivid in the differences between the West and the rest of the world.

First, young children in the West are supposed to play, whereas their peers in many non-Western countries are expected to work. As has been suggested, Japanese children in Indonesian villages, although only nine years old, already work to contribute substantially to family income. Even younger children, four or five years old, also work, though mostly taking care of younger siblings while mothers work on the farm. In many African agricultural societies, the importance of childcare givers is so keenly felt that women with infants often recruit relatives' children from distant villages to help out (Morelli and Tronick, 1991).

Second, in the West, the daily care and long-term upbringing of children are often left entirely to parents alone. Increasingly, strangers such as childcare workers take care of children for money more than affection. This kind of socialization tends to foster individualism in the charges. By contrast, in much of the rest of the world, extended family groups, clans, and even communities pitch in to care for each other's children. This kind of socialization is more likely to develop trust in others and thereby attachment to groups (Leach, 1994).

Third, Western parents start socializing their children to be self-reliant at an extremely young age—virtually right after birth. Babies are placed in a crib, often in their own room. At least initially, the trauma of being left alone causes the infant to cry at bedtime or upon waking up. By contrast, infants in many non-Western societies are spared that trauma. They

are allowed to sleep with their parents, often until age five or six (Harrison, 1992). With this sleeping arrangement, the children may have a slow start in learning to be on their own, but they are effectively socialized to develop a strong sense of security. This may partly explain why the insurance industry, supposed to meet customers' need for security about their future, is far from as prosperous in the non-West as it is in the West.

Fourth, Western parents begin earnestly socializing children to curb their impulses and behave well at a very young age—before age four. This may have much to do with Westerners' assumption that people are born bad, as suggested by the Judeo-Christian belief about being born sinners or Freud's widely accepted idea about being born with the id. By contrast, in Japan, China, and other East Asian societies, children are assumed innately good and therefore given much freedom to do what the want. This parental indulgence and permissiveness toward children usually gives way to strict disciplining after age four. From then on, the contents of Asian and Western socialization also differ. Asian parents tend to emphasize emotional control, filial piety, politeness to others, and other traits that promote social relationships and conformity. On the other hand, Western parents stress spontaneity, autonomy, assertiveness, and other characteristics that promote individual freedom and creativity (Papousek, 1991; Harrison, 1992).

Questions
For Discussion and Review

1. In what ways is childhood socialization about the same throughout the globe?
2. In what ways does childhood socialization vary from Western to non-Western societies?

ARE WE PUPPETS OF SOCIETY?

Through socialization we internalize the norms and values of society. Does this imply that we become puppets of society, individuals who basically enjoy giving up freedom and following the rules society sets down? The answer is yes and no.

In many respects, we do behave like society's puppets. We are glad to follow society's expectation that we be friendly to our friends and love our parents. We are happy to do many other similarly nice things every day as expected of us by society. It just happens

---

A GLOBAL ANALYSIS OF SOCIAL CHANGE

Social change takes place around the world. In some respects, social change differs from one society to another, and in other respects, it does not. This has therefore raised the question of whether diverse societies are converging into one world or diverging into separate worlds.

Traditions and Modernization

Modernization is the form of social change that involves the transformation of an agricultural society into an industrial one. Contrary to popular belief, such social change does not inevitably destroy tradition. There are many instances where modernization reinforces tradition or the other way around.

In India, for example, modernization reinforces tradition. When Indians of middle and lower levels seek upward mobility, they do so by "becoming more devoutly Hinduistic," by being as traditionally Indian as possible. Even among very Westernized elites, the native culture still exerts a powerful influence. Nearly all highly modernized Indian intellectuals speak a regional language as their mother tongue, are steeped in classical Sanskrit literature, are strongly tied to an extended family, and are likely to find a spouse through parental arrangements.

We can also see the positive impact of tradition on modernization in Japan. Without its traditional culture, Japan would not have become an industrial giant. The Japanese culture emphasizes the importance of social relations and collective welfare. It encourages consensus rather than conflict, deference to rather than disrespect for authority, and paternalism rather than indifference by those in authority. These cultural values saturate Japan's economic system. A business enterprise, no matter how large, is run like a household, with the accompanying interdependence and loyalty characteristic of the family. Since the company takes care of its workers by giving them lifetime employment, employees tend to identify strongly with employers and work as hard as they can. Moreover, the traditional emphasis on collective welfare serves more than just enhancing productivity through cooperation between managers and workers. It causes society to favor business and industry at the expense of individuals, transferring funds and wealth from individuals to industries. This can be seen in the fact that factories and company apartments are mostly grand and imposing, whereas private homes are cramped yet highly expensive.

Convergence and Divergence

Through modernization, many non-Western societies such as India and Japan are becoming technologically more like Western societies. But at the same time, both types of societies are getting culturally more different, with one more traditional than the other. Thus these opposite trends have led the development of two contrasting theories about the changing global society.

According to convergence theory, modernization will bring the West and the rest together by breaking down their cultural barriers to produce a one-world society. The assumption is that exposure to super-

According to convergence theory, modernization will bring the West and non-West together by breaking down cultural barriers to produce a one-world society. The assumption is that exposure to supersonic aircraft, satellite communication, the information superhighway, and multinational companies will cause non-Western societies to adopt Western ways of living and virtually all the values—even foods—of the West.

RICH AND POOR NATIONS

NEW!

CHAPTER 11, "RICH AND POOR NATIONS"

This new chapter examines the inequality among (different) nations in the world.

CHAPTER OUTLINE

STRATIFICATION OF THE WORLD

THE WORLD SYSTEM APPROACH
Social Classes in Global Society
Interclass Relations in Global Society

THE DYNAMICS OF GLOBAL STRATIFICATION

INEQUALITY AMONG NATIONS

THE COST OF GLOBAL INEQUALITY
Widespread Poverty
Female Disadvantages

Child Exploitation
Adult Slavery

SOCIAL MOBILITY IN THE GLOBAL SOCIETY
Upward Mobility
Downward Mobility

CAUSES OF GLOBAL INEQUALITY
Functionalist Perspective
Conflict Perspective
Symbolic Interactionist Perspective

Myths and Realities

MYTH: *The work done for parents by children aged 5 to 15 is good for building the youngsters' character, but the family does not need it to survive.*
REALITY: Children's work at home may not ensure the survival of families in affluent societies such as the United States, but it often does in many poor peasant societies.

MYTH: *It is economic suicide for people in poor peasant societies to have many children.*
REALITY: High birth rates are associated with poverty but children may be needed to ensure survival in poor countries where they tend to be their parents' *active partners* in struggling for survival.

MYTH: *Whenever massive famine hits a country in Africa, drought is always the only cause.*
REALITY: A drought can trigger famine, but it is usually the combatants of a civil war—both government and rebel forces—that seize food supplies from civilians as well as international relief organizations as a military strategy to starve the enemy into defeat.

MYTH: *Slavery is a social evil of the past.*
REALITY: According to Britain's Anti-Slavery International, the world's oldest human-rights organization, more than 100 million people today still suffer as slaves. That figure may be too high because it includes large numbers of child laborers, who are exploited but not really slaves. Even with a narrower definition including only chattel slavery and debt bondage, cases of involuntary servitude run well into the millions.

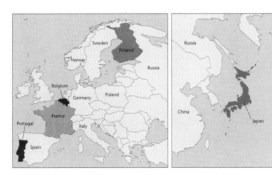

FIGURE 16.4
Countries in the Global Analysis:
Belgium, Finland, France, Japan, and Portugal

INCREASED CROSS-CULTURAL EMPHASIS THROUGHOUT

Sociology's already rich integration of cross-cultural and global issues is reinforced in this edition.

The Schools in Belgium

The Belgian educational system is unique for having proportionately larger numbers of schoolteachers than do virtually all other countries in the world. Schoolteachers make up 5.3 percent of Belgium's work force, compared with, for example, 2.6 percent for the United States and 2.4 percent for Britain. As a consequence, the average class size in Belgian schools is the smallest in the world. Belgium's student-teacher ratio is only 9.3 primary students and 6.8 secondary students per teacher, compared with 15.5 and 15.9 for the United States. But Belgian teachers' salaries are relatively low, as the country spends less per student than the United States and other industrial societies. Still, parents generally give high marks to the Belgian schools.

One major reason for the huge teacher population in Belgium is growing unemployment, which now reaches about 10 percent. This may have caused the government to raise the age of compulsory education to 18, as well as allowing children to start school as young as age 2 1/2. If the older teenagers in Belgium were not forced to stay in school longer than their U.S. counterparts, many would have wound up on the unemployment roll, pushing the nation's jobless rate even higher. In addition, the increased student enrollment helps reduce the unemployment rate by producing jobs for teachers (Brock, 1993).

The Schools in Finland

Finland is the world's most educated society. Forty percent of Finns aged 24 to 65 have a college degree, compared with 12 percent in the United States. Understandably, Finns are, per capita, the greatest consumers of literature in the world. School attendance is compulsory up to age 16, an earlier age than in Belgium. But schooling is rigorous. High school students attend classes 38 hours a week, compared with about 25 hours in the United States. Finnish students are also required to take more courses, including two foreign languages. All higher education is free, with most financial support coming from the state and the rest from private industries (Peltonen, 1993).

The Schools in France

As has been suggested, the educational bureaucracy in the United States does not give teachers the freedom to teach the way they see fit, such as choosing textbooks rather than have them chosen for them by the school board. By contrast, French teachers are free to do their job in virtually any way they want. The French government only offers general guidelines, such as giving 5-year-olds some reading instruction so that they can handle primary school lessons after having undergone a year of

NEW!

"MYTHS AND REALITIES" BOXES

Challenging students to see beyond their common-sense understanding of society, these new chapter-opening boxes present myths and realities about society to help readers employ the sociological perspective. This encourages students to think analytically about the issues to be discussed in the chapter and also to question taken-for-granted views about human behavior.

Myths and Realities

MYTH: *As the world's leading democratic society, the United States has the most equal distribution of income.*
REALITY: While the U.S. income distribution is more equal than that of developing countries, it is less so than most other industrial nations, such as England, Japan, Sweden, and Germany.

MYTH: *Given the great diversity in the U.S. population, various groups are bound to disagree on whether a particular occupation is desirable or not.*
REALITY: Virtually all groups, rich or poor, rate occupations in the same way. Even people in other countries evaluate occupations in the same way.

MYTH: *Most of the poor people in the United States are on welfare.*
REALITY: Only about one-third of the poor are on welfare.

MYTH: *As many rags-to-riches stories in the media show, it is not uncommon for a poor man's child to become a millionaire in this land of opportunity.*
REALITY: It is uncommon for a poor person in the United States to become a millionaire. The success experienced by many involves moving only a little way up the economic ladder.

CHAPTER 6   SOCIAL INTERACTION IN EVERYDAY LIFE

J ohn and Mary, a married couple, teach college in different cities. They spend three days a week far away from each other. People frequently express sympathy with remarks such as "That must be rough" or "How do you stand it?" Mary readily accepts their sympathy, saying things like "We fly a lot." Sometimes she reinforces their concern: "The worst part is packing and unpacking all the time." But John reacts differently, often with irritation. He would emphasize the advantages of his marriage: As professors, he and his wife have four-day weekends together, long vacations throughout the year, and four months in the summer. They even benefit from those days when they are separated because they can do their work without any interruption. All this is true, but Mary is surprised that her husband reacts differently than she does. He explains that he senses condescension in others' expression of concern, as if they were implying, "Yours is not a real marriage. I pity you, and look down on you, because my wife and I do not have your kind of misfortune." John tends to see others as adversaries but Mary does not (Tannen, 1990).

What John and Mary experience is **social interaction**, the process by which individuals act toward and react to others. Interactions can be classified into three types, roughly reflecting the three major perspectives in sociology. John tends to engage in **oppositional interactions**, treating others as competitors or enemies. Mary, on the other hand, is more likely to get involved in **supportive interactions**, treating others as supporters or friends. This gender difference reflects the different social worlds in which John and Mary live. Reflecting the conflict perspective, John's world is more hierarchical and dominance-oriented, in which a man must be either one-up or one-down. To men, life is more like a contest, with social interactions being an arena where "people try to achieve and maintain the upper hand if they can, and protect themselves from others' attempts to put them down and push them around" (Tannen, 1990). Reflecting the functionalist perspective, however, Mary's world is more egalitarian and sharing-oriented, in which there is a greater tendency to nurture relationships by seeking and giving confirmation and support. To women, life is more like "a community, a struggle to preserve intimacy and avoid isolation" (Tannen, 1990).

But those two perspectives are structural, suggesting that people more or less passively follow the dictates of their world. To symbolic interactionists, all interactions, whether oppositional or supportive, are also *symbolic*, involving people actively interpreting each other's action and reaction and behaving in accordance with the interpretation. Thus John and Mary react differently to the same comments from others because they *interpret* the comments differently.

In short, the three perspectives spotlight different patterns of social interaction. Functionalism focuses on the supportive nature of interaction; the conflict perspective, the oppositional nature; and symbolic interactionism, the symbolic or interpretive nature.

CHAPTER-OPENING VIGNETTES

Following each "Myths and Realities" box is a thought-provoking vignette designed to pique students' interest and their appreciation of sociology's relevance to their lives. All vignettes are entirely new to this edition.

NEW MAP PROGRAM

The addition of U.S. and global maps helps students locate countries and strengthens points made in the text.

PEDAGOGY: QUESTIONS FOR DISCUSSION AND REVIEW

Found at the ends of main sections in each chapter, these questions serve as springboards for lively class discussions and student review and encourage students to become active thinkers.

END-OF-CHAPTER REVIEW

Each chapter closes with a question-and-answer format to promote students' active involvement in the text material.

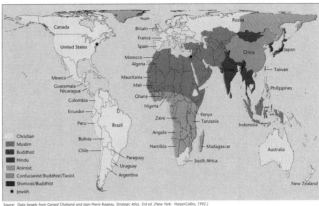

Source: Data largely from Gerard Chaliand and Jean-Pierre Rageau, Strategic Atlas, 3rd ed. (New York: HarperCollins, 1992.)

FIGURE 17.1
Religions Around the Globe

Questions For Discussion and Review

1. What does the current fundamentalist religious revival have in common with the upsurge in cults, and how do these two types of religious movements differ?

2. Why is religious television relatively popular in the United States?
3. Who are the New Agers and Muslims in the United States? What is the nature of their religions?
4. What contributes to the development of secularized religion in U.S. society?

CHAPTER REVIEW

1. *What is religion?* A religion is a unified system of beliefs and practices regarding sacred things that unites its adherents into a single community. *Must a religion focus on the worship of a god?* No, only theistic religions do so. Ethical and animistic religions define the sacred in a different way.

2. *According to Durkheim, what is God?* Durkheim argued that God is a symbolic representation of society. By their worship, members of society strengthen their bonds to each other and their accep-

tance of the society's norms. Thus, religion helps preserve social order. *What other functions does religion serve?* Supporting people, providing social control, stimulating social change, and providing individuals with a sense of identity. If these functions are carried too far, however, religion can become dysfunctional. *How did Marx view religion?* To him, religion was an oppressive illusion, which helps the rich and powerful to perpetuate their domination of the masses. He argued that religion justifies society's inequalities and gives solace to the masses, diverting their atten-

STRAIGHTFORWARD, LIVELY WRITING STYLE

Thio's fast-paced and lively writing style explains complex issues in a direct, understandable, and interesting way. Simple and vibrant, Thio's writing makes sociology come alive as it engages students' interests and enhances their comprehension.

Sports: Illustrating the Three Perspectives

The influence of sports reaches far and wide. Sports are particularly popular in our heavily leisure-oriented society. Most of us have had some experience with athletics as participants or spectators. Schools, from kindergarten to college, provide many sports opportunities. Newspapers carry more news about sports than about politics, the economy, crime, or practically any other event. Radio and television newscasts rarely go on the air without any sports report. Football, basketball, baseball, and other

games are often broadcast in their entirety, pre-empting regular programming. Sports exert so much influence on our lives that our everyday speech is full of sports imagery: "struck out," "touch base," "ballpark figure," "game plan," "teamwork," "cheap shot," "go all the way," and so on.

What, then, is the nature of this powerful aspect of our lives? From the three sociological perspectives, we can see that sports are beneficial to society in some ways, harmful in other ways, and similar to any other social interaction—governed by individuals' definitions of each other's actions.

The current high divorce rate in the United States does not mean, as common sense would suggest, that the institution of marriage is very unpopular. On the contrary, people seem to love marriage too much, as suggested by several pieces of evidence. First, our society has the highest rate of marriage in the industrial world despite having the highest rate of divorce (Census Bureau, 1994). Second, within the United States, most of the southeastern, southwestern, and

western states have higher divorce rates than the national average but also have higher marriage rates (see Figure 15.3). And third, the majority of those who are divorced eventually remarry (Cherlin, 1992). Why don't they behave like Mark Twain's cat, who after having been burned by a hot stove would not go near *any* stove? Apparently, divorce in U.S. society does not represent a rejection of marriage but only a specific partner.

NEW!

"GLOBAL VILLAGE" BOXED READINGS

"Global Village" readings feature a wealth of information about other societies throughout the world, how they fit into an emerging world system, and how they affect our lives in the United States. The boxes enhance students' understanding of how other people live and the problems they face. By learning about the rich cultural diversity in the world, students also gain special insight into their own culture and are taught how to examine it more critically and objectively.

GLOBAL VILLAGE

Before the recent political upheaval in the former Soviet Union, the Communist Party ruled that country, and sociology was forced to serve as a propaganda arm of the state. Today, sociologists are free to do objective research, and the field has experienced a dramatic rebirth. This reading describes one U.S. sociologist's recent visit to Russia and how Russians have rediscovered the work of two sociological founders discussed in this chapter, Emile Durkheim and August Comte.

The Second Coming of August Comte

In October 1991, I flew to Novosibirsk, Siberia, to teach a compressed course on sociological theory at Novosibirsk State University in Russia. This was the first course in sociology, taught by a Western academic, offered by this university for credit. Perhaps my class of 35 students and 15 faculty members in sociology and related disciplines learned something about ideas previously "forbidden." More certain is that, through them, I became acquainted with the state of contemporary Russian sociology.

For seven decades a communist totalitarian regime consistently had proclaimed that Karl Marx had provided all that one would, or should, conceptually need. But now these intelligent and highly inquisitive Russians are so tired of Marx that they simply preferred other ideas. Most surprising of all, and I believe, most instructive concerning the state of contemporary Russian sociology, was a strongly expressed interest in Emile Durkheim and August Comte, perhaps because both Durkheim and Comte favored enlightened social policy and reform, a matter of great contemporary interest to Russians.

Western sociologists, stressing the value of scientific objectivity, have emphasized Durkheim's statistically based analysis of the social conditions of suicide as a model of social scientific work. Yet, Durkheim's concluding chapter of Suicide, titled "Practical Consequences," indicates that objective analysis is preliminary to considerations of social policy. While U.S. sociologists have valued Durkheim's pioneering analysis of suicide as an outstanding instance of social scientific research, Russian sociologists are more inclined to emphasize Durkheim's final view that the purpose of objective social knowledge is enlightened social reform.

Similarly, Comte, with a far less specific, more all-encompassing agenda, indicated that a science of social life was possible and would provide the most enlightened basis for social order and progress. Indeed, as is well known in the West, Comte recommended "sociocracy," a regime in which social scientists armed with social knowledge "would institute a reign of harmony, justice, rectitude and equity." While Comte's advice that sociology should be scientific is generally accepted in the West, his desire for social scientists to become scientific high priests shepherding social order and human progress is not. On this score, Russian sociologists are less shy. They are far more likely to believe that social knowledge is relatively useless unless it leads to social reform. Professionally, they see themselves as potential contributors to social policy formation.

The pace of change within the former Soviet Union is now rapid and the future uncertain. Social science may aid the progress of liberal reform significantly; conservative reaction to social chaos may curtail intellectual endeavor, once again. Yet, one would predict that glasnost in some form will continue and that Russian sociology is destined to be influenced increasingly by the professional sociology of the West.

SOURCE: Adapted from Marvin Harris, *Our Kind*, New York: HarperCollins, 1989, pp. 344-345, 358-360, 378-379.

American Mosaic

The careful application of health care assumes that ill people understand and accept modern medical techniques. But many of the recent immigrants to the United States believe in folk or traditional medical remedies, and look with distrust at U.S. doctors. This reading reports on such a case among the Hmong in California who have immigrated from Central Vietnam.

Clash of Cultures on Illness

Officials in this Central Valley town are not sure whether to look for Lee Lor, a 15-year-old Hmong girl with cancer who ran away from home two weeks ago with a backpack full of herbal medicines but no money.

The authorities here are uncertain because the girl's parents—and the entire community of Hmong, transplants from the mountains of Southeast Asia—say they do not believe Lee has cancer and do not want her to have chemotherapy.

So strong are their objections that when the police, acting on a court order, forcibly removed her from her home to undergo treatment, they were pelted with stones and had to wrestle a knife from the father, who threatened to commit suicide if she was taken away, according to a police report.

For the 35,000 Hmong refugees who have settled in Fresno, making the city home to the largest concentration of Hmong in the nation, the issue is about more than the girl's health. It is about whether she and her family have a right to choose between using herbal remedies and using Western medicine.

The Hmong, who aided U.S. troops in the Vietnam War, were airlifted from Vietnam and Laos to Thailand after the fall of Saigon and resettled in the 1980s in cities like Fresno and St. Paul. They have been slow to embrace U.S. culture, especially Western medicine, and Fresno has been slow to accept the Hmong.

Ever since the Hmong settled in the Central Valley, the authorities have grappled with enforcing laws while respecting the culture of the Hmong. One of the thorniest issues has been how to treat sick children. The Hmong worship ancestors, whose misdeeds are said to resurface in illnesses for generations, said Lia Xiong, a Hmong and Laotian interpreter for Valley Children's Hospital in Fresno. In 1990, the parents of a Hmong child with club feet refused to seek treatment because they believed the child's feet were twisted to atone for the sins of the ancestors. In other cases, parents fought to stop operations because they believed surgery would maim the body, leaving the patients unable to be reincarnated, Mr. Xiong said.

The disappearance of Lee took hospital authorities and social service workers by surprise. They say they had been working closely with the Hmong community to combine Western medicine and the Hmong's own healing practices in helping sick children. At Valley Children's Hospital, shamans are allowed to burn incense outside a child's window or sacrifice a chicken or pig in the parking lot.

In some ways, Lee is a typical teenager, who likes to draw and write fan letters to Jonathan Brandis of the television show "Seaquest." But she is also Hmong and believes in shamanism and herbal remedies, her parents say.

Source: Excerpted from "Girl Flees After Clash of Cultures on Illness," *The New York Times*, November 12, 1994, p. 8. Copyright 1994 by The New York Times Company. Reprinted by permission.

NEW!

"AMERICAN MOSAIC" BOXED READINGS

"American Mosaic" readings highlight social diversity in the U.S.—race, ethnicity, and women and men of different classes. By giving voice to women and minorities and examining the issues in their lives, the boxes deepen students' understanding of their multicultural society—its strengths as well as its problems.

NEW!

"ENRICHING OUR LIVES" BOXED READINGS

"Enriching Our Lives" boxes focus on applied sociology—how sociology serves us. It examines relevant concerns from how to conduct research to get a job to how to improve married life, to Americans' spiritual involvement in new religious movements. By demonstrating the relevance of sociology to critical and familiar issues in students' lives, the boxes make sociology come alive.

ENRICHING OUR LIVES

Students' use of violence to resolve arguments and conflicts has become routine behavior in U.S. schools and communities. This reading reports on how conflict-resolution programs can help solve the problem by teaching alternatives to violence in schools.

The Art of Undoing Violence in Schools

For many communities, violence is a fact of life. But across the country, educators and local leaders are launching programs to teach children and families new ways to resolve conflict.

Helen Swan, a Kansas City, Mo., social worker and the creator of a conflict-resolution curriculum used in more than 100 schools, says, "Over the last three years, many schools have initiated anti-violence programs from kindergarten through high school. A lot of state departments of education have mandated programs."

What these programs have in common is the conviction that by teaching people how to improve communication and how to see issues and ideas from another perspective, violent behavior will be lessened. "What we hear from the school systems with these programs," Helen Swan says, "is more kids talking issues out and causing less problems because they have internalized some of these skills."

Swan's program, "Building Conflict Solving Skills," includes a technique called "listening contracts." "To improve relations with someone," Swan says, "a child makes a contract to improve listening skills with a specific person. Another popular devise done with humor is the story of Little Miss Muffet from the spider's perspective—a frightened, lonely spider. After hearing his side of the story, students feel differently toward him, and may not be so quick to judge others."

As a pioneer in community mediation, the Community Board Program in San Francisco has sold more than 10,000 copies of its conflict-resolution curriculum. At the school level, the program has two parts. The first is aimed at kindergarten through 12th grade and emphasizes problem-solving techniques, understanding conflict styles, communications skills, and appreciating differences.

The second is selecting students to be "conflict managers" for third grade through 12th.

Students are picked by their peers and teachers to be mediators and get special training.

"At the lower grade levels they wear T-shirts that say 'Conflict Manager,'" says Irene Cooper-Basch, a director of the mediation program. "They monitor what is happening on the playground. If there is a dispute, instead of going to the principal, the managers walk over and try to mediate the dispute. At high schools the problems are more serious and often are resolved after school by the managers."

Reprinted from David Holmstrom, "The Art of Undoing Violence is Finding Its Own Place in Classrooms and Streets," The Christian Science Monitor, September 1, 1993, pp. 1, 4.

Cutting Edge

Wrenching changes in the economy have led to a growth in joblessness and low-paid employment as well as an increase in social tensions. In this reading, Richard Sennett, a prominent sociologist, argues that the tensions reflect the conflict between the highly educated few and the less educated masses.

A New Class Warfare

Popular resentment against elites is an old story in America, perhaps as old as the nation itself. But the story twists and turns as the elite changes. In Andrew Jackson's time, the hated elite were landowners; in John D. Rockefeller's time, they were industrialists.

Today, no one would think [the billionaire] Sam Walton was an elitist; instead of great wealth, the new elite possesses rarefied skills. It has addresses on the Internet rather than on Fifth Avenue; it knows how to do global as well as local business.

Most Americans are shut out of this new world. Seventy percent of the adult population does not know how to use a computer; most high school graduates cannot read a train schedule; a large minority cannot reckon simple interest on a bill.

The elite thrives on change, the mass fears it. In a dynamic society, the mass of people are constantly threatened by becoming redundant, being passed by; all they have is their willingness to work. The new economy needs the mass of these Americans less as producers or workers than as consumers.

A new study by the Demos Institute, an opinion-research organization in London, brings this divide into focus. It shows a new attitude toward work among the young in Europe as well as America, a desire to work flexibly and individually, a loss of loyalty to corporations and a willingness to demand that employers make work more personally satisfying.

But only a fifth of young Americans have the training or skills to act on such desires; the other four-fifths, who have no personal bargaining power, can only worry about getting some job, any job, even though they share the sentiments of the elite. Under such conditions, feelings of inferiority become intensely personal. A snob doesn't appear to be someone who flings money about; instead, unlike the ordinary person, he is confident that the future belongs to him.

It's not surprising that young men form the most conservative and anti-elitist segment of the population; they are in that crucible time of life when realities—from McJobs and the necessity of living with one's parents in one's 20's to the prospect of three-job marriages—all dim hopes for self-determination.

As always, politics does symbolic duty for fundamental changes. The fear of government grown out of control is like the photographic print of a social and economic negative—a print of the fear that economic growth portends threat rather than opportunity, that the average person is likely to be left out of the spoils.

And this is a problem for us [the new elite] as well as them [the masses].

When accused of being an elite, we fudge. [Our] crocodile tears for the sufferings of others prove that we are in touch—in the certain-to-be immortal words of our President, "I feel your pain." (Others detect a certain condescension lurking in this sympathy.) Or we promise to use our skills to design solutions to make things better - public policy solutions graced almost with the complexity of modern art. In promising to solve for the masses what they have not solved for themselves, we show we believe we're what they fear we are: more competent.

Class has been the dirty secret of American history, denied by promises of individual freedom, by dreams of upward mobility and by memories of solid communities and coherent families—memories that prove on inspection only to be recovered-memory fantasies.

The plain fact is that in today's new stage of capitalism, class divides Americans as ruthlessly as it did the age of the Robber Barons; politically, America has plunged into a new round of class welfare, with a secure, confident future belonging only to the educated few.

Source: Adapted from Marvin Harris, Our Kind, New York: HarperCollins, 1989, pp.344-345, 358-360, 378-379.

NEW!

"CUTTING EDGE" BOXED READINGS

"Cutting Edge" boxes introduce students to special findings and stimulating ideas in the world of sociology. They emphasize current issues and crucial changes or movements in our society. They also help students to evaluate important controversial social thinking and provoke them to think critically about these ideas.

Table of Contents:

Supplements:

FOR THE INSTRUCTOR:

- *Instructor's Manual:* by Peter Morrill of Bronx Community College includes learning objectives, chapter summaries, lecture topics, ideas for demonstrations, projects and applications, a list of films and videotapes appropriate for each chapter, key terms and classroom discussion questions.

- *Test Bank:* also by Peter Morrill includes for each chapter approximately 65 multiple-choice, 10 true/false, 15 short-answer, and 10 essay questions. All questions are page referenced to the text.

- *TestMaster:* The *Test Bank* is available on *TestMaster* software, allowing instructors to edit existing questions and add new questions. *Quizmaster*, a feature of *TestMaster*, allows instructors to give students timed or untimed tests online; on completing tests, students can see their scores and view or print diagnostic reports listing topics or objectives that have been mastered or topics requiring further review. TestMaster is available for DOS and Macintosh.

FOR THE STUDENT:

- *Study Guide:* by Peter Morrill includes learning objectives, "strengthening what you know" (a series of questions and exercises designed to guide the student through the learning objectives), and practice tests, including multiple-choice and short-answer questions.

- *SuperShell Tutorial Software:* by Peter Morrill includes chapter outlines, sample test questions, and key term exercises.

- *HyperSoc Software:* This comprehensive sociological software combines a study guide, interactive laboratory experiences, and an online glossary of sociological terms for students, with professional lecture presentation tools for faculty.

Sociology

THINKING SOCIOLOGICALLY: A SPECIAL VISION

CHAPTER OUTLINE

Myths and Realities

MYTH: *Life must be more stressful in densely populated states such as New York and New Jersey than in wide-open areas such as Montana, Wyoming, and Alaska. Not surprisingly, people in the densely populated states are more likely to commit suicide.*
REALITY: People in the densely populated states have *lower* suicide rates (Chapter 1: Thinking Sociologically).

MYTH: *Problems, especially crises, are bad. They are sources of failures and miseries.*
REALITY: Problems, even crises, are not necessarily bad. They can be good, providing opportunities for enhancing our lives (Chapter 1: Thinking Sociologically).

MYTH: *College men who have a hard time getting dates and have little or no sexual experience are more likely than others to rape their dates.*
REALITY: Sexually active men who can easily get dates are more likely to rape their dates (Chapter 9: Sexual Behavior).

MYTH: *Because mental ability declines with age, older people are less productive than younger ones.*
REALITY: On most measures of productivity, older workers are as productive as younger ones, despite some decline in the older workers' perception and reactive speed (Chapter 14: Age and Aging).

I n 1994 the Hutu tribe in the African nation of Rwanda slaughtered some 250,000 members—about half—of the Tutsi tribe. One witness saw Hutu militiamen drag a Tutsi woman from her house and make her stand in the middle of the road. The Hutus had come to her village and hacked to death nearly all the Tutsi men, women, and children with machetes. They made two piles of bodies, one for those already dead and the other for those bleeding to death. As the lone surviving woman in the middle of the road begged for her life, the Hutu militiamen poked her with their machetes and laughed at her. Hutu bystanders also laughed. Then the militiamen picked her up, threw her on top of the pile of the still-living, and chopped all of them to pieces, scattering arms, hands, legs, and heads on the blood-stained road (Rosenblatt, 1994).

Such violence is not unique to the Hutus. The early European settlers in our country did about the same to Native Americans, so did the Turks to the Armenians and Nazi Germans to the Jews. The violence is part of the larger pattern of intergroup hostilities around the globe. What causes all these hostilities? This is only one of many questions about the world in which we live: Why do wars break out between nations? How does the economy of one nation depend on that of the other? Why are some marriages successful while others end in divorce? How will a college education affect your income? Are men naturally more aggressive than women? Do cities make people callous and rude? Answers to such questions can be found in **sociology**, the systematic, mostly scientific study of human society, as you will see in the following chapters.

THE STUDY OF SOCIAL LIFE

Virtually everybody has something to say about social behavior. Because it is the stuff of everyday life, many people assume that they know all about it. But, as Otto Larsen (1981) has noted, "Living in a family or working in an organization does not automatically make one a sociologist any more than swimming in the sea makes one an oceanographer or being an animal breeder makes one a geneticist." Sociologists have a special way of looking at human behavior and special tools for studying it.

More Than Common Sense

To many people, sociology appears to be a laborious study of the obvious, an expensive way to discover what everybody already knows. To these people, soci-

ology is merely common sense. But sociology is more than common sense because it is largely based on scientific evidence. Often ideas or beliefs derived from common sense turn out to be false, contradicted by facts from sociological research. See, for example, "Myths and Realities" at the opening of this chapter.

Sociological findings such as those that fly in the face of commonly held myths may surprise you. Of course, not every finding in sociology is surprising. In fact, some confirm what you have known all along. You should not be surprised, therefore, to learn from sociology that there is more joblessness among blacks than whites or that there are more poor people than rich people in prison. But many other commonsense ideas have turned out to be false, like the ones in the chapter-opening box. By systematically checking commonsense ideas with reliable facts, sociology can tell us which popular beliefs are myths and which are realities.

Sociology can also help clarify the confusion that sometimes arises from common sense. You may have read that "birds of a feather flock together" but also that "opposites attract." You may have heard the encouraging message that "absence makes the heart grow fonder," but you may still remember the discouraging warning, "out of sight, out of mind." When confronted with such conflicting common-sense ideas, how can we tell which are correct and which are false? We can get the answer from sociological research. It has shown, for example, that the effect of someone's absence on another depends on the strength of the initial relationship. If two people have loved each other deeply like Romeo and Juliet, absence would make their hearts grow fonder, but a high school romance tends to disintegrate, because such relationships are usually not deep and serious enough to begin with (Kohn, 1988).

In sum, it is not true that sociology is only common sense. If it were, we wouldn't want to study sociology at all. Why would we waste our time trying to learn something we already know? Common sense requires only a willingness to believe what it tells us. It cannot tell us whether those beliefs have any basis in fact. But sociology can. This is one of the reasons that sociology is exciting. It enables us to see that what has long been familiar—or just "common sense"—may turn out to be unfamiliar or uncommon. While common sense gives us familiar and untested ideas, sociology offers factually supported ideas as well as the excitement of discovering something new about ourselves.

Understanding the American Mosaic

For centuries many people have followed the ancient Greek philosopher Plato's advice, "Know thyself," by looking into themselves rather than others. But sociology suggests that we can know ourselves better by studying *others*. By doing so, we can see how others are similar to us in some ways and different in other ways, knowing that we are likely to behave similarly if we find ourselves under the same social condition. In the United States, the great diversity in race, ethnicity, class, gender, age, sexual orientation, and other social characteristics offers an excellent opportunity to know one another, thereby giving us a deeper insight into how society operates.

We can learn much from those who experience **social marginality**—being excluded from mainstream society—such as racial or ethnic minorities, women, the poor, the homeless, the elderly, gays, people with disabilities, and so on. Generally, these people are acutely aware of how powerfully their lives are affected by various social conditions such as prejudice and discrimination. Their social marginality constantly reminds them of how difficult it is for them to make it in a society that treats them as outsiders. On the other hand, we can also learn from members of mainstream society. Without their social advantages, the mainstreamers would probably have found it an uphill battle to succeed. Thus they might not owe their success to themselves as much as to favorable social conditions. In short, the study of the American mosaic can reveal the various ways in which society influences the lives of different groups and individuals.

Exploring the Global Village

We can gain further insight into ourselves and our society by going beyond our national boundary to study other societies. Today, the whole world has become a **global village**, a closely knit community of all the world's societies. Whatever happens in a faraway land can affect our lives here. Consider the various ways in which **economic globalization**—the interrelationship of the world's economies—can influence the U.S. economy and society.

First, the abundance of low-paid workers in relatively poor countries can decrease the wages of U.S. laborers by forcing their employers to reduce production costs. The abundance of low-paid foreign workers also encourages U.S. corporations to produce inexpensive products to outsell foreign competitors by building factories and hiring workers abroad. This may increase plant closing, unemployment, low-wage employment, poverty, and community breakdown in the United States. On the other hand, economic globalization can also have positive consequences for the U.S. economy. Competing with foreign firms here and abroad forces U.S. corporations to become more efficient and productive. Shifting U.S. low-skilled jobs to poor nations is likely to raise those countries' income, thereby making them bigger export markets for U.S. goods. Globalization induces each country to specialize in what it does best, a poor country, for example, making shoes and a rich country producing computer software. Finally, competition in the global market increases the availability of well-made but inexpensive products in all nations.

Given the importance of globalization in our lives, we can never emphasize enough the significance of studying other societies. As Peter Berger (1992) says, "One can be an excellent physicist without ever having stepped outside one's own society; this is not so for a sociologist . . . Thus sociologists must look at Japan in order to understand the West, at socialism in order to understand capitalism, at India so as to understand Brazil, and so on." In brief, by guiding us through the global village, sociology enables us to understand our lives better by opening our eyes to social forces that we may not see from looking at our society only.

Sociology as a Science

The goal of science is to find order in apparent chaos. Scientist search for a pattern in what, on the surface, may look like random variations. They look for regularity, something that appears over and over, across time and space. Observation is usually given the last word in this search. It is true that scientists, like everyone else, have preconceived ideas, beliefs, and values, and they use logic and intuition to understand the world. But scientific methods require scientists to put aside existing views of what the world should be like and to rely, above all, on observation. When scientists discover a pattern in the world, they describe it in the form of a **hypothesis**, a tentative statement of how various events are related to one another. Then they test the hypothesis against

Qualitative

systematic observations, producing evidence for or against it. Hypotheses, however, must be related to one another in order to explain a broader range of phenomena. A set of logically related hypotheses that explains the relationship among various phenomena is called a **theory.** A good theory will apply to a wide range of existing observations and suggest testable predictions about what can be observed in the future.

Suppose we are investigating the causes of revolutions. We find that most of the Asian and African nations gained their independence by revolting against their various European colonial rulers in the late 1940s and 1950s. Despite their differences, we come across some similarities among all those revolutions, which historians have called the revolutions of rising expectation. In those countries, the living conditions had improved but the people did not find the improvement adequate. They were enraged by the discrepancy between what was and what they felt ought to be. From these similarities, we could devise the hypothesis that revolutions are caused by a discrepancy between expectations and reality. If we test this hypothesis against systematic observations of other revolutions and find that the evidence consistently supports our hypothesis, then we have a theory of revolution.

No matter how personal our experiences may seem, they are influenced by the social forces of our society. Sociologist Emile Durkheim explored how a social force known as social integration could reduce the likelihood of suicide. (Left) As an indication of strong social integration, people are closely tied to a social group. Such people are less likely to commit suicide because if they are frustrated, they are able to receive a great deal of affection, care, and help from others. (Right) When social integration is lacking, isolated individuals tend more to commit suicide because they do not get help from others to lighten their problem.

disprove

We would, however, have proven our theory to be only tentatively rather than absolutely true. A scientific theory is always open to revision in the light of new evidence. Scientific findings are always subject to verification or refutation by other scientists. If the findings cannot be duplicated by other scientists, they are suspect. Scientists usually check whether their findings confirm or contradict those of their colleagues. This procedure increases the chances that mistakes, oversights, or biases will be detected. It ensures the objectivity of science.

The Sociological Imagination

To understand human behavior, sociologists stand back and look "from the outside" at individuals as members of society, rather than inside to examine their mind, personality, or motivation. Sociologists have long found that no matter how personal our experiences are, they are influenced by **social forces**—forces that arise from the society of which we are a part. Social forces exist outside the individual in the form of social relationships such as those we share with friends, relatives, and people in educational, economic, religious, and other institutions. C. Wright Mills (1959) referred to the ability to see the impact of social forces on individuals, especially on their private lives, as the **sociological imagination.** Through social forces, society exercises so much power on an individual that we can effectively see it through the individual's behavior.

Consider the case of suicide. It is reasonable to assume that those who kill themselves are frustrated and unhappy, since happy people rarely want to die. But suicide cannot be explained that simply. This explanation does not tell us why, for example, people who live in wide-open areas have much higher suicide rates than those who live in crowded areas (see Figure 1.1). There is no evidence that those who live in wide-open areas are more unhappy. How, then, do we account for the difference in suicide rates?

The sociological imagination leads us to look not at the individual personalities of those who commit suicide, but at social forces. When French sociologist Emile Durkheim (1951) examined suicide in the late nineteenth century, he detailed variations in the rates of suicide among various countries and groups. These rates constitute social, not individual, facts, and, to explain them, Durkheim turned to social forces. The force that he found to have a great impact on suicide was **social integration**, the degree to which people are tied to a social group. When there is either excessive or inadequate social integration, suicide rates are likely to be high.

In the past, when elderly Inuit* committed suicide, the cause was usually extreme social integration. Obedient to the values and customs of their society, they did what they were expected by others to do: killing themselves when they could no longer contribute to the economy of their community. Similarly, Hindu widows used to follow the tradition of their society by ceremoniously throwing themselves onto the funeral pyres of their husbands. These ritual suicides were called *suttee* (literally, "good

---

*Inuit are popularly called "Eskimo," which is a derogatory term meaning "eater of raw meat."

anomie

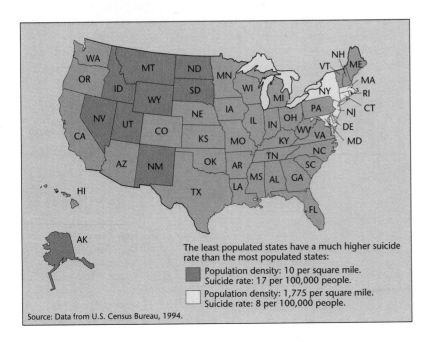

The least populated states have a much higher suicide rate than the most populated states:

■ Population density: 10 per square mile.
   Suicide rate: 17 per 100,000 people.

□ Population density: 1,775 per square mile.
   Suicide rate: 8 per 100,000 people.

Source: Data from U.S. Census Bureau, 1994.

FIGURE 1.1
Suicide More Common in Wide-Open Areas
A social cause of suicide is relative isolation from others. When having to rely on themselves to solve personal problems, people tend to be too subjective and emotional to find a viable solution. This may explain why suicide rates are generally higher in sparsely populated areas.

women"). The Hindu widows and elderly Inuit apparently felt pressured to commit suicide. If the Hindu widows did not kill themselves, they might be scorned as "bad women." If the elderly Inuit refused to kill themselves, they might be stigmatized as "selfish."

On the other hand, a lack of social integration can also be found in high suicide rates. Divorced and widowed people, for example, are more likely than married people to be isolated from others and to receive little affection or moral support when they have problems. In other words, they are more likely to experience inadequate social integration and thus are also more likely to commit suicide. Similarly, people who live in sparsely populated states such as Montana, Wyoming, and Alaska are more isolated from others than those who live in densely populated states such as New York and New Jersey (see again Figure 1.1, p. 5). Greater isolation tends to make people more individualistic, more dependent on themselves than on others. This individualism may underlie the higher rate of suicide in the wide-open areas. By relying on themselves to solve their personal problems, people tend to be too subjective and emotional to find a viable solution (Thio, 1995).

Suicide is an extreme, exceptional act, but all around us we can see ordinary actions that are also molded by social forces. The distribution of income in the United States is a social fact. Your family's position in that distribution is one of your social characteristics. And this characteristic influences your way of living and your chances in life—such as the likelihood that you will pursue a successful career. Our private worlds can never be totally sealed off from the larger world of society and global community. The technology, economy, customs, ideals, beliefs, government, and politics in the United States as well as in other countries—all are social characteristics and represent social forces that help shape our lives.

Questions for Discussion and Review

1. How does sociology differ from common sense?
2. Why is it so important to study the diversity in the U.S. and the world?
3. What is the nature of sociology as a science?
4. How does the sociological imagination clarify the influence of social forces on the experiences of individuals?

THE DEVELOPMENT OF SOCIOLOGY

Sociology has a very short history. Of course, centuries before Christ was born, thinkers such as Plato and Socrates had thought and argued about social behavior. But most of them did not make systematic observations to test their speculations against reality. They were social philosophers, not sociologists. The field of sociology emerged in the nineteenth century, when European social philosophers began to use scientific methods.

Two factors combined to convert some philosophers into sociologists: the social upheavals of nineteenth-century Europe and the advancement of the natural sciences. The Western world was radically altered during the nineteenth century as the

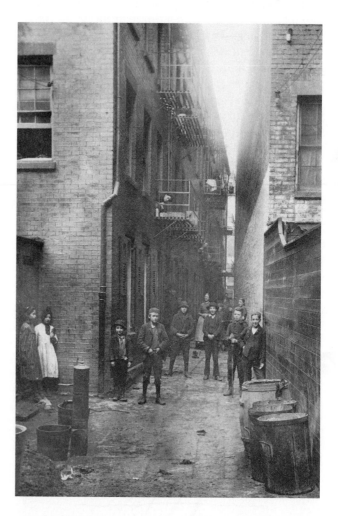

The social problems, such as urban congestion and squalid housing, that arose in the aftermath of the Industrial Revolution in the nineteenth century challenged philosophers to find explanations and solutions. Their search helped to develop sociology as a science and a profession.

Industrial Revolution brought new industries and technologies and new ways of living. Almost overnight, societies that had long been rural and stable became industrialized, urbanized, and chaotic. They confronted problems such as the exploitation of factory workers, the migration of people from farms to cities, congestion and poverty in the cities, crowded and squalid housing, broken families, and rising crime. Meanwhile, the European political order had been shaken. In the aftermath of the French Revolution, many people began to question the legitimacy of their monarchies and the authority of their churches, demanding greater freedom for the individual. Many social philosophers felt challenged to find solutions to their societies' new problems and to understand how and why such radical change could occur. At the same time, the natural sciences were highly respected because they were providing ways to both explain and control aspects of the physical world. Some social philosophers looked on natural science as a model for how they might go about understanding and controlling the social world.

As sociology developed, these two urges—to improve the world and to apply scientific methods to the study of society—continued to motivate sociologists.

The Pioneers of Sociology

The nineteenth-century French philosopher Auguste Comte (1798–1857) is sometimes called the father of sociology. He coined the word "sociology" in 1838 to refer to the scientific study of society. Comte believed that every society goes through three stages of development: religious, metaphysical, and scientific. According to Comte, reliance on superstition and speculation characterizes the religious and metaphysical stages, and neither is adequate for understanding society. What is needed, he argued, is scientific knowledge about society based on social facts, just as scientific knowledge about the physical world is based on physical facts. He envisioned a science of society with two branches: *statics*, the study of the organization that allows societies to endure, and *dynamics*, the study of the processes by which societies change. During the scientific stage, Comte believed, sociologists would develop a scientific knowledge of society and would guide society in a peaceful, orderly evolution. Such a task was soon initiated by an Englishwoman, Harriet Martineau (1802–1876). She translated Comte's writings, studied British and U.S. societies, and suggested that societal progress could be achieved by eradicating slavery, the oppression of women, and worker exploitation.

Herbert Spencer (1820–1903), an Englishman, had a different view of how society works. He believed that a society can be compared to a living organism. Each part of an animal—its heart, lungs, brains, and so on—has its own function to perform, yet all the parts are interdependent: a change in one part affects all the others. Moreover, each part contributes to the survival and health of the animal as a whole. If one organ becomes diseased, others adapt by working

Auguste Comte (1798–1857), the first to argue for the need for scientific knowledge about society, is regarded as the father of sociology.

Herbert Spencer (1820–1903) believed that society corrects its own problems because it is governed by the laws of nature. He argued that government should not intervene to solve social problems.

GLOBAL VILLAGE

Before the recent political upheaval in the former Soviet Union, the Communist Party ruled that country, and sociology was forced to serve as a propaganda arm of the state. Today, sociologists there are free to do objective research, and the field has experienced a dramatic rebirth. This reading describes one U.S. sociologist's recent visit to Russia and how Russians have rediscovered the work of two sociological founders discussed in this chapter, Emile Durkheim and Auguste Comte.

The Second Coming of Auguste Comte

In October 1991, I flew to Novosibirsk, Siberia, to teach a compressed course on sociological theory at Novosibirsk State University in Russia. This was the first course in sociology, taught by a Western academic, offered by this university for credit. Perhaps my class of 35 students and 15 faculty members in sociology and related disciplines learned something about ideas previously "forbidden." More certain is that, through them, I became acquainted with the state of contemporary Russian sociology.

For seven decades a communist totalitarian regime consistently had proclaimed that Karl Marx had provided all that one would, or should, conceptually need. But now these intelligent and highly inquisitive Russians are so tired of Marx that they simply preferred other ideas. Most surprising of all, and I believe, most instructive concerning the state of contemporary Russian sociology, was a strongly expressed interest in Emile Durkheim and August Comte, perhaps because both Durkheim and Comte favored enlightened social policy and reform, a matter of great contemporary interest to Russians.

Western sociologists, stressing the value of scientific objectivity, have emphasized Durkheim's statistically based analysis of the social conditions of suicide as a model of social scientific work. Yet, Durkheim's concluding chapter of *Suicide,* titled "Practical Consequences," indicates that objective analysis is preliminary to considerations of social policy. While U.S. sociologists have valued Durkheim's pioneering analysis of suicide as an outstanding instance of social scientific research, Russian sociologists are more inclined to emphasize Durkheim's final view that the purpose of objective social knowledge is enlightened social reform.

Similarly, Comte, with a far less specific, more all-encompassing agenda, indicated that a science of social life was possible and would provide the most enlightened basis for social order and progress. Indeed, as is well known in the West, Comte recommended "sociocracy," a regime in which social scientists armed with social knowledge "would institute a reign of harmony, justice, rectitude and equity." While Comte's advice that sociology should be scientific is generally accepted in the West, his desire for social scientists to become scientific high priests shepherding social order and human progress is not. On this score, Russian sociologists are less shy. They are far more likely to believe that social knowledge is relatively useless unless it leads to social reform. Professionally, they see themselves as potential contributors to social policy formation.

The pace of change within the former Soviet Union is now rapid and the future uncertain. Social science may aid the progress of liberal reform significantly; conservative reaction to social chaos may curtail intellectual endeavor, once again. Yet, one would predict that *glasnost* in some form will continue and that Russian sociology is destined to be influenced increasingly by the professional sociology of the West.

Excerpted from David J. Gray, "Russian Sociology: The Second Coming of Auguste Comte"; *American Journal of Economics and Sociology,* April, 1994, pp. 163–169.

---

harder to ensure the animal's survival. Similarly, in Spencer's view, each part of a society performs its own function and contributes to the survival and stability of the whole. The family, religion, the government, industry—all are parts of one "organism," society.

Spencer concluded that society, if left alone, corrects its own problems. It tends naturally toward health and stability. Social problems work themselves out through the process of natural selection called "survival of the fittest." The phrase implies that rich, powerful, or otherwise successful people—the "fittest"—deserve to enjoy their wealth, power, or success because they have been "selected" by nature to be what they are. On the other hand, poor, weak, or otherwise unsuccessful individuals—the "unfit"—should be left to fend for themselves, because nature has doomed them to failure. If government interferes with this natural process by helping the unfit, society will suffer because the efforts of its successful people will be wasted. According to Spencer, the best thing government can do about social problems is to leave them alone. The fate of society, in his view, is governed by laws of nature. If nature is left to do its job without government interference, society will not only survive but evolve to become better.

But where Spencer saw harmony and stability, Karl Marx (1818–1883) observed underlying conflict, exploitation, and the seeds of revolution. According to Marx, a German who spent much of his life writing in England, Spencer's stable, interdependent society was a myth. The primary feature of society, Marx claimed, is not stability and interdependence but conflict and competition. Every society, past and present, is marked by social conflict.

In particular, Marx claimed that the primary feature of society is **class conflict**, the struggle between capitalists, who own the means of production, and the proletariat, who do not. These two classes, he said, are inevitably locked in conflict. The laborers, far from being naturally unfit, are destined to overthrow the capitalists and establish a classless society in which everyone will work according to ability and receive according to need.

Marx did not believe, as did Spencer, that the differences between laborers and capitalists are determined by natural selection. On the contrary, Marx

believed that they are determined by the economic system. In fact, he argued, the economic system determines a society's religious beliefs, its values, and the nature of its educational system, government, and other institutions. Again unlike Spencer, he urged people not to let society evolve on its own but to change it.

Despite their differences, both Marx and Spencer, like Comte, recognized the value of science in the study of society, but they did not actually use scientific methods. They merely argued about how society worked and how its troubles might be eased. It was Emile Durkheim (1858–1917) who pioneered the systematic application of scientific methods to sociology. His ideas about suicide, discussed earlier, were not based on speculation. In his study of suicide, he made a research plan and collected a large mass of statistical data on suicide in various European countries, which he analyzed in order to discover the causes of suicide. He not only used systematic observation but also argued that sociologists should consider only what they could observe and should look at "social facts as things." They should not look, he said, to "the notions" of people in order to explain society. People's subjective experiences should not be a concern of sociologists.

In contrast, the German sociologist Max Weber (1864–1920) believed that sociologists must go beyond what people do, beyond what can be

Karl Marx (1818–1883) claimed that conflict and competition are the chief factors in social life. In his view, the primary feature of society is the conflict between capitalists and laborers.

Emile Durkheim (1858–1917) pioneered the systematic application of scientific principles to sociology. He was the first to use statistical methods to test hypotheses.

Max Weber (1864–1920) believed that an objective study of human behavior is insufficient for sociologists. In his view, sociologists must also investigate how people feel and think about their own behavior.

Jane Addams (1860–1935) conducted scientific research on social problems with the aim of eliminating or alleviating them. She was the only sociologist ever to have received the Nobel prize.

observed directly. He argued that individuals always interpret the meaning of their own behavior and act according to these interpretations. Sociologists must therefore find out how people feel or what they think about their own behavior. To do this, according to Weber, sociologists should adopt a method he called *Verstehen*—empathetic understanding of their subjects. By mentally putting themselves into their subjects' position, sociologists could obtain an "interpretive understanding" of the meanings of particular behavior. Then, he said, they should test this understanding through careful observation.

U.S. Sociology

By the turn of the twentieth century, sociology had made its way from Europe to the United States. Like their European predecessors, the first U.S. sociologists tried to understand and solve the problems of their time, problems such as crime and delinquency, broken homes, slums, and racial unrest. But they dealt with social problems differently. The Europeans were more interested in developing large-scale social theories, so they examined the fundamental issues of social order and social change, trying to discover the causes of social problems as a whole. In contrast, U.S. sociologists were more pragmatic. They were more inclined to focus on specific problems, such as prostitution or juvenile delinquency, and to treat each problem separately. To study and solve these problems, they developed scientific, quantitative methods (Ross, 1991).

A good example of those U.S. sociologists was Jane Addams (1860–1935), one of the most outstanding founders of sociology and social work. In Chicago, she set up and directed a center for social reform and research, which she named Hull House. Most of the social activists working at Hull House were women. They often exchanged ideas and interests with the

predominantly male sociologists at the University of Chicago. The chief goal of Hull House was to solve social problems using sound sociological theory. The Chicago School sociologists also were interested in applying sociological theory to social problems, but they emphasized theory and research. Thus, their achievements in social reform were not as successful as those of the truly applied sociologists of Hull House.

In their projects, Addams and her colleagues would first identify a certain problem, then gather data documenting the nature of the problem, formulate a social-action policy based on the data, and finally organize citizens and lobby political and community leaders to eliminate or alleviate the problem. They dealt with a wide array of social ills, including poverty, worker exploitation, child labor, juvenile delinquency, unjust laws, and difficulties faced by working women and the elderly. They used a new research technique called "mapping," which involved seeking information on an urban population's demographic characteristics (such as age, sex, occupations, wages, and housing conditions) and then presenting the geographic distribution of those characteristics on a map. By applying research in this way, Addams was able to play a significant role in establishing many government programs—most notably Social Security, the Children's Bureau, the Immigrant Bureau, Workers' Compensation—and various government regulations affecting health and safety standards. In 1931, Addams was awarded the Nobel Peace Prize (Deegan, 1988; Ross, 1991).

For about 40 years, after the turn of the century, most U.S. sociologists focused on studying and solving social problems. But the prosperity that followed the Second World War masked many social problems, causing the reformist fervor to begin to cool. Some sociologists turned their attention to general theories of society. The idea grew that sociology should be a *basic science*, seeking knowledge only, not an *applied science,* which puts knowledge to use. Moreover, many people believed that sociology must be objective and free of values. This left no room for a commitment to reform society according to certain values. From about 1945 to 1965, sociology was dominated by the attempt to develop scientific methods that could be applied to the study of societies and social behavior. During these two decades, sociologists developed increasingly sophisticated research techniques.

In the 1960s, however, the ideal of objective, value-free knowledge came under fire in just about all fields, including sociology. Renewed awareness of poverty and years of social unrest—marked by race riots, student revolts, and controversy about the Vietnam War—put pressure on sociologists to attack society's ills once again. Meanwhile, attitudes toward the major theoretical perspectives in sociology were also shifting. The conflict perspective, which emphasizes social conflict as a constant fact of social life, was becoming popular at the expense of the functionalist perspective, which stresses the persistence of social order.

U.S. sociology has thus developed into a diverse discipline. Today, it is both a basic and an applied science, and sociologists use both objective and subjective methods. The soaring number of sociologists—from only about 3,000 in the 1960s to about 20,000 today—has further splintered sociology into numerous specialties, such as mathematical sociology, historical Marxism, phenomenology, ethnomethodology, sociobiology, network analysis, organizational research, clinical sociology, and race and ethnic relations (see box, p. 12). Each of these specialties has itself differentiated into many subspecialties. The specialty of race relations, for example, has broken down into studies of blacks, Hispanics, Asians, and other specific minorities in the United States (Blalock, 1984; Collins, 1986; Gans, 1989). Underlying all this diversity are certain theoretical perspectives that sociologists employ to study and understand social behavior. We will examine three major ones in the next section.

Questions for Discussion and Review

1. How did Karl Marx's understanding of nineteenth-century European society differ from that of Herbert Spencer?
2. What are some of the ways in which the development of U.S. sociology differed from the work of European sociologists?

MAJOR PERSPECTIVES IN SOCIOLOGY

Sociologists approach the study of human society in different ways. They can look at the "big picture" of society to see how it operates. This is a **macro-level view**, focusing on the large social phenomena of society such as social institution and inequality. Sociologists can also take a **micro-level view**, zeroing in on the immediate social situations where people interact with one another. From these two views sociologists have developed various **theoretical perspectives**, each a set of general assumptions about the nature of society. There are three well-known theoretical perspectives in sociology: the functionalist and conflict perspectives, which view society at the macro-level, and the symbolic interactionist perspective, which sees society at the micro-level.

Functionalist Perspective

Both Spencer and Durkheim provided ideas that inspired the **functionalist perspective**, which focuses on social order. According to this perspective, each part of society—the family, the school, the economy, or the state—contributes something. Each performs certain functions for the society as a whole. Moreover, all the parts are interdependent. The family, for example, depends on the school to educate its children, and the school, in turn, depends on the family or the state to provide financial support. The state, in turn, depends on the family and school to help children grow up to become law-abiding, taxpaying citizens. Out of these interdependent parts of society comes a stable social order. If something happens to disrupt this social order, its parts will adjust in a way that produces a new stability. Suppose the economy were in bad shape, with high rates of inflation and unemployment. The family would adjust, perhaps by spending less and saving more. The school would probably offer fewer programs and emphasize vocational training. The state might try to cut its budget. As a result, there would be a new social order.

However, what holds the society together, enabling all its parts to produce social order? The answer, according to functionalists, is **social consensus**, a condition in which most members of the society agree on what would be good for everybody and cooperate to achieve it. Durkheim assumed that social consensus can come about in the form of either mechanical or organic solidarity.

American Mosaic

Sociology is as diverse as the society it studies. Sociologists thus possess ideas that can be used in a wide variety of settings. Consider how Rosabeth Moss Kanter, who teaches at the Harvard Business School, uses sociology to study U.S. corporations, to lecture on business around the world, and to engage in other activities.

Rosabeth Moss Kanter, a Corporate Sociologist

Most management gurus learn their craft by taking MBAs and serving time in business schools or consultancies. Rosabeth Moss Kanter learnt hers hanging around in the counter-culture, rubbing shoulders with the sort of gurus who believe in founding communes rather than re-inventing corporations. Her academic training was not in business or economics but in that quintessentially counter-culture subject, sociology. Her doctoral thesis dealt with 19th-century Utopian communities, such as the Shakers. Her second book expounded feminist theories of society.

Anybody who meets Ms. Kanter expecting beads and body paint is in for a surprise. She now teaches in that seminary of American capitalism, the Harvard Business School. She co-founded a Boston-based consulting firm, Goodmeasure Inc, holds several directorships and acts as an adviser to dozens of giant companies. A regular on the international lecture circuit, she spends much of her time being chauffeur-driven from airport to hotel suite.

The transformation of ponchoed sociologist into power-suited guru proved surprisingly easy. Kanter-the-sociologist was struck by the similarities between 19th-century communes and contemporary corporations in the way that both have motivated their members and transmitted their values. (Two of her communes even produced brand-name products, Amana refrigerators and Oneida silverware.) Kanter-the-guru still studies her subject with a sociologist's eye, treating the corporation not so much as a micro-economy, concerned with turning inputs into outputs, but as a mini-society, bent on shaping individuals to collective ends.

Ms. Kanter retains some of her earlier political commitments, too. A passionate Democrat, she served as chief economic advisor to Michael Dukakis during his bid for the presidency, and she continues to lend her name to good works, be they left-wing think-tanks or local regeneration schemes. She has a penchant for "people-conscious, commitment-producing work-places": the sort of fast-moving, loosely structured enterprises that the flower children founded when they tired of getting high.

Her reputation rests on a trilogy of books chronicling the way America's corporations have coped with unprecedented turbulence. *Men and Women of the Corporation* (1977) looked inside one stagnating, bureaucratic corporation. It examined the forces that locked people with routine jobs into a mood of resentful indifference, and so prevented firms from realizing talent...

The Change Masters (1983) was a study in contrasts: between established "change resisters," who saw their job as shoring up the old order, and up-and-coming "change masters," who wanted to institutionalize innovation. This squabble was taking place not only between entrepreneurial companies and their more staid rivals, but also within companies. Visiting General Motors, for example, Ms. Kanter was surprised to find not one company but two, one stick-in-the-mud, the other addicted to innovation.

When Giants Learn to Dance (1989), her best known (and best written) book, announced the birth of a new entity, the post-entrepreneurial firm. As well as repeating the well-known litany of complaints about over-bureaucratized corporate giants, Ms. Kanter pointed out that many entrepreneurial start-ups were suffering from the opposite problem: too little organization. She argued that the future lay with companies that could combine the light-footedness of entrepreneurs with the power of giants. In order to achieve this, she argued, companies of all sorts are converging on the same strategies: restructuring to create synergies between different bits of their businesses; breaking down corporate barriers to form alliances with suppliers, customers and venture partners; and devolving power to innovative business units.

Excerpted from "Moss Kanter, Corporate Sociologist," *The Economist,* October 15, 1994, p. 89.

Mechanical solidarity is a type of social cohesion that develops when people do similar work and have similar beliefs and values. It exists in relatively small-scale, traditional societies. An example is a society in which almost everyone works at farming and believes in the same gods.

In contrast, **organic solidarity** is a type of social cohesion that arises when the people in a society perform a wide variety of specialized jobs and therefore have to depend on one another. Organic solidarity is characteristic of complex, industrialized societies. The people in a U.S. city, for example, are likely to hold many very different types of jobs, to have grown up with different family customs, to hold varying beliefs and values. There are bankers, teachers, engineers, plumbers, and many other businesses, professions, and occupations. Among these people there will probably be atheists and Christians, Jews and Muslims, reactionaries and radicals, and everything in between. Thus, mechanical solidarity among the city's people is not likely to be strong. They cannot be bound together by conformity to the same ideas and ideals. But they can be more easily bound together by their need for each other. The banker needs the worker who deposits and borrows money, and both need the storekeeper, who needs the trucker who delivers food, who needs the mechanic and gas station attendant, and so on. The complex ties of dependence seem virtually endless. These people are bound together by organic solidarity.

During the 1940s and 1950s, the functionalist perspective became widely accepted by U.S. sociologists. But in its move from Europe to the United States, functionalism had been altered somewhat. Originally, it was used to help explain the society as a whole—to clarify how order and stability were maintained, but U.S. sociologists have been more interested in discovering the functions of specific types of human behavior.

The most prominent among these sociologists is Robert Merton (1957). Merton classified functions into two types: manifest and latent. **Manifest functions** are those that are intended and seem obvious; **latent functions** are unintended and often unrecognized. The manifest function of going to college, for example, is to get an education, but going to college also has the latent function of enabling many students to find their future spouses. Another latent function is to force students to learn the valuable lesson of negotiating their way through bureaucratic mazes in order to get things done. After four years of learning to master preregistration, parking permits, financial aid forms, major and general education requirements, course schedules, add-and-drop policies, and dormitory preference forms, you will find it easier to work in even the most formidable business bureaucracy (Galles, 1989).

Throughout this book we will see many examples of the usefulness of functionalism, but by itself it cannot lead to a complete picture of social events. It has also been criticized for focusing on the positive functions of a social event, such as sports, and

ignoring the negative. Similarly, the application of functionalism to analyze society has been criticized for being inherently conservative; in effect, it justifies the status quo. By emphasizing what every current aspect of society does for its citizens, functionalism encourages people to dismiss social change as "dysfunctional" (harmful), even though change may, in fact, produce a better society.

Conflict Perspective

The conflict perspective produces a portrait of society strikingly different from that offered by functionalism. Whereas functionalism emphasizes society's stability, the **conflict perspective** portrays society as always changing and always marked by conflict. Functionalists tend to focus on social order, to view social change as harmful, and to assume that the social order is based largely on people's willing cooperation. Implicitly, functionalism defends the status quo. In contrast, proponents of the conflict perspective are inclined to concentrate on social conflict, to see social change as beneficial, and to assume that the social order is forcibly imposed by the powerful on the weak. They criticize the status quo.

The conflict perspective originated largely from Karl Marx's writings on the class conflict between capitalists and the proletariat. For decades U.S. sociologists tended to ignore Marx and the conflict perspective because the functionalist perspective dominated their view of society. However, in the turbulent 1960s the conflict perspective gained popularity. Generally, those adopting the conflict perspective define conflict more broadly than did Marx. Whereas Marx believed that conflict between *economic* classes was the key force in society, conflict theorists today define social conflict to mean conflict between any unequal groups or societies. Thus, they examine conflict between whites and blacks, one religious group and another, one society and another, men and women, and so on. They emphasize that groups or societies will have conflicting interests and values and thus will compete with each other. Because of this perpetual competition, society or the world is always changing.

The conflict perspective leads sociologists to ask such questions as: Which groups are more powerful and which are weaker? How do powerful groups benefit from the existing social order, and how are weaker groups hurt? How do the powerful preserve their privileges, and how do the weaker ones challenge them? Some sociologists have in recent decades applied this kind of question to the experiences of women. As a result, they have fashioned a **feminist** theory, a form of conflict theory that explains human life from the experiences of women. Details of the theory vary from one sociologist to another, but they suggest in one way or another how women's life differs from men's (Lengermann and Niebrugge-Brantley, 1992), with the assumption that these gender differences shape the life of all of us.

First, women's experiences are *different* from those of men. There is a diversity of feminist views on what the gender differences are, but most agree that being interested in bearing and caring for infants, being gentle rather than tough, and being peaceful rather than violent toward others are among the socially learned characteristics that distinguish some women from men. To feminists, these feminine values are at least equal, if not superior, to traditional masculine values. They deserve to be respected and recognized as valuable alternatives to rather than as undesirable departures from male values. But men have long regarded these traits as less valuable, which reinforces the devaluation of women's social position.

Second, women's position in most social situations is *unequal* to that of men. Compared with men, women have less power, freedom, respect, money, or opportunities for a happy life. This gender inequality comes from the widely held sexist belief that women are inferior to men. It may also originate from the need of capitalism to enhance profits by turning women into wives, housewives, and mothers. In these roles, women serve as unpaid caregivers for husbands and children in order to ensure a productive work force, and also serve as consumers of goods and services for the household.

Third, women are *oppressed*—restrained, subordinated, controlled, molded, or abused—by men. This is the essence of **patriarchy**—"a system of domination in which men exercise power over women" (Kimmel, 1992). The oppression may involve overt physical violence against women, such as rape, wife abuse, incest, and unnecessary caesareans or more subtle forms of violence such as unpaid household drudgery, underpaid wage work, sexual harassment in the workplace, and the standards of fashion and beauty that reduce women to men's sexual playthings (Lengermann and Niebrugge-Brantley, 1992).

Feminist theory assumes that, given those negative experiences, women are bound to challenge the status quo by seeking gender equality in education, career, marriage, and other areas of life. The theory is therefore useful for understanding the changes that have been taking place in the lives of both women and men throughout society. But the theory has also been criticized for overemphasizing the oppressiveness of patriarchy. According to critics, not all men are oppressors and not all women are victims. In fact, in critics' view, most women are far from being victims of their fathers, husbands, and sons but instead receive love, assistance, and other benefits from them. In the same way, the conflict perspective itself has been criticized for overly stressing social conflict and other negative aspects of society while ignoring the order, stability, and other positive aspects of society.

Symbolic Interactionist Perspective

Both functionalist and conflict perspectives focus on larger social forces of order, conflict, and patriarchy, forces that simultaneously affect huge numbers of people across the country. In contrast, the **symbolic interactionist perspective** directs our attention to the details of a specific situation and of the interaction between individuals in that situation. The combination of these countless interactions in various situations is said to constitute society. We can trace the origins of symbolic interactionism to Max Weber's argument that people act according to their interpretation of the meaning of their social world. But it was George Herbert Mead (1863–1931), a U.S. philosopher, who introduced symbolic interactionism to sociology in the 1920s.

According to symbolic interactionism, people assign meanings to each other's words and actions. Their actions and attitudes, then, are not determined by some action in and of itself. Instead, they act according to their subjective interpretation of the action. When you speak to a friend, an observer can easily give an objective report of the words you have said. But your friend's response will depend not on the list of words you spoke but on your friend's interpretation of the entire interaction, and your friend's response is at the same time influencing what you are saying. If your friend perceives by the way you speak that you are intelligent, this interpretation may make your friend respect and admire you and, perhaps, respond more positively to what you are saying. If you, in turn, catch this interpretation, you may feel proud and speak more confidently. In short, the exchange is a symbolic interaction. It is an interaction between individuals that is governed by their interpretation of the meaning of symbols. In this case, the symbols are primarily spoken words. But a symbol can be anything—an object, a sound, a gesture—that points to something beyond itself. The marks on this paper are symbols because they point to something—they mean something—beyond black squiggles.

The symbolic interactionist perspective suggests two things. First, people do not respond directly to physical "things." Rather, they respond to their *own* interpretations of them. Second, because people constantly impose interpretations—on the world in general, other people, themselves, and even their own interpretations—and then act accordingly, human behavior is fluid, always changing. How we act is constantly being altered by how we interpret other people's actions and their reactions to our own behavior. In other words, human behavior is not real in and by itself but becomes real only after it has been subjected to **reality construction**, the process by which we interpret what a given action means and respond to it in accordance with the interpretation.

The symbolic interactionist perspective is very useful for understanding why and how we interact with others, something that we do during most of our waking hours. But the perspective has been criticized for ignoring the larger issues of national and international order and change. It has also been faulted for ignoring the influence of larger social forces such as social institutions, groups, culture, and societies on individual interactions.

But can be applied as macro

An Integrated View

After looking at those three perspectives, you may ask, "Which one is right?" The answer can be found in the following story from Elliot Liebow (1993):

> Mr. Shapiro and Mr. Goldberg had an argument they were unable to resolve. It was agreed that Mr. Shapiro would present the case to a rabbi.

The rabbi said to Mr. Shapiro, "You are right."

When Mr. Goldberg learned of this, he ran to the rabbi with his version of the argument. The rabbi said to him, "You are right."

Then the rabbi's wife said to the rabbi, "You told Mr. Shapiro he was right and you told Mr. Goldberg he was right. They can't both be right!"

The rabbi said to his wife, "You are right too."

As the rabbi would say, each of the three perspectives in sociology is right in its own way. Each shows what our world looks like, but only when viewed from a certain angle (see Table 1.1). As a worldview, each perspective consists of *general* assumptions that cannot be falsified—proven through research to be false. This is because the phenomenon of function, conflict, or symbolic interaction that the perspective assumes to exist can *always* be found somewhere in human society. But we can derive from the perspective *specific* theories or hypotheses (about, for example, how common the phenomenon is) and conduct research to see whether they are true or false.

Though different, the three perspectives are not really incompatible. To some extent, they are like different perspectives on a house. Looked at from the front, the house has a door, windows, and a chimney on top. From the back, it has a door and a chimney on top but fewer windows. From the top, it has no doors or windows, but it has a chimney in the middle. It is the same house, but it looks very different, depending on one's perspective. Similarly, whether we see functions, conflict, and interaction depends on from where we are looking. Each perspective is useful because we cannot take everything about the complex social world into account at once.

TABLE 1.1
How the Three Perspectives Differ

TYPES OF PERSPECTIVES	Subject Under Focus	Nature of Society	Maintenance of Social Order
Functionalist Perspective	Social order or stability	Consists of interdependent groups pursuing common goals	Through social consensus, whereby people agree to cooperate in order to contribute to social order
Conflict Perspective	Social conflict or change	Made up of conflicting groups, each pursuing its own interest	Through coercion, social order is imposed by the powerful on the weak
Symbolic Interactionist Perspective	Interaction between individuals	Composed of individuals whose actions depend on interpreting each other's behavior	Through constant negotiations between individuals trying to understand each other's actions and reactions

We need some vantage point. Each perspective tells us what to look for, and each brings some aspect of society and human behavior into sharper focus. Integrated into one viewing device, these diverse perspectives can enrich our sociological knowledge of the world.

Suppose we want to study the interaction between whites and blacks, or between upper- and lower-class people. Each perspective can be useful. Functionalist and conflict perspectives can lead us to analyses that clarify how the interaction is affected by larger social forces, such as the popular belief in democracy and equality, the long history of racial prejudice, or the difference in lifestyle or power between rich and poor. On the other hand, symbolic interactionism can give us a richer, more detailed view of specific interactions and an understanding of why people who are exposed to the same social forces behave in different ways. Moreover, the three perspectives can be used to check each other to see if we have overemphasized any one perspective and missed the complex reality of the world in which we live. We can see all this more clearly by analyzing sports.

Questions for Discussion and Review

1. What is a theoretical perspective, and what are the main features of the three perspectives sociologists use today?
2. How do the basic assumptions of the conflict perspective differ from those of functionalism?
3. Is any one of the three perspectives better than the others?

SPORTS: ILLUSTRATING THE THREE PERSPECTIVES

The influence of sports reaches far and wide. Sports are particularly popular in our heavily leisure-oriented society. Most of us have had some experience with athletics as participants or spectators. Schools, from kindergarten to college, provide many sports opportunities. Newspapers carry more news about sports than about politics, the economy, crime, or

Sports help to illustrate the three sociological perspectives. According to the functionalist perspective, sports contribute to success in other areas of life, enhance health and happiness, and contribute to social order and stability. According to the conflict perspective, however, sports act to numb the poor's dissatisfaction with society, encourage deviant behavior, and reinforce social, gender, and racial inequalities in society. Symbolic interactionism focuses on how athletes, fans, and coaches define situations through interaction—coaches, for example, promoting the idea that their players are winners, or parents and teachers defining certain sports as unfeminine.

practically any other event. Radio and television newscasts rarely go on the air without any sports report. Football, basketball, baseball, and other games are often broadcast in their entirety, pre-empting regular programming. Sports exert so much influence on our lives that our everyday speech is full of sports imagery: "struck out," "touch base," "ball-park figure," "game plan," "teamwork," "cheap shot," "go all the way," and so on.

What, then, is the nature of this powerful aspect of our lives? From the three sociological perspectives, we can see that sports are beneficial to society in some ways, harmful in other ways, and similar to any other social interaction—governed by individuals' definitions of each other's actions.

Sports as Beneficial to Society

According to the functionalist perspective, sports contribute to the welfare of society by performing at least three major functions.

First, sports contribute to success in other areas of life. Because they are competitive, sports inspire athletes to do their utmost to win, thereby helping them develop qualities such as skill and ability, diligence and self-discipline, mental alertness, and physical fitness which can ensure success in the larger society. In the words of General Douglas MacArthur: "Upon the fields of friendly strife are sown the seeds that, upon other fields, on other days, will bear the fruits of victory." By watching athletes perform, spectators also learn the importance of hard work, playing by the rules, and working as a team player, characteristics that help ensure success in a career and other aspects of life.

Second, sports enhance health and happiness. Participants can enjoy a healthy and long life. The health benefit is more than physical; it is also psychological. Runners and joggers, for example, often find that their activity releases tension and anger as well as relieving anxiety and depression. Moreover, many people derive much pleasure from looking upon their participation as a form of beauty, an artistic expression, or a way of having a good time with friends. Similarly, sports improve the quality of life for the spectators. Fans can escape their humdrum, boring daily routines, or find pleasure in filling their leisure time. They can further savor the aesthetic pleasure of watching the excellence, beauty, and creativity in an athlete's performance. The fans can therefore attain greater happiness, life satisfaction, or psychological well-being (Smith, 1993).

Third, sports contribute to social order and stability because they serve as an integrating force for society as a whole. Sports are in effect a social mechanism for uniting potentially disunited members of society. Through their common interest in a famous athlete or team, people of diverse racial, social, and cultural backgrounds can feel a sense of homogeneity, community, or intimacy that they can acquire in no other way. Athletes, too, can identify with their fans, their community, and their country.

Sports as Harmful to Society

According to the conflict perspective, sports are harmful to society in a number of ways, reflecting the conflict between the interests of the relatively powerful and those of the powerless (the ruling class vs. the masses, team owners vs. sports audience, whites vs. blacks, and men vs. women).

First, by serving as an integrating force, sports effectively act as an opiate, numbing the poor masses' sense of dissatisfaction with capitalist society. Involvement in sports as spectators tends to distract low-paid or unemployed workers from their tedious and dehumanizing jobs or frustrating joblessness. At the same time, they tend to develop the false consciousness that they should not question the established society but rather support it. A good example is the mostly working-class "soccer hooligans" in England. After their team loses in international soccer games, they often show "an exaggerated, embarrassing patriotism, a violent nationalism" by attacking foreigners (Buford, 1992). To divert their citizens' attention from their miserable lives, governments of many poor countries also seize any opportunity that arises to whip up the masses into a frenzy of patriotic support for their teams. Such a nationalist frenzy can be carried to the extreme as it was in 1969 when Honduras and El Salvador went to war against each other after a World Cup soccer match.

Second, sports encourage deviant behavior. This has much to do with the overemphasis on winning. *fired* In sports, as the legendary football coach Vince Lombardi said, "winning isn't everything, it's the only thing!" Not surprisingly, athletes have been known to use illicit drugs to enhance performance. In contact sports such as football, basketball, and hockey, players often gratuitously assault their opponents. Even beautiful and graceful sports like figure skating can produce violence, as the whole world saw when Tonya Harding's associate whacked rival Nancy Kerrigan's leg. All this, however, serves the interest of the powerful, such as the ruling class, wealthy team owners, and college sports administrators. They can more easily control and exploit the masses and consumers, who generally find the violence and other ruthlessly competitive actions in sports very exciting, so that they would spend a lot of time and money watching.

Third, sports reinforce social, gender, and racial inequalities in society. In regard to social inequality, the overemphasis on competition and winning has caused the loss of something that all participants can enjoy equally, namely, the original elements of play and fun in sport activities. This has turned many people into "couch potatoes," who spend more time watching than playing sports. Sports, then, have become big business, with powerful owners of professional teams exploiting the public and government. Aside from making enormous sums of money from the fans, team owners receive many tax breaks from Uncle Sam as well as enjoy the enviable position of being the only self-regulated (in effect, unregulated) monopoly in the nation. Team owners have further professionalized and bureaucratized sports. This in turn has generated an elitist system, in which a very tiny number of owners and players become tycoons and superstars and the huge number of potential players are turned into mere spectators.

It is true that over the last two decades sports participation among women has risen sharply, thanks to the women's liberation movement and the 1972 law that prohibits sex discrimination in school sports. Nevertheless, in most colleges and universities, more funds continue to be spent on men's sports, especially football and basketball, than on women's athletic programs. Because of gender bias, men are even more likely than women to get top management and coaching jobs in *women's* programs (Diesenhouse, 1990). Sports are still considered a "men's world," in which women's leadership skills are devalued. Even the skills of superb women athletes are discounted as the media often describe female athletes as "pretty," "slim," "attractive," "gracious," and "lovely," as opposed to male athletes being "brilliant," "cool," "courageous," "great," or "tough." In glorifying masculinity, sports further encourage male athletes to commit rape, sexual harassment, or wife beating (Nelson, 1994).

On the surface, the huge numbers of remarkably successful black athletes today may cast doubt on the existence of racial inequality in sports. But African Americans do suffer from racism in various ways. We can detect it in the racial patterns of playing positions in professional sports—blacks tend to be in the peripheral, less important positions, while whites are more likely to be in the central, more important positions. In football, for example, blacks tend to play the peripheral positions as offensive tackles, running backs, and defensive backs, while whites are more likely to be in the central positions of quarterbacks, centers, offensive guards, and linebackers. Racism is most visible in the virtual absence of African Americans in top positions as owners, managers, and coaches of professional teams.

Most significantly, sports help perpetuate the high rate of poverty among African Americans. Traditionally, widespread and severe job discrimination has caused many poor African American youth to work extremely hard developing athletic skills in order to make it in college and professional sports, which explains why most of the best athletes in the country are black. Today the enormous attention given by white-dominated media to black superstars further encourages many poor black youth to give their all to athletics. The media apparently have also influenced parents. As Arthur Ashe (1992) found from a survey, black families are six times more likely than white families to encourage their sons to pursue a career in sports. But such an intense concentration on sports has diverted attention from academics. And tragically so, because, given the same hard work, it is far easier to become a professional in business, government, education, or any other ordinary field. The odds of turning professional in sports are extremely small. Only one or two percent of high school players with college athletic scholarships will end up as pros, while nearly 100 percent of their non-athlete peers with scholarships for academic achievement will become professionals in other, non-athletic pursuits. This is why Ashe (1977) once urged black youth to spend two hours in the library for every hour spent on the athletic field.

Sports as Symbolic Interaction

While functionalist and conflict perspectives focus on the larger, societal issues of sports which affect most people, symbolic interactionism homes in on the smaller, immediate issue of how athletes—or other individuals involved in a sport, such as coaches and fans—behave. According to this third perspective, if we define a situation as real it is real in its consequences. This means, for example, that if athletes define a game as one that they will win, they will likely win it. Let us take a closer look at how definition influences performance.

Great coaches know that they can get their athletes to perform well by drumming certain ideas into their heads. Foremost is the idea that the players are winners so that they will think only of winning and never about the possibility of losing. Chances are great that they indeed will win, because the image of themselves as winners will force them to concentrate only on the moves that ensure winning. This is basically the technique Jack Nicklaus, perhaps the greatest golfer of all times, uses to enhance his performance. Before every shot, he forms a mental picture in which he sees three things: (1) the target area the ball lands in, (2) the flight path of the ball to the target area, and (3) himself using the appropriate swing for that particular shot (Vealey and Walter, 1993). In short, if athletes define themselves as winners, they are more likely to win. By the same token, if athletes define themselves as losers, they will very likely lose.

Whatever the content of self-definition, it does not necessarily come from within the person. It is more likely to originate from social interaction. Children under 10, for example, often evaluate how "good" or "bad" they are at a sport from what their significant others (parents, teachers, or coaches) say to them. Thus children would describe their self-definition in ways such as "I know I am a good runner because my mom says I am" or "I don't think that I'm a very good soccer player because my coach is always yelling at me" (Horn and Lox, 1993).

Indeed, how others see us when they interact with us can shape how we define ourselves. But just as we often get our self-definition from our social environment, others also get their image of us from *their* environment. In interacting with an African American athlete, for example, a coach tends to stereotype the athlete as naturally gifted in sports. This stereotype, part of the popular belief about blacks in U.S. society, has a significant impact on the coach's interaction with the black athlete. Most commonly, the coach will impose a higher standard of performance on the black athlete than on white athletes. And the black athlete will be forced to work harder in order to achieve that higher standard, which may partly explain why black athletes usually outshine their white peers on the same team. Similarly, gender bias in the larger society often leads parents and teachers to discourage young women from playing basketball, soccer, and other so-called male sports, defining women who want to compete in these games as unfeminine. As a result, many women respond by avoiding these sports and choosing the so-called female sports such as aerobic dancing, swimming, gymnastics, or tennis. The popular definition of some sports as "masculine" and others as "feminine" can also influence the spectators. "Masculine" sports such as football and soccer,

for example, are more likely to cause fan violence than are "feminine" sports such as gymnastics and swimming.

We have observed how the three sociological perspectives can shed light on different aspects of sports. Combined, the perspectives can offer not only a *fuller* but also a *balanced* view of the subject. The combination of functionalist and conflict perspectives, for example, provides the balanced view that sports are *both* beneficial and harmful—rather than either totally beneficial or totally harmful. Symbolic interactionism can also balance either of the other two perspectives. Consider, for example, the conflict perspective's assumption that the British soccer hooligans' violence is an expression of patriotism. This cannot be taken to mean that the violence *completely* or *only* reflects the hooligans' patriotism, because we know from symbolic interactionism that fans' violence may *also* reflect a unique interaction between players and spectators. In basketball, football, and other popular U.S. sports, players of both teams frequently score some points, thrilling the fans. By contrast, points are rarely scored in soccer. In a typical game, fans of the losing team are repeatedly put through the wringer of waiting with heightened expectation for a goal that never comes. The accumulation of these repeated disappointments at the end of the game is likely to trigger violence among fans, such as the British soccer hooligans, who are already frustrated by their miserable lives. Also consider the functionalist assumption that sports enable athletes to develop qualities such as skill, diligence, and self-discipline that can insure success in other areas of life. But this cannot be *always* true because symbolic interactionism suggests that some athletes define their sports as fun rather than hard work.

In conclusion, it is important to know all the three different perspectives equally well. Together, they can offer not only a fuller but a balanced view of sports.

Questions for Discussion and Review

1. What are the differences between the functionalist and conflict perspectives on sports?
2. What is the nature of sports as seen through the symbolic interactionist perspective?

HOW SOCIOLOGY CAN ENRICH OUR LIVES

Sociology can be used for at least three major purposes. First, it can be used as an *intellectual exercise*, pursued for its own sake, for the pleasure of tickling our curiosity, or for producing scientific knowledge. Second, sociology can be used as a *general guide* for understanding our lives. It encourages us to be more conscious of the society in which we live, actively participating in it while critically evaluating its popular assumptions, understanding how it operates, and appreciating its diversity in race and ethnicity, gender, sexual orientation, and other social characteristics. Third, sociology can be used for *pursuing a specific career* in government (to help fight crime, improve education, reduce poverty, or solve some other social problem) or in the private sector (as a sociology teacher, social researcher, social critic, political analyst, political lobbyist, sociological consultant, or some other position that requires sociological knowledge). However it is used, sociology can *enrich our lives* with its perspectives and insights (see box, p. 21).

One of the most useful insights is that problems, whether intellectual, personal, societal, or global, can be seen as opportunities. Common sense has long misled us into seeing problems as problems, as something bad, as sources of failures and miseries. Our society has in effect driven us into a mental prison where we can only see problems as problems. But we can break the shackles by letting the global perspective in sociology transport us to another culture. In the Chinese culture, the word for crisis consists of two characters, *wei ji*, meaning "danger" and "opportunity." Through this cross-cultural perspective, we may want to stop seeing so-called problems as problems and start looking for opportunities instead. On the surface, these opportunities may not appear real but merely a perception. However, through the symbolic interactionist perspective, sociologists have long known the self-fulfilling prophecy that if people define something as real it is real in its consequences (see Chapter 6: Social Interaction in Everyday Life). Similarly, if we believe that problems are full of opportunities, we will likely find—and use—them to solve the problems.

The same sociological perspective also offers the useful insight that *our own interpretation* of the world around us affects our lives more than what the world does to us. Suppose someone insults us. We may interpret the insult in a commonsensical way, as a justification for us to be angry at the individual; or we may define the insult in a sociological way, as a

In Chinese culture, the word for crisis consists of two characters that mean "danger" and "opportunity." Chinese view problems as being full of opportunities. In sociology, symbolic interactionists, who believe that people act in accordance with their interpretations of things, would argue that if we see problems as problems, they will be problems; but if we view problems as opportunities, we can find them to be opportunities and use them to solve the problems.

product of social circumstances—such as poverty, unemployment, family problems, or having had difficulties with work, family, or some other aspect of social life. Both interpretations affect our lives, but differently. The commonsensical one makes us feel vengeful or even violent toward the individual, but the sociological one makes us feel fortunate (for not having the problems ourselves), tolerant, or compassionate. In a larger sense, the commonsense interpretation tends to worsen social life, whereas the sociological interpretation tends to improve it. Witness how Dr. Martin Luther King improved race relations in a nonviolent way, without advocating retaliatory action against racist individuals. This is an example of sociological imagination at work. It enables us to see the individual's problem from the social-structural standpoint (as represented by the functionalist and conflict perspectives), attributing the problem to social forces rather than blaming the victim.

There are many other specific ways sociological perspectives and insights can be used to enrich our lives, as we will see in the following chapters.

Questions for Discussion and Review

1. For what purposes can sociology be used?
2. How do you apply a sociological perspective or insight to some aspects of your life?

ENRICHING OUR LIVES

Much of sociology's focus is directed toward groups and the larger patterns of society. Ultimately, though, these large social units are made up of individuals, and sociologists try to better understand and improve people's lives. This special concern for the individual, which is sometimes referred to as humanist sociology, is discussed in this reading.

Sociology for People

Concerned students like to talk about what society is like and how they may be able to relate themselves to it. If they are taking a course in sociology, they may ask each other: "Can we really use the stuff we're getting? Does it work when you try it out in life?"

Such discussions can become quite personal, even intimate. Autobiographical bits and items concerning close friends and relatives serve as illustrations. The subjects range from encounters with members of the other sex to how to reform the university, stop militarism, get a job, or build a fortune or a political constituency. The more concerned often wonder about how our jerry-built world, with all its iniquities, inequalities, and brutalities, can be made into a society that is likely to persist and be more worth living in.

There are sociologists concerned about helping people to live more effectively and satisfyingly as fuller participants in society. What they ask you to consider may at times not be pleasant, romantic, flattering, or elegant. It may mean delving into outrageous ways of life and repulsive events. But what they offer often strikes students as being relevant to their futures, as contributing, in effect, a kind of initiation into "real life."

Here, our concerns are with sociology as an awakener and stimulant and as intellectual equipment with which an individual can more effectively deal with problems of life and living. Sociologists can give people an ever-refreshing sensitivity to all kinds of other people, groups, and social problems. As consciousness-raisers, they may help to make people feel that action and change are possible and even desirable, preferable to anxious and habitual attachment to a stability that cannot and does not exist.

Sociologists can inform people about how mass-communications agencies attempt to influence them. They suggest ways to analyze, compare, and otherwise deal with such manipulative procedures. They furnish data on how to interact with and also how to use voluntary organizations in order to launch acceptable social projects that actually can serve popular interests and can gain popular support.

Sociologists can refresh people's social sensitivity through encouraging participation in constructive social actions. Sensitivity can grow quickly through participating or at least observing in ethnic, racial, or class groups other than one's own. Such groups can force us to think in terms of a subculture or culture different from our own in order to understand them, in order to deal with them. It is like learning to perceive people through another person's quite different glasses. If the contrasts are great enough, it can give us a sense of culture shock, a disturbing but unfolding and enlightening experience.

Excerpted from Alfred McClung Lee, *Sociology for People*, Syracuse, NY: Syracuse University Press, 1988, pp. 32–42. Reprinted by permission.

CHAPTER REVIEW

1. *How does sociology differ from common sense?* While common sense gives familiar and untested ideas, sociology provides factually supported ideas and the excitement of discovering something new about ourselves. *Why is it important to study groups and societies different from ours?* By studying others, we can understand our lives better, because others may open our eyes to social forces that we have not seen before.

What is the nature of sociology as a science? As a science, sociology seeks to discover relationships between one event and another, describe these relationships in the forms of hypotheses and theories, and dig out evidence to see if it supports or refutes these hypotheses and theories. *How does the sociological imagination help us understand our lives better?* By showing the influences of social forces on our private lives.

TRAVELS WITH FARLEY

2. *Plato and Socrates discussed social issues. Were they sociologists?* No, they were social philosophers, who thought and argued about the nature of the world but did not test their ideas against systematic observation. *What led to the transformation of social philosophy into sociology?* Seized with the desire to solve social problems and impressed with the contributions from the natural sciences, some nineteenth-century social philosophers tried to apply the scientific method to the study of society in the hope of curing social ills. This attempt to replace philosophical speculation with the scientific method of systematic observation transformed social philosophy into sociology.

3. *What did Spencer mean when he said society is like a living organism?* In Spencer's view, each part of society, like each organ of an animal, performs its own function. If one part of society has problems, the other parts will adapt to the situation, ensuring the survival of the entire society. *What did Marx mean by class conflict?* Marx was referring to the struggle between the class of capitalists, who own the means of production, and the proletariat, who perform the labor. *What is the difference between* Verstehen *and Durkheim's objective approach? Verstehen* requires sociologists to adopt an attitude of understanding or empathy toward their subjects in order to understand how people interpret their own behavior, whereas Durkheim, who pioneered the application of scientific methods to sociology, argued that sociologists should deal solely with observable aspects of human behavior.

4. *How did the early U.S. sociologists differ from their European predecessors?* The European sociologists were

primarily interested in explaining the nature of society as a whole—the causes of social stability and change. In the United States, interest shifted to the study of specific social problems. Later, U.S. sociologists emphasized the search for sociological knowledge rather than its application to social problems, but their interest in social reform grew again during the 1960s. *What is the nature of modern sociology?* Modern sociology is a diverse discipline, one that is both a basic and an applied science and that uses both objective and subjective methods of investigation.

5. *What are the basic ideas of the functionalist perspective?* It focuses on social order and assumes that the various parts of a society are interdependent, forming a social structure in which each part serves a function that helps ensure the survival of the whole. *How does the conflict perspective differ from functionalism?* Whereas functionalism focuses on social order and stability, the conflict perspective emphasizes social conflict and change, showing how one group dominates another. *What are the basic ideas of feminist theory?* Women are different from, unequal to, and oppressed by men, which compels women to challenge the status quo of gender prejudice and discrimination. *What is a symbolic interaction?* It is an interaction between individuals that is governed by their interpretations of each other's actions. *What is the nature of sports as seen through the three perspectives?* Sports appear to be beneficial to society in some ways, harmful in other ways, and similar to any other social interaction.

6. *How can sociology enrich our lives?* By using insights from such perspectives as the global, symbolic interactionist, and social-structural perspectives.

KEY TERMS

Class conflict Marx's term for the struggle between capitalists, who own the means of production, and the proletariat, who do not (p. 9).

Conflict perspective A theoretical perspective that portrays society as always changing and always marked by conflict (p. 13).

Economic globalization The interrelationship of the world's economies (p. 3).

Feminist theory A form of conflict theory that explains human life from the experiences of women (p. 13).

Functionalist perspective A theoretical perspective that focuses on social order (p. 11).

Global village A closely knit community of all the societies in the world (p. 3).

Hypothesis A tentative statement about how various events are related to one another (p. 4).

Latent function A function that is unintended and often unrecognized (p. 13).

Macro-level view A view that focuses on the large social phenomena of society, such as social institutions and inequality (p. 11).

Manifest function A function that is intended and seems obvious (p. 13).

Mechanical solidarity A type of social cohesion that develops when people do similar work and have similar beliefs and values (p. 12).

Micro-level view A view that focuses on the immediate social situations where people interact with one another (p. 11).

Organic solidarity A type of social cohesion that arises when the people in a society perform a wide variety of specialized jobs and therefore have to depend on one another (p. 12)

Patriarchy A system of domination in which men exercise power over women (p. 14).

Reality construction The process by which we interpret what a given action means and respond to it in accordance with the interpretation (p. 15).

Social consensus Condition in which most members of society agree on what is good for everybody to have and cooperate to achieve it (p. 11).

Social forces Forces that arise from the society of which we are a part (p. 5).

Social integration The degree to which people are tied to a social group (p. 5).

Sociological imagination C. Wright Mills's term for the ability to see the impact of social forces on individuals, especially on their private lives (p. 5).

Social marginality Being excluded from mainstream society (p. 3).

Sociology The systematic, mostly scientific study of human society (p. 2).

Symbolic interactionist perspective A theoretical perspective that directs our attention to the details of a specific situation and of the interaction between individuals in that situation (p. 14).

Theoretical perspective A set of general assumptions about the nature of society (p. 11).

Theory A set of logically related hypotheses that explains the relationship among various phenomena (p. 4).

Verstehen Weber's term for empathetic understanding of sociologists' subjects (p. 10).

SUGGESTED READINGS

Andersen, Margaret L. 1993. *Thinking About Women: Sociological Perspectives on Sex and Gender,* 3rd ed. New York: Macmillan. A sociological perspective on the lives of women, a useful counterbalance to most sociological studies, which claim to deal with people in general but in fact focus on men only.

Berger, Bennett M. 1990. *Authors of Their Own Lives: Intellectual Autobiographies of Twenty American Sociologists.* Berkeley: University of California Press. An interesting collection of stories on how sociologists get their ideas about social behavior.

Gans, Herbert J. (ed.). 1990. *Sociology in America.* Newbury Park, Calif.: Sage. A collection of essays analyzing today's sociology and its influences on U.S. society.

Ross, Dorothy. 1991. *The Origins of American Social Science.* New York: Cambridge University Press. Shows how the early U.S. sociologists, along with economists and political scientists, sought to model their new discipline on the natural sciences.

Wolfe, Alan. 1995. "Realism and Romanticism in Sociology," *Society,* January/February, pp. 56–63. An interesting discussion of the two conflicting tendencies in sociological analyses.

DOING SOCIOLOGY: RESEARCH METHODS

Myths and Realities

MYTH: *Facts speak for themselves.*
REALITY: Facts do not speak for themselves. By themselves they are meaningless. To have meaning, they must be interpreted in some way. This explains why the same fact often means different things to different people, especially in a pluralistic society like ours, let alone in a world of sharply diverse cultures.

MYTH: *Social research involves seeking facts alone. It has nothing to do with theoretical perspectives or preconceived ideas.*
REALITY: Social research is indeed concerned with seeking facts. But at the same time it is also carried out with a more or less explicit idea of what one is looking for. The idea is usually in the form of a clearly stated perspective, theory, and a set of hypotheses. Sometimes, the idea consists of nothing more than a fuzzy and indescribable sense or feeling about something.

MYTH: *Only college professors are interested in social research—and forcing their students to study it.*
REALITY: Many people outside educational institutions are also interested in social research. Research helps government officials serve people better, politicians get more votes, business people sell more products, and leaders of various organizations do their job more effectively. Moreover, average people constantly rely on research to live a better life, though they may not be aware of it. Through newspapers, television, and other media, they learn about how to choose a college, avoid getting AIDS, get a job, and do many other things, which are based on facts from social research.

rom 1984 to 1988 social researcher Elliot Liebow (1993) worked as a volunteer at an emergency shelter for homeless women just outside Washington, D.C. Along with three other volunteers, Liebow prepared and served the food, distributed towels, soap, and other things on request, socialized with the women, kept order, and kept a daily log, writing down the names of all the women present and their time of arrival. Liebow tried to identify himself with the women as much as possible, distancing himself from staff and management of the shelter. He made himself available for driving the women to a job interview, a hospital, a cemetery, someone's house, another shelter, and so on. He even loaned the women money. A genuine friendship flourished between Liebow and the women, and he enjoyed their company as much as they enjoyed his. When Liebow told them he was going to write a book about them, they welcomed it and told him much about their lives on the street. The questions he asked them were natural, arising spontaneously and directly out of the social situation at the shelter. They were not research questions, ready-made and brought from the outside.

Liebow was able to find that homeless women made an enormous effort to secure the most basic necessities of life—food, water, security, shelter, and safe sleep—which the rest of us take for granted. Even when staying at the shelter temporarily, the women had to get up every morning, no matter how they felt, and then spend all day walking the street to kill time. Liebow learned that the problems of "sleeping, fatigue, boredom, killing time, storage, health, sex, along with harassment and other unpredictable difficulties encountered on the street were some of the little murders of everyday life that confronted the homeless women." Yet they still possessed a sense of humor, with not a trace of self-pity. One evening, while Liebow was talking with several women at the shelter, one named Pauline told Liebow: "Hilda has a Ph.D." Hilda laughed, saying, "No. I don't have a Ph.D., but I do have a bachelor's degree in biology." She paused and then continued, "You know, all my life I wanted to be an M.D. and now, at the age of 54, I finally made it. I'm a Manic Depressive." In short, Liebow was struck by how valiantly the homeless struggle "to remain human in the face of inhuman conditions."

What Liebow demonstrates here is how important social research is for knowing how people actually behave in a certain social environment. It is not enough to simply think sociologically, with ideas drawn from various sociological perspectives about how social forces shape human lives as discussed in the preceding chapter. These ideas are merely idle guesswork if they are not backed up by scientific facts. Sociologists must therefore also do sociology, going out into the real world to see how people live, as Liebow did. But aside from Liebow's use of the technique known as participant observation in his study of homeless women, there are other ways of doing social research. In this chapter, we will discuss participant observation and other specific methods of gathering data. We will analyze the steps taken by sociologists to conduct research, the approaches to social research suggested by the three sociological perspectives, the emerging feminist methodology, and the ethical problems that social researchers must deal with. But first let us take a look at the basic concepts that capture the essence of what the researchers do.

BASIC CONCEPTS OF SOCIAL RESEARCH

Sociologists often do research to find out *what* is going on in society, to discover the characteristics of a social phenomenon. Thus they may take a survey, asking people about such things as their attitude toward the U.S. president, whether they smoke marijuana, and so on. This is **descriptive research** aimed at gathering information in order to simply describe a phenomenon. Sociologists also often conduct research to find out *why* or *how* some social event is happening. This is **explanatory research** designed to test a hypothesis in order to explain a phenomenon. In either case, social research must be carried out according to a well-established set of scientific rules and procedures.

Different research problems may call for different procedures, but the basic principle remains the same. All research results must be verifiable by other investigators. This goal leads to the first rule of research: we must deal with what is observable.

Operational Definition

Many social phenomena are not directly observable because they are described in the form of abstract concepts such as social integration or social class. To make specific social phenomena observable, sociologists use an **operational definition**, a specification of the action needed to translate what is abstract and unobservable into what is concrete and observable. The operational definition of social class, for example, involves asking people such concrete questions as how many years of schooling they have had, how much money they earn a year, or what they do for a living.

The answers to these questions provide something concrete that represents the concept of class. That something concrete is an **empirical indicator**, an observable representation of an abstract and unob-

servable concept. Thus education, income, or occupation is an empirical indicator of social class—in the same way as a thermometer is an empirical indicator of temperature. Empirical indicators are important tools for doing social research. Suppose some sociologists use "annual income between $30,000 and $50,000" as their empirical indicator of middle class; other researchers know exactly what they are talking about and can verify their findings about who middle-class people are.

Variable

Although we can use empirical indicators to describe the basic elements of our social world in ways that are precise and verifiable, we want more than a catalog of facts. We want to know how those elements are related to one another. Usually, we want to know which is the cause and which the effect.

Both causes and effects are known as **variables**, characteristics that vary from people to people within the population being studied. A cause is called an *independent* variable, because its presence does not depend on the effect; an effect is referred to as a *dependent* variable, because its presence does depend on the cause. Therefore, an **independent variable** may be defined as a variable that is the cause of another variable, and a **dependent variable** may be defined as a variable that is considered the effect of another variable.

Because people differ with regard to class—some are upper-class, others middle-class, and still others lower-class—social class can be treated as a variable. Gender can also be a variable, because some people are male and others female. Virtually all other social forces and human behaviors may be considered variables. If we are studying a population made up of people of different ages and both genders, with different incomes and levels of education, who express different political beliefs, all these characteristics are variables. All these social phenomena can be regarded as variables only because the population being studied is a diverse one, including people of different classes, both genders, or different characteristics of some other kind.

The same phenomena, on the other hand, can also be treated as **constants**, characteristics found in *all* members of the population being studied. Suppose we are comparing academic performance between male and female college students. Gender is a variable because our subjects differ in gender—some male and others female. The characteristic of being in college is a constant because the subjects do *not* differ in education, all being college students. But suppose we want to study social characteristics, such as education, that influence how women vote. Then gender is a constant because the subjects here do *not* differ in gender, all being women. Education is a variable because the subjects differ in education, some being college-educated and others not.

Correlation

In order to establish one variable as the cause of an effect, we must first be sure that the two variables are *correlated*, both occurring together in some regular way. If two variables are correlated, then when one changes, the other also changes and there is a pattern to these changes. Thus, a **correlation** is a consistent association between two or more variables, which may or may not be causal. A *positive correlation* exists when an increase in one variable is associated with an increase in the other variable, as is true in the case of the relationship between education and income: the more education we have, the higher the income we get. A *negative correlation* exists when an increase in one variable is associated with a decrease in the other. Education and racial prejudice, for example, are negatively correlated, in that the more education we have, the less likely we are to be prejudiced. Sometimes a correlation is *curvilinear*: as one variable is changed, another variable first changes in the same direction and then in the opposite. You may recall from Chapter 1 that both very high and very low levels of social integration are associated with high rates of suicide. That is a case of curvilinear correlation, because with the increase in integration, the suicide rate initially comes down and then goes up. (See box, p. 29, on how to read a graph, for the ways in which these variables are related.)

Correlation by itself, however, does not prove that changes in one variable are the cause of the changes observed in another. After all, there is a high correlation between hospitalization and death: many more deaths occur in the hospital than at home. But the correlation does not prove that hospitalization *causes* death. Instead, another variable, such as serious illness, may be at work, producing the high number of deaths in hospitals. Serious illness often leads to both hospitalization and death and thus may explain the relationship between these variables. Serious illness, then, is the **third variable**, a hidden variable responsible for the occurrence of a relation between two other variables that are not causally related.

In short, when two variables are correlated, it is possible that neither is having an effect on the other. Instead, a third variable, or several other variables, might be the cause of the correlation. If this is the case, we have a **spurious correlation**, an apparent but false correlation between two variables that are not causally related.

Causal Relationship

A correlation between two variables is necessary but not sufficient to establish that one variable is the cause of another. At least two additional conditions must be met before we can say that a causal relationship probably exists:

1. The independent variable must precede the dependent variable in time.
2. There must not be a third variable that causes the correlation between both of them.

Often we can determine which variable precedes another through logical assessment. If we look at the high correlation between serious illness and death, we may logically conclude that serious illness precedes death, simply because the alternative notion that death causes serious illness is logically impossible. Similarly, in the case of a high correlation between race and unemployment, we can logically conclude that being black comes first and being jobless comes later, because the alternative possibility—joblessness causes a person's skin to change color—is not logical. Unfortunately, some cases are not so simple. Trying to determine which variable precedes another is sometimes like asking, "Which came first, the chicken or the egg?" If we find that people who exercise regularly are healthier than those who do not, does this mean that regular exercise causes good health? Not necessarily, because healthy people may be more likely to exercise in the first place. Although research has found that exercise can help a person live longer, it is only one of many contributing factors. Hence, by itself, exercise cannot be said to cause good health.

H O W   T O   R E A D   A   G R A P H

A graph is a pictorial representation of a set of data. It shows measurements along two axes: a horizontal one, called the x axis, and a vertical one, the y axis. The label on each axis indicates what is being measured, and the point at which the two axes meet represents either a very low measure or a measurement of zero. As you go up the y axis or to the right on the x axis, the value of whatever is being measured increases.

Figure 2.1 provides two simple examples. The point at which the x and y axes meet is at the lower left corner of each of these graphs. Consider the graph on the left. The label on the x axis tells us that it represents social integration. The left end of the axis therefore represents very low levels of social integration, which are labeled "inadequate," and the right end represents very high, or "excessive," levels. The y axis represents the suicide rate, which increases as you go from the bottom to the top of the axis.

The curve is the part of the graph that contains the information. To see how to read it, let us take one point on the curve, the point labeled "egoistic suicide." In terms of the x axis, it is far to the left, so it shows inadequate levels of social integration. At the same time, this point is high on the y axis, so it also represents a relatively high suicide rate. Hence, the point indicates that a high suicide rate and inadequate social integration occur together.

Now let us move along the curve and see what it tells us. As we go along the x axis, social integration is increasing and the curve is sloping downward, which indicates that the suicide rate is decreasing; that is, as social integration increases, the suicide rate decreases. But that is only part of the story, because at about the middle of the x axis, the curve begins sloping upward again, which indicates that the suicide rate is increasing. According to the labels on the x axis, social integration is becoming excessive.

What the curve tells us, then, is that the suicide rate tends to be high when social integration is either inadequate or excessive. The two extreme cases—where the suicide rate is high and social integration is inadequate or excessive—are called *egoistic suicide* and *altruistic suicide*, respectively. By reading the curve in the right-hand graph, you can also see how suicide and social regulation are related.

How accurate are these graphs? Although the total suicide rate might be precisely measured and placed exactly on the y axis, social integration and social regulation are not precisely defined or measured, and the terms "inadequate" and "excessive" are value judgments. We could, however, give operational definitions of "integration" and "regulation" and substitute some measurement for the value-laden terms.

Despite this lack of precision, the graphs are valuable because they show general patterns of relationships.

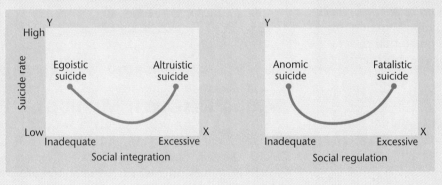

FIGURE 2.1
Social Integration and Social Regulation

Finally, in order to establish a causal relationship between two variables, we must examine the possibility that a third one is the cause of the correlation between the others. Sometimes the third variable intervenes between the other two, making them apparently rather than genuinely related. Earlier we mentioned the high correlation between race and joblessness. Although race precedes unemployment rather than the other way around, this does not necessarily mean that race is the direct cause of joblessness. Instead, it is racial discrimination or some other social problem that may have brought about the high unemployment rate among blacks. Racial discrimination (C), then, is the *intervening variable* that mediates between race (A) and joblessness (B): A→C→B. Sometimes the third variable causes the other to

People who exercise regularly are healthier than those who do not, but healthy people may be more likely to exercise in the first place. Regular exercise can contribute to good health, but it is only one of many contributing factors and should not be considered the cause of good health.

appear correlated in another way. In the previously discussed case of the high correlation between hospitalization (A) and death (B), we noted that the correlation is spurious, brought on by the third variable of serious illness (C).

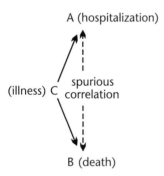

How can we find out if a correlation is spurious? Often sociologists apply *controls*, procedures for holding certain variables constant. If a correlation disappears when a third variable is held constant,

then we have good reason to believe that the correlation is spurious.

Suppose we suspect that the correlation between smoking and lung cancer is spurious and that poverty is a third variable accounting for the correlation. We may try to control the effect of poverty on the correlation by comparing cancer rates among smokers and nonsmokers who are *equally* poor. If the cancer rates of these two groups are the same, we may reason that the correlation between smoking and cancer is spurious. But if the poor smokers have higher cancer rates than poor nonsmokers, then we may conclude that smoking is probably a cause of cancer. Often, complex statistical analysis and other methods are necessary to establish the desired controls, but the specific procedure for establishing controls depends on which of several possible research methods is used. These research methods are the subject of the next section.

Questions for Discussion and Review

1. Why do sociologists attempt to define and determine relationships between variables?
2. What is the difference between descriptive and explanatory research?
3. What are dependent and independent variables, and how can sociologists establish a relationship between them?
4. How do sociologists determine whether a correlation is spurious or real?

MAJOR RESEARCH METHODS

Variables and correlations are the nuts and bolts of social research. We have examined some rules about which variables and which correlations are meaningful in research—which ones, in essence, count as scientific facts. But how do sociologists collect these facts? There are four basic methods: survey, observation, experiment, and analysis of existing data. Each has its own advantages and disadvantages.

Survey

Of the four research methods, the **survey**—a research method that involves asking questions about opinions, beliefs, or behavior—is most frequently used by

HOW TO READ A TABLE

Tables often look boring and complicated, but many sociological data are published in tables, and careful reading can yield fascinating information and ideas for further research. Table 2.1 is a simple one, but we can use it to illustrate six steps to follow in interpreting tables.

First, read the title. It should say what kind of information is in this table. It tells us the different reasons that women and men gave for having sex the first time.

Second, check the source. The source of the data is cited at the bottom of the table. Sometimes the reputation of the organization that collected the data gives a rough indication of the reliability of the source. But often we will want to know how the data were collected. The report that presents the table usually includes this information.

Third, read the labels. A table has two kinds of labels: column headings along the top of the table and labels down the left side. In this table, the column headings are "Women" and "Men" and the side labels indicate the reasons for having sex the first time.

Fourth, understand the figures. Usually, a table gives numbers, percentages, or both. The table here, for example, gives both numbers (the n subcolumn) and percentages of people interviewed. Generally, the larger the numbers, the more reliable the information.

Fifth, compare the data. Compare the figures both horizontally and vertically. The table shows the percentages of women and men who gave various reasons for their first sexual intercourse. Notice the large gender differences in regard to having first-time sex for affection, curiosity, physical pleasure, and wedding night. Almost twice as many women as men had sex out of affection for their partners, and three times as many women as men did not have their first sexual experience until their wedding night. By contrast, men are much more likely than women to have their first sexual intercourse because they were curious about sex or seeking physical pleasure.

Sixth, draw conclusions. If we read the table carefully, we should be able to draw at least a tentative

TABLE 2.1
Reasons for Having Sex the First Time

Reasons given by...	Women		Men	
	%	n	%	n
Affection for partner	48	913	25	283
Peer pressure	3	57	4	61
Curiosity/readiness for sex	24	456	51	781
Wanted to have a baby	1	19	0	0
Physical pleasure	3	57	12	184
Under influence of alcohol/drugs	0	0	1	15
Wedding night	21	399	7	107
Total	100%	1901	100%	1531

SOURCE: Adapted from Robert T. Michael, John H. Gagnon, Edward O. Laumann, and Gina Kolata, *Sex in America: A Definitive Survey* (Boston: Little, Brown, 1994), p. 93.

conclusion. According to popular belief, the sexual revolution and increased gender equality in modern society have caused women to be nearly as sexually liberal as men. But contrary to this popular belief, we may conclude from the data in the table here that women are still far more likely to be sexually conservative, preferring affectionate sex rather than impersonal sex.

sociologists. Suppose we want to know what led people to have sex for the first time. We could take a survey, and we would find, as Table 2.1 shows, that women had different reasons than men for getting their first sexual experience. (Also see box, above, on how to read the table.) Or suppose a theory suggests that students' social class and geographical background (urban, rural, or suburban) are related to their

sexual behavior. Survey data could be collected to determine whether this might be true.

Sampling To take a survey, we first select a **population**, the entire group of people to be studied. We can choose a population of any size, but all its members must have something in common. Thus a population may consist of all people above the age of

100, or all U.S. Congresswomen, or all the students at a large university, or all U.S. citizens, or all the people in the world.

If a population is relatively small, all its members can be approached and interviewed. But if a population is very large, it could cost too much time and money to contact all its members. In such a case, we need a **sample**, a relatively small number of people selected from a larger population. The sample, however, must accurately represent the entire population from which it is drawn. Otherwise the information obtained from the sample cannot be generalized to the population. Failure to heed this may produce misleading conclusions.

A famous case in point was the attempt to predict the outcome of the presidential election in 1936. A popular magazine of that era, *Literary Digest*, selected a large sample of people from telephone directories and automobile registration lists and then asked them whom they would vote for. An overwhelming majority replied that they would choose the Republican candidate, Alfred Landon, over his Democratic opponent, Franklin Roosevelt. So the editors of the magazine concluded that Landon was going to have a landslide victory. But it turned out that Landon was overwhelmingly defeated. Meanwhile, a young man named George Gallup, who had chosen a much smaller but far more representative sample of all the voters, correctly predicted the election's outcome. The *Literary Digest*'s incorrect prediction was due to the selection of a sample that did not represent the entire voting population. The sample included only middle- and upper-class people, who could afford telephones and automobiles during those Depression years and who, being largely Republicans, tended to vote for the Republican candidate. The less well-off, who later voted for the winning Democratic candidate, were excluded from the sample.

The *Literary Digest* apparently assumed that since they contacted a huge number of people (10 million), they could accurately predict the election. They did not realize, as Gallup did, that it is not the size but the representativeness of the sample that ensures accuracy. A sample as large as the *Literary Digest*'s can be misleading if it is not representative of the population, but a sample as small as Gallup's (only 300,000) can be accurate if it adequately represents the population. In fact, owing to today's increased sophistication in sampling, as few as 1500 cases can comprise a representative sample of the U.S. population. A representative sample, then, is extremely important for getting correct information on the population as a whole.

Questionnaires and Interviews   Given a representative sample, we can ask its members about their opinions, attitudes, or behavior. This is usually done by using self-administered questionnaires, personal interviews, or telephone interviews.

In using *self-administered questionnaires*, the researcher simply gives or sends the people in the sample a list of questions and asks them to fill in the answers themselves. Usually the list consists of true-false and multiple-choice questions. The respondents are asked to answer "yes," "no," or "don't know" or to check one of the answers such as "single," "married," "divorced," or "widowed." There are several advantages to this method. First, it costs the researcher relatively little time and money. Second, since the respondents are assured of their anonymity and fill out the questionnaires in privacy, they may answer the questions more honestly. Third, because they answer the same set of questions, all the respondents can easily be compared with one another as to their attitudes and reported behavior. Such comparison may enable us to know why some people do a certain thing while others do not.

The problem is that some people will not return the questionnaires. The usual way to tackle this problem is to send the subjects a follow-up letter or telephone them and ask them to please fill out the questionnaires. What if this and other remedies do not work and the amount of nonresponse remains substantial? Then the researcher must find out if

How important is a college education today—very important, fairly important, or not too important?

"We spent a lot of money educating him, so if you want Junior's opinion, you'll have to pay for it."

People usually cooperate when they are asked to participate in a personal interview. The interview can be structured, which requires respondents to choose among several standardized answers, or unstructured, which allows respondents to answer open-ended questions freely in their own words. Personal interviewing, however, may cost the researcher considerable time and money.

there is a significant difference in age, education, or some other characteristic between respondents and nonrespondents. If there is no difference, the study may be continued. If there is, the project may have to be scrapped—or modified by using some other survey method such as personal interviews.

Personal interviews may elicit greater response from the subjects than the mailed survey. Fewer people would refuse to cooperate when approached in person than when solicited by mail. Personal interviews may be either structured or unstructured. In **structured interviews** the researcher asks standardized questions that require respondents to choose from among several standardized answers. Because all the respondents are asked exactly the same questions in exactly the same way and are provided with exactly the same choice of answers, the researcher can compare the subjects with one another on the basis of which answers they choose. But some respondents may complain that it is impossible for them to answer the questions with the answers provided in the questionnaire because none of the answers adequately reflects their personal views. The researcher could get out of this problem by using an **unstructured interview,** in which open-ended questions are asked and the respondent is allowed to answer freely in the respondent's own words.

Whether structured or unstructured, personal interviews can cost much time and money. A complex study may require a bureaucracy with a swarm of administrators, field supervisors, interviewers, and sometimes even public relations personnel. Inter-

viewers must not only be paid for the hours spent in the field but also reimbursed for travel expenses. Interviews are often lengthy, and the interviewer may have to travel a long distance. In addition, the interviewer "may drive several miles to a respondent's home, find no one there, return to the research office, and drive back the next day—possibly finding no one there again" (Babbie, 1995). It is much more convenient to use *telephone interviews.* Such interviews have recently become very popular in survey research and are routinely used in many public opinion polls. An even more convenient method, computer-assisted telephone interviewing, has become increasingly popular. The U.S. Census Bureau and commercial survey firms are already using it.

Telephone interviews have certain disadvantages in comparison with face-to-face interviews. Because the interviewer cannot look the respondents in the eye, the respondents are less motivated and can more easily end the interview by simply hanging up. Another problem is that people are more distrustful when answering questions from a stranger they cannot see. They may suspect that the stranger has a hidden interest, perhaps posing as an interviewer in order to sell magazine subscriptions.

Observation

It is obvious from the preceding section that in surveys we depend on others to tell us what has happened. By contrast, in observation we rely on ourselves to go where the action is—and watch what is happening. There are two ways to observe an ongoing activity. In **detached observation** we observe as outsiders, from a distance, without getting involved. As detached observers, we may watch children playing in a schoolyard or bring them into a room and watch from behind a one-way mirror. Detached observation has the advantage of making it less likely that the subjects will be affected by the observer. But it has at least one disadvantage: the detached observer has difficulty perceiving and understanding subtle communication among the

Detached observation is one method of gathering data. From behind a one-way mirror, researchers here unobtrusively note interactions among preschool children. Since the subjects can be themselves, they behave as they would under normal circumstances, rather than changing their behavior to please the observer. This enhances the study's validity.

subjects. The detached observer behind a one-way mirror might not see some important facial expressions. The detached observer of a religious cult might never understand the emotions attached to particular symbols.

The second type of observation avoids this problem. In **participant observation** researchers take part in the activities of the group they are studying. Sometimes they conceal their identity as researchers when they join the group. This enhances the chances that the unknowing subjects will act naturally. If the subjects knew they were being observed, they might change their behavior. As members of the group, the researchers have the opportunity to observe practically everything, including whatever secret activities are hidden from outsiders. As a result, the researchers could discover some surprising facts about their subjects. Consider, for example, the following case of participant observation involving a concealed researcher identity.

Most people assume that if men engage in homosexual acts, they must be homosexuals. If you make this assumption, the results of Laud Humphreys's (1970) classic research may surprise you. Humphreys concealed his identity as a researcher by offering to serve as a lookout for men engaging in homosexual activity in public restrooms, so that the police would

not arrest them. Without being suspected of being an outsider, Humphreys also succeeded in secretly jotting down his subjects' automobile license plate numbers, which he used to trace their addresses. A year later, he disguised himself, visited those men at their homes, and found that they were mostly conservative lower-class married men who were seeking the homosexual experience as a means of releasing tension. They considered themselves straight and masculine. Humphreys has been severely criticized for being unethical in his use of deception. He has argued, though, that had he not concealed his identity, it would have been impossible to get scientifically accurate information, because his subjects would have behaved differently or would have refused to be studied.

Many sociologists do identify themselves as researchers to the people they study, as Liebow did in his study of homeless women. They do not worry that their true identity will change their subjects' behavior. They are not overly concerned that subjects would hide secrets from them. Usually they strive to minimize these problems by not getting too deeply involved with their subjects while simultaneously establishing a good rapport with them. This is not easy to accomplish, though. Nevertheless, such efforts have paid off, as can be indicated by some sociological insights that have emerged from their works. Herbert Gans (1982a), for example, became a participant observer in a poor Italian neighborhood in Boston in the late 1950s. On the surface the neighborhood looked like a badly organized place, an urban jungle. Yet Gans discovered that it was a well-organized community, an urban village, where the residents enjoyed close social relationships with one another (also see box, p. 35).

Whether carried out with detachment, with participation as a disguised member, or with participation as a known researcher, observation has the advantage of providing firsthand experience with natural, real-life situations. The wealth of findings derived from this experience are useful for developing new theories. Gans' data, for example, can be used to suggest the theory that many poor neighbor-

American Mosaic

Participant observation is one of sociology's most important research methods. Having been used from the beginning of U.S. sociology, it is the favorite method of many sociologists who are trying to understand life in the urban ghetto. This reading describes the work of one of these sociologists—Elijah Anderson—who has spent many years trying to make sense of the inner city.

Learning from the Streets

At a recent conservative conference, former New York mayor Ed Koch was berating black leaders for failing to deal with black crime and illegitimacy. As recounted in the current *New Republic,* Koch said: "When I hear the words 'root causes,' I want to go to the nearest window, as Peter Finch did in *Network,* and yell, 'I'm mad as hell and I'm not going to take it anymore!'"

Well, Ed, find yourself a window. As demands for gun control and stiffer sentences escalate, author and sociologist Elijah Anderson is Mr. Root Cause himself. A University of Pennsylvania professor, Anderson has labored for decades in the confined world of university presses. Now his sharp-edged and disturbing explorations of the ghetto's psyche are gaining attention in the current debate over crime and welfare, even from conservatives who might scorn his conclusions. While others condemn "victimization" thinking and call for ending welfare, Anderson blames the economy and racism for illegitimacy and crime. Create jobs for the poor, he argues, and you'll help break the "vicious cycle" of hopelessness and alienation—which produces the violence racking the cities.

His views sound almost old-fashioned these days, but they offer a compelling counterpoint to those arguing for the quick fix. Anderson practices what's known as the Chicago School of sociology. Instead of relying on sanitized statistics, Anderson dissects behavior the old-fashioned way—by observing. Journalist Nicholas Lemann, who writes on poverty issues, calls him one of the few prominent "street sociologists" today. In the 1970s Anderson practically lived for three years at Jelly's, a bar and liquor store in Chicago. His observations produced "A Place on the Corner," a classic in the ethnography of the black ghetto.

His latest writing, in *The Atlantic Monthly,* deconstructs how and why many inner-city residents fall into a world of drive-by shootings and seemingly unpro-

voked crime. Frustrated by the lack of jobs and desperately searching for a self-image, the ghetto poor organize their lives into an "oppositional culture," governed by what Anderson calls the "code of the streets." At the heart of this code is a pathological reverence for respect. The message youth receive from parents and friends: "Watch your back. If somebody messes with you, you got to pay them back. If someone disses [disrespects] you, you got to straighten them out."

The craving for respect, which turns into a thin-skinned quest to prove "manhood," inevitably leads to violence. While others may walk away from a slight, street youths are required under the code to show their "nerve"—by pulling a trigger or throwing a punch. "Many feel that it is acceptable to risk dying over the principle of respect," says Anderson. "In fact, among the hard-core street-oriented, the clear risk of violent death may be preferable to being 'dissed' by another."

Anderson also argues that the paucity of jobs is responsible for other urban ills, beginning with illegitimacy. Unable to financially support a family, many young men choose to wield their sexual prowess as evidence of manhood—leaving behind babies often doomed to troubled lives themselves. Conservatives like Charles Murray cite Anderson's picture of sexual wantonness to argue for eliminating welfare, an idea gaining adherents among politicians. But Anderson rejects that conclusion. He contends that young blacks don't make babies simply to get a welfare check; ending welfare would only leave inner-city residents poorer and wouldn't greatly reduce illegitimacy.

hoods in the city are actually well-organized communities. This very advantage, however, is also a disadvantage. Because rich findings from observation techniques are largely relevant to one particular case

study but not generalizable to other cases, they may not be used for testing theories. To test theories, sociologists usually use surveys, which we have discussed, or experiments.

Experiment

Actually, a theory can be tested only indirectly, not directly. It must be translated into a hypothesis or a series of related hypotheses that are directly testable—more specific statements that can be demonstrated to be either true or false. To test a hypothesis, researchers first specify what they assume to be the independent and dependent variables. Then they create a situation in which they can determine whether the *independent variable* causes the *dependent variable*. They are, in effect, conducting an **experiment**, a research operation in which the researcher manipulates variables so that their influence can be determined. Two researchers (Prerost and Brewer, 1980), for example, wanted to test the hypothesis that human crowding reduces the appreciation of humor. They assumed that if we find ourselves in a crowded situation, we tend to feel uncomfortable, which in turn makes it hard to laugh. To create a crowded condition, the experimenters put six college students in a relatively small room. They also put six other students in a larger room—a less crowded situation. Both groups were asked to rate 36 written jokes for funniness on a seven-point scale from 0 for "not funny at all" to 6 for "extremely funny." The researchers found what they had hypothesized: students under the cramped condition gave the jokes a lower rating than did those with more elbow room.

Quite often sociologists design controls to ensure that a hidden third variable is not producing the apparent effect of the independent variable. To do this, they generally select two groups of people who are similar in all respects except for the way they are treated in the experiment. One group, called the **experimental group**, is exposed to the independent variable; the second, called the **control group**, is not. If the researchers find that the experimental group differs from the control group with respect to the dependent variable, they may reasonably conclude that the independent variable is the cause of this effect.

Robert Rosenthal (1973) and his colleague Lenore Jacobson, for example, wanted to test the theory of the self-fulfilling prophecy. In applying this theory to the classroom, they hypothesized that teachers' expectations influence students' performance. That is, if a teacher considers certain students unintelligent and expects them to do poorly in class, the students will do poorly. If the teacher regards other students as intelligent and expects them to perform well, they will perform well. To test this hypothesis, Rosenthal and Jacobson gave all the children in an elementary school an IQ test. Then, *without looking at the test results*, they randomly chose a small number of children and told their teachers—falsely—that these children had scored very high on the test. The intention was to make the teachers expect these supposedly "bright" children to show remarkable success later in the year. Thus the experimental group consisted of these "bright" children, who were exposed to high teacher expectations; the control group included the rest of the pupils. Eight months later, the researchers went back to the school and gave all the children another test. They found that the experimental group did perform better than the control group. They concluded that teacher expectations (the independent variable) were indeed the cause of student performance (the dependent variable).

You may notice that the experiments just discussed were carried out in the classroom, that is, in the field. In these *field experiments*, the subjects could behave naturally. But it is still possible for the experimenter to unconsciously influence the subjects and make them behave unnaturally. This is what happened to one of the most famous field experiments in social science. It was carried out by Elton Mayo in the 1930s at the Hawthorne plant of Western Electric Company in Chicago (Roethlisberger and Dickson, 1939).

Mayo wanted to find out what kinds of incentives and work conditions would encourage workers to work harder. He first systematically changed the lighting, lunch hours, coffee breaks, methods of payment (salary versus piece rate), and the like. He was then surprised to find that no matter what changes were made, the workers increased their productivity. When the light was made brighter, they worked harder than before; but when it was made dimmer, they *also* worked harder. When they were given two or three coffee breaks, they increased their output; when they were not allowed any coffee break, they continued to increase their output. Mayo later discovered that the increased productivity was actually due to all the attention the workers were getting from the researcher. They felt that they were not mere cogs in a machine but instead respected for their work; hence, they reciprocated by working harder. The unintended impact of the researcher's presence on subjects' behavior is now known as the **Hawthorne effect**. Social scientists today strive to avoid it by using hidden cameras and tape recorders, or by using various means to prevent subjects from knowing they are being observed.

The Hawthorne effect is particularly threatening to *laboratory experiments*. Unlike the field experiment, which is carried out in a natural setting, the laboratory experiment is conducted under the artificial condition of a lab, where subjects are always aware of

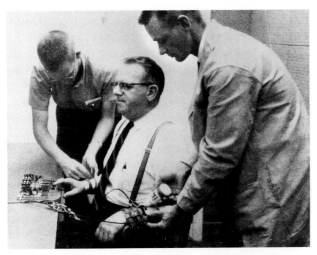

The laboratory experiment poses the problem of observing people in an artificial setting that can color their responses. In Stanley Milgram's famous experiment on obedience to authority, he devised an elaborate simulation to overcome artificiality. The subject, who activated an electric shock machine, believed that he was causing the other person to scream with pain. Actually, the machine was a fake, and the man who was screaming, shown here being attached to the machine, was acting.

being observed. A number of researchers have nevertheless managed to make their laboratory experiments as realistic as real-life situations. Stanley Milgram (1974), for example, told his subjects that he was running a test on the effects of punishment on learning. In fact, he was conducting an experiment on obedience to authority. After asking each of his subjects to assist in the experiment by taking the role of "teacher," Milgram introduced him or her to another subject playing the role of "student." Actually this "student" was Milgram's research associate. Then Milgram told the teacher to punish the student with an electric shock every time the student gave the wrong answer to a question. Whenever the subject (teacher) obeyed Milgram's command by pressing the shock machine, he or she heard the student screaming with pain. In reality, the shock machine was a fake and the student was faking, but all the subjects were led to believe that everything they did or heard was real. They trembled, sweated, and showed other signs of stress when "punishing" the student. Still, a large majority carried out Milgram's order, administering what they believed was great pain. This led Milgram to conclude that ordinary people will follow orders if they come from a legitimate authority, in the same way as the Nazi Germans did when told by their leaders to commit atrocities against the Jews.

The realism of Milgram's experiment should not blind us to the disadvantages of experiments as a whole. What happens inside a laboratory will not necessarily happen in the real world outside, where a multitude of other variables are at work. Moreover, most of the larger, important sociological issues cannot be studied through experiments. We cannot create and then study a race riot, a revolution, or a war. Nevertheless, compared with other methods, experiments give researchers more leeway to control and manipulate variables. As a result, by using experiments, they are better able to test theories by determining the relationship among variables.

Analysis of Existing Data

So far we have discussed methods for collecting data from scratch. Sometimes it is unnecessary to gather new information because there are "old" data lying around, which have been collected by someone else. Sometimes it is simply impossible to conduct an interview, observation, or experiment because the people we want to study are long dead. Thus sociologists often turn to analysis of existing data.

Secondary Analysis   In **secondary analysis** we search for new knowledge in the data collected earlier by another researcher or some public agency. Usually the original investigator has gathered the data for a specific purpose, and the secondary analyst uses them for something else. Suppose we want to study religious behavior by means of secondary analysis. We might get our data from an existing study of voting behavior conducted by a political scientist. This kind of research typically provides information on the voters' religion along with education, income, gender, and other social characteristics. The political scientist may try to find out from this research whether, among other things, men are more likely than women to vote in a presidential election and whether the more religious are more politically active than the less religious. As secondary analysts, we can find out from the same data whether women attend church more often than men.

Data suitable for secondary analysis are also available from government agencies. The use of these data has a long tradition. In his classic analysis of suicide in the 1890s, Emile Durkheim relied on official statistics in Europe. Today many U.S. sociologists employ statistics compiled by the U.S. Bureau of the Census for information on standards of living, migration, differences in incomes of ethnic and racial groups, birth and death rates, and a host of other facts about our society. The Federal Bureau of

Investigation, the National Center for Health Statistics, and the Department of Labor are among the other government agencies that provide important statistics. In addition, survey agencies such as the National Opinion Research Center, the Gallup poll, and other public opinion polls publish very useful information. The sources are practically endless. (See box, below, on understanding basic statistics.)

Sociologists can save much time and effort by using the information they need from these storehouses of existing data, but secondary analysis has at least two disadvantages. First, the available data may not be completely relevant to the subject being inves-

tigated because they have been assembled for different purposes. Data on the median U.S. income, for example, are often given for households, not individuals. If we want to compare the standard of living over the last 20 years, these data can be misleading: they are likely to show an abnormally higher standard of living in recent years because the number of two-income families has been expanding. Moreover, secondary data sometimes are not sufficiently accurate and reliable. Official statistics on crime, for example, overreport lower-class crimes and underreport crimes committed by members of the middle and upper classes.

UNDERSTANDING BASIC STATISTICS

Statistics are invaluable to sociologists. They use statistics to summarize data; to discover the characteristics of people or events as a group, rather than as separate entities; and to compare groups or events in order to find relationships between variables. To understand better how statistics are used, we will consider one type of statistic: measures of central tendency—that is, measures of what is *typical* or *average* for a group. These are among the most frequently used statistics.

Suppose we want to see whether income is related to gender and have the following information:

Income of males	Income of females
$6,000	$ 4,200
8,100	4,800
12,000	5,000
13,000	7,000
15,200	8,100
15,200	8,100
127,400	15,000

To determine whether gender and income are related, we need a measure that will tell us the typical or average income of males and of females. The three most frequently used measurements of average are the mode, the mean, and the median.

The mode is the figure that appears most often in a collection of data. Thus in this example the mode of the males' incomes is $15,200 because this figure appears twice while each of the other figures appears only once. The mode of the females' incomes is $8,100. These modes indicate that the males make more than the females.

The mode is the simplest measure of central tendency. But it gives very little information about the group as a whole, because many of the data are not

taken into account in computing it. By itself, it does not adequately represent the data. It is therefore misleading to compare these two groups on the basis of their modes of income alone.

Compared with the mode, the mean is more representative of the group, because all the data are taken into account in computing it. To calculate the mean, divide the total of all the figures by the number of cases. For example, the total of all the males' incomes is $196,900; the number of cases is 7. Dividing $196,900 by 7, we obtain the mean, $28,129. By using the same method, we find that the females' mean income is $7,457. Thus the mean incomes indicate that the male group makes much more than the female.

Like the mode, however, the mean can be misleading. Extreme values distort the picture it gives of the group. In this case, the males' much higher mean income is partly due to one unusually high income, namely, $127,400. Thus, the mean, because of this extreme case, still does not adequately represent the group as a whole.

Of the three types of average, the median is the figure most representative of the group. It characterizes the most typical person in the group. If we arrange the numbers from the lowest to highest value, as in our sample data, then the median is the number that falls in the middle of the data, with half of the numbers above (smaller than) it and the other half below (larger than) it. In this example, the males' median income is $13,000 and females' is $7,000. This clearly shows that males earn more than females, and we may tentatively conclude that there is a relationship between gender and income. For a full analysis, we would want to be sure that third variables are not producing this relationship.

Content Analysis The data for secondary analysis are usually quantitative, presented in the form of numbers, percentages, and other statistics, such as the *percentage* of women as compared to the *percentage* of men attending church once a week or the Protestants' suicide *rate* (number of suicides for every 100,000 people) as opposed to the Catholics' suicide *rate*. But some of the existing information is qualitative, in the form of words or ideas. This can be found in virtually all kinds of human communication—books, magazines, newspapers, movies, TV programs, speeches, letters, songs, laws, and so on. To study human behavior from these materials, sociologists often resort to **content analysis**, searching for specific words or ideas and turning them into numbers.

How can we carry out "this marvelous social alchemy" (Bailey, 1994) that transforms verbal documents into quantitative data? Suppose we want to know whether public attitudes toward sex have indeed changed significantly in the last 20 years. We may find the answer from comparing popular novels of today with those of the past to see if one is more erotic than the other. We first should decide what words will reflect the nature of eroticism. After we settle on a list of words such as "love," "kiss," and "embrace" to serve as indicators of eroticism, we will look for them in a novel. Finally, we will count the number of times those words appear on an average page, and the number will be used as the measure of how erotic the novel is. In repeating the same process with other novels, we will see which ones are more erotic.

Content analysis has the advantage of saving the researcher much time and money. Anybody can do a content analysis, as the materials are available in any school or public library. Even if we botch up a study, it is easier to redo it than is true with other methods. Other methods usually cost too much or are impossible to redo because the event under study no longer exists. A second advantage of content analysis is its unique suitability for historical research. It is like a time machine enabling us to visit people of another time. If we analyze the newspapers published in the last century, we can find out how the people of that period lived, which we cannot do with the other research methods. Finally, content analysis has the distinct advantage of being *unobtrusive*—the analyst cannot have any effect on the subject being studied. There is no way for a content analyst to influence, say, a novel, because it has already been written. On the other hand, the basic disadvantage of content analysis is its relative lack of validity. (**Validity** is the characteristic of a study measuring what it is supposed to measure—popularly known as accuracy.)

More specifically, the interpretation of a communication tends to be subjective and therefore does not necessarily reflect its true meaning (Babbie, 1995).

Having examined those four major research methods (summarized in Table 2.2, p. 40), let us now see how they can be used in conducting sociological studies (also see box, p. 41.)

Questions for Discussion and Review

1. Why do sociologists use surveys more than other kinds of research methods?
2. How does detached observation differ from participant observation?
3. Why does the Hawthorne effect threaten the validity of many laboratory experiments?
4. Where do sociologists find the data they use in secondary and content analysis?

STEPS IN CONDUCTING SOCIAL RESEARCH

When sociologists are doing descriptive research—trying to develop new information, they choose a problem and dig out as much information as possible. But when they are doing explanatory research—testing hypotheses—they usually follow a series of steps. Sociologists disagree about which steps should receive more attention than others, but most try to follow the sequence outlined here.

1. *Choosing a problem.* The first step is to decide what problem to investigate. To make this choice, we ask first if the problem involves something observable. How interesting is the topic? Will an investigation of this issue contribute to sociological knowledge as a whole? Can the knowledge acquired be put to practical use? Of course, researchers have different beliefs about the importance of each question, and some even consider them equally important. That is why a wide range of subjects is chosen for investigation.

2. *Formulating a hypothesis.* After choosing a subject, we formulate a hypothesis that tentatively describes a variable as the cause of some specified effect. Rosenthal and Jacobson, for example, hypothesized that teacher expectations were a cause of student performance. In looking for a hypothesis, researchers always review the existing theory and research on the problem. They may rely on their past observation of

TABLE 2.2
Major Research Methods in Sociology

Method	Characteristics	Advantages	Disadvantages
Survey	Selecting a representative sample of people and asking them to fill out questionnaires, interviewing them in person or on the phone	Self-administered questionnaires inexpensive and useful; greater response from subjects in personal interviews; phone interviews convenient	Questionnaires not returned; personal interviews costly in time and money; phone interviews discourage subjects' cooperation
Observation	Observing subjects' activities as a detached outsider, or as a participating member— identifying or concealing oneself as researcher to subjects	Providing firsthand experience with natural, real-life situations, useful for developing new theories	Findings largely relevant to one particular case, not generalizable to other cases nor useful for testing theories
Experiment	Manipulating variables to determine their influence on the subjects in the field or in a laboratory	Relatively easy to test theories by determining the relationship between independent and dependent variables	Observer's presence in the field may influence subjects; subjects may not behave the same outside the laboratory as inside
Analysis of existing data	Secondary analysis involves studying someone else's quantitative data; content analysis entails examining and converting qualitative into quantitative data	Both secondary and content analysis save much time and money; content analysis also unobtrusive to subjects and uniquely suitable for historical research	Both secondary and content analysis not sufficiently valid and reliable

the subject, or even speculate about how the phenomenon might have occurred. Still, they will review previous research so that they do not end up searching laboriously for a discovery that somebody else has already made. In formulating a hypothesis, we should make sure that it can be tested. This means that the cause of the problem (the independent variable) and the problem itself (the dependent variable) must be operationally defined. The hypothesis that demons cause suicide, for example, is not testable, because it is impossible to find an operational definition of a demon. But we could test Durkheim's hypothesis that a lack of social integration is a cause of suicide, because we can define the variables operationally. We can define the suicide rate (dependent variable) as that reported in official statistics, and we can specify the empirical indicator of a lack of social integration (the independent variable) as being divorced rather than married.

3. *Selecting a method.* To test the hypothesis, we choose a method to collect the necessary data. To make this decision, we ask questions such as: How appropriate is each method for this subject? What are the advantages and disadvantages of each? Will any of the potential methods require too much time or money? The survey method, for example, would be inappropriate for studying suicide because dead people cannot be interviewed, nor can they be observed or experimented with. Thus it is not surprising that Durkheim chose the method of secondary analysis when he studied suicide. Official records are not completely reliable because many suicides go unreported, but these records are easily available. All things considered, secondary analysis seems an appropriate method for studying suicide.

4. *Collecting the data.* Great care must be taken to ensure that the quality of the data is high. The means for ensuring quality depends on the method chosen. If the survey method is employed, the sample must be representative of the population to be studied. If we conduct an experiment, we must be careful that an artificial situation is not distorting the results. If we use secondary analysis, we must evaluate the accuracy of the information and avoid either reading too much into the data or missing relevant information. In general, controls are necessary to be sure that

ENRICHING OUR LIVES

Many sociological research strategies can be used for understanding others and improving our lives. This reading describes how college students seeking a job after graduation can undertake a wide variety of research to make a good choice. Notice how the author of the reading applies the techniques of survey research and analysis of existing data.

Researching Your Way to a Good Job

How do you begin a search for a good employer? Most books for job seekers begin with advice about the resume and cover letter. These two documents typically serve as a company's first impression of an applicant. If the impression is a good one, an invitation to a job interview may follow. Job experts often mention the importance of researching a company before going to an interview, maybe even before sending out the resume and cover letter. *Yes, researching a company is important.*

One of the benefits of research is that you begin to see how you might fit into a company and what you can offer to it. This is especially important as you begin preparing a cover letter and resume that will attract a company's attention and interest. A good cover letter can establish your interest in the company and the position available, demonstrate the value you can bring to the organization, and highlight your strengths and abilities. If you can show in the first paragraph that you have a personal interest in the company [because you are familiar with its activity], it adds an individual touch that attracts the reader's attention.

As a college student, you have a valuable advantage in researching prospective employers because campuses are filled with people dedicated to helping students make career choices. Your campus library has books and other materials containing company information; and reference librarians will guide you to the best places to start your research. Your teachers and advisors may be familiar with companies through community contacts or their research. Many faculty members have special insights as a result of consulting for a company or industry. Don't hesitate to ask for their advice.

What factors are important in evaluating a company or organization as a prospective employer?

Financial Data. Financial data are probably the most commonly sought company information. Every company researcher—and job hunters are no exception—gives this a high priority. One quick financial indication is whether a company is making a profit. But many good companies may have legitimate reasons for not making a profit. Start-up companies frequently take several years to show a profit.

Company Strategies and Goals. Look back at the company's activities over the past three to five years and look for a consistent pattern of corporate behavior. Other questions to consider might include the company's record on innovation. Does the company support new research to strengthen or broaden its product lines?

Industry Outlook. To have a full picture of a prospective employer, you must also look at the industry it competes in. Look, too, at the general economic conditions in which a company operates and how it responds to them. Start with the industry's competitive status. If it is facing tough foreign or domestic competition and has done so for several years, companies in that field are likely to be leaner and meaner than those in industries with little competition.

Excerpted from Karmen N. T. Crowther, *Researching Your Way to a Good Job.* New York: John Wiley and Sons, 1993, pp. 3 ff. ©1993 John Wiley & Sons, Inc. Reprinted by permission.

some third variables or prior causes are not responsible for a correlation.

5. *Analyzing the results.* While the popular saying holds that "the facts speak for themselves," by themselves facts are meaningless; they must be interpreted. If we find that Protestants have higher suicide rates than Catholics, we must ask why. In searching for an explanation, we should first make sure that the information is both valid and reliable. The finding that Protestants have more suicides than Catholics will be valid if Protestants do in fact have more suicides. It will not be valid if the researcher has misidentified many Catholics as Protestants or mistaken many homicides and accidental deaths for suicides. The finding will be reliable if the same result is obtained when the study is repeated. **Reliability,** popularly known as consistency, is the characteristic of a study producing the same finding when repeated. We may then explain the finding as

Durkheim did: because Protestantism encourages more individualism, Protestants are more likely to rely on themselves when faced with a personal crisis and are therefore more likely to kill themselves.

6. *Drawing a conclusion.* Finally, we must determine whether the data have confirmed or refuted our hypothesis and what this confirmation or refutation says about the theory from which the hypothesis was derived. We will also consider how the findings relate to the existing body of knowledge. If they contradict existing theories, we should suggest modifications in these theories and propose future research that might resolve the contradictions. Often, research raises new questions, which we should articulate. In the recent study of sexual behavior in U.S. society, for example, Robert Michael and his colleagues (1994) found that people are in general much less sexually liberal and active than many sex experts have assumed. The reason, according to these researchers, is that they studied a randomly selected, representative sample of U.S. adults whereas other studies had relied on biased samples of people more sexually active than average. However, more research with the same sampling technique is needed to determine the validity and reliability of Michael and his colleagues' data.

While the research process is presented as a series of steps, we should note that the sequence is usually circular (see Figure 2.2). When sociologists enter the process through step 1, they do not get their problem out of a hat. Instead, their choice is often influenced by what other researchers have done (step 6), work which they review shortly before embarking on the project or remember from graduate school. Thus, although the individual researcher completes a project at step 6, the process itself continues, starting with step 1 again.

This research process represents a deductive way of investigating social behavior. The **deductive approach** involves deriving specific observations from general ideas. Therefore, sociologists would follow these six steps only if they already have a theory or hypothesis they want to test. But the same research procedure does not apply if there is no preconceived theory. Liebow, whose study of homeless women was described at the beginning of this chapter, did not begin with an idea of what he should look for, but nonetheless ended up with some general idea about the life of homeless women. His research represents the inductive approach to social investigation. The **inductive approach** involves deriving general ideas from specific observations. Each of these two approaches reflects a strong connection between theory and research. Let us take a closer look at this connection in the following section.

Questions for Discussion and Review

1. What six steps do most sociologists use in conducting explanatory social research?
2. What should sociologists do with the conclusions they draw from a research project?

FIGURE 2.2
How Sociologists Do Research

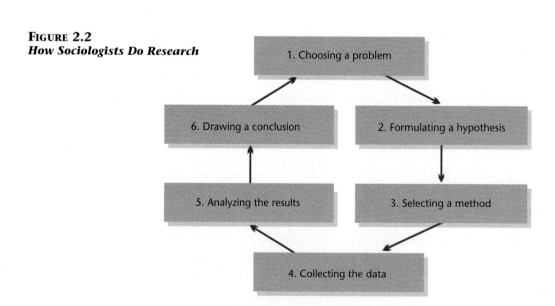

THE THEORY-RESEARCH CONNECTION

Social research may appear concerned only with seeking facts, but the real objective of social research consists of two parts. One is to *test* existing theories to see whether they are supported by data; the other is to *develop* new theories. To achieve the first, sociologists use the deductive approach. To realize the second, they use the inductive.

The Deductive Approach

In the deductive approach, sociologists start with three different types of ideas of what they expect to find in the social world. The first is *perspective,* which has the highest level of generality. The second is *theory*, which is less general or more specific. And the third is *hypothesis,* the most specific. Only hypotheses can be directly tested in research—that is, proven true or false. Thus sociologists must develop some hypotheses before they can do research. They usually derive these from a more general idea, namely, a theory. The theory in turn can be derived from an even more general idea, namely, a perspective. The relationship among the three types of ideas in a deductive process can be compared to the relationship among the three generations in a family. A perspective is like a grandparent, a theory a parent, and a hypothesis a grandchild. Just as many grandchildren can be descended from one parent, many hypotheses can be derived from one theory. Similarly, just as many parents can be descended from one grandparent, many theories can be derived from one perspective.

Consider the functionalist perspective, from which many theories can be derived. There are functionalist theories (often with other names) about different kinds of social behavior, groups, organizations, or institutions. One of these theories, found in Milgram's experiment discussed earlier, is the "obedience to authority" theory. This can be considered a functionalist theory because obedience to authority is an example of the social forces that help ensure social order, the key assumption of the functionalist perspective. From this theory many different hypotheses can be drawn. They may relate to how people obey authority in the military, in government, at home, in school, at work, on the street, and in countless other social situations. Milgram's hypothesis was that the ordinary people he recruited to be the subjects of his laboratory experiment would punish others with an electric shock when he told them to do so. The data supported the hypothesis.

This illustrates the deductive process of deriving a specific hypothesis from a general theory drawn in turn from an even more general perspective.

The Inductive Approach

Using the inductive approach, sociologists start with specific observations and then use them to develop general ideas about the social world. The researchers at Chicago's Hawthorne plant, mentioned earlier, initially used the deductive method by hypothesizing that a certain *physical* environment (in the form of incentives and working conditions) could cause employees to work harder. Instead, the researchers stumbled onto the "Hawthorne effect," the stimulating effect researcher presence has on worker productivity, suggesting that it was *social*, not physical, environment that increased productivity.

This specific observation was later taken to mean that the workers worked harder because they felt that management showed them concern and respect. Such an interpretation of the data has led to the development of the general theory of human relations, which can be applied to many different kinds of organizations (see Chapter 5: Groups and Organizations). Many of these human relations theories can in turn be developed into a general perspective similar to functionalism—because the theories share the assumption that the positive human relations in high-performing organizations reflect social consensus, interdependence, or cooperation.

The development of these perspectives and theories from the serendipitous observation of the Hawthorne effect demonstrates the inductive approach to social research. Sociologists often rely on the same approach in doing descriptive, exploratory, or qualitative research such as case studies or participant-observation studies to produce data that can be used to develop new theories and perspectives.

In short, both deductive and inductive approaches to social research reveal how general ideas lead to specific observations and vice versa (see Figure 2.3, p. 44). The three sociological perspectives also influence how sociologists conduct their research, as we will see in the next section.

Questions for Discussion and Review

1. How does theory support research?
2. How does research support theory?

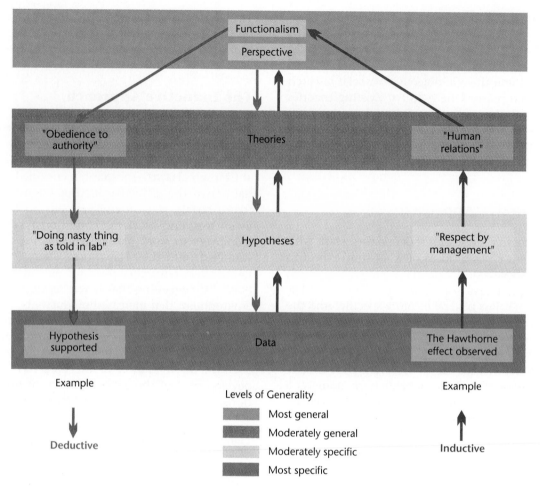

FIGURE 2.3
Deductive and Inductive Approaches

PERSPECTIVES ON SOCIAL RESEARCH

In the academic world, both the natural sciences (such as physics and biology) and the humanities (such as art and philosophy) seem to have influenced the three sociological perspectives in different ways.

Functionalist Perspective

Ever since sociology emerged as an academic discipline, functionalists have tried to adopt the scientific method, originally developed to deal with the physical world, and apply it to the study of people and their social world. The reason, according to functionalists, is that in some important ways people are like objects and nonhuman organisms. As Emile Durkheim (1895), a major founder of functionalism, proclaimed, "Social phenomena are things and ought

to be studied as things." To study social phenomena as things, the scientific method requires that the researcher be objective, just like the natural scientist. Any feelings the researcher has about the subject must be squashed. Otherwise, the study will be unscientific and distort the reality of social behavior. As Albion Small (1916), an early pioneer in U.S. sociology, stated, "to betray an emotional attitude with reference to human acts is as compromising as an exchange of mysticism for literalness would be in astronomy or physiology."

Also like natural scientists, social researchers are expected to be value-neutral, not concerned with whether the research result will help or hurt society. The fear is that such concern can distort perception, causing the researcher to see only what our life *should be* rather than what it *is*. Disagreeable facts, then, will be distorted or ignored. Social research is expected to focus only on acquiring accurate and reliable knowledge whether agreeable or not to the researcher. After the study is finished, the sociologist may use the knowledge to improve society but only as a concerned citizen, not by posing as an objective scientist.

Therefore, like natural scientists, functionalists tend to use the deductive approach by developing testable hypotheses from some theory. They then try to be as precise as possible in measuring the variables in the hypotheses. They would try to measure even complex feelings such as love and hate that cannot be meaningfully measured. Their motto seems to be "If we cannot measure, measure anyhow" (Krenz and Sax, 1986). Finally, they would use the most objective research methods, such as survey, detached observation, and experiment.

Conflict Perspective

Conflict theorists reject the notion of value neutrality as unreal. They argue that sociology cannot be value-free because the humanness of its subjects always arouses some feelings in sociologists. Unlike physical scientists, who can easily feel neutral about their nonhuman subjects, sociologists are more apt to feel positive or negative toward their human subjects. Such a feeling tends to show up in sociological research. Suppose we want to study prison life. We would look at it from the standpoint of either the prison administrators or the prison inmates, depending on where our sympathy lies. This personal value would also influence how the topic is defined, what research method is used, how the facts are collected, and what conclusions are drawn.

According to conflict theorists, the functionalist advocacy of value neutrality actually reflects tacit support for the status quo. Concerned only with studying the existing social condition *as it is*, functionalists do not bother to change it and thereby help to perpetuate it, in effect supporting it. By contrast, the conflict perspective, heavily influenced by its major founder Karl Marx (1818–1883), is critical of an existing society seen as full of exploitation of the weak by the strong (see Chapter 1: Thinking

It is easy to view those who have been jailed or imprisoned for crimes with disapproval or sympathy; either way, it is difficult to be completely neutral. Sociologists try to recognize their own biases, to keep them under control so their data are objective, and accurate. Functionalist sociologists in particular strive for objectivity in their research. While also trying to achieve reasonable objectivity, conflict sociologists reject the notion of value neutrality because of their own desire to transform the existing social order. Symbolic interactionists tend to reject the objective methods and choose instead those that are more subjective.

Sociologically). Thus social research is supposed to be *value-engaged,* designed to find ways to change the unjust social conditions.

While such activist values initiate and drive their research, conflict theorists nonetheless try to be reasonably objective in seeking facts to test their theories. Suppose it is suspected that racial discrimination in rental housing exists in a city. The conflict sociologist is likely to check out the suspicion by using an objective method to collect data. If the data turn out to be positive, the researcher will urge the victims and other advocates to end the discrimination by showing them how (Neuman, 1994). Usually, research on the negative aspects of society produces what conflict sociologists look for, but, according to functionalist critics, they are likely to exaggerate the extent or severity of the social problems they study because of what critics see as anti-establishment bias.

Symbolic Interactionist Perspective

Despite their opposition to the rigid application of natural science objectivity, conflict theorists still try to be reasonably objective. Symbolic interactionists, however, tend to reject the objective methods of studying human behavior and choose instead more subjective methods, especially participant observation. According to symbolic interactionists, scientific objectivity can only scratch the surface of human

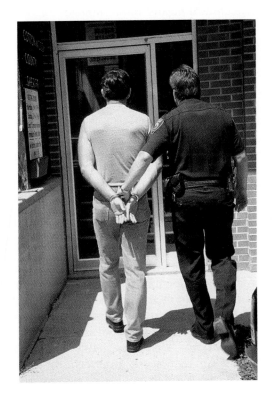

experiences, which mostly involve how people feel and look at the things that happen to them. To penetrate these experiences, *subjective interpretations* are thought to be necessary. This is why Max Weber, a major founder of interpretive sociology—similar to symbolic interactionism—advocated the use of the subjective approach, which requires understanding, empathy, intuition, sensitivity, or some other undefinable feeling for the people being studied.

Weber himself used the subjective approach to explain how early Protestantism, in particular Calvinism, led to the emergence of capitalism in Western societies. In Weber's view, the Calvinists believed in predestination but did not know whether they were predestined for salvation in heaven or punishment in hell. As a result, they felt quite anxious, which in turn caused them to believe that success through hard work was a sign of God's favor and therefore worked as hard as they could. Once they achieved success, they could not spend their money on worldly pleasures because their religion forbade it. They consequently saved and reinvested the savings in their businesses, and still worked hard to acquire new wealth. These practices and the accumulation of wealth eventually gave rise to capitalism.

How did Weber know that religious anxiety necessarily motivated the Calvinists to work hard rather than, say, become too discouraged to do anything but get drunk? Weber could only insist that good works "could be considered the most suitable means of counteracting feelings of religious anxiety. . . They are the technical means, not of purchasing salvation, but of getting rid of the fear of damnation" (Weber, 1930). But how did he know that? Apparently he *put himself in the Calvinists' shoes* and found that he could have the same fear about damnation if he believed in the same thing—predestination. The validity of this analogy from subjective experience can never be proved, but neither can it be disproved.

But today symbolic interactionists often directly interact and identify with subjects in order to understand social life from subjects' own perspective. As a result, they tend to find how different social life is from the one that typically emerges from objective research. While survey studies, for example, often suggest that unemployment causes robbery, subjective studies reveal a more personal reason. As Jack Katz (1988) found, virtually all robbers feel themselves "morally superior" to their victims, regarding their victims as fools or suckers who deserve to be robbed. If they want to rob somebody on the street, they would first ask the potential victim for the time, for directions, for a cigarette light, or for change. Each of these requests is intended to determine whether the person is a fool. The request for the time,

for example, first gives the robber the opportunity to know whether the prospective victim has an expensive watch. Compliance with the request, then, is taken to establish that the person is a fool and hence the right victim.

Questions for Discussion and Review

1. Why do functionalists insist on maintaining scientific objectivity and value neutrality?
2. What are the differences among the three perspectives on social research?

THE FEMINIST APPROACH

Since the late 1980s feminist sociologists have greatly contributed to a new way of doing social research. The motivation behind this contribution is a dissatisfaction with conventional research which, to feminists, tends to distort social reality. The basic reason is *androcentrism*—"male-centeredness" or bias against women (Harding, 1991; Reinharz, 1992). Conventional researchers often study the social world by studying only or mostly men. The failure to include women inevitably misrepresents the social world, in which women are as many and important as men. Looking at the data on occupations that often come out of androcentric research, we would see a world of work consisting mostly of men working to support their families as if they could do so *without* wives also working. The importance of women's work, including unpaid housework that makes men's paid work possible, is overlooked in androcentric research.

Related to androcentrism is *overgeneralization,* whereby the researcher unjustifiably applies the data on one gender to both genders. It would be valid to generalize from a finding about men to both men and women if both genders were socially equal, sharing the same social experiences in society. But this is not the case at all. Without taking into account the gender difference in social experiences, overgeneralization is bound to misrepresent a male-dominated society as a sexually equal one. The social realities of female exploitation through male domination, power, and privileges are therefore missing in androcentric research.

To get sociology away from androcentric research, feminists have studied various social experiences of women as well as men. Most of the research methods used are conventional ones such as survey, observation, experiment, and content analysis. But these methods are used differently in feminist research than in conventional, male-dominated research. One of the most prominent features of feminist research derives from the conflict perspective: an effort to create social change. Thus explicit policy recommendations routinely appear in feminist research. For example, after studying the continuing wage gap between women and men, Barbara Reskin (1988) recommends that the gap be narrowed by "increasing the costs men pay to maintain the status quo or rewarding men for dividing resources more equitably to reduce their resistance."

Another striking characteristic of feminist research involves using personal experiences as a valuable asset in research as well as identifying and establishing rapport with subjects. Usually, feminist researchers start with a personal problem, such as being both gainfully employed and doing housework, or a social issue that personally bothers them, such as the oppressive life of working-class women. The problem or issue is then investigated to seek understanding and solutions. As insiders to the experience of other women they study, feminist researchers believe that they can understand the subject better than "outsiders"—researchers without the experience (Reinharz, 1992).

Questions for Discussion and Review

1. According to feminists, what is wrong with conventional research?
2. What are the major characteristics of feminist research?

RESEARCH ETHICS

We have so far discussed the technical aspect of social research—the effective ways of doing research. But there is also an ethical aspect—the responsible ways of doing research. Sociologists generally follow the ethical guidelines set down by the American Sociological Association. The guidelines can be divided into three types (Singleton, Straits, and Straits, 1993).

The first guideline concerns responsibilities to *the profession*. Sociologists must report research findings fully, without leaving out significant data. They also must disclose details of their theories, methods, research designs, and data interpretations. Given these acts, it is possible to detect if the researcher tries to deceive the professional community. In short,

sociologists must be *honest*, or their profession's integrity would be in shambles.

The second type of ethical guidelines involves being responsible for the welfare of *research participants* in at least four ways. (1) Personal harm to subjects must be avoided. Subjects should not suffer personally (such as being humiliated or embarrassed), psychologically (experiencing stress or losing self-esteem), and socially (hating or losing trust in others). (2) If moderate harm is anticipated, subjects must give their informed consent. For the consent to be informed, the subject must be given enough information about the research. In Milgram's experiment, for example, subjects should have been told that they would feel stress and other similar unpleasant effects from participation in the study. (3) Subjects must not be deceived. Milgram, for example, should not have lied to his subjects by claiming to be studying the effects of punishment on learning while his real intent was to investigate obedience to authority. (4) Researchers must not invade subjects' privacy. Confidential information provided by research participants, for example, must not be divulged to others. If concealed devices such as one-way mirrors, cameras, or tape recorders are used, subjects must be kept anonymous.

The third type of ethical guidelines pertains to responsibilities to *the public*. Sociologists must refrain doing research that can be used to harm society, such as providing information for management to quiet labor unions or for the CIA to instigate or suppress revolutions in foreign countries.

While sociologists generally accept those guidelines, ethical problems can still exist. Some researchers lie to their subjects, as Humphreys and Milgram did. They justify these deceptions as necessary to their pursuit of knowledge. Otherwise, the subjects might refuse to be studied or their behavior might be altered in a way that would make the study useless. Some argue further that the knowledge gained outweighs the potential or real harm to the subjects and that the harm is insignificant. In almost all such cases, the worst that could happen to subjects of social research is only "slight embarrassment, bruised egos, umbrage, and ruffled vanity. . . the level of trauma that adults, college sophomores, infants, blacks, whites, the educated and the uneducated, the rich and the poor are able to sustain at no great cost" (Grimshaw, 1982).

But most sociologists find it morally offensive to harm or deceive subjects to achieve scientific ends. They also fear that deception by researchers can undermine public trust. Suspecting social researchers of being tricksters, subjects may lie, pretend to be naive, or do what they think the investigator expects them to do. If deception escalates, we may reach a point where there are no longer naive subjects, but only naive researchers, cranking out bogus data.

Questions for Discussion and Review

1. What ethical guidelines do most sociologists follow when conducting social research?
2. How do ethical problems still confront social researchers?

Psychiatrist Thomas Szasz once observed that when you put on a shirt, "if you button the first buttonhole to the second button, then it doesn't matter how careful you are the rest of the way." So it is with sociology. If the research is sloppy—if the sample is unrepresentative, the control inadequate, the observation biased, or the secondary data unreliable—then all the brilliant analyses in the world will not make things right. While the details of research studies are, for the most part, beyond the scope of this text, in the remaining chapters we will explore their conclusions.

CHAPTER REVIEW

1. *What are the purposes of social research?* As part of their efforts to contribute to sociological knowledge, sociologists conduct two kinds of research. One is descriptive research, intended to describe phenomena, which can stimulate new theories. The other is explanatory research, designed for testing existing theories. *What is the primary rule of social research?* All phenomena to be investigated must be observable in some way. Operational definitions are used to make unobservable phenomena observable and measurable.

2. *What are variables, and how can their causal relationship be determined?* Various events may be treated as variables if their characteristics vary from one individual or group to another within the population under investigation. The causal relationship between variables can be established if at least three conditions are met: the variables must be correlated, the independent variable must precede the dependent variable in time, and there must not be a third variable causing the correlation.

3. *What research methods do sociologists use?* Four major methods are: survey, which gathers information on a population through interviews or questionnaires; observation, which provides firsthand experience of the subject being studied; experiment, which allows the researcher to manipulate variables; and secondary and content analyses, which use existing data.

4. *What steps do social researchers follow?* Generally, they try to follow this sequence: (1) choose a problem, (2) formulate a testable hypothesis, (3) select an appropriate research method, (4) collect data, (5) analyze the result, and (6) draw a conclusion.

5. *What is the connection between theory and research?* Through the deductive approach to research, theory influences how research is to be carried out. Conversely, through the inductive approach, research influences how theory is to be developed.

6. *How do the three sociological perspectives influence social research?* The functionalist perspective encourages freedom from personal bias in research and from concern with the impact of research on society. The conflict perspective supports reasonable objectivity in social research but advocates research helpful for changing the status quo. The symbolic interactionist perspective largely focuses on the use of subjectivity in understanding social life.

7. *What is the feminist approach to social research?* It is made up of two major parts. One is a critique of conventional research as androcentric for excluding women and as unjustifiable for generalizing from data about one gender to both genders. The other is the incorporation of change-oriented values and personal experiences into most of the existing research methods.

8. *What are the ethical guidelines for conducting social research?* Researchers must protect the integrity of their profession, the welfare of their subjects, and the well-being of their society and the world.

KEY TERMS

Constant   A characteristic found in all members of the population being studied (p. 28).

Content analysis Searching for specific words or ideas and turning them into numbers (p. 39).

Control group The group that is not exposed to the independent variable (p. 36).

Correlation A consistent association between two or more variables, which may or may not be causal (p. 28).

Deductive approach Deriving specific observations from general ideas (p. 42).

Dependent variable A variable that is considered the effect of another variable (p. 27).

Descriptive research Research aimed at gathering information in order to simply describe a phenomenon (p. 27).

Detached observation A method of observation in which the researcher observes as an outsider, from a distance, without getting involved (p. 33).

Empirical indicator A concrete and observable representation of an abstract and unobservable concept (p. 27).

Experiment A research operation in which the researcher manipulates variables so that their influence can be determined (p. 36).

Experimental group The group that is exposed to the independent variable (p. 36).

Explanatory research Research designed to test a hypothesis in order to explain a phenomenon (p. 27).

Hawthorne effect The unintended impact of the researcher's presence on the subjects' behavior (p. 36).

Independent variable A variable that is the cause of another variable (p. 27).

Inductive approach Deriving general ideas from specific observations (p. 42).

Operational definition A specification of the action needed to translate what is abstract and unobservable into what is concrete and observable (p. 27).

Participant observation A method of observation in which the researcher takes part in the activities of the group being studied (p. 34).

Population The entire group of people to be studied (p. 31).

Reliability The characteristic of a study producing the same finding when repeated—popularly known as consistency (p. 41).

Sample A relatively small number of people selected from a larger population (p. 32).

Secondary analysis Searching for new knowledge in the data collected earlier by another researcher or some public agency (p. 37).

Spurious correlation An apparent but false correlation between two variables that are not causally related (p. 28).

Structured interview An interview in which the researcher asks standardized questions that require respondents to choose from among several standardized answers (p. 33).

Survey A research method that involves asking questions about opinions, beliefs, or behavior (p. 30).

Third variable A hidden variable responsible for the occurrence of a relation between two other variables that are not causally related (p. 28).

Unstructured interview An interview in which open-ended questions are asked and the respondent is allowed to answer freely in the respondent's own words (p. 33).

Validity The characteristic of a study measuring what it is supposed to measure—popularly known as accuracy (p. 39).

Variable A characteristic that varies from people to people within the population being studied (p. 27).

SUGGESTED READINGS

Harding, Sandra. 1991. *Whose Science? Whose Knowledge?* Ithaca, N.Y.: Cornell University Press. Provides an intriguing critique of conventional male-dominated research as well as a provocative argument of why feminist research is more accurate in capturing social reality.

Henry, Gary T. 1990. *Practical Sampling.* Newbury Park, Calif.: Sage. A useful guide on how to draw samples.

Hoover, Kenneth R. 1995. *The Elements of Social Scientific Thinking,* 6th ed. New York: St. Martin's. A short, readable introduction to the research process; excellent for beginning students.

Reinharz, Shulamit. 1992. *Feminist Methods in Social Research.* New York: Oxford University Press. Covers a wide range of specific methods in feminist research.

Wolcott, Harry F. 1990. *Writing Up Qualitative Research.* Newbury Park, Calif.: Sage. A small, well-written text on how to report findings from descriptive research.

3

CULTURE

Myths and Realities

MYTH: *Laws by themselves can effectively control people's behavior.*
REALITY: Without the strong backing from popular beliefs, laws are difficult to enforce.

MYTH: *People in the U.S. have given up the work ethic. They are more interested in having fun than in working hard.*
REALITY: They now work harder than before, having increased their work week from 40.6 hours 15 years ago to 46.8 hours today. While working harder, though, they also enjoy themselves more—on the job and off.

MYTH: *Language, aside from being useful for communication, is only a tool for people to express their thoughts.*
REALITY: Language is more than a tool. It can determine, or at least influence, how we think. It can be a source of our thoughts.

MYTH: *The values that the West considers highly important, such as human rights, individualism, equality, and liberty, must be popular with the rest of the world.*
REALITY: An analysis of 100 studies on cultural values in different societies concludes that "the values that are most important in the West are least important worldwide."

atoru Seo works in Toyota's Motomachi plant in Toyota City, Japan. He earns $75,000 a year. But since most things cost much more in Japan than in the United States, the standard of living for Seo—and other Japanese workers—is considerably lower. He lives with his wife and three children in a small house, which has a tiny kitchen, a postage-stamp garden, and no central heating. Nevertheless, Seo works very hard. Like most Japanese, he toils six days a week, putting in about six weeks more each year than his U.S. counterparts, 14 weeks more than West Germans, and 17 more than Swedes. He rarely takes his allotted vacation. He keeps plugging away for his company even when he suffers back pain, wrist ailments, and other invisible injuries. Working excessively, Seo risks becoming a victim of *karoshi* (death by overwork), which has happened to thousands of workers in Japan in recent years (Schor, 1991; Chipello and Templin, 1992).

Why do Seo and other Japanese work so hard? The reason has much to do with Japan's group-oriented *culture*, which considers groups more important than individuals. Thus Japanese work hard because they are socially pressured to do so—or out of a sense of obligation to their company. They are not as likely as their U.S. peers to work hard because they want to or out of a desire for self-fulfillment. Not surprisingly, a poll indicated that 11 percent of the Japanese respondents said that, given the choice they would not work, a preference chosen by only four percent of the U.S. respondents (Lehner, 1992).

What, then, is culture, which can influence people's work and attitudes about work? **Culture** is a design for living or, more precisely, a complex whole consisting of objects, values, and other characteristics that people acquire as members of society. When sociologists talk about cultures, they are not talking about sophistication or knowledge of the opera, literature, or other fine arts. While only a small portion of a population may be sophisticated, all members of a society possess a culture. Neither is culture the same as society, although the two terms are often used interchangeably. Society consists of people interacting with one another as citizens of the same country. But culture consists of (1) abstract entities—such as ideas—that influence people and (2) tangible, human-made objects that reflect those ideas. The tangible objects make up what is called the **material culture**, which includes every conceivable kind of physical object produced by humans, from spears and plows to cooking pots and houses. Objects reflect the nature of the society in which they were made. If archaeologists find that an ancient society made many elaborate, finely worked weapons, then they have reason to believe that warfare was important to that society. In their study of contemporary societies, however, sociologists are more interested in **nonmaterial culture**, the intangible aspect of culture. It includes *knowledge and beliefs* (its cognitive component), *norms and values* (normative component), and *signs and language* (symbolic component).

In this chapter, we begin by examining those three components of culture. Then we will discuss the cultural dynamics in the United States, the global aspects of culture, and sociological perspectives on culture.

THE COGNITIVE COMPONENT

Culture helps us develop certain knowledge and beliefs about what goes on around us. **Knowledge** is a collection of relatively objective ideas and facts about our physical and social worlds. Knowledge can be turned into technology, and as such it can be used for controlling the natural environment and for dealing with social problems. The high standard of living in modern societies may be attributed to their advanced knowledge and sophisticated technology. Knowledge is best exemplified by science, which we discuss more extensively in Chapter 20 (Science and Medicine). On the other hand, **beliefs** are ideas that are more subjective, unreliable, or unverifiable. They may include, for example, the idea that God controls our lives. The best example of beliefs is religion, which we discuss in Chapter 17 (Religion).

THE NORMATIVE COMPONENT

Each culture has its own idea not only about what is important in the world but also about how people should act. This is the normative component of a culture, made up of its norms and values. **Values** are socially shared ideas about what is good, desirable, or important. These shared ideas are usually the basis of a society's **norms**, social rules that specify how people should behave. While norms are specific rules dictating how people should act in a particular situation, values are the general ideas that support the norms. Thus the specific U.S. norm against imprisoning people without a trial is based on the general U.S. value of freedom. Parents are required by a norm to send their children to school because society places a high value on mass education. We are allowed to criticize our government because we value freedom of speech. Even a norm as mundane as that against pushing to the head of a line is derived from a general value, one that emphasizes fairness and equal treatment for all.

Values and norms also vary from culture to culture. Because they are subjective, a value and its norms considered good in one society may appear bad in another. If someone says to us, "You have done an excellent job!" a U.S. norm requires that we say "Thank you." This may be traced to the value our society places on fair exchange: you scratch my back and I'll scratch yours, so if you praise me I'll thank you for it. In China, however, the same praise will elicit a self-effacing response like "Oh, no, not at all" or "No, I've done poorly." The reason is that humility ranks high in the Chinese value system. Thus, we might consider the Chinese odd for being unappreciative, and the Chinese might regard us as arrogant for being immodest.

Values and norms also change together over time. Forty years ago, most people in the U.S. supported the norm of school segregation because they valued racial inequality. Today the norm has given way to school integration because the value has leaned toward racial equality. In China before the late 1970s, ideological purity ("We would rather have a poor country under socialism than a rich one under capitalism") was the country's reigning value. One of its resulting norms was to send professors, students, scientists, and other intellectuals to farms to learn equality from the peasants. After the late 1970s, the new value of pragmatism ("It doesn't matter if the cat is white or black as long as it catches mice") took over, and one of its accompanying norms has been to send many intellectuals abroad to learn modernization from the West.

Norms

Day in and day out, we conform to norms. They affect all aspects of our lives. As a result, we are usually not aware of them. If someone asked why we say "Hi" when greeting a friend, we might be inclined to answer, "How else?" or "What a silly question!" We hardly recognize that we are following a U.S. norm. This fact will dawn on us if we discover that people in other societies follow quite different customs. Tibetans and Bhutanese, for example, greet their friends by sticking out their tongues. They are simply following their own norms.

These norms are **folkways**, weak norms that specify expectations about proper behavior. It's no big

Sometimes norms persist even after the values from which they are derived have changed. The norm of showering a bride and groom with rice after a wedding can be traced back to the high value our ancestors placed on fertility. Today we hardly expect newlyweds to have numerous children, but the custom of throwing rice continues to be common.

deal if we violate folkways; nobody would punish us severely. The worst might be that people would consider us uncouth, peculiar, or eccentric—not immoral, wicked, or criminal. Often society turns a blind eye to violations of folkways. When we go to a wedding reception, we are expected to bring a gift, dress formally, remain silent and attentive during the ceremony, and so on. If we violate any of these folkways, people may raise their eyebrows, but they are not going to ship us off to jail.

Much stronger norms than folkways are mores (pronounced *mor-ayz*). **Mores** are strong norms that specify normal behavior and constitute demands, not just expectations. Violations of mores will be severely punished. Fighting with the bridegroom, beating some guests, and kidnapping the bride are violations of mores, and the offender will be dealt with harshly. Less shocking but still serious misbehaviors, such as car theft, shoplifting, vandalism, and prostitution, also represent violations of mores. In modern societies, most mores are formalized into **laws**, norms that are specified formally in writing and backed by the power of the state. Violations of these mores are also considered illegal or criminal acts, punishable under the law. Some folkways—such as driving safely, mowing the lawn, or no liquor sale on Sundays—may also be turned into laws. Laws can effectively control our behavior if they are strongly supported by popular beliefs. If there is not enough normative support, the laws are hard to enforce, as in the case of legal prohibitions against prostitution, gambling, and teenage drinking.

In fact, all kinds of norms play an important role in controlling behavior, and society has various methods of enforcing them. These enforcement measures are called **sanctions**, rewards for conformity to norms or punishments for violation of norms. Positive sanctions, or rewards, range from a word of approval for helping a child across a street to public adulation for rescuing someone trapped in a burning building. Negative sanctions, or punishments, can be as mild as a dirty look for heckling a speaker or as severe as execution for murder. Some sanctions are applied by formal agents of social control such as the police, but most often sanctions are applied informally by parents, neighbors, strangers, and so on.

Values

By regularly rewarding good actions and punishing bad ones, the agents of social control seek to condition us to obey society's norms. If they are successful, obedience becomes habitual and automatic. We obey the norms even when no one is around to reward or punish us, even when we are not thinking of possible rewards and punishments. But human beings are very complicated and not easily conditioned, as animals are, by rewards and punishments alone. Thus, sanctions are not sufficient to produce the widespread, day-to-day conformity to norms that occurs in societies all over the world. To obtain this level of conformity, something more is needed: the values of the culture.

Characteristics of Values Because norms are derived from values, we are likely to abide by a society's norms if we believe in its underlying values. If we believe in the value our society places on freedom of religion, we are likely to follow the norm against religious intolerance. If employers cling to the traditional belief that a woman's place is in the home, they will violate the norm against job discrimination by not hiring married women. In developing countries, parents often carry on the norm of producing many babies because they continue to subscribe to the traditional value of big, extended families. There are at least three reasons why values have such power over behavior: (1) our parents, teachers, and other socializing agents (see Chapter 7: Socialization) teach us our society's values so that we feel it is right and natural to obey its norms; (2) values contain an element of moral persuasion: the achievement value, for example, in effect says, "It's good to be a winner; it's bad to be a loser"; (3) values carry implied sanctions against people who reject them (Spates, 1983).

People are not always conscious of the values instilled in them, nor do they always know why they obey norms. Sometimes norms persist even after the values from which they are derived have changed. Why, for example, do we shower a bride and groom with rice after a wedding? It seems the proper thing to do, or a pleasant thing to do, or a vague sign of wishing the newlyweds well. In fact, the norm is derived from the high value our ancestors placed on fertility, which was symbolized by rice. Over time a norm can become separated from the value that inspired it and come to be valued in itself. We may follow the norm simply because it seems the right thing to do.

Values are not directly observable, but we can infer them from the way people carry out norms. When we see that the Japanese treat their old people with respect, we can safely infer that they put great value on old age. When we learn that the Comanche Indians were expected to save their mothers-in-law during a raid by an enemy before trying to save their own lives, then we conclude that the Comanche placed a high value on mothers-in-law. When we see that many U.S. women are dieting, some to the point of becoming anorexic, we know that our culture places an enormous value on slenderness as the model for feminine beauty (Mazur, 1986).

U.S. Values According to Robin Williams (1970), 15 basic values dominate U.S. culture: success, hard work, efficiency, material comfort, morality, humanitarianism, progress, science, external conformity, individualism, in-group superiority, equality, freedom, patriotism, and democracy. Most of these values, such as success, hard work, and efficiency, are clearly related to one another, showing **cultural integration**, the joining of various values into a coherent whole. But at the same time the integration is never perfect in any society. If you take another look at Williams' list of U.S. values, you will see that the value given to *efficiency and success* often clashes with considerations of *morality* in the business world: Should companies pursuing efficiency and success sell unsafe products, engage in deceptive advertising, or violate price-fixing laws? Or should they resist these immoralities and risk losing out to competitors? The conflict between efficiency/success and morality shows a lack of cultural integration. But this should not be surprising in the cultures of large, modern industrial societies generally less integrated than those of small, traditional ones (Archer, 1985).

Moreover, some of the values Williams identified have been changing. For example, people work harder than ever before. In the past 15 years, the

Values sometimes clash. Although most of us probably conform to the rule of showing respect for the flag, and many would want to see a law prohibiting flag burning, U.S. culture also values freedom and individualism.

typical adult's leisure time has shrunk by 40 percent—down from 26.6 hours to 16.6 hours a week—and the work week has swelled by 15 percent—up from 40.6 hours to 46.8 hours (Lipset, 1990b). A more recent study also shows U.S. adults working much harder as a result of the greater demands of employers and the rise of addictive consumerism (Schor, 1991). They also seem to enjoy themselves more—on the job and off. As we saw in the opening of this chapter, a large majority said they would continue to work even if they did not have to. They also spend more time in pursuit of leisure, as indicated by the significant increase in personal expenditures on recreation over the last decade (Census Bureau, 1994).

Related to working harder is a greater interest in individual success. Concern with this personal value, however, has apparently caused a decline in community life and social responsibility. In relentlessly pursuing their personal ambitions, many people have little or no time left for their families, friends, and communities, finding themselves "suspended in glorious, but terrifying, isolation" (Bellah et al., 1986). Moreover, increased concern with one's own welfare has developed a strong sense of individual rights but a weak sense of obligation to the community. In reaction, a group of social thinkers called "communitarians" have emerged to encourage social responsibility. Many individuals try to move beyond the isolated self by spending more time with the family, seeking meaningful rather than casual relationships, and working to improve community life (Etzioni, 1993).

"Ideal" and "Real" Culture

Values and norms are by themselves merely "ideal," consisting of ideas inside our heads regarding what we *believe* to be good and what we *should* do. They are not actual behavior. But most people most of the time do behave in accordance with the values and norms of their society. Thus the values and norms can also be "real," supported by actual behavior. But sometimes most people do violate their society's norms and values, failing to practice what they believe in.

Consider basic traffic rules. Virtually all of us believe that drivers should stop for a stop sign or a red light, should not exceed the speed limit, should not double park, and so on. But nearly every driver occasionally if not frequently fails to obey those rules. Sociologists call this **institutionalized deviance**, norm violation that is so prevalent it has become socially acceptable. Institutionalized deviance reflects the failure of an "ideal" culture to

turn into a "real" one. Therefore, if we want to find out whether a culture is also real rather than merely ideal, we must not simply ask people what they believe in but also must supplement the questions with observations of what they do. The questions produce the ideal, while the observations yield the real. Both are essential to understanding a culture (Whiteford and Friedl, 1992).

Questions for Discussion and Review

1. How do sociologists define "culture" differently than the general public would?
2. What are cultural values and norms, and how do they combine with sanctions to control people's behavior?
3. How do folkways differ from mores?
4. To what extent do your personal values agree with the list of cultural views identified by Williams?
5. How does real culture differ from ideal culture?

THE SYMBOLIC COMPONENT

The components of culture that we have discussed so far—norms and values as well as knowledge and beliefs—cannot exist without symbols. A **symbol** is a word, gesture, music, or anything that stands for some other thing.

The Importance of Symbols

Symbols enable us to create, communicate and share, and transmit to the next generation the other components of culture. It is through symbols that we are immersed in culture and, in the process, become fully human. We can better appreciate the importance of symbols, and particularly language, from Helen Keller's (1954) account of her first step into the humanizing world of culture. Blind and deaf, she had been cut off from that world until, at the age of seven, she entered it through a word:

Someone was drawing water and my teacher placed my hand under the spout. As the cool stream gushed over one hand she spelled into the other the word water, first slowly, then rapidly. I stood still, my whole attention fixed upon the motion of her fingers. Suddenly I felt a misty consciousness as of something forgotten—a thrill of returning thought;

and somehow the mystery of language was revealed to me. I knew that "w-a-t-e-r" meant the wonderful cool something that was flowing over my hand. The living word awakened my soul, gave it light, hope, joy, set it free! There were barriers still, it is true, but barriers that could in time be swept away.

Once Helen Keller understood that her teacher's hand sign meant water, once she understood what a word was, she could share her world with others and enter into their world, because she could communicate through symbols. All words are symbols; they have meaning only when people agree on what they mean. Communication succeeds or fails depending on whether people agree or disagree on what their words mean. Helen Keller's experience is a vivid example of the general truth that almost all human communication occurs through the use of language.

The Influence of Language

According to many social scientists, language does more than enable us to communicate. It also influences the way we perceive the world around us. Edward Sapir (1929) was the first to hold this view. Human beings, he said, live "at the mercy of the particular language which has become the medium of expression for their society." Sapir also wrote that language has "a tyrannical hold upon our orientation to the world." When societies speak a different language, "the worlds in which societies live are distinct worlds, not merely the same world with different labels attached to it."

This view was developed by Sapir's student Benjamin Whorf (1956) and became known as the *Sapir-Whorf hypothesis*. It holds that language predisposes us to see the world in a certain way. Sometimes, the hypothesis is put even more strongly: language molds our minds, determining how we think about the world. Whorf found, for example, that the language of the Hopi Indians of the southwestern United States has neither verb tenses to distinguish the past and the present nor nouns for times, days, seasons, or years. Consequently, according to Whorf, Hopi- and English-speaking people perceive time differently. Although we see the difference between a person working *now* and the same person working *yesterday*, the Hopi do not because their language makes no distinction between past and present. In his novel *1984*, George Orwell (1949) provided a dramatic presentation of the possibilities of the Sapir-Whorf hypothesis. In the dictatorship portrayed in the novel, a language called *Newspeak* has been created. Among other things, Newspeak has no word for freedom, so that people cannot even think about freedom, much less want it.

The Sapir-Whorf hypothesis has nevertheless stirred controversy. A common criticism is that the hypothesis overemphasizes the power of language. According to the critics, language only influences—rather than determines—how we think. If language determined thought, people who spoke different languages would always think differently, and it would be impossible for us to comprehend English translations of foreign languages. But the critics do admit that language does have some influence on cognition. This is why people who speak different languages sometimes think differently, so that they cannot see eye-to-eye on some issues. Virtually all social scientists, then, agree that language influences perception and thinking, though they disagree on how much the influence is.

The Sapir-Whorf hypothesis has further stimulated studies of language with the aim of understanding culture. An important finding is that the Garo of northeast India, who live in an environment full of ants, have more than a dozen words for different kinds of ants but no general term for "ant." The Garo apparently find it useful to distinguish one kind of ant from another. Ants play so small a role in our lives that our language makes no distinction between them. We lump them all together in one word, and to most of us one ant looks just like another. On the other hand, in the United States, which is full of cars, there are many different words for the automobile, such as *sedan, convertible, coupe, fastback, wagon, bus, van, truck,* and so on. To people in another society with few automobiles, a car is a car, period (Whiteford and Friedl, 1992).

Question for Discussion and Review

1. How does the language you use influence the way you see the world?

in West
opera was, + is
in Germany

U.S. POP CULTURE

Like language, popular culture is part of the symbolic component of culture. **Popular culture** consists of relatively unsophisticated artistic creations that appeal to the masses, such as movies, TV shows, musical performances, and other entertainments that attract large audiences. Popular culture reflects as well as influences society.

A Mirror of the Status Quo

In 1992 then Vice President Dan Quayle publicly criticized prime-time television for promoting single motherhood when famous TV character Murphy Brown bore a child out of wedlock. He saw moral decay in U.S. pop culture, but analysis reveals otherwise.

Unwed mothers rarely appear on prime-time TV—Murphy Brown is an exception but she does not represent most real-life unwed mothers who tend to be very young or poor. The virtual absence of poor unwed mothers as TV characters reflects the popular belief that they are immoral and thus a threat to traditional family values. A similar belief about homosexual couples also keeps them almost entirely off prime-time television. Instead, what is routinely presented is the traditional family: a heterosexual, monogamous couple and their children with considerable familial love.

"The Cosby Show," which debuted in 1984 and ended in 1992, portrays the traditional two-parent family. So do the overwhelming majority of today's TV shows, such as "Home Improvement," "Dave's World," and "All-American Girl." Even most of the main characters of such hip shows as "Beverly Hills 90210" and "The Fresh Prince of Bel-Air" have strong families. The very few single parents on TV frequently have other caring adults, such as the three fathers in "Full House," to strengthen the pro-family message. What about "Married . . . with Children," "The Simpsons," and "Roseanne?" They seem to attack the family, but actually the target of their sniping is television's sentimentalized portrayal of the family. For all the Bundys' cutting sarcasm, the Simpsons' "eat my shorts" irreverence, and Roseanne's biting wisecracks, they come through clearly as loving, cohesive families (Zoglin, 1992).

Popular movies and music may also seem morally offensive, with all their violence, sex, and raw language, but generally they reaffirm old values. Consider these top films: *Pretty Woman, Ghost, Goodfellas, Home Alone,* and *Jurassic Park.* They show, respectively, a Beverly Hills version of the old movie *My Fair Lady* starring a spirited prostitute with the proverbial heart of gold, a fantasy romanticizing widowhood, a classic gangster story, a funny kid caper, and a resurrection of the old Frankenstein movie with dinosaurs. Providing escapist entertainment, all these movies support the status quo, just as the old ones did before the rebellious 1960s. What about the extremely violent, obscene, or subversive music from the "gangsta" rapper Ice Cube, various hard-core rockers, and heavy metal? Such music is far from being really *popular* culture. It attracts considerable

Analysis of popular culture shows that television does not present a threat to our social values but often mirrors them. Even most of the main characters of a hip show such as Beverly Hills 90210 have strong families.

media attention, but its appeal to music consumers is extremely limited, compared with the popularity of Whitney Houston's love songs, Arrested Development's hip-hop, R.E.M.'s "Everybody Hurts," and other basically pleasant music (Pareles, 1994). In short, today's popular movies, series TV, and music mirror the conservative, nonrebellious times in which we live.

Patriarchal Influence

From the feminist perspective we can also see how the popular culture reflects the patriarchy of our society. At the 1993 movie award ceremony, Hollywood ostentatiously paid a special tribute to women in movies, proclaiming "Oscar Celebrates Women and the Movies" as the theme of the widely watched ceremony. But the facts showed otherwise, prompting a female film critic to say, "That Oscar theme is a joke, because men are now playing *all* the best roles. They get the macho roles *and* the sweet-sensitive roles, and they play the sexual pinups too. The best woman's role of 1992 was in *The Crying Game,* and *that* was played by a man" (Corliss, 1993). Of course, women did play strong, exemplary idealists in *Passion Fish, Lorenzo's Oil, Howard's End, Indochine,* and *Love Field.* But such movies are rare, and, more importantly, fail to become box office hits.

The reason is that the audience, under the influence of patriarchy, prefer movies that put women in their place. That's why Hollywood tends to produce blockbuster movies (such as *Basic Instinct, Single White Female,* and *Indecent Proposal*) in which women play major roles as predators or sex kittens. Explaining the predator role, Jon Avnet, director of *Fried Green Tomatoes,* observes, "The general feeling is that if a woman is bright, aggressive and successful, she's got to be a bitch." Explaining the sex kitten role, Callie Khouri, screenwriter of the feminist buddy movie *Thelma & Louise,* says, "Hollywood is trying to resexualize its women back into submission ... The women who do best in this society are the ones who are the most complacent in the role of women as sexual commodity, be it Madonna, Julia Roberts or Sharon Stone" (Corliss, 1993).

Global Reach

As a reflection of U.S. society, the pop culture exerts a powerful influence on the world. U.S. movies, television, music, novels, and fashion have never been more dominant globally than in the 1990s. U.S. movies in particular are the most popular around the world. Of the world's 100 most-attended films in 1993, for example, 88 were made in the United States. These cultural products are now the United States' second-biggest export after aircraft (Rockwell, 1994).

This U.S. dominance has stirred up some fear that it may destroy the traditional values of foreign countries. Some critics even argue that the bone-crunching, eyeball-popping violence on the screen may provoke violence on the street. But the very popularity of U.S. movies reflects the nature of foreign cultures. Apparently, foreign audiences find the U.S. movie violence highly exciting, but regard it only as pure entertainment rather than as a model for actual violence. This may partly explain why street violence is relatively rare in Hong Kong, though the movies made there are even more violent than those made in the United States. Many foreign governments also do not seem as concerned as we are about movie violence. Fundamentalist Islamic governments, for example, often deface posters of semi-clothed women but not lurid pictures of mayhem. The U.S. films would not have become hits around the world if they did not respond well to the global need for highly exciting and entertaining violence.

Another indication of how U.S. movies respond to the cultures of foreign audiences is the globalization of Hollywood in the 1990s. The U.S. movie industry is no longer as parochial as it used to be. Nowadays the French and the Japanese own some U.S. studios or invest heavily in U.S. films. Hollywood gets half of its profits from abroad, and it "boasts an Austrian named Schwarzenegger as its biggest star, a Belgian named Van Damme close behind in action films, and a Chinese, Bruce Lee, as an honorable ancestor" (Rockwell, 1994).

Questions for Discussion and Review

1. What social conditions does the U.S. pop culture reflect?
2. How does the world react to the U.S. pop culture?

CULTURAL DYNAMICS

The pop culture and other aspects of U.S. culture will not remain the same for all time. They are bound to change sooner or later. The factors that tend to cause culture to change are most likely to occur in a highly diverse society such as ours.

Subcultures

Our diverse society has many **subcultures**, cultures within a larger culture. There is no total break between subcultures and the larger culture, because members of subcultures still share characteristics with others in the larger culture. As a subculture, college students in the United States have in common certain characteristics that set them apart, but they still share with other groups values such as a belief in the importance of success and progress, norms such as those against polygamy and murder, and much the same material culture. A person can thus be a member of both a subculture and the larger, dominant culture.

In a small nonindustrial society in which people have similar backgrounds, experiences, and occupations, there are few subcultures. People in these societies are primarily differentiated by gender, age, and class, so that they have only the male and female subcultures, adult and adolescent subcultures, and upper- and lower-class subcultures. In modern industrial societies, however, people are likely to be differentiated along many lines. There are not only differences in gender, age, and class but in ethnic, linguistic, religious, racial, regional, and occupational background, all of which may provide bases for sub-cultures. As Figure 3.1 suggests, there are many linguistic subcultures in the United States, with non-English or bilingual speakers more concentrated in the West and Southwest as well as Hawaii and Alaska.

These subcultures are **variant subcultures**, which merely differ from the dominant culture in some way. Their values are still basically acceptable to the society as a whole. On the other hand, there are **deviant subcultures**, which represent values unacceptable to the dominant culture and are generally considered illegal or criminal. Examples include the subcultures of professional criminals, prison inmates, delinquent gangs, drug users, and prostitutes. Similar to and yet different from deviant subcultures are **countercultures**, which represent values unacceptable to the dominant society but generally not considered illegal or criminal. A good example is the youth movement of the late 1960s, which included hippies, flower children, political activists, and rock fans. They believed in peace, love, and cooperation as opposed to militarism, competitiveness, and self-interest. Today's countercultures include the skinheads, the Ku Klux Klan, Satanists, various religious cults, and anti-government militias (Zellner, 1995).

FIGURE 3.1
Ethnic Subcultures in the United States
There are many ethnic subcultures in the United States, with non-English or bilingual speakers more concentrated in the West and Southwest as well as Hawaii and Alaska.

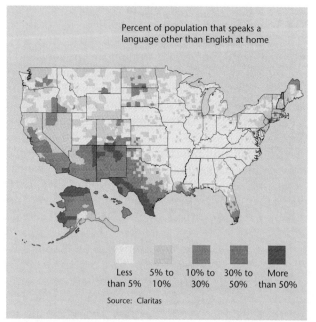

Percent of population that speaks a
language other than English at home

Less than 5% | 5% to 10% | 10% to 30% | 30% to 50% | More than 50%

Source: Claritas

Source: Time, January 30, 1995.

Multiculturalism

Various subcultures can develop into **multiculturalism**, a state in which all subcultures are equal to one another in the same society. Multiculturalism varies in degrees from one society to another. Switzerland seems to be among the most multicultural societies in view of the equality among its three subcultures—French, German, and Italian. Countries such as Bosnia where minorities are not only despised but often killed are the least multicultural. The United States is somewhere in between, perhaps closer to Switzerland than Bosnia.

Mindful of the U.S. democratic ideal of equality for all, African Americans, women, gays, and other minorities have since the early 1990s struggled to move multiculturalism closer to reality. They remind others of the fact that the United States is far from a "melting pot," where various subcultural groups are supposed to join together to form one single people as suggested by the U.S. national motto, *e pluribus unum,* or "out of many, one." Instead, the advocates of multiculturalism argue, minorities are forced to adopt the white European male subculture as if this subculture were superior to the others.

Consider, for example, U.S. history. Written mostly by white European males, it has for the last two centuries ignored minority contributions to the development of this nation and concentrated instead on the exploits of white European males. Moreover, many white European males such as Christopher Columbus were presented as heroes even though they had brought death, disease, and suffering to Native Americans, African Americans, and other minorities. To counter **Eurocentrism**, the view of the world from the standpoint of European culture, some multiculturalists have proposed the adoption of **Afrocentrism**, the view of the world from the standpoint of African culture. But most simply want better recognition of minority achievements and more realistic assessment of white-European-male actions than have so far been presented. This presumably would help create an egalitarian society where all subcultures will be treated as respectfully as the white-European-male subculture.

Some traditionalists have criticized multiculturalism for encouraging divisiveness in an already increasingly divisive society. Their reasoning is that members of each subculture would identify with only their own group rather than the whole nation. Intergroup conflict or even violence is expected to get worse. Other traditionalists have also criticized Afrocentrism for being as limiting as Eurocentrism because it is said to deprive black children of a wide range of views necessary for success in a highly diverse U.S. society.

ENRICHING OUR LIVES

The United States has become a multicultural nation, where people with diverse languages and lifestyles interact with each other. This diversity means that each of us needs to know more about other cultures. This reading describes how nurses who treat diverse patients can increase their cultural knowledge, and points to several strategies that all of us can use to better understand and serve others.

How to Enhance Our Cultural Competence

Trung Ho, an eight-year-old son of Vietnamese immigrants, was admitted for fluid and electrolyte replacement after two weeks of unremitting diarrhea. When his nurse performed an initial assessment, she noted ecchymoses on his abdomen. She reported this observation to her supervisor, expressing suspicion that the child had been physically abused. But through an interview with Trung's mother using an interpreter, the nurse determined that the boy was treated with a traditional Vietnamese folk remedy, *ventouse,* which involves placing a heated cup on the skin. It's believed that as the cup cools, it draws away excess energy or "wind" causing the illness.

Episodes like this promise to become commonplace as our patients grow more culturally and ethnically varied. As nurses, we're challenged to develop "cultural competence"—acceptance of and respect for cultural differences, sensitivity to how these differences influence relationships with patients, and the ability to devise strategies to better meet culturally diverse patients' needs.

Cross-cultural Communication

While it's important to show interest and warmth in interacting with patients, too friendly or casual a manner may be interpreted as intrusive. In many non-Western cultures, calling an elderly person by his first name is considered rude. Asking how a patient wishes to be addressed conveys respect and concern. Also be aware that in some cultures, such as Haitian, health-related matters are considered highly personal and not usually spoken of with strangers. To overcome this problem, you'll have to take the time to build rapport with the patient and establish trust.

Communication includes eye contact, facial expression, body posture, gestures, and touch, which people from different cultures may interpret differently. Cubans may appreciate physical expressions of caring such as hugging and kissing, but Native Americans or Southeast Asians may view them as intrusions into personal space. They may also consider it discourteous to make direct eye contact and stand too close to someone during conversation.

Acting as "Culture Broker"

Patients may turn to a wide variety of folk remedies prescribed or administered by family members or folk healers. How can you make sure that a patient choosing folk remedies accepts Western health care that may help him? You may need to act as a "culture broker," bridging the cultural gap by accommodating or even encouraging helpful beliefs and practices while persuading patients to reconsider harmful ones.

Consider the case of Maurice Joseph, a Haitian who had frequent episodes of headaches, dizziness, and listlessness but refused to see a neurologist. When the symptoms worsened, his daughter became quite worried and insisted he seek treatment. At a clinic visit, Mr. Joseph was interviewed by a Creole-speaking nurse, who asked him what he thought was causing his illness. Mr. Joseph explained that his symptoms resulted from a voodoo spell cast on him by a business rival, and that he had asked a voodoo priest to reverse the spell.

Knowing this, the nurse could persuade Mr. Joseph that he could see the neurologist and still seek help from the voodoo priest.

Steps to Cultural Competence

It's impossible to know the ways of life and practices of all cultural and ethnic groups you'll encounter. But you can develop cultural competence by cultivating certain knowledge and skills.

◆ *Keep an open mind.* Try to look at the world through the perspectives of culturally diverse peoples. Reading books (such as Maya Angelou's *I Know Why the Caged Bird Sings* [Bantam, 1983]) or seeing movies (such as *The Joy Luck Club*) may provide insight into other cultures.

◆ *Respect differences among peoples.* Recognize that every group has its strengths and weaknesses. Appreciate the inherent worth of diverse cultures, valuing them equally and not considering them inferior to your own.

◆ *Be willing to learn.* Cultural competence requires interest in other peoples' values, beliefs, and practices. Learn by getting to know culturally diverse peoples through traveling, reading, and attending events held by local ethnic or cultural organizations.

◆ *Learn to communicate effectively.* Cultural competence demands proficiency in verbal and nonverbal communication. Be sensitive to the nuances of language and expression, affect, posture, gestures, body movements, and use of personal space. Transcultural assessment can be performed effectively only if an atmosphere of trust exists between you and the patient.

Excerpted from Divina Grossman, "Enhancing Your 'Cultural Competence'," *American Journal of Nursing,* July 1994, pp. 59–62.

But such criticisms seem unwarranted. First, the divisiveness has largely stemmed from minority frustration born out of being treated as second-class citizens. Thus genuine recognition of minorities as equal to white European males may help reduce frustration and hence divisiveness. Second, critics are right for finding fault with Afrocentrism if it is offered as *the only* view for black school children to learn. But Afrocentrism—or any other minority-centered view—can be very useful if offered as *only one* of the many views available for learning. It not only can foster self-esteem but also can challenge Eurocentrists to stop ignoring minority contributions and exaggerating white European males' exploits.

In fact, appreciation of multiculturism has increased significantly in U.S. society. Commissioned by Congress to help bolster students' competency in core subjects, the university professors and schoolteachers of the National Standards for United States History published in late 1994 a multiculturalist teachers' guide for 5th through 12th graders. In the guide, the views and stories of blacks, Native Americans, women, and ordinary people are added to conventional history. "History comes alive with these stories," says the co-director of the project. "America's beginnings were not just a simple tale of civilization meeting savages. It was really far more messy and far more interesting" (Hancock, 1994). (Also see box, p. 61, for how all of us can better understand other cultures.)

Cultural Change

Every culture changes in order to adapt to the ever-changing physical and social environment. What, then, is in the environment that causes the growing acceptance of multiculturalism in the United States? An important cause can be found in the great increase over the last decade of non-white Americans, particularly those of Hispanic and Asian descent. But this population change itself may be related to at least three general factors in the environment that usually spark cultural change.

One is *technology*. Centuries ago improved printing technology helped decrease the cultural differences among social classes. Improved agricultural technology helped ignite the growth of U.S. cities. Modern transportation and communication make the world smaller, increase the contacts among cultures, and accelerate the pace of change. But technology also often creates **cultural lag**, the social situation in which a culture's values and beliefs fail to catch up with technology. Medical technology, for

example, is lowering death rates in many poor countries but traditional values and beliefs that favor having many children are not changing. The result of this cultural lag is overpopulation.

A second source of cultural change is *innovation*, the introduction of something new. The new thing may be an *invention*, such as the creation of the VCR or rap music, something that has not existed before. An innovation may also involve a *discovery*, something that has existed before but not known until now, such as the knowledge about HIV virus that causes AIDS. All innovations require intelligence and creativity, but even geniuses cannot innovate without the support of their culture. Einstein, for example, could not have come up with the theory of relativity if he had been born and raised in a preliterate, technologically simple society.

A third cause of cultural change is *diffusion*, the spread of things, ideas, beliefs, or some other cultural items from one society to another. Diffusion results from contact between societies. Generally, the more contacts a society establishes with others, the higher its rate of cultural change. The fast pace of change in the United States, for example, can be attributed to the numerous diverse cultures brought here by immigrants from around the world. By contrast, hunting-gathering people in South Africa and Australia have until recently survived by gathering wild plants and using spears for hunting, because they have long been isolated from the rest of the world (Chapter 4: Society).

Questions for Discussion and Review

1. What separates variant subcultures from deviant subcultures and countercultures?
2. According to advocates of multiculturalism, what is wrong with the "melting pot" concept of U.S. culture?
3. What causes cultural change?

A GLOBAL ANALYSIS OF CULTURE

The world is full of cultures. But why can't humans survive without cultures? Are cultures universally the same in some ways? Do cultural differences cause international conflict and violence? These are some of the questions of global significance that we will address here.

GLOBAL VILLAGE

"Apartheid" was a system of racial separation and domination that South Africa maintained for decades. But as the result of internal and external pressures, Apartheid has ended and South Africans are trying to create a new, integrated culture. This reading describes some of the real problems associated with this effort, including a clash of very different cultures.

A Jarring Mix of Cultures

What has happened to the Toasters?" I inquired of taxi-driver Joshua Manzini, referring to a criminal gang that terrorized Tembisa township.

"They're all dead," replied Manzini with a broad grin. "Members of the community killed each one of them with anything they could find." For Manzini, it was simple. The community had to protect itself.

Who was I to argue? The police force of the old regime had committed its share of atrocities in defense of apartheid.

While I know that part of the explanation for Tembisa's method of dealing with an external threat was a conditioned response to the violence and lack of a legitimate judicial system during the apartheid era, I was also sure part of the explanation had to do with the African sense of community and the lengths to which that community will go to preserve itself.

It is the cultural manifestations of this sense of community that have provided both the most rewarding and terrifying moments in 25 years of reporting on events in this diverse society.

Witnessing a ritual goat slaughter and feast was another jarring experience until I understood the healing role of the slaughter in the context of the African family—whether it is to celebrate a birth or wedding or to heal the wounds of a death in the family.

The sense of humanism and compassion—which is the essence of tribal values transposed into urban African culture—has often been overwhelming. Whether being received in the most modest African home, dancing in a wedding procession of a friend through Soweto, or witnessing the healing rituals of an African funeral, the sense of community is humbling for one reared in the individualistic ethic of Western culture.

How South Africans reconcile their diverse cultural influences will determine what kind of society emerges from the dramatic political transformation that culminated earlier this year in the installation of the first democratic government. "After years of (white) Afrikaner cultural domination, the challenge now is to develop an Afro-Western culture with which we can all identify," says Prof. John Makhene, development manager at the South African Broadcasting Corporation (SABC), a state-run corporation that is at the center of creating a new South African culture.

Excerpted from John Battersby, "A Jarring Mix of Cultures After Decades of Division," *The Christian Science Monitor*, September 14, 1994, p. 7.

Evolution and Culture

Culture not only surrounds all of us but becomes an important part of our very humanness. We are so dependent on culture that we cannot survive without it, though other animals can. Without culture we would not readily know how to prepare foods, work, raise children, live with other members of society, or do myriad other things. Why is culture so important to us but not to other animals? An answer can be found in our biological evolution.

About 14 million years ago, the rain forests where the apes' earliest ancestors had been living thinned out, creating a shortage of fruits and nuts. Some of the apes ventured into the savanna (grasslands) to search for new food sources such as seeds, roots, and finally the meat of other animals. The apes that remained in the forest evolved into today's chimps, gorillas, and orangutans. The savanna-dwelling apes evolved into our ancestors because the environment of the savanna forced them to develop a new set of characteristics (Leakey and Lewin, 1977).

On the savanna, it is useful to be able to stand upright in order to see over the tall grass to spot oncoming predators and to carry food to a home base. The savanna-dwelling apes who failed to develop an erect posture died out. Others became bipedal (standing on two legs), which freed their hands from walking, and so they could begin to make tools. At this time these apes began to evolve more quickly into humans. Toolmaking required intelligence and sensitive hands, and living together at a home base further required social interaction involving cooperation, sociability, and vocal communication (Rensberger, 1984). In other words, their new environment forced the erect-walking apes to develop those required physical and behavioral characteristics. Eventually, about 100,000 years ago, the apes that did not develop those characteristics became extinct, while the other apes that did survived as humans. At the same time, those very traits that made possible the emergence of humans also made possible the development of a complex culture.

The long evolutionary process has caused us to lose our **instincts**—biologically inherited traits that enable the carrier to perform complex tasks. Apparently our instincts, such as those for climbing trees like a monkey, gradually became extinct because they did not help our ancestors adapt to the radically new environment in the savanna—they were useful only for our other ancestors, left behind in the forests, to continue dealing in a fixed, automatic way with their relatively unchanging environment. Because we have no instincts, we need a culture to survive. This need is most clearly seen in human infants' long dependence on adults. Unlike newly born animals whose instincts enable them to be on their own in only a few hours or days, human infants must depend on adults for many years—until they have learned enough of the culture to fend for themselves.

We are, then, the only species that depends greatly on complex language, constant learning, sophisticated tools, and a flexible form of social organization—all of which are parts of culture—for survival. The loss of instincts has made us dependent on each other, and the resulting development of culture has also loosened our bondage to the natural environment. Thus we have adapted to vastly differing environments—from arid deserts and arctic wastelands to rugged mountains and dense rain forests—from which various forms of culture have emerged. In short, since evolution gave the human species the capacity for culture, we have moved farther and farther away from our evolutionary home. Today, we largely depend on culture rather than instincts to survive (Rindos, 1986).

Cultural Universals

Everywhere on the planet, human beings are the product of the same evolutionary process, and all of us have the same set of needs that must be met if we are to survive. Some, such as the need for food and shelter, are rooted in biology. Others—such as the need for clothing, complex communication, social order, and esthetic and spiritual experiences—are basic necessities of human social life. Human cultures are the means by which people everywhere meet these needs. Because these needs are universal, there are **cultural universals**—practices found in all cultures as the means for meeting the same human needs.

These universals appear in both material and nonmaterial culture. To meet their need for food, all peoples have some kind of food-getting technology, such as food gathering, hunting, or farming. To meet their need for shelter, people in all societies build some kind of housing, such as a grass hut, igloo, wooden house, or brick building. To meet their need for complex communication, all societies develop symbols and language. To meet their need for esthetic and religious experiences, peoples all over the world create art forms—such as music, painting, and literature—and believe in some kind of religion. In fact, George Murdock (1945) found more than 60 cultural universals, including incest taboos, myths, folklore, medicine, cooking, bodily adornment, feasting, dancing, and so on.

Since the early 1980s a new Darwinian theory called **sociobiology** has emerged to argue that human behavior is genetically determined. One of the sociobiologist's tasks is to explain how humans have acquired the cultural universals. In regard to incest taboos, for example, the leading sociobiologist Edward Wilson (1980) argues that "human beings are guided by an instinct based on genes" to avoid having sex with their mothers, fathers, or other close relatives. In order to perpetuate and multiply themselves, our genes in effect tell us to stay away from incest. If we do not, our offspring will become less fit than ourselves and less able to produce children. Through the logic of natural selection, then, individuals who avoid incest pass on their genes to more descendants than do those who practice incest. In other words, the prohibition on incest exists practically all over the world because it serves to maximize the fitness and reproductive success of humans.

Most sociologists, however, find the sociobiological argument difficult to accept. In their view, if humans were already compelled by their genes to avoid incest, why would virtually every society in the world bother to prohibit it? There are instead two

Cultural universals are practices found in all cultures as the means for meeting the same human needs. Dance, for example, has been created all over the world to meet the human need for aesthetic experiences.

sociological reasons for the incest taboo. First, the taboo brings about marital alliances among many groups that are useful for security against famine and foreign attack. Second, the taboo ensures family stability—without the taboo, sexual rivalry could tear the family apart. (More in Chapter 9: Sexual Behavior).

Culture Clash

While cultural universals reflect the *general* means by which all societies meet their common needs, the *specific* content of these means varies from culture to culture. For example, religion is a cultural universal, but its specific content varies from one culture to another, as can be seen in the differences among

Christianity, Islam, Judaism, Confucianism, and so on. These religions, along with other values, norms, and languages, constitute the specific cultures of various societies. These cultures can be classified into

JAPANESE
FOLK-HERO

FRENCH
FOLK-HERO

AMERICAN
FOLK-HERO

larger groupings called "cultural domains," popularly known as civilizations. There are, according to Samuel Huntington (1992), about eight cultural domains in the world today (see Figure 3.2).

The differences among these cultural domains can be expected to generate most of the conflict or even violence around the globe just as the culture clash within a country can (see box, p. 63). As Huntington (1993) observes, in the new world emerging from the ashes of the Cold War, the dominating source of international conflict will no longer be ideological or economic but instead will be cultural. Huntington offers a number of reasons such as the following:

First, differences among cultures are real and basic. Cultural differences do not necessarily mean conflict or violence, but differences have for centuries produced the most violent conflicts.

Second, the world is shrinking, increasing interactions between peoples of different cultures. This reinforces awareness of differences between cultures (such as U.S. and Japanese cultures) and commonalities within a culture (such as the Western culture). This partly explains why the United States reacts far more negatively to Japanese investment here than to larger investments from Canada and Western Europe.

Third, economic modernization and social changes are destroying local traditions, the long-standing source of identity for much of the world. Religion has moved in to fill the gap, often in the form of fundamentalist religious movements.

Fourth, Western values such as individualism, human rights, democracy, and the separation of church and state often run counter to Islamic, Confucian, Buddhist, Latin-American, and other cultures. As Harry Triandis (1989) found in a review of 100 comparative studies of cultural values in different societies, "the values that are most important in the West are least important worldwide." This culture clash may explain why Western efforts to promote those values often provoke charges of "human rights imperialism" from the rest of the world (Huntington, 1993).

Because of those forces, culture clash may create more conflict and violence in the world. This may not happen if peoples learn to understand each other's cultures, especially the ways people in a different culture see their own interests. But there is a strong resistance to such an understanding. It exists in the form of ethnocentrism. Let us analyze ethnocentrism and how we can deal with it.

FIGURE 3.2
Cultural Domains of the World

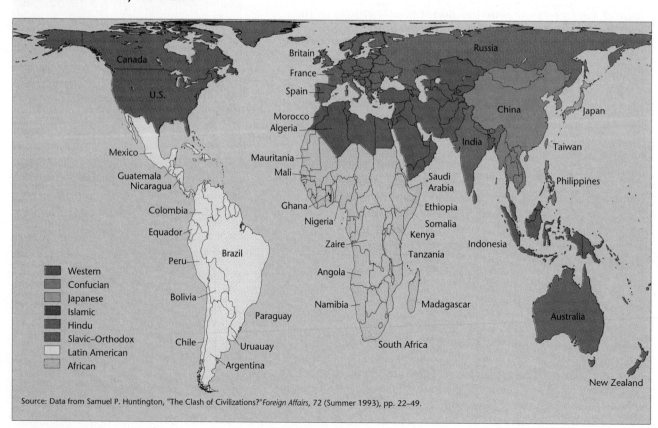

Source: Data from Samuel P. Huntington, "The Clash of Civilizations?" *Foreign Affairs*, 72 (Summer 1993), pp. 22–49.

Ethnocentrism

Almost from the time we are born, we are taught that our way of life is good, moral, civilized, or natural. At the same time we learn to feel that other people's ways of life are not. The result is **ethnocentrism**, the attitude that one's own culture is superior to that of others.

Ethnocentrism exists to one degree or another in every society. People in North America would consider it psychologically unhealthy for children in non-Western traditional countries to sleep with their parents until they reach puberty. On the other hand, people in traditional countries tend to find it cruel for North Americans to let their elderly parents live by themselves. Ethnocentrism can also become so deeply ingrained in our bodies that we can become physically ill if we eat something our culture defines as sickening. Try eating toasted grasshoppers, which Japanese relish, or ants, which some tribes in Brazil eat with gusto. But many Asians and Africans recoil from cheese, a favorite U.S. food, because they find it too smelly (Harris, 1985).

Ethnocentrism can serve as a glue to hold a society together. By declaring among themselves, "We're the greatest," people tend to feel a strong sense of unity as a nation. Usually nations keep their ethnocentrism to themselves. But ethnocentrism can go overboard, leading to global violence as suggested in the preceding section.

When he first met the Yanomamo Indians of Brazil, anthropologist Napoleon Chagnon experienced ethnocentrism, the attitude that one's own culture is superior and that other ways of life are uncivilized. Although such feelings are difficult to overcome, it is possible to enter another culture and learn its ways. Here Chagnon, wearing the tail of a black monkey as a headband, as is traditional for visitors, is seen talking with Yanomamo friends.

Cultural Relativism

Although ethnocentrism is universal, it can be suppressed with **cultural relativism**, the belief that a culture must be understood on its own terms. By looking at others' cultures from their own perspective, we can understand why they do things the way they do.

Such an understanding can bring a bonanza of profits to U.S. business operations around the globe. In our legalistic, rule-oriented culture, a written contract is usually required for conducting business. Once a contract is signed, negotiation should more or less cease. But to succeed in Greece, U.S. business people have to look at the contract from the Greek point of view: The contract is only a charter for serious negotiations, which will stop only after the work is completed. In the Arab world, success in business requires accepting the Muslim view that a person's word when given in a special kind of way is just as binding as, if not more so than, most written contracts (Morgan, 1989).

Cultural relativism can also contribute to international peace. Soon after Bill Clinton took office as President in 1993, he repeatedly pressured the Chinese government to correct its human rights abuses (which involve mistreating political dissidents). The pressure seriously strained U.S.-China relations. Clinton obviously refused to see the problem from China's perspective. To the Chinese, President Clinton should not interfere in other countries' internal affairs and should mind the United States' own human rights problems such as poverty, racism, and police brutality against African Americans. Finally, Clinton seemed to acquire cultural relativism, and came around to the Chinese view. He stopped pressuring China on its human rights problem, and started focusing on the task of increasing U.S. exports to China. The U.S.-China relations began to improve.

But Clinton has been criticized for kowtowing to China by ignoring its human rights abuses. This raises the question of how far cultural relativism should be carried out. Should ethical judgment be suspended when others engage in such horrors as infanticide, cannibalism, torture, or genocide? Only extremists would answer yes, arguing that no matter how repugnant they themselves find these horrors, their duty is only to understand them from others' perspective, without passing judgment on them. They would pursue the "live and let live" policy. But most cultural relativists would condemn the horrors, because, to them, cultural relativism requires only understanding a culture on its own terms, *not* also abandoning their moral conscience.

Cultural relativism involves judging a culture on its own terms. If carried to the extreme, cultural relativism would lead one to avoid any kind of criticism of another culture, such as that of Nazi Germany. But we still can condemn the Nazi practice of exterminating Jews because cultural relativism requires only understanding a culture on its own terms, not also abandoning our moral conscience.

Questions for Discussion and Review

1. How has the process of evolution caused humans to depend on culture for survival?
2. Could humans create culture if the theories of sociobiology were true? Why or why not?
3. Why is culture clash likely to increase global conflict in the new world order?
4. What is the nature of ethnocentrism and cultural relativism?

PERSPECTIVES ON CULTURE

We have so far taken a close-up look at various aspects of culture. We may now step back, view culture as a whole, and ask, "What is the essence of culture?" The answer is important because a few years from now you may easily forget all the details about culture but not the essence of culture. Many answers can be found in sociology as well as anthropology, but it should suffice to know three major themes of culture from the three sociological perspectives.

Functionalist Perspective

According to the functionalist perspective, culture serves the important function of meeting human needs, ranging from the basic needs for food and shelter to the higher needs for psychological security, social harmony, and spiritual fulfillment. The most central function of culture is to ensure social order and stability. As functionalists see it, without culture, human society cannot survive. All this may seem obvious, because the evidence is all around us. But the functionalist approach can help explain seemingly puzzling cultural practices. Consider how a key component of India's Hindu culture—the belief in cows as sacred—serves the function of saving human lives and therefore ensuring social order.

In India, which has the largest number of cattle in the world, there are many poor and starving people; yet the slaughter of cows is forbidden. Moreover, their 180 million cows are treated like gods and goddesses. They are given right of way in the street. They are even affectionately retired to "old-age homes" when they begin to become infirm. Why doesn't India feed starving humans by killing these animals for food? The popular explanation is simply that the Hindus consider their cows sacred. But why do they consider their cows sacred?

The reason suggested by the functionalist perspective is that the sacred cows serve several important, practical functions. First, they produce oxen, which Indian farmers desperately need to plow their fields and pull their carts. Second, when the cows die naturally, their beef is eaten by the poor lower castes and their hides are used by non-Hindu Indians to maintain one of the world's largest leather industries. Third, the cows produce an enormous amount of manure, which is used as fertilizer and cooking fuel. Fourth, the cows are tireless scavengers, eating garbage, stubble, and grass between railroad tracks, in ditches, and on roadsides. Thus it costs nothing to raise the cows, while they provide many things of value. In fact, India's peasant economy depends heavily on the cows. If the Indians ate their cows, many more people would starve to death. In short, by enabling the cows to do all those things, the Hindu belief in their sacredness ultimately serves the function of saving the lives of people, thereby helping to ensure social order and stability in India (Harris, 1985).

Conflict Perspective

While functionalism shows the positive side of culture, the conflict perspective reveals the negative side. At least two related ideas can be found in the conflict perspective.

First, culture reflects the interest of the rich and powerful in society. As Marx said, "The ruling ideas of society are the ideas of the ruling class." The value of competitiveness in our society, for example, benefits the powerful in two ways. One, it stimulates higher worker productivity, which enables employers to reap larger profit. Two, it discourages the poor and powerless from being resentful against the rich and powerful. If they believe in competition, the powerless would feel that the powerful deserve their riches and privileges because of great intelligence and hard work. Therefore, the poor are likely to envy rather than resent the rich while blaming themselves for being poor. The powerless would in effect join the powerful in supporting the status quo of social inequality.

Second, culture protects the status quo from the alienating effects of social and economic oppression. Suffering discrimination, exploitation, and poverty, some of the powerless may reject the competitive value as a hoax. But other values may still come to the rescue of the powerful. The most pertinent values are beliefs in morality and conformity, which may partly explain why most of the poor do not threaten social order by committing crime. Other, more tangible aspects of the culture further deflect the alienating impact of oppression from the powers that be. As Marvin Harris (1995) notes, such cultural artifacts as the movies, television, radio, and organized sports can effectively distract and amuse the exploited citizenry. This is similar to how the ruling elite in the ancient Roman empire controlled the masses by letting them watch gladiatorial contests and other circus spectaculars.

Symbolic Interactionist Perspective

Both functionalist and conflict perspectives provide the structural view of culture as largely capable of *constraining* us. For functionalists, culture effectively forces us to depend on it because of the important functions it performs for us. Without these functions, we can hardly survive. To conflict theorists, culture in effect oppresses the poor and the powerless by manipulating them into supporting the status quo of social inequality. Both functionalists and conflict theorists seem to offer a theme familiar to watchers of Frankenstein or Jurassic Park movies: Humans have through evolution created culture to free themselves from biological constraints, only to lose that freedom to the constraints of their own creation, namely, culture.

By contrast, symbolic interactionists are more likely to portray humans as being *free* to create and change culture. To them, culture is a set of shared understandings that people use to coordinate their activities. More specifically, culture is both a *guide* to social interaction and a *product* of interaction. As a guide to humans, culture is fixed, but as a product of humans, it is ever-changing. As Howard Becker (1982) explains, "On the one hand, culture persists and antedates the participation of particular people in it; indeed, culture can be said to shape the outlooks of people who participate in it." On the other hand, culture has "to be reviewed and remade continually, and in the remaking it changes."

As a guide, culture enables us to think and behave without first having to question the meaning of every thought and behavior. We do not, as Becker (1982) suggests, have to rack our brains for a new economic system every time we go to the grocery store. But culture has not always been a perfect or useful guide because the social environment changes continuously. A generation ago, most people bought their food at the corner grocery stores, butcher shops, or poultry and fish stores. In those days the shopping culture required the store owners or employees to serve the customers, a culture no longer today. Due to the rise of giant corporations capable of opening hundreds of stores across the country, most of us now buy our food in supermarkets, requiring a different way of shopping—we have to serve ourselves. In fact, many cultural practices in U.S. society change every 20 or 30 years. So, when new social conditions arise, people get together to create culture.

In short, while functionalist and conflict theorists are more likely to emphasize the importance of culture as a *constraint* on human behavior, symbolic interactionists tend more to stress the importance of culture as a *product* of human creation. Together, both concepts of culture contribute much more than each alone does to our understanding of culture.

Questions for Discussion and Review

1. How can the functionalist perspective be used to explain the cultural value of the "sacred cow" in India?
2. According to the conflict perspective, how is culture related to social inequality?
3. How does the symbolic interactionist view of culture differ from the two other perspectives?

CHAPTER REVIEW

1. *What is culture?* It is a design for living. It consists of material culture, which includes all the things produced by members of a society, and non-material culture, which comprises knowledge, beliefs, norms, values, and symbols.

2. *What are norms and values?* Norms are social rules dictating how to behave. There are two types: folkways, which simply expect us to behave properly, and mores, which practically force us to behave morally. Both are derived from values, socially shared ideas about what is good, desirable, or important. *What is the difference between "ideal" and "real" culture?* Ideal culture merely exists inside our heads, but real culture is more than ideal culture for being also supported by actual behavior.

3. *What is the nature of the symbolic component of culture?* It consists of symbols such as language. It influences our perception and thinking as well as reflects our social life. As an example of the influence of symbols, U.S. pop culture reflects the status quo and patriarchal influence in the United States, as well as the increasing global acceptance of U.S. culture.

4. *What are subcultures?* Subcultures are cultures within a larger culture. Some are variant subcultures, which merely differ from the dominant culture. Others are deviant subcultures, which are generally considered illegal or criminal, and countercultures, which are not illegal but still unacceptable to the larger society. *What do advocates of multiculturalism want?* An egalitarian society where all subcultures are treated equally. *What causes culture to change?* Cultural change usually stems from three factors in the environment: technology, innovation, and diffusion.

5. *What is the relationship between evolution and culture?* Our evolution from animals to culture-using humans has caused us to lose our instincts. Consequently, we must depend on culture to survive, and through cultures we have been able to adapt to widely different environments all over the world. *What are cultural universals?* Practices that are found in all cultures as a means for meeting the same human needs.

6. *Why can culture clash be expected to generate more global conflict and violence?* A number of reasons: (1) Cultural differences are real and basic. (2) The world is shrinking. (3) Modernization is destroying local traditions. (4) The West's efforts to promote its own culture have provoked resistance from non-West societies.

7. *What should we do to understand other cultures?* We should get rid of ethnocentrism, the attitude that our own culture is superior to that of others, and adopt cultural relativism, which means judging other cultures on their own terms. Cultural relativism, however, should be tempered with moral conscience.

8. *What can we learn from the functionalist perspective on culture?* Culture serves important functions for meeting human needs so as to ensure social order and stability. *What does the conflict perspective suggest about culture?* Culture reflects the interest of the rich and powerful, helping to perpetuate social inequality. Culture also protects the status quo from the alienating effects of social and economic oppression. *What is the symbolic interactionist view on culture?* While recognizing culture as a useful guide to social interaction, symbolic interactionists emphasize the importance of humans creating and changing cultures to respond to new social conditions.

KEY TERMS

Afrocentrism The view of the world from the standpoint of African culture (p. 60).

Belief An idea that is relatively subjective, unreliable, or unverifiable (p. 53).

Counterculture A subculture that represents values unacceptable to the dominant society but is generally not considered illegal or criminal (p. 60).

Cultural integration The joining of various values into a coherent whole (p. 55).

Cultural lag The social situation in which a culture's values and beliefs fail to catch up with technology (p. 62).

Cultural relativism The belief that a culture must be understood on its own terms (p. 67).

Cultural universals Practices found in all cultures as the means for meeting the same human needs (p. 64).

Culture A design for living or a complex whole consisting of objects, values, and other characteristics that people acquire as members of society (p. 52).

Deviant subculture A subculture that represents values unacceptable to the dominant culture and is generally considered illegal or criminal (p. 60).

Eurocentrism The view of the world from the standpoint of European culture (p. 60).

Ethnocentrism The attitude that one's own culture is superior to that of others (p. 67).

Folkways Weak norms that specify expectations about proper behavior (p. 53).

Instincts Biologically inherited traits that enable their carrier to perform complex tasks (p. 64).

Institutionalized deviance Norm violation that is so prevalent it has become socially acceptable (p. 56).

Knowledge A collection of relatively objective ideas and facts about the physical and social worlds (p. 53).

Laws Norms that are specified formally in writing and backed by the power of the state (p. 54).

Material culture Every conceivable kind of physical objects produced by humans (p. 52).

Mores Strong norms that specify normal behavior and constitute demands, not just expectations (p. 54).

Multiculturalism A state in which all subcultures are equal to one another in the same society (p. 60).

Nonmaterial culture The intangible aspect of culture (p. 52).

Norm A social rule that specifies how people should behave (p. 53).

Popular culture A collection of relatively unsophisticated artistic creations that appeal to the masses of a society (p. 57).

Sanction A reward for conformity to norms, or punishment for violation of norms (p. 54).

Sociobiology A new Darwinian theory that human behavior is genetically determined (p. 64).

Subculture A culture within a larger culture (p. 59).

Symbol A word, gesture, music, or anything that stands for some other thing (p. 56).

Value A socially shared idea about what is good, desirable, or important (p. 53).

Variant subculture A subculture that merely differs from the dominant culture in some way (p. 60).

SUGGESTED READINGS

Bellah, Robert N., et al. 1986. *Habits of the Heart: Individualism and Commitment in American Life.* New York: Harper & Row. Shows how we are torn between a lonely quest for our own success and a desire for close relationships with others.

Etzioni, Amitai. 1993. *The Spirit of Community: Rights, Responsibilities, and the Communitarian Agenda.* New York: Crown. Showing how individualism has adversely affected U.S. life and proposing how the society can benefit from a renewed spirit of mutuality.

Harris, Marvin. 1985. *Good to Eat: Riddles of Food and Culture.* New York: Simon & Schuster. A fun-to-read book by a leading anthropologist on why people in various cultures relish or reject such foods as cows, pigs, horses, dogs, cats, insects, and human beings.

Schor, Juliet B. 1991. *The Overworked American.* New York: Basic Books. Shows how the U.S. work ethic is more powerful than ever, evidenced by longer working hours and less leisure time.

Weinstein, Deena. 1991. *Heavy Metal: A Cultural Sociology.* New York: Lexington. An insightful sociological study of a controversial specimen of U.S. pop culture.

髮型護膚中心
The Elegance Hair & B

BEAUTY & FIGURE INSTITUTE
美容專業美肌中心
院學練訓美專容美
心中肥減容美

嘉妮安

CRYSTAL PALA

館菜川

日本式

).連利抽紗公司
& EXPORTER

宋芝
TOSHIBA

利達影音公司
LEE TAK ELECTRICAL CO.
CAMERA · VEDIO · AUDIO

中發鋼

兩替 ⑤ 找
MONEY EXCHANG

CAN

CH

藝康相機

Music

FOOCHOW ART CO., LTD.
4/F, 16 CARNARVON RD.

S & CO.
LTIES

Samsonite
Authorized Dealer
OPTICAL COMPANY

Canon Nikon
SONY National

Dust-Tex

Watson

CW 603

DF 6333

SOCIETY

Myths and Realities

MYTH: *Beauty is only skin deep. People would not consider a person competent just because he or she is good-looking.*

REALITY: Unfortunately, attractive persons are expected to be more capable than unattractive ones at most tasks. This may explain the research finding that people considered "good looking" earn more than those viewed as "homely," even though both groups have similar education and employment experiences.

MYTH: *Most college students identify strongly with their role as students.*

REALITY: Most students are not deeply committed to their role because many other roles—as a friend, date, leader, or an athlete—compete for their time.

MYTH: *Though by no means perfect, the United States is the most egalitarian society in the world.*

REALITY: Hunting-gathering societies are generally the most egalitarian because they do not attempt to accumulate food surpluses.

MYTH: *In the Middle East, the religions of Jews and Arabs are so different that they have hardly anything in common.*

REALITY: Since the Jews, who founded Judaism and Christianity, and the Arabs, who founded Islam, used to be pastoral people, we can find in each religion the image of a god who looks after his people, in the same way that a shepherd looks after his flock.

n Sheeb, Eritrea, across the Red Sea from Saudi Arabia, 18-year-old Hamida Mohammed displayed to a foreign journalist all the regalia of her recent marriage. They included elaborate gold bracelets on each wrist, a heavy steel watch, and an ornate mask—finely embroidered with metallic thread—that revealed only her eyes during the three days of her wedding feast. She is a member of the nomadic Rashaida tribe, who live in tents, move frequently, and raise goat and sheep as the main source of livelihood. Following a tribal custom, Mrs. Mohammed's husband had to "buy" her for marriage, paying a stiff bride price, of which those items were only a part. Her husband probably paid about 40,000 birr (about $7,000) in cash and several camels to her parents, in addition to jewelry and a wedding dress for her and a three-day ceremonial feast. Because of this high cost, far fewer Rashaida men today take more than one wife. The bride, however, has to be a virgin. Only on the last night of the multiday feast was Mrs. Mohammed, who had never met her husband until then, allowed to sleep with him. The tribal chief explained how the men go about ensuring chastity among female teenagers: "We try to make them marry at 15, so they are not tempted to get pregnant. If a daughter gets pregnant in the bush, we kill her. If we meet a Tigrayan man (of a neighboring tribe) playing with one of our women, we take a knife and kill him" (Perlez, 1992).

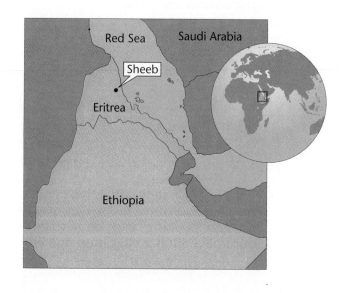

We can easily see how strikingly Mrs. Mohammed's life differs from ours in the United States. This is largely because she lives in a radically different kind of **society**, a collection of interacting individuals sharing the same culture and territory. In this chapter we examine how society shapes human life by analyzing different types of society and different sociological views on society. But first we need to look at the basic components of society: statuses, roles, groups, and institutions, which can be found in all societies.

Ascribed statuses are given to us independent of what we do. Achieved statuses result from our actions. President Clinton's status as the highest elected official of the United States is achieved. Similarly, although Hillary Rodham Clinton's traditional title of First Lady is ascribed, her status as a lawyer who has broken new ground in assisting the president in his duties is achieved.

BASIC COMPONENTS OF SOCIETY

Societies, especially large ones such as the United States, are highly complex. They have so many diverse characteristics—their cultures, religions, politics, economies, families, schools, and so on—that we may despair of making sense of what they are like. Nevertheless, sociologists have long been aware of certain patterns in the way societies operate. Most important, all societies can carry on in the face of differences and conflicts among their members because they have developed the foundation of society called statuses, roles, groups, and institutions.

Statuses

To the general public, "status" often means prestige. But to sociologists, **status** is a position in society. People usually behave in accordance with their statuses. Interacting with a friend, you are likely to be relaxed, informal, uninhibited. But talking with a professor, you are more likely to be a bit stiff and to act in a formal, inhibited way. The status of being a student differs from the status of being a friend.

In our complex society, we have so many statuses that it is impossible to name them all. Some we are born with. We are born male or female and into some racial group. These statuses of gender and race as well as age are called **ascribed statuses**, meaning they are given to us independent of what we do. All other statuses result from what we do. We earn them in some way. You must do something to gain the status of a

student or college graduate or married person or countless other things. These are called **achieved statuses**, which are attained through our own actions. In modern societies such as the United States, achieved statuses have grown in influence at the expense of ascribed statuses. In place of a king or queen who inherits the position, for example, we have a president who must win the office.

Statuses are sometimes ranked, with one being considered higher than others. In U.S. society, for example, the position of doctor is ranked higher than that of plumber. In a family, the father's status is higher than the son's. But other statuses are merely different, not higher or lower. A sociology major's status is different from but essentially equal to another student's status as a history major.

Despite our many statuses, when we interact with another person, we are usually influenced by only one status. If a woman interacts with her husband at home, she will behave primarily as a wife, not as a banker, employer, PTA leader, or athlete. Because the status of wife dominates her relationship with her husband, it is called the **master status** in this interaction. All of her other statuses—as a banker, employer, and so on—are less relevant to the interaction; hence, they are called **subordinate statuses**.

The nature of a society may determine which status becomes the master status. In an extremely racist society, race is the master status and all others are subordinate to it. A white person interacting with a black physician would therefore use race as the master status and profession as the subordinate status. As a result, the white person would not be likely to

American Mosaic

Status is defined as a position in society, and when we occupy an ascribed or achieved status others know who we are and what role we should play. However, confusion can exist when others assume we are in one status rather than another. This reading by an African American illustrates a type of status confusion that originated from some Japanese citizens' assumptions that all African American visitors to Japan are famous athletes.

Famous in the Far East

Before graduation from the University of Virginia, I sent my résumé to African embassies and consulates, trying to find a position teaching English. But I didn't find a school in all the continent that would guarantee employment. In desperation, I applied to the Japanese Ministry of Education and Ministry of Foreign Affairs to teach English in Japan, which became my only offer.

But the more I thought about going to Japan, the more apprehensive I became. I knew nothing of the history or culture, and I didn't speak the language. I worried that facing prejudice in a foreign country would be extremely frustrating.

Arriving at Sakura Nishi High School, about 40 minutes from Tokyo, I was relieved to find that everyone, from my principal to the PTA mothers, treated me with kindness and respect. But I discovered that while Japanese teens respected me as an American, they idolized me because I was Black.

While I was in Japan, trendy department stores advertised Bobby Brown posters, Cross Colours gear and *X* caps in their windows. Rappers from Ice-T to Ice Cube toured, and *Malcolm X* was at the major theaters. On Saturday nights Shibuya ward, Tokyo's hub of hip-hop and high fashion, was packed with students in baggy jeans, "Doc" Martens, Chicago Bulls caps, permed Afros and dreadlocks. To them, my being African-American meant I was *kakoi,* cool. And before long I was a star.

At a track-and-field event in Tokyo, I was one of only a few foreign spectators. I hadn't been there ten minutes when a screaming mob of young girls swarmed around me like bees, waving pens, notebooks and T-shirts in my face, shouting, "Sign, sign, sign!" I was petrified. Then it dawned on me that they thought I was an athlete. I couldn't explain in Japanese that I was only a spectator, so I surrendered.

That day was only the first of many incidents of mistaken identity and instant stardom. Nightclub managers let me in free, knowing my presence would attract patrons, and security guards at rap concerts gave me backstage passes. To be young, single and Black in Tokyo in the nineties was surely as exciting and romantic as the pre-World War II Spain Hemingway knew.

But I wanted to say to the Japanese, "You must understand, being Black is more involved than just wearing an *X* cap. It means being committed to furthering our race and nurturing our children. Being Black runs deeper than just having rhythm. It means possessing a history of more than 300 years of fighting for freedom and equality. And as a people, we are more diverse than our hairstyles. Our talents and interests vary as much as our shades of brown." I wished I could have said what I really should have been telling myself all along, rather than defining myself by our images as either sports stars and performers or criminals and victims.

Excerpted from Elizabeth Ridley, "Famous in the Far East," *ESSENCE,* August 1994, p. 38.

treat the black physician with the respect usually given doctors. In such a case, the black doctor suffers from **status inconsistency**, the experience of having two contradictory statuses, one high because of the victim's profession and the other low because of race.

In our society the master statuses of race and gender also influence the way others treat us. Research has shown that blacks in interracial groups and women in mixed company, compared with their white and male colleagues, are often given fewer opportunities to interact, are less likely to have their contributions accepted, and usually have less influence over group decisions. This "interaction disability," as imposed by the master statuses of race and gender, is difficult to overcome unless the minorities appear highly cooperative and agreeable to the majority. The influence of race and gender also appears in many other areas of social life (see Chapter 12: Race and Ethnicity, and Chapter 13: Women and Men).

Physical appearance can even function as a master status. More specifically, physical attractiveness has a profound impact on how individuals are perceived and treated by others. Research has shown, for example, that attractive individuals are expected by college students to be more capable than unattractive ones at most tasks. Similar studies have found that teachers expect attractive schoolchildren to be *new* smarter than unattractive ones and that attractive ? adults are perceived by many as more likable, friendly, sensitive, and confident. Not surprisingly, according to the latest study, people considered "good looking" earn, on average, about 10 percent more than those viewed as "homely," even though both groups have similar education, employment experience, and other characteristics. This phenomenon is not limited to occupations where looks play a big part, such as modeling or acting. It also exists in jobs where appearance cannot conceivably enhance employer profits, such as bricklaying, factory work, and telemarketing (Harper, 1993).

Roles

Every status has rights and obligations. Children enjoy the right of receiving food, shelter, and love from their parents, but they are expected to show respect, obedience, gratitude, and affection in return. In other words, every status carries with it a **role**, a set of expectations of what individuals should do in accordance with their particular status. Because of your status as a student, you act in certain ways that are part of the student role. Thus, status and role seem like two sides of the same coin. But they are distinguishable. A status is basically static, like a label on a bottle. A role is dynamic, shaped by specific situations and persons.

Consider the role of nurse. In an emergency, nurses must be cool and professional, but they are also expected to convey warmth and concern to their patients. With doctors, nurses are expected to be obedient; with patients' relatives, they may be authoritative. The behaviors demanded by the role change with the situation.

In addition, various people play the same role differently, just as various actors perform the same role on the stage in diverse ways, even though they are working from the same script. The script—the set of expectations about how a person with a particular status should behave—is the **prescribed role.** How a

For a student the prescribed role calls for attending classes, reading, thinking, and learning. But the role performance of students varies, depending, for example, on how they understand the prescribed role or how they attempt to carry it out.

person actually carries out the role is the **role performance.** The prescribed role of college student calls for attending classes, reading, thinking, and learning, but students differ in how and to what extent they fulfill these expectations. They may understand the prescribed role differently and be more or less successful in fulfilling those expectations. They may simply differ in their manner of carrying out the role. Thus, some students may expect to get straight A's while others would settle for C's and B's. The ambitious ones would study harder. No matter how each individual defines and performs the student role, however, commitment to it is far from total. In fact, most students do not strongly identify with their role as students. The reason is that many other roles—such as friend, date, leader, and athlete—compete for the student's time.

Indeed, all of us play many roles every day. Some of these are bound to impose conflicting demands. The role of judge prescribes an emotionless, objective attitude; the role of father requires emotional involvement. Usually, the conflicting demands of these roles present no particular problem because a person plays one role at a time. But if a judge found his or her daughter in court as the defendant, there would be a conflict. Similarly, if you are a student athlete, you will find yourself in conflict when your professor gives an exam on the day your coach wants you to play a game away from your school. When we are expected to play two conflicting roles at the same time, we experience **role conflict.** Even a single role may involve conflicting expectations and thus produce what is called a **role strain.** Supervisors are

Role conflict results when we are faced with opposing claims. A growing number of women find themselves caught between the traditional role of a mother and the modern role of a career woman.

expected to be friendly with their workers, to be one of them. But they are also expected to be part of management and to enforce its rules. Professors, too, are torn between the expectation to teach classes and the expectation to do research. Role conflict or strain is usually stressful, causing anxiety and other psychological aches and pains (Coverman, 1989; Voydanoff and Donnelly, 1989). But it can be resolved (see box, p. 79).

Groups

When people interact in accordance with their statuses and roles, they form a **social group**, a collection of people who interact with one another and have a certain feeling of unity. A group can be a family, a class, or two businesspersons trying to strike a deal. A group differs, though, from a **social aggregate**, a number of people who happen to be in one place but do not interact with one another, such as the audience in a theater or the pedestrians on a street. Groups are so important to our daily lives that no society can survive without them.

There are two major types of groups: primary and secondary. A **primary group** is a group whose members interact informally, relate to each other as whole persons, and enjoy their relationship for its own sake. Families, friends, neighbors, and the like are primary groups. They are durable, often lasting for years.

By contrast, a **secondary group** is a group in which the individuals interact formally, relate to each other as players of particular roles, and expect to profit from each other. A secondary group may con-

sist of a sales clerk and a customer. In such a group, there are hardly any emotional ties, the communication is bound by formalities, and each person is only interested in getting what they themselves want, such as something to sell or buy. Once this self-centered goal is accomplished, the group dissolves.

Primary groups are more common in traditional, preindustrial societies. But secondary groups are more prevalent in modern, industrial societies. (We will discuss these two types of group in greater detail in Chapter 5: Groups and Organizations.)

Tertiary groups

Institutions

Not Buildings

Society cannot survive without social institutions. A **social institution** is a set of widely shared beliefs, norms, or procedures necessary for meeting the basic needs of society. The most important institutions are the family, education, religion, economy, and politics. They have stood the test of time serving society well. The family institution leads countless people to produce and raise children to ensure they can eventually take over from the older generation the task of keeping society going. The educational institution teaches the young to become effective contributors to the welfare—such as order, stability, or prosperity—of society. The religious institution fulfills spiritual needs, making earthly lives appear more meaningful and therefore more bearable or satisfying. The economic institution provides food, clothing, shelter, employment, banking, and other goods and services that we need to live. The political institution makes and enforces laws to prevent criminal and other similar forces from destabilizing society.

In ensuring the survival of society, institutions further make life much easier for individuals. They are like the map of a country. With the map, we can easily find our way driving from one place to another. Without the map, we may have to spend much time exploring through trial and error different ways of reaching our destination. Similarly, with institutions, we know what to do in our lives. The institutions in our society help us do many things. If we want to have a family we will have a few children rather than 10 or 20. If we want to pursue a career in science, law, medicine, or some other field, we can go to school instead of studying by ourselves. If we seek spiritual fulfillment we can find guidance from various religions rather than endlessly searching for God on our own. If we need employment we are free to find the best job possible instead of being forced by government to accept a low-paid, unpleasant one. If we want to have a good government, we are allowed

Cutting Edge

Role conflict occurs when people have trouble choosing between the conflicting demands of different social roles. This situation often occurs among managers and administrators. This reading focuses on the experiences of administrators of child welfare organizations and shows how they resolve their role conflict.

Role Conflict: An Energizer

Common wisdom ties role conflict closely to high levels of burnout, but role conflict can actually be energizing and have positive effects on individuals and agencies. How individuals manage role conflict and its effect on them were questions the author explored in a recent year-long study of public child welfare directors.

This study uses an ethnographic research model to study a group of individuals operating in a situation of ongoing role conflict. The participants were all administrators of public child welfare agencies in Pennsylvania.

The findings confirmed that this group experienced professional role conflict, as well as organizational goal conflict. In fact, initial contacts with every director started with some description of the difficulties of the job and their various conflicting roles. Many stories were told about the conflicting expectations to perform police functions versus being social services providers and about the difficulty of trying to help clients who did not want to be helped.

But as they talked about their experience, these administrators stressed the importance to them of being in child welfare work for a long time. They emphasized the feeling that their work really made a difference for children and families, and they described the ways in which they made that happen, despite the various limitations they articulated so strongly. But this sense of accomplishment was not openly acknowledged, even among themselves.

Administrators' ways of dealing with role conflict took several forms. First, there was much discussion about the specific roles in conflict, which served to resolve role ambiguity by articulating the role conflict. For example, several participants explained how they clarify for their staff the multiple and conflicting roles. As one said, "I think the skill you need is the ability to work with a wide variety of people and keep everyone happy without compromising what you stand for. So of course you can't make everyone happy."

Administrators in this study spent a great deal of time networking, both within their agencies and in the larger community. Repeatedly, participants described going to an individual or group outside the agency to find out "where they are coming from." This attempt to understand the needs, frustrations, and goals of others was identified as the first step in a strategy of coalition building. This ability to span the boundaries of their own agency or profession is recognized as a way of dealing effectively in a complex and changing environment.

Excerpted from Martha L. Jones, "Role Conflict: Cause of Burnout or Energizer?" *Social Work,* March 1993, pp. 136–140.

---

to vote or run for office rather than risk our lives by starting a revolution. These are only a few of the countless benefits we can enjoy by simply following the guidance of institutions.

Because institutions are so useful, it is not surprising that they tend to be *conservative,* resisting change or supporting the status quo. People obviously support institutions with the attitude "if it ain't broke, why fix it?" Supporting the status quo, however, also involves helping to perpetuate the domination and exploitation of the powerless by the powerful and other social injustices in society. Institutions also tend to be *integrated,* in that they depend on one another as parts of a unified whole.

The family and educational institutions in the United States, for example, teach young people the values of hard work, competition, free enterprise, and democracy. These values sustain the capitalistic and democratic activities of economic and political institutions, which in turn provide the family and educational institutions with employment, income, public funding, and social order. But the degree of institutional conservatism and integration varies from one society to another.

Generally, institutions are more conservative and integrated in traditional, preindustrial societies than in modern, industrial societies. Being more conservative and integrated, the institutions in traditional societies are less likely to generate social problems such as the high rates of family violence, drug abuse, or crime. At the same time, however, the institutions in traditional societies are more likely to suppress individual freedom and creativity, forcing people to conform to age-old traditions, with threats of harsh punishment for nonconformity.

Questions for Discussion and Review

1. What are statuses, and how do they influence our behavior?
2. How do prescribed roles differ from role performance?
3. How do social groups and primary groups differ from social aggregates and secondary groups?
4. What important things do institutions do for society?

SOCIETIES IN SOCIOCULTURAL EVOLUTION

Since they first appeared on earth, most human societies have gone through different stages of **sociocultural evolution**, the process of changing from a technologically simple society to a more complex one with significant consequences for social and cultural life. In the most technologically simple soci-

eties, the methods of producing food are so primitive and inefficient that practically the whole population is forced to do the same kind of work—food production—to survive. The social and cultural opportunities—such as meeting people with various ways of life and enjoying a wide range of entertainment—are therefore extremely limited. But in the most technologically advanced societies, where highly efficient methods are used in food production, only a tiny number of farmers is needed to produce enough food to support the whole population. This frees the overwhelming majority of people to pursue numerous other kinds of work, creating a huge and complex array of social and cultural opportunities. Food-producing technology, then, is the driving force behind sociocultural evolution. Societies can be classified into different types according to the technologies they use to produce food—and the stages of sociocultural evolution they are in (Lenski, Lenski, and Nolan, 1995).

Hunting-Gathering Societies

Hunting-gathering societies hunt animals and gather plants as their primary means for survival. Throughout 99 percent of humankind's presence on earth, or until about 10,000 years ago, all societies survived by using simple tools such as spears to hunt wild animals, fishing, and using human hands to gather wild roots, fruits, birds' eggs, wild bees' honey, and the like. Today, less than 0.1 percent of the world's people live this way. Among the few

Hunter-gatherers move about in search of food. Limitations in usable food sources limit the size of the population in these societies, and division of labor is largely based on gender. Here a San woman of Africa, with children, dips for water from a tree.

remaining hunting-gathering societies are the !Kung* of South Africa, the Batek Negritos of Malaysia, and the Alyawara of central Australia.

Hunter-gatherers move about a great deal in search of food, but they cover only a small area. Because their food sources are thus so limited, hunting-gathering societies are very small, each having only 20 to 50 people. The division of labor is based on gender: men usually do the hunting; women do the gathering. Contrary to popular belief, though, hunter-gatherers do not live in total isolation, eating only wild foods. For thousands of years, they have also practiced some herding and farming or have traded with herders and farmers (Headland and Reid, 1989). But hunting and gathering remain their *primary* subsistence technology.

The lives of hunter-gatherers are not necessarily hard. In fact, because their needs are simple, they might work merely two or three hours a day. Estimates suggest that a family could easily collect enough wild cereal grain in three weeks to feed itself for a year. Sometimes the food must be processed. Some nuts, for example, require roasting and cracking. Hence, hunter-gatherers may spend more time feeding themselves than finding their food (Hawkes and O'Connell, 1981). Nevertheless, they still have so much leisure time that Marshall Sahlins (1972) has called them the "original affluent societies."

Even so, most hunter-gatherers do not attempt to accumulate food surpluses. They do not even store food for emergencies, and they tend to share their food with one another. Sharing, in fact, is a central norm and value in these societies. The more successful hunters are denied the opportunity to build prestige and wealth with their skills. Rather, they are expected to be self-deprecating about their hunting success, and boasting is met with scorn. Because no one hoards, no one acquires great wealth. And because there are few possessions to fight about, hunter-gatherers are unlikely to engage in warfare. If a strong and skilled hunter tries to dominate others or take their wives, he can be secretly killed, because there is no effective means of protection (like the police in other societies) and because everyone has easy access to poisoned arrows, spears, or other hunting weapons. As a result, hunting-gathering societies are generally the most egalitarian in the world.

Still, not all of the hunting-gathering societies are egalitarian. They fall into two categories: one with an "immediate-return system" and the other with a "delayed-return system." In the first, people go

hunting or gathering and eat the food on the same day; they do not store it for later use. In the delayed-return system, food is elaborately processed and stored. Woodburn found that the !Kung and other hunting-gathering societies with immediate-return systems are profoundly egalitarian for reasons like those discussed already. On the other hand, those with delayed-return systems, such as the aborigines of Australia, are marked by inequality because stored food can be turned into durable and exchangeable goods—hence leading to accumulation of wealth and power. Both systems, however, are patriarchal. Men exclude women from hunting activities. They even impose strict and extensive menstrual taboos on women, prohibiting them, when they are having their period, from touching any man and from handling such "male" things as bows, arrows, and fishing gear. They believe that menstruating women are dangerous to men, that the women may cause sickness, injury, or loss of magical power in the man they touch (Woodburn, 1982; Kitahara, 1982).

Pastoral Societies

Pastoral societies domesticate and herd animals as their primary source of food. In deserts, mountains, and grasslands, plants are difficult to cultivate, but animals can easily be domesticated for use as a food

---

*The ! represents a click, a speech sound not used in English.

In pastoral societies, animals are domesticated for use as a major source of food. Since pastoralists can accumulate a surplus of food, social inequality develops in their societies. Because they are on the move in search of fresh grazing grounds for their herds, pastoralists have often become fiercely independent and tend to disregard land boundaries.

source. About 10,000 years ago, some hunter-gatherers began to specialize in the domestication of animals. Today there are a number of pastoral societies, mostly in the deserts and highlands of North and East Africa, the Middle East, and Mongolia. The Africans specialize in keeping cattle; the Arabs, camels and horses; and the Mongols, various combinations of horses, cattle, camels, goats, and sheep. These peoples are different racially and far apart geographically, yet they show a considerable degree of cultural uniformity.

Unlike hunter-gatherers, pastoralists accumulate a surplus of food. One result is that pastoral societies can be far larger than hunting-gathering bands. Another result is the emergence of marked social inequality, based on the size of an individual's herd and the number of a man's wives. Some anthropologists argue that animal holdings represent an unstable form of wealth because, as a herder puts it, "Owning animals is like the wind. Sometimes it comes and sometimes it doesn't." When a disaster such as an epidemic or a severe drought strikes, the wealthy herders are assumed to suffer such great losses that social inequality cannot be maintained. But in his study of the Komachi pastoralists in south-central Iran, sociologist Daniel Bradburd (1982) found that disasters cannot wipe out inequalities in animal wealth. "While disasters befall rich and poor alike, they do not befall each with quite the same effect," Bradburd explains. "A poor man who loses half his herd frequently finds it reduced to a size from which recovery is impossible; on the other hand, a wealthy man who loses half his herd will frequently be left with enough animals to rebuild the herd without great difficulty."

Usually, pastoral peoples are constantly on the move, looking for fresh grazing grounds for their herds. Consequently, they become fiercely independent and inclined to scorn land boundaries. They also become rather warlike, and some use horses to enhance their war-making capabilities. They are just as likely to raid settled villages as they are to attack each other. The aim of such aggression is to increase their livestock as well as to warn others against encroachment. Sometimes they take captives and use them as slaves. Their religion and attitude reflect the pastoral way of life. The Hebrews who founded Judaism and Christianity and the Arabs who founded Islam used to be pastoral people, and in each religion we can find the image of a god who looks after his people in the same way that a shepherd looks after his flock. The Mongols have a religious taboo against farming, believing that plowing and planting offend the earth spirit. The African cattle herders, very proud of their pastoralism, regard horticulture as degrading toil. The non-Islamic tribes of the Hindu Kush mountains, on the borders of Afghanistan and Pakistan, treat their goats as sacred animals that are capable of appeasing the gods and mountain spirits (Parkes, 1987).

Horticultural Societies

Horticultural societies produce food primarily by growing plants in small gardens. About 10,000 years ago, while some hunter-gatherers became pastoralists, others became horticulturalists. Horticulturalists do their gardening by hand, with hoes and digging sticks. Because their soil cannot support continuous intensive farming, many horticulturalists rely on slash-and-burn cultivation. They clear an area in the forest by slashing undergrowth and cutting trees, allowing them to dry, and then burning them off, leaving ashes that help fertilize the soil. This procedure also ensures that the plot will be free of weeds. After two or three years of growing crops, the soil becomes exhausted, so new fields are slashed and burned.

Unlike pastoralists, horticulturalists live in permanent settlements. Like that of pastoralists, their society is marked by a sexual division of labor: men clear the forest, and women do the cultivation. Because horticulturalists can produce a food surplus, their societies are usually larger than those of hunter-gatherers. The existence of a surplus also gives rise to inequality in many horticultural societies, where the men can enjoy great prestige by possessing many gardens, houses, and wives.

Warfare, too, becomes common. Many tribes in a forest often raid each other, torturing, killing, or occasionally eating their captives. Victorious warriors receive great honors. They preserve and display their defeated enemies' skulls and shrunken heads, much as athletes today show off their trophies. In advanced horticultural societies, warriors hold power as well as prestige. These societies are usually divided into a small, powerful warrior nobility and a large mass of powerless common people. This social inequality is reflected in religion. Horticultural societies generally believe in capricious gods who must be worshiped. And they perform religious rituals to appease not only the gods but also the spirits of their dead ancestors, perhaps because in permanent settlements the living remain physically close to their dead. Today, there are still some horticulturalists in the tropical forests of Africa, Asia, Australia, and South America.

Agricultural Societies

Agricultural societies produce food primarily by using plows and draft animals on the farm. About 5,000 years ago, the invention of the plow touched off an agricultural revolution that radically transformed life in the Middle East and eventually throughout the world. When a field is plowed, weeds are killed and buried efficiently, fertilizing the soil. At the same time, nutrients that have sunk too deep for the plants' roots to reach are brought closer to the surface. Thus, the coming of the plow allowed peasants to obtain crop yields many times larger than the horticulturalists obtain with their hoes. If farmers use animals to pull their plows, then their productivity is increased further. As a result, unlike horticulturalists, farmers can cultivate a piece of land continuously and intensively.

The giant leap forward in food production enables large populations to emerge in agricultural societies. Because each farmer can produce more than enough food for one person, some people are able to give up farming and become tailors, shoemakers, tanners, and weavers. These people help cities emerge for the first time.

The towns, cities, and farms in an agricultural society usually come under the control of a central government, usually headed by a dictator with the power to imprison or even exterminate large numbers of people. This centralization of political control, coupled with the possession of valuable property, provides a strong stimulus for warfare. The common people who fight for their leader tend to believe that the leader has divine power. They also believe in a family of gods in which one is the high god and the others are lesser gods. This hierarchy seems to mirror the peasants' experience with various levels of government officials, from the tax collector at the bottom to the leader at the top. In fact, agricultural societies past and present have the greatest inequality of all types of society. Agricultural societies still predominate today as relatively poor countries in Africa, Asia, and Central and South America.

Industrial Societies

Industrial societies produce food for their subsistence primarily by using machinery. Since the Industrial Revolution started in England about 250 years ago, many agricultural societies have become industrialized and use machinery to till their lands. Today's industrial societies are relatively rich and can be found in Western Europe, North America, and parts of Asia (Japan, South Korea, Taiwan, and Singapore). Industrialism has been fueled by the use of increasingly powerful energy sources—flowing water, steam, internal combustion, electricity, and atomic fission—to power more and more efficient machines to do the work that had been done mostly by humans or animals in the past. Consequently, only a tiny number of farmers is needed to produce enough food for the rest of the population. This phenomenon triggers an exodus into towns and cities, creating huge urban centers across the country. There enormous masses of people work in numerous different industries, producing a cornucopia of remarkable new things and experiences. In this century alone we have seen the invention and proliferation of automobiles, telephones, radios, movies, television, jet airliners, nuclear reactors, computers, fax machines, and other high-tech devices. All these and other modern technologies have affected our lives significantly.

For one thing, the functions of institutions have changed. The family no longer provides gainful employment for adults, education for children, and religious worship for both. These functions have been taken over by business companies, schools, and churches, synagogues, mosques, or temples. The economy is vast and powerful because virtually everybody depends on this institution for survival. The educational institution is equally powerful in another way: it serves all school-age youngsters, not just a few from wealthy families, which makes for a prosperous and democratic society. Religion, however, has lost its earlier influence as the dominant, unquestioned source of moral authority, because this institution now faces challenges from varying beliefs of a more diverse population.

Secondly, human life has greatly improved. People are much healthier and live considerably longer. The standard of living has risen sharply for most people. Social inequality has declined significantly, though the income gap between rich and poor was very great in the early stages of industrialism. Gender inequality has similarly declined. And political, religious, and other freedoms have become more easily attainable.

Thirdly, war has become less likely to break out between industrial societies than between preindustrial societies. This change has much to do with the fear that modern weapons, such as nuclear bombs, can wreak massive, unthinkable destruction on warring nations. Not surprisingly, the former Soviet Union and the United States have avoided a nuclear war, choosing instead the "cold" war. But in the less industrialized world, where weapons are unlikely to destroy an entire nation, wars continue to be common. Fighting is particularly likely to erupt between tribes or ethnic groups within a nation-state, such as the recent war between the Tutsi and Hutu tribes in Rwanda or among the Serbs, Muslims, and Croats in Bosnia. In these conflicts, one party can become victorious without totally destroying itself in the process.

Fourthly, human relations have become weaker and more impersonal. Instead of working with family members on the farm, as in agricultural societies, most people in industrial societies are employed away from home and thrown into contact with others they hardly know. Their social life also revolves increasingly around secondary groups rather than primary groups. Interaction with strangers becomes more and more common. All this has led to a rise in personal concerns and a decline in social solidarity. But life has also become more interesting or

challenging because greater social diversity offers experiences of meeting new people with different ways of life and enjoying their distinctive entertainment, food, and the other aspects of their subcultures.

Postindustrial Societies

Since the early 1970s the most advanced and richest industrial countries such as the United States, Canada, the countries of Western Europe, and Japan seem to have begun emerging as **postindustrial societies**, the type that produces food for subsistence primarily by using high technology. It is impossible to predict with accuracy when those societies will become mostly postindustrial. But we can be certain that it will not take thousands or hundreds of years as it did for each of the earlier societal types to appear, because the speed of sociocultural evolution is remarkably greater today. It will only be a matter of decades, sometime in the next century, that the United States will transform into a primarily postindustrial society. Currently in transition from industrialism to postindustrialism, the United States has already shown some unmistakable signs of an emerging postindustrial society.

In recent years biotechnology has made food production far more efficient than ever. When a mass-produced hormone called BST (bovine somatotropin) is injected into cows, milk production increases by 30 or even 40 percent. By the year 2000 the use of BST will so sharply reduce the number of cows needed to meet the U.S. milk requirements that the number of commercial dairy farms could be cut in half. In the late 1980s seven genetically identical bull calves were produced from human-made embryos in Texas. This means that large numbers of cattle, pigs, and sheep can be cloned from a single embryo to produce uniformly healthier animals and higher-quality, lower-fat, and tastier meat. Fish have also been genetically altered to mature faster. Applying genetic engineering to plants has produced supertomatoes genetically programmed to have a built-in resistance to parasites, viruses, and herbicides. Various vegetables and fruits can be genetically made pest-resistant, disease-resistant, and frost-resistant. Some biotechnologists are even trying to engineer the lowly potato so that it will have better protein than beef. When these high-tech strategies become commonplace, far fewer people will be needed to farm and the United States will truly become the leading postindustrial society (Naisbitt and Aburdene, 1990).

By relieving people of physical labor, high technology has also begun to transform the nonfarm economy from one that produces things to one that

In postindustrial societies, food for subsistence is produced primarily by using high technology. Biotechnology, including genetic engineering, is part of the high-tech economy. These tomatoes were the first genetically engineered whole food to be sold in stores.

provides service or information. Over the last few decades increasing numbers of *manufacturing* jobs have been eliminated and growing numbers of *service* jobs have been created. We have increasingly allowed less industrialized societies to produce our goods largely because they can do so more cheaply, while we focus instead on designing and marketing the products. At about the same time, the proportion of people with college education has shot up to more than 50 percent, the highest in the world. Consequently, the demand for service jobs has increased sharply, and the demand has been met through an explosion of knowledge, particularly with the proliferation of computers, which creates numerous managerial, administrative, and technical jobs. These jobs, along with product design and marketing, are high-wage service jobs. However, less educated workers, who used to earn high wages in the steel, auto, and other manufacturing industries, are now left out in the cold. When they move out of manufacturing, they are forced to settle for low-paying service jobs. Obviously, higher education is

Roles for less smart?

the key to success in the increasingly postindustrial, knowledge society.

The transition to postindustrialism has begun to influence our lives in at least four ways.

First, more and more people have been moving from large cities to small towns and rural areas. In industrial societies, workers have to live close to their work, swarming into places that become larger cities. In our emerging postindustrial society, however, cities are declining because urbanites are attracted to the quality of life in less populated places: low crime rates, inexpensive housing, recreational opportunities, and a return to community values. The migration is facilitated by computers, fax machines, E-mail, and Federal Express, which enable people to work anywhere. In the United States there are now over 20 million full-time home-based businesses and as many as five million people work at home in computer-related jobs. Their numbers continue to grow (Naisbitt and Aburdene, 1990).

Second, the blind faith industrial societies place in science and technology as a religion is increasingly questioned in our emerging postindustrial society. Constant exposure to a high-tech environment has increased the realization that science is limited, especially the awareness that it may not offer us the meaning of life. This has prompted hosts of people to seek religion and spirituality. Since spiritual experience tends to be intensely personal and less dependent on an organized religion, mainstream churches that have long dominated the religious scene are declining in membership. More and more people turn inward to seek spiritual guidance, without submitting themselves to an outside authority by joining a traditional religious organization. An important reason for this shift to the individuality of faith is the fact that people who have computer and other high-tech jobs tend to spend considerable time alone.

Third, individuals enjoy more power or freedom than before. Citizens receive so much information through television and other telecommunications on government activity that they can prevent misconduct among their leaders. Computers enable individuals to keep close tabs on their government more efficiently than the government can keep tabs on all of them. With global television, fax machines, and computer networks, it seems difficult for a repressive and dictatorial government to emerge in a postindustrial society. The government can seize radio or television stations and suppress the press, but individual citizens can still get information from one another or from abroad through fax, the Internet, and other telecommunications that the government cannot control (Watson, 1995).

Fourth, there tends to be more gender equality. Postindustrialism depends on brainpower more than does industrialism. Since women are just as likely as men to attend college today, they can be expected to be as likely to command high positions in the service or information economy. Well-educated women can advance fastest in the forefront of the emerging postindustrial, information industry. At Apple Computer, for example, the proportion of women managers had risen to 30 percent in 1989 and is expected to reach 50 percent—parity with men—before the turn of the century. (Naisbitt and Aburdene, 1990).

Questions for Discussion and Review

1. What are the differences among hunting-gathering, pastoral, and horticultural societies?
2. How do industrial societies differ from agricultural societies?
3. What consequences does our emerging postindustrial society have for our lives?

A GLOBAL ANALYSIS

We can appreciate the powerful influence of our society on our lives by comparing it with societies in various stages of sociocultural evolution. (See Table 4.1 for a quick review of these societies.) Thanks to our emerging postindustrial society, most of you will earn your living in the information industry, using a computer and other high-tech equipment. You will not have to do what people in earlier societal types do: work in a factory, toil on the farm, garden with hoes, tend goats, forage wild plants, or chase wild animals with a spear.

Our society is not yet primarily postindustrial; it still has many of the features of an industrial society. Nevertheless, we are already very different from all the preindustrial societies.

Preindustrial vs. Industrial Societies

Sociologists and anthropologists have long tried to find the basic differences between these two categories of societies. As early as 1887, German sociologist Ferdinand Tönnies described the preindustrial society as a *Gemeinschaft*, or "community," meaning that people in such a society have a strong sense of community and relate to each other in a personal

way. In contrast, he described industrial society as a *Gesellschaft*, or "society." In such a society, people think of themselves as individuals first and relate to each other based on their social roles in an impersonal way that leads to alienation from one another.

Then in 1893 Durkheim used the term **mechanical solidarity** to describe the cohesion underlying preindustrial societies and **organic solidarity** to characterize industrial societies. As we saw in Chapter 1 (Thinking Sociologically), mechanical solidarity is social unity developed when people perform the same tasks and have similar values. In contrast, organic solidarity arises when people are forced to depend on one another because their jobs are very specialized.

More recently, in 1941, U.S. anthropologist Robert Redfield concluded that preindustrial societies are small, nonliterate, and homogeneous societies in which group solidarity is strong; he called them **folk societies**. On the other hand, he described industrial societies as large, literate, and heterogeneous, with very little group solidarity; these he called **urban societies**.

Four contrasting sets of traits summarize the differences between these two categories of societies:

1. *Simplicity versus complexity*. The social structure of preindustrial societies is relatively simple. There is very little division of labor, usually based only on age and gender. There tends to be only one clearly defined institution, the family, which is the center of educational, occupational, and religious activities. Technology, too, is simple. The society supports itself by a simple food-getting technique that involves human and animal power.

The social structure of industrial societies is more complex. There is an elaborate division of labor, with thousands of different jobs. There are many social institutions, each more complex than the family. They perform many of the functions of the preindustrial family, as well as new functions. Technology, too, is complex.

2. *Homogeneity versus heterogeneity*. The populations of preindustrial societies are relatively small and homogeneous. Cultural values are so widely shared that social tranquility tends to prevail. In contrast, the populations of industrial societies are larger and more heterogeneous. They include numerous diverse groups that cling to their own subcultures and often find themselves in conflict with each other.

3. *Intimacy versus impersonality*. Social life in preindustrial societies occurs mostly in *primary groups* such as the family. These are small groups in which individuals interact informally and have strong emotional ties to one another—ties that are intimate and

TABLE 4.1
Societies in Various Stages of Sociocultural Evolution

Societal Type	When First Appeared, Where Today	Food-Producing Technology	Sociocultural Life
Hunting-Gathering Societies	When human life began on earth; extremely few remain, in South Africa, Malaysia, Australia	Spears or other simple tools for hunting, hands for gathering wild plants	Gender-based division of labor, men hunting and women gathering; generally, most egalitarian in the world
Pastoral Societies	About 10,000 years ago; few today, in deserts and highlands of North and East Africa, Middle East, Mongolia	Domesticating and herding animals	Fiercely independent; warlike; religions reflecting value of pastoralists' animals; great social inequality
Horticultural Societies	About 10,000 years ago; few today, in tropical forests of Africa, Asia, Australia, South America	Simple hand tools (hoes, digging sticks)	Warlike and highly inegalitarian, warrior nobility dominating common people; inequality reflected in worship of capricious gods
Agricultural Societies	About 5,000 years ago; still numerous, relatively poor countries in Africa, Asia, Central and South America	Plows and draft animals	Create diverse occupations; cause cities to emerge; rulers believed to have divine power over common folk; many gods; most inegalitarian in the world.
Industrial Societies	About 250 years ago; many still exist, rich countries in Western Europe, North America, parts of Asia (Japan, South Korea, Taiwan, Singapore)	Machinery	Create huge urban cities; educational and economic institutions more influential than in earlier types; religion no longer dominant; living condition greatly improved; wars less likely; human relations weaker, more impersonal
Postindustrial Societies	Began to emerge about 1970; still in process of becoming fully postindustrial; led by the United States, Canada, Japan, and other richest nations	High technology (biotechnology, genetic engineering)	Increasing replacement of manufacturing by service, knowledge, information jobs; large cities in decline; blind faith in science questioned; more power and freedom for the individual; increased gender equality

enduring. From these personal relationships comes informal social control, which reinforces social order.

In industrial societies, more of the social life occurs in *secondary groups,* which consist of people who interact formally, do not know each other well, and relate to each other in a superficial way. Their relationship is temporary and impersonal. With the growing predominance of impersonal encounters, individuals are more likely to exploit each other, and informal social controls are likely to weaken. Thus, formal social control in the form of laws is instituted.
4. *Traditionalism versus modernism.* Preindustrial soci-

eties are to a large degree tied to their past and uninterested in social change. They value social stability and emphasize the group's rather than the individual's needs. In contrast, industrial societies are more likely to look to the future and to be enthusiastic about social change. They believe in social progress and tend to support individual interests above group needs.

The four characteristics of each type of society are related. Together they reflect the core nature of each. Simplicity in social structure, homogeneity in people

GLOBAL VILLAGE

An important area of sociological study is impact of technological changes and historical events on the structure of human societies. China provides a dramatic example of these changes. Following the communist victory in 1949, the government had collectivized agriculture, whereby entire villages would share the land and work together. Today, however, private property and factories are being encouraged. This article discusses the impact of these changes on the structure of China's peasant family economy.

Village Transformation in China

Since 1980 Chinese rural society has undergone profound and far-reaching changes. The government has diminished its direct control over peasant agricultural production and marketing activities. The new economic phenomena emerging among peasants include economic diversification, growth of private rural industries, and migration of rural laborers.

One example is the factory in Shenquan. It was started as a corporate enterprise in which several families pooled their capital to become shareholders. Its development has deeply affected the village's social and economic life. Those for whom work in the village factory is their main source of livelihood have become peasant-workers, and those who have their own businesses that are connected with the factory have become peasant-entrepreneurs. The relationship between the factory and the village is complex and multifaceted. The factory's management of produc-

tion, distribution and manufacture is independent of the village government. It is, however, advantageous for the factory to retain its image as a commune. Through this means, the factory obtains benefits such as the tax exemption which is granted by government policy to collective enterprises for the first year of production.

Nevertheless, some villagers have ambivalent feelings and attitudes toward the factory. They want the factory to make some sort of contribution to the village. But their lack of kinship ties with the shareholders restricts their participation in the factory, making them angry and jealous.

Excerpted from Minchuan Yang, "Reshaping Peasant Culture and Community," *Modern China*, April 1994, pp. 157ff. Copyright © 1994 by *Modern China*. Reprinted by permission of *The New Republic*, © 1994, The New Republic, Inc.

---

and values, intimacy in social relationships, and traditionalism in outlook reflect the tendency of preindustrial societies toward *social order.* Complexity in social structure, heterogeneity in people and values, impersonality in social relationships, and modernism in outlook reflect the tendency of industrial societies toward *social conflict.*

It is important not to exaggerate the differences between industrial and preindustrial societies; they exist only in degree rather than in kind. Many industrial societies, such as the United States and Japan, are not totally industrial because they still have some of the characteristics of preindustrial societies. They are considered industrial only because their industrial features seem more prominent. Nor should we exaggerate the similarities among industrial societies. Japan is just as highly industrialized as the United

States, but Japan retains to a greater extent the characteristics of a preindustrial society. Let us take a closer look at these characteristics.

Japan: A Mixed Society

First, Japan has a relatively homogeneous population. Among the world's industrial societies, the United States is the most heterogeneous, Japan the most homogeneous. Japan does have some minorities, such as the Burakumin, Ainu, Koreans, and Okinawans, but these groups make up less than one percent of the population. The society, then, is overwhelmingly Japanese. This is why Japanese culture is far more uniform than that of any other industrial society. Everywhere in Japan, schools teach the same

changing

subjects during the same weeks every year. Even most of the swimming pools open and close on the same date whether on the subarctic island to the north or on the nearly subtropical island to the south. Because practically everyone shares the same values, it is easy for Japan to be managed as a nation. To some extent, the Japanese resemble the Mormons in Utah; they have about the same orthodox family patterns, the same virtues of work and thrift, and the same emphasis on social harmony. Just as relatively homogeneous Utah is easier to govern than California or New York, Japan is easier to manage than the United States. For the same reason, Japanese companies are easier to manage than U.S. companies (Fallows, 1990).

Second, the influence of primary groups pervades Japanese society. Because they share the same values and interests, the Japanese find it more natural to develop strong social relationships than we do. This has a significant impact on Japanese business practices. Thus, most Japanese spend an enormous amount of time and energy building and nurturing intensely personal relationships. "The long hours of the Japanese businessman are legendary," Clyde Prestowitz (1989) observes. "Many of those hours are spent not working but socializing with fellow employees or members of some other group. This activity is an important part of maintaining the close personal ties that provide the group's spiritual sustenance in the same way family ties do." That business-people or employees refer to their company figuratively as *uchi*—"my house"—reflects the Japanese view of the company as a family. Actually, the tie to the company is stronger, as the Japanese often spend time with colleagues or business associates after office hours—sometimes until eleven o'clock at night. They see their families only between eleven at night and seven in the morning (Wolferen, 1990).

Third, Japan is more traditional than any other industrial society. While we value the individual's rights and interests, the Japanese emphasize the importance of the group's needs for social harmony and stability. Thus, the Japanese identify strongly with their schools, clubs, companies, and, ultimately, their nation. If asked what work they do, they would not say "plumber," "sales representative," or whatever; they would mention only the name of the company that employs them. Labor and management have a harmonious relationship, cooperating to ensure the success of their company. Government-industry relations are also mutually supportive. If an industry falls on hard times, the government will offer help. Generally, the government supports various industries with a panoply of market-protection measures against foreign imports, coupled with financial incentives such as tax credits, low-interest loans, and reserves for export losses, retirement, and price fluctuations. In return, corporations contribute heavily to politicians' election campaigns, and some business leaders become high government officials.

Although Japan may be a rich nation, the Japanese standard of living is far below that in the United States. The Japanese home, as shown here, is small, and the average Japanese house is about twice the price of one in the United States.

Ultimately, all the individuals and groups cooperate like members of a big family to turn Japan into an economic superpower.

The economic triumph, however, exacts a price from average Japanese. Japan may be a rich nation, but its people are poor. Owing to the yen's soaring value, Japan's per-capita income is now much higher than that of the United States, but when adjusted for local purchasing power, the average person's earning is lower in Japan. The standard of living is also considerably lower in Japan (see Table 4.2). Japanese houses are small and expensive, averaging about one-third smaller than U.S. homes and about twice the price. Nearly everything else also costs much more in Japan than in other industrial societies. The Japanese pay up to three times more for beef, rice, oranges, many alcoholic beverages, and imported goods, primarily because of Japan's restriction on imports of inexpensive foreign foods and products. Never-

Best buy much/newest

theless, Japanese consumers largely support government and business efforts to protect their market against low-priced imports, apparently more interested in ensuring the economic success of their nation than in buying goods at bargain prices (Prestowitz, 1989; Fallows, 1990). In short, the group takes precedence over the individual.

While Japan is as traditional as preindustrial societies in being group-centered, it is *not* as traditional in being resistant to change. Otherwise, it would not have become one of the world's most modern and richest countries. Instead, the Japanese constantly seek change in their lives through what they call *kaizen*—continuing self-improvement—as part of their Zen tradition. The application of *kaizen* has contributed a great deal to Japan's economic success. As Peter Drucker (1993) explains, "The aim of *kaizen* is to improve each product or service so that it becomes a truly different product or service in two or three years' time. . . Witness the way in which the Japanese consumer electronics manufacturer has developed one new product after the other out of the same U.S. invention, the tape recorder." Interestingly, their economic recession over the last five years may have prodded the kaizen-minded Japanese to think about changing their economic priorities from production (which has enriched corporations and the state) to consumption (which will lower prices of goods and services to benefit the individual consumer). This may explain the enormous popularity of Ichiro Ozawa's (1994) book, *Blueprint for a New Japan,* which urges Japanese to stop burying themselves in the group and start taking responsibility for themselves.

Questions for Discussion and Review

1. What are the differences between preindustrial and industrial societies?
2. What are the preindustrial features of Japanese society, and how do they contribute to its economic success?

TABLE 4.2
How Japan Compares with Others

JAPAN IS AHEAD IN NATIONAL ECONOMIC POWER:

Average GNP* per Person

Japan	$27,300
Germany	$24,700
United States	$22,200
France	$21,300
Britain	$17,600

BUT THE JAPANESE INDIVIDUAL'S WELFARE FALLS BEHIND:

Amount of housing space per person, in square meters		Average working hours per year	
United States	61.8	Germany	1,590
Germany	37.2	France	1,680
Britain	35.2	United States	1,940
France	30.7	Britain	1,950
Japan	25.0	Japan	2,210

*Gross National Product

Source: Japanese and German Government Reports, 1992.

ARE WE PRISONERS OF SOCIETY?

We have seen how society exercises considerable power over our lives through its technology, institutions, groups, statuses, and roles. Does society, in effect, resemble a prison with people as the inmates? Different answers can be found in the three major sociological perspectives. To functionalists, society operates like a prison but with popular consensus. To conflict theorists, society is run like a prison for the benefit of the ruling elite. To symbolic interactionists, society is a product of our creation, like a robot that is at our beck and call.

Functionalist Perspective

A major concern of functionalism is what makes society possible. What holds society together or keeps it from falling apart? What ensures social order or prevents social disorder? As mentioned in Chapter 1 (Thinking Sociologically), the central idea of functionalism is that the various parts of society contribute something. Each performs certain functions for the society as a whole. One of these functions is *social control*, which ensures social order by controlling the individual members of society. Political institutions control through laws, police, courts, and prisons. Less explicitly, the people we meet and interact with control us by being ready to embarrass, scold, or hurt us if we do not behave properly. Families and friends control us by threatening to withdraw their love, affection, or friendship if we fail to meet their expectations. All these social pressures push us to conform, to give up our individual freedom. They are what Emile Durkheim (1858–1917) called "social facts" or "something beyond us," which are not merely abstract concepts but real things that constrain us in the same way as a prison confines people. Social control, in effect, turns us into prisoners of society.

But social control cannot by itself hold us prisoners for long without our consent. The social consensus requires that social control be widely seen as reasonable, justifiable, or legitimate. As Durkheim suggested, we must learn to love society not only as something beyond us but also as "something in ourselves." To accomplish this goal, society relies on certain institutions—particularly the family, schools, and religion—to carry out the function of *socialization,* transmitting its values and beliefs to individuals (see Chapter 7: Socialization). Thus we are taught to believe that we should love our parents, respect the law, accept punishment for wrongdoing, defend our country, and regard many other similar things as good, proper, or positive in some way. Once all these societal beliefs become our own, society has in effect become part of us, and we, in turn, a microcosm of society. At this point we are bound to support our society, even its attempt to control us. Socialization, in effect, makes us carry out our imprisonment in society from within ourselves, betraying

ourselves into captivity with our collusion. As society's prisoners, we have developed what is called the Stockholm syndrome—we identify and cooperate with our jailer.

Conflict Perspective

Behind the functionalist notion of social consensus is the assumption that society is basically egalitarian and all members are equally subject to the same constraints. But the conflict perspective sees society as highly inegalitarian, with the powerful dominating the powerless. This perspective conjures up an image of society as a prison controlling the powerless masses for the benefit of the small ruling class.

Karl Marx (1818–1883) divided societies into three major types, and saw class domination in each. In ancient societies of the Mediterranean world, such as Greece and Rome, the patricians (slave owners) had under their thumb both the slaves and the intermediate class of plebeians (who neither owned slaves nor were slaves). In feudal, agricultural societies of the European Middle Ages, the landowning aristocracy lorded over the serfs (the servile, or slave-like, class bound to the soil) and the intermediate class of artisans and merchants. And in modern, capitalist societies, the capitalists (who own the means of production such as factories) dominate the proletariat (workers) and the intermediate class of managers, small business owners, professionals, and the like. Like a prison, society consists of the ruling class as the jailers and the dominated class as the inmates. Idealistically, Marx predicted that the proletariat would eventually overthrow the capitalists and usher in a classless, socialist society, declaring that "the proletarians have nothing to lose but their chains; they have a world to win." History has so far proven him wrong, as recently demonstrated by the collapse of the socialist governments throughout Eastern Europe and the former Soviet Union. But modern conflict theorists agree with Marx's basic belief that in all societies people with power dominate those with less or no power.

According to C. Wright Mills (1916–1962), three kinds of power are used to keep the powerless in line: coercion, authority, and manipulation. Coercion involves forcing people to do something against their will. Authority is power justified by the beliefs of the voluntarily obedient. And manipulation is power wielded without the awareness of the powerless. Since its authority is never complete, the ruling class uses coercion and manipulation to strengthen its grip on the powerless. Of these two types of power, manipulation is much more effective for controlling

According to the functionalist perspective, our society forces us to wait in lines to ensure social order. Embarrassing and scolding result if we do not patiently wait. But the conflict perspective suggests that powerful and influential people do not have to wait. And the symbolic interactionist perspective suggests that everybody can exercise freedom. If we want to move ahead in the line, we can politely ask those in front of us for a favor, offering them a credible reason why we need to move ahead.

the powerless. Through the mass media, books, education, religion, and other what Marx called "means of mental production," the ruling class can manipulate the masses into accepting its ideas, such as the idea that it deserves the right to rule. This is why Marx observed that the ruling ideas of any society are the ideas of its ruling class, with the masses acquiring **false consciousness**, the belief that justifies their domination by the ruling class to the detriment of their own interests.

Symbolic Interactionist Perspective

The central idea of symbolic interactionism is that human beings interact with each other—not by passively and rigidly following the rules imposed by society but by actively and creatively interpreting each other's actions. All these symbolic interactions form human society, making it look like a robot doing our bidding. As creators of society, we exercise considerable freedom when we interact with others.

According to Erving Goffman (1922–1982), all of us can freely manipulate our interactions, influencing each other's interpretations. We are like actors performing on a stage for an audience. In the performance, we always engage in what Goffman calls **impression management**—presenting our "self" in such a way as to make the other person form the desired impression of us. Out with a new date, we try to appear as charming as possible. Interviewed for a job, we try to appear as bright as possible. Sometimes, in order to ensure a peaceful and orderly interaction, we try to appear friendly or respectful in our encounter with obnoxious people. All this is our onstage performance. Backstage—after the date or job interview or unpleasant encounter—we may relax and drop the act. We may even ridicule or curse those obnoxious people we treated so politely.

On many occasions, we perform with one or two persons as a team. This is designed to give a third party a desired impression, such as how knowledgeable, competent, or efficient we are. Thus, teachers take care not to contradict each other in front of students. Doctors who consider each other incompetent praise each other when they are with patients. Occasionally, when a president of the United States fires a troublesome cabinet member, both tell the public how much they admire each other and how much they regret the parting.

Managing others' impressions of us is not the only freedom we have. We also have the latitude to "negotiate" for better social expectations and opportunities associated with our statuses and roles. Thus bureaucracies often operate in very unbureaucratic ways, with officials of different ranks communicating informally and directly rather than formally and through channels. Even prisoners are able to negotiate the nature of their roles with their captors. Cooperative prisoners are often allowed to exercise considerable freedom in their own affairs—as long as they do not try to escape or hold the warden and guards hostage.

In short, despite the social constraints imposed on us by society or its ruling class, we can exercise freedom in face-to-face interactions with others. We can turn a social interaction to our benefit by manip-

On an individual basis.

ulating others' behavior and by negotiating for a better deal in performing our roles.

An Evaluation

The three perspectives highlight different aspects of society. Together they give us clear insight into society as a whole. They show that society has at least three basic features: constraining us with our consent, controlling us for the benefit of our rulers, and letting us exercise our freedom. These three social forces can be found in any society. But *the extent* to which they influence our lives varies from one society to another. Generally, the more traditional and authoritarian a society is, the more powerful the first two forces and the less freedom we can get from symbolic interaction. On the other hand, the more modern and democratic a society is, the less potent the first two forces are and the more freedom we can get from symbolic interaction.

Questions for Discussion and Review

1. How do functionalist and conflict images of society differ?
2. What kinds of freedom does symbolic interaction give us?

CHAPTER REVIEW

1. *What are the basic components of society?* Statuses, roles, groups, and institutions. Statuses are the social positions occupied by individuals in a society. Roles are the expectations of what people should do in accordance with their statuses. Groups are collections of people who interact and have a feeling of unity. Institutions are sets of widely shared beliefs, norms, or procedures for meeting the basic needs of society.

2. *How do we get our statuses?* They are either ascribed or achieved. *Are status and role equivalent?* No, although they are related. Whereas a status is a static label, a role is dynamic, varying with situations and persons. Different people may understand a prescribed role in various ways and perform the same role differently. *How can roles be a source of conflict?* Role conflict occurs when we are expected to play two conflicting roles at the same time. Role strain arises when a single role imposes conflicting demands on us. *How do groups affect our behavior?* In a primary group we interact with others informally, but in a secondary group we interact formally. *Why are institutions so important to society?* Without institutions, society cannot survive, because they are necessary for meeting its basic needs.

3. *What kinds of society can be found in various stages of sociocultural evolution?* Hunting-gathering, pastoral, horticultural, agricultural, industrial, and postindustrial societies. Hunter-gatherers hunt animals and gather plants as their primary means for survival.

Pastoralists domesticate and herd animals as their primary source of food. Horticulturalists produce food primarily by growing plants in small plots of land. Agricultural societies produce food primarily by using plows and draft animals on the farm. Industrial societies produce food for their subsistence primarily by using machinery. And postindustrial societies produce food for subsistence primarily by using high technology.

4. *How does an industrial society differ from a preindustrial one?* Whereas preindustrial society is simple, homogeneous, and intimate, industrial society is complex, heterogeneous, and impersonal. Preindustrial society is traditional; it emphasizes the past, social stability, and the interests of the group. Industrial society is modern, stressing the future, social change, and the interests of the individual. Japanese society, however, is more homogeneous, less impersonal, and more traditional than other industrial societies, contributing to its economic success.

5. *Does society in effect imprison us?* Yes; it is suggested by the functionalist and conflict images of society as a prison. To functionalists, society constrains us via social control and socialization. But to conflict theorists, society controls us for the benefit of the ruling class. On the other hand, symbolic interactionists see society as a collection of symbolic interactions, providing the individual the freedom to manipulate and negotiate those interactions.

KEY TERMS

Achieved status A status attained through one's own actions (p. 75).

Agricultural society A society that produces food primarily by using plows and draft animals on the farm (p. 83).

Ascribed status A status given to us independent of what we do (p. 75).

False consciousness The belief among the masses that justifies their domination by the ruling class to the detriment of their own interests (p. 92).

Folk society Redfield's term for a society that is small, nonliterate, and homogeneous, with a strong solidarity (p. 86).

Gemeinschaft Tönnies's term for a type of society marked by a strong sense of community and by personal interactions among its members (p. 86).

Gesellschaft Tönnies's term for a type of society characterized by individualism and by impersonal interactions (p. 86).

Horticultural society A society that produces food primarily by growing plants in small gardens (p. 82).

Hunting-gathering society A society that hunts animals and gathers plants as its primary means for survival (p. 80).

Impression management The act of presenting our "self" in such a way as to make the other person form the desired impression of us (p. 92).

Industrial society A society that produces food for its subsistence primarily by using machinery (p. 83).

Master status A status that dominates a relationship (p. 75).

Mechanical solidarity Social unity that comes from people performing the same tasks and having similar values (p. 86).

Organic solidarity Social unity that arises from people being forced to depend on one another because their jobs are very specialized (p. 86).

Pastoral society A society that domesticates and herds animals as its primary source of food (p. 81).

Postindustrial society A society that produces food for subsistence primarily by using high technology (p. 84).

Prescribed role A set of expectations about how a person with a particular status should behave (p. 77).

Primary group A group whose members interact informally, relate to each other as whole persons, and enjoy their relationship for its own sake (p. 78).

Role A set of expectations of what individuals should do in accordance with their particular status (p. 77).

Role conflict Conflict between two roles being played simultaneously (p. 77).

Role performance Actual performance of a role (p. 77).

Role strain Stress caused by conflicting expectations from a role (p. 78).

Secondary Group A group in which the individuals interact formally, relate to each other as players of particular roles, and expect to profit from each other (p. 78).

Social aggregate A number of people who happen to be in one place but do not interact with one another (p. 78).

Social group A collection of people who interact with one another and have a certain feeling of unity (p. 78).

Social institution A set of widely shared beliefs, norms, or procedures necessary for meeting the basic needs of society (p. 78).

Society A collection of interacting individuals sharing the same culture and territory (p. 74).

Sociocultural evolution The process of changing from a technologically simple society to a more complex one with significant consequences for social and cultural life (p. 80).

Status A position in society (p. 75).

Status inconsistency The experience of having two contradictory statuses. (p. 76)

Subordinate status The opposite of master status (p. 75).

Urban society Redfield's term for societies that are large, literate, and heterogeneous, with little group solidarity (p. 86).

SUGGESTED READINGS

Bellah, Robert N., et al. 1991. *The Good Society.* New York: Alfred A. Knopf. Shows how U.S. social structure is in danger of crumbling from individual citizens' neglect of its institutions (families, schools, corporations, government, churches, and the law) and how it can be improved through participatory democracy.

Drew, Paul, and Anthony Wootton (eds.). 1988. *Erving Goffman: Exploring the Interaction Order.* Boston: Northeastern University Press. A collection of clearly written analyses of Goffman's important works on social interaction.

Drucker, Peter F. 1993. *Post-Capitalist Society.* New York: HarperCollins. An analysis of how an industrial, capitalist society has been changing into a postindustrial, knowledge society.

Lenski, Gerhard, Jean Lenski, and Patrick Nolan, 1995. *Human Societies,* 7th ed. New York: McGraw-Hill. The authors use the perspective of sociocultural evolution to analyze various types of societies, including those that have been briefly discussed in this chapter.

Little, Daniel. 1989. *Understanding Peasant China: Case Studies in the Philosophy of Social Science.* New Haven, Conn.: Yale University Press. A clearly written analysis of the conflicting views on changes in an agricultural society.

GROUPS AND ORGANIZATIONS

Myths and Realities

MYTH: *If two groups of people have become hostile to each other, it is impossible for friendship to develop between them.*
REALITY: If they have to work together to solve a common problem, friendship will likely emerge.

MYTH: *When we look for a job we can get more help from our close friends than from mere acquaintances.*
REALITY: Acquaintances are more effective in helping us find a job because we may already be aware of the job openings known to our friends, but we may not know of the many other job opportunities our acquaintances can tell us about.

MYTH: *In a group situation you will never accept someone else's view when you are certain it is wrong.*
REALITY: The pressure to conform can make you accept that view if it is held by the majority.

female university president was expecting a visit from a male member of the board of trustees. When her secretary told her that the visitor had arrived, she left her office to greet him at the reception area. Before ushering him into her office, the woman handed a letter to her secretary and said: "I've just finished drafting it. *Do you think you could* type it right away? I'd like to get it out before lunch. And *would you please do me a favor* and hold all calls while I'm meeting with Mr. Smith here?" After they were inside her office, with the door closed, Mr. Smith told her that he thought she had spoken inappropriately to her secretary. "Remember," he said, "*You're* the president!" To Mr. Smith, the president was self-deprecating and lacking in self-confidence, not knowing how to give orders like a man (Tannen, 1994b).

Mr. Smith didn't get it. He did not realize that many women can effectively run an organization without playing the macho game of domination with their subordinates. In fact, the egalitarian style of management, as shown by the university president's expression of respect to her secretary, has made many female managers more successful than their male counterparts who throw their weight around. To get a deeper insight into this female approach to management, let us first analyze the basic characteristics of groups and organizations.

SOCIAL GROUPS

In a classic experiment, Muzafer Sherif (1956) took a group of white, middle-class, 12-year-old boys to a summer camp at Robbers' Cave State Park in Oklahoma. Sherif pretended to be a caretaker named Mr. Musee. For the first three days, the boys lived on one site at the camp and became acquainted. Then they were separated. Half of the boys were given one cabin and one set of activities, and the other half, another. Soon each group of boys had chosen a name, one group calling themselves "Eagles" and the other, "Rattlers." Each had their own insignia on caps and T-shirts, their own jargon, and jokes and secrets.

Each band of boys, in short, had formed a **social group**—a collection of people who interact with one another and have a certain feeling of unity. A social group is more than either a social aggregate or a social category. A **social aggregate** is just a number of people who happen to be in one place but do not interact with one another, such as the boys when they first arrived at the camp. A **social category** is a

number of people who have something in common but neither interact with one another nor gather in one place. Men as a whole constitute a social category. So do women as a whole, college students as a whole, and so on. A social category becomes a social group when the people in the category interact with one another and identify themselves as members of the group. Thus, the boys at Robbers' Cave were members of a social category—12-year-old boys—but they became a social group only when they began to interact with one another and consider themselves members of the Eagles or the Rattlers. A closer look at Sherif's experiment can give us a clearer idea of the significance of groups.

In-groups and Out-groups

A few days after Sherif had put the boys in separate cabins, he arranged for the groups to compete against one another in baseball, tug of war, and other games. The winners of the games were awarded points toward a prize—camp knives. At first, the Eagles and Rattlers were very friendly with each other, but soon the games turned into fierce competitions. The two groups began to call each other stinkers, sneaks, and cheaters. They raided each other's cabins, and scuffles became common.

The boys' behavior showed that in forming each group, the youngsters set up a boundary between themselves as an in-group and the others as an out-group. An **in-group** is the group to which an individual is strongly tied as a member, and an **out-group** is the group of which an individual is not a member. Every social group defines a boundary between itself and everyone else to some extent, but a cohesive in-group has three characteristics. First, members of the in-group normally use symbols such as names, slogans, dress, or badges to identify themselves so that they will be distinguishable from the out-group. As we have seen, one group of boys in Sherif's experiment called themselves Eagles, and the other, Rattlers. Second, a characteristic of a cohesive in-group is that its members view themselves in terms of positive stereotypes and the out-group in negative stereotypes. Sherif's boys, for example, liked to say things like, "We are smart, and they are dumb!" We can also witness similar social behavior among college students: rating their own fraternities, sororities, or organizations higher in prestige than someone else's and disparaging others as "objectionable." Third, the in-group is inclined to compete or clash with the out-group.

Sherif's experiment showed how easily loyalty to an in-group can generate hostility toward an out-group and even aggression when there is competition for some resource (in this case, prizes). Competition with another group can also strengthen the unity within each group. But there was another phase in Sherif's experiment. He set up situations in which the groups had to work together to solve a common problem. When the camp's sole water tank broke down, he told the groups to work together to repair it. As they cooperated, friendships began to emerge between Eagles and Rattlers. In short, cooperation between groups eroded the hostility and divisions that competition had spurred.

Reference Groups

In-groups can become **reference groups**, a group that is used as the frame of reference for evaluating one's own behavior. Members of a street gang, for example, may evaluate themselves by the standards of the gang and feel proud about a successful mugging. This pos-

itive self-evaluation reflects the *normative effect* of a reference group whose members share the same view of themselves. If other members of your reference group (say, your parents) have high self-esteem, you too are likely to have high self-esteem. The normative effect basically involves imitating the reference group. However, reference groups can also have *comparison effects* and *associative effects* on self-appraisals. If most of your classmates shine in academic achievement, you are likely to compare yourself with them. As a result, you may have a negative self-evaluation, feeling that your academic performance is not up to par. Being associated with the brilliant group, though, you may feel proud of yourself, "basking in reflected glory" (Felson and Reed, 1986).

These reference groups are at the same time in-groups. But we do not have to be members of a group in order to use it as our reference group. As a student, you might have professional athletes as your reference group. If that is the case, you would probably judge your athletic skills to be inadequate—even if they are excellent compared with those of most amateurs—and perhaps you would work harder in an effort to meet professional standards.

Whether we are members of reference groups or not, they frequently exert a powerful influence on our behavior and attitudes, as has been suggested. In fact, their impact became well known long ago, after

"Of course you're going to be depressed if you keep comparing yourself with successful people."

Theodore Newcomb (1958) published his study of the students at Bennington College, a very liberal college in Vermont. Newcomb found that most of the students came from conservative families and that most of the freshmen were conservative. A small minority remained conservative throughout their time at the school. But most became more liberal the longer they stayed at the college. These students, Newcomb concluded, used the liberal faculty or older students as their reference group, whereas the minority continued to look to their conservative families as their reference group.

Primary and Secondary Groups

It is not at all surprising that some students used their families as a reference group. After all, families are the best examples of the groups Charles Cooley (1909) called *primary* chiefly because they "are fundamental in forming the social nature and ideals of the individual." In a **primary group** the individuals interact informally, relate to each other as whole persons, and enjoy their relationship for its own sake. This is one of the two main types of social groups. In the other type, **Secondary group**, the individuals interact formally, relate to each other as players of particular roles, and expect to profit from each other.

Families, peer groups, fraternities, sororities, neighbors, and small communities are all examples of primary groups. They are marked by what are called *primary relationships*. Communication in these relationships is not limited by formalities. The people in a primary group interact in an informal way, and they relate to each other as unique, whole persons. Moreover, they enjoy the relationship for its own sake.

These characteristics become clearer when we compare them with those of *secondary relationships*. The people in a secondary group do not know each other personally. They may have little face-to-face interaction. If they interact, they do so formally. They relate to each other only in terms of particular roles and for certain practical purposes.

Consider sales clerks and their customers. In these secondary groups, there are likely to be few if any emotional ties, and the people know little about each other. Their communications are bound by formalities. Sales clerks are not likely to kiss their customers or to cry with them over the death of a relative. The clerk will treat the customer as a customer only—not as a person who is also a mother of three, a jazz lover, a victim of an airplane hijacking, or a person who laughs easily but worries a lot. In contrast, we expect our families to treat us as whole persons, to be interested in our experiences, preferences, and feelings. The clerk is also likely to treat one customer much like another. We expect this attitude in a clerk, but the same attitude in our family or friends would hurt our feelings. Finally, the clerk and the customer have a relationship only because each has a specific task or purpose in mind: to buy or sell something. They use their relationship for this purpose. The relationship among family members, in contrast, is not oriented to a particular task but engaged in for its own sake. In fact, if we believe that a person in a primary group is interested in us only as a means to some end, we are

(Top) As members of a primary group, these high school students interact informally and relate to one another as unique persons. They also enjoy the relationship for its own sake. (Bottom) As members of a secondary group, sales clerks and their customers know little about each other, and their communication, therefore, is bound by formalities.

ENRICHING OUR LIVES

We can turn secondary relationships into primary relationships. One strategy is to schmooze, a Yiddish word meaning to befriend, to charm, to win over. This reading describes how politicians like President Clinton and his wife, Hillary, have used schmoozing to get other people to do what they want.

Schmoozing

Washington, D.C., is the schmooze capital of the world. Schmoozing, its partisans know, wins new friendships and cements the old. It stretches your database and opens new doors. It helps you avoid conflict, negotiate deals and sway even your sworn enemies. After all, when you've charmed someone she's more likely to give you what you want. You can effectively schmooze almost anyplace—on the job or at a PTA meeting, in a car pool or at a dinner party; and it works on almost anyone—your boss, your neighbor, a store clerk, your child's teacher.

You, too, can learn to schmooze like a pro—all it takes is a little practice. Here are some winning strategies from Washington's finest.

Do make time to schmooze, no matter how busy you are. Invite an associate to lunch or take an exercise class with a co-worker and pour on the charm. Hillary Clinton discovered the value of afternoon tea. She invited twenty local Washington reporters, schmoozed each in turn, and came away with twenty powerful new allies.

Do give the person you're schmoozing your undivided attention. No peeking over his or her shoulder for someone more interesting or important.

Do add that personal touch. I once knew an ambassador's wife who, to enumerate why you should do what she wanted, would gently bend down your fingers one by one as she listed the reasons—a surprising effective technique. Bob Strauss, former ambassador to the Soviet Union and Washington's very best all-time schmoozer, often puts his hand on the arm of the person he's talking to.

Be sure to do your homework. Keep track of names, faces, connections and important dates—people are flattered when you remember things about them. Before the inauguration, Hillary had an aide write to every single member of Congress, requesting the dates of birthdays and wedding anniversaries.

Don't be afraid to schmooze your foes. It's not hypocritical to ask for their point of view, to listen to what they have to say, to show you respect them even if you disagree. When Hillary went to Capitol Hill to meet with the Republican Health Care Task Force, she asked each member to "Tell me what's the most important issue to *you* in health care" and listened to all of them with rapt attention.

Don't be a snob. It's no good schmoozing some people, but not those you don't think are important enough. During his campaign, President Clinton got into a deep schmooze with a technician at a TV studio. "The second the show was over, Bill took up the discussion again and finished it," says one observer. "And the young man wasn't even old enough to vote!"

Not this time, but next perhaps. For in an often harsh, unfriendly world, a good schmooze is remembered for years.

Try it and see.

Excerpted from Diana McLellan, "How to Get Other People to Do What You Want," *LADIES HOME JOURNAL,* June 1993, pp. 118, 123. © 1993, Meredith Corporation. Reprinted from LADIES' HOME JOURNAL MAGAZINE with permission of the author.

likely to feel "used." Parents are hurt if they feel their children are interested only in the food, shelter, and money the parents provide.

Primary relationships—with our relatives, friends, or neighbors—are very precious to us. As research has shown, they are particularly helpful when we are going through stressful life events. They help ease recovery from heart attacks, prevent childbirth complications, make child rearing easier, lighten the burden of household finances, cushion the impact of job loss by providing financial assistance and employment information. However, primary relationships are not always more beneficial than secondary relationships. Our close friends cannot help us get as good a job as our acquaintances can. Our friends move in the same social circle as we do, but our acquaintances, to whom we have only weak ties, move in different circles. Hence, we may already be aware of the job openings known to our friends, but we may not know of the many other job opportunities our acquaintances can tell us about (Granovetter, 1983; Bridges and Villemez, 1986).

Instrumental leaders are primarily concerned about achieving goals. Expressive leaders are more concerned with followers' feelings, making sure that harmony and cohesiveness can prevail in the group. A small group such as this basketball team needs both types of leadership from its coach to function effectively

Group Leadership

In most groups, there are two kinds of leaders. **Instrumental leaders** are those who achieve their group's goal by getting others to focus on task performance. They may say something like "Let's get to work!" or "I think we're getting off the track." Such tactics show the leaders as overseers whose exchange with followers involves a "unidirectional downward influence" and a weak sense of common fate. Although this kind of leadership can get the group to move toward a goal, it can also rub people the wrong way. Not surprisingly, most people tend not to like their instrumental leaders. But most people are more likely to like their **expressive leaders**, who achieve group harmony by making others feel good. This second type of leaders is more concerned with members' feelings, making sure that everybody is happy, so that cohesiveness can reign in the group. The exchange between such leaders and their followers reflects a partnership, characterized by reciprocal influence, a strong sense of common fate, and mutual trust, respect, and liking. A group needs both types of leaders to function effectively.

Group Conformity

Because they are seen as competently performing certain tasks for the group, leaders are usually given an **idiosyncrasy credit**, the privilege that allows leaders to deviate from their group's norms. The rank and file, however, are expected to conform. In a group, the pressure to conform is so powerful that individual members tend to knuckle under. They will go along with the majority even though they privately disagree with it. This point has been driven home by Solomon Asch's (1955) classic experiments. Asch brought together groups of eight or nine students each. He asked them to tell him which of the three lines on a card was as long as the line on another card. In each group only one was a real subject—the others were the experimenter's secret accomplices, who had been instructed to give the same obviously wrong answer. Asch found that nearly a third of the subjects changed their minds and accepted the majority's answer even though they were sure that their own answer was correct and the others' answer was wrong (Figure 5.1).

The group to which Asch's subjects felt compelled to conform were strangers. The pressure to conform is even greater among people we know. It usually gives rise to what Irving Janis (1982) calls **groupthink**, the tendency for members of a cohesive group to maintain consensus to the extent of ignoring the truth. Groupthink may lead to disastrous decisions, with tragic consequences. It caused President Kennedy and his top advisors to approve the CIA's unsound plan to invade Cuba. It caused President Johnson and his advisors to escalate the Vietnam War. It caused President Reagan and his advisors to get involved in the Iran-Contra affair. In each case a few members had serious doubts about the majority decision but did not speak out.

It is even more difficult to voice dissent if the leader rules with an iron hand. About thirty years ago, when Nikita Khrushchev, ruler of what was then the Soviet Union, came to the United States, he met with reporters at the Washington Press Club. The first anonymous written question he received was: "Today you talked about the hideous rule of your predecessor, Stalin, who killed thousands of his political opponents. You were one of his closest aides and colleagues during those years. What were you doing all that time?" Khrushchev's face turned red. "Who asked that?" he shouted. No one answered. "Who asked that?" he shouted again. Still no answer. "That's what I was doing: keeping my mouth shut" (Bennis, 1989). Leaders can obviously prevent groupthink by encouraging and rewarding dissent. Interestingly, the greater the disagreement among group members, the better their collective decision. This is because "with more disagreement, people are forced to look at a wider range of possibilities" (Bennis, 1989).

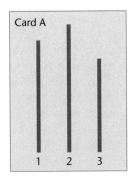 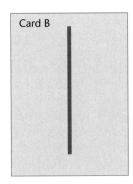

FIGURE 5.1
Would You Conform?
Asch's experiments suggest that if you are asked privately which line on card A is as long as the line on card B, there is a 99 percent chance that you would correctly pick line 2. But if you find yourself in a group where all the other members choose line 3—an obviously wrong number, there is about a 33 percent chance that you would yield to the group pressure to conform by choosing line 3.

Group Size

Aside from pressuring people to conform, social groups also cause them to behave in other ways. This has a lot to do with the specific size of groups. The smallest group is a *dyad,* which contains two people. A dyad can easily become the most cohesive of all the groups because its members are inclined to be most personal and to interact most intensely with each other. This is why we are more willing to share our secrets in a dyad than in a larger group, secrets such as our parents getting divorced or father having been committed to a mental hospital. A dyad, however, is also the most likely to break up. If just one person leaves, the group will vanish. Such a threat does not exist for a *triad,* a three-person group. If one member drops out, the group can still survive. A triad also makes it possible for two people to gang up on the third one or for one member to patch up a quarrel between the other two. But triads lose the quality of intimacy that is the hallmark of dyads; as the saying goes, "Two's company, three's a crowd."

If more people join a triad, the group will become even less personal, with each individual finding it extremely difficult to talk and relate to each of the other members. The upshot is the emergence of many different coalitions (made up of two against one, two against three, three against one, and so on) and many mediating roles for various conflicting subgroups. The reason is that even a small growth in the size of a group increases dramatically the number of relationships among its members. If a dyad, for example, grows into a seven-person group, the number of possible relationships will shoot up from

one to 966 (Hare, 1962). Generally, as a group grows larger, it changes for the worse. Its members become less satisfied, participate less often in group activities, are less likely to cooperate with one another, and are more likely to misbehave. Even the Japanese, universally known for their politeness, may become rude on a crowded train. This is because increase in group size makes it difficult to maintain interpersonal relationships and individual recognition (Mullen et al., 1989; Levine and Moreland, 1990).

There are other, more fascinating effects of group size. In a dyad or triad, the host usually has the edge over the visitor, with the host more likely to get his or her own way. Thus a businesswoman can strike a better deal if she invites the other person to her office. But such territorial dominance—the "home-court" advantage—may disappear if the group is larger than a triad. In public places, a large group may also inhibit an individual from helping someone in distress. Over 50 studies have shown consistently that people are less likely to help a victim if others are around than if they are alone with the victim. A major reason is that the knowledge that others are present and available to respond allows the individual to shift some of the responsibility to others. The same factor operates in "social loafing": as the size of a group performing a certain task increases, each member tends not to work as hard (Latané and Nida, 1981).

Questions for Discussion and Review

1. What characteristics of social groups make them different from social aggregates and categories?
2. What are some social functions of in-groups and reference groups?
3. Why are primary groups fundamental for human existence?
4. How does the concept of groupthink help explain experiences you have had in social groups?
5. How does group size affect our behavior?

SOCIAL NETWORKS

Regardless of size, groups can develop **social networks,** webs of social relationships that link individuals or groups to one another. We are all involved in numerous networks. Since birth, we have been constantly developing or expanding our networks by forming social ties with various people who come into our lives. As soon as we were born, our parents drew us into their networks, which became our own. When we began to attend school, we started to develop social ties with children in our neighborhoods, with our schoolmates and teachers, and with children in our churches, synagogues, or other places of worship. As adults, we often get into all kinds of networks, such as those at the college we attend, the place where we work, and the social organizations we belong to. These networks, however, are quite different from the ones that we joined before we turned 17 or 18. Our current adult networks are more diffuse, more loosely organized, and made up of weaker social ties.

Individuals are not the only ones joining and developing social networks. Groups, organizations, and even whole nation-states also forge ties with each other. That is why there are numerous intergroup networks (for example, among lawyers, judges, doctors, business executives, and other professional groups), intercommunity networks (such as the U.S. Conference of Mayors), and international networks (such as the United Nations).

Characteristics

To make it easier to see what networks look like, sociologists use such devices as points (technically called *nodes*) and lines (or *links*) to represent them. A point can be a person, group, or nation-state. A line can be any kind of social relationship connecting two points. The relationship can be a friendship; an exchange of visits; a business transaction; a romantic entanglement; the flow of information, resources, influence, or power; or an expression of such feelings as affection, sympathy, or hostility.

Consider what your college network may look like. Let's make A in Figure 5.2 represent you and B, C, D, and E your friends. The lines show that all five of you are *directly* connected to one another. Your college network also comprises 12 other people, namely, F through Q. This is because four of you—A, B, C, and D—are *indirectly* tied, through E, to those individuals. Because of your (A's) friendship with E and E's friendship with F, you belong to the same network as F and all the other individuals, whom you may not know. Thus, a social network can consist of both directly and indirectly connected individuals. Because each of the numerous individuals to whom you are indirectly linked knows, directly and indirectly, numerous other people, you may ultimately belong to a network involving millions of people all over the world. This is especially true today, because easily accessible air travel has made it possible for people from many different countries to establish links with one another.

Given the massive network to which we belong, we should not be surprised to meet a total stranger in some faraway city, state, or foreign country and discover that the stranger happens to know somebody that we know. On such an occasion, that stranger and we are likely to exclaim, "What a small world!" Indeed, a series of classic experiments have demonstrated how really small our world is. In one of those studies, the wife of a divinity-school student who lived in Cambridge, Massachusetts, was selected as a "target person." Her name, address, occupation, and other facts about her were printed in a booklet. Copies of this booklet were randomly distributed to a group of people in Wichita, Kansas. They were asked to send it directly to the target person only if they knew her personally. If she was a stranger to them, they were asked to send the booklet to their friends or acquaintances who they thought might know her. Interestingly, many (30 percent) of the booklets sent by strangers did finally reach the target, after passing through the hands of only about five intermediaries (Milgram, 1967; Travers and Milgram, 1969).

Effects

A social network usually acts as a support system for its members. It helps members maintain good physical and mental health or prevent physical and mental breakdown. It also reduces the risk of dying prematurely or of committing suicide. There are sev-

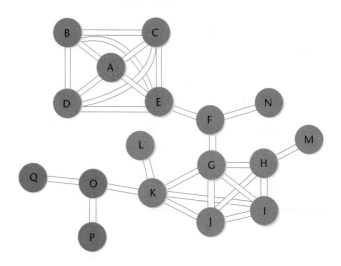

FIGURE 5.2
A Social Network.
In this network, the individuals A, B, C, D, and E are directly linked to one another. But through E's friendship with F, the other four members (A, B, C, and D) are indirectly connected to F, and all five of them (A, B, C, D, and E) are also indirectly linked too G, H, I and so on. Thus, a social network can consist of both directly and indirectly connected individuals.

eral reasons for this. Our friends, relatives, and co-workers, as part of our social network, can make us feel good by boosting our self-esteem despite our faults, weaknesses, and difficulties. Being more objective than we are about our own problems, they can open our eyes to solutions that we are too emotionally distressed to see. The companionship and camaraderie from our network, fortified by frequent participation in joint leisuretime and recreational activities, can bring us joys and pleasures while chasing away loneliness, worries, and trouble. Finally, our friends and relatives often give us "instrumental support"—money and service—to help us cope with our problems. All these social-psychological factors have a further physiological impact on our health. They keep our blood pressure and heart rate at low levels, presumably by lowering our brain's secretion of stress hormones (Lin, 1982; House et al., 1988; Pescosolido and Georgianna, 1989).

On the other hand, our intimates place many demands on our time and personal resources. They can further irritate us by criticizing us or invading our privacy. This is why in a study of the social networks of 120 widows, the women reported that more than two-thirds of the people who made their lives more difficult were their friends and relatives. In fact, these negative experiences seem to drag down people's sense of well-being more than the positive experiences of receiving social support can raise it up. Negative encounters usually have a stronger impact than positive ones, because an altercation sticks out like a sore thumb against a background of generally pleasant experiences. Thus, a pleasant exchange at a wedding that is already filled with strife between in-laws can restore only a little peacefulness, but a single heated exchange at an otherwise tranquil wedding can ruin the whole experience (Fischman, 1986).

In sum, social networks can have both positive and negative consequences for people's lives.

Questions for Discussion and Review

1. What does a social network consist of?
2. How can social networks affect our lives?

FORMAL ORGANIZATIONS

Of the various kinds of social groups that we have discussed, secondary groups are the most likely to develop into **formal organizations,** groups whose activities are rationally designed to achieve specific goals. Not all secondary groups become formal orga-

nizations, though. Some secondary groups are small and transitory, without explicitly stated goals and rules. A sales clerk and customer interact on a temporary basis to achieve a generally known but unstated objective without following any explicitly described rules for carrying out the business transaction. This is not a formal organization. Other secondary groups are large and more permanent and have explicit goals and working procedures. Government agencies, for instance, often last well beyond their members' lifetimes, and are large and complex. Their goals and rules must be stated explicitly so that the work of their many members can be coordinated. These agencies, along with hospitals, colleges, business firms, political parties, the U.S. Army, the Sierra Club, and the like, are examples of formal organizations.

Goals and Means

The importance of goals cannot be emphasized enough. Without them, organizations would not come into being. Goals can help an organization determine what to do and offer guidelines for measuring performance—how successful it is in meeting its goals. While most organizations fall by the wayside if they fail to realize their goals, some organizations continue to exist, even to thrive on their failure to achieve their goals. Government agencies that enforce drug laws, for example, continue to exist because they fail to put drug traffickers out of business.

Whether they achieve their goals or not, all organizations develop certain common means for achieving them. Generally, they engage in *rational planning.* They must decide what specific tasks are necessary to realize the goals, who are best qualified to carry out the tasks, and how to coordinate the various tasks to avoid costly conflict and achieve high efficiency.

More specifically, first, through a *division of labor,* different tasks are assigned to workers with different skills. This makes it easier for an organization to attain its goals than if all workers perform the same task. But the division of labor may get out of hand, with one worker producing an item (say, a car door) that cannot be fitted into another item (a car body) made by someone else. Thus an organization must establish a *hierarchy of control,* which makes a supervisor, a manager, and other administrators responsible for overseeing and directing workers to ensure that various activities are properly coordinated. Administrators must deal with workers in accordance with a set of *formalized rules,* without showing any favoritism. Strict adherence to the rules themselves may also explain why formal organizations typically

A formal organization is a secondary group whose activities are rationally designed to achieve specific goals, such as making a movie.

appear impersonal. The rules themselves may also explain why organizations appear to have a life of their own and can outlive original members. Because the rules stipulate how replacements are to be found, organizations do not collapse when certain personnel leave.

Power and Involvement

According to Amitai Etzioni (1975), virtually every organization includes "higher participants" (such as the administrators) and "lower participants" (the rank and file). The function of the higher participants is to exercise power over the lower participants so that the latter will help the organization achieve its goals. Three kinds of power are available to higher participants: (1) *coercive power,* the use of physical force; (2) *remunerative power,* the use of material rewards such as money and similar incentives to ensure cooperation; and (3) *normative power,* the use of moral persuasion, the prestige of a leader, or the promise of social acceptance. There are also three kinds of involvement by lower participants: (1) *alienative,* in which case they do not support the organization's goals; (2) *calculative,* which means they are moderately supportive; and (3) *moral involvement,* in which case they strongly support the organization.

From these kinds of power and of involvement, Etzioni constructed this typology of organizations:

Kinds of Power	Kinds of Involvement		
	Alienative	**Calculative**	**Moral**
Coercive	(1)	2	3
Remunerative	4	(5)	6
Normative	7	8	(9)

Of the nine types, only three—1, 5, and 9—represent the huge majority of organizations. These, then, are the most common types, and the remaining six are rare. Etzioni called the three most common types *coercive organizations* (1), *utilitarian organizations* (5), and *normative organizations* (9).

Coercive Organizations Prisons, concentration camps, and custodial mental hospitals are examples of coercive organizations. In each, force or the threat of force is used to achieve the organization's main goal: keeping the inmates in. The inmates obviously do not enjoy being imprisoned; they will run away if they have the chance. They are alienated from the organization and do not support its goals at all.

Understandably, the higher participants—prison administrators—have to act tough toward the inmates, seeking compliance by threatening solitary confinement if they try to escape. In short, in this kind of organization, coercion is the main form of power used, and the involvement by lower participants is alienative. *But they agree to obey.*

Utilitarian Organizations   Factories, banks, and other businesses are all utilitarian organizations in Etzioni's classification. The higher participants use incentives such as money to ensure that lower participants work to achieve the organization's goals. The rank and file tend to be moderately supportive of those goals. They are likely to calculate whether it is worth their while to work hard, asking "What's in it for me?" In general, the more attractive their remuneration—in money, or fringe benefits, or working conditions—the more committed lower participants are to the organization. Thus, the major form of power used in utilitarian organizations is remunerative, and the typical form of involvement by lower-level participants is calculative.

Normative Organizations   If Mormons do not pay their tithe, they may be denied access to religious services, but they are not subject to arrest and imprisonment. If a political party wants you to vote for its candidates, it may send you letters or knock on your door, and it will certainly advertise; but it does not offer you money. Churches and political parties are examples of a type of organization very different from coercive and utilitarian organizations. Their power over lower participants is based on persuasion, exhortation, social pressure, public recognition, or a leader's appeal. This normative power is sufficient because most of the participants generally want to do what the organization is asking; they are strongly committed to its goals. For this reason, normative organizations are sometimes called *voluntary associations*. In addition to religious organizations and political organizations, examples include colleges, social clubs, and charitable organizations. In Etzioni's terms, their primary form of power is normative, and involvement by the rank and file is moral.

Mixed Organizations   In fact, no organization relies entirely on just one type of power. All three types can be found in most organizations. Still the majority do use one type of power far more than the other two. Prisons, for example, may use normative power through rehabilitation programs, but still rely mostly on coercion. A business may use speeches to inspire its workers, but it depends mostly on wages to ensure their involvement.

Though rare, some organizations do depend on two types of power to about the same degree. A good example is combat units which rely heavily on both normative and coercive powers. First, they apply normative powers through basic training, military schools, and patriotic pep talks. Second, while it is not practical for the military to offer huge sums of money to induce soldiers to risk limbs and lives, it can apply effective coercion by withdrawing furloughs from uncooperative members and by imprisoning or executing deserters.

An Evaluation   The Etzioni typology is useful for knowing the characteristics of practically all organizations. It can also explain why some organizations flounder while others sail smoothly. As Etzioni suggests, organizational effectiveness depends on running an outfit for what it is. A prison managed like a coercive organization, a business firm like a utilitarian organization, or a political party like a normative organization can be expected to do well. On the other hand, a prison run like a political party or a business firm operated like a prison would likely be in trouble.

However, because Etzioni concentrates on what goes on inside organizations, his typology ignores environmental, contextual, or external influences. Outside factors do affect organizations significantly. For example, largely societal and cultural differences make Swedish prisons less coercive than U.S. prisons. Also because of social and cultural differences, Japanese firms are run more like normative organizations, whereas U.S. companies are managed more like utilitarian organizations.

Classifying Organizational Theories

All around us, we find organizations using the types of control Etzioni described. Much as we might try to stay in the warmer world of friends and family, we cannot escape these organizations and their power. How the organizations use power affects how they operate as well as our ability to achieve goals we share with them.

There have been many attempts to analyze just how organizations operate and what types of operation are most efficient. Under what circumstances, for example, can an organization do without moral persuasion? What is the most effective way to offer remunerative rewards? How should managers and workers interact if the organization is to be effective? Answers can be found in organizational theories.

A great number of theories have been proposed since the early part of this century. Some describe what organizations are like, most suggest what they *should* be like to achieve their goals. These organizational theories can be classified into three types according to how they may have been influenced by the three major sociological perspectives. (1) Theories that may be considered functionalist portray organizations as conflict-free, harmonious systems in which members can be encouraged through "scientific management" or "human relations" to work harder to achieve the organizational objective. (2) Those that may be considered conflict theories emphasize the importance of social equality for attaining organizational success. (3) Theories that may be regarded as symbolic interactionist focus on organizational culture as members' shared definitions of their life in the organization or depict bureaucracy as the embodiment of the West's "rational" worldview. We analyze these three types of theories in the following sections.

Questions for Discussion and Review

1. What are the principal features of a formal organization?
2. How do coercive, normative, and utilitarian organizations differ from each other?
3. In general, what do organizational theories tell us?

FUNCTIONALIST PERSPECTIVE

For functionalists, organizations are essentially free of human conflict. Members come together to cooperate in achieving a common goal. Given such a harmonious environment, members can be induced to increase their productivity for the betterment of everybody in the organization. Two well-known theories have been proposed to show how.

Scientific Management

Early in this century, U.S. engineer Frederick Taylor (1911) published the first systematic presentation of what was soon called *scientific management*. Taylor assumed that the primary goal of an organization is to maximize efficiency. For a manufacturing company, this means getting maximum productivity, the highest possible output per worker per hour. He further assumed that workers are not geniuses and can be manipulated. As a result, Taylor argued that the success of an organization depends on three elements: maximum division of labor, close supervision of workers, and an incentive system of piecework wages.

To obtain maximum division of labor, production must be broken down into numerous simple and extremely easy to perform tasks. Each of these is then defined down to the tiniest detail, so that it can be completed in the shortest time possible. One of Taylor's specific recommendations was that zigzag motions of the hands must be avoided; workers should begin and complete their motions with both hands simultaneously. To ensure that the task is properly carried out, the worker must be closely and continuously supervised. Taylor suggested that there be four types of supervisors—setting-up boss, speed boss, quality inspector, and repair boss—and that the supervisors in turn be controlled by a planning department. Finally, to be sure they work as hard as possible, workers should be paid by the piece: the more units each produces, the higher the pay.

Today, many companies still apply Taylor's basic principles. Productivity appears to decline if the basic points of this model are not applied to some degree. Scientific management works particularly well in the world of production, where the work is mostly routine. But the theory ignores many aspects of organizations and human behavior. It looks only at the *official* organization, the formal relationships between workers and supervisors. Most sociologists have criticized the theory for treating human beings as machines, arguing that this contributes to worker dissatisfaction and ultimately to lower productivity.

Human Relations

In the early 1930s, industrial psychologist Elton Mayo (1933) challenged practically all the assumptions of the scientific management theory. He argued that: (1) Workers' productivity is not determined by their physical capacity but by their "social capacity," their sensitivity to the work environment. No matter how fast they *can* do their job, they will not produce a lot if their fellow workers frown on the idea of working too fast. (2) Noneconomic rewards, such as friendship with co-workers and respect from management, play a central role in determining the motivation and happiness of workers. Thus, wages are less important than Taylor claimed. (3) The greatest specialization is not the most efficient division of labor. Extreme specialization creates problems for those coordinating the work. Supervisors are hard put to know all the details of very specialized tasks. (4) Workers do not react to management and its incentives as isolated individuals but as members of a group. They will reject management's offer of high pay for maximum productivity if their fellow workers are against working too hard.

The scientific management model of industrial organization suggests that a company can achieve maximum productivity if its workers do a simple repetitive task under close supervision. Scientific management works best in manufacturing companies, where the work is mostly routine; but it has been criticized for treating workers as machines.

These points make up the *human relations theory*. In contrast to scientific management, it emphasizes how productivity depends on social forces, especially the informal relations among workers. The key to increased productivity is not official organization, as Taylor assumed, but **informal organization**, a group formed by the informal relations among members of an organization—based on personal interactions, not on any plan by the organization.

Empirical support for this theory came from Mayo's studies at the Hawthorne plant in Chicago in the 1930s. As we discussed in Chapter 2 (Doing Sociology), one of these studies showed that workers increased their productivity regardless of changes in the physical environment. Productivity went up, for example, when the experimenter brightened the workplace, but it also went up when he dimmed the lights. Mayo concluded that the employees worked harder because the presence of the researcher made them feel important; management seemed to be treating them as people, not mere machines. Another study at the same plant examined whether output was determined by financial incentives. Surprisingly, it was shaped by an informal norm. The norm forbade

working too hard as well as working too slowly. Anyone working too hard was ridiculed as a "rate buster," and anyone working too slowly was scorned as a "chiseler." As a result, each worker tried to produce as much as the other workers, rather than trying to meet management's goals (Roethlisberger and Dickson, 1939). These studies have clearly shown that informal relations can increase worker productivity.

The human relations theory covers parts of the organization ignored by scientific management, but it too has limitations. First, it exaggerates the importance of the informal group life at the workplace. Most workers will not wake up every morning feeling that they cannot wait to go to work in order to be with their co-workers. They are more interested in their families and friends outside the workplace. Second, informal social relations may create more pleasant conditions in the plant, but they cannot significantly reduce the tediousness of the manual job itself. While a person may enjoy working with certain individuals, it cannot transform an inherently boring job into one that is exciting. Relations with co-workers, though, may be more significant to white-collar and professional workers, whose jobs often involve a great deal of interaction with co-workers, than to blue-collar workers.

Questions for Discussion and Review

1. What are the basic features of the scientific management theory?
2. What is the essence of the human relations theory?

CONFLICT PERSPECTIVE

According to the conflict perspective, the major problem with the scientific management and human relations theories is that they fail to take into account the reality of conflict in organizations. Given the inequality in income, status, and other rewards between management and workers, the lower participants cannot be expected to give their all to fulfill the higher participants' wish for maximum productivity. The inequality puts a severe limit on how far management can successfully use scientific management or human relations to manipulate workers into superproducers. By contrast, the practice of *equality* can help ensure organizational success. This is the main point of the collectivist and feminist models of organization, which have been influenced by the conflict perspective.

Collectivist Model

According to Karl Marx, capitalist organizations—or business corporations—are the capitalists' tool for exploiting the working class. Eventually, Marx claimed, the corporations will be abolished in a classless, communist society, replaced by collectivist organizations in which managers and workers work together as equals and for equal pay. The workers would be much more productive than the exploited ones of today. In the meantime, an approximation of this organizational model exists to some extent in the United States.

The typical U.S. corporation is bureaucratic, paternalistic, or undemocratic because those on the top dictate to those below and those at the bottom may not choose who is above them or influences their decisions. Power, then, flows from the top down. By contrast, in a collectivist organization, power flows from the bottom up. In the United States, this element of the collectivist model can be seen in some 5,000 "alternative institutions" established during the 1970s. The free schools, free medical clinics, legal collectives, food cooperatives, communes, and cooperative businesses are a legacy of movements during the 1960s against authority and "the Establishment." These enterprises are collectively owned and managed, without any hierarchy of authority. They tend to be in craft production and other special niches of the economy that exempt them from directly competing with conventional companies. Most are quite small, averaging six employees, but this size helps preserve full worker participation. The workers are highly satisfied with their jobs and strongly identify with their firms. Because they are also owners, workers tend to work too hard and often suffer stress and burnout as a result (Rothschild and Russell, 1986).

The collectivist idea of giving workers control over their jobs has also been tried on a limited basis in some 90 percent of the 500 largest U.S. corporations as a way to combat worker alienation and low productivity. In these companies small groups of employees work together as equals, similar to what is known in Japan as "quality circle." They do not await orders from the top but take the initiative. They are encouraged with rewards and recognition—merit raises, cash bonuses, and bulletin-board praises—to contribute ideas on how to increase productivity and sales. They operate with the "open door" policy, whereby employees report directly to top management, which further encourages them to work harder because it makes workers feel important and respected. Practically all these companies are in the manufacturing sector of the economy. Good examples are IBM and General Motors. The quality-circle style of worker participation has also invaded the service sector in such areas as the insurance business. All these collectivist practices can boost not only worker morale but also productivity, as demonstrated in the successful operation of a Honda auto plant and other Japanese businesses in the United States (Rothschild and Russell, 1986; Scott, 1986; Florida and Kenney, 1991).

Feminist Model

We have seen how the collectivist model of organization achieves success through social equality, also popularly known as participatory democracy. The model proposed by feminist theorists does more than simply get everybody to work together as equals. The feminist model also calls for personal, emotional support from each other as typically exists in a group of close friends. Instead of urging people to leave their personal problems behind when coming to work, as do most conventional organizations, the feminist model tolerates—even encourages—the opposite. The equality espoused in the feminist model is basically personal, subjective, or spontaneous. This is in contrast with the impersonal, objective, or rule-oriented type of equality found in organizations that have only been legally forced to hire women and minorities.

The feminist model originates from studies of predominantly female organizations and of female executives of conventional, gender-mixed organizations. An example is Judy Rosener's (1990) landmark study. Rosener compared 456 successful female executives with their male counterparts in similar positions at similar companies and found significant gender differences in leadership styles. Men tend more to prefer a "command and control" way of dealing with subordinates—relying on orders, appeals to self-interest, rational decision-making, and rewards for manipulative purposes. By contrast, women are more likely to prefer an intuitive, anti-hierarchical style. They are more willing to share power, ask for guidance from subordinates, and humanize their workplace, as demonstrated to some degree by the female university president in the vignette at the beginning of this chapter. In another study, Sandra Morgen (1994) found that the women who work at feminist health clinics generally cater to each other's *personal* needs, not just the instrumental, "bottom line" needs of the organization. Considerable "personal sharing" goes on in the organization. Members not only tend to greet each other with hugs and kisses, but also share personal problems rather than leave them at home. Not surprisingly, members identify closely with their organizations, committed with heart and soul to them.

We should be careful, however, not to stereotype all women as having the same organizational style. Personal, subjective, or spontaneous egalitarianism does not exist exclusively among women or equally among all women; some men have it, just as some women do not. It is only as a group that women are more likely than men to have that kind of organizational style. This gender difference is far from innate, but instead largely a product of socialization. Generally, females are more likely than males to have learned from parents, peer groups, schools, and various social experiences the values of supporting and nurturing others, protecting long-term relationships, seeking solutions where everyone wins, and sharing emotions. For example, boys tend more to play in packs such as hierarchical sports teams, where they learn how to compete, take criticism, and win, but girls are more likely to play in leaderless groups, where they learn to get along, be fair, and reach consensus (Heim and Golant, 1993; Rothschild and Davies, 1994).

Questions for Discussion and Review

1. What is the most important characteristic of a collectivist organization?
2. What does a feminist organization look like?

SYMBOLIC INTERACTIONIST PERSPECTIVE

The basic ideas of many organizational theories can be related to the symbolic interactionist perspective. Here we analyze two such theories. One, which is relatively new, emphasizes the significance of organizational culture, suggesting how the way people define the situations they are in shapes their organizations. The other theory, which is older and well known as Weber's theory of bureaucracy, essentially portrays bureaucracy as the embodiment of the Western—or the male—definition of rationality as the proper way to run an organization.

Organizational Culture: Shared Definitions

Over the last decade many new organizational theories have emerged, variously labeled as cultural, interpretive, or hermeneutic. All are related to the symbolic interactionist perspective, though not referred to as such. Cultural theories emphasize how organizational members' values or beliefs, which reflect how they interpret the world around them, influence their behavior in the organization. Interpretive theories focus on the individual's "perspective on life in organizations." And hermeneutic theories, largely derived from interpreting the meanings of organizational documents, regard organizations as "symbolically mediated interactions" (Morgan, 1989; Aldrich, 1992; Turner, 1992). Roughly translated into the language of symbolic interactionism, those theories essentially say that organizational culture, popularly called "corporate culture," consists of members' shared definitions of what the organization is like and therefore significantly affects what goes on in the organization.

Studies of corporate culture often reveal why some organizations succeed and others fail in achieving their goals. Tandem, a successful computer manufacturer, was found to owe its success largely to the widely shared belief among its employees that it is wonderful to work for the company. The belief is expressed in slogans such as, "It's so nice, it's so nice, we do it twice" or "Get the job done no matter what it takes." Such slogans appear on T-shirts and bulletin boards and are spread by word of mouth. A related belief is that everybody is treated equally, suggested by the absence of name tags and reserved parking spaces. Questioned by researchers, employees would also reveal the relative lack of hierarchy with comments such as, "Everyone here, managers, vice-presidents, and even janitors, communicate on the same level. No one feels better than anyone else" (Morgan, 1989). Without such a culture, organizations are more likely to go under.

Organizational culture cannot exist, though, without real support such as in the form of recognitions and rewards. If Tandem's employees were not given enough praises and salary raises for their hard work, its gung-ho culture will disappear.

Bureaucracy: Embodiment of "Rational" Worldview

According to Max Weber, modern Western society makes a specific form of organization necessary: **bureaucracy,** a modern Western organization defined as being rational in achieving its goal efficiently. "In the place of the old-type ruler who is moved by sympathy, favor, grace, and gratitude," Weber (1946) said, "modern culture requires . . . the emotionally detached, and hence rigorously 'professional' expert." In every area of modern life there is a tendency toward **rationalization,** Weber's term for the process of replacing subjective, spontaneous,

TABLE 5.1
Bureaucratic versus Collectivist Organization

Bureaucratic Organization	Collectivist Organization
1. Maximum division of labor.	1. Minimum division of labor
2. Maximum specialization of jobs—monopolization of expertise.	2. Generalization of jobs—diffusion of expertise.
3. Emphasis on hierarchy of positions—justifying reward differentials.	3. Striving for egalitarianism—restricting reward differentials.
4. Authority in individual officeholders; hierarchical control; bureaucratic elitism.	4. Authority in collectivity as a whole; democratic control; subordinate participation.
5. Formalization of fixed and universal rules.	5. Primacy of ad hoc decisions.
6. Worker motivation through direct supervision.	6. Worker motivation through personal appeals.
7. Impersonality as ideal of social relations in organization.	7. Comradeship as ideal of social relations in organizations.

informal, or diverse ways of doing things with a planned, objective, unified method based on abstract rules. Applied to organizations, rationalization means the development of bureaucracies.

What specifically is bureaucracy? It is an organization that differs sharply from a collectivist organization (see Table 5.1). It is as rational as a machine, as Weber (1946) wrote:

> The fully developed bureaucratic mechanism compares with other organizations exactly as does the machine with the non-mechanical modes of production. . . . The strictly bureaucratic administration succeeds in eliminating from official business, love, hatred, and purely personal, irrational, and emotional elements which escape calculation.

By squeezing out the human element of emotion, bureaucracy is, in Weber's view, the most efficient form of organization. This can be so as long as, as

symbolic interactionism suggests, organizational members find the machine-like rationality to be reasonable, legitimate, acceptable, or agreeable. But this definition is increasingly rejected in today's socially diverse organizations. As our previous discussion on feminist theory suggests, women are likely to define the emotionless, impersonal, or dehumanizing form of rationality as *irrational*. They tend more to define the subjective, personal, or empathetic form of rationality as *rational*. With increasing female participation in organizations, we can expect bureaucracies to become increasingly humanized like the feminist organizations that we have analyzed. The Japanese also define the Western impersonal form of rationality as *unreasonable* for running organizations. And they define their own traditional values of mutual obligations and loyalties as *reasonable*, because they help, among other things, strengthen company lifetime commitment to employee and employee commitment to company. This may explain why those traditional and emotional values, which Weber regarded as obstacles to achieving organizational efficiency, have made Japanese companies rank among the most efficient in the world.

Although bureaucracy is not the most efficient form of organization in the world, it is still most efficient in predominantly individualist cultures such as the United States. Still, bureaucracy is also deficient in some ways. Let us discuss both the efficient and deficient aspects of bureaucracy in the following section.

Questions for Discussion and Review

1. How does organizational culture contribute to corporate success?
2. What are the major characteristics of Weber's bureaucratic model of organization?

THE REALITIES OF BUREAUCRACY

All the organizational theories we have discussed are basically **normative theories**, theories that suggest what we *should* do to achieve our goals (see Table 5.2, p. 114). Here we focus on what bureaucratic organizations are really like. Despite widespread dislike of bureaucracy, this form of organization is still pervasive. Most people in the United States continue to work in bureaucracies, and, even more, must deal with bureaucratic organizations when they enroll in school, have a phone installed, pay a hospital bill, or handle any number of other countless arrangements that are part of living in a modern Western society. The prevalence of bureaucratic organization affects both the small details of everyday life and the overall function of the government and economy. The benefits and problems of bureaucracy are thus worth a closer look.

Bureaucratic Benefits

If so many people do not like bureaucracies, why does this kind of organization continue to exist? In part, it is because they are not all bad. Even red tape has its advantages: one person's "red tape" can be another person's safeguard against problems. The process of getting a government permit to open a hazardous waste dump may seem an endless, expensive obstacle course of paperwork to the company that wants to operate the dump. But to people living near the proposed site, the rules and regulations that make up that red tape may seem the best guarantee of proper precautions to safeguard their health.

Similarly, the impersonality of bureaucracies especially in government, is sometimes welcome. If you need a government-subsidized student loan, you are probably glad that impersonal rules—not political pull or personal friendships—determine whether you can obtain the loan. Bureaucracy encourages equality and discourages discrimination.

Even for employees, bureaucracies may bring some benefits. The widely held assumption that bureaucracies tend to stifle individual creativity and imagination seems groundless. Data collected by sociologist Melvin Kohn (1983) suggest that bureaucracies make their workers intellectually flexible, creative, and open-minded.

Kohn defined bureaucrats as people who work in large organizations with complicated hierarchies of authority, and nonbureaucrats as people who work in small organizations with only one level of supervision. Kohn found that, compared with nonbureaucrats, bureaucrats demonstrated a higher level of intellectual performance on tests administered by an interviewer. Bureaucrats also placed greater intellectual demands on themselves during their leisure time. They were more likely than nonbureaucrats to read books and magazines, attend plays and concerts, and go to museums. They also put greater value on self-direction, rather than conformity, and were more likely to take personal responsibility for whatever they did. Finally, they were more open-minded and more receptive to change than the nonbureaucrats.

Skeptics may argue that the bureaucrats' wonderful traits did not *result* from working in a bureaucracy. Perhaps the bureaucrats were better educated, more intellectually flexible, and more receptive to change in the first place. This argument assumes that bureaucracies hold some special attraction for people with these qualities. But because most people believe that bureaucracies suppress creativity, this assumption is far from convincing.

Kohn contended that bureaucracies themselves encourage the development of the positive traits he found in their employees. The more complex a job is, argued Kohn, the more intellectually flexible the worker becomes, and employees of bureaucracies tend to have more complex jobs than those with comparable education who work for an organization with just one or two levels of supervision.

TABLE 5.2
Organizational Theories: How to Achieve Efficiency

Functionalist Perspective

- Scientific Management: Maximize division of labor, supervision of workers, and wage incentive
- Human Relations: Foster informal relations among workers

Conflict Perspective

- Collectivist Model: Encourage workers to participate as equals in management of organization
- Feminist Model: Encourage both equality and emotional closeness among all members

Symbolic Interactionist Perspective

- Organizational Culture: Develop positive culture with recognition and reward
- Bureaucratic Theory: Squeeze out human emotion by defining for members the organization's rules and regulations regarding division of labor, differentiation of authority, and hiring based on competence

American Mosaic

U.S. society has become increasingly diverse, and more people of different cultural backgrounds participate in organizational life. Diversity helps change the U.S. corporate culture and leads to new ideas and ways of accomplishing tasks. This reading explores the potential of diversity to enhance organizational performance.

Diversification Pays

Many companies vowed to master the management of diversity. They spent huge sums for consultants to whip it into the corporate culture mix. Yet in most cases the changes never took. At some companies, downsizing became the more urgent imperative. At others, it seems, the intention was never really sincere.

But companies such as Xerox, Avon, AT&T, IBM, Grand Metropolitan's Burger King, and Levi Strauss have stuck with their commitment to work force diversity, even in the face of restructuring, rising hostilities among some ethnic groups, and blistering competition. Why? To many executives, it is just common sense. Says IBM chief Louis V. Gerstner Jr.: "Our marketplace is made up of all races, religions, and sexual orientations, and therefore it is vital to our success that our work force also be diverse." Adds Ted Childs, director of work force diversity at IBM: "We think it is important for our customers to look inside and see people like them. If they can't, it seems to me that the prospect of them becoming or staying our customers declines."

Several academic studies, while not real-world evidence, further suggest that diversity can enhance performance. At the University of North Texas last year, ethnically diverse teams of business students were pitted without their knowledge against all-white teams for 17 weeks. At first the homogeneous teams sprinted ahead, but by the study's end the heterogeneous groups were viewing situations from a broader range of perspectives and producing more innovative solutions to problems.

That seems especially likely as business moves toward management that values the intellectual contribution of every worker. No longer is the push to integrate or assimilate everyone into some homogeneous corporate type. At companies that are successfully managing diversity, different cultures and styles are embraced. The companies recognize that individuals' gender, ethnicity, and sexual orientation deeply inform the way they think about themselves. Says Robert L. Lattimer, managing director of Diversity Consultants in Atlanta, a division of Towers Perrin: "The whole point of managing diversity is to draw on the uniqueness of each employee. If people feel they must censor what they say and how they act, the major benefit of diversity is lost." Lattimer urges clients like AT&T to constantly reexamine such policies as dress codes that may tacitly support a stultifying, monolithic culture.

Excerpted from Faye Rice, "How To Make Diversity Pay," *FORTUNE*, August 8, 1994, pp. 79–80.

Bureaucratic Problems

In Weber's view, bureaucracy is inescapable but not very likable. "It is horrible," he once said, "to think that the world would one day be filled with nothing but those little cogs, little men clinging to little jobs and striving toward bigger ones" (Bendix, 1962). Finding a person to say a good word about bureaucracy is about as hard as finding a landlord who likes rent control. Why? Because of certain problems often associated with bureaucracy.

The first problem has to do with rules and regulations. Since they are based on what is already known, rules cannot tell us what to do about the unanticipated. Blind adherence to rules can therefore wreak havoc in people's lives. If we lose an important document like our I.D. card or birth certificate, bureaucrats cannot do anything for us. A more common problem is the tendency of bureaucracies to produce a seemingly endless array of rules and regulations. Public bureaucracies, in particular, are notorious for mountains of rules, all of which slow action by employees and fall like an avalanche on private citizens and businesses that must comply with them. The nation's small businesses alone spend an immense amount of money every year just to complete government forms.

Another problem is that bureaucracy tends to grow unnecessarily bigger. This problem has been called **Parkinson's Law**: "Work expands to fill the time available for its completion." The author of this law, C. Northcote Parkinson, believed that the natural tendency of bureaucracy is to grow and keep on growing by at least six percent a year. Wanting to appear busy or important or both, officials increase their workload by writing many memos, creating rules, filling out forms, and keeping files. Then, feeling overworked, they hire assistants. At the same time, there are powerful incentives—such as bigger salaries, more perquisites, higher status, and greater power—for officials to increase their agency work forces, budgets, and missions. As a result, many bureaucrats are doing the same thing at great cost to taxpayers. As the director of Vice President Al Gore's project on reducing the federal bureaucracy said, "As a rule, virtually any task being done by government is being done by 20 or more agencies."

There is yet another bureaucratic problem: deadwood tends to pile up. This problem is known as the **Peter Principle:** "In every hierarchy every employee tends to rise to their level of incompetence." Competent officials are promoted and if they prove to be competent in their new jobs, promoted again. The process continues until they are promoted to a position in which they are incompetent. And there they remain as deadwood until they retire. The bureaucracy functions only because there are always employees still proving their competence before they are promoted beyond their abilities. Like Parkinson's Law, however, the Peter Principle is based on impressionistic observation rather than rigorous scientific research. Both problems are widely thought to be common, but precisely how common is not known.

More people working at home with computers reflects the trend toward the replacement of the bureaucratic, hierarchical structure by a more egalitarian organization. The reason is that highly trained specialists resent taking orders from managers who have less technical knowledge.

The Future of Bureaucracy

Bureaucracy will probably continue to thrive. Many organizations in the United States seem to be getting larger, as suggested by the growth of big government agencies, multinational corporations, multicampus universities, and agribusinesses. Large organizational size usually leads to greater bureaucratic control, requiring numerous workers to follow standard rules and operating procedures so chaos can be avoided.

At the same time, less bureaucratic control is imposed on higher-ranked technical experts and specialists within giant organizations. There is also less administrative control throughout the corporations on the frontier of technology. In many successful corporations in the United States today, highly trained specialists already enjoy a wide range of autonomy. They resent taking orders from managers who have less technical knowledge. Because of the increasing shift from manual to knowledge work in the composition of the U.S. work force, there will be growing pressure to replace the bureaucratic, hierarchical bureaucracies with a much flatter, more egalitarian organizations made up of numerous smaller units with six to ten employees each. In fact, there is some evidence in the early 1990s that the information revolution has begun to force many centralized bureaucracies—from education to business—to give

The chief source of the efficiency of bureaucracies is reliance on impersonal rules. Rules ensure that employees treat equally all the people they serve. Unfortunately, the consequences of bureaucratic efficiency may be rigidity on the part of personnel, such as being unable to help customers with unusual needs.

way to this collectivist, egalitarian model. There are now, for example, public schools managed by teams of teachers and parents rather than bureaucrats. Increasing female participation in organizations also contributes to the replacement of bureaucratic control with egalitarian cooperation.

In short, bureaucracy appears to be moving in two seemingly opposite directions. On the one hand, bureaucracy will probably increase in *form*, with more and more organizations becoming giant bureaucracies across the United States and around the globe. On the other hand, the *content* of bureaucracy would become increasingly anti-bureaucratic, with more and more participants working as equals.

Questions for Discussion and Review

1. What are the benefits of bureaucracies?
2. What bureaucratic problems do Parkinson's Law and the Peter Principle illustrate?
3. What changes seem to be happening in today's bureaucracies?

A GLOBAL ANALYSIS

It is important to look at organizations from a global perspective. Without the perspective, we would have believed Weber's *erroneous* assumption that the traditional non-Western organization cannot be as efficient as Western bureaucracy.

Writing about organizations around 1910, Weber, like most Westerners of that time, did not have the same global sensitivity that many of us have today. Thus he tended to see in non-Western traditionalism only its *negative* aspects, such as hiring the boss's incompetent relative rather than the best-qualified person. But today, a more sensitive global analysis can reveal the *positive* aspects of non-Western traditionalism, such as the cooperation and commitment demonstrated by Japanese organizations.

Basically, the Japanese traditional culture is group-oriented rather than individual-centered as in the United States. As group members rather than independent individuals, Japanese tend to have stronger relations with one another. Therefore, at the heart of the Japanese organization is concern with group achievement. Employees begin each workday by singing their company song or reciting slogans of devotion to their company. They work in sections of eight to ten people, headed by the *kacho* (section chief). Each section, now well known as a "quality

circle," does not await orders from the top but takes the initiative, and all its members work together as equals. Personnel of different sections often get together to discuss how best to achieve company objectives. Executives, then, rubber stamp most of the decisions made by employees at the section level. Workers, moreover, look upon their company as their family because they enjoy the security of permanent employment. Executives also feel secure and regard their company as their family. Not surprisingly, both workers and executives are strongly committed to their company and work hard to make it highly efficient and productive.

Traditionalism has also contributed to organizational efficiency in other East Asian societies such as South Korea and Taiwan. But why can't it do the same in many developing countries? The answer is hard to find because most research has focused on the negative aspects of their traditionalism. If the focus of research is shifted to the positive aspects, then we may find out what prevents the clan-centeredness and personal ties from building efficient

Influenced by their society's traditional group-oriented culture, Japanese companies are often run like families, encompassing every aspect of the worker's life, even providing low-cost housing and medical care. Employees may begin each day singing their company song or reciting slogans of devotion to the company. Here a group of factory employees eat lunch—consisting of fish, rice, vegetables, and tofu soup—together in the company cafeteria.

Bureaucratic control involves requiring workers to follow standard rules and operating procedures. Some groups of workers have tried to resist this process by fighting against outside control of their work. This reading reports on the effort of New York City firefighters to resist the "proletarianization," or de-skilling, of their jobs.

Magical Work: Firefighters in New York

Firefighters in New York City have been able to avoid large-scale proletarianization, which would involve the loss of control over their own work and their having nothing to sell but their labor. They have retained control over much of their work because of the characteristic features of this hazardous occupation, which requires their routine exposure to life-threatening risks and which is associated with values celebrating such habitual exposure.

In the first place, material factors (the obvious physical dangers of the job) support resistance to proletarianization, for despite being salaried, firefighters in New York have not yet been de-skilled. De-skilling, the supplanting of skilled workers with semi-skilled or even assembly-line labor, depends on changing production methods or work requirements; its purpose, as management has always stated explicitly, is to have an easily replaceable and controllable labor force. The built-in hazards of firefighting, however, have until recently protected firefighters against losing control over their work.

The same resistance to proletarianization associated with material factors in the Fire Department of New York also applies to the social organization of work. Firefighters have been able to retain a great measure of control over the jobs they perform because of the flexibility of the work and the social structure of the firehouse. Although all members in a community have individually prescribed roles as part of the working team, the continually shifting nature of a working fire can confront firefighters with critical decisions as the fire changes. In the same way, the exclusive structure of the firehouse has promoted an autonomous, self-governing organization that has protected firefighters against external supervision.

Equally important as material and social factors in resisting proletarianization are the firefighters' values about "heroism," or routine, voluntary exposure to palpable hazards. This value system celebrates deliberate engagement with risk, and underlies firefighters' assumptions about membership in an elite occupation. Since proletarianization classically divides and demoralizes the labor force, the firefighters' beliefs about belonging to a secret and select group has been a powerful buffer between themselves as workers and penetration by management or the state.

Firefighting is dramatic. Workers race against time to rescue people and animals, buildings and forests, and they do so in an engulfing, perilous environment. The total experience—the accelerated pace that begins with the sound of the alarm and continues until the fire is under control, the focused concentration that comes with being absorbed in a dangerous physical contest, the sounds of sirens and of the fire itself, even the smell—makes each "good" fire a vivid, spectacular event.

Despite being salaried, firefighters still retain significant control over the organization, decisions, and products of their own work. Although they are required to obey their officers, they are in fact loosely regulated within the firehouse and at practice drills. Inside the firehouse there are few orders: schedules for meals, housekeeping, study for promotional exams, and recreation are flexible—especially since non-fire ground work, as well as meals and other activities, are continually interrupted by alarms.

Excerpted from Miriam Lee Kaprow, "Magical Work: Firefighters in New York." Reprinted by permission of the Society for Applied Anthropology from *Human Organization*, Spring 1991, pp. 97–100.

UNION — SAFETY

organizations in traditional African, Latin American, and other developing countries. Interestingly, in the meantime, these countries have begun to learn from the Japanese model of organization. In fact, many organizations in the United States have already done so by becoming more humanized or less impersonal.

Question For Discussion and Review

1. How can a global analysis help us understand organizations better?

CHAPTER REVIEW

1. *What is a social group?* It is a collection of people who share some characteristics, interact with one another, and have some feeling of unity. *What is an in-group and out-group?* An in-group is a group to which a person is strongly tied as a member. An out-group is a group of which an individual is not a member. *What is a reference group?* A group that people use as a guide for their behavior. *What are a primary and secondary group?* A primary group is one whose members interact informally, relate to each other as whole persons, and enjoy their relationship for its own sake. In a secondary group, the individuals interact formally, relate to each other as players of particular roles, and expect to achieve some practical purpose through the relationship.

2. *What is the nature of group leadership?* Leadership can be *instrumental*, trying to achieve goals by focusing on task performance. Leadership can also be *expressive*, being concerned with others' psychological well-being and working to enhance it. *Why are leaders less likely than followers to conform to the group?* Because leaders usually enjoy an idiosyncrasy credit. *Does the size of a group matter?* Yes. The larger a group, the more impersonal it becomes, the more difficult it is for one member to influence another, or the less likely a member is to help someone in distress.

3. *What draws us into a social network?* Friendship, business transactions, sexual contacts, expressions of admiration, or some other kind of social relationship. *Can networks affect our lives?* Yes. The smaller, denser networks of friends and relatives can help us maintain good health by giving us social support. But they can also make our lives miserable by putting many demands on our time and personal resources, criticizing us, and invading our privacy. On the other hand, the larger, looser networks of mere acquaintances are more useful than the smaller, denser networks in helping us find a job. But large networks can also spread infectious diseases to numerous people.

4. *What is a formal organization?* It is a group whose activities are rationally designed to achieve specific goals. *What are the most common types of organizations?* According to Etzioni, they are coercive, utilitarian, and normative organizations.

5. *According to scientific management theory, what must an organization do to achieve its goal?* It must have maximum division of labor, close supervision of workers, and a piecework system of wages. *How does the human relations theory differ?* Whereas scientific management focuses on the official organization and the effect of wages on efficiency, the human relations theory emphasizes the influence of social forces—in particular the informal relations among workers—on job satisfaction and productivity.

6. *What does a collectivist organization look like?* Its members participate as equals in the management of the organization. *What does a feminist organization look like?* In addition to practicing equality, the feminist organization fosters close personal relations among its members.

7. *What are the principal characteristics of a bureaucracy?* A bureaucracy is characterized by a division of labor, a hierarchy of authority, the hiring of employees on the basis of impersonal procedures and technical qualifications, and a reliance on formal, written rules. *What are some of the benefits of bureaucracy?* When tasks are stable and routine, bureaucracies are very efficient; their reliance on rules and their impersonality can protect people from the exercise of arbitrary power and favoritism. In addition, there is some evidence that bureaucracies foster among their workers intellectual flexibility, creativity, and openness to change. *What are the problems of bureaucracy?* Bureaucracies tend to produce an ever-increasing number of rules, grow unnecessarily larger, and retain incompetent officials. *What changes can be seen in bureaucracy?* Bureaucracies seem to increase in size but become more egalitarian.

8. *How does a global perspective enhance our understanding of organizations?* It enables us to see how non-Western traditionalism can contribute to organizational efficiency.

KEY TERMS

Bureaucracy   A modern Western organization defined by Max Weber as being rational in achieving its goal efficiently (p. 111).

Expressive leaders   Leaders who achieve group harmony by making others feel good (p. 102).

Formal organization   A group whose activities are rationally designed to achieve specific goals (p. 105).

Groupthink   The tendency for members of a cohesive group to maintain consensus to the extent of ignoring the truth (p. 102).

Idiosyncrasy credit The privilege that allows leaders to deviate from their group's norms (p. 102).

Informal organization A group formed by the informal relations among members of an organization—based on personal interactions, not on any plan by the organziation (p. 109).

In-group The group to which an individual is strongly tied as a member (p. 99).

Instrumental leaders Leaders who achieve their group's goal by getting others to focus on task performance (p. 102).

Normative theories Theories that suggest what we *should* do to achieve our goals (p. 112).

Out-group The group of which an individual is not a member (p. 99).

Parkinson's Law The observation that "work expands to fill the time available for its completion" (p. 114).

Peter Principle The observation that "in a hierarchy every employee tends to rise to their level of incompetence" (p. 115).

Primary group A group whose members interact informally, relate to each other as whole persons, and enjoy their relationship for its own sake (p. 100).

Rationalization Weber's term for the process of replacing the subjective, spontaneous, informal, or diverse ways of doing things with a planned, formally unified method based on abstract rules (p. 111).

Reference group A group that is used as the frame of reference for evaluating one's own behavior (p. 99).

Secondary group A group whose members interact formally, relate to each other as players of particular roles, and expect to profit from each other (p. 100).

Social aggregate A number of people who happen to be in one place but who do not interact with one another (p. 98).

Social category A number of people who have something in common but neither interact with one another nor gather in one place (p. 98).

Social group A collection of people who interact with one another and have a certain feeling of unity (p. 98).

Social network A web of social relationships that link individuals or groups to one another (p. 103).

SUGGESTED READINGS

Biggart, Nicole Woolsey. 1989. *Charismatic Capitalism: Direct Selling Organizations in America.* Chicago: University of Chicago Press. An interesting sociological study of Tupperware, Amway, Mary Kay, and other direct-selling organizations.

Czarniawska-Joerges, Barbara. 1992. *Exploring Complex Organizations: A Cultural Perspective.* Newbury Park, CA: Sage. An interpretation of what goes on within an organization from the standpoint of the participants.

Hearn, Jeff, et al. (eds.). 1989. *The Sexuality of Organization.* Newbury Park, CA: Sage. An analysis of the relationships between gender relations and organizational life, focusing on such subjects as sexual harassment in the workplace and the self-image of women managers.

Waring, Stephen P. 1991. *Taylorism Transformed: Scientific Management Theory Since 1945.* Chapel Hill: University of North Carolina Press. A historical analysis of the organizational model of scientific management.

Zeitlin, Maurice. 1989. *The Large Corporation and Contemporary Classes.* New Brunswick, N.J.: Rutgers University Press. An analysis of how managers have taken over the control of corporations from their owners.

6

SOCIAL INTERACTION IN EVERYDAY LIFE

CHAPTER OUTLINE

Myths and Realities

MYTH: *To avoid misunderstanding, especially in conversation with foreigners, it is always wise to say directly what's on our mind, such as saying "yes" to mean "yes."*
REALITY: Directness in speech may be popular in the United States, but indirectness is common in many other countries. Japanese, for example, may say "yes" to mean "no" when asked "Would you agree to do business with us?" This is their way of trying to save others from disappointment or embarrassment.

MYTH: *All over the world it is natural for people to nod their heads to mean "yes" and shake them to mean "no."*
REALITY: In the United States, we, or course, nod our heads to mean "yes" and shake them to mean "no." But in Bulgaria, head nodding means "no," and head shaking means "yes." Body language varies from one culture to another.

MYTH: *Because they speak the same language, men and women can easily understand each other.*
REALITY: They are likely to use the same language differently: men for the purpose of giving information; women for expressing feelings. Thus, men tend to misunderstand women by taking literally what women say, and women tend to misunderstand men by reading emotional meanings into what men say.

ohn and Mary, a married couple, teach college in different cities. They spend three days a week far away from each other. People frequently express sympathy with remarks such as "That must be rough" or "How do you stand it?" Mary readily accepts their sympathy, saying things like "We fly a lot." Sometimes she reinforces their concern: "The worst part is packing and unpacking all the time." But John reacts differently, often with irritation. He would emphasize the advantages of his marriage: As professors, he and his wife have four-day weekends together, long vacations throughout the year, and four months in the summer. They even benefit from those days when they are separated because they can do their work without any interruption. All this is true, but Mary is surprised that her husband reacts differently than she does. He explains that he senses condescension in others' expression of concern, as if they were implying, "Yours is not a real marriage. I pity you, and look down on you, because my wife and I do not have your kind of misfortune." John tends to see others as adversaries but Mary does not (Tannen, 1990).

What John and Mary experience is **social interaction**, the process by which individuals act toward and react to others. Interactions can be classified into three types, roughly reflecting the three major perspectives in sociology. John tends to engage in **oppositional interactions**, treating others as competitors or enemies. Mary, on the other hand, is more likely to get involved in **supportive interactions**, treating others as supporters or friends. This gender difference reflects the different social worlds in which John and Mary live. Reflecting the conflict perspective, John's world is more hierarchical and dominance-oriented, in which a man must be either one-up or one-down. To men, life is more like a contest, with social interactions being an arena where "people try to achieve and maintain the upper hand if they can, and protect themselves from others' attempts to put them down and push them around" (Tannen, 1990). Reflecting the functionalist perspective, however, Mary's world is more egalitarian and sharing-oriented, in which there is a greater tendency to nurture relationships by seeking and giving confirmation and support. To women, life is more like "a community, a struggle to preserve intimacy and avoid isolation" (Tannen, 1990).

But those two perspectives are structural, suggesting that people more or less passively follow the dictates of their world. To symbolic interactionists, all interactions, whether oppositional or supportive, are also *symbolic,* involving people actively interpreting each other's action and reaction and behaving in accordance with the interpretation. Thus John and Mary react differently to the same comments from others because they *interpret* the comments differently.

In short, the three perspectives spotlight different patterns of social interaction. Functionalism focuses on the supportive nature of interaction; the conflict perspective, the oppositional nature; and symbolic interactionism, the symbolic or interpretive nature.

FUNCTIONALIST PERSPECTIVE

According to functionalists, there are two types of supportive interaction: exchange and cooperation. An **exchange** is an interaction in which two individuals offer each other something in order to obtain a reward in return. **Cooperation** is an interaction in which two or more individuals work together to achieve a common goal.

Exchange

If you help a friend study for an exam and your friend, in turn, types a paper for you, you have engaged in an exchange. The reward we expect to get for what we have done for others may be material, such as salary or a gift, or it may be nonmaterial, such as a word of praise or gratitude. We find exchanges in all types of situations. Representatives of nations trade votes at the United Nations, employees exchange their labor for a salary, friends exchange advice and gratitude, children trade toys, and so on.

Social exchanges are usually governed by the norm of reciprocity, which requires that people help those who have helped them. If a favor has been extended to us, we will be motivated to return the favor. Conversely, if others have not been helpful to us, we are not likely to be helpful to them. Therefore, if social exchanges are fair, the social structure involved tends to be solid. The exchange reinforces the relationships and provides each party in the exchange with some needed good. But if exchanges are seen as unfair, the social structure is likely to be shaky. A friendship in which one person constantly helps another, expecting but not getting gratitude in return, is likely to be short-lived.

But friends cannot be too fussy about the fairness of exchange, unless they want the relationship to be something less than friendship. If you give someone five dollars and expect to get exactly the same amount back from that person later, chances are that he or she is not your friend. Thus, in exchanges between classmates, co-workers, or business associates who are not friends, the participants give benefits with the expectation of receiving precisely comparable benefits in return. In friendships, however, members actively avoid the exactly equitable exchange because it seems too impersonal, businesslike, or unsentimental. Instead, they work out complicated exchanges of noncomparable benefits. Such an exchange would occur if you were to offer consolation to a friend who is ill and later receive $100 from that friend when you are broke.

Cooperation

In an exchange, a task can be adequately performed by one of the parties. In cooperation, an individual needs another person's help to do a job or to do it more effectively. Within this broad category of interaction, there are some differences (Nisbet, 1970).

When neighbors come together to help a family whose house has just burned down or been destroyed by a tornado, that is *spontaneous cooperation.* This is the oldest type of cooperation, but it is unpredictable.

Over time, some forms of cooperation occur frequently enough for them to become customary in

Volunteers in Texas cooperate to build a playscape in a city park. This kind of contractual cooperation does not originate from tradition, authority, or spontaneity but from voluntary action, with some planning.

society. It was a custom in parts of the U.S. frontier, for example, for neighbors to work together to build a barn. This type of cooperation, *traditional cooperation,* brings added stability to the social structure.

Because modern societies such as the United States include people with diverse traditions, they are more likely to depend on a third type of cooperation, *directed cooperation,* based on the directions of someone in authority. We are directed by government, for example, to abide by the law and pay taxes. But in return the government provides us with such services as education, police protection, and national defense.

A fourth type of cooperation is equally useful in complex modern societies: *contractual cooperation.* It does not originate from tradition or authority but from voluntary action. Nor does it happen spontaneously; it involves, instead, some planning. In contractual cooperation, individuals freely decide, for example, whether to embark on a business project together, and they spell out the terms of the cooperation.

Questions For Discussion and Review

1. What is the difference between exchange and cooperation?
2. What are the different types of cooperation?

CONFLICT PERSPECTIVE

Oppositional interaction can be competition or conflict. **Competition** is an interaction in which two individuals follow mutually accepted rules in trying to achieve the same goal before the other does. **Conflict** is an interaction in which two individuals disregard any rules in trying to achieve their own goal by defeating the other.

Competition

In a competition, some degree of cooperation exists because the competitors must cooperate with each other by "playing the game" according to the rules. In a boxing match, for example, the fighters must cooperate by not hitting each other on certain parts of the body—by not turning it into a free-for-all. In politics, candidates competing for the same office must cooperate by following certain rules, the major one being that all contenders, especially the losers, must accept the outcome.

It is widely believed that competition brings out the best in us. The economic prosperity of Western capitalist nations, as opposed to the lower standard of living in formerly communist countries, is often attributed to the high value placed on competition. Compelled to compete fiercely with Japan and other countries in the global market, U.S. industries seem to have become more efficient and productive. It is apparently true that competition can stimulate economic growth. Certain types of professionals, such as athletes, politicians, and lawyers, are also known to thrive on competition. In our everyday life, however, we usually perform less well—or more poorly—when we are trying to beat others than when we are working with them.

Several scholars who reviewed over 100 studies conducted from 1924 to 1981 that dealt with competition and cooperation in classrooms found that in 65 of the studies, cooperation promoted higher achievement than competition. In only eight studies did competition induce higher achievement; 36 studies showed no statistically significant difference.

In competition between football teams, each team tries to achieve the same goal before the other does. But competition involves some cooperation, since competitors must cooperate with each other by playing the game according to the rules.

Research on college students, scientists, and workers has produced further data challenging the popular belief in the benefits of competition (Kohn, 1986; Azmitia, 1988). Competition seems to hamper achievement primarily because it is stressful. The anxiety that arises from the possibility of losing interferes with performance. Even if this anxiety can be suppressed, it is difficult to do two things at the same time: trying to do well and trying to beat others. Competition can easily distract attention from the task at hand. Consider a teacher asking his pupils a question. A little girl waves her arm wildly to attract his attention, crying, "Please! Please! Pick me!" Finally recognized, she has forgotten the answer. So she scratches her head, asking, "What was the question again?" The problem is that she has focused on beating her classmates, not on the subject matter (Kohn, 1986).

Conflict

In competition, the contestants try to achieve the same goal in accordance with commonly accepted rules. The most important rule is usually that competing parties should concentrate on winning the game, not on hurting each other. When competing parties no longer play by these rules, competition becomes conflict. In conflict, defeating the opponent, by hook or by crook, has become the goal. To use an extreme contrast, we can see competition in sports and conflict in wars.

Conflict exists in all kinds of social situations. It occurs between management and labor, whites and blacks, criminals and police, but also between friends, lovers, family members, and fellow workers. It can both harm and help a social structure. Wars between nations and violent confrontations between hostile groups clearly are harmful. Yet war may also unify members of a society. This is most likely to occur if various segments of society, such as leaders and the rank and file, agree that the enemy is a real menace to the entire country, that it warrants going to war and defending the nation, or that internal conflict, if any, can be resolved (Markides and Cohn, 1982). Thus, the Vietnam War divided the American people because many did not agree with their government that South Vietnam was worth defending, but the Second World War was a unifying force because virtually all Americans looked upon the threat of Nazi Germany and Japan in the same light. Conflict can also stimulate needed change. Consider the black-white conflict in the United States. Spearheaded by the civil rights movement in the 1960s, this conflict has led to greater equality between the races.

Conflict exists in all kinds of social situations. It occurs between management and labor, between races or members of the same race, and between friends, lovers, and family members. As the photo shows, it also occurs between police and lawbreakers.

Questions for Discussion and Review

1. How does competition differ from conflict?
2. How would you prevent competition from becoming conflict?

SYMBOLIC INTERACTIONIST PERSPECTIVE

Both functionalist and conflict perspectives enable us to see the different forms of interaction by watching from a distance how people interact. What we get from these perspectives is the *outside* view of interaction. We do not know what is going on *inside* people when they interact. To symbolic interactionists, we can learn much about interaction by analyzing people's interpretations of each other's actions.

Interpreting Supportive Interaction

Erving Goffman (1971) referred to supportive interactions as "supportive interchanges," "mutual dealings," or "acts of identificatory sympathy." Examples range from "the congratulations at marriage, the careful commiserations at divorce, and the doleful condolences at deaths" to "the neighborly act of lending various possessions and providing minor services" to the inquiries about "another's health, his experience on a recent trip, his feelings about a recent movie, and the outcome of his fateful business." To most people, all these acts should not be taken at face value because they are not what they appear to be.

When someone asks us "How are you?" they are not really interested in finding out the condition of our health in the same way as our doctor does. Instead, if they are strangers, they may actually mean to say "you can trust me," "I want to know you," or "I want to be your friend." If they are already our friends, they may mean to express their joy at seeing us, their desire to reaffirm our friendship. There are many other possible meanings, depending on the people and circumstances we encounter. All such meanings shape the interaction in everyday life.

Interpreting Oppositional Interaction

While supportive interaction usually involves individuals of about the same social status, oppositional interaction tends more to involve people of different statuses. In such a situation, the higher-status person tends to define a lower-status person as lacking in respectability. As a consequence, the higher-status person is likely to be disrespectful to that person. One common way of showing this disrespect involves symbolically invading the personhood of the lower-status person.

Consider, for example, the interaction between men and women in a sexist society. Since men are generally given a higher status than women, they tend more to stare at women than vice versa. Men are also more likely to touch women's bodies, such as letting their hands rest on women's shoulders, while women rarely reciprocate. When members of both sexes participate in a group discussion, men are far more likely to interrupt women than the other way around. In one study, only four percent of the interruptions in male-female conversations came from women, but 96 percent originated from men (Karp and Yoels, 1993).

Questions for Discussion and Review

1. What is the symbolic interactionist view of supportive interaction?
2. What is the symbolic interactionist view of oppositional interaction?

INTERACTION AS SYMBOLIC COMMUNICATION

We have just seen how power, respect, and other aspects of social relationships are communicated with symbols, such as words and gestures. Without symbolic communication, humans would have to interact like other animals. Symbolic communication, then, is the essence of human interaction.

The Nature of Human Communication

Animals also communicate. Try to catch a seagull and it will call out "hahaha! hahaha!" to signal its friends to watch for an intruder. A squirrel may cry out to warn other squirrels to flee from danger. But these signal systems are not symbols, and animal communication differs in fundamental ways from human communication.

First, symbols are *arbitrary*. The meaning of a word is not determined by any inherent quality of the thing itself. Instead a word may mean *whatever* a group of humans has agreed it is supposed to mean. If you do not speak Chinese, you would not know that *gou* is the Chinese word for dog. There is no inherent connection between the word and the thing itself. The Spaniards, after all, call the same animal *perro,* and the French call it *chien*. Even "dingdong" is an arbitrary symbol: a bell may sound like "dingdong" to us, but not to the Germans, to whom a bell sounds like "bimbam." The meaning of a word is "socially constructed" because it is determined by people through their social experiences as members of a specific society. It is no wonder that there are a great many different symbols in human communication to represent the same thing. Animals, on the other hand, are not free to arbitrarily produce different symbols to indicate the same thing because their communication is largely determined by instincts. This is why, for example, all seagulls throughout the world make the same sound to indicate the presence of danger. Unlike humans, they cannot express a particular thought in more than one way (Cowley, 1988).

Second, animal communication is a closed system, but human communication is an *open system*. Each animal species can communicate only a limited set of messages, and the meaning of these signals is fixed. Animals can use only one signal at a time—they cannot combine two or more to produce a new and more complex message. A bird can signal "worms" to other birds but not "worms" and "cats" together. Animal communication is also closed in the sense of being stimulus-bound; it is tied to what is immediately present in the environment. The bird can signal "worms" only because it sees them. It is impossible for an animal to use a symbol to represent some invisible, abstract, or imaginary thing. As philosopher Bertrand Russell said, "No matter how eloquently a dog can bark, he cannot tell you that his parents are poor but honest." In contrast, we can blend and combine symbols to express whatever ideas come into our heads. We can create new messages, and the potential number of messages that we can send is infinite. Thus, we can talk about abstractions such as good and evil, truth and beauty. It is this creative character of language that leads many people to believe that language is unique to humans. Language also makes possible the exchange of ideas through the information superhighway around the world (see Figure 6.1).

Human communication is not only verbal, involving the use of words. It is also nonverbal, consisting of kinesics and proxemics. **Kinesics** is "body language," the use of body movements as a means of communication, such as smiling to express happiness at seeing someone. **Proxemics** is the use of space as a means of communication. It is an example of proxemics when we snuggle up to an intimate to express affection or avoid touching a stranger to show respect.

A Global Analysis of Communication

Whether human communication is verbal or nonverbal, it is conducted differently in different societies. Let us see how people in other countries communicate differently than we.

Global Diversity in Verbal Communication In some cultures where people like to talk a lot, a listener's silence is often assumed to indicate agreement. Once an Egyptian pilot radioed ahead to the Cyprus airport for permission to land. Receiving no response, the pilot took the silence to mean "permission granted." But as the pilot brought the plane in

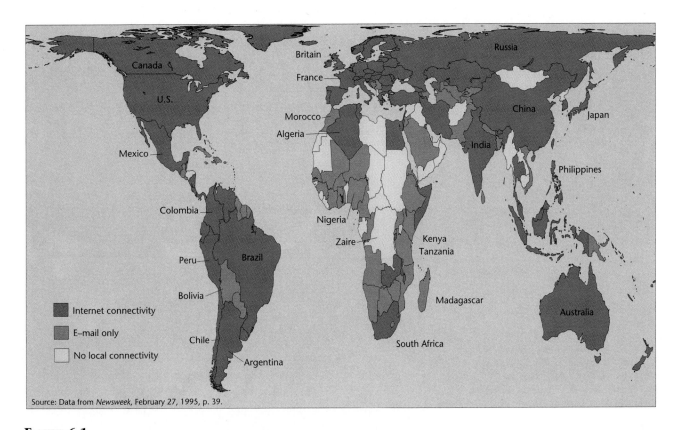

Source: Data from *Newsweek*, February 27, 1995, p. 39.

FIGURE 6.1
Modern Communication Around the World
Language is unique to humans. It enables us to create messages, and the potential number of messages that we can send is infinite. With language we can also exchange ideas through the information superhighway around the world.

for landing, the Cypriot air force opened fire. Obviously, to the Cypriots, the silence meant "permission denied" (Tannen, 1986).

But between equally talkative cultures there are also differences in conversational style. In the U.S. we tend to believe that even in casual conversation only one person should speak at a time. Yet in many other countries, it is normal for a listener to chime in when someone is talking, which is taken to mean enthusiastic participation or involvement with others. This logic seems to elude many people in the U.S. In the late 1980s, the U.S. president's wife, Nancy Reagan, complained to the press about Raisa Gorbachev, wife of the Soviet president: "From the moment we met, she talked and talked and *talked*—so much that I could barely get a word in, edgewise or otherwise." Probably unaware of the "one speaker at a time" ethic, Mrs. Gorbachev might have been wondering why her U.S. counterpart never said anything—and made her do all the conversational work (Tannen, 1990; Tannen, 1994a).

When we talk, we tend to express directly what is on our mind. People in many other cultures are more likely to speak indirectly. In Asia, if you visit an acquaintance on a hot day and feel thirsty, you would not ask your host point-blank, "Could I have a glass of water?" Instead, you would convey the same request by saying, "Isn't it hot today?" In Japan, if at the end of a lengthy business meeting you ask, "Do you then agree to do business with us?" the Japanese will always say "yes" even if they mean "no." They are reluctant to say "no" directly, in order to save others' face and spare them embarrassment. Used to directness in speech, many of us cannot understand how "yes" can possibly mean "no." But Japanese can say "yes" in a certain way to mean "yes," and in another way to mean "no."

Global Diversity in Nonverbal Communication

Like verbal communication, body language varies from one culture to another. People in the United States nod their heads to mean "yes" and shake them to mean "no." But in Bulgaria, head nodding means "no," and head shaking means "yes." The Semang of Malaya thrust their heads forward to signal "yes" and cast their eyes down to signal "no." When North Americans use a thumb and forefinger to form a circle, they mean "A-OK," but the same gesture is considered obscene in Brazil and other countries.

In proxemics, the amount of space we take up around us also varies from one society to another. In North America, when we talk to a person whom we do not know well, we ordinarily stand about three feet away. If one person moves in closer than that, the other would find it too close for comfort. This may reflect the North American values of individual independence and privacy. But South Americans are inclined to stand much closer. If we converse with Arabs, they might even get closer. In "invading" others' space, the Arabs and South Americans do not mean to be rude. On the contrary, they are expressing their predilection for human connection.

Nonverbal communication may involve proxemics, the use of space as a means of communicating. The proxemics found in Arab cultures differs from those characteristic of North Americans. When conversing with people we do not know, we usually stand about three feet away, whereas Arabs tend to maintain a closer conversational distance.

U.S. Diversity in Communication

Both verbal and nonverbal communication also vary from one group to another within our own diverse society.

Verbal Communication in the U.S. Various groups speak English with different accents. The Midwestern accent is different from the New York accent, which is distinct from the Southern accent, which is distinguishable from the New England accent, and so on, while accents also vary within each of these regional categories. Different races and classes further have their own accents. Most interestingly, there are variations in English usage and conversational style.

The middle class seldom uses the double negative ("I can't get no satisfaction"), whereas the working class often does. The middle class rarely drops the letter "g" in present participles ("doin'" for "doing," "singin'" for "singing"), perhaps because they are conscious of being "correct." The working class often drops the "g," probably to show that they are not snooty. They also tend to say "lay" instead of "lie," as in "Let's lay on the beach," without suggesting a desire for sex. On the other hand, the middle class has a weakness for euphemism. To them, drunks are "people with alcohol problems" or a prison is a "correctional facility." They also tend to go for what they consider sophisticated—"vocalist" instead of "singer," or "as of this time" rather than "now." The upper class distinguishes itself by its tendency to use such words as "tiresome" or "tedious" instead of "boring" (Fussell, 1992).

Inner-city blacks speak a dialect that their white counterparts may find hard to understand. Here is an example of how "Black English" is used to explain why God cannot be black:

> Why? I'll tell you why. 'Cause the average whitey out here got everything, you dig? And the [black man] ain't got shit, y'know? Y'understan'? So—um—for—in order for *that* to happen, you know it ain't no black God that's doin' that bullshit (Nanda, 1994).

The quote can be roughly translated into: "No way God can be black. If he was he wouldn't have screwed up our lives." To some whites, Black English is deficient, but it may be a lively, useful tool for communication in the inner city.

To Apache Indians, whites often say peculiar things in everyday conversation. Whites would say to mere acquaintances or even strangers, "Hello, my friend! How're you feeling?" Apaches would not call somebody "my friend" unless that somebody is truly a friend. They would not ask mere acquaintances

how they feel, because it is considered an invasion of personal privacy, reflecting an unnatural curiosity about others' inner feelings. Also to Apaches, whites' frequent use of the other's name ("Glad to see you, *Mary,*" "How you doing, *Joe?*) smacks of disrespect because a personal name is the individual's sacred property (Nanda, 1994).

Nonverbal Communication in the U.S. In his classic study of a Chicago slum, Gerald Suttles (1970) found some ethnic diversity in the use of body language and personal space:

> The other ethnic groups think it odd that a group of Mexican men should strike a pose of obliviousness to others, even their nearby wives and children. Puerto Ricans, on the other hand, are disparaged because they stand painfully close during a conversation... Whites say that [African Americans] will not look at them in the eye. The [African Americans] counter by saying that whites are impolite and try to "cow" people by staring at them.

But among whites themselves, when talking with members of the same sex, men are less likely than women to look at others. Researchers have observed a series of casual conversations between two subjects of the same sex. In these studies men often "looked outward, away from each other, and around the room, rather than directly at each other," while women more frequently looked straight at each other. The men did occasionally look at each other, but their eye contact did not last as long as that among women. What does this gender difference mean? It is possible that, to men, looking at others as long as women do seems like staring, hence a hostile action, a display of threat, which they try to avoid. But it is more credible that, by looking away from each other, men may be avoiding friendly connection or intimacy, which women tend more to seek and express by looking at others (Tannen, 1990; 1994a). This has much to do with the nature of the world in which men live, which differs from that of women's world. Let us explore these two worlds and see how they affect the communication between the sexes.

Questions for Discussion and Review

1. In what ways does human communication differ from animal communication?
2. How does communication differ from one society to another?
3. How do various groups in the U.S. differ in communication?

American Mosaic

Computer technology has revolutionized how we undertake our affairs and interact with other humans. Computer networks transmit knowledge, invent fantasy worlds, and create computer-based identities. This reading explores one area of digital interaction whereby Asian Americans attempt to develop an ethnic identity through the medium of computers.

Enter the Log-On

Welcome to the *otaku* generation. Tune out, plug in. Become words without body, traversing worlds without space. Ride pinwheel currents of text on a raft of silicon and glass. Feel your pupils widen as you connect across the most perfect of prophylactics, the terminal screen.

Who are the *otaku*? According to psychologists in Japan, they are a generation of youths whose social interaction is exclusively mediated by machines: computer bulletin boards, fax-modems, the Internet. Hacker-slackers who have cashed their reality checks, spurning personal contact in favor of the digital, ferreting out and trading raw data on trivial obsessions like comic books, tropical fish, and the like.

But is cyberspace really "anti-social"? What does it mean to "socialize" in an era where virtually every human act, from sex to artistic creation to murder, is mediated by technology? If digital identity is unanchored from the limits of the body—the Net being a place where author and text merge indistinguishably—then digital community, if there is such a thing, is unanchored from the limits of geography. For Asian Americans, clustered in a dozen states and spread out thinly through three dozen more, cyberspace is often the *only* place where community is possible. For the better part of a year, I've been in intimate contact with dozens of fellow Asian Americans—not in RL (real life) since I've never met them, just read them. We're neighbors in a digital suburb known as AAGPSO-L, the Asian American Graduate and Professional Student Organization mailing list.

Well, okay, not a "suburb" in the strip-mall and Sunday barbecue sense. But certainly a closed, and close, community. All of AAGPSO's members are Asian Americans. Cyberspace may be disorienting: a computer screen is a digital version of Plato's cave. Through a terminal darkly, we see but vague shadows, only what others are willing to reveal and only what the medium can transmit. No faces. No colors. No genders. Just words.

But where Asian Americans are concerned, the "dis-orientation" effect means that ethnicity is subdued: in RL, Asian Americans look different—yet, on the Net, we *do* all look the same. What we say is private to our cybernetic neighborhood; we speak over the digital equivalent of backyard fences. So read that as dis-"oriented." Orientalism, the construct that places a colonialist template over Asian American identity, isn't such an issue here. In cyberspace, Asian Americans are Asian Americans (and African Americans are African Americans, etc.) mostly because that's how we identify—essentially, because we subscribe.

So, can a postmodern community like Asian America find an anchorage in myriad data ports across the nation? Well, wasn't it Baudrillard who said, "In the future, power will belong to those peoples with no origins and no authenticity, who know how to exploit that situation to the full."

Why not?

Excerpted from Jeff Yang, "Enter the Log-On," *The Village Voice,* March 8, 1994, p. 19.

COMMUNICATION BETWEEN WOMEN AND MEN

In the world of women, connection and intimacy are the primary goals of life, and individuals cultivate friendship, minimize differences, seek consensus, and avoid the appearance of superiority. On the other hand, status and independence are the primary goals of life in men's world, so individuals seek status by telling others what to do, attain freedom from others' control, avoid taking orders, and resist asking for help. Thus, when the two sexes communicate with each other, women tend to use the language of connection and intimacy, and men the language of status and independence. Both may use the same English language, but in effect speak and hear different dialects called **genderlects**, linguistic styles that reflect the different worlds of women and men (Tannen, 1990; 1994a).

Speaking Different Genderlects

Failure to understand each other's genderlects spells trouble for intergender communication. Consider a married couple, Linda and Josh. One day Josh's old high school buddy from another city called to announce that he would be in town the following month. Josh invited him to stay for the weekend. When he told Linda that they were going to have a houseguest, she was upset. Often away on business, she had planned to spend that weekend with Josh alone. But what upset her the most was that Josh had extended the invitation without first discussing it with her. Linda would never make plans without first checking with Josh. "Why can't you do the same with me?" Linda asked. But Josh responded, "I can't say to my friend, 'I have to ask my wife for permission'!" To Josh, who lives in the men's world of status, checking with his wife means seeking permission, giving up his independence, or having to act like a kid asking his mom if it's O.K. to play with a friend. To Linda's female world of connection, checking with her husband has nothing to do with permission. In fact, Linda likes to tell others, "I have to check with Josh," because it makes her feel good to reaffirm that she is involved with someone, that her life is bound up with someone else's (Tannen, 1990). In short, Linda and Josh speak and hear different genderlects, one having to do with connection and intimacy, the other with status and independence.

There are other ways the different genderlects can throw a monkey wrench into the communication between women and men. Accustomed to speaking for the purpose of giving *information,* men tend to misunderstand women by taking literally what women say. On the other hand, women, more habituated to talking for the purpose of expressing *feelings,* tend to misunderstand men by reading emotional meanings into what men say. Thus women and men tend to communicate at cross-purposes. If a woman says to her husband, "We never go out," he is likely to upset her by responding, "That's not true. We went out last week." The husband fails to grasp the feeling the wife tries to convey. In saying "We never go out," she in effect says something like "I feel like going out and doing something together. We always have such a fun time, and I love being with you. It has been a few days since we went out." If on another occasion the woman asks her husband, "What's the matter?" and gets the answer, "I'm OK," she may respond by

saying, "I know something's wrong. What is it? Why aren't you willing to share your problem with me? Let me help you." The wife fails to understand that, by saying "I'm OK," her husband means "I am OK, I can deal with my problem. I don't need any help, thank you" (Gray, 1992). In his male world, dealing with one's own problem is a hallmark of independence, which he tries to assert, and getting help from others is a sign of weakness, which he tries to avoid.

Genderlects are not confined to communication between intimates. They also influence communication in public. Sitting alone in a dining room where bank officers had lunch, sociolinguist Alice Deakins listened to what they were talking about at adjacent tables. When no woman was present, the men talked mostly about business and rarely about people. The next most popular topics were food, sports, and recreation. When women talked alone, their most frequent topic was people, especially friends, children, and partners in personal relationships. Business was next, and then health, including weight control. Together, women and men tended to avoid the topic that each group liked best, and settle on topics of interest to both *but follow the style of the men alone.* They talked about food the way men did, focusing on the food and restaurant rather than diet and health. They talked about recreation the way men did, concentrating on sports figures and athletic events rather than exercising for weight control. And they talked about housing the way men did, dealing mostly with

In public communication between the sexes, men tend to dominate by subtly forcing women to use the male genderlect, which mostly focuses on things and activities; they ignore the female genderlect, which primarily concerns people and relationships.

location, property values, and commuting time, rather than whether the house is suitable for the family, how safe the neighborhood is for the children, and what kinds of people live next doors. In other words, in public communication between the sexes, men tend to dominate it by subtly forcing women to use the male genderlect, which mostly centers on things and activities, ignoring the female genderlect, which primarily concerns people and relationships (Tannen, 1990; 1994a).

Playing the Gendered Game of Proxemics

In gender-mixed groups, men's proxemics differs from women's. Men usually sprawl out with legs spread apart and hands stretched away from the body, taking up considerable space around them. But women are more likely to draw themselves in, using only little space with "ladylike" postures, such as closing or crossing the legs and placing the hands near the body.

A more direct way for men to dominate women in proxemics involves invading their personal space. As has been suggested, men often let their hands rest on women's shoulders but women rarely do the same to men. A similar proxemic domination prevails in interactions of mutual affection. When an intimate couple walk down the street, the man may place his arm around the woman's shoulders, but the woman is far less likely to put her arm around the man's shoulders. Doesn't this merely reflect the fact that the man is usually taller so that it would be uncomfortable for the sexes to reverse positions? No. The same ritual of man playing the powerful protector and woman the helpless protected is often observed when both are of about the same height or even when the man is slightly shorter. If the man is too short to stretch his arm around the woman's shoulders, they still will not reverse positions but will instead settle for holding hands. If a tall woman does put her arm around a shorter male's shoulders, chances are that she is a mother and he is her child (Tannen, 1990; 1994a). In the world of gender inequality, a man is likely to cringe if his girlfriend or wife treats him like a child by putting her arms around his shoulders.

Even in the most intimate moments between a man and a woman, male domination reigns. When both lie down in bed, he typically lies on his back, flat and straight, but she lies on her side, her body nestled against his. She further places her head on his shoulder, and he his arm around her. It is a picture of

unequal relationship, with the man appearing strong and protective and the woman weak and protected (Tannen, 1990; 1994).

Questions for Discussion and Review

1. What are genderlects and how do they affect the communication between women and men?
2. How do men and women play the gendered game of proxemics?

DRAMATURGY: ANALYSIS OF INTERACTION AS DRAMA

Underlying the diversity of communication that we have just analyzed is the same tendency for people everywhere to interact with others as if they were performing on the stage of a theater. Shakespeare captured the essence of social interaction as a staged drama with his famous line: "All the world's a stage, and all the men and women merely players." U.S. sociologist Erving Goffman (1922–1982) developed the theatrical analogy into **dramaturgy**, a method of analyzing social interaction as if the participants were performing on a stage.

Behaving Like Actors

When we interact, we behave like actors by following a script that we have learned from our parents, teachers, friends, and others (see Chapter 7: Socialization). The script essentially tells us how to behave in accordance with our statuses and roles (Chapter 4: Society). But the stage analogy does have limitations. On stage, the actors have a clearly written and detailed script that allows them to rehearse exactly what they will say and do. In real life, our script is far more general and ambiguous. It cannot tell us precisely how we are going to act or how the other person is going to react. It is therefore much more difficult, if possible at all, to be well rehearsed. In fact, as we gain new experiences every day, we constantly revise our script. This means that we have to improvise a great deal, saying and doing many things that have not crossed our mind before that very moment.

One example is how women used to react to a pelvic examination in the office of a gynecologist.

Many women dreaded this event, when they had to subject their most private body areas to "public" scrutiny, very often by a male physician. The occasion was potentially embarrassing to both doctor and patient. How best to minimize this risk? One way was revealed in a classic study by James Henslin and Mae Biggs (1971). They analyzed the data on several thousand pelvic examinations that Biggs had observed as a trained nurse. A typical examination unfolded like the scenes in a play.

In the prologue, the woman entered the waiting room and thus assumed the role of patient. In the first act, she was called into the consulting room, where she described her complaints. The doctor assumed his role by responding appropriately, listening closely, asking the necessary questions, and discussing the patient's problems. If a pelvic examination was indicated, he so informed the patient and then departed, leaving the patient in the nurse's hands.

The second act began as the nurse ushered the patient into an examining room and asked her to disrobe. At the same time, the nurse tried to help the patient make the transition from a dignified, fully clothed person to little more than a scientific specimen. The patient might be nervous; the nurse was sympathetic and reassuring. The nurse showed the patient where to leave her clothes, and how to put on her hospital gown. The interaction with the nurse created a strictly clinical situation.

The third act was the examination itself. Lying on the table with her body covered, the patient was transformed into a "nonperson," the object of the doctor's scrutiny. She could not see the doctor, who sat on a low stool. She also avoided eye contact with the nurse. She simply stared at the ceiling and said little or nothing. Similarly, the doctor tried to refrain from talking. All this served to desexualize the situation, reassuring everybody that it was only a medical examination.

The fourth and final act began as the examination ended. The doctor left, allowing the patient to dress in solitude. Then, fully clothed, she was ushered back into the consulting room, where both doctor and patient resumed the roles they had played in the first scene. Now the doctor again treated his patient as a person, and the patient behaved as though nothing unusual had happened. Finally, she departed, going back to her everyday roles.

This analysis suggests that, despite the lack of a script showing how doctor and patient should interact, they nevertheless managed, with the help of the nurse, to play their roles. We also learn that each participant tried to save the other's "face" with what Goffman calls *"tactful blindness"* to an embarrassing situation, acting as if it did not exist. This mutual cooperation made it possible for the performance to go on. According to Goffman, the performance is the heart of social interaction and as such involves presenting the self to the other.

Presenting the Self

As suggested in Chapter 4 (Society), we present our "self" to others to make them form a desired impression of us. We are the actors and they the audience. They also do the same, with themselves as actors and us as audience. The playing of these two opposite roles by each participant in social interaction ensures that when each performs poorly in presenting the self the audience will empathize, ignore the flaw, and

In social interaction, we present our "self" to others to make them form a desired impression. At the job interview, for example, the actor, or applicant for the job, tries to display the positive aspects of himself to persuade his audience, or the employer, to hire him.

form the impression desired by the actor. One will help the other pull off the performance because of expectation that the favor will be returned. This explains the avoidance of embarrassment through tactful blindness in many situations comparable to the pelvic examination. If our house guest stumbles on arrival or belches after dinner, we usually pretend not to see or hear the contretemps.

Although others want to help us succeed with our self-presentation, we still strive to do so on our own. Generally, we try to display the positive aspects of ourselves and conceal the negative ones. When we date someone for the first time, we will shower and dress properly and use deodorant to mask any unpleasant smell. When we listen to a story, we try to be all ears but if we become bored to the point of yawning we cover our mouth with our hand. In conversation we try to say the right thing and avoid saying the wrong thing. In fact, to ensure a smooth interaction, we often have to say or do things we truly don't want to. That is why store clerks appear friendly even to pesky customers, or a polite person laughs at bad jokes. Doesn't all this destroy our true self, self-identity, or dignity? The answer is no, because we maintain what Goffman calls **role distance**, the separation of our role playing as outward

ENRICHING OUR LIVES

Impression management is the effort to create and sustain a certain interpretation of a situation. One situation where most people are acutely aware of impression management is the job interview. This reading reports on how women, in particular, use impression management as an aid in the job search process and shows how job seekers in general can use it to secure employment.

How to Manage Impressions in a Job Search

Impression management (IM) has been defined as the conscious or unconscious attempt to construct and portray a particular image by controlling the information available to others so that they will view the actor as he or she intended. One category of IM tactics that job applicants can use might be referred to as *self-focused.* Tactics of this type allow applicants to maintain attention on themselves and concentration areas that will allow them to excel. Two impression management tactics that can be considered self-focused are *exemplification,* in which an applicant tries to convince the interviewer that his or her behavior is good enough to use as a model for others, and *self-promotion,* which is describing qualities that one possesses.

The main vehicle used by job seekers to spread the word about their availability and ability is the cover letter and resume. Because these items represent the applicant in initial contacts with the prospective employers, it should be expected that the cover letter will contain tactics to assure the reader that the applicant understands the importance of deference and will fit in with the organization's culture. Self-focused IM tactics should be found in both the cover letter and the résumé to make the job seeker appear as qualified for the job as possible.

The interview often provides the first face-to-face contact between the job seeker and the company contact. To make a favorable first impression, the job seeker may use nonverbal behavior, an activity at which women have been shown to be more adept than men. Research has found that job seekers who engaged in more eye contact were judged more favorably in terms of confidence and assertiveness and were therefore more likely to be hired. In addition, the use of positive nonverbal cues, such as smiles and nods, are often found to be successful. The appearance of the job seeker, if considered attractive by the interviewer, also has been found to result in higher ratings.

But the use of these self-focused IM strategies can backfire in certain situations. Male interviewers rate the applicant more positively when only one of the nonverbal cues is used and become overwhelmed when additional cues are added, resulting in more negative ratings. On the other hand, female interviewers are able to accurately perceive the interview information despite the addition of cues and thus rate the applicant more fairly.

Excerpted from K. Michele Kacmar and Dawn S. Carlson, "Using Impression Management in Women's Job Search Processes," *American Behavioral Scientist,* March 1994, pp. 681–692.

performance from our inner self. Thus we may outwardly appear servile to some people but inwardly scorn them.

The outward performance is similar to what the actor does *onstage*, and the inward feeling is comparable to what the actor does *backstage*. Goffman takes this stage analogy seriously in his analysis of self-presentation, which he divides into "front-region" (or "frontstage") performance and "back-region" ("backstage") behavior. In the front region, people present their selves in ways expected by others, the audience. In the back region, they reveal their true selves, with no concern for the audience. Often the backstage behavior contradicts the frontstage performance. Consider, for example, the goings-on in the funeral home. The body-preparation room is the backstage where the funeral director and staff often show no respect to the dead, such as by joking about the corpse or complaining about its size or smell. But in the frontstage interaction with the bereaved family and friends, the mortuary personnel exhibit great respect to the deceased. Even though in the back region they have drained and stuffed the corpse, in the front region the personnel never touch it, always respectfully keeping a distance from the casketed body (Turner and Edgley, 1990).

Onstage performances are not necessarily dishonest, nor intended only to manipulate or fool the audience. Often we do present who we really are. Generally, onstage performance is more honest with families and friends than with strangers. But even with strangers dishonest performance cannot be pulled off without the apparent collusion of the audience. In fact, the appearance of mutual cooperation between performer and audience is an important characteristic of interaction rituals.

Performing Interaction Rituals

In religious rituals, the worshipers perform certain acts to show reverence to the deity. Similarly, in **interaction rituals**, the participants perform certain acts to show reverence to the other. Some people may not genuinely feel reverent but only pretend to show reverence with the intent of manipulating others. But, in dramaturgy, they can be said to be engaged in an interaction ritual because the essence of interaction rituals is the *appearance* or *display* of reverence rather than actual reverence. Just as anybody can participate in religious rituals whether or not they truly believe in God, anybody can participate in interaction rituals. The only requirement is that the participant act as if the other's self is sacred, producing an action that exudes respect for the other.

In interaction rituals, the participants perform certain acts to show reverence to others. The veteran's salute is more than a gesture of his respect for those soldiers who died in the war. It also serves to communicate his respect to those around him.

Interaction rituals are performed every day. In a restaurant, on a sidewalk, or some other public place, any two strangers can be observed quickly glancing at each other and then just as quickly looking away. The split-second eye contact suggests that the two strangers consider each other worthy, important, or respectful enough to have their presence recognized. Their next-moment withdrawal of attention from each other expresses even greater respect for each other. They in effect treat each other like gods. As Goffman (1967) observed, "This secular world is not so irreligious as we might think. The individual is a deity of considerable importance. He walks with some dignity and is the recipient of many little offerings such as the fleeting eye contact from strangers."

Without the rituals, interaction in everyday life would be difficult, if not impossible. Imagine how you would feel if strangers keep staring at you. But violations of interaction rituals do occur. A common violation involves *loss of poise*, such as spilling a drink at a friend's apartment. Another form of interaction-ritual violations involves *incorrect identification*, as when we get someone's name wrong or say "How's your wife?" to a man whose wife has died. A third form of violations involves *situational impropriety*, such as dressing improperly at a social event or giving sad news to a happy couple at their wedding. When these and other ritual violations occur, everybody would pitch in by doing what Goffman called "remedial work of various kinds." The culprit is likely to say "excuse me" or "I'm sorry," or provide excuses ("The drink sure makes me a little drunk") or disclaimers ("I *don't mean* to be insensitive, but I have to tell you something"). Others would graciously accept the apologies, excuses, or disclaimers. In doing so, they help the ritual violator "save face" so that the derailed interaction can be put back on track. There are, however, strategies for preventing the problems in the first place, helping the self get the desired impression from others, as we will see in the next section.

Questions for Discussion and Review

1. What does Goffman mean by "tactful blindness"? How does it help ensure the success of a pelvic examination?
2. How do individuals present themselves to others?
3. What are interaction rituals? And how can the rituals be violated?

THE ART OF MANAGING IMPRESSIONS

In Goffman's dramaturgy, all performances in social interaction are aimed at creating a desired impression. The performer can achieve the objective by *using defensive measures* with the help of the audience. The audience assistance involves *offering protective measures*.

Defensive Measures by Performers

Goffman divides these measures into three types. The first has to do with *dramaturgical loyalty,* in which members of a team of performers support each other before an audience or keep their team secrets from outsiders. One basic technique for developing loyalty is to foster "high in-group solidarity within the team." Another is to change audiences periodically to prevent the performers from becoming so attached to a few members of the audience that other members are ignored. This is why bank managers and church ministers are often shifted from one place of operation to another.

The second defensive measure has to do with *dramaturgical discipline.* This requires self-control, such as refraining from laughing about matters that are supposed to be serious and from taking seriously matters that are supposed to be humorous. Dramaturgical discipline also involves managing one's face and voice to display appropriate feelings and conceal inappropriate ones. In dealing with a pesky customer, for example, disciplined performers suppress their annoyance with a cheerful smile and a friendly voice.

The third defensive measure is *dramaturgical circumspection.* This involves carefully looking for the right things to do to ensure success in performance. One tactic is to limit the size of the audience. As salespeople often find, it is easier to sell to an unaccompanied customer than a customer with one or more companions. Another tactic is to adapt a performance to the "information condition" at hand: relaxing the performance when we are with those we have known for a long time, while choreographing the performance when among those new to us. One should also adjust one's presentation to the nature of the thing presented to the audience. For example, clothing merchants take extreme care not to make exaggerated claims about their merchandise because customers can test it by sight and touch, but furniture salespersons need not be so careful because few customers can judge what lies behind the varnish and veneer of the product shown.

Protective Measures by Audience

By themselves those defensive techniques of impression management cannot guarantee success. The performer also needs the audience to cooperate. According to Goffman, the audience has the "tactful tendency" to act in a protective way to help the performers carry off their show.

First, audience members tend to discretely stay away from the backstage unless invited. Otherwise, the audience will know what goes on backstage and the frontstage performance will be ruined because the audience will find it unreal—contradicted by the backstage goings-on. If audience members want to enter the back region, they will give the performers some warning, in the form of a knock or a cough, so that the performers will stop activities that are inconsistent with their frontstage performance.

Second, if the performers commit a social blunder, the audience usually will tactfully "not see" it. Audience tact is so common that we may even find it among mental hospital patients, well-known for their misbehavior. To illustrate, Goffman cites this research report:

> [Once] the staff, without consulting the patients, decided to give them a Valentine party. Many of the patients did not wish to go, but did so anyway as they felt that they should not hurt the feelings of

the student nurses who had organized the party. The games introduced by the nurses were on a very childish level; many of the patients felt silly playing them and were glad when the party was over.

According to Goffman, audiences are motivated to act tactfully for one of several reasons: (1) immediate identification with performers, (2) desire to avoid a scene, or (3) ingratiating themselves with performers for purposes of exploitation. Goffman regards the third as the best explanation for audience tactfulness, citing for illustration the case of successful prostitutes "who are willing to enact a lively approval of their clients' sexual performance."

Questions for Discussion and Review

1. How can performers obtain the desired impression from the audience?
2. How does the audience help performers pull off the show?

THE SOCIAL CONSTRUCTION OF REALITY

In discussing interaction as symbolic communication or staged performance, we have focused on how people interact with *others*. But while interacting with others, people are also simultaneously interacting with *themselves*, somewhat like talking to themselves. In this internal interaction, people create in themselves an image of the other person and then interact with *this image* rather than the other person. Thus, when people are interacting outwardly with the other person, they are in reality interacting inwardly with their own image. All this refutes the popular belief that the world "out there," such as the other person, is by itself real. If the world out there is real without being defined as real by us, we will all interact in the same way with the other person, who after all is exactly the same person. But we do not, because we are not really interacting with the same person but instead with our own different images of that person. This is why different people can be seen interacting differently with the same person.

In short, reality does not exist "out there," in the form of the other person, but within ourselves, in the form of our image of that person. Nevertheless, reality cannot be created in a social vacuum, it is *socially* constructed through social interaction. Our

past as well as current encounters with others help us develop all the ideas, feelings, or attitudes that shape our image of the other person at a given moment. Let us take a closer look at this **social construction of reality**, the process by which people create through social interaction a certain idea, feeling, or belief about their environment.

Thomas Theorem: Creating Reality with Definition

After constructing reality, we just do not let the reality lie idle within ourselves. We act it out by doing something in accordance with the constructed reality. This is what sociologist W.I. Thomas (1863–1947) had in mind when he made the famous pronouncement known today as the **Thomas theorem**: "If people define situations as real, they are real in their consequences." In other words, people are able to turn their socially constructed, inner reality (perception, idea, belief, attitude, or feeling) into socially observable, outer reality (behavior, action, or activity).

If people believe that God exists, God is just as real to them as are humans, things, ideas, and other features of their social and physical world. They will *act as if God is real* by worshipping Him. Similarly, if people believe that they will become successful in the future, they will *do something to make it real*, such as working hard, which will likely lead to success. The second illustration suggests two ways in which situations defined as real are real in their consequences: working hard *now* and achieving success *later*. This is why the Thomas theorem is sometimes called "the self-fulfilling prophecy" (Chapter 1: Thinking Sociologically). But many instances also resemble the first example: definition of the situation produces only one kind of consequence, such as worshipping God now. In short, if we define something "out there" as real, we will act as if it is real or do something to make it real.

Ethnomethodology: Exposing Hidden Reality

We have just seen how the Thomas theorem focuses on the outer, observable, or behavioral consequences of defining situations. But we are not shown the inner, hidden, or subjective reality. To delve into that reality, we need **ethnomethodology**, the analysis of how people define the world in which they live. Taken from Greek, *ethno* means "folk" and *methodology* a systematic or standard method. So *ethnomethodology* literally means "folk method," implying that the method is popular, traditional, conventional, or widely shared.

But what exactly is the folk method people use to define their world in everyday interaction? To find out, Harold Garfinkel (1967), the founder of ethnomethodology, asked his students to interact with relatives, friends, and others in an "anti-folk," anti-traditional, anti-conventional manner. From such experiments, the students and Garfinkel discovered that the folk method generally involves *defining the world in a vague, ambiguous manner,* leaving out a lot of specific details. Consider the following two interactions: one involving a student and her husband; the other between a student and the student's friend.

> On Friday my husband remarked that he was tired.
>
> I asked, "How are you tired? Physically, mentally, or just bored?"
>
> "I don't know, I guess physically, mainly," he responded.
>
> "You mean that your muscles ache or your bones?" I asked.
>
> A little irritated, he said, "I guess so. Don't be so technical."

> FRIEND: How are you?
> STUDENT: How am I in regard to what? You mean my health, my finances, my school work, my sex life, my peace of mind, my. . .
> FRIEND: Look! I was just trying to be polite. Frankly, I don't give a damn how you are.

Why do people interacting with one another define things vaguely and leave out the details? The reason is *the popular assumption that people understand one another without the specific details.* But this assumption of shared understanding, or the folk method based on it, is so often employed, widely shared, and taken for granted that most people are not aware that it exists. Only when it is questioned, as in the examples given above, do they suddenly recognize not only that they have long held it, but also that it can be incorrect. As a consequence, they may become irritated, angry, dumbfounded, or embarrassed. Such negative reactions show the discomfort of having their cherished and taken-for-granted assumption taken away. The assumption has been so long and steadfastly adhered to that it has become our second nature, a part of our very being. It is hard not to lose control when someone suddenly pulls the rug from under us. Not surprisingly, Garfinkel found the same negative reactions in many

Ethnomethodology analyzes how people define the world in which they live. We tend to assume that in the many situations of everyday life, people share our understanding of the situations. People driving on an expressway, for example, assume that other drivers share their expectations about how to drive carefully. But an accident can suddenly cause people to realize that the assumption can be incorrect.

other experiments in which he instructed his students to bargain for small items in supermarkets, violate the rules in playing tic-tac-toe, or move increasingly closer to someone in conversation until being nearly nose-to-nose with them. Again, these experiments demonstrate through the subjects' negative reactions that their cherished assumption of shared understanding can be questionable.

But we may not need Garfinkel's experiments to discover the shakiness of the shared-understanding assumption. As was previously discussed, women and men often do not share the same understanding even when they use the same words to communicate. When we interact with people of different racial, ethnic, religious, or other backgrounds, we are also likely to find that they, like Garfinkel's students, do not share our definition of the situation. Generally, the more diverse the society, the more untenable the assumption of shared understanding.

This is particularly true in today's global village, where people of different cultures often interact. Without cross-cultural understanding, we may erroneously assume that people in other countries share the same definitions of situations. We may believe that it is polite to inquire about a man's wife, but to do so in Saudi Arabia would provoke an angry reaction because the Saudis consider the inquiry rude. Similarly, we may think that giving such gifts as a letter opener or a clock to a college friend is a nice gesture of friendship, but in Latin America the presentation of the letter opener may be construed as our desire to sever the relationship and in China the clock may be taken as our wish for the person to die soon. In instances such as these, people in other cultures effectively expose as untenable the hidden reality of our socially shared assumption that we understand one another. Simultaneously, we also question the same assumption held by the foreigners, in about the same manner as Garfinkel's students did to their subjects. When this happens, both interactants—we and the foreigners—may be dumbfounded, angry, irritated, or embarrassed.

Humorology: Subverting Reality With Humor

Like ethnomethodology, **humorology**—the study or practice of humor—can undermine our widely shared assumptions about our world. But, while ethnomethodologists make people feel bad, humorologists make them feel good. Consider the following joke from a Woody Allen movie:

A boy goes to a psychiatrist, saying, "Doctor, you must help us, my brother thinks he's a chicken."

The psychiatrist exclaims, "You must have him committed at once."

But the boy retorts, "We can't, we need the eggs."

With this joke, the humorologist *subverts* our conventional assumption that shared understanding exists between us and others just as it does between the psychiatrist and the boy. In addition, humorology can subvert not only the assumption about shared understanding but myriad other conventional realities, involving friendship, sex, marriage, politics, and virtually all other aspects of human life. In doing so, humorology makes us laugh.

But what is it about humor that makes us laugh? The clue can be found in the fact that almost all jokes contain an *incongruity* between two realities, usually a conventional and an unconventional one. These two realities represent conflicting definitions of the same situation. To make people laugh, we first make them clearly aware of their taken-for-granted conventional definition of a situation and then surprise them by contradicting that definition with an unconventional one. Take another look at the Woody Allen joke cited above. The first sentence sets up a situation to be defined. In the second, the psychiatrist defines the situation to mean that the boy is normal, thereby reinforcing the audience's conventional belief that people who consider their relatives mentally ill are normal themselves. But the last sentence, also aptly called the punch line, crushes the psychiatrist's definition with the unexpected reality that the boy himself is mentally ill. More generally, the punch line shatters the popular belief with the unconventional reality that people who appear normal can indeed be abnormal. About the same incongruity exists in the following joke from a study by Murray Davis (1993):

My wife comes home and says, "Pack your bags. I just won $20 million in the California lottery."

"Where are we going, Hawaii, Europe?" I ask jubilantly.

She says, "I don't know where you're going, Doug, as long as it's out of here."

The first two sentences set up in our mind the conventional assumption that the married couple will share the joy of winning the lottery. The punch line strikes down that assumption with the unexpected, unconventional reality that a presumably loving wife wants to be free from her husband.

The reality in the punch line does not always have to be unconventional. It can be any kind of reality as long as it is incongruous with the one just presented.

The punch line in the following joke, for example, is hardly unconventional but does unexpectedly contradict a reality previously defined—though with purposeful ambiguity (Davis, 1993):

> *Question:* "What is it that [the former Soviet president] Gorbachev has a long one, [the former U.S. president] Bush has a short one, the Pope has one but doesn't use it, and Madonna doesn't have one?"
> *Answer:* "A last name."

The question leads the audience to expect a risqué answer only to be contradicted by an innocent one.

Questions for Discussion and Review

1. How do people interact with themselves?
2. How can we create realities with definitions?
3. What is the hidden, socially constructed reality that guides interaction and how do ethnomethodologists expose that reality?
4. How does humor make people laugh?

CHAPTER REVIEW

1. *How do the three perspectives differ in dealing with social interaction?* The functionalist perspective focuses on the supportive types of interaction: exchange and cooperation. The conflict perspective deals with the oppositional types: competition and conflict. Both perspectives are structural, offering the outside, objective view of interaction. But the third, symbolic interactionist perspective delves into the subjective world of social interactants. While the structural perspectives concentrate on the objective, external characteristics of supportive and oppositional interactions, symbolic interactionism penetrates into the subjective, internal meanings of these interactions.

2. *How does human communication differ from animal communication?* Animal communication is largely governed by instincts. It is also a closed system, tied to the immediate present, enabling animals to communicate only a limited set of messages. In contrast, human communication is socially constructed, arbitrarily determined by people through their social experiences. It is also an open system, where people are able to create an infinite number of messages.

3. *How does communication differ globally?* Verbal communication varies from one society to another. There is, for example, a greater adherence to the "one speaker at a time" rule in the United States than in other countries. Nonverbal communication also differs; making a circle with a thumb and forefinger has a positive meaning in the United States, but negative in Brazil and other countries. *What is the U.S. diversity in communication like?* Various groups use the same language with different accents, words, and sentences as well as conversational styles. Group differences also exist in the use of body language and personal space. *How do women and men differ in communication?* They tend to use different genderlects, one emphasizing connection and intimacy and the other status and independence. The sexes also differ in proxemics, with men more likely to dominate women by invading their personal space.

4. *What is the dramaturgical view of interaction?* Interaction involves people acting toward each other as if they were performers and audiences in a theater. *How do people present themselves to others?* They display the positive sides of themselves and conceal the negative ones. This frontstage behavior, designed to create a desired impression in others, may differ from backstage activities, where the performers can reveal their true selves. *What is the essence of interaction rituals?* A show of reverence or respect among people engaged in social interaction. *What is the art of impression management?* To create a desired impression in others, we must use defensive measures but with others offering protective measures.

5. *What does the Thomas theorem mean?* If people define, see, or believe something "out there" as real, they will act as if it is real or do something to make it real. *What can we learn from ethnomethodology?* The fact that when people interact with one another they define their world in an ambiguous manner, leaving out considerable specific details. They assume that everybody understands them without the specific details. *What is the nature of humor that makes people*

laugh? Humor consists of the surprising subversion of a conventional or widely accepted reality by an unconventional or unexpected one.

KEY TERMS

Competition An interaction in which two individuals follow mutually accepted rules in trying to achieve the same goal before the other does (p. 124).

Conflict An interaction in which two individuals disregard any rules in trying to achieve their own goal by defeating the other (p. 124).

Cooperation An interaction in which two or more individuals work together to achieve a common goal (p. 123).

Dramaturgy A method of analyzing social interaction as if the participants were performing on a stage (p. 132).

Ethnomethodology The analysis of how people define the world in which they live (p. 137).

Exchange An interaction in which two individuals offer each other something in order to obtain a reward in return (p. 123).

Genderlects Linguistic styles that reflect the different worlds of women and men (p. 131).

Humorology The study or practice of humor (p. 139).

Interaction ritual The form of interaction in which the participants perform certain acts to show reverence to the other (p. 135).

Kinesics The use of body movements as a means of communication; also called body language (p. 127).

Oppositional interaction The interaction in which the participants treat each other as competitors or enemies (p. 122).

Proxemics The use of space as a means of communication (p. 127).

Role distance Separating the role-playing as outward performance from the inner self (p. 134).

Social construction of reality The process by which people create through social interaction a certain idea, feeling, or belief about their environment (p. 137).

Social interaction The process by which individuals act toward and react to others (p. 122).

Supportive interaction The interaction in which the participants treat each other as supporters or friends (p. 122).

Thomas theorem Sociologist W.I. Thomas' famous pronouncement that "If people define situations as real, they are real in their consequences" (p. 137).

SUGGESTED READINGS

Berger, Peter L., and Thomas Luckmann. 1963. *The Social Construction of Reality.* New York: Doubleday. A classic analysis of how reality is created through social interaction.

Davis, Murray S. 1993. *What's So Funny? The Comic Conception of Culture and Society.* Chicago: University of Chicago Press. A sociological study of how humor reveals various aspects of social and cultural life.

Goffman, Erving. 1959. *The Presentation of Self in Everyday Life.* New York: Doubleday. The sociological classic on the dramaturgical analysis of social interaction.

Karp, David. A., and William C. Yoels. 1993. *Sociology in Everyday Life,* 2nd ed. Itasca, Il.: Peacock. An excellent review of the current knowledge about social interaction in various situations and settings.

Tannen, Deborah. 1994. *Gender and Discourse.* New York: Oxford University Press. An insightful sociolinguistic study of the gender differences in communication.

SOCIALIZATION

CHAPTER OUTLINE

Myths and Reality

MYTH: *Infants will not die as long as they are well fed.*
REALITY: Despite being well fed, infants can become retarded and even die if deprived of human contact.

MYTH: *To be a genius, you must be born one.*
REALITY: Geniuses such as Einstein and Picasso are not only born but made. Since childhood they worked intensely to develop their potential abilities under the guidance of parents who valued learning and achievement.

MYTH: *Born with the ability to have feelings, children do not have to learn how to be happy, fearful, or anxious.*
REALITY: Emotions are not innate; they have to be learned. Through parents and other caretakers, children learn, for example, to feel happy when receiving a compliment, fearful when being threatened, or anxious when facing uncertainties.

MYTH: *Schools only help students develop their potential as creative, independent individuals by teaching them knowledge and skills.*
REALITY: Schools also mold students into social conformity. This includes the "hidden curriculum" of training students to be patriotic, to believe in their country's cultural values, and to obey its laws.

Soon after three-year-old Rebecca and her family moved to another town, her mother wanted to find a good pediatrician for her. She talked to many new neighbors and friends, and they all recommended the same doctor. After seeing Rebecca undergo a physical checkup for about five minutes, the mother was extremely pleased at how well her little girl was responding to the doctor. He was very friendly, talking gently to her and explaining everything he was doing. When it was time for him to test her reflexes, he said, "Rebecca, I'm going to hit your knee very lightly with a hammer." Immediately Rebecca let out a blood-curdling scream. Shaken and puzzled, the doctor turned to her mother and asked, "What did I do wrong?"

"Her father," said the mother, "is a carpenter" (Espinosa, 1992).

Actually Rebecca is just like all of us. To a significant degree she is a product of **socialization,** the process by which a society transmits its cultural values to its members. Socialization is carried out through society's agents, such as parents and teachers. Without socialization, Rebecca could not have become a truly human being, a person who could take part in society and its culture like most children her age. Simultaneously, though, Rebecca has developed through socialization a **personality**—a fairly stable configuration of feelings, attitudes, ideas, and behaviors that characterizes an individual—different from that of most of her peers. As we have seen, unlike other children Rebecca reacts fearfully to the word "hammer." She obviously associates the physician's harmless little hammer with the carpenter's powerful hammer, a result of being socialized by a carpenter father.

Does this mean that children are like clay waiting to be shaped in one way or another? The roles of *nature* (what we inherit) and of *nurture* (what we learn) in making us what we are have long been argued. To the seventeenth-century philosopher John Locke, the mind of a child was like a *tabula rasa* (blank slate). People became what they were taught to be. By the second half of the nineteenth century, a quite different view was popular. Instead of looking to nurture—what people are taught—to explain human behavior, many social scientists looked to nature—what people inherit. The pendulum of opinion has swung back and forth ever since. In retrospect, the debate may sometimes seem fruitless, but we have learned from it.

THE SIGNIFICANCE OF HEREDITY

Obviously, we do inherit something of what makes us who we are. But what? Physical traits such as skin color and sex are inherited, but how they affect human behavior and personality depends to a great extent on what society makes of them.

People also appear to inherit temperament—an inclination to react in a certain way. Some people are inclined to be active, nervous, or irritable, but others, although brought up in a similar environment, tend to be passive, calm, or placid. Psychologists have found that even infants show consistent temperaments. Some are active most of the time, whereas others move rather little. Some cry and fuss a lot, and others rarely. These differences may influence personality development. Very active infants, for example, are more likely than passive ones to become aggressive and competitive adults.

The role of heredity in determining intelligence and aptitude is more controversial. **Intelligence** is the capacity for mental or intellectual achievement, such as the ability to think logically and solve problems. **Aptitude** is the capacity for developing physical or social skills, such as athletic prowess. The *extent* to which intelligence in particular is inherited has been the subject of some of the most bitter, emotional debates in all of social science. Richard Herrnstein and Charles Murray (1994) assume that more than half of our intelligence comes from the genes. But most social scientists consider intelligence to be largely learned from social environment. The debate is far from settled (see box, p.146). For our

purposes, what is significant is that, although nature sets limits on what we can achieve, socialization plays a very large role in determining what we do achieve. Whatever potential is inherited may be developed or stunted through socialization.

Question for Discussion and Review

1. Can heredity influence personality? Why or why not?

THE SIGNIFICANCE OF SOCIALIZATION

What makes socialization both necessary and possible for human beings is the lack of **instincts**, biologically inherited capacities for performing relatively complex tasks. As we saw in Chapter 3 (Culture), whatever temperament and potential abilities human infants may be born with, they are also born helpless, depending on others for survival. What may be more surprising is the extent to which traits that seem very basic and essential to "human nature" also appear to depend on socialization. Evidence of the far-reaching significance of socialization comes both from case studies of children deprived of socialization and from instances in which children are socialized into geniuses.

Much of our physical makeup, including eyes, hair, and skin color, is biologically inherited. But there is much dispute over whether nonphysical characteristics such as intelligence, aptitude, and personality are also hereditary. Sociologists maintain that although nature sets limits on what we can achieve, socialization plays a large role in determining what we actually achieve.

Cutting Edge

The role of heredity in determining intelligence has long been an extremely controversial subject in social science. This reading shows how critics have challenged the Herrnstein-Murray thesis that genes largely determine I.Q. scores.

For Whom the Bell Curve Really Tolls

Rarely do 800-page books that are crammed with graphs reach best-seller lists. *The Bell Curve*, an inflammatory treatist about class, intelligence and race by the late Richard J. Herrnstein, a psychology professor at Harvard University who died last September, and political scientist Charles Murray of the American Enterprise Institute, is an exception.

The Bell Curve depicts a frightening future in which, absent strong corrective measures, a "cognitive elite" will live in guarded enclaves distant from the dull masses. This apocalyptic vision is presented as the consequence of unpalatable, undeniable "facts" about inheritance and intelligence. But the thesis rests on curiously twisted logic. Its authors have been highly selective in the evidence they present and in their interpretation of ambiguous statistics. The work is "a string of half-truths," states Christopher Jencks, a sociologist at Northwestern University.

Herrnstein and Murray's hereditarian bias is obvious in their account of a study of 100 children from varying ethnic backgrounds who were adopted into white families. The study got under way in the 1970s. At age seven, the black and interracial children scored an average of 100 on 10 tests, considerably better than the national average of black children and close to levels scored by white children. A decade later researchers Sandra Scarr of the University of Virginia and Richard A. Weinberg of the University of Minnesota found that the IQs of the black and interracial children had declined to 89 and 99, respectively, whereas those of white adoptees had fallen from 112 to 106.

Scarr and Weinberg concluded that racially based discrimination at school probably explained the drop in the black youngsters' scores. Jencks agrees: "The

results are perfectly consistent with the difference being due to something in the early home environment and, for older kids, their experience in school." But Herrnstein and Murray interpret the findings differently: "Whatever the environmental impact may have been, it cannot have been large."

The Bell Curve's most egregious failing, however, may be its bleak assessment of educational efforts to improve the intellectual performance of children from deprived backgrounds. Herrnstein and Murray cast a jaundiced eye over Head Start and other efforts for at-risk youngsters—projects that have been claimed to produce long-lasting gains in IQ, a possibility that would not square well with biological determinism. Herrnstein and Murray downplay such results, noting that such interventions are too expensive to be widely used.

Jencks is also unhappy with the book's conclusions about education. "Herrnstein and Murray are saying Head Start didn't have a profound effect. But that doesn't tell us that we couldn't do a lot better if we had a different society," he says. "In Japan, for example, children learn more math than they do in the U.S. because everybody there agrees math is important."

Scarr, who accepts a substantial role for heredity in individual IQ differences, insists that efforts to boost intellectual functioning in disadvantaged youth can deliver results. "There's no question that rescuing children from desperately awful circumstances will improve their performance," she notes.

Excerpted from Tim Beardsley, "For Whom the Bell Curve Really Tolls," *Scientific American,* January 1995, pp. 14–16.

Impairing Development

Since the fourteenth century there have been more than 50 recorded cases of "feral children"—children supposedly raised by animals. One of the most famous is "the wild boy of Aveyron." In 1797 he was captured in the woods by hunters in southern France.

He was about 11 years old and completely naked. The "wild boy" ran on all fours, had no speech, preferred uncooked food, and could not do most of the simple things done by younger children (Malson, 1972; Lane, 1976). The French boy was obviously deprived of socialization. In the United States, there have also been three well-known similar instances.

Anna was born in Pennsylvania in 1932 to a young unwed mother, a fact that outraged the mother's father. After trying unsuccessfully to give Anna away, the mother hid her in the attic and fed her just enough to keep her alive. She was neither touched nor talked to, neither washed nor bathed; she simply lay still in her own filth. When she was found in 1938 at the age of six, Anna could not talk or walk. She could do nothing but lie quietly on the floor, her eyes vacant and her face expressionless. Like Anna, Isabella was an "illegitimate" child in Ohio. Her grandfather kept her and her deaf-mute mother secluded in a dark room. When Isabella was discovered in 1938, she was six years old. She showed great fear and hostility toward people. Unable to talk, she could only make a strange croaking sound (Davis, 1947).

Genie, who was found in California in 1970, had been deprived of normal socialization for nearly 13 years—twice as long as Anna and Isabella. Since birth, Genie had been isolated in a small, quiet room. During the day she was tied to her potty seat, able only to flutter her hands and feet. At night, her father would straitjacket and cage her in a crib with an overhead cover. He would beat her if she made any noise. He never spoke to her except to occasionally bark or growl like a dog at her. Her terrified mother, forbidden to speak to Genie, fed her in silence and haste. Discovered at age 13, Genie could not stand straight, was unable to speak except whimper, and had the intelligence and social maturity of a one-year-old (Pines, 1981; Rymer, 1993).

These four cases are, to say the least, unusual. But even less severe forms of deprivation can be harmful. In 1945 researcher René Spitz (1945) reported that children who received little attention in institutions suffered very noticeable effects. In one orphanage, Spitz found that infants who were about 18 months old were left lying on their backs in small cubicles most of the day without any human contact. Within a year, all had become physically, mentally, emotionally, and socially impaired. Two years later, more than a third of the children had died. Those who survived could not speak, walk, dress themselves, or use a spoon.

Creating Geniuses

While the lack of normal socialization can destroy minds, specialized socialization can create geniuses. A young woman named Edith finished grammar school in four years, skipped high school, and went straight to college. She graduated from college at age 15 and obtained her doctorate before she was 18. Was she born a genius? Not at all. Ever since she had stopped playing with dolls, her father had seen to it that her days were filled with reading, mathematics, classical music, intellectual discussions and debates, and whatever learning her father could derive from the world's literature. When she felt like playing, her father told her to play chess with someone like himself, who would be a challenge to her (Hoult, 1979).

Like Edith, many geniuses have been deliberately subjected to a very stimulating environment. A well-known example is Norbert Wiener, a prime mover in the development of computers and cybernetics. He entered college at age 11 and received his Ph.D. from Harvard at 18. According to his father, Norbert was "essentially an average boy who had had the advantage of superlative training." Another example is Adragon Eastwood DeMello, who graduated with a degree in mathematics from the University of California at age 11. When he was a few months old, his father gave up his career as a science writer to educate him (Radford, 1990). In his study of Einstein, Picasso, Gandhi, and other world-renowned geniuses in various fields, Howard Gardner (1993) found that

Both heredity and environment play a role in the development of personality. Japanese violinist Midori may have been born with some of her musical talent, but if as a child her interest in music had been discouraged, she probably would not have grown up to perform, as she did here, with the New York Philharmonic.

they were all born into families that valued learning and achievement, with at least one loving and supportive adult.

Those people may have been born with a *potential* for becoming geniuses, but that potential was transformed into reality only through proper socialization. Without socialization, no infant can naturally grow into a genius. Consider ace test pilot Chuck Yeager. He may have been born fearless, but, if his parents had been overprotective and kept him from jumping off barns, he might never have grown up to be the first flier to break the sound barrier.

Questions for Discussion and Review

1. What would happen to children if deprived of socialization?
2. How can children become geniuses?

THEORIES OF PERSONALITY DEVELOPMENT

Children go through various processes of socialization that help them develop their personalities. We can learn much about these processes from a number of theorists and researchers.

Freud: Psychosexual Development

One of the most influential theories of how children develop their personalities is that of Sigmund Freud (1856–1939). In his view, personality consists of three parts. The **id** is the part of personality that is irrational, concerned only with seeking pleasure. The id is our inborn desire to live, enjoy ourselves, make love, or celebrate life in one way or another. But such desires cannot be successfully fulfilled unless we have learned *how* to fulfill them. Thus we have learned innumerable ways to live as best we can. The knowledge that results from this learning becomes our **ego**, the part of personality that is rational, dealing with the world logically and realistically. In trying to help us enjoy ourselves, our ego tells us that there is a limit to our id satisfaction. If we want to satisfy our sexual desire, we cannot simply make love anywhere such as on a street corner. This limit to our self-enjoyment is imposed by society in the form of rules and injunctions—"You should not do this. . . You should

not do that." Our acceptance of these rules and injunctions becomes the cornerstone of our **superego**, the part of personality that is moral, popularly known as conscience. The ego, in effect, advises the id to obey the superego so that we will enjoy life in a socially acceptable way.

Those three parts of personality develop through a series of five stages in childhood. Influenced by interaction with parents, these early experiences will have a significant impact on adult personalities. If childhood experiences are positive, adults may turn out to be normal. But a difficult childhood may later create personality problems (see Table 7.1).

While it is impossible to scientifically observe and measure the id, ego, and superego, these concepts are nonetheless useful for understanding human personality. They are also sociologically significant in at least two ways. One is the emphasis on the family as a crucial determinant of personality development. Another is the way the superego develops from acquiring society's norms and values.

Middle class, white, western

Piaget: Cognitive Development

From close observation of children, Swiss psychologist Jean Piaget (1896–1980) concluded that they pass through certain stages of cognitive (mental or intellectual) development. Today's sociologists find Piaget's studies useful for understanding how children learn new cognitive skills—such as perception, reasoning, or calculation—as they grow up. Social forces such as family and education, though, are assumed to influence cognitive development.

1. *Sensorimotor stage (birth to age 2):* Infants lack language and cannot think to make sense of their environment. In their view, something exists only if they can see or touch it. Thus a parent no longer exists when leaving the child's field of vision. Unlike older children, who interact with the world by using their brains, infants use their senses and bodily movements to interact with the environment. Infants, for example, use their hands to touch, move, or pick up objects, and put things in their mouths or suck at some objects.

2. *Preoperational stage (ages 2 to 7):* Children are not yet capable of performing simple intellectual operations. "Precausal," they cannot understand cause and effect. When Piaget asked four-year-olds what makes a bicycle move, they replied that the street makes it go. When he asked six-year-olds why the sun and moon move, the youngsters said that the heavenly bodies follow us in order to see us. These children are also animistic. They attribute humanlike thoughts

TABLE 7.1
Freud's Stages Of Psychosexual Development

	Characteristics	Personality Problems
Oral stage (birth to age 1)	Infant is at the mercy of the id because the ego and superego have not emerged; seeks pleasure through oral activity such as sucking.	If the drive for oral pleasure has been overindulged or frustrated, the adult may be excessively interested in oral pleasures, such as eating, smoking.
Anal stage (ages 1 to 3)	Infant seeks pleasure from holding in and pushing out feces. The ego emerges, aided by toilet training, through which the child learns self-control and self-dependence.	If toilet training and other self-control lessons are overly strict, the child may be either extremely messy and wasteful or too concerned with order, cleanliness, or possessions.
Phallic stage (ages 3 to 6)	Child feels sexual love for opposite-sex parent, and learns that this desire must be suppressed. Through leaning restrictions, the child internalizes the parent's ideals and morals, and thus superego develops.	If the superego fails to develop adequately, the adult is inclined to engage in unconventional or antisocial activities.
Latency stage (ages 6 to 11)	The id quiets down, and the child focuses on developing intellectual and social skills. The ego and superego become stronger.	If many problems happen in this stage, the adult may become withdrawn or extremely individualistic.
Genital stage (adolescence)	Interest in sex develops, and the habits of modesty and sympathy give way to pleasure in exhibitionism and aggressiveness; but gradually the adolescent learns to cope with these problems.	If frustrations repeatedly occur without resolution, the adult may have difficulties getting along sexually with others, and, if married, may have marital or parenting problems.

and wishes to the sun and moon. Moreover, they are egocentric, seeing things from their own perspective only. If we ask a young boy how many brothers he has, he may correctly say "One." But if we ask him, "How many brothers does your brother have?" he would say, "None." He has difficulty seeing himself from his brother's perspective.

3. *Concrete operational stage (ages 7 to 12):* By now children can perform simple intellectual tasks, but their mental abilities are restricted to dealing with concrete objects only. If children between ages 8 and 10 are asked to line up a series of dolls from the tallest to the shortest, they can easily do so. But they cannot solve a similar problem put verbally—in abstract terms, such as "John is taller than Bill; Bill is taller than Harry; who is the tallest of the three?" The children can correctly answer this question only if they actually see John, Bill, and Harry in person.

4. *Formal operational stage (ages 12 to 15):* Adolescents can think and reason formally (abstractly). They can

follow the form of an argument while ignoring its concrete content. They know, for example, that, if A is greater than B and B is greater than C, then A is greater than C—without having to know in advance whether the concrete contents of A, B, and C are vegetables, fruits, animals, or whatever can be seen or touched.

Those different stages of cognitive development, summarized in Figure 7.1 (p. 150), do *not* correspond to different levels of intelligence. Young children are not necessarily less innately intelligent than older ones. They just think about things in a different way. Contrary to Piaget's assumption, however, young children can be *taught* through intensive socialization to think like older ones. Nevertheless, Piaget has been proven right for suggesting that virtually all children go through the sequence of mental development as laid out by him. For example, children think concretely before thinking abstractly, rather than the other way around.

FIGURE 7.1
Piaget's Stages of Cognitive Development

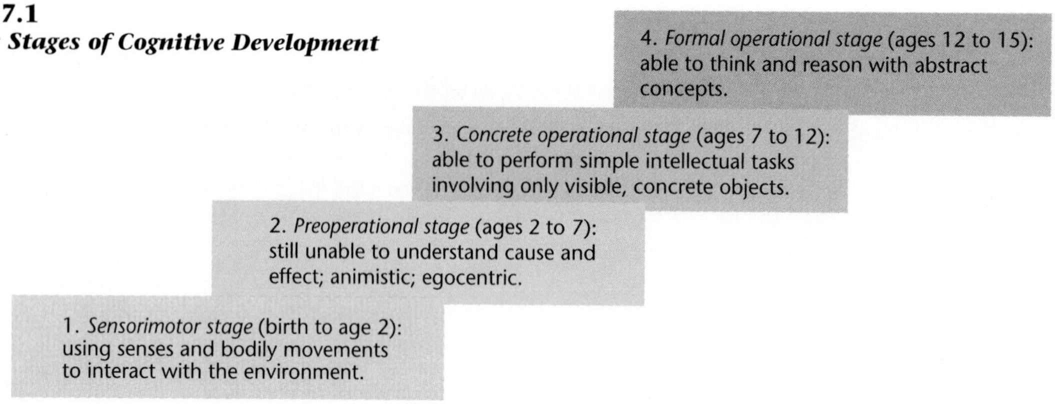

4. *Formal operational stage* (ages 12 to 15): able to think and reason with abstract concepts.

3. *Concrete operational stage* (ages 7 to 12): able to perform simple intellectual tasks involving only visible, concrete objects.

2. *Preoperational stage* (ages 2 to 7): still unable to understand cause and effect; animistic; egocentric.

1. *Sensorimotor stage* (birth to age 2): using senses and bodily movements to interact with the environment.

Kohlberg: Moral Development

According to U.S. psychologist Lawrence Kohlberg (1981), children go through three levels of moral development. This idea came from his research on how youngsters of different ages deal with moral dilemmas. The children were presented with a hypothetical situation: A man did not have the money to buy a drug that might save his dying wife. He became desperate and broke into a store to steal the drug. Should he have done that?

Some children answered yes; others no. But Kohlberg was more interested in asking further the crucial question *why* they thought so. He found three distinct patterns of response, each reflecting a certain level of moral development.

At the first level, most of the children under age 10 have a **preconventional morality**, the practice of defining right and wrong according to the *consequence* of the action being judged. The consequence involves reward or punishment. Thus some of these children said that it was all right to steal the drug because it could save the wife (reward), while others regarded the stealing as wrong because the offender could be arrested (punishment).

At the second level, children between 10 and 16 have a **conventional morality**, the practice of defining right and wrong according to the *motive* of the action being judged. Thus most of these children said that they could not blame the man for stealing the drug because of his love for his wife.

At the third level, young adults have a **postconventional morality**, the practice of judging actions by taking into account the importance of *conflicting norms*. Some of these adults supported the stealing but still believed in the general principle about the wrongfulness of stealing. They felt that the

man was justified in stealing the drug for his wife but also believed that the stealing was not really right. Other adults opposed the drug theft but were nevertheless sympathetic to the thief. To such adults, the ends do not justify the means but the compassionate husband cannot be completely blamed for stealing the drug. In short, adults are more likely than youngsters to appreciate the conflict between norms in a moral dilemma.

But this view of moral development (see Figure 7.2) has been criticized for being applicable to males more than females, as it has been derived from research on males only. According to Carol Gilligan (1982), Kohlberg focuses on men's interest in *justice*, which is impersonal in nature, and neglects women's lifelong concern with *relationships*, which are personal. In Gilligan's view, there is a different course for most females' moral development. It involves progressing from an interest in one's own survival to a concern for others. Thus women are said to have achieved a great deal of moral maturity if they have developed a compassionate concern for others.

FIGURE 7.2
Kohlberg's Levels of Moral Development

3. *Postconventional morality*: judging actions by taking account of conflicting norms

2. *Conventional morality*: defining right & wrong according to motive of action judged

1. *Preconventional morality*: defining right & wrong according to consequence of action judged

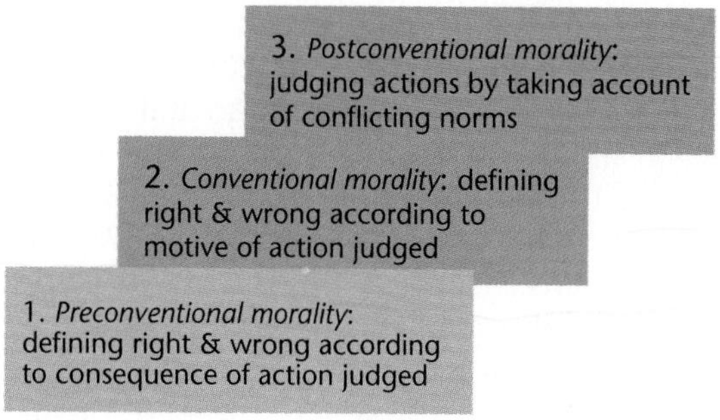

Sociology of Emotions: Affective Development

From the sociological study of emotions, we can see how children are socialized to develop their affect (emotions) so as to function well as members of society.

Human emotions abound, ranging from such basic feelings as fear, anger, and happiness to more refined emotions, such as frustration, love, and jealousy. Children are taught how to *identify* these feelings because they cannot by themselves know what they are. Suppose a little boy at a day-care center engages in such expressive behaviors as fidgeting, sulking, biting, or kicking while waiting for his mother to pick him up. He may learn from an adult that what he feels is anger. Here is how such a scenario may occur (Pollak and Thoits, 1989):

BOY [RESTLESS]: My mom is late.
STAFF MEMBER: Does that make you *mad?*
BOY: Yes.
STAFF MEMBER: Sometimes kids get *mad* when their moms are late to pick them up.

The adult, in effect, teaches the child to identify an emotion by making a causal connection between a stimulus event (mother being late) and an emotional outcome (boy being angry). Through socialization—not only by parents and other caretakers but also by television, movies, and other mass media—children learn that a compliment is expected to give pleasure, a threat is expected to arouse fear, and uncertainty is expected to give rise to anxiety. While they learn that it is logical to feel resentful toward someone who has mistreated them, they also learn that it is not logical to feel affectionate toward that person. It is crucial for children to acquire this emotional logic. Failure to do so is popularly considered a symptom of mental disorder. If 10-year-olds tell you with a big smile that their mother has just died, you may suspect them of being mentally ill (Rosenberg, 1990).

Children also learn how to *manage* their emotions in at least three ways. First, they learn how they *should* feel. For example, they should love their parents, or they should feel guilty for displeasing their parents.

Second, children learn how to *display* or *conceal* emotions. They should look happy at a wedding, look sad at a funeral, or appear reverent at a religious service. Sometimes, children learn to display an emotion that they do not have in them or conceal a feeling that they do have. If a grandparent gives them a present they do not like, they are taught to show how much they like it. If they dislike their teachers, they learn to conceal the negative feeling.

Finally, while they learn to display or conceal certain emotions, children also learn how to *change* some feelings in themselves. When children are feeling blue, they learn to manipulate that feeling by, for example, telephoning or visiting a delightful friend (Rosenberg, 1990).

Feminist Theory: Gender Development

From feminist theory we can see how boys and girls develop different **gender identities**, people's images of what they are socially expected to be and do on

Children learn how to feel in response to a specific situation. For example, through socialization, a child learns that a threat from his mother is expected to arouse fear.

the basis of their sex. Under the influence of patriarchal society, gender development involves socializing males to be dominant over females.

A major source of gender development is the family. In patriarchal society, child care is assigned primarily to the mother, and children consequently spend much time with her. During the first two years or so after birth, children of both sexes lack self-awareness, and see themselves as a part of their mothers. But beginning about age three, when children begin to see themselves as separate individuals, girls and boys start to develop different gender identities. Girls continue to identify with their mother because they are of the same sex. Girls consequently develop the traditionally feminine appreciation for relationships and nurturance. On the other hand, boys begin to differentiate themselves from their mother because of sexual difference. Further influenced by their father's dominant role in the family, boys try to suppress the feminine traits they have acquired from their mother, learn to devalue anything they consider feminine, and identify with their father by being independent and aggressive.

Another important source of gender development is the school. Also influenced by patriarchal society, teachers tend to socialize girls to see themselves as less important than boys, and boys to see themselves as more important than girls. Thus teachers praise boys' contribution more lavishly and call on boys more frequently. Teachers also tend to socialize girls to be quiet and polite and boys to be assertive and aggressive. This involves, among other things, accepting answers that boys shout out but reprimanding girls for "speaking out of turn" (Wood, 1994).

The mass media also help socialize girls to be submissive and boys to be dominant. Analyzing 80 TV series and 555 characters in 1990, the National Commission on Working Women found a preponderance of women working as secretaries and homemakers and a world of young, beautiful, and scantily dressed women. Even in advertisements that portray women as being in charge of their own lives, the women are shown "literally being carried by men, leaning on men, being helped down from a height of two feet, or figuratively being carried away by emotion" (Sidel, 1990).

Questions for Discussion and Review

1. In Freud's view, what does personality consist of and how does it develop?
2. According to Piaget, what mental abilities develop from birth through adolescence?

3. How does moral development differ between males and females?
4. How do children learn to identify and manage their emotions?
5. How does feminist theory explain the development of gender identity?

PERSPECTIVES ON SOCIALIZATION

The preceding section has focused on how children develop their personalities. Here we turn our attention to the nature of socialization.

Functionalist Perspective

To functionalists, socialization serves a number of functions for society. By far the most important is the function of ensuring social order. With socialization, the norms and values of society can be inculcated within the child. Society in effect can become a part of the individual's innermost being. It is therefore natural for socialized individuals to support their society, such as working to contribute to its prosperity and obeying the law to help ensure its stability. In addition, socialized individuals keep society going, after the older generation dies. Without socialization, anarchy would likely reign, threatening the survival of society.

Socialization also provides important psychological benefits. Most parents enjoy holding and fondling infants as well as watching and helping them play and learn. As children grow older, their love and respect for parents are also highly valued. Socialization of children further teaches parents to be patient, understanding, and self-sacrificing, qualities useful for enhancing human relations in society.

Socialization further serves an economic function for the family. While this function has sharply declined in significance in modern Western societies, it is still very important for many traditional communities around the globe. First, children are socialized to grow up to support parents in old age. Second, in many peasant villages, children are a crucial contributor to the family's economic well-being. In the Javanese villages in Indonesia, for example, girls aged 9 through 11 contribute about 38 hours of valuable work per week, while boys aged 12 to 14 put in 33 hours a week. Much of the work involves making handicrafts, processing foods for sale, and working in petty trade. Further, the children, especially girls, do most of the rearing of their younger siblings, so that their mothers can go out to work (Harris, 1995). This child labor, however, can be seen from the conflict perspective as a case of exploitation of the powerless by the powerful.

Conflict Perspective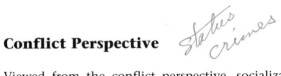

Viewed from the conflict perspective, socialization can be harmful to children because too much power is placed in the hands of parents. Because children have to depend heavily on adults to survive, an enormous power accrues to parents. Parents are therefore tempted to exploit and abuse children. Examples of child exploitation include child labor and child slavery, which are far more prevalent in poor countries (see Chapter 11: Rich and Poor Nations), and the use of children for pornographic profit, more common in rich countries. Child abuses range from beating to raping to killing them. Every year over two million children in the United States are abused, including roughly 1,300 killed by their parents (Thio, 1995).

Occupying the top of the age hierarchy, parents usually regard children as their personal possessions, denying them many rights that adults enjoy as members of society. Consider the right to physical integrity. In virtually all societies, children do not have that right, as physical punishment is widely considered appropriate for disciplining children. This contrasts with the world of adults, where, for example, army sergeants may *not* discipline recruits by beating them (Leach, 1994).

It is understandable from the conflict view that powerful people usually justify their maltreatment of subordinate individuals under their control. Not surprisingly, adults often defend physical punishment by saying "it is for their own good." In an extremely poor region in northeast Brazil, parents tend to commit infanticide by withholding medical assistance from infants who at birth have been considered not healthy or strong enough. Some of the reasons given by the parents for this infant killing are: "It is best for them to die" and "It is a blessing that the child will soon be an angel" (Harris, 1995). In Western societies, when extremely stressed or depressed parents commit suicide they tend to kill their young children first, rationalizing that the family will be happily reunited in the hereafter (McCormick, 1994).

In short, the conflict perspective reveals the dark side of socialization as exploitative and abusive, reinforcing age inequality at the expense of children. It complements the functionalist view of socialization as a positive force in society.

Symbolic Interactionist Perspective

Not concerned with the larger issue of whether socialization is a positive or negative force in society, symbolic interactionists home in on how children develop their "self"—a sense of who they are—from interaction with their parents and other people in their lives.

Cooley: The Looking-Glass Process U.S. sociologist Charles Horton Cooley (1864–1929), a founder of symbolic interactionism, viewed society as a group of individuals helping each other to develop their personalities. According to Cooley, the core of personality is the concept of oneself, the self-image. And self-image, Cooley said, is developed through the "looking-glass process":

> *Each to each a looking glass*
> *Reflects the other that doth pass.*

We in effect acquire a **looking-glass self,** the self-image that we develop from the way others treat us. Their treatment is like a mirror reflecting our personal qualities. If we have a positive image, seeing ourselves as intelligent or respectable, it is because others have treated us as such. Just as we cannot see our own face unless we have a mirror in front of us, so we cannot have a certain self-image unless others react to our behavior.

The self-image that emerges from the looking-glass process can affect our personality and behavior. If children have a favorable self-image, they tend to be self-confident, outgoing, or happy, and behave relatively well, get good grades, and even show great creativity. If youngsters have a poor self-image, they are inclined to be timid, withdrawn, or unhappy. The consequences are likely to be, among other things, delinquent behavior and lower academic achievement (Gecas, 1982).

Mead: The Role-taking Process Like Cooley, George Herbert Mead (1863–1931), the other founder of symbolic interactionism, assumed that the development of a self-concept is made possible by interaction. But while Cooley stressed the importance of using others as mirrors by observing their reactions to our behavior, Mead emphasized the significance of getting "under the skin" of others by taking their roles.

According to Mead, children develop their self-concept in three stages. First, during their initial two years, they go through *the preparatory stage by simply*

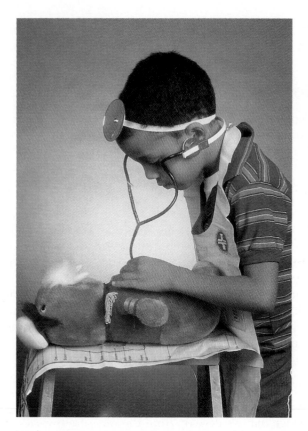

Mead emphasized role-taking, by which children internalize the values and attitudes of significant others, in socialization. Children first imitate their parents without actually knowing the meanings of their actions. Then, in play, they pretend to be their parents, thus internalizing their values. The boy in the picture is taking the role of a doctor, a generalized other, thus beginning to be a part of the larger society.

imitating other people in their immediate environment. When they see their mother reading a newspaper, they will pretend to read it too. When they see their father talk on the phone, they may later pick up the phone and talk on it. In this imitation stage, however, they are not yet playing the role of father or mother, because they do not have any idea of what they are doing. They simply learn to act like others without knowing the meanings of those actions.

Then, at about age three, children begin to go through *the play stage by taking the roles of* **significant others**—people who have close ties to the child and exert a strong influence on the child. Children will pretend to be their mother and father, examples of their significant others, while they play. In this world of make-believe, they learn to see themselves from their parents' perspective. In the process, they internalize their parents' values and attitudes, incorporating them into their own personalities. When they tell their baby dolls not to be naughty, they, in effect, tell themselves not to be naughty.

As they grow older, they also come into contact with doctors, nurses, bus drivers, sales clerks, and so on. These people outside the family circle are not as significant as the parents, but they are representative of society as a whole. Mead called them **generalized others,** people who do not have close ties to the child but do influence the child's internalization of the

values of society. By this time, children pass through *the game stage by playing the roles of the generalized others*. In this third stage, they learn to internalize the values of society as a whole. Participation in organized games such as baseball and basketball also promotes this internalization. These games involve a complex interaction among the players that is governed by a set of rules. When they play such games, children are, in effect, playing the game of life. They are learning that life has rules too.

Internalized social values become only one part of our personality, which Mead called the *me*. Whenever we feel like obeying the law, following the crowd, and the like, we are sensing the presence of the me. It represents society within our personality. On the other hand, a portion of our personality cannot be easily "invaded" by society, no matter how often we have played childhood games. Mead referred to this part of our personality as the *I*. It is basically spontaneous, creative, or impulsive. Unlike the me, which makes all of us look alike in our behavior, the I makes each of us unique. These two aspects of personality are complementary: without the I, there would be no individual creativity or social progress; without the me, there would be no social order or individual security. Both are inevitable and necessary.

With his concept of the me, Mead has greatly advanced the sociological understanding of how human personality emerges from social interaction. But he has been criticized for failing to explain where the I comes from. According to Norbert Wiley (1979), the I develops from both the me and the *we*. Infants first develop the me in about the same way as Mead indicated, except at a younger age. Through this me infants identify with their parents so totally that they feel themselves an inseparable part of their parents. Then, through a tactile, giggly love experience between parents and infants, which Wiley calls a *we experience*, the adults are, in effect, saying to the youngsters, "You exist; you are a different person;

FIGURE 7.3
Stages of Self-Development

6. The I
5. The we
4. The me
3. Playing roles of generalized others
2. Taking roles of significant others
1. Imitating others without understanding

and I love the person you are." The infant then learns to see itself as independent from its parents, at which point it develops the I (see Figure 7.3).

Questions for Discussion and Review

1. In what ways can socialization be functional?
2. In what ways can socialization be exploitative or abusive?
3. How do children develop their I and me?

AGENTS OF SOCIALIZATION

Every society tries to socialize its members. It slips the task into the hands of several groups and institutions, which sociologists call the *socializing agents* of

society. Some of them, including the family and school, are in a sense appointed by society to transmit its cultural heritage to the young. Other agents, including the peer group and mass media, are not appointed by society. Their socialization of children is mostly unintentional.

The Family

The family is the most important socializing agent, especially during the first few years of life. A review of various studies has concluded that warm, supportive, moderately restrictive family environments usually produce happy and well-behaving children; whereas cold, rigid, and overly restrictive families cause youngsters to become rebellious, resentful, and insecure (Gecas, 1981).

Various social forces, however, influence the way parents socialize their children. The most significant is social class. Research has long shown that lower-class families tend to be more authoritarian and strict than middle-class families. In authoritarian families, parents tend to train children to respect and obey parental authority. On the other hand, middle-class parents are more permissive and lenient, emphasizing the value of independence. Compared with lower-class mothers, middle-class mothers are also more child-centered and sensitive to the child's feelings. For example, they spend considerably more time in mutual play with their three-year-olds. And if a child while playing makes a toy puppy bite off a larger toy dog's head, they would refrain from jumping in with the accusatory remark, "Oh, that's terrible!" They would instead respect the child's feeling by saying something like "Wow! It looks as if

The cultural heritage is passed on directly from parents to children, which is why the family is the prime socializing agent of society. The family teaches the child to behave as the society expects. Since their parents follow Navajo traditions, these children are socialized to behave differently than if they were raised in a city where Navajo traditions had been set aside.

the baby doggy is really angry at the daddy doggy" (Farran and Haskins, 1980; Crossen, 1991).

As an agent of socialization, the family has changed a great deal over the last 30 years. In the past, young children were regarded as innocent and teenagers immature, so that they were protected from what were considered the evils and temptations of the world outside the family. Today, young children are considered competent rather than innocent. Thus, even four- or five-year-olds are taught about AIDS and child abuse and provided with "toys" that simulate pregnancy. Similarly, teenagers are no longer considered immature, but sophisticated in the ways of the world, knowledgeable about sex, drugs, crime, and much more. Teenagers are consequently left to fend for themselves, with little guidance or supervision from adults (Elkind, 1992). This is particularly true for children whose parents seem more committed to career than parenting. But these children are more likely than traditional children to learn understanding and mature behavior instead of unthinking obedience (Greenberger and Goldberg, 1989).

The School

At home children are treated as unique, special persons. At school, they are treated more impersonally, the same as all their schoolmates. They may learn to fit in by getting along with others. In fact, the schools often provide children with their first training in how to behave in secondary groups.

Whereas socialization by families often contributes to the diversity of society, the schools are more likely to contribute to uniformity. Society, in effect, officially designates schools as its socializing agents. They are expected both to help children develop their potential as creative, independent individuals and to mold them into social conformity—two goals that seem contradictory. To meet the first goal, the school teaches its formal curriculum of academic knowledge and skills. The pursuit of this goal becomes increasingly important as students rise to progressively higher educational levels. By cultivating their intellectual capabilities, students are expected to turn into intelligent citizens capable of making a living and contributing to the prosperity of their society.

The pursuit of the second goal—social conformity—is more earnest at the lower grade levels. It involves teaching history and civics. But also important is the "hidden curriculum," training students to be patriotic, to believe in their country's cultural

As the chief socializing agency outside the family, the school teaches a "hidden curriculum." Children learn to acquire public virtues, such as patriotism, obedience to laws, and respect for authority.

values, and to obey its laws. It is also implicit in classroom rituals (such as the Pledge of Allegiance), in demands that classroom rules be obeyed, in the choice of books to be assigned in English classes, and in a host of other activities (such as glorification of the competition and discipline of sports).

The Peer Group

As children grow older, they become increasingly involved with their **peer group**, a group whose members are about the same age and have similar interests. As a socializing agent, the peer group differs from the family and school. While parents and teachers have more power than children and students, the peer group is made up of equals.

The peer group teaches its members several important things. First, it teaches them to be independent from adult authorities. Second, it teaches social skills and group loyalties. Third, the peer group teaches its members the values of friendship and companionship among equals—values that are relatively absent in the socialization received from authority figures like parents and teachers. On the other hand, a peer group can socialize its members to thumb their noses at authorities and adults. If there is a rule against bringing toys from home to nursery school, some children will ignore it. Some may end up getting into trouble with the law one day. But many others may only innocently poke fun at adults behind their backs (Elkin and Handel, 1988; Corsaro and Eder, 1990).

Freeing themselves from the grip of parental and school authorities, peer groups often develop distinctive subcultures with their own values, symbols, jargon, music, dress, and heroes. Whereas parents and teachers tend to place great importance on scholastic achievement, adolescent peer groups are likely to put a higher premium on popularity, social leadership, and athletic attainment (Corsaro and Rizzo, 1988). The divergence between parental and peer values does not necessarily lead to a hostile confrontation between parents and teenagers.

In fact, most youngsters are just as friendly with parents as with peers. They simply engage in different types of activities—work and task activities with parents but play and recreation with peers. Concerning financial, educational, career, and other serious matters, such as what to spend money on and what occupation to choose, they are inclined to seek advice from parents. When it comes to social activities, such as whom to date and what clubs to join, they are more likely to discuss them with peers (Sebald, 1986). This reflects the great importance placed by the peer group on "other-directed behavior," looking to others for approval and support as opposed to reliance on personal beliefs and traditional values. Peer groups, in effect, demand conformity at the expense of independence and individuality. Early adolescents are most willing to accept conformity; hence, they are most deeply involved with peer groups. As the young people grow into middle and late adolescence, their involvement with peers gradually declines because of their growing predilection for independence. When they reach the final year of high school, they tend more to adopt adult values, such as wanting to get good grades and good jobs.

The Mass Media

The mass media include popular books, magazines, newspapers, movies, television, and radio. Today, television has become the prime source of information about the world, more than parents or teachers. It has been found to affect children in certain ways.

First, children may come to expect their lives, their parents, and their teachers to be as exciting as those portrayed on television. Even the widely praised Sesame Street makes children expect their schools to

An important function of the peer group is to teach its young members the value of friendship and companionship among equals. These values are relatively absent in the socialization by authority figures, such as parents and teachers.

be fast-paced and entertaining. Thus, children are likely to be disappointed, finding their parents inadequate and their teachers boring. Second, television tends to impoverish its young viewers' creative imagination. If they watch TV frequently, they may find it difficult to create pictures in their own minds or to understand stories without visual illustration. This is because watching television usually makes people feel passive. Third, through its frequent portrayal of violence, television tends to stimulate violence-prone children to actual violence, to make normal children less sensitive to violence in real life, and to instill the philosophy that might makes right. Television violence can further heighten children's senses of danger and vulnerability as well as their feelings of alienation and doom. Finally, television destroys the age-old notion of childhood as a discrete period of innocence. It reveals the "secrets" of adulthood that have been hidden from children for centuries. The spectacle of adults hitting each other, killing each other, and breaking down and crying teaches them that adults do not know any better than children (Cullingford, 1993).

On the other hand, television has the redeeming quality of enlarging young children's vocabulary and knowledge of the world (Josephson, 1987). Moreover, whatever negative effects TV may have on young children, they are likely to dissipate with older children. Thus, beginning at age 12, youngsters will increasingly find commercials unreal and misleading. With more sophistication, older teenagers also take TV violence for what it is—fake and for entertainment only (Freedman, 1986; Rice et al., 1990).

Questions for Discussion and Review

1. Why is the family the most important agent of socialization?
2. What is the hidden curriculum of the school, and how does it help ensure social order?
3. Why are many adolescents more influenced by their peer group than by their family?
4. How does television influence children?

ADULT SOCIALIZATION

The socialization process does not stop at the end of childhood. It continues with the emergence of adulthood and stops only when the person dies.

Locher/Reprinted by permission: Tribune Media Services.

GLOBAL VILLAGE

The drug trade and underdevelopment have caused the South American country of Colombia to experience a wave of street violence, but some Colombian leaders have identified television as one potential contributor to the problem. This reading explores the efforts to rid Colombia's television of violent TV shows.

The Streets Are Murder But the Tube Is Safe

Tired of being bombed on the streets, blown out of the sky, tortured, kidnapped and assassinated in war-zone numbers every year, Colombians are campaigning to eliminate violence—from television.

Blaming the likes of Rambo for contributing to the country's high level of mayhem, major business and political figures have organized what has turned out to be a popular crusade to purge TV of excessive violence and sex in order to throw a little cold water on the country's violent passions.

After being victimized by guerrillas, narco-traffickers and other assorted criminals, says Carlos Delgado, the president of an organization of Colombia's advertisers, Colombians shouldn't have to put up with the violence of the "Rambo" movies or the sex of films like "9 1/2 Weeks." In November, Mr. Delgado persuaded his membership not to advertise in programs deemed exceedingly violent or sexual.

Since he began his campaign, Mr. Delgado has gotten a flood of letters expressing support. One poll in El Espectador, a leading daily, said 80% of the public doesn't want programs with excessive violence and sex.

Indeed, violence is so endemic here that Colombian universities have made it an academic specialty. Violence professionals are known as *violentologos*. Rather than sneering at the anti-TV violence campaign, some violentologos find merit in it.

"There are a lot of television shows and films, such as 'The Terminator,' whose theme is that of private justice," says Eduardo Pizarro, another violentologo at the National University. Private justice is a problem in Colombia. Five years ago, says Mr. Pizarro, the government said there were 125 paramilitary groups or death squads active in Colombia.

Most of the groups were alliances of military men, landowners and drug traffickers who joined forces to kill guerrilla sympathizers. Almost all these groups had names derived from U.S. films and TV shows, such as Rambo, the Terminators or the A-Team. "In Switzerland such a show wouldn't do any damage," says Mr. Pizarro, whose brother Carlos, a former guerrilla, was one of four presidential candidates assassinated during the course of the 1990 election. "In Colombia, unfortunately, it could have a lot of damage."

For Colombian TV executives, the controversy has become a big headache. Having agreed to more stringent self-policing, they were just coming to grips with Mr. Delgado's campaign. Then, in late March, affairs took an unexpected turn. A Barranquilla widow convinced a judge that her three adolescent children were being perverted by television. The judge gave the government agency that regulates TV air time 48 hours to clean it up.

The widow, Deisy Porto de Vargas, told reporters that her son, imitating a TV character who often defuses bombs in the U.S.-produced show "MacGyver," was starting to take apart her appliances. She worried that things could only get worse when she saw a Venezuelan soap opera in which a mother threw her daughter down the stairs after the daughter refused to get an abortion.

But a TV production chief thinks it's all pretty silly. After all, he says, Colombia was violent before television arrived here in 1954.

Excerpted from Jose de Cordoba, "Streets are Murder, But the Tube is Safe: Colombia Tames TV," *The Wall Street Journal,* May 12, 1993, p. 1 ff.

Learning New Roles

Being socialized includes learning new roles. Like children, adults learn many new roles as they go through various stages of life. At the same time, adults' specific socialization experiences do differ from those of children. We can see this in the three types of socialization that all of us undergo.

One is **anticipatory socialization**, the process by which people learn to assume a role in the future.

Many young children learn to be parents in the future by playing house. Young adults prepare themselves for their future professions by attending college. Generally, as people get older, they tend to be less idealistic or more practical. Many first-year medical students, for example, expect to acquire every bit of medical knowledge and then to serve humanity selflessly. Toward the end of their medical schooling, they usually become more realistic. They will strive to learn just enough to pass exams and look forward to a lucrative practice as a reward for their years of hard work. In short, as people get closer to the end of their anticipatory socialization, their earlier idealism gradually dies out, to be replaced by realism.

Like children, adults also go through **developmental socialization**, the process by which people learn to be more competent in playing their currently assumed role, much like receiving on-the-job training. Children learn their currently acquired roles as sons or daughters, students, and members of their peer groups. Adults learn their newly assumed roles as full-time workers, husbands, wives, parents, and so on. The learning of these roles can mold adult personality. For example, the more complex the worker's job, the more likely the worker will experience self-direction in the workplace and end up valuing autonomy in other aspects of life. On the other hand, the more simple and routine the work, the more likely the individual will be supervised by some higher-up and eventually will value conformity (Kohn, 1980).

A third form of socialization is less common: **resocialization**, the process by which people are forced to abandon their old self and develop a new self in its place. It happens to adults more often than to children. Resocialization can take place in prisons, mental institutions, POW camps, military training centers, and religious cults. Such settings are **total institutions**, places where people are not only cut off from the larger society but also rigidly controlled by the administrators. Resocialization in total institutions is usually dehumanizing.

In a state mental institution, for example, the staff tends to treat patients as if they were objects rather than humans. The staff may verbally or physically abuse them, or prevent them from talking to the staff unless spoken to first. The staff may also enter the patients' rooms and examine their possessions at any time. The staff may even monitor the patients' personal hygiene and waste evacuation in the bathroom. Such dehumanization is intended to strip the patients of whatever self-concept they have brought into the institution from their prior social life. Then rewards and punishments are used to mold them into docile conformists. Such patients usually develop "institutionalism"—a deep sense of hopelessness, pervasive loss of initiative, deterioration of social skills, and an inability to function in larger society (Thio, 1995).

Continuing Development

As we saw earlier, Freud suggested that once adult personality has been molded by childhood experiences it stops growing or changing. But his student, Erik Erikson (1902–1994), theorized that personality continues to develop throughout the life span. According to Erikson, personality development goes through eight stages (see Figure 7.4). In each stage, people are faced with a crisis that must be resolved, with either a positive or a negative result.

The first five, pre-adult stages parallel Freud's. According to Erikson, the child normally develops a sense of *trust* during what Freud called the oral stage, *autonomy* during the anal stage, *initiative* during what Freud called the phallic stage, *industry* during the latency stage, and *identity* during adolescence. Negative childhood experiences, however, lead to mistrust, doubt, guilt, inferiority, and confusion. Consider as an example how trust and mistrust develop. During the oral stage, from birth to age one, the totally helpless infant must depend on an adult to survive. If the infant's need for life-sustaining care is well met, he or she will develop a sense of trust in others; otherwise, mistrust will develop.

After people enter adulthood, they will, in Erikson's view, go through three more stages of development. In early adulthood, which lasts from ages 20 to 40, people face the crisis of having to resolve the conflicting demands for love and work. They usually meet the demand for love by falling in love, getting married, and raising a family. If they are too attached to their families, they may not be able to achieve great success in their careers. But if they are too eager to work extremely hard, they risk losing intimacy with and incurring isolation from their families. In this stage, the young adult is confronted with the conflict between enjoying *intimacy* and suffering *isolation*.

In middle adulthood, which lasts from ages 40 to 60, people become acutely aware that their death will come, that their time is running out, and that they must give up their youthful dreams to start being more concerned with others rather than themselves. Usually, they choose to be what Erikson calls "generative"—nurturing or guiding the younger generation. This would give them an elevating sense of productivity and creativity, of having made a significant contribution to others. On the other hand, they are

Changes with circumstances

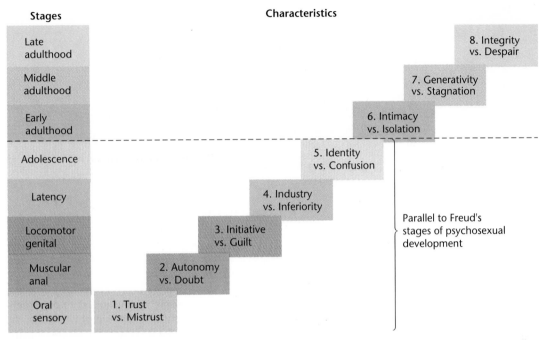

Stages **Characteristics**

Late adulthood — 8. Integrity vs. Despair

Middle adulthood — 7. Generativity vs. Stagnation

Early adulthood — 6. Intimacy vs. Isolation

Adolescence — 5. Identity vs. Confusion

Latency — 4. Industry vs. Inferiority

Locomotor genital — 3. Initiative vs. Guilt

Muscular anal — 2. Autonomy vs. Doubt

Oral sensory — 1. Trust vs. Mistrust

Parallel to Freud's stages of psychosexual development

FIGURE 7.4
Erikson's Stages of Psychosocial Development

also inclined to continue hanging on to their youthful dreams, to try to be active and feel young again. Because this is difficult to fulfill at this stage, the individuals risk getting weighed down with a depressing sense of disappointment, stagnation, and boredom. In short, the middle-aged adult is faced with the conflict between *generativity* and *stagnation*.

In late adulthood, from age 60 until death, people find themselves in conflict between achieving *integrity* (holding oneself together) and sinking in *despair* (emotionally falling apart). Those who are able to maintain the integrity of the self are likely to have accepted whatever they have attained so far. But those who sink in despair regret that their lives have been full of missed opportunities and that the time is just too short for them to start another life. Therefore, death loses its sting for those who have learned to hold themselves together and to accept death as the ultimate outcome of life. But those who fall apart emotionally cannot accept death and are gripped with fear of it.

Feminists have criticized Erikson's theory for applying to men more than women. The crisis of having to choose between intimacy and isolation, for example, is less likely to confront women in early adulthood because they have long been socialized to appreciate personal relationships. But research has established that most people do experience the two conflicting forces in most of the stages (Varghese,

1981; Ochse and Plug, 1986). Especially significant to sociology is Erikson's emphasis on society's influence on personality development. He observes, for example, that teenagers in modern societies have a hard time solving their identity crisis because they are bombarded with a staggering array of lifestyle and

When people reach middle adulthood, from ages 40 to 60, they begin to become more concerned with others. They choose to be "generative," guiding and nurturing the younger generation.

ENRICHING OUR LIVES

As we have noted, Erikson suggests that it is difficult for young people in the United States to know who they are because they are bombarded with a staggering array of life-style and career choices. This reflective reading provides a way of solving that problem.

Embrace Multiple Identities

Every culture has its preferred description of the human distinction. In our culture, the preferred descriptions have included: the soul, the self, the ego, the person. In our time, the preferred description: identity. In America we are choking on identity. And not only on the identity of others; we are choking also on the identity of our own.

Identity, according to Erik Erikson, writing in the 1950s, is "vague," "ambiguous," "unfathomable," "colloquial," "naive," "all-pervasive." Identity was certainly one of the most repercussive contributions of the social sciences to American culture. But what was it? For many intellectuals in post-war America, identity was what alienation was not. Erikson's influence on the American obsession with identity was less a theory than a mood. He made identity into a romance.

Private identity is an oxymoron. Identity is public; it is how one is known. Identity is toasty. It imparts a feeling of the inside; but this feeling is imparted to us from the outside. The inside and the outside should be correctly mapped. The outside is vast. The country to which I belong is outside. The people to which I belong is outside. The family to which I belong is outside. Inside, there is only my body and my soul.

It is important to distinguish between identifying oneself and justifying oneself. Identity in America is so fitful and so flexible not least because it is so often cobbled together for the purpose of self-justification; and this constant clamor for self-justification is a drain on American dignity. One must defend oneself, of course, if one is attacked for being a black or a homosexual or a woman or a Jew or a Catholic, but one must dream of being more than a defender of oneself. To assert your right to be something is not yet to be something.

The lure of identity is the lure of wholeness. It proposes to bind up the parts and the pieces of a life and transform them into a unity, into a life that adds up. The idea provides a mixture of psychological and aesthetic satisfaction. But is there really nothing worse than a life that does not add up? Surely the life that does add up is the easeful one. In the modern world, the cruelest thing that you can do to people is to make them ashamed of their complexity. A life that does not add up is not a life of irony. Quite the contrary. Its accomplishment is to contain within itself many things that do not go together. This is an age in which inconsistency is an occasion for pleasure. Not my identity, but my identities. There is greater truth in the plural. There is also a greater likelihood of decency.

Excerpted from Leon Wieseltier, "Against Identity," *The New Republic,* November 28, 1994, pp. 24 ff. Excerpted by permission of *The New Republic,* © 1994, The New Republic, Inc.

career choices unimaginable in traditional societies (see box, above).

Aging and Dying

Also unlike traditional societies, modern societies do not adequately socialize individuals for old age. In traditional societies, old people are more valued and respected. It is quite an accomplishment to survive into old age in a traditional society, where most people die relatively young. Further, the experiences that the elders have accumulated over the years are invaluable to younger generations, because their societies change so little and so slowly that old knowledge and values do not seem to lose their relevance. Since the aged live with their children and grandchildren, are given an honored role, and are often observed to dispense wisdom and advice, young people are easily socialized to accept old age when they themselves become old.

In modern societies, old people typically live alone. By not living with their old parents and grandparents, younger people have little chance of learning how to grow old gracefully. Although they may visit their old relatives often, they do not relish

In traditional societies, people see their loved ones die at home, handle their corpses, and personally bury them. But in modern societies, we seldom witness a dying scene at home because most deaths take place in hospitals. It is therefore difficult for us to accept death as the natural culmination of life.

the prospect of growing old themselves, because they believe that the aged live an unrewarding, lonely, or even degrading life.

Modern societies also have come up short in socialization for death. In traditional societies, people see their loved ones die at home, handle their corpses, and personally bury them. But in modern societies, we seldom witness a dying scene at home because most deaths occur in hospitals. As Sherwin Nuland (1994) says, "We have created the method of modern dying. Modern dying takes place in the modern hospital, where it can be hidden, cleansed of its organic blight, and finally packaged for modern burial." The method of modern dying has in effect robbed us of the important realization that death is the natural culmination of life. Not surprisingly, many of us find death frightening, as research by Elisabeth Kübler-Ross (1969) has suggested.

Kübler-Ross found that terminally ill patients usually go through five stages of reaction, from the time when they discover they are dying to the final moment of their death. She refers to the first stage as *initial denial* because upon being told that they are dying, patients usually express disbelief: "No, not me; it just can't be me." At the second stage—*anger*—they believe they are dying but get angry with family, doctor, and God, protesting, "Why me?" When they move into the third stage—*bargaining*—they are no longer angry and ask God to let them live just a little longer in return for good behavior. In the fourth stage—*depression*—they can no longer postpone their death, so they sink into deep depression. Finally, in the fifth stage—*acceptance*—they feel calm and ready to die. But most patients do not make it to the final stage.

Because our elderly population is increasing, we will see many more deaths in our lives. Common sense would suggest that this should make us less afraid of the "horsemen of death." But it is not the number of deaths but *how society treats death* that affects our feelings about the end of life. We will likely continue to fear death as long as our society continues to depersonalize it, rendering it more distant and more forbidding than in traditional societies (Nuland, 1994).

Questions for Discussion and Review

1. How do anticipatory and developmental socialization differ from resocialization?
2. What are Erikson's three development stages of adult life, and what personal crisis does each stage contain?
3. Why is the fear of death relatively common in modern societies?

A Global Analysis

All over the world, socialization appears largely the same in some ways and different in other ways. Researchers rarely study socialization with a global approach, but the existing findings reveal some interesting similarities and differences.

In a study of three significantly different cultures (U.S., French, and Japanese), researchers found some similarities in how mothers respond to their five-month-olds. When infants cry, mothers respond with nurturance. If the babies simply vocalize, showing no distress, mothers will respond with imitation. Mothers generally respond more to infants' vocalizing than to infants' looking (Bornstein et al., 1991). Such uniformities across different societies suggest the influence of biological factors on socialization.

But most of the studies that have been conducted suggest the powerful influence of culture on socialization. This is most vivid in the differences between the West and the rest of the world.

First, young children in the West are supposed to play, whereas their peers in many non-Western countries are expected to work. As has been suggested, Javanese children in Indonesian villages, although only nine years old, already work to contribute substantially to family income. Even younger children, four or five years old, also work, though mostly taking care of younger siblings while mothers work on the farm. In many African agricultural societies, the importance of child caregivers is so keenly felt that women with infants often recruit relatives' children from distant villages to help out (Morelli and Tronick, 1991).

Second, in the West, the daily care and long-term upbringing of children are often left entirely to parents alone. Increasingly, strangers such as childcare workers take care of children for money more than affection. This kind of socialization tends to foster individualism in the charges. By contrast, in much of the rest of the world, extended family groups, clans, and even communities pitch in to care for each other's children. This kind of socialization is more likely to develop trust in others and thereby attachment to groups (Leach, 1994).

Third, Western parents start socializing their children to be self-reliant at an extremely young age—virtually right after birth. Babies are placed in a crib, often in their own room. At least initially, the trauma of being left alone causes the infant to cry at bedtime or upon waking up. By contrast, infants in many non-Western societies are spared that trauma. They are allowed to sleep with their parents, often until age five or six (Harrison, 1992). With this sleeping arrangement, the children may have a slow start in learning to be on their own, but they are effectively socialized to develop a strong sense of security. This may partly explain why the insurance industry, supposed to meet customers' need for security about their future, is far from as prosperous in the non-West as it is in the West.

Fourth, Western parents begin earnestly socializing children to curb their impulses and behave well at a very young age—before age four. This may have much to do with Westerners' assumption that people are born bad, as suggested by the Judeo-Christian belief about being born sinners or Freud's widely accepted idea about being born with the id. By contrast, in Japan, China, and other East Asian societies, children are assumed innately good and therefore given much freedom to do what they want. This parental indulgence and permissiveness toward children usually gives way to strict disciplining after age four. From then on, the contents of Asian and Western socialization also differ. Asian parents tend to emphasize emotional control, filial piety, politeness to others, and other traits that promote social relationships and conformity. On the other hand, Western parents stress spontaneity, autonomy, assertiveness, and other characteristics that promote individual freedom and creativity (Papousek, 1991; Harrison, 1992).

Questions for Discussion and Review

1. In what ways is childhood socialization about the same throughout the globe?
2. In what ways does childhood socialization vary from Western to non-Western societies?

ARE WE PUPPETS OF SOCIETY?

Through socialization we internalize the norms and values of society. Does this imply that we become puppets of society, individuals who basically enjoy giving up freedom and following the rules society sets down? The answer is yes and no.

In many respects, we do behave like society's puppets. We are glad to follow society's expectation that we be friendly to our friends and love our parents. We are happy to do many other similarly nice things every day as expected of us by society. It just happens that we enjoy doing all these things because others have made us happy by responding positively. It is only that, living in a highly individualistic society, we do not see ourselves as society's puppets.

But we may also do things differently than dictated by society. We may get drunk, fool around a bit too much, protest what we perceive to be a social injustice, or do other similar things that raise others' eyebrows. By engaging in such activities, we express the unsocialized aspect of our "self," no longer behaving like puppets.

Dennis Wrong (1961) has suggested that we can never be puppets all the time because it is impossible to be entirely socialized. There are at least four reasons why socialization can never turn us into total puppets.

First, we have certain "imperious biological drives" that always buck against society's attempt to mold us in its image.

Second, the socializing influences are not always consistent and harmonious with one another. Our ethnic group, social class, and professional and occupational associations may not socialize us in the same way. They may teach conflicting roles, norms, and values.

Third, even if society could consistently and completely socialize us, we would still violate its laws and rules. In the very process of learning to obey the rules, we may also learn how to break them without getting caught, which is a great temptation for most if not all people. Even some of the most "respectable" citizens have committed crimes.

Finally, if we were completely socialized, we would become extremely unhappy and probably neurotic or psychotic. This is why, as Sigmund Freud said, civilization tends to breed discontent in the individual. No normal persons want their drives for self-expression, freedom, creativity, or personal eccentricity to be totally suppressed.

Questions for Discussion and Review

1. In what ways do we behave like society's puppets?
2. What aspects of human life prevent socialization from turning us into total puppets?

CHAPTER REVIEW

1. *What is socialization?* It is the process by which a society transmits its cultural values to its members. *Can either nature or nurture alone explain human behavior?* No. Both heredity and environment make us what we are. The importance of heredity can be demonstrated by how our temperament, intelligence, and aptitude influence the development of our personality. The significance of socialization can be seen in the case studies of children who are feral, isolated, institutionalized, or gifted.

2. *How do various theories explain the development of personality?* To Freud, personality develops from the interaction of the id, ego, and superego during childhood. To Piaget, children develop mentally in stages from using sensorimotor skills in infancy to thinking abstractly in adolescence. To Kohlberg, children develop morally from a low, preconventional level of judging right and wrong to higher levels. The sociology of emotions demonstrates how children learn to develop emotionally by identifying and managing their feelings through interaction with others. And feminist theory shows how children develop different gender identities under the influence of patriarchal society.

3. *What do the three sociological perspectives tell us about socialization?* According to functionalists, socialization helps ensure social order as well as provide psychological and economic benefits. To conflict theorists, socialization reinforces age inequality, leading to child exploitation and abuse. And the symbolic interactionist perspective suggests how children learn to see themselves from the way others see them and from the roles of others with whom they interact.

4. *What is distinctive about each of the major socializing agents?* The family is the most important socializing agent for the child. The school is charged both with

helping children develop their potential as independent individuals and with securing their conformity to social norms. The peer group socializes its members as equals, offering a set of values largely different from that presented by adult authorities. The mass media, particularly television, influence the child's values and behavior, but this influence tends to wear off as the child grows up.

5. *Does socialization stop with the end of childhood?* No. Adults continue to experience socialization as children do. They go through anticipatory socialization, developmental socialization, and resocialization. According to Erikson, adults continue to go through three more stages of psychosocial development after having come out of five pre-adult stages. Each stage involves struggling to resolve a crisis. *How does modern society deal with aging and dying?* Not very well. Generally, the aged are not as highly respected in modern societies as in traditional ones. Death is also not treated as a normal, eventually inevitable part of life to be accepted.

6. *What can a global analysis of socialization reveal?* Socialization is similar and different from society to society, suggesting the influence of both biological and cultural factors.

7. *Are we puppets of society?* Yes, to the extent that we enjoy doing many things in accordance with social norms, but no, to the extent that we occasionally engage in activities frowned on by others.

KEY TERMS

Anticipatory socialization   The process by which people learn to assume a role in the future (p. 159).

Aptitude   The capacity for developing physical or social skills (p. 145).

Conventional morality   Kohlberg's term for the practice of defining right and wrong according to the *motive* of the action being judged (p. 150).

Developmental socialization   The process by which people learn to be more competent in playing their currently assumed role (p. 160).

Ego   Freud's term for the part of personality that is rational, dealing with the world logically and realistically (p. 148).

Gender identity   People's image of what they are socially expected to be and do on the basis of their sex (p. 151).

Generalized others   Mead's term for people who do not have close ties to the child but do influence the child's internalization of the values of society (p.154).

Id   Freud's term for the part of personality that is irrational, concerned only with seeking pleasure (p. 148).

Instincts   Biologically inherited capacities for performing relatively complex tasks (p. 145).

Intelligence   The capacity for mental or intellectual achievement (p. 145).

Looking-glass self   Cooley's term for the self-image that we develop from the way others treat us (p. 153).

Peer group   A group whose members are about the same age and have similar interests (p. 156).

Personality   A fairly stable configuration of feelings, attitudes, ideas, and behaviors that characterizes an individual (p. 144).

Postconventional morality   Kohlberg's term for the practice of judging actions by taking into account the importance of *conflicting norms* (p. 150).

Preconventional morality   Kohlberg's term for the practice of defining right and wrong according to the *consequence* of the action being judged (p. 150).

Resocialization   The process by which people are forced to abandon their old self and to develop a new self in its place (p. 160).

Significant others   Mead's term for people who have close ties to the child and exert a strong influence on the child (p. 154).

Socialization   The process by which a society transmits its cultural values to its members (p. 144).

Superego   Freud's term for the part of personality that is moral, popularly known as conscience (p. 148).

Total institutions   Places where people are not only cut off from the larger society but also rigidly controlled by the administrators (p. 160).

SUGGESTED READINGS

Bornstein, Marc H. (ed.). 1991. *Cultural Approaches to Parenting*. Hillsdale, N.J.: Lawrence Erlbaum Associates. A collection of empirical studies on how parents in various societies socialize their children.

Gardner, Howard. 1993. *Creating Minds: An Anatomy of Creativity Seen Through the Lives of Freud, Einstein, Picasso, Stravinsky, Eliot, Graham, and Gandhi*. New York: Basic Books. Shows how the family and other social forces affect the development of these seven geniuses.

Gilligan, Carol, et al. (eds.). 1990. *Making Connections*. Cambridge, Mass.: Harvard University Press. A series of research reports on how U.S. society encourages adolescent girls to change from being confident about what they know and see to being uncertain and hesitant.

Nuland, Sherwin B. 1994. *How We Die: Reflections on Life's Final Chapter*. New York: Knopf. Offers a sharp insight into how death has become frightening and lonely to modern society.

Rymer, Russ. 1993. *Genie: An Abused Child's Flight from Silence*. New York: HarperCollins. Details how the atrocious deprivation of socialization affected Genie and how her case led to conflicts among linguists, psychologists, social workers, and others who claimed to help her.

DEVIANCE

Myths and Realities

MYTH: *Strangers don't care about us as much as our relatives, friends, and acquaintances. No wonder that strangers are more likely to kill us.*
REALITY: Strangers are less likely to kill us. Most murder victims were related to or knew their killers.

MYTH: *"Guns don't kill, people do." Therefore, it is futile to outlaw the possession of guns.*
REALITY: Of course, guns by themselves cannot kill, nor can their absence reduce the motivation to kill. But, were guns less available, potential murderers would use less-lethal weapons, which would result in fewer deaths.

MYTH: *Drug abuse is common in the United States, involving all kinds of people such as the rich and the poor as has been the case for many years.*
REALITY: Since the early 1980s drug abuse has worsened among the lower classes, particularly the socially and economically oppressed minorities, but it has declined among the middle classes.

MYTH: *Deviance is always harmful to society.*
REALITY: Deviance can bring benefits to society if it occurs within limits.

MYTH: *The U.S. criminal justice system is by any measure soft on criminals.*
REALITY: Our country appears soft on criminals because extremely few criminals are apprehended and punished. But compared with other democracies, the U.S. is tougher for imprisoning proportionately more criminals and imposing longer prison terms.

hen you thumb through a newspaper or magazine, you might come across a story such as this: In 1988 Jeffrey Dahmer murdered three people. He first met a 14-year-old boy at a bus stop and asked him to pose in the nude for photos. Soon after they arrived at Dahmer's apartment, Dahmer had sex with the boy, drugged him, strangled him, dismembered him, and smashed his bones with a sledgehammer. Several months later, Dahmer picked up a 23-year-old man at a gay bar, had oral sex with him, drugged him, and butchered him. Later in the same month, Dahmer strangled another, 24-year-old man and then kept his head after having boiled it to remove the skin and painted the skull. Dahmer later told the police that he only saved skulls of the most handsome victims so that he would not forget them. He also said that he ate the flesh of three young men "like filet mignon." By 1991, when he was arrested, the police found in his apartment at least 15 dismembered bodies, a head in the refrigerator and a heart in the freezer, and a blue barrel of acid for leftovers (Matthews, 1992a).

When crimes such as this pop up in the media, we may regard the perpetraters as deviants who are foreign to us. But deviance is widespread, though most is far from as gruesome as Dahmer's. In the United States virtually everybody has committed one or more offenses, such as those listed in Table 8.1. Even in a society of saints, as Durkheim long ago suggested, its rules would be broken. What exactly is deviance?

TABLE 8.1
Common Offenses Punishable by Fines or Jail Terms

- Gambling illegally, such as betting on a sport event or political election.
- Evading taxes, such as failing to report or exaggerating deductible expenses.
- Committing computer crime, such as copying software illegally.
- Serving alcohol to minors.
- Drinking in public, where prohibited.
- Possessing marijuana in small quantities for personal use.
- Committing adultery in states where illegal.
- Patronizing a prostitute.
- Appearing nude in public, such as nude sunbathing, where prohibited.
- Stealing TV signals, such as with a satellite dish.
- Speeding or other moving-traffic violations.
- Parking illegally.
- Smoking in public, where ordinance prohibits it.
- Failing to recycle where required.

SOURCE: Adapted from Stephen J. Adler and Wade Lamber, "Common Criminals: Just About Everyone Violates Some Laws, Even Model Citizens," *Wall Street Journal,* March 12, 1993, p. A6.

WHAT IS DEVIANCE?

Deviance is generally defined as any act that violates a social norm. But the phenomenon is more complex than that. How do we know whether an act violates a social norm? Is homosexuality deviant—a violation of a social norm? Some people think so, but others do not. There are at least three factors involved in determining what deviance is: time, place, and public consensus or power.

First, what constitutes deviance varies from one historical period to another. In the last century in the United States, opium and cocaine were legal and easily available common drugs; today their use is a criminal offense. Nowadays in most countries cigarette smoking is legal, but in the seventeenth century it was illegal and, in some countries, smokers were punished harshly: in Russia their noses were cut off and in Hindustan their lips sliced off (Goode, 1989).

Second, the definition of deviance varies from one place to another. A polygamist is a criminal in the United States but not in Saudi Arabia and other Muslim countries. Prostitution is illegal in the United States (except in some counties in Nevada), but legal

Cutting Edge

Crime statistics help sociologists gain a better perspective on crime, but sometimes the numbers are not accurate. This reading explores the assembly of crime statistics in Britain and the U.S. and shows how they sometimes distort the true extent and patterns of crime.

Measuring Crime

Most Americans and Britons think crime has risen over the past two decades, opinion polls show. Yet, according to the most reliable measure available, total levels of crime in the United States have fallen, not risen, over that time.

To understand why such conflicting assertions can be made about crime rates, the place to start is with police statistics, the most common source of published data quoted by politicians and headline writers. In the United States, the number of crimes recorded by the police has risen by more than 60% since 1973. But police figures often say as much about police practices and procedures as they do about the underlying crime rate. Two hurdles must be crossed before a crime makes it into police records. First, victims or bystanders must report the crime to the police. Second, the police must note the crime in their books. In most countries, only a minority of crimes make it that far.

Police are unlikely to hear at all about most "victimless crimes," such as drug-taking and prostitution. Victims of more serious offenses might, in principle, be expected to turn more readily to the police. Yet even here, reporting can be surprisingly haphazard. In the United States, four out of ten violent crimes are committed by relations or acquaintances of the victim, a fact which may weigh against involving outsiders—such as the police. The next stage of the process is the entry of the crime on to police records. Sometimes a record will not be made because of a simple failure in book-keeping. But a police station or police force may also have a positive interest in keeping hard-to-solve crimes off its books, since clear-up rates are a common way to measure efficiency and so to judge which officers should be promoted and which departments receive more resources.

It is also observable that, when crime rates are calculated from police records, by and large an increase in the number of policemen will produce an increase in the recorded rate of crime, as more policemen have more time available to deal with crimes that might otherwise have passed without official notice.

Fortunately, police figures are not the only source of systematic information about crime. A handful of governments sponsor crime surveys in which respondents are asked whether they have been victims of crime. Victim surveys have a huge advantage over police statistics, in that they do a much better job of picking up the "dark figure" of crimes which victims do not report or the police do not record. Victim surveys in the United States suggest that roughly two and a half times as many crimes occur there as the police record.

But as a general rule, the public mood is at least as sensitive to information about how fast crime is supposedly rising (or falling) as it is to information about absolute levels of crime. And in Britain and the United States, two countries that conduct regular victim surveys, the trends revealed in such surveys are less worrying than those derived from the much more widely publicized police figures.

Excerpted from "Measuring Crime," *The Economist*, October 15, 1994, pp. 21–22.

Deviant behavior is any act considered by public consensus or by the powerful at a given time and place to be a violation of some social rule. This suggests that deviance is relative, a matter of definition. To many, the performances and lyrics of some rappers are deviant, whereas others see these works merely as forms of self-expression. In any case, rappers are not put in prison for being rappers.

in Denmark, Germany, France, and many other countries.

Third, whether a given act is deviant depends on public consensus. Murder is unquestionably deviant because nearly all people agree that it is. In contrast, long hair on men is not deviant because hardly anybody considers it so. Public consensus, however, usually reflects the vested interests of the rich and powerful. As Marx would have said, the ideas of the ruling class tend to become the ruling ideas of society. Like the powerful, the general public tends, for example, to consider bank robbery to be a serious crime but not fraudulent advertising, which serves the interests of the powerful.

In view of those three determinants of deviant behavior, we may more precisely define **deviance** as an act considered by public consensus or by the powerful at a given time and place to be a violation of some social rule.

Question for Discussion and Review

1. What determines whether a person has violated a social norm?

EXAMPLES OF DEVIANCE

There exists a wide gamut of deviance, ranging from the relatively trivial, such as bad manners at the dinner table, to the extremely serious, such as murdering a person. Here we discuss the more serious ones.

Homicide

Homicide is mostly a "personal" crime far more likely to be committed against acquaintances, friends, or relatives than against strangers (see Figure 8.1). Common sense may suggest this is incredible. But as

FIGURE 8.1
Most Victims Know Their Killers

Relationship of homicide victim and offender
(cases of unknown relationship excluded)

Killed by an acquaintance or a friend

Killed by a family member

22%

58%

20%

Killed by a stranger

Source: Data from Kathleen Maguire and Ann L. Pastore, (eds.), *Source of Criminal Justice Statistics* - 1993 (Washington, D.C.: Government Printing Office, 1994), pp. 380 – 381.

The most personal crime, homicide, is mostly committed against relatives, friends, and acquaintances rather than strangers. It is also most often carried out with a gun. Here is a typical victim—shot after an argument at a stadium.

sociologists Donald Mulvihill and Melvin Tumin (1969) explained, "Everyone is within easy striking distance from intimates for a large part of the time. Although friends, lovers, spouses, and the like are a main source of pleasure in one's life, they are equally a main source of frustration and hurt. Few others can anger one so much." As a crime of passion, homicide is usually carried out under the overwhelming pressure of a volcanic emotion, namely, uncontrollable rage.

Homicide occurs most frequently during weekend evenings, particularly Saturday night. This holds true largely for lower-class murderers, but not for middle- and upper-class offenders, who tend more to kill on any day of the week. One apparent reason is that higher-class murders are more likely than lower-class homicides to be premeditated, hence less likely to result from alcohol-induced quarrels during weekend sprees. Research has also often shown that most U.S. murderers are poor, including semiskilled workers, unskilled laborers, and welfare recipients (Parker, 1989).

Whatever their class, murderers most often use handguns to kill. Perhaps seeing a gun while embroiled in a heated argument incites a person into murderous action. As Shakespeare wrote, "How oft the sight of means to do ill deeds, makes ill deeds done." Of course, firearms by themselves cannot cause homicide, nor can their absence reduce the motivation to kill. It is true that "Guns don't kill, people do." Still, were guns less available, less dangerous weapons such as fists or knives might have been used. Thus many heated arguments might result in aggravated assaults rather than murders, thereby reducing the number of fatalities. But given

the enormous number of guns in private hands, it is not surprising that far more deaths result from gun attacks in this country than in Canada, Britain, and other industrialized countries, where there are considerably fewer guns per person.

The easy availability of guns has contributed to a stunning upsurge in killings by teenagers. Since 1985 the homicide rate has declined among older adults, but soared 121 percent among 17-year-olds, 158 percent among 16-year-olds, and 217 percent among 15-year-olds (see Figure 8.2). Most of these killings take

FIGURE 8.2
Soaring Rates of Teen Homicide

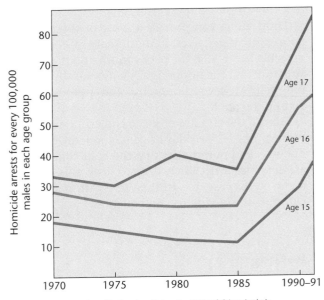

Source: Data from Northeastern University, National Crime Analysis Program, 1992.

place in poor inner city neighborhoods, where many teenagers carry guns, a new phenomenon since 1985.

Drug Abuse

In the United States drug abuse has steadily declined since the early 1980s among the middle class. But it has increased in the lower classes, particularly the socially and economically oppressed minorities. The obvious reasons include lack of education, lack of jobs, and despair from being poor or discriminated against. Less obvious is the experience of being treated as the enemy in their own society's war on drugs. Instead of being provided with drug education and treatment, poor and minority drug users are often arrested or imprisoned. In 1989, for example, African Americans constituted only 12 percent of the U.S. population, but they made up 40 percent of all arrests for various drug offenses (Currie, 1993).

But why would the poor abuse drugs in the first place? Reviewing various studies, Elliott Currie (1993) found at least four reasons. First, drugs can fulfill the need for *status*. In the larger, conventional society, the poor are denied legitimate avenues for attaining esteem and respect. Therefore in the poor neighborhood a drug culture that serves as an alternative source of respect has developed. "Being in the drug culture is just like being a movie star. So many people depend on you, want to stop you in the street. . . You are a very important person" (Currie, 1993).

Second, drugs can help the user *cope* with the harsh, oppressive realities of poverty. As Currie writes, "drugs become a way of getting away from daily problems, medicating emotional anguish, relieving stress, escaping pain."

Third, drugs can provide a sense of *structure* (purpose) to shattered lives. In the absence of steady work or stable family life, the poor cannot find the sense of structure that the nonpoor have. As a substitute, drug use helps relieve monotony and purposelessness among the poor.

Fourth, the absence of social and economic opportunities has for decades or generations made life so hopeless and purposeless that the poor communities are *saturated* with illicit drugs. Given this environment, it is easy to drift passively into drug use without considering its consequences.

Pornography

It is against the law to distribute **pornography**, sexually explicit materials in the media. The general public also opposes the distribution as well as the use of pornography. Yet pornography can be found everywhere, and most people, especially men, have used it. But is pornography harmful?

According to some conservatives, pornography is harmful to society. The studies most often cited to support this view, conducted in laboratories, suggest that exposure to pornography increases aggression. In these studies, male subjects were first made to feel irritated, angry, or ready to behave aggressively. Then they were exposed to pornographic materials. Mostly their level of aggression increased significantly (Linz and Malamuth, 1993). But the artificial laboratory setting is quite different from the real world outside. At home, pornography users may not become more aggressive because they can do something—such as masturbating or copulating—to satisfy their sexual arousal.

According to some liberals, pornography is harmless. To support this view, studies that fail to show a connection between pornography and rape are often cited. Cities with high circulation of sexually oriented magazines, for example, have largely the same rates of rape as cities with low circulation. But the pornography in such studies is mostly *nonviolent*, depicting merely nudity and consensual sex (Linz and Malamuth, 1993).

Other studies suggest that *violent* pornography is harmful, as some feminists assert. For example, research often finds that men who see slasher movies, in which a female rape victim is cut up, show less sympathy for rape victims in general. Studies on rapists suggest that men who lack rape sympathy are more likely to assault women (Linz and Malamuth, 1993). We may therefore conclude that nonviolent pornography is harmless but violent pornography is harmful.

Corporate Crime

Corporate crimes are committed by company officials without the overt use of force, and their effect on the victims is not readily traceable to the offender. If a miner died from a lung disease, it is difficult to prove beyond reasonable doubt that he died *because* the employer violated mine safety regulations. Corporate crimes may be perpetrated not only against employees but also against customers and the general public. Examples include disregard for safety in the workplace, consumer fraud, price-fixing, production of unsafe products, and violations of environmental regulations. Compared with traditional "street crime," corporate crime is more rationally executed, more profitable, and less detectable by law enforcers. In addition, crime in the executive suite is distinguished from crime in the street by three characteristics that help explain the prevalence of corporate crime.

The Criminal's Noncriminal Self-Image   Corporate criminals often see themselves as respectable people rather than common criminals. They maintain their noncriminal self-image through *rationalization.* Violators of price-fixing laws, for example, may insist that they are helping the nation's economy by "stabilizing prices" and serving their companies by "recovering costs." There is no such crime as price-fixing in their book.

The noncriminal self-image is also maintained through *seeing oneself as a victim rather than an offender.* Corporate criminals would argue that they are just unlucky enough to get caught for doing something that practically everyone else does. As a convicted tax offender said, "Everybody cheats on their income tax, 95 percent of the people. Even if it's for $10 it's the same principle. I didn't cheat. I just didn't know to report it" (Benson, 1985).

The noncriminal self-image is further maintained through *denial of criminal intent.* Corporate criminals may admit that they committed the act that landed them in prison, but regard their acts only as mistakes, not something motivated by a guilty, criminal mind. As a convicted tax offender said, "I'm not a criminal. That is, I'm not a criminal from the standpoint of taking a gun and doing this and that. I'm a criminal from the standpoint of making a mistake, a serious mistake" (Benson, 1985).

The Victim's Unwitting Cooperation   Primarily due to lack of caution or knowledge, many victims unwittingly cooperate with the corporate criminal. In a home improvement scheme, victims do not bother to check the work history of the fraudulent company that solicits them, and sign a contract without examining its contents for such matters as the true price and the credit terms. Some victims purchase goods through the mail without checking the reputation of the firm. Doctors prescribe untested dangerous drugs, relying only on the pharmaceutical company's salespeople and advertising. It may be difficult for victims to know they are victimized, even if they want to find out the true nature of their victimization. Average grocery shoppers, for example, are hard put to detect such unlawful substances as residues of hormones, antibiotics, pesticides, and nitrites in the meat they buy.

Society's Relative Indifference   Generally, little effort is made to catch corporate criminals, and, on the rare occasions when they are caught, they seldom go to jail. Their pleas for mercy are heard after they promise to repay their victims and to cooperate in prosecutions against others. They insist that a long prison term will do no good because their lives are

Deliberately violating environmental, health, or safety regulations can cost society money, cause injuries, and claim lives. Illegally dumping wastes, as shown here, can pollute air and water supply, causing health problems, even death. Compared with "street crime," however, such corporate crimes as these may be difficult to detect, are easily rationalized by the corporate criminals, and seldom elicit much concern from society.

already in ruins. Thus, in the more than a dozen convictions for Wall Street insider trading in the late 1980s, most defendants were merely put on probation or sentenced to prison for less than six months. From 1987 through 1992, federal agents charged a staggering 95,045 white-collar and corporate executives with various bank and S&L frauds, but more than 75 percent of these charges were dropped from prosecution (Pizzo and Muolo, 1993). Even when convicted of crimes that caused the deaths of many workers or customers, corporate offenders have never been sentenced to death, let alone actually executed, though numerous lower-class criminals have been executed for killing only one person.

Mental Disorder

Mental disorder is far more common than popularly believed. According to the latest surveys, about 19 percent of U.S. adults suffer from a mental disorder serious enough to require psychiatric help or hospitalization, and the figure for adolescents is ten percent (Myers et al., 1984; Robins et al., 1984; Lewinsolhn et al., 1993). The most common disorder is phobia (such as fear of heights or enclosed spaces), followed by depression and alcoholism (Regier et al., 1993). In fact, all of us have been or will be mentally ill in one way or another. Of course, most of our mental disorders are not serious at all. We occasionally come down with only a brief anxiety or depression, "the common cold of mental ailments." But the types of mental disorder that sociologists—and psychiatrists—study are rather serious. They include **psychosis**, typified by loss of touch with reality, and **neurosis**, characterized by a persistent fear, anxiety, or worry about trivial matters. A psychotic can be likened to a person who thinks incorrectly that 2 plus 2 is equal to 10 but strongly believes it to be correct. On the other hand, a neurotic can be compared to a person who thinks correctly that 2 plus 2 is equal to 4 but constantly worries that it may not be so (Thio, 1995).

Sociologists have long suspected that certain social forces are involved in the development of mental disorder. The one that has been most consistently demonstrated by many different studies to be a key factor in mental illness is social class: the lower the social class, the higher the rate of mental disorder.

This finding, however, has prompted two conflicting explanations. One, known as *social causation,* suggests that lower-class people are more prone to mental disorder because they are more likely to have the following experiences: being subjected to social stress, such as unemployment, family problems, or threat of criminal victimization; suffering from psychic frailty, infectious diseases, and neurological impairments; and lacking quality medical treatment, coping ability, and social support. The other explanation, called *drift,* suggests that the heavy concentration of mental disorder in the lower-class neighborhood results from the downward drift of mentally ill people into the neighborhood coupled with the upward movement of mentally healthy people out of it. This means that being a member of the lower class is a consequence rather than a cause of mental illness. Both explanations have been found to have some basis in fact. In general, the evidence for the drift theory comes from studies of major mental illnesses, especially schizophrenia. The early onset of such illnesses can cause job loss and downward mobility (Jones et al., 1993; Rodgers and Mann, 1993; Fox, 1993). But the evidence for social causation comes from studies of less severe disorders such as depression and phobia. These problems are more likely to result from the social stresses of lower-class lives (Kessler, Price, and Wortman, 1985; Link, Lennon, and Dohrenwend, 1993).

Questions for Discussion and Review

1. What does it mean to call homicide a personal crime?
2. Why do the poor abuse drugs?
3. Is pornography harmful? Why and why not?
4. What distinguishes corporate crime from street crime?
5. How common is mental disorder in the United States, and what does social class have to do with the disorder?

FUNCTIONALIST PERSPECTIVE

Most scholars other than sociologists generally attribute deviance to certain biological or psychological abnormality in the individual. But sociologists have long assumed that there is nothing physically or mentally wrong with most deviants. This assumption is a legacy of French sociologist Emile Durkheim (1858–1917), one of the founders of functionalism in

One positive function of deviant behavior is to bring about social change. The refusal of Rosa Parks (at left) to move to the back of the bus in Montgomery led to a citywide bus boycott in 1955 led by Martin Luther King Jr.

the discipline. For him, deviance is not only normal but also beneficial to society.

Durkheim: Functionalist Theory

According to Durkheim, deviance can serve a number of functions for society.

First, deviance helps *enhance conformity* in society as a whole. Norms are basically abstract and ambiguous, subject to conflicting interpretations. Even criminal laws, which are far more clear-cut than other norms, can be confusing. The criminal act a deviant commits and is punished for provides other citizens with a concrete example of what constitutes a crime. From deviants we can learn the difference between conformity and deviance, seeing the boundary between right and wrong more clearly. Once aware of this boundary, we are more likely to stay on the side of righteousness.

Second, deviance *strengthens solidarity* among law-abiding members of society. Differing values and interests may divide them, but collective outrage against deviants as a common enemy can unite them. Because deviance promotes social cohesion that decreases crime, Durkheim (1966) described it as "a factor in public health, an integral part of all healthy societies."

Third, deviance *provides a safety valve* for discontented people. Through relatively minor forms of deviance, they can strike out against the social order without doing serious harm to themselves or others. As Albert Cohen (1966) suggested, prostitution may serve as a safety valve for marriage in a male-dominated society, because the customer is unlikely to form an emotional attachment to the prostitute. In contrast, a sexual relationship with a friend is more likely to develop into a love affair that could destroy the marriage.

Fourth, deviance can *induce social change*. Martin Luther King, Jr., and other civil rights leaders were jeered and imprisoned for their opposition to segregation, but they moved the United States toward greater racial equality.

There is a limit, however, to the validity of Durkheim's functionalist theory. If deviance is widespread, it can threaten social order in at least two ways. First, it can destroy interpersonal relations. Alcoholism can tear many families apart. If a friend flies into a rage and tries to kill us, it will be difficult to maintain a harmonious relationship. Second, deviance can undermine trust. If there were many killers, robbers, and rapists living in our neighborhood, we would find it impossible to welcome neighbors into our home as guests or babysitters. Nevertheless, Durkheim's theory is useful for demolishing the commonsense belief that deviance is always harmful. Deviance can bring benefits if it occurs within limits.

Merton: Strain Theory

In the 1930s U.S. sociologist Robert Merton agreed with Durkheim that deviance is "an integral part of all healthy societies." However, rather than seeing deviance as a *cause* of social solidarity, as Durkheim did, Merton regarded deviance as a normal *consequence* of a culture's contribution to a prosperous social order.

According to Merton, U.S. culture places too much emphasis on success as a valued goal. From kindergarten to college, teachers prod students to achieve "the American Dream." Parents and coaches even pressure Little League players not just to play well but to win. The media often glorify winning not only in sports but in business, politics, and other arenas of life. All this motivates hard work, thereby contributing to society's prosperity. But at the same time not all people are provided with equal opportunities (such as good jobs) for success. There is, then, an inconsistency between too much emphasis on the success *goal* and too little emphasis on the availability of legitimate *means* for achieving that goal. Such inconsistency produces a strain among people in the lower classes, pressuring them to achieve success through what Merton calls *innovation*—using illegitimate means of achieving success, such as committing robbery or selling drugs.

But most people do not resort to innovation as a response to the goal-means inconsistency. In addition to innovation, four other responses are possible, depending on whether the cultural goal of success and institutionalized means are accepted or rejected (see Table 8.2).

1. *Conformity,* the most popular form of response, involves accepting both the cultural goal of success and the use of legitimate means for achieving that goal.

2. *Innovation,* the response described earlier, involves accepting the goal of success, but rejecting the use of socially accepted means to achieve it, turning instead to unconventional, illegitimate methods.

3. *Ritualism* occurs when people no longer set high success goals but continue to toil as conscientious, diligent workers.

4. *Retreatism* is withdrawal from society, caring neither about success nor about working. Retreatists include vagabonds, outcasts, and drug addicts.

5. *Rebellion* occurs when people reject and attempt to change both the goals and the means approved by society. The rebel tries to overthrow the existing system and establish a new system with different goals and means. An example would be attempting to replace the current U.S. competitive pursuit of fame and riches with a new system that enhances social relations through cooperation.

TABLE 8.2
Merton's Typology of Responses to Goal-Means Inconsistency
In U.S. society, according to Merton, there is too much emphasis on success but too little emphasis on the legitimate means for achieving success. Such inconsistency may cause deviant behavior, yet various people respond to it differently.

Response	Success goal	Legitimate means
1. Conformity	+	+
2. Innovation	+	−
3. Ritualism	−	+
4. Retreatism	−	−
5. Rebellion	− +	− +

NOTE: + signifies accepting; − rejecting; and − + rejecting the old and introducing the new.

SOURCE: By permission of The Free Press, a Division of Macmillan, Inc., from *Social Theory and Structure* by Robert K. Merton. Copyright 1957 by The Free Press; copyright renewed 1985 by Robert K. Merton.

Merton's theory is useful for explaining the higher rates of robbery, theft, and other property crimes among lower-class people. But the theory fails to explain embezzlement, tax fraud, and other white-collar crimes. As a functionalist, Merton assumes that the same value—belief in *material* success—is shared throughout our society. But this runs counter to the pluralistic and conflicting nature of U.S. society, where many groups differentiated by class, gender, ethnicity, or religion do not share the same values. Some groups are more interested in pursuing strong relationships than "big bucks."

Hirschi: Control Theory

A functionalist like Merton, U.S. sociologist Travis Hirschi (1969) assumed that the family, school, and other social institutions can greatly contribute to social order by controlling deviant tendencies in all of us. If such control is lacking or weak, in Hirschi's view, people will commit deviant acts.

According to Hirschi, the best control mechanism against deviance is our bond to others or, by extension, society. There are four types of bond.

The first bond is *attachment* to conventional people and institutions. Teenagers, for example, may show this attachment by loving and respecting their parents, making friends with conventional peers, liking school, or working hard to develop intellectual skills.

The second is *commitment* to conformity. This commitment can be seen in the time and energy devoted to conventional activities—getting an education, holding a job, developing an occupational skill, improving professional status, building a business, or acquiring a reputation for virtue.

The third is *involvement* in conventional activities. Following the maxim that "idleness is the devil's workshop," people keep themselves so busy doing conventional things that they do not have time to take part in deviant activities or even to think about deviance.

The fourth is *belief* in the moral validity of social rules. This is the conviction that the rules of conventional society should be obeyed. People may show this moral belief by respecting the law.

Many studies have supported Hirschi's theory that the lack of social bond *causes* deviance, but most of these studies have ignored, as does the theory, the fact that the lack of bond can also be the *effect* of delinquency. Just as the loss of bond can cause the youth to commit delinquency, delinquency can cause the youth to lose their bond to society.

Braithwaite: Shaming Theory

While Hirschi sees how society controls us through bonding, Australian sociologist John Braithwaite (1989) looks at how society controls us through shaming. Shaming involves an expression of disapproval designed to invoke remorse in the wrongdoer. There are two types of shaming: disintegrative and reintegrative. In **disintegrative shaming**, the wrongdoer is punished in such a way as to be stigmatized, rejected, or ostracized, in effect, banished from conventional society. It is the same as stigmatization. **Reintegrative shaming** is more positive; it involves making wrongdoers feel guilty while showing them understanding, forgiveness, or even respect. It is the kind of shaming that affectionate parents administer to their misbehaving child. It involves "hating the sin but loving the sinner." Thus reintegrative

shaming serves to reintegrate—welcome back—the wrongdoer into conventional society.

Reintegrative shaming is more common in communitarian societies (marked by strong social relationships or interdependence) such as Japan. Disintegrative shaming is more prevalent in less communitarian societies (characterized by weaker social relationships) such as the United States. While reintegrative shaming usually discourages further deviance, disintegrative shaming encourages more deviance. This is why crime rates are higher in the United States than in Japan. Braithwaite concludes by arguing that the United States can significantly reduce its crime rates if it emphasizes reintegrative shaming rather than stigmatization in dealing with criminals as Japanese society does.

Braithwaite may be correct that reintegrative shaming can reduce crime, especially if it is applied to first-time offenders who have committed relatively minor crimes. But it can hardly have the same positive impact on hardened criminals with little sense of shame for their crimes.

Questions for Discussion and Review

1. According to Durkheim, in what ways can deviance benefit society?
2. How did Merton explain the high crime rate in the United States?
3. How does Hirschi's control theory explain deviance?
4. In Braithwaite's view, how is shaming related to society and deviance?

CONFLICT PERSPECTIVE

Functionalists assume the importance of social consensus for explaining deviance. Thus, for Durkheim, deviance is functional to society as a whole and hence to virtually all groups in it. To Merton, nearly all people worship money as their god. To Hirschi, bond to society is always a desirable goal for everybody if they want to avoid deviance. And to Braithwaite, shaming is a widely shared value in communitarian societies. By contrast, conflict theorists assume the importance of social conflict—as in the form of inequalities or power differentials—for explaining deviance.

According to conflict theory, firms unable to compete with giant corporations, are likely to shore up their sagging profits by illegal means, such as hiring illegal immigrants from Mexico at wages below the legal minimum.

Conflict Theory

Many people assume that the law is based on the consent of citizens, that it treats citizens equally, and that it serves the best interest of society. If we simply read the U.S. Constitution and statutes, this assumption may indeed be justified. But focusing on the *law on the books,* as William Chambliss (1969) pointed out, may be misleading. The law in the books does indeed say that the authorities ought to be fair and just. But are they? To understand crime, Chambliss

FIGURE 8.3
Quinney's Conflict Theory

Four factors influence one another, helping to produce and maintain a high level of crime in society.

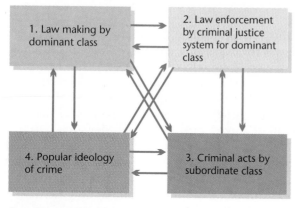

Source: Data from Richard Quinney, *The Social Reality of Crime* (Boston: Little, Brown, 1970).

argued, we need to look at the *law in action,* at how legal authorities actually discharge their duty. After studying the law in action, Chambliss concluded that legal authorities are actually unfair and unjust, favoring the rich and powerful over the poor and weak.

Richard Quinney (1974) blamed the unjust law directly on the capitalist system. "Criminal law," said Quinney, "is used by the state and the ruling class to secure the survival of the capitalist system." This involves the dominant class doing four things: First, it defines as criminal those behaviors (robbery, murder, and the like) that threaten its interests. Second, it hires law enforcers to apply those definitions and protect its interests. Third, it exploits the subordinate class by paying low wages so that the resulting oppressive life conditions force the powerless to commit what those in power have defined as crimes. Fourth, it uses these criminal actions to spread and reinforce the popular view that the subordinate class is dangerous, in order to justify its concerns with making and enforcing the law (see Figure 8.3). The upshot is the production and maintenance of a high level of crime in society (Quinney, 1975).

To Marxists, the capitalists' ceaseless drive to increase profit by cutting labor costs has created a large class of unemployed workers. These people become what Marxists call **marginal surplus population**—superfluous or useless to the economy. They are compelled to commit property crimes to survive. The exploitative nature of capitalism also causes violent crimes (such as murder and assault) and noncriminal deviances (such as alcoholism and mental illness). As Sheila Balkan and her colleagues (1980) explained, economic "marginality leads to a lack of self-esteem and a sense of powerlessness and alienation, which create intense pressures on individuals. Many people turn to violence in order to vent their frustrations and strike out against symbols of authority, and others turn this frustration inward and experience severe emotional difficulties."

Marxists further contend that the monopolistic and oligopolistic nature of capitalism encourages corporate crime, because "when only a few firms dominate a sector of the economy they can more easily collude to fix prices, divide up the market, and eliminate competitors" (Greenberg, 1981). Smaller firms, unable to compete with giant corporations and earn enough profits, are also motivated to shore up their sagging profits by illegal means.

Conflict theory is useful for explaining why most laws favor the rich and powerful and why the poor and powerless commit most of the unprofitable crimes in society (such as murder, assault, and robbery). The theory is also useful for explaining why crime rates began to soar after the formerly communist countries in Russia and Eastern Europe embraced capitalism. But the theory has been criticized for implying that all laws are unjust and capitalism is the source of all crimes.

Power Theory

It seems obvious that power inequality affects the quality of people's lives. The rich and powerful live better than the poor and powerless. Similarly, power inequality affects the quality of *deviant* activities likely to be engaged in by people. Thus the powerful are more likely to perpetrate profitable crimes, such as corporate crime, while the powerless are more likely to commit unprofitable crimes, such as homicide and assault. In other words, power—or lack of it—largely determines the *type* of crime people are likely to commit.

Power can also be an important *cause* of deviance. More precisely, the likelihood of powerful people perpetrating profitable crimes is greater than the likelihood of powerless persons committing unprofitable crimes. It is, for example, more likely for bank executives to peacefully rob customers than for jobless persons to violently rob banks. Analysis of the deviance literature suggests three reasons why deviance is more common among the powerful (Thio, 1995).

First, the powerful have a *stronger deviant motivation*. Much of this motivation stems from **relative deprivation**—feeling unable to achieve a relatively high aspiration. Compared with the powerless, whose aspirations are typically low, the powerful are more likely to raise their aspirations so high that they cannot be realized. The more people experience relative deprivation, the more likely they are to commit deviant acts.

Second, the powerful enjoy *greater deviant opportunity*. Obviously, a rich banker enjoys more legitimate opportunities than a poor worker to make money. But suppose they both want to acquire *illegitimately* a large sum of money. The banker is bound to have access to more and better opportunities that make it easy to defraud customers. The banker also has a good chance of getting away with it because the kind of skills needed to pull off the crime comes from the kinds required for holding the bank position in the first place. In contrast, the poor worker would find his or her illegitimate opportunity limited to crudely robbing the banker, an illegitimate opportunity further limited by a high risk of arrest.

Third, the powerful are subjected to *weaker social control*. Generally, the powerful have more influence in the making and enforcement of laws. The laws against higher-status criminals are therefore relatively lenient and seldom enforced, but the laws against lower-status criminals harsher and more often enforced. Not a single corporate criminal, for example, has ever been sentenced to death for marketing some untested drug that "cleanly" kills many people. Given the lesser control imposed on them, the powerful are likely to feel freer to use some deviant means to amass their fortunes and power.

There is some evidence to support this theory, presented in greater detail elsewhere (Thio, 1995). In the United States, for example, there are about six industrial deaths caused by corporate violation of safety regulations for every one homicide committed by a poor person. In Great Britain, the ratio of industrial deaths to homicides is seven to one (Box, 1983). It is difficult, however, to get more data on powerful deviants. Compared with their powerless counterparts, powerful deviants are more able to resist divulging their deviant activities and to carry out such activities in sophisticated and consequently undetectable fashion.

Feminist Theory

Many theories about deviance are meant to apply to both sexes, but feminists argue that those theories are actually about men only. Consequently, the theories may be valid for male behavior but not necessarily for female.

Consider Merton's strain theory. First, this theory assumes that people are inclined to strive for material success. This may be true for men but not necessarily for women. In a patriarchal society, women have been socialized differently from men. Thus women are traditionally less interested in achieving material success, which often requires one-upmanship, and more given to attaining emotional fulfillment through close, personal relations with others. Second, strain theory assumes that women who have a strong desire for economic success but little access to opportunities would be as likely as men in similar circumstances to commit a crime. Nowadays, given the greater availability of high positions for women in the economic world, the number of ambitious women in the "men's" world is on the rise. But, faced with the lack of opportunities for greater economic success, these women are not as likely as men to engage in deviant activities. And finally, strain theory explicitly states that people in the United States are likely to commit a crime because their society overemphasizes the importance of holding high success goals while failing to provide the necessary opportunities for all of its citizens to realize those goals. But this may be more relevant to men than to women. Despite their greater lack of success opportunities, women still have lower crime rates than men (Beirne and Messerschmidt, 1995).

The lack of relevancy to women in strain and other conventional theories stems from a male-biased failure to take women into account. In redressing this problem, feminist theory focuses on women. First, the theory deals with women as *victims*, mostly of rape and sexual harassment. The crimes against women are said to reflect the patriarchal society's attempt to put women in their place so as to perpetuate men's dominance.

Feminist theory also zeroes in on women as *offenders*. It argues that the recent increase in female crime has not been great enough to be significant. This is considered to reflect the fact that gender equality is still far from being a social reality. Like employment opportunities, criminal opportunities are still much less available to women than men, hence women are still much less likely to engage in criminal activities. When women do commit a crime, it tends to be the types of crime that reflect their continuing subordinate position in society, namely minor property crimes, such as shoplifting, passing bad checks, welfare fraud, and petty credit-card fraud. In fact, recent increases in female crime primarily involve these minor crimes, largely reflecting the increasing feminization of poverty—more women living below the poverty line. Not surprisingly, most women criminals are unemployed, without a high

school diploma, and single mothers with small children. They hardly fit the popular image of the newly empowered, liberated women, who benefit from any increase in gender equality. There is no increase in female involvement in more profitable crimes, such as burglary, robbery, embezzlement, and business fraud (Day and Chesney-Lind, 1988; Weisheit, 1992; Miller, 1995).

Feminist theory is useful for understanding female deviance. But its focus on female deviance cannot be generalized to male deviance.

Questions for Discussion and Review

1. How does conflict theory explain the nature of laws and the cause of deviance?
2. How does power theory explain why deviance is more prevalent among the powerful?
3. How does feminist theory differ from other theories?

SYMBOLIC INTERACTIONIST PERSPECTIVE

Both the functionalist and conflict perspectives portray deviance as a *product* of society. In contrast, symbolic interactionists see deviance as a *process* of interaction between the supposed deviant and the rest of society. And that process of interaction involves subjective interpretations that shape the world of deviance.

Differential Association Theory

According to Edwin Sutherland (1939), deviance is learned through interactions with other people. Individuals learn not only how to perform deviant acts but also how to define these actions. Various social groups have different norms, and acts considered deviant by the dominant culture may be viewed positively by some groups. Each person is likely to be exposed to both positive and negative definitions of these actions. An individual is likely to become deviant if the individual engages in **differential association**, the process of acquiring through interaction with others "an *excess* of definitions favorable to violation of law over definitions unfavorable to violation of law" (Sutherland, 1939).

ENRICHING OUR LIVES

Gang violence has become one of the most worrisome forms of deviant behavior in the United States today, and sociologists and others are involved in efforts to understand and solve this social problem. Luis Rodriquez is a former gang member who works with youth gangs in Chicago and who has written about the problem of gang violence. In this reading, he analyzes the gang problem and shows some ways to turn youth gangs around.

Turning Youth Gangs Around

Pedro is a thoughtful, articulate and charismatic young man; he listens, absorbs and responds. His movements are quick, well-developed during his years surviving in the streets of Chicago. Pedro is a 20-year-old gang leader. For most of his life, he has lived off and on between his welfare mother and an uncle. He has been kicked out of schools and has served time in youth detention facilities. He is also a great human being.

I've long recognized that most youths like Pedro aren't in gangs to be criminals, killers, or prison inmates. For many, a gang embraces who they are, gives them the initiatory community they seek and the incipient authority they need to eventually control their own lives. These are things other institutions, including schools and families, often fail to provide. Yet without proper guidance, support and means to contribute positively to society, gang involvement can be disastrous.

A media storm was created recently when 11-year-old Robert Sandifer of Chicago, known as "Yummy" because he liked to eat cookies, allegedly shot into a crowd and killed a 14-year-old girl. A suspected member of a Southside gang, Yummy disappeared; days later he was found shot in the head. Two teenage members of Yummy's gang are being held in his death. This is a tragedy, but without a clear understanding of the social, economic and psychological dynamics that would drive an 11-year-old to kill, we can only throw up our hands. Yet it isn't hard to figure out the motive forces behind much of this violence.

Sandifer was a child of the Reagan years, of substantial cuts in community programs, of the worst job loss since the Great Depression, of more police and prisons and of fewer options for recreation, education or work. Here was a boy who had been physically abused, shuttled from one foster home to another, one juvenile facility after another. At every stage of Robert's young life since birth, he was blocked from becoming all he could be. But there was nothing to stop him from getting a gun. From using it. And from dying from one.

It's time the voices for viable and lasting solutions be heard. The public debate is now limited to those who demonize youth, want to put them away, and use repression to curb their natural instincts to re-create the world.

I have other proposals. First, that we realign societal resources in accordance with the following premises: that every child has value and every child can succeed. That school teach by engaging the intelligence and creativity of all students. That institutions of public maintenance—whether police or social services—respect the basic humanity of all people. That we rapidly and thoroughly integrate young people into the future, into the new technology. And finally, that we root out the basis for the injustice and inequities that engender most of the violence we see today.

Excerpted from Luis J. Rodriquez, "Turning Youth Gangs Around," *The Nation,* November 21, 1994, pp. 605–609. Reprinted with permission from *The Nation* magazine. © The Nation Company, L.P.

Suppose a father tells his children that "it's all right to steal when you are poor," he is giving them a pro-deviant definition. On the other hand, if the father tells his children that "it's wrong to steal," it is an anti-deviant definition. If the youngsters pick up a greater number of pro-deviant definitions, they are likely to become deviant.

While definitions play a crucial role in becoming deviant, Sutherland emphasized more the importance of social interaction because it is the source of definitions. Thus Sutherland also stressed that deviance would arise if interactions with those who define deviant behavior positively outweigh interactions with those who define it negatively. Which definitions are most influential depends not just on the frequency and duration of the interactions but also on the strength of the relationship between the interactants.

Sutherland developed his theory to explain various forms of deviance, including white-collar crimes such as tax evasion, embezzlement, and price-fixing. All these misdeeds were shown to result from some association with groups that viewed the wrongdoings as acceptable. Still it is difficult to determine precisely what differential association is. Most people cannot identify the persons from whom they have learned a pro-deviant or anti-deviant definition, much less whether they have been exposed to one definition more frequently, longer, or more intensely than the other.

Labeling Theory

Most theories focus on the *causes* of deviance. In contrast, labeling theory, which emerged in the 1960s, concentrates on *societal reaction* to rule violation and the impact of this reaction on the rule violator.

According to labeling theorists, society tends to react to a rule-breaking act by labeling it deviant. Deviance, then, is not something that a person does

According to labeling theory, tagging a person as deviant can make the person deviant. A social drinker who gets labeled as "a man who can hold his liquor" can become an alcoholic because people begin to pressure him to live up to that image.

but merely a label imposed on that behavior. As Howard Becker (1963) said, "Deviance is *not* a quality of the act the person commits, but rather a consequence of the application by others of rules and sanctions to an 'offender.' The deviant is one to whom that label has successfully been applied; deviant behavior is behavior that people so label." The label itself has serious and negative consequences for the individual—even beyond any immediate punishment.

Once a person is labeled a thief or a delinquent or a drunk, the individual may be stuck with that label for life and be rejected and isolated as a result. Finding a job and making friends may be extremely difficult. More important, the person may come to accept the label and commit more deviant acts. Labeling people as deviants, in short, can push them toward further and greater deviance.

Much earlier, Frank Tannenbaum (1938) had noted this process of becoming deviant. According to him, children may break windows, annoy people, steal apples, and play hooky—and innocently consider these activities just a way of having fun. Edwin Lemert (1951) coined the term **primary deviance** to refer to these violations of norms that a person commits for the first time and without considering them deviant. Now suppose parents, teachers, and police consider a child's pranks to be a sign of delinquency. They may "dramatize the evil" by admonishing or scolding the child. They may even go further, hauling the child into juvenile court and labeling the child as bad, a delinquent—a deviant. The child may develop a bad self-image and try to live up to this self-image by becoming increasingly involved in deviant behavior. Lemert used the term **secondary deviance** to refer to such repeated norm violations, which the violators themselves recognize as deviant. Secondary deviants are, in effect, confirmed or career deviants.

Labeling theory helps us understand how secondary deviance might develop, and it sensitizes us to the power of labels, but the theory has been criticized for at least two reasons. First, it cannot explain why primary deviance occurs in the first place. Second, it cannot deal with deviance that occurs in secret; unknown to others, it cannot be labeled deviance. Without the label, logically the theory cannot define it as deviance.

Phenomenological Theory

Phenomenologists delve into people's subjectivity (called *phenomenon*) including their consciousness, perception, feelings, and opinions about deviance. To really understand deviance, phenomenologists say, we must study people's subjective interpretations of their own deviant experiences.

Generally, phenomenological studies have revealed that deviants tend to see themselves and their deviance in some positive way and then behave accordingly. This is what Harold Garfinkel (1967) found in his classic study of Agnes, a hermaphrodite, who has both male and female sex organs. Agnes was 19, and had been born as a male and raised as a boy until high school. At 17 she had developed an attractive female figure. By then she dropped out of school, left home, moved to another city, and tried to begin a new life as a woman. A year later, she went to the UCLA medical center to request a sex-change operation. Before any surgery could be approved, Agnes had to be thoroughly investigated to ensure that she

really felt like a woman. As a participant in this investigation, Garfinkel interviewed her extensively.

Garfinkel found that she saw herself as a normal woman and did her best to convince others that she was. She told Garfinkel that she was merely a normal woman who happened to have a physical defect comparable to any other deformity such as a harelip or clubfoot. Like any other normal person with a deformity, she felt that it was only natural for her to want to have hers—the male organ—removed. Her self-concept as a normal woman further led her to claim that, as a sexual organ, her penis was "dead," that she had no sexual pleasure from it nor felt any sexual attraction to women. She wanted it to be replaced by a surgically constructed vagina. Her self-concept as a normal woman also caused her to make sure that others would not suspect her of having the

TABLE 8.3
Perspectives and Theories of Deviance

Functionalist Perspective

- *Durkheim's functionalist theory:* Deviance benefits society by enhancing conformity, strengthening social solidarity, safely releasing discontent, and inducing social change.

- *Merton's strain theory:* U.S. crime rate is high because the society emphasizes the importance of success without providing equal opportunities for achieving it.

- *Hirschi's control theory:* The absence of social bonds causes deviance.

- *Braithwaite's shaming theory:* Disintegrative shaming causes deviance.

Conflict Perspective

- *Conflict theory:* For Chambliss, law enforcement favors the rich and powerful over the poor and weak. For Quinney, the dominant class produces crime by making laws, enforcing laws, oppressing subordinate class, and spreading crime ideology. For Marxists, deviance and crime stem from the exploitative nature of capitalism.

- *Power theory:* Because of stronger deviant motivation, greater deviant opportunity, and weaker social control, the powerful are more likely to engage in profitable deviance than the powerless in unprofitable deviance.

- *Feminist theory:* Critical of conventional theories for being largely inapplicable to women, while suggesting that the status of women as victims and offenders reflects the continuing subordination of women in patriarchal society.

Symbolic Interactionist Perspective

- *Differential association theory:* Deviance arises if pro-deviant definitions outweigh anti-deviant definitions acquired in social interactions.

- *Labeling theory:* Being labeled deviant by society leads people to see themselves as deviant and live up to this self-image by committing more deviance.

- *Phenomenological theory:* Looking into people's subjective interpretation of their own experiences is key to understanding their deviant behavior.

male organ, so she always wore a bathing suit with a skirt and she never undressed in her female roommate's presence.

In his more recent analysis of murderers, robbers, and other criminals, Jack Katz (1988) also found a similarly positive self-perception that conflicts with society's negative view of the deviant. Murderers, for example, tend to see themselves as morally superior to their victims. In most cases of homicide, after the victims have humiliated the killers, the killers have felt outraged and considered the killing a justifiable way of defending their identity, dignity, or respectability.

Phenomenological theory is useful for understanding the subjective world of deviants. But it is doubtful that all, or even most, deviants have a positive view of themselves and their deviance. Some are bound to develop negative self-image from having been condemned or ridiculed by society, as suggested by labeling theory.

Questions for Discussion and Review

1. How does differential association lead to deviance?
2. What occurs when some people move from primary to secondary deviance?
3. What does phenomenological theory tell us about deviants?

CONTROLLING DEVIANCE

After discussing various perspectives and theories about deviance (summarized in Table 8.3, p 185), we need to deal with the more practical issues that concern many people today, namely, how to control deviance. As discussed in the preceding chapter, society transmits its values to individuals through socialization. If families, schools, and other socializing agents do their jobs well, then individuals internalize the values of their society, accepting society's norms as their own. They tend to become conformists and law-abiding citizens.

Internalization through socialization is the most efficient way of controlling deviance. It produces unconscious, spontaneous self-control. As a result, most people find it natural to conform to most social norms most of the time. Violating the norms makes them feel guilty, ashamed, or at least uncomfortable. They act as their own police officers.

Nevertheless, for reasons suggested by various theories that we have discussed, a few people commit serious crimes, and everyone deviates occasionally, at least from some trivial norms. Thus, control by others is also needed to limit deviance and maintain social order.

Social Control

Social control is the process by which individuals are pressured by society to conform to social norms. It may be either informal or formal. Teachers, peer

Society controls individuals informally and formally. Informal control is enforced through gossip, criticism, or ridicule by parents, teachers, or, as shown here, peer groups. But formal control comes from police, judges, and similar government agencies.

groups, and even strangers enforce *informal* controls through frowning, gossip, criticism, or ridicule. When deviant acts are serious, *formal* controls are usually imposed by police, judges, prison guards, and other law-enforcement agents.

In small, nonindustrialized societies, informal control is the primary or only means of handling deviance. It may involve such mild expressions of disapproval as a frown, scowl, or scolding, as in modern industrialized societies. But it may also call for more serious punishment, such as beating, maiming, or killing. Such informal control is administered on a private basis, usually by the aggrieved party. The Mayan Indians of South Mexico believe that you should kill a person who has wronged you. The Ifugao of the Philippines consider it necessary for any "self-respecting man" to do away with an adulterer caught red-handed. Violence in these societies is nonetheless quite rare—so are adultery and other deviances—apparently a testament to the effectiveness of informal control. The deterrent effect of informal control in traditional societies is at least greater than that of formal control in modern societies. As Donald Black (1983) pointed out, in the 1950s the rape incidence among the Gusii of Kenya shot up after the British colonial government prohibited traditional violence against the rapist and started to use British law to deal with the criminal.

But in large, industrialized societies, there is an extensive system of formal control. Perhaps formal control has become more important in modern nations because they have become more heterogeneous and more impersonal than traditional societies. This societal change may have increased social conflicts and enhanced the need for formal control, popularly called the "criminal justice system."

Criminal Justice

The criminal justice system is a network of police, courts, and prisons. These law enforcers are supposed to protect society, but they are also a potential threat to an individual's freedom. If they wanted to ensure that not a single criminal could slip away, the police would have to deprive innocent citizens of their rights and liberties. They would restrict our freedom of movement and invade our privacy—by tapping phones, reading mail, searching homes, stopping pedestrians for questioning, and blockading roads. No matter how law-abiding we might be, we would always be treated like crime suspects—and some of us would almost certainly fall into the dragnet.

To prevent such abuses, the U.S. criminal justice system is restrained by the Constitution and laws. We

"And if you want to talk to your attorney, you'll find him in the next cell."

have the right to be presumed innocent until proven guilty, the right not to incriminate ourselves, and many other legal protections. The ability of the police to search homes and question suspects is limited. Thus, our freedom, especially from being wrongly convicted and imprisoned, is protected.

In short, the criminal justice system faces a dilemma: If it does not catch enough criminals, the streets will not be safe; if it tries to apprehend too many, people's freedom will be in danger. Striking a balance between effective protection from criminals and respect for individual freedom is far from easy. This may be why the criminal justice system is criticized from right and left, by one group for coddling criminals and by the other for being too harsh.

Both criticisms have some merit. Most criminals in the United States are never punished. Of the 35 million crimes committed every year, less than half—about 15 million more serious crimes—are reported to the police. Out of these serious crimes, only 20 percent (3 million) result in arrest and prosecution. Of these three million prosecuted, two million are convicted, out of which 25 percent (500,000) are sent to prison. Ultimately, then, *less than 2 percent* of the original 35 million offenders are put behind bars (Anderson, 1994). Moreover, most of these prisoners do not serve their full terms because they are released on parole. The average prisoner serves only about one-third of the sentence (Census Bureau, 1994).

Does this mean that the U.S. criminal justice system is soft on criminals? Not necessarily. The

FIGURE 8.4
Imprisonment: A Global View

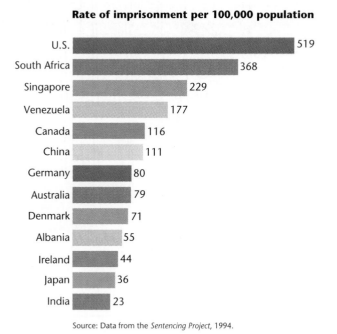

Rate of imprisonment per 100,000 population

U.S.	519
South Africa	368
Singapore	229
Venezuela	177
Canada	116
China	111
Germany	80
Australia	79
Denmark	71
Albania	55
Ireland	44
Japan	36
India	23

Source: Data from the *Sentencing Project*, 1994.

United States treats convicted criminals more severely than any other democratic nation. It has the dubious distinction of being the No. 1 jailer in the world (see Figure 8.4, next page). Since the early 1980s the U.S. prison population has more than doubled to over one million inmates. With the 1994 "three strikes and you're out" law (which mandates life sentences for a third violent crime), the prison population is expected to continue growing. Imprisonment is also generally longer than in other democratic countries. The length of imprisonment is

FIGURE 8.5
Recidivists Outnumber First-Timers in Prison

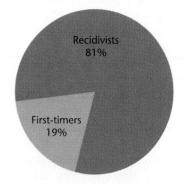

Recidivists
81%

First-timers
19%

Source: Data from U.S. Bureau of Justice Statistics, 1994.

generally measured in months and weeks in Sweden, but years in the United States. The United States is also the only industrialized nation in the West that still executes convicted murderers.

Does the comparatively harsh treatment in the United States help to decrease crime rates? Apparently not. Although the number of people behind bars has more than doubled since the early 1980s, the rate of crime has remained about the same (Census Bureau, 1994). In addition, the rate of **recidivism**—repeated commission of crimes—is extremely high. As Figure 8.5 shows, about eight out of every ten prisoners have served time before. Although these recidivists constitute a small minority of the criminal population, they have committed most of the crimes in society. The prisons are in effect "crime schools," producing tougher, more motivated criminals. Such schools are expensive, though: it costs more to send a person to prison than to college. A number of states have hired private companies to run some of their prisons at far lower costs. Nonetheless, because of widespread belief that crime is getting out of control, there is increased outcry to "lock 'em up and throw away the key." The general public today is far more interested in using prisons to punish criminals than to deter crime.

The War on Drugs

Over the last 15 years or so, the drug problem in the United States has become considerably worse. In 1981, there were about three million drug addicts, but today the figure is around six million. The numbers of drug-overdose deaths and drug-related homicides have soared in cities across the country, even in the midst of an eightfold increase in the federal budget for the war on drugs (Massing, 1993). The drug war is obviously a colossal failure. Most drug experts attribute the failure to the government's emphasis on law enforcement over drug education and treatment. But why the emphasis on law enforcement? A likely reason is lack of concern for the welfare of the poor and minorities. Witness the fact that the drug war is waged largely against poor African Americans and Hispanics, who are much more likely than affluent whites to be arrested and convicted for drug offenses.

Failure of the law-enforcement approach has led to calls for legalization of drugs. Advocates of legalization contend that, like Prohibition (of alcohol) in the 1920s, the current drug laws do more harm than good. They are said to generate many crimes, including homicides, and to encourage police corruption. By legalizing drugs, the proponents argue,

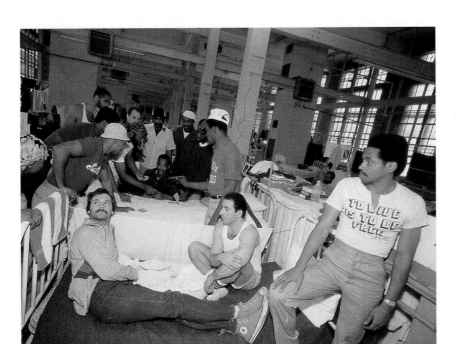

Prisons are in effect "crime schools." Such schools are costly, producing tougher, more motivated criminals, yet there is an increased outcry in society to "lock 'em up and throw away the key." The general public today is far more interested in using prisons to punish criminals than to deter crime.

the government can take away obscene profits from drug traffickers, end police corruption, and reduce crime drastically. Finally, legalizers believe that with legalization the huge amount of money currently spent on law enforcement can be used for drug treatment and education, which will dramatically reduce drug abuse.

Those who oppose legalization respond that, if drugs are legalized, drug use and addiction will sky-rocket. As William Bennett (1989), a former national drug-control policy director, says, "After the repeal of Prohibition, consumption of alcohol soared by 350%." Sociologist Elliott Currie (1993) also argues that legalization cannot solve the problem of wide-spread drug abuse and crime, because legalizers, just like the drug warriors, ignore the root cause of the problem, which is poverty, racism, or inequality. Thus Currie proposes that the government eradicate the cause of the problem by providing employment to all, increasing the minimum wage, expanding the Job Corps, increasing health care for the poor, offering paid family leave, providing affordable housing, and reducing social inequality.

Questions for Discussion and Review

1. What is the difference between formal and informal control?

2. In what ways can the criminal justice system balance the need to catch criminals with the need to respect individual freedom?
3. Can the war on drugs be won?

A GLOBAL ANALYSIS

Analysis of deviance around the world reveals societal differences in a number of deviant activities (Thio, 1995).

First, homicide is generally more likely to occur in poor than rich countries, suggesting that poverty is a major contributing factor. Among rich countries, the United States has the highest homicide rate largely because the poverty rate is considerably higher than in Western Europe, Canada, and Japan. But the ratio of property crimes to violent crimes is generally higher in rich than poor countries. While poverty serves as a strong *motivation* for committing a crime, property crimes cannot occur without the necessary *opportunities*, namely, properties being available as targets for robbery or theft. Since such opportunities abound in more prosperous countries, more property crimes can be expected.

Second, prostitution has recently become a fast-growing global industry. Many unemployed women in formerly communist Russia and Eastern Europe

GLOBAL VILLAGE

Organized crime groups have operated in U.S. society for over a hundred years, and they remain a major source of crime and violence. But organized crime is now an international problem, as crime groups have grown in power in Russia, Italy and other countries. This reading explores the extent and impact of organized crime in many countries.

International Organized Crime

In 1991 and 1992 the disruptive influence of organized criminal activity rocked the foundations of political stability in Italy. Since World War II organized crime has carried out a wide range of domestic activities, using violence, extortion, bribery, and murder to advance its interests. More recently the Sicilian Mafia specifically has been locked in a murderous struggle with the government, assassinating judges, policemen, and those seen as interfering in its operations, and, more ominously, using its economic power to try to corrupt the political process itself.

All over Asia, organized criminal groups, Pakistani, Thai, Chinese, or Japanese, operate vast international organizations trafficking in drugs or engaging in a wide variety of other criminal activities, in many cases with the complicity of local government and military officials. In the former Soviet Union and in the struggling states of Eastern Europe, criminal organizations, long held in check, are beginning to grow. They have developed international links to improve their own organizational abilities and marketing contacts. Of more concern, these criminal groups are penetrating local governments (which are often struggling for cohesion and lacking resources) by using bribery and violence to win protection for their expanding operations.

In a New York courtroom in 1992, Clark Clifford, an adviser to presidents and one of the most respected men in the United States, was called as a defendant in a case involving a vast illegal international financial enterprise, The Bank of Credit and Commerce International (BCCI). So far, BCCI is the biggest such case, but it illustrates only too graphically the extent to which banking and financial systems are vulnerable to penetration, manipulation, and fraud by criminal groups. The mechanisms whereby the incredible sums of illegal proceeds—perhaps $300 billion in drug money alone—are laundered and massive frauds are perpetrated through the world's financial markets are still only dimly understood.

Whether in the developed or in the developing world, criminal organizations' scope of action and range of capabilities are undergoing a profound change. Decline in political order, deteriorating economic circumstances, a growing underground economy that habituates people to working outside the legal framework, easy access to arms, the massive flow of emigrants and refugees, and the normal difficulties involved in engendering meaningful state-to-state cooperation are working to the advantage of criminal organizations. The rise of better-organized, internationally based criminal groups with vast resources is creating a new threat to the stability and security of the international system.

Excerpted from Roy Godson and William J. Olson, "International Organized Crime." Published by permission of Transaction Publishers, from *Society*, Vol. 32, No. 2, pp. 18–19. Copyright © 1995 by Transaction Publishers.

---

have flocked to more prosperous Western Europe to sell sex. Some of these women, however, have been tricked into prostitution with promises of singing, dancing, modeling, or waitressing jobs from pimps posing as businessmen in their home countries. More women from poor Asian countries have been lured with promises of legitimate jobs into Japan and Western Europe only to be sold to brothels. Large numbers of Thai and Filipino prostitutes that remain in their home countries cater to local men as well as hordes of Japanese and Western men on organized sex tours. Most of these prostitutes come from poor villages. Thus, poverty, along with exploitation by richer countries, contributes to the sex trade.

Third, suicide is generally more common in modern than in traditional societies. But among modern societies, countries such as Finland, Denmark, and Austria suffer higher rates of suicide than do the United States, Spain, and Italy. The higher suicide rate seems to relate to greater social equality. In societies with greater equality, people are less subjected to social regulation, a key contributor to suicide. As Durkheim (1966) suggested, less regulated individuals are more encouraged to expect too much from life and thus become more liable to greater frustration when expectations fail to materialize.

Fourth, organized crime differs cross-societally in some ways. Members' loyalty to the crime organization seems stronger in Japan and Hong Kong than in the United States and Italy. The syndicates in Hong Kong, Japan, Italy, and Russia have penetrated legitimate business and politics more deeply, compared with those in the United States. Not surprisingly, anti-syndicate measures fail more frequently in those countries than in the United States. There is one important similarity between the U.S. Mafia and its counterparts in other countries. They all serve as a "crooked ladder of upward mobility" for the ambitious poor, who can become rich by joining a syndicate (also see box, p. 190).

Question for Discussion and Review

1. How do some deviances vary from society to society?

————————

CHAPTER REVIEW

1. *What is deviance?* It is an act considered by public consensus or by the powerful at a given time and place to be a violation of some social rule.

2. *In what ways does homicide occur?* Homicide involves nonstrangers more than strangers. It most frequently takes place during weekend evenings, especially for lower-class offenders. Guns are often used to commit homicide, and their easy availability has contributed to a startling upsurge in teen homicide.

3. *Who is more likely to abuse drugs and why?* The poor, for several reasons: drugs can meet their need for status, help them cope with their harsh lives, and provide them a sense of purpose. An additional reason is easy access to drugs.

4. *Is pornography harmful?* Merely erotic, nonviolent pornography is not harmful, but violent pornography is, according to current research.

5. *How does corporate crime differ from street crime?* Corporate crime is more rationally executed, more profitable, and less detectable. Corporate offenders do not see themselves as criminals, their victims unwittingly cooperate with them, and society does little to punish them.

6. *Who is more likely than others to be mentally ill?* The poor. But there are two conflicting explanations. One is the stressful life of the poor. The other is that the mentally ill move into lower-class neighborhoods and the healthy ones, out of them.

7. *What does Durkheim's functionalist theory tell us about deviance?* Deviance helps enhance conformity, strengthen social solidarity, provide safe release for discontent, and induce social change. *According to Merton's strain theory, what is the cause of deviance?* U.S. society emphasizes the importance of success without providing equal opportunities for achieving it. One possible response to this inconsistency is deviance. *How are Hirschi's and Braithwaite's theories similar and how are they different?* Both assume that social control leads to conformity, and, therefore, the absence of control causes deviance. According to Hirschi, the absence of control arises from a lack of social bonds, but to Braithwaite, the absence of control comes from disintegrative shaming.

8. *What does conflict theory say about deviance?* According to Chambliss, law enforcement favors the rich and powerful over the poor and weak. In Quinney's view, the dominant class produces crime by making criminal laws, hiring enforcers to carry out the law, oppressing the subordinate class into deviance,

and spreading the ideology that the lower class is crime-prone and dangerous. Marxists argue that the exploitative nature of capitalism produces violent crimes and noncriminal deviances. *How does power theory explain deviance?* The powerful are more likely to engage in profitable deviance than the powerless in unprofitable deviance because the powerful have a stronger deviant motivation, greater opportunity, and weaker social control. *What is the feminist theory of deviance?* Conventional theories may be relevant to men but not women. Women are likely to be victims of rape and sexual harassment, which reflects men's attempt to put women in their place. Although female crime has recently increased it is not significant because most of the increase involves minor property crimes with very little profit, reflecting the continuing subordinate position of women in a patriarchy.

9. *How does differential association lead to deviance?* Deviance occurs if interactions with those who define deviance positively outweigh interactions with those who define it negatively. *How is being labeled deviant likely to affect people?* The label may cause them to look upon themselves as deviant and to live up to this self-image by engaging in more deviant behavior. *What insight about deviance does phenomenological theory offer?* We can understand deviance better by looking into people's subjective interpretation of their own deviant experiences.

10. *How does society control deviance?* Through socialization, supplemented by formal and informal social control. Informal control is more common in traditional societies, and formal control is more common in modern societies. Informal control, however, seems more effective in deterring deviance. *Is the U.S. criminal justice system soft on criminals?* It appears so because extremely few criminals are apprehended and punished, but compared with other democracies, the United States imprisons proportionately more people and imposes longer prison terms. *How does the government wage the war on drugs?* It focuses its efforts on law enforcement against drugs rather than treatment and education. Failure of the drug war has led some to advocate legalizing drugs, arguing it would take away obscene profits from drug traffickers, end police corruption, and reduce crime drastically. Opponents respond that legalization will cause rampant drug use and addiction without reducing crime.

11. *How does deviance differ cross-societally?* Homicide is more likely to occur in poor countries or rich coun-

tries with high rates of poverty. Property crimes are more prevalent in rich countries because targets for such crimes are more abundant. Prostitution flourishes in poor countries both as a result of poverty and exploitation by richer countries. Suicide is more common in the more modern and egalitarian societies. Organized crime is stronger and more a part of legitimate business and politics in other countries than in the United States, but similarly serves as an avenue to success for the ambitious poor in all countries.

KEY TERMS

Deviance   An act that is considered by public consensus or by the powerful at a given place and time to be a violation of some social rule (p. 172).

Differential association   The process of acquiring through interaction with others "an *excess* of definitions favorable to violation of law over definitions unfavorable to violation of law" (p. 182).

Disintegrative shaming   The process by which the wrongdoer is punished in such a way as to be stigmatized, rejected, or ostracized (p. 179).

Marginal surplus population   Marxist term for unemployed workers who are superfluous or useless to the economy (p. 180).

Neurosis   The mental disorder characterized by a persistent fear, anxiety, or worry about trivial matters (p. 176).

Pornography   Sexually explicit materials in the media (p. 174).

Primary deviance   Norm violations that a person commits for the first time and without considering them deviant (p. 184).

Psychosis   The mental disorder typified by loss of touch with reality (p. 176).

Recidivism   Repeated commission of crimes (p. 188).

Reintegrative shaming   Making wrongdoers feel guilty while showing them understanding, forgiveness, or even respect (p. 179).

Relative deprivation   Feeling unable to achieve a relatively high aspiration (p. 181).

Secondary deviance   Repeated norm violations that the violators themselves recognize as deviant (p. 184).

Social control   The process by which individuals are pressured by society to conform to social norms (p. 186).

SUGGESTED READINGS

Braithwaite, John. 1989. *Crime, Shame, and Reintegration.* Cambridge: Cambridge University Press. Explains how "reintegrative shaming" prevents deviance, while "disintegrative shaming" encourages deviance.

Friedman, Lawrence M. 1993. *Crime and Punishment in American History.* Reveals how the United States has repeatedly lost the "war against crime" from the colonial period to today.

Goode, Erich, and Nachman Ben-Yehuda. 1994. *Moral Panics: The Social Construction of Deviance.* Cambridge, MA: Blackwell. Explains why people react with unreasonable fear to a nonexistent threat or a relatively harmless threat.

Sterling, Claire. 1994. *Thieves' World: The Threat of the New Global Network of Organized Crime.* New York: Simon & Schuster. Showing how criminal organizations around the world engage in such activities as massive credit card scams, weapon deals, drug-running, and contract killings.

Thio, Alex. 1995. *Deviant Behavior,* 4th ed. New York: HarperCollins. A comprehensive and, according to a UCLA professor writing in the journal *Teaching Sociology,* "remarkably well-written text that takes the student two steps beyond most extant texts."

SEXUAL BEHAVIOR

CHAPTER OUTLINE

Myths and Realities

MYTH: *People are likely to masturbate if they do not have a sex partner or have not had one for a long time. Not surprisingly, young adults or singles masturbate more often than older, married people.*
REALITY: Surprisingly, it is the other way around: older, married people masturbate more often.

MYTH: *Marriage is the wrong place to find a lot of sexual pleasure. It is the footloose and fancy-free who enjoy the greatest amount of sex.*
REALITY: Compared with singles, married people have more sex as well as more satisfaction with their sex lives.

MYTH: *Most people in the United States have a huge sexual appetite and enjoy a great variety of sex partners.*
REALITY: U.S. society is overwhelmingly monogamous. Every year a large majority (about 83 percent) have only one or no sexual partner.

MYTH: *A great majority of married people have had at least one affair over their lifetime.*
REALITY: In their lifetime a minority—15 percent of married women and 25 percent of married men—have ever been unfaithful.

MYTH: *Since sexually active men can easily get sex, they are unlikely to rape their dates.*
REALITY: Sexually active men are more likely to rape their dates than men with little or no sexual experience.

single, unmarried woman told a sex researcher what she thought about one-night stands, with which she had had considerable experience:

It's too demeaning. Making love to someone you don't even know is like Sylvester Stallone punching a piece of meat in his movie *Rocky*. . . Many of these men like to exaggerate, even lie about, their sexual expertise. . . It may seem cruel, but I once spotted one of these men that [I had had sex with] giving his same spiel to another young woman. I walked up to him, said a loud hello, turned to the young woman and said in an even louder voice, "He's a premature ejaculator!" Sweet revenge was mine (Janus and Janus, 1993).

Like this woman, a large majority of people of either sex do not find one-night stands appealing (Michael, 1994). But among the few who do like this kind of impersonal sex, men outnumber women. Why? The reason, according to popular belief, is that men are born with a stronger sexual appetite. But evidence suggests a sociological reason: society does not condemn men as much as women for engaging in casual sex (Janus and Janus, 1993).

THE SOCIOLOGICAL NATURE OF SEX

People seem to believe that sex comes naturally, that everybody instinctively knows how to have sex. Such a popular belief, however, is false. Only animals are born with a **sex instinct**, an innate biological mechanism that causes its carrier to have sex in a certain way and at a certain time only. All dogs, for example, are instinctively programmed to use the same coital position, with the male mounting and entering the female from behind. They also instinctively copulate for reproduction only. They do not have sex unless the female is in heat—the period when she is ovulating and susceptible to pregnancy.

Humans, in contrast, do not have a sex instinct. This is why humans, unlike lower animals, are able to have sex in many different ways and all year round—in fact, most of the time when the female is not ovulating. What we have is only a **sex drive**, a biological potential for, rather than a determinant of, sexual desire or action. Whether, when, where, or how we will turn our sex drive into a certain sexual act

depends on the nature of our socialization. Because the way we are socialized is subject to the influence of social and cultural forces, human sexuality tends to vary from society to society and from group to group within the same society.

Domestic Diversity

In the United States, certain sexual practices vary with gender, age, education, race, religion, class, and location (Michael, et al., 1994). First, women masturbate less than men of a similar age. But older people—above age 24 and mostly married—masturbate *more* than those who are 18 to 24 years old and mostly unmarried. This fact undermines the popular belief that people are more likely to masturbate if they do not have a sex partner. The general public erroneously assumes that masturbation is only an outlet for sexual tension, a substitute for the sexually deprived. But the fact is that masturbation is more a part of being sexually active, so that the more sex people have the more likely they will masturbate.

Whether, when, where, or how we turn on our sex drive depends on our socialization. Because the way we are socialized is subject to the influence of social and cultural forces, human sexuality varies from society to society and from group to group within the same society.

Additional data show that people who masturbate seek out a greater variety of sexual experiences. In short, masturbation is largely a part of sexually active, older, and married people's erotic repertoire that also includes watching the partner undress, lengthy foreplay, genital sex, and oral sex.

Second, regardless of gender, the more educated people are, the more likely they have engaged in oral sex at some time in their lives. Whites are also more likely to have done so when compared with Hispanics and African Americans. The apparent discomfort with oral sex among the less well educated, Hispanics, and African Americans may owe much to their religious conservatism.

Third, for both women and men, the more religiously conservative, the less interest in oral sex. As Michael and his colleagues (1994) found, the percentage of conservative Protestants having had oral sex in their lifetime is the lowest among various religious groups.

Fourth, the poorer segments of the U.S. population tend to use a no-nonsense, quick, silent approach to sex, while those who are richer are more likely to practice an elaborate sexuality. The affluent are inclined to use a greater variety of sexual techniques, such as lengthy foreplay, oral sex, mutual masturbation, and different coital positions.

Fifth, the rate of homosexuality (identifying oneself as gay) is higher among people who live in large cities than among those who live in small towns and rural areas. The rate is also higher among the relatively well-educated and affluent than among the less educated and less affluent. Moreover, a higher percentage of whites than African Americans identify themselves as gay (Michael et al., 1994).

Global Diversity

Sexual behavior differs even more significantly among societies. In Western societies some form of kissing accompanies sexual intercourse. The Balinese of Indonesia do not kiss at all, and the Thonga of East Africa, to whom kissing is also unknown, said with disgust when they first saw Europeans kiss: "Look at them—they eat each other's saliva and dirt."

In the United States, most married couples make love about once or twice a week, but the frequency of sex is much higher or lower in other societies. On one side, the Mangaians of Polynesia make love and reach orgasm at least once every night, and the Aranda of Australia copulate as often as three times every night. On the other side, the Hindus in India make love less frequently than the people in the United States. This has much to do with many Hindu men's belief that semen is a source of strength and therefore should not be wasted (Ford and Beach, 1951; Harris, 1995).

In our society, where premature ejaculation is considered a problem, men strive for prolonged intercourse. But in more male-dominant societies, such as East Bay in Melanesia, where *delayed* ejaculation is considered a hang-up, men try to reach orgasm in 15 to 30 seconds or less (Reiss, 1986).

Homosexuality is far from prevalent in Western societies, but it is widely practiced in some preindustrial societies, such as the Etoro of Papua New Guinea and the people on the Caribbean island of Carriacou. Male homosexuality flourishes among the Etoro, largely because semen is believed to be the source of manhood—in addition to babies. The Etoro believe that every man has only a limited supply of semen, but boys can boost their supply by having oral intercourse with older men. On the other hand, the female homosexuality that is common on the island of Carriacou has to do with the migration of men in search of work. For most of the year when migrant husbands are away from home, older married women seek sexual favors and emotional support from younger single women while sharing with them the absent husband's remittance (Harris, 1995).

There is, however, a limit to the domestic and global variation in human sexuality, revealed particularly in the abhorrence of incest throughout the world. Because incest avoidance is virtually universal, does it mean that it is biologically based?

Questions for Discussion and Review

1. How do humans and other animals differ in regard to their sexuality?
2. In what ways does human sexuality vary within and across societies?

THE INCEST TABOO

Practically all societies abhor and prohibit sexual intercourse between close relatives, such as between father and daughter, mother and son, and brother and sister. There are exceptions. In the royal families of ancient Egypt, Hawaii, and Peru, siblings were required to marry. A famous example is Cleopatra, who was married to two of her brothers at different times while she was herself the product of a brother-sister marriage. But as these cases have been extremely rare, sociologists generally regard the **incest taboo**—the social norm that strongly prohibits sexual relations between close relatives—as universal.

Biological Explanations

The universality of the taboo poses a challenge to the sociological perspective. If social and cultural *differences* in sexual behavior are taken as proof that human sexuality is sociological rather than biological in origin, how can the sociological perspective account for the universality of the incest taboo? It cannot, argue sociobiologists, who assume that if certain behavior is universal it must be biologically based. This assumption is at the heart of three biological explanations for the existence of the taboo.

According to one biological theory, the incest taboo is the result of our natural, instinctive revulsion against sexual relations with close relatives. If this were true, critics argue, not a single society would have found it necessary to enact strict laws to prevent incest. To suggest, as instinct theory does, that all societies would legislate against something that everyone will not do anyway is like arguing that they would make laws to prohibit people from eating dirt.

According to a second biological theory, incest is prohibited because inbreeding causes physical degeneration and mental retardation in the offspring. But this explanation does not hold water, either. Inbreeding does not necessarily cause biological defects. It only intensifies the inheritance of traits, good or bad, rather than bad only. If two incestuous relatives are of superior stock, the quality of their children would be better. As agricultural experts have long known, inbreeding can improve the strains of already superior plants and livestock.

A third biological theory attributes the incest taboo to **negative imprinting**, a biological mechanism that suppresses erotic feelings for individuals with whom one has been familiar since early childhood. Two cases are often used to support this theory. One shows that, in the Israeli kibbutzim, young men and women who are unrelated but have been raised together in the same children's house never marry each other. Another case concerns a village in northern Taiwan, where it is customary for rich families to adopt a poor baby girl and raise her as their son's future bride. When these children grow up, they always refuse to marry each other, despite strong parental pressure.

These findings are taken to mean that childhood familiarity breeds sexual indifference. Actually, it is the incest taboo that encourages sexual indifference. Under the influence of the taboo, people who have developed a strong "familial bonding" with others in the same household generally refrain from incest. But where there is an absence of familial bonding, as in the case of dysfunctional or unstable family life, incest is more likely to occur (Erickson, 1989).

Sociological Explanations

More satisfactory explanations for the incest taboo are sociological. According to one such explanation, the taboo came into being because it enabled different family groups to work together, thereby enhancing their chances of survival. The early preindustrial societies are believed to have been confronted with the serious choice of either marrying out or dying out. The incest taboo had evolved into a device for forcing the children of a family to marry out—into other families. The resulting cooperation among different families became all-important, not only in making daily living easier but also in ensuring survival against famine and security against enemy attack. Although people today, particularly those in highly industrialized societies, no longer marry for interfamily cooperation but for love, the norm against incest remains.

According to another sociological explanation, the incest taboo exists because it serves to keep the family intact. Without the taboo, sexual rivalry and tension would make it impossible for the family to function as an effective unit. If the father has an affair with the daughter, the mother is bound to be jealous and resentful. Consequently, the mother can no longer love and care for the daughter. The father will not be able to perform his fatherly duty as his daughter's disciplinarian while, at the same time, being her lover. Moreover, incest can create a great deal of status confusion within the family. As Kingsley Davis (1949) said, "The confusion of statuses would be phenomenal. The incestuous child of a father-daughter union, for example, would be a brother of his own mother; the son of his own sister; a stepson of his own grandmother; possibly a brother of his own uncle; and certainly a grandson of his own father."

Sociologists assume that the incest taboo has made most people feel it unnatural to have sex with close relatives. Without the taboo, incest might have been common. As Dorothy Willner (1983) pointed out, brothers and sisters usually avoid physical contact in cultures with stern sibling incest prohibitions but engage in sexual play in cultures with lax or no prohibitions. No matter how strong the taboo, though, it cannot totally prevent incest. Thousands of cases of incest occur annually in the United States, mostly involving fathers molesting daughters.

Questions for Discussion and Review

1. What is the incest taboo?
2. What caused the development of the incest taboo?

SEXUAL BELIEFS AND PRACTICES

We are constantly bombarded by the mass media with movies, TV talk shows, books, and magazine articles about sex in the United States. Along the way we pick up many myths.

Popular Myths

One myth is that most teenagers start having sexual intercourse for the first time at a very young age—about *13 or 14*. Most studies, however, report that a majority of the young people have their first intercourse at about age *17*. A second myth is that *most*

In the United States we are constantly bombarded with movies, TV talk shows, books, and magazine articles about sex . Along the way we pick up a number of popular myths. One myth is that most teenagers have sexual intercourse for the first time at a very young age—about 13 or 14. Most studies, however, report that a majority of young people have their first intercourse at about 17.

married people have been unfaithful at least once. The fact is that only a *minority* have been unfaithful. A third myth is that it is easy to tell whether people are homosexual by their appearance or gestures. In fact, it is difficult to tell, because homosexual men can appear extremely masculine, average, or effeminate and can be football players, political leaders, truck drivers, or in any other type of occupation— just like heterosexual men. Similarly, homosexual women can be extremely feminine, average, or masculine and can have any kind of job—just like heterosexual women (Reinisch, 1990).

A recent highly scientific study of sex revealed a long list of other myths (Michael et al., 1994):

1. Most people are having a considerable amount of sex, and the few who are not must be frustrated and miserable.
2. Most people have a huge sexual appetite, enjoying a wide variety of partners and practices.
3. Marriage is the wrong place to find a great deal of sexual pleasure. It is the footloose and fancy-free who enjoy the greatest amount of sex.
4. Masturbation is an inferior substitute for sex with a partner. It is therefore more popular with partnerless, unhappy, frustrated people who have gone too long without having sex with somebody.
5. Ten percent of the U.S. population identify themselves as gay.
6. Everyone who is sexually active is at great risk of getting AIDS. The deadly disease will spread inexorably throughout the U.S. population.

The general myth is that the United States is a "golden land of eroticism where everybody who is young and beautiful has a hot sex life," and "a land where vast hordes of miserable people, kicked out of the sexual banquet, lick their wounds in silence and resentment" (Michael et al., 1994).

All the beliefs above run counter to findings from the latest sex survey by Robert Michael and his colleagues (1994). This survey is the most scientific and accurate of its kind. Other studies tend to be biased, because they have largely recruited their subjects from volunteers, who are more sexually active than average persons. But the study by Michael and his colleagues is based on a randomly selected sample of the U.S. population between ages 18 and 59. Let us look at the major findings from the study.

Sexual Practices

Being sexually active is far from common in the United States. Love-making averages only about 6.4

times a month, or less than twice a week. About a third of the U.S. adult population have sex at least twice a week. Another third have sex a few times a month. And the final third have sex a few times a year or not at all. If most people have so little sex, are they not frustrated and dissatisfied? On the contrary. They appear happy, even thrilled with their sex lives. As the researchers point out, a vast majority (over 88 percent) of U.S. adults are either *very* or *extremely* satisfied with their sex lives. Satisfaction is particularly high among people who are married and those who live together. They are not only more satisfied with their sex lives but also have sex more often, compared with singles. This fact throws cold water on the popular belief that the unmarrieds have the hottest sex.

There is also an *absence* of close relationship between orgasm and satisfaction. Seventy-five percent of men always reach orgasm during sex, but less than 50 percent are extremely pleased. On the other hand, while only 29 percent of women always have orgasm, a higher percentage are extremely physically pleased. All this suggests that one can have a satisfying sex life without orgasm and that having orgasm does not guarantee sexual satisfaction.

The United States is an overwhelmingly monogamous society. Every year a large majority (83 percent) have only one or no sexual partner. Over a lifetime, as Figure 9.1 shows, the average number of partners is three (two for women, and six for men). Married people are even more monogamous. Eighty-five percent of wives and 75 percent of husbands have been faithful during the entire length of their marriage. Similar patterns are found in other Western societies, such as Britain, France, and Finland.

Of the various forms of sexual practices, such as vaginal intercourse, masturbation, oral sex, anal intercourse, or group sex, vaginal intercourse is by far the most popular in the United States. Ninety-five percent of U.S. adults have had vaginal intercourse the last time they made love. Our society is also con-

FIGURE 9.1
Number of Sex Partners in One Year and Lifetime

Median number of sex partners since age 18

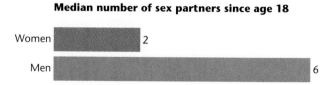

Source: Data from Robert T. Michael, John H. Gagnon, Edward O. Laumann, and Gina Kolata, *Sex in America: A Definitive Survey* (Boston: Little, Brown, 1994).

ventional in another way: next to vaginal intercourse, *watching the partner undress* ranks second among the sex acts found appealing. It beats oral sex, group sex, or other sexual activities that the media often portrays as exciting.

Many people believe that 10 percent of the U.S. population are gay. This figure comes from the pioneer sex researcher Alfred Kinsey, who in 1950 claimed to have found that one-tenth of adults had had at least six homosexual experiences in their life-

time. But Kinsey did not consider these people *exclusively* homosexual. To be exclusively homosexual, people have to identify themselves as gay, be sexually attracted only to members of the same gender, and engage only in homosexual acts. In fact, Kinsey found only about 2.5 percent of U.S. adults to be exclusively gay. This is not much different from the latest finding that about *2 percent* of the popular (1.4 percent women and 2.8 percent men) identify themselves as gay.

GLOBAL VILLAGE

AIDS now affects every country in the world as millions of persons are infected with this life-ending virus. But different groups and government agencies are trying to develop more AIDS awareness and wider use of condoms. This reading reports on a unique program in Argentina, where spray-painting students use graffiti to promote safe sex.

With Spray Paint, Students Wage 'Safe Sex' War

For Love, Use a Condom," reads graffiti scrawled across walls in almost every neighborhood of this genteel city in Argentina. The spray-painted message may be the most effective tool yet in the fight against AIDS.

But oddly enough, the Government wants nothing to do with the graffiti slogan. It was written by scores of high-school students who went on a graffiti-writing rampage last year, scribbling the message on every available wall they could find.

The youths said they were frustrated with the refusal of the Government to use the word condom in its AIDS prevention campaign. "We have to do something because our friends and lovers are becoming infected and dying because the Government is too prudish to even mention the very device that can save them," said Baltizar Álvarez, a 17-year-old student.

Concepción Mateo, 16, whose brother died of AIDS two years ago, said she had written the slogan on at least 20 walls across the city.

The police arrested her last year when she was writing on a building in the fashionable Recoleta district, she said, "but they let me go after I cried and told them that my brother would be alive today if he had used a condom."

Nongovernmental AIDS groups and AIDS activists here fault the federal Government for running what they say is an anti-AIDS campaign straight out of the Middle Ages because it does not mention condoms. The critics say they believe the federal Government has bowed to pressure from the Catholic Church not to promote condom use openly.

Government health officials acknowledge that the weight of the Catholic Church has prevented them from actively promoting condoms, but they say the control is more covert than overt. Dr. Laura Astarloa, who is in charge of the national AIDS program, said that while she would prefer to include condoms in the Government's AIDS program, she did not believe that it would make a big difference because "it's extremely difficult to change people's behavior."

A Gallup poll commissioned by the Argentine Government in August found that 90 percent of those surveyed knew the risk factors for contracting AIDS but that only one in 10 said they used condoms.

Dr. Astarloa said her main concern was convincing the Government to spend more money on AIDS programs. Last year, the Government spent $13 million on AIDS, including medical assistance, education, blood screening, prevention, H.I.V. testing, and training of health personnel.

She said that the Government had increased AIDS financing to about $20 million for 1995 but that that amount would still not go very far. Until the situation changes, Dr. Astarloa said, Argentines will have to depend on efforts of courageous teen-agers who take to the street to help in the fight against the deadly disease.

AIDS can spread easily among people with multiple sex partners. But recent research suggests two reasons why the disease is not likely to spread like wildfire throughout the entire U.S. adult population. One reason is that most sex is monogamous; another is that most people find partners who are like themselves, monogamous rather than sexually indiscriminate.

Research has suggested that AIDS can spread easily among people with multiple sex partners. But contrary to popular belief, the disease is not likely to spread like wildfire throughout the entire adult population. Michael and his colleagues (1994) offer two reasons based on their survey data. One is that most sex is monogamous. The most sexually active are marrieds, not singles. Even among singles, having multiple partners is far from the rule. Another reason is that most people find sex partners who are like themselves, monogamous rather than sexually indiscriminate.

Changes in Sexual Attitude

Although most people in the United States appear far more sexually conservative than widely believed, they are nevertheless more liberal than a generation or two ago. Today, sex is no longer the hush-hush matter it used to be. Nudity can be seen in theaters, in movies, and on television. Pornographic magazines and films are easily available. Homosexuality has become more open. Cohabitation, oral sex, and even the number of partners have increased, though not to a great extent as the media would have us believe. These are the obvious consequences of the sexual revolution that has swept the United States over the last three decades. The revolution has also brought about some basic changes in our sexual attitude.

First, there is more tolerance for various forms of sexual behavior. Consider the tolerance for homosexuality, for example. As much as half of the general public believes that homosexual acts between con-

senting adults should be legal, although only about two percent identify themselves as homosexual (Reinisch, 1990; Michael et al., 1994). This suggests that many believe it is all right for others to do what we may not want to do ourselves. The same kind of tolerance extends to premarital sex. Those who want to postpone sexual relations until they are married do not mind if their friends engage in premarital sex. As Mary Meyer, founder of the National Chastity Association for singles who, like herself, desire to preserve sex for marriage, says, "Recreational sex might work for other people. That's fine with me. I only know what works for me" (D. Johnson, 1990).

Second, the **double standard** of sexual behavior— the social norm that allows males, but not females, to have certain sexual experiences—is not as pervasive as it was in the past. One indication has been the increase in women's premarital experience. Moreover, more women than before expect to enjoy sex and reach orgasm. This means that there are now more women who enjoy sexual freedom that has traditionally been "for men only." But the double standard has not disappeared completely. While women may no longer be condemned for losing their virginity before marriage, they may be condemned for having multiple sex partners. They are likely to be called "sluts." Men with the same experience, however, are more likely to be called "studs," a term that connotes far more approbation than opprobrium (Rubin, 1990).

Third, there is some evidence of a sexual counter-revolution in the 1990s. Although premarital sex has become more prevalent today than a generation ago, increasing numbers of young people have in recent years begun to abstain from sex before marriage. The

American Mosaic

The large number of teenage pregnancies may suggest that nearly all U. S. teenagers are sexually active, but that is not true. More and more young people recognize the problems of teen sexuality and are adopting a more careful lifestyle. This reading explores the rise of interest in sexual abstinence, and how teachers are helping teenagers say "no" to sex.

Virgin Cool

Fredda Chalfin's students drag their chairs into a circle, joking and jostling until, finally, 31 pairs of baggy-jeaned legs are sitting knee to knee. Here, in a basement classroom at DeWitt Clinton High School in the Bronx, Chalfin leads a daily encounter group, and the box of Kleenex on the floor is just the most visible sign that, for the next 45 minutes, there will be no routine academics. Chalfin, casual in jeans and ankle boots, grew up in the age of peace and love, and her rules are gentle but firm: no lateness, no gum, no breaking confidences. No one needs a reminder. Three weeks into the term, her 14- to 18-year-olds are already each other's protectors, offering enough security to reveal an early-childhood sexual abuse, to applaud a schoolyard refusal to smoke some weed—and to support a choice to forego sex in a teenager's sex-crazy world.

With a note of innocence—or maybe it's shyness—they recite the affirmation scrawled on the board: I LOVE MY SEXUALITY ♥ I AM AT PEACE ♥ I AM FREE TO MAKE MY OWN DECISIONS REGARDING SEX♥.

Even here, in a corner of the Bronx that runs the economic and social gamut, it's obvious that abstinence is looking good to a lot more kids. "If you don't want to give it up, you don't have to," says Myra. "If that's what he wants, tell him to forget about it."

"What happens when he gets hot and horny and you're a virgin?" Chalfin asks. "How are you gonna work it out? It's like you're a vegetarian and he loves steak—where are you going to eat?"

"If your relationship is based on sex, you don't *have* a relationship," says Sweeney.

"I want to be different from other girls," says Betsy. "I want a guy to look at me in another way. I want to have respect for myself. I see girls getting into trouble, and I don't want to get hurt. I *want* to be a virgin."

School teachers, counselors, and social scientists say more teens are waiting, though these changes in attitudes and behavior won't show up in statistics for years. The question is, why now? One reason is the fear of AIDS. As Damien Ritter, a 15-year-old from Missoula, Mont., who wears his virginity as defiantly as the ponytail that sticks straight up from his head, says, "A person can have sex once and be *dead* six months later." ...

Even if they're not scared of AIDS, kids are worried about diseases that could leave them infertile or babies that could weigh them down with adult responsibilities. By the age of 21, according to the Centers of Disease Control, one in four young people is already infected with a sexually transmitted disease like chlamydia, syphillis or gonorrhea. And though teen-pregnancy rates are higher among the poor, it burdens all kids.

median age for first intercourse is 17.4 for girls and 16.6 years for boys, but nearly *one-fifth* of 19-year-olds have remained virgins throughout their teenage years (see Figure 9.2). The survey by Michael and his colleagues (1994) also indicates an increase in virginity among 20-year-olds. All this may reflect the fear of AIDS as well as the increased conservatism and puritanism of the 1990s.

Fourth, there is a fundamental change in the perceived purpose of sex. In the past, the primary motive for sex was reproduction. Today, most people want more than procreation from sex. They also

want recreation. Although vaginal intercourse is still their number one choice, couples are now much more inclined to engage in a variety of sex acts, such as prolonged foreplay and oral sex, that are aimed at giving pleasure rather than reproduction.

Fifth, a new sexual morality has largely replaced the old. In the past, people were more concerned with the "location" of sex, whereas today they emphasize the quality of the partners' relationship. According to the old ethic, a sex act that occurs within marriage is moral, and a sex act that takes place outside marriage is immoral. But, according to

FIGURE 9.2
Teens Who Remain Virgins
A growing number of teenagers have in recent years begun to abstain from sex before marriage. Now nearly one-fifth (18 percent) of 19-year-olds have remained virgins.

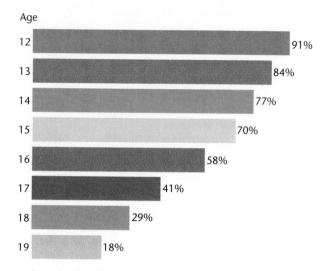

Age

12	91%
13	84%
14	77%
15	70%
16	58%
17	41%
18	29%
19	18%

Source: Data from Alan Guttmacher Institute, *Sex and America's Teenagers,* 1994.

the new ethic, regardless of whether a sex act is marital or nonmarital, it is moral if the couple love each other and immoral if they sexually exploit each other. Thus, in the old days, premarital sex was widely condemned but marital rape condoned. Today, marital rape is more likely to be condemned and premarital sex condoned.

In their survey, Michael and his colleagues (1994) refer to supporters of the new sex ethic as *relationalists* for believing in sex as part of a loving relationship. Supporters of the old ethic are called *traditionalists,* who regard premarital sex as wrong. The researchers discover that relationalists now make up nearly half of the U.S. adult population. Traditionalists have become a minority, constituting about a third of the population. The rest of the population, roughly a fifth, are *recreationalists,* who believe that sex need not have anything to do with love.

Related to those various changes in sexual attitude is the larger issue of gender equality. Most people believe that women should have the same right as men to choose how to live their lives and that this includes, among other things, their right to have an abortion. Supporters of this view, however, have been encountering serious opposition. Let us then take a closer look at the continuing battle over abortion.

The Battle over Abortion

In 1973, the U.S. Supreme Court made its landmark decision, known as *Roe* v. *Wade*, to legalize abortion. More specifically, the law allows women to have an abortion before the fetus is viable—able to survive outside the womb, which is about six months after conception, or three months before birth. The Supreme Court based its decision mainly on the grounds that the constitutional protection of individual rights to privacy should extend to women as well as men.

The desire for gender equality is what drives the abortion-rights activists. As Kate Michelman, president of the National Abortion Rights Action League, says, "Reproductive choice is the cornerstone of women's equality—if the right to have an abortion is eroded in any way, so are all other rights—the right to work, the right to have a family, the right to dignity, the right to economic security, the right to good health" (Steinmetz et al., 1990). By contrast, antiabortion activists believe that fetuses are unborn babies and, as such, have the same right to live as any human being does. As Congressman Henry Hyde, a leading opponent of abortion, says, "The pro-life argument assumes that fertilization creates a new member of the human family. . . . From the moment of conception forward, the principle of the sanctity of human life ought to apply. Under our Constitution, equal protection applies to every person" (Steinmetz et al., 1990).

Most people in the United States support the legalization of abortion. But, ever since the Supreme Court legalized abortion in 1973, antiabortion forces have repeatedly managed to chip away at abortion rights through various laws, federal regulations, and other judicial decisions. Today, for example, many women on welfare can no longer receive Medicaid for abortions and many public hospitals refuse to perform abortions for fear of losing federal funds. Antiabortion protesters and terrorists have further discouraged visits to abortion clinics. Consequently, abortion has dropped significantly—to its lowest level since 1979, which has in turn contributed to an increase in young single mothers (Lewin, 1994).

Today there are about six million pregnancies in the United States. Slightly more than half are unintended, and about half of these—1.5 million—are terminated by induced abortions. Even though abortion is legal, most women do not choose it casually. Instead, their decision is based on such overwhelming reasons as being too poor or too young to raise the child. Moreover, abortion does not necessarily leave a woman with a sense of relief, but rather a sense of loss. The woman's husband or boyfriend may also feel guilty, anxious, and powerless. It is thus fairly common for couples to split up as a result of the stress, guilt, and conflict that result from abortion (Strong and DeVault, 1989; Steinmetz et al., 1990).

Since most of the women who seek abortions are poor, young, and unmarried, it has been suggested that both abortion-rights advocates and antiabortion activists call off their battle over abortion and work together toward eliminating the need for abortion, namely, the causes of unwanted pregnancy. These efforts could include providing sex education, encouraging contraception, improving schools, reducing poverty, and offering other programs to better the lives of the young and the poor—the casualties of the current battle over abortion (Rosenblatt, 1992).

Questions for Discussion and Review

1. What are the popular myths regarding sex in the United States? What data refute them?
2. In what ways has the sexual attitude in the United States changed?
3. How do the views of abortion-rights advocates and abortion opponents differ?

HETEROSEXUALITY

We have so far discussed sexual attitudes and practices in general. Let us now analyze the more specific nature of heterosexuality, divided into three major types: premarital, marital, and extramarital sex.

Premarital Sex

An overwhelming majority of societies around the world approve of **premarital sex**—sex before marriage. About 70 percent permit it for both sexes and nearly all the rest for males only. Most of the permissive societies are quite different from ours. They do not merely condone premarital sex; they encourage it. As a father in such a society told his adolescent son, "Don't be discouraged by a girl's rebuffs or running away; chase her down. Follow her—it's well worth your while." While our society may not be that permissive—and sexist, it is not as restrictive as the handful of societies (about five percent) that *completely* prohibit premarital sex (Murdock, 1967).

Why is one society permissive and another restrictive? The reason, according to George Goethals (1971), is either male dominance or societal complexity. As for the first reason, Goethals observed that sanctions against premarital sex are likely to be severe in patrilineal and patrilocal societies, marked by male dominance. In some of these societies, premarital sex is allowed, but for males only. Premarital sex for both sexes is more likely to be permitted in matrilineal and matrilocal societies, where male dominance is less prevalent. As for societal complexity, Goethals noted that sexually permissive societies tend to be small, simple, or preliterate. Most are tribal communities in developing, preindustrial countries. More restrictive societies are usually large, complex, or modern.

The United States is one of the comparatively restrictive societies. It is true that a majority of young people in the United States engage in premarital sex, but most of this sex is far from indiscriminate or wild, unrestrained by the restrictive culture. Instead, it operates in accordance with the sexual code that

TABLE 9.1
Dating Stages and Sexual Intercourse

	INTERCOURSE	
	Females	**Males**
Stage 1: Dating with no particular affection	2%	23%
Stage 2: Dating with affection but not love	77%	33%
Stage 3: Dating and being in love	16%	60%
Stage 4: Dating one person only and being in love	59%	80%
Stage 5: Engaged	75%	89%

SOURCE: Data from John P. Roche and Thomas W. Ramsbey, "Premarital Sexuality: A Five-Year Follow-Up Study of Attitudes and Behavior by Dating Stage," *Adolescence*, 28 (Spring 1993), p. 70.

has been described as "permissiveness with affection." Thus premarital sex is often between future spouses. Even if there is no intention for marriage, the sexual relations reflect a commitment between the partners. As a 16-year-old woman explains, she and her boyfriend are not going to get married, but "we won't date anybody else as long as we're together. That's a commitment, isn't it? Just because we don't expect to get married doesn't mean we're not in love, does it?" (Rubin, 1990). Young men are less monogamous than women, but only a minority of men engage in casual sex. In short, premarital sex is strongly tied to emotional involvement (see Table 9.1, p. 205).

Marital Sex

Sex in marriage declines in frequency with increasing age. Still, aging is only a small factor; a larger one is sociological: the arrival of children and growing career demands. Marital sex has undergone significant changes over the last 30 years. The duration of coitus has increased impressively. In the past it took married men only about two minutes to ejaculate after intromission (vaginal penetration), but now it takes about ten minutes. Because of increased foreplay, the entire process takes between 15 minutes and one hour for most couples. There is also a greater willingness today to experiment with a great variety of sex acts. In regard to oral sex, for example, more than 75 percent of married people today, as compared with fewer than 50 percent in the past, have tried it (Blumstein and Schwartz, 1983; Jasso, 1985; Michael et al., 1994).

It is clear that married couples today have stronger interest in sex and engage in it more often. The latest research even found them to be the most sexually active group. But do they enjoy it more? Apparently, they do. As has been suggested, a vast majority of married people are "very" or "extremely" satisfied with their sex lives (Michael et al., 1994).

Extramarital Sex

Unlike premarital sex, which is prohibited by only a few societies, **extramarital sex**—having sex with a person who is not one's spouse, popularly called adultery or infidelity—is condemned by most societies (Murdock, 1967). Adulteresses, though not adulterers, have often been stoned to death in some places. In the United States, adultery is still widely disapproved of and still legally considered a sufficient ground for divorce. Given the great social pressures

against infidelity, it is understandable that extramarital sex is relatively rare. As Figure 9.3 shows, in their lifetime only 15 percent of wives and 25 percent of husbands have been unfaithful, and in the past year only about six percent of married people have had an affair (Michael, 1994).

An affair typically involves another married person, is usually confined to one or two partners, and often lasts only a year or less. It is widely believed that extramarital sex is highly exciting, satisfying, or refreshing, but data show otherwise. Perhaps because extramarital copulation is mostly carried out in secret and frequently charged with tension and guilt, the experience is far from gratifying. According to one study, two-thirds of married men rated their marital sex "very pleasurable," but fewer than half of the unfaithful husbands gave the same rating to their extramarital coitus. In the same study, the proportion of straying wives regularly reaching orgasm in extramarital intercourse is significantly lower than the percentage of nonstraying wives having orgasm with their husbands (Katchadourian, 1985). Another study indicates that older men are more likely to suffer a heart attack and die during extramarital sex than during sex with their wives (Reinisch, 1990). This apparently suggests that the illicit sex can induce a dangerously high level of stress.

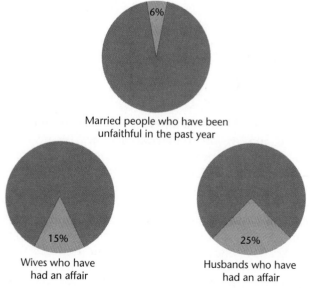

FIGURE 9.3
The Prevalence of Infidelity

6%

Married people who have been
unfaithful in the past year

15%

Wives who have
had an affair

25%

Husbands who have
had an affair

Source: Data from Robert T. Michael, John H. Gagnon, Edward O. Laumann, and Gina Kolata, *Sex in America: A Definitive Survey* (Boston: Little, Brown, 1994).

Extramarital sex—sex with a person other than one's spouse—is condemned by most societies. Studies on the extramarital sex that does occur show that the experience is far from gratifying and that older men are more likely to suffer a heart attack and die during extramarital sex than during sex with their wives. Apparently illicit sex induces a high level of stress.

It is also popularly believed that "people have affairs because they are oversexed." Research, however, shows that people who have affairs are much less sexually active, having much less sex, than monogamous couples (Pittman, 1993).

Questions for Discussion and Review

1. What is the nature of premarital sexuality in the United States?
2. How is marital sex today different than 30 years ago?
3. What are the prevalence and characteristics of extramarital sex?

HOMOSEXUALITY

Homosexuality may involve having the *feeling* of sexual desire for members of the same sex, the *experience* of having sex with persons of the same sex, or the *identification of oneself* as a homosexual. Because of prejudice and discrimination against homosexuality, most people with homosexual feelings or experiences do not identify themselves as homosexual. This is why the latest sex survey shows that only about 1.4 percent of U.S. women and 2.8 percent of men identify themselves as homosexual even though considerably more people (four percent for women and nine percent for men) have had the experience. The prejudice against homosexuality has also generated a number of myths about gays, just three of which are discussed below.

Myths

According to one popular myth, as suggested earlier, gays (male homosexuals) are typically effeminate and lesbians (female homosexuals) masculine. Gays are believed to walk like women, talk like women, or look like women, and lesbians are believed to walk, talk, or look like men. In reality it is difficult to differentiate most homosexuals from heterosexuals. Research has shown that most gays are just as masculine as conventional men, and that most lesbians are just as feminine as straight women (Dunkle and Francis, 1990).

A second myth is that homosexuals like to molest or seduce young children. The fact is that the great majority of gay men have no more sexual interest in young boys than the great majority of straight men have in little girls. Actually, most child molesters are *heterosexual* males. For one year between 1991 and 1992 at the Children's Hospital in Denver, Colorado, there were 387 cases of suspected child molestation. Only one case involved a gay perpetrator; all the rest involved boys and girls abused by heterosexual men (Marcus, 1993).

A third myth is that most people are either completely homosexual or completely heterosexual. In reality, as biologist-turned-sexologist Alfred Kinsey (1948) wrote,

> [People] do not represent two discrete populations, heterosexual and homosexual. The world is not to be divided into sheep and goats. . . It is a fundamental of taxonomy that nature rarely deals with discrete categories. Only the human mind invents categories and tries to force facts into separate pigeon holes. The living world is a continuum in each and every one of its aspects.

The difference between the sexes is mostly a matter of *kind*: people are either male or female. But the difference between sexual orientations is a matter of *degree*: some people are more, or less, homosexual (or heterosexual) than others. Thus Kinsey assigned people varying positions on a scale from one extreme of

Money

FIGURE 9.4
The Kinsey Heterosexual-Homosexual Scale

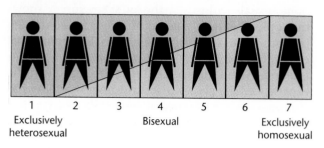

| 1 | 2 | 3 | 4 | 5 | 6 | 7 |
| Exclusively heterosexual | | | Bisexual | | | Exclusively homosexual |

1. Exclusively heterosexual
2. Predominantly heterosexual, only incidentally homosexual
3. Predominantly heterosexual, but more than incidentally homosexual
4. Equally heterosexual and homosexual
5. Predominantly homosexual, but more than incidentally heterosexual
6. Predominantly homosexual, but incidentally heterosexual
7. Exclusively homosexual

Source: Adapted from Alfred C. Kinsey et al., *Sexual Behavior in the Human Male* (Philadelphia: W.B. Saunders, 1948).

being exclusively heterosexual to the other extreme of being exclusively homosexual (see Figure 9.4).

Presumably only about two percent of the U.S. population are exclusively homosexual—identifying themselves as gay (Michael et al., 1994). Many more people *appear* to be exclusively heterosexual because they do not define themselves as gay at all. But just because people do not define themselves as gay does not necessarily mean that they are 100 percent straight, without any feeling of attraction to same-sex others. Given the widespread fear of homosexuality and prejudice against gays, most people would have easily banished their homosexual feelings—especially weak ones—into the unconscious part of their mind. It is thus possible that most people are predominantly rather than exclusively heterosexual (2 or 3 on the Kinsey scale).

Causes

Researchers in various disciplines have tried to explain why some people become homosexual. Their explanations may be classified into three major types: biological, psychiatric, and sociological theories.

Biological Theories   Homosexuality has been linked to at least three kinds of biological factors: hormones, genes, and brain.

According to the *hormone theory,* gay men have lower levels of male sex hormones than nongay men,

and lesbians have less female sex hormones than male sex hormones. But most studies have found no hormonal difference between gays and straights.

According to the *genetic theory*, people are born rather than bred to be homosexual. Studies have suggested that the probability of two siblings becoming homosexual together is significantly higher among *identical* twins than among *fraternal* twins. This is taken to mean that homosexuality is largely determined by genes, because identical twins are more genetically alike than fraternal twins. But the findings do not necessarily mean that homosexuality can be traced to genes. Social environment may contribute to the development of homosexuality because, when compared with fraternal twins, identical twins are more likely to elicit similar responses from others. A different kind of study claims to have found the "gay gene" somewhere on the X chromosome of gays (Bishop, 1993). But the researchers studied only gay men, and it is quite possible that the so-called gay gene also appears in these gays' *heterosexual* brothers.

The *brain theory* comes from a study in which Simon LeVay (1991) examined brain tissues from deceased gays and straights. The researcher found, among other things, that the gays' hypothalamus was less than half the size of the straights'. (The hypothalamus is the cluster of neurons, or nervous tissues, in the brain's lower area, which controls sex drive and body temperature.) It was concluded that a relatively small brain could make a person gay. But it could be the other way around, namely, that homosexuality may affect the brain structure. There is evidence that the brain's neural networks can change in response to certain experiences. In people reading Braille after becoming blind, for example, the area of the brain controlling the reading finger usually grows larger.

Psychiatric Theories   For many years most psychiatrists assumed that homosexuality was a form of mental illness. But in 1973 the American Psychiatric Association (APA) decided to define homosexuality as normal. Still today the APA continues to find some, though not most, homosexuals to be suffering from what it calls *sexual orientation disturbance*. Most psychiatrists would help these troubled gays to accept their homosexuality and feel comfortable with themselves. But some psychiatrists would try to "cure" the "patients" of their homosexuality. Such psychiatrists continue to hold the old belief that homosexuality is characterized by "hidden but incapacitating fears of the opposite sex."

This pathological fear is often attributed to an abnormal parent-son relationship. A young boy is said to become homosexual later in life if he has a domineering, overprotective, or seductive mother and a weak, detached, or hostile father. Alienated from his father, the boy will not look upon him as a model for learning the masculine role. Instead, being driven by his hostile father into the arms of his loving mother, the boy will learn to identify himself with her. As a consequence, the boy will likely grow up to become homosexual, according to this theory.

Many psychiatrists have found most of their homosexual patients to have had disturbed relationships with their parents, but these patients do not represent the majority of the gay population. Numerous studies on average, *non*patient homosexuals have found them to be no different from heterosexuals in parent-child relationships (Ross, 1988).

Sociological Theories   A basic problem with biological theories is their assumption that homosexuality is universally the same. Were this true, we should expect various societies to have about the same rate of homosexuality. But the reality is that homosexuality varies greatly in form and frequency from one society to another. Though relatively rare in many Western societies today, homosexual practices have been and are common in other societies such as ancient Greece, ancient Japan, the Azande of Africa, and New Guinea societies. In these societies, male teenagers have sex regularly with older men as a normal way of growing up but later in their adulthood marry women and have children (Herdt, 1990). This suggests that society has much to do with the development of homosexuality. To most sociologists, then, homosexuality is largely social behavior, no different from heterosexuality. Both are assumed to develop from past social experiences. Only the specific nature of their social experiences differs.

Most sociologists assume that gays, like straights, are born with a diffuse, neutral sexual desire. They do not naturally develop the sexual orientation toward members of the same sex. As young children, they are not particularly attracted to the homosexual object choice or to the heterosexual object choice—a same-sex playmate may be just as sexually exciting or unexciting as a different-sex playmate. Only through constant interaction with parents and other socializing agents of society are they gradually conditioned to confine their sexual interest to a particular sexual choice—a person of the same sex. A few sociologists, however, hold the sociobiological assumption that homosexuals are born with a biological predisposition in their genes and hormones that makes them more likely than other children to be attracted to members of the same sex. By itself, though, the biological proclivity does not automatically cause them

to become homosexual. As suggested by societal variations in the incidence of homosexuality, society can check—or encourage—it through a socializing process.

That process may involve children acquiring sexual orientation from physical contact with parents during the sensitive period between birth and age three. If a mother kisses, touches, or caresses her little girl more than her little boy, as expected by the predominantly heterosexual society, then both the girl and the boy are likely to become heterosexual. But if, contrary to the expectation of heterosexual society, the mother has more physical contact with the boy than the girl, both children have a greater chance of growing up to be homosexual (Fleishman, 1983).

But as suggested in Chapter 7 (Socialization), nobody can be completely socialized to become anything. Similarly, socialization cannot completely determine sexual orientation. Even if all the identical twins in a study have gone through the same childhood socialization, a large number of them still will not develop the same sexual orientation (Bailey et al., 1993; Bailey and Pillard, 1991). This suggests that some other unknown factors are also involved in the development of homosexuality.

Homophobia

A major factor that strongly affects gay life is **homophobia**, prejudice and discrimination against homosexuals. Like other minorities, gays often encounter prejudice and discrimination simply because their sexual orientation differs from that of most people in society. Not all straights are homophobic, but some are more so than others. The homophobic ones have been found to have certain characteristics that distinguish them from others. They are generally:

1. less likely to personally know someone who is gay or lesbian;
2. more conservative—socially, politically, religiously, and sexually;
3. less educated and less well-off;
4. older, except in cases of extreme violence against gays, known as "gay bashing" or "hate crimes," which are more common among young men;
5. more likely to be influenced by their peers; and
6. more likely to stereotype as homosexual a man they consider to be "feminine" in some way (Berrill, 1992; Blumenfeld and Raymond, 1993).

It is difficult to assess the extent of homophobia in the United States. But if homophobia involves only a visceral discomfort with gay life, then a slight

O.K
Practice

Society has much to do with the development of homosexuality. A major social factor that affects gay life is homophobia—prejudice and discrimination against homosexuals. Most Americans can be considered homophobic if homophobia involves only a visceral discomfort with gay life or opposition to such emotional issues as allowing gays to be legally married. But if homopobia involves denying homosexuals the same civil rights enjoyed by heterosexuals, then most Americans do not appear to be homophobic.

majority of the U.S. population may be considered homophobic. Asked in a 1992 *Newsweek* poll whether homosexuality is an acceptable alternative lifestyle, 53 percent of the respondents said "no," compared with 41 percent saying "yes." Most were also antigay in regard to other highly emotional issues. Fifty-eight percent did not want gays to be legally married, and 61 percent did not want gays to adopt children. However, if homophobia involves denying homosexuals some of the same civil rights enjoyed by heterosexuals, then most people do not appear to be homophobic. As shown in the same survey, a large majority say that gay people should have equal rights in job opportunities, health insurance, inheritance, and social security. In short, U.S. society is deeply ambivalent about gays and lesbians, torn between an uneasy feeling about their homosexuality and a democratic tolerance for homosexuals as fellow citizens.

Questions for Discussion and Review

1. What are the common myths about homosexuality?
2. How do different theories explain the causes of homosexuality?
3. What are the characteristics of homophobia in the United States today?

COERCIVE SEX

Rape is basically coercive sex, involving the use of force to get someone to do something sexual against their will. It is a common problem in the United States, but exactly how common? And why is it common? Let us find the answers.

Incidence and Characteristics

Every year only about 110,000 cases of rape in the United States are reported to the police, but the actual number of rapes is considerably higher, running into the millions. According to the latest survey, 22 percent of women aged 18 to 59 have been forced to have sex at least once since age 13 (Michael et al., 1994). This 22 percent translates into about 15 million women as victims of forced sex. Most of these incidents are not even legally defined as rapes, let alone reported to the police. A key reason is that the overwhelming majority of the cases involve intimates such as lovers and close friends (see Figure 9.5), while rape is popularly associated with strangers or mere acquaintances.

In the same survey, while 22 percent of the women said they had been forced to have sex, only about 3 percent of the men admitted to having committed forced sex. Why do the overwhelming majority of men fail to see what some women see as forced sex?

FIGURE 9.5
The Men Who Force Sex on Women

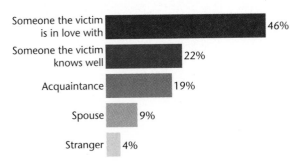

Source: Data from Robert T. Michael, John H. Gagnon, Edward O. Laumann, and Gina Kolata, *Sex in America: A Definitive Survey* (Boston: Little, Brown, 1994).

The apparent reason, again, has much to do with the fact that most cases of forced sex involve intimates. Consider the two scenarios given by Michael and his colleagues (1994).

One involves a married man coming home late after drinking a lot of beer with the guys. He wants sex, but his wife cringes when he gets near. She obviously does not want sex. He does, and has his way. He does not think it was forced, but she does. Another illustration involves two young people on a date. She touches his hand, his arm, then even his thigh while they are talking at dinner. She thinks she is only trying to get to know him. But he thinks she wants sex. Later, when he makes his move, she says "no." But he thinks she means "yes." He believes the sex was consensual. To her, it was forced.

But why do such husbands and dates fail to see they have committed forced sex? The reason seems to lie in the traditional, patriarchal belief that men should be aggressive to win a woman's heart. Resulting from such aggression gone out of control, forced sex is an extension of the traditional pattern of male sexual behavior. The belief about the importance of male aggressiveness is embedded in the culture that encourages rape.

The Culture of Rape

The culture of rape reveals itself through at least three prevailing attitudes toward women.

First, women are treated like men's property. If a woman is married, she is, in effect, her husband's property. Thus in most countries and some states in the U.S. a man cannot be prosecuted for raping his wife. The reasoning seems to be: How can any man steal what already belongs to him? The property logic may also explain the difficulty of getting a man con-

victed for raping a "cheap, loose woman" or a known prostitute. Such a female is considered as if she were every man's property, because she has had sex with many men. If a "good" woman is raped, we often say that she has been "ravaged," "ravished," "despoiled," or "ruined," as if she were a piece of property that has been damaged.

Globally, when conquering armies destroy the conquered population's property, they also tend to rape the women as if they were part of that property. During World War II, German soldiers raped massive numbers of Jewish and Russian women after occupying many villages and cities in Europe, and the Japanese army systematically raped women and girls as it invaded Korea, China, and various Southeast Asian countries. In 1971, when the Pakistani army marched into Bangladesh, as many as 200,000 women were raped. Most recently, in 1992, the Serbian soldiers in Bosnia raped thousands of Muslim women as part of their "ethnic cleansing" campaign (Thio, 1995).

Second, women are treated as if they were objects of masculinity contests between men. To prove his manhood, a man is culturally pressured to "make out" with the largest number of women possible. The pressure to play this masculinity game often comes from friends who ask things like: "Did you score?" "Had any lately?" If the answer is "no," they may say, "What's the matter? Are you gay or something?" Such social pressure tends to make young men want to show off their "masculine" qualities, such as aggressiveness, forcefulness, and violence. Even without peer pressure, the popular belief in sexual conquest as a badge of masculinity already encourages men to be aggressive toward women. If women say "no," men are expected to ignore this response or even translate it into really meaning "yes." Such lessons in sexual conquest often come from the stereotype of the movie or television hero who forcefully, persistently embraces and kisses the heroine despite her strong resistance and is rewarded when she finally melts in his arms.

In real life, such sexual aggression can easily lead to rape. This is why many sociologists regard rape as an extension of the socially approved, conventional pattern of male sexual behavior. It is also not surprising that members of the Spur Posse, a group of high school boys in California who compete with one another by scoring points for sexual conquests, were jailed for a few days in 1993 on charges of molesting and raping girls as young as 10. It is also no wonder that other winners of the masculinity game, such as college men with considerable sexual experiences, are more likely to rape their dates than

ENRICHING OUR LIVES

Public awareness of the extent and impact of date rape has greatly increased, and many colleges have developed new policies to heighten campus awareness. But what if it happens to you or someone you know? This article, written to assist doctors whose patients might be victims of date rape, provides useful advice to help victims regain a sense of control over their lives and avoid confrontations in the future.

Dealing With Date Rape

Most date rape victims believe the myth that a sexual attack is a rape *only* when a stranger violently attacks a woman and injures or kills her while she is fighting him off. In fact, rape is what happens anytime a victim is forced to have sex against her will. Moreover, if sex takes place when the woman is unconscious, or if she is under the age of consent or is physically or mentally incapacitated, the act meets the legal definition of rape in most jurisdictions. Similarly, rape occurs if the victim capitulates to sex out of fear for his or her physical safety.

All patients, male as well as female, need relevant medical and legal information about rape. Adolescent boys need this information especially urgently, since they may commit date rape without thinking they are doing anything wrong. Many grow up believing that a woman's "no" never really means "no" and that if the man persists, he will get what he wants.

Three typical behavior patterns may be observed in rape victims, either immediately after the rape or years afterwards, according to one researcher:

- Withdrawal from social interactions. The victim does not feel she can trust her own judgment, because she once chose to date a rapist. Therefore, she stops making any decisions requiring judgment and withdraws from social interactions.

- Repression of the rape memory. In the attempt to get back to normal, the victim may repress her memory of the rape; once under stress and reminded of the rape, however, she may explode emotionally.

- Nondiscriminatory sexual behavior. If the victim was a virgin before the rape, she may conclude that she is now "a bad person" and has no legitimate reason to refuse any requests for sex. She may therefore adopt a sexually indiscriminate behavior pattern.

If the victim shows any of these behavior patterns, she needs counseling that will help her overcome feelings of guilt and self-blame. Such feelings often play havoc with the woman's interpersonal relationships and her self-esteem.

Your patient can overcome her rape experience by taking some of the following actions. She may want to confront the assailant after the event (when she is feeling strong, to tell him her reactions to what he did to her. She may prefer to do this in a safe, public place and with a support person present.) She can give information to the police without being obliged to give her name or press charges, or she can press criminal charges against her assailant. She may also sue him in civil court for pain and suffering and for the recovery of therapy costs.

If the rapist is a student, the victim can report the rape to the school authorities. If both victim and assailant attend the same institution, the rapist may be transferred, suspended, or expelled so she will not have to see him every day in her classes.

The most important thing a victim can do to regain control over her life is to place blame and responsibility for the rape where it belongs—with the rapist.

Excerpted from Andrea Parrot, "Date Rape," Medical Aspects of Human Sexuality, April, 1990, pp. 28–31.

the so-called losers, who have little or no sexual experiences (Kanin, 1983; Schur, 1984).

Third, there is a popular myth that, deep down, women want to be raped. This myth is often expressed in various ways: "she asked for it;" "she actually wanted it;" "she lied about it (or consented to sex but later decided to 'cry rape');" and "she was not really hurt (or it was only a form of sex, though without her consent)." In essence, the victim is held

responsible for the rape. The victim is assumed to have done something that provoked the man to rape her. That "something" involves being in the "wrong" place (going to a bar or walking alone at night); wearing the "wrong" clothes (short shorts, miniskirts, or some other sexy dress); turning the man on (letting him kiss or pet her); or having "an attitude" (behaving assertively or independently) (Brinson, 1992).

Because of this blame-the-victim assumption, defense attorneys for alleged rapists tend to portray the victim as a willing partner. In one case, the victim was accused of having a "kinky and aggressive" sex life. In another case, the victim was said to be "sexually voracious" and to have "preyed on men" (Lacayo, 1987). The willing-victim myth is a major motivating force behind many rapes. In a study of convicted rapists, 59 percent deny their guilt and blame their victims instead. They insist that their victims seduced them, meant "yes" while saying "no" to the sexual assault, and eventually relaxed and enjoyed the rape. Not surprisingly, men who believe this dangerous myth about women are likely to rape them (Scully and Marolla, 1984).

Questions for Discussion and Review

1. How prevalent is rape and what kinds of people are most likely to commit it?
2. What is the culture of rape and how does it encourage rape?

COMMERCIAL SEX

Prostitution, the exchange of sex for money, is legal in Europe and many other countries. By contrast, it is not legal in the United States, except in some counties of Nevada. Nonetheless, prostitution has long been big business here. Every year billions of dollars are spent on the sexual favors of prostitutes. The number of prostitutes has been estimated to range from 84,000 to 336,000 (Potterat et al., 1990). Despite the threat of AIDS, the sex business continues to grow. In New York City, the prostitution capital of the United States, the selling of sex through escort services (which supply prostitutes to customers' hotel rooms, homes, or offices) has multiplied over 400 percent in the last 10 years (Janus and Janus, 1993). Three theories may explain why prostitution exists or why some women become prostitutes.

Functionalist Theory

For thousands of years there have been attempts in various societies to eradicate prostitution and yet it continues to exist. Why? The answer, according to functionalist Kingsley Davis (1971), is that prostitution serves an important function for society by,

ironically, strengthening its moral system. More specifically, prostitution is said to "protect the family and keep the wives and daughters of the respectable citizenry [morally] pure." Given the availability of prostitutes, men will likely go to them rather than persuade or pressure respectable women to engage in premarital sex, extramarital sex, anal intercourse, or kinky sex—namely, what society considers "immoral" sex. If multitudes of conventional women, who make up half of the nation's population, are not involved in these sexual "immoralities," the level of the society's sexual morality will be high.

There is some evidence to support the theory. The level of premarital and other "immoral" sex seems lower in many traditional non-Western societies where prostitution flourishes—than in modern Western societies where there is less prostitution. According to feminists, however, there is a problem with functionalist theory. It defines the moral system in sexist terms, implying that only women are immoral for engaging in the same sex act as men.

Conflict Theory

To conflict theorists, prostitution reflects the exploitation of a group by a more powerful group. More specifically, as feminists would say, prostitution reinforces the patriarchal system of male dominance over women. In selling their bodies as a commodity, prostitutes effectively remind people that men can buy or use women as an object (Miller, 1991; Overall, 1992).

At the same time, the patriarchal system encourages prostitution by creating demand and supply for it. On the demand side, boys are socialized to be dominant over girls, and to desire, as adults, sexual domination of women by patronizing prostitutes. If a young man does not want to visit a prostitute, his peers will pressure him to do so. On the supply side, girls are socialized to be submissive to boys and, later as adults, to men in work, play, or sex. In addition, women are relegated to the "job ghetto"—low-status employment, including prostitution. All this explains why prostitution usually prevails in traditional societies marked by great gender inequality.

By emphasizing the power of patriarchy, feminists assume that there is no free choice in becoming a prostitute. But leaders of the prostitutes' rights movement disagree, arguing that prostitution is no different from other jobs held by straight women, such as cooking, nursing, or child care. If these straight women, who are just as exploited by men as are prostitutes, can be said to have freely chosen their jobs, so can prostitutes (Jenness, 1993).

Symbolic Interactionist Perspective

The functionalist and conflict theories are designed to explain why prostitution exists as a social phenomenon. The symbolic interactionist theory explains why some individuals become prostitutes while others do not.

Emphasizing the influence of personal perception as well as social interaction on human behavior, symbolic interactionists may argue that some women are likely to become prostitutes for three reasons. First, the women see prostitution as a job better than any other that they can get. Second, they define sexual intercourse with strange men as a commercial transaction, not an intimate involvement. And third, they are led into prostitution through interaction with people such as pimps, prostitutes, or men who offer to pay for sex. There is some evidence to support those three points (Thio, 1995).

The most intriguing is the sociological implication of the finding that most prostitutes have been abused by their fathers. Psychologists generally assume that the abuse has made the prostitutes abnormal. But to sociologists, most prostitutes are *normal* for being able to detach themselves emotionally from sex with strange men. Though an abnormal form of socialization, parental abuse in effect teaches the young victim *not* to feel affectionate toward her abusive father. This emotional detachment can carry over into prostitution, where the woman does *not abnormally* feel affectionate toward her customer. That's why many prostitutes *normally* feel contempt for their customers as they do for their fathers. There is no definitive study, though, to determine how common is the impact of child abuse on the victim's ability to define commercial sex for what it is—impersonal rather than personal.

Question for Discussion and Review

1. How do the theories derived from the three sociological perspectives differ in explaining prostitution?

CHAPTER REVIEW

1. *What is the sociological nature of sex?* Human sexuality is a product of socialization under the influence of social and cultural forces, as suggested by the variations in sexual behavior between and within societies.

2. *Why is the incest taboo universal?* Because, according to biological theories, revulsion against incest is instinctive, inbreeding causes physical and mental weaknesses in offspring, and negative imprinting results from childhood familiarity. But to sociologists the incest taboo exists because it has been necessary for securing interfamily cooperation and keeping the family intact.

3. *What are the popular myths about sex?* In the United States, people start having sex at a very young age. Too many married persons are unfaithful. It is easy to identify homosexuals by their appearance or gestures. Most people, particularly the unattached, have a lot of sex with a wide variety of partners. Many people are homosexual. All sexually active people are very likely to get AIDS, and the disease will spread inexorably throughout the United States.

4. *How do people in the United States conduct themselves sexually?* They do not have a very active sex life but are highly satisfied with what they do have. They are overwhelmingly monogamous. They greatly prefer vaginal intercourse over other sex acts. Only about two percent of the U.S. population identify themselves as gay. AIDS is unlikely to spread widely throughout the United States because most sex is monogamous.

5. *How has the sexual attitude changed?* There is more tolerance for various forms of sexual behavior. The double standard has weakened. Increasing numbers of teenagers have remained virgins in the 1990s. There is more interest in using sex for recreation. Support has risen for the new ethic that emphasizes the importance of love in sex.   *What is the battle over abortion about?* Abortion-rights advocates want women's rights protected but abortion opponents want to protect the unborn.

6. *Why does one society allow premarital sex while another does not?* Male dominance or societal complexity has been linked to sexual restrictiveness; their

absence, to permissiveness. *What is the nature of premarital sex in the United States?* Most premarital sex involves some commitment between sex partners. *How is marital sex today compared with that in the past?* The volume and variety of marital sex have increased, while a vast majority of people are very or extremely satisfied. *What is extramarital sex like?* It is far from gratifying because it is carried out in secret and charged with tension.

7. *What are some of the myths about homosexuals?* Gays are typically effeminate and lesbians masculine. Homosexuals like to molest children. Most people are either completely gay or completely straight. *How do various theories explain homosexuality?* Biological theories attribute homosexuality to hormonal imbalance, genetic inheritance, and small hypothalamus. Psychiatric theories explain homosexuality as the result of abnormal parent-child relationships. Sociological theories regard homosexuality as the product of socialization. *What is the nature of homophobia in the United States?* The feelings toward gays are ambivalent, rejecting gay lifestyle but supporting gays' civil rights.

8. *How common is rape in the United States?* Rape is very common. About 22 percent of women, or 15 million, have been forced to have sex. Most of these rapes are committed by lovers and other intimates rather than strangers. *What is the culture of rape?* It encourages men to rape women by treating women as if they were men's property, as if they were the trophies of men's masculinity contests, and as if they want to be raped.

9. *How do the three sociological perspectives explain prostitution?* To functionalist Kingsley Davis, prostitution exists because it serves a very useful function by keeping the level of sex moralities high. To conflict theory, prostitution reinforces the patriarchal system of male dominance over women. And to symbolic interactionists, entry into prostitution depends on three factors: perceiving prostitution as better than other available jobs, defining sex with strange men as purely business, and interacting with others such as pimps and prostitutes.

KEY TERMS

Double standard The social norm that allows males, but not females, to have certain sexual experiences (p. 202).

Extramarital sex Having sex with a person who is not one's spouse, popularly called adultery or infidelity (p. 206).

Homophobia Prejudice and discrimination against homosexuals (p. 209).

Incest taboo The social norm that strongly prohibits sexual relations between close relatives (p. 198).

Negative imprinting A biological mechanism that suppresses erotic feelings for individuals with whom one has been familiar since early childhood (p. 198).

Premarital sex Sex before marriage (p. 205).

Prostitution The exchange of sex for money (p. 213).

Rape Basically coercive sex, involving the use of force to get someone to do something sexual against their will (p. 210).

Sex drive A biological potential for, rather than a determinant of, sexual desire or action (p. 196).

Sex instinct An innate biological mechanism that causes its carrier to have sex in a certain way and at a certain time only (p. 196).

SUGGESTED READINGS

Blumenfeld, Warren J., and Diane Raymond. 1993. *Looking at Gay and Lesbian Life.* Boston: Beacon. Discusses many different issues about homosexuality, including gay sex, causes of homosexuality, homophobia, gay rights movement, and AIDS.

Janus, Samuel S., and Cynthia L. Janus. 1993. *The Janus Report on Sexual Behavior.* New York: John Wiley & Sons. Analyzes various forms of sexual behavior, including the very deviant and not so deviant sex acts.

Michael, Robert T., John H. Gagnon, Edward O. Laumann, and Gina Kolata. 1994. *Sex in America: A Definitive Survey.* Boston: Little, Brown. The first sex survey that is based on a randomly selected, representative sample of U.S. adults, exploding many widely held beliefs about sexuality.

Reinisch, June M. 1990. *The Kinsey Institute New Report on Sex: What You Must Know to Be Sexually Literate.* New York: St. Martin's. A comprehensive, authoritative source of information about sex.

Rubin, Lillian B. 1990. *Erotic Wars: What Happened to the Sexual Revolution?* New York: Farrar, Straus & Giroux. An insightful analysis of how the sexual revolution has influenced people between ages 13 and 48 in the United States.

10

STRATIFICATION AND CLASS

CHAPTER OUTLINE

Myths & Realities

MYTH: *As the world's leading democratic society, the United States has the most equal distribution of income.*
REALITY: While the U.S. income distribution is more equal than that of developing countries, it is less so than most other industrial nations, such as Japan, Sweden, and Germany.

MYTH: *Given the great diversity in the U.S. population, various groups are bound to disagree on whether a particular occupation is desirable or not.*
REALITY: Virtually all groups, rich or poor, rate occupations in the same way. Even people in other countries evaluate occupations in the same way.

MYTH: *Most of the poor people in the United States are on welfare.*
REALITY: Only about one-third of the poor are on welfare.

MYTH: *As many rags-to-riches stories in the media show, it is not uncommon for a poor man's child to become a millionaire in this land of opportunity.*
REALITY: It *is* uncommon for a poor person in the United States to become a millionaire. The success experienced by many involves moving only a little way up the economic ladder.

obert Swanson was already relatively rich 10 years ago, but since then he has became even richer. A decade ago, when he founded a semi-conductor firm, he paid himself $125,000 in salary. Today, the 53-year-old California entrepreneur earns $360,000 a year, and his net worth has soared to $15 million. He revels in being a very rich man, often riding around in a 1992 Porsche. By contrast, Mary Huntley found the 1980s a time of stagnation rather than success. In 1982, the 41-year-old medical technologist from Fort Wayne, Indiana, took home $24,000 a year. Today, she makes only $34,000, which, because of inflation, is less than what she earned a decade ago. An avid moviegoer, she has to skip evening shows in favor of half-price matinees. "For me," says Huntley, "50 cents is 50 cents" (Hawkins, 1992).

"Those who have, get." This old saying suggests that in every society some people, like Robert Swanson, get more rewards than others, like Mary Huntley. The specific nature of the rewards may vary from one society to another. The rewards could be in the form of wealth, power, prestige, or whatever is highly valued by the society. All over the world, these rewards are distributed unequally. This patterned inequality is called **social stratification**, the division of society in such a way that some people get more rewards than others.

THE BASES OF STRATIFICATION

Of the many different rewards people can receive in life, sociologists have long identified three as the most important bases of stratification in the United States: wealth, power, and prestige. These three are, respectively, economic, political, and social rewards. They usually go together. If we are rich, we are also likely to have considerable political power and social prestige. But possession of one reward does not guarantee enjoyment of others. Compared with teachers, some garbage collectors may make more money but have less prestige and power.

Wealth

In the last century Karl Marx divided industrial society into two major classes and one minor class: the *bourgeoisie* (capitalists), the *proletariat* (workers), and the *petite bourgeoisie* (small capitalists). Marx differentiated them on the basis of two criteria: whether they own the "means of production"—tools, factories, offices, and stores—and whether they hire others to work for them. Capitalists are those who

own the means of production and hire others. Workers neither own the means of production nor employ others. Hence they are forced to work for capitalists. As for small capitalists, they own the means of production but do most of the work themselves. Examples are shopkeepers, doctors, lawyers, and other self-employed persons. Marx considered these people a minor, transitional class because he believed that they would eventually be forced down into the working class when their means of production are taken over by giant corporations.

In Marx's view, exploitation characterizes the relationship between the two major classes: capitalists and workers. Capitalists, bent on maximizing profit, compel workers to work long hours for little pay. Such exploitation was indeed extreme in Marx's time. Consider his description of child laborers:

> Children of nine or ten years are dragged from their squalid beds at two, three, or four o'clock in the morning and compelled to work for a bare subsistence until ten, eleven, or twelve at night, their limbs wearing away, their frames dwindling, their faces whitening, and their humanity absolutely sinking into a stone-like torpor, utterly horrible to contemplate (Marx, 1866).

Karl Marx believed that capitalists sought to maximize profit by exploiting workers. He had seen the appalling working conditions in factories in the mid-nineteenth century in England, where women and children were employed for long hours at low pay. Conditions in the United States were not much better, as shown here in a famous photograph of child laborers taken by Lewis Hine in the early twentieth century.

Marx believed that eventually workers would rise in revolt and establish a classless society of economic equals. But his prophecy of revolution has not materialized in any highly developed capitalist economy. Writing in the 1860s, Marx failed to foresee that the exploitation of workers would ease and that a large, prosperous class of white-collar workers would emerge as in the United States.

Even so, the United States still suffers from glaring economic inequalities. According to the latest data available, the richest 20 percent of the population earns nearly 45 percent of the nation's total income. In contrast, the poorest 20 percent has only about four percent of the national income (see Figure 10.1). In fact, the U.S. income inequality ranks among the greatest in the industrial world. The ratio of the richest fifth's share of national income to the poorest fifth's is higher in the United States than in most other industrial countries.

Power

Power—the ability to get people to do things they otherwise would not do—is associated with wealth. Most sociologists agree that people with more wealth tend to have more power. This is evident in the domination of top government positions by the wealthy. Higher-income persons are also more likely to feel a strong sense of power. Thus they are more likely to be politically active, working to retain or increase their power. Meanwhile, lower-income people are more likely to feel powerless to influence major political decisions. They are therefore more indifferent to politics and less likely to participate in political activity—a reaction likely to exacerbate their lack of power.

It is clear that power is distributed unequally. To what extent? A lot? A little? Power cannot be identi-

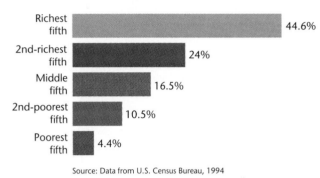

Share of nation's income

Source: Data from U.S. Census Bureau, 1994

FIGURE 10.1
Unequal Income Distribution in the United States

fied and measured as easily as wealth because people with power do not always express it. As a result, sociologists disagree about how it is distributed.

Both Marxist and elite theorists argue that a very small group of people holds most of the power in the United States. According to *Marxist theorists,* that group consists of capitalists. Even if they do not hold office, say Marxists, capitalists set the limits of political debate and of the government's actions, protecting their own interests. This is why large corporations, through heavy political campaign contributions and congressional lobbying, are able to hold down their taxes and avoid regulation. According to *elite theorists,* a great amount of power resides in the **power elite**, a small group of individuals who hold top positions in the federal government, military, and corporations and have similar backgrounds, values, and interests.

In contrast to both Marxist and elite theorists, *pluralist theorists* argue that power is not tightly concentrated, but widely dispersed—more or less equally distributed among various competing groups. The power of big business, for example, is balanced by that of big labor, and government actions are ultimately determined by competition and compromise among such diverse groups. Even ordinary citizens have the power to vote anyone into office or out of it.

In short, while Marxists and elitists see a great deal of inequality in power distribution, pluralists see very little. Both views may be correct. Most of the power in U.S. society is concentrated at the top, but the elite is not all-powerful. It is subject to challenge by voters from below. It is true that the general public is usually powerless—because it does not get organized. But occasionally, when people feel strongly enough about an issue to make their wishes known, as they did in opposition to the Vietnam War in the 1960s, the government does change policy to follow public opinion.

Prestige

A third basis of social stratification is the unequal distribution of prestige. Following Max Weber, sociologists call this kind of stratification a **status system,** a system in which people are stratified according to their social prestige.

There is a difference between prestige, on the one hand, and wealth and power, on the other. Wealth and power are objective entities: an individual can have them regardless of what other people think of the individual. But prestige is subjective, depending

on how the individual is perceived by others. If the individual is rich and powerful but is seen by others as unworthy of respect, the individual has low prestige. The boss of an organized crime syndicate may make millions and exercise awesome power, but he might never acquire prestige because most people refuse to hold him in esteem—and they cannot be forced to do so. On the other hand, many college professors may not be rich and powerful, but they do enjoy more prestige than the crime boss. Why the difference? The answer has much to do with occupation.

For many years, sociologists have found that people have very definite ideas about the prestige of various occupations. In 1947 a team of sociologists asked a large random sample of the U.S. population to evaluate 90 occupations on a scale from "excellent" to "poor." Since then, similar surveys have been periodically taken on different representative samples. The result has always been the same: occupations that require more *education* and offer higher *income* than others are generally given higher prestige scores (see Figure 10.2). Almost everybody, rich or poor, has rated the occupations in the same way.

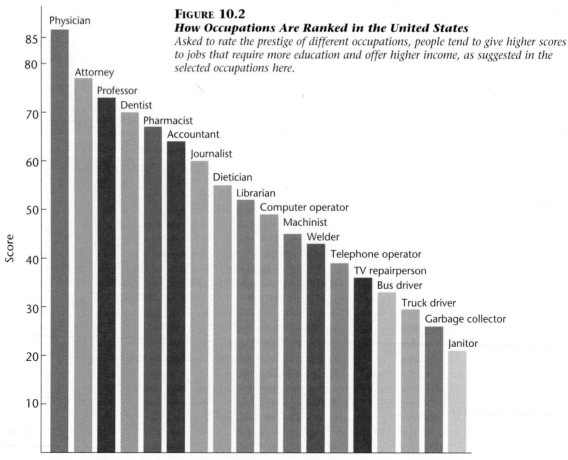

FIGURE 10.2
How Occupations Are Ranked in the United States
Asked to rate the prestige of different occupations, people tend to give higher scores to jobs that require more education and offer higher income, as suggested in the selected occupations here.

Source: Data from NORC, *General Social Surveys, 1972–1994*, pp. 881–889.

Even people in many other countries—some industrialized and some not—have been found to rank occupations in the same way (Hodge, Siegel, and Rossi, 1964; Treiman, 1977).

Occupation is only one of a person's many statuses, among those based on age, race, and gender. These statuses may create **status inconsistency**, the condition in which the same individual is given different rankings, such as being high in occupation but low in ethnicity. An African American lawyer or a female executive, for example, have high occupational status, but they may have less prestige because of prejudice against their race or gender. People plagued with status inconsistency usually experience considerable stress. They resent the source of their status inconsistency. They think of themselves in terms of their higher status and expect others to do the same. But others may treat them in reference to their lower status. Consequently, people with status inconsistency are likely to support liberal and radical movements designed to change the status quo.

Questions for Discussion and Review

1. What is social stratification?
2. How are economic rewards distributed in the United States?
3. In what ways is the power basis of stratification different from the system of prestige?

Status inconsistency is the condition in which the individual is given a different ranking in various social categories, such as a high ranking due to occupation but a low ranking because of prejudice against one's race. An African American lawyer may experience status inconsistency.

STRATIFICATION SYSTEMS: A GLOBAL VIEW

Stratification exists around the globe, but differs in form from one society to another.

The Egalitarian System

The least stratified of societies are those where social inequality is minimal. As has been discussed in Chapter 4 (Society), hunting-gathering societies are the most egalitarian. Still, they are not totally free of inequalities. Men and adults enjoy higher status than women and children. Shamans (comparable to priests) and better hunters are held in higher esteem than others. But such inequalities pale in significance when compared with those in most other societies.

Hunters-gatherers tend to be egalitarian primarily because there is hardly any opportunity in their small-scale environment for anyone to accumulate wealth. Similarly, large-scale societies without wealth-accumulating opportunities, such as communist countries, tend to be more egalitarian than capitalist societies. Deprived of those opportunities, segments of the population within a large-scale society, such as peasants, industrial workers, or pastoral laborers, are also more likely than others to practice equality among themselves (Howard, 1993).

The Master-Slave System

In sharp contrast to the egalitarian society is the master-slave system, in which some people are held in servitude as someone else's property. It used to be common in ancient Egypt, Rome, and Athens as well as in the United States. Most of the slaves were poor people, ethnic groups considered inferior, war captives brought home from conquered nations, or foreigners imported for sale. They did most of the manual labor in society. The emergence of slavery has partly been attributed to the great accumulation of wealth in those ancient societies that could produce huge food surpluses with improved technology (Lenski, Lenski, Nolan, 1995).

Today slavery is outlawed in virtually all societies, but it still persists in certain areas. Some of this modern slavery is similar to the ancient form of human bondage called chattel slavery. It exists, for example, in the Northern African country of Mauritania. But most slaves today fall victim to *debt bondage*, which forces whole families to work in fruitless efforts to pay off loans. These debt slaves can be found in parts of India, Pakistan, Thailand, Peru, and

Haiti. This subject will be discussed more in Chapter 11 (Rich and Poor Nations).

The Feudal System

Compared with the master-slave system, the feudal system is less extreme in practicing inequality. It used to be prevalent in the agrarian societies of medieval Europe, Asia, and Latin America. These societies were stratified into two groups: those who worked the land and those who appropriated some of the produce and labor of the other. The first group is called serfs or peasants, and the second, lords or landlords.

The feudal system emerged largely because the collapse of centralized political authority had caused considerable chaos as well as struggles for power among warlords. To survive, various segments of the farming population were compelled to give part of their products to different lords for military protection.

Today the feudal system persists only in a few places in Latin America. In highland Peru, the feudal system, called the *hacienda,* consists of three classes of people: the landlord, the tenant-workers, and the administrators hired by the landlord. To pay for the use of the land, tenant-workers work on the landlord's farm, work as a servant in the landlord's house, do repairs on the landlord's house, or perform other services for the landlord. All this leaves tenant-workers little time to work for themselves. The landlord does pay them some money, but the amount is too small to keep them from falling into deep poverty (Howard, 1993).

In a caste system, people's positions are ascribed—primarily determined by such factors as race, ethnicity, or sex. These positions are also fixed: people must marry within their caste, children are born into their parents' caste, and movement from one caste level to another almost never occurs. The man shown here, an "untouchable" of India's caste system, (which is now breaking down), would likely never become a member of the sports club, nor probably would his children.

The Caste System

The feudal and slave-master systems have one thing in common. Both are similar to the **caste system,** a relatively rigid stratification system in which people's positions are ascribed and fixed. "Being ascribed" means that positions in this hierarchy are primarily determined by ascription, such as one's race, ethnicity, or sex. The positions are also fixed: people must marry within their caste, children are born into their parents' caste, and movement from one caste to another almost never occurs.

A clear-cut example can be found in India, where people are stratified into five castes on the basis of occupation. The highest caste consists of (1) *Brahmins*—priests and scholars—considered the most spiritually pure. These are followed by (2) *warriors,* (3) *merchants,* (4) *artisans* and *menial workers,* and (5)

untouchables, whose work is considered too spiritually unclean. The untouchables are in effect outcasts, and could almost never become members of a higher caste. Members of higher castes fear that they would suffer ritual pollution if they touched an outcast or passed through the shadow of an outcast. Although the caste system still dominates the lives of millions in India, it is breaking down as the society is becoming increasingly industrialized.

The Indian caste system is associated with *religion*—the Hindu belief that people's castes reflect the moral quality of their actions in a previous life, namely, the worse the actions, the lower the castes. But until recently the caste system in South Africa has been based on *race.* Black, white, and "colored" groups were rigidly segregated by law as well as custom. In many other societies, a caste system exists to some degree because people are treated unjustly on the basis of not only their race but their sex, as will be discussed in Chapters 12 (Race and Ethnicity) and 13 (Women and Men).

The Class System

Less rigidly segregated than the caste system is the **class system**, a relatively open stratification system in which people's positions are achieved and changeable. Since achieved characteristics such as education and skill can change, people can be socially mobile— moving from one position to another. The class system is the primary form of stratification in virtually all societies around the globe. But the inequality between classes varies in degree from one society to another.

The amount of social inequality in a society depends on its economic development. More precisely, a curvilinear, inverted-U relationship exists between development and inequality. As a country develops, inequality initially increases, then peaks, levels off, and finally declines (see Figure 10.3). This changing relationship between development and inequality is known as the **Kuznets curve**, named after its discoverer Simon Kuznets.

As preindustrial societies develop, economic surplus increases to make available the opportunity for some groups to accumulate wealth more than others, which spurs increases in social inequality. When

In a developing country, such as those in Asia that are in the process of transforming from agricultural to industrial, economic productivity and population growth surge, pushing inequality to the peak. Only when societies begin to become predominantly industrial does inequality begin to decrease.

these societies are in the midst of a transformation from agricultural to industrial, economic productivity and population growth surge, pushing inequality to the peak. Only when societies begin to become predominantly industrial does inequality start to decrease. Reasons include educational expansion and political democracy. As more people are educated, pressure for democracy increases, causing inequality to diminish.

However, since 1970, there have been signs of a resurgence of inequality in many industrial societies, including the United States, Canada, Sweden, Australia, and Germany. Contributing factors include increases in global competition, the shift from a manufacturing to a service economy, the decline of unionization, and increases in female-headed households, all of which have caused the masses to fall farther behind the rich (Nielsen, 1994; Morris, Bernhardt, and Handcock, 1994).

Questions for Discussion and Review

1. Why are hunters-gatherers and other groups relatively egalitarian?
2. How do the master-slave and feudal systems differ?
3. What are the differences between the caste and class systems?
4. What is the Kuznets curve?

FIGURE 10.3
The Kuznets Curve

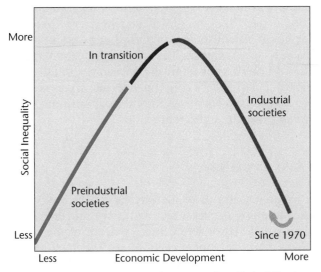

Source: Data from Francois Nielson, "Income Inequality and Industrial Development: Dualism Revisited," *American Sociological Review*, 59 (October 1994), pp. 654– 677.

THE U.S. CLASS STRUCTURE

The inequality in the United States can be observed in the way the society is divided into different social classes, forming a distinctive class structure.

Identifying Classes

Sociologists have long defined **social class** as a category of people who have about the same amount of income, power, and prestige. But how do we know who is in which class? There are three different methods for identifying a person's class.

Reputational Method   One way of finding out which classes people belong in is through using the **reputational method**, identifying social classes by selecting a group of people and asking them to rank others. These selected individuals, or informants, typically have been living in the community for a long time and can rank many other residents on the basis of their reputation. If these "judges" are asked to rank a man whom they know to be a public drunk, they would put him in a lower-class category. If they are asked to rank a woman whom they know as a respectable banker, they would place her in an upper-class category.

The reputational method is useful for investigating the class structure of a small community where everybody knows practically everybody else. But it has several disadvantages. First, the reputational method cannot be applied to large cities because it is impossible to find individuals who know thousands of other people. Second, it is impossible to generalize the findings from one community to another because the informants can judge only their own community. Third, it is impossible to find unanimity among the reputation judges in a community. There are always cases in which an individual is considered upper class by one judge but lower class by another.

Subjective Method   To find out the class structure of a large population, we can use the **subjective method**, identifying social classes by asking people to rank themselves.

In using this method, sociologists have long discovered that, if asked whether they are upper, middle, or lower class, the overwhelming majority of people will identify themselves as middle class. Both "upper class" and "lower class" have connotations offensive to democratic values. To call oneself upper class is to appear snobbish. To call oneself lower class is demeaning. As a result, many millionaires would call themselves middle rather than upper class; meanwhile, many low-income people such as maids and laborers would also regard themselves as middle class. But, if given "working class" as a fourth choice, many people will identify themselves as working class rather than as middle class.

Thus, the weakness of the subjective method is twofold. The result depends heavily on how the question is asked, and respondents may lie about their social class. Despite these problems, the subjective method has at least two advantages. First, it can be used to investigate large cities or even an entire society. Second, it is useful for understanding and predicting behaviors that are strongly affected by attitudes. If self-employed auto mechanics, electricians, and plumbers identify themselves with the upper class, they can be expected to hold politically conservative views and to vote Republican, just as upper-class people tend to do.

Objective Method   Both subjective and reputational methods rely on people's perception of class. The third method depends on objective criteria, such as how much people earn annually. The **objective method** involves identifying social classes by using occupation, income, and education to rank people.

Like the subjective method, the objective method is useful for identifying the classes of a large population. It has another advantage as well: sociologists can easily obtain the needed data on occupation, income, and education from the Bureau of the Census or by mailing questionnaires to the people themselves.

The objective method has at least one disadvantage, though. In using objective criteria such as income and education, we can distinguish clearly between the top and the bottom of the class ladder, but it is difficult to differentiate the huge number of people near the middle. Researchers are therefore forced to establish an *arbitrary* boundary between classes—say, choosing 12 years of education rather than 11 or 13 to distinguish between the middle and working classes. As a consequence, many people who are said to be *middle* class in one study turn out to be *working* class in a different study.

Class Profiles

The three methods of identifying classes have been used in many studies with roughly the same result: in the United States, about 3 to 5 percent of the population are in the upper class, 40 to 50 percent in the middle class, 30 to 40 percent in the working class, and 15 to 20 percent in the poor, lower class. Sociologists disagree about the precise boundaries of these classes, but most accept these broad estimates of their sizes.

 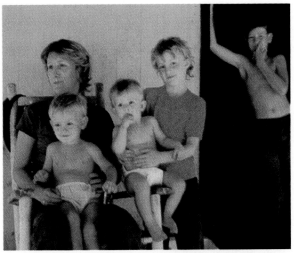

Left: In the middle class, people are distinguished from those above them (the upper class) primarily by their lesser wealth and power, and from those below them (the working class) by their white-collar, nonmanual jobs. Right: The lower class—including the chronically unemployed, welfare recipients, and the impoverished aged—is characterized by joblessness and poverty. A new lower class has emerged in recent decades: workers skilled in mechanized industry who have become unskilled workers in electronically run factories. But many are now unemployed and poor.

The Upper Class   Though it is a mere three to five percent of the population, the upper class possesses at least 25 percent of the nation's wealth. This class has two segments: upper-upper and lower-upper. Basically, the upper-upper class is the "old rich"—families that have been wealthy for several generations—an aristocracy of birth and wealth. Their names are in the *Social Register,* a listing of acceptable members of high society. A few are known across the nation, such as the Rockefellers, Roosevelts, and Vanderbilts. Most are not visible to the general public. They live in grand seclusion, drawing their income from the investment of their inherited wealth. In contrast, the lower-upper class is the "new rich." Although they may be wealthier than some of the old rich, the new rich have hustled to make their money like everybody else beneath their class. Thus, their prestige is generally lower than that of the old rich. The old rich, who have not found it necessary to lift a finger to make their money, tend to look down on the new rich.

However its wealth is acquired, the upper class is very, very rich. They have enough money and leisure time to cultivate an interest in the arts and to collect rare books, paintings, and sculpture. They generally live in exclusive areas, belong to exclusive social clubs, rub elbows with one another, and marry their own kind—all of which keeps them so aloof from the masses that they have been called the *out-of-sight class* (Fussell, 1992). More than any other class, they tend to be conscious of being members of a class.

They also command an enormous amount of power and influence in government and business, affecting the lives of millions.

The Middle Class   The middle class is not as tightly knit as the upper class. Middle-class people are distinguished from those above them primarily by their lesser wealth and power, and from those below them by their white-collar, nonmanual jobs.

This class can be differentiated into two strata by occupational prestige, income, and education. The *upper-middle class* consists mostly of professional and business people with high income and education, such as doctors, lawyers, and corporate executives. The *lower-middle class* is far larger in size and much more diverse in occupation. It is made up of people in relatively low-level but still white-collar occupations, such as small-business owners, store and traveling salespersons, managers, technicians, teachers, and secretaries. Though having less income and education than the upper-middle class, the lower-middle class has achieved the middle-class dream of owning a suburban home and living a comfortable life.

The Working Class   The working class consists primarily of those who have little education and whose jobs are manual and carry little prestige. Some working-class people, such as construction workers, carpenters, and plumbers, are skilled workers and may make more money than those in the lower reaches of the middle class, such as secretaries and teachers. But their jobs are more physically demanding and, especially in the case of factory workers, more dangerous. Other working-class people are unskilled, such as migrant workers, janitors, and dishwashers. There are also many women in this class working as domestics, cleaning ladies, and waitresses, and they are the sole breadwinners in their households. Because they are generally underpaid, they are often called the *working poor*.

The Lower Class This class is characterized by joblessness and poverty. It includes the chronically unemployed, the welfare recipients, and the impoverished aged. These people suffer the indignity of living in run-down houses, wearing old clothes, eating cheap food, and lacking proper medical care. Very few have finished high school. They may have started out in their youth with poorly paying jobs that required little or no skill, but their earning power began to drop when they reached their late twenties. A new lower class has emerged in recent decades: skilled workers in mechanized industry who have become unskilled workers in electronically run factories. They have first become helpers, then occasional workers, and finally the hard-core unemployed. Most members of the lower class are merely poor. But they are often stigmatized as "the underclass," a term conjuring up images of poor people as violent criminals, drug abusers, welfare mothers who cannot stop having babies, or able-bodied men on welfare who are too lazy to work.

The Influence of Class

One of the most consistent findings in sociology is that people in different classes live differently. In fact, the influence of class is so great and pervasive that it is taken into account in nearly every sociological study. This is why we have discussed, for example, the impact of class on childhood socialization, mental illness, and sexual behavior in previous chapters. We will also examine class differences in religion, politics, and other human behaviors in later chapters. Here we focus on how social class affects life chances and lifestyles.

Life Chances Obviously, the rich have better houses, food, and clothes than the middle class, who, in turn, live in more comfortable conditions than the poor. The upper classes can also devote more money, and often more time, to nonessentials like giving lavish parties; some rich people even spend more money on their pets than most people earn from their jobs. Their choices are often wider, their oppor-

tunities greater, than those of the lower classes. In other words, the upper classes have better **life chances**—the likelihood of living a good, long, or successful life in a society.

We can see the impact of class on life chances in the *Titanic* tragedy, which took 1,500 lives in 1912. On the night when the ship sank into the Atlantic Ocean, social class was a major determinant of who survived and who died. Among the females on board, three percent of the first-class passengers drowned, compared with 16 percent of the second-class and 45 percent of the third-class passengers. All passengers in first class had been given the opportunity to abandon ship, but those in the third class had been ordered to stay below deck, some of them at the point of a gun (Lord, 1981; Hall, 1986).

Less dramatic but just as grim is the common finding in many studies that people in the lower classes generally live shorter and less healthy lives than those above them in the social hierarchy. An infant born into a poor family is much more likely to die during its first year than an infant born into a nonpoor family. For adults, too, mortality rates are higher among men and women of the lower classes than among those of the higher classes. People of the lower classes are also more likely to die from syphilis, tuberculosis, stomach ulcers, diabetes, influenza, and many other diseases (Gilbert and Kahl, 1993).

Lifestyles Lifestyles—tastes, preferences, and ways of living—may appear trivial in comparison to life chances. But studying lifestyle differences among people also shows the importance of social class in our lives. Let us see how class shapes lifestyles.

Upper- and middle-class people are likely to be active outside their homes—in parent-teacher associations, charitable organizations, and various community activities. They are also likely to make friends with professional colleagues or business contacts, with their spouses helping to cultivate the friendship. In fact, they tend to combine their social and business lives so much that friendships are no longer a personal matter but are used to promote careers. In contrast, working-class people tend to restrict their social life to families and relatives. Rarely do they entertain or visit their friends from work. Although male factory workers may "stop off for a beer with the guys" after work, the guys are seldom invited home. Many working-class men and women are also quite reluctant to form close ties with neighbors. Instead, they often visit their parents, siblings, and other relatives, which has prompted Lillian Rubin (1976) to describe the extended family as "the heart of working-class social life." Some observers believe that this kin-oriented sociability arises because working-class people feel less secure in social interactions, fearing or distrusting the outside world (Gilbert and Kahl, 1993).

People in different classes also tend to prefer different magazines, newspapers, books, television programs, and movies. Whereas the working class and lower-middle class are more likely to read the *National Enquirer* and watch soap operas or professional wrestling, the upper-middle class is more likely to read *Time* and *Newsweek* and watch public television programs. The upper class does not go for TV viewing at all. When the richest 400 persons were asked what they thought about TV's evening entertainment offerings, their typical responses were condescending: "very mediocre," "99 percent hogwash," "juvenile, boring and insulting" (Hacker, 1983). More generally, compared with higher classes, working-class people read less; attend fewer concerts, lectures, and theaters; participate less in adult education; and spend less on recreation and are more likely to watch television, work on their cars, take car rides, play cards, and visit taverns.

Questions for Discussion and Review

1. What methods can be used to study social class, and what are their strengths and weaknesses?
2. What are the distinguishing features of various social classes in the United States?
3. How does social class influence life chances and lifestyles?

POVERTY

Consider the case of a single mother with three children. Suppose she earns $15,000. Is she poor? The government says no, because her income is above the official poverty line of $14,763 for a family of four. But critics would say that the woman is definitely poor. Who is right depends on which definition one chooses to accept.

What Is Poverty?

To determine the number of poor people, the U.S. government first defines poverty as the lack of minimum food and shelter necessary for maintaining life, which sociologists call **absolute poverty.** The government then decides what income is needed to sustain that minimum standard of living and sees how many people fall below it. This method of determining poverty originates from the research that Mollie Orshanksy did for the Social Security Administration in the early 1960s. Because she found that the average family then spent a *third* of its income on food, she determined the poverty line by multiplying the cost of the Agriculture Department's cheapest recommended food plan by *three.* Her resulting figures, which varied with family size, were officially adopted in 1969. Since then, those figures have been simply raised every year to take inflation into account. Thus, for 1993, the "poverty line" for a four-person family was $14,763, and 15.1 percent of the population—over 39 million of the U.S. population—were considered poor (see Figure 10.4).

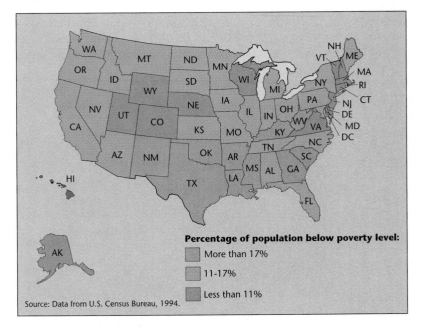

Percentage of population below poverty level:

More than 17%

11-17%

Less than 11%

Source: Data from U.S. Census Bureau, 1994.

FIGURE 10.4
The U.S. Poverty Rate
According to the federal government's definition of poverty, about 15 percent of the U.S. population in 1993 were poor. The poverty rate, however, varied from one state to another, with many southern states having higher rates than the national average.

Those figures have stirred a controversy. Conservative critics argue that the figures overestimate the extent of poverty because they do not count as income many noncash benefits, such as food stamps, housing subsidies, and medical assistance, which the poor receive from the government. These noncash benefits account for two-thirds of government programs for the poor. If these benefits were added to cash incomes, many "poor" people would rise above the poverty line—and hence no longer be poor.

Liberal critics, on the other hand, contend that the official rate *underestimates* the extent of poverty because it is based on the outdated assumption that the average U.S. family today spends a third of its income on food, as it did more than 30 years ago. Actually, it now spends only a fifth of its income on food, largely because of increases in the cost of housing and child care. In other words, the family today needs a much higher income than the family of 30 years ago in order to stay out of poverty. Failing to take this into account, the government excludes from its poverty statistics many families that are actually poor. The poverty rate is not only reported as lower than it actually is, it is even reported as *lower* for today than 30 years ago, flying in the face of

today's lower standard of living and higher incidence of homelessness.

Poverty can also be found more prevalent than officially reported, if it is defined in terms of how people live relative to—in comparison with—the majority of the population. According to a widely accepted relative definition of poverty, those who earn less than half of the nation's median income are poor because they lack what is needed by most people to live a decent life. By this definition, for more than 30 years the percentage of the nation living in poverty has been much higher than what has been reported by the government. These poor people are said to live in **relative poverty,** a state of deprivation resulting from having less than what the majority of the people have. The psychological impact of relative poverty seems far greater in the United States than in other countries. In many developing countries, the poor may not find themselves too bad off because most people around them are just as poor. But it is tougher to be poor in a sea of affluence, such as the United States, where many people blame the poor for their poverty, stereotyping them as lazy. In a poll taken by New York Times/CBS News (1994), for example, more people attributed poverty to "lack of effort" than to "circumstances beyond one's control."

Feminization of Poverty

Poverty affects women more than men, creating a social phenomenon that sociologists call the **feminization of poverty,** a huge number of women bearing the burden of poverty, mostly as single mothers or heads of families. Compared with other industrial nations, the United States has the largest gender gap in poverty (see Figure 10.5). The reason is that U.S. women are much more likely than their for-

Absolute poverty is the lack of minimum food and shelter necessary for maintaining life. Poverty can also be relative: a state of deprivation resulting from having less than what the majority has. Poor people find their poverty all the more disheartening when they see the vivid contrast between their lives and the lives of the wealthy.

FIGURE 10.5
Gender Gap in Poverty: A Global View

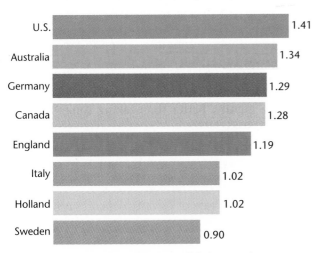

Ratio of women's to men's poverty rate*

U.S.	1.41
Australia	1.34
Germany	1.29
Canada	1.28
England	1.19
Italy	1.02
Holland	1.02
Sweden	0.90

*If a ratio exceeds 1, women are more likely than men to be poor. 1.41, for example, means that women are 41% more likely than men to be poor.

Source: Data from Lynne M. Casper, Sara S. McLanahan, Irwin Garfinkel, "The Gender-Poverty Gap: What We Can Learn from Other Countries," *American Sociological Review*, Vol. 59 (August 1994), p. 597.

eign counterparts to be both unemployed and heads of families with children (Casper, McLanahan, and Garfinkel, 1994). In fact, single mothers constitute the largest proportion of the poor adult population in the United States. In 1993, about 46 percent of single-mother families were poor, compared with only seven percent of two-parent families (Census Bureau, 1994). Thus, the feminization of poverty mostly involves poor women maintaining a household.

The problem can be attributed to several changes in U.S. society. Increases in divorce, separation, and out-of-wedlock birth have caused a growing number of women to become heads of poor households. The increase in divorced fathers not paying child support, along with reduction in government support for welfare, has caused many more female-headed households to fall below the poverty line. Living longer than men has further contributed to a growing number of elderly women living in poverty alone.

But most important, according to feminists, women as a group are more vulnerable than men to poverty because of the sexist and patriarchal nature of the society. Unlike men, who often can escape poverty by getting a job, women tend to remain poor even when being employed. This is because in the gender-segregated labor market, women are much more likely to work in low-paid, low-status jobs. By socializing women to become wives and mothers, the patriarchal society further discourages them from developing educational and occupational skills. This is likely to cause poverty among divorced women or widows, even those from relatively affluent families (Gimenez, 1990; Pearce, 1993). What about poverty in general?

Causes of Poverty

There are two kinds of theories about general poverty. One essentially blames the poor for their poverty. The other is sociological in nature.

"Blame the Poor" Theories   These are based on the assumption that there are plenty of opportunities for making it in the United States. Therefore, the poor are believed to have failed to grab the opportunities by not working hard. Attempts have long been made to find the source of this self-defeating behavior. Political scientist Edward Banfield (1974) claimed to have found it in the present-oriented outlook among the poor. They were said to live for the moment, unconcerned for the future. Earlier, anthropologist Oscar Lewis (1961) had found about the same lifestyle among the poor families that he studied. He found that the poor were fatalists, resigning themselves to being poor and seeing no way out of their poverty. They were said to have developed a "culture of poverty," characterized by a series of debilitating values and attitudes, such as a sense of hopelessness and passivity, low aspirations, feelings of powerlessness and inferiority, and present-time orientation. According to Lewis, this culture of poverty is passed on from one generation to another. All this, then, was assumed to discourage the poor from working hard, which, in turn, continues to keep them poor.

But there are holes in the blame-the-poor theories. For one thing, the poor are not necessarily averse to working hard. They are likely to work hard if given the opportunity. But the problem is that, even if they have the opportunity, they are likely to remain poor because of low wages. In fact, the "working poor" account for 40 percent of those who fall below the poverty line. Also, in fully 60 percent of all poor families, at least one person works (Roberts, 1993). Another flaw in the blame-the-poor explanation is that it confuses cause and effect. The self-defeating values that Banfield and Lewis found among the poor may well be the effect, not the cause, of poverty.

Sociological Theories   According to a functionalist theory, society creates and maintains poverty because benefits can be derived from it. Poverty is assumed to

Functionalist

perform some positive functions for society, such as the following:

1. Poverty makes it possible for society's "dirty work" to be done. Most people would stay away from many boring, underpaid, or unpleasant jobs such as washing dishes, scrubbing floors, and hauling garbage. Poor people are compelled to take such jobs because they cannot find better ones.
2. By working as maids and servants, poor people make it easier for the affluent to pursue their business and professional careers.
3. Poverty creates jobs for social workers and other professionals who serve the poor. It also produces jobs for police and other law enforcers who protect others from the poor (Gans, 1971).

But this functionalist theory still cannot explain how society has created poverty in the first place. Such an explanation can be found in conflict theory. It suggests that the inegalitarian nature of society makes inevitable the unequal distribution of economic opportunities, with the poor getting the short end of the stick. Receiving few or no opportunities, the poor are bound to be poor and to remain so.

Why Poor Become Poorer   In recent years the poor have gotten *poorer,* particularly in big cities. Again, there are two contrasting explanations. One is sociological, attributing the increase in poverty to forces beyond the control of the individual. Over the last 30 years the middle class has largely left the cities for the suburbs, taking much of the tax base with them. Many well-paying, low-skilled jobs in manufacturing industries have also left the cities. As a result, the poor who are left behind jobless have become poorer.

According to another explanation, a new version of the old "blame the victim" theory, poor people have gotten poorer because they do not want to work. There are still many jobs that match their skills, such as working in sweatshops, in fast-food restaurants, and as maids or servants, but poor people today consider these jobs demeaning and prefer to be on welfare instead. Such an attitude is said to scorn the traditional view that almost any honest job, however unpleasant, confers independence and therefore dignity, better than taking something for nothing (Mead, 1992).

Questions for Discussion and Review

1. How does the rate of poverty depend on its definition?
2. What are characteristics and causes of the feminization of poverty?
3. How do different theories explain the causes of poverty?

HOMELESSNESS

No one is sure about the number of homeless in the United States. There are only estimates and they vary widely or wildly. Former President Bush's administration estimated the homeless to be only about 300,000 in the late 1980s, but for the same period the Clinton administration put the estimate at seven mil-

In recent years the poor have gotten poorer, especially in the city. According to the sociological explanation, the increase in poverty is a result largely of forces beyond the control of the individual, such as the middle class leaving the cities for the suburbs, taking much of the tax base with them, and manufacturing plants closing down or leaving the cities, creating joblessness.

lion (Filer, 1990; DeParle, 1994). Generally, conservatives give low estimates, while liberals provide high estimates. But a careful, nonpartisan analysis by sociologist Christopher Jencks (1994) shows the number to be between 300,000 and 400,000.

Who Are the Homeless?

The homeless are among the extremely poor. They are by definition people who sleep in streets, parks, shelters, and places not intended as dwellings, such as bus stations, lobbies, or abandoned buildings.

According to Peter Rossi's (1989) study of the Chicago homeless, most of the subjects are African American men in their middle thirties with an educational attainment largely similar to that of the general population. Most have never married; if they have, their marriage has failed. Most held their last steady job more than four years ago. Although a third of the homeless studied had worked for some time in the previous month, the jobs were only temporary, involving low skills and paying low wages (Rossi, 1989). Other studies have further indicated that only about one-sixth of the homeless are female-headed families with children, one-fourth of the homeless

GLOBAL VILLAGE

Many homeless people in cities around the world beg in order to survive. But this article, written from a British perspective, shows how begging can make life more difficult for the beggars.

The Dysfunctions of Begging

Begging is bad for you. Charity and handouts are no route out of poverty. And those who dole out alms to the needy are doing nothing to help them to deal with their problems. Giving alms to the needy has never changed anything. It may salve the consciences of those who do it, but it does nothing to help those who are the recipients.

Relying on the beneficence of the passing public is at best an unreliable source of income. It rarely does more than provide the price of a cup of tea and a take-away. "Professional" beggars may exist (and some people, in some locations, at some times, may make as much as the average white-collar worker after tax), but the vast majority don't even make ends meet in one of the most demanding and dispiriting activities open to the destitute.

Standing around in all weathers asking for spare change from strangers is more typically resorted to only after all other options have been exhausted. It represents a level of desperation that can only be guessed at by those who have never done it. Ask anyone who has begged for any length of time what it is like. The first week is the worst. The average beggar does not turn to their task resolutely. It's not like the first day at a new job: all those people out there, a sea of alternately hostile, sympathetic, pitying and—most common of all—blank or inattentive faces, is enough to make one recoil. Suddenly, you have become an object on the street. Whereas the destitute

can disappear into the background, once you stick out a hand and mumble for alms you almost become street furniture.

Declaring that you are incapable of supporting yourself is like finally accepting that you are nothing—worthless. It never gets any better. But gradually you begin to adapt, the trauma begins to numb and you find it difficult to remember that once you were a part of the sea of faces from which you are now trying to extract some cash. To survive begging, it is necessary to suppress—in time, actually to forget—almost all your feelings.

Begging destroys whatever self-confidence and sense of well-being survived your fall into the abyss. It keeps you held locked into the generosity and pity of people who temporarily take on your plight. But it changes nothing for you and it changes nothing for the people who give you a handout.

If you are desperate, then receiving handouts can be explained away as maybe making the best of a bad job. But the more you beg, the more unhappy you become. You begin to resent those who dispense their charity to you, and to hate those who do not. You become aggressive—aggression becomes a defense mechanism. And you are definitely going nowhere.

Excerpted from John Byrd, "Beggars Can Be Choosers," *New Statesman and Society*, September 30, 1994, p. 17.

are mentally ill, and one-third are alcohol or drug abusers (Jencks, 1994).

Homelessness is not new. There have always been homeless people in the United States. But the homeless today differ in some ways from their counterparts of the 1950s and 1960s. More than 30 years ago, most of the homeless were old men, only a handful were women, and virtually no families were homeless. Today, as has been suggested, the homeless are younger, and include more women and families with young children. Today's homeless are also more visible to the general public because they are much more likely to sleep on the streets or in other public places in great numbers. They also suffer greater deprivation. Although the past homeless men on Skid Row were undoubtedly poor, their average income from casual and intermittent work was three to four times more than what the current homeless receive. In addition, many of the elderly homeless men in the past had small but stable pensions, which today's homeless do not have (Rossi, 1989).

Causes of Homelessness

The causes of homelessness can be categorized into two types: larger social forces and personal characteristics. One social force is the shortage of inexpensive housing for poor families and poor unattached persons. This shortage began in the 1970s and accelerated in the 1980s. Another social force is the decreasing demand for unskilled labor in the 1980s, which resulted in extremely high unemployment among young men in general and blacks in particular. A third social force is the erosion of public welfare benefits over the last two decades. These three social forces do not directly cause homelessness. They merely enlarge the ranks of the extremely poor, thereby increasing the chances of these people becoming homeless.

Certain personal characteristics may explain who among the extremely poor are more likely to become homeless. These characteristics have been found to include chronic mental illness, alcoholism, drug addiction, serious criminal behavior, and physical health problems. Most of the extremely poor do not become homeless because they live with their relatives or friends. But those who suffer from any of the personal disabilities just mentioned are more likely to wear out their welcome as dependents of their parents or as recipients of aid and money from their friends. After all, their relatives and friends are themselves extremely poor and already living in crowded housing (Rossi, 1989; Baum and Burnes, 1993). We should be careful, though, not to exaggerate the

impact of personal disabilities on homelessness. To some degree, personal disabilities may be the consequences rather than the causes of homelessness (Snow and Anderson, 1993).

Questions for Discussion and Review

1. Who are the homeless?
2. What causes homelessness?

WELFARISM

Contrary to popular belief, most of the poor in the United States are not on welfare. Only about one-third are. Moreover, most people on welfare are children. There are about 14 million, of whom five million are single mothers and 10 million their children. Thus the large majority—two-thirds—of the welfare recipients are children. Since the economic recession began in 1989, the welfare roll has increased steadily (Census Bureau, 1994: Dowd, 1994). This has in turn increased taxpayer and government opposition to the welfare system.

Beliefs About Welfare

In a recent survey, a national sample of people in the United States were asked, "Do you think government spending on *welfare* should be increased, decreased, or kept about the same?" The most popular response was *"decreased."* But many people do not realize that the proposed welfare cut will affect mostly children. This is why, asked about government spending on *poor children,* far more people said they wanted the government to *increase* it (Dowd, 1994).

If the real target of public opposition is not the children, it is their single mothers. In the same survey just mentioned, a large majority (87 percent) of the general public want welfare recipients to be required to work. It is widely assumed that welfare encourages dependency, that most welfare recipients are so dependent on the system that they will never leave it (Toner, 1992).

But the fact is that most recipients (about 70 percent) stay on welfare less than two years. Moreover, welfare benefits do not seem generous enough to encourage dependency. An average three-member family on welfare receives only about $380 a month, and the benefit has declined over the last 20 years (Bane and Ellwood, 1994).

Reforming Welfare

Nevertheless, efforts have been made to end welfare dependency. The Clinton administration has proposed that single mothers who have been on welfare for more than two years be required to join a work program. Those who stay in the program may continue to receive aid as long as they are seeking pri-vate-sector jobs. By contrast, Republican leaders want the federal government to abolish its welfare programs and replace them with grants to state governments. The states are expected to eliminate welfare within two years even if the recipients cannot find private jobs. Republican leader Newt Gingrich has also proposed that unmarried mothers under 18 be denied benefits and their children be placed in orphanages.

According to a recent survey, only 20 percent of U.S. citizens like the orphanage idea while 72 percent would rather have the children remain with their

ENRICHING OUR LIVES

After years of trying, changes in the U.S. welfare program are now under way. But some proposals seem more intended to hurt, not help, the poor. Many experts argue that the poor need more, not less support from government programs. This reading explores some practical ways to actually help women and children who must receive welfare.

Real Welfare Reform

Everyone seems to want to force poor people to get a job. Any job. It will be good for their character. That's the mantra of neoliberals and others in the Clinton administration pursuing the chimera of "welfare reform." The self-styled New Democrats added fuel to the old conservative charge that the welfare system causes rather than fights poverty.

This theory says that the welfare system lures its recipients into a pattern of dependence that makes them impervious to upswings in the business cycle. Jobs open up but the poor don't take them. A new Census Bureau study tells why: It's not that welfare is attractive but that the job market is so dismal.

Work doesn't pay—at least for poor people. According to the Census Bureau, 24 percent of working women fall below the poverty line by earning less than $13,091 a year. The vast majority of welfare recipients are single mothers and their children. Why should they leave home to take full-time jobs that don't improve the family's income?

Neoliberals show no respect for the parenting that poor people do, so they feel nothing is lost when mothers are forced into the workplace. Isn't it time for us to challenge that contemptuous notion? And to make certain that welfare reform leaves poor women and their children in better, not worse, circumstances?

Four actions could move us toward that goal:

♦ Increase the earned-income tax credit to guarantee President Clinton's goal that no one who works should be poor. The current maximum tax credit of $3,370 is woefully insufficient to reverse the mathematics of poverty. No parent should be forced off welfare and into a job that leaves the family poor.

♦ Raise the minimum wage at least to the level of 15 years ago in purchasing power. When Labor Secretary Robert Reich floated that notion late last year, he received no support from the administration or from citizen action groups.

♦ Guarantee proper child care to poor working parents. There is no job more difficult than raising a child in the Other America. Schools are lousy, streets are crazy, and drug dealing represents the only jobs program left—except, of course, the dead-end fast-food industry. If the government is going to force single parents into the workforce, it must provide a safe, nurturing environment for their kids.

♦ Guarantee health insurance for those who risk losing coverage by entering the workforce. A recent study shows that 49 percent of those living below the poverty level were without insurance for a month or more between 1990 and 1992. Coverage for the working poor must be in place *before* people are forced off the welfare rolls into low-wage jobs.

Excerpted from Robert Scheer, "Real Reform," *The Nation,* April 25, 1994, p. 34. Reprinted with permission from *The Nation* magazine. © The Nation Company, L. P.

mothers on welfare (Dowd, 1994). Many experts have also observed that the cost of running orphanages will be too high. A mother with two children now receives benefits of about $15,000 a year in cash, food stamps, Medicaid, housing, and other services. By contrast, the cost of keeping two children in an orphanage would be at least $72,000 (Besharov, 1994). It is thus unlikely that millions of poor children will be sent to orphanages.

It is far more likely that the welfare program will be sharply reduced, with many poor families being denied benefits or losing what they now have. But will all this spur poor adults to lead more productive lives and provide their children with better role models, as the reformers assume? Critics do not think so. They argue that the government continues to avoid solving the real problem. The solution lies in providing "good job training, adequate child care, and decent wages at the end of the road," which would enable many poor single mothers to leave welfare. But such programs would cost more than $50 billion, which the government is not willing to spend (Abramovitz and Piven, 1994).

Questions for Discussion and Review

1. What does the public think about welfare?
2. What do you think is the best idea for solving the welfare problem?

SOCIAL MOBILITY

In virtually all societies there is some **social mobility**—movement from one social standing to another. The amount of mobility, though, varies from one society to another. Generally, there is more mobility in the more industrialized societies than in less developed societies. Sociologists have long discovered certain patterns and causes of mobility.

Patterns

Social mobility can take several forms. **Vertical mobility** involves moving up or down the status ladder. The upward movement is called *upward mobility* and downward movement, *downward mobility*. The promotion of a teacher to principal is an example of upward mobility, and demotion from principal to

teacher is downward mobility. In contrast to vertical mobility, **horizontal mobility** is movement from one job to another within the same status category. If a teacher leaves one school for the same position at another, the teacher is experiencing horizontal mobility.

Mobility can also be intragenerational or intergenerational. When an individual moves from a low position to a higher one, it is called **intragenerational mobility** (or *career mobility*)—a change in an individual's social standing. A manager who becomes the vice president of a company illustrates intragenerational mobility. When a person from a lower-class family gets a higher-status job, as in the case of a factory worker's daughter becoming company vice president, it is called **intergenerational mobility**—a change in social standing from one generation to the next.

Of those various forms of mobility, upward intergenerational mobility has attracted the most attention from sociologists. Their research has primarily focused on the degree to which such mobility exists in the United States. This interest is understandable because we revel in stories about the son of a poor farmer becoming president, as politicians and journalists proclaim, "Only in America." This may be an exaggeration, but it reflects the high place that upward mobility holds in U.S. values. Rags-to-riches tales make people feel good about their country, and they make interesting stories. By publicizing them, the media reinforce the vision of the United States as a land of opportunity, where through sheer hard work the son of a janitor can become a millionaire. This view of the United States is further reinforced by the experience of those who have achieved moderate, but real, upward mobility.

But is this picture accurate? Is upward mobility common? Until the 1970s, the answer was "yes" and "no": "yes" because numerous people climbed a little way up the social ladder; "no" because very few people rose from rags to riches. Since the early 1970s, however, the rich have gotten richer and the poor poorer. As Figure 10.6 shows, the share of national income in the hands of the richest portions of the U.S. population has gone up but the income share of the poorest groups has gone down. The middle classes have been hurting, too. While corporate presidents and chairpersons have been riding high, many mid-level management and technical jobs have been lost. Middle managers and highly educated technicians are said to have become insecure and to feel incredibly hurt—"they feel like slaves on an auction block." They have increasingly shared with high-school-trained assembly-line workers and office clerks the same feelings of uncertainty, insecurity,

FIGURE 10.6
The Rich Get Richer.

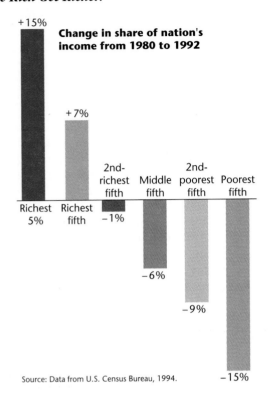

Change in share of nation's income from 1980 to 1992

+15% Richest 5%

+7% Richest fifth

-1% 2nd-richest fifth

-6% Middle fifth

-9% 2nd-poorest fifth

-15% Poorest fifth

Source: Data from U.S. Census Bureau, 1994.

tried to be "lean and mean" by greatly reducing their size and cost.

In the earlier part of this century, however, most of the structural mobility was upward rather than downward. This kind of structural mobility can be traced to at least four sources. First, there was a tremendous expansion of the industrial economy. In 1900, agricultural workers made up nearly 40 percent of the labor force, but massive industrialization reduced the proportion to only four percent today. At the same time, many unskilled jobs were gradually taken over by machines, but replaced by numerous higher-status jobs—clerical, service, business, and professional jobs. This created the opportunity for large numbers of people from farming and blue-collar families to get into those higher-status occupations (Blau and Duncan, 1967; Kerckhoff et al., 1985).

A second source of structural mobility has been the dramatic increase in the educational attainment of the population. High school enrollment exploded from a mere 7 percent of the appropriate age group in

and anxiety about their jobs and incomes. They have become what Secretary of Labor Robert Reich (1994) calls "the anxious class."

Sources

Why, in the pursuit of the American Dream, are some people upwardly mobile while others stay or fall behind? There are two major factors determining the chances for upward or downward mobility: structural changes in the society and individual characteristics.

Structural Mobility Sometimes large changes in society enable many people to move up or down the social ladder at the same time. The result is **structural mobility**, social mobility related to changes in society. As we have suggested, much of the downward mobility of blue-collar workers over the last two decades is the decline of manufacturing industries and labor unions, which have long shored up wages and benefits for workers without much education and high-level skills. As for the downward mobility of many well-educated managers and technicians in recent years, it can be attributed to the increased globalization of the U.S. economy. Pressured by international competition, many U.S. corporations have

One source of structural mobility in the United States has been the large influx of immigrants. Immigrants usually take lowly jobs as laborers on the farm, in factories, and in mines, which pushes many native-born people up into higher-status occupations.

1900 to over 90 percent today. College enrollment jumped from only a quarter of a million in 1900 to over 12 million today. Thus, more people achieved the knowledge and skills needed to fill higher-status jobs (Featherman and Hauser, 1978; Davis, 1982).

A third source of structural mobility has been the lower birth rates in the higher classes than in the lower classes. In the early part of this century, professional and other white-collar workers had relatively few children, but manual workers, especially farmers, had many. As the economy expanded, there were many more new professional positions. Because there was a shortage of higher-status people to fill all those higher-status jobs, it provided the lower classes with an opportunity to take them.

A fourth source of structural mobility has been the large influx of immigrants into this country. Immigrants usually have taken lowly jobs as laborers on the farm, in factories, and in mines, pushing up many native-borns into higher-status occupations. When children of immigrants grew up, they too had the opportunity as native-borns to become upwardly mobile. It is no accident that the world's most prosperous societies—Israel, Canada, Australia, and the United States—have had unusually large numbers of immigrants (Tyree et al., 1979; Tyree and Semyonov, 1983).

In short, as a result of a rapidly industrializing economy, increasing education, lower birth rates in the higher classes, and considerable immigration, many people whose parents were factory or farm workers came to fill higher-status jobs. In today's increasingly postindustrial society, however, higher-status jobs require much more education and skill than before.

Individual Mobility   Even when structural mobility opens up higher-status positions, some people move up and some do not. Let us take a closer look at this **individual mobility**, social mobility related to an individual's personal achievement and characteristics.

Among the characteristics that influence individual mobility are racial or ethnic background, gender, education, occupation, place of residence, and sheer luck. More specifically, being African American, Mexican American, Puerto Rican, Native American, or female decreases the chances for

upward mobility (in later chapters we look at these inequalities in detail). College graduates are much more likely than the uneducated to be upwardly mobile. White-collar workers are more likely than blue-collar workers to experience upward career mobility. People who live in urban areas have a greater chance of upward mobility than those who live in rural areas. Finally, sheer luck often acts as the force pushing a person up the status ladder.

Some of the personal characteristics are *achieved,* such as education, talent, motivation, and hard work. Others are *ascribed,* such as family background, race, and gender. As has been suggested, both achieved and ascribed qualities have a hand in determining who gets ahead in U.S. society. But the popular belief in equal opportunity would lead us to expect career success to be attained through achievement more than ascription. Is achievement, then, really the more powerful determining force in upward mobility? According to most sociological studies, achievement may appear on the surface to be the predominant factor, but it is at bottom subject to the influence of ascription. It is well-known that the more education people have, the more successful they are in their careers. But the amount of education people have is related to their family background. Thus, compared with children from blue-collar families, white-collar children can be expected to get

Even when structural mobility opens up higher-status positions, some people move up and some do not. Being white, male, and college educated increases one's chances for upward mobility.

more education—and then have a better chance for career mobility.

Questions for Discussion and Review

1. What are the different patterns of mobility?
2. What structural and individual characteristics influence social mobility?

PERSPECTIVES ON STRATIFICATION AND CLASS

Social stratification is in essence social inequality, contrary to the American belief in equality. Functionalists argue that it is necessary. Conflict theorists disagree. Symbolic interactionists, however, are more interested in how differences in status and power influence social interaction.

Functionalist Perspective

Kingsley Davis and Wilbert Moore (1945), in the most influential statement of the functionalist view, said that stratification is necessary. Davis and Moore were trying to explain why stratification exists in all societies. The reason, they said, is that stratification serves a useful, positive function—in effect, a function necessary for the survival of a society.

What is this function? According to Davis and Moore, stratification motivates people to work hard by promising them such rewards as money, power, and prestige. The amount of rewards depends on two things: how important a person's job is to society and how much training and skill are required to perform that job. A physician, for example, must receive more rewards than a garbage collector, not only because the physician's job is more important than the garbage collector's but also because it requires more training and skill. Without this system of unequal rewards, many jobs important to society would never be performed. If future physicians knew they would be paid and respected just as much as garbage collectors, they would not bother to spend years studying long hours at medical school. In short, stratification is necessary for society because it ensures that "the most important positions are conscientiously filled by the most qualified persons."

Conflict Perspective

The Davis-Moore theory has been subjected to many criticisms. Some critics argue that it is difficult to see why such large inequalities are necessary to fulfill the functions Davis and Moore described. Why is it functional to pay a corporate executive two or three times more than the president of the United States? The functionalist theory would suggest that the corporate executive's job is more important. But is it really? Many people may disagree. Even the physician's job is not necessarily more important than the garbage collector's, because uncollected refuse can present a serious problem to a society. The functionalist theory also fails to take into account the inherent interest of certain jobs. The intrinsic satisfaction of being a doctor far outweighs that of being a garbage collector. Why, then, should the doctor be given more rewards?

In addition, according to Melvin Tumin (1953), stratification is dysfunctional rather than functional. First, by limiting the opportunities of those who are not in the privileged class, stratification restricts the possibility of discovering and exploiting the full range of talent in society. When some intelligent teenagers are too poor to stay in school and never develop their talents fully, society loses. Second, stratification helps maintain the status quo of social injustices, such as denying the poor, minorities, and women the opportunities for good jobs. Third, because the stratification system distributes rewards unjustly, it encourages the less privileged to become hostile, suspicious, and distrustful. The result may be social unrest and chaos.

Symbolic Interactionist Perspective

According to symbolic interactionists, social inequality largely determines how people interact with one another. Generally, when interacting with a lower-status person, higher-status people tend to show off their power, either consciously or unconsciously. A common example involves calling lower-status persons by their first names. At work, our bosses call us by our first names, but we do not call them by their first names unless we get their permission first. When we go to see a doctor, he or she calls us by our first names, but we address him or her as "doctor." By readily using lower-status persons' first names, higher-status people try to be personal, but in doing so they disregard whether the lower-status persons may prefer to be shown respect instead (Karp and Yoels, 1993).

Cutting Edge

Wrenching changes in the economy have led to a growth in joblessness and low-paid employment as well as an increase in social tensions. In this reading, Richard Sennett, a prominent sociologist, argues that the tensions reflect the conflict between the highly educated few and the less educated masses.

A New Class Warfare

Popular resentment against elites is an old story in America, perhaps as old as the nation itself. But the story twists and turns as the elite changes. In Andrew Jackson's time, the hated elite were landowners; in John D. Rockefeller's time, they were industrialists.

Today, no one would think [the billionaire] Sam Walton was an elitist; instead of great wealth, the new elite possesses rarefied skills. It has addresses on the Internet rather than on Fifth Avenue; it knows how to do global as well as local business.

Most Americans are shut out of this new world. Seventy percent of the adult population does not know how to use a computer; most high school graduates cannot read a train schedule; a large minority cannot reckon simple interest on a bill.

The elite thrives on change, the mass fears it. In a dynamic society, the mass of people are constantly threatened by becoming redundant, being passed by; all they have is their willingness to work. The new economy needs the mass of these Americans less as producers or workers than as consumers.

A new study by the Demos Institute, an opinion-research organization in London, brings this divide into focus. It shows a new attitude toward work among the young in Europe as well as America, a desire to work flexibly and individually, a loss of loyalty to corporations and a willingness to demand that employers make work more personally satisfying.

But only a fifth of young Americans have the training or skills to act on such desires; the other four-fifths, who have no personal bargaining power, can only worry about getting some job, any job, even though they share the sentiments of the elite. Under such conditions, feelings of inferiority become intensely personal. A snob doesn't appear to be someone who flings money about; instead, unlike the ordinary person, he is confident that the future belongs to him.

It's not surprising that young men form the most conservative and anti-elitist segment of the population; they are in that crucible time of life when reali-

ties—from McJobs and the necessity of living with one's parents in one's 20's to the prospect of three-job marriages—all dim hopes for self-determination.

As always, politics does symbolic duty for fundamental changes. The fear of government grown out of control is like the photographic print of a social and economic negative—a print of the fear that economic growth portends threat rather than opportunity, that the average person is likely to be left out of the spoils.

And this is a problem for us [the new elite] as well as them [the masses.]

When accused of being an elite, we fudge. [Our] crocodile tears for the sufferings of others prove that we are in touch—in the certain-to-be immortal words of our President, "I feel your pain." (Others detect a certain condescension lurking in this sympathy.) Or we promise to use our skills to design solutions to make things better – public policy solutions graced almost with the complexity of modern art. In promising to solve for the masses what they have not solved for themselves, we show we believe we're what they fear we are: more competent.

Class has been the dirty secret of American history, denied by promises of individual freedom, by dreams of upward mobility and by memories of solid communities and coherent families—memories that prove on inspection only to be recovered-memory fantasies.

The plain fact is that in today's new stage of capitalism, class divides Americans as ruthlessly as it did in the age of the Robber Barons: politically, America has plunged into a new round of class warfare, with a secure, confident future belonging only to the educated few.

In short, interaction between unequals tends to involve "superiors" using various symbols of power to put "inferiors" in their place.

Questions for Discussion and Review

1. How does the functionalist theory of stratification differ from the conflict approach?
2. How do status differences affect symbolic interaction?

TOWARD SOCIAL EQUALITY

Both functionalist and conflict theorists assume that inequality is here to stay. Functionalists believe that stratification will persist because it is necessary. Conflict theorists also believe that inequality will continue, but because the powerful will not give up their privileged positions. Mickey Kaus (1992) argues that social equality can be achieved.

According to Kaus, it is futile to pursue equality of money, income, or wealth in a capitalist society such as the United States unless capitalism is eliminated. But so long as we want to preserve capitalism, we are inevitably saddled with income inequality, selfishness, or even greed. These nasty aspects of capitalism are the price for enjoying the prosperity that capitalism brings to the country. In fact, capitalism can generate prosperity only because it depends on money inequality as a spur to work—the more you work, the more money you make. The success of capitalism also depends on *vast* inequality as a spur to risk-taking—people, especially greedy ones, will gamble their money on an economic venture because they will get rich if it succeeds. Finally, capitalism thrives on income inequality because most people do not resent the rich for they have their own dreams of getting rich themselves. It is, therefore, impossible to get rid of income inequality in order to achieve equality.

Although income equality cannot be achieved, *social* equality can. To Kaus, social equality is a situation where people respect one another regardless of their wealth or lack of it. They have equal pride of being a citizen and treat one another as equals. There are no feelings of superiority among the rich, and there is no servile behavior among the nonrich. But "money talks," especially in a capitalist society, where wealth exerts a great influence on the other two aspects of inequality—prestige and power. Recognizing this problem, Kaus calls for government action "to *restrict the sphere of life in which money matters*, and enlarge the sphere in which money *doesn't* matter." The aim is to restrain the influence of wealth to prevent money inequality from translating into social inequality.

The primary way to do this is through social institutions, where the capitalist principle of the marketplace ("rich beat poor") is replaced by the principle of equality of citizenship. Thus Kaus would create, or reinforce, essentially egalitarian institutions, such as military draft; mandatory national service (caring for the infirm elderly, tutoring the illiterate, maintaining or patrolling public spaces); more public financing of political campaigns; a national health care system; expanded day care (where toddlers of ordinary workers mix with those of company executives); revived schools, parks, museums, post offices, libraries, and mass transit. In these spheres of life the rich and nonrich interact, so that they can rediscover "the esthetics of democracy"—the joy of mingling with people of all classes while feeling equal as simply citizens.

Questions for Discussion and Review

1. According to Kaus, what is social equality?
2. How can it be achieved?

CHAPTER REVIEW

1. *What are the bases of social stratification?* Wealth, power, and prestige. The unequal distribution of these social rewards constitutes social stratification.

2. *How equal is the distribution of wealth in the United States?* Very unequal. The richest 20 percent of the population earns about 45 percent of the total national income, and the poorest 20 percent earns less than 5 percent. *How is power distributed in the United States?* Very unequally, according to Marxist and elite theorists. They argue that power is concentrated in the hands of a very few people. In contrast, pluralist theorists contend that power is widely

dispersed among competing groups. *What is an important source of prestige in the United States?* Occupation.

3. *How does social stratification vary from one society to another?* Different societies have different kinds of stratification, including the egalitarian, master-slave, feudal, caste, and class systems.

4. *How do we know who is in which social class?* We may use the reputational method, asking a selected group of people to rank others; the subjective method, asking people how they rank themselves; or the objective method, ranking people according to such criteria as income, educational attainment, and occupation. *How is the U.S. population distributed into social classes?* About three to five percent are in the upper class, 40 to 50 percent in the middle class, 30 to 40 percent in the working class, and 15 to 20 percent in the lower class. *How does social class affect our lives?* People of different classes have different life chances and lifestyles.

5. *What is poverty?* Poverty can be absolute or relative. Absolute poverty is the lack of minimum food and shelter necessary for maintaining life. Relative poverty is having less than the majority of the people. *What is the feminization of poverty?* A huge number of women bearing the burden of poverty, mostly as single mothers. *What causes poverty?* To some social scientists, personal weaknesses and the "culture of poverty" cause people to be poor. To sociologists, however, society's need for "dirty work" to be done and its inegalitarian nature cause poverty. *Why have the poor gotten poorer in large cities?* Sociologists find the cause in forces beyond the control of the individual, but others blame the poor for not wanting to work.

6. *Who are the homeless?* Extremely poor, most are African American men in their middle thirties, but a few are single mothers with children, mental patients, or alcohol or drug abusers. *What causes homelessness?* A combination of social forces, such as housing shortage, and personal disabilities, such as mental illness.

7. *What does the public think of the welfare system?* A large segment of the public do not like welfare because they believe that it encourages dependency. *What has been proposed to deal with the welfare problem?* The Clinton administration wants welfare recipients to work and Republicans want to turn welfare programs back to the states.

8. *Is upward mobility common in the United States?* Before the 1970s, upward mobility was common, but mostly within the middle segment rather than from "rags to riches." In the last two decades, however, most people have experienced downward mobility. *What factors influence the opportunity for social mobility?* There are structural factors, including the decline of manufacturing industries in recent decades, and an expanding economy, increasing education, low fertility among higher classes, and massive immigration in earlier periods. There are also individual characteristics, such as social and ethnic background, gender, education, occupation, and luck.

9. *Why do functionalists think that social stratification is useful for society to have?* Because stratification ensures that relatively important jobs are performed by competent people. *How do conflict theorists view stratification?* As harmful to society—limiting opportunities for those not in the privileged class, preserving the status quo of injustices, and producing social unrest. *How do symbolic interactionists view stratification?* Stratification influences how higher-status people show off their power in social interaction.

10. *Is it possible to achieve social equality?* Yes, according to Kaus. It involves the government encouraging citizens of all classes to mingle in public spheres of life.

KEY TERMS

Absolute poverty   The lack of minimum food and shelter necessary for maintaining life (p. 227).

Caste system   A relatively rigid stratification system in which people's positions are ascribed and fixed (p. 222).

Class system   A relatively open stratification system in which people's positions are achieved and changeable (p. 223).

Feminization of poverty   A huge number of women bearing the burden of poverty, mostly as single mothers or heads of families (p. 228).

Horizontal mobility   Movement from one job to another within the same status category (p. 234).

Individual mobility   Social mobility related to an individual's personal achievement and characteristics (p. 236).

Intergenerational mobility   A change in social standing from one generation to the next (p. 234).

Intragenerational mobility   A change in an individual's social standing (p. 234).

Kuznets curve   The changing relationship between economic development and social inequality (p. 223).

Life chances   The likelihood of living a good, long, or successful life in a society (p. 226).

Lifestyles   Tastes, preferences, and ways of living (p. 226).

Objective method   The method of identifying social classes by using occupation, income, and education to rank people (p. 224).

Power   The ability to get people to do things they otherwise would not do (p. 219).

Power elite   A small group of individuals who hold top positions in the federal government, military, and corporations and have similar backgrounds, values, and interests (p. 219).

Relative poverty   A state of deprivation resulting from having less than what the majority of the people have (p. 228).

Reputational method   The method of identifying social classes by selecting a group of people and asking them to rank others (p. 224).

Social class   A category of people who have about the same amount of income, power, and prestige (p. 224).

Social mobility   Movement from one social standing to another (p. 234).

Social stratification   The division of society in such a way that some people get more rewards than others (p. 218).

Status inconsistency   The condition in which the same individual is given different rankings, such as being high in occupation but low in ethnicity (p. 221).

Status system   A system in which people are stratified according to their social prestige (p. 220).

Structural mobility   Social mobility related to changes in society (p. 235).

Subjective method   The method of identifying social classes by asking people to rank themselves (p. 224).

Vertical mobility   Moving up or down the status ladder (p. 234).

SUGGESTED READINGS

Allen, Michael Patrick, 1987. *The Founding Fortunes: A New Anatomy of the Super-Rich Families.* New York: E. P. Dutton. A data-supported investigation into the various strategies used by the rich to preserve their wealth from generation to generation.

Bane, Mary Jo, and David T. Ellwood. 1994. *Welfare Realities: From Rhetoric to Reform.* Cambridge, MA: Harvard University Press. A collection of the authors' articles describing and explaining various aspects of the welfare problem.

Henry, William A., 3rd. 1994. *In Defense of Elitism.* New York: Doubleday. A popular version of the functionalist theory of stratification, defending inequality and attacking equality.

Jencks, Christopher. 1994. *The Homeless.* Cambridge, MA: Harvard University Press. A careful, objective analysis of homelessness in the United States.

Kaus, Mickey. 1992. *The End of Equality.* New York: Basic Books. Details a proposal on how to reform welfare and achieve social equality in the United States.

11

RICH AND POOR NATIONS

CHAPTER OUTLINE

Myths and Realities

MYTH: *The work done for parents by children aged 5 to 15 is good for building the youngsters' character, but the family does not need it to survive.*
REALITY: Children's work at home may not ensure the survival of a family in affluent societies such as the United States, but it often does in many poor peasant societies.

MYTH: *It is economic suicide for people in poor peasant societies to have many children.*
REALITY: High birth rates are associated with poverty but children may be needed to ensure survival in poor countries where they tend to be their parents' active partners in struggling for survival.

MYTH: *Whenever massive famine hits a country in Africa, drought is always the only cause.*
REALITY: A drought can trigger famine, but it is usually the combatants of a civil war—both government and rebel forces—that seize food supplies from civilians as well as international relief organizations as a military strategy to starve the enemy into defeat.

MYTH: *Slavery is a social evil of the past.*
REALITY: According to Britain's Anti-Slavery International, the world's oldest human-rights organization, more than 100 million people today still suffer as slaves. That figure may be too high because it includes large numbers of child laborers who are exploited but not really slaves. Even with a narrower definition including only chattel slavery and debt bondage, cases of involuntary servitude run well into the millions.

MYTH: *The United States and other rich countries spend too much on foreign aid. Spending much of that money on their own poor and homeless people would go a long way toward relieving their problems.*
REALITY: The rich industrial nations allocate far less than 1 percent of their income to foreign aid, compared with about 15 percent for domestic welfare programs.

he baby boy is less than 24 hours old. He was born at the Central Hospital in Quagadougou, the capital city of the African nation of Burkina Faso. Brain damaged, he weighs only half of what he should. His tiny form, cradled in a doctor's two hands, is convulsing. The mother waits with apprehension in the dusty courtyard outside. Apparently she did not have any prenatal consultation nor did she eat sufficiently. According to the doctor, it is common for women like her from the countryside to cut down on food during pregnancy (Darnton, 1994b). Heartrending scenes of human suffering like this can frequently be found in many poor nations not only in Africa but also in Asia and Latin America. The widespread misery reflects the brutal reality of **global stratification**, a system in which all the countries of the world find themselves in various positions, some getting less—or more—in life than others.

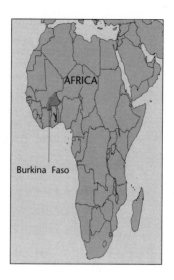

STRATIFICATION OF THE WORLD

Like the general public, some sociologists have traditionally divided the world into three parts: the "First World," "Second World," and "Third World." The First World consists of the rich, industrialized, capitalist countries, such as the United States, Canada, Japan, and Western European countries. The Second World includes the former socialist countries, namely, the former Soviet Union and its Eastern European satellites. And the Third World is made up of mostly poor, agricultural societies in Africa, Asia, and Latin America.

This view of the world is a legacy of the Cold War, which is now over. After the disappearance of socialism in the Soviet Union and Eastern Europe, it seems unrealistic to talk about the Second World. Moreover, some Third World countries, such as South Korea and Taiwan, have over the last decade become highly industrialized, nearly to the same degree as the First World. It is therefore also unrealistic to place these newly rich countries in the Third World with poor and predominantly rural countries. In addition,

the very term "Third World" connotes that developing countries are backward. Most importantly, dividing countries into those three worlds implies that the countries have little to do with one another. It is more realistic to look at the world today as a *system of relationships* among various societies.

THE WORLD SYSTEM APPROACH

Today's **world system**—a network of commercial and other relationships among all the members of the world's community—includes three broad classes of countries that correspond to the upper, middle, and lower classes within a society. Sociologist Immanuel Wallerstein (1987) refers to those three classes of countries in terms having to do with their position of economic power and influence in the world system. Thus countries with the greatest influence are said to be in the *core* of the world system, those with less influence are in the *semiperiphery* of the system, and those with the least influence are in the *periphery*.

Social Classes in Global Society

The United States, Western European countries, and Japan are **core countries**, the world's upper class, the most industrialized and richest societies, popularly known as industrial or developed countries. They have highly diversified economies, producing practically anything from corn to microchips. They also have a very high standard of living, stable governments, and a great deal of individual freedom. Countries with the least influence in the world are called **peripheral countries**—the world's lower class, relatively poor societies, popularly known as developing countries. These are the predominantly agricultural countries in Africa, Asia, and Latin America. Their economies are highly specialized, producing and exporting to core countries only a few raw materials or foodstuffs, such as oil, copper, sugar, or coffee. Their governments tend to be unstable.

In between those two types of societies are **semiperipheral countries**, the world's middle class, relatively affluent societies in the middle of global stratification, also known as newly industrialized countries. Examples are South Korea, Taiwan, Mexico, and Brazil. These countries are more industrialized and richer than peripherals but less industri-

alized and rich than cores. Their economies are also more diversified than those of peripherals but less diversified than those of cores. What about the former Soviet Union and Eastern Europe, which have splintered into many independent nations? Most, such as Russia, Ukraine, and Poland, appear more industrialized than the typical peripheral country. These countries may be considered semiperipheral. But a few, such as Tajikistan and Uzbekistan, are more like peripheral countries and may be considered as such. (See Figure 11.1 for the distribution of these three classes of countries in the world.)

Interclass Relations in Global Society

Traditionally, core countries exploit peripheral countries in the world system just as the upper class exploits the lower class within a given society. The cores often buy raw materials from the peripherals at a considerably low price and then use these raw materials to manufacture goods to sell back to the peripherals for a large profit. The profit, however, is mostly sent back to the cores rather than invested in the peripherals. Consequently, the peripherals remain poor and economically underdeveloped. The

FIGURE 11.1
Global Stratification

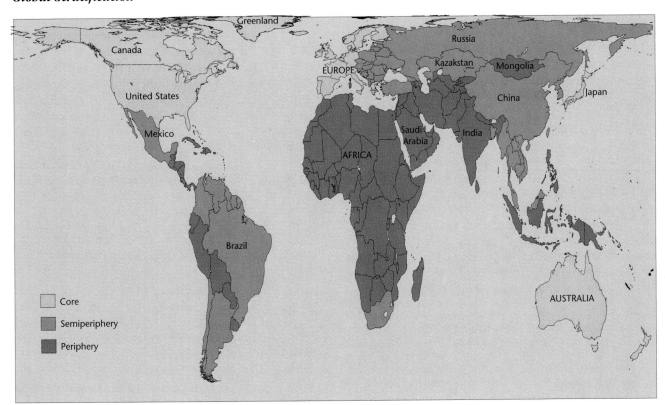

The world system—a network of relationships among all the members of the world's community—comprises three broad classes of countries. Countries with the greatest influence make up the core of the world system, those with less influence are in the semiperiphery, and those with the least are in the periphery. Traditionally, according to the world system theory, core countries exploit peripheral countries, though they may also be involved in transferring technology to the peripherals by building and operating factories there, helping the peripherals to industrialize.

semiperipherals also exploit the peripherals in about the same way. Brazil, for example, gets cheap oil, gas, and agricultural commodities from Bolivia, a poor peripheral; Bolivia in turn buys more expensive manufactured goods from Brazil.

This kind of exploitative trading has been going on for a long time—even centuries in some cases. But, according to the world system theory, in the last 40 years new forms of exploitation have emerged under the guise of generosity or commercial cooperation. They have, however, served the latent function of enabling some peripheral countries to industrialize and improve their economies. By taking advantage of the cheap labor, core countries have transferred technology to the peripherals by building and operating factories there, helping the peripherals to industrialize. Moreover, eager to turn peripherals into markets for products from the cores, the rich countries have instituted foreign aid programs to help the poor countries increase their agricultural and industrial productivity. All this has significantly helped Japan, South Korea, Taiwan, and others to transform into affluent core or semiperipheral countries.

In short, as members of the stratified world system, various classes of nations are interrelated and influence each other's fortunes. The ability of one country to influence another suggests that the class structure of the world system is dynamic rather than static, fluid and changing rather than rigid and fixed.

Question for Discussion and Review

1. How are the social classes in global society related to each other?

THE DYNAMICS OF GLOBAL STRATIFICATION

To move up or down in the global class system depends not only on foreign influence but also on the domestic conditions of a country.

Let us first consider how *peripheral countries can turn into semiperipherals.* One condition is that the peripherals must already have a number of factories that manufacture goods rather than only farms and mines that produce food and raw materials. Examples are some Latin American countries. When the price of their primary exports (raw materials) declines so as to cause high unemployment and other economic problems, the peripherals that have already established adequate industrial bases are able to expand these bases to produce more goods and sell them to core and semiperipheral countries. This is partly how Brazil and Argentina, already relatively industrialized as early as the 1950s, have changed from peripherals to semiperipherals. Another condition for becoming semiperipherals is the ability to attract foreign investment with an abundance of cheap labor, thus broadening the industrial base with the addition of many more manufacturing plants. This is partly how South Korea and Taiwan, which used to be poor peripherals, have moved up into the semiperipheral class. The third condition for peripherals is a nationwide pursuit of economic development through social or political changes. China, for example, has just become semiperipheral largely because its socialist government has turned largely capitalist and given its citizens the freedom to create personal wealth, an opportunity seized with a vengeance.

Semiperipheral countries can transform into cores if they meet at least two requirements. First, they must have developed an advanced technology that can turn out products at a lower cost than their competitors. Second, they must have large affluent markets, such as North America and Western Europe, for their products. This is how Japan, Spain, and Italy have achieved the status of a core country over the last 30 years or so. On the way to joining them are some newly industrialized countries such as East Asia's "four small tigers" (South Korea, Taiwan, Hong Kong, and Singapore), which have penetrated the rich core markets with their electronics, cars, computers, and other high-tech goods.

Finally, *core countries may lose their upper-class status in the world system.* In recent decades the United States seems to have fallen a notch or two from its preeminent core status. One major source of this slip is **deindustrialization,** the loss of numerous factory jobs as a result of relocating a massive number of manufacturing plants to peripheral countries. Deindustrialization peaked in the midst of a deep economic recession in the early 1980s. As deindustrialization slowed significantly by the mid–1980s, **reindustrialization**—the proliferation of unstable, low-skilled, or low-paying jobs—swept across the economy. Most victims of deindustrialization are forced to seek such jobs, in effect having to compete with poorly paid workers in labor-cheap countries (So, 1990). This has raised the specter of the United States eventually becoming a poor country (Chomsky, 1993; Luttwak, 1994). This downward mobility of the United States and the upward mobility of other societies will be discussed in greater detail later.

Question for Discussion and Review

1. What are the general forces that push some nations up or down in the global stratification system?

INEQUALITY AMONG NATIONS

Global stratification clearly suggests inequality among nations. This inequality appears in many different forms, the most important of which have to do with economic condition and quality of life.

By definition, the economic condition is better in relatively rich countries than in poor ones, but the disparity between rich and poor appears extreme. Although they constitute only about 20 percent of the world's population, richer countries have well over 80 percent of global income and other economic opportunities. These disparities reflect other disparities such as those in productivity, trade, savings, and investment. The richest 20 percent of the world population have 84.7 percent of the world's GNP (gross national product—the total value of all the goods and services produced by a nation, including those exported). In sharp contrast, the bottom 20 percent of the world population have only 1.4 percent of the GNP. The global inequality appears even worse in other economic indicators: the poorest fifth have less than one percent of world trade, domestic savings, and domestic investment, way below the over–84 percent enjoyed by the richest fifth (United Nations, 1994).

Such global disparities are indeed extreme. Even so, they are expected to get even worse. Over the last 30 years, the share of world income for the richest fifth has risen from 70 to 85 percent, while the meager share for the poorest fifth has dropped from 2.3 to 1.4 percent. To appreciate how much the gap between the global rich and poor has widened, let us turn to Figure 11.2. Here we can see that in 1960 the world's top fifth was 30 times richer than the bottom fifth, but by 1991 the top fifth became 61 times richer. In other words, the gap between the world's rich and poor has widened by more than 100 percent.

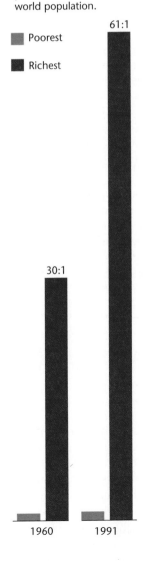

Ratio of income shares
Richest 20% compared to poorest 20% of the world population.

■ Poorest
■ Richest

61:1

30:1

1960   1991

FIGURE 11.2
The Widening Gap Between the World's Rich and Poor

SOURCE: *United Nations, Human Development Report 1994.*

Cutting Edge

Capitalism has become a global economic system that widens the gap between rich and poor nations. This reading analyzes how this global division of wealth has increased over the last three decades.

The Wealth and Poverty of Nations

The third annual report of the United Nations Development Program deals with a familiar theme: the widening gap between rich and poor. But rather than being a purely American problem, the report asserts, the growing gap is a world-wide trend. And far from being limited to the excess-ridden 1980s, such income disparities actually have more than doubled over the past 30 years.

In fact, the UNDP calculates that as of 1988, the top one fifth of nations in terms of income—38 countries, ranging from Switzerland to the former U.S.S.R.—laid claim to 65 times as much in per capita income as the poorest one fifth, or the 30 nations ranging from Mozambique to India. Leaving aside nationality, the income gulf between rich and poor individuals around the world was more than 140 to 1. The report singles out two prime causes for the growing divide. The nations with educated, healthy workers increasingly dominate the most lucrative economic activities, such as trade or high-tech research. And through such steps as erecting protectionist barriers, rich countries have isolated poor ones from global markets—even as the latter reinforce their detachment through bad policies of their own.

Education pays. The result is a vicious cycle in which the rich increasingly prosper while the poor stagnate—or emigrate. Around the world, educating workers produces growing payoffs. From 1985 to 1990, Thailand's heavy investments in technical training triggered a 65 percent increase in labor productivity. Marrying skilled workers to advanced technology only raises the rewards: the report cites a 17 percent average rate of return for investments in rich countries, versus just 12 percent for the best projects

in the developing world. The difference suggests that both brains and money will increasingly flow to the wealthiest nations. Indeed, this is just what occurred in the 1980s, when more than 80 percent of foreign direct investment was ploughed into the richest nations, while one-third of Africans with post-secondary education emigrated to Europe.

Poor policy. National policies only worsen the problem. Noting that only seven percent of world trade is conducted more or less freely—in full compliance with the General Agreement on Tariffs and Trade—the report asserts that industrialized nations' protectionism helps to deprive developing countries of $500 billion in income each year. A prime example is the notorious Multifiber Arrangement, which restricts exports of textiles and clothing from poorer nations and which the United States has pushed to renew four times in the past 19 years. Developing nations' tactics are no better. Impoverished sub-Saharan countries still spend two to three times as much on arms as on education. And wasteful state-owned enterprises in oil-rich Cameroon lost more money during the 1980s than the country earned from petroleum exports.

The report suggests that a top priority for the U.S. and its wealthy peers is to scuttle roadblocks to increased world trade. But dismantling trade barriers would force the industrialized nations to train their own low-skilled workers to advance to higher-tech industries lest they be displaced by new competition from abroad.

Excerpted from Susan Dentzer, "The Wealth of Nations," *U.S. News & World Report,* May 4, 1992, p. 54. Copyright, May 4, 1992, U.S. News and World Report.

A similar gap exists in regard to the quality of life. The United Nations (1994) finds that, compared with poor developing countries, affluent industrial countries have considerably higher income per person, far greater longevity, and a much higher rate of literacy. While the world's affluent enjoy a better life, the poor bear the cost of global inequality.

Question for Discussion and Review

1. How do economic condition and quality of life differ among nations?

Reflections of global stratification seen in the contrast between Rodeo Drive in Los Angeles and a dump in Guatemala City, Guatemala, where scavengers search for food. Inequality between rich and poor countries exists in economic conditions, such as global income and economic opportunity, and in quality of life, as indicated by income, longevity, and education.

THE COST OF GLOBAL INEQUALITY

The cost of this inequality among countries is high. We can see it in the form of widespread poverty, extensive female disadvantages, relatively prevalent child exploitation, and a shocking extent of slavery in the relatively poor, mostly peripheral countries.

Widespread Poverty

Most of the world's poor live in Africa, Asia, and Latin America. The extent of poverty in these areas' peripheral countries appears extremely great compared with that of affluent, core countries in the West. About 30 percent of the people in the peripherals live in *absolute poverty* (unable to meet their most basic needs), in sharp contrast with only three percent in the core countries. In other words, the peripherals' poverty rate is about *10 times* higher than in the cores. The extent of poverty is even worse in some peripheral countries. As shown in Table 11.1, in peripherals such as Rwanda, Bangladesh, and Somalia over 70 percent of their population live in poverty, over 20 times the poverty rate of core countries.

Poverty is most widespread in Africa's peripheral countries south of the Sahara, where there are 18 of the world's 20 poorest countries. Close to 50 percent of their population are poor, compared with about 30 percent for all developing countries. To under-

TABLE 11.1
Poverty Rates: A Global View

	Percentage of population in poverty
Core Countries	
United States	13.3
Canada	7.0
Australia	6.7
United Kingdom	5.2
France	4.5
Sweden	4.3
Netherlands	3.4
Germany	2.8
Peripheral Countries	
Rwanda	88
Bangladesh	78
Somalia	71
Ethiopia	60
Bolivia	58
Vietnam	54
El Salvador	51
Nigeria	40

SOURCES: Data from United Nations, *Human Development Report 1994* (New York: Oxford University Press, 1994); *Statistical Abstract of the United States, 1993.*

stand how difficult it is for the Africans to meet their basic needs, consider this fact: the gross national product of all sub-Saharan African countries (excluding South Africa), home to *600 million* people, is about the same as the gross national product of Belgium, which has a population of *only 10 million.* Even more tragically, when there is a civil war widespread poverty can easily turn into a massive famine, as happened over the last 10 years in such countries as Ethiopia, Sudan, and Somalia. Both government and rebel forces usually seize food supplies from civilians as well as international relief organizations as a military strategy to starve the enemy into defeat (Keen, 1994). Drought can also trigger a large-scale famine, because agricultural production has plummeted over the last 20 years while population has soared. Even when there is no famine, the combination of food shortages and population explosion often causes malnutrition, increasing susceptibility to disease, particularly among children. According to the United Nations Children's Fund,

> The overall status of children is getting worse in sub-Saharan Africa. We have 10,000 children dying every day from preventable causes. And another 10,000 crippled for life. So every 24 hours, 20,000 children are being wasted (Darnton, 1994).

African countries are not unique, however. Their counterparts in other regions of the world share with them certain characteristics.

First, poverty tends to be worst in rural areas. Although the urban poor are more visible, the rural poor suffer greater problems of malnutrition, lack of education, low life expectancy, and substandard housing. For the poor in cities, the problems arise from being housed in slums or squatter settlements, and from appalling overcrowding, bad sanitation, and contaminated water.

Second, poor families tend to be large, averaging 7.7 members. Because food is scarce, it is difficult to feed a large family. Malnutrition is therefore common, especially among the children. Child labor is also common, although it contributes significantly to the family's survival.

Third, the poor have too few or no assets. They are typically landless or own land too small or too unproductive to ensure family survival. Many are forced to seek low-paid farm employment or rural nonfarm employment.

Fourth, most of the poor try to survive by engaging in many different earning activities: working as small farmers, hunters and gatherers, small artisans, petty traders, and wage laborers every now and then. Still, they are rarely self-sufficient, and frequently have to borrow money or things from one another. Some, particularly in the city, become so desperate that they turn into full-time beggars, garbage sifters, prostitutes, or pickpockets.

Fifth, the poor usually fall victim to their government's neglect. Deprived of educational opportunities, clean water, and health care services, the poor end up with high rates of illiteracy, morbidity, and mortality (World Bank, 1990).

Female Disadvantages

Associated with widespread poverty is the prevalence of disadvantages for women in the poor, peripheral countries. According to the United Nations, the women's "human development index," a measure of the quality of life or living standard, is significantly

Associated with widespread poverty is the prevalence of female disadvantages in the poor, peripheral countries. In these countries, such as India, women face social, cultural, legal, and economic disadvantages that men do not.

lower in poor countries where women face all kinds of social, cultural, legal, and economic disadvantages that men do not.

Compared to men equally as poor, women have much lower literacy rates. In South Asia, female literacy rates are only around 50 percent of males'. The figure is even lower in some sub-Saharan African countries, only 39 percent in Somalia and 28 percent in Sudan, for example. Concentrated in poor countries, women make up two-thirds of the world's illiterates (United Nations, 1994).

Women lag far behind in education. The female rates for secondary education represent 72 percent of the men's rates and, for college education, only 51 percent (United Nations, 1994).

Women have many fewer opportunities for paid employment. There are only 58 women employed for every 100 men and they are paid considerably less. Women not gainfully employed are far from idle, however. In fact, they usually work an average of 12 hours a day while men work only 8 hours. Women not only do domestic chores, care for children and the elderly, but also work on the farm, gather firewood, weave baskets, or engage in petty trade such as selling small quantities of produce or food (United Nations, 1994).

Women generally live longer than men, but due to neglect of their health or nutrition, are sick more often. One of their greatest health risks is childbirth. The average rate of maternal mortality in poor countries is about 420 per 100,000 live births, more than 16 times higher than the rate (only 26) in affluent countries (United Nations, 1994).

Child Exploitation

Another cost of global inequality is the greater prevalence of child exploitation in relatively poor countries. There are three different types of child exploitation: work at home, labor outside the home, and slavery.

Working at Home   Children's work at home includes housekeeping, taking care of younger siblings, helping parents with such activities as working on the farm, hawking on the street, or running errands. The child workers, usually aged 5 to 15, are not paid. At first glance, these children may not appear to be exploited. After all, children in the United States do all kinds of chores for their parents, who see chores as an important part of socialization—useful for teaching diligence, discipline, and other positive values that will ensure success in the child's future. This may be true for the children in affluent societies,

but children's work in poor countries is far different. The economic well-being of most families in a rich country does not depend on children's work, but without it, many families in a poor country can hardly survive.

In poor villages around the world children as young as five routinely perform such chores as babysitting, fetching water, or looking after small livestock. By the age of eight, they often contribute as much as their parents to the family's survival. They may help their parents with their occupational activities such as weaving baskets, spinning yarns, fishing, or selling fruits and vegetables (Nieuwenhuys, 1994). Thus, contrary to popular belief, children in poor countries are not their parents' dependents but *partners* in a common struggle for survival. This may partly explain why parents in poor societies want to have many children. However, since the children must work as hard as their parents, school attendance is often impossible. Apparently exploited by their own parents, these children are actually victims of the stratification system of domestic and global society.

Child labor   If children's work at home cannot help keep the family afloat, poor parents are compelled to send their children to work for pay as farmers, miners, factory workers, or domestic servants. Such paid employment, known as child labor, is widely condemned, because it is well-known to be harmful to children, particularly children in poor countries. The children's health is often ruined for life, and they are deprived of education as well as robbed of the normal enjoyment of their early years. Consider the hazards children face working in a cloth-making factory in the North African nation of Morocco:

> Wool dust, created by the spinning machinery, pervades the air, covering the children's clothes and hair. The children also constantly breathe in the dust. The factory is intolerably cold and noisy. The children, mostly between ages 5 and 10, work fast under the watchful eyes of their supervisors. When the children emerge from the factory at the end of the day, their complexions are pale and eyes bleary, many developing colds or sores on their faces. The children work like this six days a week (Sawyer, 1986).

The exploitation of children who work as domestic servants is no less horrendous. The child servants not only work long hours for a pittance, but are often sexually or physically abused.

Child labor is in great demand for several reasons. Children are more docile, easier to discipline, and more often too frightened to complain. Their small

One of the costs of global inequality is the prevalence of child exploitation in relatively poor countries. Parents are sometimes compelled to send their children to work for pay, as shown here in Pakistan, where a young child works at making bricks. The health of child workers is often ruined, and they are deprived of an education. Because they are paid so little, they are never able to pay off the heavy debts imposed by employers for food, housing, and the use of work tools.

frames and nimble fingers are considered an asset for certain kinds of work. Though only seven to 10 years old, they are forced to work 12 to 14 hours a day. Most important, child labor is extremely cheap; children are generally paid less than one-third of the adult wage. Not surprisingly, when children are given jobs, their parents are likely to be laid off (United Nations, 1991).

Child Slavery Some child laborers are slaves. In 1993, the International Labor Organization reported that child slavery is relatively common. In Sudan, extremely poor peasants sell their young sons to merchants for as little as $70. In Thailand many poverty-stricken peasants sell or lease their young daughters to urban employment agencies, which in turn sell them to work in homes, restaurants, factories, and brothels. In Haiti more than 100,000 children have been sold or given away by their poor parents and most toil as domestic servants. In Pakistan some 7.5 million children work as bonded laborers in factories, on farms, or on construction projects. These young workers are virtual slaves, because they are paid so little that they will never pay off the heavy debts imposed by employers for food, housing, and even the use of work tools. In fact, children are not alone in being enslaved. Slavery is far more common than popularly believed.

Adult Slavery

Shocking as it may be, adult slavery is not uncommon today. According to Britain's Anti-Slavery International, the world's oldest human-rights organization, there are more than 100 million slaves. This figure includes a large number of child laborers and slaves. Still, cases of adults being in servitude can safely be assumed to reach well into the millions.

Like their ancient counterparts, some of these slaves are held as someone's property. This old-fashioned human bondage, called chattel slavery, can be found in the North African country of Mauritania,

where some 100,000 black Africans live as the property of Arab-descended Berbers. As chattel, these slaves are used for labor, sex, and breeding or can be exchanged for camels, trucks, guns, or money (Jacobs and Athie, 1994).

Most slaves today, however, are victims of debt bondage, which forces whole families to work, sometimes for generations, in fruitless efforts to pay off loans. Typical are Sadram and his wife, who have worked in a stone quarry outside India's capital city of New Delhi for eight years. Sadram breaks large rocks into smaller ones and loads them into trucks. His wife carries soil in a basket. The couple are paid $25 a month, nearly all of which goes for food and the explosives needed for the job. In the meantime, the $46 loan they took out eight years ago has grown to $88. When they told someone that they wanted to go home without paying off the debt, four men broke into their mud house and beat them with iron bars. After recovering from the wounds, Sadram and his wife returned to work. They simply have no way out. The same kind of debt slavery exists in such poor countries as Pakistan, Thailand, Peru, Haiti, and the Dominican Republic (Masland, 1992). Such human bondage will cease only if poor countries are able to achieve social mobility in the global stratification system.

Questions for Discussion and Review

1. How poor are the countries in sub-Saharan Africa? What are the common characteristics they share with poor countries in other regions of the world?
2. What disadvantages do women have in the world's poor, peripheral countries?
3. What is the nature of child exploitation in poor countries?
4. What kinds of life do slaves have today? How have most of them become slaves in the first place?

SOCIAL MOBILITY IN GLOBAL SOCIETY

Over the last 30 or 40 years a number of poor and not-so-poor nations have moved from a lower global status to a higher one. At the same time some other nations have gotten poorer.

Upward Mobility

Among those that have been socially mobile are Japan and other East Asian countries as well as Spain and Brazil.

East Asian Societies Japan is the world's best-known success story. It has risen like a meteor from the devastation of World War II to the ranks of prosperous core nations. In Chapter 4 (Society) we discussed how Japan's preindustrial characteristics—population homogeneity, emphasis on primary relations, and group orientation—may have to do with the nation's economic success. There are other, more direct contributing factors. One is the huge economic aid provided by the United States to rebuild Japan after the War. Another is an uncompromising attitude toward work; the Japanese toil longer hours than in other industrial countries. Their attitude stems from the Confucian culture that emphasizes the supreme importance of hard work as an obligation to the family. A third contributing factor is the strong government support to business. Through the Ministry of International Trade and Industry (MITI), government leaders often cajole businesspeople into new and risky enterprises, help them get the necessary capital, and sometimes even provide them with government subsidies (Harrison, 1992).

Similar factors contributed to the four small dragons' upward mobility. South Korea and Taiwan received massive economic and military aid from the United States in the 1950s and 1960s. The aid provided nearly 40 percent of the capital needed to build and expand Taiwan's industries. U.S. advisers urged Taiwan's government to open up the economy to foreign imports, expand exports, and encourage foreign investment. Similarly, U.S. aid helped change South Korea's traditionally inward-looking economic policy to one that emphasized the external market, triggering the explosive, export-driven growth of the economy as it did in Taiwan. The same Confucian culture that inculcates the Japanese uncompromising

American aid to South Korea helped change that country's traditionally inward-looking economic policy to one that emphasized the external market. The Confucian culture that inculcates an uncompromising attitude toward work and the government's role in guiding and promoting investment and exports also contributed to the country's transformation into an affluent semiperipheral nation. Shown here is a view of Seoul, South Korea, at night.

attitude toward work also contributed to the Korean and Taiwanese economic success. The governments of both countries further played an active role in guiding and promoting investment and exports. About the same three factors helped the current British colony of Hong Kong and the former British colony of Singapore become affluent semiperipheral societies, although the foreign aid came from Britain rather than the United States (Harrison, 1992).

Spain and Brazil   Like Japan, Spain has become a prosperous core nation over the last 20 years. In 1950, Spain was a relatively closed, isolated, and poor country run with an iron fist by Generalissimo Francisco Franco's highly authoritarian government. Its economy was so underdeveloped that its per capita income was lower than that of many of its former colonies in Latin America. But in the early 1970s the economy began to take off, and by the early 1990s Spain was an open democracy with the highest rate of economic growth in Europe. The impetus for this upward mobility came largely from a sweeping economic policy reform coupled with substantial U.S. financial aid. Massive U.S. air and naval bases, built in the 1950s during Cold War hostilities with the Soviet Union, helped stimulate the Spanish economy, developing a wide range of public and private industries. With U.S. encouragement, Spain further dismantled state regulations that restricted trade and capital investment, curtailed government spending, encouraged industrial growth, and attracted foreign investment (Harrison, 1992).

Like Spain, Brazil is upwardly mobile, though still a semiperipheral rather than core country. A former Portuguese colony, Brazil has one of the fastest growing economies in the world. In the past few decades the export of its manufactured goods has skyrocketed to a value today more than 100 times higher than in 1965. Several factors may explain Brazil's upward mobility. First, there has been a huge influx of enterprising immigrants from Europe and Japan. Second, social power in Brazil derives largely from commerce, industry, and capital, not from politics and land-owning as in many poor Latin American countries. And third, the government has concerned itself with economic growth more than those of poor countries.

But the single-minded pursuit of fast economic growth in Brazil has left its social conditions by the wayside. Although it now has the richest economy in Latin America, Brazil has one of the world's most unfair income distributions. The top 20 percent of its population earn *32 times* what the bottom 20 percent earn. The poverty rate is also unusually high, with

47 percent of its population being poor (Harrison, 1992; United Nations, 1994).

Downward Mobility

Over the last 20 or 30 years many poor countries have become poorer, while some rich countries have gotten less rich.

Poor Countries   The living standards of the poor countries in Latin America are now lower than in the early 1970s. The living standards have fallen even more—to levels last seen in the 1960s—among the poor nations in sub-Saharan Africa.

There are several reasons for the downward mobility. One is rapid population growth, which far exceeded the increase in GDP (gross domestic product—the total value of all the goods and services produced by a nation *minus* those sold abroad). Another is a large drop in global commodity prices; since 1980 the prices of oil as well as non-fuel commodity exports from poor countries fell by about 40 percent. Because they traditionally rely only on a few raw materials rather than manufactured goods to export, poor countries are most adversely affected. A third reason is the failure of rich countries to provide them with an adequate flow of capital, especially low-interest loans, for developing their economies. Instead, saddled with heavy debts to rich countries, poor countries have paid considerably more to rich countries than they have received from them, a large portion for interest alone (Angelopoulos and Fagen, 1993).

The economic decline among poor countries is expected to continue as long as those three reasons exist. Unfortunately, they are not about to disappear soon. In fact, a new problem makes it even more difficult to stop the slide into deeper poverty. With the ending of the Cold War, the United States and the former Soviet Union no longer have to compete for the favor of poor nations by showering them with military hardware, projects such as dams and steel mills, and boatloads of subsidized food and other goods. Moreover, rich countries are now preoccupied with tackling their own slumping economies and other domestic ills. Aid programs for poor nations have consequently been greatly reduced (Greenberger, 1992; Angelopoulos and Fagen, 1993).

The United States   Among rich countries, the United States seems to have suffered the greatest loss of economic status. In 1970 the United States was *by far* the most productive, boasting a GNP (gross national product) of $4,950 per person. In that same year, the figure was only $1,950 for Japan and $2,360 for Western Europe as a whole. In other words, the United States was *more than twice* as productive as Japan and Western Europe in 1970. But 10 years later, the U.S. lead had been reduced by *more than two-thirds*, with $12,000 for the United States compared to $9,870 for Japan and $9,760 for Western Europe (Luttwak, 1994). Today the U.S. lead has *disappeared*, with the United States losing the edge to Japan and showing virtual parity with Western Europe (see Table 11.2). The United States has also fallen from being the world's largest creditor to being the world's largest debtor. Once having the highest standard of living in the world, the United States is now only average among industrial nations.

TABLE 11.2
Productivity Among Rich Nations

Nation	Per capita GNP*
Switzerland	$33,710
Japan	26,840
Sweden	25,180
Norway	24,090
Finland	23,930
Denmark	23,760
Iceland	23,230
United States	22,340
Western Europe	22,310
Canada	20,510
Germany	20,510
France	20,460
Austria	20,200
Belgium	19,010
Netherlands	18,840
United Kingdom	16,600

*GNP is gross national product, the total value of all the goods and services of a nation, including those exported.

SOURCE: Data from United Nations, *Human Development Report 1994* (New York: Oxford University Press, 1994).

Victims of job cuts owing to a recession in the United States. The United States has suffered downward mobility since the 1970s as a result of deindustrialization, an increase in consumption, a decrease in savings, and efforts to make corporations "mean and lean," which brings worker layoffs.

The United States' downward trend has many different causes, of which only a few major ones can be identified here. Most important is probably deindustrialization, the massive loss of manufacturing jobs as many U.S. corporations move their production to poor, labor-cheap countries. But deindustrialization hurts mostly low-skilled manufacturing workers. Most of the well-educated, high-skilled employees in service industries are left unscathed. Deindustrialization alone is therefore not enough to explain the economic decline. Another major factor is the great increase in consumption and decrease in savings. Like their government, people spend more than they earn and become deeply in debt. Those who do practice thrift still have an average rate of savings significantly lower than in countries with fast-growing economies. The habits of high consumption and low savings may have resulted from the great affluence after the Second World War up until the early 1970s (Harrison, 1992).

Ironically, the increased economic hardships could bring back great prosperity to the United States if all sectors of U.S. society are compelled to cut down on spending. Most visible have been the efforts to reduce the federal budget deficit and government programs and to make corporations "lean and mean." As contradictory as it may seem with so many people laid off, pay increases frozen, and the poor getting poorer, the U.S. economy has begun to

American Mosaic

Changes in the world economy have presented special challenges to the United States. Millions of jobs have left the country, producing an increase in unemployment or low-paid employment. This reading analyzes whether the United States can solve this problem.

Is U.S. Well-Prepared for the New Century?

Although debates about the future of this and that country occur from France to Japan, perhaps nowhere are they more widespread than in the United States. In this large, decentralized, media-rich society, all sorts of controversies from abortion to "the end of History," from race to education, are vigorously debated. Characteristic of this thinking is the assumption that somehow the American people have taken a wrong path. Many Americans are worried by the growing evidence that *general* levels of precollege public education are relatively mediocre. Despite the opportunities offered by the free mass public education system, pupils are abandoning it in record numbers; between 600,000 and 700,000 drop out of high school each year.

To other experts, technical alternations in education are less significant than the social culture within which American education has to operate. The "trivialization" of U.S. culture, meaning the emphasis upon consumer gratification, pop culture, cartoons, noise, color, and entertainment over serious reflection, is portrayed as a self-inflicted wound. This anti-intellectual youth culture—continued later by the fascination with sports or "soap" shows—is not helped by the disintegration of the family. The average American child is said to be picking up the value system of a shallow entertainment industry rather than the moral standards, discipline, and intellectual curiosity that equip a person to learn.

How will U.S. society in its present condition interact with the broad forces for global change? How well-prepared is the United States for the twenty-first century? Since the 1970s, the composition of the work force has changed significantly. While manufacturing cut many skilled and relatively high-paying jobs, the boom in services created ever more low-paid, low-skilled jobs (cleaners, restaurant personnel, drivers, healthcare assistants, and the like), most of which paid less than $15,000 a year. The other trend was the growth in white-collar, technical jobs, especially in information and research sectors of the economy, requiring advanced training and higher education. According to the Hudson Institute survey *Workforce 2000*, by the end of this century as many as 52 percent of *new* jobs may require at least some college education. Yet the supply of so many educated individuals is in doubt.

Demographic trends suggest the worst is yet to come. During the 1990s the number of entrants into the work force will grow more slowly than in past decades, unless boosted by a great influx of immigrants. The point here is educational access. Of the new entrants into the work force, white males—currently the best-educated sector of the population, especially in science, technology, and engineering—will constitute only 15 percent, and the rest will be women, minorities, and immigrants. Since the latter two categories have generally gone into low-paid, unskilled jobs, there exists a potentially enormous mismatch between educational levels and the forecast demand for jobs requiring advanced technical or higher education.

If the above analysis is generally accurate, the United States may not be a "loser" in the face of global changes, as many desperate societies in the developing world will be; but because of its social and economic structure—its educational and social deficits, its fiscal problems—it could be less than a clear "winner." What emerges instead is a mixed picture: some industries rising as others fall, consultants flourishing as blue-collar workers have fewer opportunities, the slow growth in overall per capita GNP barely concealing the widening gap between those whose skills are in demand and those whose are not.

Excerpted from Paul Kennedy, *Preparing for the Twenty-First Century*, New York: Random House, 1993, pp. 290 ff.

grow faster. Widespread cost-cutting practices can produce the huge savings and investment needed to get the U.S. economy humming again. Will the pursuit of fast economic growth reduce social inequality as it does in East Asia or increase it as in Brazil? Only the future can tell.

Questions for Discussion and Review

1. What similarities and differences do socially mobile countries show in achieving economic success?
2. What causes the downward mobility among poor nations?
3. What are the signs that the United States has lost its enormous economic leadership of more than two decades ago?

CAUSES OF GLOBAL INEQUALITY

Sociologists have long tried to explain global inequality, or more specifically, why many countries in Africa, Asia, and Latin America are poor and most Western countries are rich. Under the influence of the functionalist perspective, in the 1950s and 1960s, some sociologists argued that increased contact with rich countries can benefit poor countries by helping them modernize and prosper. Conversely, according to the same argument, lack of contact perpetuates poverty. Then, in the 1970s and 1980s, other sociologists, influenced by the conflict perspective, argued just the opposite: that contact with rich countries is harmful, keeping poor countries poor. In the 1990s a third theory has emerged to explain a different but related phenomenon: the transformation of some poor countries into rich ones. Derived from the symbolic interactionist perspective, the explanation is that people in those countries attach special meanings to the importance of family, hard work, and other values of the past.

Functionalist Perspective

According to functionalists, society is made up of interdependent parts that cooperate to ensure social order. If one part is strong and another weak, the strong is expected to help the weak. Similarly, in global society, rich nations are expected to assist poor ones, otherwise the plight of the poor will lead to wars, mass migrations into rich countries, and other problems that threaten world order. Thus rich nations such as the United States have tried to help poor nations improve their economies.

This functionalist logic led to the development of **modernization theory,** namely that contact with rich nations can enrich poor ones but lack of contact keeps them poor. The contact may involve rich nations providing poor countries with various forms of assistance. They include offering family-planning services to slow population growth; assistance in mass education; fertilizers, irrigation projects, biological engineering, and other modern agricultural techniques to boost food production; loans and technical expertise to establish infrastructure (such as roads, embankments, and power stations) and transport and communication systems; modern machinery to increase industrial production; and loans and investment capital to expand businesses, imports, and exports.

Those foreign aid programs, according to modernization theory, should help poor countries develop the following conditions necessary for modernization:

1. A technological revolution in agriculture, which permits, even forces, workers to move off the farms and into industry.
2. An accumulation of capital and of money that can

In the functionalist perspective, contact with rich nations can modernize poor ones. Foreign aid programs offered by rich nations to the poor, according to modernization theory, can help people in poor countries develop their agriculture, accumulate capital, expand foreign trade, and encourage entrepreneurs willing to take risks to invest in new business ventures. Shown here is a banana export enterprise in Peru.

be loaned to exploit natural resources and manufacture consumer goods.

3. An expansion of foreign trade, which provides an export market for the country's manufactured goods as well as attracting foreign funds and technology.

4. The emergence of entrepreneurs—people who are willing to take risks to invest in new business ventures (Rostow, 1960).

However, many poor countries with foreign aid still fail to develop those conditions for modernization. The main reason, according to modernization theory, is deep reverence for the past and strong attachment to the family. This is assumed to cause many poor countries to resist technological innovations and other modern ideas from the West. The consequence is continuing poverty.

Modernization theory has for decades influenced the foreign policy of the United States and other Western nations. The massive assistance given to a few countries such as Spain and the four East Asian "dragons" has indeed helped produce impressive prosperity to validate modernization theory. But the theory has also drawn criticisms from sociologists and other social scientists who are influenced by the conflict and symbolic interactionist perspectives.

Conflict Perspective

Contrary to functionalists, conflict sociologists are critical of the rich and powerful for exploiting the poor and weak. Thus the rich nations are blamed for the development failure of most poor nations. To conflict sociologists, rich nations may appear interested in providing poor nations with adequate assistance but actually are not. For evidence they point to

the fact that aid to poor nations represents a negligible portion of the rich nations' income, namely, *only 0.3 percent* of their combined GNPs (United Nations, 1994). Conflict sociologists suspect that rich nations are more interested in exploiting poor nations. This suspicion has led to the development of **dependency theory,** which says that rich nations exploit poor ones for power and commercial gain, thereby perpetuating poverty, underdevelopment, or dependency on rich nations. The theory suggests various ways the exploitation is carried out.

First, much of the exploitation is a legacy of colonialism. Many of today's poor nations used to be colonies of rich nations in the West. As the Western countries were industrializing, they used their colonies as a source of cheaply priced raw materials and a market for their higher priced manufactured goods. These colonies have been independent nations for more than three decades, but are still very much under the thumb of their former masters. The control is in the form of **neocolonialism,** the economic control exercised by rich nations over their former colonies. Thus a similar pattern of unequal trading continues to this day; the rich nations import raw materials at a low price from their former colonies and then send them manufactured goods for a large profit.

Rich nations also use their powerful banks, particularly the International Monetary Fund and the World Bank, to control the economies of poor nations. Desperate for financial aid from these banks, many poor nations are forced to accept whatever conditions the banks impose upon them. Basically, they are required to practice Western-style capitalism: maximizing free-market enterprise with minimum government interference. This may stimulate production but it imposes unbearable costs on people's lives. For example, in the African nation of Ghana,

In the conflict perspective, rich nations are more interested in exploiting poor nations for power and commercial gain than in helping them. Rich countries, for example, can use their powerful banks to control the economies of poor nations. Supported by these banks, foreign corporations can exploit cheap labor to manufacture goods and can even get farmers to switch from growing food for local consumption to producing commodities for export.

an aid recipient, gold production has tripled since 1986, but many miners skip lunch because they cannot afford it (Darnton, 1994a). Moreover, most of the aid money does not go to the poor masses but instead ends up in the pockets of the local elite. The banks are far from charitable. In 1993 the World Bank issued loans worth $16 billion to support 1,900 projects but collected nearly $20 billion in repayment and other charges from borrowers. The $4 billion profit seems excessive for a bank created to assist poor nations. Nonetheless, the large profit is expected to continue because, since the late 1980s, poor countries have been repaying debts plus interest faster than they receive new loans (Zagorin, 1994).

With support from those banks, huge corporations from rich countries engage in many projects in poor countries. Considerable profit is made from the local policy that allows foreign corporations to maximize production without any governmental restrictions, as has been applied to gold mining in Ghana. Many foreign corporations can also exploit cheap labor to manufacture goods. They can even get farmers to switch from producing food for local consumption to producing commodities (such as coffee, sugar, fruits, or palm oil) for export. The consequence is often disastrous for local people. In Central America, for example, for the last 30 years huge increases in production of beef for export to the United States have sharply increased hunger by reducing production of staple foods such as corn and beans, damaged the environment by cutting and clearing millions of acres of forests for cattle to graze, and produced more poverty by forcing countryfolk onto considerably smaller pieces of land (Darnton, 1994a).

Dependency theory is useful for understanding how foreign exploitation helps perpetuate poverty in many poor nations in Africa, Asia, and Latin America. But the theory fails to explain the rapid economic ascendancy of the formerly poor East Asian societies.

Symbolic Interactionist Perspective

Earlier we suggested that the East Asian prosperity validated modernization theory because substantial foreign aid has played a significant part in contributing to the prosperity. But substantial foreign aid does not appear to be the only or most important factor. If it were, the Philippines, which has received as much if not more military and economic assistance from the United States, would have prospered. In fact, in the 1950s, when modernization theory was first proposed, many of its proponents considered the Philippines the most likely to succeed. But the

country has turned out to be an economic disaster.

Modernization theory further suffers from a serious defect, harboring a Western bias against non-Western countries. As we have observed, the theory assumes that the non-Western traditions of deep reverence for the past and strong attachment to the family are a barrier to modernization in many poor nations. If all this were true, the deeply traditional societies in East Asia would not have achieved extraordinary prosperity. In fact, as Peter Berger (1992) points out, supporters of modernization theory in the 1950s wrongly assumed that the ancient Confucian tradition of ancestor worship and family attachment was one of the most formidable obstacles to development in now-modernized Korea and Taiwan. Apparently, modernization theorists embrace the ethnocentric belief that, just because individualism works in the West, poor non-Western nations can develop only if they drop their traditional reverence for authority and adopt the Western respect for the individual. Modernization theorists fail to see that the traditional culture of reverence for the past, authority, or family can inculcate a strong sense of *obligation to others,* which can serve as a powerful motivation for hard work and cooperative action. Consider how those traditional values contribute to economic success in Japan.

The Japanese culture emphasizes the importance of social relations and collective welfare. It encourages consensus rather than conflict, deference to rather than disrespect for authority, and paternalism rather than indifference by those in authority. These traditional values saturate Japan's economic system. A business enterprise, no matter how large, is run like a household, with the accompanying interdependence and loyalty characteristic of the family. The traditional emphasis on collective welfare does more than just enhance productivity through cooperation between managers and workers. It causes society to favor business and industry at the expense of individuals, transferring funds and wealth from individuals to industries. This can be seen in the fact that factories and company apartments are mostly grand and imposing, whereas private homes are cramped yet highly expensive. Still, given the enormous prosperity of the society as a whole, the Japanese enjoy one of the highest living standards in the world.

Since modernization theory, like dependency theory, cannot explain the economic success of the East Asian societies, some sociologists have recently turned to **cultural theory,** namely that cultural values of discipline, thrift, education, and the family contribute to economic success. These Confucian values pervade East Asian societies. Cultural theory is derived from the symbolic interaction perspective

Some sociologists have recently turned to cultural theory—a derivative of the symbolic interactionist perspective—to explain the economic success of East Asian societies. For example, in countries such as Taiwan, shown here, where Confucianism is freely expressed, the economy flourishes. Confucianism is seen as encouraging hard work as an obligation to others, thus contributing to economic success.

because it implies that values reflect how people see and interpret the world around them and that this powerfully affects their behavior and activities.

According to cultural theorists, in countries such as Japan, South Korea, and Taiwan where Confucianism is freely expressed, the economy flourishes. But in countries such as Communist China and North Korea where Confucianism has been suppressed, there has been widespread poverty. According to some cultural theorists, the Confucian

values are actually similar to the Calvinist values— the old Protestant ethic—which fueled the early U.S. industrial revolution (Harrison, 1992; Kotkin, 1992). There is a difference, though: Confucianism encourages hard work as an obligation to others, whereas the Protestant ethic encourages hard work as an obligation to oneself—a way of attaining what is known in U.S. society as self-fulfillment. Yet these two value systems are similar in that they both contribute to economic success. In short, cultural values can shape a nation's economy, hence its position in global stratification.

Cultural theory may be useful for explaining the economic success in East Asia, but values are not the only factor. After all, as we have observed, Spain and Brazil have achieved upward mobility without the same values. Other, noncultural factors are also at work. They may include foreign assistance, as modernization theory suggests, or freedom from foreign exploitation, as dependency theory implies.

Questions for Discussion and Review

2. How do modernization, dependency, and cultural theories reflect the major sociological perspectives?
3. According to modernization theory, why do some nations fail to develop economically while others succeed?
4. According to dependency theory, how do poor nations get stuck in poverty?
5. According to cultural theory, why do some societies prosper?

CHAPTER REVIEW

1. *What is the world system approach to global stratification?* The world is divided into three classes. The most industrialized and wealthy nations make up the upper class known as the core of the world system, the poor countries constitute the lower class known as the periphery, and nations that are in between are the middle class known as the semiperiphery. *What is the dynamic nature of global stratification?* It is fluid rather than rigid, with nations moving up or down, depending on foreign influence and domestic conditions.

2. *What is global inequality?* The extreme disparity in economic condition and life quality between rich and poor nations. *What is the cost of global inequal-*

ity? Poor countries suffer from widespread poverty, extensive female disadvantages, relatively prevalent child exploitation, and large-scale slavery.

3. *What did Japan and the four East Asian "tigers" have in common that can explain their social mobility in the world?* Huge foreign assistance, an uncompromising attitude toward work, and active government support for privately owned businesses. *How has Spain achieved its upward mobility?* Through a sweeping economic reform that opened up the economy for unrestricted trade, foreign investment, and industrial growth, along with massive U.S. aid. *What factors may explain Brazil's upward mobility as one of the world's fastest growing economies?* A huge influx of

enterprising immigrants from Europe and Japan; social power deriving from commerce, industry, and capital rather than politics and land-owning; and relatively great government concern with economic growth.

4. *What seems to cause downward mobility among sub-Saharan African nations?* Several factors including rapid population growth, a huge drop in global commodity prices, and inadequate flow of capital from rich countries. *What may have caused the United States to suffer a loss of economic status in the world over the last 20 years?* Deindustrialization, or mass loss of manufacturing jobs; great increase in consumption; and substantial decrease in savings.

5. *How does modernization theory explain why some poor countries develop economically while others fail?* Contact with rich countries, especially in the form of foreign aid, can help poor countries develop. But many poor countries that receive foreign aid still fail to develop, because they do not have the proper conditions for modernization. *What is dependency theory?* Derived from the conflict perspective, dependency theory is critical of rich nations, arguing that their exploitation of poor countries tends to perpetuate poverty, underdevelopment, or dependency. *How does cultural theory explain the economic ascendancy in East Asia?* The ascendancy arises from the traditional, Confucian values of discipline, thrift, education, and the family.

KEY TERMS

Core countries The world's upper class, the most industrialized and richest societies, popularly known as industrial or developed countries (p. 245).

Cultural theory The theory that cultural values of discipline, thrift, education, and the family contribute to economic success (p. 259).

Deindustrialization The loss of numerous factory jobs as a result of relocating a massive number of manufacturing plants to peripheral countries (p. 247).

Dependency theory The theory that rich nations exploit poor ones for power and commercial gain, thereby perpetuating poverty, underdevelopment, or dependency on rich nations (p. 258).

Global stratification A system in which all the countries of the world find themselves in various positions, some getting less—or more—in life than others (p. 244).

Modernization theory The theory that contact with rich nations can enrich poor ones but lack of contact keeps them poor (p. 257).

Neocolonialism The economic control exercised by rich nations over their former colonies (p. 258).

Peripheral countries The world's lower class, relatively poor societies, popularly known as developing countries (p. 245).

Reindustrialization The proliferation of unstable, low-skilled, or low-paying jobs (p. 247).

Semiperipheral countries The world's middle class, relatively affluent societies in the middle of global stratification, also known as newly industrialized countries (p. 245).

World system A network of commercial and other relationships among all the members of the world's community (p. 244).

SUGGESTED READINGS

Angelopoulos, Angelos, and Melvin Fagen. 1993. *The Third World and the Rich Countries: Proposals to Combat the Global Economic Crisis.* Lanham, Maryland: University Press of America. Shows how poor countries sink deeper in poverty and how both the poor and affluent countries can work together to promote economic development in the Third World.

Guillermoprieto, Alma. 1994. *The Heart That Bleeds: Latin America Now.* New York: Alfred A. Knopf. An inside look into how Latin America creates pervasive inequality in its struggle for modernity and prosperity.

Harrison, Lawrence E. 1992. *Who Prospers: How Cultural Values Shape Economic and Political Success.* New York: Basic Books. Presenting a cultural theory of how certain countries achieve prosperity in the modern world.

Hayter, Teresa. 1990. *The Creation of World Poverty.* London: Pluto Press. An analysis of how the core, wealthy nations in the West have enriched themselves by exploiting the peripheral, poor nations.

Luttwak, Edward N. 1994. *The Endangered American Dream: How to Stop the United States From Becoming a Third World Country and How to Win the Geo-Economic Struggle for Industrial Supremacy.* New York: Simon & Schuster/Touchstone. An examination of how the United States has begun to develop such conditions as the declining earnings for the majority, the spectacular enrichment of the few, and the increasingly violent desperation of the poor.

RACE AND ETHNICITY

Myths and Realities

MYTH: *When people move from one country to another their racial characteristics, such as skin color and facial features, do not change. Therefore, if African Americans go to another country, they will be considered blacks there, as in the United States.*

REALITY: It is true that people's physical features do not change when they move to another country. But their racial identification as blacks or whites may change. Most African Americans in the United States, for example, would be considered whites in some Latin American countries.

MYTH: *As "model Americans," Asian Americans are more economically successful than other groups, including whites.*

REALITY: The family income is higher for Asians than whites, but this is because the average Asian family is larger and more persons in the family work, compared with the average white family. Individual income is lower for Asians than for whites.

MYTH: *Since Jewish Americans as a whole are prosperous, they tend to be conservative or to vote Republican, like other prosperous U.S. citizens.*

REALITY: On the contrary, they tend more to be liberal, supporting welfare, civil rights, women's rights, and the like. They are also more likely to vote Democratic.

MYTH: *If a white person discriminates against blacks, he or she must be prejudiced.*

REALITY: Not necessarily. Many whites discriminate without being prejudiced, primarily because of social pressure. Unprejudiced white men, for example, might not date black women for fear of being ostracized.

n the summer of 1992 a deluge of horror stories about human cruelties shocked the world. The reports poured out of newly independent Bosnia, the most ethnically diverse republic of what used to be Yugoslavia. The Serbs were reported to be carrying out an "ethnic cleansing" campaign, driving Muslims and Croats from their homes, torturing and killing some, and abusing and terrorizing the rest. In a northern Bosnian town, armed Serbs rounding up 100 prisoners for a move from one detention camp to another pulled out about 30 prisoners and shot them. At one camp, the family of one starving prisoner tried to bring him some food, but the guards took it away and then beat the prisoner in front of his relatives. Near Tuzla in eastern Bosnia, three Muslim girls were stripped and chained to a fence "for all to use." After being raped for three days, they were doused with gasoline and set on fire. Other Muslim and Croatian girls had been used as sex slaves for months, and if they became pregnant they were set free to "have Serbian babies." While most reports focused on Serbian cruelties, some Muslims and Croats struck back with atrocities of their own in areas where they predominate (Watson, 1992).

Mistreatment of minorities is not limited to Bosnia. It occurs in other parts of Eastern Europe and Russia as well. In Western Europe, Pakistanis, Turks, Algerians, and other non-European minorities are often subjected to random insults and hostile stares, which sometimes escalate into gang attacks or firebombs thrown from the streets. In Japan, the Koreans, Burakumin, and Konketsuji (American-Japanese mixed bloods) are also targets of considerable prejudice and discrimination. In the United States, African Americans are given poor service in stores or restaurants, have racial epithets hurled at them, are harassed by white police, and are attacked by white supremacists (Feagin, 1991). These are only a few of the countless cases of mistreatment minorities suffer around the world.

In this chapter we take a closer look at the problem.

SOCIOLOGICAL DEFINITIONS

People are accustomed to thinking of a **minority** as a category of people who are physically different and who make up a small percentage of the population. But this is not the way sociologists define a minority. Consider the Jews in China and in the United States and the blacks in South Africa. The Jews in China do not "look Jewish"—they look like other Chinese. Similarly, the Jews in the United States do not "look Jewish"—they look like other white Americans. Jews cannot be differentiated from the dominant group on the basis of their physical characteristics, but they are sociologically considered a minority. In South Africa, blacks are also sociologically a minority, although they make up a majority of the population. Neither physical traits nor numbers alone determines whether people constitute a minority. To understand the sociological idea of minority, we need first to look at race and ethnicity.

Race

As a biological concept, race refers to a large category of people who share certain inherited physical characteristics. These may include particular skin color, nasal shape, or lip form. The popular classification of human races recognizes three groups: Caucasoid, Mongoloid, and Negroid. Caucasoids have light skin, Mongoloids yellowish skin, and Negroids dark skin—and other physical differences exist among the three groups.

There are at least two problems with this classification of races. First, some groups fit into none of these categories. Natives of India and Pakistan have Caucasoid facial features but dark skin. The Ainu of Japan have Mongoloid faces but white skin. The Vogul of Siberia have Caucasoid faces but yellowish skin. Some aboriginal groups in Australia have dark skin and other Negroid features but blond hair. The Polynesians of Pacific Islands have a mixture of Caucasoid, Mongoloid, and Negroid characteristics (Jacquard, 1983).

Another problem with the biological classification of races is that there are no "pure" races. People in these groups have been interbreeding for centuries. In the United States, for example, about 70 percent of blacks have some white ancestry and approximately 20 percent of whites have at least one black ancestor (Sowell, 1983; Davis, 1991; Kilker, 1993). Biologists have also determined that all current populations originate from one common genetic pool—one single group of humans that evolved about 30,000 years ago, most likely in Africa. Today, about 95 to 99 percent of the DNA molecules (which make up the gene) are the same for all humans, and only the remaining 1 to 5 percent are responsible for all the differences in appearance (Vora, 1981; Shipman, 1994). Even these outward differences are meaningless because the differences among members of the same "race" are greater than the average differences between two racial groups. Some U.S. blacks, for example, have lighter skins than many whites, and some whites are darker than many blacks.

Since there are no clear-cut biological distinctions—in physical characteristics or genetic make-up—between racial groups, sociologists define race as a social rather than biological phenomenon. Defined sociologically, a **race** is a group of people who are *perceived* by a given society to be biologically different from others. People are assigned to one race or another, not necessarily on the basis of logic or fact but by public opinion, which, in turn, is molded by society's dominant group. Consider a boy in the United States whose father has 100 percent white

In Brazil, the definition of race differs from that in the United States. According to Brazil's popular perception of a black as a person of African descent who has no white ancestry at all, about three-fourths of all American blacks would not be considered blacks. Instead, they would be considered white, since they have some white ancestry.

ancestry and whose mother is the daughter of a white man and black woman. This youngster is considered "black" in our society, although he is actually more white than black because 75 percent of his ancestry is white. In many Latin American countries, however, this same child would be considered "white." In fact, according to Brazil's popular perception of a black as a person of African descent who has no white ancestry at all, about three-fourths of all U.S. blacks would *not* be considered blacks (Denton and Massey, 1989). The definition of race, then, varies from one society to another. Sociologists use this societal definition to identify "races" because it is the racial status to which people are assigned by their society—rather than their real biological characteristics—that has profound significance for their social lives.

Ethnicity

Jews have often been called a race, but they have the same racial origins as Arabs—both are Semites—and through the centuries Jews and non-Jews have interbred extensively. As a result, as noted earlier, Jews are often physically indistinguishable from non-Jews. Besides, a person can become a Jew by conversion to Judaism. Jews do not constitute a race, but are instead, a religious group or, more broadly, an ethnic group.

Whereas race is based on popularly perceived physical traits, ethnicity is based on cultural characteristics. An **ethnic group**, then, is a collection of people who share a distinctive cultural heritage. Members of an ethnic group may share a language, religion, history, or national origin. They always share a feeling that they are a distinct people. In the United States, members of an ethnic group typically have the same national origin. As a result, they are named after the countries from which they or their ancestors came. Examples are Polish Americans, Italian Americans, or Irish Americans.

For the most part, ethnicity is culturally learned. People learn the language, values, and other characteristics of their ethnic group. Members of an ethnic group are usually born into it, but the cultural traits of the group are passed from one generation to the next.

Minority

A **minority** is a racial or ethnic group that is subjected to prejudice and discrimination. **Prejudice** is a negative attitude toward a certain category of people. It includes ideas and beliefs, feelings, and predispositions to act in a certain way. For example, whites prejudiced against blacks might fear meeting a black man on the street at night. They might resent blacks who are successful. They might plan to sell their houses if a black family moves into the neighborhood.

Whereas prejudice is an attitude, discrimination is an act. More specifically, **discrimination** is an unfavorable action against individuals that is taken because they are members of a certain category. When a landlord will not rent an apartment to a family because they are African American or Hispanic, that is discrimination.

A minority is not necessarily a small percentage of the population. Blacks are considered a minority in South Africa, even though they make up about 70 percent of the population, because they are the subordinate group. Similarly, the dominant group need

not make up a large part of the population. People of English descent in the United States today constitute only about 13 percent of the population, but because of their continuing social and cultural influence, they are still considered the dominant group—as they were more than 200 years ago.

Questions For Discussion and Review

1. Why do sociologists define race as a social rather than a physical phenomenon?
2. When does a racial or ethnic group become a minority group?

RACE AND ETHNICITY IN THE UNITED STATES

The United States is a nation of immigrants (see Figure 12.1). The earliest "immigrants" were the American Indians, who arrived from Asia more than 20,000 years ago. Long after the Indians had settled down as Native Americans, other immigrants began to pour in from Europe and later from Africa, Asia, and Latin America. They came as explorers, adventurers, slaves, or refugees—most hoping to fulfill a dream of success and happiness. The English were the earliest of these immigrants and, on the whole, the most successful in fulfilling that dream. They

FIGURE 12.1
Ancestry of U.S. Population

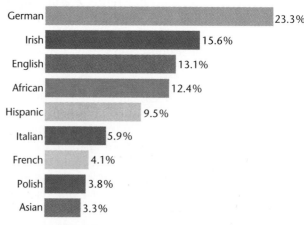

German 23.3%
Irish 15.6%
English 13.1%
African 12.4%
Hispanic 9.5%
Italian 5.9%
French 4.1%
Polish 3.8%
Asian 3.3%

All other Europeans 19.5% Southwest Asian 0.6% West Indian 0.4%

(Figures add up to more than 100% because some people reported multiple ancestries.)

Source: *Statistical Abstract of the United States, 1994.*

American Mosaic

Arab Americans make up a new and growing ethnic group in the United States. Coming from many diverse countries, they are becoming deeply involved in U.S. business and social life. This reading explores some features of this diverse group and why they are often misunderstood.

The Arab Americans

Real Arab Americans don't fit into media stereotypes. They are people we know and respect, like consumer advocate Ralph Nader. Singer Paula Abdul and deejay Casey Kasem prove that Arab Americans can be as American as rock and roll. Heart surgeon Michael De Bakey and Heisman Trophy winner Doug Flutie place Arab Americans among our heroes. Secretary of Health Donna Shalala, Senate majority leader George Mitchell, and many other Arab Americans rank among our leaders.

The vast majority of Arab Americans are citizens. They are much like other Americans, except younger, more educated, more affluent, and more likely to own a business. The demographics of Arab Americans make them an important consumer market.

According to the Census Bureau's definition, Arab Americans are people who trace their ancestry to northern Africa and western Asia. While nations in these areas vary somewhat in their cultures and traditions, the common ground is an "Arabic heritage" and the Arabic language.

Arab Americans tend to be younger than the overall U.S. population. Again, this is probably because younger people are more likely than older people to immigrate. As a result, a large proportion of Arab Americans are in their childbearing years, and another large proportion are native-born children and teenagers.

As with many other minorities, Arab Americans are a geographically concentrated group. Over two-thirds live in 10 states; one-third live in California, New York and Michigan. They are also more likely than other Americans to live in metropolitan areas. Thirty-six per- cent of Arab Americans live in 10 metros, led by Detroit, New York, and Los Angeles-Long Beach.

In general, Arab Americans are better educated than the average American. The share who did not attend college is lower than average, and the share with master's degrees or higher is twice the average. Because a larger-than-average share of Arab Americans are highly educated people of working age, their work force rates are high. Eighty percent of Arab Americans aged 16 and older were employed in 1990, compared with 60 percent of all American adults.

Sixty percent of Arab Americans work as executives, professionals, salespeople, administrative support, or service personnel, compared with 66 percent of the general American population. Arab Americans are more likely than average to work in sales and less likely to work in most other broad occupational categories, particularly administrative support and service jobs. Although many large companies are laying people off, Arab Americans may be better able to survive a changing economy. They are more likely than average to be entrepreneurs or self-employed (12 percent versus 7 percent).

In short, Arab Americans are productive citizens, concentrated in a few geographic areas, and bound by a common heritage and language. They are tired of the negative press surrounding international issues. and they are tired of thoughtless portrayals in the media.

Excerpted from Samia El-Badry, "The Arab Americans," *American Demographics* magazine, January, 1994, pp. 22–30. © 1994. Reprinted with permission.

became the dominant group. Eventually, they founded a government dedicated to the democratic ideal of equality, but they kept African Americans as slaves and discriminated against other racial and ethnic groups. This "American dilemma"—the discrepancy between the ideal of equality and the reality of discrimination—still exists, though to a lesser degree than in the past. Let us look at how the major minority groups have fared under the burden of the American dilemma.

Native Americans

Native Americans have long been called Indians— one result of Columbus's mistaken belief that he had landed in India. The explorer's successors passed down many other distorted descriptions of the Native Americans. They were described as savages, although it was whites who slaughtered hundreds of thousands of them. They were portrayed as scalp hunters, although it was the white government that

offered large sums to whites for the scalps of Indians. They were stereotyped as lazy, although it was whites who forced them to give up their traditional occupations. These false conceptions of Native Americans were reinforced by the contrasting pictures whites painted of themselves. The white settlers were known as pioneers rather than invaders and marauders; their conquest of the Native Americans' land was called homesteading, not robbery.

When Columbus "discovered" what would later become the United States, there were more than 300 Native American tribes with a total population of over a million. Of the natives he encountered around the Caribbean, Columbus wrote: "Of anything they have, if it be asked for, they never say no, but do rather invite the person to accept it, and show as much lovingness as though they would give their hearts" (Hraba, 1979). In North America, too, the earliest white settlers were often aided by friendly Native Americans.

As the white settlers increased in numbers and moved westward, however, Native Americans resisted them. But the native population was decimated by outright killing, by destruction of their food sources, and by diseases brought by whites, such as smallpox and influenza. With their greater numbers and superior military technology, the whites prevailed. Sometimes they took land by treaty rather than by outright force—and then often proceeded to violate the treaty.

By 1992, there were about two million Native Americans. Slightly more than half lived on 278 reservations, mostly in the Southwest, the rest in urban areas. After more than two centuries of colonial subjugation, Native Americans today find themselves at the bottom of the socioeconomic

ladder—the poorest minority in the United States. Their unemployment and poverty rates are much higher than those among other Americans and their family income is considerably lower (see Figure 12.2). Moreover, they suffer from much higher rates of pneumonia, influenza, diabetes, tuberculosis, suicide, alcoholism, and car accidents compared with the general U.S. population.

Under constant pressure by Native Americans, the U.S. government has since 1988 instituted a policy "to promote tribal economic development, tribal self-sufficiency, and strong tribal government." Today, on some reservations Native Americans are exempted from paying taxes and further allowed to sell gasoline, cigarettes, and other items tax-free to non-Indians. About 59 percent of the reservations are also permitted to run highly profitable gambling operations that cater to non-Indians. At least seven tribes have recently been allowed to govern themselves virtually as sovereign nations. These tribes may set their own budgets, run their own programs, and negotiate directly with the federal government for services, functions that have long been performed by the U.S. Bureau of Indian Affairs. If this experiment in self-government succeeds, the U.S. government may extend it to all the other tribes (Gartner, 1990; Verhovek, 1990; Egan, 1991).

All this has sparked a national movement to recapture traditions, to make Native Americans feel proud of their cultural heritage. Virtually every tribe places a heavy emphasis on teaching the younger generation its native language, crafts, tribal history, and religious ceremonies. There used to be a lack of unity among the 300 tribes, but today intertribal visiting and marriage are common occurrences. Moreover, in the last 15 years, many Native American men and

FIGURE 12.2
Native Americans: Poorest Minority

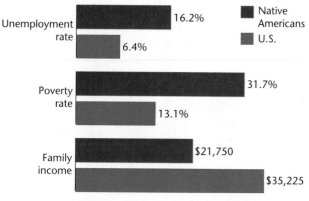

Source: U.S. Census Bureau, 1994.

After more than 200 years of subjugation, Native Americans find themselves at the bottom of the socioeconomic ladder in the United States. Unemployment and poverty rates are much higher than among other Americans, and many live without electricity, heat, or plumbing.

women have successfully established themselves in business, law, and other professions. Of course, the majority of Native Americans still have a long way to go. Without a viable economic base to draw on, they still find themselves powerless, mired in high unemployment, deep poverty, and other problems. The last 15 years have not been long enough to overcome two centuries of government oppression.

African Americans

There are more than 31 million African Americans, constituting about 12 percent of the U.S. population. They are the largest minority in the nation. In fact, there are more blacks in the United States than in any single African nation except Nigeria.

Their ancestors first came from Africa to North America as indentured servants in 1619. Soon after

that they were brought here as slaves. Most lived in the South, where they worked on cotton, tobacco, or sugar-cane plantations. Slavery ended during the Civil War in 1865, but soon after federal troops withdrew from the South, white supremacy returned. Many **Jim Crow** laws were enacted to segregate blacks from whites in all kinds of public and private facilities—from restrooms to schools. A more basic tactic to control blacks was terror. If an African American man was suspected of killing a white or of raping a white woman, he might be lynched, beaten to death, or burned at the stake.

Lynchings occurred in the North, too. Still, the North did offer more opportunities to African Americans. Since the early 1900s, as southern farms were mechanized and as the demand for workers in northern industrial centers rose during the two World Wars, many southern African Americans migrated north. When the wars ended and the demand for workers decreased, however, they were often the first to be fired. Even in the North, where there were no Jim Crow laws, African Americans faced discrimination and segregation.

A turning point in U.S. race relations came in 1954 when the U.S. Supreme Court ordered that public schools be desegregated. The order gave momentum to the long-standing campaign against racial discrimination. In the late 1950s and 1960s, the civil rights movement launched marches, sit-ins, and boycotts to end political and economic discrimination. The price was high: many civil rights workers were beaten and jailed; some were killed. Eventually Congress passed the landmark Civil Rights Act of 1964, prohibiting segregation and discrimination in virtually all areas of social life, such as public facilities, schools, housing, and employment.

In the last 30 years, the Civil Rights Act has put an end to many forms of segregation and paved the way for some improvement in the position of African Americans. Various studies have shown a significant decline in white opposition to such issues as school integration, integrated housing, interracial marriage, and voting for an African American president. The number of African Americans elected to various public offices has sharply increased since 1980. The proportion of African Americans with college degrees has also grown significantly. An affluent middle class has emerged among African Americans.

Full equality, however, is still far from being achieved. Most evident is the continuing large economic gap between blacks and whites. The latest figures on median family income are $21,161 for blacks and $38,909 for whites—with blacks earning only about 54 percent of the amount made by whites, a decline from 57 percent in 1980. Over 33 percent of

Poet and novelist Alice Walker , who took part in the civil rights movement of the 1960s that paved the way for improvements in the position of African Americans, receives an award at Radcliffe College. Though the proportion of African Americans today contributing to the nation's cultural, political, and educational life is greater than ever before, full equality is still far from achieved.

blacks live in poverty, compared with fewer than 12 percent of whites (Census Bureau, 1994). More glaring racial inequality shows up in housing. Over the last decade there has been some decline in residential segregation, especially in relatively small metropolitan areas with active housing construction in the South and West, but the decline has been very modest (Figure 12.3). Most blacks continue to reside in segregated neighborhoods and are more likely than whites with similar incomes to live in overcrowded and substandard housing (Hacker, 1992).

In short, progress has been significant in education and politics, but not in housing and economic conditions. The economic situation is a little complicated, though. Unemployment and poverty have soared in the black working class, primarily because of numerous plant shutdowns caused by the shift from a manufacturing to service economy in the face of increased global competition. On the other hand, the black middle class has become more prosperous,

largely because of their advanced education and skills required by the technological changes in the U.S. economy (Takaki, 1993). Still it is difficult for middle-class blacks to enjoy the rewards of their success. They are often outraged by being treated like the "black underclass," which involves being stopped and questioned as crime suspects by police, getting bad or no service in shops and restaurants, having difficulty flagging down a taxi, and being falsely charged with shoplifting (Feagin, 1991; Close, 1993).

Hispanic Americans

In 1848 the United States either won in war or bought from Mexico what would become Texas, California, Nevada, Utah, Arizona, New Mexico, and Colorado. Many Mexicans consequently found themselves living in U.S. territories as U.S. citizens. The vast majority of today's Mexican Americans, however, are the result of immigration from Mexico since the turn of the century. At first immigrants came largely to work in the farmlands of California and to build the railroads of the Southwest. Later a steady stream of Mexicans began to pour into the United States, driven by Mexico's population pressures and economic problems and attracted by U.S. industry's need for low-paid, unskilled labor.

In 1898 the United States added Puerto Rico to its territory by defeating Spain in the Spanish-American War. In 1917 Congress granted all Puerto Ricans citizenship , but they may not vote in presidential elections and are not represented in Congress. Over the years, especially since the early 1950s, many Puerto Ricans, lured by job opportunities and cheap plane service between New York City and San Juan, have migrated to the mainland. In the last two decades, though, more have returned to Puerto Rico than have come here.

Thus, a new minority group emerged in the United States—Hispanic Americans, also called Latinos. Today the category actually includes several groups. Besides Mexican Americans and Puerto Ricans, there are Cuban immigrants who began to flock to the Miami area when their country became communist in 1959. There are also the "other Hispanics"—immigrants from other Central and South American countries who have come here as political refugees and job seekers. By 1992, the members of all these groups totaled about 24 million, constituting over nine percent of the U.S. population, the second largest minority. Because of high birth rates and the continuing influx of immigrants, Hispanic Americans may outnumber African Americans in the next decade (Census Bureau, 1994).

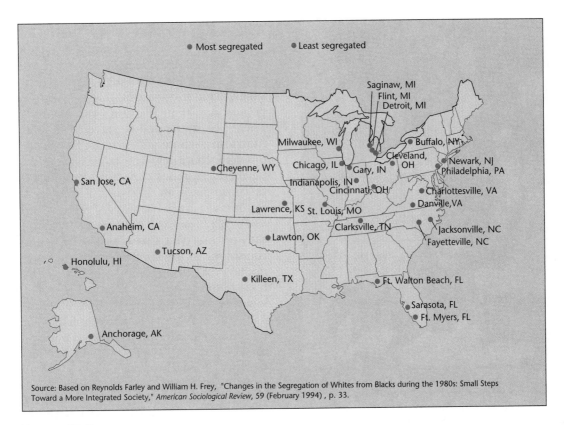

Source: Based on Reynolds Farley and William H. Frey, "Changes in the Segregation of Whites from Blacks during the 1980s: Small Steps Toward a More Integrated Society," *American Sociological Review*, 59 (February 1994), p. 33.

FIGURE 12.3
Residential Integration
Out of 232 cities, 194 have shown a modest decline in residential segregation since 1980. The largest decreases in segregation took place in small southern and western metropolitan areas with significant housing construction. Here are the most and least segregated cities.

The Spanish language is the unifying force among Hispanic Americans. Another source of common identity is religion: at least 85 percent are Roman Catholic. There are, however, significant differences within the Hispanic community. Mexican Americans are by far the largest group, accounting for 64 percent of the Hispanics. They are heavily concentrated in the Southwest and West. Puerto Ricans make up 11 percent and live mostly in the Northeast, especially in New York City. As a group, they are the poorest among the Hispanics (Figure 12.4), which may explain why many have gone back to Puerto Rico. The Cubans, who constitute five percent of the Hispanic population, are the most affluent and therefore have the greatest tendency toward integration with "Anglos"—white Americans. The remaining Hispanics are a diverse group, ranging from uneducated, unskilled laborers to highly trained professionals (Census Bureau, 1994).

Hispanics in general lag behind both whites and blacks in educational attainment. Among those age 25 or older, only nine percent have completed college, compared with 23 percent for whites and 12

percent for blacks. But some Hispanic groups are more educated than others. Cubans are the best educated, primarily because most of the early refugees fleeing communist Cuba were middle-class and professional people. Mexican Americans and Puerto Ricans are less educated because they consist of many recent immigrants with much less schooling. The

FIGURE 12.4
Poverty Rates Among Hispanic Groups

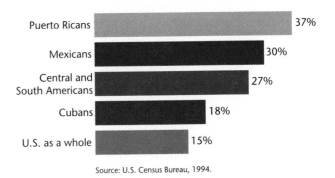

Source: U.S. Census Bureau, 1994.

Henry Cisneros, a Hispanic (also sometimes known as Latino), was appointed head of the Department of Housing and Urban Development under President Clinton. Hispanics, a diverse population unified by the Spanish language and Catholicism, make up the second largest minority group in the United States.

young, U.S.-born Hispanics usually have more education. Lack of proficiency in English has retarded the recent Hispanic immigrants' educational progress. As much as 25 percent of Hispanics in public schools speak little or no English, which has resulted in higher dropout rates than non-Hispanic students (Bernstein, 1990; Census Bureau, 1994).

Hispanics are primarily clustered in lower-paying jobs. They earn about 60 percent of the amount made by Anglos. They also have a higher rate of unemployment and poverty. However, the higher educational achievement of young Hispanics provides hope that more Hispanics will be joining the higher paid white-collar work force in the future. Recent research shows that, if Hispanics speak English fluently and have at least graduated from high school, their occupational achievement is close to that of non-Hispanics with similar English fluency and schooling (Stolzenberg, 1990). Nationwide, Hispanics are also already a growing force in politics. They now have more members of Congress, more state governors, and more mayors of large cities than before.

Asian Americans

Since 1980, Asian Americans have been the fastest growing minority, although they remain a much smaller minority—about three percent of the U.S. population—than Hispanics and African Americans. There is tremendous diversity among Asian Americans, whose ancestry can be traced to over 20 different countries. The larger groups are Chinese, Japanese, Filipinos, Koreans, and Vietnamese; the first two have the longest history in the United States.

The Chinese first came in 1849 during the gold rush on the West Coast, pulled by better economic conditions in the United States and pushed by economic problems and local rebellions in China. Soon huge numbers of Chinese were imported to work for low wages, digging mines and building railroads. After these projects were completed, jobs became scarce, and white workers feared competition from the Chinese. As a result, special taxes were imposed on the Chinese, and they were prohibited from attending school, seeking employment, owning property, and bearing witness in court. In 1882 the Chinese Exclusion Act restricted immigration to the United States, and it stopped all Chinese immigration from 1904 to 1943. Many returned to their homeland (Kitano, 1981; Henry, 1990).

Immigrants from Japan met similar hostility. They began to come to the West Coast somewhat later than the Chinese, also in search of better economic opportunities. At first they were welcomed as a source of cheap labor, but soon they began to operate small shops and anti-Japanese activity grew. In 1906 San Francisco forbade Asian children to attend white schools. In response, the Japanese government negotiated an agreement whereby the Japanese agreed to stop emigration to the United States, and President Theodore Roosevelt agreed to end harassment of the Japanese who were already here. But when the Japanese began to buy their own farms, they met new opposition. In 1913 California prohibited foreign-born Japanese from owning or leasing lands; other Western states followed suit. In 1922 the U.S. Supreme Court ruled that foreign-born Japanese could not become U.S. citizens.

Worse events occurred during World War II. All the Japanese, aliens and citizens, were rounded up from the West Coast and confined in concentration camps in isolated areas. They were forced to sell their homes and properties. The action was condoned even by the Supreme Court as a legitimate way of ensuring that the Japanese Americans would not help Japan defeat the United States. Racism, however, was the real source of such treatment. There was no evi-

Many Asian Americans have become successful in education, business, and the professions. However, Korean storeowners in the large cities of the United States, as shown here, as well as other Asian Americans, continue to experience prejudice and discrimination in the United States. Contrary to popular belief, Asian Americans still have not attained real income equality with whites, even though they have more education.

dence of any espionage or sabotage by a Japanese American. Besides, German Americans were not sent to concentration camps, although Germany was at war with the United States and there were instances of subversion by German Americans. In 1987, when the survivors sued the U.S. government for billions of dollars in compensation, the solicitor general acknowledged that the detention was "frankly racist" and "deplorable." And in 1988 the Senate voted overwhelmingly to give $20,000 and an apology to each of the surviving internees (Molotsky, 1988).

Despite this history of discrimination, the Asians *seem* to be educationally and economically among the most successful minorities in the United States today. As Figure 12.5 shows, a higher percentage of Asians than whites have a college degree and an annual family income of $50,000 or more. But the same figure indicates more poverty among Asians than whites. Moreover, the Asians' higher family income is misleading for two reasons. First, the average Asian family is larger and more members of the family work compared with the average white family. *Individual* income is actually lower for Asians than for whites. Second, most Asians live in California, Hawaii, and New York, where the cost of living is higher than the national average (Takaki, 1993). Contrary to popular belief, then, Asian Americans still have not attained real income equality with whites, even though they have more education.

Discrimination against Asians is subtle. Many well-educated Asian Americans can get work as professionals and technicians, but they rarely become officials and managers. White bosses often cite language deficiencies as an excuse for denying promotions. Privately, they stereotype the Asians as weak

and incapable of handling people, although Japanese-managed companies are well known for out-performing U.S. companies. It is assumed that Asian talents can flourish in the classroom or laboratory but not in senior management. The Asians are in effect victims of the **glass ceiling**, the prejudiced belief that keeps minority professionals from holding high, leadership positions in organizations. Thus, many Asian professionals are prevented from joining the top ranks of corporations.

The stereotype of Asians as a "model minority" also hurts. It implies that *all* Asians do well, which of

FIGURE 12.5
How Asian Americans Fare

Education
Percentage of persons in each group having graduated from college

42%
23%

Family Income
Percentage of families with annual income of $50,000 or more

40.9%
35.8%

Poverty Rate
Percentage of persons below the poverty level

12.5%
11.6%

Asians
Whites

Source: U.S. Census Bureau, 1994

course is not true because there is still much poverty among, for example, Filipinos and Chinatown residents. By suggesting that Asian Americans are not victims of discrimination, the model-minority stereotype further shuts Asians out of affirmative action programs. The stereotype is similarly used against Hispanics and African Americans who are told directly or indirectly that they do not need racial preferences because "the Asians have made it, so why can't you?" This provokes resentment and even hostility against Asians, as blacks have shown against Korean stores in some cities. Finally, the model-minority stereotype puts undue pressure on young Asian Americans to succeed in school, particularly in mathematics and science classes, which may lead to mental health problems and even teen suicide (U.S. Commission on Civil Rights, 1992).

Jewish Americans

The first Jews came here from Brazil in 1654—their ancestors had been expelled from Spain and Portugal. Then other Jews arrived directly from Europe. Their numbers were very small, however, until the 1880s, when large numbers of Jewish immigrants began to arrive, first from Germany, then from Russia and other Eastern European countries. Here they were safe from the *pogroms* (massacres) they had faced in Europe, but not from prejudice and discrimination.

During the 1870s, many colleges in the United States refused to admit Jewish Americans. At the turn of the century, Jews often encountered discrimination when they applied for white-collar jobs. During the 1920s and 1930s, they were accused of being part of an international conspiracy to take over U.S. business and government, and **anti-Semitism**—prejudice or discrimination against Jews—became more widespread and overt. The president of Harvard University called for restrictive quotas for Jewish Americans. Large real estate companies in New Jersey, New York, Georgia, and Florida refused to sell property to Jews. The Chamber of Commerce of St. Petersburg, Florida, announced its intention to make St. Petersburg "a 100 percent American gentile city" (McWilliams, 1948). Many country clubs and other social and business organizations barred Jewish Americans from membership.

But since the 1960s anti-Semitism has declined sharply. Today Jewish Americans are widely recognized as hard-working, family-oriented, religious, and friendly. Their contributions to U.S. cultural life are appreciated. Vandalism and violence against Jewish Americans are rare; the membership of anti-Semitic hate groups is extremely small; economic and

Physicist Albert Einstein was one of the large number of Jewish immigrants who left Germany with the rise of fascism in that country in the 1930s. Today many Jews have become successfully integrated into U.S. society.

social discrimination against Jews has practically disappeared; and non-Jews have elected a growing number of Jews to high public office (Lipset, 1987).

Jewish Americans are so highly regarded largely because they have become the most successful minority. Their levels of education, occupation, and income are higher than those of any other group. Their success may stem from the emphasis Jewish culture gives to education, from a self-image as God's chosen people, and from parental pressure to succeed. Not all are successful, though; there is still significant poverty in their midst. Being rich or poor has much to do with the recency of arrival in the United States. Most of the poor Jews are Orthodox, the most recent immigrants in the United States. The more successful are Conservative Jews, who have been in this country longer. The wealthiest are Reform Jews, who have been here the longest.

Although Jewish Americans as a whole are prosperous, they are not conservative or inclined to vote Republican, as other prosperous U.S. citizens are. Instead, they tend more to be liberal—supporting welfare, civil rights, women's rights, civil liberties, and the like—and to vote Democratic, perhaps reflecting an ability to identify with the dispossessed and oppressed. It also reflects the impact of Jewish norms underlying *tzedekah* ("righteousness"), which requires the fortunate and the well-to-do to help individuals and communities in difficulty (Lipset, 1990).

Jewish Americans, however, are in danger of losing their traditional identity. Today, about half of all Jewish Americans are not affiliated with a synagogue, and only a small minority (about 20 percent) attend synagogue regularly. Marriage with non-Jews has increased greatly; over half of all Jewish marriages involve a non-Jew and most children from such marriages are brought up as non-Jews. The Jewish birth rate has also declined. All this has caused consternation among some rabbis and Jewish communal workers. But Jewish sociologists point out that, despite all those changes in their lives, Jews "have been able to maintain a stronger sense of group identity than most other ethnic groups" in the United States (Waxman, 1990). A major reason is that the Jewish cohesion does not derive from traditional Jewish values, but rather from occupational and residential concentration. By sharing similar neighborhoods, schools, occupations, organizations, and friends, Jewish Americans have been and continue to be able to maintain the highest level of cohesion (Zenner, 1985; Waxman, 1990).

European Americans

The majority of the U.S. population are descendants of immigrants from Europe.

WASPs and other Western and Northern European Americans   Western and Northern European Americans are the dominant group in the United States. They include WASPs (white Anglo-Saxon Protestants), Germans, Irish, and others whose ancestors came from western and northern Europe. Most WASPs are English and a few are Scottish and Welsh. With the exception of Native Americans, WASPs have a longer history in the U.S. than any other racial or ethnic group. However, since 1990 WASPS have been outnumbered by Germans and Irish.

Still, WASPs continue to dominate U.S. society with their English language, English laws, and Protestant religion. WASPs also continue to control U.S. political and economic institutions, since most high government officials, large business owners, and corporate executives are WASPs. WASP dominance has faced vigorous challenges from other European

Americans, such as the Irish, Germans, and Italians, who have rapidly moved up the success ladder in education, professions, politics, and business. The WASP culture, into which various minorities have long been forced to assimilate, has also been under siege by multiculturalism, which emphasizes the equal importance of various minority ways of life. Average, middle-class WASPs, along with other European Americans, now feel that minorities are getting special advantages in jobs and education at their expense (Brookhiser, 1991; Baltzell, 1991; Baltzell, 1994).

White Ethnics: Southern and Eastern European Americans   Toward the end of the nineteenth century a new wave of immigrants came from southern and eastern Europe. Many native-born citizens proclaimed these new immigrants to be inferior people and treated them as such. This belief was reflected in the National Origins Act of 1924, which set quotas that greatly restricted immigration from southern and eastern Europe—a policy that was not altered until 1965.

Today, the descendants of those immigrants are called **white ethnics**, Americans of eastern and southern European origins. Although they have made their mark in education, business, professions, and politics, they are often stereotyped as ultraconservative, uneducated blue-collar workers. In fact, there are more middle-class people among white ethnics than other minorities, and about half have attended college, the same proportion as other European Americans. According to several surveys, white ethnics largely favor liberal policies, such as welfare programs, antipollution laws, and guaranteed wages. They are also relatively free of racial prejudice, perhaps because they can easily identify with African Americans since, like blacks, many have held low-paying manual jobs and been subjected to discrimination (Feagin, 1989; Farley, 1995).

White ethnics by and large can no longer speak their immigrant parents' language, no longer live in ethnic neighborhoods, and routinely marry into the dominant group. In short, they have become such an integral part of mainstream U.S. society that it is difficult to tell them apart. Traces of prejudice toward some white ethnics still exist, though. Italian Americans, for example, continue to be associated with organized crime, although people of Italian background make up less than one percent of the 500,000 individuals involved in such activities. In general, the young and highly educated white ethnics are particularly sensitive to ethnic stereotypes, because they identify themselves strongly with their ethnicity (Giordano, 1987; Alba, 1990).

Putting It All Together

Put in perspective, the status of all the minorities is generally better today than before. Getting closest to the American dream of success are Jews, Asians, and white ethnics, followed by blacks and Hispanics. Ironically, the original owners of this land—Native Americans—have experienced the least improvement in their lives. Of course, we still have considerable prejudice and discrimination. But it is less than before, especially less than in South Africa, where racism has until recently been an official policy (see Figure 12.6) and less serious than in Bosnia, Rwanda, and other countries, where a single incident of ethnic conflict often takes hundreds or thousands of lives. Therefore, as black sociologist Orlando Patterson (1991) notes, "The sociological truths are that America, while still flawed in its race relations, is now the least racist white-majority society in the world; has a better record of legal protection of minorities than any other society, white or black; offers more opportunities to a greater number of black persons than any other society, including all those of Africa; and has gone through a dramatic change in its attitude toward miscegenation over the last 25 years."

However, we tend to focus on our own current racial problems, without comparing them with how they were in the past or with similar problems in other societies. Interestingly, although the lack of historical and cross-cultural concern may limit our understanding of race relations, it can intensify our impatience with our own racial inequality. This may be good for our society because it compels us—especially the minorities among us—to keep pushing for racial equality. On the other hand, the historical and cross-societal analysis in this chapter, which does reveal improvement in our race relations, is also useful. It counsels against despair, encouraging us to be hopeful that racial equality can be achieved.

Questions For Discussion and Review

1. Why have Native Americans become the poorest minority in their own land?
2. What is the social condition of African Americans today?
3. Who are the different groups of Hispanic Americans, and what factors unify all of them?
4. What is the nature of prejudice and discrimination against Asian Americans?
5. How have the experiences of Jewish Americans differed from those of other white ethnic groups?
6. Are European Americans a homogeneous group?
7. What is the status of U.S. minorities as a whole?

RACIAL AND ETHNIC RELATIONS

Racial and ethnic relations appear in different forms, from violent conflict to peaceful coexistence. The functionalist perspective emphasizes peaceful coexistence and other positive forms of intergroup relations because they are functional to society, contributing to social order and stability. In contrast, the conflict perspective focuses on violent conflict and other negative aspects of intergroup relations, in which the powerful, dominant group mistreats powerless minorities. On the other hand, the symbolic interactionist perspective focuses on how perceptions influence intergroup interactions and vice versa.

Functionalist Perspective

According to the functionalist perspective, various racial and ethnic groups can contribute to social order through assimilation, amalgamation, or cultural pluralism. **Assimilation** is the process by which a minority adopts the dominant group's culture as the culture of the larger society. **Amalgamation** is the process by which the subcultures of various groups are blended together, forming a new culture.

FIGURE 12.6
Disparity Between Blacks and Whites

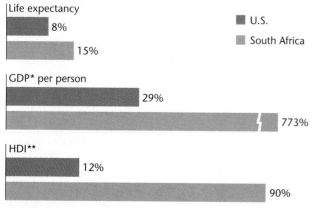

In the U.S. and South Africa, whites are better off than blacks by the following percentages.

Life expectancy
- 8% — U.S.
- 15% — South Africa

GDP* per person
- 29%
- 773%

HDI**
- 12%
- 90%

*GDP(Gross Domestic Product) is the total amount of goods and services produced.

**HDI (Human Development Index) is a combined measure of longevity, adult literacy, years of schooling, and standard of living.

Source: Based on United Nations, *Human Development Report 1994* (New York: Oxford University Press, 1994).

Cultural pluralism is the peaceful coexistence of various racial and ethnic groups, each retaining its own subculture.

Assimilation   Assimilation can be expressed as A + B + C = A, where minorities B and C lose their subcultural traits and become indistinguishable from the dominant group A (Newman, 1973). But there are two kinds of assimilation. The first is **behavioral assimilation**, the social situation in which the minority adopts the dominant group's language, values, and behavioral patterns. Behavioral assimilation, however, does not guarantee **structural assimilation**, the social condition in which the minority is accepted on equal terms with the rest of society. A white Russian immigrant who speaks halting English may find it easy to get structurally assimilated in the United States, but this is less the case with a black middle-class American. Nevertheless, most members of the disadvantaged minorities look upon assimilation as a promise of their right to get ahead—economically and socially—in the United States (Hirschman, 1983).

Amalgamation   In a society that encourages assimilation, there is little respect for the distinctive traits of minority groups. By contrast, a society that seeks amalgamation as an ideal has a greater appreciation for the equal worth of various subcultures. Amalgamation is popularly compared to a "melting pot," in which many subcultures are blended together to produce a new culture, one that differs from any of its components. It can be described as A + B + C = D, where A, B, and C represent different groups jointly producing a new culture—D—unlike any of its original components (Newman, 1973).

More than 80 years ago, a British-Jewish dramatist portrayed the United States as an amalgamation of subcultures. "There she lies," he wrote, "the great melting pot—listen! . . . Ah, what a stirring and seething—Celt and Latin, Slav and Teuton, Greek and Syrian, Black and Yellow—Jew and Gentile" (Zangwill, 1909). Indeed, to some extent the United States is a melting pot. In popular music and slang you can find elements of many subcultures. And there has been considerable intermarriage among some groups, particularly among those of English, German, Irish, Italian, and other European backgrounds. But such amalgamation is less likely to involve white and nonwhite groups.

Cultural Pluralism   Switzerland provides an example of yet a third way in which ethnic groups may live together. In Switzerland, three major groups—Germans, French, and Italians—retain their own languages while living together in peace. They are neither assimilated nor amalgamated. Instead, these diverse groups retain their distinctive subcultures while coexisting peacefully. Unlike either assimilation or amalgamation, cultural pluralism encourages each group to take pride in its distinctiveness, to be conscious of its heritage, and to retain its identity. Such pluralism can be shown as A + B + C = A + B + C, where various groups continue to keep their subcultures while living together in the same society (Newman, 1973). To some extent, the United States has long been marked by cultural pluralism. This can be seen in the Chinatowns, Little Italies, and Polish neighborhoods of many U.S. cities.

Conflict Perspective

To conflict theorists, racial and ethnic relations can be negative, marked by **racism**, the belief that one's own race or ethnicity is superior to that of others. Racism tends to cause the dominating group to *segregate*, *expel*, and *exterminate* minorities.

Segregation   Segregation means more than spatial and social separation of the dominant and minority groups. It means that minority groups, because they are believed inferior, are compelled to live separately, and in inferior conditions. The neighborhoods, schools, and other public facilities for the dominant group are both separate from and superior to those of the minorities.

The compulsion that underlies segregation is not necessarily official, or acknowledged. In the United States, for example, segregation is officially outlawed, yet it persists. In other words, **de jure segregation**—segregation sanctioned by law—is gone, but **de facto segregation**—segregation resulting from tradition and custom—remains. This is particularly the case with regard to housing for African Americans. Like the United States, most nations no longer practice de jure segregation. Even South Africa finally ended its official policy of *apartheid*—racial separation in housing, jobs, and political opportunities—in 1992. But apartheid has become so entrenched that it will continue in the form of de facto segregation for many years to come.

Expulsion   In some cases, the dominant group has expelled a minority from certain areas or even out of the country entirely. During the nineteenth century, Czarist Russia drove out millions of Jews, and the U.S. government forced the Cherokee to travel from their homes in Georgia and the Carolinas to reservations in Oklahoma. About 4,000 Cherokee died on this

Cutting Edge

Tens of millions of people from other countries have come to the United States during the last decade and are faced with the crucial decision of whether to assimilate. This reading, using the case of Haitian Americans, looks at a reason not to assimilate.

Should Immigrants Assimilate?

Growing up in an immigrant family has always been difficult. Individuals are torn by conflicting social and cultural demands, while facing the challenge of entry into an unfamiliar and frequently hostile world. Yet the difficulties are not always the same. The process of "growing up American" ranges from smooth acceptance to traumatic confrontation, depending on the characteristics that immigrants and their children bring along, and the social context that receives them. We believe that something quite disturbing is happening to the assimilation or, if you will, the "Americanization" of the second generation of new immigrants.

In Miami, Florida, the Haitian community is composed of some 75,000 legal and clandestine immigrants, many of whom sold everything in order to buy passage to the United States. Haitians of the first generation are strongly disposed to preserve a robust national identity, which they associate both with community solidarity and with social networks promoting individual success. But in trying to instill in their children national pride and an orientation toward achievement, they often clash with the youngsters' everyday experiences in school. Little Haiti is adjacent to Liberty City, the main black inner-city area of Miami, and Haitian adolescents attend predominantly inner-city

schools. Native-born black youth stereotype the Haitian youngsters as docile and subservient to whites, and make fun of the Haitians' French and Creole as well as their accents. As a result, second generation Haitian children find themselves torn between conflicting ideas and values: to remain "Haitian," they must endure ostracism and continuing attacks in school; to become "American" (black American in this case), they must forgo their parents' dreams of making it in the United States through the preservation of ethnic solidarity and traditional values.

As the Haitian example illustrates, adopting the outlook and cultural ways of the native born does not necessarily represent the first step toward social and economic mobility. It may, in fact, lead to exactly the opposite. Meanwhile, immigrant youth who remain firmly ensconced in their ethnic communities may, by virtue of this fact, have a better chance for educational and economic mobility.

Excerpted from Alejandro Portes and Min Zhou, "Should Immigrants Assimilate?" *The Public Interest,* Summer, 1994. reprinted with permission of the authors and *The Public Interest,* Number 116, Summer 1994, pp. 18–33. ©1994 by National Affairs, Inc.

"Trail of Tears." During the 1970s, Uganda expelled more than 40,000 Asians—many of them Ugandan citizens—and Vietnam forced 700,000 Chinese to leave the country (Schaefer, 1988).

Extermination The most drastic action against minorities is to kill them. **Genocide**, wholesale killing of a racial or ethnic group, has been attempted in various countries. During the nineteenth century, Dutch settlers in South Africa exterminated the native Khoikhoin, or "Hottentots." During the pioneer days of the United States, white settlers slaughtered Native Americans. On the island of Tasmania, near Australia, British settlers killed the entire native population, whom they hunted like wild animals.

Between 1933 and 1945, *[or 2 million gypsies + others]* the Nazis systematically murdered six million Jews. More recently, in 1992, the Serbs in Bosnia killed and tortured numerous Muslims and Croats as part of their campaign of "ethnic cleansing." In 1993 and 1994 thousands of minority members were massacred in the African state of Rwanda.

Symbolic Interactionist Perspective

According to this perspective, if the dominant group defines a minority as inferior, undesirable, or dangerous, interaction between them will be greatly affected. There is likely to be segregated interaction,

"Gypsies" in Eastern Europe were among those whom Nazis systematically murdered during World War II. Wholesale killing of a racial or ethnic group is called genocide.

with members of each group interacting mostly with others of the same group (Charon, 1992). If dominant group members do interact with minority members, the interaction will likely be tense or superficial. The nature of intergroup interaction, then, can be determined by the dominant group's definition of minorities.

The definition is not based on reality. Instead, it is a **stereotype**, an oversimplified, inaccurate mental picture of others. Consider the stereotype of blacks as dangerous. Many whites seem to carry this picture in their heads, after having been repeatedly fed by the media with images of black violence and criminality. The reality is that the vast majority (over two-thirds) of blacks are law-abiding, hard-working middle-class people. The remaining third fall below the poverty line, but most are, for the most part, far from being violent criminals; rather they are young children and single mothers. The small minority that commits violence rarely targets whites; most of their victims are fellow blacks. Still, many whites are fearful of blacks.

The stereotype of blacks as dangerous often causes African Americans—including highly successful middle-class blacks—to suffer legal harassment in the hands of white police officers as well as other indignities as suggested earlier. The stereotype can also bring about grotesque consequences for whites themselves. As a white man said,

My wife was driving down the street in a black

neighborhood. The people at the corners are all gesticulating at her. She was very frightened, turned up the windows, and drove determinedly. She discovered, after several blocks, she was going the wrong way on a one-way street and they were trying to help her. Her assumption was they were blacks and were out to get her. Mind you, she's a very enlightened person. You'd never associate her with racism, yet her first reaction was that they were dangerous (Terkel, 1992).

While stereotypic definitions can shape intergroup interaction, the interaction can also change the definitions. If the interaction is cooperative, in which two groups work or play together, negative definitions may dissolve into positive definitions, such as definitions of African Americans as helpful and friendly. Similar positive definitions are also likely to emerge if the interactants from different groups are of equal status, such as being equally well-educated (See and Wilson, 1988). Although such interactions may improve the dominant group's definition of minorities, they may have little impact on African Americans' distrust of whites. In recent decades, many blacks have studied, worked, and lived in predominantly white settings, but they still feel that many whites they interact with do not accept them as equals (Jones, 1994). In other words, such whites are defined by many blacks as prejudiced although they may interact respectfully with blacks.

Questions For Discussion and Review

1. What kinds of racial and ethnic relations can we see better through the functionalist and conflict perspectives?
2. How is intergroup interaction related to the dominant group's definition of a minority?

PREJUDICE AND DISCRIMINATION

Is it possible for a prejudiced person to act in a respectable, nondiscriminatory way toward a minority person as suggested above? Don't prejudiced people always discriminate? In this section we will find answers to these and other similar questions by analyzing the characteristics, causes, and consequences of prejudice and discrimination as well as attempted solutions to the problem.

Characteristics

Prejudice and discrimination can be the characteristics of both individual persons and social institutions.

Individual Responses to Minorities As we have said, prejudice is an attitude; discrimination is an act. Robert Merton (1976) found that the two do not nec-

essarily go hand in hand. Analyzing the possible combinations of prejudice and discrimination, Merton developed a typology of four dominant-group members on the basis of their responses to minorities (see Table 12.1).

First are the *unprejudiced nondiscriminators*. These people believe in the U.S. creed of equality and put their belief into action—their attitude and behavior are consistent. They are also called *all-weather liberals* because they are likely to abide by their belief regardless of where they are—even if their friends and neighbors are bigots.

The second type of dominant-group member in Merton's analysis is the *unprejudiced discriminator*. These people's discriminatory behavior is inconsistent with their unprejudicial attitude. Although free from prejudice themselves, they practice discrimination because of social pressure. Hence, they are also called *fair-weather liberals*. Unprejudiced homeowners are fair-weather liberals if they refuse to sell their house to a minority family for fear of offending the neighbors. An unprejudiced executive may also hesitate to promote minority employees to managers lest other employees be resentful.

Merton's third category is the *prejudiced nondiscriminator*, the prejudiced person who is afraid to express his or her prejudice through discrimination. Like the fair-weather liberals, these people do not practice what they believe in. They allow social pressure to keep them from doing what they want to do. But, since they are prejudiced despite their nondiscriminatory behavior, they are called *fair-weather illiberals* rather than liberals. Under the pressure of

TABLE 12.1
A Typology Of Dominant-Group Members

	Nondiscriminator	**Discriminator**
Unprejudiced	1. Unprejudiced nondiscriminator (all-weather liberal)—is not prejudiced and does not discriminate, whatever the social pressure might be.	2. Unprejudiced discriminator (fair-weather liberal)—is not prejudiced but, because of social pressure, does discriminate.
Prejudiced	3. Prejudiced nondiscriminator (fair-weather illiberal)—is prejudiced but, because of social pressure, does not discriminate.	4. Prejudiced discriminator (all-weather illiberal)—is prejudiced and does discriminate, whatever the social pressure might be.

SOURCE: Data from Robert K. Merton, *Sociological Ambivalence and Other Essays* (New York: Free Press, 1976).

Prejudice is a negative attitude toward a certain category of people, and discrimination is unequal treatment of people because they are members of some group. A member of the Ku Klux Klan would most likely be, in Merton's classification, an example of a prejudiced discriminator: someone who both is prejudiced and discriminates.

antidiscrimination laws, prejudiced people will hire or work with minorities.

Finally, there is the *prejudiced discriminator* who is deeply prejudiced against minorities and practices discrimination. Like all-weather liberals, these *all-weather illiberals* are consistent: their actions match their beliefs. Members of the Ku Klux Klan or neo-Nazis provide an example.

Institutionalized Discrimination   Even if every single white were no longer prejudiced and discriminating, discrimination would still exist for some time. Over the years it has been built into various social institutions, so that discrimination can occur

even when no one is aware of it. When blacks and whites have long lived in separate neighborhoods, neighborhood schools will remain segregated, even though no one tries to discriminate against blacks. If employers prefer to hire people who graduated from their own universities that have long denied entrance to blacks, then blacks will not have much chance of being hired. When fire and police departments continue to use the height requirements in hiring that *women* were originally intended for evaluating white applicants, then many otherwise qualified Mexican and Asian Americans—who are generally shorter than whites—will not get the job (Kimmel, 1986).

These are all cases of **institutionalized discrimination**, the persistence of discrimination in social institutions, not necessarily known to everybody as discrimination. They are traceable to the long history of discrimination by educational, economic, and other social institutions, not to individual prejudice. African Americans suffer the most from institutionalized discrimination. Long victimized by racial oppression, many African Americans lack adequate education and job skills. Many colleges and companies, then, have unintentionally practiced discrimination by denying them college admission and professional or managerial positions only because of their inadequate scholastic and occupational performance, failing to recognize that these are largely the effects of the long history of slavery and discrimination.

Causes

Prejudice and discrimination are far from unique to the United States. They are found throughout the world and there are many causes.

One cause is *social-psychological*. It involves **scapegoating**, blaming others for one's own failure. Through prejudice and discrimination, dominant-group members who have suffered failures in life make themselves feel superior to minorities and so build up their self-image. Hostility against minorities is likely to mount when many dominant-group members are beset with unemployment, poverty, and other problems, which threaten to deflate their self-image. In the last century, anti-black mob violence usually increased in the Deep South during an economic downturn. In the Middle Ages, when thousands of Europeans died in a plague, "rioters stormed Jewish ghettos and burned them down, believing that Jews were somehow responsible for the epidemic" (Beck and Tolnay, 1990; Coleman and Cressey, 1993).

A protest against discrimination on a college campus. Many colleges have unintentionally practiced institutionalized discrimination, such as denying African Americans college admissions only because of their inadequate scholastic perform-ance, without recognizing that this is largely the effect of the long history of slavery and discrimination.

A second cause is *sociological*. It involves socialization, namely, if our parents, teachers, and peers are prejudiced, we are likely to follow their lead. If minorities are often portrayed in the media as inferior or violent, we are likely to be prejudiced and to discriminate against them. Even parents opposed to racism may unknowingly plant seeds of racist thought when they select for their children such popular books as *Mary Poppins* and *The Story of Little Black Sambo,* which contain disparaging images of African Americans (Madsen, 1982).

A third cause is *economic.* It involves the desire for job security and business profit. Historically, given widespread prejudice and discrimination, minorities were prevented from competing for employment, thereby helping to ensure job security for the dominant group's middle and working classes. Prejudice and discrimination also brought profits to the dominant group's upper class. Racism created a huge supply of cheap labor from among oppressed minorities, and prevented much competition from minority businesses.

A fourth cause is *political*. It involves maintaining governmental power. This is why for so many years the white regime in extremely racist South Africa denied black people the right to vote. In the United States in the past, many state and local governments used various means to keep minorities out of the political process, primarily to prevent blacks from voting. When these efforts became unconstitutional, some states continued to discourage minorities from political participation by charging a poll tax, by requiring a literacy test, or by printing ballots only in English in areas where many minority people did not know the language.

Consequences

Prejudice and discrimination have costly consequences for minorities.

First, minorities generally have a lower quality of life than the dominant group. As we have observed, Native Americans, African Americans, and Hispanics have lower income, more unemployment and poverty, fewer years of schooling, and lower life expectancy than whites. There are exceptions. West Indian blacks—immigrants or descendants of immigrants from the Caribbean, such as Colin Powell—have suffered discrimination, but they have achieved higher educational and economic levels than the national average (Harrison, 1992; Sowell, 1994)

Second, partly because of prejudice and discrimination, the "black underclass" has grown larger and more desperate. Deep poverty persists from generation to generation, the rate of unemployment continues to remain distressingly high among young people, and the number of poor female-headed families is soaring. All this has in turn generated a dramatic rise in violent crime, especially among the youth (Chapter 8: Deviance). Occasionally, riots erupt, as they did in South-Central Los Angeles in 1992. In many other cities the underclass's rage simmers just below the surface.

Third, young victims of prejudice and discrimination tend to develop a negative self-image. In 1947 Kenneth and Mamie Clark did a study that helped influence the Supreme Court to desegregate schools in 1954. In the study, 253 black children were asked to choose between four dolls, two black and two white. Two-thirds of the children chose white dolls. In 1985 Darlene Powell-Hopson updated the Clarks' experiment and found essentially the same result: about 65 percent of the black children preferred white dolls. Powell-Hopson believes that the result is likely to be the same if the study is repeated today. One reason is the pervasive real-life reminders that blacks are still regarded less highly than whites. Another reason is that television, movies, and children's books seem to link everything beautiful with whiteness. But most black parents try to shield their children from this racial bias and instill ethnic pride (White, 1993).

Attempted Solutions

Under the pressure of the civil rights movement, the Supreme Court first outlawed school segregation in 1954. To achieve school integration, students were often bused from predominantly black to white schools. But mandatory busing provoked strong protests from white parents and some "white flight" from cities to suburbs. As a result, mandatory busing programs have largely been dismantled. Today most of the busing programs are voluntary. In addition, the schools that need to be desegregated are turned into "magnet schools." Since these schools offer better education, many white parents are eager to have their children bused to them.

Also under the pressure of the civil rights movement, federal legislators passed a series of anti-discrimination laws in the 1960s. But because of institutionalized discrimination, Congress instituted **affirmative action**, a policy that requires employers and colleges to make special efforts to recruit qualified minorities for jobs, promotions, and educational opportunities. Given equal qualifications, the opportunity must be given to the minority. Sometimes, a less qualified black may have to be chosen over a more qualified white. President Lyndon Johnson summarized the reasoning behind special opportunities for blacks in a 1965 speech: "You do not take a person who for years has been hobbled by chains, and liberate him, bring him up to the starting line, and then say, 'You are free to compete with all the others'" (Hacker, 1992). Since then affirmative action has enabled mostly middle-class African Americans to enter higher education and gain professional and managerial positions. But it has failed to help the masses of poor African Americans, who have instead become poorer (Wilson, 1990).

Affirmative action has also aggravated racial tensions because many whites see it as "reverse discrimination" against them. They demand that opportunities be open without regard to race or ethnicity. A growing number of African American scholars are also opposed to racial preference. They view it as contrary to Dr. Martin Luther King's belief that people should be judged by the content of their character, not the color of their skin. The scholars also observe that affirmative action tends to revive racist beliefs about blacks being inferior by suggesting to whites that blacks are incapable of competing for college or jobs unless they are given preference (Wilson, 1990; Steele, 1990).

Prejudice and discrimination can have extremely negative consequences for the victims, as in the former Yugoslavia, where Serbians have waged war against Bosnian Muslims. Here Muslims are being evacuated in a United Nations truck from the city of Srebrenica.

A proposed alternative to affirmation action is that the government improve the educational and economic conditions of disadvantaged people. Regardless of race or ethnicity, disadvantaged children should have better schools, job training, safer neighborhoods, and more financial assistance for education (Steele, 1990). Sociologist William Julius Wilson (1990) also favors similar race-neutral programs: full employment, job skills training, comprehensive health care, educational reforms in public schools, child care, and crime and drug abuse prevention programs. All these programs are, in effect, based on need rather than on race but can significantly help poor minorities. Since they are meant for all racial and ethnic groups, the programs will be more acceptable to most people than racial preference. They are also more likely to get approved by Congress, which has increasingly turned thumbs-down on racial preference policies.

Questions for Discussion and Review

1. How do dominant-group members react to minorities?
2. What is institutionalized discrimination?
3. What causes prejudice and discrimination?
4. What consequences do prejudice and discrimination have for minorities?
5. How have the attempts to end discrimination turned out?

A GLOBAL ANALYSIS

For more than 200 years, the United States has faced the "American dilemma," proclaiming equality yet practicing discrimination. As we have observed, gov-ernment efforts have not put an end to discrimination. Nevertheless, the problem seems much more severe in other parts of the world. In the 1992 Los Angeles race riot, one of the most destructive in recent U.S. history, about 44 people died, but some 250,000 were killed in the ethnic conflict in Rwanda in 1994 (Rosenblatt, 1994).

Why the difference? As a democratic state, our nation at least officially encourages respect for ethnic differences while providing aggrieved minorities with legal recourse. But many other countries with more severe ethnic problems are mostly authoritarian states that outlaw diverse ethnic expressions. In such societies, the state is defined as the preserve of only one ethnic group, with other groups made to feel like outsiders (Maybury-Lewis, 1994). Thus numerous members of these other groups have in recent years been attacked or killed, not only in Africa, but also in many countries that had been part of the former Soviet Union.

There are at least three other reasons why ethnic conflict is so fierce in some countries. First, the hostile group has an excessive ethnic identity (Williams, 1994). The strength of this identity usually comes from a shared history of victimization. In Rwanda, for example, the Hutus who slaughtered the Tutsis in 1994 had kept alive the memory of how Tutsis had killed some 100,000 Hutus in 1972. Second, those countries are experiencing enormous political and economic problems, especially high rates of inflation, unemployment, and poverty. Third, politicians seek power by blaming the problems on minorities and inciting destructive action against them (Lemarchand, 1994).

Question for Discussion and Review

1. Why is ethnic conflict more deadly in countries outside of the United States?

CHAPTER REVIEW

1. *Do racial classifications mean anything?* Biologically, they have little significance. They do not correspond to genetically distinct groups. Socially, however, racial classifications have had profound meaning, because people often think of themselves and respond to others in terms of race. *How does an ethnic group differ from a race?* People are categorized into races on the basis of their popularly perceived physical characteristics, but ethnic groups are based on shared cultural characteristics. *How do racial and*

GLOBAL VILLAGE

Conflict and wars between diverse ethnic and national groups occur frequently around the world. Civil wars in the former Yugoslavia and Rwanda are two examples of harsh, violent conflicts between traditional ethnic rivals. This reading explores the origins of these conflicts and why they continue to create death and hardship.

The Roots of Ethnic Conflict

When Vamik Volkan was growing up in a Turkish family on the island of Cyprus, he heard rumors that each knot in the local Greek priest's cincture stood for a Turkish child the priest had strangled. Young Vamik also heard, in tones of dismay, that his Greek Cypriot neighbors ate pigs, considered too dirty to eat in Islamic culture.

Now a psychiatrist at the University of Virginia, Dr. Volkan, who came to the United States in 1957, cites these Turkish Cypriot attitudes as examples of how ethnic hatreds can be kept simmering from generation to generation. Dr. Volkan proposes that a reservoir of hostile biases like these, as well as bitter memories of historical grievances, are shared by members of an ethnic group, and can set off active antagonism in times of group hardship or under the prodding of ambitious leaders.

Dr. Volkan's theory of the roots of ethnic conflict is part of a concerted effort by psychiatrists, anthropologists and political scientists to find the common patterns that might help explain why ethnic identities have become ascendant in the post-cold war world, and how those identities can lead to brutal battles between neighbors.

That question is more compelling than ever at a time when Hutus battle Tutsis in Rwanda, Bosnians struggle with Serbs, Azerbaijanis fight Armenians, and new ethnic tensions seem to flare up weekly around the world.

"These conflicts have always been there—history can document them wound by wound," said Joseph Montville, director of a conflict resolution project at the Center for Strategic and International Studies in Washington. "But the cold war was a containing structure. With its collapse, people are freer to act on these ancient grievances. It's as though the cops had gone home, and there's no one to answer at 911."

Ethnicity, unlike race, is less a matter of a common gene pool than of shared history, perceptions and group identity. A potent source of a people's ethnic identity is a collective memory of their past glories and traumas, Dr. Volkan said. Passing on these memories to the next generation feeds ethnic animosity but helps keep the group's identity alive.

For the Serbs, one historical trauma that has persisted with freshness in the collective memory is the 1389 defeat of the Serbs and their Christian allies at the hands of the Muslim Turks in the Battle of Kosovo. "Every Serbian child learns about Kosovo," Dr. Eugene Hammel, an anthropologist at the University of California at Berkeley, said. "It was the beginning of 500 years of Turkish occupation, which the Serbs remember as oppression." Likewise, the Muslims of Bosnia remember "the massacres of Muslims by Serbs in World War II, and dating back to the 19th century."

The immediate spark for ethnic conflict is typically a sudden hardship for a group, often caused by larger events like economic hard times. "When there is a great external stress and a sense you are losing control over your own security, you have the urge to strike out at a scapegoat to try to assert some sense of control," Dr. Montville said.

A plunge in world coffee prices indirectly led to a slaughter of Hutus by Tutsis in 1972 in Rwanda, next to Burundi. At the time 85 percent of Rwanda's foreign exchange was from coffee exports, and the drop was calamitous for the economy, said Dr. Montville. In April of that year a group of Hutus tried to overthrow the ruling Tutsis, who were suffering much less than Hutus from the country's depression. In retaliation the Tutsis killed 100,000 Hutus, particularly those who were educated, whom they saw as a political threat.

ethnic groups become minorities? They become minorities when subjected to prejudice and discrimination by the dominant group.

2. *Are there indications that Native Americans still experience discrimination?* Their income and health fall below the national average, while their unemployment and poverty are higher. But they have been recapturing their proud traditions.

3. *Have the civil rights laws of the 1960s made a difference?* Yes, but they have not ended inequality. They have made significant strides in education and politics, but not in housing and economic condition.

4. *What are the origins of Hispanic Americans?* The category lumps many people together—from the descendants of Mexicans and Puerto Ricans who became citizens because the United States took their lands in wars, to recent immigrants from Cuba and other Central and South American countries. Mexican Americans are the largest group.

5. *How do Asian Americans fare today?* They seem to have achieved more than other groups in education and family income, but they have a relatively high poverty rate and continue to face discrimination.

6. *What is the position of Jewish Americans today?* Their educational, occupational, and economic status is very high. Their affluence, however, has not weakened their traditionally liberal stand on social and political issues.

7. *Who are European Americans?* Most have their national origins in western and northern Europe, among whom WASPs are the dominant group. A much smaller group of European Americans are white ethnics whose ancestors immigrated from southern and eastern Europe. Though successful in various arenas of U.S. life, white ethnics still encounter traces of prejudice.

8. *How is the status of U.S. minorities today?* Though still experiencing prejudice and discrimination, the minorities are faring better today than before and better in the U.S. than in other countries.

9. *What do racial and ethnic relations look like from the three sociological perspectives?* Seen from the functionalist perspective, intergroup relations appear in the form of assimilation, amalgamation, and cultural pluralism, all of which contribute to social order. Viewed from the conflict perspective, intergroup rela-

tions appear in the form of segregation, expulsion, and extermination, all of which harm society. According to symbolic interactionists, intergroup relations and definitions influence each other.

10. *Can a person be prejudiced without being discriminatory or be discriminatory without being prejudiced?* Yes, because prejudice and discrimination are not the same—one is an attitude and the other an act. Although the two are related, they do not always go together. *What is institutionalized discrimination?* It is the practice of discrimination in social institutions that is not necessarily known to everybody as discrimination. *What causes prejudice and discrimination?* Scapegoating, socialization, and desire for jobs, profits, or power. *What are the consequences of prejudice and discrimination?* Lower quality of life for minorities, larger and more desperate "black underclass," and negative self-image in black children. *What efforts have been officially made to combat prejudice and discrimination?* School segregation has been outlawed and anti-discrimination laws have been made, with some but not complete success.

KEY TERMS

Affirmative action A policy that requires employers and colleges to make special efforts to recruit qualified minorities for jobs, promotions, and educational opportunities (p. 283).

Amalgamation The process by which the subcultures of various groups are blended together, forming a new culture (p. 276).

Anti-Semitism Prejudice or discrimination against Jews (p. 274).

Assimilation The process by which a minority adopts the dominant group's culture as the culture of the larger society (p. 276).

Behavioral assimilation The social situation in which the minority adopts the dominant group's language, values, and behavioral patterns (p. 277).

Cultural pluralism The peaceful coexistence of various racial and ethnic groups, each retaining its own subculture (p. 277).

De facto segregation Segregation resulting from tradition and custom (p. 277).

De jure segregation Segregation sanctioned by law (p. 277).

Discrimination An unfavorable action against individuals that is taken because they are members of a certain category (p. 266).

Ethnic group A collection of people who share distinctive cultural heritage (p. 266).

Genocide Wholesale killing of a racial or ethnic group (p. 278).

Glass ceiling The prejudiced belief that keeps minority professionals from holding high, leadership positions in organizations (p. 273).

Institutionalized discrimination The persistence of discrimination in social institutions, not necessarily known to everybody as discrimination (p. 281).

Jim Crow A set of laws that segregate blacks from whites in all kinds of public and private facilities (p. 269).

Minority A racial or ethnic group that is subjected to prejudice and discrimination (p. 266).

Prejudice A negative attitude toward a certain category of people (p. 266).

Race A group of people who are perceived by a given society to be biologically different from others (p. 265).

Racism The belief that one's own race or ethnicity is superior to that of others (p. 277).

Scapegoating Blaming others for one's own failure (p. 281).

Stereotype An oversimplified, inaccurate mental picture of others (p. 279).

Structural assimilation The social condition in which the minority is accepted on equal terms with the rest of society (p. 277).

White ethnics Americans of eastern and southern European origins (p. 275).

SUGGESTED READINGS

Dinnerstein, Leonard. 1994. *Anti-Semitism in America.* New York: Oxford University Press. An account of anti-Semitism from its colonial origins to the present.

Hacker, Andrew. 1992. *Two Nations: Black and White, Separate, Hostile, Unequal.* New York: Scribner's. Shows the continuing presence of racial inequality with an analysis of statistical data.

Kotkin, Joel. 1993. *Tribes: How Race, Religion and Identity Determine Success in the New Global Economy.* New York: Random House. An interesting story of how Jews, Britons, Japanese, Chinese, and Indians have prospered in countries far away from their ancestral homes.

Nabokov, Peter (ed.). 1992. *Native American Testimony: A Chronicle of Indian-White Relations from Prophecy to the Present, 1492–1992.* Includes hundreds of stories about the relations between Native and white Americans told by the Indians themselves.

Sowell, Thomas. 1994. *Race and Culture: A World View.* New York: Basic Books. A controversial analysis of the differences among racial and ethnic groups.

13

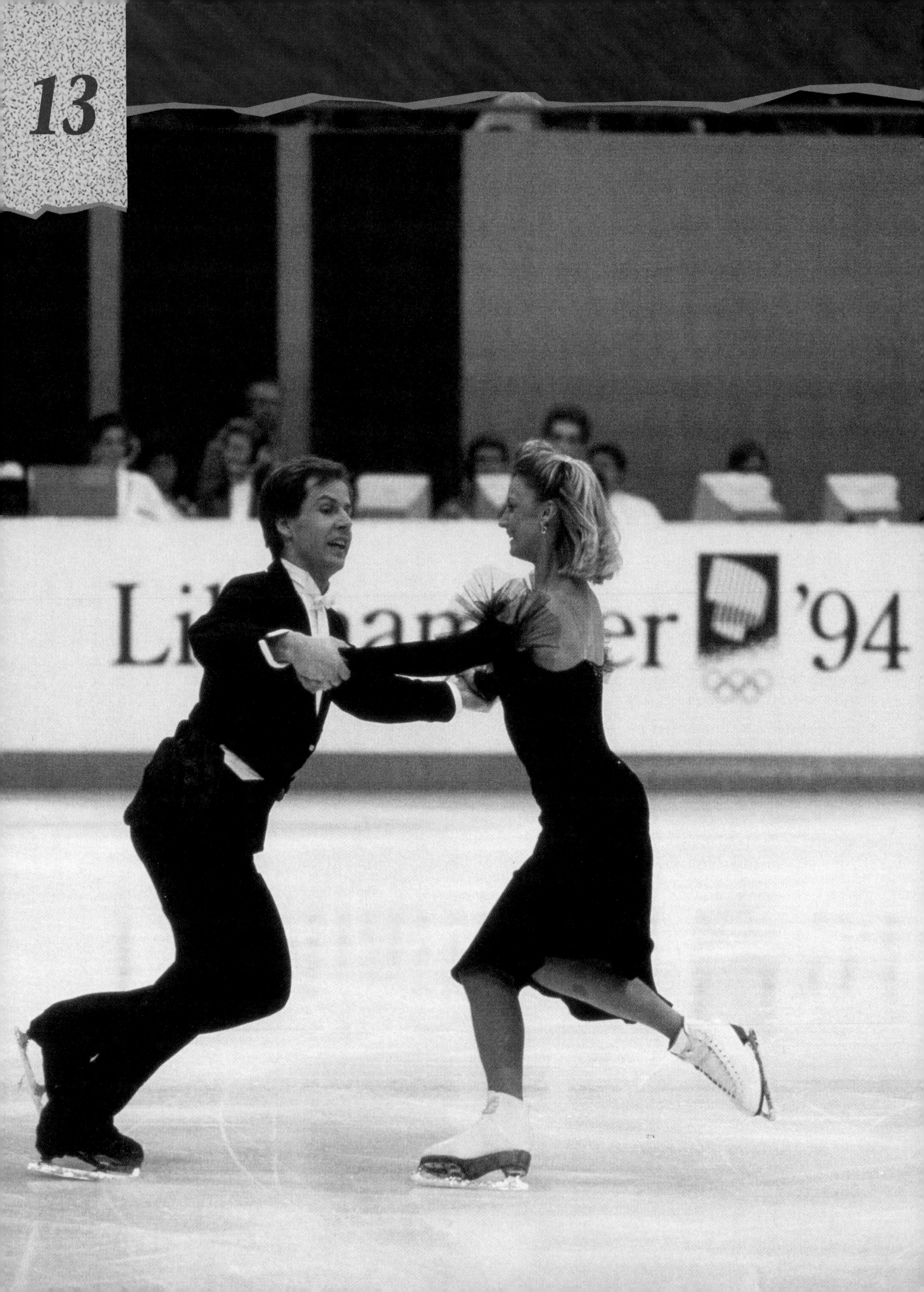

WOMEN AND MEN

CHAPTER OUTLINE

Myths and Realities

MYTH: *As a group, women are more emotional than men in every way.*
REALITY: Women are more likely than men to express such emotions as sympathy, sadness, and distress, but they are more inhibited when it comes to anger and sexual desire.

MYTH: *Physicians are among the highest paid professionals solely because of the importance of their work to society.*
REALITY: There is an additional reason: Most doctors in the United States are men. In the former Soviet Union, where medicine was considered a "feminine" occupation because most physicians were women, they were paid less than skilled blue-collar workers.

MYTH: *Nowadays, with the women's movement influencing most aspects of U.S. life, parents usually bring up their sons and daughters in the same way.*
REALITY: Girls and boys are still treated differently. Usually, girls are given dolls and boys are given action figures. Mothers also tend to fuss about how pretty their little girls should look, but are less concerned about their little boys' appearance.

MYTH: *Women receive lower pay than men simply because their jobs typically require fewer skills and less training.*
REALITY: Sexism is also a factor, because, even when women hold the same jobs as men, they tend to earn less.

n 1991 a plane packed with businesspeople and tourists took off from a southern city in India to the country's capital, New Delhi. On that flight a 10-year-old Indian girl named Ameena sat sobbing, her hands covering her tears. Beside her was a 60-year-old Arab man staring blankly out of the window. A flight attendant came over and asked her what was wrong. Appearing afraid of the man, she did not answer and kept on weeping. After the attendant and several passengers ushered her away from him, she said, "This man came to our house. He found my elder sister dark and ugly. My father, who drives an autorickshaw, made me marry this man. He is taking me to Saudi Arabia. I don't want to go with him." When the plane landed in New Delhi, the police arrested the man and took the girl into protective custody. It turned out that the man had been bride shopping in southern India, buying the girl from her poor father for 6000 rupees ($240). Selling young daughters into marriage is common among lower-class Indians (Gargan, 1991).

This incident is part of the larger, common problem of prejudice and discrimination against females around the globe. In this chapter we analyze various aspects of the problem.

GENDER ROLES

There are basic differences in what societies expect of women and men. These differences are made explicit in **gender roles:** patterns of attitude and behavior that a society expects of its members because of their being female or male. What is the nature of these gender roles? Are they the same in other societies? Where do the roles come from? Let us analyze each of these issues.

Feminine and Masculine in the U.S.

In the United States women have traditionally been assigned the role of homemaker and men the role of breadwinner. The "woman's world" was the home; her job was to comfort and care for husband and children, maintain harmony, and teach her children to conform to society's norms. The man was expected to work out in the world, competing with other men in order to provide for his family. The "man's world" outside the home was viewed as a harsh and heartless jungle in which men needed to be strong, ambitious, and aggressive.

This basic division of labor has been accompanied by many popular stereotypes—oversimplified mental images—of what women and men are supposed to be, and to some extent these stereotypes persist. Women are supposed to be shy, easily intimidated, and passive; men, bold, ambitious, and aggressive. Women should be weak and dainty; men, strong and athletic. It is not bad form for women, but it is for men, to worry about their appearance and aging. Women are expected to be emotional, even to cry easily, but men should hold back their emotions and must not cry. Women are expected to be sexually passive and naive; men, aggressive and experienced. Women are believed to be dependent, in need of male protection; men are supposed to be independent, fit to be leaders. Women are expected to be intuitive and inconsistent; men, logical, rational, and objective.

These are the traits that have long been associated with each gender in the United States. They represent both *stereotypes* about how men and women behave and *expectations* about how they should behave. Today, some people are more likely than others to hold or reject them. Among women, those who are relatively young, unmarried, well educated, gainfully employed, or who have strong feelings of personal competence tend to reject the traditional gender-role attitudes. Among men, the working and lower classes are more traditional in gender-role outlook than the middle and upper classes.

Although people may consciously reject the traditional gender roles, they tend to behave otherwise. Research has shown that women are more likely to be passive and men aggressive in a number of ways. In interactions between the sexes, the male is more likely to initiate interactions and the female to respond. During a conversation, men tend more to touch women than vice versa. When a man opens the door for women, women tend to say "thank you" or smile their appreciation. But men tend to look confused if a woman opens the door for them, because they are not accustomed to being women's passive beneficiaries. Women are also more likely than men to express feelings of sympathy, sadness, and distress, but more inhibited with regard to anger and sexual desire (Tannen, 1990; Campbell, 1993). All this reflects the powerful influence of traditional gender roles, which make men and women behave differently.

Gender Roles in Other Societies

The traditional gender roles in the United States are not necessarily the same in all societies. Many years ago, anthropologist Margaret Mead (1935) found striking differences among three tribes in the south-west Pacific island of New Guinea. Among one of them, the Arapesh, *both* women and men behaved in what many people in the United States would consider a *feminine* way. They were passive, gentle, and home-loving. The men were just as enthusiastic as the women about taking care of babies and bringing up children. The second tribe, the Mundugumor, were just the opposite: *both* sexes showed what many people in our society would consider *masculine* traits. Both women and men were competitive, aggressive, and violent. In the third tribe, the Tchambuli, there was a sharp difference between female and male roles, and they were the *opposite* of those traditional in the West. Tchambuli women were the bosses at home. They were the economic providers, doing the hunting, farming, and fishing. Tchambuli men were emotional, passive, and dependent. They took care of children, did housework, and used cosmetics.

But the traditional U.S. gender roles can be found in most societies, with men assigned the primary role of breadwinner and women the secondary role of homemaker. The public world is considered a man's domain and the private world a woman's. "Men's work" is more highly valued than "women's work." Even in most of the egalitarian hunting-gathering societies, where women often contribute more than half the food supply by gathering nuts, fruits, and plants, men may dominate women. Thus, male dominance over females is nearly universal. As Kay Martin and Barbara Voorhies (1975) have observed, "A survey of human societies shows that positions of authority are almost always occupied by males." Since this gender difference appears to be universal, is it biologically determined?

Biological Constraints

What makes one person female and another person male has to do with their **chromosomes,** the materials in a cell that transmit hereditary traits to the carrier from the carrier's parents. Females have two similar chromosomes, XX, one inherited from each parent. Men have two different chromosomes, XY, the X inherited from the mother and the Y from the father.

Whether a person will develop the appropriate sex characteristics—say, breasts or facial hair—depends on the proportion of female and male sex **hormones**, chemical substances that stimulate or inhibit vital biological processes. If a woman has more male than female hormones, she will have facial hair rather than breasts. If a man has more female than male hormones, he will end up with breasts instead. But in most females the proportion of female hormones is greater, and in most men the proportion of male hormones is greater. It is clear that women and men differ chromosomally and hormonally.

The chromosomal and hormonal differences underlie other biological differences between the sexes. Stimulated by the greater amount of male sex hormones, men are on the average bigger and stronger than women. Yet due to their lack of a second X chromosome, men are less healthy. Men are susceptible to more than 30 types of genetic defects, such as hemophilia and color blindness, which are very rare in women. At birth, males are more likely to die. Throughout life, males tend to mature more slowly. They are more physiologically vulnerable to stress. They are stricken with heart disease at a younger age. And they die sooner (Stoll, 1978; Gorman, 1992).

There are also sex differences in brain structure. Neuroscience research has long established that the left hemisphere, or half, of the brain controls speech and the right hemisphere directs spatial tasks such as object manipulation. There is less specialization in the female's brain, so that she tends to use both hemispheres for a given task at the same time, whereas the male tends to use only one hemisphere. For example, women are more likely to listen with both ears and men with the right ear. Moreover, the female experiences greater cell growth in her language-dominated hemisphere, while the male's greater growth is in his spatial perception-dominated hemisphere (Restak, 1979; Goy and McEwen, 1980; Gorman, 1992).

The differences in brain structure and hormonal production may have contributed to some behavioral differences between the sexes. Thus female babies are more sensitive than males to certain sounds, particularly their mother's voices, and are more easily startled by loud noises. Female infants are also more quiet and males more vigorous and inclined to explore, shout, and bang in their play. Female infants talk sooner, have larger vocabularies, and are less likely to develop speech problems—stuttering, for example, is several times more prevalent among males. Girls are superior not only in verbal abilities but also in overall intelligence, while boys excel in spatial performances such as mental manipulation of objects and map reading. When asked how they have mentally folded an object, boys tend to say simply "I folded it in my mind," but girls are more likely to produce elaborate verbal descriptions. Women are more sensitive to touch, odor, and sound. They show

The traditional gender roles in the United States are not necessarily the same in all societies. Because U.S. culture has defined being a physician as men's work, the majority of our doctors are males and are among the highest paid professionals. By contrast, in the former Soviet Union, where medicine was a "feminine" profession, most doctors were women and generally were paid "women's wages."

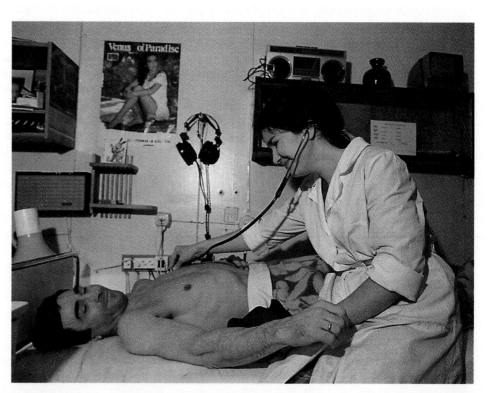

greater skill in picking up peripheral information as well as nuances of facial expression and voice. They are six times more likely than men to sing in tune (Rossi, 1984; Trotter, 1987).

In short, nature makes women and men different, but these differences do not add up to female inferiority or male superiority. On some measures—such as physical health and early verbal ability—females as a group seem superior to males, and by other measures—especially size and strength—males as a group are superior.

The Role of Culture

The biological differences between males and females seem logically related to the division of labor between the sexes. If men are bigger and stronger, then it makes sense for them to do the work that requires strength. And assigning women the care of the home and children may be a logical extension of their biological ability to bear and nurse children.

However, there are limitations to biological constraints on gender roles. Since women generally have smaller hands and greater finger agility than men, they are logically more fit to be dentists and neurosurgeons. Yet men dominate these high-paying professions because our culture has long defined them as "men's work." Indeed, the cultural definition of gender roles exercises awesome power. Because U.S. culture has defined being a physician as men's work, the majority of our doctors are males, and they are among the highest paid professionals. By contrast, in the former Soviet Union, where medicine was a "feminine" profession, most of the doctors were women, and they were generally paid "women's wages"—less than what skilled blue-collar workers made.

Undeniably, biology sets females and males apart. But it can only predispose—not force—us to behave in certain ways. Society does much to accentuate gender differences. As Alice Rossi (1984) points out, women may have the natural tendency to handle an infant with tactile gentleness and soothing voice and men may have the natural tendency to play with an older child in a rough-and-tumble way, but these tendencies are often exaggerated through socialization—under the guidance of culture. Also, boys may have been born with a *slightly* greater spatial ability than girls, but as adults, males can perform *much* better on spatial tasks, largely due to socialization. As Beryl Benderly (1989) explains: "Most boys, but few girls, grow up throwing baseballs, passing footballs, building models, breaking down engines—activities that teach about space." Thus, we are born female or male, but we learn to become women or men. We

take a closer look at this learning process in the next section.

Questions for Discussion and Review

1. What are gender roles, and what traits does U.S. society associate with them?
2. How are gender roles different or similar in various societies?
3. How do biology and culture influence the development of gender roles?

GENDER SOCIALIZATION

However a society defines gender roles, its socializing agents pass that definition from generation to generation. The family, peer group, school, and mass media all teach important lessons about these roles.

The Family

Newborn babies do not even know their gender, much less how to behave like girls or boys. Influenced by parents, children quickly develop their sexual identity and learn their gender roles. Right from birth, babies are usually treated according to their gender. At birth, girls tend to be wrapped in pink blankets and boys in blue. Baby girls are handled more gently than boys; girls are cuddled and cooed over but boys are bounced around and lifted high in the air. Girls are given dolls, whereas boys are given action figures. Mothers tend to fuss about how pretty their little girls should look, but they are less concerned about their little boys' appearance.

When they learn to talk, children become more aware of the gender difference. They are taught to differentiate "he" and "his" from "she" and "hers." Gender cues are also available. Both parents use more words about feelings and emotions with girls than with boys, so that by age two, girls use more emotion words than boys do. Mothers further tend to talk more politely ("Could you turn off the TV, please?"), but fathers use more commanding or threatening language ("Turn off the TV"). By age four, girls and boys have learned to imitate those conversational styles: talking among themselves, girls emphasize agreement and mutuality, and boys use more threatening, dominating language (Shapiro, 1990).

Girls are taught to be "ladylike," to be polite, to be gentle, and to rely on others—especially males—for

Influenced by their family, children generally quickly develop their sexual identity and learn their gender roles. Often, for example, boys grow up with a fear of being feminine. In recent years, though, there has been a trend toward more gender-neutral socialization.

help. They are allowed to express their emotions freely. Observing their mothers' focus on fashion and cosmetics, they learn the importance of being pretty, even that they must rely more on their beauty than on intelligence to attract men. On the other hand, boys are taught to behave "like men," to avoid being "sissies." They are told that boys don't cry. If they put on makeup and wear dresses, though in play, their parents are horrified. Growing up with a fear of being feminine, young men learn to maintain a macho image as well as an exploitative attitude toward women. Boys are also encouraged to be self-reliant and assertive, to avoid being "mama's boys" (Elkin and Handel, 1988; Power and Shanks, 1989).

In recent years, though, there has been a trend toward more gender-neutral socialization. Young parents, female professionals, and well-educated parents are particularly inclined to socialize their children into egalitarian gender roles.

The Peer Group

The socialization of girls and boys into their gender roles gets a boost from their same-sex peers, as Barrie Thorne (1993) found in her research. First, girls engage more often in cooperative kinds of play. They jump rope and count in unison, swing around the bars one after another, or practice dance steps in a synchronized fashion. Girls further tend more to say "let's . . ." or "we gotta . . ." to generate collaborative action. By contrast, boys engage more in competitive rough-and-tumble play and physical fighting. Older boys like to play competitive sports. Boys also like to appear tough by issuing verbal threats: "Shut up or I'll bust your head" or "I'm gonna punch you." Such threats are sometimes given in annoyance or anger, but also in a spirit of play.

Second, girls like to spend time with only one or two best friends, while boys tend more to hang around with a larger group of mere friends. With best friends, girls often show gestures of intimacy, such as combing each other's hair and borrowing each other's sweaters. By contrast, boys express their solidarity in a rough way, with, for example, "giving

five" handslaps, friendly teasing, or mock violence such as pushing and poking.

Third, far from "sugar and spice and everything nice," girls do occasionally suffer a breakdown in group harmony, experiencing considerable tension and conflict. But girls are not as direct and confrontational as boys in expressing their conflict. The offenses of others are usually talked about behind their back rather than to their face. A dispute among girls is consequently more protracted, much of if carried out through reports to and by third parties (Thorne, 1993).

In short, girls are more likely than boys to learn cooperation, intimacy, and indirectness in dealing with conflict. But, as Thorne cautions, these gender differences should not be exaggerated. Not all of the youngsters show the same gendered characteristics. Those traits are less common among nonwhite and working-class youth. For example, African American girls are just as skilled in direct verbal conflict as boys, and white working-class girls value "being tough" as much as boys do.

The School

Until recently, schools usually segregated courses and sports on the basis of gender. Secretarial courses and home economics were for girls; business and mechanics courses, for boys. Girls played softball; boys, hardball. High school counselors were not very likely to encourage girls to go on to college, because

American Mosaic

Adolescent girls from widely different cultural backgrounds experience strong social pressures, harassment, and sometimes violence from boys and men. Today, many people, especially women, are more aware of these problems and are actively working to help girls develop in a healthy way. This reading looks at life from the viewpoint of girls, and describes how the problems they face can be solved.

What Do Girls See?

At last count, there were 10 million adolescent girls in the United States. Too often teachers ignore them, boys and men harass them, women lie to them, and society downplays their needs as well as the challenges they face. What if, even for a day, everyone dropped whatever they were doing and focused on girls? Take Our Daughters to Work (TODTW)—the Ms. Foundation for Women's public education campaign to make girls "visible, valued, and heard"—captured the imagination of the country with this simple, compelling concept. As project manager coordinating the first TODTW campaign, I experienced firsthand the roller coaster of responses to making girls the center of attention. Girls were thrilled, women energized, fathers proud, employers welcoming, teachers appreciative, and the media fascinated. Those were the good days. Other times, mothers of sons were furious, fathers indifferent, employers rigid, columnists reactive, boys hostile, and teachers too overwhelmed to hear us out. The most disheartening reaction was the outcry, "What about the boys?"

The pervasive sexism that keeps attention rooted on boys and men is the foundation of many of the barriers and challenges facing young women. Adolescence is the critical point when they start reflecting on their chances as adults. "What girls see is a very powerful force in motivating and shaping their behavior," says Ruby Takanishi, executive director of the Carnegie Council on Adolescent Development.

What *do* girls see? Less opportunity in the workplace for women than for men and greater responsibility in the home, the degradation of women in the media, an absence of girls and women in school curricula, conflicting messages about female sexuality, the prevalence of racism and violence, and adults enforcing gender roles. At this juncture, girls—documented originally by Carol Gilligan and Harvard University's project on women and girls—tend to lose their self-esteem.

The good news is that women can make a fundamental difference. That message came across loud and clear when I talked to girls for this report. Those who seemed self-confident each had a strong, confiding relationship with a woman who talked with her openly and listened to her respectfully. But girls whose responses to my queries were painfully inaudible or simply "I don't know" tended to have little support from the adults in their lives.

The best news is that an exciting new girls' movement is taking shape, based on the premise that by learning to resist limiting social messages, girls can become strong, healthy young women. Fostering this movement is clearly feminist work. By listening to what girls say about their lives and becoming familiar with the terrain, we can begin to leverage resources and ensure that girls have access to the full range of life's options.

Excerpted from Kristen Golden, "What do Girls See?" *Ms. Magazine,* May/June, 1994, pp. 53 ff. Reprinted by permission of Ms. Magazine, © 1994.

they were expected to get married and stay home to raise children. If a girl was going to college, counselors tended to steer her toward traditionally feminine careers, such as teaching, nursing, and social work. While these overtly differential treatments are no longer prevalent, more subtle lessons of gender-role differences are still common. Consider just two examples that follow:

Girls are often led to believe that they are not as proficient in mathematics as boys. If a gifted female student builds a robot, her achievement may be trivialized with questions like "Did you build it to do housework?" Since math is stereotyped as a male domain, boys benefit more than girls from math classes. They are spoken to more, are called on more, and receive more corrective feedback, social interaction, individual instruction, and encouragement. They learn more than what is in the textbook. By contrast, girls are mostly consigned to learning by rote the math in the text, with little exposure to extracurricular math and science. Not surprisingly, girls usually end up scoring lower on standardized math tests, though they may receive better grades on classroom exams—which largely require memorization of course material (Kimball, 1989).

Another subtle lesson of gender-role differences inheres in the structure of the school. In virtually all elementary and secondary schools, men hold positions of authority (principals and superintendents), and women are in positions of subservience (teachers and aides). In such a male-dominant atmosphere, children are led to believe that women are subordinate, needing the leadership of men. As Laurel Richardson (1988) observes, "Children learn that although their teacher, usually a female, is in charge of the room, the school is run by a male without whose strength she could not cope; the principal's office is where the incorrigibles are sent."

The Mass Media

The media are pervasive sources of gender-role socialization. In such traditional magazines as *Good Housekeeping* and *Family Circle,* until recently the tendency has been to talk down to women as if they were children needing endless reiterations of basics on how to take care of the family. Today, the publications are more sophisticated, but they still tend to

define the female role in terms of homemaking and motherhood, and to offer numerous beauty tips to help attract men or please husbands. There are now relatively new, less traditional magazines, such as *New Woman* and *Working Woman,* which show fewer gender stereotypes. But they are dwarfed in circulation by the traditional "seven sisters"—*Better Homes and Gardens, Family Circle, Woman's Day, McCall's, Ladies' Home Journal, Good Housekeeping,* and *Redbook.* These traditional magazines have a combined circulation of 37 million, compared with only three million for the new magazines (Carmody, 1990; Peirce, 1990).

Women's magazines are not alone in perpetuating gender stereotypes. Television commercials have until recently presented women as sex objects and dedicated housewives. Young sexy women were shown admiring an old cigar smoker who used an air freshener. Housewives were shown in ecstasy over their shiny waxed floors or stricken with guilt for not using the right detergent to rid their husbands' shirts of "ring around the collar." Prime-time television programs also reinforced traditional gender roles. Women were generally typecast as lovers, mothers, or weak, passive sidekicks to powerful, effective men. Today, the media are more likely to present women as successful and able to support themselves and their families, but the traditional stereotypes of women are still there. On television and in movies, women are

Today the media have begun to present women as successful, able to support themselves, but the traditional stereotypes of women are still there. In many magazines women are told that it's all right to be successful but they shouldn't forget that they should be provocative and sexy because "looks are crucial."

still often depicted as sex objects, even when they are successful professionals. In men's as well as general-interest magazines, women are told that it's all right to be successful in the workplace but they shouldn't forget that they should also be provocative and sexy because "looks are crucial" (Sidel, 1990).

The Learning Process

We may know much about what a socializing agent teaches, but we still have to know how the child learns the gender role in the first place. According to social learning theory, such social-psychological factors as *conditioning* and *imitation* lie in the process of learning gender roles. Children are rewarded for behaving in ways that parents and others consider appropriate for their gender—and punished for not doing so, so they eventually conform to their society's gender roles. A little boy, for example, learns to hide his fears or pain because he has been praised for being brave and scolded for crying. Children also learn by imitation. They tend to imitate their same-sex parent and other adult models because these adults are powerful, nurturant, and able to reward or punish them. Through reinforcement and imitation, children engage in certain gender-typed activities, which lead to the development of a stable gender identity—"I do girl things. Therefore I must be a girl."

But according to cognitive development theory, gender *identification* is the cause rather than the product of gender-role learning. Children first learn to identify themselves as a male or female from what they observe and what they are told. Then they seek to act and feel like one: "I am a boy, therefore I want to do boy things." Thus, children are not passive objects in the acquisition of gender roles. They are active actors developing their gender identities and performing their gender roles. How clear their identities are and how well they perform their gender roles depend significantly on their *cognitive skills* as, for example, a fast or slow learner.

Apparently, all the processes discussed here—conditioning, imitation, identification, and cognition—play a part in the learning of gender roles. They are also interrelated. Children cannot rely on their cognition alone to distinguish what is masculine from what is feminine. They have to depend on their parents to serve as models of masculinity and femininity. In serving as models, the parents are likely to reinforce specific gender-typed behavior. Identification with the same-sex parent may also result from—as well as influence—the parents' tendency to reinforce certain gender-typed behavior (Basow, 1986).

Questions for Discussion and Review

1. How do the family, peer group, school, and mass media contribute to gender-role socialization?
2. How do girls and boys learn gender roles through the processes of conditioning, imitation, identification, and cognition?

GENDER INEQUALITY

At one time or another, laws have denied women "the right to hold property, to vote, to go to school, to travel, to borrow money, and to enter certain occupations" (Epstein, 1976). In recent years, there has been significant movement toward gender equality, but large inequalities remain, even in the United States. They are evident in education, in the workplace, in politics, and in religion. Underlying these inequalities is **sexism**—prejudice and discrimination based on the victim's gender. Sexism also involves sexual abuses against women, of which the most common is sexual harassment.

Sexism

A fundamental characteristic of sexism is the belief that women are inferior to men. Even when a male and a female have the same personalities or are equally competent in performing the same task, the woman is still likely to be considered inferior to the man. We can see this sexist attitude even in psychiatry, a profession that is supposed to be scientific and objective in analyzing human traits. Normal men tend to be described positively—as independent, courageous, and the like—but normal women are more likely to be described negatively, as having "sexual timidity" and "social anxiety." What if women lose their sexual timidity and become sexually active, typically considered normal for men? Then they are likely to be diagnosed as abnormal (Goleman, 1990a).

Such a "damned if you do, damned if you don't" attitude toward women is revealed in a study of college students asked to evaluate men and women with various characteristics. Women with "feminine" traits, such as compassion and sensitivity to others' needs, were rated more poorly than men with "masculine" characteristics, such as assertiveness. But women with the "masculine" traits were also rated

Sexism is characterized by the belief that women are inferior to men. When sexism takes the active form of discrimination against women, it obviously creates inequality. At each level of occupational skill, for example, men receive higher pay than women.

less favorably than men with the "feminine" traits (Gerber, 1989).

Sexism has long exerted a negative impact on women, making them believe they were inferior to men. In a classic study by Matina Horner (1969), most college women were afraid to pursue successful careers because sexism had caused them to believe that success by women would ruin their lives—making them unpopular, unmarriageable, lonely, or otherwise miserable. This "fear of success" is far less common among bright women today, a consequence of the women's movement, which vigorously attacked sexism in the 1970s and 1980s. Nevertheless, sexism is still powerful enough to make many women reluctant to pursue careers as men do. In fact, over the last 10 years women have become less willing to pursue careers and more willing to stay home to care for the family. A major reason, according to Susan Faludi (1991), is the exaggerated, negative portrayal of career women in the mass media: suffering depression and burnout from the rat race, being confronted with fewer opportunities for marriage, and running up against infertility from postponing childbearing.

Sexism may produce inequality between the sexes in two ways. When sexism takes the active form of discrimination against women, it obviously creates inequality. At each level of occupational skill, for example, men receive higher pay than women. Sexism may also foster inequality in a less direct way. If women have been socialized to feel inferior or abnormal, they may lower their expectations, aiming to achieve less than they otherwise might. Whether through overt discrimination or traditional gender-role socialization, sexism has brought gender inequalities in education, employment, politics, and religion.

Education

Before the turn of this century it was widely believed that "schoolwork would make women sick, diverting blood from their wombs to their brains" (Manegold, 1994). Thus women were long deprived of the opportunities for higher education. They were barred from many colleges and universities, especially graduate and professional schools, far into the 1960s. In general, the more prestigious the institutions, the more strongly they discriminated against women. Harvard, for example, was one of the last to give up sex discrimination. It began to admit women to its graduate business program only in 1963.

In 1973, the federal government, under pressure from the women's movement, began to pass laws against sex discrimination in schools. As a result, women have made impressive gains in education. As Figure 13.1 shows, more women than men are now attending and graduating from college. Although still fewer women than men receive medical and law degrees, the proportion of women earning these degrees has increased enormously since 1970. Women are expected to achieve parity with men in receiving these and other advanced degrees in the near future. Apparently, education has become the most equal institution in the United States with opportunity for both sexes.

But there is still substantial inequality in other aspects of education. First, from preschool through high school, girls are given less attention than boys. Teachers call on boys more often, offer boys more detailed and constructive criticism, and allow boys to shout out answers but reprimand girls for doing so, especially in math and science classes. Receiving less

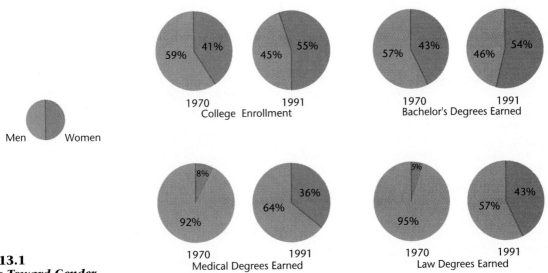

FIGURE 13.1
Progress Toward Gender Equality in Education

Source: *Statistical Abstract of the United States*, 1994, pp. 180, 188, 191.

attention from teachers, girls further suffer a drop in self-esteem when reaching high school. At age nine a majority of girls are confident, assertive, and feel positive about themselves, but by age 14 less than one-third feel that way (Sadker and Sadker, 1994). As a result, high school girls score lower on most subjects on standardized tests (see Figure 13.2).

Significant inequalities also persist on the faculties of numerous colleges and universities. As anthropologist Judith Shapiro (1994) points out, women make up less than 30 percent of full-time college faculty. The figures are even lower in the higher ranks of faculty and at prestigious universities. Various studies have consistently shown that, compared with their male colleagues, female academics are less likely to be hired, less likely to be promoted, and more concentrated in the lower ranks of institutions. They are also paid substantially less. Because there is no evidence that women faculty are less competent in teaching or research, this treatment can be attributed to gender discrimination.

Employment

Since laws were passed to prohibit sex discrimination in employment more than 30 years ago, women have made some gains in the workplace. More women are gainfully employed than before, and their pay is also higher. Still women are far from economically equal to men.

Women typically hold lower-status, lower-paying jobs, such as nursing, public school teaching, and secretarial work (see Table 13.1, p. 300). These traditionally female occupations, known in sociology as

women's ghettos, are subordinate to positions usually held by men. Thus, nurses are subordinate to doctors, schoolteachers to principals, and secretaries to executives.

FIGURE 13.2
Gender Gap in Academic Achievement

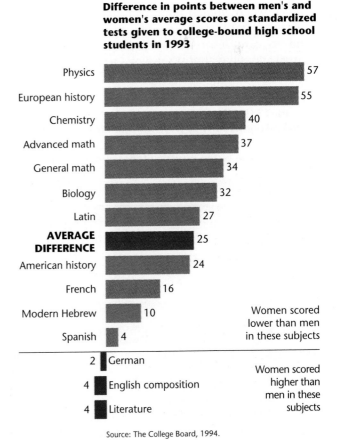

Difference in points between men's and women's average scores on standardized tests given to college-bound high school students in 1993

Source: The College Board, 1994.

TABLE 13.1
The Women's Ghettos

Percent of women in lower-status, lower-paying positions.	Percent of women
Secretaries	99
Dental hygienists	99
Receptionists	97
Childcare workers	97
Cleaners and servants	94
Registered nurses	94
Bank tellers	88
Librarians	88
Billing clerks	86
Elementary school teachers	86
Waiters	80

SOURCE: *Statistical Abstract of the United States, 1994*, pp. 407–409.

TABLE 13.2
Where Women Count

Women as a percentage of officials and managers in major industry in 1992:	Percent of Women
Finance, insurance, real estate	41.4
Services	38.9
Retail trade	38.5
Transportation, communication	25.6
Wholesale trade	20.9
Manufacturing	15.9
Agriculture	14.5
Construction	10.4
Mining	9.8
Average	24.0

SOURCE: Rochelle Sharpe, "The Waiting Game," *Wall Street Journal*, March 29, 1994, p. A8.

Even when women hold the same jobs as men or have comparable skills, training, and education, they tend to earn less. Among industrial nations, the United States has almost the worst record in women's earnings (see Figure 13.3). The state of Washington

FIGURE 13.3
Gender Gap in Earnings: A Global View

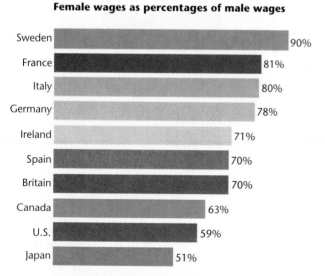

Female wages as percentages of male wages

Sweden	90%
France	81%
Italy	80%
Germany	78%
Ireland	71%
Spain	70%
Britain	70%
Canada	63%
U.S.	59%
Japan	51%

Source: *United Nations Human Development Report 1994*, p. 185.

has tried to solve this problem by instituting the comparable-worth program, which means that women are paid the same as men for doing different but equally demanding work, such as office cleaning as compared to truck driving. Some other states have followed Washington's lead by developing similar programs (Kilborn, 1990). But the gap in earnings continues to be large. Gender gap is even more striking when it comes to higher-management positions. As Table 13.2 shows, women make up about 24 percent of officials and managers in various industries as a whole. At the higher, vice presidential level, women make up an even smaller proportion—less than five percent (Sharpe, 1994).

Politics

Theoretically, women can easily acquire more political power than men. After all, women voters outnumber men, and most of the volunteer workers in political campaigns are women. Yet, until recently, most women felt that politics was a male activity, and that women should not plunge into the dirty world of politics. Sexism also tended to trap women in a "Catch–22" situation to squash their political ambition. If a woman campaigned vigorously, she would likely be regarded as a neglectful wife and mother. If she was an attentive wife and mother, she was apt to be judged incapable of devoting energy to public office. But in a man comparable qualities—a vigorous campaigner or a devoted husband and father—were considered to be political assets.

In recent years, more and more women have assumed political leadership, but they still have a long way to go. Although they make up over 50 percent of the voting population, women capture no more than five percent of all public offices. As Figure 13.4 shows, even in 1993, the year of "genderquake" when a greatly increased number of women were elected to the U.S. Congress, women still occupied only 47 House seats (10.8 percent) and seven Senate seats (seven percent). Globally, the United States also lags behind most other industrial nations in female political leadership (see Figure 13.5, p. 302). Why don't U.S. women recognize their power as a majority of the voting population and put it to work? A major reason, Naomi Wolf (1993) suggests, is lack of unity. Wolf has found many women who wrongly assume that in order to exert their influence they must become liberal feminists and promote abortion rights.

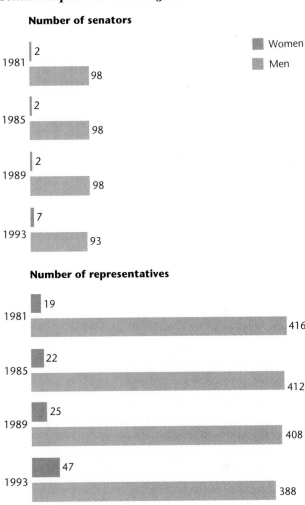

FIGURE 13.4
Gender Gap in the U.S. Congress

Number of senators

Women
Men

1981 — 2 / 98
1985 — 2 / 98
1989 — 2 / 98
1993 — 7 / 93

Number of representatives

1981 — 19 / 416
1985 — 22 / 412
1989 — 25 / 408
1993 — 47 / 388

Source: *Statistical Abstract of the United States.* 1994. p. 281.

Traditionally, most women felt that politics was a male activity. In recent years, a growing number of women, among them Senator Carol Moseley Braun, have assumed political leadership, though they still have a long way to go before reaching equality with men.

Wolf therefore calls for a broadly inclusive "power feminism" that helps all kinds of women, whether liberal or conservative, to win more political offices.

Religion

Long used to justify male dominance, the sexist notion of female inferiority can be found in the sacred texts of all the world's major religions. Buddhism and Confucianism instruct wives to obey their husbands. The Muslim Koran states, "Men are superior to women on account of the qualities in which God has given them preeminence." The Christian Bible says that after Eve ate the forbidden fruit and gave it to Adam, God told her: "In pain you shall bring forth children, yet your desire shall be for

FIGURE 13.5
Gender Gap in Politics: A Global View

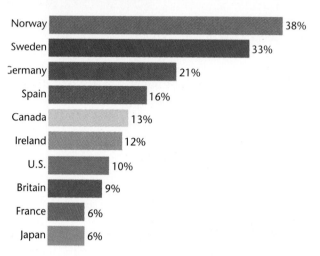

Percentage of seats in congress or parliament occupied by women

Norway	38%
Sweden	33%
Germany	21%
Spain	16%
Canada	13%
Ireland	12%
U.S.	10%
Britain	9%
France	6%
Japan	6%

Source: United Nations, *Human Development Report 1994*, p. 189.

your husband, and he shall rule over you" (Genesis 3:16). The daily Orthodox Jewish prayer for men includes this sentence: "I thank Thee, O Lord, that Thou has not made me a woman."

All this should *not* be taken to suggest that religion *always* puts women down. In the four Gospels of the New Testament, for example, "there is a total of 633 verses in which Jesus refers to women, and almost none of these is negative in tone" (Van Leeuwen, 1990). But sexist ideas can be found in other parts of the Bible. Even the most central concept of religion—God—is spoken and thought of as belonging to the male sex. To some feminists, the notion of the Supreme Being as male is the quintessence of sexism. Because of this, some liberal church leaders have begun purging hymnals and liturgies of references to God as male (such as "God the Father") and preaching about a genderless deity (called the Creator or Great Spirit). But many bishops, pastors, and laypeople have protested the changes (Niebuhr, 1992).

Sexism is hardly confined to sacred texts. It also shapes contemporary religious organizations and practices. For the past 20 years in the United States, under the increasing influence of the women's movement, more women have been enrolling in theological seminaries and becoming ordained ministers. But they are still a small minority and have limited

opportunities. Compared with their male counterparts, women clergy are more likely to be underemployed, be paid low salaries, serve merely as assistant or associate pastors, and be relegated to small congregations, and less likely to be promoted. Moreover, Conservative and Orthodox Jews and the Missouri Synod Lutherans are still opposed to ordaining women. The Roman Catholic and Eastern Orthodox churches, which represent over half of all Christians, also continue to prohibit ordination for women (Anderson, 1993). These church hierarchies are at odds with the rank-and-file, though. Two-thirds of lay Catholics, for example, favor opening the priesthood to women (Goldman, 1992).

In sum, gender inequalities in religion can be found both in the sacred texts and the contemporary practices. These two subjects will continue to be a focus of debate as the world's religions confront gender-related issues.

Sexual Harassment

Most sociologists define **sexual harassment** as an unwelcome act of a sexual nature. But in 1993 the Supreme Court provided a more precise definition: sexual harassment is any sexual conduct that makes the workplace environment so hostile or abusive to the victims that they find it hard to perform their job. This definition came with the Court's ruling on the suit that Teresa Harris filed against her former boss, Charles Hardy. In 1987 Harris quit her job in despair because she felt she had been sexually harassed by Hardy. According to Harris, Hardy often asked her—and other female employees—to retrieve coins from the front pockets of his pants. He once asked Harris to go with him to a hotel room to negotiate her raise. And he routinely made such remarks to her as "You're a woman; what do you know?" and called her "a dumb-ass woman." She had spent six years trying to convince judges that she was sexually harassed in violation of federal law, but to no avail. The judges found Hardy's conduct not severe enough to "seriously affect her psychological well-being." But the Supreme Court ruled that sexual harassment does not have to involve inflicting "severe psychological injury" on the victim. As the Court says, federal law "comes into play before the harassing conduct leads to a nervous breakdown" (Sachs, 1993).

The Harris case was the second on sexual harassment to reach the Supreme Court. In the first, in 1986, the Court ruled that sexual harassment was a form of gender discrimination prohibited by the

Civil Rights Act of 1964. Since that first ruling, the number of harassment charges has increased substantially. In 1992 alone the figure was about 13,000, nearly double the previous year. To avoid being sued, many companies as well as universities and colleges have instituted anti-harassment policies, guidelines, or educational programs (Sachs, 1993).

But the problem is too prevalent to go away soon. About half of all working women have been sexually harassed at some point in their careers. One study shows that on college campuses some 28 percent of female graduate students and 40 percent of undergraduate women have been harassed. Examples of harassment are, in descending order of frequency, unwanted sexual remarks, leers and suggestive looks, deliberate touching, pressure for dates, pressure for sexual favors, and attempted or actual rape. According to another study on high school and junior high students, more than two-thirds of girls and 42 percent of boys have been touched, groped, or pinched on school grounds (Kantrowitz, 1991; Henneberger and Marriott, 1993).

Generally, sexual harassment reflects the men's attempt to preserve their traditional dominance over women. Men are therefore more likely to harass a woman if they feel threatened by her "invasion" into their male-dominated world. This may explain why sexual harassment seems to occur most frequently in heavily male-dominated occupations such as the navy, surgery, and investment banking (Goleman, 1991). At bottom, sexual harassment is an expression of power, involving a more powerful person victimizing the powerless. It is possible, for example, for a female boss to sexually harass her male underling. But, given the prevalence of men being more powerful than women, men are the offenders in most cases.

Questions for Discussion and Review

1. What are the characteristics and consequences of sexism?
2. What is the current status of women in educational institutions?
3. Why have jobs traditionally reserved for women led to the creation of women's employment ghettos?
4. How have women fared in politics in recent years?
5. What impact does sexism have on religion?
6. How did the Supreme Court define sexual harassment? And why do you think sexual harassment is so common?

PERSPECTIVES ON GENDER INEQUALITY

We have just seen how gender inequality manifests itself in various aspects of society. But why the inequality in the first place? Functionalists and conflict theorists provide different answers. On their part, symbolic interactionists are not interested in the origin of gender inequality but are more concerned with how gender inequality and the interaction between genders influence each other.

Functionalist Perspective

According to functionalists, it is functional for society to assign different tasks to men and women. This division of labor was originally based on the physical differences between the sexes. For thousands of years when hunting-gathering societies predominated, men were more likely to roam far from home to hunt animals because men were larger and stronger, and women were more likely to stay near home base to gather plant foods, cook, and take care of children because only women could become pregnant, bear and nurse babies. Today, muscle power is not as important as brain and machine power. Contraceptives, baby formula, childcare centers, and convenience foods further weaken the constraints that the childbearing role places on women. Yet traditional gender roles persist.

The reason for this persistence, functionalists assume, is that these roles continue to be functional to modern societies. How? Talcott Parsons and Robert Bales (1953) argued that two basic roles must be fulfilled in any group. One is the **instrumental role**, which requires performance of a task. The other is the **expressive role**, which requires taking care of personal relationships. In the modern family, the instrumental role is fulfilled by making money; playing this role well requires competence, assertiveness, dominance. The expressive role requires offering love and affection, and it is best filled by someone warm, emotional, nonassertive. When men are socialized to have the traits appropriate for the instrumental role and women are socialized to have the traits suitable for the expressive role, then the family is likely to function smoothly. Each person fits into a part, and the parts fit together.

The role differentiation may have worked well for many traditional families, especially in traditional societies in Asia, as suggested by their lower rates of divorce. But functionalists may have exaggerated the

According to some feminists, surrogate motherhood has emerged as the ultimate exploitation of women by men because it turns women into mere breeding machines. In the photo, a man claims "Baby M" after the 1987 trial that awarded him and his wife custody of the baby which they had paid the surrogate mother $10,000 to have with his sperm.

role differentiation because women do perform the instrumental role to a large degree. In the United States every day many women still spend hours on such instrumental tasks as cooking, housecleaning, laundering, and shopping. Even in many highly sex-segregated preindustrial societies, women perform a significant instrumental role. As Joel Aronoff and William Crano's (1975) research shows, in nearly half the preindustrial societies women contributed at least 40 percent of their societies' food supply. If women perform at least some of the instrumental tasks as men do, it is not role differentiation alone that determines gender inequality. There must be something else that also contributes to gender inequality. That something else can be found in the conflict perspective.

Conflict Perspective

Conflict theorists argue that gender inequality arose because men were able to exploit women. According to the classic Marxist view, gender inequality is part of the larger economic stratification. By restricting women to childbearing and household chores, men ensured their own freedom to acquire property and amass wealth. They also used their power over women to obtain heirs and thus guarantee their continued hold on their economic power. Moreover, men have directly exploited women by getting them to do much work with little or no pay. Thus, married women are not paid for doing housework and child care, which would cost about half of most husbands' income if they had to be purchased from others.

Gainfully employed wives also do most of the housework and child care, although they work as much as their husbands outside the home. In addition, as we have seen, they are usually paid less than men for their work outside the home (Hochschild 1989; Shellenbarger, 1991). In short, economic exploitation of women helps bring about gender inequality.

Some conflict theorists give greater weight to sexual exploitation as the source of gender inequality. Randall Collins (1975) argues that "the fundamental motive is the desire for sexual gratification, rather than for labor per se; men have appropriated women primarily for their beds rather than their kitchens and fields, although they could certainly be pressed into service in the daytime too." More recently, according to some feminists, surrogate motherhood has emerged as the ultimate exploitation of women by men because it turns women into mere breeding machines. To conflict theorists, female exploitation of one type or another contributes greatly to the development of gender inequality.

Symbolic Interactionist Perspective

According to symbolic interactionists, interaction between the sexes reflects as well as reinforces gender inequality.

When women interact with men, the interaction tends to reflect their inequality. Suppose a group of women and men discuss some issues at a meeting. Men usually talk more often than women, and tend to interrupt women more than the other way around. Men are also more likely to boast about their accomplishments and take credit for others'. On the other hand, women tend to speak more softly and politely, and to say more often "please," "thank you," or "I'm sorry." Such interaction between men and women, while reflecting gender inequality, also reinforces it. Because of their verbal aggression men are more likely to end up being considered highly competent, having their arguments and decisions accepted, and getting promotions or larger salary raises. By contrast, the less verbally aggressive women tend to lose out, even if they may really be more competent, be the ones who actually get the job done, or contribute more to the company (Tannen, 1994).

Nonverbal interactions between the sexes also reflect and reinforce gender inequality. Women talking to a man typically give such low-status signals as smiling, nodding, holding their arms to their bodies, or keeping their legs together. Men are more likely to use high-status gestures by smiling only occasionally, holding their heads still, and sprawling out with legs spread apart, taking up substantial space around them, as has been observed in Chapter 6 (Social Interaction in Everyday Life). Because of such an unequal interaction, a mutually aggravated spiral is likely to occur: the woman's conciliatory and nonaggressive gestures lead the man to see her as weak, which makes him more overbearing and aggressive, which intimidates her so as to make her more conciliatory (Cory, 1979; Tannen, 1994). Ultimately, gender inequality is reinforced, with the man's power enhanced at the woman's expense.

Questions for Discussion and Review

1. According to the functionalist and conflict perspectives, what is the origin of gender inequality?
2. What insight about gender inequality can be learned from the symbolic interactionist perspective?

TOWARD GENDER EQUALITY

As we have seen, there has been significant progress toward gender equality in the last two decades, due largely to the women's rights movement. Women's attempts to liberate themselves from the constraints of female-role stereotypes have further induced a growing number of men to free themselves from male-role stereotypes.

The Women's Movement

The women's movement for gender equality in the United States can be divided historically into three waves. The first wave began in the middle of the last century, developing out of the larger social movement to abolish slavery. The women who participated

NOW President Patricia Ireland at a rally. NOW has been the most successful feminist organization. Its aim is to end sexual discrimination in education, work, politics, religion, and all the other institutions.

in the abolitionist movement came to realize that they themselves also lacked freedom. Initially, they attempted to eradicate all forms of sexual discrimination, but gradually focused their attention on winning the right for women to vote. When women's suffrage finally became a reality in 1920, the feminist movement came to a complete halt.

But in the mid-1960s, the movement was put back into action, and thus began the second wave of feminism. Two factors seem to have brought it on. First, after the end of World War II, more and more women were going to college. After having so much education, the women were unhappy to be mere housewives or to hold low-status, low-paying jobs outside the home. Second, many young women participating in various social movements (including the civil rights movement, the student movement, and the antiwar movement), supposedly fighting for the freedom of the oppressed, found themselves oppressed by the male freedom fighters. These women, wrote Annie Gottlieb (1971), "found themselves *serving* as secretary, mother and concubine, while men did all the speaking, writing, and negotiating—and these were men who professed to reject the 'oppressive' ritual machinery of their society."

Out of this background emerged a number of all-female organizations. Some might be considered very radical because they hated men, rejected marriage, and vowed to tear down the whole gender-role system. They gave their organizations such names as SCUM (Society for Cutting Men) or WITCH (Women's International Terrorist Conspiracy from Hell). Other feminist groups were more moderate, the most famous being NOW (National Organization for Women). NOW has been the most successful feminist organization and continues to have a strong influence on women's positions today. NOW's aim is to end sexual discrimination in education, work, politics, religion, and all the other institutions. Consequently, many states have passed laws requiring equal pay for equal work, government departments have issued affirmative-action guidelines to force universities and businesses to hire more women, and, in many cases, court decisions have supported women's charges of sexual discrimination in hiring, pay, and promotion.

Now, in the 1990s, a new generation of young women in their teens and twenties have started the third wave of feminism. These women have grown up taking equality for granted, because of their mothers' victories for women's rights. A series of events in the early 1990s awakened them to the fact that the fight for equality is not over. The most jolting event was probably the spectacle of an all-

men committee grilling Anita Hill on her charges of sexual harassment against Supreme Court nominee Clarence Thomas. The hearings, broadcast widely, revealed how political institutions still grossly disadvantage women with their paucity of female members and their old-boy rules. The proliferation of negative reaction against women's progress, detailed in Susan Faludi's controversial 1992 book, *Backlash*, has further demonstrated that equality is far from being attained.

But the third wavers are different from their mothers. The young feminists today are more inclusive, welcoming men to join them in addressing not only women's concerns but also problems that affect both sexes, such as racism, pollution, and poverty (Schrof, 1993). By being inclusive in organization and concern, these young feminists can achieve goals that the older generation has largely ignored. Made up largely of highly educated white women, the older feminists have made great strides for women in college education, professional schools, and white-collar jobs. But less attention has been paid to the plight of poor and minority women (Guttman, 1994).

Men's Quiet Revolution

A quiet revolution has been going on among some men who want to free themselves from the demands of the traditional male role. As we have observed, men are expected to be tough, aggressive, and competitive and to suppress their emotions even if they feel like crying when sad. It can be difficult for men to relate closely to their wives and children, because such a close relationship requires sensitivity, warmth, and tenderness—the very qualities discouraged by the masculine role. It also can be difficult to develop deep friendships with other men because of the pressure to be competitive and to put up a tough, impersonal front.

Consequently, a growing number of men support gender equality. They can see how equality helps reduce the burden of being male. They can also see the benefit of encouraging their wives to pursue careers outside the home if that is their choice. Imprisoning a bored and frustrated wife in the homemaking role is believed likely to cause the marriage to fall apart. Moreover, the working wife can boost the family income. A working wife makes it possible for men to change careers, if they wish, rather than being trapped in a boring job. The significant financial contributions from their working wives relieves the pressure on men. If they do not have to work so hard to make a living, they can take more time for

ENRICHING OUR LIVES

Many men have been influenced by the women's movement and have come to question and change their feelings and behavior regarding gender. This reading describes some ways Canadian men are attempting to redefine themselves and shows ways men can get in touch with their feelings and fantasies.

Feelings and Fantasies

Two decades after the launch of modern feminism, men are forming their own movement. The men's groups have been dismissed as drum beaters doing silly things in the woods. But Cory Bretz, a member of Vancouver M.E.N. (Men's Evolvement Network) and the Wisdom Council, says drumming and other rituals are a small part of what those organizations do. They are primarily support groups in which men talk about their feelings without pressure to conform to male stereotypes. If men are going to change their roles in society, Bretz maintains, they must first find out more about themselves—"and that's a feminine characteristic." The group, he says, has changed his life. "I'm much more able to engage in a relationship. I have a sense of peace and calmness."

Changed Men

They sport the same paisley ties and pressed dress shirts they have always worn. But make no mistake: the four supervisors slurping coffee in the bus drivers' lounge at the headquarters of the Halifax area's Metro Transit Division are changed men. In fact, when purchasing manager Peter Ross, 38, tells a visitor, "We were always sensitive guys," the table explodes with laughter loud enough to startle the nearby bus drivers out of their card games.

It was no laughing matter when Metro Transit's manager resigned two years ago after several female employees accused him of sexual harassment. The manager denies the allegations, and the case is still before the Nova Scotia Human Rights Commission. But the incident led to a crash course in gender politics that has left many in the mostly male organization confused. "We went from no rules," says support services supervisor Moss Mombourquette, 42, "to not being sure if we could compliment a female co-worker on how she looked without overstepping the bounds." Adds Mike Hartlen, 33, a quality-control analyst: "For a while, it seemed we had a target painted on our chests and it was open season."

A Stay-at-Home Father

Mister Mom—the very phrase pokes fun at fathers who stay at home to care for their kids. But men who tie on the apron strings say there is nothing amusing about the social disapproval they sometimes endure.

Three years ago, Ken and Judy Toews of suburban Ottawa decided that their two sons, then one and seven years old, were suffering because both parents were too busy with their careers. Ken, now 36, quit his planning job at an Ottawa defense contractor because Judy, a 37-year-old teacher, was less likely to be laid off. When he resigned—after 17 years of continuous employment—Toews was on the verge of panic, wondering if he had done the right thing. "It's been a sweet and sour experience," he says now. "My father and a number of older relatives think I'm a bum. They say Judy should stay home. But I think it's the best thing I've ever done."

According to informed estimates, less than one percent of Canadian fathers fit the Mr. Mom description. But Toews speaks warmly of the intensity of his new relationship with his children. Raising his youngest son from infancy, he adds, has created a bond between them that is "weirdly powerful." There are also more tangible benefits. "We used to eat very poorly because we were always rushing," he says. "I've found that I enjoy cooking, and now there are always homemade cookies or muffins in the house and good food at every meal."

Despite those rewards, Toews still struggles with negative feelings. "In our society, your identity is your job," he says. "When I was employed, I felt like a somebody. Bringing up children is not something that society values." In other words, Toews now empathizes with stay-at-home mothers. "I get so angry because I see how little these women are appreciated. When their husbands are rude to them, I find myself shouting at the men." In fact, Toews says, looking after others has altered his own character. "Constant giving generally doesn't suit the male psyche, which is more self-centered," he muses. "Looking back, I can see that I'm a much more caring person than I was."

Excerpted from Patricia Chisholm, et al., "Feelings and Fantasies," *Maclean's*, January 31, 1994, pp. 45–46.

Cutting Edge

The women's movement of the 1960s pushed for egalitarian feminism, insisting that women and men be treated exactly alike. But today more women are advocating protectionist feminism, insisting that working women be granted special benefits such as prenatal care and maternity leave. In this reading, a leading writer on feminism, Wendy Kaminer, reflects on the social meanings of this new feminist view.

A New Feminist View

My favorite political movement of the 1960s was a Black Panther rally in a quadrangle of Smith College on a luxuriant spring day. Ramboesque in berets and ammunition belts, several young black males exhorted hundreds of young white females to contribute money to Bobby Seale's defense fund. I stood at the back of the crowd watching yarn ties on blonde ponytails bobbing up and down while the daughters of CEOs nodded in agreement with the Panthers' attack on the ruling class.

It was all so girlish—or boyish, depending on your point of view. Whatever revolution was fomenting posed no apparent threat to traditional gender roles. Still, women who were not particularly sensitive to chauvinism in the counterculture or the typical fraternity planned to attend graduate or professional school and pursue careers that would have been practically unthinkable for them ten years earlier. Feminism was altering their lives as much as draft avoidance was altering the lives of their male counterparts.

Today, three decades of feminism later, a majority of American women agree that feminism has altered their lives for the better. In general, polls conducted over the past three years indicate strong majority support for feminist ideals. But these same polls suggest that a majority of women hesitate to associate themselves with the movement. As Karlyn Keene, a resident fellow at the American Enterprise Institute, has observed, more than three-quarters of American women support efforts to "strengthen and change women's status in society," yet only a minority, a third at most, identify themselves as feminists.

Many feminists take comfort in these polls, inferring substantial public support for economic and political equality, and dismissing women's wariness of the feminist label as a mere image problem (attributed to unfair media portrayals of feminists as a strident minority of frustrated women). But the polls may also adumbrate unarticulated ambivalence about feminist ideals, particularly with respect to private life. If widespread support for some measure of equality reflects the way women see, or wish to see, society, their unwillingness to identify with feminism reflects the way they see themselves, or wish to be seen by others.

To the extent that it challenges discrimination and the political exclusion of women, feminism is relatively easy for many women to embrace. It appeals to fundamental notions of fairness; it suggests that social structures must change but that individuals, particularly women, may remain the same. For many women, feminism is simply a matter of mommy-tracking, making sure that institutions accommodate women's familial roles, which are presumed to be essentially immutable. But to the extent that feminism questions those roles and the underlying assumptions about sexuality, it requires profound individual changes as well, posing an unsettling challenge that well-adjusted people instinctively avoid. Why question norms of sex and character to which you've more or less successfully adapted?

Of course, the social and individual changes demanded by feminism are not exactly divisible. Of course, the expansion of women's professional roles and political power affects women's personality development. Still, many people manage to separate who they are in the workplace from who they are in bed, which is why feminism generates so much cognitive dissonance. As it addresses and internalizes this dissonance, and women's anxiety about the label "feminism'" as it embarks on a "third wave," the feminist movement today may suffer less from a mere image problem than from a major identity crisis.

Excerpted from Wendy Kaminer, "Feminism's Identity Crisis," *The Atlantic Monthly*, October, 1993, pp. 51–53, 68.

their family and discover the joys of fatherhood.

Many of these men, however, do not support total equality between the sexes. They are what Kathleen Gerson (1993) calls "autonomous men." They like to enjoy freedom from the traditional burden of being the family's sole breadwinner but refuse to share equally with their wives the responsibility of housework and childcare. As a result, while these autonomous men can have it all, their working wives tend to do it all, coming home after a day of work to a "second shift" of doing housework and caring for children (Hochschild, 1989). The younger generation of men, though, are more inclined to do domestic chores. According to a survey, already nearly half of the young men—ages 18 to 24—interviewed said they would be interested in staying home with their young children so that their wives could succeed in their careers (Gibbs, 1990). (See box, p. 307).

The Future of Gender

As we have seen, women have made some advances in education, employment, and politics but they still have a long way to go before winning the battle for equality.

Nevertheless, equality will come sooner if large numbers of U.S. women move into male-dominated, higher-status occupations. As research by Janet Chafetz (1984) suggests, the more women are involved in socially valued economic production, the more equality there is between the sexes. Similarly, Joan Huber (1989, 1990) has found that the increasing participation of educated women in the labor force generally leads to greater gender equality. Huber also believes that, with more women becoming highly paid doctors, lawyers, business executives, and other professionals, more husbands will need only "a little friendly persuasion" to share housework.

But all this by itself is not likely to translate into real equality. As suggested, most working wives still do most of the housework, while they, along with unmarried career women, still receive less pay and less likelihood of promotion than their male peers. To achieve genuine equality, women may have to resort to force—such as legal action and political pressure, not only to get equal pay for equal work, but to get special benefits such as maternity leave and child-care services. Moreover, the women's movement should raise a new consciousness for the 1990s: working mothers cannot "make it" alone; they need help from their husbands or government or companies to achieve their goals. Actually, there is nothing new about this need to depend on others. Most successful men have not made it alone, either. As Ruth Sidel (1990) says, men have "had women beside them every step of the way—women to iron their shirts, press their pants, mend their socks, cook their meals, bring up their children, and soothe them at the end of a hard day. . . They did not do it alone. They *still* don't do it alone." In short, women are

pushing for both egalitarian and protectionist feminisms (also see box, p. 308).

There are signs that women's lives are moving in those directions. Today more young women than young men are graduating from college with bachelor's or master's degrees (Census Bureau, 1994). This will increase further the significant growth of women in high-paid professions over the last two decades. Young women's salaries are fast reaching parity with those of young men with similar job experiences (O'Neill, 1994). Women are also becoming a powerful political force. One result is the passage of federal family leave law, which requires larger companies to offer workers three months of unpaid leave in the event of a child's birth or family medical emergency (Gerson, 1993). But too many poor and minority women are still either unemployed or crowded into traditionally women's low-paid occupations. Without better job training, child care, and other programs for these women, the progress toward gender equality will likely continue to be uneven.

Questions for Discussion and Review

1. What is the history of the women's rights movement?
2. What is the nature of men's quiet revolution?
3. In what ways can gender equality be achieved?

A GLOBAL ANALYSIS

While the women's rights movement has produced significant gains in the United States, discrimination against women is still rampant in many developing countries.

The abuse of women is by no means unique to developing countries. As the United Nations (1994) found, every single country in the world today still treats its women less well than its men. The problem only seems more serious and widespread in developing countries than in industrial societies. As suggested in Chapter 11 (Rich and Poor Nations), the gender gap in literacy, education, employment, income, and health is significantly larger in developing than in industrial countries.

But some forms of gender discrimination appear unique to certain countries. As the U.S. State

Department reported in 1994, many women in China are forced to undergo sterilization and abortion so that they will not have more than one child, young village girls in Burma and Thailand are sold by their parents to brothel owners, maids are beaten in Saudi Arabia, and girls in the Sudan and Somalia are ritually subjected to "female circumcision," during which their clitoris is cut off (Greenhouse, 1994). In China and India the tradition of female infanticide continues in small pockets of the huge countries, and the availability of ultrasound machines that can detect the sex of a fetus has resulted in widespread abortions of females. In India, every year over one thousand young wives are burned to death by their husbands or in-laws because their parents cannot pay any more dowries. In Russia, business etiquette calls for female secretaries to sleep with their boss (MacFarquhar, 1994; Pope, 1994).

Questions for Discussion and Review

1. In what ways is gender discrimination similar and different around the globe?

CHAPTER REVIEW

1. *What are the traditional gender roles of men and women in the United States?* Men are expected to be breadwinners, aggressive, and ambitious. Women are expected to be homemakers, passive, and dependent. Consequently, the sexes tend to behave differently. *Are these gender roles the same all over the world?* No. They are different in some societies, though similar in most other societies. *Do biological differences between the sexes make women inferior to men?* No. In some ways women seem biologically superior and in other ways inferior. *How does culture influence gender-role differences?* Culture defines what the gender differences should be, and through socialization we develop those differences.

2. *How do we learn our gender roles?* Through socialization by the family, peer group, school, and media. *What is the process by which children learn gender roles?* Gender roles are learned through conditioning, imitation, identification, and cognition.

3. *What is sexism?* It involves prejudice and discrimination against women, based on the belief that women are inferior to men. *Do women today match men in educational attainment?* Yes in attending and graduating from college. But high school girls still score lower than boys on most subjects. *Have women in the workplace achieved equality with men?* No. Women still tend to hold lower-status jobs and to be paid less than men. *How do U.S. women fare in politics?* Better than before, but they are still far from achieving political parity with men. *What is the impact of sexism on women in religion?* Women are generally accorded low status and refused ordination in conservative churches. *What is the sociological nature of sexual harassment?* It reflects an attempt of the powerful to put the powerless in their place.

4. *According to functionalists, why are gender roles still functional in industrial societies?* With men playing the instrumental role and women the expressive role, the family's smooth functioning can be ensured. *How do conflict theorists explain gender inequality?* It stems from economic or sexual exploitation of women. *How does symbolic interactionism enhance our understanding of gender inequality?* By showing how interaction between women and men reflects as well as reinforces gender inequality.

5. *How has the women's movement changed over time?* Before 1920 the movement fought for women the right to vote. Since the 1960s the aim has been to end all forms of gender discrimination, but the plight of poor and minority women has been largely ignored. The young feminists of today deal with such issues while inviting men to join them. *What is the quiet revolution?* An increasing number of men have rejected the traditional male role and supported gender equality. But many of these men still have not shared equally with women the responsibility of housework and childcare. *How can greater equality be achieved?* By increasing women's educational attainment, professional careers, and political power, while also solving the problems of poor and minority women.

6. *How is gender inequality apparent around the world?* Gender inequality exists in all countries, except that

the problem seems more serious and widespread in developing countries. Some forms of female abuse also appear unique to some societies.

KEY TERMS

Chromosomes The materials in a cell that transmit hereditary traits to the carrier from the carrier's parents (p. 291).

Expressive role Role that requires taking care of personal relationships (p. 303).

Gender role The pattern of attitudes and behaviors that a society expects of its members because of their being female or male (p. 290).

Hormones Chemical substances that stimulate or inhibit vital biological processes (p. 292).

Instrumental role Role that requires performance of a task (p. 303).

Sexism Prejudice and discrimination based on the victim's gender (p. 297).

Sexual harassment An unwelcome act of a sexual nature (p. 302).

Women's ghettos Traditionally female occupations that are subordinate to positions usually held by men (p. 300).

SUGGESTED READINGS

Faludi, Susan. 1991. *Backlash: The Undeclared War Against American Women*. New York: Crown. A provocative analysis of how the movies, television, journalists, and politicians blame the feminist movement for "every woe besetting women, from mental depression to meager savings accounts, from teenage suicides to eating disorders to bad complexions."

French, Marilyn. 1992. *The War Against Women*. New York: Summit Books. A hard-hitting analysis of how patriarchal institutions, culture, and men are involved in dominating, exploiting, or abusing women.

Gerson, Kathleen. 1993. *No Man's Land: Men's Changing Commitments to Family and Work*. New York: HarperCollins. An empirical analysis of how traditional and nontraditional men respond to gender equality.

Hochschild, Arlie. 1989. *Second Shift: Working Parents and the Revolution at Home*. New York: Viking. A well-written, compassionate account of how working mothers do most of the housework.

Wolf, Naomi. 1993. *Fire with Fire*. New York: Random House. Presents the concept of "power feminism," showing how women achieve more by recognizing their power as a majority in society.

AGE AND AGING

Myths and Realities

MYTH: *It is natural for old people to be senile—experience serious memory loss, confusion, and loss of reasoning ability.*
REALITY: Old age does not inevitably lead to senility. Senility is an abnormal condition, not a natural result of aging. The large majority of old people are not senile.

MYTH: *Because older people experience mental deterioration, they are bound to become less effective workers.*
REALITY: Elders may lose some mental speed, but their accumulated experience more than compensates for the loss of quickness. Not surprisingly, as shown by many studies, the quality of job performance improves with age.

MYTH: *If older people like their jobs, they will not look forward to retirement.*
REALITY: A large majority of workers are relatively satisfied with their jobs, but most still have favorable attitudes toward retirement. Only a few dread it, mostly blue-collar workers who are only moderately rather than profoundly satisfied with their employment.

MYTH: *Elder abuse is similar to child abuse. That's why* physical *abuse is the most common when elders are victimized by their younger relatives.*
REALITY: While child abuse usually takes the form of physical assault, elder abuse often involves financial exploitation.

hen 70-year-old Margaret Embrey was brought into the emergency room of a hospital in Houston, her condition appalled the doctors and nurses. She was covered with bedsores, some as large as a hand. Maggots were gnawing at her wounds, which had cut into her bones. She also suffered from dehydration and malnutrition. Five-foot-seven tall, she weighed only 95 pounds, having lost 40 pounds over the previous six months. The old woman's 19-year-old granddaughter and her husband, age 22, were later charged with criminal abuse (Rosado, 1991).

This is an extreme case of elder abuse, but it reflects the larger problem of mistreatment of older people. Elder abuse has also become more common today partly because of the "graying" of our society: the number of elderly persons—aged 65 or older—has risen sharply, and they now make up over 12 percent of the U.S. population, about the same proportion as African Americans (see Figure 14.1).

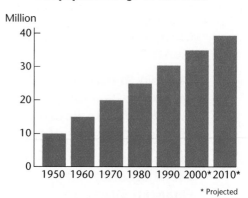

FIGURE 14.1
An Aging Boom

U.S. population age 65 and older

* Projected

Source: Data from Census Bureau, 1994.

THE AGING PROCESS

The Heinz ketchup company once tried to market dietetic food to older people under the name "Senior Foods." It turned out to be a flop. A perceptive observer explained, "People didn't want to be seen eating the stuff. It was labeling them old—and in our society, it is still an embarrassment to be old." Another company, Johnson & Johnson, made a similar mistake when it introduced Affinity shampoo. Its first TV commercial featured a chance meeting between a middle-aged woman and an old boyfriend. He says, "You still look great." By emphasizing age, the commercial failed to sell the product and was soon pulled off the air (Gilman, 1986). The bottom line is that our culture is youth-oriented. Growing old bothers many people. This feeling has much to

do with the biological and psychological effects of aging. But social forces, such as our society's tendency to define the elderly as a national burden rather than a national treasure, also play an important role. These social forces can aggravate or diminish biological and psychological effects.

Biological Consequences of Aging

Sooner or later, all of us gradually lose our energies and our ability to fight off diseases. This natural physical process of aging is called **senescence.** Biologists have been trying to crack the mystery of why it occurs, but without much success. Some believe that humans are genetically programmed to age; others point to the breakdown of the body's immunological system, cells, or endocrine and nervous systems. In any event, it is clear that senescence involves a decline in the body's functioning, increasing the vulnerability to death. It is a gradual process in which the changes come from within the individual, not from the environment. It is also both natural and universal, occurring in all people.

Old age has many biological consequences. The skin becomes wrinkled, rough, dry, and vulnerable to malignancies, bruises, and loss of hair. Because aging also causes the spinal disks to compress, most elderly people lose one to three inches in height. Another result of aging is a loss of muscular strength. More important, blood vessels harden as we age, creating circulatory problems in the brain and heart, problems that raise the incidence of stroke and heart disease among older people. Functioning of the kidneys shows the greatest decline with advancing age. Although aging has all those deteriorative effects, they do not cause disability in most of the elderly.

Psychological Consequences of Aging

Aging affects such psychological processes as sensory perceptions, psychomotor responses, memory, and personality. By the time they are 65, more than 50 percent of men and 30 percent of women in the United States suffer hearing losses severe enough to hinder social interaction. Visual acuity also declines with age: 87 percent of those over age 45 wear glasses, compared with only 30 percent of those under 45. For most people, though, hearing and visual problems are generally inconveniences, not disabilities. The elderly further tend to have slower though more accurate psychomotor responses—such as being able to type at lower speeds but with fewer errors—than young people (Butler, 1984; Kart, 1990).

Short-term memory—recall of recent events for a brief time—seems to decline with age, although memory of remote events does not. Old age, however, does not inevitably lead to **senility,** an abnormal condition characterized by serious memory loss, confusion, and loss of the ability to reason. Aging does not necessarily lead to a decline in intellectual performance, either. In fact, **crystalline intelligence**—wisdom and insight into the human condition, as shown by one's skills in language, philosophy, music, or painting—continues to grow with age. Only **fluid intelligence**—ability to grasp abstract relationships as in mathematics, physics, or some other science—tends to stabilize or decline with age (Butler, 1984).

Much of the decline in psychomotor and intellectual performance amounts to only a slowing in work, not a drop in quality. The elderly may lose some mental speed, but their accumulated experience more than compensates for the loss of quickness. In fact, compared with youngsters, older people may take longer to make a decision, but it is usually a better one. Therefore, contrary to the stereotyped assumption about the aged automatically experiencing mental deterioration, many studies have shown the quality of job performance to improve with age.

With advancing age, people also tend to change from an active to a passive orientation to their

Aging does not necessarily lead to a decline in intellectual performance, as these performers prove. In fact, crystalline intelligence, such as artistic skills, continues to grow with age. From left to right are Connie Stevens, George Burns, Betty White, and Carol Channing.

environment, becoming less inclined to bend the world to their own wishes and more likely to conform and accommodate to it (Butler, 1984).

Social Effects on Aging

Biological aging does not affect all people in the same way. The speed of aging, for example, varies greatly from one individual to another. Some people at age 75 look 60, and others who are 60 look 75. A number of social factors may determine the disparities. The older look, characterized by the sagging and wrinkling of the skin, may stem from too much sun exposure in earlier years, a legacy of an active, outdoorsy lifestyle. Lack of exercise, another lifestyle, may also speed up the aging process. Thus those who sit in a rocking chair waiting for the Grim Reaper usually look and feel older than those who are physically active. Social isolation and powerlessness further enhance aging. These largely social, environmental factors suggest that, if aging can be accelerated, it can also be retarded (Gelman, 1986; Begley, 1990).

Psychological aging does not affect all people in the same way, either, because of the intervention of social factors. Elderly persons who are well educated, and thus presumably accustomed to flexing their

minds, maintain strong mental abilities. So do those elderly who have a complex and stimulating lifestyle. By contrast, deterioration of the intellect is more likely to occur among those whose lifestyle is marked by a lack of mental activity, a rigid adherence to routine, and a low satisfaction with life.

Societal definition of aging also influences the impact of aging on mental ability. In their cross-societal study, Becca Levy and Ellen Langer (1994) gave a memory test to comparable samples of young and old people in the United States and China. They found that the U.S. youth turned in a slightly better performance than the Chinese youth. But the elderly in China were found to have a sharper memory than their U.S. counterparts (see Figure 14.2). A self-fulfilling prophecy is apparently at work here: widely respected in Chinese society for being wise, elders are often asked for advice, thus creating considerable opportunities for keeping the aging mind active and sharp. But the elderly in U.S. society are less respected and less often given those opportunities. More

FIGURE 14.2
Societal Impact on Elderly's Memory

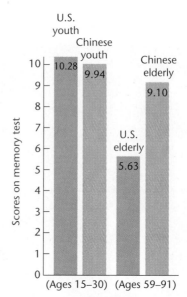

Source: Data from Becca Levy and Ellen Langer, "Aging Free from Negative Stereotypes", *Journal of Personality and Social Psychology*, Vol. 66 (June 1994), p. 994.

ENRICHING OUR LIVES

Sociologists and anthropologists have frequently studied how different cultures interpret the passage of the years, and psychologists have examined the individual experience of time. This article uses these insights to explain the nature of time and offer advice on how to slow down the pace of life and live longer.

How to Manage Time

The belief that time is a resource that must be monitored closely and managed carefully is one of the basic laws of our time-crunched world, as is the imperative to do more and do it quicker. Is it any wonder our culture favors the young and energetic? Who else can accomplish the hundreds of tasks each of us must master in a typical day, as well as process the thousand bits of information rushing at us every hour?

In my workshops at Omega and around the country on time-shifting—learning how to toggle between hyperproductivity and an awareness of the world around you—the first question I pose is "Do you feel that you have enough time in your daily lives?" Invariably, more than 90 percent declare an overwhelming sense of "time-poverty"—part of an epidemic of anxiety and pressure in our society.

Ironically, in response, methods to improve our management of time have gained in popularity, along with new, speedier technology that helps us develop greater efficiency. Yet while these initially seem to help, they ultimately serve only to increase the speed of our lives. We learn to go faster and get more done—only to take on more work and responsibility.

As a result, the future arrives that much quicker, and it begins to predominate. The "now" becomes a prelude to the "next." We do this so we can get to that. We work for the weekend, rush through lunch to get back to our desks, worry about next month's deadline before this month is completed. We divide our attention and awareness between the task at hand that we're rushing to complete and the next item on our day-planner.

So, what is needed is to come into the present moment. Instead of rushing, take your time, let your rhythm slow down. You can rush later if you need to, but for now, simply perform the task that is in front of you, whether it's washing the dishes or commuting to work.

We spend our lives waiting for the important events to take place, rushing through these "in-between" moments. Yet the reality is that these interims actually make up a significant portion of our lives. Allowing ourselves to be present in them and experience them fully is what makes us alive—and helps to keep us young.

This involves developing a sense of mindfulness, a way of being that puts you fully in the moment without pressure or anxiety about staying on schedule. It is a quality that each of us needs to learn how to cultivate more in our lives, awakening all of our senses and being comfortable in the present—to feel rooted, with no need to rush.

Some will read this and wonder why they should slow down. Isn't it okay to keep moving along with the progress of modern times? Isn't it, in fact, necessary to do so?

There really is no right or wrong answer; rather it is a question of how we feel about our lives. My experience has taught me that there is too much stress caused by the frantic pace at which most of us exist. The result is a disconnection from the world around us and our sense of being alive in it. People report feeling trapped, powerless to effect any meaningful change, coping as best as they can yet knowing they don't feel the way they would like to feel.

The key is to step back from the edge, learn to get involved in the *process* rather than constantly longing for the end result. This does not mean giving up our goal-oriented lives—simply modifying them, finding a balance between our productive and our emotional selves. This enables us to live as whole beings, fully alive.

In response to the pace of our modern world, learning how to successfully shift time can be one of the keys to achieving both health and longevity as we continue to age.

Excerpted from Stephen Rechtschaffen, M.D., "Time," *Psychology Today*, November/December, 1993, pp. 32–36.

analysis of aging around the globe can further demonstrate the strong influence of social forces on the elderly, to which we turn in the next section.

Questions for Discussion and Review

1. What are some of the biological and psychological consequences of aging?
2. How do social factors blunt or worsen the biological and psychological effects of aging?

A GLOBAL ANALYSIS

Elders generally enjoy higher status in traditional societies than in modern industrialized societies. Part of the reason is that it is no mean feat to grow into old age in traditional societies, which typically have far fewer elderly than modern societies (see Figure 14.3). Thus, by merely living to be old at a time when few survive past middle age, the elderly earn a certain respect. In addition, because traditional societies change slowly, the knowledge and skills of the aged remain useful. Their experience is greatly valued. They are the community's "experts." Not surprisingly, throughout Africa growing old results in rising status and increased respect. Among the Igbo, old people are widely regarded as wise, consulted for their wisdom, and accorded great respect. The male Bantu elder is known as "the Father of His People" and revered as such. In Samoa, too, old age is considered "the best time of life," and elders are highly respected. Similar respect for older people has also been observed in various other countries, from Thailand to rural Mexico (Cowgill, 1974).

In many societies, however, the norm changed with the arrival of industrialization. Older people lost their previous role and status. No longer were they the storehouses of a community's knowledge or the guardians of its traditions, because the knowledge important to the community was changing and traditions were losing their hold. Thus, in many modern societies today, elders lose status because their skills have become obsolete. The loss of status can also be found in rural areas that have been touched by modernization. In a remote community in the Nepal Himalayas, for example, the elderly are unhappy with their lot, wishing that they were dead, complaining that their children have abandoned them, and trying to drown their sorrows in home-brewed liquor every day. The reason is that many of

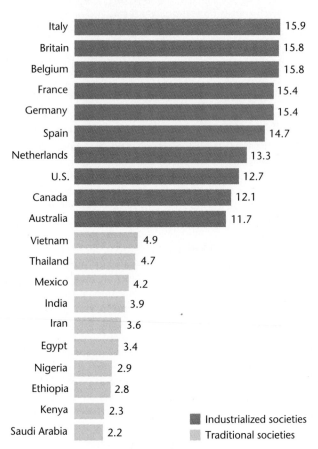

FIGURE 14.3
Fewer Elderly in Traditional Societies

Percentage of each country's population age 65 and older

Italy	15.9
Britain	15.8
Belgium	15.8
France	15.4
Germany	15.4
Spain	14.7
Netherlands	13.3
U.S.	12.7
Canada	12.1
Australia	11.7
Vietnam	4.9
Thailand	4.7
Mexico	4.2
India	3.9
Iran	3.6
Egypt	3.4
Nigeria	2.9
Ethiopia	2.8
Kenya	2.3
Saudi Arabia	2.2

■ Industrialized societies
□ Traditional societies

Source: Data from Census Bureau, 1994.

their young men have gone to India to work on construction projects and brought back ideas and attitudes that have no room for the traditional value of filial devotion (Goldstein and Beall, 1982; Gilleard and Gurkan, 1987).

Modernization does not always have such adverse effects on the elderly, though. Faced with an extremely high level of industrialization, Japan nonetheless continues to embrace its long-standing tradition of respect for old people. This tradition is derived from the Confucian principle of filial duty, which requires children to repay their parents a debt of gratitude for bringing them up. It is further supported by a sharply inegalitarian social structure, which requires inferiors, like servants, students, and children, to respect superiors, like masters, teachers, and parents (Palmore and Maeda, 1985). Nevertheless, the case of Japan is only an exception to the rule that modernization reduces the elderly's status.

In contrast to Japan, the United States is founded on the ideology of equality and individualism. With egalitarianism opposing the traditional inequality between old and young, the elderly began to lose their privileged status when independence was declared in 1776. The emphasis on individualism also helped loosen the sense of obligation between young and old (Fischer, 1977). Assisted by this ideological background, extreme industrialization has decisively brought down the status of elderly. Today, it sometimes seems as if the elderly are expected to do nothing but wait to die. The elderly can be imprisoned in a **roleless role**, being assigned no role in society's division of labor, a predicament of the elderly in industrial society.

Questions for Discussion and Review

1. Why are elders more respected in traditional societies?
2. Why has there been a shift in this respect in modern societies?

THE ELDERLY'S HEALTH

Health has special importance for older people, because aging most often brings an increase in health problems.

Chronic Ailments

It is well-known that the elderly are more likely than younger people to suffer from chronic (long-term) ailments, such as heart problems, arthritis, rheumatism, and hypertension. In fact, a majority of elderly have these ailments. But these ailments are far from disabling. Most of the elderly with the chronic problems can and do continue to work or manage their own households. Only about 18 percent are forced to significantly scale down their everyday activities (Kart, 1990).

Chronic ailments affect men more seriously than women. Men with chronic ailments are three times more likely to lose their capacity to carry on an active life (Atchley, 1988). This may partly explain why elderly men are far more likely than elderly women to kill themselves. At the same time, though, chronic ailments do not cause a high suicide rate among elderly *African American* men. In fact, their suicide

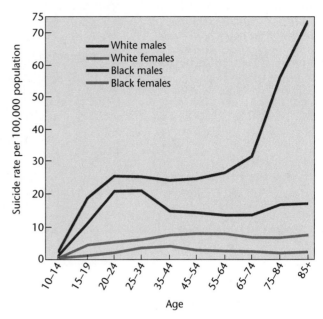

FIGURE 14.4
Suicide Soars Among Elderly White Males

Source: Data from Census Bureau, 1994.

rates are very low. It is elderly white men who have extremely high rates, considerably higher than other groups (see Figure 14.4). A major reason is that white men's self-identity tends to derive from performance in the business or professional world. Chronic ailments tend to threaten such self-identity. By contrast, the self-identity of elderly white women and elderly black men and women is less performance-oriented because sexism and racism have long denied them entry into business or professional careers. They are instead more intrinsically oriented, defining their self-worth as a caring family person or a religious person, and thus less likely to be threatened by the physical decline of old age (Girard, 1994). In short, social forces such as gender and race can aggravate or alleviate the impact of chronic problems on elders.

Mental Disorders

People may believe that since it is no fun to be old the elderly must be most likely to suffer from mental illness, especially depression, but the truth is just the opposite. According to a national survey (Kessler et al., 1994), it is relatively young persons, aged 25 to 34, who have the highest rate of mental illness. While elders are less likely than most younger groups to become emotionally disturbed, they are significantly more likely to suffer from brain disorders.

Victims of Alzheimer's disease, a disease of the brain, progressively lose their memory and other mental abilities. But despite the higher frequency of serious and less serious illnesses among elders, old age itself is not a disease.

According to one study, brain disorders occur in only about two percent of those under age 65 but in 20 percent of those aged 80 or older (Shanas and Maddox, 1976). The most familiar of these disorders is senility. As we noted earlier, senility is not a natural part of being old but instead an abnormal condition. In 80 percent of the cases the symptoms of senility—confusion and forgetfulness—result from *non*neurological problems that can be treated. Malnutrition, fever, and medication can make a person appear senile. If these underlying problems are not treated, the symptoms of senility may persist.

In contrast to these cases of nonneurological problems, about four million U.S. elders do suffer from neurological diseases. Most of these people are stricken with **Alzheimer's disease**, a disease of the brain characterized by progressive loss of memory and other mental abilities. Scientists suspect that it is hereditary, because half the immediate family members of the patient may develop the mental disorder if they live into their nineties. The disease can also strike the middle-aged, but the symptoms usually do not appear before the age of 50. The victims gradually lose their abilities to remember, think, reason, and count, until finally they cannot perform the simple chores of everyday life.

Despite the higher frequency of such serious and other less serious illnesses among the elderly, old age itself is not a disease. Old people cannot die of old age—just as young people cannot die of young age. There are great differences in the health of individuals among the elderly, just as among younger

people. This is why, as Matilda Riley (1982) points out, "even at the oldest ages there are some who can see as well, run as far, and perform as well on mental tests as younger people can."

Questions for Discussion and Review

1. Why do chronic ailments have a greater impact on elderly white males than on other groups?
2. Is old age a disease? Why or why not?

WORK AND RETIREMENT

Over the last 40 years, the elderly have become less likely to join the labor force. Today, only about 12 percent of the elderly are employed. In many other industrialized nations, the elderly have similarly low rates of employment (Census Bureau, 1994).

Factors in Declining Employment

Several factors have contributed to the drop in employment among the elderly. First, industrialized economies increasingly demand more and more highly educated workers with the latest skills and knowledge, placing older workers at a competitive disadvantage with younger workers. Changing technology tends to make older people's skills obsolete, adding to their difficulties in retaining jobs or finding new ones. With the coming of nonmechanical watches, for example, the demand for skilled watchmakers who could repair the delicate mechanisms of conventional watches has dropped.

Second, older workers are often stereotyped as less efficient and productive than younger workers. Coupled with this myth is the reality that it costs more to pay older employees because of seniority. Consequently, a system of mandatory retirement has been instituted to force workers to quit at a certain age so that their jobs could be given to younger people. Age discrimination, then, makes it difficult for elders to get and keep jobs.

Finally, employment rates have dropped because retirement has become an established institution. The emergence of pension programs allowed workers to retire, and changing attitudes made it socially acceptable to do so. For the majority of U.S. workers, retirement has become economically feasible since Social Security was established in 1935 for older people. Later, programs offering early retirement benefits further encouraged the exodus of older workers from the labor force.

"*Last month, I reached mandatory retirement age. I am still here. Anybody want to make something of it?*"

Drawing by Joe Mirachi; © 1977 The New Yorker Magazine

The Decision to Retire

People may be forced to retire because of poor health, inability to find a job after being laid off, or the mandatory retirement policy. When retirement is a matter of choice, both *moderate job satisfaction* and *adequate retirement income* seem to play an important part in the decision (Atchley, 1988; Dychtwald, 1989).

It might seem that if we like our jobs now, we will not look forward to retirement. Yet some evidence seems to refute this presumption. According to surveys, more than 80 percent of the U.S. labor force are relatively satisfied with their jobs, but most still have favorable attitudes toward retirement. Actually, most of these workers, particularly the blue-collar workers, are only moderately rather than profoundly satisfied with their jobs (Atchley, 1988).

On the other hand, professionals, managers, and others in high-status occupations overall like their jobs better than those in lower-status occupations, and these higher-status workers are less likely to retire early. Physicians are more than three times as likely as nurses and other health-service people to

keep working past age 65. A judge or lawyer is seven times as likely as the laborer to keep working. College professors are four times as likely as cafeteria employees to continue working. When they do retire early, higher-status people may continue to be involved in their professions. The majority of retired scientists, for example, spend time on scientific research. In contrast, people with lower-status, more physically demanding, and less intellectually stimulating work are more likely to retire as soon as they can afford to (Dychtwald, 1989).

The most important factor in deciding when to retire, however, is income. Most workers who are eligible for adequate pay during retirement, choose to retire early.

The Consequences of Retirement

Retirement has been blamed for a variety of physical and psychological problems, including death. But research has shown that there is no causal relationship between retirement and illness or death. Of course, some people become ill and die after retirement, but usually they have been in poor health before retirement. Indeed, they may have retired because of their poor health (Palmore, 1981; Minkler, 1981). In one survey, about a third of the workers reported that retirement *improved* their health, and only about 3 percent thought their health worsened (Rosenberg, 1970). Another study suggests that health is especially likely to improve if retirement provides a release from the stress and strain of a job (Ekerdt, Bosse, and LoCastro, 1983).

In recent years, growing numbers of retirees have begun to return to work. The desire to return to work arises largely from insufficient pension and Social Security benefits. Older workers such as this one are now visible at restaurants that have traditionally hired teenagers. They can be found working other places, too, but, no matter what jobs they have, the pay and status are generally low.

But retirement can adversely affect people's lives, and it affects some groups more than others. It often increases feelings of economic deprivation, because incomes usually drop when people retire—mostly to about half of preretirement earnings. Retirement is also more likely to produce poverty and social isolation among women and the working class than among men and the middle class. Generally, blue-collar workers tend to be less satisfied with retirement than white-collar workers, even though they have been more eager to retire. On the other hand, men and white-collar workers are better adjusted to retirement because of their superior financial situation (Atchley, 1988; Dychtwald, 1989).

In recent years, growing numbers of retirees have begun to return to work. The desire to return to work arises largely from insufficient pension and Social Security benefits. Many retirees with these problems have been able to find work because of labor shortages that result from fewer young people in the population. Older workers are now visible at fast-food restaurants, which have traditionally hired teenagers. But older people can also be found working in banks, hotels, travel agencies, hardware stores, grocery stores, and other retailers. The pay and status are generally low, though. Many of these jobs are part-time, so older workers can still collect full Social Security benefits by keeping their earnings low. Still not all older workers are stuck with bottom-of-the-barrel positions. Some have higher positions, but their new jobs are typically a step down from their career work, sometimes involving a reversal of roles—from being a supervisor to being supervised. This may produce

problems between older workers and their much younger bosses. Giving orders to older workers, according to a vice president of the fast-food chain Rax Restaurant, is "sort of like telling your grandma to clear off the table" (Hirsch, 1990).

Questions for Discussion and Review

1. What keeps elders' unemployment rate low?
2. What factors enter into older workers' decision to retire?
3. Why does retirement benefit some people more than others?

ECONOMIC CHALLENGES

Once out of the labor force, the elderly are faced with new economic challenges in their lives. Here we focus on two issues: The nature of their new source of income and their financial security.

Social Security

Most retirees depend on Social Security as a major source of income. It is a popular program. But a widely held myth is that Social Security works like a

American Mosaic

In the United States many social services are devised to help the elderly, but they tend to miss the Native Americans who live in urban areas. This reading offers some reasons for this problem.

Native American Elderly in Cities

For many years, American Indian organizations in Los Angeles county have recognized that the reality of their lives and their view of the world are not understood or accommodated by the human services system. As a result, essential human services have not been reaching the American Indian community—particularly its frail elderly population. Even well-meaning service providers are ignorant of American Indian culture and values.

Many people are surprised to learn that American Indian elderly live in cities, since it is commonly assumed that they return to their reservations. In fact, half of all American Indian elders live in urban areas. Los Angeles has an American Indian population of 100,000, the highest concentration of city-living Indians in the country.

There are an estimated 11,000 American Indian elders living in Los Angeles. Most were part of a larger American Indian federal relocation project following World War II, in which thousands of American Indians came to work in the city's factories. This population has now reached retirement age. While some live on pensions, many are frail, lonely, and unable to enjoy their retirement years.

Widely dispersed throughout a 4,000 square mile area, lacking transportation and a centrally located intergenerational center, the American Indian elders have been deprived of social contact with each other and with younger members of their tribes. Through their churches, neighborhood bulletin boards, or by chance, they might hear of a food bank or legal aid office, but culturally and socially isolated, they have not been receiving the kinds of geriatric services which, as elderly Americans, they are entitled to under the Older Americans Act.

Unlike other ethnic groups, city-living American Indians have not congregated in neighborhoods, as has been suggested. While young American Indians maintain a strong shared cultural tradition, they have not been able to share that culture or make a visible imprint on the urban scene around them. Although this may be partly due to the fact that they account for only one percent of the population, it is more a matter of style. The American Indian community is typically not activist, and does not engage in political protests or other highly visible public demonstrations of power. They usually do not wear braids or clothing that would identify them as American Indians. Their last names are often Hispanic. Thus they tend to become an "invisible minority" in the city.

Most important, American Indians are reluctant to approach a bureaucratic system that they perceive as disrespectful at best or outright hostile at worst. Thus, in the highly diverse and pluralistic ethnic and cultural matrix of Los Angeles, American Indians—particularly American Indian elders—have been greatly underserved.

Excerpted from Josea B. Kramer, "Serving American Indian Elderly in Cities: An Invisible Minority," *Aging Magazine*, 1992, pp. 48–52.

pension fund: Social Security payroll taxes are deposited in individual accounts in a trust fund, where they earn interest and eventually are used to pay benefits upon retirement. In reality, Social Security schemes are income transfer operations. As soon as the taxes are collected they are used as benefits for today's retirees. In other words, the Social Security taxes people pay do not go toward their future retirement.

This means there is no guarantee that today's workers will, upon retirement, get back from future workers what they are now putting into the system. They will be able to get Social Security benefits only if future workers pay enough taxes. Whether that will

happen depends on demographic and economic factors: How many people will retire to claim benefits? How many people will be working and for what wages? How strong will economic growth be? What will the rate of inflation be? If the future work force is small (because of slow population growth or high unemployment) or if wages are low (because of weak economic growth), Social Security funds will diminish. If, in addition to these unfavorable factors, the number of future retirees or the rate of inflation soars, the Social Security system will go broke and be unable to pay benefits to retirees.

In fact, in about 20 years, when the huge baby-boom generation begins to retire, there will be far more retirees than workers. *Each worker* will have to pay a much higher tax to support *more than one retiree*. This will be in sharp contrast to the situation of 40 years ago, when there were 50 workers sharing the cost of supporting one retiree, or to today's situation where three workers support one retiree. Will young workers of the small baby-bust generation in 2015 pay the heavy taxes needed to support the hordes of elderly people? Optimists argue that they will, for the following reasons. First, young adults will realize that government benefits from taxes will go to their own parents and grandparents, whom they might have to support by themselves if the government did not. Second, the baby-bust generation will be in great demand as workers, so they will be well-off enough to accept the tax increases necessary for supporting the elderly. And third, due to improved health, a growing number of elderly will work past normal retirement, and these workers will pay taxes into the Social Security fund rather than draw benefits from it (Otten, 1987).

However, these are mere speculations about the future, and so cannot be predicted accurately. In the meantime, the government may reduce Social Security benefits to help shrink its enormous budget deficit, although older citizens are fighting to prevent that from happening.

Financial Situation

In some ways the elderly are financially better off than younger people. Usually they have fewer expenses. Most do not need to furnish a large new home, raise children, and pay their education expenses. Their expenses for work clothes and transportation are lower. They are also likely to have financial assets that younger people do not have. The majority own their homes, free from mortgage payments, have money in the bank, and often own some U.S. savings bonds, stocks, and corporate bonds. At the same time, however, the elderly are more likely than younger people to face huge medical bills, beyond what government programs cover. And financial hardship is particularly difficult for the aged who have been accustomed to a better financial situation in their younger days.

The majority of elders receive most of their income from Social Security benefits, personal assets, and private or public pensions. Of these programs, Social Security is by far the most important source of income. For many of the elderly, this income is supplemented by other government benefits such as Medicare, special property tax exemptions, public housing, and Supplemental Security Income for the

FIGURE 14.5
Mean Monthly Income by Age Group

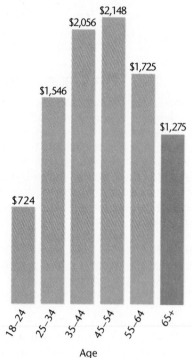

Source: Data from Census Bureau, 1994.

elderly poor. Thus, the elderly are not so poor that they will pilfer food and medicine from a store (Kart, 1990).

Until recently, the elderly were much more likely to be poor than most other age groups. In 1970 the proportion of the elderly living in poverty was nearly 25 percent, compared with 13 percent for the general population. A change came in the late 1970s: Congress tied Social Security to increases in the consumer price index, so benefits rose automatically as the cost of living rose. As a result, the poverty rate among the elderly declined from 25 percent in 1970 to 12.9 percent in 1993—compared with 14.5 percent for the general population (Census Bureau, 1994).

The elderly are not exactly well-off, though. They still have less income than most of the younger age groups (see Figure 14.5). It is true that the elderly do not need much money to live comfortably—because they no longer have children to support, high mortgage payments, and other expenses that younger people have. But a substantial proportion of the elderly—at least one-third—are living *near* the poverty line, though they are not officially considered poor. Poverty is especially common among those elderly who live alone, who are women, and who are members of minority groups (Census Bureau, 1994).

Questions for Discussion and Review

1. Will today's workers receive adequate Social Security benefits when they retire?
2. In what ways are elders richer or poorer than others?

PERSONAL RELATIONSHIPS

A large majority of the elderly say they are never or hardly ever lonely. They often see close relatives, socialize with friends, go to church, and participate in voluntary organizations. At any one time, less than 5 percent of elders are living in a nursing home or other institution. Less than a tenth of older people have never married and, as lifelong loners, they are not likely to find old age a time of special isolation. About 30 percent of the elderly—mostly women—live alone. Most elderly live with their spouses, and their family relationships tend to be far more satis-

fying than stereotypes suggest (Kart, 1990; Census Bureau, 1994). In short, the personal lives of most elderly are better than popularly believed. Let us take a closer look.

Sex and Marriage

More than half of the elderly are married and living with their spouses. Men are much more likely than women to be living with their spouses, because more than 74 percent of older men but only about 40 percent of older women still have a spouse alive (Census Bureau, 1994). One reason for this difference is that women tend to live longer than men; another is a greater tendency for men to marry younger women than for women to marry younger men.

The rate of divorce is extremely low among older people—about 5 percent. In one study, 95 percent of the elderly rated their marriage as happy or very happy. Even more impressive is the finding that a majority (55 percent) reported that the happiest period of their marriage was the present (Decker, 1980).

Contrary to popular stereotypes, most men and many women remain sexually active during their seventies and eighties. The availability of a partner and sexual experience in earlier life are the most important factors determining sexual activity among the aged. Those who are sexually active in old age generally were active when they were younger, and those who are less active sexually are likely to have shown this pattern, too, when younger. Other significant determinants of sexual frequency are health and socioeconomic status: better-educated, higher-income, and healthier elderly persons tend to be more sexually active. Although sexual activity does not guarantee longevity, it does tend to maintain or enhance both health and happiness among the elderly (Palmore, 1981).

A continuing interest in sexuality does not occur only among the married elderly; it is also a significant part of their unmarried peers' dating experience. As a 77-year-old woman says, "Sex isn't as important when you're older, but in a way you need it more." Single elders need the intimacy provided by sex because it helps raise their self-esteem, making them feel desired and needed. They also find their sexual

A large majority of elders see their children and grandchildren often. In the middle and upper classes, elderly parents often give advice, money, and other assistance to their offspring.

experience different from what it used to be. As a man in his seventies explains, "When you're young, sexuality is heavily oriented toward proving yourself, a kind of immature showmanship. Now it's different. It's more loving, more playful, more of a nourishment between two people" (Dychtwald, 1989).

Relationships with Children

When the last child leaves home, most parents do not find the "empty nest" lonely or meaningless. They have anticipated their children's leaving, and they appreciate their own increased freedom. As a result, fewer than 10 percent of U.S. elderly live with their grown children, while more than 60 percent of Japanese elderly live this way (Dentzer, 1991). Nonetheless, U.S. elderly tend to maintain close ties with their children.

About 85 to 90 percent of the elderly who have children live less than an hour away from them, so they can visit each other easily. Indeed, they do see each other often, "maintaining intimacy at a distance." A large majority of older parents have seen one of their children within the last day or week. Elderly parents often give advice, gifts, even money. They are more likely to give money to their children than to receive it. Their generosity often "takes the form of helping with college tuition, down payment on a house, furniture—not just a check every Christmas" (Gibbs, 1988). According to most estimates, about 10 percent of the elderly *receive* cash from their adult children, but half *give* cash to their children or grandchildren. There is a class factor in all this: the flow of aid from parents to adult children occurs more often in the middle and upper classes, but the flow of aid from children to old parents happens more frequently in the working class (Atchley,

1988). In short, the fact that few of the elderly live with their grown children does not reflect an absence of emotional and physical connection.

Although most people in the United States have traditionally rejected the idea of two or three generations living in the same household, more people today than before consider it a good idea for old parents to live with their grown children (see Figure 14.6). There are several reasons for the increasing support for multigenerational residence. First, the rising number of old people has increased sensitivity to elderly's needs. Second, the decreased dependence of older individuals because of improved health and financial status has made them much easier to live with. And third, young people trying hard to succeed in their careers welcome the benefits of pooled economic resources and the help with child rearing and other domestic tasks (Okraku, 1987). But most elderly are still reluctant to move in with their children, which reflects the importance that the U.S. culture attaches to independence and self-reliance.

Gender and Widowhood

There are nearly five times as many widows as widowers. But women adjust to widowhood more easily than men do. Although widows are more likely to suffer severe financial setbacks, they usually have a great number of close friends to provide emotional support. In addition, adult children tend more to rally around the mother than the father (Otten, 1990; Census Bureau, 1994).

For men, losing a spouse can have serious consequences. When their wives die, men lose the only intimate confidante they ever had. They also have difficulties doing unaccustomed household chores. Elderly widowers are seven times more likely than

FIGURE 14.6
Growing Support for Multigenerational Residence

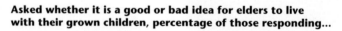

Asked whether it is a good or bad idea for elders to live with their grown children, percentage of those responding...

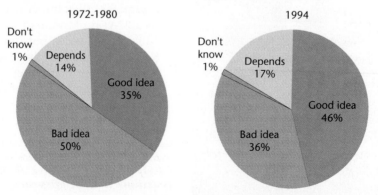

Source: Data from National Opinion Research Center, *General Social Survey*, 1972-1994.

Aging, of course, brings the end of life closer and closer. Most people prefer not to think about death but to focus on how to live as long as possible. Lifestyle is a major influence on the age of death: diet, smoking, and drinking are all factors that can prematurely end life. In this reading, we see how our relationships with others also influence how long we live.

Death Comes Knocking When You're Alone

If you want to cheat death, form friendships, studies suggest. People—including the chronically ill—who have good social networks tend to outlive others who lack that support.

A new, six-year study involving 2,503 Finnish men, ages 42 to 60, provides more details about the relationship between social involvement and longevity.

Not being involved in clubs or volunteer organizations, having poor quality relationships, giving or receiving little social support, and being single increased the men's risk of dying during the six years, reports coauthor George A. Kaplan of the California Department of Health Services' Human Population Laboratory in Berkeley. During the study, 167 of the participants died.

For example, those who didn't participate in any organizations were twice as likely to die as the men most involved in groups, the team reports in the September *Epidemiology*. People who were most dissatisfied with the quality of their relationships had a 1.8 times greater chance of dying than the most satisfied men.

Unlike in other studies, the frequency of interactions with friends appeared unrelated to risk of death, suggesting quality may prove more important than quantity, Kaplan says.

Some researchers question which comes first—the good health or the social involvement? Perhaps people with better social lives are healthier to start. Kaplan's team found that the association between social satisfaction and involvement and risk of death held up even when they looked only at men who rated themselves as in average or better-than-average health.

Money helps ward off death. Men with higher incomes had a lower chance of dying. They also were more involved in organizations and were more likely to be married, Kaplan says.

Excerpted from "Death Comes Knocking When You're Alone," *Science News*, September 3, 1994, p. 159.

married men in the same age bracket to die. They are also three times more likely to die in a car accident, four times more likely to commit suicide, six times more likely to die from a heart attack, and ten times more likely to die from a stroke (Kucherov, 1981; Seligmann, 1994).

For women, widowhood also brings problems. Although widows have more friends than widowers, the most serious problem that widows face is nonetheless loneliness. This is mostly because they were accustomed to the traditional role of wife, having derived one's identity from being the wife of so-and-so. Widows who have been more independent are better able to cope with their loneliness. There are other factors that influence women's reactions to widowhood. Widows who live in large cities are more lonely than those who live in small towns. Compared with middle-class women, working-class women tend to be more lonely and isolated, because they have fewer friends and less money. Younger widows are more lonely than older ones. As Robert Atchley (1988) explains, "If [a woman] is one of the first in her group of friends to become widowed, she may find that her friends feel awkward talking about death and grief. . . if the widow is one of the last to become widowed in a group of friends, then she may find great comfort among friends who identify very well with the problems of grief and widowhood."

Elder Care and Abuse

Although most older people are capable of taking care of themselves, a significant minority of them have difficulty doing so. Today, about 25 percent of elders require long-term care. A few live in nursing homes, but the vast majority live at home, most often cared for by their daughters (Kart, 1990).

Helping aging parents is for the most part a highly stressful job. It is particularly hard on the 40 to 50 percent of daughters who work outside the home and are still raising children of their own. Consider the case of Sandy Berman, a 47-year-old schoolteacher. One day she discovered that her parents, ages 83 and 74, had been living with trash in their home for almost a year. She convinced them to move closer to where she lived. Her father had become forgetful, and her mother could not find her way from the bedroom to the bathroom. For months, Berman called them every morning before going to work, and stopped by to see them every afternoon. She worried that she was neglecting her husband and son. Consequently, she lost 30 pounds and had fantasies of running away. Finally, her father died, and she put her mother in a board-and-care home and enrolled her in an adult day-care center. Today, Berman visits her mother twice a month, and calls once a week, but she still worries that she might not be doing the right thing for her mother (Beck, 1990).

Many other women find that the trap between child care and elder care prevents them from working outside the home. Having been on the "mommy track" but assuming that they could get back to their careers, they now find themselves on an even longer "daughter track." Because the elderly population continues to get larger and older, chronic and disabling conditions will become more common, so that many more daughters will care for aged parents. A government study has estimated that the average woman in the United States will spend 17 years raising children and 18 years caring for aged parents (Beck, 1990).

Is the stress that comes from elder care likely to cause elder abuse? The answer is no. Most of the stressed caregivers do not abuse their elders, and most abusers do not suffer from stress because they do not spend long hours caring for their aged relatives. Elder abusers tend to have severe personal problems, including alcoholism, drug addiction, antisocial behavior, and emotional instability. Elder abusers also tend to be chronically beset with money problems. This explains why elder abuse differs from child abuse. It rarely takes the form of physical abuse but often involves financial exploitation (Pillemer and Finkelhor, 1989).

While most caregivers are free from those personal and financial problems, many are overburdened with the stress of taking care of their parents. Nevertheless, they don't abuse their elders. Why? A clue can be found in the fact that three-fourths of the caregivers are daughters. Women seem to have been socialized to feel closer to their parents and to take family responsibilities more seriously than men. As caregivers, they "see their efforts as a chance to repay the time and care their parents gave them—a

chance to say, again, *I love you*, before it's too late" (Beck, 1990).

Questions for Discussion and Review

1. What is the elderly's marital and sex life like?
2. How do elders get along with their grown children?
3. Do women and men react differently to widowhood? Why or why not?
4. What causes elder abuse?

PERSPECTIVES ON AGING

There are different views on the later stages of a person's life, represented in, among others, disengagement theory, minority theory, activity theory, and subculture theory. These theories appear related to the three major perspectives in sociology.

Functionalist Perspective: Functions of Disengagement

According to **disengagement theory**, aging causes people to disengage from society. Although elders hardly withdraw like hermits, their social interaction does decline. The disengagement is mutual—both aged and younger members of society withdraw from each other. As Elaine Cumming (1963) explains: "The disengagement theory postulates that society withdraws from the aging person to the same extent as the person withdraws from society. . . the process is normatively governed and in a sense *agreed upon by all concerned*." In other words, social consensus, as the functionalist perspective emphasizes, is crucial, otherwise disengagement cannot take place. Thus, disengagement occurs when older people retire; when their grown children leave home; when their spouses, friends, and relatives die; when they lose contact with friends and fellow workers; and when they turn their attention to personal rather than societal concerns.

Disengagement theory further holds, as the functionalist perspective suggests, that this mutual withdrawal serves useful functions for society. It is as if two friends, knowing that separation is imminent, gradually drift apart, easing the pain of separation. Society benefits in at least two ways: disengagement renders the eventual death of the elderly less disruptive to the lives of friends and relatives, and precludes

Minority theory suggests that the elderly are treated in society as an oppressed minority. Discrimination against the aged can in fact be seen in mandatory retirement laws, substandard nursing homes, and domestic neglect and abuse. Yet in some respects, elders are far from oppressed. In fact, they participate in powerful organizations, such as the Gray Panthers and The American Association of Retired Persons.

the harmful economic effects of the older workers' increasing incompetence or sudden death, because younger people have already replaced them in the workplace. The elderly themselves also benefit because disengagement relieves them of responsibilities, making their lives easier, and encourages them to begin preparing for their inevitable death. Being "well adjusted" to old age, then, means accepting that one is outside the mainstream of life and coming to terms with one's mortality. Therefore, according to the theory, disengaged elders tend to be happier and healthier than those who try to ignore their age and remain as active as before (Cumming and Henry, 1961; Cumming, 1963).

Critics, however, have challenged the assumption that disengagement is universal or inevitable. They point, for example, to many older members of the U.S. Congress who are far from disengaged from society. Critics have also contended that disengagement may be harmful to both society and the individual: it may mean losing the talent, energy, and expertise of the disengaged elders, and, among some, it could contribute to poor health, poverty, and loneliness (Levin and Levin, 1980).

Conflict Perspective: The Elderly as an Oppressed Minority

Derived from the conflict perspective, **minority theory** suggests that older people are treated in

society as an oppressed minority. In other words, they are victims of **ageism**, prejudice and discrimination against the aged. Like race and gender, age is used as the basis for judging and reacting to people, regardless of their individual characteristics.

Prejudice against older people is often expressed in various ways. When an 82-year-old man went to visit a doctor with the complaint that his left knee was stiff and painful, the physician examined it. Then he said, "Well, what do you expect? After all, it's an 82-year-old knee." The patient retorted, "Sure it is. But my right knee is also 82, and it's not bothering me a bit" (Dychtwald, 1989). In fact, age prejudice with its underlying stereotype of elders as frail or weak, as shown by that doctor, has become so ingrained in many people that they are unaware of its existence. Consider the popular AT&T commercial in which the elderly woman's son calls "just to say I love you, Ma." It has won the hearts of many television viewers because they were apparently touched by how sweet the son was to his mother. But they did not realize that it also implied that older people waste their time doing nothing. As one older person says about the commercial, "What do you think we do—just sit around waiting for someone to call?" (Beck, 1990).

Prejudice is also evident in the common belief that old people are set in their ways, old-fashioned, forgetful, or spend their days dozing in a rocking chair. Some of these ageist beliefs are expressed in jokes such as "Old college presidents never die; they just lose their faculties." Prejudice can further be found in mass communication: in prime-time television shows, the aged tend to be depicted as evil, unsuccessful, or unhappy. Stereotypes about the aged being accident-prone, rigid, dogmatic, and unproductive are often used to justify firing older workers, pressuring them to retire, or refusing to hire them (Levin and Levin, 1980; Meer, 1986).

Discrimination against the aged can be seen in mandatory retirement laws, substandard nursing homes, and domestic neglect and abuse of elders. Even well-intentioned people may unconsciously practice discrimination by patronizing the elderly, treating them like children. This often comes across in the "baby talk" directed to the elderly. As the famous psychologist B. F. Skinner (1983) observed from his perspective as a 79-year-old: "Beware of those who are trying to be helpful and too readily flatter you. Second childishness brings you back within range of those kindergarten teachers who exclaim, 'But *that* is very *good!*' Except that now, instead of saying, 'My, you are really growing up!' they will say, 'You are not really getting old!'"

But in some respects the elderly are far from oppressed. Especially in government and politics, many leaders are aged 65 or older. And older people are such a powerful political force that many elected officials are afraid to anger them by cutting Social Security.

Symbolic Interactionist Perspective: Continuing Interaction

In direct opposition to functionalists' disengagement theory is **activity theory**, which suggests that most of the elderly maintain a great deal of interaction with others, even in vigorous physical activities. People do lose certain roles when they retire or when their children leave home, but, according to activity theory, this loss does not necessarily produce disengagement. Instead, the elderly can invest more of their energies in the roles they retain, or in new activities. They might, for example, deepen relationships with grandchildren, make new friends, or join volunteer organizations. By keeping socially active, say activity theorists, older people remain physically and psychologically fit—healthy, happy, and able to live a long life (Havighurst, 1963; Lemon, Bengtson, and Peterson, 1972).

But, according to **subculture theory**, the elderly interact mostly with one another, sharing interests and experiences with members of the same age group. Several factors increase interaction among the elderly. First are social and demographic trends, including the increasing size of the elderly popula-

tion, the growing concentration of older people in areas such as retirement communities and public housing for the elderly, and the proliferation of social services for the aged. Second, because of widespread prejudice against the aged and discomfort with aging, the elderly may find it difficult to interact with younger persons. For example, when older people want to talk about their impending death, their 40-year-old children are likely to change the conversation. The result, according to subculture theory, is that elders interact with their peers more than with younger people (Rose, 1965).

Critics have argued that activity theory presents elders with an often unattainable goal by urging them to cling to an active role in life. Because their activities may not seem meaningful in comparison to their previous roles as workers or parents, older people are likely to feel like failures, useless, and worthless (Atchley, 1988). However, because of increased longevity, elders are becoming more and more active than their counterparts of the past. Not surprisingly, many today engage in a wide variety of activities, even as strenuous as marathon running, that two decades ago would have been considered beyond their reach. As for subculture theory, it is not clear whether there is truly an elderly subculture with values, beliefs, and lifestyles different from the rest of society.

Questions for Discussion and Review

1. What is disengagement theory and why has it been criticized?
2. What is ageism and how does it support the theory that the elderly are an oppressed minority?
3. According to activity and subculture theories, how do elders live their lives?

THE FUTURE OF AGING

What will it be like to age in the United States 20 or 30 years from now? Elders will probably have a higher educational level and occupational status, perhaps destroying the stereotype of doddering, senile oldsters. The divorce rate of the elderly will probably increase, too, because as people expect to live longer, they may demand more from their marriages. Social pressure against taking early retirement and receiving Social Security will probably increase because of the high cost of providing income to retirees.

GLOBAL VILLAGE

A major consequence of better medical care is a vast increase in the number of the world's elderly. This reading discusses the social changes that will likely result from the global aging.

Aging Around the World

We are growing old—older than we ever imagined.

By the turn of the century, for the first time, there will be nearly 500-million people in the world who are older than 65.

In the United States, the number will have doubled from today's 32 million to 60 million. There will be more Americans in retirement homes than in junior high schools. One in three retirees will be older than 80.

The graying of the world is bound to change the way we live and the way we view aging. How old will "old" be if one in five Americans is older than 65?

The definition of family may continue to change. People in their 40s may care not only for their children but for two or three older generations.

And if so many people are drawing pensions, what will that do to the national budget, already saddled with a $3 trillion debt? The United States survives by borrowing, mostly from Europe and Japan. But in the future, Europe and Japan will be caring for larger numbers of older citizens, too. They likely will spend money on themselves before lending to others.

Perhaps economic necessity will force us to stretch the retirement age beyond 65, so people can continue to work, or hold off drawing pensions.

With so many older people, we may be spending more on health care. The United States already spends eight times more on the health care of older citizens than it does on its children. We won't be likely to say no to spending hikes, because the electorate will have grown older.

We won't notice this change in the next 10 years, even 15 years. But after that, it will crash on us, carrying the large number of baby boomers born after World War II. This change will touch every nation in the world. Consider Sweden, China, and India.

Sweden is the oldest country; 18 percent of Swedes are older than 65. Its birth rate plunged long before other developed countries', so it began to feel the onset of aging 50 years ago. In a way, Sweden gives us a peek at our future, because our population will resemble its population in about 15 years. Its socialist economy allows it to spend generously on social programs for every age group. The majority of old Swedes live at home, rather than in institutions, and their government pays a network of social workers to deliver home care. But the Swedish economy is feeling the burden of the high cost of social spending, and the government has begun to trim many programs.

China and India will have millions of very old and very young people to care for. China's 80 million elderly will almost quadruple to 300 million in another 35 years. India's elderly population will nearly quadruple to 150 million. The majority of people in both countries live in villages and aren't covered by any health care or pension plans.

Their social security is their children—and the number of children that families traditionally have has dropped dramatically in the last 30 years.

China's government has had to promise support in old age to induce people to stick to the country's one-child policy, but it isn't wealthy enough to carry through on such a promise.

In India, large numbers of young people migrate to cities in search of better-paying jobs, leaving parents and older relatives behind. Large, extended families cemented by tradition are melting away. And the nuclear family doesn't include grandparents.

Excerpted from Reena Shah, "Aging Around the World," *St. Petersburg Times,* August 2, 1992, p. 1A+.

The prediction that can be made with the most confidence, however, is that the size of the elderly population will grow. If present trends continue, by the year 2020 the elderly will make up more than 20 percent of the population, as opposed to about 12 percent today. There will be more geriatric day-care centers offering part-time supervision and care, including medical treatment, rehabilitation, and counseling. The political power of the elderly, already considerable, is likely to increase.

Other consequences of the growth in the elderly population are less certain. Some people argue that it will decrease prejudice against the aged. But prejudice against a minority often increases as the size of the group grows because its members are more likely to be seen as a threat. If unemployment increases as

Because of the significant growth in the older population, there are numerous geriatric day-care centers offering part-time supervision and care, including medical treatment, rehabilitation, and counseling.

it did in the early 1990s, younger unemployed workers may resent older people who hold jobs. Even those who are employed may see older, high-status workers as obstacles to their own upward mobility. However, if the economy becomes strong, age conflict is unlikely to break out. One reason is that jobs would be abundant. Another reason is that as a result of low birth rates during the 1960s and 1970s, labor would be scarce. Thus, employment opportunities for the elderly may increase, and workers young and old should enjoy greater bargaining power with employers.

Questions for Discussion and Review

1. What kind of life do you think the elderly will have 20 or 30 years from now?
2. What economic factors could minimize conflict between young and old?

CHAPTER REVIEW

1. *What are the biological and psychological consequences of aging?* With age, people become more vulnerable to disease. There are many more specific changes that typically accompany old age—from wrinkled skin to declining visual acuity and slowing of psychomotor responses. *How do social forces influence aging?* By slowing down or speeding up the biological and psychological processes of aging. *Why are elders in traditional societies more respected than their peers in modern societies?* Because few can survive into old age and society changes slowly, the elderly are admired and their knowledge and skills remain useful.

2. *Generally, how is the elderly's health?* The elderly are more likely than younger people to suffer from chronic ailments and brain disorders. But elderly individuals vary widely in falling victim to these health problems.

3. *What causes the decline in elderly employment?* The causes include increasing demand for new skills, age stereotypes and discrimination, and popular acceptance of retirement. *What factors enter into the decision to retire?* Moderate job satisfaction and adequate

retirement income. *What are the consequences of retirement?* Retirement is far more likely to improve health than worsen it. Relatively well-off elderly are more satisfied with retirement than others with less income.

4. *How does the Social Security system work?* Retirees collect Social Security benefits not from the payroll taxes they paid as workers many years ago, but from the taxes paid by current workers. *What is the financial situation of the elderly?* In some ways, the elderly are better off because of fewer expenses, compared with younger people. But their income is relatively low, and poverty is prevalent among women, minorities, and those who live alone.

5. *What is the marital and sex life among the elderly like?* Most are happily married and still remain sexually active during their seventies and eighties. *How do the elderly get along with their children?* Very well. Though living apart from their children, the elderly often see them and give them advice, gifts, and money. *How does gender affect an elderly person's adjustment to widowhood?* Losing a spouse creates more problems for men than for women. *Does care-*

giver stress often lead to elder abuse? No. Elder abuse is likely to result from the caregiver's personal and financial problems rather than from stress.

6. *Generally, what is the life of the elderly like?* According to disengagement theory, which is influenced by functionalist perspective, the elderly and society withdraw from each other. Influenced by the conflict perspective, minority theory suggests that elders are an oppressed minority victimized by ageism. Influenced by symbolic interactionism, activity theorists argue that, instead of withdrawing from society, the elderly continue to interact with others although mostly with one another as members of subculture.

7. *What is the status of aging likely to be a few decades from now?* The elderly are likely to make up a larger share of the U.S. population, and their educational level and occupational status are likely to be higher. But social pressure against early retirement and Social Security will likely increase, unless the economy becomes strong.

KEY TERMS

Activity theory The theory that most elders maintain a great deal of interaction with others, even when it requires vigorous physical activities (p. 330).

Ageism Prejudice and discrimination against the aged (p. 329).

Alzheimer's disease A disease of the brain characterized by progressive loss of memory and other mental abilities (p. 320).

Crystalline intelligence Wisdom and insight into the human condition, as shown by one's skills in language, philosophy, music, or painting (p. 315).

Disengagement theory The theory that aging causes people to disengage from society (p. 328).

Fluid intelligence Ability to grasp abstract relationships, as in mathematics, physics, or some other science (p. 315).

Minority theory The theory that older people are treated in society as an oppressed minority (p. 329).

Roleless role Being assigned no role in society's division of labor, a predicament of the elderly in industrial society (p. 319).

Senescence The natural physical process of aging (p. 314).

Senility An abnormal condition characterized by serious memory loss, confusion, and loss of the ability to reason (p. 315).

Subculture theory The theory that the elderly interact mostly with one another, sharing interests and experiences with members of the same age group (p. 330).

SUGGESTED READINGS

Bengtson, Vern L., and W. Andrew Achenbaum. 1993. *The Changing Contract Across Generations.* Hawthorne, N.Y.: Aldine de Gruyter. A collection of articles on various aspects of the conflict between the elderly and the young and middle-aged.

Chudacoff, Howard P. 1989. *How Old Are You? Age Consciousness in American Culture.* Princeton, N.J.: Princeton University Press. An interesting analysis of how age consciousness has developed into a prominent feature of U.S. culture.

Dychtwald, Ken. 1989. *Age Wave: The Challenges and Opportunities of an Aging America.* Los Angeles: Jeremy Tarcher, Inc. An upbeat view of aging in the United States, with numerous interesting examples and research findings.

Friedan, Betty. 1993. *The Fountain of Age.* New York: Simon & Schuster. Analyzing the often unrecognized positive side of aging among business and professional people.

Qureshi, Hazel, and Alan Walker. 1989. *The Caring Relationship: Elderly People and Their Families.* Philadelphia: Temple University Press. A study of how families care for their elderly parents, based on a survey of about 300 elderly people and interviews with some of their caregivers.

15

FAMILY

Myths and Realities

MYTH: *The popularity of romantic love in the United States causes young people to choose their mates emotionally and thus irrationally.*
REALITY: U.S. youth do not irrationally fall in love with undesirable characters. Most make sound choices, using their heads more than their hearts in choosing whom to love.

MYTH: *There is no difference between dating and marriage in the choice of mates. In both cases people are equally likely to choose someone close to their own level of attractiveness.*
REALITY: The similarity in attractiveness is greater among married couples than dates. In marriage people usually choose someone whose looks match theirs, but this is less true in dating.

MYTH: *High divorce rates in the U.S. mean that fewer people want to get married.*
REALITY: Despite high divorce rates, marriage remains popular. The U.S. has the highest marriage rate in the industrial world.

riving home from work, Janice Edwards, a 27-year-old single mother, tells a journalist interviewing her how she felt when her husband left her five years ago, just after their second child was born: "I thought we'd fall apart with no man there. There was a time I had no money for formula, no gas, no water, no electricity, and I didn't know what in the world we would do." But she has managed for all those years to work at least two jobs at a time to keep her family going. She has most often had an office job during the day and another job at Kmart in the evening. At one point, she even delivered newspapers from 2 to 5 in the morning. She says proudly, "I'm going to work 17 jobs if I have to, but I'm going to take care of my children. I'm not going to listen to people who tell me single mothers are bad. I'm not single by choice; I'm single by force, and I'm not going to listen to those negative things." Like many single mothers, Ms. Edwards is indeed doing reasonably well for her family (Lewin, 1992).

The traditional image of the average U.S. family shows Mom tending her two kids and a house in the suburbs while Dad drives off to work. In fact, such a family is relatively rare today. Meanwhile, new forms of the family unit, such as single-parent families like the one just described, have become increasingly common. In this chapter, we discuss various forms of family not only in the United States, but around the world.

THE FAMILY: A GLOBAL ANALYSIS

People who marry have, in effect, two families. One is the **family of orientation,** the family in which one grows up, consisting of oneself and one's parents and siblings. The other is the **family of procreation,** the family that one establishes through marriage, consisting of oneself and one's spouse and children. As the abundance of jokes about mothers-in-law illustrates, the relationships between these two families can be complicated. Societies need norms that govern this relationship as well as norms that assign roles within each family. Societies must offer the answers to questions like these: Who is part of my family? Who lives with whom? Who is an acceptable spouse? Who makes that decision?

Around the world, societies have given varied answers to questions such as: Who is part of my family? Who lives with whom? Who is an acceptable spouse, and who makes that decision?

All over the world, societies have given varied answers to these and other questions. The answers have much to do with family composition, norms of mate selection, rules of residence and descent, and rules of authority.

Family Composition

Who makes up a family? Societies' definitions of a family can be classified into two basic types. In the United States, a "family" has long been defined as a **nuclear family**, consisting of two parents and their unmarried children. It is also called a *conjugal family,* because its members are related by virtue of the marriage between the parents. This type of family is quite common in Western industrial societies.

Another type of family is more prevalent in less industrialized societies. It includes not only the nuclear family, but grandparents, uncles, aunts, and cousins. When a nuclear family lives in close proximity to other relatives, interacting with them frequently and acting together as a unit for some purposes, it becomes an **extended family**, consisting of two parents, their unmarried children, and other relatives. This kind of family is also called a *consanguine family,* because the blood tie among relatives is considered more important than the marital bond. In traditional Chinese and Japanese extended families, for example, the tie between a married man and his mother is much stronger than his bond to his wife. In fact, if a mother does not like her son's wife, she can force him to divorce the wife.

Mate Selection

Societies differ, too, in their norms specifying who selects the marriage partner and who is an appropriate partner. In many traditional societies, **arranged marriages**—marriages in which partners are selected by their parents—are the rule. The young couple may not even know each other until the wedding day, but they are expected to learn to love each other during the marriage. They are considered too emotional to choose the "right" compatible mates. Usually the parents base their choice of a spouse on how financially secure the other family is, how agreeable the prospective daughter-in-law is to the young man's mother, and how compatible the couple's personalities are.

The selection of a partner depends, too, on the society's norms regarding which partners are appropriate. In most societies, people are required to prac-

tice **exogamy** (literally, "marrying outward"), the act of marrying someone from outside one's group—such as clan, tribe, or village (for an extreme form of exogamy, see box, p. 338). Contrasted with exogamy is **endogamy** ("marrying within"), the act of marrying someone from one's own group. Endogamy, however, stops short of violating the incest taboo, because endogamous societies do not encourage marriage between close relatives.

There are also norms governing the number of spouses a person may have. **Monogamy**—the marriage of one man to one woman—is the most common form in the world. But many societies, especially small, preindustrial ones, approve of **polygamy**, marriage of one person to two or more people of the opposite sex. It is rare for a society to allow the practice of **polyandry**, marriage of one woman to two or more men. But many societies permit **polygyny**, marriage of one man to two or more women. A new variant of polygamy has become increasingly common in the United States. Rather than having several spouses at the same time, many have one spouse at a time, going through a succession of marriage, divorce, and remarriage. Such practice is not really polygamy, but **serial monogamy**, marriage of one person to two or more people but only one at a time.

Residence and Descent

In the United States, when most couples marry, they establish a home of their own, away from both families of orientation. They are in effect having a **neolocal residence**, a home where the married couple live by themselves, away from both husband's and wife's families. Although this is the most common rule of residence in the United States, it is the least common in the world. People in most societies have a **patrilocal residence**, a home where the married couple live with the husband's family. People in other societies have a **matrilocal residence**, a home where the married couple live with the wife's family.

There are similar rules about who are supposed to be our close relatives. The most common of such rules in the world is **patrilineal descent**, the norm that recognizes only the father's family as a child's close relatives. The children belong to their father's family of orientation, not that of their mother, and they adopt their father's family name. But daughters lose their family name when they marry, and their tie to their father's family is not permanent. Only sons, not daughters, may inherit property from the father in patrilineal societies.

GLOBAL VILLAGE

Russia's worsening economic problems have led many women to seek marriage to wealthy men from other countries. This article describes the experiences of Russian women who have tried to find husbands through a large international marriage agency.

Brides for Foreigners

Russia seems to be turning into a major exporter of brides. Almost 1,500 marriages with foreigners are registered in Moscow every year. According to a poll, 23 percent of Russian mothers would like their daughters to marry foreign citizens. Tens of thousands of Russian women dream of an advantageous marriage and look for foreign husbands. How? One way is through personal ads in newspapers. I responded to one of them: "Man from Australia (37, 5 feet 5, 132 pounds) seeks short (5 feet 2 to 5 feet 5) slender woman 22–29 for marriage." The man is from Sydney. His mother advised him to marry a Russian woman because Australian women are very liberated, change men like gloves, and do not do housework. Russian women, in the opinion of the placer of the ad, love to clean, cook, stay home, and have children. In two days, he got 100 calls.

Many women are not shy about going to dating agencies. The agency Alliance is one of the largest in Moscow, with branches in Russia's large cities and abroad. It has been flourishing for more than five years. Each day, about 10 girls go to the agency. But only two or three of them are put in the files. There are criteria for selection. First, you must be successful in your professional milieu. Second, you must know a foreign language. And third, you must meet a standard of "European looks": blond with blue eyes, slender with long legs. Of the 2,000 girls a year who get into the files, only 10 percent get married. Of the 200 who have married recently, one was lucky enough to become the wife of a millionaire.

There are 700 foreign men in the files, mostly from the United States, Germany, and Britain. Up to 300 men apply annually. They must meet only one requirement—being well-to-do. The information on the man's passport is checked, and a call is made to his place of work.

Once a husband is found, the next step is Wedding Palace Number 4, the only place in Moscow that registers marriages to foreigners. Each year, 1,200 couples get married there. In 1992, the bridegrooms came from 96 countries. The greatest number came from the United States; in second place was Israel, followed by Turkey and Bulgaria.

The Wedding Palace requires confirmation that, in the given country, a marriage to a citizen of another state is valid. After all, in a number of countries, a foreign wife and her children could find that they have no property rights. In Syria, for example, marriage to a foreigner is considered invalid without special permission.

Many Russian girls who marry foreigners quickly get divorced and come back. The reasons are well known: a sense of second-class status, a language barrier, financial difficulties. Deceptions are frequent: One "sweetheart" described his home as a palace with a fountain, but, in reality, it turned out that he lived in a small cottage without a bathtub.

Excerpted from S. Kuzina, "70 Brides for 7 Foreigners," *Komsomolskaya Pravda.* Reprinted in the *World Press Review,* July, 1993, p. 47.

Much less common is **matrilineal descent**, the norm that recognizes only the mother's family as a child's close relatives. Even in matrilineal societies, however, daughters rarely have the right to inherit property. Usually, sons inherit property from their mother's brother.

The influence of patrilineal traditions seems to exist in U.S. society. Wives and children mostly adopt only the husband's family name. But there is an observance of **bilateral descent**, the norm that recognizes both parents' families as the child's close relatives. Children feel closely related to both their father's and their mother's kin, and both sons and daughters may inherit property from their mother's and their father's families.

Authority

Societies differ in defining who has authority in the family. In most societies, authority rests with the eldest male. Thus, the **patriarchal family**, in which the dominant figure is the eldest male, is the most prevalent around the world. In such a family, the eldest male dominates everyone else. He allocates tasks, settles disputes, and makes other important decisions that affect family members.

There are also the **matriarchal family**, in which the dominant figure is the eldest female, and an **egalitarian family**, in which authority is equally distributed between husband and wife. Globally, these two types of family are rare. A variant of the matriarchal family, however, has appeared in many industrial countries. In the United States, for example, many poor families are matriarchal by default. Either the father is not present, or he has lost his dominant status because of chronic unemployment. Many other U.S. families, though still dominated by husbands, are also becoming increasingly egalitarian, thanks to the women's movement, as suggested in Chapter 13 (Women and Men).

Questions for Discussion and Review

1. How do family composition and mate selection differ from society to society?
2. How do the world's families differ in regard to residence, descent, and authority?

PERSPECTIVES ON THE FAMILY

The three perspectives in sociology shed light on different aspects of the family. Together, they can give us a deeper understanding of the family than each alone can.

Functionalist Perspective

According to the functionalist perspective, the family performs certain functions for virtually all societies. The more important functions include sexual regulation, reproduction, socialization, economic cooperation, and emotional security. *+ inheritance –* *Care for children) preservation of wealth, etc.*

Sexual Regulation   No society advocates total sexual freedom. Although societies have different sexual norms, all impose some control on who may have sex with whom. Even societies that encourage premarital and extramarital sex restrict and channel these activities so that they reinforce the social order. The Trobrianders of the South Pacific, for example, use premarital sex to determine whether a girl is fer-

tile and to prepare adolescents for marriage. Traditional Inuit society condones extramarital sex, but under conditions that do not disrupt family stability: as a gesture of hospitality, husbands offer their wives to overnight guests.

Traditionally, Western sexual norms have been relatively restrictive, demanding that people engage in sex only with their spouses. Tying sex to marriage seems to serve several functions. First, it helps minimize sexual competition, thereby contributing to social stability. Second, it gives people an incentive to marry. Even today, most young adults eventually feel dissatisfied with unstable, temporary sexual liaisons and find a regular, secure sexual relationship in marriage an attractive prospect. Even most of the divorced, who usually find their postmarital sex lives pleasurable, eventually remarry because sex with commitment is available in marriage. Finally, encouraging people to marry and confining sexual intercourse to those who are married tends to ensure that children will be well cared for.

Reproduction   In order to survive, a society must produce children to replace the adults and elders who die, and practically all societies depend on the family to produce these new members. In some traditional societies, such as the Baganda in the African nation of Uganda, children are considered so precious that a marriage must be dissolved if the wife turns out to be barren. In many industrial nations like the United States, families with children are rewarded with tax deductions. *Tax rates/privileges vary with state of economy in Europe.*

Socialization   To replace members who die, a society needs not only biological reproduction, but "sociological reproduction." It needs, in other words, to transmit its values to the new generation, to socialize them. As we saw in Chapter 7 (Socialization), the family is the most important agent of socialization. Because parents are likely to be deeply interested in their own children, they are generally more effective socializing agents than other adults.

Economic Cooperation   Besides socialization, children also need physical care—food, clothing, and shelter. Fulfilling these needs is the core of the family's economic function, and it can facilitate effective socialization. Generally, however, the family's economic role goes beyond care for children and embraces the whole family. Family members cooperate as an economic unit, working to earn income or doing household chores to minimize expenditure. Each person's economic fate rises and falls with that of the family as a whole. *# children varies with economic value + role of mother.*

The family's economic role goes beyond care for children and embraces the whole family. Family members cooperate as an economic unit, working to earn income or doing household chores to minimize expenses.

Emotional Security   Finally, the family is the center of emotional life. As we saw in Chapter 7 (Social-ization), the relationships we form in our families as children shape our personalities and create hard-to-break patterns for all our relationships. Throughout life, the family is the most important source of pri-mary relationships, the most likely place for us to turn to when we need comfort or reassurance.

Conflict Perspective

Through the functionalist perspective, we see the bright side of the family. But the family also has a dark side, which the conflict perspective reveals.

First of all, the family, because of the strong feel-ings it generates, is a powerful source not just of love and care but also of pain and conflict. According to a major study, the family is the most violent institu-tion in U.S. society, except the military in time of war (Gelles and Cornell, 1990). In most families, there are instances of conflict and violence, such as anger, physical punishment of children, or spouses poking and slapping each other. In fact, the family is one of the few groups in society empowered by law or tradi-tion to hit its members. It is, for example, legal for parents to spank their children as a form of punish-ment. Moreover, many husbands who strike their wives to "keep them in line" are not arrested, prose-cuted, or imprisoned.

From the conflict perspective, we can also see the family as a tool for men's exploitation of women

(Delphy and Leonard, 1992). Homemakers and mothers have greatly contributed to the rise and maintenance of capitalism with such forms of labor as reproduction and care of children, food prepara-tion, daily health care, and emotional support. Without this "household production," men would not have been free to go out working. Yet, while men are paid for their jobs outside the home, women do not get any wages for their work in the home. Ironically, women's household work is on the average worth more than men's paid employment. If a woman were paid for services as mother and home-maker according to the wage scale for chauffeurs, baby-sitters, cooks, and therapists, she would earn more than most men do. By demeaning women's housework, however, the family serves the interests of male domination. Even in families where both spouses are gainfully employed, wives generally do most of the housework.

In short, the family is far from "a haven in a heart-less world." It is an extension of that world, full of violence and female exploitation.

Symbolic Interactionist Perspective

Both the functionalist and conflict perspectives deal with the larger issue of what the family is like as a social institution. The symbolic interactionist per-spective focuses on more immediate issues, such as how certain interaction between husband and wife can bring marital happiness or unhappiness.

In a family, symbolic interaction occurs between husband and wife, between parent and child, between one sibling and another, or among all these individuals. Using the symbolic interactionist perspective as a guide, researchers can focus on any of these interactions and find how the interaction affects the group. Let us see what John Gottman (1994) finds out in his study of marital interaction.

Gottman has observed many couples interact in his lab, concentrating not only on what the spouses say to each other but on the tone of voice in which they verbally interact. He finds three different types of interaction. One is *validating* interaction, in which the partners compromise, showing mutual respect and accepting their differences. The second is *volatile* interaction, in which conflict erupts, resulting in a vehement, loud dispute. And the third is *conflict-avoiding* interaction, in which the partners agree to disagree, making light of their differences rather than trying to confront and resolve them. But these three interacting styles do not by themselves determine marital happiness or unhappiness. What is conducive to happiness is an *excess of positive interactions over negative interactions*. Positive interactions involve touching, smiling, paying compliments, and other acts of thoughtful friendliness. Negative interactions involve ignoring, criticizing, calling names, and other acts of thoughtless nastiness. Gottman discovers that among happy couples there are at least five positive interactions for every one negative interaction, but among unhappy couples the ratio is less than 5 to 1.

Questions for Discussion and Review

1. What functions does the family perform for society?
2. How does the family appear from the conflict perspective?
3. How can the symbolic interactionist perspective be used to understand the quality of family life?

PATTERNS OF U.S. MARRIAGES

In the United States the family is by and large nuclear and monogamous and increasingly egalitarian. Its cornerstone is the relationship between husband and wife. In this section, we discuss how people prepare for marriage, how they choose their spouse, and how most U.S. couples achieve marital success.

Preparing for Marriage

Most people do not consciously prepare themselves for marriage or diligently seek a person to marry. Instead, they engage in activities that gradually build up a momentum that launches them into marriage. They date, they fall in love, and in each of these steps they usually follow patterns set by society.

The Dating Ritual   Developed largely after World War I came to an end in 1918, the U.S. custom of dating has spread to many industrial countries. It has also changed in the United States in the last two decades. Before the 1970s, dating was more formal. Males had to ask for a date at least several days in advance. It was usually the male who decided where to go, paid for the date, opened doors, and was supposed to be chivalrous. The couple often went to an event, such as a movie, dance, concert, or ball game.

Today, dating has become more casual. In fact, the word "date" now sounds a bit old-fashioned to many young people. Usually you do not have to call somebody and ask for a date. "Getting together" or "hanging around" is more like it. Spontaneity is the name of the game. A young man may meet a young woman at a snack bar and strike up a brief conversation with her. If he bumps into her a day or two later, he may ask if she wants to go along to the beach, to the library, or to have a hamburger. Males and females are also more likely today than in the past to hang around—get involved in a group activity—rather than pair off for some seclusive intimacy. Neither has the responsibility to ask the other out, which spares them much of the anxiety of formal dating. Getting together has also become less dominated by males. Females are more likely than before to ask a male out, to suggest activities, pay the expenses, or initiate sexual intimacies. Premarital sex has also increased, but it tends to reflect true feelings and desires rather than the need for the male to prove himself or for the female to show gratitude (Strong and DeVault, 1992).

The functions of dating, however, have remained pretty constant. It is still a form of entertainment. More important, dating provides opportunities for learning to get along with members of the opposite sex—to develop companionship, friendship, and intimacy. Finally, it offers opportunities for courting, for falling in love with one's future spouse. "Playing the field" does not lead to a higher probability of marital success, though. Those who have married their first and only sweetheart are just as likely to have an enduring and satisfying marriage as those who have married only after dating many people (Whyte, 1992).

For most people, dating provides opportunities for learning to get along with members of the opposite sex. It also offers opportunities for courting, and falling in love with one's future spouse.

Romantic Love   Asked why they want to get married, people usually say, "Because I am in love." In U.S. society, love between husband and wife is the foundation of the nuclear family. In fact, young people in the United States are most reluctant to marry someone if they do not love the person even though the person has all the right qualities they desire (see Figure 15.1). Many people in traditional societies, though, believe that love is too irrational to form the basis for a marriage and that intense love between husband and wife may even threaten the stability of the extended family. To them, it is more rational to marry for such pragmatic considerations as economic security and good character.

But does romantic love really cause people to choose their mates irrationally? Many studies have suggested that the irrationality of love has been greatly exaggerated. An analysis of these studies has led William Kephart and Davor Jedlicka (1988) to reach this conclusion: "Movies and television to the contrary, U.S. youth do not habitually fall in love with unworthy or undesirable characters. In fact, [they] normally make rather sound choices." In one study, when people in love were asked, "Does your head rule your heart, or does your heart rule your head?" 60 percent answered, "The head rules." Apparently, romantic love is not the same as infatuation, which involves physical attraction to a person and a tendency to idealize that person. Romantic love is less emotionalized, but it is expected to provide intrinsic satisfactions, such as happiness, close-

FIGURE 15.1
No Love, No Marriage

Percentage of college students who say they would *not* marry someone with all the right qualities if they didn't love the person

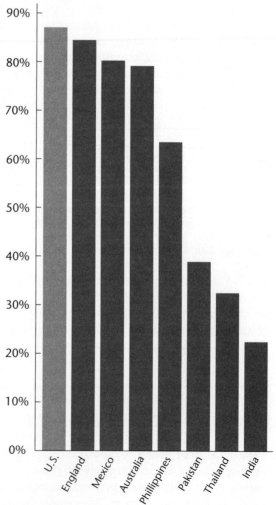

Source: Data from Robert Levine et al., "Love and Marriage in Eleven Cultures," *Journal of Cross-Cultural Psychology*, in press.

Love is a powerful emotion that helps create and sustain the family. This reading provides a unique view of love, based on findings from observations in bars and at parties as well as from the field of ethology—the scientific study of animal behavior.

Humans and Beasts Share Language of Love

With the same ethological methods they have long used in studies of animals, scientists are turning their attention to the nuances of human courtship rituals—otherwise known as flirting.

By turning the ethologist's lens on human courtship, scientists are finding striking similarities with other species, suggesting that the nonverbal template used by Homo sapiens for attracting and approaching a prospective mate is to some extent part of a larger, shared animal heritage.

A woman parades past a crowded bar to the women's room, hips swaying, eyes resting momentarily on a man and then coyly looking away just as she notices his look. This scenario exemplifies a standard opening move in courtship, getting attention, said Dr. David Givens, an anthropologist in Washington. "In the first phase of courting, humans broadcast widely a nonverbal message that amounts to 'notice me'" said Dr. Givens. "They do it through movement, through their dress, through gesture."

From hundreds of hours of observations in bars and at parties, Dr. Givens discovered that women, more than men, tend to promenade, making numerous trips to the women's room, for instance, both to scout and to be seen.

Perhaps the first serious study of flirting was done in the 1960s by Dr. Irenaus Eibl-Eibesfeldt, an eminent ethologist, who traveled to cultures around the world with a camera that took pictures from the side so he could stand near couples and take their pictures without their realizing they were being observed. In research in Samoa, Brazil, Paris, Sydney and New York, Dr. Eibl-Eibesfeldt discovered an apparently universal nonverbal human vocabulary for flirting and courtship.

In humans, one such gesture is a palm-up placement of the hand, whether on a table or a knee, a reassuring sign of harmlessness. Another submissive display is the shoulder shrug, which, ethologists suggest, derives from an ancient vertebrate reflex, a posture signifying helplessness. A posture combining the partly shrugged shoulder and a tilted head—which displays the vulnerability of the neck—is commonly seen when two people who are sexually drawn to each other are having their first conversation, Dr. Givens said.

Being playful and childish is another way potential lovers often communicate harmlessness. "You see the same thing in the gray wolf," said Dr. Givens.

When wolves encounter each other, they usually give a show of dominance, keeping their distance. But in a sexual encounter, they become playful and frisky, "like puppies," said Dr. Givens, "so they can accept closeness." The next step is a mutual show of submission, all of which paves the way for physical intimacy.

From this view, the coyness of courtship is a way to "test a prospective partner for commitment," said Dr. Jane Lancaster, an anthropologist. "Women, in particular, need to be sure they're not going to be deserted."

Coyness is not seen in species where the female does not need the sustained help or resources of a male to raise her young, said Dr. Lancaster. But in species where two parents appreciably enhance the survival of offspring, "females don't want to mate with a male who will abandon them," said Dr. Lancaster.

ness, personal growth, and sexual satisfaction. These differ from the extrinsic rewards offered by a pragmatic loveless marriage—rewards such as good earnings, a nice house, well-prepared meals, and overt respect.

In the United States over the last 20 years, the belief in romantic love as the basis for marriage has grown more fervent than before. In several studies in the 1960s, 1970s, and 1980s, college men and women were asked, "If a person had all the other qualities you desired, would you marry this person if you were not in love with him/her?" Today, as opposed to earlier decades, a greater proportion of young people say no (Simpson et al., 1986).

Marriage Choices

Romantic love is far from blind, but it also does not develop in a social vacuum. It depends heavily on the partners' support from others, particularly family and friends. Such support is usually available if the couple are involved in **homogamy**, marrying someone with social characteristics similar to one's own.

Most marriages occur within the same social class because of shared values, expectations, tastes, goals, and occupations. People also tend to choose mates of the same religious faith. The more cohesive and smaller the group is in a community, the more homogamous the group. Jews are therefore more likely to marry Jews than Catholics are to marry Catholics. Most marriages further involve members of the same race.

There is also a tendency to marry people very close to one's own age. Most couples are only two years apart. But most men who marry at 25 have a wife who is three years younger; at 37, most men marry a woman six years younger. A major reason that older men tend to marry much younger women is that men generally place greater importance on physical attractiveness than women. But the age difference between brides and grooms increases only until the men reach age 50. After this, most men marry women close to their own age again (Schulz, 1982; Mensch, 1986).

Since people of similar race, religion, and class are likely to live close to one another, there is a strong tendency to marry someone who lives nearby. This tendency may be weakening as cars and airplanes continue to increase mobility, yet most couples still come from the same city, town, or even neighborhood. According to many studies, there is more than a 50–50 chance that one's future spouse lives within walking distance (Kephart and Jedlicka, 1988). As James Bossard (1932) said, "Cupid may have wings, but apparently they are not adapted for long flights."

We have seen how homogamy applies to the *social* characteristics of couples. What about their individual characteristics, such as aggressive personalities and talkativeness? Do they also follow the same pattern? The answer is no, according to Robert Winch's (1971) well-known theory of complementary needs. Winch argues that people with *different* personality traits are attracted to each other if these traits complement each other. This theory resembles the popular belief that "opposites attract." Thus, aggressive men tend to marry passive women; weak men like strong women; talkative women go for quiet men; emotional men find rational women attractive; and so on. Winch's own research has supported the com-

plementarity theory, but more recent studies by other investigators have backed the social psychological version of homogamy—the theory that people with *similar* traits are attracted to each other, much as "birds of a feather flock together" (Wilson, 1989; Morell et al., 1989). Perhaps, given increasing gender equality in recent decades, the sexes may have become more alike. For example, men now seem more sensitive than before and women more assertive.

Homogamy also reigns in regard to physical attractiveness. Everybody prefers the person of their dreams, but most people end up marrying someone close to their own level of attractiveness. Interestingly, the similarity in attractiveness is greater among deeply committed couples than among casual ones. When people are playing the field, their looks may not match their dates'. But they are more likely to get serious with the dates who have about the same level of attractiveness (Kalick and Hamilton, 1986; Stevens et al., 1990).

Marital Happiness

With time, both the physical attraction and the idealization of romantic love are likely to fade, so that marital love involves mostly commitment. Love may be less exciting after marriage, but, as William Kephart and Devor Jedlicka (1988) observe, it "provides the individual with an emotional insight and a sense of self-sacrifice not otherwise attainable," qualities that may be keys to marital success.

How successful are U.S. marriages? The answer obviously depends on how we define "successful." Gerald Leslie and Sheila Korman (1989) suggest that in a successful marriage the couple have few conflicts, basically agree on major issues, enjoy the same interests during their leisure time, and show confidence in and affection for each other. To others, this sounds like a static, spiritless relationship. Instead, some argue, a successful marriage is one that is zestful and provides opportunity for personal growth. Such disagreement among scholars suggests that a "successful marriage" is basically a value judgment, not an objective fact (Strong and DeVault, 1992).

It is, therefore, best to simply look at whether people themselves consider their marriages successful, however experts might judge them. By this standard, most U.S. marriages are a success. Several studies have shown that the overwhelming majority (over 90 percent) of people say they are either "very happy" or "pretty happy" with their marriages. In fact, married couples are much more likely than

Questions for Discussion and Review

1. What roles do dating and romantic love play in preparing individuals for marriage?
2. What are the distinguishing characteristics of homogamy?
3. What accounts for marital happiness?

single people to say that they are happy, whether it is about love, sense of recognition, personal growth, or even job satisfaction (Strong and DeVault, 1992; NORC, 1994). Marriage, however, rather than parenthood, is the focal point of marital happiness. As research has suggested, the presence of children often detracts from marital happiness because the couple see their relationship less as a romance and more as a working partnership. In fact, these working partners often find parenting so stressful that they feel relieved or happy after their children reach adulthood and leave home (White and Edwards, 1990).

What makes for marital happiness? By comparing happily married with unhappily married couples, researchers have come up with a long list of characteristics associated with happy marriages. Among these are having happily married parents; knowing the prospective spouse for at least two years; being engaged for at least two years; getting married at an age above the national average (about 25 for men and 23 for women); being religious or adhering to traditional values; regarding one's spouse as a friend; being of the same religion and race; having the same level of education; and having good health, a happy childhood, emotional stability, parental approval of the marriage, and an adaptable personality (Kephart and Jedlicka, 1988; Hatch et al., 1986). But why are couples with these characteristics likely to be happy? Perhaps they engage in positive interactions far more frequently than negative interactions (Gottman, 1994) as discussed earlier.

FAMILY PROBLEMS

While most couples are happy with their marriages, many do have serious problems. One is family violence. Another is divorce, the culmination of marital problems.

Violence

Family violence is relatively common in the United States. Its exact incidence is hard to pin down, because various researchers do not define family violence in the same way. There is, of course, little disagreement about extreme cases where a family member is killed or seriously injured by another. But there is disagreement over what kinds of behavior are acceptable for disciplining children or dealing with spousal conflict. Some researchers consider spanking, for example, an act of violence, whereas others do not (Klaus and Rand, 1984; Dobash et al., 1992). Thus, there have been different estimates of the extent of family violence in the United States. The estimates on the proportion of families where violence occurs at least once in a year range from 10 to 20 percent, and anywhere between 25 and 50 percent of all couples have been estimated to suffer serious family violence at least once during the course of their marriage (Straus et al., 1988; Gelles and Cornell, 1990). All this may make family violence appear an enormous problem because the family is supposed to be "home sweet home."

Why does family violence occur? A major reason is stress. Research shows that the incidence of violence is highest among groups most likely to feel under stress, such as the urban poor, families with a jobless husband, and those with four to six children (Straus et al., 1988). Stress by itself, however, does not necessarily cause violence. People would not resort to violence as a way of relieving stress if they were not culturally encouraged to do so. There seems to be a "culturally recognized script for behavior under stress" in U.S. society (Straus et al., 1988). The violence on television, corporal punishment in schools, and the death penalty, for example, convey the idea that violence is an acceptable solution to problems. Research further suggests the tendency for marital violence to be transmitted from one generation to another. It has been found that most of the violent couples have, as children, seen their parents hit each other (Kalmuss, 1984).

Ironically, though, as many as half of the battered women do not leave their husbands who continue to abuse them. Why? Most do not have money and cannot earn enough to support themselves or their children. Moreover, if they leave, their husbands may stalk them to inflict more serious violence. These reasons, along with repeated abuse, cause the victims to feel helpless, which forces them to survive in the same way as hostages, prisoners of war, or concentration camp victims do: by accommodating their captors and living from hour to hour (Brody, 1992).

(handwritten in margin: No place to go, shelters)

Divorce

Divorce is common in the United States. About half of the people who marry for the first time will eventually get a divorce. Although the divorce rate has begun to dip slightly since 1980, it is still more than twice as high as it was in 1960 —the year when the rate began to rise (see Figure 15.2). It is also the highest in the world (Census Bureau, 1994).

Why do so many marriages end in divorce? Numerous studies have compared divorced couples with nondivorced couples and found a number of personal problems and social characteristics to be associated with divorce. They include infidelity, incompatibility, financial difficulties, lower socioeconomic status, and marrying too young (Strong and DeVault, 1992; Goode, 1982, 1993). But these data cannot explain why industrial Western societies have higher divorce rates than traditional Eastern societies, or why the U.S. divorce rate today is far higher than it was a century ago. A cross-cultural analysis may suggest at least five larger social forces behind the current high divorce rate in U.S. society.

1. *Decreased social disapproval of divorce.* In many traditional societies, unhappily married couples stay married because of the stigma attached to divorce. In the U.S., there is virtually no stigma. Divorce has gained wide acceptance as a solution to marital unhappiness, and it has become easier to obtain from the courts.

2. *Greater availability of services and opportunities for the divorced.* In traditional societies, men depend heavily on marriage for sexual gratification and housekeeping, and women look to it for financial security. Such services and opportunities are more easily available to U.S. adults without being married. The men can get sexual gratification outside marriage, and the women can become financially independent without husbands. In addition, the high divorce rate today has expanded the pool of eligible new partners. All this can make divorce more attractive to unhappily married couples.

3. *The family's increased specialization in providing love and affection.* In U.S. society, the family has become specialized in offering love and affection, while the importance of its other functions has declined. When love and affection are gone, a couple are likely to

FIGURE 15.2
U.S. Divorce Rate

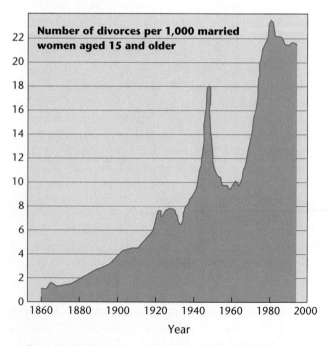

Number of divorces per 1,000 married women aged 15 and older

Source: Data from Census Bureau, 1994; Andrew J. Cherlin, *Marriage, Divorce, Remarriage* (Cambridge, MA: Harvard University Press, 1992).

break up their "empty shell" marriage. By contrast, in traditional societies with low divorce rates, the family's other functions—especially socializing children and providing economic security—remain highly important. Thus, even when love has disappeared from marriage, there are still other reasons for keeping the family together.

4. *High expectations about the quality of marital relationship.* Young people in traditional societies do not expect an exciting romantic experience with their spouses, especially if their marriages are arranged by their parents. But young people in the U.S. expect a lot, including an intense love relationship. These expectations are difficult to fulfill year after year, and the chances of disillusionment with the partner are therefore great. Since young people have higher expectations than older ones, it is not surprising that most divorces occur within the first four years of marriage (Cherlin, 1992).

5. *Increased individualism.* The rights of the individuals are considered far more important in the U.S. than in traditional societies. Individualism encourages people to put their own needs and privileges ahead of those of others including their spouse and to feel that if they want a divorce, they are entitled to get one. In traditional societies, people are more likely to subordinate their needs to those of the kinship group and thus to feel they have no right to seek a divorce.

The current high divorce rate in the United States does not mean, as common sense would suggest, that the institution of marriage is very unpopular. On the contrary, people seem to love marriage too much, as suggested by several pieces of evidence. First, our society has the highest rate of marriage in the industrial world despite having the highest rate of divorce (Census Bureau, 1994). Second, within the United States, most of the southeastern, southwestern, and western states have higher divorce rates than the national average but also have higher marriage rates (see Figure 15.3). And third, the majority of those who are divorced eventually remarry (Cherlin, 1992). Why don't they behave like Mark Twain's cat, who after having been burned by a hot stove would not go near *any* stove? Apparently, divorce in U.S. society does not represent a rejection of marriage but only a specific partner.

FIGURE 15.3
How Divorce and Marriage Go Together

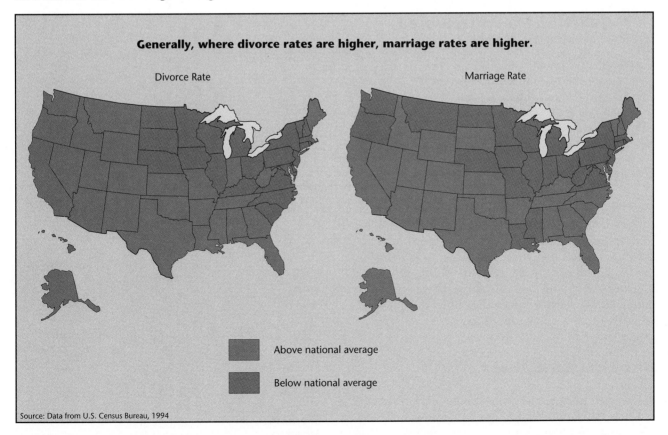

Source: Data from U.S. Census Bureau, 1994

Western societies such as the United States have higher divorce rates than traditional Eastern societies such as Japan. One of the reasons for this difference is the increased individualism in the United States. In traditional societies, by contrast, people are more likely to subordinate their needs to those of the kinship group.

Questions for Discussion and Review

1. What causes family violence?
2. What are the social causes of divorce?

CHANGES IN THE U.S. FAMILY

The traditional nuclear family, which consists of two parents living with children, is no longer the typical U.S. family. As far back as 1970, the proportion of traditional families had already declined to 40 percent. By 1993 it was only 26 percent (see Figure 15.4). Increasingly, people are choosing new patterns of family life. To see how much the family has changed, let us first take a quick tour of its past.

Historical Background

Before the industrialization of this country in the last century, the family had long consisted of husband, wife, and children, with no other relatives. One

reason for the popularity of the nuclear family in those days is that few people lived long enough to form an extended, three-generation family. Another reason is that impartible inheritance practices—which allow for only one heir to inherit all the property—forced sons who did not inherit the farm to leave and set up their own households (Cherlin, 1983).

On colonial farms, men, women, and children helped produce the family's livelihood. The wife was typically an essential economic partner to the husband. If her husband was a farmer, she would run the household; make the clothes; raise cows, pigs, and poultry; tend a garden; and sell milk, vegetables, chickens, and eggs. If the husband was a skilled craftsman, she would work with him. Thus, weavers' wives spun yarn, cutlers' wives polished metal, tailors' wives sewed buttonholes, and shoemakers' wives waxed shoes (Tilly and Scott, 1978).

But, as the United States became industrialized in the nineteenth century, the "household ceased to be a center of production and devoted itself to child

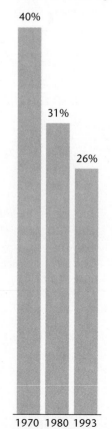

Percentage of married couples with children under age 18

40%

31%

26%

1970 1980 1993

FIGURE 15.4 Traditional Nuclear Families: A Shrinking Minority

Source: Data from U.S. Census Bureau, 1994.

In colonial days the wife was typically an essential economic partner to the husband. If they had a craft, she would work with her husband as a skilled craftsperson. For example, if the husband were a weaver, the wife would shear the sheep and dye and spin the yarn.

rearing instead" (Lasch, 1979). Industrialization took production out of the home. Initially husbands, wives, and children worked for wages in factories and workshops to contribute to the common family budget. But, due to the difficulty of combining paid employment with the domestic tasks imposed on them, married women tended to work for wages irregularly. As wages rose, growing numbers of families could earn enough without the wife's paid work. Then, increasingly, the home was seen as the emotional center of life and a private refuge from the competitive public world. The woman's role became emotional and moral rather than economic. Women were expected to rear their children and comfort their husbands. This became the stereotype of a typical and ideal U.S. family.

Thus, after industrialization had been in full swing, women lost their status as their husbands' economic partners and acquired a subordinate status as housewives (Cherlin, 1983). But over the last few decades there have been significant increases in gender equality, female independence through paid employment, and personal freedom for everybody. As a result, a diversity of family types has emerged, causing the traditional nuclear family to become less popular. Some of these new family types are discussed in the following sections.

Two-Career Families

In the last 30 years, there has been a tremendous surge of married women into the labor force. As Figure 15.5 shows, the proportion of gainfully employed wives shot up from only 31.9 percent in 1960 to about 59.4 percent in 1993. Their employment has increased family income significantly. In 1993 the median income of two-career families ($56,000) was more than 34 percent higher than the income for one-career families ($37,000). At the low end of the income scale, the wife's contribution is so

FIGURE 15.5
The Surge of Employment Among Married Women

Percentage of married women in the labor force

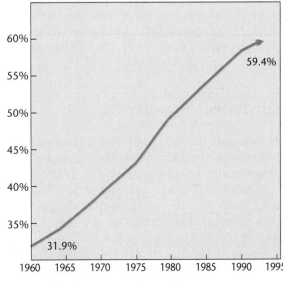

Source: Data from U.S. Census Bureau, 1994.

great that relatively few dual-earner families fall below the poverty line (Census Bureau, 1994).

Does this economic gain bring marital happiness? Apparently it does for *most* two-career couples. But research comparing them with one-career families has produced conflicting results. Some studies found that the wife's employment benefited her but not her husband. In one such study, employed wives reported more marital happiness, more communication with husbands, fewer worries, and better health, while their husbands were less content with their marriage and in poorer health (Burke and Weir, 1976). But other studies found more strain in two-career marriages because the wife was still expected to be a homemaker rather than a career seeker (Skinner, 1980). The strain is much heavier for the employed wife than for her husband, because she does most of the housework, as already observed.

The effect of a wife's employment seems to depend on how much support she gets from her husband. Many husbands still find it difficult to render total support to their wives' careers, particularly if their wives earn more than they do. Consequently, in cases where the wife outperforms the husband, sex lives are more likely to suffer, feelings of love are more likely to diminish, and marriages are more likely to end in divorce. Lack of support for the wife's career may also explain why premature death from heart disease is 11 times more frequent among husbands whose wives outshine them professionally (Rubenstein, 1982).

On the other hand, in cases where the husbands fully support their wives' employment by doing their share of house cleaning and child care, the couples do head off marital stress and achieve marital happiness (Cooper et al., 1986). Generally, supportive husbands have long been exposed to egalitarian ideologies and lifestyles. They have accepted the value of gender equality. They have also seen their mothers as competent and influential individuals who shared equal status with their fathers (Rosin, 1990).

Single-Parent Families

With increased divorce, there has been a phenomenal rise in the number of children growing up in households with just one parent. From 1970 to 1993, the proportion of single-parent families increased from 13 to 30 percent. A large majority (80 percent) of such families are headed by women. About a quarter of the children today live for some time in female-headed families. It has been estimated that more than half of all children born in the 1990s will live with their mothers alone before they reach age 18 (Strong and DeVault, 1992; Census Bureau, 1994).

Most (about 70 percent) single mothers today are women who have been divorced, separated, widowed, or abandoned by their husbands (Lewin, 1992). Most of these families live below or near the poverty level. Even women of higher-income groups tend to suffer a sharp drop in household income as a result of marital breakup. African American mothers are more likely to reside with the children's grandmothers, who provide free child care. But they are far from well prepared to cope with the challenges of single parenthood (Hogan et al., 1990).

Since the early 1980s there has been a significant increase in *never-married* women having children. As shown in Figure 15.6, 23.7 percent of all never-married women had children in 1992, a 57 percent increase over the 15.1 percent of just ten years earlier. Figure 15.6 also shows that the most dramatic increase is among women in managerial and professional jobs, whites, and college graduates. This increase may be attributed to growing middle-class acceptance of unwed motherhood, women's rising earning power, and women's higher standards for choosing husbands (Seligmann, 1993). Nevertheless, the number of these more affluent unwed mothers is still much smaller than that of other groups.

Compared with two-parent families, female-headed families are more likely to experience social and psychological stress, such as unemployment, job change, lack of social support, negative self-image, and pessimism about the future (McLanahan, 1983). Children from single-parent families also have a larger share of such problems as juvenile delin-

"I now pronounce you a two-career family."

**Percentage of never-married women
aged 18 to 44 who have children**

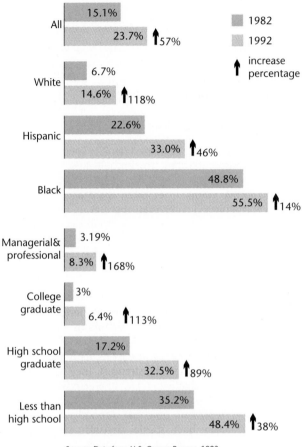

| | 1982 |
| | 1992 |

↑ increase
  percentage

All
15.1%
23.7% ↑57%

White
6.7%
14.6% ↑118%

Hispanic
22.6%
33.0% ↑46%

Black
48.8%
55.5% ↑14%

Managerial&
professional
3.19%
8.3% ↑168%

College
graduate
3%
6.4% ↑113%

High school
graduate
17.2%
32.5% ↑89%

Less than
high school
35.2%
48.4% ↑38%

Source: Data from U.S. Census Bureau, 1993

FIGURE 15.6
Never-Married Women with Children

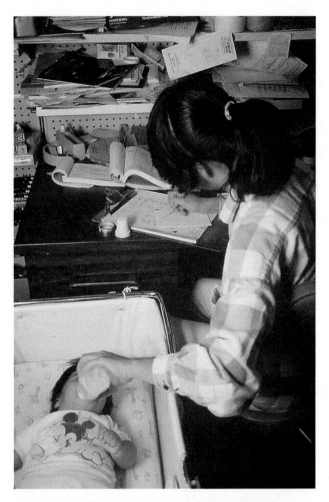

Compared with two-parent families, female-headed families are more likely to experience social and psychological stress, and the children of these families have a larger share of problems. Their problems, however, do not result directly from the absence of a father but from factors such as low income, poor living conditions, and lack of parental supervision.

quency, truancy, and poor school work. Whatever problems these children may have, however, they do not result directly from the absence of a father in a female-headed home, as popularly believed, but from factors that can also be found in a two-parent family, such as low income, poor living conditions, and lack of parental supervision (Cherlin and Furstenberg, 1983; Cherlin, 1992).

Stepfamilies

Given the high rates of divorce and remarriage, stepfamilies have become quite common. They number some 7.3 million and account for 16 percent of all married couples with children under age 18. Because women usually win custody of children in divorce cases, most stepfamilies—also called "blended families"—consist of mothers, their biological children,

and stepfathers. Nine out of ten stepchildren live with their biological mothers and stepfathers (Census Bureau, 1994).

The happiness of stepfamilies depends largely on how well the stepfather gets along with the children. It is extremely tough to be a stepfather. Society has not yet provided a script for performing the stepfather role as it does for the father role. Thus it is much more difficult for stepfathers to develop intimate and durable bonds with their stepchildren than for other fathers to do so with their biological children (Cherlin and Furstenberg, 1994).

Accustomed to living with their biological fathers, children tend to regard their stepfathers as interlopers or as distant, unwanted relatives overstaying

ENRICHING OUR LIVES

Remarriage, or the marriage of persons who have been married before, has become increasingly common. This article discusses an innovative program to enrich the lives of remarried families, based on recognizing and improving on family strengths.

Strengthening Remarried Life

The remarried family has become an increasingly common family form. The United States has the highest remarriage rate in the world; more than 40 percent of marriages are remarriages for one or both partners.

Family professionals most often focus on problems within remarried families, often ignoring possible or potential strengths. RENEW is an innovative program to help remarried families recognize and build upon their strengths. Five major strength domains and their descriptions were identified, which formed the foundation for RENEW.

Family Caring: Strong, remarried families strive to be sensitive to members' needs and to affirm, support, and trust one another. Affection is shared in ways family members find mutually acceptable and is not dependent upon the successes or failures of individuals.

Family Communication: Family members can communicate frequently, openly, clearly, and directly. They share important personal feelings, daily experiences, goals, dreams, joys, and sorrows. Because remarried parents are often more mature, experienced, and motivated to be successful, they are likely to strive to be good communicators.

Family Pride: Members of strong remarried families are committed to one another and value the traits that make their family unique. They have the realistic expectations that their family will be different from first-marriage families, but they are proud to be a member of a remarried family.

Family Unity: Strong remarried families spend time together in shared activities. The amount and kind of activities are determined by how much closeness a remarried family wants. They often share a commitment to something greater than themselves and the recognition of a higher power. They have developed or are developing shared values and goals.

Community and Family Ties: Strong remarried families are connected to other individuals and institutions that support them emotionally and practically. But the kind and amount of help are selected carefully in order to maintain privacy. These families tend to be closely involved with community institutions such as the school and church.

A family-strengths approach helps remarried families identify and build upon the strengths they already have. From this perspective, many characteristics of remarried families frequently cited as problematic are "reframed" to represent potential strengths. When families realize they have special strengths and are responsible for their enhancement, they are more likely to feel capable and motivated to achieve the kind of family life they want.

Excerpted from Stephen F. Duncan and Geneva Brown, "RENEW: A Program for Building Remarried Family Strengths," *Families in Society,* March, 1992, pp. 149–151. Published by *Families International, Inc.*

their visits. They may resent having to change their lifestyle, as a 15-year-old girl sobs to her mother, "I can't stand it. I have to put on my bathrobe at 10 o'clock at night in 'our' own house to go downstairs to get an apple from the refrigerator because he's there in 'our' living room." Aside from running into such conflicts over territoriality, stepfathers are likely to have problems with discipline. If they tell a 13-year-old stepson that he should not watch an R-rated cable movie, he may retort: "My dad lets me watch them. Besides, it's Mom's television set" (Nordheimer, 1990).

Conflicts over territoriality and discipline are most likely to erupt with teenagers. Young children can quickly accept a stepfather's love and discipline because of their physical and emotional dependence on adults. But teenagers are striving to break free of adult authority, as they are preoccupied with their developing sexuality, schoolwork, friends, and sports. They accept parental discipline only out of love and respect, which the stepfather initially does not or may never have. During an argument, they are likely to shout at their stepfathers: "You're not my real father!" Not surprisingly, the presence of stepchildren has been found to be a major reason why second marriages fail at a higher rate than first marriages. Nevertheless, most stepfamilies are relatively free of serious trouble and conflict (Nordheimer, 1990; Strong and DeVault, 1992). *fail over small things?*

Questions for Discussion and Review

1. Why did the traditional nuclear family made up of the breadwinner husband and homemaker wife emerge in the last century?
2. How has the entry of large numbers of married women into the labor force changed the family?
3. What special problems do single mothers and stepfathers face in raising children?

ALTERNATIVE LIFESTYLES

There are always people who reject conventional family life and pursue different lifestyles. Some of these lifestyles have in recent decades become more popular.

Staying Single

Of various alternatives to marriage, staying single is by far the most common. In 1990 about 10 percent of people lived alone, accounting for 24 percent of all U.S. households. This represents an increase of more than 112 percent over the last 20 years, from just less than 11 million singles in 1970 to 23 million today, many in their thirties and forties. But most are younger adults, who postpone marriage into their late twenties. More significant, a growing number of young adults live with their parents and will also stay single for some time (Crispell, 1990; Nemy, 1991; Gross, 1991).

Most singles are not actually opposed to marriage and do expect to be married sooner or later. In fact, they are likely to be married within five years. One reason they often give for their current singlehood is that they have not met the right person. But increasing numbers of men and women choose to stay single. Some studies have found them to be happier than their married counterparts. They are also more likely to see themselves as very romantic. If asked why they are single, they are likely to say that "marriage entails too much commitment and responsibility" or "I prefer the life-style" (Simenauer and Carroll, 1982; Harayda, 1986; Janus and Janus, 1993). There are, however, two sociological reasons for the increase in committed singlehood.

First, the social pressure to get married has declined. This is particularly true for city dwellers, who face far less pressure to marry than small town residents. And second, the opportunity for singles to have a good life has expanded. This is especially true for women. As educational and career opportunities open up for them, along with the freedom to choose

Most singles are not actually opposed to marriage and do expect to be married sooner or later. But increasing numbers of men and women choose to stay single. Sociological reasons for the increase in committed singlehood include a decline in social pressure to get married and an expanded opportunity for singles to have a good life.

to be a single mother, marriage stops being the only avenue to economic security, emotional support, social respectability, and meaningful work. Although singles are generally happy and respected, our society, like most others, still relegates them to a diminished status, treating their way of life as less desirable than that of married couples (Nemy, 1991).

Living Together

In the past, very few couples lived together without a formal wedding ceremony or marriage license. These couples were said to be "living in sin." They were mostly the very rich, who could afford to ignore society's rules, and the very poor, who had little to lose by ignoring them. But today cohabitation has spread to other sectors of U.S. society, including college students and young working adults. The result is a dramatic rise in cohabitation. In 1970, the number of unmarried couples living together was only slightly over half a million. But since then it has soared to 3.5 million (Census Bureau, 1994). Social disapproval has vastly diminished, and courts have stepped in to protect couples' rights as if they were legally married (Lewin, 1982; Bumpass and Sweet, 1989).

Since the incidence of cohabitation continues to rise, there is some fear that it may undermine the institution of marriage. In Sweden, where cohabitation is four times as prevalent as in the United States, living together does not pose a threat to marriage at all. Most cohabitants live like married couples, and intend to marry eventually. The situation in the United States is similar. Often called common-law marriage, cohabitation as a permanent alternative to marriage is relatively rare today. It occurs mostly among the very poor. For most of the cohabitants, living together is a temporary arrangement, which usually lasts for fewer than two years. Although it does not imply a commitment to marry later, cohabitation often leads to marriage. It is a modern extension of the courtship process, comparable to the traditional custom of "going steady" (Spanier, 1983; Gwartney-Gibbs, 1986; Tanfer, 1987).

Does living together lead to more marital happiness than traditional courtship? Couples who live together often argue that cohabitation works like a trial marriage, preparing them for marital success. But research has mostly shown less marital satisfaction or more divorces among couples who have cohabited than those who have not. The reason for marital failure, however, is not the prior experience of cohabitation. It is the lack of strong commitment to marriage, which often exists among couples who have lived together (Watson and DeMeo, 1987; Barringer, 1989; Trussell and Rao, 1989; Whyte, 1992).

Gay and Lesbian Marriages

More gay men and lesbians live together today than before. Same-sex couples now number over 1.6 million in the United States (Seligmann, 1992). Gay marriages have recently been legalized in only a few countries such as Denmark, Norway, and Sweden. But they are not in the United States, where gay couples do not have the same legal protections and financial benefits as "straight" couples, such as tax exemptions and deductions or Social Security survivor's benefits. In recent years, though, a number of cities have granted unmarried couples, both gay and straight, a legal document called "domestic partnership agreement." Some gay couples have used it to gain family benefits from employers, insurance companies, health clubs, and other commercial establishments. Also, in 1993 the Supreme Court of Hawaii ruled that the ban on same-sex marriages violates the state constitution's ban against sex discrimination. Hawaii could well be the first state in the United States to legalize gay marriages. — Congress against

Like heterosexuals, most gay men and lesbians want to get married when they are in love. Though denied the legal right to marry, they tie the knot in about the same way as their "straight" counterparts. Gay weddings range from simply exchanging rings in private to pulling out all the stops, such as having "the church ceremony, matching tuxedos or dresses, traditional vows, formal reception for two hundred, and a four-tiered wedding cake topped with two grooms or two brides" (Marcus, 1993). Sociologically, the wedding serves to strengthen the couple's relationship. By expressing their vows and love for each other in the presence of their significant others, the same-sex couple tend to feel a stronger sense of commitment and security.

Also like their heterosexual counterparts, many gay and lesbian couples have children. Most of these children come from earlier, heterosexual relationships. But an increasing number of the children are adopted or born through artificial insemination.

Gay couples are far more egalitarian in their relationship than heterosexual couples. Heterosexual men and women usually have been socialized to play different gender roles, with the husband expected to do "masculine" things such as fixing the family car and the wife "feminine" things such as preparing the family meal. Such gender-role differences often make men dominant over women. By contrast, gay partners have been socialized to the same gender role, so that they tend to have an egalitarian relationship. If a gay couple works, as most do, both partners would do about the same amount of housework. One would not do more housework than the other, as is often the case with heterosexual couples (see Chapter 13: Women and Men).

Questions for Discussion and Review

1. Why do some people stay single?
2. Does the great increase in cohabitation threaten the institution of marriage? Why or why not?
3. In what ways are gay and lesbian families similar to and different from conventional families?

ETHNIC DIVERSITY OF U.S. FAMILIES

The discussion so far is mostly based on studies of European American families. Here we focus on families of other ethnicities.

Native American Families

Before the emergence of the United States as a nation, some Native American tribes had been patrilineal, but most were matrilineal, including the better known tribes like the Zuni and Hopi in the southwest and the Iroquois in the northeast. Despite their tribal differences, various Native American families shared certain characteristics. Infants were born in special birth huts. During the years of breastfeeding, mothers refrained from sex. Physical punishment was rarely used to discipline children, who were taught instead by example. Children learned adult roles at an early age, so that most girls were married between ages 12 and 15 and boys between ages 15 and 20. Most tribes were monogamous. Only a few allowed men to have two wives or engage in extramarital sex when their wives were pregnant or breastfeeding. Extended family networks predominated, and kinship ties and obligations to relatives flourished (Strong and DeVault, 1992; Wilkinson, 1993).

Today this traditional family life has disappeared among many Native Americans. Between 1870 and 1930 the U.S. government embarked on a program of destroying the Native American culture. It involved assimilating Native Americans to the white culture by, among other things, sending their children to white-run boarding schools. Today only a small minority of Native Americans have successfully resisted assimilation and kept alive their traditional values, particularly the importance of kinship ties and obligations. The rest have either adopted white values completely or a mixture of white and Indian values, including the third of all Native Americans who marry outside their race. Compared with other ethnic groups, Native Americans suffer from higher rates of poverty, alcoholism, suicide, and other problems, all of which create severe difficulties for many Native American families (Strong and DeVault, 1992; Harjo, 1993).

African American Families

When in slavery, African Americans were prohibited from marrying. They created their own marriages, developing strong family ties similar to those in the traditional African extended family. These emotional bonds helped African Americans cope with the daily indignities of servitude. Still, slavery made it difficult for many African American families to be stable, because family members were often sold. After slavery was abolished, African Americans continued to suffer, this time as victims of racism and poverty. Throughout their travails, the mutual aid and emotional support that characterized the early family system has survived (Strong and DeVault, 1992; Wilkinson, 1993).

Since the early 1970s many African American families have been dealt a devastating blow from deindustrialization. As suggested in Chapter 11 (Rich and Poor Nations), deindustrialization involves a massive loss of blue-collar jobs from many U.S. cities to labor-cheap countries. One consequence has been rampant unemployment among African Americans in inner cities. As their poverty rate soared, the traditional African American family, which consists of a married couple with children, declined sharply. Today about 52 percent of African American families have only one parent, mostly a single mother, and 67 percent of African American babies are born to unmarried women under age 35 (Chideya et al., 1993; Census Bureau, 1994).

It has been observed that ironically "the traditional family system that slavery could not destroy

Most Hispanic families are nuclear, with only parents and children living together. But they do have the characteristics of an extended family. Like the families of Native Americans, African Americans, and Asian Americans, Hispanic families emphasize the importance of kinship ties.

during 200 years may be dismantled in a few short years by the modern industrial transition" (Billingsley, 1993). Still the African American family is most likely to survive, because it continues to draw its strength from the legacy of mutual assistance among relatives, friends, neighbors, and church members (Taylor et al., 1992).

Hispanic American Families

Most Hispanic families are nuclear, with only parents and children living together. But they do have the characteristics of an extended family. There exist strong kinship ties, as various relatives live close to one another and often exchange visits, emotional support, and economic assistance (Vega, 1992).

Hispanic families tend to have large numbers of children, generally more than families of other ethnicities. Children typically occupy the center of family life. They are taught to respect the elders, to appreciate family unity, and to assume family responsibilities. The father tends to be very affectionate and easygoing toward younger children, but becomes more authoritarian and strict as they get older. His role as the head of the family is often described as *machismo*, being "manly" in protecting

and providing for the family, exercising authority fairly, and respecting the role of the wife (Becerra, 1988). The wife is in charge of the day-to-day matters of child rearing and homemaking. Gender equality increases with the length of residence in the United States, with families started by younger generations being more egalitarian than families of older generations (Wilkinson, 1993; Chilman, 1993).

Imbued with strong family values, Hispanics generally have lower divorce rates compared with Anglos. The exception is Puerto Ricans, who have a much higher rate as a result of a greater prevalence of poverty. Hispanics are also likely to marry outside their group, especially among those with a higher socioeconomic status. Generally, the longer their families have been in the United States, the higher their rates of interethnic marriage (Wilkinson, 1993).

Asian American Families

Compared with other U.S. families, Asian American families—particularly Chinese, Japanese, Korean, and Vietnamese— generally are more stable, having lower divorce rates, fewer female-headed households, fewer problems with child rearing, greater familial solidarity, and stronger kinship associations (Wilkinson,

1993). These are often attributed to the Asians' Buddhist or Confucian culture, which emphasizes the subordination of the individual to the family.

Instead of stressing the importance of the individual's independence and autonomy, Confucianism emphasizes the individual's obligation to the family. The nature of the obligation varies with the status of each family member. The father is the head of the family, and thus must provide for the economic welfare of his family. The mother is expected to be the nurturant caretaker of both her husband and children. And the children are supposed to practice *hsiao*, or filial piety. This essentially involves showing gratitude toward parents by performing two tasks: (1) providing parents with economic and emotional support, such as aid, comfort, or affection, especially in their old age, and (2) bringing parents reflected glory by achieving success in educational and occupational activities (Shon and Ja, 1992; Lin and Liu, 1993).

The influence of this traditional culture declines with succeeding generations of Asian Americans. Thus, among the third or fourth generations, the family has fewer children, the father is less authoritarian, the mother is more likely to be gainfully employed, interracial marriage has increased significantly, and divorce is more common. But the Confucian culture still has a residual effect on many Asian American families, making them more stable than other U.S. families (Lin and Liu, 1993; Wilkinson, 1993).

Questions for Discussion and Review

1. What are the similarities among Native American, African American, Hispanic American, and Asian American families?
2. What are the differences?

THE FUTURE OF THE FAMILY

The death of the family has been predicted for decades. In 1949 Carle Zimmerman concluded from his study on the family that "We must look upon the present confusion of family values as the beginning of violent breaking up of a system." By the "confusion of family values," Zimmerman (1949) referred to the threat that individualism presented to the tradition of paternalistic authority and filial duty. He assumed that individualism would eventually do the family in. Today, many continue to predict the demise of the family, pointing out as evidence the increases in divorce, out-of-wedlock births, cohabitation, and singlehood. But the family is alive and well. The flaw in the gloomy forecast is that it confuses change with breakdown.

Many of the traditional families—with husbands as breadwinners and wives as homemakers—have merely changed into two-career families, which still hang together as nuclear families rather than disintegrate. Despite the increased number of people staying single, an overwhelming majority of those who now live alone will eventually marry. Although divorce rates have doubled over the last two decades, three out of four divorced people remarry, most doing so within three years of their marital breakup. Most of the young adults who live together before marriage will also marry eventually. It is true that single-parent families, especially those resulting from out-of-wedlock births, do pose problems for many mothers and their children. But the problems stem more from economic deprivation than from single parenthood as a new form of family.

Evidence from public opinion polls also points to the basic health of the U.S. family. Asked to describe their marriages in a recent national survey, 60 percent of married individuals said "very happy," 36 percent said "pretty happy," and only 3 percent said "not too happy" (NORC, 1994).

What will the U.S. family be like in the next 20 years? Most likely it will be much the same as it is today: manifesting *diversity* without destroying the basic family values. The continuing acceptance of these values comes through clearly in two studies. One shows that, compared with Europeans, people in the United States are more likely to tie the knot, to marry at an earlier age, and to have slightly larger families, despite their higher incidence of divorce and single-parent families (Sorrentino, 1990). Another study is longitudinal, having tracked changes in U.S. family attitudes and values from the 1960s to the 1980s. It shows that the vast majority of young people in the United States still value marriage, parenthood, and family life, and plan to marry, have children, and be successful in marriage (Thornton, 1989).

Question for Discussion and Review

1. What will the family be like in the future?

CHAPTER REVIEW

1. *In what ways does the family vary from one society to another?* Key variations occur in the definition of who makes up the family, in norms regarding who selects a marriage partner and who is an appropriate partner, and in rules of residence, descent, inheritance, and authority.

2. *What is the family like as seen through the three sociological perspectives?* Seen through the functionalist perspective, the family is functional to society for providing sexual regulation, reproduction, socialization, economic cooperation, and emotional security. Seen through the conflict theory, the family is full of violence and female exploitation. Symbolic interactionism focuses on how certain interaction between a couple leads to marital happiness.

3. *How do people in the U.S. prepare for marriage?* Usually, they do not prepare for marriage intentionally, but dating and falling in love are the traditional preparatory steps in the United States. *Is there any truth to the saying that opposites attract?* Winch believes so, but most studies support the contrary view, saying that birds of a feather flock together. The theory that people of similar personality traits are attracted to each other gains further support from the norm of homogamy, namely that a person is likely to marry someone of the same class, race, religion, and other social characteristics. *Are most marriages successful?* An overwhelming majority of individuals say they are very or pretty happy with their marriages.

4. *What causes family violence?* One reason is the popular acceptance of violence as a solution to problems. Another reason is the history of violence in the offender's family of orientation. *Why is the divorce rate so high?* Among the likely social causes are (1) decreased social disapproval of divorce, (2) greater availability of services and opportunities for the divorced, (3) increased specialization of the family in providing love and affection, (4) higher expectations about the quality of marital relationships, and (5) increased individualism.

5. *What changes have taken place in the U.S. family in recent decades?* The family has taken on diverse forms, such as two-career families, single-parent families, stepfamilies, cohabitation, singlehood, and gay or lesbian families. *How is ethnic diversity revealed among U.S. families?* The families of Native Americans, African Americans, Hispanic Americans, and Asian Americans are basically alike in emphasizing the importance of kinship ties, which contrasts with European American families' emphasis on the individual's independence. But differences in history and culture bring about different types of family life.

6. *What is the future of the U.S. family?* The diversity of family forms will continue while the basic family values, such as marrying and having children, will remain very much alive.

KEY TERMS

Arranged marriage   The marriage in which partners are selected by their parents (p. 337).

Bilateral descent   The norm that recognizes both parents' families as the child's close relatives (p. 338).

Egalitarian family   The family in which authority is equally distributed between husband and wife (p. 339).

Endogamy   Literally, "marrying within," the act of marrying someone from one's own group (p. 337).

Exogamy   Literally, "marrying outward," the act of marrying someone from outside one's group—such as clan, tribe, or village (p. 337).

Extended family   The family that consists of two parents, their unmarried children, and other relatives (p. 337).

Family of orientation   The family in which one grows up, consisting of oneself and one's parents and siblings (p. 336).

Family of procreation   The family that one establishes through marriage, consisting of oneself and one's spouse and children (p. 336).

Homogamy   Marrying someone with social characteristics similar to one's own (p. 344).

Matriarchal family   The family in which the dominant figure is the eldest female (p. 339).

Matrilineal descent   The norm that recognizes only the mother's family as a child's close relatives (p. 338).

Matrilocal residence   The home where the married couple live with the wife's family (p. 337).

Monogamy   The marriage of one man to one woman (p. 337).

Neolocal residence   The home where the married couple live by themselves, away from both husband's and wife's families (p. 337).

Nuclear family   The family that consists of the parents and their unmarried children (p. 337).

Patriarchal family   The family in which the dominant figure is the eldest male (p. 338).

Patrilineal descent   The norm that recognizes only the father's family as a child's close relatives (p. 337).

Patrilocal residence   The home where the married couple live with the husband's family (p. 337).

Polyandry   The marriage of one woman to two or more men (p. 337).

Polygamy   The marriage of one person to two or more people of the opposite sex (p. 337).

Polygyny   The marriage of one man to two or more women (p. 337).

Serial monogamy   The marriage of one person to two or more people but one at a time (p. 337).

SUGGESTED READINGS

Billingsley, Andrew. 1993. *Climbing Jacob's Ladder: The Enduring Legacy of African-American Families.* New York: Simon & Schuster. A rare analysis of the resourcefulness and resilience of African American families.

Cherlin, Andrew J. 1992. *Marriage, Divorce, Remarriage.* Cambridge, MA: Harvard University Press. Analyzes the trends, explanations, and consequences of divorce and remarriage.

McAdoo, Harriette Pipes (ed.). 1993. *Family Ethnicity: Strength in Diversity.* Newbury Park, CA: Sage. A collection of articles offering insight into families of various ethnic minorities.

Stacey, Judith. 1991. *Brave New Families: Stories of Domestic Upheaval in Late Twentieth Century America.* New York: Basic Books. Provides an intimate look into the lives of people confronted with changes in their traditional nuclear family.

Sweet, James A., and Larry L. Bumpass. 1987. *American Families and Households.* New York: Russell Sage Foundation. A study of the changes in U.S. families and households, dealing with such issues as divorce, cohabitation, and single-parent families.

16

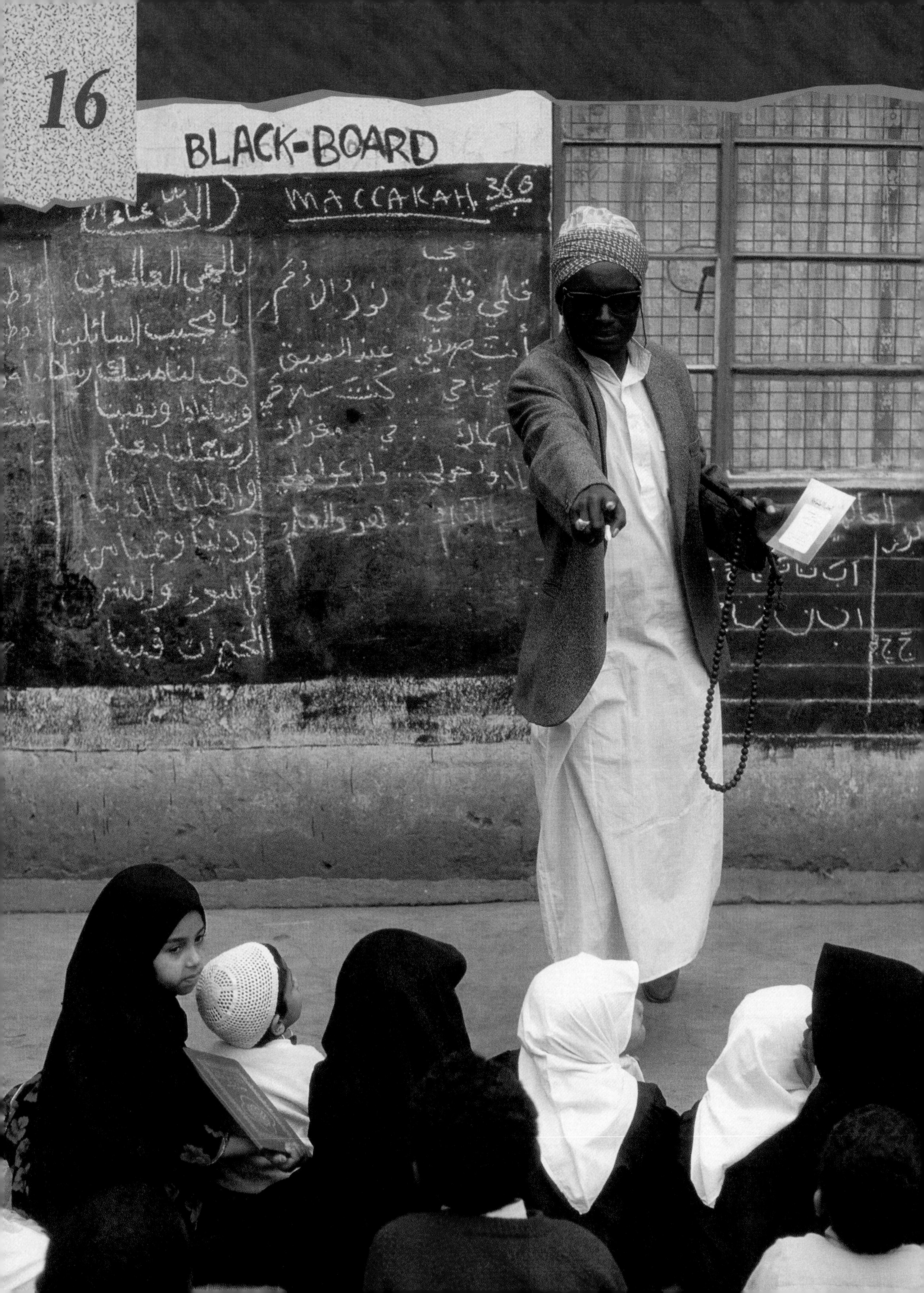

EDUCATION

Myths and Realities

MYTH: *Because college education provides abstract knowledge rather than practical training, college graduates find it increasingly difficult to find well-paid jobs in today's highly competitive economy.*
REALITY: Due to the increasing reliance of modern industries on highly educated workers, the value of college education has risen dramatically. In 1980 college graduates earned about 32 percent more than high school graduates, but ten years later the earnings difference had increased to 61 percent.

MYTH: *Because it is expensive to start a mass education program, a country must industrialize to produce wealth first. Not surprisingly, industrialization has caused the proliferation of schools in many modern societies such as the United States.*
REALITY: Mass schooling has contributed to modernization more than the other way around. The reason is that education expansion can increase worker productivity, develop more productive technology, and create a stable political climate.

MYTH: *A major function of schools is to teach children nothing but the truth about their country.*
REALITY: A major function of schools is to foster national unity. Therefore, the nation's glorious achievements are played up, but its shameful acts are often watered down or left out.

O n a school day, a group of six-year-old pupils gathered around a small pond in Ron Helmer's backyard, collecting water samples and aquatic plants for study. A second, older group was in Helmer's living room, playing a computer game called SimCity 2000. They were in effect struggling with urban planning, such as whether to build a highway or where to put the power plants. A third group was in Helmer's garage, trying to make kid-size furniture of their own design.

What we have here is a new kind of public school in action. The school consists of Helmer as the principal, two teachers, and 39 students ages six to 12. It is an autonomous "charter school," which gets funding from Michigan's state lottery and sales taxes. The principal is free to spend the money to run the school in any way he wants, without interference or oversight from the local board of education. Minnesota was the first to pass laws permitting the creation of charter schools in 1991, and by the fall of 1994 ten other states had passed similar laws and 12 additional states were planning to do so (Wallis, 1994). The charter-school movement reflects one of diverse attempts to improve the U.S. educational system. In this chapter we will see what schools are like in the United States as well as in other societies.

FUNCTIONALIST PERSPECTIVE

According to the functionalist perspective, education performs many functions for society. Here we discuss only the most important functions: teaching knowledge and skills, enhancing social mobility, promoting national unity, and providing custodial care.

Teaching Knowledge and Skills

The most obvious function of education is to provide a new generation with the knowledge and skills necessary to maintain the society. It is true that family background does have an impact on student learning. Given their greater learning resources— such as a daily newspaper, dictionary, and encyclopedia in their homes—upper- and middle-class students do have higher educational attainment than their lower-class peers (Teachman, 1987). Nevertheless, when researchers take family background into account, they still find that schools make a difference in how much their students learn.

Students from lower-income families attending "good" high schools, for example, have been found to learn more and have a better chance of going to college than other lower-income students attending "bad" schools. Moreover, studies conducted during summer months and teacher strikes have shown that inner-city and minority youngsters are most likely to suffer sharp drops in learning skills and knowledge when not in school. Studies in developing countries, where schooling is not available to all children, have also shown that whether or not children attend school has a significant impact on their cognitive development. In fact, an extensive review of relevant studies concludes that schools can and do make a big difference in transmitting knowledge and skills to students (Rutter, 1983; Heyneman and Loxley, 1983; Mortimore, 1988; Griffith et al., 1989).

Enhancing Social Mobility

Most people value the knowledge and skills transmitted by the schools because they hope to translate

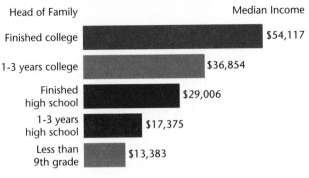

The more education people have, the bigger their earnings

Head of Family		Median Income
Finished college		$54,117
1-3 years college		$36,854
Finished high school		$29,006
1-3 years high school		$17,375
Less than 9th grade		$13,383

Source: Data from U.S. Census Bureau, 1994.

FIGURE 16.1
How Education Raises Income

those skills into good jobs and money. Does education really enhance the opportunity for social mobility? The answer is apparently yes. As Figure 16.1 shows, the more education people get, the higher their incomes are. Today, due to the increasing reliance of modern industries on highly educated workers, the value of a college education has risen dramatically. In 1980 college graduates earned about 32 percent more than high school graduates, but 10 years later the earnings difference had gone up to 61 percent (Kosters, 1990).

Education also makes social mobility available throughout the society by stimulating economic growth. This is what, as Pamela Walters and Richard Rubinson (1983) have found, the expansion of education in the United States since 1933 has done for the nation's economy. The reason is that educational expansion can increase worker productivity, develop more productive or labor-saving technology, and create a stable political climate. Studies in other industrial societies as well as developing countries have further shown that mass schooling contributed to modernization (Ramirez and Meyer, 1980).

Promoting National Unity

To foster national unity, schools—chiefly primary and secondary schools rather than colleges and universities—play an important role in transmitting the culture to a new generation. Students are taught to become good citizens, to love their country, to cherish their cultural values, and to be proud of their nation—Mexico, Japan, Nigeria, Russia, or whatever it may be. Teaching good citizenship may involve the performance of certain rituals. In the United States, for example, schoolchildren are taught to recite the

Pledge of Allegiance to the flag and to stand at attention to the playing of "The Star-Spangled Banner" before a ball game.

Schools also plant seeds of patriotism in their young charges by teaching civics, history, and other social studies. In these courses, the glorious national achievements are played up, but often the shameful acts are watered down or left out for fear of a negative effect on children. Thus, U.S. children are taught that their European ancestors came to this country as heroic pioneers, even though they slaughtered massive numbers of Native Americans and stole their lands. In Japan, school textbooks do not contain information or pictures showing Japanese wartime atrocities in China, such as massacring 200,000 Chinese civilians in the city of Nanjing, bayoneting Chinese civilians for practice, or burying Chinese civilians alive (Sayle, 1982; Kim, 1983).

Providing Custodial Care

Another major but latent function of schooling is to offer custodial care of children—providing a place to put them and having someone to watch them. Schools keep children off the streets, presumably out of trouble. The importance of this function has increased, as there have been many more two-career and single-parent households. Schools have traditionally been effective in performing their custodial role. In the past many schools were run under strict discipline, with teachers diligently enforcing rules and regulations and students obeying without question. But since the middle of this century a growing number of schools fit the description of "blackboard jungle," where violence and drugs are rampant. Nevertheless, an orderly routine still prevails in most schools.

The custodial function of schools is important for yet another reason: it keeps the young out of the job market. The nation's unemployment rate would shoot up dangerously if there were no compulsory school attendance. The need to keep young people out of the job market, though, requires that they spend more years in school than necessary for acquiring basic knowledge and skills. Thus, most students take 12 years—from grades 1 through 12—to acquire basic reading and mathematical skills that could be achieved in about three years of intensive training between ages 15 and 18 (White, 1977). Given the enormous bulk of time left over from learning those basic skills, how can students be kept so long in school without getting too restless? They are given ample opportunities for recreational,

ENRICHING OUR LIVES

Students' use of violence to resolve arguments and conflicts has become routine behavior in U.S. schools and communities. This reading reports on how conflict-resolution programs can help solve the problem by teaching alternatives to violence in schools.

The Art of Undoing Violence in Schools

For many communities, violence is a fact of life. But across the country, educators and local leaders are launching programs to teach children and families new ways to resolve conflict.

Helen Swan, a Kansas City, Mo., social worker and the creator of a conflict-resolution curriculum used in more than 100 schools, says, "Over the last three years, many schools have initiated anti-violence programs from kindergarten through high school. A lot of state departments of education have mandated programs."

What these programs have in common is the conviction that by teaching people how to improve communication and how to see issues and ideas from another perspective, violent behavior will be lessened. "What we hear from the school systems with these programs," Helen Swan says, "is more kids talking issues out and causing less problems because they have internalized some of these skills."

Swan's program, "Building Conflict Solving Skills," includes a technique called "listening contracts." "To improve relations with someone," Swan says, "a child makes a contract to improve listening skills with a specific person. Another popular device done with humor is the story of Little Miss Muffet from the spider's perspective—a frightened, lonely spider. After hearing his side of the story, students feel differently toward him, and may not be so quick to judge others."

As a pioneer in community mediation, the Community Board Program in San Francisco has sold more than 10,000 copies of its conflict-resolution curriculum. At the school level, the program has two parts. The first is aimed at kindergarten through 12th grade and emphasizes problem-solving techniques, understanding conflict styles, communication skills, and appreciating differences.

The second is selecting students to be "conflict managers" for third grade through 12th.

Students are picked by their peers and teachers to be mediators and get special training.

"At the lower grade levels they wear T-shirts that say 'Conflict Manager,'" says Irene Cooper-Basch, a director of the mediation program. "They monitor what is happening on the playground. If there is a dispute, instead of going to the principal, the managers walk over and try to mediate the dispute. At high schools the problems are more serious and often are resolved after school by the managers."

Excerpted from David Holmstrom, "The Art of Undoing Violence is Finding Its Own Place in Classrooms and Streets," *The Christian Science Monitor*, September 1, 1993, pp. 1, 4.

---

extracurricular, or nonacademic activities. In fact, the schools play their custodial role so well that many students end up considering games, sports, and friends—not books, classes, and teachers—the most important features of their school experience (Goodlad, 1984).

Questions for Discussion and Review

1. How does education promote social mobility and national unity?
2. What benefits does society gain from having the schools provide custodial care?

CONFLICT PERSPECTIVE

While the functionalist perspective focuses on the positive side of education, the conflict perspective sheds light on the negative side.

Education as Cultural Imperialism

Like other societies, the United States has long recognized the importance of using education to unify its people by teaching history from its own viewpoint. Schoolchildren can therefore be "Americanized," thinking of themselves as U.S. citizens, supporting the American democratic idea, and becoming assimilated into the mainstream of U.S. culture.

To functionalists, schools play an important role in the Americanization of young people, enabling the nation to enhance its unity and minorities to improve their life chances. But conflict theorists see the so-called Americanization as a threat to the cultural heritage of minorities.

Seen from the functionalist perspective, Americanization is not only necessary for the nation as a whole, but it is also useful to immigrants and minorities. It enables the nation to enhance its unity and the minorities to improve their life chances. Viewed from the conflict perspective, however, Americanization looks like **cultural imperialism**, the practice of making the minorities accept the dominant group's culture. It involves forcibly imposing much of the WASP (White Anglo-Saxon Protestant) culture on U.S. citizens of other cultural backgrounds. The typical U.S. history textbook is written from the WASP's point of view so that it presents mostly whites as heroes—very few of the heroes are from minority groups. Americanization also forces minority children to give up their cultural heritage, such as the Spanish language, and expect to be taught in English only. Thus, the so-called Americanization not only threatens to destroy minority cultures but also encourages teachers to stereotype minority students as "culturally deprived."

Reinforcing Social Inequality

Functionalists assume that schools serve to reduce social inequality in the larger society by improving the life chances of the poor and minorities. But conflict theorists argue just the opposite—that schools reinforce the existing social structure of inequality.

Education in the United States is therefore seen as supporting the capitalist system by producing an array of skills and attitudes appropriate for maintaining social inequality. In elementary and secondary schools, lower-class children are trained to respect authority and obey orders—characteristics that employers like in manual laborers. In high school, higher-income youths are usually channeled into college preparatory courses, and thus eventually into higher-status jobs, while lower-income students are typically guided into vocational courses, which lead to lower-status jobs. After graduating from high school, higher-income students are more likely to attend college than lower-income students. Those in elite universities learn independent thinking and decision-making skills, which are useful for leadership positions. Meanwhile, in average universities and colleges, middle-class youth are taught responsibility, dependability, and the ability to work without close supervision—qualities needed for middle-level professions and occupations. In short, education teaches youth to know their place and fill it (Bowles and Gintis, 1976; Carnoy and Levin, 1985; Weis, 1988).

There is evidence to support the conflict argument. In the United States, a majority of elementary and secondary schools practice **tracking**, the system of sorting students into different groups according to ability (Strum, 1993). In his study of nearly 900 high school classes throughout the United States, John Goodlad (1984) found that higher-income students tend to be in higher-track (higher-ability) classes and lower-class and minority students in lower-track classes. Goodlad further discovered that higher-track students were taught "a more independent type of thinking—self-direction, creativity, critical thinking, pursuing individual assignments, and active involvement in the process of learning." By contrast, lower-track students were taught "a more conforming type of classroom behavior—working quietly, punctuality, cooperation, improving study habits, conforming to rules and expectations, and getting along with others." Higher-income students were, in effect, taught to be high-paid professionals, while lower-class and minority students are taught to become low-paid manual workers.

Questions for Discussion and Review

1. What does "Americanization" mean?
2. How does the conflict perspective on education differ specifically from the functionalist perspective?

SYMBOLIC INTERACTIONIST PERSPECTIVE

According to a key tenet of symbolic interactionism, in social interaction we tend to behave in accordance with how we think others see us. Thus, in classroom interaction, how the teacher defines a student can have powerful consequences for the student's academic performance. If a student is viewed as intelligent, the student will likely perform well. If another student is considered less intelligent, that student will likely perform less well. Such power held by the teacher reflects the **Pygmalion effect**, the impact of a teacher's expectations on student performance.

The Pygmalion Effect

In Greek mythology, Pygmalion is a sculptor who created Galatea, an ivory statue of a beautiful woman. Pygmalion fell in love with his creation and prayed to the goddess of love, who brought the statue of Galatea to life. In a sense, by bringing their expectations to life, teachers behave like Pygmalion toward their students as if they were Galatea. Basically, if a teacher expects certain students to fail, they are likely to do so. If a teacher expects them to succeed, then they are likely to succeed. Thus, the Pygmalion effect is an example of a self-fulfilling prophecy. Robert Rosenthal and numerous other researchers have demonstrated the Pygmalion effect in a series of experiments, one of which was described briefly in Chapter 2 (Doing Sociology).

The teachers' expectations do not affect the students' performance directly, but they do influence the teachers' behavior, which in turn directly affects

students. Teachers tend to give attention, praise, and encouragement to students they consider bright. If the students fail to perform as well as expected, the teachers work extra hard to help them live up to expectations. But teachers tend to be uninterested in, critical toward, or impatient with those they expect to do poorly in school. When these students have difficulty, teachers are likely to think it would be a waste of time trying to help them. As a result of this differential treatment, the differences in students' performances tend to match teachers' expectations: the "bright" students do better than the "poor" ones (Rosenthal, 1973; Harris and Rosenthal, 1985).

Pygmalion and Tracking

In view of the Pygmalion effect, it is not surprising that school tracking generally benefits higher-track students more than lower-track students. Tracking raises teacher expectations for higher-track students and lowers teacher expectations for lower-track students.

This may explain why, as research by John Goodlad (1984) indicates, teachers in higher-track classes spend more time on instruction, expect students to study more at home, and are seen by students as more enthusiastic in teaching, more concerned about them, and less punitive toward them, when compared with teachers in lower-track classes. Thus, the good students tend to get better and the poor students poorer. As many studies have shown, higher-track students are more likely to go to college, and lower-track students are more likely to have low self-esteem, drop out of school, or become delinquents (Alexander and Cook, 1982; Goodlad, 1984; Strum, 1993).

Questions for Discussion and Review

1. What is the Pygmalion effect?
2. What is the connection between the Pygmalion effect and school tracking?

THE U.S. EDUCATIONAL SYSTEM

For some time now, many critiques of education in the United States have documented a decline in educational standards and achievement compared with the past and with other countries. As Figure 16.2

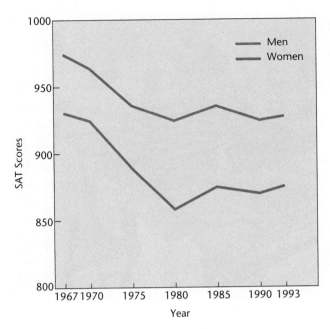

Source: Data from U.S. Census Bureau, 1994.

FIGURE 16.2
Declining SAT Scores

shows, scores on Scholastic Aptitude Tests (SAT) taken by college-bound high school seniors fell continuously from 1967 to 1980. Although the SAT scores have inched upward since 1980, they still appear inadequate. Compared with their counterparts in other countries, U.S. high school students also score lower on math tests (see Figure 16.3). As a result, the media as well as many national task forces on education have raised the alarm about a crisis in

U.S. schools, said to threaten our very future as a nation and a people (Lord and Horn, 1987; Gleick, 1995). Is U.S. education really in a state of crisis? The answer is probably "no" if we put the discouraging data in proper perspective.

Problems in Perspective

First, the decline of SAT scores may have partly resulted from the increasing democratization of U.S. education. In contrast to the continued elitism of foreign educational systems, the U.S. system has included growing numbers of poor, minority, and immigrant students. Because of inadequate academic preparation or the tests' cultural bias or both, the socially disadvantaged students do not do as well on the SAT as the socially advantaged, helping bring down the average score for the entire group. But the investment in equal education has begun to pay off. Since 1980 the national SAT averages have begun to level off or pick up, partly a result of the steady improvement in test scores among African American, Hispanic, and other minority students. On other standardized tests, minorities have even shown greater gains in scores than whites (Grissmer, 1994).

Second, the United States is not alone in having educational problems. Japan, which is often touted as being a world leader in science and technology, has serious problems with its higher education. Although Japanese schoolchildren are under enormous pressure to study hard, university students are allowed to take it easy, as if in reward for having beaten their brains out before college. As Robert Christopher (1983) observes, "the great majority of Japanese universities are extraordinarily permissive: once you get into one, it takes real effort to get kicked out . . . Japanese university authorities do not regard a student's failure to attend classes or even to pass courses as a ground for dismissal." Moreover, Japanese leaders have grown concerned that their schools' emphasis on conformity, such as finding the "single right answer" to a problem, is depriving their society of much needed creativity, especially in the current age of rapid change (Fiske, 1987).

Third, U.S. schools are not to blame for the lower achievement of their students compared with the Japanese. For one thing, our schools are expected to

FIGURE 16.3
Comparative Math Test Scores of High School Students

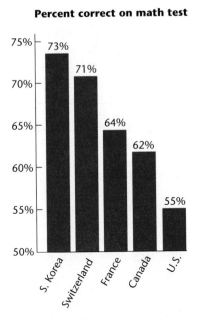

Source: Data from National Center for Education Statistics, 1991

Unlike U.S. schools, Japanese schools do not spend time dealing with such problems as alcohol, drug abuse, or teenage pregnancy. Japanese mothers make sure their children study three to four hours a night, and Japanese adolescent peer culture pressures teenagers to study hard.

dilute their teaching resources by dealing with such social problems as alcohol and drug abuse and teenage pregnancy, which Japanese schools do not have. Given the high rates of divorce, single parenthood, and two-career couples, U.S. parents are too stressed, tired, or self-absorbed to do what Japanese mothers do—help with their children's homework and make sure they study three or four hours a night. Moreover, many U.S. teenagers hold part-time jobs, significantly reducing their ability to hit the books after school. By contrast, working during the school year is virtually unheard of in Japan. Finally, U.S. teenagers are under great pressure from their peers to look good, drink, socialize, date, or even have sex. In contrast, the Japanese adolescent peer culture pressures teenagers to study hard. Japanese students like to say, though a little facetiously, "Four you score; five you die," meaning "If you sleep five hours a night instead of four, you won't pass the exams" (Steinberg, 1987). In short, it is largely social problems, the lack of support from parents, and the adolescent subculture that make it hard for U.S. schools to compete with their Japanese counterparts.

Finally, while many problems can be found in U.S. schools, there is a lot of good in them, particularly in their mission of providing quality with equality (Goodlad, 1984). Although education researcher and reformer Theodore Sizer (1984) criticizes the nation's high schools for being rigid and impersonal, he still finds that "they are, on the whole, happy places, settings that most adolescents find inviting, staffed by adults who genuinely care for youngsters." In con-

trast, most Japanese students do not enjoy their school experience, because they feel like robots or prisoners in a rigidly controlled environment. Moreover, some Japanese professors who have taught in the United States have observed that U.S. students are more creative than their Japanese counterparts (Tharp, 1987). Japanese schools, like their society, stress extreme conformity, pressuring students to do what everybody else is doing while discouraging them from sticking out by taking risks. In contrast, U.S. schools, like U.S. society, place a high premium on individuality, prodding students to think for themselves. This is why there are proportionately more original thinkers in the United States, as shown by the numerous U.S. scientists who have won the Nobel prize. The U.S. education system may turn out to be the ace in the hole in our economic competition with Japan. We may do well to keep all this in mind as we analyze the various aspects of the U.S. educational system in the following sections.

Bureaucracy

In the United States, state governments are largely responsible for providing primary and secondary education. They pay about 50 percent of school expenses, compared with 44 percent from local school districts and 6 percent from the federal government. States regulate such things as the number of school days per year, grade-level curricula, and graduation requirements. But they leave the operations of schools to local school districts. School districts, which have the power to levy taxes, are governed by elected school boards (Griffith et al., 1989).

Today, school administrators, teachers, and students constitute more than a fifth of the entire U.S. population. If it is considered one unit, the school system has become the largest bureaucracy in the country. Within this giant bureaucracy, schools of various sizes and types are in a way remarkably similar. They all have "the *framework* of grades, schedules, calendar, courses of study, even rituals" (Sizer, 1984).

Like other bureaucracies, the schools have a clear-cut division of labor and hierarchy of authority. They are also largely impersonal, run in accordance with a set of formal rules. These rules dictate that administrators have authority over teachers, who, in turn, have authority over students. Teachers must be assigned to teach certain subjects on the basis of skills rather than personal preferences. Students must be placed in classes according to age and ability. Usually, textbooks are chosen by a state educational committee according to prescribed rules rather than by individual teachers. Even detailed curricula may be dictated to teachers by the educational bureaucracy.

All this is for the sake of efficiency, and the bureaucracy does have some advantages. The bureaucratic system ensures the provision of education for huge masses of children rather than only the few privileged ones. The larger school systems make it more likely that pupils can choose from a wide range of courses. The standardization that arises from bureaucracies allows children to adjust more easily to a new school, even when it is in a different part of the country. And bureaucratic rules offer administrators, teachers, and even students some protection from political pressures, racial and sexual prejudice, and the personal whims of those in authority.

The negative effects of bureaucracy, however, are more apparent. Parents often complain that the bureaucracy leaves them out in the cold, frequently unable to influence their children's schooling. Students, too, may feel that they are treated like numbers—a situation that is not likely to inspire either respect for the school's authority or eagerness to learn. Some administrators may even find that they cannot fire incompetent teachers, and teachers, in turn, may occasionally throw up their hands in frustration at being mired in red tape. To the extent that the organization of a school system is bureaucratic, everyone is likely to lose the freedom to try innovations or to respond creatively to the unique aspects of a particular school or situation. The most serious problem seems to be the rapidly increasing size of administration. Aside from school superintendents and principals, there are now all kinds of administrators, ranging from curriculum specialists and guidance counselors to "instruction supervisors," who observe how teachers teach, and assistant principals, who help with yearly evaluations of teachers. It is not surprising that half of our education spending goes to administration, compared with only 20 percent in many European countries (Hood, 1990).

All this has caused an increasing number of teachers to complain that they have lost control over their jobs. Agreeing that teachers are now largely governed by rules made by administrators who outrank them, the Carnegie Foundation has suggested that these conditions be radically altered to give teachers more leeway over how they teach (Solorzano, 1987). Other researchers have suggested that states, school boards, and superintendents give more power to each school so that it can take care of its own business, without having to do exactly what other schools are doing. This is, in fact, a major characteristic of the better schools in Goodlad's (1984) massive study of schooling in the United States. A more recent study further shows that relatively autonomous schools perform much better than schools closely controlled by external bureaucrats. The reason is that the principals and teachers, having been trained to teach and deal with students every day, know the business of teaching better than the bureaucrats (Chubb and Moe, 1990). Thus, in a number of states teachers are now permitted to join administration in designing curricula, choosing textbooks, deciding discipline policy, and setting budgets (Chira, 1990).

Teachers

Teachers play an important role in the educational system. As many studies have indicated, teachers constitute the one single element of schooling that most influences students' learning (Goodlad, 1984).

Public school teachers appear quite qualified for their jobs. Nearly all of the primary and secondary teachers have a bachelor's degree and over half have a master's degree (Census Bureau, 1994). Very few have the most advanced degrees. Ironically, these teachers—with the doctorates—tend not to teach but gravitate toward administration or out of the school system completely, for higher pay. As Goodlad (1984) writes, "Teaching is perhaps the only profession where the preparation recognized as most advanced almost invariably removes the individual from the central role of teaching."

It is difficult to make a living as a schoolteacher. The salary for teaching is notoriously low. Yet most teachers are quite satisfied with their career. According to one survey, 74 percent of teachers said that their career expectations had been fulfilled. Another study shows that 92 percent take pride in their profession.

What do teachers learn while obtaining their college degrees? The curriculum for education majors includes a teaching practicum, as well as many courses on teaching methods. In fact, the method courses are often emphasized at the expense of courses in the specific subjects the prospective teachers will eventually teach. As a result, many English, science, and mathematics teachers are not qualified to teach these subjects. Apparently, many teachers have learned from those teaching methods how to raise students' self-esteem by making students feel good about themselves, but at the expense of teaching a subject competently. By contrast, teachers in Korea tend to concentrate on imparting knowledge in an authoritative manner. It is no coincidence that in a standardized math test given to 13-year-olds in six countries, U.S. youngsters did the worst while Koreans did the best. In the same test, all were also asked whether they agreed with the statement: "I'm good at mathematics." Koreans came in last, with only 23 percent of them answering yes. But U.S. youngsters were number one, with an impressive 68 percent in agreement, suggesting widespread self-esteem. (Krauthammer, 1990).

It is difficult to make a living as a schoolteacher. The salary for teaching is notoriously low, lower than for trucking and other occupations that require much less education. Many teachers are compelled to supplement their income with part-time and summer employment. Yet most are quite satisfied with their teaching career. According to one survey, 74 percent of the teachers said that their career expectations had been fulfilled, and 69 percent reported that if they had it to do over again they would choose teaching as a career. Another study shows that 92 percent of the teachers take pride in their profession and consider the quality of education to be either good or excellent. Actually, all this need not be surprising, because, for most teachers, money is not the primary reason they enter the profession. Instead, the major reasons have to do with the nature of teaching itself: desire to teach in general or a particular subject, perception of teaching as a good and worthy profession, and desire to be of service to others (Goodlad, 1984; Carmody, 1989).

Given the low pay, teachers do want higher salaries, along with more respect for their professionalism, more professional autonomy, and less administrative work, which they believe can help them do their jobs better. Thus, powerful teachers' unions—to which over 90 percent of the nation's teachers belong—often negotiate for higher pay, smaller class size, fewer classes taught, and greater influence over hiring standards and textbook selection. Unions may resort to strikes as a way of enhancing their bargaining power. Private school teachers are generally happier with their working conditions, despite their lower pay and lack of job security. The reason is their

Cutting Edge

It is popularly assumed that psychological stress is common among students in Asia because they are made to study very hard. But a study reviewed in this reading shows that U.S. students who achieve high academic success experience more stress than their Asian counterparts because of pressure to participate in nonacademic activities.

Teen Students in U.S.: Stressed for Success

A current school of thought holds that teenagers living in Asian countries pay a psychological price for their mathematical superiority to adolescents in the United States. Some U.S. parents and teachers suspect that high-achieving Asian students feel more nervous, depressed, and overburdened in response to the pressures of maintaining academic eminence.

A cross-cultural study now supports a link between mathematics success in high school and frequent psychological distress—but only for U.S. students, not those in Japan or Taiwan.

"High academic achievement, such as that exhibited by students in Taiwan and Japan, can be attained without necessarily increasing students' reports of psychological distress," contend David S. Crystal and Harold W. Stevenson, both psychologists at the University of Michigan in Ann Arbor, and their coworkers.

A teenager's peers and family in the two Asian countries typically help to maintain academic achievement through various forms of support, Crystal's team asserts. But U.S. high achievers get torn between the desire to spend extra time on their studies and to pursue myriad nonacademic interests touted by peers and parents, they argue. These include socializing with friends, playing sports, dating, and working at a part-time job.

Moreover, the same researchers have found that parents and children express lower expectations for academic success in the United States than in Japan and Taiwan.

Crystal and his colleagues administered questionnaires to 1,386 U.S., 1,633 Taiwanese, and 1,247 Japanese eleventh graders, who averaged 17 years old. Participants rated the frequency with which they felt stressed or pressured, depressed, aggressive (such as wanting to hit someone or destroy something), and anxious about school work. They also noted anxiety-related physical complaints, such as headaches, stomachaches, and sleep troubles.

The researchers interviewed approximately 200 additional eleventh graders in each country. Native speakers of each language asked these students to explain when and why they felt stressed or depressed at home, at school, and in other situations.

All volunteers took a challenging mathematics test. Items ranged from calculating fractions and percentages to the solution of problems of limits and the addition of tangents and secants.

Although students in Japan and Taiwan noted greater parental dissatisfaction with their school work and higher parental expectations for academic performance than did U.S. students, the former groups also cited less frequent stress, anxiety, and aggression, the researchers report in the June *Child Development*.

Japanese teenagers reported the fewest instances of depressed mood and physical problems, whereas Taiwanese youngsters noted the greatest frequency of those conditions. But in a comparison of those with high and low scores on the math test, Asian high scorers reported less emotional and physical distress than low scorers. In contrast, U.S. high scorers cited these symptoms more frequently than low scorers.

Interviews indicated that more students in the United States and Taiwan than in Japan regarded school as a source of stress. Only U.S. teens mentioned sports and part-time jobs as additional causes of tension. Japanese students most often cited peers as stressful.

High achievers in the United States devoted much more time to studying than low-achieving peers but expressed the same level of interest in out-of-school activities, the scientists note. "Adolescent culture" in the United States may present academic achievers with the most conflict over how to arrange daily activities, they argue.

Excerpted from B. Bower, "Teen Students in U.S.: Stressed for Success," *Science News*, October 10, 1994, p. 38.

greater sense of identity and belonging. In contrast, most public school teachers "must sustain their commitment to their profession on their own, with little support from their school organizations" (Johnson, 1990). Given a satisfying educational environment, teachers can teach more effectively.

The youth culture in high school tends to denigrate scholarship. It also receives unintended support from teachers and parents who demand little of students. In private schools, however, compared with public schools, there is more emphasis placed on homework and academic programs.

Students

Conflicting interests create a wide gulf between teachers and students. Unlike teachers, children are forced to be in school. Whereas teachers are duty-bound to press academic work on students, students are likely to resist. Over 30 years ago, James Coleman (1961) found that high school boys aspired to be star athletes and girls wanted to be popular; neither wanted to be brilliant students. These attitudes were part and parcel of a youth culture. More recently, John Goodlad (1984) asked high school teenagers to choose from six categories of students they considered the most popular. A large majority (79 percent) selected "good-looking students" or "athletes," but very few (only 7 percent) picked "smart students." This and other similar data led to the conclusion that the youth "are excessively preoccupied with physical appearance, popularity in the peer group, and games and athletics." Why are most high school students far from fired up over their books, teachers, or the classes they are attending?

In its denigration of scholarship, the youth culture receives considerable, though unintended, support from teachers and parents. In many urban high schools, teachers do not demand much of students. According to a survey, more than one-fifth of eleventh graders do not do any homework. In suburban high schools, college-preparatory courses are often watered down to accommodate students' desires. Often parents do not stress enough the importance of studying hard. In a survey, 63 percent of eighth graders reported that their parents rarely or never limit how much TV they may watch. The stu-

dents also said that they spend an average of 21.4 hours a week watching television but only 5.6 hours doing homework and 1.8 hours on outside reading. Moreover, half of the students rarely discuss school with their parents (Maeroff, 1990; Bacon, 1990).

The situation is brighter, though, in U.S. private schools. Coleman and his associates (1982a, 1982b) surveyed tens of thousands of students in public and private schools and gave achievement tests to tenth and eleventh graders. They discovered that although the typical private school (a Catholic parochial school) had larger classes, lower-paid teachers, and substantially fewer resources than the average public school, the private school students achieved far more in vocabulary and mathematics. The investigators attribute this to private schools' "educational climate." Compared with public schools, private schools are more rigorous—their students do more homework every night. Private schools impose stricter disciplinary rules and maintain more order in their classrooms. Most important, they put more emphasis on academic subjects, enrolling nearly 70 percent of their students in academic programs, compared with only 34 percent for public schools. A larger proportion of private school students rated their teachers' interest in them as "excellent" than did public school students (40 versus 10 percent).

Compared with primary and secondary school students, college students are more interested in intellectual pursuits. But they are not all cut from the same cloth. Burton Clark and Martin Trow (1966) found four distinct college subcultures that still exist on today's campuses. The **collegiate subculture** revolves around fraternities, sororities, parties,

The collegiate subculture revolves around fraternities, sororities, parties, drinking, football, and similar activities. It is similar to the youth culture in high school. Its members come from middle-class homes where parents are not particularly interested in intellectual matters.

drinking, football, and similar activities. This subculture is similar to the youth culture in high school. Its members tend to come from middle-class homes, and their parents are not particularly interested in intellectual matters. More serious, the **vocational subculture** emphasizes hard work in order to get good jobs after graduation. Students in this subculture are likely to major in science, engineering, law, and business. Today, they can be divided into "careerists" and "strivers." Careerists come largely from middle-class families, while strivers are mostly minority members or whites from lower-income homes (Katchadourian and Boli, 1986). Less utilitarian, the **academic subculture** stresses the pursuit of scholarly achievement largely for its own sake. Its members tend to have upper-class or highly educated parents who are physicians, lawyers, or corporate executives. Repudiating the values of those three subcultures, the **nonconformist subculture** advocates rebellion from conventional society. These rebels come from all ethnic groups, from both high and low social statuses, but rarely from the middle class.

Questions for Discussion and Review

1. What is the nature of educational problems in the United States?
2. What are the major characteristics of educational bureaucracies?
3. What are modern public school teachers like?
4. How do private school students differ from public school students?

A GLOBAL ANALYSIS

To understand the U.S. educational system better, we can compare it with the schools in other industrial societies. Let us take a quick tour of the schools in five countries, focusing on their most distinctive features or problems. We will see that given different social environments the schools in various societies produce different results.

Schools in Belgium

The Belgian educational system is unique for having proportionately larger numbers of schoolteachers than virtually all other countries in the world. Schoolteachers make up 5.3 percent of Belgium's work force, compared with, for example, 2.6 percent for the United States and 2.4 percent for Britain. As a consequence, the average class size in Belgian schools is the smallest in the world. Belgium's student-teacher ratio is only 9.3 primary students and 6.8 secondary students per teacher, compared with 15.5 and 15.9 for the United States. But Belgian teachers' salaries are relatively low, as the country spends less per student than the United States and other industrial societies. Still, parents generally give high marks to the Belgian schools.

One major reason for the huge teacher population in Belgium is growing unemployment, which now reaches about 10 percent. This may have caused the government to raise the age of compulsory education to 18, as well as to allow children to start school as young as age two-and-a-half. If the older teenagers in

FIGURE 16.4
Countries in the Global Analysis: Belgium, Finland, France, Japan, and Portugal

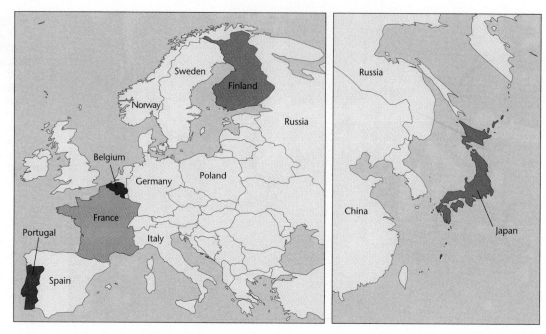

Belgium were not forced to stay in school longer than their U.S. counterparts, many would have wound up on the unemployment rolls, pushing the nation's jobless rate even higher. In addition, increased student enrollment helps reduce the unemployment rate by producing jobs for teachers (Brock, 1993).

Schools in Finland

Finland is the world's most educated society. Forty percent of Finns aged 24 to 65 have a college degree, compared with 12 percent in the United States. Understandably, Finns are, per capita, the greatest consumers of literature in the world. School attendance is compulsory up to age 16, an earlier age than in Belgium, but schooling is rigorous. High school students attend classes 38 hours a week, compared with about 25 hours in the United States. Finnish students are also required to take more courses, including two foreign languages. All higher education is free, with most financial support coming from the state and the rest from private industries (Peltonen, 1993).

Schools in France

As suggested, the educational bureaucracy in the United States does not give teachers the freedom to teach the way they see fit, such as choosing their own textbooks rather than having the school board do it.

By contrast, French teachers are free to do their job in virtually any way they want. The French government only offers *general* guidelines, such as suggesting that five-year-olds be given some reading instruction so that they can handle primary school lessons after their year of preschool games. But the teachers are free, for example, to pick the books for their classes or even not to use any books. The teachers are given so much freedom because their government assumes that they know their job better than anybody else. The assumption turns out to be correct: 14-year-olds in France, along with those in Finland, are the most proficient readers, compared with their peers in other industrial countries (Riding, 1993).

Schools in Japan

The Japanese schools are world-famous for producing high achievers. According to researcher Thomas Rohlen (1983), the average high school graduates in Japan have learned as much basic knowledge in all fields, especially math and science, as have the average college graduates in the United States. A major reason is that the school occupies a much larger place in Japanese teenagers' life. They spend far more hours in education-related activities in school and at home, which leaves much less free time for play, when compared with U.S. teenagers. The very intensity of the educational experience, however, has increased school violence and truancy. Moreover, the Japanese schooling emphasizes rote learning far more

American Mosaic

The United States. has experienced a vast wave of immigration, and new arrivals have brought along innovative social activities. This reading reports on some immigrants sending their children to "cram schools," where students receive extra schooling to insure admission to top colleges.

Cram Schools: Immigrants' Tools for Success

On a brisk Saturday morning, while most of their friends were relaxing at home, 16-year-old Jerry Lee and eight other Asian teenagers huddled over their notebooks and calculators for a full day of math and English lessons.

During the week they all attend public schools in the city. But every Saturday, they go to a Korean *hagwon*, or cram school, to spend up to seven hours immersed in the finer points of linear algebra or Raymond Chandler.

"I complain, but my mom says I have to go," said Jerry, a Stuyvesant High School student from Sunnyside, Queens, who has already scored a 1520 on the Scholastic Assessment Test for college, but is shooting for a perfect 1600. "It's like a habit now."

Long a tradition in the Far East, where the competition to get into a top university borders on the fanatic, the cram schools of Asia have begun to appear in this country too, in Queens and New Jersey and Los Angeles and elsewhere, following the migration of many Koreans, Japanese, and Chinese over the last two decades.

In the last 10 years, the cram schools—called *juku* in Japanese and *buxiban* in Chinese—have become a flourishing industry, thriving on immigrant parents' determination to have their children succeed. Only a handful of cram schools existed here when the hagwon that Jerry attends, the Elite Academy, opened in 1986. Today, the Korean-language yellow pages list about three dozen Asian cram schools in the New York area. In Los Angeles, the Chinese yellow pages list about 40.

While the pressure to get into a good school is not nearly so extreme in the United States, the cram schools, such as the ambitiously named Nobel Education Institute in Arcadia, a heavily Asian suburb of Los Angeles, have nonetheless found a burgeoning niche in Asian communities. Chinese and Korean newspapers bulge with cram school advertisements. Some schools simply print lists of their graduates who have been accepted to New York City's specialized high schools, as well as to Harvard, Stanford, and M.I.T.

For many busy parents, the schools have become a kind of academic baby-sitting service. But most see them as a way of insuring that their children excel in spite of public schools that they perceive as lax and unchallenging compared with those in Asia.

Since language and cultural barriers prevent many of them from moving easily in U.S. society, they are willing to invest whatever is required to insure that their children, armed with diplomas from the best universities, will not face the same hardships. Tuition averages about $200 a month.

The rigor and discipline of the cram schools have even begun to attract a growing number of non-Asian parents who want their children to excel.

"The Asian people are willing to invest in their children," said Miri Kessar, an Israeli immigrant who sent her 11-year-old daughter to a Flushing *hagwon* to study. "They want the best for them. They want Harvard, Yale, and Princeton."

than original thinking, while the reverse is more common with U.S. schools.

The Japanese youngsters' academic excellence cannot be attributed to the schools alone. Japanese mothers play a crucial role in their children's education, not only constantly encouraging hard work but also rendering help with homework. After-school classes, called *jukus* ("cram shops"), also contribute substantially, as they are attended by more than one-quarter of all primary pupils and more than one-half of all secondary students. Since so many students are involved in this supplementary learning, Francis

McKenna (1993) concludes that the quality of Japanese schooling is actually lower than popularly believed.

Schools in Portugal

Before the 1960s education in Portugal had long been largely reserved for the rich and, as a consequence, illiteracy was widespread. Since then schools have been made accessible to large masses of children, triggering an explosion in enrollment. But school financing has remained low. Today, schools are overcrowded, money for books and equipment is scarce, and there is a shortage of teachers. As a result, the levels of student achievement are among the lowest in Europe.

Portugal is particularly concerned about its students' poor performance in math. Scores on standardized math tests are lower than in most other industrial countries. The reasons include a lack of discipline among students and teachers as well as inadequate support from parents. The nation has recently tried to overhaul its mathematics curriculum. Greater emphasis is placed on ways of applying math skills rather than concentrating on learning abstract knowledge. Efforts are also made to individualize teaching and to augment teaching with computers (Howe, 1993).

Questions for Discussion and Review

1. How do the schools in the five societies differ from one another?
2. How are those schools different from U.S. schools?

TRENDS IN U.S. EDUCATION

There are always ideas about how to improve U.S. schools. On the surface, it sometimes seems as if ideas about educational reform change much like hemlines going up, then down, then up again. Discipline has been in fashion, then out of fashion, then "in" again. These shifts are often more than fads, though. They frequently reflect changing needs and changing problems. In the 1960s, many people believed that the schools' main task was to promote individual development, but since the early 1980s it has been widely believed that schools should prepare students for jobs and that the nation's economy should be strengthened. In the 1960s, people awoke to the problem of educational inequalities, but by the 1980s a general decline in academic performance became a pressing problem. Among the main reforms and trends that emerged over the last two decades were Head Start, alternative or charter schools, "back to basics," school choice, home schooling, and life-long learning.

Head Start

Sociologists in the 1960s often found that trying to equalize the quality of the nation's schools and educational opportunities would not produce educational equality, because children's family backgrounds could handicap them even from the start of school. Some youngsters never see a book at home and are never encouraged to do well at school. There seemed to be a need for **compensatory education**, a school program intended to improve the academic performance of socially and educationally disadvantaged children. So in the mid–1960s the federal government began funding Head Start, a compensatory education program for disadvantaged preschoolers across the nation. It was not run by public school administrators, but rather mostly by pediatricians and child psychologists working for poverty agencies. The aim was to prepare poor children aged three and four for kindergarten. These children were taught the skills and vocabulary that many of their middle-class peers absorb at home. Their parents were also brought in to learn child care, health care, and nutrition.

Earlier studies of the results were not encouraging. They showed that, although the training did raise children's I.Q. scores and scholastic achievement, the benefits were temporary. In the first grade, disadvantaged pupils who had had preschool training might perform better than those who had not, but by the third grade this difference tended to disappear, and both disadvantaged groups were equally likely to fall behind their grade level (Stearns, 1971). This is the kind of evidence that conservative politicians in the 1990s often point to in their call for abolishing Head Start.

Why did the benefits disappear, and why did students not respond better to remedial programs? In the 1970s, researchers were not able to find a definitive answer. Most argued that the continuing influence of a poor family environment was the cause—it simply overwhelmed the influence of any educational program. Others contended that the preschool programs had been doomed to failure because of inadequate funding. A few argued that they had been unfairly evaluated before they had time to prove their effectiveness. The last argument turns out to be the one that hit the nail on the head.

In the 1980s and 1990s, many studies showed that the preschool programs do benefit low-income students in the long run. When poor youngsters who were in the preschool programs reach age 9 to 19, they do better in school than peers who did not participate. They are also more likely to graduate from high school, attend college, and have higher rates of employment (Celis, 1993b). Head Start is still far from being fully funded, though. Only about half of eligible children can enroll. The quality of the staff—teachers, nutritionists, social workers, and psychologists—is not uniformly adequate in all Head Start programs. The average staff salary is only $12,000 a year, compared with about $30,000 for an average public school teacher. Low salaries have led to shortages of well-trained staff at some places. President Clinton and other liberal politicians want to increase government support for Head Start, but conservatives want to abolish it (Schweinhart and Weikert, 1990, Kantrowitz and Wingert, 1993).

Alternative Schools

During the 1950s and much of the 1960s, rote learning and discipline were prominent features of many U.S. classrooms. Students generally had little if any choice about what they would be taught or how they should go about learning it. To some critics of the 1960s, the schools were repressive organizations that resembled boot camps: teachers were obsessed with rules and regulations, and students were forced to obey without question. The schools, said these critics, "destroy the hearts and minds of children" and in most, "children are treated, most of the time, like convicts in a jail" (Kozol, 1968; Holt, 1968). Their capacity for curiosity, creativity, self-direction, and learning itself was being stifled.

Thus emerged the **alternative school**, which encourages student creativity by allowing the freedom to choose learning materials within the classroom. Basically, the alternative-school movement maximizes personal choice for students. Its supporters believed that children would learn best if, rather than being processed from one structured program to another, they were free to choose to work on projects that interested them. Teachers do not lead, direct, or control the children. They are expected to "facilitate" activities that the child initiates and to help interpret materials that the child chooses. The classroom is supposed to be a "resource center," with

In the 1960s the federal government began funding Head Start, a compensatory education program for disadvantaged preschoolers. Though earlier studies of the benefits of Head Start were not encouraging, many studies in the 1980s and 1990s showed that the preschool programs do benefit low-income students in the long run.

Among the different kinds of alternative schools are those that use a particular culture to increase minority children's scholastic achievement. In the Malcolm X Academy, Detroit, Michigan, young African Americans are taught black history and culture so that they will develop a strong sense of pride in their ethnic heritage.

a rich variety of educational materials, such as tools, paints, musical instruments, writing materials, and books. It is supposed to be a place that pupils enjoy and that encourages them to be creative and to learn to direct their own lives. But, once the students have decided to study a given subject, the teacher will give personal attention to each of them, creating a mentor system that emphasizes depth over breadth.

From small beginnings in the mid-1960s, the alternative-school movement has grown to be a force with some influence in the 1990s. Today there are about 10,000 alternative schools, up from a few hundred in 1972. These schools are either private or public. Many of these public schools, called "magnet schools," are operated with some control by the school board. But some have become *charter schools,* which are totally autonomous. Among these schools are those that use culture to increase minority chil-

dren's scholastic achievement by giving them a strong sense of pride in their ethnic heritage (Wallis, 1994).

Because of the focused, personal attention given to each student, made possible by the small size of the schools, alternative schools have generally produced gratifying results. The results can even be dramatic for students from educationally disadvantaged backgrounds. Consider the case of Edith Casimir, who dropped out of a traditional high school in the tenth grade. She explained, "School was such a strain on my system. I thought I was being degraded every day, treated like a sheep—hall monitors, passes. I was always being considered a troublemaker, talking back." Now, at 16, after switching to an alternative school, she bubbles with enthusiasm for school, saying, "It's brought new hope to me. I don't have such a sense of desperation. I'm free to make my own decision. I'm now planning to go to college" (Gruson, 1986).

Back to Basics

Educators and intellectuals have spearheaded most educational reforms, but during the late 1970s, parents and politicians began to take the lead in pushing for major changes in U.S. education. Angry about declining student achievement and discipline, functional illiteracy, and teacher incompetence, they blamed the educators, and sought to gain some control over their children's education. What this movement proposed was a "return to the basics"—to basic subjects such as arithmetic and what they considered basic values such as obedience and respect for authority.

Around the country, many schools have adopted at least some of the changes related to the back-to-basics movement. Many have placed greater emphasis on teaching basic skills in reading, writing, and arithmetic. They have reduced the students' freedom to choose elective courses, required students to take tests in basic skills, and stiffened the standards for grading. They have raised their graduation standards, which include more academic subjects such as mathematics, science, social studies, and English, but fewer vocational electives, physical education courses, and other less rigorous subjects. Discipline, too, has been intensified in some schools—partly just to bring order to the classroom and partly in hopes of thereby raising academic standards. Some schools have ended the policy of passing students from grade to grade whatever their achievement (the "social promotion" policy) and brought back the old practice of flunking students. In some states, students must now pass standardized tests of minimum achievement before they can graduate from high school.

The back-to-basics movement has been sweeping the country since the early 1980s. Many schools have begun to produce more orderly classrooms and higher test scores. But if this movement is carried too far, we will, in a decade or so, likely hear that the schools are turning children into unthinking, conforming robots, and reforms will be called for. There is no final solution to educational problems, because schools have to maintain a constantly shifting balance between the competing needs of the individual and society, the needs for creativity and conformity, and the needs for freedom and discipline.

School Choice

In the late 1960s, a new idea began to receive considerable publicity. It was vintage USA: if there were more competition among schools, perhaps schools would be better. After all, people were entitled to more freedom in choosing where their children would be educated. This idea inspired proposals for voucher plans. Public schools have a virtual monopoly on public funds for education, and children attend schools depending, for the most part, on where they live. A voucher plan can change this situation. In a sense, parents, not schools, receive public money. They receive it in the form of a voucher, which they use to pay for their children's attendance at the schools of their choice. The schools receive money from the government in return for the vouchers. The greater the number of parents who choose a particular school, the more money it receives. The idea is to force the public schools to compete with each other, and with private and parochial schools, for "customers." Presumably, good schools would attract plenty of students, and poor schools would be forced either to improve or to close.

But the majority of teachers and their unions, along with some civil rights groups, opposed vouchers for several reasons: Vouchers would encourage white parents to choose schools on the basis of racial or ethnic prejudice. They would promote economic and racial segregation and, eventually, greater divisiveness in U.S. society generally. If vouchers stimulated competition, they would probably also stimulate hucksterism, such as offering field trips to Disneyland. Moreover, because a voucher plan would mean giving government money to religious schools, it would violate the separation of church and state required by the Constitution (Hegedus, 1976). In any event, the voucher plan

never caught on, and finally the government let it die in the late 1970s.

In the 1990s, however, popular support has grown significantly because many schools continue to have such problems as overcrowding, violence, and poor test scores. The federal government has considered providing vouchers in the form of tuition tax credits for enrolling children in any schools, including private or parochial schools. A number of states have already started "school choice" programs. One immediate impact has been the proliferation of TV commercials and other ads promoting various schools (Newman, 1994). But will school choice greatly improve poor schools as its advocates believe? It is still too early to tell.

Home Schooling

There has been phenomenal growth in the number of children who receive their formal education at home. Today there are about 500,000 such children, compared with only 12,500 in the late 1970s (Gibbs, 1994). Most of the home schooling parents are fundamentalist Christians who believe that religion is either abused or ignored in the public school. Other parents reject public education because of poor academic standards, overcrowding, or lack of safety. Most homeschooling parents have some college, with median incomes between $35,000 and $50,000. Over 90 percent are white (McArdle, 1994).

There are different kinds of home-based curricula. One is the back-to-basics approach, which emphasizes the three R's, patriotism, and Bible studies. It is free of sex education, drug abuse programs, AIDS education, self-esteem exercises, and other nonacademic programs that are often provided in public schools. Most back-to-basics programs teach reading phonetically; use fact-rich history, geography, and science texts; and emphasize simple repetition and drill methods.

Another type of home teaching is the "unschooling" approach, similar to the alternative-school philosophy discussed previously. It offers children the freedom to pursue their interests, without adult interference. But the parent provides various educational resources such as encyclopedias, dictionaries, and atlases. The parent also teaches concepts related to the activities in which the children have chosen to get involved.

A third type of home curriculum emphasizes classical learning. Children are taught to read "great books," to memorize important facts, and to think logically and express their ideas effectively. They study not only classical literature but also history, geography, and Latin or some other foreign language in the early grades. This kind of curriculum has long been popular with missionary and diplomatic families stationed abroad. Famous figures of the past such as Abraham Lincoln, Thomas Edison, Leo Tolstoy, and John Stuart Mill had this kind of home schooling during their childhood. Because it largely concentrates on academic lessons, home schooling requires only about three hours a day, as opposed to six hours in public schools (Seuffert, 1990).

Home schooling has been criticized for depriving children of the opportunity to interact with their peers. Such criticism is based on the popular assumption that children need to socialize with their peers in order to learn how to get along with people. But many home schoolers are taught to develop social skills by associating with people of different ages and backgrounds rather than with mostly their peers (Seuffert, 1990).

What about the quality of home education? There are stories about successful home schoolers. Sociologist David Colfax and his wife Micki have been teaching their four sons at home since 1973. Their oldest son has graduated from Harvard with high honors, two younger brothers are now attending Harvard, and the youngest will eventually go to the same university. There is some evidence that home schoolers score higher on standardized tests than students in conventional schools. Undoubtedly, some home schools turn out to be dis-

asters, but their advocates argue that public schools are no better—they already are disasters (Allis, 1990, McArdle, 1994).

Lifelong Learning

Yet another trend in education has involved not children and adolescents but adults who have been out of school for some time. The appeal of "lifelong learning" has led many adults to return to the classroom, often for formal college credits. Most of these lifelong learners are enrolled in two-year community colleges. But seeing the popularity of adult education in community colleges and facing declining enrollments of traditional students, many four-year colleges and universities have offered their own continuing education programs. Today, adults aged 35 and older make up over 16 percent of total enrollment, nearly twice the figure of 20 years ago (Figure 16.5). And adults older than 24 account for about 44 percent of total enrollment, and are expected to represent half of all undergraduates by the year 2000 (Levine, 1993).

Among the students in continuing education programs are blue-collar workers seeking a promotion, a raise, or a new career; homemakers preparing to enter the job market at middle age; retired people seeking to pursue interests postponed or dormant during their working years; and people who want to enrich

Adult students on the campus of the University of North Carolina, Asheville. The appeal of "lifelong learning" has led many adults to return to the classroom, often for formal college credits.

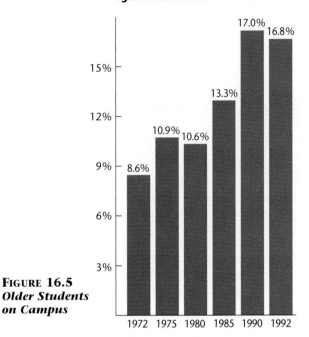

Percentage of college students aged 35 and older

17.0%
16.8%

15%

13.3%

12%
10.9% 10.6%

9%
8.6%

6%

3%

FIGURE 16.5
***Older Students
on Campus***

1972 1975 1980 1985 1990 1992

Source: Data from Census Bureau, 1994.

unusual times, even weekends, and sometimes outside conventional classrooms, in various community facilities such as libraries. Their requirements are flexible, too. Some programs allow students to earn college credits without taking a course, by passing an examination or by proving their competency through their job, hobby, writing, and so on. In the future, the students will also take courses by audiocassette, videocassette, CD-ROM, and independent study. Many courses offered on the campus will be shorter and more focused than typical college courses. Since most of the students will be over age 25 and working full time, most of the courses currently designed for lifelong learners may well become the standard curricula at most colleges and universities.

Questions for Discussion and Review

1. How can Head Start improve academic performance?

2. What are the differences between the alternative-school and back-to-basics movements?

3. What is a voucher plan, and why do many teachers and some civil rights groups oppose this kind of educational practice?

4. Can home schooling eventually replace the existing school system? Why or why not?

5. How have community college and continuing education programs tried to meet the educational needs of adults?

the quality of their personal, family, and social lives. Most of these adults are serious students, as 60 percent are enrolled in a degree program (Cohen and Brawer, 1982; *Futurist*, 1989).

To accommodate their students' diverse responsibilities and interests, continuing education courses tend to be flexible. The courses may be offered at

CHAPTER REVIEW

1. *What are the functions of education?* The main functions are teaching knowledge and skills, enhancing social mobility, promoting national unity, and providing custodial care.

2. *Does "Americanization" mean preserving all cultures brought to the United States by immigrants from all over the world?* The answer, according to the conflict perspective, is no, because much of the WASP culture is imposed on U.S. minorities. *Does education reduce social inequality?* According to the conflict perspective, education does the opposite, reinforcing inequality by channeling students of different socioeconomic backgrounds into different classes and colleges.

3. *According to symbolic interactionism, how does the Pygmalion effect work?* Certain expectations about students lead teachers to behave in a particular way that causes the students to live up to what the teachers have expected of them. *What does the Pygmalion effect have to do with school tracking?* Because of tracking, students who are perceived positively or negatively are treated accordingly so that they end up doing well or poorly in school.

4. *Does the decline in standardized test scores mean that there is a crisis in U.S. education?* Not necessarily. The drop in test scores may have reflected the opening up of educational opportunities for the poor and minorities. Lower achievement scores in the United

States compared to other industrialized countries may have also reflected the impact of democratization. The United States is not the only country having some problems with its schools. Thus U.S. education is not as bad as it appears though it always needs improvement.

5. *What are the main features of U.S. educational bureaucracy?* The bureaucracy is huge, and schools across the country are remarkably similar. It is operated with formal rules that dictate who has authority over whom. It is efficient in rendering education to masses of people, but its impersonality makes it difficult to deal with individuals' unique needs and problems. *What are U.S. teachers like?* In view of their college degrees, they appear quite qualified for their jobs. Most teachers teach primarily because they like to do so rather than because they expect to earn much money.

6. *What is the nature of the youth culture in high school?* It emphasizes the importance of looks, popularity, or athletics at the expense of intellectual pursuit. *Why do private school students have higher academic achievement than their peers in public schools?* A major reason is that private schools demand much more of their students. *What are college subcultures like?* There are four college subcultures: collegiate, vocational, academic, and nonconformist.

7. *How do the schools in different societies vary from one another?* In Belgium, there are proportionately more teachers than in virtually all other countries. In Finland, schooling is rigorous and all higher education is free, making the nation the most educated in the world. In France, teachers are allowed to teach in any way, without interference from bureaucrats. In Japan, schooling is intense and pervasive so as to produce a high-achieving society, but it has also generated student violence and truancy. In Portugal, students' math performance is poor, partly because of a lack of discipline among students and teachers and inadequate support from parents.

8. *What are the major educational trends that have emerged in the United States?* One is Head Start, designed to help young disadvantaged children become better students. Another is alternative schools, which foster student initiative and creativity. A third trend is the back-to-basics movement, which teaches discipline and basic skills. A fourth trend is school choice, which reflects an effort to improve schools by establishing competition among

them for students. A fifth trend is home schooling, where children are taught by parents. And a sixth trend is lifelong learning, involving adults who want to continue their education by attending college.

KEY TERMS

Academic subculture The college subculture that stresses the pursuit of scholarly achievement largely for its own sake (p. 373).

Alternative school A school that encourages student creativity by allowing the freedom to choose learning materials within the classroom (p. 377).

Collegiate subculture The college subculture that revolves around fraternities, sororities, parties, drinking, football, and similar activities (p. 372).

Compensatory education A school program intended to improve the academic performance of socially and educationally disadvantaged children (p. 376).

Cultural imperialism The practice of making the minorities accept the dominant groups culture (p. 365).

Nonconformist subculture The college subculture that advocates rebellion from conventional society (p. 373).

Pygmalion effect The impact of a teacher's expectations on student performance (p. 366).

Tracking The system of sorting students into different groups according to ability (p. 365).

Vocational subculture The college subculture that emphasizes hard work in order to get good jobs after graduation (p. 373).

SUGGESTED READINGS

Chubb, John E., and Terry M. Moe. 1990. *Politics, Markets, and America's Schools.* Washington, D.C.: Brookings Institution. Shows how excessive bureaucracy has ruined public education, and proposes that schools be run entirely by teachers and that parents be allowed to choose schools for their children.

Eckert, Penelope. 1989. *Jocks and Burnouts: Social Categories and Identity in High School.* New York: Teachers College Press. An analysis of middle-class and working-class high school students, showing how social class influences the culture of adolescent peer groups.

Goodlad, John I. 1984. *A Place Called School: Prospects for the Future.* New York: McGraw-Hill. Presents a wealth of research findings about what goes on in U.S. elementary and secondary schools.

McKenna, Francis R. 1993. *Schooling in America.* Dubuque, Iowa: Kendall/Hunt. A collection of articles dealing with reform, power, and equity in the U.S. educational system.

Sizer, Theodore R. 1984. *Horace's Compromise: The Dilemma of the American High School.* Boston: Houghton Mifflin. A remarkable research report on 80 high schools throughout the United States; highly enjoyable to read because of its personal and lively style of writing.

RELIGION

Myths and Realities

MYTH: *A belief in God is present in all religions.*
REALITY: A belief in God is present only in *theistic* religions, such as Christianity and Islam. Other religions that do not involve a belief in God are *ethicalism,* such as Buddhism or Confucianism, which emphasizes moral principles as guides for living a righteous life, and *animism,* such as shamanism or totemism, which believes in spirits capable of helping or harming people.

MYTH: *It is always beneficial for the faithful to identify as strongly as possible with their religion.*
REALITY: History has shown that when people identify too strongly with their religion, they tend to end up believing that there is only one true religion, namely, their own. Consequently, they are likely to be intolerant of others' religions, which they consider false.

MYTH: *People who are affiliated with a successful, respectable, or popular religion must be very religious. Otherwise, their religion cannot be successful.*
REALITY: The more successful a religion is, the less religious its members become.

n St. Anthony's Roman Catholic Church in the South Bronx of New York City, congregants sway back and forth with their arms above their heads to a Caribbean rhythm. Amid the sounds of an amplified guitar and tambourine filling the crowded church, shouts of "Blessed be God. Alleluia, Alleluia!" can be heard. Other voices offer thanks to God or beseech God for help with loneliness, illness, and other problems. At the end of the mass, some worshipers are crying; others embracing (Newman, 1992).

The influence of religion reaches far beyond the walls of this church. In fact, religion is everywhere. Some form of religious belief can be found all over the world (see Figure 17.1), ranging from belief in an invisible deity to worship of an animal. Some people may see religion as a carryover from the superstitious past, hence highly important only for "primitive" or "backward" societies. Actually, religion is also very much a part of modern social life. Although the United States is one of the world's most scientifically and technologically advanced societies, it is also one of the most religious. An overwhelming majority of us believe in God. Most (78 percent) pray at least once a week, and more than half (57 percent) pray at least once a day. Even among the 13 percent of U.S. adults who are atheists or agnostics, one in five prays daily, wagering that there is a God listening to them (Woodward, 1992).

FIGURE 17.1
Religions Around the Globe

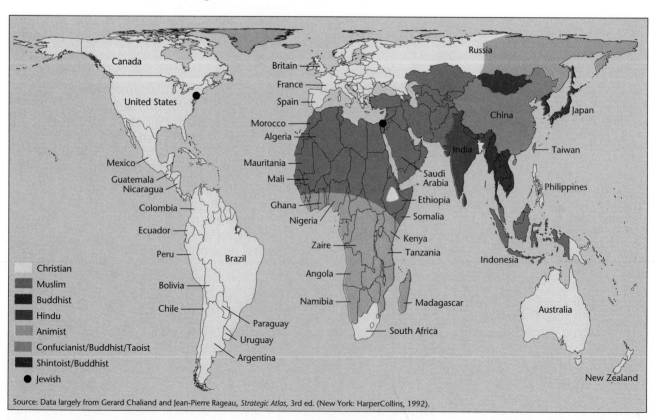

Source: Data largely from Gerard Chaliand and Jean-Pierre Rageau, *Strategic Atlas*, 3rd ed. (New York: HarperCollins, 1992).

What exactly do religious people believe? What can religion do for people? Why does religion continue to play a vital role in modern society? In trying to answer questions such as these, sociologists do not analyze religious beliefs for their truth or falsity. As a science, sociology can neither support nor undermine the validity of any religion. What sociologists do is study religion as a social institution—an institution that, like the family or education, is created by human beings and fulfills human rather than divine needs. Thus, in this chapter, we deal with the human dimensions of religion.

A GLOBAL ANALYSIS OF RELIGION

According to some native religions of Africa, one god created the world, but he then withdrew. The spirits of ancestors and other gods now influence the world. These gods, as well as the creating god, are neither good nor evil, but they require animal sacrifices (Curtin et al., 1978). Christians hold that there is one all-powerful and all-good God and that one sacrifice—the death of Christ—was sufficient to redeem all people. Different as these religions are, they have several elements in common, elements characteristic of all religions.

These elements can be found in Emile Durkheim's (1915) classic definition of **religion** as a unified system of beliefs and practices regarding sacred things that unites its adherents into a single moral community. Thus, religion consists of (1) something that is considered **sacred**, which transcends the everyday world and inspires awe and reverence, (2) a set of beliefs about the sacred thing, (3) the affirmation of beliefs through **rituals**—a ceremonial form of religious activity, and (4) an organization of believers who participate in the same rituals.

These four elements are present in theistic or god-related religions such as Christianity, Judaism, and Islam. But the same elements can also be found in beliefs that do not involve a deity. Democracy, socialism, Confucianism, and humanism are just as sacred to their adherents as God is to believers. These also have their own beliefs, rituals, and communities. Thus, they can be considered religions in the same way as Christianity, Judaism, and Islam are. In fact, religion appears in many different forms, each with what it regards as sacred along with its own beliefs, rituals, and community. They can be classified into three major types: **theism**, the type of religion that centers on the worship of a god or gods; **ethicalism**, the type of religion that emphasizes moral principles as guides for living a righteous life; and **animism**, the belief in spirits capable of helping or harming people.

Theism

Theistic religions define the sacred as one or more supernatural beings. These religions center on the worship of a god or gods. There are two subtypes of theism: **monotheism**, or belief in one god, and **polytheism**, belief in more than one god.

Christianity, Judaism, Islam, and Zoroastrianism are all monotheistic. With over a billion followers, Christianity is the world's largest religion. It is split into three principal groups—Roman Catholic, Protestant, and Eastern Orthodox—but these groups share a belief in God as the creator of the world and in Jesus as its savior. Judaism worships Yahweh, the God of the Old Testament, as the creator of the universe and teaches that he chose the people of Israel as witness to his presence. Islam, the world's second-largest religion, was established by the prophet Muhammad in the seventh century A.D. It emphasizes that believers must surrender totally to the will of Allah (God), the creator, sustainer, and restorer of the world. Zoroastrianism is an ancient, pre-Christian religion, which still has a quarter of a million followers known as Parsees in India. Parsees believe in one supreme God whose omnipotence is, however, temporarily limited by an ongoing battle with evil—although God is ensured of eventual victory. The faithful join forces with God by keeping themselves pure through ablution, penance, and prayers.

The best-known polytheistic faith is Hinduism. The great majority of Hindus live in India. In small villages throughout India, countless gods are worshiped, each believed to have a specific sphere of influence, such as childbirth, sickness, the harvest, or rain. These local deities are often looked on as manifestations of higher gods. Hinduism also teaches that we are *reincarnated*—born and reborn again and again—into new human or animal bodies. People may escape the cycle of reincarnation and achieve salvation by practicing mystical contemplation and

Islam, like Judaism, Christianity, and Zoroastrianism, is a monotheistic religion. Shown here, Muslim worshipers in Mauritius, an island in the Indian Ocean, wearing hooks and needles as part of the ritual, form a procession to mark the anniversary of the battle that took the life of the prophet Muhammad's grandson in A.D. 680.

steadfast endurance and by following traditional rules of conduct for their castes, families, and occupations.

Ethicalism

Some religions do not focus on supernatural beings. Instead, *ethicalist religions* ascribe sacredness to moral principles. The heart of these religions is a set of principles they offer as guides for living a righteous life. The best examples are Buddhism, Confucianism, Taoism, and Shintoism.

Buddhism was founded in India in the sixth century B.C. by Gautama, who is known as the Buddha ("enlightened one"). It is today the largest ethical religion. According to Buddhism, there is no independent, unchanging "self" and no physical world—both are illusions. Belief in their reality, attachment to them, and craving for human pleasures are, according to Buddhism, the source of human misery. To escape this misery is to attain Nirvana (salvation). It requires meditation—freeing one's mind from all worldly desires and ideas—and right thinking, right speech, right action, and the right mode of living. Buddhism is widely practiced in many Asian societies.

Confucianism was founded by Confucius (551–479 B.C.) in China. For well over 2,000 years, it was practically the state religion of China. Confucianism stresses personal cultivation through learning and self-examination, so that the individual becomes imbued with confidence and serenity. It also urges harmony between individuals. Confucius

described proper social conduct as "reciprocity," which means, in his words, "Do not do to others what you would not want others to do to you."

Like Confucianism, Taoism has shaped the Chinese character for more than 2,000 years, but today has a much smaller following. Whereas Confucianism compels its adherents to be austere and duty-conscious, Taoism encourages joyful, carefree quietism, nonintervention, or "not overdoing." According to Taoism, every deliberate intervention in the natural course of events sooner or later turns into the opposite of what was intended. In essence, in a mystical manner, Taoism tells people to yield totally to the Tao ("the Way"), accepting what is natural and spontaneous in people. Actually, Taoism and Confucianism pursue the same goal—the subordination of individuals to groups, such as families and society. They differ only in the means of achieving that goal. While Confucianism urges *activism* through performance of one's social duties, such as obeying one's parents and being polite to others, Taoism teaches *passivity* through avoidance of self-indulgence, power seeking, and self-aggrandizement.

Shintoism has always been a part of Japanese culture. It teaches that people should strive for *magokoro*—a "bright and pure mind" or "truthfulness, sincerity, or uprightness." This means that individuals must be sincerely interested in doing their best in whatever work they have chosen, and they must be truthful in their relationships with others. Purification, physical and spiritual, is the path to these goals. To remove the dust of humans' wickedness believed to cover their divine nature, purification rites are performed at Shinto shrines.

Animism

Animists believe that spirits, whether helpful or harmful to people, may reside in humans, animals, plants, rivers, or winds. They are not gods to be worshiped, but supernatural forces that can be manipulated to serve human ends. Rituals such as feasting, dancing, fasting, and cleansing are often performed to appease the spirits so that crops can be harvested, fish caught, illness cured, or danger averted. Animism is prevalent in sub-Saharan Africa.

Among indigenous peoples in North and South America, a common type of animism is called **shamanism**, the belief that a spiritual leader can communicate with the spirits by acting as their mouthpiece or letting the soul leave the leader's body and enter the spiritual world. By communicating with the spirits, the shaman ("one who knows") heals the sick, discovers lost animals, sees events in distant places, foresees those in the future, and forecasts prospects for farming, fishing, and hunting.

Another form of animism, popular among native peoples of Australia and some Pacific islands is **totemism**, the belief that a kinship exists between humans and an animal (or, less commonly, a plant). The animal, called a *totem*, represents a human family, a clan, or a group of ancestors. It is thought of as a person—but a person with superhuman power—and it must be treated with respect, awe, and fear. Killing, eating, touching, and even seeing the animal are often prohibited. The totem is relied on as a helper and protector, but it also punishes those who breach a taboo.

Questions for Discussion and Review

1. What are the four basic elements of religion?
2. How do theistic religions differ from ethical and animistic beliefs?

FUNCTIONALIST PERSPECTIVE

According to the functionalist perspective, a religion is of immense importance to society as well as to individuals. Exactly why is religion so important? One answer can be found in Durkheim's classical functionalist theory, another in modern sociologists' functionalist analyses.

Society as Representation of God

Emile Durkheim presented his functionalist view of religion in *The Elementary Forms of Religious Life*, first published in 1912. It was Durkheim's aim to refute the popular view that God—or whatever is worshiped as sacred—is merely an illusion, a figment of human imagination. According to Durkheim, if religion were an illusion, it would have disappeared in rational modern societies. But it has not. "It is inadmissible," said Durkheim, "that systems of ideas like religion, which have held so considerable a place in history, and to which people have turned in all ages for the energy they need to live, should be mere tissues of illusion." If God were merely a product of the individual's imagination, Durkheim also argued, it would occupy the same status as any other idea—a part of the profane world incapable of inspiring reverence, awe, and worship. Instead, God must be sacred and

Among Native Americans, a common type of animism is called shamanism, the belief that a spiritual leader can communicate with the spirits by acting as their mouthpiece or letting the soul leave the leader's body and enter the spiritual world. Here a shaman performs at a Ute ceremony in Utah.

far above humans, as demonstrated by the fact that the deity is widely worshiped.

If this revered entity is both real and superior to us, then what is God? Durkheim's answer: society. Society is more powerful than any of us and beyond our personal control. It is separate from us, yet we are part of it, and it is part of our consciousness. It outlives each of us, and even our children. We are dependent on it, and it demands our obedience to it. It is neither a person nor a thing, yet we feel and know its reality. These attributes of society are also characteristics of the sacred—in Western religions, of God. In short, the sacred, according to Durkheim, is the symbolic representation of society. By worshiping God, we in effect are worshiping society.

Such a view of religion led Durkheim to emphasize that religion functions to preserve social order. Every religion, he argued, possesses both rituals and moral norms. Through their religion's rituals, people sanctify and renew their bonds to one another. Their belief in the sacred and their acceptance of common norms are strengthened. Thus, religion binds the society and helps maintain it.

Functions and Dysfunctions

While Durkheim made the general statement that religion helps to preserve social order, today's functionalist sociologists are more specific on the functions of religion. They also find a paradox in each of these functions: namely, if it were to be too successful in carrying out a positive function, religion could become a negative force in society (O'Dea and Aviad, 1983).

Supportive Function Religion often performs a supportive function by providing consolation, reconciliation, and relief from anxiety. By praying, believers may become less anxious about losing their jobs or about old age and death. Faith may console those who have lost a loved one or are beset by loneliness, disappointment, frustration, or sorrow. Religion can reconcile people to the sinfulness of others, the hostility of enemies, the injustices of society, or other unpleasant aspects of this world. Not surprisingly, as research has shown, religiously active people are healthier and happier (Myers, 1993).

However, if religion offers *too much* support and consolation, it can impede useful social change. Many religions urge their believers to see all worldly things as trivial compared with the life of the spirit. Others perceive this world as a mere way station, or a "vale of tears" that is meant to be a test of love and faith, or even as an illusion. All these beliefs can

encourage the faithful, not only to be consoled but also to endure their suffering docilely. Thus, religions can discourage people from confronting the sources of their suffering, from joining a social or revolutionary movement that may help to alleviate their suffering.

Social Control Function Religion performs a social control function by strengthening conformity to society's norms in at least two ways. First, religion helps to sacralize (make sacred) the norms and values of established society with such commandments as "Thou shalt not kill" and "Thou shalt not steal." Thus religious people are less likely to violate the laws of the state if the laws are taken to be the laws of God. Not surprisingly, as over 50 research studies have shown, religious participation inhibits crime, delinquency, and deviant behavior in general (Ellis, 1985; Peek et al., 1985). Second, religion encourages good, friendly, or cooperative behavior illustrated through the story of the Good Samaritan, the proverb "do unto others as you would have others do unto you," and other such teachings. As a result, as research has indicated, more religious people seem more friendly and cooperative—more likely to stop and comfort a crying child, to be good listeners, and even to get along with loud-mouthed, obnoxious people (Morgan, 1983, 1984).

However, religion's power to reinforce social control may set up yet another roadblock to useful change. Some of the state's laws and values sacralized by religion are unjust and harmful, such as those supporting racial or gender inequality. But the extremely faithful may consider them too sacred to question or change, perhaps saying, for example, "It is God's will that women should stay home and be wives and mothers only."

Prophetic Function Acting as a source of social change, religion may perform the prophetic function. It does this through some leaders who, like the ancient Jewish prophets, challenge the unjust political authorities of their day in order to bring a better life to the people. In the 1950s and 1960s, for example, Dr. Martin Luther King, Jr., led the fight against racial discrimination in the United States. During the 1980s, Anglican Archbishop Desmond Tutu played an important role in the blacks' struggle against the white racist government in South Africa. Similarly, the leader of the Philippines' Roman Catholic church, Jaime Cardinal Sin, helped bring down President Marcos' repressive government.

Sometimes, however, prophetic calls for reform may produce violent fanaticism. During the seventeenth century, some 20,000 peasants in Russia were inspired to burn themselves as a way of protesting

Religion performs the prophetic function through its leaders who challenge the unjust political authority of their day to bring a better life to the people. In this photo, a group of Native Americans are drumming at an environmental rally to save James Bay, in Canada. By viewing ecology as a spiritual issue, Native Americans have tied their religious beliefs to efforts to make social change.

liturgical reforms in the Russian Orthodox Church. In 1420 the Adamites, a religious cult of Bohemians in Europe, set about making holy war to kill the unholy. They believed that they must continue killing until they could make the blood fill the world to "the height of a horse's head" (Morrow, 1978). Today, Muslim terrorists in the Middle East who try to kill their enemies welcome death as God's blessing for themselves.

Identity Function   Religion may perform the identity function by enabling individuals to know who they are, what they are, and what the purpose of their lives is. In modern societies marked by imper-

sonal relations and a confusing variety of values and norms, this function of providing self-identity may be especially important to individuals. Without an identity, people may fall into an existential vacuum, finding life meaningless and merely muddling through.

Intense social conflict, however, is likely to erupt if people identify too strongly with their own religion. Such people tend to believe that there is only one true religion—their own—and become intolerant of all other, "false" religions. Indeed, history is filled with persecutions and wars related to religious differences. Consider the medieval Christian Crusades against Muslim "heathens," the Thirty Years' War

between Catholics and Protestants in seventeenth-century Europe, the persecution and slaughter of Mormons in the United States during the last century, the Hindu-Muslim conflicts that resulted in the creation of mostly Hindu India and a separate Islamic Republic of Pakistan in 1947, the strife between Protestants and Catholics in Northern Ireland, and the clash between Buddhists and Hindus that plagues the Asian nation of Sri Lanka today.

Questions for Discussion and Review

1. Why did Emile Durkheim argue that society is a representation of God?
2. How can positive functions of religion turn into negative forces in society?

CONFLICT PERSPECTIVE

Unlike Durkheim, Karl Marx considered religious beliefs to be mere illusions. Nevertheless, Marx believed those illusions to be a powerful force in society.

A Supporter of the Ruling Class

Marx presented the conflict theory that in a society divided into classes, the dominant religion usually represents the interests of the ruling class. The religion disguises and justifies the power of that class, though. The deception is not deliberate. The ruling class is not conscious of the true state of things. Yet religion, argued Marx, is nonetheless a real and an oppressive illusion, one that helps the ruling class perpetuate its domination of the masses. In medieval Europe, the Roman Catholic Church bolstered the feudal system by promoting the notion that kings ruled by divine right. In India the Hindu religion for thousands of years has provided religious justification for the caste system. Religion supports the ruling class by justifying existing inequalities.

The Opium of the Masses

If religion is merely an oppressive illusion, why would the masses support and even cling to it? The reason, according to Marx, is the prevailing social inequality and oppression, which drive the masses to seek solace somewhere. "Religion," Marx declared, "is

the sigh of the oppressed creature, the heart of a heartless world, the soul of soulless circumstances. It is the opium of the people" (Acton, 1967). Opium offers relief and escape, and it drains one's will to find the source of problems. Similarly, religion brings relief to oppressed workers, dulls their sensitivity to suffering, and diverts them from attacking the root of their pain—their exploitation by the wealthy and powerful. Religion accomplishes all this by emphasizing the superiority of spiritual over earthly matters or promising eternal bliss in the afterlife with such doctrines as "Blessed are the poor." As a result, religion ends up "alienating" workers from themselves by acquiring a harmful power over them—causing them to develop a "false consciousness," an acceptance of the dominance of their oppressors.

Many studies have supported Marx's assumption that poverty or oppression tends to make people embrace religion for consolation (Wimberley, 1984). This serves as a useful counterbalance against the functionalist analysis. But at the same time it should be noted, as discussed earlier, that sometimes religion does fight oppression through its prophetic function.

Questions for Discussion and Review

1. According to Karl Marx, how does religion support the ruling class?
2. What did Marx mean when he wrote that religion is the opium of the people?

SYMBOLIC INTERACTIONIST PERSPECTIVE

Marx's analysis suggests that religion in general induces a passive resignation to poverty. But Max Weber saw that at least one religion—Protestantism—could promote an active pursuit of wealth.

An Interpretation of the World

As a symbolic interactionist, Weber regarded religion as an interpretation of the world around us that powerfully influences our behavior toward that world. He noticed that the early Protestants in Europe, especially those of the Calvinist sect, had a unique belief. The belief was that long before they were born, God had predestined them to either salvation in heaven or damnation in hell. But they could not know which would be their eternal destiny. This generated a great deal of anxiety. To relieve anxiety, the Calvinists turned to constant self-control and work. They further believed that, whether saved or damned, the faithful must work hard for the glory of God so as to establish God's kingdom on earth. Work came to be seen as a "calling" from God, and the worldly success that work brought came to be interpreted as a sign of election to heaven. Inevitably, the Calvinists worked extremely hard.

The Rise of Capitalism

But the Calvinists also had a unique definition of hard work. To them, the purpose of hard work was to glorify God, not to produce wealth to enable people to indulge in their own pleasures. Thus the Calvinists believed that they should not spend their wealth on worldly pleasures. Instead, they invested and reinvested their profits to make their businesses grow. The constant accumulation of wealth—the continual investment of profit—lay a foundation for capitalism to emerge in the Protestant societies.

Weber further argued that capitalism did not emerge in predominantly Catholic countries or China or India because their world views differed from the Protestant ethic. Catholicism does not teach predestination. It encourages people to seek their rewards in heaven, and it does not view earthly success as a sign of God's favor. Confucianism values social harmony, not individualistic strivings. Taoism teaches acceptance of the world as it is and withdrawal from it. Buddhism views worldly things as

illusory and encourages escape from them through meditation. Hinduism requires its believers to endure the hardships of life and fulfill the obligations of their respective castes. These religions, Weber argued, did not offer ideas and habits favorable to the development of capitalist industrialism, as Calvinist Protestantism did.

But it is difficult to see how Weber's theory can be valid today. The Catholics in the United States are now economically better off than many Protestants, such as Methodists and Baptists (see Figure 17.2). Capitalism is also booming in such non-Protestant countries as Japan, South Korea, and Taiwan. Nevertheless, Weber's theory sounds convincing in explaining the *emergence* of capitalism in Europe.

Questions for Discussion and Review

1. How did the early Protestants in Europe interpret the world?
2. How did the Calvinist view of the world help develop capitalism?

DEALING WITH THE SECULAR WORLD: CONFRONTATION OR COMPROMISE?

A religion is concerned with the sacred, but it exists in this world, an earthly rather than heavenly society. It must stand in some relation to that society—in harmony or disharmony, as an integral part of other institutions or apart from them, or in some position between these extremes. Even within Christianity, different groups have established different relations to society.

Church and Sect

Christian organizations can be divided into two categories: the church and the sect. The church compromises with society; the sect confronts it. Many groups do not quite fit into either of these extreme categories, but we can think of mainline Protestant groups, such as the Episcopal and Presbyterian churches, as examples of a church, whereas Pentecostals and Jehovah's Witnesses are examples of a sect.

A **church** is a relatively large, well-established religious organization that is integrated into the society and does not make strict demands on its members. It has a formalized structure of belief, ritual and

FIGURE 17.2
How Religions Rank in Income

Median annual household income

Jewish	$36,700
Episcopal	$33,000
Presbyterian	$29,000
Roman Catholic	$27,700
Methodist	$25,100
Evangelical	$21,900
Jehovah's Witness	$20,900
Baptist	$20,600
Pentecostal	$19,400

Source: Data from Barry A. Kosmin and Seymour P. Lachman, *One Nation Under God* (New York: Harmony Books, 1993).

authority. It is also an inclusive organization, welcoming members from a wide spectrum of social backgrounds. Thus, members often have little but their religion in common, and they may hardly know one another. Members tend to be born into the church, and the church sets up few if any requirements for membership. Its demands, on both its members and society, are far from exacting. Over the years, the church has learned to take a relatively tolerant attitude toward its members' failings. It has learned to reconcile itself one way or another with the institutions of the society, coexisting in relative peace with society's secular values.

The church's compromises do not satisfy the **sect,** a relatively small religious group that sets itself apart from society and makes heavy demands on its members. It begins with a relatively small religious movement that has broken away from an established church. Time and again, groups have split off from Christian churches because some members believed the church had become too worldly. The sect that results holds itself separate from society, and it demands from its members a deep religious experience, strong loyalty to the group, and rejection of the larger society and its values. The sect is a tightly knit community, offering close personal relations among its members.

Dilemmas of Success

Most pure sects do not last long. They either fail to maintain their membership and disappear, or they undergo change. Consider Methodism, which was founded in opposition to the Church of England. It was at first a sect that sought to correct social injustices and to aid the poor. Then Irish immigrants brought it to the United States, where it was initially associated with the lower classes. But it has become a highly institutionalized religion today—successful, respectable, middle class, and less demanding of its members.

A paradoxical relation exists between religiosity and success. The more "successful" a religion is—in the sense of being more popular and more respectable in society as well as having more members—the less religious its members tend to be. Established churches, such as the Episcopal, Methodist, and Catholic, are more successful than sects such as the Amish and Jehovah's Witnesses. But members of sects tend to be more religious, devoting more of their time to such religious matters as reading the Bible, praying, and door-to-door evangelizing. They may even show greater willingness to suffer or even die for their beliefs, as did their ancient counterparts such as Jesus, his disciples, and early

The more successful religions, such as the Roman Catholic church, need a large organization to function smoothly. But such an organization has an elaborate hierarchy of authority, with some members occupying higher positions than others that is, in effect, a form of social inequality. This becomes a dilemma for the church because it professes that all people are equal before God. Sects such as the Jehovah Witnesses, with fewer members and less organization, do not have the same dilemma.

Christians. Success presents a religion with at least five dilemmas (O'Dea and Aviad, 1983).

1. *The dilemma of mixed motivation.* The success of a church offers its leaders new, self-centered motives for their careers—motives such as power and prestige. A similar change may occur among the rank and file. Once a religion is institutionalized, its members may be born into the church rather than converted to it. The security, friendship, or prestige that the church offers may become a more important motive for membership than religious conviction. These motives may be useful for ensuring the success of a church, but they are basically secular, opposed to the religious doctrines that stress single-minded devotion to God and that emphasize God-centered rather than human-centered needs.

2. *The dilemma of administrative order.* The organization that emerges with institutionalization brings another problem as well: bureaucracy. The Roman Catholic Church, for example, has a vast bureaucracy, with an elaborate hierarchy including the pope, cardinals, archbishops, bishops, monsignors, priests—plus many other ranks and lines of authority. Such an administrative order is necessary for maintaining the success of the church. But its hierarchy of positions—which is essentially a practice of social inequality—is contrary to the religious idea that all people are equal before God and should be treated as such.

3. *The symbolic dilemma.* At the heart of religions are symbolic expressions of the sacred. They are necessary for ensuring the success of a church, because they can make profound, complex religious concepts comprehensible and help people relate to God better. But people may end up misusing the symbols and missing the message behind them. The cross, for example, is a Christian symbol of God's love for humanity, which should cause us to accept and worship Christ with fervor. But illiterate Christians in traditional societies may be so awed by the cross that they worship it as an idol or use it as a talisman to ward off evil spirits. Better-educated Christians in traditional and industrial countries may find the cross so beautiful that they use it as a mere ornament. In short, the sacred symbols of a popular religion can lead to such irreligious behaviors as idolatry and vulgarization of God.

4. *The dilemma of oversimplification.* This is similar to the symbolic dilemma. In order to ensure the success of its religion, the institutionalized church oversimplifies its teachings to make them easily comprehensible. To make people understand how much God still loves us even though we are sinful or worthless, Christian preachers may tell the story about the prodigal son or about the lost sheep. God is com-

pared to the prodigal son's father, who still loves us despite our sins like those of the prodigal son, or God is portrayed as the shepherd who is still looking everywhere for his one lost sheep, though he still has many sheep left. Just as symbols may be transformed into idols, however, the stories, parables, fables, and other preaching techniques of oversimplification may become mere objects of admiration and awe, causing the faithful to miss the message behind the stories. For example, some Christians may say "Oh, how moving the prodigal son story is!" but they continue to sin.

5. *The dilemma of power.* In societies where there is no separation of religion and state, religious organizations use the state to enforce religious conformity and in turn lend their authority to sanctify what the state does. Coercion may replace faith. In many places in the past, heresy was punished by torture and even death. All this may ensure the success of the church but is basically irreligious, because the church is supposed to show compassion, love, and forgiveness instead.

Today a more subtle form of power—radio and television—is employed to capture the souls of prospective followers. Preachers with easy access to the media are more successful than others. But the success is usually bought at the price of irreligiosity. TV evangelists tend to sell God like household goods, transforming the holy into the profane. Urging his viewers to send in money ("donation") to buy his product (God), televangelist Richard Roberts once asked them to "sow a seed on your MasterCard, your VISA, or your American Express, and then when you do, expect God to open the windows of heaven and pour you out a blessing" (Woodward, 1987).

Church and State

In 1978, when the whole world was shocked by the Jonestown bloodbath in which over 900 U.S. cult members committed suicide, President Jimmy Carter commented, "I don't think we ought to have an overreaction because of the Jonestown tragedy by injecting government into trying to control people's religious beliefs." This is testimony to the unusually high degree of religious tolerance in the United States. Without this tolerance, the diversity of U.S. religions would not be possible.

This diversity would have appalled some of the earliest settlers of this country. They came to the New World in order to establish a "Holy Commonwealth," a community that would be ruled by church officials. In the Puritans' republic, "theology was wedded to politics and politics to the progress of the kingdom of

God" (Bercovitch, 1978). Even after independence was won, some of the states had official religions. But the Constitution guarantees religious freedom by forbidding government interference in religious activities. Eventually, the courts interpreted this guarantee to mean that church and state must be kept separate and that the government, including state governments, must refrain from promoting religion.

Thus, the United States has no official religion. But, in practice, the separation of church and state is far from complete. In a sense, the U.S. government does support religion in general, by exempting religious organizations from taxation. Every day in public schools students salute the flag with the affirmation of "one nation, *under God.*" Even at the opening of legislative sessions, presidential inaugurations, and other public ceremonial occasions, ministers, priests, and rabbis offer their religious invocations or benedictions. The state occasionally even intervenes in religious affairs. Thus church activities are investigated if a church is suspected of abusing its tax-exemption privileges or otherwise violating the law. The government has even forbidden activities that some groups consider religious, such as prohibiting Mormons from practicing polygamy or forcing Christian Scientists in some cases to accept blood transfusions.

There is, then, no strict separation between church and state in our society. According to a recent poll, only slightly over half of U.S. adults agree with the statement that "we have to keep church and state completely separate" (Sheler, 1994). Other surveys show that most people do not object to the inclusion of religion in the public realm as long as the religion involved represents all faiths rather than one particular faith. A majority of people also favor *voluntary* prayer by public school students themselves (NORC, 1994).

Civil Religion

Instead of being formally separated, church and state are fully integrated in the form of **civil religion**, a collection of beliefs, symbols, and rituals that sanctify the dominant values of a society. The civil religion is a hybrid of religion and politics. The state takes up certain religious ideas and symbols, and religion sacralizes certain political principles, backing up the government's claim to a right to rule with its own moral authority. Thus a civil religion can unify the citizens of a country by heightening their sense of patriotism.

The U.S. civil religion includes faith in what is popularly known as the American way of life, with freedom, democracy, equality, individualism, effi-

ciency, and other typically U.S. values as its creeds. The "American way of life," said Will Herberg (1983), is the common religion of our society by which we define ourselves and establish our unity. Protestantism, Catholicism, and Judaism are its "sub-faiths."

God plays an important role in this civil religion. God is cited on our coins ("In God We Trust") and in national hymns ("God Bless America"). References to God are made in all oaths of office, in courtroom procedures, at political conventions, in the inaugural address of every president, and on practically all formal public occasions.

But the God of U.S. civil religion is not the god of any particular church. Adherence to U.S. civil religion requires only our belief in God, however we choose to define the deity—as a personal God, an impersonal force, a supreme power, an ideal, or whatever. We do not have to believe in Moses, Jesus, the Bible, heaven and hell, or any other doctrine of a particular religion. We are instead exhorted to go to any church of our choice. As President Eisenhower said, "Our government makes no sense, unless it is founded on a deeply felt religious faith—*and I don't care what it is.*" The civil religion does not favor one particular church but religion in general. Everyone is expected at least to pay lip service to religious principles, if not to join a church or synagogue. It is considered un-American to be godless or, worse, to attack religion.

Like a genuine religion, U.S. civil religion contains symbols, rituals, and scriptures. Its sacred writings are the Declaration of Independence and the Constitution. George Washington is seen as the Moses who led his people out of the hands of tyranny. Abraham Lincoln, our martyred president, is seen as the crucified Jesus; his Gettysburg Address is a New Testament. The civil religion's holy days are the Fourth of July, Thanksgiving, Memorial Day, and Veterans Day, when we sing sacred hymns such as "The Star-Spangled Banner" and "America the Beautiful," invoke the name of God, listen to sermonlike speeches, and watch ritualistic parades. The U.S. flag, like the Christian cross, is supposed to inspire devotion.

Questions for Discussion and Review

1. What is the difference between church and sect?
2. What problems are likely to occur when a church becomes highly successful?
3. Do you support the separation of church and state? Why or why not?
4. What is the nature of the U.S. civil religion?

RELIGION IN THE UNITED STATES

As early as 1835, Alexis de Tocqueville observed that "there is no country in the world in which the Christian religion retains a greater influence over the souls of men" than in the United States. Still today, religion is pervasive in our society. According to several surveys, about 95 percent of U.S. adults believe in God, 90 percent pray, and 88 percent believe that God loves them. Some 56 percent also consider religion "very important" in their lives. By contrast, far smaller proportions of Italians, Spaniards, Belgians, Germans, Britons, and other Europeans believe in God or regard religion as very important in their lives (Gallup and Castelli, 1989; NORC, 1994)

Just what is it that all these people in the United States believe? There is an amazing diversity of religions in the U.S. The diversity reflects not only the faithful's differences in religious affiliations but also their differences in social characteristics such as residence, social and political values, social class, and age, as we see in this section.

Religious Affiliation

There are more than 280 religious denominations in the country, but a few large churches have the allegiance of most people. Protestants constitute the largest group, although Catholics outnumber the largest Protestant denomination—the Baptists.

FIGURE 17.3
Religious Affiliations in the United States

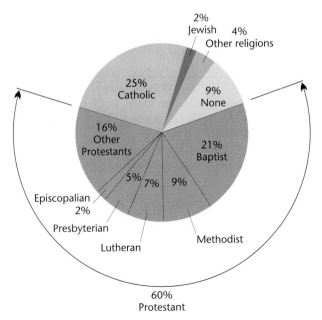

Source: Data from National Opinion Research Center, 1994.

According to the latest survey, 92 percent of the U.S. adult population have a specific religious preference, with 60 percent saying they are Protestants, 25 percent Catholics, and 2 percent Jews. Among the Protestants, the Baptists are the largest group (see Figure 17.3).

The correlation between affiliation with an organized religion and religious belief and practice is far from perfect. Although 91 percent of the U.S. population claim to have a religious preference, only a small minority (about 20 percent of Protestants and 28 percent of Catholics) attend religious services regularly (Hadaway et al., 1993). Among those who do go to church, very few do so for strictly religious reasons. As a survey of Minnesota Christians has shown, less than 10 percent cited worship as the primary reason they attend church (Bilheimer, 1983). Apparently, religious affiliation reflects something besides religious belief and practice. Belonging to a church can also afford a way of conforming to social norms or a way of enjoying fellowship.

Residential Patterns

Catholics and Jews are more likely than other religious groups to live in cities; Protestants tend more to live in small towns and rural areas. Catholics, Jews, Episcopalians, and Presbyterians can be found mostly in the Northeast. Baptists, Methodists, and Lutherans predominate in the South and West. The largest proportions of other religions, such as the Mormons and Disciples of Christ, are in the Midwest. Religiosity varies also by region. Southerners seem to be the most religious, and westerners the least, with midwesterners ranking second and easterners third (Gallup and Castelli, 1989).

Social and Political Values

Most religious groups favor the Democratic party over the Republican, just as the majority of the U.S. population do. But Protestants are not as overwhelmingly Democratic as Catholics and Jews. In fact, Protestants as a group are more Republican than Democratic. In general, Protestants are more socially conservative and less supportive of civil liberties than Catholics and Jews. Among Protestants, higher-income groups such as Episcopalians and Presbyterians are most likely to be socially liberal and pro-civil liberties, whereas lower-income groups such as Baptists and Pentecostals are most likely to be socially conservative and least supportive of civil liberties (Lipset and Raab, 1978; Gallup and Castelli, 1989; NORC, 1994).

Class Backgrounds

Although they may consider themselves equal before God, various religious groups are far from equal socioeconomically. They have different statuses, and they tend to attract people from different educational and income levels. Usually, Jews, Episcopalians, and Presbyterians top the status hierarchy. They are followed by Catholics and Methodists, and trailed by Baptists and Pentecostals (see again Figure 17.2, p. 393).

Social class also influences people's religious participation. In general, the higher their classes, the more likely they are to attend church regularly, join Bible study groups, and provide their children with religious education. Moreover, people of higher classes hold most of the leadership positions, such as membership on a church's board of trustees. But these facts do not mean that higher-status people are more religious. In fact, belief in God is more widespread among the poor than among the rich. The lower classes are also more likely to believe in the literal interpretation of the Bible, to believe in a personal God, and to be emotionally involved in religion. The higher rate of participation by higher-status people seems to reflect a greater inclination to participate in *all* kinds of voluntary organizations. For many higher-status people, religious participation appears to be a public activity required for social respectability.

The Age Factor

Adults above age 24 are also more active in their church than younger people. Religious involvement normally begins to escalate by age 25, first with marriage and then with parenthood. Adults are also more involved in a variety of social, political, and charitable activities—more likely, for example, to be registered to vote. Church involvement, then, reflects a broader pattern of social involvement (Gallup and Castelli, 1989).

The same age factor in religious involvement emerges in a study of baby boomers, who are now in their thirties and forties. During their teens or early twenties, two-thirds dropped out of their churches and synagogues. Now older in the 1990s, nearly 40 percent of these dropouts have returned to religious practice. Why do they return to organized religion? One reason is their feeling that religion is important for bringing up children. Another is their personal quest for meaning, triggered by feelings of emptiness and loneliness (see box, p. 399). A third reason is

their need to belong to a community—to be with others, share faith, and do things together (Roof, 1993). In short, religious involvement tends to increase with age.

Questions for Discussion and Review

1. What are the traditional religious affiliations in the United States?
2. How do residence, politics, class, and age relate to religion?

TRENDS IN U.S. RELIGION

There is already a great deal of diversity in U.S. religion. Yet the diversity continues to increase. We see this in a number of new religious trends, including the fundamentalist revival, the proliferation of cults, the popularity of religious television, the New Age movement, the rise of Islam, and the secularization of religion.

The Fundamentalist Revival

Although religious membership throughout the United States remains high, the growth in church membership has not kept pace with the growth of the general population. Since the early 1970s, the U.S. population has grown by over 12 percent, but religious institutions have expanded by only 4 percent. Some churches have actually lost members. Others, however, have gained many members (Naisbitt and Aburdene, 1990).

Generally, the large mainline churches—Episcopal, Methodist, Presbyterian, and Congregational—have lost many members. Those churches that have registered large gains tend to be smaller, less established religious groups. They are also the more conservative groups. Among them are various fundamentalists (see Table 17.1, p. 400). In contrast to mainline Protestants, fundamentalists emphasize a literal interpretation of everything in the Bible. Evangelical, "born again" Christians also stress emotional demonstrativeness rather than quiet devotion at church services. Through the experience of being "born again," they believe that their lives have been dramatically changed. Some of these groups, known as charismatics or pentecostals, also speak in tongues, utter prophecies, and heal the sick.

Cutting Edge

U.S. culture has become very secularized; most important decisions are based on science, not religion. But we still search for the sacred. This article describes the various ways we construct religious meanings to enrich our lives.

On the Road Again

For most of human history, no one had to search for the sacred. At the core of every culture was a cult, with sacred times and places set aside for public rituals that enabled everyone to commune with the divine. Religion was the womb of civilizations. The real world was the realm of the gods, whose cosmic power and mysterious presence gave the mundane cycle of birth, work, sex and death its meaning. Periodic religious festivals brought secular activities to a welcome halt so that the populace could celebrate its identity as a people. Every tribe, every village and eventually every city set aside public space for sacred worship.

Today it is otherwise. Work defines the "real" world; we move in secular time and space. The sacred is experienced—if at all—as a private, usually weekend option. Science long ago desacralized the cosmos: the gods have fled their lofty pedestals and been domesticated in diverse houses of sectarian worship. Detached from the sacred, culture has become a human construct we labor to create.

But the yearning for a sacred dimension to life is far from extinct. In a secular culture where nothing is sacred, anything can be sacralized. What Americans seem to be searching for is some sense of harmony with a cosmic order and communion with its source—the experience other societies have celebrated as the presence of the sacred.

Searching for the sacred is scarcely new in the American experience. To the Pilgrim Fathers, the American continent itself was sacred soil—a new promised land uniquely blessed by God and reserved by him for a newly chosen people. By the middle of this century, however, all that remained of the Pilgrims' foundation myth was the quintessential American belief in the sacredness of the individual person. Disguised in the secular language of psychotherapy, the search for the sacred turned sharply inward—a private quest. The goal, over the last 40 years, has been variously described as "peace of mind," "higher consciousness," "personal transformation" or—in its most banal incarnation—"self-esteem."

Forging another path to the sacred, the religious wing of U.S. feminism seeks to ground women's liberation in a God stripped of masculine traits. . . . What is at stake is a total redefinition of sacred time and space. No longer is God to be worshiped as a transcendent authority figure: that's taboo masculine theory. Instead, she is to be experienced as the power that makes spiritual and physical communion possible. . . .

For other searchers, the quest for the sacred is inspired by the simple need to connect their lives to something larger. To many Americans who find conventional religion alienating . . . that quest begins with a heightened concern for the environment. Nature, of course, has always prompted feelings of transcendence. But to many environmental enthusiasts, the evolution of the earth and its interlocking ecosystems provide a new context for encountering the sacred. . . .

Apart from spiritual tourists, the purpose of every journey is to arrive at a destination. Unlike the ancients, we now know that the sacred is no longer up there, out there or even in there. Rather, it is to be found wherever—and whenever—the pilgrim learns to recognize the mystery in each moment. That takes spiritual discipline, detachment and discernment. In the traditions of the West, every serious sojourner arrives at the still point of an abiding Presence, who sustains the seeker and justifies the search.

Southern Baptists, Jehovah's Witnesses, Mormons, members of the Church of God, and Catholic Pentecostals are among the groups participating in this revival. In the past, fundamentalist and evangelical Christianity was associated with the poor and uneducated. Today, however, its appeal has spread, and business executives and prominent politicians can be found among its advocates. The revival has also spawned most of the new 43 superchurches, each accommodating 5,000 or more worshipers every

TABLE 17.1
Winners and Losers Among Churches

	1970	Latest	Change
Over the last two decades, fundamentalist churches have gained members:			
Southern Baptist Convention	11,628,032	14,907,826	Up 28%
Church of Jesus Christ of Latter-Day Saints (Mormons)	2,073,146	4,370,690	Up 11%
Assemblies of God	625,027	2,137,890	Up 242%
Seventh-Day Adventists	420,419	701,781	Up 67%
Church of the Nazarene	383,284	561,253	Up 46%
In that same period, many mainline churches have declined:			
United Methodist Church	10,509,198	8,979,139	Down 15%
Presbyterian Church (U.S.A.)	4,045,408	2,886,482	Down 29%
Episcopal Church	3,285,826	2,433,413	Down 26%
Lutheran Church in America	2,788,536	2,609,025	Down 6%
Christian Church (Disciples of Christ)	1,424,479	1,052,271	Down 26%

Source: *The Universal Almanac*, 1993.

Sunday. The growing strength of fundamentalism has further helped many African American churches to hold their own in the midst of various social ills, such as rising drug use, unemployment, crime, and family disintegration. Like white fundamentalism and evangelicalism, black Christianity preaches the reality of flesh-and-blood Jesus and the urgency of spiritual rebirth. But it also includes social and economic liberation in its gospel (Lincoln and Mamiya, 1990; Ostling, 1991).

The fundamentalist revival is a reflection of the conservative trend in society. It is also a culmination of a number of factors. First is the aggressive, skillful use of television, as illustrated by the popularity of such fundamentalist preachers as Jerry Falwell and Pat Robertson. A second factor is the social changes of the last two decades that have driven many conservative people into fundamentalist churches. These social changes have involved the women's movement, gay rights movement, unmarried mothers, legalization of abortion, and court decisions against school prayer. And a third factor is the highly personal style of worship in fundamentalist churches, which tends to attract the casualties of this fast-changing, high-tech age—individuals who are socially isolated, alienated, and dehumanized by

modern society (Moberg, 1984; Hammond, 1985; Marty and Appleby, 1992).

The Proliferation of Cults

A **cult** is a religious group that professes a new belief system, totally rejects society, and consists of members with extreme devotion to their leader. Like evangelical groups, U.S. cults have been growing. In the 1980s there were already about 2,500 cults but most were very small (Levine, 1984).

An example of a cult is the Branch Davidians in Waco, Texas. Led by David Koresh in the late 1980s and early 1990s, members gave up all their bank accounts and personal possessions. They also let Koresh take their wives and daughters as his concubines. Koresh claimed that he was Jesus Christ, and convinced his followers that he was destined to lead them in bringing about the end of the world. In 1993, after he was charged with gun law violations, Koresh refused to come out of the compound where he and his followers lived. Nearly all the Branch Davidians died when their residence was torched in response to an attempt by government agents to force them out with tear gas (also see box, p. 401).

GLOBAL VILLAGE

A poison gas attack on a Japanese subway during rush hour in 1995 caused alarm throughout the world. The apparent perpetrators of this attack are members of the religious sect Aum Shinrikyo ("Supreme Truth"), which is a rigid, secretive cult operating in Japan and other countries.

Aum Shinrikyo: An Apocalyptic Cult

Religious fanaticism, not militant politics, is emerging as the primary motive behind the nerve-gas attack on Tokyo subway riders.

Aum Shinrikyo is one of several groups that are called Japan's "new-new religions," a label that distinguishes them from the now well-established "new religions" that arose between 1800 and the period following World War II.

The new religions generally have a "this-worldly" focus, according to Susumu Shimazono, a professor religion at Tokyo University. They promise to make people's lives happier, more prosperous, and healthier.

The more recently founded sects, by contrast, provide their adherents with an "other-worldly" focus, Professor Shimazono said. "The new-new religions tend to regard life in the world as less important," adding that many urge followers to believe in reincarnation.

The new-new religions tend to appeal to young people who experiment with the sects for a few years before familial and professional duties begin.

Aum Shinrikyo adherents live communally, apart from their families, and take part in rigorous forms of meditation and asceticism modeled on the practices of Buddhist monks and Hindu yogis. Six people found by police at one of the sect's facilities were hospitalized for malnutrition and dehydration, and dozens of others were in a weakened state.

The group's founder, Shoko Asahara, claims to have achieved special powers through his own meditation. Experts estimate there may be 1,000 to 2,000 full-time members of this sect, but the group claims 10,000 members in Japan and 30,000 overseas. Although reliable information about the group is hard to obtain, it seems clear that it subscribes to pessimistic views of the future.

The Japanese scholar says Mr. Asahara's writings speak of an impending catastrophe sometime between 1996 and 1998—"They say a big event will happen and a large part of the urban population in Japan will die"—but he adds that apocalyptic views are not uncommon in the new-new religions.

The Asahi newspaper reported that the group planned to declare itself an independent nation in 1997, and has named its divisions "ministries"—in the bureaucratic, not the religious, sense. The newspaper said the group is behind a project to build utopian villages in Japan that would be a basis for world salvation.

"The group is technologically sophisticated," Shimazono says, and has discussed methods "to protect themselves against nuclear attack." Media reports in Japan say that Asahara has sometimes spoken of poison gas, including sarin, the substance used in the subway attack. The group has been linked to previous incidents involving gas.

The group has also stirred allegations of forcing young members to stay in the sect, spurring parental protests. And it has been linked to two disappearances, including that of a Tokyo notary for whom the police are searching.

Excerpted from Cameron W. Barr, "How Sect, Spotlighted in Tokyo Attack, Thrives." *The Christian Science Monitor*, March 23, 1995, pp. 1, 7.

The Unification Church has been more successful. Its founder, Sun Myung Moon, a South Korean businessman, declares himself the New Messiah. According to him, Jesus has appeared to him, telling him that he has been chosen by God to complete the mission that Jesus could not finish because of the crucifixion. Moon's mission is to combine all the world's religions and nations into one, to be headed by Moon himself. Members of the cult, most of whom are young, must break all ties with their families, work 18 hours a day soliciting donations, and give all their possessions to the church. All the while Moon lives in splendor on a huge estate, owns several yachts, and controls an enormous business empire.

A cultist's life is not at all easy. Why, then, would anyone want to join a cult? Contrary to popular belief, the young people who join a cult are mostly normal and come from stable, religious families that uphold traditional values of family life, morality, and decency. Most have maintained good relationships with their parents and have done particularly well in school. Indeed, their warm, concerned parents have

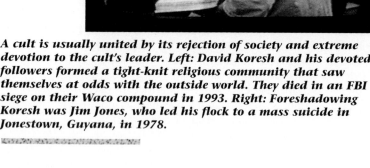

A cult is usually united by its rejection of society and extreme devotion to the cult's leader. Left: David Koresh and his devoted followers formed a tight-knit religious community that saw themselves at odds with the outside world. They died in an FBI siege on their Waco compound in 1993. Right: Foreshadowing Koresh was Jim Jones, who led his flock to a mass suicide in Jonestown, Guyana, in 1978.

given them every material, social, and intellectual benefit (Barker, 1984; Wright and Piper, 1986). What possible rewards can *they* find from joining a cult?

After studying at least 100 cults and interviewing more than 1,000 individual members, Saul Levine (1984) concludes that the cults provide the youth with "desperate detours to growing up." Like most of their peers, the youthful joiners must grow up to be free and independent by leaving their parents. But lacking the skill, confidence, or courage to strike out on their own in the harsh, cold world outside, they find it too painful to leave their warm families. For these youngsters, a cult provides separation without the accompanying pain, because the communal group typically operates like an exaggerated and idealized family that offers an enormous amount of love and care. It even gives careful attention to serving good, nutritious food, an emphasis that rivals a mother's care in ensuring a wholesome diet for her children.

Serving as a halfway house between the parental home and the outside world, the cult enables the young joiners to pick up skills for living an independent life. Once they have learned to take care of themselves, cult members usually leave the groups, resuming their previous lives and finding gratification in the middle-class world. In fact, more than 90 percent of the cult joiners return home within two years, and virtually all joiners eventually abandon their groups (Levine, 1984).

The Popularity of Religious Television

According to a Gallup survey, 49 percent of the U.S. population has watched a religious program on television at some time in their lives, and 25 percent (61 million) does so every week (Gallup and Castelli, 1989). Who are these people, particularly the regular viewers? The same survey finds that the viewers are more likely than nonviewers to be relatively old (over age 50), female, low-income, and poorly educated. They are also more religiously active and conservative. They are more likely to attend church regularly, to consider religion very important in their lives, to have tried to encourage nonbelievers to accept Jesus Christ as their savior, and to believe the Bible to be the literal word of God.

Ironically, they are highly satisfied with their experience of worshiping in church. Why, then, do they turn to religious television? One reason is that most TV evangelists are conservative, and their messages are compatible with those of the audience. Another reason is that religious television serves as a supplement to, rather than a replacement for, church life. Feeling deeply religious, the regular viewers of religious television apparently hunger for more than what they get from their church. But because their church remains the main source of their religious experience, they do not expect as much from television. They only expect a little extra benefit from it. Hence, they do not feel put off by the fact that religious television is less effective than church service in satisfying the needs of the faithful.

These people can choose between two kinds of TV evangelists. Some evangelists, such as Robert Schuller and Oral Roberts, focus their messages on achieving personal needs like success and miracles. Other evangelists, such as Jerry Falwell and Pat Robertson, are more socially oriented and political—condemning the sinful ways of life in today's society (Frankl, 1987). Given their unique styles and messages, individual evangelists appeal to different audiences. Billy Graham has the largest percentage of viewers who are women, white, and over 50. Jimmy Swaggart's viewers include the highest percentage of men, rural dwellers, and southerners. Oral Roberts' followers are especially likely to be divorced, widowed, or single. Pat Robertson has the highest percentage of viewers who are relatively young and married and who attend church most frequently (Gallup and Castelli, 1989).

The New Age Movement

A new religious phenomenon that has attracted a great deal of attention is known as the New Age movement. In every major city, its devotees can be seen seeking insight or personal growth with spiritual teachers, at a metaphysical bookstore, or at an edu-

cational center. But only about 28,000 people regard themselves as New Agers. Despite their small number, they have been given far more attention than any other new group on the U.S. religious landscape because they represent the most affluent, well-educated, and successful individuals. Ninety-five percent of the readers of *New Age Journal,* for example, are college educated, with average incomes of $47,500 (Goldman, 1991).

New Agers are unorganized (without an organization like the United Methodist Church or the Southern Baptist Convention). They do not have a coherent philosophy or dogma, either. But many do believe in a number of phenomena, two of which have been widely publicized as the major characteristics of the New Age. One is the belief in *reincarnation*—a person's being reborn, after death, in a new body or life form. The other is *channeling*—using one's body and voice as a vehicle for some wise person from the great beyond.

Running through these beliefs is a strong sense that the divine resides in humanity. Thus New Agers seek to realize the limitless potential of humanity for themselves. They are not interested in transforming the world, but themselves. Many New Agers used to be Christians who attended church regularly but who were left spiritually hungry. "They wanted God, not to hear God," as a Harvard theologian said. In the New Age movement, they find God within themselves. Some Christians say that the notion of a person being God is blasphemous. They believe that only through Christ can humanity be *united* with the divine—humanity alone cannot *be* divine. Actually, the New Age's concept of human divinity is similar to the Christian belief that people are made in the image and likeness of God, therefore possessing a divine spark. But New Agers prefer to seek God in their own way—such as through meditation—rather than with the help of an organized Western religion. They regard Jesus as merely an enlightened teacher like Buddha, Muhammad, or Gandhi, rather than as the only savior of humanity (Hoyt, 1987; Naisbitt and Aburdene, 1990; Bloom, 1992).

Religious programs on TV, viewed regularly by 25 percent of the U.S. population, find their viewers among the relatively old, female, low-income, and poorly educated. They are also highly satisfied with worshiping in church. The Reverend Jerry Falwell is one kind of TV evangelist; he focuses on socially oriented and political issues—condemning the ways of life in today's society that he sees as sinful.

The Rise of Islam

Islam in the United States has considerably more adherents than most people might suspect. Their number is estimated to be anywhere between three million and 6 million. This figure includes virtually all immigrants from predominantly Muslim Arab countries. But most of these Arab Americans are Christians rather than Muslims. Actually, only about 1.4 million U.S. adults identify themselves as Muslims (Goldman, 1991). Still, U.S. Muslims are one of our fastest-growing religious groups.

Slightly over half of all Muslims are immigrants, a number which has doubled in the past two decades. But a steadily increasing number of native-born U.S. citizens are converts, many of them African Americans. Most of them used to espouse a militant, antiwhite, and separatist philosophy, but now embrace orthodox, mainstream Islam. African Americans make up about 40 percent of the U.S. Muslim population (Sheler, 1990).

Muslims must follow a strict code of ethics and diet. They must not consume alcohol, illicit drugs, or pork. They must refrain from premarital and extramarital sex and dating. They are forbidden to gamble or pay or accept interest on loans or savings

Slightly more than half of all Muslims in the United States are immigrants, but a steadily increasing number of native-born U.S. citizens have been converted. The Islamic community includes large numbers of African Americans, including former heavyweight boxing champion Muhammad Ali, who prays at a mosque in Chicago.

accounts. These religious rules bring Muslims into conflict with the dominant U.S. culture. Many Muslims are compelled to pay interest on bank loans needed for purchasing homes and cars. Devout Muslims find U.S. society shockingly permissive, riddled with what they consider moral problems, such as sexual freedom, drug use, crime, and lack of respect for authority. Immigrant parents often clash with their teenage children over dating and drinking (Ostling, 1988; Sheler, 1990).

The conflict between Islamic and Western cultures may ultimately produce a distinctively U.S. brand of Islam. In many ways, some U.S. mosques already function more like Christian churches than traditional mosques in Islamic countries. The Toledo center—the most impressive U.S. mosque—located in Perrysburg, Ohio, has 22 nationality groups among its members. Weddings and funerals are held in the mosque. There are Sunday classes for children and teenagers as well as "lectures" for adults. After the afternoon prayer service, the faithful get together for a meal in a lower-level dining room. The problem is that there is still a lack of Western-trained imams (Muslim prayer leaders, comparable to Christian pastors or Jewish rabbis) and Islam scholars. Nearly all imams come from the Middle East with little first-hand experience in Western culture. There are also no Islamic "divinity schools" in North America (Sheler, 1990).

The Secularization of Religion

Common sense suggests that the more secular a society is, the less likely religion is to thrive. But the United States, as Will Herberg (1983) said, is "at once the most religious and the most secular of nations." The churches have retained large memberships despite the secularization of society. One reason may be the nature of U.S. religion: it is, to a great extent, "secularized religion"—in effect, nonreligious religion. The religious elements are easy to see. But what are the nonreligious?

First, the high rate of religious affiliation does not reflect a strong commitment to religion. Close to half of Christian church members reject such traditional articles of faith as Christ's miracles, the resurrection, life after death, the virgin birth, and the second coming of Christ. Most Catholics also support birth control, the use of condoms to prevent AIDS, and legal abortion, all of which their church opposes (see Figure 17.4, p. 406). In other words, many religious people hold the same beliefs as secular, nonreligious people do. Yet they still consider themselves to be religious. As one poll shows, an overwhelming 93

American Mosaic

Islam has become one of the fastest growing religions in the United States, and its followers have established centers throughout the country. Its members largely come from African Americans who have converted to this religion and immigrants from Islamic countries. This reading describes the growth and way of life of a Muslim group in one area of the deep South.

Dixie Islam

From the top of a square brick building, an amplified voice sings the Islamic call to prayer, as it does five times each day. The voice echoes over a boarded-up shopping mall, overgrown vacant lots, bleak housing projects.

Inside, about 60 men and boys stand side by side. They face Makkah, or Mecca, as it is more commonly known in English, the holy city of Islam, now in Saudi Arabia. Behind and separated from the men by a wooden lattice screen, two dozen women and girls clad in green robes and white scarves wrapped around their heads follow the Friday service.

It's Friday night at the Jamaat Ibad Ar-Rahman *masjid*, or mosque, on Fayetteville Street in Durham, North Carolina.

In recent years Muslims have become a presence in the Raleigh-Durham area, as they have throughout the United States, establishing communities and centers of worship. The Islamic faithful, immigrants as well as American-born converts, number in the thousands in the area, though accurate figures aren't available.

There are two *masjids* in Durham and one in Raleigh, and Muslims have established university student groups, private schools, and a network of other organizations and businesses. At Shaw University in Raleigh, a $1 million International Studies Center, paid for by the Kingdom of Saudi Arabia, also includes a mosque. The Ar-Razaq *masjid* in Durham produces a weekly cable TV program, *Al-Islam in Focus*, to spread the word of Islam.

Except for the distinctive dress of many of the women, Muslims here are largely indistinguishable from other citizens. They are students, business people, computer programmers, city planners, mechanics. Nazeh Abdul-Hakeem, for example, works during the day as a planner in Durham. At night, he conducts the daily business of the Jamaat Ibad Ar-Rahman *masjid*. A tall, imposing man with a white lace skullcap and a long squarish beard, Abdul-Hakeem does not mince words when he is talking about the dangers Muslims face in the United States. Drugs, alcohol, crime, promiscuity, and divorce all pose a great threat to the family, the basic unit of Islamic society.

Abdul-Hakeem came to Islam 13 years ago, in reaction to what he calls "shallowness and hollowness" in the lives of other African Americans. After he converted, he divorced his wife and waited three years before seeking a Muslim wife. His present marriage was arranged in the traditional Islamic way.

If Allah is willing and the two have children, they will raise them in accordance with Islamic child-raising tenets. Abdul-Hakeem considers an Islamic education essential. "In public school, [Muslim] families would lose their children. Some kids don't make it."

The three-year-old Iban Ar-Rahman school is accredited by the state and currently enrolls about 40 students with as many as 10 teachers. Classes are small; students wear uniforms and are segregated by gender in the classroom. Students learn Arabic and Islamic teachings, in addition to traditional subjects. "The main difference is that we stress discipline." For Abdul-Hakeem, this return to discipline is a reaction to a chaotic society. The structures dictated by the Koran for families, *masjids*, schools, businesses, and charities provide stability and continuity.

Excerpted from James Eli Shiffer, "Dixie Islam: Praising Allah in Raleigh-Durham," *The Independent*, January 6, 1993. Reprinted with permission.

---

percent of Catholics believe that "it is possible to disagree with the Pope and still be a good Catholic" (Bilheimer, 1983; Ostling, 1987).

Secularism can further be found in religious television. To have an authentic religious experience, people usually have a special place for the performance of a religious service, such as a church, synagogue, temple, or mosque. Such places suffuse anything that happens there with a religious aura. Other places, such as a gymnasium or dining hall, are sometimes used for religious purposes, but they are usually first decontaminated—divested of its secular, profane uses. Then the place is sacralized with a cross on a wall, candles on a table, or a sacred document in

Catholics Speak Out

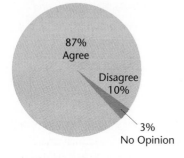

"The church should permit couples to make their own decisions about birth control."

87% Agree

Disagree 10%

3% No Opinion

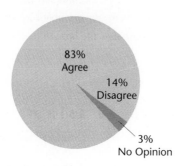

"U.S. bishops should approve the use of condoms to prevent the spread of AIDS."

83% Agree

14% Disagree

3% No Opinion

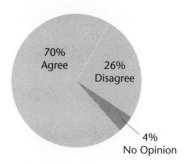

"Catholics can, in good conscience, vote for political candidates who support legal abortion."

70% Agree

26% Disagree

4% No Opinion

Source: *New York Times.* June 19, 1992, p.A8.
Copyright © 1992 by the New York Times Company. Reprinted by permission.

FIGURE 17.4
Catholics Speak Out
Most Catholics disagree with the Pope on many issues, including birth control, condom use, and abortion.

public view. Moreover, worshipers' behavior is supposed to befit the otherworldliness of the place. This can be attained by sitting quietly, meditating, kneeling down at appropriate moments, wearing a skullcap, or some other religious conduct. But in watching a religious television program most people can hardly derive a real religious experience. They do not separate the sacred from the profane. They eat and drink and talk and occasionally walk to the refrigerator for more refreshments or to the bathroom for bodily relief—all these right in the middle of a religious service. What they get from the TV religious program is, in effect, secularized religion—the experience similar to watching a secular program (Postman, 1985).

Questions for Discussion and Review

1. What does the current fundamentalist religious revival have in common with the upsurge in cults, and how do these two types of religious movements differ?
2. Why is religious television relatively popular in the United States?
3. Who are the New Agers and Muslims in the United States? What is the nature of their religions?
4. What contributes to the development of secularized religion in U.S. society?

CHAPTER REVIEW

1. *What is religion?* A religion is a unified system of beliefs and practices regarding sacred things that unites its adherents into a single community. *Must a religion focus on the worship of a god?* No, only theistic religions do so. Ethical and animistic religions define the sacred in a different way.

2. *According to Durkheim, what is God?* Durkheim argued that God is a symbolic representation of society. By their worship, members of society

strengthen their bonds to each other and their acceptance of the society's norms. Thus, religion helps preserve social order. *What other functions does religion serve?* Supporting people, providing social control, stimulating social change, and providing individuals with a sense of identity. If these functions are carried too far, however, religion can become dysfunctional. *How did Marx view religion?* To him, religion is an oppressive illusion, which helps the rich and powerful to perpetuate their domination of the masses.

He argued that religion justifies society's inequalities and gives solace to the masses, diverting their attention from the source of their oppression. *According to Weber, how did Calvinist Protestantism help develop capitalism?* By encouraging believers to work hard and accumulate money.

3.`*What is the basic difference between church and sect?* A church is well integrated into society, but a sect sets itself apart from society. *How can success be harmful to religion?* Success of a religion tends to make its followers become less religious. *How are church and state related in the U.S.?* There is no official church, and freedom of religion is guaranteed by the Constitution, but the separation of church and state is not absolute. *What is the U.S. civil religion?* It includes belief in God, support for religion in general—but not for any particular religion—and celebration of the "American way of life."

4. *What are some distinguishing characteristics of religion in the United States?* There is great diversity in U.S. religion, with most people belonging to some church. Such social characteristics as residence, social and political values, class backgrounds, and age are related to religious affiliation and involvement.

5. *What are the new trends in U.S. religion?* Fundamentalist churches have grown larger while mainline churches have suffered a decline. Religious cults, religious television, New Age, and Islam have also surged in numbers, size, or influence. But there are some signs of religion becoming secularized.

K E Y T E R M S

Animism   The belief in spirits capable of helping or harming people (p. 387).

Church   A relatively large, well-established religious organization that is integrated into the society and does not make strict demands on its members (p. 393).

Civil religion   A collection of beliefs, symbols, and rituals that sanctify the dominant values of a society (p. 396).

Cult   A religious group that professes a new religious belief, totally rejects society, and consists of members with extreme devotion to their leader (p. 400).

Ethicalism   The type of religion that emphasizes moral principles as guides for living a righteous life (p. 387).

Monotheism   The belief in one god (p. 387).

Polytheism   The belief in more than one god (p. 387).

Religion   A unified system of beliefs and practices regarding sacred things that unites its adherents into a single moral community (p. 387).

Ritual   A ceremonial form of religious activity (p. 387).

Sacred   Whatever transcends the everyday world and inspires awe and reverence (p. 387).

Sect   A relatively small religious group that sets itself apart from society and makes heavy demands on its members (p. 394).

Shamanism   The belief that a spiritual leader can communicate with the spirits by acting as their mouthpiece or letting the soul leave the leader's body and enter the spiritual world (p. 389).

Theism   The type of religion that centers on the worship of a god or gods (p. 387).

Totemism   The belief that a kinship exists between humans and an animal or, less commonly, a plant (p. 389).

S UGGESTED R EADINGS

Bloom, Harold. 1992. *The American Religion: The Emergence of the Post-Christian Nation.* New York: Simon & Schuster. An analysis of how the Mormons, the Southern Baptists, and other made-in-America religions reflect the U.S. preoccupation with the self.

Gallanter, Marc. 1989. *Cults: Faith, Healing, and Coercion.* New York: Oxford University Press. Shows how cults effectively use rewards and benefits rather than coercion to gain loyalty from members.

Greeley, Andrew M. 1989. *Religious Change in America.* Cambridge, Mass.: Harvard University Press. A data-packed analysis of how people continue to be as religious as ever despite all the social changes around them.

Marty, Martin E., and R. Scott Appleby (eds.) 1992. *Fundamentalism Observed.* Chicago: University of Chicago Press. A collection of articles by scholars from various disciplines dealing with a wide range of fundamentalists.

Roof, Wade Clark 1993. *A Generation of Seekers: The Spiritual Journeys of the Baby Boom Generation.* New York: HarperCollins. An analysis of how the baby boomers, now in their thirties and forties, feel about religion.

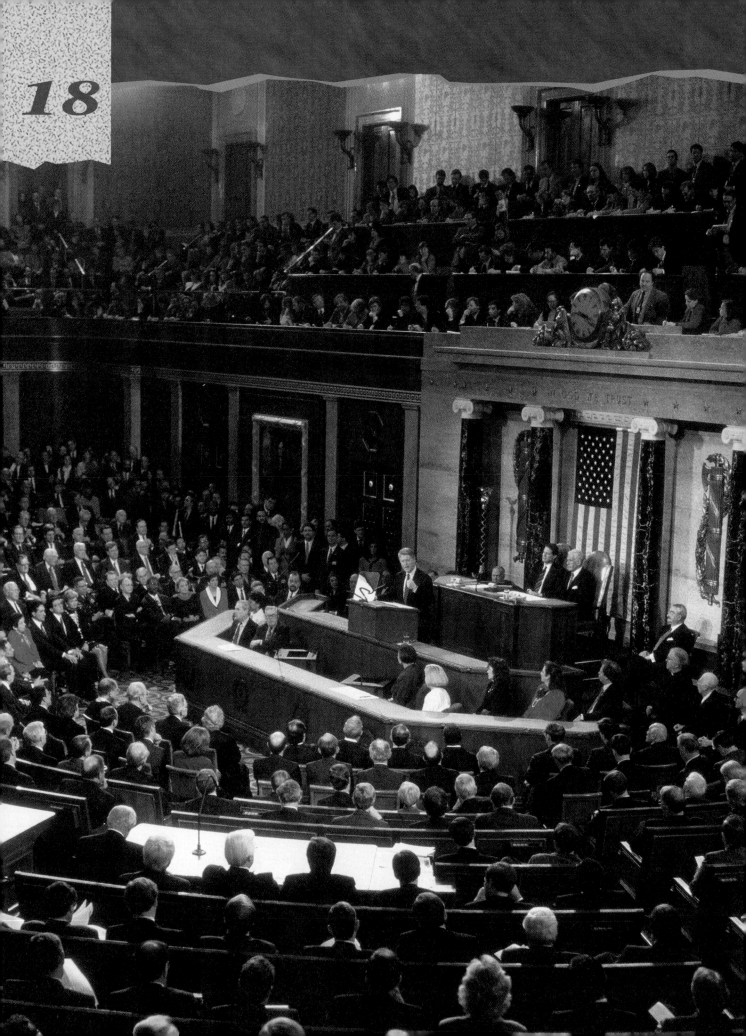

POLITICS

Myths and Realities

MYTH: *There are big differences between the Republican and Democratic parties. The Republicans are much more conservative while the Democrats considerably more liberal.*
REALITY: Party differences are not very great because the two-party system requires that each party represent as many citizens as possible if it is to win election. Both parties usually aim for the center of political opinion, trying to appeal to everyone and offend no one and taking in a broad coalition of politicians with many viewpoints.

MYTH: *Many conservatives dislike "big government," wanting to "get government off our backs" in all aspects of our lives.*
REALITY: Many conservatives are ideologically opposed to government intervention in people's private lives, but at the same time support school prayer and antiabortion laws, which, in effect, represent government intervention in private lives.

MYTH: *In the 1992 presidential election, Bill Clinton was reported to receive 43 percent of "the popular vote." That is, about 43 percent of all U.S. citizens who were eligible to vote cast their ballots for Clinton.*
REALITY: Of all eligible voters, only about 24 percent voted for Clinton, far less than the 50 percent who did not bother to register to vote.

wo weeks before the 1992 election, presidential candidates George Bush and Bill Clinton continued to hammer each other on the issues that had dominated their final televised debate the night before. Campaigning by passenger train in several small towns in Georgia and South Carolina, Bush attacked Clinton's record as Arkansas governor, assailed his "tax and spend" economic proposals, warned repeatedly that he "flip flops" on difficult issues, and emphasized his inability to tell the truth about his avoiding the Vietnam war draft. Meanwhile, Clinton, campaigning in Illinois and Wisconsin, assured voters that he would not raise taxes on the middle class, which he insisted had been seriously hurt by Republican "trickle down" economic policies. He also counterattacked Bush on the issue of character and trust, saying that Bush was the one who said "read my lips," in reference to Bush's later-broken 1988 promise not to raise taxes. While Clinton and Bush were out on the hustings, the third candidate, Ross Perot, returned to his home base in Dallas to launch a series of advertising offensives that would later appear on the three major television networks (Harwood and Noah, 1992).

Like those three presidential candidates and the millions of U.S. citizens who supported them, people everywhere are "political animals." Because valued resources such as jobs and money are scarce, people are compelled to play politics to determine who gets what, when, and how. **Politics** is the type of human interaction that involves some people acquiring and exercising power over others. In most societies, however, the state steps in to dictate how politics should be played. The **state** is a political institution that regulates conflict and allocates resources among the citizens of a country. We often equate the state with the government, but the two words have somewhat different meanings. The state is an *abstract entity*, such as the U.S. presidency, Congress, and Supreme Court combined. The **government** is a group of *specific individuals* who run the affairs of the state, such as the U.S. president, members of Congress, Supreme Court justices, and so on. Government officials come and go, but the state remains.

THE NATURE OF POWER

The state can do its job of regulating conflict and allocating resources only because it has a tremendous amount of power. In some societies, the government has the power to tell citizens what work they will do and what god, if any, they can worship. Governments take their citizens' money and spend it to educate children or to overthrow a foreign government or to do many other things. Max Weber (1954) argued that the modern state is distinguished from other institutions by its power to monopolize the use of physical force. To understand the state, we therefore begin by taking a closer look at what power is.

Power is the ability to control the behavior of others, even against their will. If a robber forces us to hand over our wallet, that is an example of power. If our friends convince us to cancel a dinner and help them move, that is power. Power is at work when we pay taxes. It is an aspect of all kinds of social interaction, but obviously there are important differences in the types of power people can exercise.

The most basic difference is between illegitimate and legitimate power. *Illegitimate power* is control that is exercised over people who do not recognize the right of those exercising the power to do so. Weber referred to the use of such power as **coercion**, the illegitimate use of force or threat of force to compel obedience. In contrast, *legitimate power* is control that is exercised over people with their consent; they believe that those exercising power have the right to do so.

Exercising power through coercion requires constant vigilance. If this is their only source of power, leaders are not likely to be able to sustain their power for long. In contrast, legitimate power can often be exercised with little effort, and it can be very stable. Employers, for example, often need do little more than circulate a memo in order to control their employees' behavior. A memo goes out telling workers to stop making personal telephone calls or to request vacations in writing a month in advance, and, at least for a while, workers are likely to obey.

There are at least two kinds of legitimate power. One is **influence**, the ability to control others' behavior through persuasion rather than coercion or authority. Frequently, those who wield other types of power also exercise influence. They may acquire influence because of wealth, fame, charm, knowledge, persuasiveness, or any other admired quality. Business executives may use their wealth to achieve influence over politicians through campaign contributions. Television reporters may acquire the ability to influence public opinion because of their personal attractiveness and journalistic skill. In general, influence is less formal and direct, and more subtle, than other forms of power. A second type of legitimate power is **authority**, legitimate power institutionalized in organizations. When authority exists, people grant others the right to power because they believe that those in power have the right to command and that they themselves have a duty to obey. Authority is essential to the state.

Questions for Discussion and Review

1. How can we tell the difference between legitimate and illegitimate power?
2. How do some people become influential?

TYPES OF AUTHORITY

What is the source of the state's authority? For an answer, we turn again to Weber (1957). He described three possible sources of the right to command as traditional, charismatic, and legal.

Traditional Authority

In many societies, people have obeyed those in power because, in essence, "that is the way it has always been." Thus, kings, queens, feudal lords, and tribal chiefs did not need written rules in order to govern. Their authority was based on tradition, on long-standing customs, and it was handed down from parent to child, maintaining traditional authority from one generation to the next. Often, traditional authority has been justified by religious tradition. For example, medieval European kings were said to rule by divine right, and Japanese emperors were considered the embodiment of heaven.

Charismatic Authority

People may also submit to authority, not because of tradition, but because of the extraordinary attraction of an individual. Napoleon, Gandhi, Mao Zedong, and Ayatollah Khomeini all illustrate authority that derives its legitimacy from **charisma**—an exceptional personal quality popularly attributed to certain individuals. Their followers see charismatic leaders as persons of destiny endowed with remarkable vision, the power of a savior, or God's grace. Charismatic authority is inherently unstable; it cannot be transferred to another person. If a political system is based on charismatic authority, it will collapse when the leader dies. Otherwise, it will go through a process of "routinization," in which the followers switch from "personal attachment" to "organizational commitment," with their personal devotion to a leader being replaced by formal commitment to a political system (Madsen and Snow, 1983). In essence, charismatic authority is transformed into legal authority.

Legal Authority

The political systems of industrial states are based largely on a third type of authority: legal authority, which Weber also called *rational authority*. These systems derive legitimacy from a set of explicit rules and

There are three types of authority. Traditional authority, as usually held by African chiefs, derives from long-standing customs and is handed down from parent to child. Charismatic authority, as illustrated by the Indian nationalist leader Mahatma Gandhi, is based on an exceptional personal quality popularly attributed to certain individuals. Legal authority, as held by U.S. presidents such as John F. Kennedy, comes from explicit rules and procedures that spell out the leader's rights and duties, although Kennedy is often said to have possessed charisma as well.

procedures that spell out the ruler's rights and duties. Typically, the rules and procedures are put in writing. The people grant their obedience to "the law." It specifies procedures by which certain individuals hold offices of power, such as governor or president or prime minister, but the authority is vested in those offices, not in the individuals who temporarily hold the offices. Thus, a political system based on legal authority is often called a "government of laws, not of men." Individuals come and go, as U.S. presidents have come and gone, but the office, "the presidency," remains. If individual officeholders overstep their authority, they may be forced out of office and replaced.

In practice, these three types of authority occur in combinations. The U.S. presidency, for example, is based on legal authority, but the office also has considerable traditional authority. Executive privilege, whereby a president can keep certain documents secret, even from Congress, acquired its force from tradition, not through the Constitution or laws. Some presidents, like Abraham Lincoln, Franklin Roosevelt, or John F. Kennedy, have also possessed charismatic authority. Still, the primary basis of the power of the president is legal authority. In general, when societies industrialize, traditional and charismatic authority tend to give way and legal authority becomes dominant.

Questions for Discussion and Review

1. How does traditional authority differ from charismatic authority?
2. What is the nature of legal authority?

PLAYING POLITICS IN THE UNITED STATES

The U.S. government consists of three branches: the executive (including the president), the legislative (Congress), and the judiciary (the Supreme Court). The three check and balance each other so that no

Political parties are designed to gain government offices. But they also perform functions vital to democracy, such as formulating and promoting policies that reflect public opinion.

one can become too powerful. Thus, gross abuse of power can be avoided and democracy preserved. But how all this happens depends on the nature of political parties and interest groups in this country.

Political Parties

Political parties are not mentioned in the U.S. Constitution, but it is difficult to imagine the government functioning today without them. A **political party** is a group organized for the purpose of gaining government offices. In seeking this goal for themselves, political parties also perform several functions vital to the operation of a democracy. First, parties recruit adherents, nominate candidates, and raise campaign money to support their choices for public office. Without the parties, the process of electing officials would be chaotic, as hundreds of people might offer themselves as candidates for each office. Second, parties formulate and promote policies. The desire to seek voters' support ensures that these policies reflect public opinion. This is one way in which the parties serve as a link between the people and their government. Finally, the parties help organize the main institutions of government. Leadership positions in the legislature and its committees are parceled out on the basis of which party holds the allegiance of most members of Congress.

The Two-Party System The U.S. political party system is quite different from its counterpart in European democracies, each of which often has 10 or more political parties. But we have only two major parties. For more than a century, the Democratic and Republican parties have held unquestioned dominance over the political system. Of course, there are many other parties, which we collectively call "third parties." Occasionally, a third-party candidate wins a local or even a state election, as some Socialist party candidates have done. But no third party has had much of a chance of winning the presidency. No third party has any influence in Congress, either. By contrast, "third parties" in other countries hold seats in the national parliaments, and they may have a strong influence on policy.

Generally, the Republicans are more conservative than the Democrats. The Republicans tend to advocate tax breaks for the wealthy, reduction in government spending, more local control, and less government interference with the economy. Consequently, the Republican party usually gets more support from the economically advantaged, Anglo-Saxon whites, members of major Protestant churches, and suburban and small-town residents. The Democrats, on the other hand, are inclined to emphasize the government's role in promoting social welfare and institute programs to combat unemployment and relieve poverty. Therefore, the Democratic party tends to gain more support from the economically disadvantaged, minority groups, and residents of the central-city areas in large metropolitan regions.

But party differences, when all is said and done, are actually not very great. Consider tax policies, for example. In 1954 the Republican administration offered large tax breaks to big business, but in 1969, 1974, 1975, and 1976 Republican presidents also signed rather than vetoed bills that gave tax credits to low-income people and increased payroll taxes for high incomes. In a similar zigzag, compromising manner, Democratic administrations enacted tax cuts for low incomes in 1964 but also cuts for the rich in 1962 and 1978. In the early 1980s, the Democrats even tried to out-Reagan Reagan by offering more lucrative tax breaks to business (Page, 1983).

In fact, the two-party system requires that each party represent as many citizens as possible if it is to win election or reelection. Thus, both parties usually aim for the center of political opinion, trying to appeal to everyone and offend no one. They take in a broad coalition of politicians with many viewpoints. We can find such strange bedfellows as conservatives and liberals in each party. When it's time to nominate presidential candidates, both parties usually look to their party's center. This has led to the charge that there is "not a dime's worth of difference" between them. Yet, if the Republican party overemphasizes its conservatism and the Democratic party its liberalism, both parties are certain to turn off many voters and get a severe beating at the polls. This is what happened when the conservative wing seized control of the Republican party and nominated ultraconservative Barry Goldwater for president in 1964; Democratic liberals did the same with ultraliberal George McGovern in 1972. Both choices led to landslide defeats in the general election.

Declining Party Influence   For more than 20 years, U.S. political parties have suffered a decline in influence. More and more voters identify themselves as "independents" rather than as Democrats or Republicans (Census Bureau, 1994). Even those who say they are Democrats or Republicans often split their vote, choosing some candidates from one party and some from another. Most politicians still call themselves Democrats or Republicans, but they often act like independents, refusing to follow the direction of party leaders in Congress, or even the president from their party. Several possible forces seem to have caused this decline.

One is television, which enables candidates, if they have the money, to reach voters directly rather than through an organized army of volunteers and party activists knocking on doors. Another is the spread of party primaries, which increasingly put the choice of candidates in the hands of voters rather than party leaders and activists. A third factor is the increasing cost of elections and the rise of political action committees (PACs) as a big source of that campaign money. **PACs** are political organizations that funnel money from business, labor, and other special-interest groups into election campaigns to help elect or defeat candidates. PACs act independently of the parties, so party leaders can no longer whip recalcitrant members into line by threatening to cut off their campaign funds. Finally, politicians have increasingly turned to pollsters and political consultants rather than local or state party leaders for data on what the public is thinking and feeling. In short, whatever the

parties can offer, politicians can find elsewhere. The parties have fewer carrots and sticks to control politicians. But if politicians do not follow a party's position, then the party labels mean less and less, and voters have little reason to pay attention to them.

Interest Groups

For those people who find neither party to be an effective representative of their concerns, there is another alternative: interest groups. An **interest group** is an organized collection of people who attempt to influence government policies. If you are a hog farmer interested in keeping the price of hogs high, there is a group for you. If you are a hunter interested in preventing the regulation of firearms or a baseball bat manufacturer interested in breaking into the Japanese market, there are groups for you, too. There are business groups like the U.S. Chamber of Commerce and the National Association of Manufacturers; labor groups like the AFL-CIO; professional groups like the American Medical Association; as well as civil rights groups, civil liberties groups, environmental groups, consumer groups, religious groups and more.

All these groups use the same basic methods in trying to influence the government's policies. First, they try to influence public opinion. They advertise in the media, collect petitions, and send out letters urging people to write or call their legislators. Second, they help elect sympathetic candidates by endorsing them, urging their members to support those candidates, and donating money to their campaigns. Third, interest groups frequently file lawsuits

NATIONAL RIFLE ASSOC.

SILENCER

American Mosaic

During the last several decades, U.S. politics has been greatly influenced by a combination of traditional Democrats, racial minority groups, and white liberals, who are sometimes called the "rainbow coalition." Recent elections, however, have shown that this old alliance is breaking up and a new, more pragmatic leadership is emerging. This reading analyzes the end of the old rainbow coalition and some new directions in politics.

The End of the Rainbow

On a trip to Israel in July, 1993, New York Mayor David Dinkins' eyes welled with tears as he recalled a close friendship with his accountant of many years, a Jew, in which racial differences had mattered so little that "one didn't know what the other was." It was a moment emblematic of the healer New Yorkers hoped Dinkins would be when they elected him in 1989. It was emblematic, too, of the promise of black "Rainbow" mayoralties in multiracial cities in the 1970s and 1980s. Yet, just as other rainbows have faded, the ecumenical side of Dinkins on display in Jerusalem has been eclipsed in the years since his "Vote your hopes, not your fears" victory.

What went wrong? There are two reasons for the decay of Dinkins' rainbow politics, neither peculiar to New York. First, a deep recession and economic upheaval demanded a "reinventing" of local government. Second, Dinkins' failures of leadership during a long, black boycott of Korean stores and amid black rioting against Hasidic Jews in Crown Heights are only the best-known of many abdications to the politics of victimization.

It's a familiar pattern. Beyond New York, the Rainbow habit of crying racism has found itself discounted by voters of all colors who want better governance and less rhetoric. Politically centrist mayoral candidates, many of them, ironically, white men, have drawn substantial numbers of nonwhite voters into new coalitions—call them Rainbow II—by touting a can-do pragmatism and a common civic identity that is more than the sum of skin tones, genders, sexual orientations and resentments. The truth they've grasped remains obscure only to some in liberal Democratic circles and the academy: The more genuinely multicultural and racially diverse a city becomes, the less "liberal" it is in the Rainbow sense of the term.

The pattern emerges from half a dozen donnybrooks of the last three years, including Houston, Philadelphia, Los Angeles and Jersey City. In each, the liberal candidate, usually a person of color, had the mantle of the civil rights movement, the support of a multiracial, multicultural coalition and the endorsement of Jesse Jackson. He was militantly pro-choice, anti-death penalty and in favor of the most expansive gay rights and immigrant rights agendas around. The white male opponent, who typically had never held elective office, posed as a businesslike reformer, promising to clean house and create new jobs through commercial deregulation, better public safety, less onerous taxation and tougher union contracts. Preaching tolerance rather than correctness and touting endorsements from prominent Latinos and other minority leaders who had broken with the civil rights establishment, he vowed to unite the city across racial and partisan lines.

It is here, in the interaction of shifting civil rights strategies and changing urban demographics, that Rainbow I meets its end. In the years after 1970, 10 million immigrants, the vast majority of them nonwhite, entered U.S. cities. Today, 40 percent of Angelenos and 30 percent of New Yorkers are foreign-born. These Mexican and Filipino laborers, Chinese and Puerto Rican seamstresses, Pakistani and Haitian cabbies, and Korean and Dominican merchants often bring with them notions of race that are more fluid and ecumenical than those of U.S. blacks or whites. They don't necessarily embrace a Rainbow I agenda of affirmative action and group rights-oriented litigation that presumes victimization by white racism. They rely more heavily on family and communal ties in order to achieve success.

Excerpted from Jim Sleeper, "The End of the Rainbow," *The New Republic,* November 1, 1993, pp. 20–23. Excerpted by permission of *The New Republic,* ©1993, The New Republic, Inc.

to further their goals. Finally, interest groups hire lobbyists, people who deal directly with government officials, attempting to influence them on behalf of the groups. There are over 31,000 lobbyists in Washington, which averages out to nearly 62 lobbyists working on each member of Congress (Borger, 1990).

Interest groups serve some useful functions. First, they provide a way for millions of citizens to make their voices heard. Civil rights and environmental issues are but a few examples of issues that were first put on the political agenda by interest groups. To the political parties and those in office, these issues were either unimportant or too controversial to warrant action until interest groups forced the politicians to address them. Second, interest groups inform and advise lawmakers. Being masters of their subject, lobbyists, in effect, become technical advisers to legislators and their staffs, supplying them with information vital to wise decision making and to the writing of workable laws. Of course, lobbyists are likely to slant the information they present to favor their interest group. But hopefully lawmakers rely on a multitude of lobbyists with different views that counterbalance one another.

If interest groups appear so useful, why do so many people fear and criticize them? Why do Democrats and Republicans both rail against the "special interests"? One concern is that interest groups are corrupting the process of government through back room dealings of one sort or another—through secret meetings between lobbyists and regulatory officials, or through outright bribery of members of Congress. Such explicit deals seem to be an infrequent exception in the political process, however. More serious is the concern that through relentless pursuit of their narrow goals, some interest groups are thwarting the will of the majority and harming the public good. Although polls have consistently shown broad support for gun control, for example, the National Rifle Association (NRA) has often successfully persuaded Congress to reject gun-control bills.

Money is another powerful tool. Interest groups have increasingly used PACs to give contributions to candidates considered most likely to win an election. They heavily favor incumbents over challengers because incumbents are much more likely to win. Donations continue even after elections. Thus, as the power of interest groups grows, the government may end up being for sale to whatever group has the most money to contribute. Federal tax policy, for example, favors business more often than labor because business donates much more money to legislators (Berke, 1990).

Questions for Discussion and Review

1. What is the nature of the U.S. political party system?
2. What may have caused the declining influence of the parties?
3. What are the functions and dysfunctions of interest groups?

WHO REALLY GOVERNS IN U.S. SOCIETY?

The emergence of political parties and interest groups in the United States has brought us a long way from the government envisioned by James Madison, the fourth U.S. president from 1809 to 1817. It was his hope to exclude "interests" and "factions" from the government. Legislators were to represent and vote for the public good, not one interest or the other. Where has this evolution brought us? Are the interest groups and parties mechanisms through which the people gain more effective control of government, or have the people lost control? Who in fact has **political power**, the capacity to use the government to make decisions that affect the whole society?

The Pluralist View

A pluralist looking at the U.S. government sees many centers of power and many competing interest groups. Government reflects the outcome of their conflict. In this view, the interest groups are central to U.S. democracy. Together they create a mutually restraining influence. No one group can always prevail. Thus, through their competition the interests of the public are reflected in government policy.

But, as we have seen in Chapter 10 (Stratification and Class), there are large inequalities of wealth, power, and prestige. How, in the face of such inequality, can pluralism be maintained? Cannot one group marshal its resources to dominate others? *Why doesn't one group or one coalition of groups gradually achieve a concentration of power?*

The reason, according to Robert Dahl (1981), is that inequalities are *dispersed*, not cumulative. Inequalities would be cumulative if a group rich in one resource (wealth, for example) were also better off than other groups in almost every other resource—political power, social standing, prestige,

According to C. Wright Mills, the United States is governed by a power elite. This elite consists of top military leaders, such as Chief of Staff John Shalikashvili, in close alliance with top government and corporate leaders.

legitimacy, knowledge, and control over religious, educational, and other institutions. In the United States, however, one group may hold most of one of these resources, but other groups may have the lion's share of others. What the upper middle class lacks in wealth, for example, it makes up for in knowledge and legitimacy. Power over economic institutions may be concentrated in the hands of corporations, but U.S. religious institutions elude their grasp.

This dispersal of power in society is reflected in a dispersal of political clout. The country's many competing groups vie for control over government policy and end up dominating different spheres. Corporations may dominate the government's decisions on taxes but not on crime. Even tax policy is not dictated solely by corporations, because labor unions and other groups fight with the corporations for influence on politicians and voters. The structure of the government, with its separation of powers, promotes this pluralism. What civil rights groups could not win in Congress in the 1950s, they sometimes won in the courts. Corporations that have lost a battle in Congress may win the war by influencing regulations issued by the executive branch. In the end, in Dahl's view, competing groups usually com-

promise and share power. Thus, there is no ruling group in the United States. It is instead a pluralist democracy dominated by many different sets of leaders.

David Riesman (1950) and Arnold Rose (1967) have developed a somewhat different analysis. In their view, the U.S. has become so pluralistic that various interest groups constitute *veto groups* in that they are powerful enough to block each other's actions. To get anything done, the veto groups must seek support from the unorganized public. The masses, then, have the ultimate power to ensure that their interests and concerns are protected. The bottom line is that the overall leadership is weak, stalemate is frequent, and no one elite can emerge to dominate the others.

The Elitist View

It is true that there are many competing groups in the United States. But does their competition actually determine how policy is made? Is the government merely the neutral arbitrator among these conflicting interests? According to power-elite theorists, the answer is no.

Many years ago, Italian sociologists Vilfredo Pareto (1848–1923) and Gaetano Mosca (1858–1941) argued that a small elite has governed the masses in all societies. Why should this be so? If a nation is set up along truly democratic lines, isn't control by an elite avoidable? According to German sociologist Robert Michels (1915), there is an "iron law of oligarchy" by which even a democracy inevitably degenerates into an oligarchy, which is rule by a few. A democracy is an organization, and according to Michels, "who says organization says oligarchy."

In Michels' view, three characteristics of organizations eventually produce rule by the elite. First, to work efficiently, even a democratic organization must allow a few leaders to make the decisions. Second, through their positions of leadership, the leaders accumulate skills and knowledge that make them indispensable to the rank-and-file. Third, the rank-and-file lack the time, inclination, or knowledge to master the complex tasks of government, and they become politically apathetic. Thus, in time, even a democracy yields to rule by an elite.

How does this view apply to the United States? According to C. Wright Mills (1916–1962), there are three levels of power in this country. At the bottom are ordinary people—powerless, unorganized, fragmented, and manipulated by the mass media into believing in democracy. In the middle are Congress, the political parties, interest groups, and most political leaders. At this level, pluralism reigns. The middle groups form "a drifting set of stalemated, balancing forces" (Mills, 1959a). Above them, however, ignored by pluralist theorists, is an elite—what Mills called the *power elite*—that makes the most important decisions. This elite consists of the top leaders in three institutions (the federal government, the military, and the large corporations). These leaders cooperate with one another in controlling the nation. Government leaders can allocate billions to defense to strengthen the military and enrich the corporations from which the weapons are purchased. Big business can support political leaders with campaign money. The politicians can aid business with favorable legislation.

If Mills is correct, all the hoopla of political campaigns and debates is but so much sound and fury because the power elite determines who gets elected and how the government is run. There is some evidence, though, to support Mills' view that a cohesive elite exists. Time and again researchers have found, for example, that top officials in both Democratic and Republican administrations previously held high positions in corporations, that they return to corporations after leaving the government, and that leaders come disproportionately from upper-class backgrounds (Domhoff, 1978, 1983; Barlett and Steele, 1992).

The Marxist View

According to the Marxists, Mills' analysis confuses the issue. They argue that his political and military elites are not free to act in their own interests—they are merely agents of the corporate elite. What we have are not three elites that come together but one ruling class.

Marxist sociologist Albert Szymanski (1978) provides an example of this approach. According to Szymanski, there are four classes in the United States. The first is the capitalist class, which owns and controls the major means of production and is commonly known as big business. The second is the petty bourgeoisie, which includes professionals, small-business people, and independent farmers. Some of these people own the "means of production," but they must work with it themselves. The third class is the working class, including industrial, white-collar, and rural workers; they must sell their physical or mental labor to live. The fourth is the lumpenproletariat, which consists of the unemployed, welfare recipients, criminals, and down-and-outs. Szymanski argues that the capitalist class uses the state as an instrument for exploiting the other three economically subordinate classes.

To control the state, capitalists may use the same methods employed by interest groups, such as lobbying and supporting sympathetic candidates. In using these tools, however, the capitalist class has a big advantage over the run-of-the-mill interest group: they have more money. The capitalist class also uses the media, schools, churches, and other institutions to permeate society with its values, such as free enterprise, economic growth, and competition. Violations of these capitalist values are often taken to be "un-American," giving capitalist interests a potent weapon against unsympathetic politicians. Understandably, few U.S. politicians want to be branded as antigrowth, antibusiness, or socialist. In addition, if the government acts against the capitalists' interests, big business can refuse to put its capital to work. The corporations may close plants or stop investing or send their money abroad (Greider, 1992). As a result, "business can extort favors, virtually without limit, from the political authorities" (Walzer, 1978).

Thus, politicians of all stripes have often talked about molding an economic policy that would "send a message" to "reassure Wall Street." In state after state in recent years, gubernatorial and mayoral cam-

Sparked by computers and other information-related technologies, the United States. seems to have changed from a mass society to a more individualist, more fragmented, and less cohesive society. This reading discusses how the change calls for a transformation of our political life.

21st Century Democracy: An Idea Whose Time Has Come

It seems only last night that we were in the midst of triumphal celebrations, dancing on the coffin of the "evil empire," proclaiming the end of ideology, the end of history, and the ultimate victory of liberal democracy. Yet here we are, in the light of a cold dawn, wondering whether liberal democracy itself can survive into the 21st century.

Like U.S. car dealers shipping their used cars for sale south of the border, the liberal democracies of the West are busy merchandising their used political systems to Central Europeans, Russians and anyone else who will listen. Yet like broken-down jalopies, our political systems are sputtering, rattling and threatening to stall.

Leaders everywhere face plunging polls. Throughout Europe, the United States and Japan we find festering alienation, worsening inter-group conflict and a deepening contempt for all political parties. These, in our opinion, do not just reflect the economic recession, or even the post-Cold War blues. They are indisputable signs for a malignancy that cannot be cured with aspirin and that cannot be diagnosed in terms of left or right, liberal or conservative—and least of all Democrat or Republican.

The central fact of our time is the rise of a new postmodern civilization. Just as the agrarian revolution unleashed a first wave of social transformation, and the industrial revolution a second, we are now being carried into the future by a third historic wave of change.

At its core, this torrent of change brings a radically new system for wealth creation based on the manipulation of symbols. But the Third Wave goes far beyond economics. Internally, it throws industrial-style institutions into terminal crisis. Under these conditions it is hardly surprising that our political institutions are also plunging into crisis. All the arrangements identified with liberal democracy—voting, representation, multiparty competition, separation of powers between legislative and executive branches, and independent judiciary—were designed for a slower and less socially complex time before computers, satellites, television, jet aviation or a global economy.

The first, heretical principle of Third Wave government is that of minority power. It holds that majority rule, the key legitimating principle of the modern era, is increasingly obsolete. Mass democracy as we know it is the political expression of societies based on mass production, mass consumption, mass media, mass entertainment and mass education. The postmodern or Third Wave revolution, however, destroys the underlying conditions for majority rule by de-massifying the mass society.

Therefore, to reconstitute democracy in Third Wave terms we need to jettison the frightening, but false, assumption that increased diversity automatically brings increased tension and conflict. The answer is not to stifle dissent but to develop imaginative new arrangements for accommodating and legitimating diversity—new institutions that are sensitive to the rapidly shifting needs of changing and multiplying minorities.

Excerpted from Alvin and Heidi Toffler, "21st Century Democracy: An Idea Whose Time Has Come," *New Perspectives Quarterly,* Fall, 1992, pp. 13–16.

paigns have been fought over the issue of whether a particular candidate would create a good or bad "business climate," over which candidate had the best plan of subsidies and tax breaks to lure business into the city or state. The public interest is identified with business interests, and political choices thus become hostages to the decisions of capitalists.

The issue of who really governs in U.S. society boils down to three questions: Which group holds the most power? Where does it get the power? And what role do the masses play in the government? The three views that we have discussed are different in some respects and similar in others. Both elitists and Marxists see power concentrated in the hands of a

TABLE 18.1
Who Really Governs?

	Pluralist View	Elitist View	Marxist View
1. Who holds the most power?	Various competing groups.	Top leaders in business, government, and military.	Capitalists; top leaders of the corporate world.
2. Where does the power come from?	The authority vested in elected officials.	Key positions in business, government, and military.	The control of the nation's economy.
3. What role do the masses play?	Choose political leaders in competitive elections.	Are exploited or manipulated by the power elite.	Are exploited or manipulated by the capitalists.

small group and hardly any influence by the masses on the government. These theorists differ, however, in regard to the key source of power. To elitists, the ruling elite's power comes from its leadership in business, government, and the military, whereas to Marxists, the ruling class gets its power from controlling the economy. On the other hand, pluralists disagree with both. They argue that political leaders ultimately derive their power from the citizenry, and they must compete among themselves to stay at the top (see Table 18.1).

Which view, then, most accurately represents the reality of the U.S. government? It is difficult, if not impossible, to answer the question because relevant data are unavailable. But it seems obvious that each of the three views captures only a small portion, rather than the complex whole, of the political reality. Pluralists are most likely to hit the bull's eye in regard to most domestic issues, such as jobs and inflation, about which the public feels strongly. In these cases the government tries to do what the people want. Elitists and Marxists are more likely to be correct on most foreign and military policy matters, about which the masses are less concerned and knowledgeable. This explains why defense contractors are able to sell the U.S. government far more arms than are needed (Page, 1983). The three views may be oversimplistic and one-sided, but they are basically complementary, helping to enlarge our understanding of the complex, shifting nature of political power (also see box, p. 419).

Questions for Discussion and Review

1. How does the elitist view of who exercises political power differ from the pluralist view?

2. According to the Marxist view, which elite makes the most important decisions, and how does this elite exercise power?

U.S. CITIZENS AND POLITICS

Each of the three theories we have discussed focuses on the decision makers. Here we turn to those who are governed. What influences their attitudes toward government, and what are those attitudes? Are most U.S. citizens as powerless and passive as the power-elite and Marxist views suggest, or do they take an active part in government?

Political Socialization

In politics as in other spheres of life, socialization is one key to behavior. **Political socialization** is a learning process by which individuals acquire political knowledge, beliefs, and attitudes. It begins at a very young age, when the family is the major socializing agent. As children grow up, schools, peer groups, and the media also become important agents of political socialization.

What is it that children learn? Before they are nine years old, most know who the U.S. president is, and they are aware of the Democratic and Republican parties. Childhood socialization also appears to shape several important political attitudes. Schools and parents begin to influence children's sense of political efficacy—their belief that they can participate in politics and that their participation can make a difference. In addition, parents often transmit their party

Voting is the easiest form of political participation, yet the percentage of people who bother to vote in the United States is lower than in nearly all other Western nations. One reason is that it is not as easy to vote in the United States as in most other Western countries.

identification (their support of a political party) to their children. If both their parents support the same party, children are likely to support that party. With age, however, their identification with their parents' party tends to decline. Parental influence is generally stronger among conservative Republicans than liberal Democrats. As sociologist Frederick Koenig (1982a) explains, conservative children feel more strongly about preserving traditions across generations and have greater respect for authority figures like parents.

Socialization continues in adulthood, because our social environment can affect our political beliefs. Our neighborhood, for example, tends to influence our choice of a political party. Thus people who live in predominantly Democratic neighborhoods are mostly Democrats themselves, but the likelihood of their becoming Republicans increases significantly if they move into Republican neighborhoods. Also, the conservative nature of today's political climate has made many people more conservative than before—more likely to oppose welfare and other government programs that help the poor and other less fortunate individuals (Sears et al., 1991).

Political Attitudes

Social class seems to play a leading role in shaping attitudes toward government and its policies. Members of the working class tend to be economic liberals and social conservatives. They are, for example, likely to support intervention in the economy by the government but to oppose gay

rights. In contrast, higher-income groups tend to be economic conservatives, opposing government intervention, and social liberals, supporting gay rights (Lipset, 1981).

There is more consensus in public opinion, however, than those statements may suggest. Surveys have found wide support among all classes for government spending to clean up the environment, improve the nation's health, combat crime, strengthen the educational system, improve the situation of minorities, and provide medical care and legal assistance for the poor. But while they support all these government services, they are highly critical of the government itself, which they believe has become too powerful, too intrusive, and too wasteful—spending too much taxpayers' money (Lipset and Schneider, 1983; NORC, 1994).

In short, most citizens are angry over "big government," yet they support big government by demanding more services. This inconsistency reflects a uniquely U.S. political character. There is a strong tendency to be **ideological conservatives**, who, in theory, are opposed to big government because of their belief in free enterprise, rugged individualism, and capitalism. Simultaneously, the same individuals tend to be **operational liberals**, who, in effect, support big government by backing government programs that render service to the public. Such mixed, ambivalent attitudes do not only pertain to economic issues. They also involve social issues. Many conservatives, for example, want to "get government off our backs," but at the same time support school prayer and antiabortion laws, which, in effect, represent government intervention in private lives (Ladd, 1983).

ENRICHING OUR LIVES

How our national leaders think about the government has a great impact on our lives. This reading provides two different views, one from President Clinton and the other from House Speaker Newt Gingrich.

What Good Is Government?

Response by Bill Clinton

There were many many times when I thought the national government was doing things that didn't make sense. When I was attorney general, for instance, I saw that because of federal law, the appeals process in death penalty cases took, on average, eight years. That was crazy, cost a lot of money, and didn't serve the ends of justice.

There are some things the government does quite well. One, of course, is national security. We have the finest military in the world. And with the FBI, the Drug Enforcement Administration and the crime bill that we passed last year, the government can help make people feel safer in our streets and schools.

The government is also good at what is known in the policy world as "income transfers." In other words, it's good at taking in tax money from the population as a whole and redistributing it to people with special needs. The Social Security system has worked quite well, with a very low overhead. Medicare has problems due to the general inflation in health care costs, but its overhead is low too and compares favorably with any system in the world.

Government has successfully set up institutions that protect economic markets from their own worst excesses. The Federal Reserve System, which regulates banks, and the Securities and Exchange Commission, which oversees the stock markets, have been crucial in fostering economic growth in this country.

Carefully targeted government action can also work in other areas. Our family leave law, the Brady Bill, the school lunch program, and the proposed minimum wage increase are good examples.

Finally, the government has done well when it sets out to provide education to a broad base of Americans. Perhaps the single most important thing the government did to improve opportunity during my childhood was the GI Bill, which helped millions of young men go to college. Since then, other college loan programs, including our new direct loan program, have helped so many more students. And the Head Start program has helped disadvantaged kids become more prepared for school.

Response by Newt Gingrich

Government does some things very well. It defends the nation. It keeps the peace. It freed the slaves. It builds useful things, like the Panama Canal, and enables valuable research, like discovering the cure for polio. It can shape market forces creating the right incentives for saving or investing. Those are things government can do.

But government, as a general rule, does a very poor job at fine-grained, detailed decisions. It's too slow, too political; it just doesn't have the capacity. The idea of the government in Washington trying to decide where to put a bridge in a Georgia county is just crazy. It's insane. Government can run very small, very elite bureaucracies very well. But the longer government stays in charge of something, the more bureaucratic, the slower, the more cumbersome, the more inefficient it becomes.

Federal agencies that stay in touch with reality every day—the FBI and the military, the Treasury and the Federal Reserve—have a different rhythm, a different flavor, a different style. They have to be responsive to real-world problems in real time. They're worth keeping. But in the case of the ones that don't touch reality every day, we ought to consider whether they have served their purpose. In the Department of Labor, the Department of Commerce, the Department of Education, people sit around in large rooms reading paper reports from people they've never met on topics they've never seen involving towns they've never visited. Why would you think such a system could possibly work?

Our modern leaders have forgotten that government cannot substitute for private initiative, personal responsibility, or faith. The role of a national leader is, first, to nurture the culture, second to encourage civic duty, and third, to strengthen the private sector. Managing the bureaucracy comes last. Thomas Jefferson understood this; so did FDR. Where Lyndon Johnson went wrong was that he thought government could do it all. In the 1960s, government crowded out private sector volunteerism. Secular bureaucracy crowded out spiritual commitment.

I would replace this degenerative system. Let's restore our church-and-synagogue-based system of volunteer help for the poor. Where government is still necessary to provide a safety net, I would return the responsibility to states and local government.

Political Participation

Individuals can participate in government and politics in numerous ways. They can attend a rally or run for office, form an interest group or send money to a candidate, write to their representatives or work for their opponents. But few U.S. citizens choose to take an active role in their government, even when it comes to the easiest form of political participation—voting.

The percentage of people who bother to vote is lower in the United States than in nearly all other Western nations. Usually, only 50 to 55 percent of all eligible voters in the U.S. go to the polls, compared with over 80 percent in Belgium, Sweden, Italy, Germany, and other European countries. As a consequence, our officials are usually put into office by a minority of citizens. In the 1992 presidential election, which was widely reported to attract enormous voter interest, only 24 percent of the eligible electorate voted for Clinton (Clymer, 1992). Earlier, in the 1980 election, Reagan's victory was often called a landslide because he beat Carter by a wide margin. But most citizens either voted for someone else or did not bother to vote at all. Only about 20 percent of eligible voters chose to vote for Reagan (Ranney, 1983). Why the low turnouts?

One reason is that it is not as easy to vote in the United States as in most other Western countries. In the United States, citizens must meet residency requirements and must register to vote some time before an election. The biggest obstacle to voting is the requirement that every time people change residence they must sign up all over again. The nuisance of re-registration reduces voting turnout, because a great many people move. By contrast, in other democracies voter registration is automatic or public officials go out to register citizens at their homes (Wines, 1993).

There are other reasons for nonvoting in the United States. First, many U.S. citizens simply get tired of voting because many more elections are held here than in other countries. Second, many regard political campaigns as mean-spirited, lacking in substance. The profusion of negative political advertising launched by two candidates against each other makes *both* look like liars and crooks. Third, even in regard to substantive issues such as jobs and taxes, voters see little or no difference between candidates, who are equally inclined to promise the same things that voters like to hear. Fourth, the long-standing political stability of this country makes it seem unnecessary to vote, so we can usually forget about politics and focus on the serious business of living—our education, jobs, families, and the like.

Those reasons, though, cannot explain the significant differences in the voting turnout of various groups of U.S. citizens. In general, those who are poorer, younger, or less educated are less likely to vote. African Americans also have lower voting rates than whites, but blacks and whites of similar education and income have about the same rates (Kourvetaris and Dobratz, 1982; Glass et al., 1984). In other words, class is a more significant factor in voting rates than race.

Does the low voting turnout pose a threat to democracy? Most political scientists say yes. They assume that a true democracy requires citizens' full participation because the people are supposed to rule. Without adequate support from its citizens, the government lacks legitimacy and therefore tends to be unstable. The government is also likely to ride roughshod over the people. But there is a contrary view: the low voting turnout means that people are relatively contented with their lives. They "see politics as quite marginal to their lives, as neither salvation nor ruin" (Krauthammer, 1990). Nonvoting, then, reflects a preference against politics, which is assumed to be healthy because it reminds politicians that our country was founded on the belief that the government is best when it governs least.

Questions for Discussion and Review

1. What is political socialization?
2. How are U.S. citizens' attitudes toward their government contradictory?
3. Do you think that lower voter turnouts threaten democracy? Why or why not?

POLITICAL VIOLENCE: A GLOBAL ANALYSIS

Throughout U.S. history, various groups that believed the government would not respond to their needs have resorted to one form of violence or another. Analyzing 53 U.S. protest movements, William Gamson (1975) found that 75 percent of those groups that used violence got what they wanted, compared with only 53 percent of those that were nonviolent. Violence, it seems, can pay off.

But much of the violence in U.S. history has taken the form of riots, or brief violent seizures of property for limited aims, inspired by specific grievances. Violent as our history is, we have seen rather little of

The revolutions in Eastern Europe and the former Soviet Union occurred under the kinds of conditions that trigger most revolutions. The conditions include the political dissatisfaction of well-educated leaders, the masses' rising expectations, a worsening economic crisis, and an increasingly weak government.

the two forms of political violence—revolution and terrorism—both more broadly aimed at overthrowing the government.

Causes of Revolution

If a protest movement turns to violence, it may produce a **revolution**—the violent overthrow of the existing government and drastic change in the social and political order. The numerous studies on revolutions in many different societies differ in explaining the causes of revolution, but they all suggest in one way or another that a revolution is likely to occur if the following conditions are met (Goldstone, 1982):

1. *A group of rather well-off and well-educated individuals is extremely dissatisfied with the society.* They may be intellectuals or opinion leaders such as journalists, poets, playwrights, teachers, clergy, and lawyers. These people would withdraw support from the government, criticize it, and demand reforms. Discontent may also exist within such elites as wealthy landowners, industrialists, leading bureaucrats, and military officials. It is from among all these people that most revolutionary leaders emerge.

2. *Revolutionary leaders rely on the masses' rising expectation to convince them that they can end their oppression by bringing down the existing government.* By itself, poverty does not produce revolution. Most of the world, after all, is poor. When people have long lived with misery, they may become fatalists, resigned to

their suffering. They may starve without raising a fist or even uttering a whimper against the government. But, if their living conditions improve, then fatalism may give way to hope. They may expect a better life. It is in times of such a *rising expectation* that revolutionary leaders may succeed in attracting mass support.

3. *A deepening economic crisis triggers peasant revolts and urban uprisings.* In a social climate of rising expectations, large masses of peasants and workers tend to respond explosively to serious economic problems. When the state raises taxes too high, and landlords, in turn, jack up the dues of tenant farmers or take over their lands, the peasants are likely to revolt. When the cost of food and the rate of unemployment soar, food riots and large-scale antigovernment protests tend to erupt in the cities.

4. *The existing government is weak.* Usually, before a government is overthrown, it has failed to resolve one problem after another and has gradually lost legitimacy. As the crisis mounts, the government often tries to initiate reforms. But the effort tends to be too little or too late. This only reinforces people's conviction that the regime is flawed, and encourages demands for even bigger reforms. All this can quicken the government's downfall. As Machiavelli (1469–1527) said in his warning to rulers, "If the necessity for [reforms] comes in troubled times, you are too late for harsh measures. Mild ones will not help you, for they will be considered as forced from you, and no one will be under obligation to you" (Goldstone, 1982).

Revolution in Eastern Europe

The four conditions described above can be found in the revolution that brought down the communist governments, one after another, in Eastern Europe in late 1989 (Echikson, 1990).

1. *Most of the revolutionary leaders were well educated.* They included writers, professors, journalists, and college students. The most famous was playwright Vaclav Havel, who later became president of Czechoslovakia. An exception was electrician Lech Walesa, who organized his fellow workers into a politically powerful force in Poland. This was extraordinary because "everywhere else the initial pressure for revolution came from intellectuals, with workers providing back-up support." Nevertheless, Walesa felt it necessary to have intellectuals as his advisors. As he told them, "We are only workers. These government negotiators are educated men; we need someone to help us" (Echikson, 1990).

2. *Expectations of freedom rose significantly after 1985.* Before Mikhail Gorbachev became the Soviet leader in 1985, Eastern Europeans had long lived in fear under communism. They knew that if they spoke out against the communist rule, they could lose their jobs, cars, and homes, even face prison or death. The 1956 Soviet invasion of Hungary, the 1968 invasion of Czechoslovakia, and the 1981 suppression of Solidarity in Poland further showed how dangerous it was to question the status quo. Soon after 1985, however, Gorbachev removed this fear. He refused to interfere with the internal affairs of Eastern European nations, and decided to thin out Soviet forces in those countries. Consequently, the masses of Eastern Europe were no longer afraid. Their expectation for freedom rose, and they took to the streets to demonstrate against their repressive governments.

3. *Economic crisis added impetus to the revolution.* After Eastern Europe turned communist in 1945, its traditionally impoverished, rural societies underwent significant modernization. A whole generation of workers who were mostly peasants' children could live in apartments with running water and toilets. But beginning in the early 1980s, incomes and living standards plummeted, inflation and foreign debt accelerated, and economic growth and innovation went downhill. Even worse, after 1985, Eastern Europe began to lose the subsidy of vital resources such as oil and gas that it had long received from the former Soviet Union. Beset by his own country's economic problems, Gorbachev refused to supply the precious raw materials to Eastern Europe in exchange for its low-quality and obsolete products that could not be sold on the world market. The worsening economic crisis provoked many antigovernment strikes and protests, especially among the workers in Poland.

4. *The communist governments in Eastern Europe became weak.* For a long time, those governments had largely been controlled by the Soviet Union. They had been able to rule with an iron hand because of the tremendous military force that the Soviet Union had used to prop them up. But after 1985 the Soviet Union, under Gorbachev, decided that it would no longer use its troops to squash any uprising in Eastern Europe. Without the Soviet support, the Eastern European regimes became weak, which encouraged a fast-growing number of people to join the revolution.

The Collapse of the Soviet Union

The forces that had caused the revolution in Eastern Europe finally toppled the Soviet government itself in late August 1991:

1. Boris Yeltsin and other revolutionary leaders are all well-educated people who chafed at the slowness of the liberal reforms started by Gorbachev.

2. Under Gorbachev's liberal leadership, the expectation for freedom soared throughout the Soviet Union.

3. Like the Eastern Europeans, the Soviets were hit with a worsening economic crisis.

4. The Soviet government, which had long derived its power from the Communist Party, had become increasingly weak. Not surprisingly, when the Party's hard-liners staged a coup to take over the government, they failed quickly after only two days of resistance by the people. With the collapse of the Communist Party, the Soviet Union disintegrated, and all 15 of its republics declared independence one after another.

Most of the U.S. media have regarded the collapse of communism in the Soviet Union—as well as in Eastern Europe—as the failures of socialism. But the socialism that has been practiced in the Soviet Union was not the real socialism expounded in Marxist theory. According to Marx, a socialist state is supposed to reduce social inequality by freeing the poor

Some terrorists are powerless individuals who are futilely fighting a government while other terrorists are actually carrying out their government's policies. Shown here are Irish terrorists on the 29th anniversary of the siege of Londonderry by Protestants.

masses from exploitation by the rich. But the communist regimes have merely turned this Marxist idea into slogans such as "All power to the people," while creating a privileged elite to exercise absolute power over the masses. It is true that the capitalist practices of private ownership and enterprise were eliminated to end the exploitation of the poor by the rich. But the communist rulers took over the exploitation themselves, causing even more misery to the masses than in capitalist countries. In fact, there is arguably more socialism in the United States today than there ever was in the Soviet Union, as there is more power for ordinary people, who have more opportunity to influence U.S. government and economy.

The Nature of Terrorism

What if the masses do not support a revolutionary movement and the government is not vulnerable? In that case, a violent protest is likely to produce not revolution but terrorism. The would-be leaders of a revolution become terrorists, trying on their own to destabilize, if not to topple, the government through violence. Their methods include bombing, kidnapping, airplane hijacking, and armed assault. Terrorist groups include the Palestinian extremists in Isreal, Neo-Nazi extremists in Germany, and right-wing extremists in the United States. Most terrorists are in their early twenties and have attended college. They almost always come from middle-class rather than poor families. In short, their background resembles that of leaders of revolutions—but the terrorists are self-styled leaders without followers.

These terrorists are basically powerless individuals futilely fighting a government. Some are international terrorists, who leave their country to attack a foreign government. An example is the Islamic radicals from the Middle East who bombed New York's World Trade Center in 1993 because of U.S. support for Israel. Other international terrorists, however, carry out policies of their own government. Examples of such a government are the militant regimes in Libya, Syria, and Iran—known as the "League of Terror" to the U.S. State Department—which have sent terrorists to foreign countries to assassinate their opponents. Other terrorists fight their own government. Examples of these domestic terrorists include Timothy McVeigh and his associates, who were accused of bombing the federal office building in Oklahoma City in 1995.

Responses to Terrorism

U.S. and European governments have generally adopted hard-line, "no ransom, no concessions" policies on terrorism. Since 1986, they have also stepped up their cooperative efforts against terrorism. They have imposed arms embargoes, improved extradition procedures, reduced the size of diplomatic missions of terrorism-supporting countries, and refused to admit any person expelled from another country because of suspected involvement in terrorist activities.

But it has been difficult to implement the "get tough" policies against terrorists who held hostages. Before 1986 the Reagan administration declared a no-concessions all-out war against terrorists. But in 1986 the plight of the U.S. hostages held in the Middle East and the appeals of their families finally compelled the Reagan administration to secretly swap arms with Iran for the hostages. The Iranians got the weapons but most of the hostages were not released.

In early 1986, the prime minister of France also compromised his strong public position against concessions to terrorists. He secured the release of French hostages by agreeing to return to Iran the late Shah's billion-dollar investment in France (Oakley, 1987). Finally, toward the end of 1991, all U.S. hostages were released. A major reason was the conciliatory stance expressed by the Bush administration telling the terrorist governments that "good will begets good will" (Dowell, 1991).

The response to home-grown terrorism has been different. In countries where incidents of terrorism are relatively common, law enforcers are given considerable powers to prevent terrorist acts. In Britain, for example, the police have the legal authority to detain suspects for seven days without charge, which would probably violate U.S. law. But similar authority may be given to U.S. law enforcement agencies because the 1995 Oklahoma bombing has heightened concern for domestic security. In fact, the Clinton administration has proposed to grant the FBI more power in dealing with suspected terrorists, such as monitoring their telephone calls or infiltrating their organizations. But this has caused concern that it may unintentionally end up infringing the civil liberties of innocent citizens (Lewis, 1995; Lacayo, 1995).

Questions for Discussion and Review

1. What social conditions usually exist before a revolution occurs?
2. Who are the terrorists and how have Western governments responded to them?

WAR AND PEACE

War is the most destructive force in the world. Yet humans have more often been at war than they have lived in peace. In the last 5,600 years peace has reigned in the world only in 292 of them (Farley, 1987). This means that for 95 percent of that long history war has occurred somewhere in the world.

The Power to Declare War

In getting the United States involved in a war, the president plays an important role. But it is not always clear how much power the president has, because the Constitution is subject to different interpretations. This problem came to a head when former President Bush was contemplating military action against Iraq in late 1990. The president believed that he had the power to declare war. As his Secretary of State told the Senate Foreign Relations Committee, "We should not have a constitutional argument about whether or not the president, as commander in chief, has the constitutional authority to commit forces. It's been done going all the way back, I think, to World War II." Many members of Congress disagreed. They believed that only Congress has the power to authorize war. Hence, according to them, President Bush could not plunge us into offensive war in the Persian Gulf without congressional approval.

But, like Bush, other U.S. presidents had claimed the right to declare war. President Truman involved the United States in the Korean War in 1952 and Presidents Kennedy and Johnson got the country into the Vietnam War in the 1960s—without seeking congressional authorization. President Reagan did not get authorization, either, before he sent U.S. troops to liberate Grenada in the 1980s. Even if Congress had not voted, as it eventually did, to authorize him to wage war against Iraq, President Bush would have gone ahead and ordered U.S. troops into battle.

Thus, presidents usually believe that, as commander in chief, they have the power to make war—and they have often carried out that power. They also think that they know foreign policy better than anybody else because of their direct contact with foreign leaders. They therefore resent what they consider to be congressional interference. But Congress may insist on exercising what it believes is its constitutional prerogative to deny the president the power to make war. Congress may choose to use its constitutional power of the purse to cut off funds to stop the president from waging war, as it did eventually during the Vietnam War (Crovitz, 1991).

Causes of War

The scope of presidential authority is limited because this is a democratic country governed by the will of the people. But a totalitarian state such as the former Soviet Union exercises nearly total control over the politics, economics, and other aspects of its citizens' lives. This totalitarian policy may encourage domination over other countries as well. And the totalitarian state is likely to use war as an instrument to subjugate countries that do not willingly submit to this domination. As the nineteenth-century military strategist Karl von Clausewitz said, "War is simply the continuation of state policy by other means."

But war is a complex phenomenon. It cannot be attributed to totalitarianism alone. After all, as a democratic society, the United States has engaged in so many wars that it is said to have a "warrior culture." What, then, are other reasons for nations going to war? Recent history suggests the following:

1. If two countries are *traditional, long-standing enemies,* as in the case of Israel and its Arab neighbors, they are likely to attack each other every now and then.

2. If nations have become polarized into *two hostile camps,* a single incident may trigger a world war. Given the already existing polarization of Germany, Austria, and Hungary on one side and Great Britain, France, and Russia on the other, World War I broke out when an Austrian duke was assassinated.

3. A combination of *an inflammatory ideology and a charismatic leader* can be a powerful recipe for war. Nazi Germany started World War II by invading its neighbors because the Germans, under Hitler's strong, mesmeric leadership, came to believe that they were the "master race," destined to rule the world.

4. If nations are *militarily prepared* to defend themselves or their allies, they are likely to engage in war. Fortified with huge armies and enormous stockpiles of weapons, the United States and the former Soviet Union have until recently stood ready to "defend" themselves against each other. The United States did so by sending troops to Vietnam in the 1960s and, more recently, by supporting Israel in its conflicts with Syria and aiding the Contra rebels in their attempt to overthrow the pro-Soviet Sandinista government of Nicaragua. Similarly, the former Soviet Union dispatched troops to Afghanistan, supported Syria and Nicaragua, and aided the rebels in El Salvador in their effort to topple pro-U.S. governments.

Achieving Peace

As history suggests, it is relatively easy to start a war, but considerably harder to achieve peace. But there are many ways in which peace can be achieved. Among these are two well-known strategies: "GRIT" and third-party mediation.

GRIT stands for "graduated reciprocation in tension reduction." It involves *one side taking the initiative to make small concessions* as a way of seducing the other side into making reciprocal concessions. The gesture of tension reduction by one side is necessary to trigger a positive reaction from the other side. This is what the United States did for the Soviet Union during the Cold War era. In the early 1960s, President

Kennedy first unilaterally ended nuclear tests in the atmosphere. Then a series of mutual diplomatic concessions followed, leading to such tension-reducing moves as U.S. wheat sales to the Soviets, direct air traffic between Moscow and New York, and a direct "hot line" between the two national leaders to avoid an accidental nuclear attack. As a result, nuclear war between the two nations has never occurred (Sears et al., 1991).

Another strategy for achieving peace is through *thirty-party mediation.* A good example is President Jimmy Carter's success in mediating the conflict between Israel and Egypt in the late 1970s. He brought the leaders of the two warring nations together at the presidential retreat at Camp David. After a series of negotiations between the two foreign leaders with Carter serving as their mediator, they finally signed a peace treaty and other historic agreements (Sears et al., 1991).

Questions for Discussion and Review

1. In the United States, who has the power to declare war?
2. What factors help explain why wars occur?
3. How can peace be achieved?

SOCIOLOGICAL PERSPECTIVES ON WAR

Additional insight into the nature of war can be gained from the three major sociological perspectives. According to the functionalist perspective, war occurs because it serves some useful functions for society. According to the conflict perspective, war reflects an exploitation of the masses by the ruing elite. According to the symbolic interactionist perspective, war is the culmination of a series of interpretations that the leaders of two hostile nations impute to each other's actions.

Functionalist Perspective

To functionalists, war serves a number of functions. First, it enhances social solidarity by focusing people's attention on fighting a common enemy. Consider the 1991 Persian Gulf War between Iraq and the United States and its allies, which resulted in Iraq being driven out of Kuwait. Arabs in the Middle

East who supported Iraq felt strongly united against the United States and its allies. The United States, in turn, joined forces with various nations, including traditionally anti-U.S. Russia and Syria.

Second, war stimulates scientific and technological development. The Gulf War in effect serves as a live laboratory for testing new high-tech weapons. Before the war, it was uncertain, for example, whether Tomahawk cruise missiles and stealth fighter-bombers could fly undetected and hit their targets with pinpoint accuracy. Because the high-tech weapons were guided by computer systems, knowledge gained from their use in the war benefited the computer industry.

Third, war tends to bring about positive changes in society. The Gulf War brought pressures for democratic reforms in Kuwait, Saudi Arabia, and other Gulf states that had long been governed by kings or sheiks with an iron hand. After the war, Kuwait's autocratic ruler, for example, promised democratic reforms. He acknowledged that without popular support from his subjects in exile as well as military help from the United States and other democratic countries, his tiny nation could still be under Iraq's thumb.

Conflict Perspective

The conflict perspective suggests that war often involves the ruling elite exploiting the masses. Political leaders have been known to whip up a war frenzy against some foreign enemy as a way of

regaining popular support or diverting the citizenry's attention from domestic problems. Other members of the power elite also benefit, as military brass become heroes and business tycoons reap profits from sales of military hardware. More important, members of the ruling elite do not have to suffer the heart-rending familial consequences of war. During the Gulf War, for example, no one in the president's cabinet had a son or daughter being sent to the front line. Of the 535 members of Congress, only two had sons involved in the war against Iraq (Lacayo, 1990). It is mostly poor, working-class, and minority families whose children do the fighting and dying.

Symbolic Interactionist Perspective

According to symbolic interactionism, the way that the leaders of two hostile nations interpret each other's actions may lead to war. A good example is how George Bush and Saddam Hussein interpreted each other's actions leading up to the Gulf War.

Before the Iraqi invasion of Kuwait, Bush regarded Saddam as a potential force for stability in the Middle East. Bush therefore refrained from strongly criticizing Saddam for using chemical weapons against Iran or for spreading poison gas on Iraq's Kurdish minority. A week before the Iraqi invasion of Kuwait, the U.S. ambassador in Iraq assured Saddam that President Bush wanted to seek better relations with Iraq and that the United States would not intervene in Saddam's border dispute with Kuwait, though

To functionalists, war occurs because it serves useful functions, such as enhancing national unity or stimulating technological progress. But to conflict theorists, war primarily serves the interests of the ruling class. On the other hand, to symbolic interactionists, war is the culmination of a series of interpretations that the leaders of two hostile nations impute to each other's actions.

urging that violence not be used. All this, however, was taken by Saddam as a green light to invade Kuwait.

The invasion outraged Bush, who threatened Saddam with war if he did not withdraw from Kuwait. But Saddam shrugged off the threat, apparently believing that the U.S. experience of losing the Vietnam war in the 1960s would deter it from going to war against Iraq. Even when he finally realized that Bush would carry out his threat, Saddam did not pull out of Kuwait. He was hoping for a "victorious defeat." As an Arab diplomat who had dealt personally with the Iraqi dictator on numerous occasions explained, "If there is no war and Saddam withdraws, then he looks like a coward, an idiot, who's lost everything. He is thinking, 'If I go to war, there is a chance that I will survive it, and at least I will be looked on by the Arabs as a hero who went against the whole world because of right and justice'"

(Dickey, 1991). Saddam expected to lose the war and be forced out of Kuwait, but he still considered the war his triumph for having fought and survived against the mighty United States and its allies. Thinking that Saddam did not appreciate the awesomeness of the military power arrayed against him, Bush finally decided to show it to him by starting the war.

In short, a sequence of interpretations by two national leaders of each other's actions may culminate in the outbreak of a war.

Questions for Discussion and Review

1. How do the three sociological perspectives differ in explaining the occurrence of war?
2. How can the Gulf war be explained from the symbolic interactionist perspective?

CHAPTER REVIEW

1. *How is legitimate power different from illegitimate power?* When power is exercised over people with their consent, the power is called legitimate, otherwise it is illegitimate. The legitimate power institutionalized in the state is called authority. *Where does authority come from?* It may be derived from tradition, from the charisma of a leader, or from a set of legal rules.

2. *What is the nature of the U.S. political parties?* Two parties dominate national politics, and they each usually avoid adhering to an extreme ideology because they want to appeal to people with a wide range of interests and opinions. But the two parties have suffered a decline in influence, challenged by independent voters and politicians. *How do interest groups influence government?* They try to sway public opinion, support sympathetic candidates, or hire lobbyists to deal personally with government officials.

3. *According to pluralist theory, who really governs in the United States?* Diverse interest groups share power. *Who controls the government according to C. Wright Mills?* A power elite made up of those who hold top positions in the federal government, the military, and corporations. *According to Marxists, what is wrong with Mills' power-elite theory?* It does not recognize that the power elite serves as the agent for the capitalist class. In Marxists' view, capitalists use the state to maintain their dominance over the other classes.

4. *What is the nature of political socialization during childhood?* Children acquire both political information and political attitudes from their families, schools, peers, and the media. *How are political attitudes in the United States divided?* Along class lines. People of the higher classes are generally more conservative on economic issues and more liberal on social issues. But there is wide support among all social classes for a great variety of government programs—and widespread opposition to big government. Thus, there is a tendency, across class lines, for U.S. citizens to be ideological conservatives but operational liberals. *Are U.S. citizens active participants in their government?* No. Many limit their participation to voting, and the percentage of those who bother to vote has been low.

5. *What conditions make revolution likely?* There are four: (1) some disgruntled, well-off, and well-educated individuals; (2) the masses' rising expectation; (3) a sudden economic crisis; and (4) weak government. These four conditions can be found in the 1989 revolution in Eastern Europe and the 1991 collapse of the Soviet Union. *When is terrorism likely to occur?* When the would-be leader of a revolution does not have the support of the masses against a strong government. *How do Western governments respond to terrorism?* By adopting hard-line policies against international terrorists while being willing to compromise to save the lives of hostages. But the response to domestic terrorists is tougher.

6. *Does the U.S. Constitution grant the president the authority to declare war?* U.S. presidents usually think so, but others believe that the authority belongs to Congress. *What causes war?* There are many causes, including totalitarianism, the history of hostility between enemies, the polarization of nations into two hostile camps, a combination of an inflammatory ideology and a charismatic leader, and military buildup. *How can peace be achieved?* Through one side making small concessions on its own and through third-party mediation.

7. *What is the nature of war as seen through the major sociological perspectives?* To functionalists, war can be useful for society. To conflict analysts, war reflects an exploitation of the masses by the ruling elite, and to symbolic interactionists, war culminates a series of interpretations the leaders of two hostile nations impute to each other's actions.

KEY TERMS

Authority Legitimate power institutionalized in organizations (p. 411).

Charisma An exceptional personal quality popularly attributed to certain individuals (p. 411).

Coercion The illegitimate use of force or threat of force to compel obedience (p. 411).

Government A group of specific individuals who run the affairs of the state, such as the U.S. president, members of Congress, Supreme Court justices, and so on (p. 410).

Ideological conservatives U.S. citizens who, in theory, are opposed to big government because of their belief in free enterprise, rugged individualism, and capitalism (p. 421).

Influence The ability to control others' behavior through persuasion rather than coercion or authority (p. 411).

Interest group An organized collection of people who attempt to influence government policies (p. 414).

Operational liberals U.S. citizens who, in effect, support big government by backing government programs that render service to the public (p. 421).

PACs Political organizations that funnel money from business, labor, and other special-interest groups into election campaigns to help elect or defeat candidates (p. 414).

Political party A group organized for the purpose of gaining government offices (p. 413).

Political power The capacity to use the government to make decisions that affect the whole society (p. 416).

Political socialization A learning process by which individuals acquire political knowledge, beliefs, and attitudes (p. 420).

Politics The type of human interaction that involves some people acquiring and exercising power over others.(p. 410).

Power The ability to control the behavior of others, even against their will (p. 410).

Revolution The violent overthrow of an existing government and drastic change in the social and political order (p. 424).

State A political institution that regulates conflict and allocates resources among the citizens of a country (p. 410).

SUGGESTED READINGS

Echikson, William. 1990. *Lighting the Night: Revolution in Eastern Europe.* New York: Morrow. A personal account of the facts and faces behind the series of events that culminated in the collapse of the communist regimes throughout Eastern Europe.

Gans, Herbert J. 1988. *Middle American Individualism: The Future of Liberal Democracy.* New York: The Free Press. *An analysis of how liberal intellectuals and politicians fail to understand the individualist values of average U.S. citizens.*

Maoz, Zeer. 1990. *Paradoxes of War: On the Art of National Self-Entrapment.* Boston, Mass.: Unwin Human. *Explains why wars occur and how they end, with emphasis on the unintended consequences of wars.*

Osborne, David, and Ted Gaebler. 1992. *Reinventing Government: How the Entrepreneurial Spirit Is Transforming the Public Sector.* Reading, Mass.: Addison-Wesley. Shows how government can serve its citizens better by decentralizing authority, reducing bureaucracy, and promoting competition.

Witt, Linda, Karen M. Paget, and Glenna Matthews. 1993. *Running as a Woman: Gender and Power in American Politics.* New York: The Free Press. An interesting analysis of the inroads women are making in U.S. politics.

ECONOMY

Myths and Realities

Myth: Industrialization can be a boon to the world by helping all nations to prosper, so that international peace can be achieved.
Reality: According to a 50-nation study, industrialization creates global inequality, with highly industrialized nations enjoying higher status and more power than the less industrialized nations, thereby threatening world peace.

Myth: In the United States and Japan, the world's most capitalist societies, the government pursues a strict laissez-faire, free-enterprise policy by not interfering in economic affairs at all.
Reality: Governments in even the most capitalist societies do not follow a strict laissez-faire policy. They often step in to regulate business.

Myth: Most U.S. adults work for large companies, such as GM and IBM, which have more than 1,000 employees each.
Reality: Most adults work in relatively small firms with fewer than 100 employees.

Myth: In the U.S. most workers would rather pursue leisure than work.
Reality: Most workers are satisfied with their jobs. Even if they inherited enough money to live comfortably without having to lift a finger, they would still want to work.

I n 1981, after Morris Shanks left the navy at age 37, he could not find work except a low-wage job as a security guard. At that time the U.S. economy was in deep recession, and had a very high rate of unemployment. Besides, Shanks only had a high school equivalency diploma and had been trained to fix fighter planes with hand tools, a skill that does not pay well in an increasingly high-tech society. But today the economy has slowly turned around, with more "Help Wanted" signs than before. Over the last 14 years Shanks has obtained more education, including completion of several computer courses. He now works as a maintenance technician earning a middle-class salary and living a middle-class life (Levinson, 1995).

Like Shanks, people everywhere experience the importance of their nation's economy, as they work to fulfill even their simplest needs. Beyond basic needs of survival, we have developed countless others—needs for clothing, housing, schooling, medical care, entertainment, and innumerable other goods and services. To meet these needs, societies develop an **economic institution**, a system for producing and distributing goods and services. In studying this institution, economists tend to focus on impersonal things such as productivity, wages, prices, and profits. Sociologists are more interested in people such as Shanks and how they work or how their occupations affect their lives, as well as how the economy relates to other aspects of society.

THE INDUSTRIAL REVOLUTION

To understand the economic world today, we need to look back at least to the eighteenth century, when a momentous event took hold in England. It was the **Industrial Revolution**, the drastic economic change brought about by the introduction of machines into the work process about 200 years ago. The revolution transformed not only the world's economies but also its societies.

Characteristics

For 98 percent of the last 10,000 years, the pattern of economic life changed rather little: practically all our ancestors eked out a mere subsistence living from relatively simple economies such as hunting and gathering (see Chapter 4: Society). During all those years, as sociologists Raymond Mack and Calvin Bradford (1979) pointed out, "the whole economic process was

wrapped up in the individual." This was especially true for craftsworkers: they owned their own tools, secured their own raw materials, worked in their own homes, set their own working hours, and found their own markets for finished products.

But gradually, as the population grew and the demand for goods increased, individual craftsworkers became more and more dependent on intermediaries to find raw materials and to sell their finished products. Some of these intermediaries took over the economic process, telling craftsworkers what to produce and how much. In essence, these intermediaries became capitalists, and the formerly independent craftsworkers became employees. Craftsworkers, however, still worked separately in their own homes, forming what is called a *cottage industry*.

As the Industrial Revolution was about to dawn in England, cottage industry began to give way to a *factory system*. Capitalists found it more economical to hire people to work together in one building than to collect goods from many scattered cottages. They

Sparked by the invention of spinning jennies and other machines, which made mass production possible, the Industrial Revolution began in England around 1760. It has brought great wealth to the West, while changing work patterns, population characteristics, human relations, and social values. It has also brought about global inequality.

began to own every part of the manufacturing process: the factory, the tools, the raw materials, and the finished products. In effect, they even owned the landless workers, who had only their labor to sell in order to survive. To make the process more efficient, capitalists increased the division of labor. Some individuals were hired to spin thread, others to weave cloth, and one person to oversee all the workers as their supervisor.

Then, with the invention of steam engines, spinning jennies, and other machines, mass production became possible, and the Industrial Revolution was under way. It began in England around 1760, and during the following century profoundly changed the economic structure of Western Europe and North America. The Industrial Revolution substituted machines for human labor to perform many tasks, greatly improved the getting and working of raw materials, developed widespread railroad and steamship systems to transport huge quantities of raw materials and manufactured goods, and moved labor and resources from agriculture to industry. All this created tremendous wealth in the West. At the same time, small machines were replaced by large ones, little mills became giant factories, and modest partnerships changed into large corporations.

Consequences

Industrialization has far-reaching results. *First, it changes the nature of work.* The mechanization of agriculture calls for few operators, leading most farmers

into industrial work. Bigger and better machines in the factory, in the mines, and at construction sites also require fewer workers, reducing the number of blue-collar jobs. But, because technology is highly productive, it brings prosperity which increases the demand for all kinds of services, from education and health to entertainment and money management. Thus, white-collar occupations proliferate. Even in manufacturing companies, white-collar workers outnumber blue collars. The General Electric Company, for example, produces numerous different items from turbines to light bulbs, but the majority of its employees are engaged in services from accounting to marketing.

Second, industrialization brings about demographic changes—changes in the characteristics of a population. In general, as a society industrializes, cities grow, and fewer people live on farms, but the population as a whole increases. Once a society has developed an industrialized economy, population growth tends to slow, and the percentage of elderly people in the population rises.

Third, industrialization changes human relations. In industrial societies, people usually spend much of their time in huge, bureaucratic organizations. They interact with a broad range of people, but their relationships with these people tend to be formal, fragmentary, and superficial. Ties to primary groups loosen. Industrialization alters other institutions as well. Formal schooling tends to become more important, and functions once served by the family are taken over by other institutions, such as business and government. According to a study of 50 countries, industrialization also creates global inequality, with highly industrialized nations enjoying higher status and more power than the less industrialized, thereby threatening world peace (Rau and Roncek, 1987).

Fourth, industrialization changes the values of a society. Traditional values and ways of living are discredited. People learn to view change as natural and to hope for a better future. Thus, industrialization brings a dynamism into society. It produces greater energy and open-mindedness but also restlessness and discontent. Social and political conflict often follows.

Toward a Postindustrial World

Many developing countries have been trying to achieve in a few years the industrialization that took the West over 200 years to develop. Thus they can realize modernization only partially. These countries have imported Western technology that has lowered death rates but not birth rates, so that population growth has eaten up or outstripped any gains in income. They have instituted Western-style education, enough to let people dream of a better life but not enough to create and operate a modern economy. They have seen the rewards of an industrial technology—and developed a craving for what they believe to be a material paradise—but they do

not have the means to satisfy their appetite. As a result, widespread poverty, high rates of unemployment, and other social problems tend to ensue.

Meanwhile, the developed countries continue to industrialize and to take the process a step further. During industrialization, machines take over tasks from humans and people control the machines. Now the task of controlling the machines is increasingly given over to computers. A growing number of factory workers sit at computer terminals in clean, quiet offices, monitoring tireless, precise robots doing the kind of work that assembly-line workers do with dirty, noisy machines. Along with computers, other related technological breakthroughs, such as electronics, microchips, and integrated circuits, are ushering in a postindustrial age.

Postindustrialism has brought many developed countries a high degree of affluence and leisure. It has also made it possible for everyone on the globe to be in instant communication with everyone else. Consequently, the spread of high technology throughout the world will likely mean greater output per worker and hence a higher standard of living in more and more societies. Instant communication may further undermine authoritarian controls, as it has in Eastern Europe, and keep democratic governments on their toes with a new degree of scrutiny. In short, we are likely to see more economic wealth and political freedom in the postindustrial world (Bartley, 1991).

During industrialization, machines take over tasks that humans have performed in the past, but people control the machines. Now, in the postindustrial world, the task of controlling the machines is increasingly given over to computers.

Questions for Discussion and Review

1. How did the Industrial Revolution change economic institutions?
2. What impact did the Industrial Revolution have on societies?

PERSPECTIVES ON CAPITALISM

No factory functions on its own. It must buy raw materials and sell its products. It is enmeshed in a complicated network of exchanges. This network must be organized in some way. One way is through markets. A market economy is driven by the countless decisions individuals make to buy and sell. This is **capitalism**, an economic system based on private ownership of property and competition in producing and selling goods and services. To functionalists, capitalism can bring about a prosperous and stable social order. But to conflict theorists, capitalism threatens society by allowing a powerful wealthy class to exploit a weak poor class. On the other hand, symbolic interactionists focus on how people's definition of their world creates or supports capitalism.

Functionalist Perspective

The functionalist ideas about the contributions of capitalism to a prosperous society can be traced to Adam Smith (1732–1790). Although Smith was an economist, his theory of capitalism has become a part of economic sociology. At the core of the theory lies a belief about the psychology of human beings: we are inherently selfish and act to serve our own interests. Capitalism works by allowing this pursuit of self-interest to flourish. It does so through two key characteristics: (1) *private ownership* of property and (2) *free competition* in buying and selling goods and services. Without these, capitalism does not exist.

Private ownership is considered functional for society's economic health because it motivates people to be efficient and productive. This may explain why Federal Express and other private companies in the United States are generally more successful than the U.S. Postal Service and other government agencies. Private ownership may also explain why private lands in China are far more productive than state-owned farms. In that country, the private plots once constituted only 4 percent of all cultivated land but produced some 33 percent of the country's meat and dairy products and 50 percent of its potatoes (Naisbitt and Aburdene, 1990).

Free competition is also considered beneficial to society's economic health because it compels businesses to make the most efficient use of resources, to produce the best possible goods and services, and to sell them at the lowest price possible. Only by doing so can they expect to beat their competitors. Competition, then, acts as an "invisible hand," as Smith called it, bringing profits to the efficient producers and putting the inefficient ones out of business.

Doesn't the pursuit of self-interest reduce society to a jungle and harm the public good? On the contrary, Adam Smith argued that because of free competition the self-serving decisions of individuals to buy and sell end up promoting the public good. Competition forces people to take account of others' interests in order to serve their own. If Apple Computer does not meet your needs, you can buy a product from Texas Instruments or IBM—and Apple knows it. It is in their interest to serve your interests. Since many businesses strive to serve their own interests by serving those of the public, the whole society will benefit. There will be an abundance of high-quality, low-priced goods and services, which will entice many people to buy. Businesses will then produce more to meet consumers' increased demand, which will create more jobs and raise wages. The result is a prosperous economy for the society as a whole.

Conflict Perspective

The conflict ideas about the harmfulness of capitalism can be traced to Karl Marx (1818–1883). He saw as inevitable private property owners' exploitation of their laborers by paying them as little as possible. Marx also disagreed with Smith on the specialized division of labor in industrial capitalism. To Smith, specialization enhances *efficiency* in the generation of wealth. But when Marx looked at specialization, he saw a source of **alienation of labor**, the laborers' loss of control over their work process. Because workers own neither their tools nor the products they make and because they cannot exercise all their capacities as they choose but are forced to perform an isolated, specific task, their work is no longer their own. Instead, it becomes a separate, alien thing.

Marx further saw severe contradictions within the capitalist system, contradictions that would serve as "its own gravediggers." One contradiction grows from capitalism's devotion to individualism. As

Heilbroner (1972) said, "*capitalism* had become so complex that it needed direction, but *capitalists* insisted on a ruinous freedom." Marx saw another contradiction as well. Capitalists depend on profit, but their profit comes from the fact that workers put more value into products than they are given in the form of wages. To increase their profits, capitalists often hold down wages, and, whenever possible, substitute machines for human labor as well. As a result, the poor get poorer from lower wages or job loss. This, in turn, reduces the demand for the capitalists' products, thereby decreasing their profits. The economy can work itself out of this crisis, but such crises will recur, with each one getting worse until the workers revolt.

Ultimately, Marx believed, the contradictions of capitalism would lead to communism, a classless society that would operate on the principle of "from each according to his ability, to each according to his needs." In this society, the state would wither away. First, however, the destruction of capitalism would be followed by a temporary era of **socialism**, an economic system based on public ownership and government control of the economy.

No state, including the so-called communist countries, such as the former Soviet Union and China, has ever reached communism, but many have tried socialism. In a socialist economy, the state owns and operates the means of production and distribution, such as land, factories, railroads, airlines, banks, and stores. It determines what the nation's economic needs are and develops plans to meet those goals. It sets wages and prices. Individual interests are subordinate to those of society.

Symbolic Interactionist Perspective

As a symbolic interactionist, Max Weber (1864–1920) concentrated on how subjective meanings affect economic action. To Weber, subjective meanings involve "taking into account the behavior of others," which in turn leads the individual to engage in certain activities (Weber, 1968). As suggested in Chapter 17 (Religion), Weber saw how the early Protestants in Europe acquired from their interactions with each other some shared beliefs that gave rise to capitalism.

First, the Protestants defined hard work as a sign that God would send them to heaven rather than hell. They in effect equated toil with God's work. By working hard, they were able to produce wealth. Second, they defined play as the devil's temptation. They were thus afraid to spend the fruit of their labor on amusements and other worldly pleasures (Biggart, 1994). The wealth, then, was used as capital to start a business or to be reinvested in an existing business. The continuing accumulation of capital and growth of business led to the development of capitalism.

After capitalism had emerged, it could continue to operate for a long time because the early Protestants had learned to restrain themselves from behaving in an irrational or unsystematic manner. The early Protestantism helped discipline an unruly working class, restraining its members from consuming alcohol, from engaging in disorderly conduct, and even from taking breaks or walking off their jobs, thus turning them into a docile labor force (Wuthnow, 1994). Simultaneously, the same religion encouraged the capitalist class to run its business rationally. As a result, these capitalists developed bureaucracy as the most rational form of organization to perpetuate capitalism. As suggested in Chapter 5 (Groups and Organizations), bureaucrats must restrain themselves from the subjective, personal ways of doing things, ways that the early Protestants considered irrational. Instead, bureaucrats must rigidly, joylessly follow impersonal rules like ascetic Protestants.

Questions for Discussion and Review

1. How does capitalism affect society?
2. How did the early Protestantism produce and support capitalism?

A GLOBAL ANALYSIS

The economic system varies from one society to another. In theory, as we have observed, there are two major systems: capitalism and socialism. But in the real world do we really have purely capitalist economies or purely socialist economies? What are the economies around the globe really like? We explore these issues next.

Mixed Economies

All economic systems are **mixed economies**, containing elements of both capitalism and socialism. No state has a purely socialist or purely capitalist economy. In all socialist economies, there is still some buying and selling outside of government control and some individual ownership of property. In pre–1990 communist Poland, independent-minded

Most people assume that money is only useful for buying things. But, in this reading, sociologist Viviana Zelizer shows how people tend to attach certain meanings to money and behave accordingly.

A Buck Is Not A Buck

People constantly convert various objects into the equivalent of currency. It might be cigarettes; sometimes it's postage stamps, subway tokens, poker chips, baseball cards. They create physically distinct markers such as gift certificates or food stamps, or they make distinctions in the way they use existing currencies. Think of how people who win the lottery will treat that money very differently from their wages or an inheritance. Found money, a windfall, is different from a stolen dollar or earnings; payment to a prostitute is different from a loan to a daughter or a tip to a waitress. It's all cash, it's all that physically indistinct, anonymous dollar, and yet people care deeply about those differences.

This phenomenon is probably most apparent within families, where money is carefully (and often passionately) differentiated and segregated. Families set food money apart from rent money, school money or charity money, as well as funds for burial, weddings, Christmas or recreation. Sometimes these behaviors are highly idiosyncratic. I found a case of one father, for example, who would set aside every quarter bearing the year of his son's birth for his education. The process of personalizing currency is often ingenious.

It's no accident that we use the expression "an honest dollar." We distinguish morally reputable earnings from "dirty money," which is stained by its ethically dubious origins. There was a remarkable study of Oslo prostitutes, which revealed that the women perceived and practiced two distinct economies. One had to do with the money they received from health benefits or welfare subsidies, legitimate kinds of income, in their minds. They would be very careful with this money, counting every penny and budgeting meticulously. By contrast, they would just blow their prostitution earnings on drugs, alcohol and clothes.

If money were truly neutral, there never would have been the moral uproar that occurred when Teddy Roosevelt removed "In God We Trust" from the dollar. Supporters of the ban argued that money was a medium of secular, not sacred, transactions and that as such it needed no religious inscription. But in the end, the inscription was put back on because people basically protested, "We don't want a Godless currency."

farmers produced much of the country's food supplies on private plots. Similarly, in Hungarian cities, taxi drivers, artisans, shopkeepers, and restaurants operated almost as freely as their counterparts in the capitalist West. Even in the former Soviet Union, perhaps the most anticapitalist before 1992, some service industries kept the profits they earned, rather than turning them over to the government. This **second economy**—a free market operating within and parallel to the state-controlled economy—continues to exist in countries that remain communist, such as Cuba, Vietnam, and Angola (Los, 1990). Nevertheless, in all the communist countries, the state still owns and controls key industries, such as steel and oil, and bans large, privately owned companies.

On the other hand, no government in capitalist societies has followed a strictly laissez-faire policy. In the United States, for example, government policies provided the canals, roads, railroads, cheap land, and education that laid the foundation for the nation's economic growth. When the U.S. public became disgusted with outrageous railroad freight fares, contaminated meat, and similar problems around the turn of the century, the government stepped in with new laws to regulate business. When capitalism failed in the Great Depression of the 1930s, the government established an array of programs to regulate business practices and to provide people with a cushion against the impact of hard times. When people realized that Adam Smith's "invisible hand" did not prevent business from producing dangerous levels of pollution, environmental regulations were passed. To protect workers against gross exploitation, the government passed laws governing wages, hours, and working conditions. Most of these socialist elements of government ownership and control still exist in the United States today (Friedman, 1989b).

The Economic Continuum

Although all economic systems are mixed economies, the "mix" between the capitalist and socialist elements varies considerably. Thus, we can arrange economies along a continuum from most capitalist to most socialist.

The United States and Japan are among the most capitalist. Yet, as we have seen, the United States does not follow a laissez-faire policy, and competition is limited in many ways. In Japan the government takes a leading role in planning investment for the future, in turning corporations toward industries that are likely to grow.

Ranging along the middle of the continuum are the European democracies. From time to time, several of these democracies have had socialist governments. In general, these nations have combined capitalist enterprise with wide-ranging government control—and high taxes. They tend to establish stricter controls on business and more extensive social services than the United States. All these states, for example, provide a national system of health insurance. Over the years, their governments have

owned and managed many industries. Great Britain, for example, has had the coal, steel, automobile, and television industries under government control at various times. Even before France elected a socialist government in 1981, its government had created subway and aerospace industries. Nevertheless, these European democracies are so much more capitalist than socialist that they are usually considered capitalist.

At the socialist end of the continuum we find countries such as North Korea, Vietnam, China, and Cuba. Their governments largely control their economy. But some have recently tried to introduce a new economic arrangement in which centralized direction of the economy by the government is reduced. China has adopted some free enterprise practices. It has abolished most rural communes, restored family farms, established a free market for agricultural and consumer goods, granted state-owned enterprises wide autonomy in running their businesses, and opened up its coastal regions to foreign investors. This free enterprise, however, is still more limited than in other countries.

Economic Performance

The socialist economies have a decidedly mixed record. Their total wealth is generally far below that of capitalist countries (see Figure 19.1). True, under socialism, nations such as Cuba and China have improved the standard of living for vast numbers of

China is found at the socialist end of the economic continuum. The Chinese government has largely controlled the economy of the country. But some free-enterprise practices, such as the selling of silk by these private citizens on the streets, have recently been permitted.

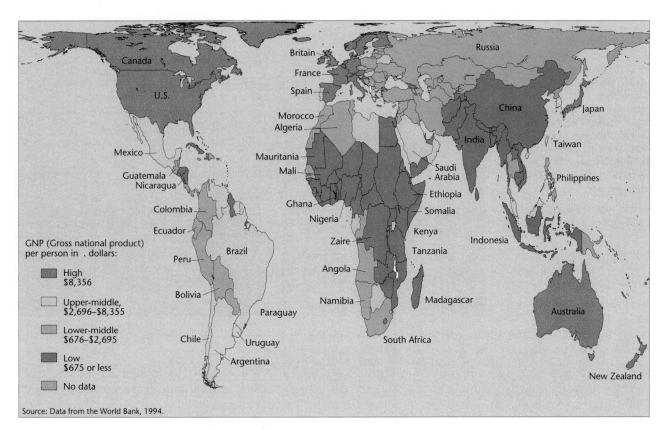

FIGURE 19.1
Economic Performance Around the World
Socialist economies such as those in China, the former Soviet Union, and formerly communist Eastern Europe are generally poor. But, under socialism, these countries have reduced the extremes of inflation, unemployment, or poverty. On the other hand, capitalist economies such as those in the United States, Western Europe, and Japan are considerably more prosperous, but have suffered periodic bouts of extreme inflation and unemployment.

people who had been destitute. In general, socialist nations have reduced the extremes of poverty, inflation, or unemployment that occasionally hit capitalist states. But significant economic inequalities still remain. Managers make much more money than ordinary workers. They also have special privileges and access to luxury goods that ordinary citizens cannot get. Furthermore, the central planning of socialist states often creates inefficiencies and bottlenecks. Perhaps their greatest problem is production. Severe shortages often plague socialist states. The absence of adequate incentives comparable to private-property ownership is the major cause of the low productivity of the state-run farms in socialist countries (Benjamin et al., 1992).

In the meantime, capitalist economies in the West have little trouble producing ample quantities of goods, although they have faced periodic bouts of extreme inflation and unemployment, as in the late 1970s and early 1980s. Moreover, their social peace to a great extent has depended on economic growth,

which gives even the poor some hope of improving their standard of living. Their ability to sustain this growth may not be certain all the time. Around 1980, the U.S. economy, for example, seemed to get stuck, unable to continue up the spiral that Adam Smith predicted would generate more productivity and more wealth. In fact, its productivity went down, increasing unemployment as well as inflation. But in 1983 the U.S. economy began to make a dramatic comeback, showing a substantial growth in productivity and a decline in unemployment and inflation. The economies in Canada, Western Europe, and Japan also rebounded. In 1991 another worldwide economic recession hit these capitalist countries, and again there have been some signs of recovery since then.

Despite the ups and downs of their economic conditions, the capitalist countries tend to remain considerably more productive than their socialist counterparts. According to a study by the WorldWatch Institute, Western European countries'

The bright spots in the U.S. economy today are lower unemployment and lower inflation. Some people have become fabulously rich. Yet our standard of living has mostly failed to improve. Largely because of a slowdown in productivity growth, income has been relatively stagnant for most people.

labor productivity rates were often twice as high as those of formerly socialist Eastern Europe, and the United States was nearly 20 times more productive than the former Soviet Union. The capitalist system's higher efficiency can be attributed to the freedom for pursuing personal gain or the absence of socialist-style government control (Rheem, 1986).

The U.S. Economy Today

There are both bright and dark spots in the U.S. economic picture. For about 10 years now, the U.S. economy has been producing an abundance of jobs. Massive numbers of women and immigrants have joined the baby-boom generation in entering the labor force without causing a bulge in unemployment. Inflation has also gone down to a level that generates only little discomfort. But our standard of living is now lower than before. Although some people have become fabulously rich, the majority of U.S. workers earn little, if any, more in real take-home pay than they did before 1980. Low-income people have suffered more, with real incomes falling, more persons dropping below the poverty line, and homelessness rising (also see box, p. 443).

Throughout most of the 1980s, only about 5 percent of our work force was unemployed. This was a remarkable achievement. The U.S. economy has managed to create jobs for huge numbers of baby-boomers, women, and immigrants. By contrast, in Europe, few new jobs have been generated, so that unemployment there has increased sharply. During

the 1992 recession the U.S. jobless rate went up to 7.6 percent, causing profound distress and fear among millions of unemployed and employed workers. But that rate was still far lower than the 10.8 percent of a decade before, and now (in 1995), with the recession over, it has come down to about 5 percent again (Hershey, 1995). Another success story is that the inflation rate came down from 12 percent in 1980 to about 5 percent today (Krugman, 1990; Gwynne, 1992).

Despite lower unemployment and lower inflation over the last 10 years, our living standard has mostly failed to improve. Income has remained relatively stagnant for most people. Significantly more workers have to moonlight to meet regular household expenses or to pay off debts. A key reason is that since 1970 we have suffered a slowdown in productivity growth. Although the U.S. economy has grown significantly since 1983, its growth is still much smaller today than 30 and 40 years ago. Since 1970 U.S. output per worker has risen an average of only 1.2 percent a year, compared with 2.8 percent in the 1950s and 1960s. This has made it impossible for most people to improve their living standard. If the productivity growth continues to remain low, today's young families will live no better than their parents (Krugman, 1990).

Related to our slowdown in productivity growth is our large **trade deficit**—buying more goods and services from foreign countries than selling to them. Before 1984 there was a **trade surplus**—selling more goods and services to foreign countries than buying from them. But since 1984 we have annually spent

ENRICHING OUR LIVES

The new world economy is creating wealth but also poverty. This reading, which comes from a lecture by a foremost U.S. economist, John Kenneth Galbraith, discusses the rise of a new class system and suggests how to help the underclass share the good life with the upper class.

The Good Life Beckons

We must begin by considering the very great changes that have occurred in the social and economic structure of the economically advanced lands in modern times. Once all economic and social thought turned on a bilateral economic and social structure. There were capital and labor, the capitalists and the worker. This is no longer the case in the advanced industrial countries. The great political dichotomy between the capitalists and the working masses has retreated into the shadows. Politically dominant now are the managerial bureaucracy, the public-sector bureaucracy and the lawyers, physicians, educators, members of the many other professions, the large pensioned and *rentier* community.

We have now a new class structure that embraces, on the one hand, the comfortably situated we have just mentioned, who have replaced the once-dominant capitalist, and on the other, a large number of less affluent or often impoverished people who do the work that makes life pleasant, even tolerable, for the culture of contentment. The modern equivalent of the one-time industrial proletariat is an underclass in the service of the comfortably situated. This underclass does much of the heavy repetitive industrial work that still survives. In the United States, we have a modern reserve army of the masses consisting of the poverty-stricken population in the big cities.

In the good society there cannot, must not, be a deprived and excluded underclass. Those who heretofore have made it up must become fully a part of the larger social community. There must be full democratic participation by all, and from this alone can come the sense of community that accepts and even values diversity. But full participation by the now-excluded will not be brought about by plea or prayer or lectures. It requires some very practical, very concrete steps on the part of the modern state.

There is, first, the absolute, inescapable requirement that everyone in the good, even decent, society should have a basic source of income. And if this is not available from the market system, it must come from the state.

Next, there must be opportunity for people to escape from the underclass—for upward social and political mobility. Political tranquility is best served by the hope of such upward movement, if not for this generation, then for the next. There is no novelty as to what is required here; it is education—human investment. Nothing else is so important. In the U.S., our approach to this is far from satisfactory. We have excellent universities and good suburban and private schools for the comfortable class, but the underclass in our cities is condemned to an education that perpetuates their poverty.

There remains a final requirement of the good society. It must have an effectively working economy. A central step is to ensure a more equitable distribution of income than the market system provides. I do not foresee or even advocate any rigid equality in economic reward. I accept the inevitable; I urge that a reasonably equitable distribution of income is not only socially right, but also economically functional. It is a mark of a good society; it contributes notably to economic stability.

Excerpted from John Kenneth Galbraith, "The Good Life Beckons," *New Statesman & Society,* January 28, 1994, pp. 14–16.

over $100 billion more on foreign imports than we earned from our exports abroad. As a result, foreign companies have been using their profits to buy a steady stream of U.S. assets, such as stocks, bonds, real estate, and whole corporations. This further causes a drain on our national income, because the United States has to pay interest to foreign bondholders, dividends to foreign stockholders, and rents to foreign landowners. We are also running the risk that foreigners will precipitate an economic crisis here by liquidating their U.S. assets and taking their profits home. This is likely to occur if their confidence in the U.S. economy wavers or their own economies worsen considerably.

Another economic problem is the huge federal budget deficit. Every year the government spends much more than it takes in. Many fear that the government may someday be unable to pay the debt and become as bankrupt as many Latin American countries were in the 1980s. Traditionally, most Democrats have wanted to reduce the budget deficit by raising taxes but have failed to take the lead for fear of alienating voters. Most Republicans have wanted to eliminate the deficit by cutting government spending but have feared alienating voters by cutting popular social insurance programs (primarily Social Security), which account for 40 percent of the federal expenditure. Today the Republican-controlled Congress may pass the balanced-budget amendment, but it will require ratification by at least 38 states, which can take years (Alter, 1995).

The Economies in Other Countries

We now live in a global economy, with the economies of different countries affecting one another. We can see this in the current economic trends around the world. As the U.S. economy, the most powerful in the world, started to climb out of the worldwide recession in 1992, the economies in many other countries followed suit, producing significant growth in 1994. Today's hottest economies—in Southeast Asia and Latin America—have attracted considerable foreign investment. Free from domination by the former Soviet Union, Eastern Europeans have in recent years been heavily influenced by capitalist nations. They not only have received a great deal of foreign investment but also have got rid of many government-controlled industries. Being part of the same global economy, various nations have also experienced similar problems such as the budget deficit, inflation, or unemployment. But the economies in most countries are doing better than several years ago.

Canada Canada has become the most successful exporting country in the industrial world. Along with sharply increasing exports, surging corporate investment and job growth have significantly pushed down its unusually high unemployment. But consumer spending cannot go up much because of both tax increases and higher borrowing costs. The government plans to raise taxes, as well as reduce spending, to tackle a huge budget deficit, the second highest among industrialized countries (Farnsworth, 1995).

Latin America With runaway inflation under control and foreign investors pouring in capital, Latin America is likely to maintain its position as the world's second fastest-growing region—after Southeast Asia. Traditional export commodities, from coffee to copper, are also expected to bring in higher profits because of improved prices. To stimulate their economies, most Latin American countries are removing trade barriers and using private capital to build roads and power plants. The region's exception is Venezuela, whose gross national product fell 3 percent and where annual inflation hovered around 70 percent in 1994, while for the region as a whole the GNP went up 4 percent and inflation was 10 percent (Brooke, 1995).

Western Europe Economies from Italy to Scandinavia have just passed through their worst recession since the end of the Second World War in the 1940s. Growth has picked up and is expected to be 3 percent or higher for 1995 and 1996. Inflation remains low, less than 3 percent. Corporate profits have gone up more than 50 percent. Confident of further successes, companies have begun to increase their capital investment. All these signs of recovery since 1993 have largely resulted from a surge in demand for European goods from rapidly growing economies such as those of Asia and North America (Nash, 1995).

Eastern Europe and Russia In their transition from socialist to capitalist economies, most Eastern European nations have shown significant growth, with their GNPs increasing over 4 percent. Foreign investment is expected to continue expanding, but the extent of the increase will depend on how fast and extensively the state industries are privatized. Foreign investors are wary of Poland, for example, because its government, dominated by two parties with past communist influence, has been reluctant to implement the long-awaited program of mass privatization. But foreign investors are more interested in the Czech Republic, which has forged ahead with its privatization program by selling state industries cheaply to Czech citizens. While Eastern Europe is improving economically, Russia continues to suffer high unemployment and inflation because of political instability (Perlez, 1995; Erlanger, 1995).

China and Southeast Asia Since 1992 China has turned in an extraordinary economic performance, with annual growth rates of over 13 percent, by far the highest in the world. The growth has partly been fueled by foreign investment, which continues to flood into the country. But the economy remains mostly socialist. State-owned factories continue to soak up most of the capital (investment and bank loans) in China, although they contribute only a

GLOBAL VILLAGE

Many Asian countries are experiencing a major economic transformation as the world economy expands and national borders become less important. As the media and information travel around the world, consumers increasingly want the same goods, regardless of where they live. This article describes this process of economic globalization through the efforts of the Avon Corporation to sell cosmetics in China.

China's 600,000 Avon Ladies

On old economic maps, the most important cartographic facts had to do with things like the location of raw material deposits, energy sources, navigable rivers, deep-water ports, railroad lines, paved roads—and national borders. On today's maps, by contrast, the most salient facts are the footprints cast by TV satellites, the areas covered by radio signals and the geographic reach of newspapers and magazines. Information has replaced both propinquity and politics as the landscape feature most likely to shape the flows of economic activity. Physical terrain and political boundaries still matter, of course, but they—especially political boundaries—do not matter as much as what people know or want to value.

For example, girls in Guangzhou, the capital of the state of Guangdong in China, are eager to get hold of Avon lipstick. There is a reason for this. Avon ran a TV commercial called "Hong Kong Girls" about two years ago. It implied that Cantonese girls, if they became rich, could look as pretty as Hong Kong girls. The girls in the TV commercial, clad in mini skirts, dancing the go-go and wearing this American lipstick, looked very attractive indeed.

Today, after just three years in operation in Guangdong, Avon has mobilized more than 30,000 door-to-door Avon ladies in Guangdong alone. The Avon people thought door-to-door sales were necessary, but demand is so great that the customers come right to the distribution points for more products. It is estimated that more than 600,000 Avon ladies will be needed in all of China by the turn of the century.

Although Avon just opened its Shanghai operation, it has already hired 6,000 Avon ladies. Those girls snatching up lipstick probably don't remember how to spell "communism" anymore. Nor do they care about it. The promise of prosperity has completely and irreversibly changed their priorities and agenda.

What is happening in China today is a case in point of how the power of information has become the key determinant of the future shape of the world. It has tumbled walls. It is erasing borders and undoing the traditional19th-century model of the nation state.

Excerpted from Kenichi Ohmae, "China's 600,000 Avon Ladies," *New Perspectives Quarterly,* Winter, 1995, pp. 14–17.

---

small percentage to the nation's industrial output (Tyler, 1995).

As a region, Southeast Asia (especially Indonesia, Malaysia, Singapore, and Thailand) continues to have the world's most vibrant economy as it had in the last several years, boasting an annual growth rate of 7 percent or more. This remarkable growth has largely been attributed to the region's large numbers of low-wage but relatively well-educated workers. Huge foreign investment, notably from Japan, has also been an important factor. But with the unrestrained economic boom many cities are now overbuilt, congested, and polluted. The vast disparity

between rich and poor has also become a common sight (Shenon, 1995).

Questions for Discussion and Review

1. What is a mixed economy?
2. How can economies be classified? How well has each type performed in recent history?
3. What is the condition of the U.S. economy today?
4. What is the nature of today's global economy? What is the current status of various economies in the world?

THE DOMINANCE OF BIG CORPORATIONS

There is an inherent contradiction in the competitive market system: the more efficient it is, the more it threatens to destroy itself. Through free competition, the best producers gain more resources, which gives them an edge on their competitors. They may use this edge to drive their competitors out of business or to buy them out and prevent other potential producers from entering the market. Eventually, just one firm might dominate production of a product, achieving a **monopoly**—the situation in which one firm controls the output of an industry. It is far more likely that a handful of firms would control a certain market, forming an **oligopoly**—the situation in which a very few companies control the output of an industry. Indeed, today, a small number of big corporations dominate the economy in many countries. In the United States, for example, 2,000 corporations, which represent only 0.1 percent of all companies in the country, own 40 percent of all company assets and 88 percent of all business income (Useem, 1980; Census Bureau, 1994).

The Nature of Big Corporations

A big corporation does not have a single owner. Instead, it has thousands or even hundreds of thousands of stockholders. They do not communicate with one another, much less organize to control the corporation. But they can exercise their right to vote—usually for electing a board of directors to run the corporation. The directors make overall plans for the company. They may decide how to raise money, how to expand the company, or what dividends are to be paid to shareholders. The directors also appoint the president, vice president, and other officers to conduct the company's day-to-day operations. In corporations, then, ownership and control are separated.

The big corporation is a far cry from what Adam Smith expected. To him, a typical company would be small, started by one or a few individuals with their personal savings. These entrepreneurs would personally manage it and reap profits or suffer losses, depending on how well they would do in a competitive market. Thus, the rise of giant corporations today can have serious consequences that Smith did not anticipate.

First, the few dominant companies, relatively free from competitive challenges, can force consumers to pay high prices for their products. They may slow down production and then increase the prices for their "scarce" goods. This is what the oil, steel, and

other mining and manufacturing companies did in the 1970s. Price hikes can generate inflation, and production slowdowns can cause unemployment, both of which can throw society into an economic crisis, as they did in the 1970s.

Moreover, given their control over large shares of the market, giant corporations may *not* have the incentives to build new plants, increase research and development of new products, make themselves more efficient, and offer consumers better goods and services. This may partly explain why in recent decades some giant U.S. companies—especially in the car and steel industries—could not compete with Japanese and other foreign firms.

But big corporations also contribute to the well-being of society. By combining the capital of millions of investors and the talents of numerous workers, giant corporations make it possible for many to enjoy a relatively high standard of living. Large corporations also contribute heavily to universities and colleges, charitable organizations, and public service projects. Corporate philanthropy may be intended to stimulate sales by generating good will, but it does help improve the nation's health, education, and welfare (Burt, 1983). Since corporations are considered vitally important, they receive a great deal of help from the government, as we will see in the next section.

Welfare for the Rich

There are two welfare systems in the United States. One is the well-known welfare system for the poor and the other is that for the rich. The government help for rich individuals and big corporations may be in the form of *special tax breaks* called tax credits or deductions or other "loopholes." Some of the government help for corporations may also be in the form of direct payments or loans, usually called, not welfare, but a *subsidy*. Welfare for rich individuals and big corporations is far more generous than welfare for the poor.

Big corporations seem to get the greatest amount of government benefits. Corporate income taxes have always been proportionately smaller than personal income taxes. Over the last 30 years, the corporate income tax as a fraction of the federal revenue has steadily declined, from 23.0 percent in 1966 to 10.5 percent in 1992 (Auerbach, 1983; Census Bureau, 1994). The government also supplies big business with more dollars in direct loans and loan guarantees than all the commercial and industrial loans provided by private banks. Every year the government further pays an enormous sum for research and development projects in areas such as the mili-

The U.S. government sometimes bails out huge corporations on the verge of bankruptcy, such as Chrysler in 1979. Thus our "free enterprise" system looks like corporate socialism. To some extent, risk has been "socialized"—borne by all of us—but profit remains "privatized," claimed by corporate stockholders.

tary, space, and atomic energy. After developing the technology at taxpayers' expense, corporations are allowed to use it to earn a profit.

The government can even bail out a corporation on the verge of bankruptcy. Generally, the larger a corporation, the larger the number of people who would be hurt by its failure, and the more likely the government is to rescue the corporation from its own mistakes. In 1979, for example, Chrysler had a $4.1 billion payroll, with about 130,000 workers in the United States. In addition, the economic fate of automobile suppliers and dealers scattered across the country was tied to Chrysler. Hundreds of companies fail every year, but when Chrysler seemed about to go under, the government offered a helping hand with $1.5 billion in loan guarantees (Gregg, 1980). Thus, our free enterprise system might be called "corporate socialism." To some extent, risk has been "socialized"—borne by all of us—but profit remains "privatized," claimed by corporate stockholders.

Multinational Corporations

In many big corporate mergers, a corporation buys others that operate different kinds of business to form a **conglomerate**, a corporation that owns companies in various unrelated industries. A striking example is the International Telephone and Telegraph Corporation (IT&T). In the last two decades, IT&T has bought a long string of companies that had nothing to do with telephones and telegraphs. Its acquisitions included Sheraton Hotels, Avis car rentals, Bobbs-Merrill publishers, Hartford Insurance, Levitt and Sons builders, Continental bak-

eries, and Smithfield hams, as well as firms that manufacture cellulose, vending machines, and other products (Clairmonte and Cavanagh, 1983).

Most of these conglomerates have further expanded by becoming **multinational corporations**, corporations that have subsidiaries in many countries. IT&T, for example, employs over 425,000 workers in at least 70 countries. Many multinationals have more economic power than a medium-sized nation. One way to measure their power is to compare the annual sales of a corporation with the gross national product of a nation. By this standard, in 1990, General Motors was more powerful than Ireland, Greece, Pakistan, and Nicaragua combined, and Exxon was more powerful than Israel, Jordan, the Philippines, and Guatemala (*Forbes,* 1991; *World Factbook,* 1990).

In search of lower labor costs, lower taxes, and larger markets, many multinational corporations have shifted their assets out of their industrialized birthplaces into the developing world. From these foreign investments, U.S. corporations can earn as much as 70 percent of their total profits. For these profits, multinational corporations pay very little in taxes because of the much lower tax rates in foreign countries. Even for earnings that come from goods manufactured in the United States, multinational corporations often avoid paying the high U.S. taxes by selling the merchandise at cost to their subsidiaries abroad. Suppose an item is produced in the United States at a cost of $100 and sold to an Irish subsidiary for $100. Because there is no profit from this transaction, no U.S. tax is paid. But suppose the subsidiary turns around and resells the item for $200 to another U.S. subsidiary, earning a $100 profit. The company pays only a 4 percent tax ($4) in Ireland, thereby evading the 48 percent tax in the United States (Martz, 1991).

Multinational corporations can have far-reaching effects on developing nations. They can promote social conflict by bringing in elements of a foreign culture. They can promote dangerous practices such as smoking. They can control a small nation's most important industry such as copper production. But most developing countries still welcome multinationals. They often try to attract more foreign investment with a wide array of incentives, ranging from extensive tax benefits to subsidized labor, including the elimination of trade unions. Apparently, they appreciate the fact that multinationals usually create many badly needed jobs, transfer modern technology to them, and stimulate their economic growth.

Questions for Discussion and Review

1. How can a competitive market system lead to oligopoly or monopoly?
2. What are the characteristics of big corporations?
3. What is welfare for the rich?
4. How do multinational corporations earn their profits?

WORK IN THE UNITED STATES

When we meet strangers, one of our first questions is likely to be, "What do you do?" They might answer, "I am a salesperson" or "I am a cabdriver" or a doctor or lawyer, or whatever. Work is not just a way to make enough money to pay the bills. For many of us, work helps define our identity and our sense of self-worth. Just what it is that we are able to do, however, depends to a great extent on the economic institutions we have described. As we see in the following sections, the kinds of workers needed by our complex economy have implications for job satisfaction and the workplace.

Occupations

With the industrialization of the farm—a process that accelerated greatly after World War II—the stage was set for the appearance of today's labor force. Thanks to technological innovations ranging from new

machinery to new fertilizers to new breeding techniques, agricultural productivity has soared during this century. In 1900 one U.S. farmer on average produced enough food to support seven other people. Today, one farmer produces enough for more than 60 people.

This increasing agricultural productivity pushed many workers off the farm. Now only about 1 percent of the U.S. labor force works on the farm, compared with nearly 60 percent in 1870 and 30.2 percent in 1920. The continuing exodus also reflects the failure of many small family farms to survive. Government subsidies and other "save the family farm" programs, such as crop insurance and production control, have largely come to naught. What remains is an increasingly smaller number of highly efficient farms that need only a few workers to produce enough food for the whole nation. In fact, these farms are capable of producing so much food that the federal government has to pay them about $10 billion a year *not* to produce more than necessary (Robbins, 1990).

Many of those who left the farm in earlier decades went to work in manufacturing industries, producing clothes, furniture, or cars. But major changes were under way in manufacturing as well. Just as in agriculture, new machines decreased the number of people needed to produce things. Since World War II, the share of *jobs in manufacturing held by white-collar workers*—managers, professionals, clerical workers, salespersons—has increased greatly. Before 1945, blue-collar workers had long outnumbered white-collar workers, but then white collars began to grow so fast in numbers that today they are three times as numerous as blue collars in manufacturing companies. At General Motors Corporation, for example, 77.5 percent of the work force is white collar, compared with 22.5 percent blue-collar workers (Rosecrance, 1990).

Meanwhile, the growth in jobs in manufacturing and other goods-producing industries has slowed, but *jobs in service industries*—education, health care, banking, real estate, insurance—have increased. In 1900 about 75 percent of the labor force was employed in production and fewer than 25 percent in service. But by 1982 the situation was reversed—74 percent in service and 26 percent in production. In the 1990s, the largest job growth in service industries will be among retail salespeople, janitors and maids, waiters and waitresses, and registered nurses, along with doctors, lawyers, teachers, accountants, and other professionals (Crispell, 1990). The rapid growth in the service sector as a whole results largely from an increased demand for health care, entertainment, and business and financial services.

The Workers

The composition of the U.S. labor force has changed, too. The most publicized change has occurred in gender. In 1984 the U.S. Department of Labor announced that since 1960 the number of women in the labor force had nearly doubled. Today, about 58 percent of women are in the labor force, compared with just 38 percent in 1960. The number of women workers will continue to rise, and women are projected to account for about two-thirds of the entire labor force *growth* between 1982 and 1995 (Census Bureau, 1994). By publicizing and legitimizing the rights and needs of women to earn enough money to support themselves and contribute to total family income, the feminist movement has largely aided the increase (see Chapter 13: Women and Men).

Important changes have also occurred in the age and racial composition of the work force. In the last two decades, the employment rate for men older than 65 declined significantly. Age discrimination and retirement programs, such as Social Security and private pension plans, have probably played a part in this decline. But in recent years, a growing industrial demand for cheaper labor—stimulated by global competition—has fueled a dramatic increase in labor-force participation among minorities and immigrants. These groups will account for 88 percent of work-force *growth* between 1989 and 1999. Meanwhile, there will be proportionately fewer white men in the labor force (Solomon, 1989).

These breakdowns by gender, race, and age do not tell us much about what is actually going on in the U.S. economy. We have a **dual economy**, an economy that comprises a *core* of large corporations dominating the market and a *periphery* of small firms competing for the remaining, smaller shares of business. In addition, there is a *third sector*, consisting of various government agencies. About 30 percent of the U.S. labor force work in the third, state sector, and the rest are employed in the private core and peripheral sector. Contrary to popular belief, most of the privately employed individuals do not work in the core's large companies (with more than 1,000 employees each). Only 30 to 40 percent do so. Most work in the peripheral sector, especially in small firms with fewer than 100 employees (Granovetter, 1984). Whatever sector they work in, U.S. workers are now better educated than before. In 1940 most workers had just slightly more than a grade school education. Today, more than half have some college and three out of four are high school graduates (Granovetter, 1984; Census Bureau, 1994). Unfortunately, they are faced with problems that did not exist before.

In today's fiercely competitive global economy, many U.S. companies have begun to minimize production costs by paying their employees low wages, comparable to those received by skilled but low-paid workers in the fast developing economies of Asia and Eastern Europe. A popular way to keep payroll costs low involves hiring temporary, contingent, part-time, or contract workers. In fact, since 1982 temporary employment has soared by nearly 250 percent, compared with a less than 20 percent increase in all employment. Temporary workers now compose one-third of the U.S. labor force, and their ranks are growing so fast that they are expected to outnumber permanent full-time workers by the end of this decade (Castro, 1993).

Labor Unions

As an individual, the worker usually has little, if any, power. Of course, workers at least theoretically can leave their jobs if they don't like them, but many cannot afford to take that risk, especially when

To balance the scale of power in the workplace, millions of workers have joined labor unions. Business and government long fought the establishment of unions in the United States, sometimes, as shown here, violently. Between 1933 and 1936, more than 100 workers were killed while striking for union recognition. Toward the late 1930s, the federal government began to back the right of workers to join unions and bargain collectively with their employers.

unemployment is high. A few workers may have some bargaining power with their employers if their skills are rare and in great demand. When labor is very scarce, employers may compete to offer the best conditions and salaries. More often, workers compete for jobs, and employers have the upper hand.

To balance the scales of power in the workplace, millions of workers have joined labor unions. Both business and government long fought their establishment in the United States, sometimes violently. Between 1933 and 1936, for example, more than 100 workers were killed while striking for union recognition. Only toward the late 1930s did the federal government change sides and back the right of workers to join unions and bargain collectively with their employers. After that, unions organized more and more workers, so that the percentage of the work force that was unionized climbed from only 12 percent in the 1930s to a peak of 35 percent in the 1950s. Unions won for their workers higher wages, shorter working hours, safer working conditions, and fringe benefits such as health insurance, pensions,

and vacations. All these did cost individual companies by eating into their profits, but that cost was more than offset by the beneficial results of collective bargaining—better morale and increased productivity (Freeman and Medoff, 1984).

In the early 1970s, however, unions began to decline in membership and power. The proportion of workers who joined unions fell from 31 percent in 1970 to 16 percent in 1990. While losing members, unions have also been losing their traditional power to gain concessions from employers. From the 1950s through the 1970s, employers could rarely operate during labor strikes. This is no longer the case today. In 1986, for example, when 150,000 communication workers struck the American Telephone and Telegraph Company, service continued with little disruption because, along with supervisors filling in, new workers were hired to replace the strikers (Clark, 1990; Sheets, 1990). It is no wonder that the frequency of major strikes has fallen sharply (see Figure 19.2). Why have unions been losing members and power?

FIGURE 19.2
A Declining Number of Strikes

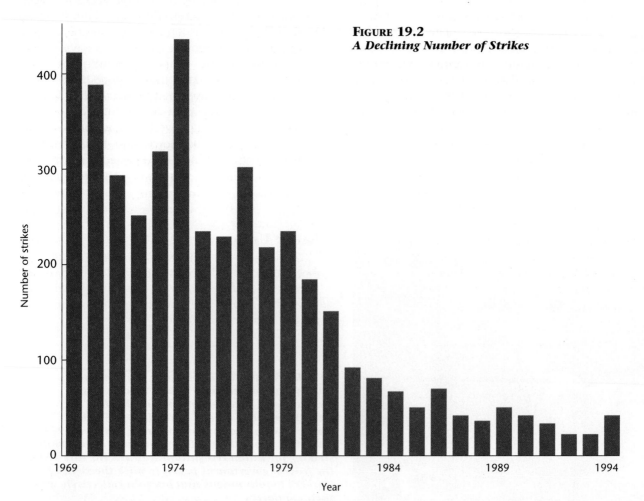

Source: Bureau of Labor Statistics, 1994

There are a number of reasons. First, unions were born among blue-collar workers, and such workers have long been the bulwark of the unions. But, as we have seen, it is white-collar employment that has been growing while blue-collar jobs have been increasingly scarce. Second, many blue-collar workers have lost their jobs to their lower-paid counterparts in foreign countries. Third, U.S. employers have been facing tougher competition in the global market. To be more competitive, they are compelled to reduce costs by hiring permanent replacements at lower wages to fill the jobs of union members who strike. They are able to do so because, given the increased difficulty of making a comfortable living in today's economy, replacement workers are happy to earn the wages and benefits spurned by strikers.

Unemployment

Unemployment is especially likely to hit blue-collar workers. The jobless rate of blue collars is usually three times as high as that of white collars. As we have observed, industrial reorganization has diminished production industries and hence blue-collar jobs. The loss of such jobs will continue. The already small blue-collar work force is expected to shrink from its present 25 percent of the labor market to only 10 percent in the next two decades. Already manufacturing companies have been more likely to lay off their mostly blue-collar workers, firing more than five times as many employees as have service companies, where white collars predominate. Joblessness is also higher among teenagers, minorities, and others with less than three years of high school (Young, 1983; Devens, 1984; Lee, 1990).

Aside from economic deprivation, joblessness can produce emotional, physical, and social problems. Many studies have shown that the unemployed typically suffer a loss of self-esteem. They feel ashamed and humiliated, avoid seeing friends, and sink into depression. The cumulative effect of unemployment on society is great. Being unemployed is associated with an increase in a broad range of other problems, from burglary and alcoholism to heart attacks and suicide. Unemployment may not be a direct cause of these problems, but rather serve as a trigger for problem-prone people (Brenner, 1976; Hamilton et al., 1990).

To soften the impact of unemployment, the government provides unemployment compensation, food stamps, and other transfer payments. There are also programs to train laid-off blue-collar workers for high-tech reemployment as machinists, data processors, aerospace equipment builders, and the like. Training for high-skilled jobs is increasingly important these days. Since the early 1980s, there has been a substantial growth in jobs that require higher skills.

Job Satisfaction

It may be depressing to be laid off, but does having a job bring happiness? Are U.S. workers really happy with their jobs? In many studies during the last two decades, representative samples of workers have been asked whether they would continue to work if they inherited enough money to live comfortably without working. More than 70 percent replied that they would. Asked how satisfied they were with their jobs, even more—from 80 to 90 percent—replied that they were very or moderately satisfied. But asked whether they would choose the same line of work if they could begin all over again, most said no. Only 43 percent of white-collar workers and 24 percent of blue collars said yes. And when asked, "Do you enjoy your work so much that you have a hard time putting it aside?" only 34 percent of men and 32 percent of women answered affirmatively (Glenn and Weaver, 1982; Burtless, 1990; Lipset, 1990b; NORC, 1994). In short, most people seem to like their jobs but are not too excited about them.

American Mosaic

A number of scholars have argued that it is difficult for government programs to redevelop the inner city, but that entrepreneurship and other self-help activities could play a more effective role, as discussed in this reading.

Race, Entrepreneurship, and the Inner City

Throughout the U.S., on talk shows and in newspapers, discussions are ongoing concerning the condition of blacks within inner-city America. These people represent less than one-third of the black population, yet get nearly 100 percent of the publicity about blacks in the United States Every four years, presidential candidates promise to change their conditions. The questions always are: How can this population establish a degree of economic security or how can the central cities be rebuilt? How can hope be created in a sea of seeming hopelessness?

Research in the area of race, ethnicity, and mobility is providing a revised picture of what it takes to be successful in U.S. society. For decades, academics, as well as the general public, viewed the picture of success by race and ethnic groups as going through a process that began with them starting on the bottom of the economic ladder in bad jobs, then working up to better ones.

While this model has been dominant, research is starting to show some interesting results that relate to another model of incorporation into society. The new model is not new at all, but takes as its inspiration from research in the 1800s and early 1900s on self-help among ethnic groups. In *The Protestant Ethic and the Spirit of Capitalism*, sociologist Max Weber noted that national or religious minorities are likely—because they are excluded from opportunities in the larger society—to be driven with peculiar force into private, self-determined economic activity.

Weber's ideas serve as the intellectual springboard for scholars who study groups that incorporate themselves into countries through self-help activities. In-cluded are the importance of small enterprises, development of community organizations, building and maintaining private schools, and an emphasis on the higher education of children. It is the presence of prejudice and discrimination that drives the victimized groups to concentrate on self-help activities.

The key to rebuilding portions of black America, especially the central cities and other places where hope is low, lies in the often-forgotten self-help tradition of African Americans, the group that created this phenomenon in U.S. society. That history is not forgotten by all blacks, especially those who were reared in the self-help tradition. Like today's Koreans and generations of Jewish Americans, they understand the importance of business enterprise and education in a society where race can be problematic. In order to rebuild many black communities, they have to be grounded in the self-help tradition. That means that, if the public education system has turned into a detention center, rather than a place of learning, private schools should be created. It means that when an individual does not have the credentials to find an excellent job in the competitive market, the person must concentrate on the establishment of small enterprises. The lessons that were noticed by ethnic scholars such as Weber once again are being played out in an advanced society.

Excerpted from John Sibley Butler," Race, Entrepreneurship, and the Inner City," *USA Today* magazine, January, pp. 26–29, copyright 1995 by the Society for the Advancement of Education.

Job satisfaction varies from one group to another. Generally, older workers are more satisfied than younger ones. One reason is that older workers, being more advanced in their careers, have better jobs. Another is that younger workers are more likely to expect their jobs to be highly interesting and stimulating, hence are more likely to be disillusioned because of the difficulty in realizing their high aspirations. White-collar workers, especially professionals and businesspeople, are also more likely than blue collars to feel genuinely satisfied with their jobs.

Among blue-collar workers, union members report significantly *less* job satisfaction than nonmembers, which reflects job dissatisfaction as the primary reason for joining unions in the first place (Schwochau, 1987).

Generally paid less and having less prestigious jobs than men, women may be expected to be less satisfied with their work. But research has shown just the opposite: women are equally or more satisfied when compared with men. Why? One reason is that, because of gender discrimination, women expect less

Compared to men, women are equally or more satisfied with their work. Because of gender discrimination, they expect less from the job market and so can more easily fulfill their lower expectation. They also tend to compare themselves to homemakers and consequently find their own jobs far more satisfactory.

than men from the job market and so can more easily fulfill their lower expectations. If they get jobs that are as good as men's, going beyond their expectation, they are likely to express more satisfaction than men. Another reason is that, in evaluating their jobs, working women tend to compare themselves to traditional homemakers and consequently feel more satisfied with their jobs. This is why working women whose mothers have never worked outside the home like their jobs better than their female counterparts whose mothers have been gainfully employed (Hodson, 1989; Weaver and Matthews, 1990).

The Changing Workplace

In a survey, only 26 percent of U.S. workers still held the traditional view that it is all right to accept even an unpleasant job as long as it pays well. Some of these workers said "the more I get paid, the more I do." Others agreed that "work is one of life's unpleasant necessities. I wouldn't work if I didn't have to." A bumper sticker says it all: "Work sucks, but I need the bucks." In another survey, only 7 percent said they "work only as hard as they have to." By contrast, large majorities of the respondents expressed more positive attitudes toward work. Many agreed with the statement: "I have an inner need to do the very best I can, regardless of pay." They most frequently rated as "very important" certain non-

monetary, inherent qualities of work, such as interesting jobs, developing their own skills, and seeing how good the results of their work are (Yankelovich and Immerwahr, 1984; NORC, 1994). In short, most people in the U.S. still like to work hard, but their work ethic has taken on a new quality.

The traditional work ethic is imbued with the early Protestant belief in work as a moral duty—a way of sacrificing for others. Thus until recently most have believed that "a man with a family has a responsibility to choose the job that pays the most, rather than one that is more satisfying but pays less." They would work hard to support their families, disregarding how unpleasant and boring their work might be. But today a majority reject that view and attitude. Most are more interested in jobs that allow for personal growth, self-fulfillment, and other post-materialist values. There is, then, a shift in the work ethic, from an emphasis on self-sacrifice to a stress on self-development as the primary motive for hard work (Cramer, 1989; Schor, 1991).

How has this new ethic come about? As we have observed, the number of white-collar workers and the amount of average workers' education have increased substantially over the last several decades. It is these white-collar and better-educated workers who value autonomy and personal growth in the workplace. As a result, attempts have been made to reorganize the workplace. They usually include offering workers more interesting jobs, more autonomy, and increased participation in decision making. A growing number of companies give workers some freedom to set their own working hours within specified limits. Some have introduced mechanisms that allow workers to take part in decisions about production methods, promotions, hiring, and firing. Some companies have even raised wages by sharing profits with workers. These efforts have boosted productivity by 5 to 40 percent. Apparently, workers are more productive when management treats them as equal partners (Yankelovich and Immerwahr, 1984; Gwynne, 1990; Wartzman, 1992).

Questions for Discussion and Review

1. What occupations make up the U.S. labor force today, and what kinds of people fill these positions?
2. Why do so few workers join labor unions today?
3. What is the overall impact of unemployment on individuals and society?
4. What kinds of people are more satisfied with their jobs and why?
5. How and why has the U.S. work ethic changed?

CHAPTER REVIEW

1. *How did the Industrial Revolution change the economic process?* Machines replaced much human labor, mass production in factories displaced cottage industry, and agriculture lost ground to industry. *What are some effects of industrialization?* Industrialization speeds up production, shrinking blue-collar employment and enlarging white-collar work. It further changes demographic features, human relations, and the values of society.

2. *What are the major sociological perspectives on capitalism as an economic system?* To functionalists, capitalism serves a useful function by bringing about a prosperous and stable society. To conflict theorists, capitalism threatens society by allowing the rich to exploit the poor. Symbolic interactionists focus on how people's definition of their world creates or supports capitalism.

3. *What kinds of economic systems exist around the globe?* Some are capitalist and others socialist, but they all are mixed economies, with elements of both capitalism and socialism. They differ only in degree, ranging on a continuum from the most capitalist to the most socialist. *Which economic system is generally more productive?* Capitalist economies are more productive than socialist ones. *What is the current condition of the U.S. economy?* The rates of unemployment and inflation are relatively low, but the productivity growth and living standard are largely at a standstill, while the trade and budget deficits remain high. *What is the status of economies in other countries today?*

Most economies have started to recover from the worldwide recession of several years ago, with some showing greater growth than others. One of the major forces behind this growth is foreign investment.

4. *What is a big corporation like?* The numerous shareholders who own the corporation do not run it. A small group of directors and managers do. Owners and managers may profit from corporate assets but may not be held responsible for its liabilities. Corporations tend to grow into giants through mergers and acquisitions. The rise of giant corporations has both positive and negative consequences for the economy and society. *What is welfare for the rich?* The government provides special tax breaks for rich individuals and big corporations as well as direct payments to big corporations. *What are some characteristics of multinational corporations?* They reap huge profits from abroad, are more powerful than some governments, and can create problems for some peoples. But they are still welcomed in many developing countries.

5. *How has the U.S. labor force changed in recent years?* The number of jobs in agriculture has dropped sharply, the number in service industries has risen, and the population of white-collar workers has expanded. Meanwhile, the employment rate for women, blacks, and other minorities has increased, while the rate for older men has declined significantly. At the same time, temporary employment has increased sharply. *Why has union membership dwin-*

dled? The traditional source of unionization—blue-collar employment—has shrunk.

6. *How does unemployment affect the individual and society?* The effects are more than economic. The individual usually suffers a loss of self-esteem, and the rates of such social problems as crime, alcoholism, and suicide rise. *Who are more likely to be satisfied with their work?* Older and white-collar workers. Given the same kinds of jobs, women are happier than men. *How has the U.S. workplace changed?* Workers are less willing to accept unpleasant jobs and more likely to expect meaningful ones. Thus efforts have been made to give employees more interesting jobs, more freedom, and more power in the workplace.

Multinational corporations   Corporations that have subsidiaries in many countries (p. 447).

Oligopoly   The situation in which a very few companies control the output of an industry (p. 446).

Second economy   A free market operating within and parallel to the state-controlled, command economy (p. 439).

Socialism   An economic system based on public ownership and government control of the economy (p. 438).

Trade deficit   Buying more goods and services from foreign countries than selling to them (p. 442).

Trade surplus   Selling more goods and services to foreign countries than buying from them (p. 442).

KEY TERMS

Alienation of labor   Marx's term for laborers' loss of control over their work process (p. 437).

Capitalism   An economic system based on private ownership of property and competition in producing and selling goods and services (p.437).

Conglomerate   A corporation that owns companies in various unrelated industries (p. 447).

Dual economy   An economy that comprises a *core* of giant corporations dominating the market and a *periphery* of small firms competing for the remaining, smaller shares of business (p. 449).

Economic institution   A system for producing and distributing goods and services (p. 434).

Industrial Revolution   The dramatic economic change brought about by the introduction of machines into the work process about 200 years ago (p. 434).

Mixed economy   An economic system that contains elements of both capitalism and socialism (p. 438).

Monopoly   The situation in which one firm controls the output of an industry (p. 446).

SUGGESTED READINGS

Erikson, Kai, and Steven P. Vallas (eds.). 1990. *The Nature of Work: Sociological Perspectives.* New Haven, Conn.: Yale University Press. A collection of insightful articles by well-known researchers on the subject.

Etzioni, Amitai. 1988. *The Moral Dimensions: Toward a New Economics.* New York: Free Press. Discusses how, contrary to traditional economic assumptions, people do not maximize only their self-interests, often make irrational rather than rational decisions, and are an integral part of social groups rather than isolated individuals.

Granovetter, Mark. 1992. *The Sociology of Economic Life.* Boulder, CO: Westview. A collection of articles on the sociological study of the economy.

Krugman, Paul. 1990. *The Age of Diminished Expectations: U.S. Economic Policy in the 1990s.* Cambridge, Mass.: MIT Press. An evenhanded presentation of the arguments and facts about the major problems facing the U.S. economy today.

Schwartz, Barry. 1994. *The Costs of Living: How Market Freedom Erodes the Best Things in Life.* New York: Norton. A critical analysis of how the pursuit of wealth weakens the bonds of religion, family, friendship, and other aspects of human life.

20

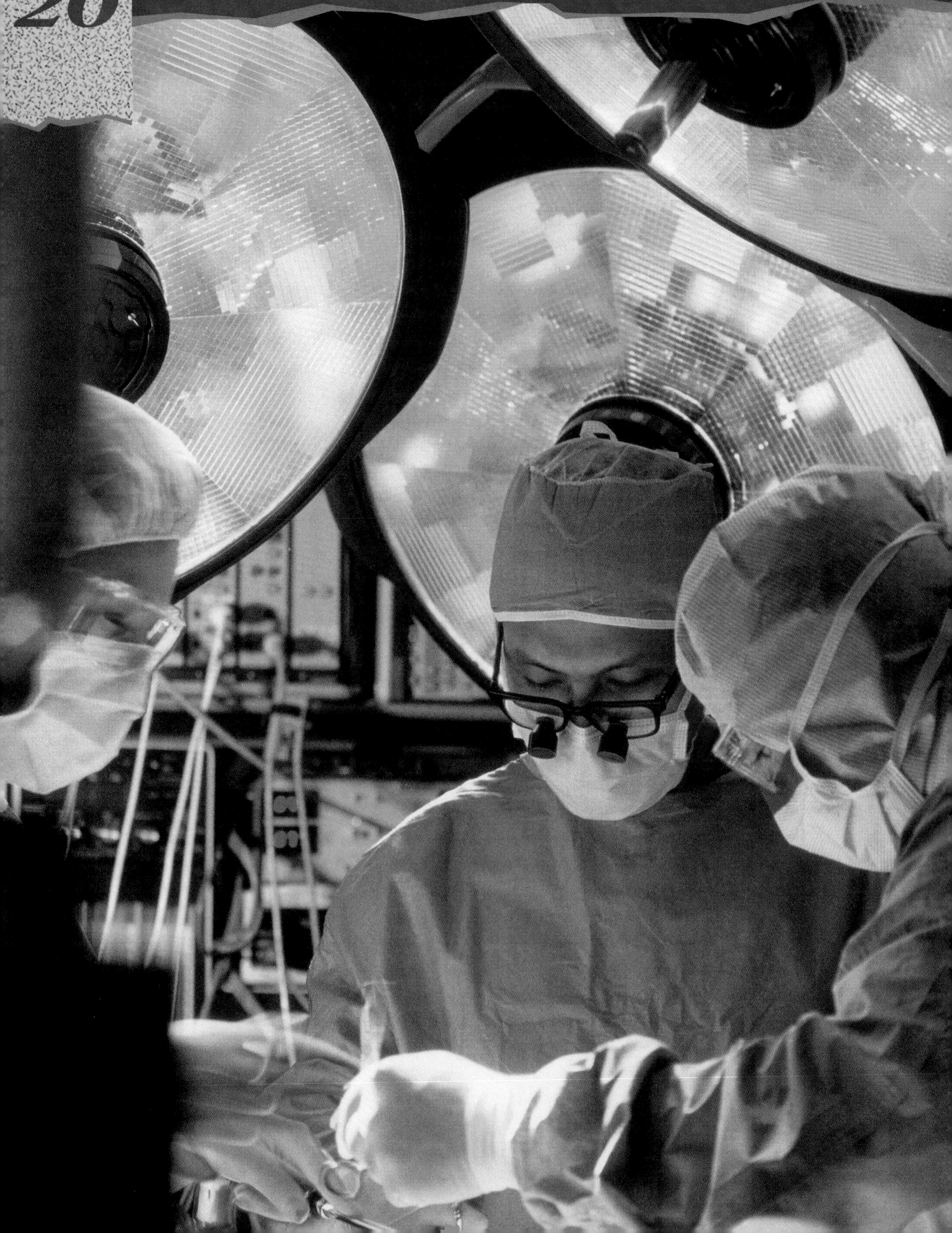

SCIENCE AND MEDICINE

CHAPTER OUTLINE

Myths and Realities

MYTH: *Because they reject the use of faith to accept ideas, scientists often repeat each other's experiments before they will accept their colleagues' findings as valid.*
REALITY: Most scientists rarely replicate others' experiments. They often make certain assumptions, taking certain things on faith, just like everybody else.

MYTH: *The scientist who discovered the theory of evolution was Charles Darwin.*
REALITY: Alfred Russel Wallace also independently developed the theory of evolution. Science is full of multiple discoveries—the same discoveries made independently by different scientists.

MYTH: *Scientists are single-mindedly objective. They would reject scientific ideas for objective reasons only.*
REALITY: Scientists are just as human and emotional as the rest of us. Strict objectivity is more a scientific ideal than a reality. Scientists are far from objective and are much more intent on confirming their own ideas than those of others.

MYTH: *Being frail, old people are more likely than younger people to fall victim to virtually all kinds of illness.*
REALITY: While they are more likely to suffer from such chronic illnesses as arthritis, heart disease, and cancer, older people are less susceptible to acute and infectious illnesses, such as measles and pneumonia.

everal years ago, Francine Vogler went to see a neurosurgeon when she suffered a neck injury. After a quick examination, the doctor was cruelly blunt as he prescribed immediate surgery: "You have a 5 percent chance of dying or becoming a quadriplegic." Immediately Vogler began to cry, but the surgeon walked briskly out of the room. "I was totally shocked," she says today. A physician herself, Vogler teaches medicine at the University of Southern California, where she can make sure that her students learn how to treat patients more humanely (Nazario, 1992). This real-life story suggests a relationship between science and medicine: the more scientific physicians are, the less sensitive they are in dealing with patients. Not surprisingly, highly specialized physicians such as neurosurgeons, who have been trained to be rigorously scientific, objective, and dispassionate toward medical problems, are more likely than general practitioners to lack a warm bedside manner. Let us take a closer look at the nature of science and medicine to understand better, among other things, how they are connected.

SCIENCE AND SOCIETY

The family, religion, economy, and other institutions have existed for thousands of years. But science began to emerge as a social institution only 300 years ago. Only then did it begin to become widely accepted as a necessary means of satisfying societal needs. This acceptance came about when scientific knowledge was used to improve technology, which in turn led to improvements in daily life. Today, science and technology are so intertwined that we often use the words interchangeably, but they do refer to different things. **Science** is a body of knowledge developed through systematic observation. **Technology** can mean any kind of tool or practical know-how, but it has come to mean the practical application of scientific principles. If science did not have practical uses, it would probably have little influence or prestige. It has become an important social institution primarily through its marriage to technology. How did this come about?

The First Scientists

Science can be traced back to Greeks such as Plato, who advocated mathematics as a means of disciplining the mind, and Aristotle, who classified animals and plants. But their science was not based on what is now called the scientific method. It was not until the seventeenth century that the seed of modern science began to grow in Western Europe, especially in England. Then "a growing habit of testing theories against careful measurement, observation, and upon occasion, experiment" spurred rapid progress in the natural sciences (McNeill, 1963; Lindberg, 1992).

A radical change in philosophical ideas about nature was a key factor stimulating scientific growth. Earlier students had seen nature as a living cosmos, filled with spiritual or human qualities. The new scientists treated the universe as a dead thing. Natural phenomena were no longer believed to act randomly, on their own whim, or by the will of a supernatural power. Instead, *scientists now regarded nature as an object* that behaves predictably, like a machine. Nature could be studied through direct observation, measured, and controlled. Respect for nature gave way to the quest to dominate, control, and use it.

Another factor in the development of modern science was the emergence of *cooperative scholarship* among those who regarded themselves as scientists. Through cooperative communication, scientists can expand their knowledge more easily and quickly and avoid repeating the work and mistakes of others. The world's first example of cooperative scholarship among scientists came in 1662 when the Royal Society of London was organized. Its members, being gentlemen of wealth and leisure, could afford to spend long hours studying nature and discussing their findings with each other. But unlike their scholarly predecessors, they were not prejudiced against "dirtying their hands with anything but ink" (McNeill, 1963). They not only shared the new, mechanistic philosophy of nature but also believed that experiments provided the path to knowledge.

These early scientists were also for the most part *deeply religious Protestants.* We might expect that their dedication to science would clash with their religion. But two characteristics allowed them to maintain fidelity to both religion and science. First, the potential for conflict was eased by the fact that the early scientists "were content with striving to understand only a small segment of reality at a time, leaving the great questions of religion and philosophy to one side" (McNeill, 1963). A second characteristic reconciling their religion and their science was the Protestant ethic. They believed that their scientific activity fulfilled the demands of this ethic, which, as we have seen, required them to work hard for the glory of God. They reasoned that "the scientific study of nature enables a fuller appreciation of His works and thus leads us to admire and praise the Power, Wisdom, and Goodness of God as manifested in His creation" (Merton, 1973).

The Institutionalization of Science

The members of the Royal Society had a committee devoted to improving "mechanical inventions," but for many years science did little to aid technology. In fact, it was technology that aided science. Galileo, for example, was able to make his astronomical observations because a Dutchman playing with lenses had invented the telescope. The modern technological age did not begin until around 1832, when a huge water turbine was perfected as a result of scientific studies (Mumford, 1963). This singular event marked the emergence of a new pattern, one in which science drives technology onward.

Today, science and technology depend on each other, as we depend on both of them. Modern technological developments such as computers and nuclear reactors could not have been invented through trial and error. Their invention required an understanding of scientific principles. Current technological advances in computer chips, tiny semiconductor lasers, the liquid crystals of computer displays, optic devices, composite materials of extraordinary strength, and so on would not have existed without scientific knowledge of condensed-matter physics, which studies such phenomena as proton and electron transport (Broad, 1990a).

To carry on their work, however, most scientists require extremely complicated technology. Biologists use electron microscopes, physicists use particle accelerators, and astronomers use NASA's satellites—all extremely sophisticated technology. Without having the advanced X-ray astrophysics laboratory satellite in outer space, scientists would find it difficult to investigate black holes, dark matter, and the age of the universe (Goldberger and Panofsky, 1990). Although it enables scientists to do their research,

For many years in its early history, science did little to aid technology. It was technology that aided science. Galileo, shown here before the Court of the Holy Office in 1633, was able to make his astronomical observations because of the invention of the telescope.

technology can also by itself suggest new scientific ideas. For example, the search to eliminate a technological problem—static in radiotelephony—led to the birth of the science of radio astronomy and hence to the discovery of quasars and other astronomical phenomena. Thus, the flow of knowledge goes not only from science to technology but also from technology to science.

There would not have been much progress in both science and technology if they had been differentiated—one being highly developed to the neglect of the other. Scientific ideas, especially mathematics and logical proof, reached great heights in ancient Greece, but science never flourished there for want of interest in technical problem-solving. The technology in ancient China was highly sophisticated, bringing forth papermaking, gunpowder, iron casting, and many other inventions long before they appeared in the West. But these technical innovations later fell far behind Western technology because the Chinese failed to pursue conceptual abstraction and theoretical generalization—the essence of science (Munch, 1983). By contrast, as we have seen, Westerners have shown much interest in both science and technology since the seventeenth century, which may explain why both are so highly advanced in the West today.

Scientific Progress

Scientists are supposed to subject everything to the test of observation and experiment. Taken literally, however, this would mean that scientists would be repeating each other's experiments endlessly. In fact, scientists often find replication an impractical undertaking. One reason is the incompleteness of many published descriptions of experiments. Just as cookbook recipes cannot include all the tiny details that every good cook knows, neither can scientists be exhaustive in describing their experiments. But these little technical points are often necessary for a successful replication. Thus many scientists would rather do original research. Besides, in science, the prizes go for originality, not for repeating someone else's experiment. And replication may require just as much time, effort, and money as original research. Contrary to popular belief, then, most scientists seldom repeat each other's experiments (Broad and Wade, 1983).

If they do not constantly replicate experiments, scientists must make certain assumptions, taking certain things on faith, just like everyone else. Most biologists today accept as a basic assumption Darwin's theory of natural selection. Physicists use the theory of quantum mechanics as a working assumption. Each of these constitutes what Thomas Kuhn (1970) calls a **paradigm**, a model for defining, studying, and solving problems in accordance with certain basic assumptions. For hundreds of years, for example, astronomers shared the Ptolemaic system of the heavens as their paradigm. They believed that the earth was the center of the universe and the sun revolved around it. Most scientists work within the paradigm of their discipline. They are not inclined to doubt its basic assumptions. How, then, does science advance? How do innovations—new facts and ideas—appear?

Scientists are supposed to subject everything to the test of observation and experiment. This would mean repeating each other's experiments. In fact, scientists often find replication impractical, because many published descriptions of experiments are incomplete. Many scientists would rather do original research.

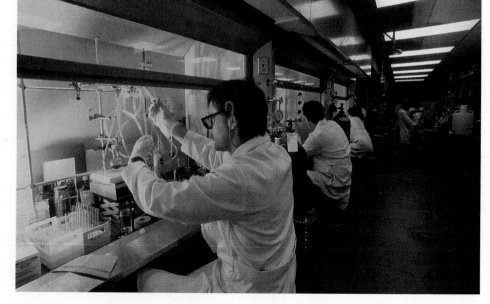

Left: The era of "little science" is seen in the relatively simple working conditions of chemist Percy Julian shown in his lab in the 1940s. This era ended in the United States with World War II, the development of the atomic bomb, and the beginning of the Cold War with the former Soviet Union. Right: In the era of "big science," scientists have joined the "team" of a bureaucracy, gaining access to expensive, sophisticated equipment. Here scientists conduct human genome research with light microscopes and video monitors.

Kuhn divides innovation into two types: ordinary innovation and scientific revolution. Ordinary innovation is the product of everyday research, such as Foucault's discovery in 1850 that light travels faster in air than in water, or the invention of the transistor in 1949 by a team of scientists at Bell Labs. Journeymen scientists routinely conduct research that produces such innovations all the time, and Kuhn calls those scientists' routine research **normal science.** As normal science keeps producing new ideas and data, however, some of these create problems for the existing paradigm. They are **anomalies,** ideas and data incompatible with or unexplainable by the paradigm. If these anomalies keep piling up, they generate a "crisis" that compels some very innovative scientists to develop a new paradigm. The scientists, in effect, initiate a **scientific revolution,** replacing an old paradigm with a new one, such as Newton's law of gravity or Einstein's theory of relativity (Kuhn, 1970).

All this suggests the importance of cultural accumulation. Normal science does not operate in an intellectual vacuum but through the guidance of a paradigm. The paradigm itself is a product of an earlier scientific revolution, which in turn resulted from the accumulation of anomalous theories and data,

the fallout of routine research. At each stage of cultural accumulation, there is a storehouse of scientific ideas and facts that can be used to fashion an innovation. Even Isaac Newton acknowledged a debt to this cultural storehouse, claiming in great modesty, "If I have seen farther, it is by standing on the shoulders of giants." This cultural accumulation explains why science is full of multiple discoveries—the same discoveries made independently by different scientists. The theory of evolution, for example, was developed independently by Charles Darwin and Alfred Russel Wallace.

Modern Science

As science advanced over the years, its methods were applied to more and more areas of life, and it achieved great prestige in Western society. As recently as 40 years ago, however, scientists were poorly paid, worked alone on shoestring budgets, and were popularly viewed as eccentric characters. This era of "little science" ended in the United States with World War II and the development of the atomic bomb. In a sense, scientists had enabled the United States to end the war. The Cold War and the arms race with the Soviet Union that followed ensured that the government, like industry, would continue to have a large interest in fostering scientific development. When, in 1957, the Soviet Union surprised the world by launching the first satellite into space, the U.S. government intensified its role in science. It poured new money into research and scientific education.

The billions of dollars that the government, industry, and private foundations spent on research after the war gave birth to the era of "big science." The number of scientists and the prestige and influence of science have soared. Increasingly, scientists work as narrow specialists within huge bureaucracies. In Jacques Ellul's (1964) words, "The research worker is no longer a solitary genius." For the most part, scientists work as members of teams. Only by joining the "team" of a bureaucracy can they gain access to the expensive, sophisticated equipment most scientists require.

Big science will become even bigger in this decade. The U.S. government has already embarked on the most ambitious array of gigantic science projects ever. Some of these projects are the $1.15 billion Hubble Space Telescope now orbiting high above the earth, the $3 billion Human Genome Initiative designed to map out the entire human genetic code, and the $30 billion space station Freedom for conducting scientific experiments and possibly serving as the stepping stone to Mars. These and other similarly huge projects now planned for completion in the 1990s will cost more than $60 billion to build, and more than $100 billion will be needed to operate them over their lifetimes (Goldberger and Panofsky, 1990).

Critics, however, warn that this enormous cost could cripple vital parts of U.S. scientific effort by reducing support for smaller projects. Smaller projects have contributed much more to scientific advances than have large projects, as shown by the greater number of Nobel prizes awarded to scientists working on smaller projects. The great contribution from small science can be found in the field of superconducting materials that promises to revolutionize electric devices. In 1987 Dr. Paul Chu, a University of Houston physicist, made a key breakthrough in superconductivity, and in that year his laboratory ran on only $130,000, a pittance compared with the billions spent on big science projects. But more scientific discoveries can be expected to come out of the big science projects of the 1990s. The reason is that small science projects cannot produce information on big questions, such as the origin of our universe and its stars, galaxies, black holes, and quasars (Goldberger and Panofsky, 1990).

Nuclear waste burial site, Washington State. The benefits of scientific advances are apparent, often immediately attainable. But the costs, such as burying nuclear wastes in our soil, may not be understood until years later.

Social Consequences of Science

Scientific advances can produce both beneficial and harmful effects. The benefits are apparent, often immediately attainable. In contrast, the costs may not be understood until years later.

Thanks to science, we can pamper ourselves with cultural delights provided by radio, stereo, and video. We can get in touch instantly with someone far away through a telephone, a fax machine, and e-mail. We can transport ourselves speedily and comfortably over vast distances by jet. Many dramatic advances have burst on the scientific scene in the last decade. Electronics has given us pocket calculators, electronic games, and sophisticated home computers; it may soon radically change everything from the way we study, work, and think to how we travel, shop, vote, and play. Another scientific revolution is under way in genetics. Scientists are learning to manipulate genes and create new organisms, such as genetically reprogrammed bacteria that are able to produce insulin for use by diabetics, to manufacture antibiotics, to devour oil slicks, or to turn chemical wastes into usable plastics. Scientists may soon be able to cure some genetic diseases such as sickle cell anemia and thalassemia. To ward off death, more and more human organs are being transplanted from one person to another.

The same scientific innovations that improve our lives, however, also threaten us with their unintended harmful effects. The spread of computers throughout society is eroding our long-cherished right to privacy because our personal records are easily accessible to the curious. If we sue a doctor for medical malpractice, we are likely to go onto a computer blacklist and suffer more than the loss of privacy rights. One woman in Joliet, Illinois, filed a malpractice suit and later found that 30 other doctors refused to treat her when she became ill again (Elmer-DeWitt, 1986). Another example of the harmful consequences of our scientific breakthroughs is the threat of nuclear wastes buried in our soil, asbestos-dust particles in our schools and workplaces, and other cancer-causing pollutants in our air, water, and food.

Questions for Discussion and Review

1. How does technology differ from science?
2. Who were the first scientists, and what happened when the activities of scientists became institutionalized?
3. What are the characteristics of "big science"?
4. What effects can science have on our lives?
5. How does science advance?

THE SCIENTIFIC PROFESSION

Most U.S. scientists work in business and industry and a lesser number in universities and colleges (see Figure 20.1). Those working in educational institutions are much more likely to do basic research ("pure science") than scientists in government or business, many of whom work on technology, often called "applied research." Wherever they work, scientists tend to share certain norms and activities.

FIGURE 20.1
Where U.S. Scientists Work

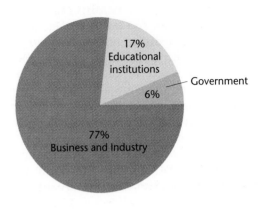

Source: Data from U.S. Census Bureau, 1994.

Scientific Ideals

From the outset of their training, scientists are socialized to consider science worthy of their dedication for its own sake and to keep it "pure": "Science must not suffer itself to become the handmaiden of theology or economy or state" (Merton, 1973). The self-confident insistence on autonomy attests to the power and influence of science today. Robert Merton argues that the autonomy and purity of science are maintained through four norms.

The first is **universalism**, the norm that requires scientists to evaluate ideas or findings in accordance with impersonal criteria. In evaluating ideas, scientists should not consider the author's personality, race, age, sex, or other personal characteristics. Instead, they should consider only their consistency with logic and observations. Scientists should be passionless, unbiased by emotion, and intellectually cold.

A second norm, **organized skepticism**, requires scientists to be critical of any scientific idea or finding. Whereas the church and the state often ask people to bow to their authority, and may see skepticism as a sign of disloyalty, science elevates skepticism to the status of a virtue. According to this norm, scientists should take nothing in science at face value and should carefully scrutinize all findings, even those by the most respected scientists, for faulty logic or factual error.

A third norm, **communality**, requires scientists to share their knowledge freely with one another. They should regard their discoveries as public property, not as private property that they might keep secret or sell to the highest bidder. As a result, their discoveries can provide springboards for further knowledge, just as past discoveries made today's advances possible. The only "property right" scientists may claim is professional recognition and esteem.

A final norm, **disinterestedness**, requires scientists to pursue truth rather than self-interest. Scientists should not expect to gain great wealth, fame, or power. Seeking these rewards may be appropriate for businesspeople, politicians, lawyers, and others—but not for scientists. They must seek the truth and only the truth, and they should consider the thrill of making a discovery sufficient reward for their work. So long as scientists follow this norm, it is unlikely that they will be tempted to falsify data.

Scientific Realities

Contemplating his colleagues' denial of any interest in fame, one modern scientist wondered, "Why do even the greatest minds stoop to such falsehood? For, without being conscious lies, these denials are undoubtedly false" (Merton, 1973). The denials suggest that the norm of disinterestedness does influence scientists, but they are ambivalent toward it. Scientists do not totally reject this and the other norms Merton identified, but they do not enthusiastically support them either. In fact, they find these norms irrelevant to their everyday scientific activities and tend to break all of them.

Consider the norm of universality. Ian Mitroff (1974) found clear violations of this norm by the scientists who analyzed lunar rocks brought back by Apollo astronauts. Instead of being impersonal, objective, or emotionally neutral, the Apollo scientists, especially the best ones, "were emotionally involved with their ideas, were reluctant to part with them, and did everything in their power to confirm them." Every one of the scientists considered it naive and nonsensical to say that scientists are objective. Science is an intensely personal enterprise.

Scientists often violate those norms not only by preferring their own ideas but also by bowing to authority. A common example is the **Matthew effect,** the tendency to praise famous scientists and to ignore the contributions of those who are not well known. This tendency is named after the New Testament gospel of Matthew 25:29—"For to everyone who has, more shall be given, and he shall have plenty. But from him who has not, even that which he has shall be taken away from him." When two scientists independently make the same discovery, for example, the more famous one is likely to get most if not all the credit.

Violations of the norms, however, do not bring science to a halt. In fact, they sometimes promote scientific progress. Being emotionally involved with one's work, for example, may pay off. In Mitroff's lunar rocks study, the three scientists perceived by their colleagues to be the most emotionally committed to their own hypotheses were also judged the most outstanding and creative of those in the program. "Without emotional commitment," one of the scientists said, "one couldn't have the energy, the drive to press forward, sometimes against extremely difficult odds."

Scientific Competition

Since the birth of science in the seventeenth century, scientists have sought to advance their own interests as well as those of science. Three hundred years ago the English mathematician Newton and the German Leibniz battled each other to claim the glory of being recognized as the first to discover calculus. They attacked "each other with injurious epithets" and encouraged "their partisans to publish scurrilous innuendos in learned journals" (Merton, 1973). They eventually accused each other of plagiarism—stealing the idea of calculus from each other and then publishing it as their own (Collins and Restivo, 1983).

A similar incident erupted in the last decade between U.S. and French medical scientists. In 1983 Dr. Luc Montagnier and his French colleagues reported that they had discovered the virus that causes AIDS. Then, in 1984, Dr. Robert Gallo and his U.S. colleagues discovered an apparently different virus, and quickly used this finding to develop AIDS test kits. But the French filed a lawsuit, claiming that the U.S. scientists had used the French virus samples to develop the test. The court later dismissed the suit, which the French appealed to a higher court. But finally, in 1987, President Reagan and French Prime Minister Jacques Chirac announced that both countries had agreed to share profits from the blood test—while leaving it to historians to decide who had discovered the AIDS virus first.

For a scientist wishing to gain recognition from the scientific community, making a breakthrough is not enough. The work must be published first. If two or more scientists make the same discovery independently, the one who publishes first gets the credit. Scientists, then, often compete fiercely to be the one who "got there first." Such competition can bring benefits by motivating scientists to work harder. Researchers have found that stiff competition in U.S. universities, and in German universities during the

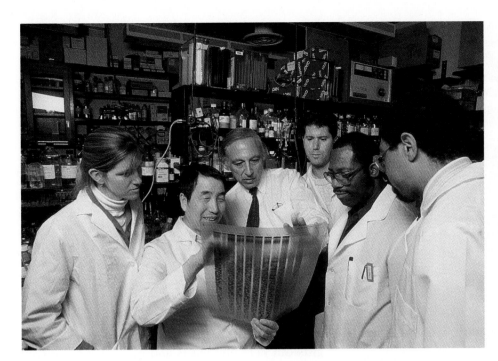

Laboratory where early work was done on HIV, the AIDS virus. In 1984 Dr. Robert Gallo (wearing tie) began using his discovery of a virus to develop AIDS test kits. The French filed a lawsuit, claiming that the U.S. scientists had used the virus discovered by the French to develop the test. Both countries now share profits from the blood test, but the incident illustrates the kind of competition that exists among scientists.

nineteenth century, helped make them more productive than French and British universities (Hagstrom, 1974; Fuchs, 1993). Competition can also discourage scientists from delaying the publication of their findings. After considering his theory for 20 years, Charles Darwin finally published his ideas about evolution when he learned that Alfred Russel Wallace had independently reached the same conclusions. By spurring scientists to publish their work quickly, competition may promote the diffusion of ideas and thus hasten the advance of science.

On the other hand, competition can deter this diffusion by inhibiting cooperation and communication. Scientists eager for recognition and afraid of being beaten into print often keep their work secret until it is published. Before winning a Nobel prize, biophysicist Maurice Wilkins was so possessive of an X-ray study of DNA that James Watson, his Nobel co-winner, used his sister's charms and other devious means to gain entrance to Wilkins's lab (Watson, 1968).

Questions for Discussion and Review

1. What four key norms make up the ideals of science?
2. How do scientists often disobey the scientific norms?
3. What does scientific competition involve?

HEALTH AND SOCIETY

As a social phenomenon, health varies from one society to another and from one group to another within the same society. From these variations, we can see how social factors affect health and what consequences an outbreak of illness has for society. We can also track down the origin of a disease by examining all its victims for something that they have in common as a social group.

Social Factors

In the United States older people are less likely than young people to suffer from acute and infectious illnesses such as measles and pneumonia. But they are more susceptible to chronic illnesses such as arthritis, heart disease, and cancer. Cancer deaths, in particular, have been climbing steeply and steadily among people aged 55 and older (Census Bureau, 1994).

Health also varies with gender. Women have higher rates of both chronic and acute illnesses than men of the same age, yet women live longer than men. Why? One reason is biological superiority. Women are more able to endure sickness and survive. They also are less likely to develop hemophilia and other diseases linked to the X chromosome. Their sex hormones further protect them from cardiovascular morbidity up to the time of menopause. A second reason is that women maintain stronger emotional

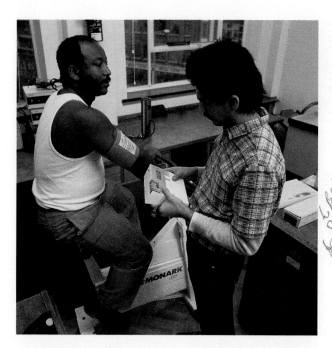

Social factors figure strongly in health. Poverty can aggravate the problem of hypertension suffered by minorities. Because they sometimes cannot deal with the sociopsychological stress induced by racism in the United States, poor African Americans are significantly more likely than middle-class blacks to have high blood pressure.

ties with others than men do. By offering social support and deterring loneliness, intimate human relationships can reduce the severity and duration of illness. A third reason is the greater tendency of men to smoke, drink, and drive. Such behaviors increase the risk of serious chronic diseases and physical injuries (Verbrugge, 1985).

Race and ethnicity are also correlated with health. African Americans, Hispanic Americans, and Native Americans all have shorter life expectancies than do Anglo-Americans. Minorities are far more likely to suffer or die from many diseases such as influenza, pneumonia, and AIDS. Both Hispanics and Native Americans, however, are less likely than Anglos to die from heart disease and cancer, partly because Anglos live longer and those chronic illnesses typically increase with age (Cockerham, 1995; Johnson et al, 1991).

These racial and ethnic differences may reflect another social factor that influences health: social class. The diseases that hit minority groups the hardest are those associated with poverty. In particular, acute and infectious diseases, such as tuberculosis and influenza, are more prevalent among the lower social classes. Researchers have attributed the higher rates of disease among the lower classes to several related factors: toxic, hazardous, and unhygienic environments; stress resulting from life changes, such as job loss and divorce; and inadequate medical care (Syme and Berkman, 1987). More recent research has found another problem: unhealthy eating habits. Poor people are much more likely than others to eat high-sugar, high-salt, and high-fat food (Freedman, 1990). Poverty can also aggravate the problem of hypertension suffered by minorities. Because they may be less able to deal with the sociopsychological stress induced by racism in the United States, poor African Americans are significantly more likely than middle-class blacks to have high blood pressure (Klag et al., 1991).

Epidemiology

In analyzing the social forces behind illness, sociologists can help physicians and public health workers track down the cause of a disease. This requires a kind of detective work called **epidemiology**, the study of the origin and spread of disease in a given population. As epidemiologists, sociologists and medical scientists first hunt down all the people who already have the disease. Then they ask the victims where they were and what they did before they got sick. The epidemiologists also collect data on the victims' age, gender, marital status, occupation, and other characteristics. The aim is to find out what all the victims have in common besides the disease so that its cause can be identified and eliminated. Usually, the common factor that ties all the victims together provides the essential clue.

Epidemiology emerged as an applied science in 1854, when the English physician John Snow discovered the source of one of London's periodic cholera epidemics. He had gone to the neighborhoods where the victims lived and asked them what they did every day, where they worked, what they ate and drank, and many other questions about their lives and activities. Finally, after sifting through this huge pile of information, Snow hit upon the clue to the origin of the disease. He found that all the victims had one thing in common: they had drunk water from a particular pump on Broad Street. Snow simply shut off the pump and, with that single act, stopped the epidemic in its tracks. Not till many years later, with the discovery of germs, could anyone explain why shutting down the pump was effective: he had removed the source of the cholera bacteria (Cockerham, 1995).

Since then, epidemiology has been used to trace the origins of many different diseases such as cancer and heart disease. In investigating heart disease, for example, epidemiologists have discovered that the majority of victims have eaten high-cholesterol foods, smoked or drunk heavily, and failed to get enough exercise. Thus avoiding these habits can reduce the risk of heart disease.

AIDS

Directly caused by a virus called HIV, AIDS is a deadly disease that destroys the body's immune system, leaving the victim defenseless against other diseases. The disease first came to the attention of U.S. physicians in early 1981. Since then, it has spread rapidly.

Social Causes In searching for the cause of the AIDS virus, epidemiologists have found clues in the social characteristics and behaviors of the victims. So far *In the U.S.* most of the victims have been gay or bisexual men. The second largest group has been intravenous drug users. The rest are non-drug-using heterosexuals, of whom most have caught the AIDS virus through sex and a few have been infected through blood transfusions or being born to mothers with AIDS (see Figure 20.2).

New cases of AIDS among gay men declined or leveled off in the late 1980s and early 1990s because of increasing practice of safer sex. But now the disease among gay men is on the rise again, a result of the return to unsafe sex (Signorile, 1995). AIDS has also increased among non-drug-using heterosexuals. But new infection among intravenous drug users has increased the most. These people are mostly poor, African American, and Hispanic heterosexuals in the inner city. They often share contaminated needles when shooting drugs, thus passing the AIDS virus from one to another.

All these epidemiological facts clearly suggest that AIDS spreads mostly through sexual intercourse with an infected person and through the sharing of a hypodermic needle that has been contaminated with the virus. Studies in other societies can also be useful. For example, epidemiologists have discovered some similarities and differences between African AIDS victims and their U.S. counterparts. Unlike the U.S. victims, the African patients do not have histories of intravenous drug use, homosexuality, or blood transfusion. But like U.S. gays with AIDS, African heterosexuals with the disease mostly live in large cities, and have had sex with many different partners. Thus, AIDS has spread among Africans in the same way as it has among gays in the United States: through sex with multiple partners. By itself, though, promiscuity is not the source of the AIDS virus. It is unprotected sex that increases the risk of infection.

FIGURE 20.2
The AIDS Epidemic in the United States

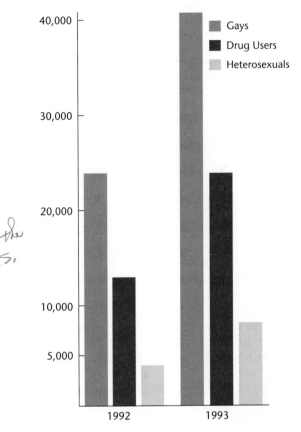

Source: Data from Centers for Disease Control and Prevention, 1994.

Social Consequences Unlike such familiar killers as cancer and heart disease, AIDS is mysterious and has had an unusual impact on our society. As we have seen, the disease is not only lethal but can be transmitted through life's most basic human interaction—sex and procreation. Understandably, the general public is gripped with the fear of contagion. The initial appearance of AIDS among two groups of which the larger society disapproves—gays and drug addicts—has added to the fear, as prejudice discourages any understanding of "their" disease.

According to a series of surveys by the U.S. Public Health Service, a growing number of people have quickly learned the risk factors for AIDS, but misinformation about the disease's transmission remains a problem. Many still fear that they can get AIDS by donating blood or through casual contact with an infected person. Though such fears are groundless, they have spawned strange, sad, or hostile actions against AIDS victims.

In 1987, for example, the school board in Arcadia, Florida, barred three hemophiliac brothers—Richard,

Infection by the AIDS virus has increased the most among intravenous drug users, who often share contaminated needles when shooting drugs and pass the virus on to another. There has been some controversy about distributing free needles to drug addicts as a way of stopping the spread of AIDS. Prejudice against drug addicts, as well as against gays, the two groups among whom AIDs first appeared in the United States, makes it difficult to resolve such issues.

Robert, and Randy Ray—who had been infected with the virus through blood transfusions. When the boys were ordered admitted to class by a court, many parents boycotted the school. The Ray family received telephone threats and lost their home to arson, forcing them to leave the town. Parents in many other places have also demanded mandatory testing of all schoolchildren and segregation of those with AIDS. The parents are not the only ones that discriminate against AIDS victims. There are many instances where people with AIDS are prevented from keeping jobs or getting housing, insurance coverage, or medical care. Such acts of discrimination sometimes are directed against those who are not already infected with AIDS but are only perceived to be at risk for the disease. Those who care for AIDS patients are also likely to encounter discrimination (Hilts, 1990).

A Global Analysis of Health

People in the United States are much healthier than ever before. Since 1900 our life expectancy has increased by more than 50 percent, from about 49 years in 1900 to 75 today. At birth we can expect to live 26 more years than did our counterparts in

1900—more than one-and-a-half times as long as they did then. Another indicator of our health, the infant mortality rate, has shown even more dramatic improvement. While about 15 percent of all U.S. babies died during the first year of life at the turn of this century, only 1 percent die today (Census Bureau, 1994). All this can be chalked up to healthier living conditions, better diet, immunization, and penicillin and other antibiotics.

But our increased life expectancy loses its impressiveness if compared with that of other industrial countries, where people live longer than we. Our standing in regard to infant mortality is the same. Proportionately more babies die in the United States than in other industrial nations (see Table 20.1). This seems ironic, because we spend more money on health care than any of these nations. But the

TABLE 20.1
Health Among Industrial Countries
The United States has the lowest life expectancy and highest infant mortality in the industrial world. This seems ironic because we spend more money on health care than does any of the other countries.

Country	Life Expectancy	Country	Infant Mortality Rate
Japan	79.3	Japan	4.3
Sweden	78.3	Sweden	5.7
France	78.2	Netherlands	6.1
Canada	78.1	Germany	6.5
Netherlands	77.8	France	6.6
Australia	77.6	Canada	6.9
Italy	77.6	Britain	7.2
Britain	76.8	Australia	7.3
Germany	76.3	Italy	7.6
U.S.	75.9	U.S.	8.1

SOURCE: Data from U.S. Census Bureau, 1994.

problem cannot be attributed totally to the lack of efficiency in our health care system. Unhealthy lifestyles, such as eating high-cholesterol food and smoking, may also be a contributing factor (Grubaugh and Santerre, 1994). Only when compared with poor, developing countries does the United States have a much higher life expectancy (see Figure 20.3) and a considerably lower infant mortality rate.

Questions for Discussion and Review

1. How do social factors like age, gender, ethnicity, and class influence a person's health?
2. What is epidemiology, and how does it help doctors locate the causes of disease?
3. Where have epidemiologists discovered the sources of the AIDS virus?
4. What are the social consequences of the AIDS epidemic?
5. What is the status of health in the United States today?

THE MEDICAL PROFESSION

Before 1870, doctoring was a lowly profession. Many of the doctors were more like quacks than true medical scientists. They had little knowledge of how the various body systems worked or of how diseases developed. In the face of such ignorance, doctors could be a menace. For numerous ailments, they bled patients profusely; evacuated their bowels, often until they passed out; stuffed them with dangerous drugs; and tormented them with various ghastly appliances. One treatment for syphilis involved roasting the patient in an oven. Sometimes the patients survived despite all this assistance, but more often they died. Either way, the doctors learned a great deal from them. In time, they developed a store of knowledge that eventually enabled them to practice a highly respectable profession (Blundell, 1987).

The Emergence of Modern Medicine

Before 1870 medical knowledge largely consisted of the theories that the Greek physician Hippocrates formulated some 2,500 years ago. According to

FIGURE 20.3
Life Expectancy Around the Globe

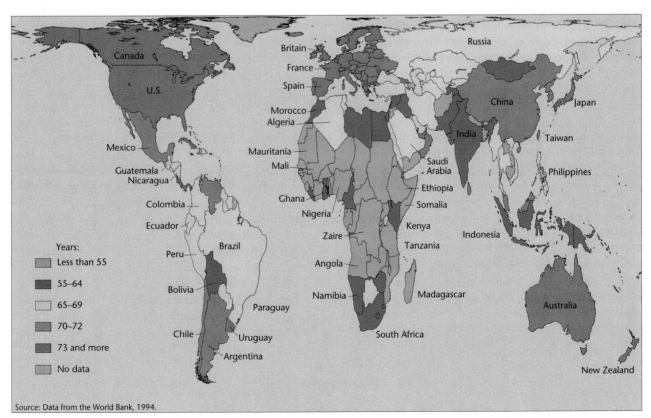

Source: Data from the World Bank, 1994.

Hippocrates, a person's health depended on a delicate balance among four "humors": blood, phlegm, yellow bile, and black bile. If these bodily fluids were in equilibrium, the individual was healthy. But any imbalance, with one fluid being more abundant than the others, led to illness. Thus, fever, a common symptom of many diseases, was attributed to an excess of "hot blood." Logically, the patient should be bled. Bloodletting, then, became a popular method of treatment, although it did more harm than good.

For centuries doctors never suspected that germs could cause disease. They were thus generally unconcerned about the sanitary condition of their practice. They did not bother to scrub before they operated on a patient. After patching up wounds or dissecting corpses, they would proceed to deliver babies—without first washing their hands. Hospitals were filthy places where patients were left unwashed on vermin-infested beds. Indeed, hospitals were more notorious for spreading diseases than curing them. Not surprisingly, most people turned to family members for care at times of sickness, and hospitals operated mostly as charity wards for those urban poor who had no families to care for them (Rosenberg, 1987).

In 1867, however, French chemist Louis Pasteur revolutionized medicine with his discovery of germs as the cause of cholera, anthrax, chicken pox, and other common infectious diseases. Surgeons then began to scrub and hospitals became sanitary. To further stop the infection and spread of diseases, people were immunized against them. Toward the end of the last century, physicians were able to treat many more ailments, thanks to the introduction of medical technology like X-ray examinations and of synthetic drugs like barbital and quinine.

It was, however, in this century that the medical profession took a quantum leap in fighting diseases. By the 1920s, the hospital had supplanted the home as the preferred place in which to receive medical care. Most people no longer regarded the hospital as a refuge for the poor but as a place where genuine medical treatment was offered. In the 1930s, the development of penicillin and sulfa drugs began to give physicians their first true power to cure. They would soon be able to eliminate nearly every infectious disease. Tending the wounds of combat during World War II, they received ample opportunity to hone their skills and develop new techniques. In the 1950s and 1960s, vaccines became available for preventing polio and measles, and high medical technology—respirators, dialyzers, and CAT scans—began to appear everywhere. By now these vaccines and medical machines, along with antibiotics, have trans-

formed our image of doctors. They are expected to heal their patients. As a consequence, medicine has become the most respected profession (Starr, 1983; Easterbrook, 1987).

Training for a Medical Career

About half of all applicants to medical schools in the United States are being admitted. Traditionally, nearly all of these students were white males, but in recent years they have been increasingly joined by women and minorities.

The first two years of medical school are taken up with basic sciences: anatomy, physiology, biochemistry, pharmacology, microbiology, and pathology. The next two years are devoted to clinical training. Under the supervision of interns, residents, and faculty, students serve as junior physicians, learning to collect samples for laboratory analysis, examine patients, diagnose diseases, and suggest treatments. In these four years, students acquire the scientific knowledge and clinical skills they will need as doctors. But their attitudes and values also change significantly. During the first year, they bubble with idealism, determined to learn it all so that they can later serve humanity. Soon they realize that there is too much information for them to absorb. After feverishly trying to memorize everything—to no avail—they throw in the towel. They begin to study only that fraction of the material that they think will appear on the exams (Becker et al., 1961).

Medical students also learn to avoid emotional involvement with patients. They learn to maintain professional objectivity, seeing disease and death as medical problems rather than emotional issues. Because this means suppressing empathy and compassion, it is bound to throw cold water on their earlier fiery enthusiasm for serving humanity. Having lost much of their idealism, doctors-to-be begin to think more about making money. Thus, many would not choose to help the poor by providing basic medical care or to practice medicine in the small towns and rural areas where doctors are needed desperately. After graduation, they learn doctoring by serving as interns for a year, after which they take an exam leading to a license to practice medicine.

An increasing number of these new physicians continue their training by taking a residency at a hospital for one to five years. Typically, they work 12 hours straight each day, not by sitting behind desks but by doing the hard labor of tending people in pain. In addition, every third night or so they must interrupt their sleep to answer the dreaded emergency calls. Despite their overwork, young doctors are paid only about $22,000 yearly, much less than the average physician's salary of $113,000. Then, after spending a small fortune on medical school, residents are further burdened with an average debt of $42,000. Even more significant, they must forgo their young adulthood, because the brutalizing learning process does not stop until age 30. Thus, many are determined to make up for lost youth by earning high fees when they set up their own medical practice. Still they may not like what they find in the medical profession, which has recently changed a great deal (Easterbrook, 1987; Altman, 1990).

The Changing Medical Profession

Over the last 10 years, there have been significant changes in the medical profession. Today, doctors often find their autonomy eroded, their prestige reduced, and their competence challenged by everyone from insurance companies to patients.

Before 1980 most doctors practiced alone. Today more than half are salaried employees, working in group practices or health maintenance organizations (HMOs). One reason is that the cost of starting a private practice is too high for most young doctors, whose medical training has landed them deeply in debt. Another reason is that doctors get most of their payments from the government and insurance companies, not from the patients as they did in the past. To be paid, doctors must fill out numerous forms to

justify their fees, which often proves too burdensome for a private doctor to handle (Altman, 1990).

Efforts by the employers, government, and insurance companies to control costs have caused many doctors to complain about losing their professional autonomy. Physicians must seek permission from outside regulators—government agencies or insurance companies—for major but nonemergency hospitalization and surgeries. If the regulators do not approve a case in advance, they will not pay. They occasionally refuse to authorize a treatment that they consider too costly or unnecessary (Kramon, 1991). While chafing at these outside regulators, doctors also complain of internal controls from their employers. HMOs routinely pass around lists ranking their physicians on the time spent with patients. This is intended to give the doctors the subtle but clear message that those highest on the list cause a financial drain on the organization (Belkin, 1990).

The general public also seems to hold less esteem for doctors than before. According to a Gallup poll, 57 percent of the people questioned agreed that "doctors don't care about people as much as they used to." Sixty-seven percent said that doctors are too interested in making money. Seventy-five percent complained that "doctors keep patients waiting too long." And 26 percent said that they have less respect for doctors than they did 10 years ago (Kolata, 1990). Many patients do not fully trust their doctors, and the better educated often feel obliged to make themselves as informed as possible about their illness so

The recent dropoff in the number of applicants to medical school has come from white males, who have traditionally dominated the medical profession. At about the same time, the number of women and minority applicants has increased. Because of the more moderate income expectations among these groups, this demographic change may more effectively meet the cost-conscious needs for health care in the future.

March for federal funding for breast cancer research, Boston. There is a lack of knowledge about breast cancer, which kills about 44,000 women every year. Yet research institutes have not studied these female diseases as much as they have studied diseases that also afflict men.

that they can get the best treatment. This has led many doctors to complain that some patients challenge their expertise after only learning about medical advances on television or in newspapers and magazines (Altman, 1990).

The growing discontent among doctors has apparently discouraged many college students from pursuing a medical career. The number of applicants to medical school fell from 35,944 in 1985 to only 26,915 in 1990. But this drop-off has come only from white males, who have traditionally dominated the medical school and profession. There have been great increases in women and minority members among medical school applicants. In 1988–89, for the first time ever, there were more women and minorities than white men in the first-year class. These demographic changes will make the medical profession more representative of U.S. society and, as suggested by a more moderate income expectation among today's minority and women doctors, will perhaps more effectively meet the cost-conscious needs for health care in the future (Altman, 1990).

Sexism in Medical Research

With more and more women entering the medical profession, there have been an increasing number of discoveries that some well-accepted treatments may be dangerous to women patients. The reason is that the treatments may be based on knowledge from research on men only.

In 1988 the medical profession, along with the general public, was informed that aspirin reduces the risk of heart attacks. But this was based on a study of 22,071 men. Because the study did not include women, nobody knows whether aspirin also benefits women. If it does not, it could spell trouble for women with heart disease who rely on aspirin for treatment. In 1990 a similar study showed that heavy coffee intake did not increase the risk of heart attacks or strokes. Is it safe, then, for women with a heart problem to drink coffee heavily? Not necessarily, because the 45,589 subjects of the study, aged 40 to 75, were all men (Ames, 1990; Purvis, 1990).

It is not necessary to include women in a study on heart disease if their hearts do not differ from men's. But they do. For one thing, cardiovascular disease strikes women later in life, and women are much more likely to die after undergoing heart-bypass surgery. Another thing is that blood cholesterol levels seem to affect female patients differently. Women seem less vulnerable than men to high levels of LDL (the so-called bad cholesterol) but more vulnerable to low levels of HDL (the "good" cholesterol). Diets that reduce *both* levels, as promoted by the American Heart Association, may end up harming women (Ames, 1990; Purvis, 1990).

The bias against women further shows up in the lack of research on health problems that affect women only. The medical profession therefore knows very little about how any of the 19 million women with osteoporosis could have prevented the bone-breaking condition. Doctors also do not know for sure whether it is wise to supply women with replacement hormones when they go through menopause. There is also a serious lack of knowledge about breast cancer, which kills about 44,000 women *every year* (for comparison, the Vietnam War, which lasted *more than 10 years,* cost 58,000 U.S. lives). Still, research institutes have not studied these female diseases as much as they have studied diseases that also afflict men (Silberner, 1990; Beck, 1990c).

However, increased awareness of the medical research bias against women, coupled with mounting pressure from various women's health groups, has begun to produce positive results. The National Institutes of Health, for example, has issued new guidelines that applications for research grants should include women as subjects. At least 20 bills have also been introduced in Congress to fund projects that are aimed at improving women's health (Silberner, 1990).

Questions for Discussion and Review

1. How does modern medicine differ from medicine before 1870?
2. What experiences during and after medical school shape the practice of medicine?
3. What are some recent changes in the medical profession?
4. How is sexism reflected in medical research?

MEDICAL CARE

When people feel sick, they obviously want to get well again, but they do not automatically go to see a doctor. Some may simply shrug off their illness, feeling that it is not serious enough. But more than the severity of illness motivates people to seek medical care. Social factors such as age, gender, ethnicity, and class, which reflect the social diversity in the United States, are also involved. They help determine who is likely to see a doctor and who is not.

Social Diversity

It is common knowledge that the elderly are more often ill than are younger people. It is, therefore, not surprising that they are most likely of all age groups to seek medical care.

Women are more likely than men to use health services. But women are less likely to obtain proper care. Under the influence of sexual prejudice, doctors tend to dismiss women's complaints with such terms as "overstress," "back strain," "could be just the heat," or "nothing to worry about." Even when a patient presents complaints such as chest pains and other symptoms of heart disease, the doctor is less likely to take them seriously coming from a woman than from a man. As Jonathan Tobin and his colleagues (1987) found, doctors are twice as likely to label women's chest pains as a psychiatric complaint

Folk healers with believers, Mexico. Because many Mexican Americans turn to folk healers for medicines, herbs, and teas as well as the performance of religious ritual, they tend to see a doctor as a last resort.

American Mosaic

The careful application of health care assumes that ill people understand and accept modern medical techniques. But many of the recent immigrants to the United States believe in folk or traditional medical remedies, and look with distrust at U.S. doctors. This reading reports on such a case among the Hmong in California, who have immigrated from Central Vietnam.

Clash of Cultures on Illness

Officials in this Central Valley town are not sure whether to look for Lee Lor, a 15-year-old Hmong girl with cancer who ran away from home two weeks ago with a backpack full of herbal medicines but no money.

The authorities here are uncertain because the girl's parents—and the entire community of Hmong, transplants from the mountains of Southeast Asia—say they do not believe Lee has cancer and do not want her to have chemotherapy.

So strong are their objections that when the police, acting on a court order, forcibly removed her from her home to undergo treatment, they were pelted with stones and had to wrestle a knife from the father, who threatened to commit suicide if she was taken way, according to a police report.

For the 35,000 Hmong refugees who have settled in Fresno, making the city home to the largest concentration of Hmong in the nation, the issue is about more than the girl's health. It is about whether she and her family have a right to choose between using herbal remedies and using Western medicine.

The Hmong, who aided U.S. troops in the Vietnam War, were airlifted from Vietnam and Laos to Thailand after the fall of Saigon and resettled in the 1980s in cities like Fresno and St. Paul. They have been slow to embrace U.S. culture, especially Western medicine, and Fresno has been slow to accept the Hmong.

Ever since the Hmong settled in the Central Valley, the authorities have grappled with enforcing laws while respecting the culture of the Hmong. One of the thorniest issues has been how to treat sick children. The Hmong worship ancestors, whose misdeeds are said to resurface in illnesses for generations, said Lia Xiong, a Hmong and Laotian interpreter for Valley Children's Hospital in Fresno. In 1990, the parents of a Hmong child with club feet refused to seek treatment because they believed the child's feet were twisted to atone for the sins of ancestors. In other cases, parents fought to stop operations because they believed surgery would maim the body, leaving the patients unable to be reincarnated, Mr. Xiong said.

The disappearance of Lee took hospital authorities and social service workers by surprise. They say they had been working closely with the Hmong community to combine Western medicine and the Hmong's own healing practices in helping sick children. At Valley Children's Hospital, shamans are allowed to burn incense outside a child's window or sacrifice a chicken or pig in the parking lot.

In some ways, Lee is a typical teenager, who likes to draw and write fan letters to Jonathan Brandis of the television show "Seaquest." But she is also Hmong and believes in shamanism and herbal remedies, her parents say.

or something other than a sign of heart disease. Among those who suffer from kidney failures, women are also less likely than men to receive kidney transplants (Blakeslee, 1989). Nevertheless, when they feel ill, women are still more likely than men to consult doctors.

Some ethnic groups tend less to visit doctors. When ill, Mexican Americans tend more to see the doctor as a last resort, preferring to try Mexican folk medicine first. Their relatives, friends, neighbors, or *curanderos* (folk healers) are generally ready to pro-

vide certain patent medicines, herbs, and teas along with the performance of religious rituals. Native Americans also have a similar system of folk medicine, which they believe to be capable of restoring health by restoring a harmonious balance among various biological and spiritual forces in the sick person's life. Similar principles of harmonious balance can be found in traditional Chinese medicine, which is popular with residents in America's Chinatowns. According to the Chinese, illness results from an imbalance between *yin* (the female, "cold" force) and *yang* (the male, "hot" force). If illness results from an excess of (cold) yin over (hot) yang, certain herbs and foods that are classified as hot should be taken to bring back the balance between yin and yang—and hence health. If illness results from too much (hot) yang, "cold" herbs and foods should be taken (Cockerham, 1995).

African Americans, without the folk medicine available to other minorities, are nearly as likely as whites to visit physicians. But blacks are more likely than whites to receive treatment in hospital outpatient clinics or emergency rooms, which are more often public than private. Whites are more likely to go to a private doctor's office. This is largely because a greater proportion of blacks than whites are poor. The poor are indeed more likely than the rich to get medical treatment in public clinics and emergency rooms (Dutton, 1978; Cockerham, 1995).

Health Care Delivery

One major problem with the health care system in the United States is unequal access. There is no scarcity of medical resources. In fact, we have more doctors per person than many other industrial countries, as well as an abundance of medical technology and hospitals. But the distribution of these resources is very unequal. Doctors are plentiful in affluent areas but often scarce in poverty-stricken parts of the inner cities and countryside.

Another problem with our health care system is soaring costs. In the last 20 years, medical costs have gone up faster than the rate of inflation for other goods and services. According to a 1994 government report, the cost for 1993 came to $884 billion (or $3,299 for every person), compared with $75 billion in 1970. Our yearly medical expenditure amounts to over 10 percent of our gross national product—a higher percentage than any other nation spends on medical care (Toufexis, 1990).

Why have health care costs escalated so rapidly? The aging of the U.S. population may be one contributing factor. The proliferation of expensive medical technology may be another. There have also been significant advances in keeping coma and stroke victims alive—but these patients may then require extremely expensive medical care for years.

There are also other reasons for rising costs. The medical establishment has emphasized curing illness rather than preventing it and maintaining health. This may explain why the United States does not do as good a job as most other industrial countries in low-cost preventive medicine, such as providing free prenatal care, free infant care, and free exams for the middle-aged and elderly. Most significant, medical care in the United States is organized as a business, but it is quite different from other businesses. Medical "customers" do not have much say about what they buy because they usually cannot judge what they need. They rely on doctors to tell them what they need and how much they must pay. Meanwhile, consumers have few incentives to keep prices down. They pay only a small share (about a third) of the cost directly. Most of it is passed on to third parties—insurance companies, employers, and the government.

The Right to Die

Advanced medical technology can prolong life. But, ironically, the same technology can also prolong the agony of dying for the hopelessly ill—and the suffering of the families who have to live with their loved one's living death. Today, about 10,000 patients lie irreversibly comatose in hospital beds across the United States, kept alive by machines such as respirators and feeding tubes. Many have been living in the vegetative, semi-death state for years. Most of their loved ones would like to let them die in dignity. But they cannot have the treatment halted unless they first get authorization from a court. The problem is that the court is likely to deny them the right to let the patient die.

Usually, a physician is required to obtain *informed consent* from the patient (or the patient's parent or guardian) before carrying out surgery or some other important treatment. **Informed consent** is the

From *The Wall Street Journal*, Reprinted with Permission from Cartoon Feature Syndicate.

"I don't use chemical anesthetics anymore. I just give them an estimate of their hospital bill."

approval that a patient gives to the doctor for a treatment after receiving adequate information on it. This clearly implies that the patient has the right to *refuse* treatment. Formally, courts support the principle of informed refusal. But since comatose patients cannot possibly provide informed refusal, the courts have to determine the patient's fate. Normally, they would not let the patient die if the doctor or prosecutor wants the patient kept alive, as they often do (Capron, 1990).

But in 1990 the U.S. Supreme Court ruled that a person has a constitutional right to die but only if the wish to die is clearly known. This has stirred a great deal of interest in **living wills**—advance instructions on what people want their doctors to do in the event of a terminal illness. Still, only the rich and well educated are likely to draw up a living will. Even among this group, young people are the least interested in living wills. They are unlikely to anticipate suffering major brain damage, although they are the most likely of all age groups to be involved in automobile accidents (Davis, 1990). In view of these factors, many hopelessly ill patients can expect to be unable to exercise their right to die.

Questions for Discussion and Review

1. How do social factors determine who might seek medical care?
2. Why has the cost of health care risen so dramatically over the last 20 years?
3. Is it easy for hopelessly ill patients to die? Why or why not?

PERSPECTIVES ON HEALTH AND MEDICAL CARE

From the functionalist perspective, we can see the positive aspects of medical care and even the positive functions of sickness for society. By contrast, the conflict perspective directs our attention to the negative side of health and medical care. While these two perspectives deal with the larger issues of health, symbolic interactionism focuses on the direct interaction between doctor and patient.

Functionalist Perspective

Many people make money have jobs

According to functionalists, both physicians and patients play roles that contribute to social order.

Patients must play the **sick role**, a set of social expectations regarding how an ill person should behave. As discussed in Chapter 4 (Society), role is associated with status, which in turn presents the person with a set of rights and obligations. In his classic definition of the sick role, Talcott Parsons (1964) essentially laid out what rights the sick can claim and what obligations the sick should discharge.

First their rights: (1) They have the right to be taken care of by others, because they do not choose to be sick and thus should not be blamed for their illness. (2) They have the right to be exempted from certain social duties. They should not be forced to go to work. In the case of students, they should be allowed to miss an exam and take it later. Then their obligations: (1) They are obligated to want to get well. They should not expect to remain ill and use the illness to take advantage of others' love, concern, and care for them and to shirk their work and other social responsibilities. (2) They are obligated to seek technically competent help. In seeing a doctor, they must cooperate to help ensure their recovery.

On the other hand, doctors have their own rights and obligations in playing the **healing role**, a set of social expectations regarding how a doctor should behave. Basically, doctors are obligated to help the sick get well, as required by the Hippocratic Oath, which they take when embarking on their medical careers. At the same time, they have the right to receive appropriate compensation for their work. Because their work is widely regarded as highly important, they may expect to make a great deal of money and enjoy considerable prestige.

Seen from the functionalist perspective, both the sick and healing roles serve a social control function. They help to prevent illnesses from disrupting economic production, family relations, and social activities. Moreover, the functionalist perspective suggests that the system of medical care helps maintain the health of people in the society. Thus functionalists tend to attribute an improvement in the nation's health to medicine, the physician, the medical profession, or some new technology of treatment. Such medical discoveries as the germ theory and such medical interventions as vaccines and drugs are credited for our great victory over infectious diseases. All this, however, is a myth to conflict theorists.

Conflict Perspective

According to conflict theorists, improvements in the social environment contribute far more than medical interventions to the reduction of illness and mortality. As one study shows, only about 3.5 percent of

ENRICHING OUR LIVES

Many diseases facing modern societies are likely to come from inactive life styles. Doctors and fitness experts have urged people to lead more healthy lifestyles through exercise and better diet. This reading describes a program created in Canada to promote more active lifestyles.

Active Living: Promoting Healthy Lifestyles

Physical fitness is a well-known concept in modern society. Many leisure services professionals are involved in the fitness boom because of an increasing demand for programs that offer the opportunity to improve physical fitness. Activities such as jogging, cycling, aerobic dance, rope jumping, and walking have become standard offerings of recreation departments.

The approach in the fitness industry has always been bifocal. The first approach concerns testing physical fitness and then prescribing specific activities to improve areas where individuals showed weaknesses. The second approach involves offering activity programs in which the participants could become physically fit. Thus, many health, physical education, and recreation professionals have viewed physical fitness as an end in itself. But a growing number of these professionals consider the means as important as the end. In Canada this "means" is becoming known as Active Living.

Active Living is anchored in physical activity, yet acknowledges that there is more to physical activity than achieving a state of physical fitness. Physical activity, in its broadest context, engages the whole person—the body, the mind, the spirit, the emotions, and social life. Three fundamental principles provide the foundation for Active Living:

Active Living is individual. While external, arbitrary, normative definitions of a certain "state" of health or fitness are important, physical activity choices should correspond to personal interests, needs, abilities, environment, age, health status, financial resources, and related circumstances. Individuals decide how to incorporate physical activities into daily living.

Active Living is social. Participation in physical activity is significantly influenced by the presence or absence of support from family, friends, and colleagues within schools, workplaces, neighborhoods, and communities. The development of both social and physical environments that encourage and support Active Living is an important consideration.

Active Living is inclusive. The concept embraces all positive forms of physical activity. Included are activities of daily living, physical labor, and recreation. It is encased in the full spectrum of physical activity, from mild to vigorous. The nature, intensity, and frequency of the activity depend on each individual's interests, needs, aspirations, abilities, and environment.

The idea of Active Living is already stimulating changes in a variety of ways. Previously, individuals who needed "get fit" programs the most tended to shy away from them. With the advent of Active Living, individuals are beginning to understand that the real goal for their activity is the pleasure they receive from participating. There is no need to be a superstar, and the activity does not have to be one which has been traditionally viewed as an acceptable fitness activity. Bird watching, playing a musical instrument, using the stairs at work, or having a picnic exemplify the broader approach. Indeed, all activities with a physical component and a positive effect on well-being are included.

Excerpted from Randy B. Swedburg and Bill Izso, "Active Living: Promoting Healthy Lifestyles," *Journal of Physical Education, Recreation, and Dance,* April, 1994, pp. 32–35. Reprinted with permission from the *Journal of Physical Education, Recreation, and Dance.* JOPERD is a publication of the American Alliance for Health, Physical Education, Recreation and Dance, 1900 Association Drive, Reston, VA 22091.

the total decline in mortality from five infectious diseases (influenza, pneumonia, diphtheria, whooping cough, and poliomyelitis) since 1900 can be attributed to medical measures. In many instances, the new chemotherapeutic and prophylactic measures to combat those diseases were introduced several decades *after* a substantial decline in mortality from

the diseases had set in (McKinlay and McKinlay, 1987). According to the conflict perspective, this decline in mortality has been brought about mostly by several social and environmental factors: (1) a rising standard of living, (2) better sanitation and hygiene, and (3) improved housing and nutrition (Conrad and Kern, 1994).

According to the conflict perspective, the profit motive has driven corporations to oversell many expensive technological advances, even though they benefit only a limited number of patients and have not significantly improved the nation's health.

Conflict theorists, however, do not mean to suggest that modern clinical medicine does not alleviate pain or cure disease in *some individuals*. Their point is that the medical institution fails to bring about significant improvements in the health of *the population as a whole*. Why, then, does our society continue to spend such vast sums of money on medical care? This, according to conflict theorists, has much to do with the pursuit of private profit in our capitalist society.

In his Marxist analysis of coronary care technology, for example, Howard Waitzkin (1987) finds that, since its introduction in the 1960s, the expensive coronary care units have become so popular that today they can be found in half of all the acute care hospitals in the United States. But the intensive care provided by that medical technology has not been proven more effective than simple rest at home. Waitzkin argues that the proliferation of this expensive but relatively ineffective form of treatment can be traced to the profit motive. He finds that corporations such as Warner-Lambert Pharmaceutical Company and the Hewlett-Packard Company have participated in every phase of the research, development, promotion, and dissemination of today's coronary care technology, which produces huge profits for them. Waitzkin also points out that the same profit motive has driven corporations to oversell many other expensive technological advances, such as computerized axial tomography and fetal monitoring, even though these devices have not significantly improved the nation's health; they have

benefited only a limited number of patients.

The conflict perspective further suggests that the unequal distribution of health and medical care reflects the larger social inequality. The poor suffer from higher rates of most diseases than do the rich. The poor are also more likely to receive inadequate or no medical care.

Symbolic Interactionist Perspective

An important aspect of medical practice is the symbolic interaction between doctor and patient. As suggested by research, patients tend to evaluate warm, friendly doctors favorably even when these doctors have not provided successful treatment. By contrast, patients are most likely to sue for malpractice those physicians who are the most highly trained and who practice in the most sophisticated hospitals. Although these physicians are not intentionally negligent, they are most likely to be viewed by their patients—not just the ones that sue them—as cold and bureaucratic (Twaddle and Hessler, 1987). It is the friendly doctor's "affiliative style" of communication that enhances patient satisfaction, and it is the highly competent but bureaucratic doctor's "dominant style" that alienates patients. "Affiliative style" involves behaviors that communicate honesty, compassion, humor, and a nonjudgmental attitude. "Dominant style" involves the manifestation of power, authority, professional detachment, and status in the physician's interaction with the patient (Buller and Buller, 1987).

Why does the doctor's communication style affect patient satisfaction? From the symbolic interactionist perspective, we can assume that, in interacting with patients, friendly doctors are more likely than dominant doctors to take into account the views, feelings, and expectations held by the patients about themselves, their illnesses, and their doctors. To the patients, the illness is unusual, as it does not happen to them every day, and their suffering is a highly intimate, emotional reality. Thus, they expect their doctors to show a great deal of concern. They obviously want a cure, but they also crave emotional support. If doctors attune themselves to these expectations, they can develop a warm relationship with their patients. But this is no easy task because physicians have been trained to take an objective, dispassionate approach to disease. They have learned to view patients unemotionally, especially when performing surgeries, which involves sticking their hands inside diseased strangers without flinching or losing their nerves (Easterbrook, 1987).

Such emotional detachment often intrudes into the medical interview as well. According to the National Task Force on Medical Interviews, "In the typical doctor-patient encounter, all too often the doctor dominates with questions based on his technical understanding of the cause and treatment of the illness, while the patient, often in vain, tries to get the doctor to pay attention to his very personal sense of the illness" (Goleman, 1988). In one study, average patients were found to have three different problems on their minds when they went to see their doctors, but their efforts to tell their stories were cut off by the doctors within the first 18 seconds of the interview. In fact, most patients never got beyond the first question. In cases where patients were allowed to talk, the physician often responded only with an "um hum." Such a response is noncommittal and indicates only minimal interest (Goleman, 1988). Detached professionalism tends to exact a price by alienating patients, making them feel that they are being treated as mere diseases rather than as people. Such patients are also likely to suffer other consequences. As one study shows, about 60 percent of patients leave their doctors' offices confused about medication instructions, and more than half of new prescriptions are taken improperly or not at all (Winslow, 1989; Nazario, 1992).

Questions for Discussion and Review

1. How do the roles played by patients and physicians contribute to the social order?
2. What facts about U.S. health care do conflict theorists emphasize?
3. What is the nature of the doctor-patient relationship?

CHAPTER REVIEW

1. *When did modern science begin to develop?* In seventeenth-century Europe. Its development was nurtured by the mechanistic philosophy of nature, cooperation among the new scientists, and the scientists' Protestantism. Science became established as a social institution. *How are science and technology related today?* They are virtually inseparable. Science is routinely applied to technological problems, and most current technological advances could not occur without science. But to carry on their work, most scientists today require complicated technology, and the flow of knowledge goes from technology to science as well as from science to technology. *When did the era of "big science" begin?* After World War II. Billions of dollars were poured into scientific research, and the number and prestige of scientists

soared. Increasingly, scientists worked as narrow specialists with huge bureaucracies. *What are the benefits and costs of science?* The benefits are often attainable right away. They include physical comforts and conveniences from technological innovations. But the same innovations can also produce unintended harmful effects.

2. *What norms help preserve the integrity of science?* Robert Merton identified four: universalism, organized skepticism, communality, and disinterestedness. *Do scientists follow these norms?* The norms are frequently violated. Scientists are often emotional about their work, more enthusiastic about their own discoveries than those of others, strongly motivated to seek recognition, and ready to accept or reject new

ideas for nonscientific reasons. *Does competition benefit science?* Competition can benefit science by stimulating hard work and discouraging delay in publication of new ideas. But competition can also discourage cooperation. *How is scientific knowledge advanced?* Cultural accumulation is fundamental. Most scientists work within the reigning paradigm of their discipline. The paradigm is a cultural product, a heritage scientists share as a result of the work of earlier scientists. Normal research produces an accumulation of scientific ideas and findings. Some of these will be anomalies, from which a new paradigm is eventually fashioned, and thus a scientific revolution occurs.

3. *What social factors influence our health?* One is age: old people are more likely to suffer chronic illnesses. Another factor is gender: women are more likely than men to experience chronic and acute illnesses, though they do live longer. African, Hispanic, and Native Americans also have lower life expectancies and higher illness rates than whites. Poor people, too, are more likely than higher-income groups to become ill. *Can epidemiology track down the social causes of diseases?* Yes. It can do so by finding out who has the disease and what all the victims have in common. *How has AIDS spread?* Mostly through unprotected sex and intravenous drug use. *What social consequences have ensued from the AIDS epidemic?* There is a lot of fear about the disease and discrimination against AIDS victims. *How does the health in the United States compare with that in other industrial nations?* We have the lowest life expectancy and highest infant mortality.

4. *What triggered the emergence of modern medicine?* The discovery of the germ theory by French chemist Louis Pasteur in the middle of the last century. *What have doctors learned from their medical training?* The first two years of medical school are devoted to courses in the basic sciences, and the next two years focus on clinical training. As freshmen, medical students are eager to learn everything about medicine so as to be able, eventually, to serve humanity. But many later lose their idealism and develop an emotionless professionalism. *How has the medical profession changed over the last decade?* Doctors' autonomy has eroded, their prestige has declined, and their competence is more open to challenge by laypersons. *How does gender bias in medical research affect women?* Because it produces medical knowledge from studying men only, the treatment based on this knowledge can be inappropriate, even dangerous, to women. The lack of research on women's diseases further prolongs their suffering.

5. *Who is likely to seek medical care when ill?* Those who have higher rates of physician utilization are the elderly, women, African Americans, and whites. Mexican Americans, Native Americans, and the residents of Chinatowns are less likely to visit physicians because they can rely on folk medicine. The poor are more likely than others to go to public clinics and emergency rooms. *What is wrong with the health care system?* One problem is the unequal access to medical care, with the poor receiving inadequate and poor-quality care and the affluent getting better care. Another problem is the soaring cost of health care. *Do terminally ill patients have the right to die?* In principle, they do. But in reality, it is difficult to exercise that right, because the courts would not let the patients die if the doctor or prosecutor wants to keep them alive.

6. *How do functionalists and conflict theorists view health and medical care?* To functionalists, the sick role and the healing role contribute to social order, and the system of medical care significantly maintains health or reduces illness. But to conflict theorists, better social environment reduces mortality from diseases much more than medicine does. In this view, medical care and technology reflect the pursuit of private profit in our capitalist society. *How can symbolic interactionism shed light on the doctor-patient relationship?* If doctors take into account the patients' own views about themselves, their illnesses, and their doctors, patients are likely to be happy with the medical treatment they receive.

KEY TERMS

Anomaly Kuhn's term for an idea or data incompatible with or unexplainable by the existing paradigm (p. 461).

Communality The norm that requires scientists to share their knowledge freely with one another (p. 463).

Disinterestedness The norm that requires scientists to pursue truth rather than self-interest (p. 464).

Epidemiology The study of the origin and spread of disease within a population (p. 466).

Healing role A set of social expectations regarding how a doctor should behave (p. 476).

Informed consent The approval that a patient gives to a doctor for a treatment after receiving adequate information on it (p. 475).

Living will Advance instructions on what people want their doctors to do in the event of a terminal illness (p. 476).

Matthew effect The tendency to praise famous scientists and to ignore the contributions of those who are not well known (p. 464).

Normal science Kuhn's term for routine research (p. 461).

Organized skepticism The norm that requires scientists to be critical of any scientific idea or finding (p. 463).

Paradigm A model for defining, studying, and solving problems in accordance with certain basic assumptions (p. 460).

Science A body of knowledge developed through systematic observations (p. 458).

Scientific revolution Kuhn's term for the replacement of an old paradigm by a new one (p. 461).

Sick role A set of social expectations regarding how an ill person should behave (p. 476).

Technology Any kind of tool or practical know-how, but also the practical application of scientific principles (p. 458).

Universalism The norm that requires scientists to evaluate ideas or findings in accordance with impersonal criteria (p. 463).

SUGGESTED READINGS

Barber, Bernard. 1990. *Social Studies of Science.* New Brunswick, N.J.: Transaction. A collection of articles about various social aspects of science written over the last 35 years by a founder of the sociology of science.

Cozzens, Susan E., and Thomas F. Gieryn (eds.). 1990. *Theories of Science in Society.* Bloomington: Indiana University Press. A collection of articles discussing, with interesting case studies, various theories about the relationship between science and society.

Polednak, Anthony P. 1989. *Racial and Ethnic Differences in Disease.* New York: Oxford University Press. An extensive review of the data on the influences of race and ethnicity on various diseases, such as cancer, heart disease, infectious diseases, and chronic disorders.

Proctor, Robert N. 1995. *Cancer Wars: How Politics Shapes What We Know and Don't Know About Cancer.* New York: Basic Books. A revealing look at the way such groups as corporations, environmentalists, and scientists use and abuse the knowledge about cancer to advance their own interests.

Ratcliff, Kathryn Strother (ed.). 1989. *Healing Technology: Feminist Perspectives.* Ann Arbor: University of Michigan. A collection of articles about how health care, environmental, and occupational technologies affect women's health.

POPULATION AND ENVIRONMENT

CHAPTER OUTLINE

Myths and Realities

MYTH: *The world's total population has become very large today, because it has taken many thousands of years to grow gradually into its present size.*
REALITY: Most of the world's population growth has occurred only in relatively recent years. Before the modern era began in 1600, the global population had taken more than 500,000 years to reach only about half a billion. But since then it has taken less than 400 years to skyrocket to more than 5.6 billion today.

MYTH: *The tremendous population growth in today's poor countries depends almost entirely on their high birth rates.*
REALITY: The high birth rates are obviously a major factor. But a sharp decline in death rates due to the introduction of modern medicine also contributes significantly to the population growth.

MYTH: *Sterilization is a drastic birth control method. It has often been recommended to the peasants in poor countries. It is not likely to become popular in the United States.*
REALITY: Of all the birth control methods used in the United States, the most popular is sterilization.

MYTH: *The U.S. law that prohibits hiring of undocumented workers can effectively discourage poor foreigners from coming here illegally, as was intended.*
REALITY: The sanctions against employers for hiring illegals have failed to be an effective deterrent. Besides, they have produced widespread discrimination against Americans of Hispanic or Asian origin.

I t was a hot day in Bardera, a small town in southern Somalia in Africa. A crowd of starving, emaciated people gathered at a United Nations feeding center. They were waiting for a meal of brown gruel. A five-year-old boy passed out. Two relief workers rushed over, picked him up, and put him down under a shade tree. The child was suffering from severe dehydration. A nurse quickly inserted an intravenous tube, hooking the bottle to a branch. But it was too late. The boy's eyes rolled back beneath quivering eyelids, which an older woman gently shut with her fingers. The boy had come from a village 34 miles away, where both his parents and eight brothers and sisters had also died from starvation in the past six months. Weak and hungry, the boy had walked for four days to this town with his last relative, an elder brother. Now his sibling was rocking and weeping quietly by his lifeless body (Purvis, 1992).

POPULATION

The mass starvation in Somalia and other African countries, though triggered by marauding armies or drought, can be traced partly to population explosion. Even hard-won advances in food production cannot catch up with the continuing enormous growth in population. Increased population pressure has made many of Africa's farms and fields barren through overuse. In addition, demands for heating and cooking fuel have run so high that woodlands—firewood is Africa's chief source of energy—have virtually disappeared. The resulting deforestation has damaged flood control, sped up erosion, and increased the hardship of simply staying alive. It is therefore important to study population.

Demography

The scientific study of population is called **demography**. More than any other area of sociology, demography is based on a large body of reasonably accurate data. Most of these data come from censuses and vital statistics. **Vital statistics** consist of information about births, marriages, deaths, and migrations into and out of a country. Since 1933, the U.S. government has required all states to record these data. The other source of population information, the **census**, is a periodic head count of the entire population of a country. It includes a wealth of data,

such as age, sex, education, occupation, and residence.

Census taking has been with us for a long time. As early as 3000 B.C., China conducted a census in some parts of the country for tax purposes. In biblical times, after the Israelites escaped from Egypt, they listed all men aged 20 and older to assess their military strength. These and other ancient censuses were intended to control particular categories of people—to identify who should be taxed, drafted into military service, or forced to work on certain government projects, such as building the Great Wall in China. Early censuses did not seek to count the entire population—only such categories of people as family heads or males of military age.

By contrast, the modern census, which started to evolve in the seventeenth century, is designed to count all people within a country for governmental, scientific, and commercial purposes. A good example is the U.S. census, which has been taken every 10 years since 1790. It is used for determining the number of congressional seats for each state and allocating federal and state funds to local governments. It is also used for scientific analyses of the nation's demographic traits and trends, economic development, and business cycles. As for its commercial use, orthodontists, for example, would find the census data worthwhile, because they can learn where there are a lot of teenagers in high-income households. But how does one take a census in a large, complex society like the United States?

The U.S. Census

Taking the latest U.S. census in 1990 was a massive task. It required the orchestration of some 500,000 workers and the delivery of 106 million forms to people throughout the United States, Puerto Rico, Guam, the U.S. Virgin Islands, Samoa, and other U.S.-held Pacific locales. Using a decentralized approach, the U.S. Bureau of the Census, which is part of the Department of Commerce, set up about 484 computer-equipped district offices, hiring mainly local people from a wide variety of backgrounds. Most of the census takers worked part-time only. But they all had received special training as office managers, data-entry people, payroll clerks, regular enumerators, and Special Place enumerators (who went to such places as bus depots and abandoned buildings to count the homeless). They compiled and checked address lists, marked census questionnaires, followed up on non-respondents, and reported results (Roberts, 1990; Little, 1991).

Problems appeared in all these operations, but in most cases the Census Bureau had anticipated them and had developed solutions from six years of planning the project. The most common problem was the public's fear that their personal data would fall into the hands of the Internal Revenue Service, Immigration, and other government agencies. Thus, the Census Bureau waged massive national and local public relations campaigns via television, radio, newspapers, fliers, and posters to convey repeatedly the message that strict confidentiality had been ensured by law for 72 years, with census workers being sworn to secrecy. But some 10 percent of the potential respondents remained skeptical. They were typically minorities—the poor and nonwhites—ironically, the very people who stand to benefit the most from government funds if they are counted.

The Census Bureau tried to solve this nonresponse problem by door-to-door canvassing, with enumerators making three or more personal visits. As Barbara Bryant, the Census Bureau's director, said, "Eighty or 90 percent of our effort is targeted at the 10 percent we're most likely to miss" (Little, 1991). This effort included the first-ever attempt to count the homeless in the 1990 census. Special Place enumerators fanned out to where the homeless were known or suspected to stay. In addition to established shelters, the places included rail, bus, and air depots; hidden spots under viaducts; abandoned buildings; laundromats; heating grates; and shanties.

The census put the 1990 U.S. population at 249,632,692—an increase of more than 23 million people, or 10.2 percent, over the 1980 total. Is this number, and the numbers for various subgroups, accurate? Probably not; the census could not be perfect. Some African American leaders have already accused the Census Bureau of undercounting minorities. Cities that were shown to have suffered population decline have also complained of an undercount. But, given the extraordinary efforts to enumerate the population accurately, the 1990 census must be more accurate than any of the past decennial censuses. It is a far cry from earlier censuses. In the 1890 census,

Photo 21.1
The latest U.S. census in 1990 made the first ever attempt to count the homeless. Census takers fanned out even to such places as heating grates, where the homeless were known or suspected to stay.

families were asked if they had any "idiots" and whether their heads were larger or smaller than average. The 1910 census missed most of the numerous immigrants in Chicago who hid from the counters for fear of being deported. The 1910, 1920, and 1930 censuses classified female homemakers as "idlers" despite protests by women who asked that "housewife" be included as an occupation. And the 1960 and 1970 censuses seriously undercounted people in many cities despite the great migration from rural to urban areas that had begun 20 and 30 years earlier (Roberts, 1990).

But from today's considerably more accurate census, demographers can tell as a great deal about population characteristics and changes. These variables are greatly influenced by social factors, and they vary from one society to another.

Questions for Discussion and Review

1. What is demography?
2. How are demographic data collected?

A GLOBAL ANALYSIS

The world's population increases enormously. About 94 million new babies are added every year, a number equal to the size of Mexico's population (Elliott and Dickey, 1994). Moreover, given the same yearly growth rate, population does not increase linearly, with the *same* number of people added annually. Instead, it grows exponentially, with an *increasingly larger* number of new people appearing in each succeeding year. It works like your savings account, which earns an increasingly larger rather than the same interest in each succeeding year.

Increases in population are therefore far more dramatic in modern times of large populations than in ancient times of small populations. Before the year 1600, it took more than 500,000 years for the human population to reach about 0.5 billion. Thereafter, the population skyrocketed to 5.4 billion in less than 400 years. Today it takes only five or six years, in contrast to the 500,000 years before 1600, for the world to produce 500 million people. (See Figure 21.1 for the remarkable population growth in the modern era.)

In general, populations are growing much faster in poor, developing countries than in rich, developed ones. Rich nations generally have an annual growth rate of less than 1 percent. By contrast, poor nations

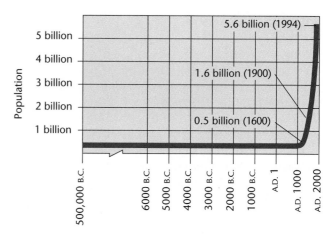

Source: Population Reference Bureau, "How Many People Have Ever Lived on Earth?" *Population Bulletin.* Feb. 1962. p. 5., *The Statistical Abstract of the United States,*1994. p. 850.

FIGURE 21.1
How the World's Population Grows
In recent history, the world's population has experienced exponential growth. Before the modern era began in A.D. 1600, it had taken more than 500,000 years for global population to reach only about half a billion. But since then it has taken less than 400 years for the population to skyrocket to more than 5.6 billion today.

typically grow at a rate of above 2 percent (see Figure 21.2). The growth of a nation's population is determined by the number of births minus the number of deaths plus the net immigration rate—the excess of people moving into a country (immigrants) over those leaving it (emigrants). Let us take a closer look at these three determinants of population growth.

Birth Rates

The **birth rate** is the number of babies born in a year for every 1,000 members of a population:

$$\frac{\text{Births}}{\text{Total population}} \times 1000$$

For many years the birth rates of most industrialized nations have been far lower than 20 per 1,000 population, whereas those of most agricultural countries have far exceeded 30 per 1,000.

Indeed, people in poor countries do tend to have larger families—an average of four or more children—than people in rich countries, who have an average of about two children per family. Because of high birth rates in past years, poor countries also have a very large number of women entering their childbearing years. As a result, even if these women average fewer children than their mothers did, their nations' birth rates will remain high. Meanwhile,

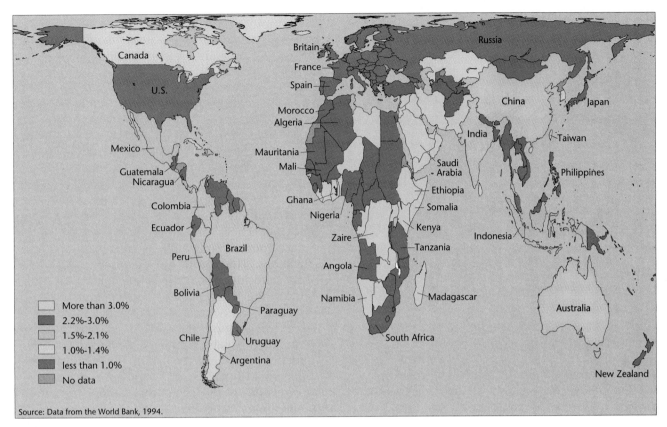

Source: Data from the World Bank, 1994.

Legend:
- More than 3.0%
- 2.2%-3.0%
- 1.5%-2.1%
- 1.0%-1.4%
- less than 1.0%
- No data

FIGURE 21.2
Population Growth Around the Globe

developed countries are close to or already experiencing *zero population growth,* a situation in which the population stops growing. Consequently, well over 90 percent of the world's population increase in coming decades will occur in the poorest nations. By the year 2000, the United States will probably account for only about 4 percent of the total population (Census Bureau, 1994).

Why do people in rich nations have fewer babies? One reason is access to effective and convenient methods of birth control. Another is the nuclear family system. Unlike the married couple in the extended family with many relatives to help raise their children, couples in nuclear families must assume all the responsibility for their children's care. More fundamental than these two reasons is a third—industrialization. In agricultural societies, children are economic assets; they can help with the farmwork. In industrialized societies, however, children have become economic liabilities. They depend on their families for financial support, but they cannot contribute significantly to the family's income. Industrialization is in turn associated with two other related factors that hold down fertility: the entrance of women into the work force, and a prefer-

ence for small families. If women join the labor force outside the home, they may find the prospect of raising children too difficult. A preference for small families is then more likely to take hold.

Death Rates

The **death rate** is the number of deaths in a year for every 1,000 members of a population. Rich nations have an average of 10 deaths per 1000 population, and the poor nations have 13. The difference is surprisingly small. In fact, death rates obscure the large gap between rich and poor nations in health and living conditions. Because the percentage of young people is much higher in developing countries than in developed ones and the percentage of old people much lower, the death rates in these two kinds of nations are more similar than we might expect.

To compare the health and living conditions of nations, demographers therefore use refined rates, especially the **infant mortality rate**, which shows the number of deaths among infants less than one year old for every 1,000 live births. In many developed countries, the infant mortality rate is far lower

"You figure it. Everything we eat is 100 percent natural yet our life expectancy is only 31 years."

than 20. In many developing countries, it is far higher than 30 (Census Bureau, 1994). Another indicator of health conditions is **life expectancy**, the average number of years that a group of people can expect to live. If the group being considered is a nation's newborn infants, then the average life expectancy in developing nations is 63, compared with 75 for industrialized nations (United Nations, 1994).

At least two factors shape death rates or life expectancies. One is medical practice. Immunization of children, for example, has greatly reduced the number of deaths resulting from infectious diseases, and death rates in many poor nations today are being reduced because modern medical practices have been brought into these countries. But early in this century the U.S. life expectancy improved *before* modern medicine could make a substantial contribution to health. The improvement came about because of a second factor that often leads to better health: wealth. As living standards rose, nutrition and sanitation improved, and the life expectancy in the United States rose.

International Migration

International migration—movement of people from one country to another—obviously does not increase or decrease the world's population, but it may greatly alter the population of a specific country. Israel is a case in point. For several years after it was established in 1948, Israel experienced a tremendous annual population growth of 24 percent. Ninety percent of this growth was a result of immigration by European

Jews. Another notable example is the United States. Between 1880 and 1910, more than 28 million European immigrants settled in the United States. During the 1970s, many European countries attracted millions of immigrants from the Middle East, North Africa, Asia, and the Caribbean region (Wrong, 1990).

The effect of immigration goes beyond the immediate addition to the population. Most immigrants are young adults from lower-class families—categories with relatively high fertility rates. As a result, through their children and grandchildren the immigrants multiply population growth, producing an effect that echoes through the years.

Both "pushes" and "pulls" stimulate international migrations. The "push" typically comes from economic hardship, which compels people to leave their country; the "pull" comes from economic opportunity elsewhere. A hundred years ago, nearly half of Ireland's population was "pushed" out of the country by its great potato famine and "pulled" into the United States by its reputation for providing economic opportunity. Nowadays, there is a worldwide mass movement of people from various poor countries to more prosperous ones. Why is this happening now? After all, poverty has been around from time immemorial. The answer is that we have had two revolutions. One is the information revolution, which enables people, even the very poor, to know what life is like in other parts of the world. Another is the transportation revolution, which makes it much easier than before for people to travel long distances.

Economics, however, does not motivate all migrations. Political and religious oppression has pushed many people to brave the uncertainties of a new land. Some 50 years ago, millions of Jews fled persecution in Nazi Germany. More recently, hundreds of thousands of Vietnamese and Cubans escaped communist oppression in their homelands. In the last decade, many Jews left behind their oppressive lives in the former Soviet Union, immigrating to Israel and the United States. Similarly, since 1990 hostility toward ethnic minorities throughout Eastern Europe has recently spurred migration, with, for example, Romania's ethnic Hungarians fleeing to Hungary and Bulgaria's ethnic Turks going to Turkey.

Age, Gender, and Marriage

Other characteristics of a population influence its growth. Among the most important are the age structure, sex ratio, and marriage rate.

The **age structure**—the pattern of the proportions of different age groups within a population—shapes birth rates. Compared with industrialized countries, developing countries generally have a very low percentage of old people and a high percentage of children. Since the current large numbers of children will grow up to produce children themselves, future birth rates in these nations are likely to be high. The age structure also affects death rates. If two nations have equally healthy populations and living conditions, the country with the higher percentage of older people will have a higher death rate.

The **sex ratio** indicates the number of males per 100 females. A sex ratio of more than 100 means there are more males than females. If the sex ratio is 100, the number of males equals the number of females. In most societies, slightly more boys are born than girls, but males have higher death rates. As a result, there are more females than males in the population as a whole. The sex ratio for young adults is about even in normal times, but it falls in wartime because wars are waged mainly by men. In the United States, about 105 males are born for every 100 females each year (giving a sex ratio of 105), but because males die sooner than females, the sex ratio for the entire population is 95 (Census Bureau, 1994).

If the sex ratio is close to 100, then the **marriage rate**—the number of marriages for every 1000 people in a given year—is likely to be high. Because most babies are born to married rather than unmarried couples, a high marriage rate will likely bring a high birth rate. When soldiers came home from World War II, for example, our marriage rate went up, and the "baby boom" followed. Since 1960 the numbers of unmarried adults, late marriages, and divorces in the United States have all increased, partly helping to bring down our birth rates.

Questions for Discussion and Review

1. What influences birth rates, death rates, and international migration?
2. What are the age structure, sex ratio, and marriage rate of a population?

PATTERNS OF POPULATION CHANGE

Demographers can tell us a great deal about how populations are changing. The most influential explanations of population change are the Malthusian theory and the theory of demographic transition. Demographers also can offer insight into the consequences of population change.

Malthusian Theory

In 1798 the English clergyman and economist Thomas Malthus (1766–1834) published a truly dismal portrait of population dynamics in *An Essay on the Principles of Population*. He argued that population grows much faster than the production of food supplies, because a population *multiplies* itself but food production increases only by *addition*—through the cultivation of land. Thus, population typically increases geometrically (2, 4, 8, 16), but food supplies increase only arithmetically (2, 3, 4, 5). As a population outstrips food supplies, it will be afflicted by war, disease, and poverty. Eventually, population growth will stop.

People might halt this growth through what Malthus called "preventive checks," by which he meant late marriage and sexual restraint, which would reduce birth rates. But Malthus doubted that people, especially the lower classes, had the will to exercise this restraint. Instead, he argued, population growth would eventually be stopped by nature. Its tools would be what Malthus called "positive checks"—disease and famine.

Malthus failed to foresee three revolutions that undermined his theory: the revolutions in contraception, agricultural technology, and medicine. He did not anticipate the development of effective and convenient contraceptives such as the pill and the IUD (intrauterine contraceptive device). He did not expect that birth control would become widespread. Especially in the West, the use of contraceptives has helped bring birth rates down to a point lower than Malthus thought possible. Meanwhile, the technological revolution has allowed farmers to increase production by raising the yield of their land, not just by adding farmland. Finally, medical advances have given us an arsenal of effective weapons against the contagious diseases that Malthus expected would devastate overpopulated nations. As a result, instead of being reduced by disease, overpopulated nations continue to grow more crowded. Thus, the awful fate Malthus predicted has not come to pass—or, at least, not yet. His theory, however, has served as a warning to nations that populations cannot expand indefinitely, because natural resources are finite.

The Demographic Transition

Most demographers subscribe to the **demographic transition** theory, namely, that human populations tend to go through specific, demographic stages and that these stages are tied to a society's economic development. This theory is based on the population

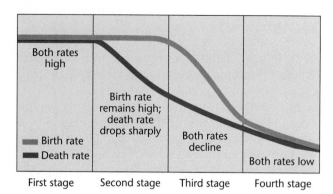

FIGURE 21.3
The Demographic Transition

changes that occurred in Western Europe during the past 200 years. According to the theory, there are four demographic stages (see Figure 21.3).

In the first stage, both birth rates and death rates are high. Because the two rates more or less balance each other, the population is fairly stable, neither growing nor declining rapidly. This was the stage of the populations in Western Europe in 1650, before industrialization.

During the second stage, the birth rate remains high but the death rate declines sharply. This stage occurred in Western Europe after it had become industrialized, and it is occurring today in many developing nations. The introduction of modern medicine, along with better hygiene and sanitation, has decreased death rates in developing countries. But their economies and values are still essentially traditional, so their birth rates remain high. As a result, their populations grow rapidly.

During the third stage, both birth rates and death rates decline. Western countries found themselves in this stage after they reached a rather high level of industrialization. Today, Taiwan, South Korea, and Argentina are among the developing nations that have reached this stage. Their birth rates have declined significantly. The population still grows because the birth rate continues to exceed the death rate, but growth is slower than during the second stage.

The fourth stage is marked by a low birth rate and a low death rate. Only the most industrialized nations of Western Europe, the United States, and Japan have reached this stage. They have fairly stable populations and are moving close to zero population growth. Some countries, such as Japan, France, and Italy, have fallen below zero growth, with birth rates lower than death rates.

To proponents of the demographic transition theory, the future of human populations looks bright. They believe that developing countries will

eventually join the industrialized world and have stable populations. To critics of the theory, the future is far less certain. There is at least one major difference between the developing countries of today and the European nations of 200 years ago. Thanks to modern medicine, death rates in developing countries have declined far more rapidly than they did in nineteenth-century Europe. While it took Europe 200 years to lower its mortality, it takes developing countries today only a year or so to lower theirs. At the same time, their birth rates remain high. As a result, the population is exploding in the developing world today, a condition that did not occur in nineteenth-century Europe.

The fallout from the population explosion can be seen in the oppressive poverty of many of the developing nations. Cities, such as the Asian city shown here, are filled with people who live in overcrowded shacks, and others who live on the streets, sidewalks, vacant lots, and other undesirable locations.

GLOBAL VILLAGE

In many places around the world, birth rates have soared, making it difficult for poor countries to feed or house their populations. This reading reports on the population explosion in Central America, and its impact on the region.

The Population Explosion

I was walking through the streets of Cartago, Costa Rica, some 20 years ago when the bells rang and the elementary schools let out. A thousand scrubbed and uniformed children flooded the streets. That Lilliputian world was a dramatic reminder that Costa Rica, like the rest of Central America, is a nation of children. Nearly half the population is under the age of 15.

Central America's population explosion—and the population explosion taking place throughout the Third World—was captured for me in that incident. Today, ever-larger numbers of children are pressing hard on small and, in some cases, shrinking economies.

In one lifetime, Central America's population is not just doubling or tripling. It is rising by a factor of seven—if the ecology can support it.

Overwhelming population growth is wreaking havoc on the region's cultures, economies, social systems, and natural-resource base. Forget the failure of political systems and civil wars as the leading issue. Forget economic depression and unemployment, affecting as much as half the labor force. Forget old debates over land-holding systems where power is concentrated in the hands of a few export-crop producers. Forget low standards of living and miserable urban slums.

Focus instead on the rise in population as the single basic issue. It has put an incredible burden on attempts to resolve old problems and has, meanwhile, created new ones. In Central America today, you truly must run faster and faster just to stay in place.

The concept of "economic development" has dominated, for the most part, the Third World's view of its future since the 1960s. A fast pace of economic growth was expected to more than offset rapid population gains. Population growth was still considered a given. The idea of slowing it down offended many—for religious and political reasons—and grated deeply on personal convictions. But it was always recognized that economic growth has to keep pace with population growth. If the economies faltered, the continuing population gains would slip right by, producing lower and lower standards of living. This is precisely what has happened.

Central America offers a typical case of the demographic forces working in the Third World. Demographers have informed politicians that they see a very major problem emerging for which there is no short-term solution. Further, the problem is guaranteed to continue to intensify for the next half century and longer.

Slowly but surely, the soundness of these alarming population projections is being recognized. These projections, accompanied by common-sense observations in the increasingly crowded streets outside, are convincing politicians that a serious and intractable problem has emerged.

The Third World's demographic future contains hard messages that are difficult to swallow. But, with rapid population growth still accelerating, neither Central America nor other developing nations are likely to stabilize and take the pressures off their social, ecological, and economic systems.

Excerpted from Robert W. Fox, "The Population Explosion: Threatening the Third World's Future," *The Futurist,* January-February 1992, p. 60.

Demographic "Fallout"

The fallout from the population explosion can be seen in the oppressive poverty of many of the developing nations. Their cities are filled with people who live in overcrowded shacks, and others who must live on the streets, sidewalks, vacant lots, rooftops, and cemeteries. In these poor countries, most are undernourished, and malnutrition is devastating 200 million children under age five, weakening their bodies and their minds. Some 15 million children die of starvation every year (Ehrlich, 1984; United Nations, 1994).

The rapidly growing populations of developing nations greatly complicate their efforts to fight poverty. Instead of climbing up the economic ladder, they find themselves standing on a treadmill, constantly in danger of slipping backward to the

Malthusian famine. Economic investment can barely keep up with the rapid population growth. More than half of Africa's economic expansion has been used just to maintain the expanding population at a subsistence level. More than 40 percent of Africa's population are already living below the region's poverty line. Some African countries, such as Ethiopia, Somalia, and the Sudan, have experienced and will continue to face massive starvation. Other developing countries in Asia and Latin America, though, have made significant progress against poverty by slowing population growth and hastening economic growth. Indonesia, for example, over the last two decades has reduced its poverty rate from nearly 60 percent to less than 20 percent today (Farnsworth, 1990).

Questions for Discussion and Review

1. How would a Malthusian theorist's view of current world population patterns differ from that of a demographic transitionist?
2. What is the demographic "fallout" of population explosion?

COMBATING POPULATION GROWTH

For thousands of years, there have been individuals who practiced birth control, but many nations at various times in their histories have sought to *increase* their population because they associated a large population with great military power and national security. Religious, medical, and political authorities have often argued against birth control. For more than a century, the United States even had laws that prohibited the mailing of birth control information and devices. During the 1950s and 1960s, however, many governments began to see population growth as a social problem. By 1984 most countries, representing about 95 percent of the world's population, had formulated official policies to combat population

In India it has been difficult to control relentless population growth because of low literacy and a dearth of sustained family planning information and services. Shown here is an attempt to promote voluntary family planning on a placard on the back of a bus.

growth (Davis, 1976; Russell, 1984). These policies can be classified into two types: encouragement of voluntary family planning and compulsory population control.

Voluntary Family Planning

A number of governments make contraceptives available to anyone who wants them. They encourage birth control, but they do not try to impose a limit on how many children a couple may have. For this voluntary family planning to work, however, people must *prefer small families* to large ones—otherwise they will not use birth control.

This is the heart of the problem with family planning. Family planning programs have reduced birth rates significantly in advanced developing countries such as Taiwan and South Korea, because these societies value small families. Family planning is even more successful in the more industrialized nations of the West, where the preference for small families is strong. However, many less advanced developing countries retain the preference for large families typical of agricultural societies. In these societies, having many children is a status enhancer, particularly for the less educated. Children are also considered a form

of old-age pension because there are no social welfare systems like the ones we have in the United States. Because many children die early, parents are even more anxious to have a large family to increase their chances of being looked after in their senior years (Francis, 1987).

As a result, voluntary planning programs in these poor societies have failed to reduce birth rates significantly. This has led the governments of some of these countries to resort to compulsory programs.

Compulsory Population Control

In the early 1970s, India forced government employees who had more than two children to undergo sterilization. With the encouragement of the central government, some states in India also forced men to be sterilized after their second child was born. If the men refused, they could be fined $250 and imprisoned for up to a year. In some villages, overzealous government officials rounded up and sterilized all the men, without checking how many children they had. The program stirred up widespread opposition. Demographer Frank Notestein had predicted in 1971 that if a developing country tried to force its people to practice birth control, it "would be more likely to bring down the government than the birth rate." Indeed, the sterilization program apparently contributed to the fall of Prime Minister Indira Gandhi's government in 1977. Since then, India has returned to a voluntary program. But it has been difficult to control the relentless population growth because of low literacy and a dearth of sustained family planning information and services. India now has a fertility rate of four children per woman (compared with two in the United States), and it will become the world's most populous nation by about 2045 (Crossette, 1990; World Bank, 1994).

China has had more success with a program that combines rewards and punishments. For a couple with only one child, rewards are substantial. The parents get a salary bonus, and the child receives free schooling, priority in medical care, admission to the best schools and universities, and preference in employment. By contrast, multichild parents are severely penalized. They must pay all costs for each additional child, are taxed about 10 percent of their income, and are often denied promotion for two years. Since starting this "one-child family" campaign in 1979, China has halved its birth rate, a record unmatched by any other developing nation.

Beginning in 1986, though, the birth rate began to rise again because the government relaxed its one-child policy—by allowing rural couples to have a second baby if their firstborn was a girl. One reason for the relaxation has been the increasing prosperity among the Chinese, many of whom are willing to pay the fines for having more than one child. Another reason is the international criticism that China has received for pressuring women to abort fetuses even late in pregnancy. A third reason is that the one-child policy has encouraged, albeit unintentionally, the killing of female infants by parents who hope to have sons. Nevertheless, China continues to exhort couples to have only one child, though it now focuses on persuasion, education, and publicity campaigns rather than coercion and penalties. All this has been quite successful with urban couples, though it tends to fall on deaf ears in the countryside (Kristof, 1990).

U.S. Population Policy

In the 1960s, the U.S. government began to recognize global population growth as a potential problem; by 1968 it had spent several hundred million dollars to help developing countries. During the conservative Reagan and Bush administrations in the 1980s and early 1990s, however, the U.S. government suspended aid to countries that advocated abortion as a family planning operation. More liberal, the Clinton administration has restored the aid. Similar assistance is given to family planning in the United States.

FIGURE 21.4
Contraceptive Choices in the United States

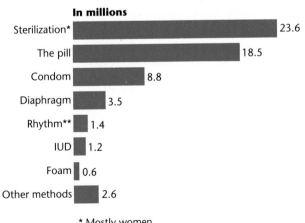

In millions

Sterilization*	23.6
The pill	18.5
Condom	8.8
Diaphragm	3.5
Rhythm**	1.4
IUD	1.2
Foam	0.6
Other methods	2.6

* Mostly women
** Periodic abstinence

Source: Data from the U.S. Census Bureau, 1994.

Birth Control The federal government has been spending over $100 million a year to assist family planning centers. But our population growth has slowed, primarily because of social and economic factors, not government action. In fact, family planning has become the norm rather than the exception. Even the majority of U.S. Catholics practice forms of birth control forbidden by their church. Today, sterilization is the most popular type of birth control in the United States, followed by the pill and the condom (see Figure 21.4). The use of sterilization and the condom has increased faster than most other methods, because of concern and controversy over the side effects of the pill and the IUD.

But all these contraceptives are antiquated; the pill and the IUD, for example, were introduced 30 years ago. They are also less convenient and less effective than the ones coming out in Western Europe. Only as late as December 1990 was the innovative Norplant device—introduced in Europe 20 years earlier—approved for use in the United States. Norplant, when properly implanted in a woman's upper arm, can protect against pregnancy for five years. But, since it is very expensive, it will likely be of little use to the poor, who have the highest incidence of unwanted pregnancy. Owing to the lack of modern and inexpensive contraceptives, more than half of all U.S. pregnancies every year are accidents or unwanted—more than in Western Europe. This may explain why our rate of abortion as a form of birth control is among the highest in the industrialized world, despite restrictions by the federal government and many state governments on the use of Medicaid funds for abortions (Elmer-DeWitt, 1991).

Nevertheless, the use of contraception is prevalent enough. And given the added prevalence of abortion, the Census Bureau (1994) believes that within 15 years U.S. women in their childbearing years will average just 1.8 births—less than the replacement rate of 2.1. (Demographers determine the replacement rate at 2.1 rather than 2.0 to take into account young people who die before reaching their reproductive age.) It seems inevitable that if the "birth dearth" continues, the United States will rely increasingly on immigration to stop the population from declining.

Immigration Today, both legal and illegal immigration accounts for about 26 percent of the nation's population growth. But that proportion is expected to rise to 50 percent early in the next century, and then immigration will provide the bulk of the nation's population growth in the second half of the twenty-first century (Census Bureau, 1994). History has shown how immigration has contributed to the prosperity of this country. Hoping to benefit the U.S. economy more quickly, Congress has passed a bill to admit larger numbers of highly educated and skilled immigrants, such as scientists, engineers, and medical technicians, as Canada and Australia have done for years. But opposition to admission of poor and unskilled immigrants, especially illegals, has sharply increased in recent years, as shown by the 1994 passage of Proposition 187 in California, denying most government services to illegal immigrants. There is widespread fear that immigrants take jobs from U.S. workers. But supporters of immigration suspect racism because most of the immigrants come from nonwhite countries rather than Europe.

Nonetheless, every year more people enter this country illegally than legally. In 1986, Congress passed a law that offers amnesty—in effect, legal residency status—to illegals who have been living in this country since January 1, 1982. But at the same time the United States will beef up its efforts to stop illegal immigration. Because the small number of agents from the U.S. Immigration and Naturalization Service (INS) cannot by themselves prevent the vast number of aliens from flooding illegally into this country, Congress has also passed a law that prohibits employers from hiring illegals. This law has, in effect, forced the nation's seven million employers to work for free as agents of the INS. But such sanctions have 500failed to be an effective deterrent in the United States and 20 other nations. Moreover, the sanctions have produced widespread discrimination against minorities, particularly Americans of Hispanic and Asian origin. Some employers practice "preventive discrimination" by refusing to hire *any* foreign-sounding job applicants in order to avoid the possibility of hiring illegal aliens. Other employers simply use the sanctions as an excuse for not hiring people who have a "foreign appearance or accent" (Solis et al., 1987; Yoshihashi, 1990).

Questions for Discussion and Review

1. How does family planning differ from population control?
2. What has been the result of compulsory birth control programs in overpopulated countries like India and China?
3. What kinds of contraceptives are commonly used to keep birth rates low in the United States?
4. How has the U.S. government dealt with the immigration issue?

ENVIRONMENT

To understand how the growth of population can damage the environment and thus endanger us, we look to **ecology.** It is a study of the interactions among organisms and between organisms and their physical environment.

Elements of Ecology

Like all organisms, humans exist within a thin layer of air, soil, and water surrounding the earth known as the **biosphere.** Within the biosphere we can isolate countless **ecosystems,** self-sufficient communities of organisms depending for survival on one another and on the environment. An ecosystem may be as small as a puddle in a forest or as large as the biosphere itself. But whatever ecosystem we choose to look at, we find that the organisms within it depend on one another and on the physical environment for their survival. They are bound together by mutual interdependence. Energy and matter are constantly being transformed and transferred by the components of an ecosystem, providing the organisms with the essentials of life. Plants, for example, take in carbon dioxide and give off oxygen, which humans and other animals require for survival, and animals exhale carbon dioxide. Plants, in turn, use carbon dioxide in photosynthesis, the process by which they convert solar energy into carbohydrates and become food for animals. When animals die, their decomposed bodies provide nutrients to the soil, which plants then use.

From analyzing ecosystems we can isolate two simple principles. First, natural resources are finite. Every ecosystem therefore has a limited *carrying capacity,* a limited number of living things that it can support. Second, we can never do just one thing, because everything is related to everything else. If we try to alter one aspect of an ecosystem, we end up changing others as well. When farmers used DDT, for example, they meant merely to kill pests. But DDT also got into the soil and water, from there into plankton, into fish that ate plankton, and into birds that ate the fish. The chemical also found its way into our food.

Despite all the amazing things humans have managed to do, we are still limited by these ecological principles. We are still living organisms, dependent like other organisms on ecosystems. However, we have tried to ignore that dependence and act in defiance of nature's limits. Two environmental problems result: a depletion of natural resources and environmental pollution.

Diminishing Resources

Although we make up less than 6 percent of the world's population, each year we consume about 30 percent of the world's energy and raw materials. If this high level of consumption continues, the world will soon run out of resources. According to some estimates, the world's reserves of lead, silver, tungsten, mercury, and other precious resources will be depleted within 40 years. Even if new discoveries increase oil reserves fivefold, the global supply of oil will last only 50 years. Poor nations fear that by the time they become fully industrialized, the resources they hope to enjoy will be gone. In the meantime, their cropland is literally disappearing—running down the rivers or blowing away with the wind (Wald, 1990).

Closer to home, we are endangering our own supplies of arable land and water. We are losing topsoil to erosion at an alarming rate. In the worst cases, an inch of topsoil, which nature takes 100 to 1,500 years to form, is being destroyed in 10 to 20 years. At the same time, homes and stores and businesses are taking over millions of acres of farmland each year. Meanwhile, in the western United States, underground water reservoirs are being depleted. In the East, thousands of gallons of water are wasted because of leaking city pipes. Even wetlands and marshes, which help control shoreline erosion and act as filtering systems to purify water, are disappearing at a rate of 450,000 acres a year (Carpenter, 1990).

In short, we are fast running out of natural resources. "Barring revolutionary advances in technology," concludes the *Global 2000 Report,* "life for most people on earth will be more precarious in 2000 than it is now." Economist Julian Simon (1990), however, disagrees. He argues that the future is likely to be better "because our powers to manage our environment have been increasing throughout human history." To Simon, if nonrenewable resources such as minerals, metals, coal, or oil are used up, they can always be replaced through technology. Solar energy can be captured to replace coal and oil. We can also find substitutes for metals, such as plastics and aluminum for tin cans, and use satellites and fiber-optic lines instead of copper telephone wires. But to produce substitutes may require the use of materials that will themselves eventually run out. More ominous,

Pollution of the air has many sources. Throughout the world, power-generating plants, oil refineries, chemical plants, steel mills, and the like spew about 140 million tons of pollutants into the air every year. Air pollution is especially bad in Eastern Europe, as this Romanian woman illustrates by her darkened hand.

the production process for the substitutes may contribute to the pollution of the environment.

Environmental Pollution

To consume more, we must produce more and thereby create more wastes. These by-products of our consumption must go somewhere. Nature has many cycles for transforming wastes to be used in some other form, but we are overtaxing nature's recycling capacity. We put too much waste, such as automobile emissions, in one place at the same time, and we have created new toxic substances, such as dioxin, that cannot be recycled safely. The result is pollution.

Pollution of the air has many sources. Throughout the world, power-generating plants, oil refineries, chemical plants, steel mills, and the like spew about 140 million tons of pollutants into the air every year. The heaviest polluter is the automobile, which accounts for at least 80 percent of air pollution. The pollutants irritate our eyes, noses, and throats; damage buildings; lower the productivity of the soil; and may cause serious illnesses, such as bronchitis, emphysema, and lung cancer. Air pollution is especially bad in Eastern Europe. As many as 10 percent of the deaths in Hungary are attributed directly to air pollution; the problem is even worse in parts of Czechoslovakia, Poland, and former East Germany (Nelson, 1990).

Throughout the world, a growing concentration of industrial gases (carbon dioxide, methane, nitrous oxides, and chlorofluorocarbons) in the atmosphere is retaining more and more radiation from sunlight and thus will substantially raise the temperature of the earth's surface in the next century. A number of scientists expect this global warming to cause worldwide flooding, climatic change, and social disruption (Shabecoff, 1990). Some of the industrial gases—especially chlorofluorocarbons, used in refrigeration and air conditioning—have already weakened the ozone layer in many areas of the globe, thereby letting in more of the sun's ultraviolet light, which may cause skin cancer, harm the human immune system, and damage some crops and wild plants (Lemonick, 1992).

Another kind of air pollution, called *acid rain*, has also aroused concern. When sulfur and nitrogen compounds are emitted by factories and automobiles, chemical reactions in the atmosphere may convert them to acidic compounds that can be carried hundreds of miles and then fall to the earth in rain and snow. Rain as acidic as vinegar has been recorded. This acid rain can kill fish and aquatic vegetation. It damages forests, crops, and soils. It corrodes buildings and water pipes and tanks because it can erode limestone, marble, and even metal surfaces. Because of acid rain, thousands of lakes and rivers in North America and Europe are now "dead," unable to support fish and plant life. Worst is the acid rain in Russia's Siberia, which has ruined more than 1,500 square miles of timber, an area half as large as Rhode Island (Feshbach and Friendly, 1992).

A Primary Cause

Polluting our environment and depleting its resources may amount to a slow form of suicide. Sometimes the cause is ignorance; sometimes it is poverty. In many developing nations, rivers and streams are polluted by human wastes. Poor people desperate for fuel in developing countries have stripped mountainsides of trees, clearing the way for massive erosion. Overgrazing is expanding the deserts of Africa.

Neither ignorance nor poverty, however, can explain much of the environmental damage now being done around the world. After all, affluent societies consume much more resources. Although inhabitants of the United States make up only about 6 percent of the world's population, they consume more than 30 percent of the world's energy and raw material. By burning far more fossil fuel in power plants, factories, and family cars, each U.S. resident contributes to air pollution five times as much as does the average Brazilian (Easterbrook, 1989; Census Bureau, 1994).

A primary source of the environmental problem is the fact that clean air, clean rivers, and other environmental resources are public, not private, goods. In Aristotle's words, "What is common to the greatest number gets the least amount of care." Garrett Hardin (1993) has used a parable called the "Tragedy of the Commons" to illustrate why this is so and how damage to the environment results. Suppose you are raising sheep, and you and your neighbors share a commons, a common piece of land for grazing. To increase your income, you want to raise more sheep and graze them on the commons. If you do, you may damage the commons by overgrazing, but you will gain the entire benefit of raising additional sheep and share only part of the cost of the damage done to the commons. So you add another sheep to your herd, and then perhaps another. Everyone else using the commons makes the same calculation, however, and in their own self-interests, add to their herds. Eventually, overgrazing is severe enough to destroy the commons.

Without government intervention, the physical environment is much like this grazing commons. Individuals gain by using, even polluting, it, but society as a whole bears the cost of the damage. When people act on the basis of their individual self-interests, they end up degrading the environment. How, then, can the environment be saved?

Saving the Environment

Since 1970 a number of methods have been used to bring environmental problems under control.

First, various *antipollution laws* have been passed. Initially, industry tended to resist them because of their expense. Unions sometimes opposed them because of fear that jobs would be lost as a result of the cost to industry. Some consumers objected to the laws because they feared prices would rise too high if industry was forced to reduce pollution. Therefore, state governments were often reluctant to make or enforce their own pollution-control laws for fear that

Conservation provides one method of reducing humans' negative impact on the environment. This photo shows a form of recycling: about four to six million tires are burned for electricity by a California plant that supplies 3,500 homes.

companies would move their business elsewhere. But as pollution continued to get worse, popular support for the laws increased significantly (Wald, 1990).

Conservation provides a second method of reducing our negative impact on the environment. During the late 1970s, the federal and state governments took many steps to encourage the conservation of energy. People were urged to insulate their homes, turn down the thermostat in cold months, drive smaller cars at lower speeds, and ride buses and trains. The government began to offer tax credits and direct subsidies to encourage energy conservation. We were reminded that most European countries use far less energy than the United States while maintaining a high standard of living. Conservation efforts combined with rising energy prices and economic recession to produce a drop in our energy use from 1979 to 1982 that was greater than experts had thought possible. Recycling, aside from combating pollution, provided another means of conserving energy and raw materials. Today, conservation has become popular. According to one poll, for example, more than 80 percent of people are willing to separate their trash for recycling, to give up plastic containers and superfluous packaging to reduce waste, and to favor a ban on disposable diapers (Rosewicz, 1990).

A third approach to dealing with environmental problems focuses on the development of *new, alternative technology* that is efficient, safe, and clean.

Changes in automobiles illustrate this approach. Since the early 1970s, the fuel efficiency of cars has been increased and their polluting emissions have been reduced. Especially in the last 10 years, the widespread use of catalytic converters in cars has greatly reduced two types of pollutants emitted by tailpipes: carbon monoxide and nitrogen oxide. Industrial scrubbers have also been used to remove much of the sulfur dioxide—the major ingredient of acid rain—from the process of producing energy from coal. More recently, scientists have been trying to develop photovoltaic cells to produce electricity directly from the sun, without releasing any pollutants into the air. The solar cells are expected to be in widespread use in the sunny Southwest later this decade, when they become cheaper than conventional power sources. By using energy more efficiently and at less cost, the new technology would make U.S. economy more productive and more competitive internationally (Wald, 1990; Stevens, 1992)

Limiting both population and economic growth is a fourth way of solving environmental problems. As John Firor (1990) observes, nearly every environmental problem, be it acid rain, global warming, or ozone depletion, is first driven and then exacerbated by growth in the world's population. By stemming population growth, we will go a long way toward reducing environmental pollution and resource depletion. Rich countries have done much better than poor countries in curbing population growth.

ENRICHING OUR LIVES

The movement to save the environment has traditionally used the slogan, "Think Globally, Act Locally," to encourage people to save the globe through local efforts. This reading, using the example of native Canadians, reverses the slogan, and shows how people can express their local environmental concerns by taking action against global corporations that damage their environment.

Think Locally, Act Globally

Conflicts over resource use and development projects in northern Canada are being played out increasingly in the international arena. Foreign investment in resource projects can trigger wider-ranging interactions, as in the case of Japanese involvement in large-scale, clear-cut logging and pulp mill construction in northern Alberta. Canadian aboriginal peoples and environmental groups, concerned about the impacts of logging in the northern forest, have attempted to gain support in the "end-user" country (where the wood or wood products are used) by forging links with Japanese environmentalists and by developing an information campaign aimed at Japanese tourists visiting Canada.

The James Bay hydroelectric power scheme in Quebec has also generated conflicts featuring pervasive transnationalization. The government of Quebec and the provincial power utility, Hydro-Quebec, are committed to harnessing 28,000 megawatts of hydroelectric capacity from northern rivers. The end-users—consumers of electricity generated from dams—live in southern Quebec, New York, and the New England states. Ultimately, Europeans and the Japanese may also be end-users if electricity-based hydrogen production and liquid hydrogen export prove to be feasible.

The project is greatly modifying the hydrological regime including water volumes, discharge rates, temperature patterns and ice formation of the rivers flowing into James Bay and thus should result in substantial changes to the inland waters and coastal region. The affected people are mostly Cree Indians and Inuit living on the northern fringe of the project area.

Aboriginal people have called for independent assessment by international bodies, prepared factual documentation of perceived impacts, performed acts of disobedience in Canada and abroad, organized lobbying activities overseas, run information campaigns abroad by linking their causes to highly symbolic events, such as the 500th anniversary of Columbus's landing, participated in foreign legal and administrative procedures, and formed alliances with supporter groups abroad.

Clearly, the interplay among marginalized groups in the north, southern domestic proponents, and foreign end-users has turned the conflict over the James Bay hydroelectric power project into transnational, rather than purely Canadian, issues. When marginal groups lack power, believe that existing institutions and decision-making processes are not sufficiently responsive, and feel that their rights are not recognized or protected, some try to gain bargaining power by seeking support in the international arena. The strategy is to "think locally" but "act globally."

Excerpted from Mary L. Barker and Dietrich Soyez, "Think Locally, Act Globally?" *Environment*, June 1994, pp. 12 ff.

This is achieved primarily by abandoning the traditional value that favors having many children.

But most countries, rich or poor, have not abandoned the traditional value that favors economic growth with little regard to its cost to the environment. Gross national product (GNP) is still measured the old-fashioned way: adding the total value of goods and services *without* subtracting the value of clean air, water, ground, trees, fish, animals, human health, and other ecological elements that have been harmed by the production process, as if these were free goods rather than assets that are being lost. Thus, a large economic growth measured as a great increase in GNP does not truly represent a country's wealth, the welfare of its citizens, or the value of its goods and services. Environmentalists have therefore called on governments and industries to stop pursuing this old kind of economic growth, which harms the environment, and to start seeking a "green," ecologically safe economic growth (Simon, 1990; Commoner, 1990).

Questions for Discussion and Review

1. What major environmental problems now challenge the ecosystems of modern industrial societies?
2. Why can't technology solve all the problems of diminishing resources and environmental pollution?
3. How does the "Tragedy of the Commons" help explain environmental destruction?
4. How can environmental destruction be brought under control?

PERSPECTIVES ON POPULATION AND ENVIRONMENT

Functionalists have a positive view of population and the environment. Even population growth and environmental degradation are seen as serving a useful, though latent, function for developing a stable, prosperous society. By contrast, conflict theorists see overpopulation and environmental pillaging as problems but attribute them to the exploitation of developing countries by wealthy industrialized countries. Symbolic interactionists, however, are more interested in analyzing how human interpretation influences population and the environment.

Functionalist Perspective

To functionalists, human society consists of different parts with each contributing in its own way to the well-being of the system. If one part creates what appears to be a problem, it will stimulate other parts to solve the problem so that the system as a whole can function well or even better. Thus, a large population with little natural resources may look like a problem but it serves the latent function of stimulating economic development. The likely consequence is a well-functioning, prosperous society. A good example is Japan. While having few natural resources, it has a high population density—about 850 people per square mile, compared with 70 in the United States. Yet it is one of the world's most prosperous and stable nations. A similarly well-functioning social system can be found in Singapore, a nation with hardly any natural resources and sardine-packed with 11,800 people per square mile.

To functionalists, overpopulation may be functional rather than dysfunctional, because it helps stimulate the economy by providing a large supply of labor and a large market for its goods. Thus, the functionalist suggests, a poor country with a population explosion should focus on economic development rather than on birth control. This will stimulate the educational institution to enhance the nation's human capital through education and training. Once the society prospers, birth control will increase and the birth rate will decline as have happened in most industrialized countries.

Functionalists do not see diminishing resources and environmental pollution as a problem, either. It is believed that while natural resources are limited, human ingenuity is unlimited. Thus the depletion of natural resources can stimulate the search for substitutes, such as fiber optics that are now widely used to replace copper wire in communications. Similarly, environmental pollution can stimulate the development of an appropriate technology, such as catalytic converters in cars, to produce a cleaner environment.

Conflict Perspective

While functionalists present one side of the reality about population and environmental problems, conflict theorists show a different side.

According to the conflict perspective, many developing countries are poor not because they have high rates of population growth but because they have long been exploited by Western colonial or neocolonial powers. As suggested in Chapter 11 (Rich and Poor Nations), wealthy industrialized nations have long enriched themselves by getting an abundance of cheaply priced raw materials from poor countries or pressuring farmers in poor countries to produce commodities for foreign corporations rather than food for local consumption. As a result, the rich nations become richer while the poor nations poorer.

But such unpleasant facts are routinely covered up through speeches that emphasize overpopulation as the cause of the poverty in developing countries. By blaming poverty on overpopulation, the rich nations in effect play the "blame the victim" game. They avoid holding themselves responsible for having caused the poverty in the first place. Instead, the developing countries are held responsible for making themselves poor by producing too many babies. Moreover, the granting of relatively small foreign aid for birth control to poor countries serves as a smoke screen for foreign exploitation. According to the logic of conflict theory, the rich nations should first acknowledge having contributed to the poverty of poor nations. Only then will they stop exploiting the poor nations and start providing them with a genuine, far more substantial aid to develop their economy. This, rather than the foreign aid for birth control, will greatly reduce poverty. The economic development will also bring down population growth, as it has done in industrialized countries.

Like poverty, the environmental degradation in developing countries is often attributed to their enormous population growth. But, to conflict theorists, the real cause of the problem is that wealthy nations have long exploited developing countries' natural resources to meet their own excessive consumption needs (Ross, 1994).

Symbolic Interactionist Perspective

To symbolic interactionists, overpopulation has much to do with certain interpretations of what family and children mean. In many developing countries, large families are favored because having many children is perceived as proof of a man's virility. A high birth rate can often be found in societies where many accept the religious view that one should "be fruitful, and multiply." Because of high infant death rates, high birth rates are also seen as useful for ensuring against childlessness.

Especially in Africa, having many children is interpreted as a status enhancer, particularly for the less educated. Children are further pragmatically viewed

as a form of old-age pension because there are no social welfare systems like those in the United States and other industrialized countries.

As for the environmental problems in industrialized nations, they have much to do with the Western, white view of nature. Traditional Asians and Native Americans generally see themselves as an integral part of nature and try to live in harmony with it. By contrast, Westerners have long viewed themselves as masters over nature, so that they have no qualms about exploiting it. The exploitative attitude toward nature freed the early settlers of this country to cut across and conquer the continent. Considering the white settler, Chief Luther Standing Bear mused, "One portion of the land is the same to him as the next, for he is a stranger who comes in the night and takes whatever he needs. The earth is not his brother but his enemy, and when he conquers it he moves on" (Hayden, 1980).

Questions for Discussion and Review

1. What is the difference between the functionalist and conflict perspectives on population and environmental problems?
2. How do people's interpretations of the world around them influence population and the environment?

CHAPTER REVIEW

1. *Why is the modern census better than the earlier ones?* The modern census does something the earlier ones did not: seeking to achieve its governmental, scientific, and commercial objectives by employing an enormous number of trained census takers and by making extra efforts to reach the typically hard-to-reach people, such as the poor.

2. *What determines a nation's growth rate?* The birth rate plus the net immigration rate minus the death rate. *What social factors hold down birth rates?* Access to effective birth control methods, substitution of nuclear for extended families, industrializa-

tion, movement of women into the labor force, and a preference for small families are all significant factors. *What social factors lower death rates?* The availability of modern medicine and wealth or high living standards. *What motivates migrations?* The "push" of deprivation and oppression and the "pull" of opportunity and freedom elsewhere are often the key motives.

3. *What are two prominent theories regarding population patterns?* Malthusian and demographic transition theories. According to Malthus, human populations tend to grow faster than food supplies. As a popula-

tion outstrips its supply of food, it is afflicted by war, disease, poverty, and even famine, which eventually stop population growth. Malthus's predictions have been derailed by contraceptive, technological, and medical revolutions. According to the theory of demographic transition, human populations go through specific stages, which are tied to economic development.

4. *How do governments control population growth?* By encouraging voluntary family planning and setting up compulsory population programs. But family planning programs work only if people prefer to have small families, and compulsory programs may meet stiff opposition. China, however, has reduced its birth rate through a basically compulsory program that combines rewards for small families and punishments for large families. *Does the U.S. government control population growth?* No, but it does give some aid to family-planning centers. Social and economic factors, not government action, keep birth rates low.

5. *Why are sociologists interested in ecology?* Humans, like other organisms, live within ecosystems, dependent on other organisms and on the physical environment. Thus, we are limited by two ecological principles. One, natural resources are finite. Two, if we alter one aspect of our environment, we end up changing others as well. *What are our basic environmental problems?* The depletion of natural resources and pollution. *How is pollution related to consumption?* To consume we must produce, and both production and consumption create waste materials that must go somewhere. When our creation of wastes exceeds nature's capacity to recycle the material, pollution results. *What are the main causes of environmental problems?* Poverty, ignorance, and overconsumption are among the causes. *What are the main methods of saving the environment?* Antipollution laws, conservation, development of more efficient, less polluting technology, and a slowing of traditional economic and population growth.

6. *What can the three sociological perspectives tell us about population and the environment?* Functionalists have a positive view of population and the environment. Even population growth and environmental degradation are seen as serving a useful, though latent, function for society. Conflict theorists see overpopulation and environmental degradation as problems but attribute them to the exploitation of

developing countries by wealthy industrialized countries. Symbolic interactionists analyze how human interpretation influences population and the environment.

KEY TERMS

Age structure The pattern of the proportions of different age groups within a population (p. 488).

Biosphere A thin layer of air, water, and soil surrounding the earth (p. 495).

Birth rate The number of babies born in a year for every 1,000 members of a given population (p. 486).

Census A periodic head count of the entire population of a country (p. 484).

Death rate The number of deaths in a year for every 1,000 members of a population (p. 487).

Demographic transition The theory that human populations tend to go through specific, demographic stages and that these stages are tied to a society's economic development (p. 489).

Demography The scientific study of population (p. 484).

Ecology A study of the interactions among organisms and between organisms and their physical environment (p. 495).

Ecosystem A self-sufficient community of organisms depending for survival on one another and on the environment (p. 495).

Infant mortality rate The number of deaths among infants less than one year old for every 1,000 live births (p. 487).

Life expectancy The average number of years that a group of people can expect to live (p. 488).

Marriage rate The number of marriages for every 1,000 people in a given year (p. 489).

Sex ratio The number of males per 100 females (p. 489).

Vital statistics Information about births, marriages, deaths, and migrations into and out of a country (p. 484).

SUGGESTED READINGS

Commoner, Barry. 1990. *Making Peace with the Planet.* New York: Pantheon. Shows the importance of harmonizing our technologies with our environment to prevent pollution.

D'Antonio, William V., Masamichi Sasaki, and Yoshio Yonebayashi (eds.). 1994. *Ecology, Society & the Quality of Social Life.* New Brunswick, N.J.: Transaction. A collection of articles on how the way a society handles its environment affects the quality of life.

Firor, John, 1990. *The Changing Atmosphere: A Global Challenge.* New Haven, Conn.: Yale University Press. A clear analysis of various environmental problems, especially acid rain, global warming, and ozone holes.

Hardin, Garrett. 1993. *Living Within Limits: Ecology, Economics, and Population Taboos.* New York: Oxford University Press. A collection of essays discussing the danger of population growth and environmental destruction while suggesting solutions to the problems.

Simon, Julian L. 1990. *Population Matters: People, Resources, Environment, and Immigration.* New Brunswick, N.J.: Transaction. A collection of controversial articles about population and the environment, presenting an optimistic view of the issue.

URBANIZATION AND CITY LIFE

Myths and Realities

MYTH: *Most of the world's large cities—like New York or Los Angeles—are in prosperous, industrialized countries.*
REALITY: Generally, the poorer the country, the faster its urban growth. As a result, more than half of the world's megacities are now in developing countries.

MYTH: *Living in an impersonal world of strangers, city dwellers are more lonely than rural and small-town people.*
REALITY: Those who live in the city are no more lonely than those who live in small towns and rural areas. Urbanites visit friends and relatives as often as do rural people.

MYTH: *New York City is well-known for its crime, poverty, homelessness, racial tension, exorbitant rents, and official corruption. It is no wonder that most New Yorkers dislike living in the city.*
REALITY: Most New Yorkers are ambivalent about their city. On the one hand, they consider their city an urban hellhole. On the other hand, they like living in "the Big Apple" very much.

MYTH: *All suburbs are basically alike. If you have seen one, you have seen them all.*
REALITY: There is a diversity of suburbs. There are predominantly upper-class suburbs, middle-class suburbs, blue-collar suburbs, poverty-ridden suburbs, and various ethnic suburbs, much like the different neighborhoods within a large city.

even years ago farmer Yang Yufu left his village to find work in a large city in China. Unable to get a job, he has eked out a living by repairing shoes, fixing appliances, and selling glasses and plastic buckets. The most he can earn in a month is only $100. Yet he has to support his mother, brother, and sister, who live with him in two rented rooms. His father is left in the village to farm the tiny family plot (Tefft, 1993).

Like Yang, millions of poor rural Chinese as well as their counterparts in many developing countries are moving into cities. What we have here is **urbanization**, the migration of people from the countryside to the city, increasing the percentage of the population that lives in the city.

A GLOBAL ANALYSIS

In 1693 William Penn wrote that "the country life is to be preferred for there we see the works of God, but in cities little else than the work of man." Most people at the time probably agreed with him. Less than 2 percent of the world's population then were urban dwellers. But, today, about 39 percent of the world's population lives in urban areas, and more than 50 percent will do so by the end of the century (Fischer, 1984; Linden, 1993).

While urban populations have grown, the cities themselves have changed. We can identify three periods in their history: the preindustrial, industrial, and metropolitan-megalopolitan stages.

The Preindustrial City

For more than 99 percent of the time since human beings appeared on earth, our ancestors roamed about in search of food. They were able to hunt, fish, and gather edible plants, but they could never find enough food in one place to sustain them for very long. They had to move on, traveling in small bands from one place to another.

Then, about 10,000 years ago, technological advances allowed people to stop their wandering. This was the dawn of what is called the Neolithic period. People now had the simple tools and the know-how to cultivate plants and domesticate animals. They could produce their food supplies in one locale, and they settled down and built villages. The villages were very small—only about 200 to 400 residents each. For the next 5,000 years, villagers produced just enough food to feed themselves.

By about 5,000 years ago, humans had developed more powerful technologies. Thanks to innovations like the ox-drawn plow, irrigation, and metallurgy, farmers could produce more food than they needed to sustain themselves and their families. Because of this food surplus, some people abandoned agriculture and made their living by weaving, pottery, and other specialized crafts. Methods of transporting and storing food were also improved. The result was the emergence of cities (Childe, 1952).

Cities first arose on the fertile banks of such rivers as the Nile of Egypt, the Euphrates and Tigris in the Middle East, the Indus in Pakistan, and the Yellow River in China. Similar urban settlements later appeared in other parts of the world. These *preindustrial cities* were small compared with the cities of today. Most had populations of 5,000 to 10,000 people. Only a few cities had more than 100,000 people, and even Rome never had more than several hundred thousand.

Several factors prevented expansion of the preindustrial city. By modern standards, agricultural techniques were still primitive. It took at least 75 farmers to produce enough of a surplus to support just one city dweller. For transportation, people had to depend on their own muscle power or that of animals. It was difficult to carry food supplies from farms to cities, and even more difficult to transport heavy materials for construction in the cities. Poor sanitation, lack of sewer facilities, and ineffective medicine kept death rates high. Epidemics regularly killed as much as half of a city's population. Moreover, families still had a strong attachment to the land, which discouraged immigration to the cities. All these characteristics of preindustrial society kept the cities small (Davis, 1955).

The Industrial City

For almost 5,000 years, cities changed little. Then their growth, in size and number, was so rapid it has been called an urban revolution or urban explosion. In 1700 less than 2 percent of the population in Great Britain lived in cities, but by 1900 the majority of the British did so. Other European countries and the United States soon achieved the same level of urbanization in an even shorter period.

The major stimulus to this urban explosion was the Industrial Revolution. It triggered a series of related events that sociologist Philip Hauser (1981) has termed a population explosion, population displosion, population implosion, and technoplosion. Industrialization first causes a rise in production growth, and the mechanization of agriculture brings about a farm surplus. Fewer farmers can support more people—and thus larger urban populations (*population explosion*). Workers no longer needed on the farms move to the city. There is, then, displacement of people from rural to urban areas (*population displosion*) and a greater concentration of people in a limited area (*population implosion*). The development

of other new technologies (a *technoplosion*) spurs urbanization on. Improved transportation, for example, speeds the movement of food and other materials to urban centers.

The outcome of these events was the *industrial city*. Compared with the preindustrial city, the industrial city was larger, more densely settled, and more diverse. It was a place where large numbers of people—with different skills, interests, and cultural backgrounds—could live and work together in a limited space. Also, unlike the preindustrial city, which had served primarily as a religious or governmental center, the industrial city was a commercial hub. In fact, its abundant job opportunities attracted so many rural migrants that migration accounted for the largest share of its population growth. Without these migrants, the city would not have grown at all, because of its high mortality rate brought about by extremely poor sanitary conditions.

Metropolis and Megalopolis

Early in this century, the large cities of the industrialized nations began to spread outward. They formed **metropolises**, large urban areas that include a city and its surrounding suburbs. Some of these suburbs are politically separate from their central cities, but

Above: Food surpluses, which enabled a number of people to abandon agriculture and practice specialized crafts, as well as improved methods of transporting and storing food, allowed for the emergence of the preindustrial city, represented here by the Aztec capital city of Tenochtitlán. Left: The emergence of the industrial city came about largely as a result of the Industrial Revolution.

socially, economically, and geographically, the suburbs and city are tied together. The U.S. Census Bureau recognizes this unity by defining what is called a *Standard Metropolitan Statistical Area,* which cuts across political boundaries. Since 1990 most people have been living in metropolitan areas with a million residents or more (Suro, 1991).

In the United States, the upper and middle classes have usually sparked the expansion of cities outward. As migrants from rural areas moved into the central city, the better-off classes moved to the suburbs. The automobile greatly facilitated this development. It encouraged people to leave the crowded inner city for the more comfortable life of the suburbs, if they could afford it. As the number of cars increased, so did the size of suburbs and metropolises. In 1900 there were only 8,000 cars in the United States, but by 1930 the number had soared to more than 26 million. Meanwhile, the proportion of the U.S. population living in the suburbs grew from only 15.7 percent in 1910 to 48.6 percent in 1950 (Glaab and Brown, 1983).

Since 1950, virtually all the growth in metropolitan areas has occurred in the suburbs. During the 1960s, U.S. suburbs grew four times faster than inner cities, and stores and entertainment facilities followed the people there. Suburban jobs increased 44 percent, while inner-city employment dropped 7 percent. This pattern of suburban growth at the expense of the urban core continued in the 1970s and 1980s. Today, suburbanites outnumber city residents three to two (Jaret, 1983; Gottdiener, 1983; Census Bureau, 1994).

As the suburbs expanded, they combined with the suburbs of adjacent metropolitan areas to form a **megalopolis,** a vast area in which many metropolises merge. For hundreds of miles from one major city to the next, suburbs and cities have merged with one another to form a continuous region in which distinctions between suburban, urban, and rural areas are blurred. The hundreds of miles from Boston to Washington, D.C. form one such megalopolis, another stretches from Detroit through Chicago to Milwaukee in the Midwest, and another goes from San Francisco to San Diego.

FIGURE 22.1
Megacities Around the Globe
Generally, the poorer the country, the faster its urban growth. Today more than half of the world's megacities (cities with 5 million or more people) are in developing countries.

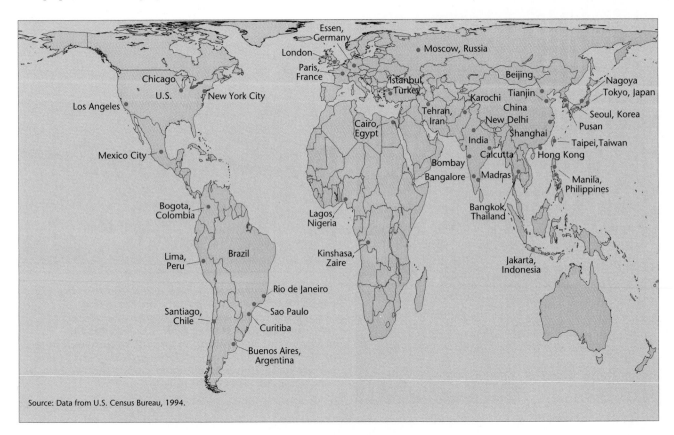

Source: Data from U.S. Census Bureau, 1994.

The World's Megacities

The world's urban population has grown so fast that today there are about 40 "megacities," with populations of five million or more. Generally, the poorer the country, the faster its urban growth. Thus today only three of the world's megacities are in the United States, and more than half are already in developing countries (see Figure 22.1). Many more in the developing world will soon become megacities.

Ever since the emergence of the preindustrial city 5,000 years ago, great cities have risen and fallen. The same is true today. One city that is collapsing is Kinshasa, the capital of Zaire (see again Figure 22.1). Although the country is endowed with abundant natural resources such as gold, diamonds, copper, and rich agricultural land, Kinshasa has produced massive miseries under the corrupt 27-year-reign of President Mobutu. Government officials have routinely looted fuel, manufactured goods, food, and medical supplies, even most of the emergency food aid sent by foreign countries. As a result, the annual inflation rate often goes up more than 3,000 percent and the jobless rate stands at 80 percent, posing serious threats of starvation and epidemics. By contrast, the city of Curitiba in Brazil is a success story. The city is not rich but its government makes the most of its resources. One example is recycling: parks are lit with lamps made from soda bottles, and some government offices were built in part with old telephone poles. The city further delivers excellent services, including a highly efficient bus system and well-constructed housing projects for the poor (Linden, 1993).

In between those two contrasting types, most megacities are saddled with serious problems but manage to cope reasonably well, usually in ways that reflect the nature of their societies. Consider three cities. (1) Tokyo, the world's largest city, with 28.4 million people, faces such enormous problems as traffic-choked streets, sky-high housing costs, and overwhelming waste. But the technologically advanced Japanese have, among other things, developed the "Urban Heat System" to extract heat from sewage, which is then used to regulate temperatures in several of Tokyo's buildings. (2) Mexico City, the world's second largest city, has grown so fast that air pollution is a severe problem. But the Mexican devotion to community will likely solve the problem as it saved the city from collapse after the 1985 earthquake. And (3) New York City, the world's fifth largest, is full of poverty, crime, and other signs of urban decay. But the city is likely to survive because it has a history of rising from its ashes. After losing its pre-eminence as a port and a manufacturing center,

New York City has now become a leader in finance, the media, design, advertising, and arts (Linden, 1993).

Questions for Discussion and Review

1. What accounted for the emergence of the preindustrial city?
2. How does the industrial city differ from the preindustrial city?
3. What forces have led to the development of suburbs, metropolises, and, finally, megalopolises?
4. What problems do megacities have and how can the problems be tackled?

CITIES IN THE UNITED STATES

Cities around the world are similar in some ways, such as being overcrowded and polluted and in need of ways to solve the problems. But the cities also vary from one society to another. Here we focus on the cities in the United States.

A Demographic Profile

In general, the poor and minority groups concentrate in the inner cities and more affluent people live in the suburbs. A closer look, however, led sociologist Herbert Gans (1968) to find five types of people in many cities:

1. Cosmopolites—artists, intellectuals, professionals
2. Unmarried individuals and childless couples
3. "Ethnic villagers"—immigrants from other countries
4. The deprived—the poor, including many African Americans, and other minorities
5. The trapped—poor elderly people.

These groups are not likely to feel strong ties to each other or to the city as a whole. The deprived and the trapped are too poor to move—they live in the city by necessity, not choice. The ethnic villagers are likely to be strongly tied only to fellow immigrants in their neighborhoods. The unmarried and childless have ties mostly to those who share their lifestyle. Cosmopolites associate primarily with those who share their interests.

The movement of African Americans into the central city has been especially striking. Just 50 years ago, less than half of the black population was urban. Today, a large majority live in urban areas, and most of these in the inner cities. Several large cities are already predominantly black. For years African Americans entering the city have come from the rural South, but now most of these migrants come from other urban areas. Compared with the inner-city natives, these later migrants rank higher in education and employment and have lower rates of crime. Some middle-class African Americans have joined the exodus to the suburbs, but they move mostly to black suburbs.

The number of cosmopolites, young professionals, adult singles, and childless couples in the inner city has also grown significantly. Increasing numbers of these affluent people now choose to remain in the inner city. They buy run-down buildings and renovate them into elegant townhouses and expensive condominiums. This urban revival is called **gentrification**, the movement of affluent people into poor urban neighborhoods. It has transformed poor neighborhoods into such stylish enclaves as Capitol Hill in Washington, Philadelphia's Queen Village, Boston's South End, Cincinnati's Mount Adams, and Chicago's New Town. To a large extent, urban rehabilitation programs have stimulated gentrification by selling abandoned homes and stores for the price of a few dollars and offering low-interest mortgage loans. Ironically, though, gentrification tends to drive up rents and property taxes, forcing poor and elderly residents to give up their homes to the well-off gentrifiers. However, gentrification has

not been extensive enough to transform most of the city. In the last decade, nearly twice as many people have been moving from central cities to suburbs as those moving in the opposite direction. Central cities continue to lose residents, a trend that began in the early 1970s.

Edge Cities

Most suburbs still offer better schools, more living space, less pollution, and less crime than the central city, so people continue to "vote with their feet" and head for suburbia. More than a decade ago, most suburbs were largely bedroom communities; their residents commuted to the nearby cities to work. But in the last 10 years, a new kind of suburbanization has taken place—involving not only people and homes but offices and jobs—that has transformed many suburbs into economic centers.

In these suburbs, new office buildings, factories, and warehouses have sprung up alongside the housing subdivisions and shopping malls. Developers have already created vast clusters of big buildings, people, and cars. Thus, many suburbs, in effect, have become cities in their own right. Unlike the traditional U.S. city, where diverse businesses operate, the new suburban cities, also popularly called "edge cities," are typically focused on a principal activity, such as a collection of computer companies, a large regional medical center, or a sports or recreation complex. The growth of edge cities, there-

Revival of a Boston neighborhood. The movement of affluent people into poor urban neighborhoods is known as gentrification. Many cosmopolites, young professionals, adult singles, and childless couples in the inner city buy run-down buildings and renovate them into elegant townhouses and expensive condominiums.

fore, has taken away many jobs from the urban cores. Despite the arrival of some nonwhite residents, the edge cities are generally "whiter" than the inner cities (Suro, 1991).

Recent Trends

The latest U.S. census revealed a number of significant changes in U.S. cities over the last decade. As long expected by sociologists, many cities in the West and Southwest, particularly California, have grown significantly larger, while many northeastern and midwestern cities have experienced a decline in population. However, there are some changes that have largely gone unnoticed.

First, older industrial cities in the South have fallen into the same cycle of decline as their northern counterparts. These cities include Atlanta, Georgia; Birmingham, Alabama; and Chattanooga, Tennessee. They represent half of all the big U.S. cities that have lost population since 1980.

Second, immigration has served as a brake against population decline in major cities such as New York, Miami, and New Jersey's Elizabeth and Jersey City. With a large influx of immigrants from countries such as India, China, the Philippines, and the

Dominican Republic, these cities have registered some population gain rather than decline (Salins, 1991).

Third, although California's growth was expected to be significant, it has turned out to be astonishing. Of the 29 U.S. cities that have surpassed the population mark of 100,000, most are in California. Seven of the ten fastest growing, large U.S. cities are in Southern California: Bakersfield, Irvine, and Escondido, for example.

Fourth, a large majority (two-thirds) of state capitals have gained population, even though the states themselves have stagnated. North Dakota, for example, lost 1.7 percent of its population, but its capital, Bismarck, had a gain of 10.7 percent. Most cities that are within a declining state but that have a college or university have also grown larger. Examples are Lawrence, Kansas, home of the University of Kansas, and West Lafayette, Indiana, the site of Purdue University (Barringer, 1991b).

Questions for Discussion and Review

1. What kinds of people are most likely to live in U.S. cities?
2. How do today's edge cities differ from the traditional suburb?
3. How have U.S. cities changed over the last decade?

THE URBAN ENVIRONMENT

As we observed in the previous chapter, ecologists study the natural world to see how everything in it is related to everything else. Organisms affect other organisms and they all affect the environment, which in turn affects them. During the 1920s and 1930s, some sociologists at the University of Chicago began to look at the urban world in a similar way. They initiated a new approach to the study of cities called **urban ecology**, the study of the relationship between people and their urban environment.

The influx of immigrants into a number of U.S. cities has caused these cities to register some population gain rather than decline. Latinos (Hispanic Americans) in southern California cities have added greatly to their growth.

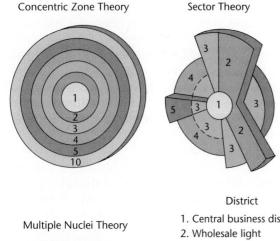

Concentric Zone Theory

Sector Theory

Multiple Nuclei Theory

District

1. Central business district
2. Wholesale light manufacturing
3. Lower-class residential
4. Middle-class residential
5. Upper-class residential
6. Heavy manufacturing
7. Outlying business district
8. Residential suburb
9. Industrial suburb
10. Commuters' zone

Source: Reprinted from "The Nature of Cities," by Chauncy D. Harris and Edward L. Ullman, in *Annals of the American Academy of Political and Social Sciences*, Nov. 1945, p. 13.

FIGURE 22.2
Cities' Spatial Patterns
A diagram of the three theories about the shapes and locations of various districts within a typical American city.

Spatial Patterns

Like a natural environment, the urban environment is not a random arrangement of elements. Walking around a city, you rarely see a mansion next to a poor neighborhood, or an apartment next to a factory. Different areas tend to be used for different purposes. As a result, the people, activities, and buildings within a city are distributed in a certain pattern. The urban ecologists tried to describe what this pattern is and how it arose. Three prominent theories came out of their efforts (see Figure 22.2).

Concentric Zone Theory   In the 1920s, Ernest Burgess presented the **concentric zone theory**, the model of land use in which the city spreads out from the center in a series of concentric zones, each of which is used for a particular kind of activity. The heart of the city is the central business district. The innermost zone is occupied by shops, banks, offices, hotels, and government buildings. The next zone is the transition zone, characterized by shabby rooming houses, deteriorating apartments, and high crime

rates. The third zone is in better shape. It is made up of working people's homes. Beyond it is a zone that houses mostly middle-class people, and beyond that is the commuters' zone, with large homes and plenty of open space. The rich live here, and commute to the city to work (Burgess, 1967).

According to this theory, social class has a lot to do with spatial distribution: the farther a piece of land is from the center of the city, the higher the status of those using it. But land values tend to *drop* with distance from the center of the city. Thus, the pattern of land use has a rather perverse result: the poor live on expensive land and the rich on relatively cheap land (Alonso, 1964).

The concentric zone theory describes some U.S. cities fairly well, especially those such as Chicago and St. Louis that grew rapidly early in this century under the stimulus of intense industrialization and the automobile. But many cities do not have concentric zones.

Sector Theory   San Francisco and Minneapolis illustrate a pattern described by Homer Hoyt in the late 1930s in his **sector theory**, the model of land use in which a city grows outward in wedge-shaped sectors from the center. Hoyt agreed with concentric zone theorists that a city grows outward from the center, and that the center is occupied by the central business district. But, Hoyt said, growth occurs, not in concentric circles, but in wedge-shaped sectors that extend outward from the city. As a result, low-class housing occurs not just close to the business district but in a band extending from the center outward, perhaps to the rim of the city. The key to the extension of a sector is transportation. If, say, warehouses are built along a railroad, they tend to expand along the length of the railroad toward the periphery of the city. Similarly, a retail district might expand along a highway. The poor tend to live along transportation lines near factories, whereas the rich tend to choose areas that are on the fastest lines of transportation and occupy high ground, safe from floods and offering a beautiful view (Hoyt, 1943).

Multiple Nuclei Theory   Boston is one of many cities that do not show either wedge-shaped sectors or concentric zones. It seems to be described better by yet a third theory, which was proposed by Chauncy Harris and Edward Ullman in the 1940s. Unlike the concentric and sector theories, which suggest how each city is built around one center, Harris and Ullman's **multiple nuclei theory** is the model of land use in which a city is built around many discrete nuclei, each being the center of some specialized activity. There are centers of finance and commerce, which are separate from the political center, which in turn is separate from the center of heavy industries, and so on.

These separate nuclei, according to Harris and Ullman, arise as a result of at least three factors. First, some activities require specialized facilities. Manufacturing districts must be located on large blocks of land with easy connections to railroads or water transportation, or a port district must be attached to a suitable waterfront. Second, similar activities often profit from being grouped together. If retail stores are concentrated in one district, they all profit from an increased number of potential customers, who are usually attracted by the chance to compare the offerings of various stores. Third, putting dissimilar activities together in one location often harms them. Factories and homes do not mix well. Wholesale districts, which require street loading and rail facilities, stay away from retail districts, which need many pedestrians, cars, and buses (Harris and Ullman, 1945).

These three theories are largely valuable for depicting the major patterns of some of our cities, such as Chicago, San Francisco, and Boston. But because the theories were based on studies of U.S. cities, they are less applicable to land-use patterns in other countries, where, for example, upper-class residences are close to the center of the city rather than far away from it. The theories are also less accurate in describing many U.S. cities today. Most of the middle and white working classes no longer live in inner cities but in edge cities. Many factories, office complexes, wholesale and retail trade, and jobs involving people (retail sales, medical services, food service) have further moved out of the urban center.

Ecological Processes

How do these spatial patterns come about? Nowadays, city governments often use zoning laws and building codes to determine the patterns of land use and to segregate activities. But many patterns arose without anyone planning them, forming what are called *natural areas* of segregated activities. Urban ecologists believed that two forms of human behavior are most important in shaping the urban environment: dominance and competition. A group of people typically concentrate in a particular area of the city for a specific purpose, dominating that area. Businesses, for example, usually dominate the center of U.S. cities. Sometimes, a group achieves dominance only after competing with others to determine how the land will be used. Businesses and residents

often clash over land use in a city. Businesses can usually win by buying out the land at a high price, forcing residents to move. Universities often engage in a similar competition with residents. Thus, the use of land in a city is determined directly by *dominance* and indirectly by *competition*.

The city, however, is not static. Instead, over time a new group or type of land use will move into an established area, a process called *invasion*. If the new group forces others out, *succession* has occurred. The process of gentrification discussed earlier is an example: young professionals invade an urban neighborhood, raising land values and rents, and eventually they push out its lower-income residents, who can no longer afford the neighborhood. This reverses the traditional pattern of succession that shaped many U.S. cities. As industries, immigrants, and minorities moved into the cities, those who were better off moved out to the suburbs, and their neighborhoods "filtered down" to the lower class.

Dominance, competition, invasion, and succession constitute what are called the **ecological processes**, processes in which people compete for certain land use, one group dominates another, and a particular group moves into an area and takes it over from others.

Questions for Discussion and Review

1. According to the three theories of land use, what do cities look like?
2. How do the ecological processes shape a city?

THE NATURE OF CITY LIFE

In 1964 people were horrified by a story that many took as typical of life in New York City—or any large city. A young woman named Kitty Genovese was walking home from work in the early morning hours when she was attacked. Her murderer stabbed her repeatedly for more than half an hour. Thirty-eight neighbors heard her screams or witnessed the attack. But no one helped or even called the police. Most of the neighbors later explained that they did not want to "get involved."

What could cause such cold-bloodedness? Many commentators of the time blamed the city. Living in a city, they believed, changes people for the worse. This charge echoed what some sociologists had long been saying. Louis Wirth, for example, contended in the 1930s that the conditions of the city produce a distinctive way of life, *urbanism*, and that the urban

TABLE 22.1
The Nature of City Life

Urban anomie theory	City people have a unique way of life, characterized by alienation, impersonal relations, and stress.
Compositional theory	City dwellers are as involved with small groups of friends, relatives, and neighbors as are noncity people.
Subcultural theory	The city enriches people's lives by offering diverse opportunities and developing various subcultures.

environment harms the people who live there. His analysis represented the ecological approach of the Chicago school. Since Wirth's time, some sociologists have supported his view. Richard Sennett (1991), for example, criticizes city life for insulating people from others who are racially, socially, or economically different. But many other sociologists have rejected Wirth's view. Some have argued that the city does not make much difference in people's lives, and others contend that the urban environment enriches people's lives by creating and strengthening subcultures. These three theories about the nature of urban life are called urban anomie theory, compositional theory, and subcultural theory (see Table 22.1).

Urban Anomie Theory

In 1938 Louis Wirth presented his **urban anomie theory,** arguing that city people have a unique way of life, characterized by alienation, impersonal relations, and stress. According to Wirth, the urban environment has three distinctive features: huge population size, high population density, and great social diversity. These characteristics, Wirth argued, have both a sociological and a psychological impact, producing social and personality disorders.

In the city, people are physically close but socially distant. Every day they encounter strangers. They become accustomed to dealing with people only in terms of their roles. Their relationships tend to be impersonal. In other words, much of their lives are filled, not with primary relations with neighbors, who are also relatives and friends, but with secondary relations. Moreover, these people are separated by diverse religious, ethnic, and racial backgrounds. It is difficult for people in the city to form friendships across these lines or to develop a moral consensus. Under these circumstances, people can no longer ensure social order by relying on informal controls such as tradition and gossip. Instead, they turn to formal controls, such as the police. Rather than talking to a young troublemaker's parents, they call the police. But formal controls, Wirth argued, are less effective than informal controls, so crimes and other forms of deviance are more frequent in the city than in the countryside.

The size, density, and diversity of the city, according to Wirth, also damage the psychological health of its residents by making life stressful. Much of the stress comes from being bombarded with various kinds of stimuli. Sights, sounds, and smells assault urbanites virtually every minute of their waking hours. Wherever they turn, they must contend with the actions of others. They are jostled on the street and in the elevator. They wake to the sound of their neighbor's radio and fall asleep despite screaming sirens. Panhandlers, staggering inebriates, and soliloquizing mental patients are a common sight. All may make people feel irritable, nervous, anxious. The result, Wirth claimed, is that mental disorders are more common in the city than in rural areas.

People in ethnic neighborhoods in large cities have a strong sense of community loyalty. Sociologist Herbert Gans has found the solidarity in these neighborhoods impressive enough to call them "ethnic villages."

American Mosaic

Urban violent gangs often use graffiti to mark their territory and influence. This reading reports on how groups of concerned citizens use a new type of graffiti to combat violence.

American Graffiti

Like empty seed envelopes placed on a stick to tell the gardener what lies below, billboards in the ghetto mark the terrain, reminding residents and passers-by alike that here is a special kind of ground, a place set apart from the more pedestrian territory of simple consumers and producers. In sections of Chicago, Newark, Detroit and New York City where the murder rate has reached record highs, there are dozens of billboards designed solely to urge people to stop killing and to avoid getting killed. Mostly they are sponsored by churches and civic organizations—public service announcements for populations so dangerous and endangered that they constitute their own macabre advertising niche.

One popular sign admonishes, "Don't Let Your Child Be the Next Victim of Violent Crime" and urges people to get a booklet. Another, referred to as "the peace sign," proclaims, "It's Time for Peace, Stop the Killing," these words framed by the symbols of Chicago's major gangs. A billboard in Detroit, using red letters dripping blood, reads: "Cease Fire," an injunction underscored in small print with the statement "Hundreds of our children are dying."

Greg Turner, who manages a day shelter on Chicago's West Side, argues that these billboards, which began popping up in the late 1980s, were long overdue. "We should have been hollering a long time ago in our communities to stop this kind of behavior," he says. "Those are our offspring, those are our next generation and now they are killing each other. That is our future, and if we don't let them know how they should live, there will be no future for us."

For the Reverend John Porter, whose organization placed "peace signs" in the Englewood section of Chicago, this is a way to communicate with the gangs. He explains: "The community has one of the highest homicide rates in the country. Young men cannot find meaningful work, and they [society] expect them to be functional. Men are in a position out there where they face other angry men, and angry men who are frustrated take their frustration out on the nearest target. And the nearest target to these men is not some social system that is very abstract, it is somebody that looks like them. White people don't have the same need for these signs." Indeed, white neighborhoods never display such billboards—not even those that preach brotherly love and urge an end to bigotry.

Excerpted from Camilo José Vergara, "American Graffiti," *New Statesman & Society,* November 18, 1994, p. 15.

Compositional Theory

Wirth's description of the urban environment and its effects sounds reasonable. But is it accurate? Many empirical studies of cities have shown that his portrait amounts to an overdrawn stereotype. Some sociologists have therefore proposed a **compositional theory,** arguing that city dwellers are as involved with small groups of friends, relatives, and neighbors as are noncity people.

Perhaps the crucial difference between the urban anomie and compositional theorists concerns the influence of the urban environment on primary relations. Wirth argued that city life is impersonal, that the city erodes primary relations. But compositional theorists contend that no matter how big, how dense, how diverse the city is, people continue to be deeply involved with a small circle of friends and rel-

atives and others who have similar lifestyles, backgrounds, or personalities. In this small social world, they find protection from the harsher, impersonal world of strangers.

Many studies show that there is indeed a significant amount of social cohesion within cities, as compositional theorists contend. Herbert Gans (1982a), for example, has found that people in ethnic neighborhoods of large cities have a strong sense of community loyalty. He found the solidarity in these neighborhoods impressive enough to call them "ethnic villages." Other researchers have also found that city residents carry on their personal lives much as people in rural areas do, such as visiting relatives at least once a week (Palisi and Canning, 1983). What about studies that show higher rates of crime and mental illness in urban than in rural areas? According to compositional theorists, these disorders are not created by the urban environment itself. Instead, they result from the demographic makeup of the city—from the fact that the urban population includes a high percentage of those categories of people likely to suffer from social and mental disorders. Examples are young unmarried individuals and the lower classes.

Subcultural Theory

Claude Fischer (1984) presents his **subcultural theory**, arguing that the city enriches people's lives by offering diverse opportunities and developing various subcultures. While urban anomie theorists emphasize the negative impact of city life, Fischer stresses the positive. In his view, the urban environment creates and strengthens various groups of people. These groups are, in effect, *subcultures*—culturally distinctive groups, such as college students, African Americans, artists, corporate executives, and so forth. These subcultures are able to emerge because of the great population size, density, and diversity of the city, and the clash of subcultures within a city may strengthen each of them. When people come in contact with individuals from other subcultures, Fischer (1984) wrote, they "sometimes rub against one another only to recoil, with sparks flying. . . . People from one subculture often find people in another subculture threatening, offensive, or both. A common reaction is to embrace one's own social world all the more firmly, thus contributing to its further intensification."

Fischer has also argued that the urban experience brings some personal benefits to city dwellers. Urban housing, when compared to rural housing, generally has better plumbing facilities and is less crowded. Compared with people in the country, city people have access to far more facilities, services, and opportunities. As Harvey Cox (1966) noted, "Residents of a city of 10,000 may be limited to one or two theaters, while people who live in a city of a million can choose among perhaps 50 films on a given night. The same principle holds for restaurants, schools, and even in some measure for job opportunities or prospective marriage partners."

Each of the three theories presents only a partial truth about city life. As urban anomie theory suggests, residents of large cities are usually much less satisfied with their neighborhoods than are their counterparts in small towns (Lee and Guest, 1983). At the same time, city life is not as bad as popularly believed. People do lead a normal, pleasant life in the city with friends and subcultural groups, as compositional and subcultural theories suggest. But all the theories fail to capture the ambivalence people feel toward the city. According to a survey, most New Yorkers consider their city an urban hellhole, with all its crime, poverty, homelessness, racial tension, heavy taxes, exorbitant rents, filth, and official corruption. Still, they like living in the Big Apple very much. To them, "the pulse and pace and convenient, go-all-night action of the city, its rich ethnic and cultural stew, still outweigh its horrors" (Blundell, 1986). Indeed, many urbanites throughout the United States seem to consider the horrors a fair price for the freedom of expression they enjoy in the city. But others find the price too high, choosing to leave the city for the suburb (Lapham, 1992).

Questions for Discussion and Review

1. According to urban anomie theory, how does the city affect people's life?
2. In what ways are compositional and subcultural theories similar and different?

THE SUBURBAN EXPERIENCE

About 2,000 years ago, the Roman poet Horace expressed feelings familiar to many of us: "In Rome you long for the country; in the country—oh inconstant!—you praise the city to the stars." Many people in the United States have tried to solve this ancient dilemma by moving to the suburbs. They hope to leave noise, pollution, crowds, and crimes behind—but to keep their jobs in the city and their access to its stores and museums and nightlife. They hope in the suburbs to find the best of both worlds—the open space, quiet, comfort, and wholesomeness of the country and the economic and recreational opportunities of the city. Thus more than half of the U.S. population now live in the suburbs.

Past Stereotypes

In the past, particularly in the 1950s, it was common to criticize the suburbs as wastelands of bland, shallow conformity. Suburbanites, the critics said, are a homogeneous lot, and their lives are ruled by the need to conform. Their houses are all the same, inside and out. They are consumed by efforts to impress one another with their spic-and-span homes and perfect lawns. They seem friendly enough, but form no deep friendships. They are bored, lonely, and depressed. The women are domineering housewives, the husbands absent breadwinners, and the children spoiled. Behind the green lawns, barbecue pits, and two-car garages lurk marital friction, adultery, divorce, drunkenness, and mental breakdown (Gans, 1982b).

Then, in the 1960s and 1970s, those notions about suburbia were discredited as either gross exaggerations or totally unfounded. It was observed that suburbs are not all alike. There are predominantly white-collar suburbs, blue-collar suburbs, and various ethnic suburbs, much as there are different neighborhoods within a central city. Even within a suburb, total homogeneity is very rare—there are almost always a few families of different ethnic, religious, or occupational backgrounds. But there was a tendency to stereotype suburban life as far better than city life. According to this view, the move to the suburb increases the time that parents spend with children and spouses spend with each other. Suburbanites are thus less lonely and bored after the move (Berger, 1971). But today suburban life has become more complicated and less idyllic.

Current Realities

Many suburbs are now less "suburban" and more "urban." As previously suggested, these suburbs have turned into edge cities, where the availability of jobs makes it unnecessary to work in the city far away from home. As edge cities, suburbs are now faced with problems once considered the special burden of cities. Particularly in the larger, sprawling suburbs, the way of life has become much less centered on community, and much more on work, entrepreneurship, and private life, with neighborhood groceries and gathering spots giving way to superstores and fast-food franchises. The potential for being lonely and friendless is therefore considerably greater (Morris, 1987).

Many suburbs have also developed problems once considered "urban," such as congestion, pollution, and crime. Rapid, unregulated growth has created some of these problems. When industry and stores move to the suburbs to be near people's homes, they often bring with them traffic jams and noise, air and water pollution, not to mention landscape "pollution." Although most suburbs are prosperous, increasing numbers are not. The Los Angeles suburbs have more poor families than the city, and there is more substandard housing in the suburbs of Pittsburgh than in the city itself (McCormick and McKillop, 1989).

Still, suburban homes remain the overwhelming choice of most people in the United States. Moreover, these problems—suburban sprawl, traffic congestion, and lonely existence—may not haunt carefully planned suburbs of the future. Near Sacramento, California, Tacoma, Washington, and Tampa, Florida, preparations are under way to build new suburbs that resemble a small town. Single-family homes, rental apartments, townhouses, day-care centers, parks, and commercial buildings will be clustered around a town center, where residents can stroll, shop, relax, and socialize (Thomas, 1990).

Questions for Discussion and Review

1. How was suburban life viewed in the past?
2. How have the suburbs changed in recent years?

Many suburbs are now less "suburban" and more "urban." Particularly in the larger, sprawling suburbs, the way of life has become much less centered on community. Many suburbs have also developed such problems as congestion, pollution, and crime.

CAUSES OF URBAN PROBLEMS

Almost every problem in U.S. society—drug abuse and crime, racism and poverty, poor education and environmental pollution—seems more severe in the cities, particularly in the older and more congested ones. Even as newer cities grow and age, their problems will probably become more severe. The difficulties the cities face and their ability to deal with them are shaped to a great extent by the intertwining effects of various social forces. We discuss some of them here.

Population Decline

In the last 10 years Detroit, Cleveland, Pittsburgh, St. Louis, and other big cities have lost more than 10 percent of their population. In fact, most of the cities that have more than 200,000 people have suffered population declines (Census Bureau, 1994). On the face of it, this may look like good news for the cities' finances. Fewer people should mean less demand for, and less spending on, police protection, fire protection, education, and other public services. In reality, however, population decreases have created serious problems.

As the years go by, a city must spend more on maintaining its road, sewer, and water networks, even if it has fewer residents to pay for those services. Similarly, when families abandon the central city, the need for police and fire protection increases, because

abandoned homes can become magnets for vandalism and crime. They become fire hazards, and finally must be torn down at the city's expense. Furthermore, behind the statistics of declining populations lies the fact that those who move out of the cities are largely middle-class whites, and with them go many businesses. Thus, the cities have fewer private-sector jobs and declining revenues. Those left behind in the city are typically less educated, poorer, and older, the people most in need of government spending for education, housing, health services, and welfare.

Fiscal Squeeze

In large part, urban problems stem from the city government's inability to generate sufficient income to provide various kinds of service to the public. Cities get most of their revenues from taxes on property, income, sales, and corporations. Some money can come from charging fees for services. But all these revenues have shrunk over the last decade, because the suburbs have drained off much of the cities' tax base by attracting industries and stores and middle-class and upper-class people.

There are other potential sources of revenue that cities cannot tap. In many states cities are prohibited from raising as much in taxes as they wish. Cities are also deprived of other revenue-producing opportunities. When federal and state governments use city property, they are exempted from paying city taxes

One reason for the financial trouble of cities is their inability to tap many potential sources of revenue. For example, suburbanites may often come into Atlantic City to gamble at Taj Mahal, adding to traffic congestion while benefiting from police protection, but the city cannot tax them.

worth billions of dollars. Suburbanites come into town, adding to traffic congestion, garbage, and wear and tear on roads and parks, while benefiting from police protection and other urban resources, but pay no taxes to the city. Consequently, since the 1960s cities have come to depend increasingly on the state and federal governments to help pay their bills. Since the late 1980s, however, the federal government has been forced by its huge budget deficit to end its revenue-sharing program.

Political Dilemma

Part of the cities' fiscal problem originates with elected officials' unwillingness to raise taxes even if they have the power to do so and their citizens have the ability to pay. Given the unpopularity of tax increases, politicians tend to avoid risking taxpayers' anger even when taxes are low and necessary. But this political dilemma seems to have forced the cities to increasingly rely on private enterprise to tackle urban problems.

With their eyes on economic development, cities compete with one another to keep or attract businesses and industries. Low taxes and tax exemptions are used as lures. Although this may undermine the current tax base, the cities hope to build a larger tax base, through an increase in jobs, for the future.

Cities also set up **enterprise zones**, economically depressed urban areas that businesses, with the help of generous tax credits, try to revive by creating jobs.

In the late 1980s, the U.S. Congress voted against a bill designed to create 75 enterprise zones around the country. A majority of states have nonetheless proceeded on their own, creating thousands of jobs for the poor residents of the special zones (Carlson, 1991). A similar effort to solve public ills with private cures has appeared. Grass-roots entrepreneurs known as CDCs (short for community development corporations) have rehabilitated abandoned homes, creating commercial enterprises, and organizing social services in various large cities. Their objective is to succeed where governments have failed—by reclaiming city streets from crime and economic decline (*New York Times*, 1991).

Housing Segregation

Every year billions of dollars are spent on housing in the United States. The government helps out by granting billions of dollars in tax deductions to landlords and homeowners. As a result, we are among the best-housed people in the world, with most of the nation's families owning their own homes. But it has become increasingly difficult to own or rent a home. At the same time, large numbers of houses are dilapidated. Most of these housing problems are concentrated in the poorest sections of cities, where jobs and public services are few, and crime, drugs, and homelessness are common.

Housing problems are most severe for the nation's minorities. For one thing, minorities, especially

While most whites living in metropolitan areas are spread out in the suburbs, most of the metropolitan African Americans are concentrated in the inner cities. Thus, some major cities, such as Washington, D.C., shown here, have become predominantly black.

ENRICHING OUR LIVES

Public housing projects seem to embody the worst urban nightmare in the United States. But this reading shows how the projects can become islands of hope in the city.

Saving Kids in the Projects

Mention public housing and many people think: racial segregation, welfare dependency, a permanent underclass, neglect, violence, crack addiction, marauding adolescent "wolf packs." However, four years of work with young people in Harlem tells us that housing projects can be good places to raise children and adolescents. Projects should be viewed as centers of neighborhood renewal, islands of hope in beleaguered urban communities.

Martin Luther King Jr. Towers in Harlem was notorious during the late 1960s and into the mid-1970s. Efforts by tenant organizations and the Housing Authority to turn this complex around proved successful in the late 1980s, making King a safer place than many other uptown projects. The children did better in school than children elsewhere in Harlem, and tenant participation in supporting the project manager was high. King was known in the Housing Authority as a project where efforts to work with local leadership paid off, where there was a sense of community and political cohesion.

But children in other housing projects continue to experience declining education and increasing frustration, alienation, and violence. Because of the high concentration of teenagers and young adults in the projects, there are a limited number of jobs open to them in local neighborhood stores and businesses. Parents in the projects need help in the struggle to make their children qualified and competitive in years to come.

So what is to be done? First, society's efforts to make the projects a stage in upward mobility should be renewed—if not for adult residents, then at least for their children. This would entail upgrading community centers in the projects so that both adults and children can learn new skills and better avail themselves of the programs that already exist to serve them. Such initiatives should grow out of the bootstrap programs lovingly nurtured by community leaders. Their heroic efforts cry out for more resources.

Second, as a response to the present youth crisis, experienced youth workers should be assigned to each project. They would work the street, parks and school yards afternoons and nights to help steer kids away from drugs and violence and into constructive activities in local community centers. Youth workers could foster a new sense of pride in Harlem's most troubled and jaded young people. They in turn would pass on the message to friends and siblings—and not just the negative message, against drugs and violence, but also a positive one, about the importance of African American, Latino and family heritage in New York and the world.

Excerpted from Terry Williams and William Kornblum, "Saving Kids in the Projects," *The Nation,* April 11, 1994, pp. 484–488. Reprinted with permission from *The Nation* magazine. ©The Nation Company, L.P.

African Americans, make up a high percentage of the population of the inner cities, where good housing at reasonable prices is increasingly scarce. While most blacks living in metropolitan areas are concentrated in the inner cities, most of the metropolitan whites are spread out in the surrounding suburbs. In both the inner cities and in the suburbs, blacks are frequently segregated from whites, with the housing of blacks being inferior to that of whites.

Economics may be a factor in the segregation. Because African Americans tend to have lower incomes, they often cannot afford to move into more expensive white neighborhoods. But racial discrimination is a bigger factor. Many blacks would not move into white neighborhoods because they wish to avoid rejection by whites. Real estate agents tend to steer potential black buyers and renters away from white neighborhoods, perpetuating segregation. Banks are often more cautious in granting loans to blacks than to whites, making it difficult for blacks to own or rehabilitate homes and thus encouraging the deterioration of black neighborhoods (Hayes, 1990).

Questions for Discussion and Review

1. What impact does population decline have on a city?
2. Why do many cities have serious financial problems?
3. How have cities dealt with the political dilemma of raising taxes?
4. What factors contribute to housing segregation?

PERSPECTIVES ON URBANIZATION

Both the functionalist and conflict perspectives have been used to explain the forces behind the urbanization of U.S. society. To functionalists, the masses of ordinary people seek, and benefit from, urbanization as a way of adapting to their changing environment. But to conflict theorists, the real driving force and beneficiary of urbanization is big business. Symbolic interactionists, however, are more interested in explaining how strangers interact with each other in the city.

Functionalist Perspective

A key concept in the functionalist perspective is interdependence. Thus the nature of a city can be said to depend on a complex of interrelationships among its different parts. If a city is modern, its most important parts may be people, organization, environment, and technology. Consider how these different parts are interrelated:

> In Los Angeles a favorable natural environment was conducive to large-scale population growth, which brought with it organizational problems (civic and governmental) and technological changes (freeways and factories). These in turn led to environmental changes (smog), which resulted in organizational changes (new pollution laws), which in turn resulted in technological changes (antipollution devices on automobiles) (Palen, 1981).

The same concept of interdependence can also explain the process of urbanization in the United States. First, technology increased agricultural production so much that considerably fewer people were needed to work on the farm. Second, seeking better job opportunities, throngs of people left the farm for the city, which led to its explosive growth. Third, since these former farmers were mostly manual laborers, their huge numbers in the city helped expand the manufacturing industry, mass-producing everything from shoes to clothes to cars. Fourth, as cities became crowded, increasing numbers of people moved to the outskirts while commuting to work in the inner city, thanks to the mass production of cars. Fifth, as suburbs became increasingly populated, various businesses emerged to cater to the shopping needs of the suburbanites, eventually leading to the proliferation of shopping malls. Finally, a cornucopia of jobs was created in the suburbs, so that suburbanites need not commute to the inner city. At this late stage of urbanization, metropolises and megalopolises began to emerge.

All these social changes are assumed to benefit the masses by raising their standard of living.

Conflict Perspective

The conflict perspective provides a different picture of urbanization. This perspective stresses the role played by big business in the growth and expansion of cities (Gottdiener, 1985).

First, in the pursuit of profit, large corporations are said to have bought up huge farmlands and mass-produced food, driving many small family farms into bankruptcy and forcing huge numbers of farmers to leave for the city. In doing so, big business has received considerable assistance from big government as a partner of the ruling elite. The assistance included direct subsidies to business, grants for research and development, low-interest loans, and support of farm-related education.

Second, the expansion of cities into suburbs has resulted from big business making a killing in real estate, construction, and banking industries. Again, with considerable government subsidies and tax deductions, numerous single-family homes were built in the suburbs in the 1950s and 1960s. To induce people to buy these houses, the government guaranteed mortgages as well as provided tax deductions for interest payments. The result was massive suburbanization.

Third, from the 1970s to today, large corporations have helped turn many suburbs into edge cities by moving their businesses and factories there from central cities. The move has been motivated by profit. By building new plants in the suburbs, corporations have intended to avoid problems in central cities such as labor unrest, high city taxes, and other financial costs—or have expected to receive such benefits from the suburbs as cheap land, lower taxes, a local industry-friendly government, and the lack of organized labor.

Cutting Edge

Economic globalization and political decentralization are now going on around the world. This reading discusses how these social changes may soon be transforming some cities into city-states like those that used to flourish in the Middle Ages (AD 500–1500).

The Return of the City-State

Throughout much of history, cities were modestly sized, compact, and to a large extent self-governing. While they were fiercely territorial and boasted an enormous pride of place, they were also the first human communities to look far beyond their borders. Located on navigable waterways or land trade routes, cities became the hearing posts on the world's first information highways, gathering news of distant lands from travelers and merchants. A number of cities attained a degree of civilization and vitality from which we can learn a great deal today, and achieved an artistic and architectural beauty that continues to dazzle us.

The nation-state, of course, succeeded and supplanted the city-state. Most traditional historians view this as an inevitable result of economic and technological evolution. The nation-state did preempt the authority of the cities. For hundreds of years, cities continued to spur scientific and technological innovation, but they were no longer masters of their own destinies. Through the centuries they were stripped of significant authority.

The pendulum of power may be swinging again. The 300-year dominance of the nation-state is ebbing. As sociologist Daniel Bell has observed, "The nation-state is becoming too small for the big problems of life and too big for the small problems of life." At the twilight of the 20th century two phenomena are sweeping the planet: the globalization of economies and the localization and regionalization of politics. Products and services are moving around the world in ever greater quantities at ever greater speeds. But at the same time people are demanding more direct participation at the local level in the decisions that affect their future.

Cities are moving to center stage, gaining a self-awareness and self-direction unknown since the Middle Ages. Federations and alliances of cities are redrawing geopolitical maps. In Europe, the rise of the European Union and the accompanying centralization of authority in continental agencies has been accompanied by the emergence of "entrepreneurial city regions." Vancouver, Seattle, and Portland, the economic engines of the American Pacific Northwest, have joined in an alliance to form a new city-region called Cascadia.

Resolving the tension between globalism and localism may be our greatest challenge. We are losing control over important decisions to planetary corporations and global institutions even while we demand more control over our lives in our communities. We are becoming ever more enmeshed in a planetary electronic web while we increasingly insist on the importance of place. This is a time of profound change and fluidity. The old structures are dying and a new order is being born. Kind of like the early Middle Ages. And in this historical moment the emerging city-states may play an equally crucial role in defining and shaping the future.

Excerpted from David Morris, "The Return of the City-States," *UNTE Reader*, September/October, 1994, pp. 78–81.

Symbolic Interactionist Perspective

We can learn much from symbolic interactionists about how people interact in the city as a world of strangers (Karp, Stone, and Yoels, 1991).

First, city people tend to interact with one another in a superficial, impersonal way. Given the density of the urban population and hence a huge number of potential interpersonal contacts, urbanites have learned to protect themselves from "psychic overload" by shutting out as many sensations as possible, sometimes even the call of a neighbor for help. Thus most interactions with strangers are brief. An example is one person asking another for a street direction and the other person responding by pointing at a street and saying "over there."

Second, city people tend to interact through "civil inattention" as a way of respecting others' desire for privacy in public places. This involves avoiding eye or physical contact in an elevator, a bus, or some other public place. But conversations with strangers do occur under unusual circumstances, as when people are stuck in a stalled elevator or traffic jam.

Third, city people tend to be tolerant of others' alternative lifestyles, such as different sexual orientations or religious practices. When such people interact, they usually refrain from imposing their values on others or showing disapproval of others' behavior.

Questions for Discussion and Review

1. How do the functionalist and conflict perspectives differ in explaining urbanization?
2. According to symbolic interactionism, how do strangers in the city interact?

THE FUTURE OF U.S. CITIES

Most cities, particularly those in the Northeast and Midwest, will continue to lose population to the suburbs and the country. Most of these migrants are whites and middle class, leaving behind in inner cities a large concentration of black, poor, and elderly people. The trend is toward racially separate communities. Gentrification will continue, but it will not be enough to revive the decaying inner cities. The gentrifiers will only create small enclaves of residential wealth—luxury apartments, townhouses, and condominiums—segregated from the urban poor.

Central cities will suffer more than the loss of population. As the nation's economy shifts from manufacturing to service, informational, and high-technology industries, businesses will build their plants in edge cities, where most white-collar workers live. But if enterprise zones and other similar programs in inner cities succeed, the loss of blue-collar jobs will stop and unemployment and poverty will decline.

Finally, the federal government will continue to cut its financial support for the cities. Especially if the budget deficit remains enormous, the government can hardly be expected to pump much money into urban programs. On the other hand, the federal government cannot leave the cities out in the cold. There will always be a tension between the conservative impulse toward local control and the liberal tendency toward federal intervention. The federal government will probably continue to tackle problems that are essentially national in scope, such as welfare, Medicaid, and long-term health care, though to a reduced degree. But programs that are local in nature will probably be returned to state and local governments. Such programs may include community-development block grants, mass transit, rural waste-water grants, and vocational education. Some cities may become so independent that they turn into city-states (see box, p. 522).

Question for Discussion and Review

1. What does the future hold for U.S. cities?

CHAPTER REVIEW

1. *What are the main stages in the history of cities?* Preindustrial, industrial, and metropolitan-megalopolitan. Preindustrial cities began developing about 5,000 years ago. They were very small, and people lived where they worked. The industrial city developed when the Industrial Revolution triggered urbanization. During the twentieth century the industrial city spread outward, and the city and its suburbs became interdependent, forming a metropolis and megalopolis. *What is the condition of megacities*

around the globe? Megacities have grown faster in the developing world than in the developed world. All are faced with problems but most are able to solve the problems in ways that reflect the nature of their societies.

2. *Who usually lives in the city, and who lives in the suburbs?* Generally, more affluent people live in the suburbs. The poor and minority groups tend to concentrate in central cities. But typical urban resi-

dents also include immigrants, professionals, unmarried individuals, and childless couples. *How have suburbs changed over the last decade?* Many suburbs that used to be residential communities have turned into edge cities, economic centers like central cities. *What changes have occurred in U.S. cities over the last 10 years?* Many western and southwestern cities have grown larger, while many northeastern, midwestern, and southern cities have lost population. Some large cities have been rescued from decline by substantial immigration from foreign countries. Most state capitals and college towns have grown larger even in the midst of their states' decline.

3. *Is there a pattern behind land use in a city?* Yes, but no one pattern characterizes all cities. Three theories explain the patterns found in many U.S. cities. According to concentric zone theory, cities spread outward from a central business district, forming a series of concentric zones. According to sector theory, cities expand from a central business district, not in concentric circles, but in wedge-shaped sectors. By contrast, multiple nuclei theory holds that a city is not built around one center but around discrete nuclei, each of which is the center of specialized activities. *What determines the spatial pattern of a city?* Dominance, competition, invasion, and succession.

4. *Does the urban environment make city people different from other people?* Three theories offer different answers. According to urban anomie theory, city life is filled with alienation, impersonal relations, and reliance on formal social control as well as emotional stress and mental disorders. By contrast, compositional theorists argue that city dwellers' social lives, centered in small groups of friends, relatives, and neighbors, are much like those of people outside the city. Subcultural theorists contend that the city enriches people's lives by offering them diverse opportunities and by promoting the development of subcultures.

5. *How was the suburban life viewed in the past?* The views ranged from the stereotype of suburbs as lonely places to the stereotype of suburbs as happy places. *What are the realities of suburbia today?* Many suburbs have become more urban, facing typically urban problems such as congestion, pollution, and crime.

6. *If large U.S. cities have been losing populations, why have their budgets increased?* The costs of maintaining streets, sewers, public buildings, and so on have risen as the cities age. Many of those who remain in the city are the ones who depend most on its services to survive. *Why is it difficult for a city to be financially independent?* One reason is that a city often receives no tax revenues from suburbanites and other nonresidents who use its services. *What is the political dilemma in running a city?* Elected officials are not willing to raise taxes for fear of antagonizing voters. *Why has housing remained segregated?* Reasons include lower minority income, racial prejudice in white neighborhoods, and racial discrimination among real estate agents and banks.

7. *What insight do the three sociological perspectives provide about urban growth and city life?* According to functionalists, ordinary people contribute to and benefit from urbanization. But to conflict theorists, big business, with help from big government, is the driving force behind urban expansion. Symbolic interactionists, however, focus on how strangers interact in the city.

8. *What is the future of U.S. cities?* Separation between whites and minorities and between rich and poor will continue within cities. Population and job loss will also continue. The federal government will continue to expect cities to solve their own problems by themselves.

KEY TERMS

Compositional theory The theory that city dwellers are as involved with small groups of friends, relatives, and neighbors as are noncity people (p. 515).

Concentric zone theory The model of land use in which the city spreads out from the center in a series of concentric zones, each of which is used for a particular kind of activity (p. 512).

Ecological processes Processes in which people compete for certain land use, one group dominates another, and a particular group moves into an area and takes it over from others (p. 513).

Enterprise zone The economically depressed urban area that businesses, with the help of generous tax credits, try to revive by creating jobs (p. 519).

Gentrification The movement of affluent people into poor urban neighborhoods (p. 510).

Megalopolis A vast area in which many metropolises merge (p. 508).

Metropolis   A large urban area that includes a city and its surrounding suburbs (p. 507).

Multiple nuclei theory   The model of land use in which a city is built around many discrete nuclei, each being the center of some specialized activity (p. 512).

Sector theory   The model of land use in which a city grows outward in wedge-shaped sectors from the center (p. 512).

Subcultural theory   The theory that the city enriches people's lives by offering diverse opportunities and developing various subcultures (p. 516).

Urban anomie theory   The theory that city people have a unique way of life, characterized by alienation, impersonal relations, and stress (p. 514).

Urban ecology   The study of the relationship between people and their urban environment (p. 511).

Urbanization   Migration of people from the countryside to city, increasing the proportion of the population that lives in the city (p. 506).

SUGGESTED READINGS

Baumgartner, M.P. 1988. *The Moral Order of a Suburb.* New York: Oxford University Press. A case study of an upper-middle-class suburb whose residents strive to maintain a facade of social order while ignoring the conflicts within their community and families.

Fischer, Claude. 1982. *To Dwell Among Friends: Personal Networks in Town and City.* Chicago: University of Chicago Press. Marshals data to drive home the subcultural theory that city life is highly rewarding.

Kelly, Barbara M. (ed.). 1989. *Suburbia Re-examined.* New York: Greenwood. A collection of articles presenting diverse views of suburban life.

Peirce, Neal R. 1993. *Citistates: How Urban America Can Prosper in a Competitive World.* Washington, D.C.: Seven Locks Press. Analyzes how U.S. cities deal with their problems in the new world economy.

Shelton, Beth Anne, et al. 1989. *Houston: Growth and Decline in a Sunbelt Boomtown.* Philadelphia: Temple University Press. An analysis of the social, political, and economic forces behind the eye-catching changes of a U.S. metropolis.

23

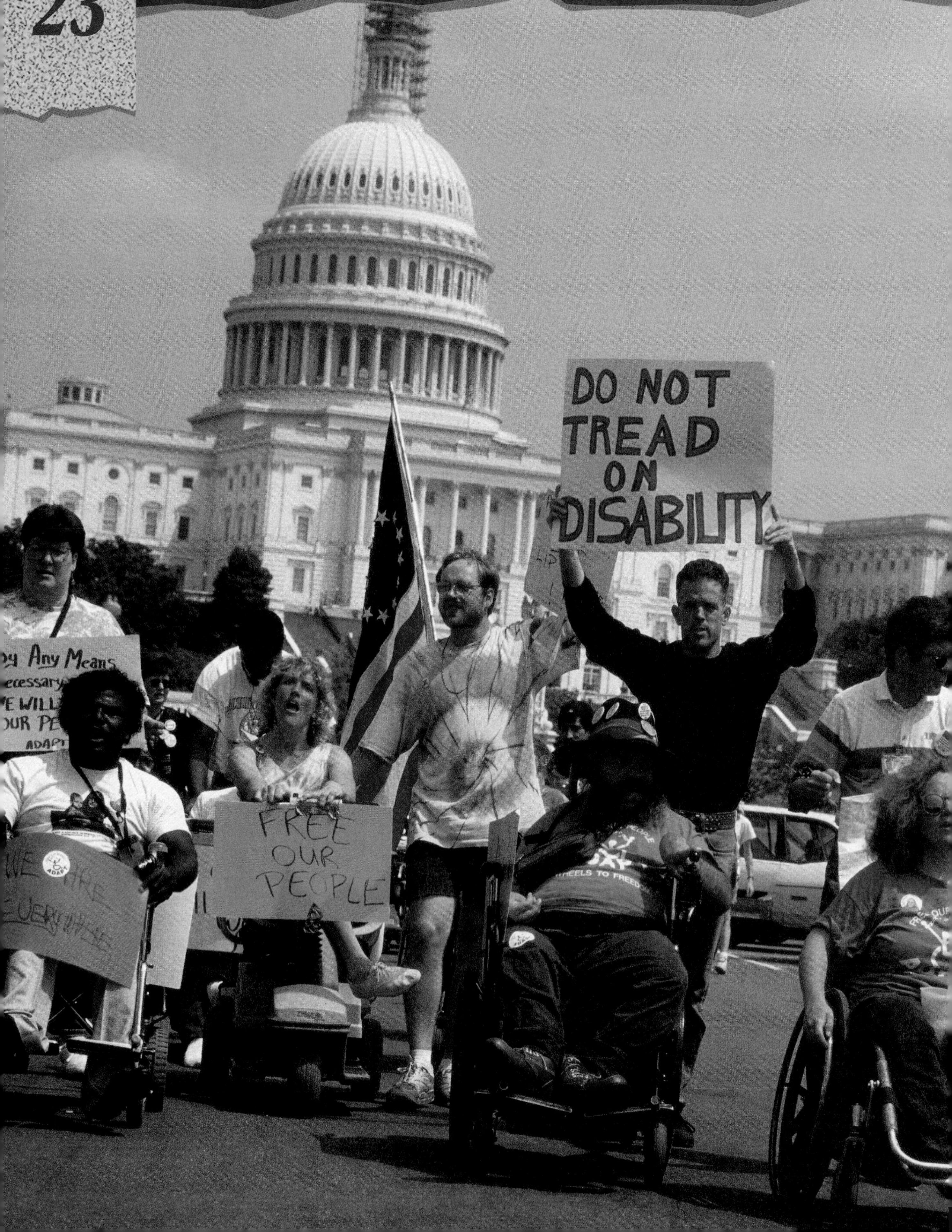

COLLECTIVE BEHAVIOR, SOCIAL MOVEMENTS, AND SOCIAL CHANGE

CHAPTER OUTLINE

Myths and Realities

MYTH: *If you are watching a humorous movie in a theater, how often you laugh depends solely on how funny you think the movie is.*
REALITY: The size of the audience also has a significant impact. The larger the audience, the more frequent your laughter will be.

MYTH: *Violence in most riots is contagious—virtually all participants are involved.*
REALITY: Not all participants in riots engage in violence. Many simply watch others commit the violence.

MYTH: *It's better not to listen to rumors, because they are always false.*
REALITY: Rumors are not necessarily false; they may turn out to be true. They are merely unverified stories spread from one person to another—unverified because people do not bother to check them against facts.

he long ideological conflict between the United States and the former Soviet Union is finally over. But, like many people of his generation, 42-year-old John Driscoll still holds many Cold War memories. One of his most vivid memories is the fear that came with the air raid drills at school. All the students learned to crawl under their desks, practicing for the day when the Soviet hydrogen bombs were expected to fall. "It seems surreal now," he said soon after the Soviet Union formally announced its end as a nation in 1991. "Every summer, when I heard lightning over the city and the sky would light up, I was convinced it was over. My whole childhood was built on the notion that the Soviets were a real threat." Today, Driscoll teaches economics and government at a high school just outside Washington, D.C. He is helping an organization to coordinate food shipments to Moscow, the capital of the "evil empire" that terrified him as a child. He found on a recent visit to Moscow that "these folks have absolutely no confidence in themselves" (Brinkley, 1992).

Like Driscoll, we can expect to witness great changes in our lives. The reason is that **social change**—the alteration of society over time—is nothing new. We can see it in the emergence of space travel, heart transplants, ubiquitous computers, omnipresent foreign cars, large shopping malls, the increased gap between rich and poor, widespread homelessness, and the many great events that make our society different from what it was a decade or two ago. Where will all this social change take us? Is there some general pattern behind the way societies change? Where can we expect future changes to come from, and do we have any control over them?

To understand these issues better, we look in this chapter at several theories of social change. We will also examine modernization—a particular type of social change that shaped many features of our society and is now reshaping societies around the world. But let us first take a look at collective behavior, which can be an impetus to social change.

COLLECTIVE BEHAVIOR

Collective behavior is relatively spontaneous, unorganized, and unpredictable social behavior. It contrasts with institutionalized behavior, which occurs in a well-organized, rather predictable way. Institutionalized behavior is frequent and routine. Every weekday, masses of people hurry to work. On every campus, groups of students walk to classes. These predictable patterns of group action are basically governed by social norms and are the bedrock of social order. Collective behavior, however, operates largely outside the confines of these conventional norms.

Characteristics

Sociologists who study collective behavior face a problem. While scientific analysis seeks out predictable, regular patterns, collective behavior is relatively unstructured, spontaneous, and unpredictable.

Nevertheless, sociological analysis of collective behavior has been fruitful. Although collective behavior is relatively unstructured, it does have a structure that sociologists have been able to illuminate. Even rumor, for example, includes a structure for division of labor; some people are messengers, others interpreters, skeptics, or merely an audience. The difference between institutionalized and collective behavior is not absolute. Instead, the behaviors can be classified according to the relative degree of control exercised by traditional norms. Thus, we can arrange social behaviors on a continuum like that shown in Figure 23.1. As we move from left to right in the figure, the behavior noted is increasingly subject to traditional norms. Thus, institutionalized behavior is at the far right of the continuum and collective behavior lies to the left.

Only the main forms of collective behavior are shown on the continuum. At the far left, for example, is panic, the least structured, most transitory, and rarest form of mass action. When people in a burning theater rush to the same exit, losing their capacity to cooperate and reducing their chance of escape, that is a panic. Next on the continuum are crowds, somewhat more structured than panics and more subject to the influence of social norms. As a result, members of a crowd can be persuaded to work toward a common goal. Moving further to the right on the continuum, we see that social movements are even more structured than crowds; their members consciously work together to achieve a common objective.

Social Factors

Despite their diversity, all forms of collective behavior are basically an attempt to deal with a stressful situation, such as danger to life, threat of loss of money, or social injustice. The specific form such behavior takes depends largely on how the people involved define the problem. If they see it as a simple matter, they are likely to engage in such "clumsy" or "primitive" behavior as a panic or riot. If they believe the problem is complex enough to require an elaborate analysis, they are more prone to respond through a social movement. Thus, the more complex the situation of strain is believed to be, the more structured the collective behavior. Whatever the form of the collective behavior, according to Neil Smelser (1971), six factors are necessary to produce the behavior. By itself, no one of these factors can generate collective behavior. Only the combination of all six factors, occurring in sequence, creates the conditions necessary for any kind of collective behavior to occur. Let us examine these six factors, illustrated by some facts about the 1992 riot in South-Central Los Angeles.

1. *Structural conduciveness.* Individuals by themselves cannot start a collective action. The social organization must permit collective action to occur. Some condition, such as living in the same neighborhood, must exist in order for them to assemble and communicate with each other before they can take part in collective behavior. In South-Central Los Angeles, the African American residents who joined the riot were brought together by media reports that a nearly all-white jury had found four white policemen not guilty for savagely beating black motorist ·Rodney King.

2. *Social strain.* The strain may arise from a conflict between different groups, from the failure of a government to meet citizens' needs, or from the society's inability to solve a social problem. The strain that existed in the black community stemmed from many cases of police brutality against blacks.

FIGURE 23.1
A Continuum of Normative Regulation
There are two kinds of social behavior, collective and institutionalized. The difference is not absolute but relative to normative regulation. Collective behavior is less strongly controlled by traditional norms. Collective behavior may further be divided into different forms, which vary from one another in the degree to which they are regulated by traditional norms.

Degrees of normative regulation

Collective behavior						Institutionalized behavior	
Panics	Crowds	Fashions	Rumors	Public opinion	Social movements	Small groups	Large organizations
Behavior less regulated by traditional norms						Behavior more regulated by traditional norms	

Riots, such as the uprising in Los Angeles in 1992, occur under six conditions: structural conduciveness, social strain, the growth and spread of a generalized belief, a precipitating factor, the mobilization of participants for action, and inadequate social control.

3. *The growth and spread of a generalized belief.* Participants in a collective action come to share some belief about the social strain. The rioters in South-Central Los Angeles shared the belief that the local police had often brutalized and mistreated blacks.

4. *A precipitating factor.* Some event brings the social strain to a high pitch and confirms the generalized belief about it. The King verdict clearly touched off the riot.

5. *The mobilization of participants for action.* Leaders emerge to move people to take a specific action. Some leaders in the Los Angeles riot urged people on the street to follow them, saying something like "Come with us. Let's burn." Others set an example for others by initiating the burning or looting of stores.

6. *Inadequate social control.* Agents of control such as the police fail to prevent the collective action. The Los Angeles police department was slow to respond to the riot. The police were virtually absent in the early hours of rioting, allowing many looters to smash storefronts and burn buildings with impunity.

If we look at other riots, such as those in the Liberty City section of Miami in 1980 and in the Overtown section in 1982, we find a similar sequence of events (Porter and Dunn, 1984).

Questions for Discussion and Review

1. What makes collective behavior different from institutionalized behavior, and why is it difficult to study?
2. According to Smelser, what six factors together generate collective behavior?

PANICS

On a December afternoon in 1903, a fire broke out in Chicago's Iroquois Theater. According to an eyewitness,

> Somebody had yelled "Fire!" . . . The horror in the auditorium was beyond all description. . . . The fire-escape ladders could not accommodate the crowd, and many fell or jumped to death on the pavement below. Some were not killed only because they landed on the cushion of bodies of those who had gone before. But it was inside the house that the greatest loss of life occurred, especially on the stairways. Here most of the dead were trampled or smothered, though many jumped or fell to the floor. In places on the stairways, particularly where a turn caused a jam, bodies were piled seven or eight feet deep. . . . An occasional living person was found

in the heap, but most of these were terribly injured. The heel prints on the dead faces mutely testified to the cruel fact that human animals stricken by terror are as mad and ruthless as stampeding cattle (Schultz, 1964).

The theater did not burn down. Firefighters arrived quickly after the alarm and extinguished the flames so promptly that no more than the seats' upholstery was burned. But 602 people died and many more were injured. Panic, not the fire itself, largely accounted for the tragedy. Similarly, on a July morning in 1990 in the holy city of Mecca, Saudi Arabia, when the lights accidentally went out in a 600-yard-long tunnel through which thousands of Muslim pilgrims were walking, panic triggered a stampede, killing 1426 people.

The people in the Iroquois Theater and the Mecca tunnel behaved as people often do when faced with unexpected threats such as fires, earthquakes, floods, and other disasters: they exhibited panic behavior. A **panic** is a type of collective behavior characterized by a maladaptive, fruitless response to a serious threat. That response generally involves flight, but it is a special kind of flight. In many situations, flight is a rational, adaptive response: it is perfectly sensible to flee a burning house or an oncoming car. In these cases, flight is the only appropriate way of achieving a goal—successful escape from danger. In panic behavior, however, the flight is irrational and uncooperative. It follows a loss of self-control, and it increases, rather than reduces, danger to oneself and others. If people in a burning theater panic, they stampede each other, rather than filing out in an orderly way, and produce the kind of unnecessary loss of life that occurred in the Iroquois Theater or the Mecca tunnel.

Preconditions

When five knife-wielding hijackers took over a Chinese airplane bound for Shanghai in 1982, the passengers did not panic. Instead, they cooperated and, with mop handles, soda bottles, and other objects, overpowered the hijackers. About 20 years earlier, during a performance of *Long Day's Journey into Night* in Boston, word spread through the audience that there was a fire. But the audience did not stampede to the exits. One of the actors "stepped to the footlights and calmly said, 'Please be seated, ladies and gentlemen, nothing serious has happened. Just a little accident with a cigarette. . . . The fire is out now and if you will sit down again we can

resume.'" The audience laughed and sat down (Brown, 1965). In this case, as in the Iroquois fire, the audience had an impulse to flee for their lives. But, because the crisis had been defused, a contradictory impulse, to follow the norms of polite society and remain calm and quiet, won out.

In short, the existence of a crowd and a threat does not ensure that people will panic. There are several social-psychological preconditions for the development of a panic. First, there must be a *perception* that a crisis exists. Second, there must be *intense fear* of the perceived danger. This fear is typically compounded by a feeling of *possible* entrapment. If people believed they were *certainly* trapped, as in the case of prisoners who are about to be executed by a firing squad, they would give in to calm resignation rather than wild panic. Third, there must be some *panic-prone individuals*. Typically, they are overly self-centered persons whose frantic desire to save themselves makes them oblivious to the fate of others and to the self-destructive consequences of their panic. Fourth, there must be *mutual emotional facilitation*. The people in the crowd must spread and enhance each other's terror. Finally, there must be a *lack of cooperation* among people. Cooperation typically breaks down in a panic because no norms exist to tell people how to behave appropriately in an unusual, unanticipated situation. But most crowds are made up of many small, primary groups of relatives or friends rather than strangers. Constrained by the bonds of these primary groups, members of crowds usually do not panic and stampede each other to death (Schultz, 1964; Johnson, 1987).

Mass Hysteria

Panic sometimes takes the form of **mass hysteria**, in which numerous people engage in a frenzied activity without bothering to check the source of their fear. A classic case occurred in 1938, when the play *War of the Worlds* was broadcast on the radio. Many people thought that they were hearing a news report. Tuned in to music on the radio, they suddenly heard an announcement that Martians had invaded the earth:

Ladies and gentlemen, I have a grave announcement to make. Incredible as it may seem, both the observations of science and the evidence of our eyes lead to the inescapable assumption that those strange beings who landed in the New Jersey farmlands tonight are the vanguard of an invading army from the planet Mars. The battle which took place tonight . . . has ended in one of the most startling defeats ever suffered by an army in modern times; seven thousand men armed with rifles and machine guns pitted against a single fighting machine of the invaders from Mars. One hundred and twenty known survivors. The rest strewn over the battle area . . . and trampled to death under the metal feet of the monster, or burned to cinders by its heat ray (Cantril, 1982).

Long before the broadcast ended, at least a million of the six million listeners were swept away by panic. Many prayed, cried, or fled, frantic to escape death from the Martians. Some hid in cellars. Young men tried to rescue girlfriends. Parents woke their sleeping children. People telephoned friends to share the bad news or to say good-bye. Many called hospitals for ambulances; others tried to summon police cars.

But not everyone panicked. Hadley Cantril directed a study to find out who panicked, who didn't, and why. Those who did not were found to have what Cantril called *critical ability*. Some of these people found the broadcast simply too fantastic to believe. As one of them reported, "I heard the announcer say that he saw a Martian standing in the middle of Times Square and he was as tall as a sky-scraper. *That's all I had to hear*—just the word Martian was enough even without the fantastic and incredible description." Others with critical ability had sufficient specific knowledge to recognize the broadcast as a play. They were familiar with Orson Welles's story or recognized that he was acting the role of Professor Pierson. Still others tried to check the accuracy of the broadcast by looking up newspaper listings of radio schedules and programs. These people, on the whole, had more years of education than those who did panic. The less educated, aside from lacking critical ability, were found to have a feeling of personal inadequacy and emotional insecurity (Cantril, 1982).

Questions for Discussion and Review

1. What preconditions usually exist before a panic occurs?
2. Why are some people more vulnerable than others to mass hysteria?

CROWDS

A **crowd** is a collection of people temporarily doing something while in proximity to one another. They may be gathered on a street corner, watching a fire.

They may be in a theater, watching an opera. They may be on a street, throwing rocks at police.

Traits and Types

Nearly all crowds share a few traits. One is *uncertainty:* the participants do not share clear expectations about how to behave or about the outcome of their collective behavior. Another element common to most crowds is a *sense of urgency.* The people in the crowd feel that something must be done right away to solve a common problem. The third characteristic of crowds is the *communication* of mood, attitude, and ideas among the members, which pressures them to conform. Crowds are also marked by *heightened suggestibility.* Those in a crowd tend to respond uncritically to the suggestions of others and to go along impulsively with their actions. Finally, crowds are characterized by *permissiveness,* freedom from the constraint of conventional norms. Thus, people tend to express feelings and take actions that under ordinary circumstances they would suppress (Turner and Killian, 1987).

Beyond these similarities, there are significant differences. Sociologist Herbert Blumer (1978) has classified crowds into four types: casual, conventional, acting, and expressive. The *casual crowd* is the type with the shortest existence and loosest organization. It emerges spontaneously. People collecting at a street corner to watch a burning building, a traffic accident, or a street musician constitute a casual crowd. The *conventional crowd,* unlike the casual crowd, occurs in a planned, regularized manner. Examples include the audience in a theater and the spectators at a football game. Whereas the conventional crowd assembles to observe some activity, the *acting crowd* is involved in an activity that enables its members to focus their energy on one particular goal. Rioters, a lynch mob, and a revolutionary crowd are all acting crowds. The *expressive crowd* has no goal. Its members plunge themselves into some unrestrained activity, releasing emotions and tensions. Examples include people at a rock concert or at a religious revival.

Social Contagion

Some acting and expressive crowds are irrational or destructive. Consider the lynch mobs in the United States before 1900. Thousands of whites and blacks were lynched. The number of lynchings dropped during this century, but still, between 1900 and 1950 there were more than 3,000 victims, nearly all of them black. The alleged crimes of the black victims

LeBon argued that, as a result of the anonymity of a crowd, people give up their individuality and act irrationally, even violently. But to Turner and Killian, the seemingly irrational behavior results more from conformity to a new norm that emerges so that the crowd can deal with the unconventional problem facing it.

were often trivial, such as trying to act like a white man, making boastful remarks, winking at a white man's wife, or being too ambitious (Raper, 1970). Why did the members of lynch mobs behave so irrationally and destructively? In particular, why did otherwise civilized whites act like beasts as members of a lynch mob?

According to French social psychologist Gustave Le Bon (1841–1931), a crowd is homogeneous in thought and action. All the people in a crowd think, feel, and act alike. As a crowd, they possess a "collective mind." This mind is emotional and irrational, stripped bare of all civilizing restraints. Beneath those restraints, Le Bon believed, hides a barbarian. All the members of a crowd bring to the situation this hiding barbarian with its primitive instincts. Normally, they suppress these instincts, wearing the mask of civilized behavior. But a crowd provides them with a different sort of mask: the large numbers of people give individuals a cloak of anonymity that weakens their restraining sense of responsibility and releases primitive emotions.

But why do individuals give up their individuality and transform themselves into a collective mind? The reason, in Le Bon's view, is **social contagion**—the spreading of a certain emotion and action from one member of the crowd to another. Research has uncovered factors that can facilitate contagion. Among these factors are *crowd size* and *noise*. When people are viewing a humorous movie in a theater, the larger the audience, the more frequent the laughter. If a person coughs in a room full of people, others are more likely to cough than if there were only a few people around. Watching a videotaped arm-wrestling match, the subjects' tendency to imitate the wrestlers increases with higher levels of audi-

ence noise (Levy and Fenley, 1979; Pennebaker, 1980; Markovsky and Berger, 1983).

The Emergent Norm

To most sociologists today, Le Bon's notion of a collective mind is valid only as a loose metaphor for what happens in crowds. Members of a crowd may appear homogeneous. They may seem to have given up their individuality and become absorbed into a "collective mind." But beneath these appearances, the members of a crowd are basically just individuals engaged in a particular kind of interaction. Whereas Le Bon set the behavior of crowds apart from normal social interaction as a sort of bizarre regression to almost subhuman behavior, other sociologists have found that routine and orderly behavior prevails in most crowds (McPhail and Wohlstein, 1983).

U.S. sociologists Ralph Turner and Lewis Killian (1987), for example, accept Le Bon's fundamental idea that a crowd appears to act as a homogeneous group, but they have argued that Le Bon exaggerated its homogeneity. In a lynch mob, for example, not all the members think or act in the same way. Some individuals storm the jail, others drag out the prisoner, others bring ropes, others hang the victim, and some just stand by and watch. Even those engaged in the same act may have different feelings, attitudes, or beliefs, and they participate because of diverse motives. How, then, does the apparent unanimity among the participants develop?

The answer can be found in Turner and Killian's **emergent-norm theory**, the theory that members of a crowd develop, through interaction, a new norm to deal with the unconventional situation facing them.

Because of the norm, people feel pressed to conform with the crowd's outward behavior, even if they disagree with the action. The result is the appearance of unanimity, which may be more illusion than reality. Indeed, many studies have found the "illusion of unanimity" in most crowds (McPhail and Wohlstein, 1983).

Questions for Discussion and Review

1. What are the traits and types of crowd?
2. Why do individuals in a crowd tend to lose their individuality and act irrationally?

FASHIONS

Compared with crowds, fashions are more subject to traditional norms. Practically all aspects of human life—clothes, hairstyles, architecture, philosophy, and the arts—are influenced by fashions. A **fashion** is a great though brief enthusiasm among a relatively large number of people for a particular innovation.

Most fashions, which are a great but brief enthusiasm among a large number of people for a particular innovation, are related to clothes. But any artifact that strikes people's fancy can become a fashion.

Because their novelty wears off quickly, fashions are very short-lived. Most are related to "the latest" in clothes, but as long as there is something new about any artifact that strikes many people's fancy, it can become a fashion.

Sources of Fashions

Why do fashions occur in the first place? One reason is that some cultures, like ours, *value change*: what is new is good, even better. Thus, in many modern societies clothing styles change yearly, while people in traditional societies may wear the same style for generations. A second reason is that many industries *promote* quick changes in fashions to increase sales. A third reason is that fashions usually *trickle down from the top*. A new style may occasionally originate from lower-status groups, as blue jeans did. But most fashions come from upper-class people who like to adopt some style or artifact as a badge of their status. But they cannot monopolize most status symbols for long. Their style is adopted by the middle class, maybe copied or modified for use by lower-status groups, offering many people the prestige of possessing a high-status symbol (Turner and Killian, 1987).

Fads and Crazes

Similar to fashions but less predictable and shorter-lived are fads and crazes. **Fad** is a temporary enthusiasm for an innovation less respectable than a fashion, while **craze** is a fad with serious consequences. Examples of fads include hula hoops, goldfish-swallowing, telephone booth-stuffing, streaking, pet rocks, yo-yos, and Air Jordans. (If these things mean nothing to you, it is testimony to how fast the magic of fads can fade.) Fads are basically trivial, but they can be a source of status to some people. Carrying a beeper, for example, is a status symbol for teenagers in New York City. Certain individuals also get a sense of being part of an in-group by wearing ripped jeans.

More bizarre and harmful than fads, crazes are a kind of contagious folly with serious consequences. Usually crazes are economic in nature, including a *boom,* in which many people frantically try to buy something of wildly exaggerated value, and a *bust,* in which many frantically try to sell a worthless thing. The most famous craze is probably the tulip mania that swept Holland in 1634. For some unknown reason, the Dutch developed a passion for tulips. Eventually, one bulb would cost as much as a large house. Soon the Dutch were more interested in

Cutting Edge

Hipness is basically an anticonventional attitude. Like fashion and fad, hipness can last only for a short period of time. Ironically, hipness disappears when it becomes too popular. This reading suggests how hipness becomes widely accepted and dies.

If Everyone Is Hip, No One Is Really Hip

In the years right after World War II, there emerged from the bohemias of San Francisco, New York City and a few other metropolises a loose disposition, a convergence of moods, disaffections, ecstasies and unconventional conclusions, a willful refusal to act sensibly, that could be collected under the catchall term hip.

Though it was always a little hard to pin down, hip was a notion roomy enough to describe flower children in tie-dye as well as bikers in black leather. All of it was admissible on the principle that it represented a heartfelt rejection of the mainstream. The mainstream was understood to be all-powerful and wrong about everything: politics, art, religion, sex, drugs, and music.

In the course of four decades, the poses and postures of hip have moved outward from the back rooms of a few cities to the great plains of America's cultural space. Ideas and style statements that 40 years ago might have languished for a while in jazz clubs and coffeehouses now move in nanoseconds from the dance clubs and gangsta corners. Through MTV and the trendier magazines, and whatever other express routes the mass media command, they get passed over to mass-marketers who shear off the rough edges and ship them to the malls. So body piercing and ambient technomusic and performance art and couture motorcycle boots and the huggie drug Ecstasy are shipped overnight throughout the merchandise mart that is America.

In its infinite pliancy, capitalism proved itself well suited to absorb whatever it was in hip that might fascinate consumers, while discarding the uncomfortable parts. For every counter-culture, there emerged a corresponding sales counterculture. The appurtenances of hip—Ray-Bans, leather jackets, this or that haircut—are constantly sent scattership across America, blurring the lines between the hip and the square. It was only a matter of time before espresso moved from Greenwich Village bongo bars to McDonald's. But when hipness is embraced by the mainstream, much of the life gets squeezed from it. If the signs of hip—goatees, pierced nipples and calf tattoos—are everywhere, what's so hip about them?

Excerpted from Richard Lacayo, "If Everyone's Hip ... Is Anyone Hip?" *Time,* August 8, 1994, pp. 50–51. Copyright 1994 by The Time Inc. Magazine Company. Reprinted by permission.

---

making a fortune out of tulips than in growing them. People bought bulbs only to sell them for a huge profit. They were astonished when people who returned from long trips abroad did not share this appreciation of the bulbs at all. It was widely known that a sailor mistook a valuable bulb for an onion and ate it with his herring. Eventually, people began to realize that the price of tulips could not keep rising forever. Thus, the boom was broken, and the price of tulips fell sharply, bankrupting thousands.

Questions for Discussion and Review

1. Where do fashions come from?
2. What is the nature of fads and crazes?

RUMOR

On the face of it, rumor may appear as unreal as a craze. But it is not necessarily false.

Characteristics

A **rumor** is an unverified story that is spread from one person to another. As the story circulates, each person distorts the account by dropping some items and adding his or her own interpretation. But a rumor is not necessarily false. It may turn out to be true. It is unverified *not* because it is necessarily a distortion but because people do not bother to check it against facts.

Everyday we all act on the basis of unverified reports. Sociologists therefore view rumors as a normal form of communication. According to

Tamotsu Shibutani (1966), for example, rumor is a communication people use in an effort to comprehend what is going on in a situation where information is lacking. Rumor, then, is a process in which many individuals try together to construct a definition of an ambiguous situation.

Contributing Factors

A rumor is likely to develop and circulate if people's demand for news about an ambiguous situation is not met by institutionalized channels of communication, such as newspapers, government announcements, and television and radio newscasts. The more *ambiguous* a situation, the greater the chance a rumor will develop. Thus, rumor is much more a part of interpersonal communications in police states and totalitarian societies where people do not trust the government-controlled media.

Anxiety also plays a significant role. Not long ago, widespread anxiety over economic problems made the United States ripe for the rumor mill. People who had lost or were afraid of losing their jobs were especially likely to believe or pass on damaging rumors about big companies. Seeing a corporate giant in trouble seemed to make them feel better. All this provided fertile ground for the growth of the rumor in 1978 that McDonald's added earthworms to its hamburgers. In 1982 another rumor had it that Procter & Gamble's logo, showing 13 stars and a man in the moon, was a sign of devil worship. In 1991 it was rumored that Liz Claiborne, the clothing company, gave 30 percent of its profits to the Church of Satan. In that same year, Tropical Fantasy—a soft drink marketed to minorities in Northeastern cities, became the target of a rumor that the Ku Klux Klan owned the company and that they added to the drink an ingredient that would make black men sterile (Koenig, 1982; Goleman, 1991). Although all these rumors were false, they spread like a prairie fire.

Questions for Discussion and Review

1. What is the nature of rumor?
2. What causes rumor to emerge?

PUBLIC OPINION

When we talk about "the public," we usually mean the population at large. In sociology, however, **public** is a dispersed collection of people who share a partic-ular interest or concern. The interest may involve environmental issues, or civil rights, or outlawing pornography. Thus, there are a great many publics within the population at large.

Whenever a public comes into being, it forms an opinion. **Public opinion** is the collection of ideas and attitudes shared by the members of a particular public. As measured by polls and surveys, public opinion often seems fickle, changing easily even while values appear constant. This fickleness may reflect the difference between private and public opinion. "What a person says only to his wife, himself, or in his sleep," wrote Turner and Killian (1987), "constitutes his private opinion. What he will say to a stranger is public opinion." In private, many people will express doubts about an opinion. In public, they might state an opinion shared by others.

Propaganda

Politicians want to win our hearts and minds, and businesses want to win our dollars. Both use the media to try to gain mass support by manipulating public opinion. In other words, they generate **propaganda**—communication tailored to influence opinion. Propaganda may be true or false. What sets it apart from other communications is the intent to change opinion. Alfred and Elizabeth Lee (1979) have identified seven methods that are frequently used to sway public opinion:

1. *Name calling,* or giving something a negative label. This method is designed to make the audience reject an idea or person or product without analysis. If a candidate is "ultraconservative," "ultraliberal," "flaky," or a "big spender," why bother to consider his or her qualifications seriously? If abortion is "murder," who can support its legalization?

2. *Glittering generality,* the opposite of name calling. An idea or product is associated with a general, ambiguous, but extremely popular concept or belief. If a war represents the defense of democracy and freedom, who can oppose it?

3. *Transfer,* or associating an idea or product with something else that is widely respected, admired, or desired. Beautiful, scantily clad actresses sell cars and mattresses on television commercials. Presidents give television speeches with the U.S. flag prominently displayed behind them.

4. *Testimonial,* or having a famous person endorse or oppose some idea or product. Top athletes tell us to

use a certain shampoo or shaving cream. Famous politicians travel to towns they never heard of to urge people to vote for obscure candidates.

5. *Plain folks,* or identifying the propagandist with the average person. While President, Jimmy Carter made sure people saw him playing softball and going fishing—doing what ordinary people do. He frequently presented himself as a mere peanut farmer, not much different from an average-income person, even though he was a wealthy man.

6. *Card stacking,* in which one fact or falsehood supporting a point of view is piled on top of another. Commercials do not tell us both the strengths and the weaknesses of a product or a candidate. Instead, we read that a brand-new car, for example, is "Quiet. Smooth riding. Full size. With comfort and luxury for six passengers. . . . Rich velour fabrics, thick carpeting and warm woodtones. . . . A truly fine automobile."

7. *Bandwagon,* creating the impression that everyone is using a product or supporting an idea or person. Soft-drink companies use commercials to show a horde of young, happy people drinking their product and singing its praises. Political candidates are usually quick to announce favorable poll results. Thus, the propagandist creates pressure to conform to a real or illusory norm.

Media Influence

Despite those manipulations, the effect of propaganda, like the effect of any communication, is limited. Because we are not computers to be programmed or clay to be molded, neither propagandists nor the media can simply insert opinions into our heads or erase previously held beliefs.

In general, at least three factors limit the influence of the media on public opinion. First, a multitude of independent organizations *present diverse viewpoints,* canceling each other's impact on the audience. Second, because most of the media are interested in making a profit, they often *present what the audience wants to see or hear.* Third, communication frequently occurs through the *two-step flow* of influence. We may hear an analysis of an issue on television ("the first step"), but we often accept or reject it after *being influenced by our* **opinion leaders** ("the second step"), individuals whose opinion is respected by others and influences them (Turner and Killian, 1987).

The media do influence public opinion to some degree. Their power comes largely from their role as gatekeepers—determining what information will be passed on to large numbers of people. There are at least five ways in which the media affect opinion. First, they *authenticate* information, making it more credible to the audience. A news item reported in the mass media often seems more believable than one

Although there are limitations, the U.S. media does have the power to influence opinion. This power comes largely from the media's role as gatekeepers—determining what information will be passed on to large numbers of Americans.

passed by word of mouth. Second, the media *validate* private opinions, preferences, and values. If a famous commentator offers a view similar to our own, we are likely to feel more confident of our own opinion. Third, the media *legitimize* unconventional viewpoints. The wildest idea may eventually sound reasonable, or at least worth considering, if we read it repeatedly on the editorial pages of newspapers or hear it on the evening news. Fourth, the mass media *concretize* free-floating anxieties and ill-defined preferences. By supplying such labels as "the crime wave" and "population explosion," the media in effect create a world of objects against which feelings can be specifically expressed. Fifth, the mass media help *establish a hierarchy* of importance and prestige among persons, objects, and opinions. If the national media never interview the senators from your state, the public is not likely to consider them important, even if they are very influential among their colleagues in the Senate (Turner and Killian, 1987).

Questions for Discussion and Review

1. How do people use propaganda and the media to mold public opinion?
2. How can the media influence public opinion and what is the limitation of its influence?

SOCIAL MOVEMENTS

A hundred years ago, women in the United States could not vote. Fifty years ago, paid vacations for workers were almost unheard of. A little more than two decades ago, George Wallace took office as governor of Alabama, declaring "segregation now, segregation tomorrow, segregation forever." These features of U.S. society were transformed through **social movements**, conscious efforts to bring about or prevent change.

Compared with the forms of collective behavior we have so far discussed, social movements are far more purposive. A bank run or stock market crash, for example, unfolds without plan, but a social movement develops as a result of purposeful effort. Social movements are also far more structured than other forms of collective behavior, even if they are not centrally coordinated. A lynch mob may develop a division of labor, but it is an informal division with a very short life. By contrast, the civil rights movement has within it numerous organizations, recognized leaders, and sets of roles and statuses. Finally, a social movement is also more enduring than other forms of collective behavior. A crowd may stay together for a few hours, but a movement may endure for years. These characteristics give social movements the potential to build a membership in the thousands or even millions.

The resistance movement is a type of social movement that cherishes an existing system and tries to reverse trends that threaten to change that system. Pro-life groups have tried to resist the legalization of abortion.

Types

Most social movements aim to change society, but they seek varying degrees of change. They can be classified into four types on the basis of their goals.

1. *Revolutionary movements* seek total, radical change in society. Their goal is to overthrow the existing form of government and replace it with a new one. Revolutionary movements typically resort to violence or some other illegal action. Examples include the revolution for independence in the United States, the Bolshevik revolution in Russia, the Chinese Communist revolution, and the Castro-led revolution in Cuba.

2. *Reform movements* seek only a partial change in society. They support the existing social system as a whole and want to preserve it, but they aim to improve it by removing its blemishes, typically through legal methods. Each reform movement usually focuses on just one issue. The civil rights movement seeks to rid society of racial discrimination. The women's movement seeks to eliminate gender inequality. The ecology movement seeks to put a stop to environmental pollution.

3. *Resistance movements* seek to preserve an existing system by resisting social change. The Ku Klux Klan and the U.S. Nazi party, for example, try to stop racial integration. In Muslim countries, the Islamic revolution seeks to protect the traditional Islamic ways of life against Western influences.

4. *Expressive movements* seek to change the individual, not society. Many are religious, aimed at converting individuals to a particular faith. These movements enable their members to express a sense of guilt, their joy of redemption, and their devotion to a religion. Examples include the "Moonies," Hare Krishnas, and other sects.

Causes

There are so many things to do in this world. We can spend our time making money, or fishing, or whatever. Why would people instead spend their time pushing a social movement? According to Eric Hoffer (1966), those who participate in social movements are frustrated and troubled. They use social movements as a diversion, enabling them to hide from themselves their personal problems, such as a sense of inadequacy and inferiority. Furthermore, through such a social movement they can gain a sense of

being noble and magnanimous, as they fight a good cause beyond their own self-interest. A social movement can also provide a sense of belonging and a way of identifying oneself. Members are therefore, in Hoffer's view, strongly dedicated to their movement's objective, following their leaders blindly as "true believers."

There are, however, some holes in Hoffer's psychological theory. For one thing, he in effect blames movement participants rather than society for their frustration. It is often the unpleasant social conditions, such as social injustice or racial discrimination, that have brought about the discontent in the first place, as is obvious in the case of the civil rights movement. Another problem with Hoffer's view is that, although frustration may motivate people to join a social movement, it cannot explain why some participate in the *pro*-abortion rights movement, while others take part in the *anti*-abortion movement. Nevertheless, some sociologists have argued that frustration among masses of people may be the first condition necessary for the emergence of a movement. But other social factors are also considered important, such as discontented individuals identifying a common frustration, working out a plan to change the offending conditions, and banding together to carry out that plan (Turner and Killian, 1987).

Other sociologists have proposed the **resource mobilization theory**, arguing that social movements result from the availability of resources for mobilization. According to this theory, what sparks a movement is not discontent but the availability of such mobilization resources as strong organization, effective leadership, money, and media access. But these theorists have in turn been criticized for virtually ignoring the place of discontent in social movements. In fact, both resource mobilization and discontent can be found in practically all movements. But the importance of each varies from one movement to another. As Harold Kerbo (1982) notes, discontent plays a larger role in "crisis movements" involving African Americans, the unemployed, or poor people, while resource mobilization figures more in "affluence movements," such as environmental movements, which involve mostly affluent Americans.

Questions for Discussion and Review

1. How do sociologists define and categorize social movements?
2. What causes social movements?

ENRICHING OUR LIVES

The relentless pursuit of material prosperity can have harmful consequences for our lives. This reading suggests that we learn from a traditional culture the importance of pursuing nonmaterial goals such as developing healthy families and strong communities.

Lessons from Traditional Culture

Why is the world teetering from one crisis to another? Has it always been like this? Were things worse in the past—or better?

For the past 16 years, I have spent half of each year in Ladakh, a harsh but wildly beautiful desert land high in the western Himalayas. This place, also known as "Little Tibet," is home to one of the last traditional cultures to remain essentially uninfluenced by the Western world.

My experiences in Ladakh have dramatically changed my response to these questions about Western civilization. I have come to see my own industrial culture in a very different light.

Before I went to Ladakh, I used to assume that the direction of "progress" was somehow inevitable, not to be questioned. As a consequence, I passively accepted a new road through the middle of the park, a steel-and-glass bank where the 200-year-old church had stood, a supermarket instead of the corner shop, and the fact that life seemed to get harder and faster with each day.

I do not accept that anymore. Ladakh has convinced me that there is more than one path into the future and given me tremendous strength and hope.

Western society today is moving in two distinct and opposing directions. On the one hand, mainstream culture led by government and industry moves relentlessly toward continued economic growth and technological development, straining the limits of nature and all but ignoring fundamental human needs. On the other hand, a countercurrent, comprising a wide range of groups and ideas, has kept alive the ancient understanding that all life is inextricably connected, which is widely shared in Ladakh.

At present, this countercurrent is a minority in the United States, but it is growing in strength as more and more people begin to question society's definition—and the whole notion—of progress. Individual consumers are beginning to realize their power to bring about change in the economic system, and businesses are competing with each other to appear more socially conscious or "environmentally friendly."

These changes can greatly enrich our lives. Yet, they are often treated as sacrifices. The emphasis is on giving things up and making do with less, rather than recognizing how much we stand to gain. We forget that the price of never-ending economic growth and material prosperity has been spiritual and social impoverishment, psychological insecurity, and the loss of cultural vitality.

In Ladakh, however, I have seen how human-scale structures nurture intimate bonds with the earth and an active and participatory democracy, while supporting strong and vital communities and healthy families. These structures in turn provide the security needed for individual well-being and, paradoxically, for a sense of freedom.

Excerpted from Helena Norberg-Hodge, "Lessons from Traditional Cultures," *The Futurist,* May-June, 1992, p. 60.

A GLOBAL ANALYSIS OF SOCIAL CHANGE

Social change takes place around the world. In some respects, social change differs from one society to another, and in other respects, it does not. This has therefore raised the question of whether diverse societies are converging into one world or diverging into separate worlds.

Traditions and Modernization

Modernization is the form of social change that involves the transformation of an agricultural society into an industrial one. Contrary to popular belief, such social change does not inevitably destroy tradition. There are many instances where modernization reinforces tradition or the other way around.

In India, for example, modernization reinforces tradition. When Indians of middle and lower levels seek upward mobility, they do so by "becoming more devoutly Hinduistic," by being as traditionally Indian as possible. Even among very Westernized elites, the native culture still exerts a powerful influence. Nearly all highly modernized Indian intellectuals speak a regional language as their mother tongue, are steeped in classical Sanskrit literature, are strongly tied to an extended family, and are likely to find a spouse through parental arrangements.

We can also see the positive impact of tradition on modernization in Japan. Without its traditional culture, Japan would not have become an industrial giant. The Japanese culture emphasizes the importance of social relations and collective welfare. It encourages consensus rather than conflict, deference to rather than disrespect for authority, and paternalism rather than indifference by those in authority. These cultural values saturate Japan's economic system. A business enterprise, no matter how large, is run like a household, with the accompanying interdependence and loyalty characteristic of the family. Since the company takes care of its workers by giving

them lifetime employment, employees tend to identify strongly with employers and work as hard as they can. Moreover, the traditional emphasis on collective welfare does more than enhance productivity through cooperation between managers and workers. It further causes society to favor business and industry at the expense of individuals, transferring funds and wealth from individuals to industries. This can be seen in the fact that factories and company apartments are mostly grand and imposing, whereas private homes are cramped yet highly expensive.

Convergence and Divergence

Through modernization, many non-Western societies such as India and Japan are becoming technologically more like Western societies. But at the same time, both types of societies are growing apart culturally, with one valuing tradition more than the other. These opposite trends have led to the development of two contrasting theories about the changing global society.

According to **convergence theory**, modernization will bring the West and non-West together by breaking down cultural barriers to produce a one-world society. The assumption is that exposure to supersonic aircraft, satellite communication, the information superhighway, and multinational companies will cause non-Western societies to adopt Western ways of living and virtually all the Western values. Under the influence of modernization, technocrats and leaders in Asia, Africa, and South America will become a "cosmopolitan elite." They will abandon their own traditional cultures, thereby dissolving the cultural differences between their countries and the West.

But this view runs counter to **divergence theory**, which emphasizes the growing separation between Western and non-Western cultures. Especially in many Asian and Muslim societies, the tides of cultural nationalism are rising, rejecting Western culture. Saudi Arabia and other mideastern countries, for example, preserve their traditional Islamic way of

According to convergence theory, modernization will bring the West and non-West together by breaking down cultural barriers to produce a one-world society. The assumption is that exposure to supersonic aircraft, satellite, communication, the information superhighway, and multinational companies will cause non-Western societies to adopt Western ways of living and virtually all the values—even foods—of the West.

life despite their embrace of modernization. Thus, in Saudi Arabia, gambling, movies, and dancing are forbidden, and Western videos, books, and publications are heavily censored. Islamic laws are also strictly enforced: thieves' hands are chopped off, adulterers are stoned to death, murderers and rapists are beheaded, and lesser offenders are flogged; all such punishments are carried out in the city squares for the public to see (Beyer, 1990).

Is the U.S. in Decline?

The convergence and divergence theories essentially deal with the issue of whether non-Western societies are more like or unlike the West. Now let us examine the same issue from the standpoint of the West: Is the United States, widely seen as the epitome of all that is Western, becoming more like the developing countries by losing its status as the world's leader?

According to Paul Kennedy, the United States has not actually suffered a serious decline. But he warns that "if the trends in national indebtedness, inadequate productivity increases, mediocre educational performance, and decaying social fabric in the United States are allowed to continue at the same time that massive U.S. commitments of men, money and materials are made in different parts of the globe" in order to maintain our international status as the foremost military power, we will lose that very power in a decade or so down the road (Kennedy, 1988; 1991). Kennedy is concerned that the United States cannot solve its economic problems, improve

its public education, and eliminate its social problems, such as crime, drugs, and homelessness. All these problems are assumed capable of driving the United States into the developing world.

But other social scientists are more optimistic. Joseph Nye (1990) agrees with Kennedy that U.S. decline will occur if those domestic issues are not soundly addressed, but Nye has faith in the U.S. ability to deal with those problems. One reason is that, according to Nye, the United States, for all its problems, continues to be the world's largest economy and has the highest level of absolute productivity. Another reason is that the United States still has a great deal of what Nye calls "hard" and "soft" power to lead the world. Hard power is economic and military strength. Soft power is the ability to persuade rather than command, which comes from intangible sources, such as the worldwide popularity of U.S. movies and the admiration and good will that U.S. citizens often enjoy abroad. The 1991 Gulf War has shown how the United States possesses those two kinds of power. It succeeded in using its military's hard power to defeat Iraq swiftly and with remarkably few U.S. casualties. It succeeded in using its soft power to persuade the United Nations to pass resolutions forcing Iraq to withdraw from Kuwait; the United States further used its soft power successfully to mobilize an international coalition to wage war against Iraq. Increasingly, the soft, noncoercive power will be more effective than the hard, military power in leading the world, and here Nye believes the United States has a clear edge over any other nation.

The United States' position as a superpower derives from more than military and economic strength. It also comes from "soft power"—the ability to persuade rather than command—as shown by the worldwide popularity of U.S brand names.

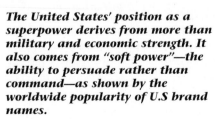

Questions for Discussion and Review

1. How are tradition and modernization related in India and Japan?
2. Are various societies converging into one world?
3. Is the United States in danger of joining the developing world?

FUNCTIONALIST PERSPECTIVE

Modern sociology was born in a period of great social tumult, and its founding fathers developed many of their ideas as a result of trying to understand the vast social changes of their time. Anthropologists and historians, too, were intrigued by the question of how societies change. Most of them were basically functionalists. To some, human society seemed like a well-functioning one-way train, headed toward eventual Utopia. To others, it was like a healthy human body, growing from innocent childhood to old age. To yet others, it was rather like an ocean tide, rising and falling and then rising again. To more recent sociologists, it was a social system, with its different parts cooperating to make it function properly. All these social scientists seemed to consider society a harmonious, peaceful system, without pointing out any chaos, exploitation, or conflict within the system.

Evolutionary Theory

Human horizons expanded greatly during the nineteenth century, as Europeans "discovered" and studied peoples of other lands and of the distant past. The early anthropologists believed that these peoples offered a portrait of their own ancestors. Most agreed that all societies progressed, or evolved, through three stages of development: savagery, barbarism, and civilization. Western societies, of course, were deemed civilized. All other peoples were considered savages or barbarians.

This was the origin of **evolutionary theory**, the theory that societies change gradually from simple to complex forms. One of its early exponents was functionalist Herbert Spencer (1820–1903), who believed that all societies followed uniform, natural laws of evolution. These laws decreed "survival of the fittest": those aspects of society that worked well would survive; those that did not would die out.

Thus, over time, societies would naturally and inevitably improve. Behind this old theory were several questionable assumptions, including the extremely ethnocentric belief that Western culture represents the height of human civilization.

Modern evolutionary theorists have discarded several of these assumptions. In general, they argue that societies tend to change gradually from simple to complex forms. Pastoral societies may be considered simple; modern industrial societies, complex. But evolutionary theorists no longer imply that the change represents an improvement (Lenski et al., 1995). Evolving complexity can be seen in the change Durkheim described from mechanical solidarity to organic solidarity (see Chapter 4: Society). But organic solidarity is not necessarily "better" than mechanical solidarity. A modern lifestyle is not always an improvement over a traditional one.

Cyclical Theory

Evolutionists assume that social change has only one direction. They believe that when societies change they, in effect, burn their bridges behind them—they cannot return to their previous states. In contrast, proponents of **cyclical theory** believe that societies move forward and backward, up and down, in an endless series of cycles.

Spengler's "Majestic Cycles" German historian Oswald Spengler (1880–1936) was the first to make this assumption explicit. He wrote in 1918 that Western civilization was headed downhill and would soon die out, just as the Greek and Egyptian civilizations had. "The great cultures," he explained, "accomplish their majestic wave cycles. They appear suddenly, swell in splendid lines, flatten again, and vanish, and the face of the waters is once more a sleeping waste." More often, Spengler likened a culture to an organism. Like any living thing, a culture, he believed, went through a life cycle of birth, youth, maturity, old age, and death. Western civilization, as he saw it, had reached old age and was tottering toward death.

Spengler's theory was very popular for a time. But to modern sociologists, there is too much poetry and too little science in his argument, and the analogy between societies and biological organisms is more misleading than useful. Nevertheless, Spengler's basic idea that social change is cyclical has influenced social science. Arnold Toynbee and Pitirim Sorokin, for example, offered famous theories based on this view.

Toynbee's "Challenge" and "Response" Like Spengler, British historian Arnold Toynbee (1889–1975) believed that all civilizations rise and fall. But in his view, the rise and fall do not result from some inevitable, biologically determined life cycle. Instead, they depend both on human beings and on their environments. Environments present "challenges," and humans choose "responses" to those challenges. The fate of a civilization, according to Toynbee, depends on both the challenges presented to a civilization and the responses it devises.

The challenge may come from the natural environment or from human sources. Barren land, a frigid climate, and war, for example, all represent "challenges." A civilization declines if the challenge it faces is either too weak or too severe. Suppose food is extremely abundant; people may become lazy, and their civilization will decline. But if food is very scarce, starvation may kill the people, and their civilization as well. A moderate challenge is likely to stimulate a civilization to grow and flourish. The relatively large population and relatively scarce natural resources of Japan might represent a "moderate" challenge.

The fate of a civilization, however, depends not just on the challenge from the environment but also on the people's response. Whether a successful response comes about usually hinges on the actions of a creative minority, which involve developing new ideas and leading the masses to meet the challenge. Without such leaders, the civilization will decline.

Toynbee's theory provides an interesting way of looking at the history of civilizations, but it does not give us a means of predicting how societies will change. What, after all, is a "severe" challenge? Will the depletion of oil and minerals represent a "moderate" or an overly "severe" challenge for Western civilization? We know the answer only after the fact. If a civilization falls, we may assume that the challenge was too severe and the response was inadequate. *Before* a civilization rises or falls, we have no way of testing Toynbee's theory. But it still can be considered a useful theory. According to French sociologist Raymond Boudon (1983a, 1983b), social change is so complex that the best we can expect from a theory is whether it can help us understand what has happened rather than predict what will happen. That's what Toynbee's theory does.

Sorokin's Principle of Immanent Change According to Pitirim Sorokin (1889–1968), a Russian American sociologist, societies fluctuate between two extreme forms of culture, which he called ideational and sensate. **Ideational culture** emphasizes faith or religion as the key to knowledge and encourages people to value spiritual life. **Sensate culture** stresses empirical evidence or science as the path to knowledge and urges people to favor a practical, materialistic, and hedonistic way of life.

External forces such as international conflict or contact with another culture may force change on a society, but Sorokin believed in the **principle of immanent change**, the notion that social change is the product of the social forces that exist *within* a society. When the time has come for a society's "inwardly ordained change," all the main aspects of the culture change. Thus, society eventually reacts against one extreme form of culture and swings to the other extreme. Sorokin regarded the Western culture of his time, for example, as sensate, and, like Spengler, thought it was declining. In the widespread pursuit of pleasure, proliferation of fraud and crime, and deterioration of the family, Sorokin saw signs that Western culture was "overripe" and ready to swing to the other extreme—ideational culture.

To most sociologists today, Sorokin's theory is too speculative, and impossible to test scientifically. Although Sorokin supported his theory with a mountain of historical data, he seems to have selected those facts that supported his view and ignored those that did not. Nevertheless, Sorokin's theory, like Toynbee's, can help us understand some of the changes in our history, such as the rise of fundamentalist religion in the last decade (see Chapter 17: Religion). It can be interpreted as a reflection of the shift from a sensate to an ideational culture.

Equilibrium Theory

U.S. sociologist Talcott Parsons (1902–1979) developed yet another theory of social change, one that remains influential today. According to his **equilibrium theory**, all the parts of society serve some function and are interdependent. As a result, a change in one part produces compensatory changes elsewhere. It has recently become necessary, for example, for both parents to work in order to earn enough income to support a family. But if both parents must leave the home, who will care for their children? Society has responded with the increased availability of day-care services. Such changes keep the various parts of the social system in balance, ensuring social order and stability.

In this view of society, social change triggers the social system to make adjustment. If there is a change in one part of society, other parts will change to keep society functioning smoothly. To Parsons, social change is not the overthrow of the old and the creation of something wholly new. Instead, new elements are integrated with aspects of the old society through a "moving equilibrium," or movement toward a new harmonious system.

Parsons's theory is useful for describing gradual change. According to its critics, though, it fails to explain why social change occurs, does not deal with *revolutionary* change, and portrays societies as far more stable and harmonious than they are.

Questions for Discussion and Review

1. How does today's evolutionary theory differ from the older one?
2. How do the separate versions of cyclical theory differ from each other, and how does each contribute to sociology's understanding of social change?
3. What is the equilibrium theory of social change?

CONFLICT PERSPECTIVE

According to **conflict theory**, societies are always marked by conflict and that conflict is the key to change. Karl Marx (1818–1883) is the father of this theory. We have discussed aspects of his work in previous chapters, especially his prediction of the downfall of capitalism.

According to Marx, a capitalist society includes two classes: the owners of the means of production (the bourgeoisie or capitalists) and those who must sell their labor (the proletariat or workers). These classes are in constant conflict with each other. The capitalists are determined to keep wages low in order to maximize their profits, while the workers resist this exploitation. The capitalists have the upper hand, but they unwittingly sow the seeds of their own destruction. By completely controlling the labor of workers, capitalists further their alienation. By exploiting workers mercilessly, capitalists fuel rage and resentment among workers, and lead them to feel that they have nothing to gain from the present system. And through factories and improved transportation and communication, the capitalist society brings workers together and helps them share their sufferings with one another. As a result, the workers develop a consciousness of themselves as a class. According to Marx, the alienation, resentment, and

class consciousness eventually lead workers to revolt against capitalist society.

History has not fulfilled these predictions. Marx failed to anticipate the emergence of a large middle class, made up largely of white-collar workers. He also failed to see that governments might respond to social conflict by improving the condition of workers. In fact, Marx's dire predictions about the future of capitalism helped spur governments to ease the suffering of workers. In a sense, by predicting that capitalism carried the seeds of its destruction, Marx sowed seeds that would help destroy his own prediction. Through the emergence of the welfare state as well as the growth of the middle class, workers in capitalist societies have grown richer, not poorer as Marx predicted. They have thus gained a stake in the system and are not likely to overthrow it by supporting revolution.

Other aspects of Marx's work have stood up better against the test of time. Marx did accurately predict the rise of large-scale industry, the emergence of multinational corporations, and the continuous squeeze of technology on employees. His analysis further implied the concentration of capital in a few giant corporations, which is evident in the United States today. Moreover, many social scientists agree with Marx that material conditions—economic production in particular—shape intellectual, political, and social life. They also accept his view that "the innermost nature of things" is dynamic and filled with conflict (Heilbroner, 1980).

Question for Discussion and Review

1. What are the strengths and weaknesses of Marx's approach to social change?

SYMBOLIC INTERACTIONIST PERSPECTIVE

According to symbolic interactionism, human beings actively interpret the world around them and then act—or interact with others—in accordance with the interpretation. Imbedded in this interpretation is how the individuals see themselves and want others to see them, which itself also influences the social interaction. Thus, when society changes to create a new social life, people will define their world differently than they have in the past. If the individuals are young and therefore familiar only with the current world, their worldview will differ from their parents' view of the earlier world. Therefore, through the symbolic interactionist perspective, we can gain insight into how social change shapes our definition of the world, our selves, and our interaction with others.

There seem to be two major types of social change around the globe today. In most societies the change has involved modernization, transforming from being agricultural to being industrial. In the fewer industrial societies, the modernization has involved transforming from being industrial to postindustrial. Both types of social change have a great impact on the individual's worldview, self-perception, and social interaction. This point can be illustrated with just two examples.

First, people in traditional societies have a relatively clear concept of who they are because their social statuses have been familiar to them since childhood. They thus know themselves as farmers, carpenters, and the like, just like their parents, which determines how they interact with others. By contrast, people in modern societies tend to achieve their statuses as teachers, lawyers, businesspersons, and so on, which they have not learned to live with since childhood. As a result, these people tend to be less self-confident, more anxious, and more inclined to ask who they are.

Second, people in traditional societies tend to define themselves as an integral part of a group and seek happiness from developing close relationships with others. By contrast, people in modern societies tend to define themselves as being free and independent of others so that they are more likely to engage in superficial interactions.

Question for Discussion and Review

1. According to symbolic interactionism, how does social change influence our personal life?

MAJOR CHANGES IN OUR FUTURE

What is in store for us in the remainder of this century? Demographic changes should have a marked impact on U.S. society. Working adults and the elderly will each make up a larger share of the population, while the young will constitute a smaller

share. With fewer youth, we can expect crime and competition for entry-level jobs to decrease. With more working and elderly adults, productivity and political conservatism will increase. The conservatism may find expression in toughness toward criminals, in heartlessness toward the poor, and in resistance to efforts by women and minorities to achieve social and economic equality. Brought up in such an environment, the young may also become more conservative. Political conflict between the young and the old may increase, as the interests of those receiving Social Security and those paying to support it clash.

Technology will continue to stimulate change. We are now entering the postindustrial age, which seems as momentous as the Industrial Revolution. A postindustrial society is largely based on services, particularly information-related services. Today, more than two-thirds of the U.S. labor force already work in the information-related service industry, such as health care, retail trade, and financial services.

The computer-driven technologies have also begun and will continue to dismantle the traditional industrial principle of mass production aimed at a mass society. By using computers, companies are increasingly customizing their goods and services for niche markets. The new technologies are also making local production as competitive as national mass production. Many supermarkets, in addition to selling national brands of bread, have begun to bake their own. Photos, which used to be sent to Rochester, New York, to be processed centrally by Kodak, can now be developed and printed anywhere in the United States. The same demassification process has taken away much of the audience from the three giant TV networks, as cable and other media have proliferated to serve new niche markets. Similar changes have also weakened the mass-production labor unions (Toffler, 1990).

With demassification, however, our society will become more individualistic, more fragmented, and less cohesive. We will consequently have more social conflicts. There are already signs of how demassification has made us more aware of our individual rights. Our society has become awash with almost as many different rights as there are many different individuals. There are criminal rights, victim rights, animal rights, pro-abortion rights, anti-abortion rights, housing rights, privacy rights, the right to own AK–47s (powerful assault rifles) for hunting purposes, a damaged fetus' right not to be born, and airline pilots' right not to be randomly tested for alcohol, which presumably leaves passengers the right to crash every now and then (Leo, 1991). With many different groups demanding that only their rights be protected, social responsibility or civic obligation will decline, and national consensus will be harder to sustain. Thus, more social conflict will occur.

Finally, the end of the Cold War may temporarily make us less interested in foreign affairs because the Soviet threat to our national security no longer exists. But new international problems will goad our nation into action. The United States will help to contain the inter-ethnic conflict unleashed by the disintegration of the Soviet empire. Our nation will try to control the spread of missiles and nuclear technology, which the former members of the Soviet Union are eager to sell to developing countries. And our government will make sure that U.S. companies can more easily sell their products in foreign countries (Friedman, 1992).

CHAPTER REVIEW

1. *According to Smelser, what are the preconditions for the appearance of collective behavior?* Six conditions must appear in this sequence: (1) structural conduciveness, (2) social strain, (3) the spread of a generalized belief, (4) a precipitating factor, (5) mobilization of participants, and (6) inadequate social control.

2. *What conditions create a panic?* There must be a perception of a crisis, intense fear of possible entrapment, some panic-prone individuals, mutual emotional facilitation, and a lack of cooperation among people. *What type of people are most likely to succumb to mass hysteria?* People with little critical ability and little education. *Why do crowds sometimes act irrationally, even violently?* Le Bon argued that as a result of the anonymity of a crowd, people give up their individuality and release their primitive instincts. Then as a result of social contagion, they become part of a collective mind that is irrational. Many sociologists today believe that Le Bon's "collective mind" is a fiction and that crowds are not as homogeneous as they appear. Instead, as Turner and Killian have argued, crowds appear homogeneous because they conform to a new norm that emerges to deal with the unconventional situation in which the crowd finds itself.

3. *Do fashions affect many aspects of life?* Yes. In fact, almost all aspects of life are influenced by fashion. *How do fashions, fads, and crazes differ?* Fashions occur more predictably, last longer, and are more socially respectable than fads and crazes. Fads are less outrageous and less harmful than crazes. *Are rumors always distortions?* No. They are merely unverified.

They, or parts of them, may turn out to be true. *When are rumors likely to develop?* If a situation is ambiguous and institutionalized channels of communication do not satisfy the demand for news about it, then a rumor is likely to emerge.

4. *How does propaganda differ from other types of communication?* It is designed to influence opinion. *Why is the influence of the U.S. media limited?* There are several reasons: the multitude of viewpoints the media present; the tendency to tell people what they want to hear; and the frequency with which communication occurs by a two-step flow—from the media to opinion leaders and only then to the public. *What influence do the media have?* They frequently authenticate information; validate private opinions, preferences, and values; legitimize unconventional viewpoints and behavior; concretize ill-defined anxieties and preferences; and establish a hierarchy of importance and prestige among people, objects, or ideas.

5. *What are the aims of social movements?* In general, they seek some sort of change. Revolutionary movements seek total, radical change of society. Reform movements seek a partial change. Resistance movements try to turn back some ongoing social change. Expressive movements seek to change individuals, not society. *What are the social causes of social movements?* According to the traditional perspective, social conditions must first frustrate masses of people; then people must identify a common frustration and work out a plan and band together to change the offending conditions. But resource mobilization theory emphasizes the importance of the

availability of certain resources more than discontent as the cause.

6. *Does modernization necessarily destroy tradition?* No. It may even reinforce tradition. *Will modernization produce a one-world society?* Not necessarily. Modernization of non-Western countries may actually increase their cultural differences with the West. *Is the United States really in decline?* Not really, but if its various problems remain unsolved, decline can be expected.

7. *How do modern evolutionary theorists describe social change?* They argue that societies tend to change gradually from simple to complex forms. *What is a primary difference between evolutionary and cyclical theorists?* Evolutionary theorists see social change as moving in one principal direction: toward increased complexity. Cyclical theorists portray social change as reversible: societies may move "forward" and "backward," they may rise and fall, in cycles. *What is equilibrium theory?* It holds that the various parts of society are all interdependent and that a change in any one part stimulates compensatory changes in other parts of the system. *What does conflict theory say about social change?* Social change stems from conflict, which always characterizes societies. *What does symbolic interactionism reveal about social change?* Social change shapes the individual's self-perception and interaction with others.

8. *What effects are demographic changes in the United States likely to produce in the near future?* The aging of the population seems likely to lead to lower crime rates and increased productivity and conservatism. Political conflict between racial and ethnic groups, sexes, and generations may increase. *How is technology changing society?* It is carrying us into the postindustrial age in which information is the most important product. Computer technology will produce goods and services more efficiently, but its tendency to demassify production for individual needs will encourage more social conflict.

KEY TERMS

Collective behavior Relatively spontaneous, unorganized, and unpredictable social behavior (p. 528).

Conflict theory The theory that societies are always marked by conflict and that conflict is the key to change (p. 545).

Convergence theory The theory that modernization will bring the West and non-West together by breaking down cultural barriers to produce a one-world society (p. 541).

Craze A fad with serious consequences (p. 534).

Crowd A collection of people temporarily doing something while in proximity to one another (p. 532).

Cyclical theory The theory that societies move forward and backward, up and down, in an endless series of cycles (p. 543).

Divergence theory The theory that emphasizes the growing separation between Western and non-Western cultures (p. 541).

Emergent-norm theory The theory that members of a crowd develop, through interaction, a new norm to deal with the unconventional situation facing them (p. 533).

Equilibrium theory The theory that all the parts of society serve some function and are interdependent (p. 544).

Evolutionary theory The theory that societies change gradually from simple to complex forms (p. 543).

Fad A temporary enthusiasm for an innovation less respectable than a fashion (p. 534).

Fashion A great though brief enthusiasm among a relatively large number of people for a particular innovation (p. 534).

Ideational culture Sorokin's term for the culture that emphasizes faith or religion as the key to knowledge and encourages people to value spiritual life (p. 544).

Mass hysteria A form of collective behavior in which numerous people engage in a frenzied activity without checking the source of their fear (p. 531).

Modernization The form of social change that involves the transformation of an agricultural society into an industrial one (p. 540).

Opinion leader A person whose opinion is respected by others and influences them (p. 537).

Panic A type of collective behavior characterized by a maladaptive, fruitless response to a serious threat (p. 531).

Principle of immanent change The notion that social change is the product of the social forces that exist within a society (p. 544).

Propaganda   Communication tailored to influence opinion (p. 536).

Public   A dispersed collection of people who share a particular interest or concern (p. 536).

Public opinion   The collection of ideas and attitudes shared by the members of a particular public (p. 536).

Resource mobilization theory   The theory that social movements result from the availability of resources for mobilization (p. 539).

Rumor   An unverified story that is spread from one person to another (p. 535).

Sensate culture   Sorokin's term for the culture that stresses empirical evidence or science as the key to knowledge and urges people to favor a practical, materialistic, and hedonistic way of life (p. 544).

Social change   The alteration of society over time (p. 528).

Social contagion   The spreading of a certain emotion and action from one member of a crowd to another (p. 533).

Social movement   A conscious effort to bring about or prevent change (p. 538).

SUGGESTED READINGS

Harris, Marvin. 1989. *Our Kind: Who We Are, Where We Came From, and Where We Are Going.* New York: Harper & Row. An interesting narration of how humans have been changing from prehistoric times to the present.

Inkeles, Alex. 1983. *Exploring Individual Modernity.* New York: Columbia University Press. A well-integrated collection of articles that reports and analyzes findings from the author's famous studies on becoming modern in developing countries.

Kennedy, Paul M. 1988. *The Rise and Fall of the Great Powers.* New York: Random House. A Spenglerian, cyclical analysis of how past great powers such as Spain and Britain eventually declined, spiced with a controversial comparison between those former superpowers and the United States of today.

Nye, Joseph, Jr. 1990. *Bound to Lead: The Changing Nature of American Power.* New York: Basic Books. An anticyclical analysis of how in the new international order the United States will lead the world with its social and cultural resources more than with its military power.

Toffler, Alvin. 1990. *Powershift.* New York: Bantam Books. Argues that industrialism is losing world dominance to new forces of power.

Glossary

Absolute poverty The lack of minimum food and shelter necessary for maintaining life.

Academic subculture The college subculture that stresses the pursuit of scholarly achievement largely for its own sake.

Achieved status A status attained through one's own actions.

Activity theory The theory that most of the elderly maintain a great deal of interaction with others, even when it requires vigorous physical activities.

Affirmative action A policy that requires employers and colleges to make special efforts to recruit qualified minorities for jobs, promotions, and educational opportunities.

Afrocentrism The view of the world from the standpoint of African culture.

Age structure The pattern of the proportions of different age groups within a population.

Ageism Prejudice and discrimination against the aged.

Agricultural society A society that produces food primarily by using plows and draft animals on the farm.

Alienation of labor Marx's term for laborers' loss of control over their work process.

Alternative school A school that encourages student creativity by allowing the freedom to choose learning materials within the classroom.

Alzheimer's disease A disease of the brain characterized by progressive loss of memory and other mental abilities.

Amalgamation The process by which the subcultures of various groups are blended together, forming a new culture.

Animism The belief in spirits capable of helping or harming people.

Anomaly Kuhn's term for an idea or data incompatible with or unexplainable by the existing paradigm.

Anticipatory socialization The process by which people learn to assume a role in the future.

Anti-Semitism Prejudice or discrimination against Jews.

Aptitude The capacity for developing physical or social skills.

Arranged marriage The marriage in which partners are selected by their parents.

Ascribed status A status given to us independent of what we do.

Assimilation The process by which a minority adopts the dominant group's culture as the culture of the larger society.

Authority Legitimate power institutionalized in organizations.

Behavioral assimilation The social situation in which the minority adopts the dominant group's language, values, and behavioral patterns.

Belief An idea that is relatively subjective, unreliable, or unverifiable.

Bilateral descent The norm that recognizes both parents' families as the child's close relatives.

Biosphere A thin layer of air, water, and soil surrounding the earth.

Birth rate The number of babies born in a year for every 1,000 members of a given population.

Bureaucracy A modern Western organization defined by Max Weber as being rational in achieving its goal efficiently.

Capitalism An economic system based on private ownership of property and competition in producing and selling goods and services.

Caste system A relatively rigid stratification system in which people's positions are ascribed and fixed.

Census A periodic head count of the entire population of a country.

Charisma An exceptional personal quality popularly attributed to certain individuals.

Chromosomes The materials in a cell that transmit hereditary traits to the carrier from the carrier's parents.

Church A relatively large, well-established religious organization that is integrated into the society and does not make strict demands on its members.

Civil religion A collection of beliefs, symbols, and rituals that sanctify the dominant values of a society.

Class conflict Marx's term for the struggle between capitalists, who own the means of production, and the proletariat, who do not.

Class system A relatively open stratification system in which people's positions are achieved and changeable.

Coercion The illegitimate use of force or threat of force to compel obedience.

Collective behavior Relatively spontaneous, unorganized, and unpredictable social behavior.

Collegiate subculture The college subculture that revolves around fraternities, sororities, parties, drinking, football, and similar activities.

Communality The norm that requires scientists to share their knowledge freely with one another.

Compensatory education A school program intended to improve the academic performance of socially and educationally disadvantaged children.

Competition An interaction in which two individuals follow mutually accepted rules in trying to achieve the same goal before the other does.

Compositional theory The theory that city dwellers are as involved with small groups of friends, relatives, and neighbors as are noncity people.

Concentric zone theory The model of land use in which the city spreads out from the center in a series of concentric zones, each of which is used for a particular kind of activity.

Conflict An interaction in which two individuals disregard any rules in trying to achieve their own goal by defeating the other.

Conflict perspective A theoretical perspective that portrays society as always changing and marked by conflict.

Conflict theory The theory that societies are always marked by conflict and that conflict is the key to change.

Conglomerate A corporation that owns companies in various unrelated industries.

Constant A characteristic found in all members of the population being studied.

Content analysis Searching for specific words or ideas and turning them into numbers.

Control group The group that is not exposed to the independent variable.

Conventional morality Kohlberg's term for the practice of defining right and wrong according to the *motive* of the action being judged.

Convergence theory The theory that modernization will bring the West and non-West together by breaking down cultural barriers to produce a one-world society.

Cooperation An interaction in which two or more individuals work together to achieve a common goal.

Core countries The world's upper class, the most industrialized and richest societies, popularly known as industrial or developed countries.

Correlation A consistent association between two or more variables, which may or may not be causal.

Counterculture A subculture that represents values unacceptable to the dominant society but is generally not considered illegal or criminal.

Craze A fad with serious consequences.

Crowd A collection of people temporarily doing something while in proximity to one another.

Crystalline intelligence Wisdom and insight into the human condition, as shown by one's skills in language, philosophy, music, or painting.

Cult A religious group that professes a new religious belief, totally rejects society, and consists of members with extreme devotion to their leader.

Cultural ecology The theory that emphasizes physical environment as the determinant of human culture.

Cultural imperialism The practice of making the minorities accept the dominant group's culture.

Cultural integration The joining of various values into a coherent whole.

Cultural lag The social situation in which a culture's values and beliefs fail to catch up with technology.

Cultural pluralism The peaceful coexistence of various racial and ethnic groups, each retaining its own subculture.

Cultural relativism The belief that a culture must be understood on its own terms.

Cultural theory The theory that the cultural values of discipline, thrift, education, and the family contribute to economic success.

Cultural universals Practices that are found in all cultures as the means for meeting the same human needs.

Culture A design for living or a complex whole consisting of objects, values, and other characteristics that people acquire as members of society.

Cyclical theory The theory that societies move forward and backward, up and down, in an endless series of cycles.

De facto segregation Segregation resulting from tradition and custom.

De jure segregation Segregation sanctioned by law.

Death rate The number of deaths in a year for every 1,000 members of a population.

Deductive approach Deriving specific observations from general ideas.

Deindustrialization The loss of numerous factory jobs as a result of relocating a massive number of manufacturing plants to peripheral countries.

Demographic transition The theory that human populations tend to go through specific, demographic stages and that these stages are tied to a society's economic development.

Demography The scientific study of population.

Dependency theory The theory that rich nations exploit poor ones for power and commercial gain, thereby perpetuating poverty, underdevelopment, or dependency on rich nations.

Dependent variable A variable that is considered the effect of another variable.

Descriptive research Research aimed at gathering information in order to simply describe a phenomenon.

Detached observation A method of observation in which the researcher observes as an outsider, from a distance, without getting involved.

Developmental socialization The process by which people learn to be more competent in playing their currently assumed role.

Deviance An act that is considered by public consensus or by the powerful at a given place and time to be a violation of some social rule.

Deviant subculture A subculture that represents values unacceptable to the dominant culture and is generally considered illegal or criminal.

Differential association The process of acquiring through interaction with others "an *excess* of definitions favorable to violation of law over definitions unfavorable to violation of law".

Discrimination An unfavorable action against individuals that is taken because they are members of a certain category.

Disengagement theory The theory that aging causes people to disengage from society.

Disintegrative shaming The process by which the wrongdoer is punished in such a way as to be stigmatized, rejected, or ostracized.

Disinterestedness The norm that requires scientists to pursue truth rather than self-interest.

Divergence theory The theory that emphasizes the growing separation between Western and non-Western cultures.

Double standard The social norm that allows males, but not females, to have certain sexual experiences.

Dramaturgy A method of analyzing social interaction as if the participants were performing on a stage.

Dual economy An economy that comprises a *core* of giant corporations dominating the market and a *periphery* of small firms competing for the remaining, smaller shares of business.

Ecological processes Processes in which people compete for certain land use, one group dominates another, and a particular group moves into an area and takes it over from others.

Ecology A study of the interactions among organisms and between organisms and their physical environment.

Economic globalization The interrelationship of the world's economies.

Economic institution A system for producing and distributing goods and services.

Ecosystem A self-sufficient community of organisms depending for survival on one another and on the environment.

Egalitarian family The family in which authority is equally distributed between husband and wife.

Ego Freud's term for the part of personality that is rational, dealing with the world logically and realistically.

Emergent-norm theory The theory that members of a crowd develop, through interaction, a new norm to deal with the unconventional situation facing them.

Empirical indicator A concrete and observable representation of an abstract and unobservable concept.

Endogamy Literally, "marrying within," the act of marrying someone from one's own group.

Enterprise zone The economically depressed urban area that businesses, with the help of generous tax credits, try to revive by creating jobs.

Epidemiology The study of the origin and spread of disease within a population.

Equilibrium theory The theory that all the parts of society serve some function and are interdependent.

Ethicalism The type of religion that emphasizes moral principles as guides for living a righteous life.

Ethnic group A collection of people who share a distinctive cultural heritage.

Ethnocentrism The attitude that one's own culture is superior to that of others.

Ethnomethodology The analysis of how people define the world in which they live.

Eurocentrism The view of the world from the standpoint of European culture.

Evolutionary theory The theory that societies change gradually from simple to complex forms.

Exchange An interaction in which two individuals offer each other something in order to obtain a reward in return.

Exogamy Literally, "marrying outward," the act of marrying someone from outside one's group—such as clan, tribe, or village.

Experiment A research operation in which the researcher manipulates variables so that their influence can be determined.

Experimental group The subjects in an experiment who are exposed to the independent variable.

Explanatory research Research designed to test a hypothesis in order to explain a phenomenon.

Expressive leaders Leaders who achieve group harmony by making others feel good.

Expressive role Role that requires taking care of personal relationships.

Extended family The family that consists of two parents, their unmarried children, and other relatives.

Extramarital sex Having sex with a person who is not one's spouse, popularly called adultery or infidelity.

Fad A temporary enthusiasm for an innovation less respectable than a fashion.

False consciousness The belief among the masses that justifies their domination by the ruling class to the detriment of their own interests.

Family of orientation The family in which one grows up, consisting of oneself and one's parents and siblings.

Family of procreation The family that one establishes through marriage, consisting of oneself and one's spouse and children.

Fashion A great though brief enthusiasm among a relatively large number of people for a particular innovation.

Feminist theory A form of conflict theory that explains human life from the experiences of women.

Feminization of poverty A huge number of women bearing the burden of poverty, mostly as single mothers or heads of families.

Fluid intelligence Ability to grasp abstract relationships, as in mathematics, physics, or some other science.

Folk society Redfield's term for a society that is small, nonliterate, and homogeneous, with a strong solidarity.

Folkways Weak norms that specify expectations about proper behavior.

Formal organization A group whose activities are rationally designed to achieve specific goals.

Functionalist perspective A theoretical perspective that focuses on social order.

Gemeinschaft Tönnies's term for a type of society marked by a strong sense of community and by personal interactions among its members.

Gender identity People's image of what they are socially expected to be and do on the basis of their sex.

Gender role The pattern of attitudes and behaviors that a society expects of its members because of their being female or male.

Genderlects Linguistic styles that reflect the different worlds of women and men.

Generalized others Mead's term for people who do not have close ties to the child but do influence the child's internalization of the values of society.

Genocide Wholesale killing of a racial or ethnic group.

Gentrification The movement of affluent people into poor urban neighborhoods.

Gesellschaft Tönnies's term for a type of society characterized by individualism and by impersonal interactions.

Glass ceiling The prejudiced belief that keeps minority professionals from holding high, leadership positions in organizations.

Global stratification A system in which all the countries of the world find themselves in various positions, some getting less—or more—in life than others.

Global village A closely knit community of all the societies in the world.

Government A group of specific individuals who run the affairs of the state, such as the U.S. president, members of Congress, Supreme Court justices, and so on.

Groupthink The tendency for members of a cohesive group to maintain consensus to the extent of ignoring the truth.

Hawthorne effect The unintended effect of the researcher's presence on the subjects' behavior.

Healing role A set of social expectations regarding how a doctor should behave.

Homogamy Marrying someone with social characteristics similar to one's own.

Homophobia Prejudice and discrimination against homosexuals.

Horizontal mobility Movement from one job to another within the same status category.

Hormones Chemical substances that stimulate or inhibit vital biological processes.

Horticultural society A society that produces food primarily by growing plants in small gardens.

Humorology The study or practice of humor.

Hunting-gathering society A society that hunts animals and gathers plants as its primary means for survival.

Hypothesis A tentative statement about how various events are related to one another.

Id Freud's term for the part of personality that is irrational, concerned only with seeking pleasure.

Ideational culture Sorokin's term for the culture that emphasizes faith or religion as the key to knowledge and encourages people to value spiritual life.

Ideological conservatives U.S. citizens who, in theory, are opposed to big government because of their belief in free enterprise, rugged individualism, and capitalism.

Idiosyncrasy credit The privilege that allows leaders to deviate from their group's norms.

Impression management The act of presenting our "self" in such a way as to make the other person form the desired impression of us.

Incest taboo The social norm that strongly prohibits sexual relations between close relatives.

Independent variable A variable that is the cause of another variable.

Individual mobility Social mobility related to an individual's personal achievement and characteristics.

Inductive approach Deriving general ideas from specific observations.

Industrial Revolution The dramatic economic change brought about by the introduction of machines into the work process about 200 years ago.

Industrial society A society that produces food for its subsistence primarily by using machinery.

Infant mortality rate The number of deaths among infants less than one year old for every 1,000 live births.

Influence The ability to control others' behavior through persuasion rather than coercion or authority.

Informal organization A group formed by the informal relations among members of an organization—based on personal interactions, not on any plan by the organization.

Informed consent The approval that a patient gives to a doctor for a treatment after receiving adequate information on it.

Instincts Biologically inherited capacities for performing relatively complex tasks.

Instincts Fixed traits that are biologically inherited and enable their carrier to perform complex tasks.

Institutionalized deviance Norm violation that is so prevalent it has become socially acceptable.

Institutionalized discrimination The persistence of discrimination in social institutions, not necessarily known to everybody as discrimination.

Instrumental leaders Leaders who achieve their group's goal by getting others to focus on task performance.

Instrumental role Role that requires performance of a task.

Intelligence The capacity for mental or intellectual achievement.

Interaction ritual The form of interaction in which the participants perform certain acts to show reverence to the other.

Interest group An organized collection of people who attempt to influence government policies.

Intergenerational mobility A change in social standing from one generation to the next.

Intragenerational mobility A change in an individual's social standing.

In-group The group to which an individual is strongly tied as a member.

Jim Crow A set of laws that segregate blacks from whites in all kinds of public and private facilities.

Kinesics The use of body movements as a means of communication; also called body language.

Knowledge A collection of relatively objective ideas and facts about the physical and social worlds.

Kuznets curve The changing relationship between development and inequality.

Latent function A function that is unintended and often unrecognized.

Laws Norms that are specified formally in writing and backed by the power of the state.

Life chances The likelihood of living a good, long, or successful life in a society.

Life expectancy The average number of years that a group of people can expect to live.

Lifestyles Tastes, preferences, and ways of living.

Living will Advance instructions on what people want their doctors to do in the event of a terminal illness.

Looking-glass self Cooley's term for the self-image that we develop from the way others treat us.

Macro-level view A view that focuses on the large social phenomena of society, such as social institutions and inequality.

Manifest function A function that is intended and seems obvious.

Marginal surplus population Marxist term for unemployed workers who are superfluous or useless to the economy.

Marriage rate The number of marriages for every 1,000 people in a given year.

Mass hysteria A form of collective behavior in which numerous people engage in a frenzied activity without checking the source of their fear.

Master status A status that dominates a relationship.

Material culture Every conceivable kind of physical object produced by humans as members of society.

Matriarchal family The family in which the dominant figure is the eldest female.

Matrilineal descent The norm that recognizes only the mother's family as a child's close relatives.

Matrilocal residence The home where the married couple live with the wife's family.

Matthew effect The tendency to praise famous scientists and to ignore the contributions of those who are not well known.

Mechanical solidarity A type of social cohesion that develops when people do similar work and have similar beliefs and values.

Mechanical solidarity Social unity that comes from people performing the same tasks and having similar values.

Megalopolis A vast area in which many metropolises merge.

Metropolis A large urban area that includes a city and its surrounding edge cities and suburbs.

Micro-level view A view that focuses on the immediate social situations where people interact with one another.

Minority A racial or ethnic group that is subjected to prejudice and discrimination.

Minority theory The theory that older people are treated in society as an oppressed minority.

Mixed economy An economic system that contains elements of both capitalism and socialism.

Modernization The form of social change that

involves the transformation of an agricultural society into an industrial one.

Modernization theory The theory that contact with rich nations can enrich poor ones but lack of contact keeps them poor.

Monogamy The marriage of one man to one woman.

Monopoly The situation in which one firm controls the output of an industry.

Mores "Strong" norms that specify normal behavior and constitute demands, not just expectations.

Multiculturalism A state in which all subcultures are equal to one another in the same society.

Multinational corporations Corporations that have subsidiaries in many countries.

Multiple nuclei theory The model of land use in which a city is built around many discrete nuclei, each being the center of some specialized activity.

Negative imprinting A biological mechanism that suppresses erotic feelings for individuals with whom one has been familiar since early childhood.

Neocolonialism The economic control exercised by rich nations over their former colonies.

Neolocal residence The home where the married couple live by themselves, away from both husband's and wife's families.

Neurosis The mental disorder characterized by a persistent fear, anxiety, or worry about trivial matters.

Nonconformist subculture The college subculture that advocates rebellion from conventional society.

Nonmaterial culture The intangible aspect of culture.

Norm A social rule that specifies how people should behave.

Normal science Kuhn's term for routine research.

Normative theories Theories that suggest what we *should* do to achieve our goals.

Nuclear family The family that consists of two parents and their unmarried children.

Objective method The method of identifying social classes by using occupation, income, and education to rank people.

Oligopoly The situation in which a very few companies control the output of an industry.

Operational definition A specification of the action needed to translate what is basically unobservable into what can be observed and measured.

Operational liberals U.S. citizens who, in effect, support big government by backing government programs that render service to the public.

Opinion leader A person whose opinion is respected by others and influences them.

Oppositional interaction The interaction in which the participants treat each other as competitors or enemies.

Organic solidarity A type of social cohesion that arises when people in a society perform a wide variety of specialized jobs and therefore have to depend on one another.

Organic solidarity Social unity that arises from people being forced to depend on one another because their jobs are very specialized.

Organized skepticism The norm that requires scientists to be critical of any scientific idea or finding.

Out-group The group of which an individual is not a member.

PACs Political organizations that funnel money from business, labor, and other special-interest groups into election campaigns to help elect or defeat candidates.

Panic A type of collective behavior characterized by a maladaptive, fruitless response to a serious threat.

Paradigm A model for defining, studying, and solving problems in accordance with certain basic assumptions.

Parkinson's Law The observation that "work expands to fill the time available for its completion."

Participant observation A method of observation in which the researcher takes part in the activities of the group being studied.

Pastoral society A society that domesticates and herds animals as its primary source of food.

Patriarchal family The family in which the dominant figure is the eldest male.

Patriarchy A system of domination in which men exercise power over women.

Patrilineal descent The norm that recognizes only the father's family as a child's close relatives.

Patrilocal residence The home where the married couple live with the husband's family.

Peer group A group whose members are about the same age and have similar interests.

Peripheral countries The world's lower class, relatively poor societies, popularly known as developing countries.

Personality A fairly stable configuration of feelings, attitudes, ideas, and behaviors that characterizes an individual.

Peter Principle The observation that "in a hierarchy every employee tends to rise to their level of incompetence."

Political party A group organized for the purpose of gaining government offices.

Political power The capacity to use the government

to make decisions that affect the whole society.

Political socialization A learning process by which individuals acquire political knowledge, beliefs, and attitudes.

Politics The type of human interaction that involves some people acquiring and exercising power over others.

Polyandry The marriage of one woman to two or more men.

Polygamy The marriage of one person to two or more people of the opposite sex.

Polygyny The marriage of one man to two or more women.

Polytheism The belief in more than one god.

Popular culture A collection of relatively unsophisticated artistic creations that appeal to the masses of a society.

Population The entire group of people to be studied.

Pornography Sexually explicit materials in the media.

Postconventional morality Kohlberg's term for the practice of judging actions by taking into account the importance of *conflicting norms.*

Postindustrial society A society that produces food for subsistence primarily by using high technology.

Power The ability to control the behavior of others, even against their will.

Power The ability to get people to do things they otherwise would not do.

Power elite A small group of individuals who hold top positions in the federal government, military, and corporations and have similar backgrounds, values, and interests.

Preconventional morality Kohlberg's term for the practice of defining right and wrong according to the *consequence* of the action being judged.

Prejudice A negative attitude toward a certain category of people.

Premarital sex Sex before marriage.

Prescribed role A set of expectations about how a person with a particular status should behave.

Primary deviance Norm violations that a person commits for the first time and without considering them deviant.

Primary group A group whose members interact informally, relate to each other as whole persons, and enjoy their relationship for its own sake.

Principle of immanent change The notion that social change is the product of the social forces that exist within a society.

Propaganda Communication tailored to influence opinion.

Prostitution The exchange of sex for money.

Proxemics The use of space as a means of communication.

Psychosis The mental disorder typified by loss of touch with reality.

Public A dispersed collection of people who share a particular interest or concern.

Public opinion The collection of ideas and attitudes shared by the members of a particular public.

Pygmalion effect The impact of a teacher's expectations on student performance.

Race A group of people who are perceived by a given society to be biologically different from others.

Racism The belief that one's own race or ethnicity is superior to that of others.

Random sample A sample drawn in such a way that all members of the population had an equal chance of being selected.

Rape Basically coercive sex, involving the use of force to get someone to do something sexual against their will.

Rationalization Weber's term for the process of replacing the subjective, spontaneous, informal, or diverse ways of doing things with a planned, formally unified method based on abstract rules.

Reality construction The process by which we interpret what a given action means and respond to it in accordance with the interpretation.

Recidivism Repeated commission of crimes.

Reference group A group that is used as the frame of reference for evaluating one's own behavior.

Reindustrialization The proliferation of unstable, low-skilled, or low-paying jobs.

Reintegrative shaming Making wrongdoers feel guilty while showing them understanding, forgiveness, or even respect.

Relative deprivation Feeling unable to achieve a relatively high aspiration.

Relative poverty A state of deprivation resulting from having less than what the majority of the people have.

Reliability The extent to which a study produces the same findings when repeated by the original or other researchers; popularly known as "consistency".

Religion A unified system of beliefs and practices regarding sacred things that unites its adherents into a single moral community.

Reputational method The method of identifying social classes by selecting a group of people and asking them to rank others.

Resocialization The process by which people are forced to abandon their old self and to develop a new self in its place.

Resource mobilization theory The theory that social movements result from the availability of resources for mobilization.

Revolution The violent overthrow of an existing government and drastic change in the social and political order.

Ritual A ceremonial form of religious activity.

Role A set of expectations of what individuals should do in accordance with their particular status.

Role conflict Conflict between two roles being played simultaneously.

Role distance Separating the role-playing as outward performance from the inner self.

Role performance Actual performance of a role.

Role strain Stress caused by conflicting expectations from a role.

Roleless role Being assigned no role in society's division of labor, a predicament of the elderly in industrial society.

Rumor An unverified story that is spread from one person to another.

Sacred Whatever transcends the everyday world and inspires awe and reverence.

Sample A relatively small number of people selected from a larger population.

Sanction A reward for conformity to norms, or punishment for violation of norms.

Scapegoating Blaming others for one's own failure.

Science A body of knowledge developed through systematic observation.

Scientific revolution Kuhn's term for the replacement of an old paradigm by a new one.

Second economy A free market operating within and parallel to the state-controlled, command economy.

Secondary analysis Searching for new knowledge by analyzing mostly quantitative data that have been collected by somebody else such as another researcher or some public agency.

Secondary deviance Repeated norm violations that the violators themselves recognize as deviant.

Secondary group A group whose members interact formally, relate to each other as players of particular roles, and expect to profit from each other.

Sect A relatively small religious group that sets itself apart from society and makes heavy demands on its members.

Sector theory The model of land use in which a city grows outward in wedge-shaped sectors from the center.

Semiperipheral countries The world's middle class, relatively affluent societies in the middle of global stratification, also known as newly industrialized countries.

Senescence The natural physical process of aging.

Senility An abnormal condition characterized by serious memory loss, confusion, and loss of the ability to reason.

Sensate culture Sorokin's term for the culture that stresses empirical evidence or science as the key to knowledge and urges people to favor a prac-

tical, materialistic, and hedonistic way of life.

Serial monogamy The marriage of one person to two or more people but one at a time.

Sex drive A biological potential for, rather than a determinant of, sexual desire or action.

Sex instinct An innate biological mechanism that causes its carrier to have sex in a certain way and at a certain time only.

Sex ratio The number of males per 100 females.

Sexism Prejudice and discrimination based on the victim's gender.

Sexual harassment An unwelcome act of a sexual nature.

Shamanism The belief that a spiritual leader can communicate with the spirits by acting as their mouthpiece or letting the soul leave the leader's body and enter the spiritual world.

Sick role A set of social expectations regarding how an ill person should behave.

Significant others Mead's term for people who have close ties to the child and exert a strong influence on the child.

Social aggregate A number of people who happen to be in one place but who do not interact with one another.

Social category A number of people who have something in common but neither interact with one another nor gather in one place.

Social change The alteration of society over time.

Social class A category of people who have about the same amount of income, power, and prestige.

Social consensus Condition in which most members of society agree on what is good for everybody to have and cooperate to achieve it.

Social construction of reality The process by which people create through social interaction a certain idea, feeling, or belief about their environment.

Social contagion The spreading of a certain emotion and action from one member of a crowd to another.

Social control The process by which individuals are pressured by society to conform to social norms.

Social forces Forces that arise from the society of which we are a part.

Social group A collection of people who interact with one another and have a certain feeling of unity.

Social institution A set of widely shared beliefs, norms, or procedures necessary for meeting the basic needs of society.

Social integration The degree to which people are tied to a social group.

Social interaction The process by which individuals act toward and react to others.

Social marginality Being excluded from mainstream society.

Social mobility Movement from one social standing to another.

Social movement A conscious effort to bring about or prevent change.

Social network A web of social relationships that link individuals or groups to one another.

Social stratification The division of society in such a way that some people get more rewards than others.

Socialism An economic system based on public ownership and government control of the economy.

Socialization The process by which a society transmits its cultural values to its members.

Society A collection of interacting individuals sharing the same culture and territory.

Sociobiology A new Darwinian theory that human behavior is genetically determined.

Sociocultural evolution The process of changing from a technologically simple society to a more complex one with significant consequences for social and cultural life.

Sociological imagination C. Wright Mills's term for the ability to see the impact of social forces on individuals, especially on their private lives.

Sociology The systematic, mostly scientific study of human society.

Spurious correlation The appearance of a correlation between two variables that are not causally related.

State A political institution that regulates conflict and allocates resources among the citizens of a country.

Status A position in society.

Status inconsistency The condition in which the same individual is given different rankings, such as being high in occupation but low in ethnicity.

Status inconsistency The experience of having two contradictory statuses.

Status system A system in which people are stratified according to their social prestige.

Stereotype An oversimplified, inaccurate mental picture of others.

Structural assimilation The social condition in which the minority is accepted on equal terms with the rest of society.

Structural mobility Social mobility related to changes in society.

Structured interview An interview in which the researcher asks standardized questions that require respondents to choose from among several standardized answers.

Subcultural theory The theory that the city enriches people's lives by offering diverse opportunities and developing various subcultures.

Subculture A culture within a larger culture.

Subculture theory The theory that the elderly interact mostly with one another, sharing interests and experiences with members of the same age group.

Subjective method The method of identifying social classes by asking people to rank themselves.

Subordinate status The opposite of master status.

Superego Freud's term for the part of personality that is moral, popularly known as conscience.

Supportive interaction The interaction in which the participants treat each other as supporters or friends.

Survey A research method that involves asking questions about opinions, beliefs, or behavior.

Symbol A word, gesture, music, or anything that stands for some other thing.

Symbolic interactionist perspective A theoretical perspective that directs our attention to the details of a specific situation and of the interaction between individuals in that situation.

Technology Any kind of tool or practical know-how, but also the practical application of scientific principles.

Theism The type of religion that centers on the worship of a god or gods.

Theoretical perspective A set of general assumptions about the nature of society.

Theory A set of logically related hypotheses that explains the relationship among various phenomena.

Third variable A hidden variable responsible for the occurrence of a relation between two other variables that are not causally related.

Thomas theorem Sociologist W.I. Thomas' famous pronouncement that "If people define situations as real, they are real in their consequences".

Total institutions Places where people are not only cut off from the larger society but also rigidly controlled by the administrators.

Totemism The belief that a kinship exists between humans and an animal or, less commonly, a plant.

Tracking The system of sorting students into different groups according to ability.

Trade deficit Buying more goods and services from foreign countries than selling to them.

Trade surplus Selling more goods and services to foreign countries than buying from them.

Universalism The norm that requires scientists to evaluate ideas or findings in accordance with impersonal criteria.

Unstructured interview An interview in which open-ended questions are asked and the respondent is allowed to answer freely in the respondent's own words.

Urban anomie theory The theory that city people have a unique way of life, characterized by alienation, impersonal relations, and stress.

Urban ecology The study of the relationship between people and their urban environment.

Urban society Redfield's term for societies that are large, literate, and heterogeneous, with little group solidarity.

Urbanization Migration of people from the countryside to city, increasing the proportion of the population that lives in the city.

Validity The characteristic of a study measuring what it is supposed to measure—popularly known as accuracy.

Value A socially shared idea about what is good, desirable, or important.

Variable A characteristic that varies from people to people within the population being studied.

Variant subculture A subculture that merely differs from the dominant culture in some way.

Verstehen Weber's term for empathetic understanding of sociologists' subjects.

Vertical mobility Moving up or down the status ladder.

Vital statistics Information about births, marriages, deaths, and migrations into and out of a country.

Vocational subculture The college subculture that emphasizes hard work in order to get good jobs after graduation.

White ethnicss Americans of eastern and southern European origins.

Women's ghettos Traditionally female occupations that are subordinate to positions usually held by men.

World system A network of commercial and other relationships among all the members of the world's community.

References

Abramovitz, Mimi, and Frances Fox Piven. 1994. "Scapegoating women on welfare." *New York Times,* September 2, p. A13.

Acton, H. B. 1967. *What Marx Really Said.* New York: Schocken.

Ainsworth, Martha. 1984. "Population policy: Country experience." *Finance & Development,* 21, pp. 18–20.

Alba, Richard D. 1990. *Ethnic Identity: The Transformation of White America.* New Haven, Conn.: Yale University Press.

Aldrich, Howard E. 1992. "Incommensurable paradigms? Vital signs from three perspectives." In Michael Reed and Michael Hughes (eds.), *Rethinking Organization: New Directions in Organization Theory and Analysis.* Newbury Park, Calif.: Sage.

Alexander, Karl L., and Martha A. Cook. 1982. "Curricula and coursework: A surprise ending to a familiar story." *American Sociological Review,* 47, pp. 626–640.

Allis, Sam. 1990. "Schooling kids at home." *Time,* October 22, pp. 84–86.

Alonso, William. 1964. "The historic and the structural theories of urban form: Their implications for urban renewal." *Journal of Land Economics,* 40, pp. 227–231.

Alter, Jonathan. 1995. "Decoding the contract." *Newsweek,* January 9, pp. 26–27.

Altman, Lawrence K. 1990. "Changes in medicine bring pain to healing profession." *New York Times,* February 18, pp. 1, 20–21.

Ames, Katrine. 1990. "Our bodies, their selves." *Newsweek,* December 17, p. 60.

Andersen, Margaret L. 1993. *Thinking About Women,* 3rd ed. New York: Macmillan.

Anderson, David C. 1994. "The crime funnel." *New York Times Magazine,* June 12, pp. 57–58.

Angelopoulos, Angelos, and Melvin Fagen. 1993. *The Third World and the Rich Countries.* Lanham, MD: University Press of America.

Archer, Margaret S. 1985. "The myth of cultural integration." *British Journal of Sociology,* 36, pp. 333–353.

Aronoff, Joel, and William D. Crano. 1975. "A re-examination of the cross-cultural principles of task segregation and sex role differentiation in the family." *American Sociological Review,* 40, pp. 12–20.

Asch, Solomon E. 1955. "Opinions and social pressure." *Scientific American,* 193, pp. 31–35.

Ashe, Arthur. 1977. "An open letter to black parents: Send your children to the libraries." *New York Times,* February 6, section 5, p. 2.

———. 1992. "A zero-sum game that hurts blacks." *New York Times,* February 27, p. A10.

Atchley, Robert C. 1988. *Social Forces and Aging,* 5th ed. Belmont, Calif.: Wadsworth.

Auerbach, Alan J. 1983. "Welfare aspects of current U.S. corporate taxation." *American Economic Review Papers and Proceedings,* 73, pp. 76–81.

Azmitia, Margarita. 1988. "Peer interaction and problem solving: When are two hands better than one?" *Child Development,* 59, pp. 87–96.

Babbie, Earl R. 1995. *The Practice of Social Research,* 7th ed. Belmont, Calif.: Wadsworth.

Bacon, Kenneth H. 1990. "Many educators view involved parents as key to children's success in school." *Wall Street Journal,* July 31, p. B1.

Bailey, J. Michael, and Richard C. Pillard. 1991. "A genetic study of male sexual orientation." *Archives of General Psychiatry,* 48, pp. 1089–1096.

Bailey, J. Michael et al. 1993. "Heritable factors influence sexual orientation in women." *Archives of General Psychiatry,* 50, pp. 217–223.

Bailey, Kenneth D. 1994. *Methods for Social Research,* 4th ed. New York: Free Press.

Balkan, Sheila, Ronald J. Berger, and Janet Schmidt. 1980. *Crime and Deviance in America: A Critical Approach.* Belmont, Calif.: Wadsworth.

Baltzell, E. Digby. 1991. *The Protestant Establishment Revisited.* New Brunswick, N.J.: Transaction.

———. 1994. *Judgment and Sensibility: Religion and Stratification.* New Brunswick, N.J.: Transaction.

Bane, Mary Jo, and David T. Ellwood. 1994. *Welfare Realities: From Rhetoric to Reform.* Cambridge, Mass.: Harvard University Press.

Banfield, Edward C. 1974. *The Unheavenly City Revisited.* Boston: Little, Brown.

Barker, Eileen. 1984. *The Making of a Moonie.* New York: Basil Blackwell.

Barlett, Donald L., and James B. Steele. 1992. *America: What Went Wrong?* Kansas City: Andrews and McMeel.

Barringer, Felicity. 1989. "Doubt on 'trial marriage' raised by divorce rates." *New York Times,* June 9, pp. 1, 23.

Barringer, Felicity. 1991b. "Population grows in state capitals." *New York Times,* January 26, pp. 1, 10.

Bartley, Robert L. 1991. "Beyond the recession." *Wall Street Journal,* January 2, p. A6.

Basow, Susan A. 1986. *Sex-Role Stereotypes.* Monterey, Calif.: Brooks/Cole.

Baum, Alice S., and Donald W. Burnes. 1993. *A Nation in Denial: The Truth about Homelessness.* Boulder, Colo.: Westview.

Becerra, Rosina. 1988. "The Mexican American family." In Charles Mindel et al. (eds.), *Ethnic Families in America: Patterns and Variations,* 3rd ed. New York: Elsevier.

Beck, E. M., and Stewart E. Tolnay. 1990. "The killing fields of the deep South: The market for cotton and the lynching of blacks, 1882–1930." *American Sociological Review,* 55, pp. 526–539.

Beck, Melinda. 1990a. "Trading places." *Newsweek,* July 16, pp. 48–54.

———. 1990b. "The politics of cancer." *Newsweek,* December 10, pp. 62–65.

Becker, George. 1984. "Pietism and science: A critique of Robert K. Merton's hypothesis." *American Journal of Sociology,* 89, pp. 1065–1090.

Becker, Howard S. 1963. *Outsiders.* New York: Free Press.

———. 1982. "Culture: A sociological view." *The Yale Review,* 71, pp. 513–527.

———, et al. 1961. *Boys in White: Student Culture in Medical School.* Chicago: University of Chicago Press.

Begley, Sharon. 1990. "The search for the fountain of youth." *Newsweek,* March 5, pp. 44–48.

Beirne, Piers, and James Messerschmidt. 1995. *Criminology,* 2nd ed. San Diego: Harcourt Brace Jovanovich.

Belkin, Lisa. 1990. "Many in medicine are calling rules a professional malaise." *New York Times,* February 19, pp. A1, A9.

Bellah, Robert N., et al. 1986. *Habits of the Heart: Individualism and Commitment in American Life.* New York: Harper & Row.

Benderly, Beryl Lieff. 1989. "Don't believe everything you read … " *Psychology Today,* November, pp. 67–69.

Bendix, Reinhard. 1962. *Max Weber: An Intellectual Portrait.* Garden City, N.Y.: Anchor.

Benjamin, Daniel, et al. 1992. "Shock of reform." *Time,* February 17, pp. 38–40.

Bennett, Stephen Earl, and David Resnick. 1990. "The implications of nonvoting for democracy in the United States." *American Journal of Political Science,* 34, pp. 771–802.

Bennett, William J. 1989. "A response to Milton Friedman." *Wall Street Journal,* September 19, p. A32.

Bennis, Warren. 1989. "The dilemma at the top." *New York Times,* December 31, p. F3.

Benson, Michael L. 1985. "Denying the guilty mind: Accounting for involvement in a white-collar crime." *Criminology,* 23, p. 594.

Bercovitch, Sarcan. 1978. *The American Jeremiad.* Madison: University of Wisconsin Press.

Berger, Bennett M. 1971. *Working-Class Suburb: A Study of Auto Workers in Suburbia.* Berkeley: University of California Press.

Berger, Peter L. 1992. "Sociology: A disinvitation?" *Society,* November/December, pp. 12–18.

Berke, Richard L. 1990. "Lawmakers accept PAC money while urging finance changes." *New York Times,* September 25, pp. A1, A12.

Bernstein, Richard. 1990. "In U.S. schools a war of words." *New York Times Magazine,* October 14, pp. 34, 48–52.

Berrill, Kevin T. 1992. "Anti-gay violence and victimization in the United States: An overview." In Gregory M. Herek and Kevin T. Berrill, eds., *Hate Crime.* Newbury Park, Calif.: Sage.

Besharov, Douglas J. 1994. "Orphanages aren't welfare reform." *New York Times,* December 20, p. A19.

Beyer, Lisa. 1990. "Lifting the veil." *Time,* September 24, pp. 38–44.

Biggart, Nicole Woolsey. 1994. "Labor and Leisure." In Neil J. Smelser and Richard Swedberg (eds.), *The Handbook of Economic Sociology.* Princeton, N.J.: Princeton University Press.

Bilheimer Robert S. (ed.). 1983. *Faith and Ferment: An Interdisciplinary Study of Christian Beliefs and Practices.* Minneapolis, Minn.: Augsburg.

Billingsley, Andrew. 1993. *Climbing Jacob's Ladder: The Enduring Legacy of African-American Families.* New York: Simon & Schuster.

Bishop, Jery E. 1993. "Research points toward a 'gay' gene." *Wall Street Journal,* July 16, pp. B1, B4.

Black, Donald. 1983. "Crime as social control." *American Sociological Review,* 48, pp. 34–45.

Blakeslee, Sandra. 1989. "Race and sex are found to affect access to kidney transplants." *New York Times,* January 24, pp. 19, 23.

Blalock, Hubert M. 1984. *Basic Dilemmas in the Social Sciences.* Beverly Hills, CA: Sage.

Blau, Peter M., and Otis Dudley Duncan. 1967. *The American Occupational Structure.* New York: Wiley.
Bloom, Harold. 1992. *The American Religion: The Emergence of the Post-Christian Nation.* New York: Simon & Schuster.

Blumenfeld, Warren J., and Diane Raymond. 1993. *Looking at Gay and Lesbian Life.* Boston: Beacon.

Blumer, Herbert. 1978. "Elementary collective groupings," in Louis E. Genevie (ed.), *Collective Behavior and Social Movements.* Itasca, Ill.: Peacock.

Blumstein, Philip, and Pepper Schwartz. 1983. *American Couples: Money, Work, and Sex.* New York: Morrow.

Blundell, William E. 1986. "Gripe session." *Wall Street Journal,* May 9, pp. 1, 9.

——. 1987. "When the patient takes charge." *Wall Street Journal,* April 24, pp. 5D–6D.

Borger, Gloria. 1990. "Out of order!" *U.S., News & World Report,* October 22, pp. 28–32.

Bornstein, Marc H. et al. 1991. "Parenting in cross-cultural perspective: The United States, France, and Japan." Pp. 69–90 in Marc H. Bornstein (ed.), *Cultural Approaches to Parenting.* Hillsdale, N.J.: Lawrence Erlbaum Associates.

Bossard, James. 1932. "Residential propinquity as a factor in marriage selection." *American Journal of Sociology,* 38, pp. 219–244.

Boudon, Raymond. 1983a. "Individual action and social change: A no-theory of social change." *British Journal of Sociology,* 34, pp. 1–18.

——. 1983b. "Why theories of social change fail: Some methodological thoughts." *Public Opinion Quarterly,* 47, pp. 143–160.

Bowles, Samuel, and Herbert Gintis. 1976. *Schooling in Capitalist America.* New York: Basic Books.

Box, Steven. 1983. *Power, Crime, and Mystification.* London: Tavistock.

Boyd, Monica, Mary Ann Mulvihill, and John Myles. 1991. "Gender, power and postindustrialism." *Canadian Review of Sociology & Anthropology,* 28, pp. 407–436.

Bradburd, Daniel. 1982. "Volatility of animal wealth among Southwest Asian pastoralists." *Human Ecology,* 10, pp. 85–106.

Bradshaw, York W. 1987. "Urbanization and underdevelopment: A global study of modernization, urban bias, and economic dependency." *American Sociological Review,* 52, pp. 224–239.

Braithwaite, John. 1981. 1989. *Crime, Shame and Reintegration.* New York: Cambridge University Press.

Brenner, Harvey. 1976. *Hearings of the Joint Congressional Economic Committee.* Washington, D.C.: U.S. Government Printing Office.

Bridges, William P., and Wayne J. Villemez. 1986. "Informal hiring and income in the labor market." *American Sociological Review,* 51, pp. 574–582.

Brinkley, Joel. 1992. "U.S. looking for a new path as superpower conflict ends." *New York Times,* February 2, pp. 1, 8.

Brinson, Susan L. 1992. "The use and opposition of rape myths in prime-time television dramas." *Sex Roles,* 27, pp. 359–375.

Broad, William J. 1990a. "Small-scale science feels the pinch from big projects." *New York Times,* September 4, pp. B5, B8.

——. 1983. *Betrayers of the Truth.* New York: Simon & Schuster.

Brock, Fred. 1993. "Belgium: Keeping spending high and guaranteeing jobs." *New York Times,* December 9, p. A8.

Brody, Jane E. 1992. "Personal health." *New York Times,* March 18, p. B8.

Brooke, James. 1995. "Higher growth seen for Latin America." *New York Times,* January 3, p. C10.

Brookhiser, Richard. 1991. *The Way of the WASP: How It Made America, and How It Can Save It, So to Speak.* New York: Free Press.

Brown, Roger. 1965. *Social Psychology.* New York: Free Press.

Buford, Bill. 1992. *Among the Thugs.* New York: Norton.

Buller, Mary Klein, and David B. Buller. 1987. "Physicians' communication style and patient satisfaction." *Journal of Health and Social Behavior,* 28, pp. 275–388.

Bumpass, Larry, and James Sweet. 1989. "National estimates of cohabitation." *Demography,* 26, pp. 615–625.

Burgess, Ernest W. 1967/1925. "The growth of the city: An introduction to a research project," in R. E. Park, E. W. Burgess, and R. D. McKenzie (eds.), *The City.* Chicago: University of Chicago Press.

Burke, Ronald J., and Tamara Weir. 1976. "Relationship of wives' employment status to husband, wife, and pair satisfaction and performance." *Journal of Marriage and the Family,* 38, pp. 279–287.

Burt, Ronald S. 1983. "Corporate philanthropy as a cooptive relation." *Social Forces,* 62, pp. 419–449.

Burtless, Gary. 1990. "It's better than watching Oprah." *Wall Street Journal,* January 4, p. A14.

Butler, Robert. 1984. Interviewed in *U.S. News & World Report,* July 2, pp. 51–52.

Campbell, Anne. 1993. *Men, Women, and Aggression.* New York: Basic Books.

Cantril, Hadley, with Hazel Gaudet and Herta Herzog. 1982/1940. *The Invasion from Mars.* Princeton, N.J.: Princeton University Press.

Capron, Alexander Morgan. 1990. "The burden of decision." *Hastings Center Report,* May/June, pp. 36–41.

Carlson, Eugene. 1991. "Impact of zones for enterprise is ambiguous." *Wall Street Journal,* April 1, pp. B1, B2.

Carmody, Deirdre. 1989. "Teachers taking more pride in profession, survey finds." *New York Times,* September 22, pp. 9, 13.

———. 1990. "Identity crisis for 'Seven Sisters.'" *New York Times,* August 6, p. C1.

Carnoy, Martin, and Henry M. Levin. 1985. *Schooling and Work in the Democratic State.* Stanford, Calif.: Stanford University Press.

Carpenter, Betsy. 1990. "Living with our legacy." *U.S. News & World Report,* April 23, pp. 60–65.

Casper, Lynne M., Sara S. McLanahan, and Irwin Garfinkel. 1994. "The gender-gap: What we can learn from other countries." *American Sociological Review,* 59, pp. 594–605.

Castro, Janice. 1993. "Disposable workers." *Time,* March 29, pp. 43–47.

Celis, William 3rd. 1993a. "International report card shows U.S. schools work." *New York Times,* December 9, pp. A1, A8.

———. 1993b. "Study suggests Head Start helps beyond school." *New York Times,* April 30, p. A11.

Census Bureau. 1994. *Statistical Abstract of the United States.* Washington, D.C.: Government Printing Press.

Chaefetz, Janet Saltzman. 1984. *Sex and Advantage: A Comparative, Macro-Structural Theory of Sex Stratification.* Totowa, N.J.: Rowman & Allanheld.

Chambliss, William J. 1969. *Crime and the Legal Process.* New York: McGraw-Hill.

Charon, Joel M. 1992. *Symbolic Interactionism,* 4th ed. Englewood Cliffs, N.J.: Prentice-Hall.

Cherlin, Andrew J. 1992. *Marriage, Divorce, Remarriage.* Cambridge, Mass: Harvard University Press.

———, and Frank F. Furstenberg, Jr. 1983. "The American family in the year 2000." *Futurist,* 18, June, pp. 7–14.

———, and Frank F. Furstenberg, Jr. 1994. "Stepfamilies in the United States: A reconsideration." *Annual Review of Sociology,* 20, pp. 359–381.

Chideya, Faria, et al. 1993. "Endangered family." *Newsweek,* August 30, pp. 17–27.

Childe, Gordon. 1952. *Man Makes Himself.* New York: New American Library.

Chilman, Catherine Street. 1993. "Hispanic families in the United States: Research perspectives." In Harriette Pipes McAdoo (ed.), *Family Ethnicity: Strength in Diversity.* Newbury Park, Calif.: Sage.

Chipello, Christopher J., and Neal Templin. 1992. "Two worlds: Work ethic aside, some U.S. employees still live very well." *Wall Street Journal,* February 24, pp. A1, A10.

Chira, Susan. 1990. "Efforts to reshape teaching focus on finding new talent." *New York Times,* August 28, pp. A1, A14.

Chomsky, Noam. 1993. *The Prosperous Few and the Restless Many.* Berkely, CA: Odonian.

Christopher, Robert C. 1983. *The Japanese Mind: The Goliath Explained.* New York: Linden/Simon & Schuster.

Chubb, John E., and Terry M. Moe. 1990. *Politics, Markets, and America's Schools.* Washington, D.C.: Brookings Institution.

Clairmonte, Frederick F., and John H. Cavanagh. 1983. "Transnational corporations and the struggle for the global market." *Journal of Contemporary Asia,* 13, pp. 446–480.

Clark, Burton R., and Martin Trow. 1966. "The organizational context," in Theodore M. Newcomb and Everett K. Wilson (eds.), *College Peer Groups.* Chicago: Aldine.

Clark, Kenneth B., and Mamie P. Clark. 1947. "Racial identification and preferences in Negro children," in Theodore M. Newcomb and Eugene L. Harley (eds.), *Readings in Social Psychology.* New York: Holt, Rinehart and Winston.

Clark, Lindley H., Jr. 1990. "U.S. unions did too well for themselves." *Wall Street Journal,* June 13, p. A14.

Close, Ellis. 1993. *The Rage of a Privileged Class.* New York: HarperCollins.

Clymer, Adam. 1992. "Turnout on election day '92 was the largest in 24 years." *New York Times,* December 17, 1992, p. A13.

Cockerham, William C. 1995. *Medical Sociology,* 6th ed. Englewood Cliffs, N.J.: Prentice-Hall.

Cohen, Arthur M., and Florence B. Brawer. 1982. "The community college as college." *Change,* March, pp. 39–42.

Coleman, James S. 1961. *The Adolescent Society.* Glencoe, Ill.: Free Press.

———, Thomas Hoffer, and Sally Kilgore. 1982a. "Cognitive outcomes in public and private schools." *Sociology of Education,* 55, pp. 65–76.

———, Thomas Hoffer, and Sally Kilgore. 1982b. *High School Achievement: Public, Catholic, and Private Schools Compared.* New York: Basic Books.

Coleman, James William, and Donald R. Cressey. 1993. *Social Problems,* 5th ed. New York: HarperCollins.

Collins, Randall. 1975. *Conflict Sociology.* New York: Academic Press.

———. 1986. "Is 1980s sociology in the doldrums?" *American Journal of Sociology,* 91, pp. 1336-1355.

———, and Sal Restivo. 1983. "Robber barons and politicians in mathematics: A conflict model of science." *Canadian Journal of Sociology,* 8, pp. 199–227.

Commoner, Barry. 1990. *Making Peace with the Planet.* New York: Pantheon.

Conrad, Peter, and Rochelle Kern (eds.). 1995. *Sociology of Health and Illness: Critical Perspectives,* 4th ed. New York: St. Martin's.

Cooley, Charles H. 1909. *Social Organization.* New York: Scribner's.

Cooper, Kristina, et al. 1986. "Correlates of mood and marital satisfaction among dual-worker and single-worker couples." *Social Psychology Quarterly,* 49, pp. 322–329.

Corliss, Richard. 1993. "A few good women." *Time,* April 15, pp. 58–59.

Corsaro, William A., and Donna Eder. 1990. "Children's peer cultures." *Annual Review of Sociology,* 16, pp. 197–220.

Cory, Christopher T. 1979. "Women smile less for success." *Psychology Today,* March, p. 16.

Coverman, Shelley. 1989. "Role overload, role conflict, and stress: Addressing consequences of multiple role demands." *Social Forces,* 67, pp. 965–982.

Cowgill, Donald O. 1974. "Aging and modernization: A revision of the theory," in J. F. Gubrium (ed.). *Late Life: Communities and Environmental Policy.* Springfield, Ill.: Thomas.

Cowley, Geoffrey. 1988. "The wisdom of animals." *Newsweek,* May 23, pp. 52–59.

Cox, Harvey. 1966. *The Secular City.* New York: Macmillan.

Cramer, Jerome. 1989. "Where did the gung-ho go?" *Time,* September 11, pp. 52–56.

Crispell, Diane. 1990. "Workers in 2000." *American Demographics,* March, pp. 36–40.

Crossen, Cynthia. 1991. "Kids acting up? Don't yell, validate their tiny feelings." *Wall Street Journal,* December 10, pp. A1, A4.

Crossette, Barbara. 1990. "India to shake up birth-control bureaucracy." *New York Times,* March 14, p. A4.

Crovitz, L. Gordon. 1991. "How Bush outflanked Iraq and liberated the Constitution." *Wall Street Journal,* March 6, p. A9.

Cullingford, Cedric. 1993. "Children's social and moral claims." *Society,* November/December, pp. 52–54.

Cumming, and William E. Henry. 1961. *Growing Old: The Process of Disengagement.* New York: Basic Books.

Cumming, Elaine. 1963. "Further thoughts on the theory of disengagement." *International Social Science,* 15, pp. 377–393.

Currie, Elliott. 1993. *Reckoning: Drugs, the Cities, and the American Future.* New York: Hill and Wang.

Curtin, Philip D., et al. 1978. *African History.* Boston: Little, Brown.

Dahl, Robert A. 1981. *Democracy in the United States: Promise and Performance,* 4th ed. Boston: Houghton Mifflin.

Darnton, John. 1994a. "In decolonized, destitute Africa bankers are the new overlords." *New York Times,* June 20, pp. A1, A6–7.

——. 1994b. "'Lost decade' drains Africa's vitality." *New York Times,* June 19, pp. 1, 5.

Davis, Bernard D. 1990. "Right to die: Living wills are inadequate." *Wall Street Journal,* July 31, p. A12.

Davis, James F. 1991. *Who Is Black?: One Nation's Definition.* University Park, Penna.: Pennsylvania State University Press.

Davis, James. 1982. "Up and down opportunity's ladder." *Public Opinion,* June/July, pp. 11–15, 48–51.

Davis, Kingsley. 1947. "Final note on a case of extreme isolation." *American Journal of Sociology,* 52, pp. 432–437.

——. 1949. *Human Society.* New York: Macmillan.

——. 1955. "The origin and growth of urbanization in the world." *American Journal of Sociology,* 60, pp. 429–437.

——. 1971. "Sexual behavior." In Robert Merton and Robert Nisbet, (eds.), *Contemporary Social Problems,* 3rd ed. New York: Harcourt Brace Jovanovich.

——. 1976. "The world's population crises," in Robert K. Merton and Robert Nisbet (eds.), *Contemporary Social Problems,* 4th ed. New York: Harcourt Brace Jovanovich.

——, and Wilbert E. Moore. 1945. "Some principles of stratification." *American Sociological Review,* 10, pp. 242–249.

Davis, Murray S. 1993. *What's So Funny? The Comic Conception of Culture and Society.* Chicago: University of Chicago Press.

Day, Kathleen, and Meda Chesney-Lind. 1988. "Feminism and criminology." *Justice Quarterly,* 5, pp. 101–143.

Decker, David L. 1980. *Social Gerontology.* Boston: Little, Brown.

Deegan, Mary Jo. 1988. *Jane Addams and the Men of Chicago School.* New Brunswick, N.J.: Transaction.

Delphy, Christine, and Diana Leonard, 1992. *Familiar Exploitation: A New Analysis of Marriage in Contemporary Western Societies.* Cambridge, U.K.: Polity Press.

Denton, Nancy A., and Douglas S. Massey. 1989. "Racial identity among Caribbean Hispanics: The effect of double minority status on residential segregation." *American Sociological Review,* 54, pp. 790–808.

Dentzer, Susan. 1991. "The graying of Japan." *U.S. News & World Report,* September 30, pp. 65–73.

DeParle, Jason. 1994. "Report to Clinton sees vast extent of homelessness." *New York Times,* February 17, pp. A1, A10.

Devens, Richard M., Jr. 1984. "Employment in the first half: Robust recovery continues." *Monthly Labor Review,* 107, August, pp. 3–7.

Dickey, Christopher. 1991. "Not just a case of trying to save face." *Newsweek,* January 21, p. 22.

Diesenhouse, Susan. 1990. "More women are playing, but fewer call the shots." *New York Times,* December 11, pp. B11-B12.

Dobash, Russell P., et al. 1992. "The myth of sexual symmetry in marital violence." *Social Problems,* 39, pp. 71–91.

Domhoff, G. William. 1978. *The Powers That Be: Processes of Ruling-Class Domination in America.* New York: Random House.

——. 1983. *Who Rules America Now? A View for the Eighties.* Englewood Cliffs, N.J.: Prentice-Hall.

Dowd, Maureen. 1994. "Americans like G.O.P. agenda but split on how to reach goals." *New York Times,* December 15, pp. A1, A14.

Dowell, William. 1991. "Freedom is the best revenge." *Time,* December 16, pp. 24–29.

Drucker, Peter F. 1992. *Managing for the Future: The 1990s and Beyond.* New York: Truman Talley/Dutton.

——. 1993. *Post-Capitalist Society.* New York: HarperCollins.

Dunkle, John H., and Patricia L. Francis. 1990. "The role of facial masculinity/femininity in the attribution of homosexuality" *Sex Roles,* 23, pp. 157–167.

Durkheim, Emile. 1895/1938. *Rules of the Sociological Method.* Chicago: University of Chicago Press.

——. 1897/1951. *Suicide.* New York: Free Press.

Dutton, Diana B. 1978. "Explaining the low use of health services by the poor: Costs, attitudes, or delivery system?" *American Sociological Review,* 43, pp. 348–368.

Dychtwald, Ken. 1989. *Age Wave: The Challenges and Opportunities of an Aging America.* Los Angeles: Jeremy Tarcher.

Easterbrook, Gregg. 1987. "The revolution in medicine." *Newsweek,* January 26, pp. 40–74.

Echikson, William. 1990. *Lighting the Night: Revolution in Eastern Europe.* New York: Morrow.

Egan, Timothy. 1991. "7 Indian tribes seeking end to shackles of dependency." *New York Times,* January 16, pp. A1, A11.

Ehrlich, Anne. 1984. "Critical masses: World population 1984." *Sierra,* July/August, pp. 36–40.

Ehrlich, Paul R., Anne H. Ehrlich, and John P. Holdren. 1977. *Ecoscience: Population, Resources, Environment.* San Francisco: Freeman.

Ekerdt, David J., Raymond Bosse, and Joseph S. LoCastro. 1983. "Claims that retirement improves health." *Journal of Gerontology,* 38, pp. 231–236.

Elkin, Frederick, and Gerald Handel. 1988. *The Child and Society,* 5th ed. New York: Random House.

Elkind, David. 1992. "The future of childhood." *Psychology Today,* May/June, pp. 38–81.

Elliott, Michael, and Christopher Dickey. 1994. "Body politics: Population wars." *Newsweek,* September 12, pp. 22–27.

Ellis, Lee. 1985. "Religiosity and criminality." *Sociological Perspectives,* 28, pp. 501–520.

Ellul, Jacques. 1964. *The Technological Society.* Translated by John Wilkinson. New York: Vintage Books.

Elmer-DeWitt, Philip. 1986. "An electronic assault on privacy?" *Time,* May 19, p. 104.

——. 1991. "Why isn't our birth control better?" *Time,* August 12, pp. 52–53.

Epstein, Cynthia Fuchs. 1976. "Sex roles," in Robert K. Merton and Robert Nisbet (eds.), *Contemporary Social Problems.* New York: Harcourt Brace Jovanovich.

Erickson, Mark. 1989. "Incest avoidance and familial bonding." *Journal of Anthropological Research,* 45, pp. 267–291.

Erikson, Erik H. 1963. *Childhood and Society.* New York: Norton.

Erlanger, Steven. 1995. "Russia faces plenty of disappointment." *New York Times,* January 3, p. C10.

Espinosa, P. K. 1992. "Life in these United States." *Reader's Digest,* January, p, 68.

Etzioni, Amitai. 1975. *A Comparative Analysis of Complex Organizations,* rev. ed. New York: Free Press.

——. 1993. *The Spirit of Community: Rights, Responsibilities and the Communitarian Agenda.* New York: Crown.

Fallows, James. 1990. *More Like Us: Making America Great Again.* Boston: Houghton Mifflin.

Faludi, Susan. 1991. *Backlash: The Undeclared War Against American Women.* New York: Crown

Farley, John E. 1987. *American Social Problems: An Institutional Analysis.* Englewood Cliffs, N.J.: Prentice-Hall.

——. 1995. *Majority-Minority Relations,* 3rd ed. Englewood Cliffs, N.J.: Prentice-Hall.

Farley, Reynolds, and William H. Frey. 1994. "Changes in the segregation of whites from blacks during the 1980s: Small steps toward a more integrated society." *American Sociological Review,* 59, pp. 23–45.

Farnsworth, Clyde H. 1990. "Report by World Bank sees poverty lessening by 2000 except in Africa." *New York Times,* July 16, p. A3.

——. 1995. "Canada's momentum expected to continue." *New York Times,* January 3, p. C10.

Farran, D. C., and R. Haskins. 1980. "Reciprocal influence in the social interactions of mothers and three-year-old children from different socioeconomic backgrounds." *Child Development,* 51, pp. 780–791.

Feagin, Joe R. 1989. *Racial and Ethnic Relations,* 3rd ed. Englewood Cliffs, N.J.: Prentice-Hall.

——. 1991. "The continuing significance of race: Antiblack discrimination in public places." *American Sociological Review,* 56, pp. 101–116.

Featherman, David L., and Robert M. Hauser. 1978. *Opportunity and Change.* New York: Academic Press.

Felson, Richard B., and Mark D. Reed. 1986. "Reference groups and self-appraisals of academic ability and performance." *Social Psychology Quarterly,* 49, pp. 103–109.

Feshbach, Murray, and Alfred Friendly, Jr. 1992. *Ecocide in the U.S.S.R.* New York: Basic Books.

Filer, Randall K. 1990. "What we really know about the homeless." *Wall Street Journal,* April 10, p. 22.

Firor, John. 1990. *The Changing Atmosphere: A Global Challenge.* New Haven, Conn.: Yale University Press.

Fischer, Claude. 1984. *The Urban Experience,* 2nd ed. San Diego: Harcourt Brace Jovanovich.

Fischer, David Hackett. 1977. *Growing Old in America.* New York: Oxford University Press.

Fischman, Joshua. 1986. "What are friends for?" *Psychology Today,* September, pp. 70–71.

Fisher, Helen E. 1992. *Anatomy of Love: The Natural History of Monogamy, Adultery, and Divorce.* New York: Norton.

Fleishman, Ellen Gerschitz. 1983. "Sex-role acquisition, parental behavior, and sexual orientation: Some tentative hypotheses." *Sex Roles,* 9, pp. 1051–1059.

Florida, Richard, and Martin Kenney. 1991. "Transplanted organizations: The transfer of Japanese industrial organization to the U.S." *American Sociological Review,* 56, pp. 381–398.

Forbes. 1991. "Forbes Sales 500." April 29, pp. 75–78.

Ford, Clellan S., and Frank A. Beach. 1951. *Patterns of Sexual Behavior.* New York: Harper & Row.

Fox, John W. 1993. "The conceptualization and measurement of social mobility differences: A brief reply to Rogers and Mann." *Journal of Health and Social Behavior,* 34, pp. 173–177.

Francis, David R. 1987. "Despite concern, black Africa's population picture grows worse." *Christian Science Monitor,* November 7, p. 22.

Frankl, Razelle. 1987. *Televangelism: The Making of Popular Religion.* Carbondale: Southern Illinois University Press.

Freedman, Alix M. 1990. "Deadly diet." *Wall Street Journal,* December 18, pp. A1, A4.

Freedman, Jonathan L. 1986. "Television violence and aggression: A rejoinder." *Psychological Bulletin,* 100, pp. 372–378.

Freeman, Richard B., and James L. Medoff. 1984. *What Do Unions Do?* New York: Basic Books.

Friedman, Milton. 1989. "We have socialism, Q.E.D." *New York Times,* December 31, p. E11.

Friedman, Thomas L. 1992. "Rethinking foreign affairs: Are they still a U.S. affair?" *New York Times,* February 7, pp. A1, A7.

Fuchs, Stephan. 1993. "A sociological theory of scientific change." *Social Forces,* 71, pp. 933–953.

Fussell, Paul. 1992. *Class: A Guide Through the American Status System.* New York: Touchstone.

Futurist. 1989. "Adult education: Beyond 'night school'." January/February, pp. 43–44.

Galles, Gary M. 1989. "What colleges really teach." *New York Times,* June 8, p. 23.

Gallup, George, Jr., and Jim Castelli. 1989. *The People's Religion: American Faith in the '90s.* New York: Macmillan.

Gamson, William A. 1975. *The Strategy of Social Protest.* Homewood, Ill.: Dorsey.

Gans, Herbert J. 1968. *People and Plans.* New York: Basic Books.

——. 1971. "The uses of poverty: The poor pay all." *Social Policy,* 2, pp. 20–24.

——. 1982a. *The Urban Villagers.* New York: Free Press.

——. 1982b. *The Levittowners: Ways of Life and Politics in a New Suburban Community.* New York: Columbia University Press.

——. 1989. "Sociology in America: The discipline and the public." *American Sociological Review,* 54, p. 1–16.

Gardner, Howard. 1993. *Creating Minds: An Anatomy of Creativity Seen Through the Lives of Freud, Einstein, Picasso, Stravinsky, Eliot, Graham, and Gandhi.* New York: Basic Books.

Garfinkel, Harold. 1967. *Studies in Ethnomethodology.* Englewood Cliffs, N.J.: Prentice-Hall.

Gartner, Michael. 1990. "Indian tribes shouldn't bet their future on casinos." *Wall Street Journal,* June 28, p. A15.

Gecas, Viktor. 1981. "Contexts of Socialization," in Morris Rosenberg and Ralph H. Turner (eds.), *Social Psychology: Sociological Perspectives.* New York: Basic Books.

Gelles, Richard J., and Claire Pedrick Cornell. 1990. *Intimate Violence in Families,* 2nd ed. Beverly Hills, Calif.: Sage.

Gelman, David. 1986. "Why we age differently." *Newsweek,* October 20, pp. 60–61.

Gerber, Gwendolyn L. 1989. "The more positive evaluation of men than women on the gender-stereotyped traits." *Psychological Reports,* 65, pp. 275–286.

Gerson, Kathleen. 1993. *No Man's Land: Men's Changing Commitments to Family and Work.* New York: Basic Books.

Gibbs, Nancy R. 1988. "Grays on the go." *Time,* February 22, pp. 66–75.

———. 1990. "The dreams of youth." *Time,* Fall, pp. 10–14.

———. 1994a. "Home sweet home." *Time,* October 31, pp. 62–63.

———. 1994b. "Why? The killing fields of Rwanda." *Time,* May 16, pp. 57–63.

Gilbert, Dennis, and Joseph A. Kahl. 1993. *The American Class Structure,* 4th ed. Belmont, Calif.: Wadsworth.

Gilleard, Christopher John, and Ali Aslan Gurkan. 1987. "Socioeconomic development and the status of elderly men in Turkey: A test of modernization theory." *Journal of Gerontology,* 42, pp. 353–357.

Gilligan, Carol. 1982. *In a Different Voice: Psychological Theory and Women's Development.* Cambridge: Harvard University Press.

Gilman, Hank. 1986. "Marketers court older consumers as balance of buying power shifts." *Wall Street Journal,* April 23, p. 37.

Gimenez, Martha E. 1990. "The feminization of poverty: Myth or reality?" *Social Justice,* 17, pp. 43–69.

Giordano, Joseph. 1987. "The Mafia mystique." *U.S. News & World Report,* February 16, p. 6.

Girard, Chris. 1993. "Age, gender, and suicide: A cross-national analysis." *American Sociological Review,* 58, pp. 553–574.

Glaab, Charles N., and A. Theodore Brown. 1983. *A History of Urban America,* 3rd ed. New York: Macmillan.

Glass, David, Peverill Squire, and Raymond Wolfinger. 1984. "Voter turnout: An international comparison." *Public Opinion,* December/January, pp. 49–55.

Gleick, Elizabeth. 1995. "The costly crisis in our schools." *Time,* January 30, pp. 67–68.

Glenn, Norval D., and Charles N. Weaver. 1982. "Enjoyment of work by full-time workers in U.S., 1955 and 1980. *Public Opinion Quarterly,* 46, pp. 459–470.

Goethals, George W. 1971. "Factors affecting permissive and nonpermissive rules regarding premarital sex," in James M. Henslin (ed.), *Studies in the Sociology of Sex.* New York: Appleton-Century-Crofts.

Goffman, Erving. 1967. *Interaction Ritual.* New York: Random House.

———. 1971. *Relations in Public: Microstudies of the Public Order.* New York: Basic Books.

Goldberger, Marvin L., and Wolfgang P. K. Panofsky. 1990. "All science, great and small." *New York Times,* December 22, p. 15.

Goldman, Ari L. 1991. "Portrait of religion in U.S. holds dozens of surprises." *New York Times,* April 10, pp. A1, A11.

Goldman, Ari L. 1992. "Catholics are at odds with bishops." *New York Times,* June 19, p. A8.

Goldstein, Melvyn C., and Cynthia M. Beall. 1982. "Indirect modernization and the status of the elderly in a rural third-world setting." *Journal of Gerontology,* 37, pp. 743–748.

Goldstone, Jack A. 1982. "The comparative and historical study of revolutions." *Annual Review of Sociology,* 8, pp. 187–207.

Goleman, Daniel. 1988. "Physicians may bungle part of treatment: Medical interview." *New York Times,* January 21, p. 12.

———. 1990. "Stereotypes of the sexes said to persist in therapy." *New York Times,* April 10, pp. B1, B7.

———. 1991a "Anatomy of a rumor: Fear feeds it." *New York Times,* June 4, pp. B1, B7.

———. 1991b. "Sexual Harassment: About Power, Not Sex," *New York Times,* October 22, p. C12.

Goode, Erich. 1989. *Drugs in American Society,* 3rd ed. New York: Knopf.

Goode, William J. 1982. *The Family,* 2nd ed. Englewood Cliffs, N.J.: Prentice-Hall.

———. 1993. *World Changes in Divorce Patterns.* New Haven, Conn.: Yale University Press.

Goodlad, John I. 1984. *A Place Called School: Prospects for the Future.* New York: McGraw-Hill.

Gorman, Christine. 1992. "Sizing up the sexes." *Time,* January 20, pp. 42–51.

Gottdiener, Mark. 1983. "Understanding metropolitan deconcentration: A clash of paradigms." *Social Science Quarterly,* 64, pp. 227–246.

———. 1985. *The Social Production of Urban Space.* Austin: University of Texas Press.

Gottlieb, Annie. 1971. "Female human beings." *New York Times Book Review,* February 21, sec. 2, p. 1.

Gottman, John. 1994. *Why Marriages Succeed or Fail.* New York: Simon & Schuster.

Gouldner, Alvin W. 1979. *The Future of Intellectuals and the Rise of the New Class.* New York: Seabury.

Goy, R. W., and B. S. McEwen. 1980. *Sexual Differentiation of the Brain.* Cambridge, Mass.: MIT Press.

Granovetter, Mark. 1983. "The strength of weak ties: A network theory revisited," in Randall Collins (ed.), *Sociological Theory 1983.* San Francisco: Jossey-Bass.

———. 1984. "Small is bountiful: Labor markets and

establishment size." *American Sociological Review,* 49, pp. 323–334.

Gray, John. 1992. *Men Are From Mars, Women Are From Venus.* New York: HarperCollins Publishers.

Greenberg, David. 1981. *Crime and Capitalism: Readings in Marxist Criminology.* Palo Alto, Calif.: Mayfield.

Greenberger, Ellen, and Wendy A. Goldberg. 1989. "Work, parenting, and the socialization of children." *Developmental Psychology,* 25, pp. 22–35.

Greenberger, Robert S. 1992. "North-south split: With cold war over, poorer nations face neglect by the rich." *Wall Street Journal,* May 14, pp. A1, A7.

Greenhouse, Steven. 1994. "State dept. finds widespread abuse of world's women." *New York Times,* February 3, pp. A1, A6.

Greer, Scott. 1956. "Urbanism reconsidered: A comparative study of local areas in a metropolis." *American Sociological Review,* 21, pp. 19–25.

Gregg, Gail. 1980. "Chrysler aid cleared in final day's session." *Congressional Quarterly Almanac 1979,* pp. 285–292.

Greider, William. 1992. *Who Will Tell the People: The Betrayal of American Democracy.* New York: Simon & Schuster.

Griffith, Jeanne E., et al. 1989. "American education: The challenge of change." *Population Bulletin,* December, pp. 2–39.

Grimshaw, Allen D. 1982. "Whose privacy? What harm?" *Sociological Methods and Research,* 11, pp. 233–247.

Grissmer, David W. 1994. *Student achievement and the changing American family: An executive summary.* Santa Monica, Calif.: Rand Corp.

Gross, Jane. 1991. "More young single men clinging to apron strings." *New York Times,* June 16, pp. 1, 10.

Grubaugh, Stephen G., and Rexford E. Santerre. 1994. "Comparing the performance of health care systems: An alternative approach." *Southern Economic Journal,* 60, pp. 1030–1042.

Grusky, David B., and Robert M. Hauser. 1984. "Comparative social mobility revisited: Models of convergence and divergence in 16 countries." *American Sociological Review,* 49, pp. 19–38.

Gruson, Lindsey. 1986. "Alternative schools' revisited." *New York Times,* April 8, p. 17.

———. 1990. "Political violence on the rise again in Guatemala, tarnishing civilian rule." *New York Times,* June 28, p. A3.

Guttman, Monika. 1994. "Separating the sisters." *U.S. News & World Report,* March 28, pp. 49–50.

Gwartney-Gibbs, Patricia A. 1986. "The institutionalization of premarital cohabitation: Estimates from marriage license applications, 1970 and 1980." *Journal of Marriage and the Family,* 48, pp. 423–434.

Gwynne, S. C. 1992. "The long haul." *Time,* September 28, pp. 34–38.

Hacker, Andrew. 1983. "What the very rich really think." *Forbes,* Fall, pp. 66–70.

———. 1992. *Two Nations: Black and White, Separate, Hostile, Unequal.* New York: Scribner's.

Hadaway, C. Kirk, et al. 1993. "What the polls don't show: A closer look at U.S. church attendance." *American Sociological Review,* 58, pp. 741–752.

Hagerty, Bob. 1993. "Trainers help expatriate employees build bridges to different cultures." *Wall Street Journal,* June 14, pp. B1, B6.

Hagstrom, Warren O. 1974. "Competition in science." *American Sociological Review,* 39, pp. 1–18.

Hall, Wayne. 1986. "Social class and survival on the *S.S. Titanic.*" *Social Science and Medicine,* 22, pp. 687–690.

Hamilton, V. Lee, et al. 1990. "Hard times and vulnerable people: Initial effects of plant closing on autoworkers' mental health." *Journal of Health and Social Behavior,* 31, pp. 123–140.

Hammond, Phillip E. 1985. "The curious path of conservative Protestantism." *Annals of American Academy of Political and Social Science,* 480, July, pp. 53–62.

Hancock, LynNell. 1994. "Red, white—and blue." *Newsweek,* November 7, p. 54.

Harayda, Janice. 1986. *The Joy of Being Single.* Garden City, N.Y.: Doubleday.

Hardin, Garrett. 1993. *Living Within Limits: Ecology, Economics, and Population Taboos.* New York: Oxford University Press.

Harding, Sandra. 1991. *Whose Science? Whose Knowledge?* New York: Cornell University Press.

Hare, A. Paul. 1962. *Handbook of Small Group Research.* Glencoe, Ill.: Free Press.

Harjo, Suzan Shown. 1993. "The American Indian experience." In Harriette Pipes McAdoo (ed.), *Family Ethnicity: Strength in Diversity.* Newbury Park, Calif.: Sage.

Harper, Lucinda. 1993. "Good Looks Can Mean a Pretty Penny on the Job ... " *Wall Street Journal,* November 23, p. B1.

Harris, Chauncy D., and Edward L. Ullman. 1945. "The nature of cities." *Annals of the American Academy of Political and Social Science,* 242, pp. 7–17.

Harris, Marvin. 1980. *Cultural Materialism.* New York: Vintage.

——. 1985. *Good to Eat: Riddles of Foods and Culture.* New York: Simon & Schuster.

——. 1995. *Cultural Anthropology,* 4th ed. New York: HarperCollins.

Harris, Monica J., and Robert Rosenthal. 1985. "Mediation of interpersonal expectancy effects: 31 meta-analyses." *Psychological Bulletin,* 97, pp. 363–386.

Harrison, Lawrence E. 1992. *Who Prospers? How Cultural Values Shape Economic and Political Success.* New York: Basic Books.

Harwood, John, and Timothy Noah. 1992. "Candidates head down campaign trail … " *Wall Street Journal,* October 21, p. A18.

Hatch, Ruth C., Dorothy E. James, and Walter R. Schumm. 1986. "Spiritual intimacy and marital satisfaction." *Family Relations,* 35, pp. 539–545.

Hauser, Philip M. 1981. "Chicago-urban crisis exemplar," in J. John Palen (ed.), *City Scenes,* 2nd ed. Boston: Little, Brown.

Havighurst, Robert J. 1963. "Successful aging," in Richard H. Williams, Clark Tibbitts, and William Donahue (eds.), *Processes of Aging,* vol. 1. New York: Atherton.

Hawkes, Kristen, and James F. O'Connell. 1981. "Affluent hunters? Some comments in light of the Alyawara case." *American Anthropologist,* 83, pp. 622–626.

Hawkins, Dana. 1992. "A very rich dessert." *U.S. News & World Report,* March 23, pp. 52–53.

Hayden, Tom. 1980. *The American Future: New Visions Beyond Old Frontiers.* Boston: South End Press.

Hayes, Arthur S. 1990. "Suburban dilemma." *Wall Street Journal,* October 4, pp. A1, A16.

Headland, Thomas N., and Lawrence A. Reid. 1989. "Hunter-gatherers and their neighbors from prehistory to the present." *Current Anthropology,* 30, pp. 43–51.

Hegedus, Rita. 1976. "Voucher plans," in Steven E. Goodman (ed.), *Handbook on Contemporary Education.* New York: Bowker.

Heilbroner, Robert L. 1972. *The Worldly Philosophers: The Lives, Times, and Ideas of the Great Economic Thinkers,* 4th ed. New York: Simon & Schuster.

——. 1980. *Marxism: For and Against.* New York: Norton.

Heim, Pat, and Susan Golant. 1993. *Hardball for Women.* New York: Plume.

Henneberger, Melinda, and Michel Marriott. 1993. "For Some, Youthful Courting Has Become a Game of Abuse," *New York Times,* July 11, pp. 1, 14.

Henry, William A., III. 1990. "Beyond the melting pot." *Time,* April 9, pp. 28–31.

Henslin, James M., and Mae A. Biggs. 1971. "Dramaturgical desexualization: The sociology of the vaginal examination." In James M. Henslin (ed.), *Studies in the Sociology of Sex.* New York: Appleton-Century-Crofts.

Herberg, Will. 1983. *Protestant-Catholic-Jew: An Essay in American Religions.* Chicago: University of Chicago.

Herdt, Gilbert. 1990. "Developmental discontinuities and sexual orientation across cultures," in David P. McWhirter et al., *Homosexuality/Heterosexuality.* New York: Oxford University Press.

Herrnstein, Richard J., and Charles Murray. 1994. *The Bell Curve: Intelligence and Class Structure in American Life.* New York: Free Press.

Hershey, Robert D. Jr. 1995. "U.S. closed year with employment growing sharply." *New York Times,* January 7, pp. 1, 29.

Heyneman, Stephen P., and William A. Loxley. 1983. "The effect of primary-school quality on academic achievement across twenty-nine high- and low-income countries." *American Journal of Sociology,* 88, pp. 1162–1194.

Hilts, Philip J. 1990. "AIDS bias grows faster than disease, study says." *New York Times,* July 17, pp. 1, 14.

Hirsch, James. 1990. "Older workers chafe under young managers." *Wall Street Journal,* February 26, pp. B1, B6.

Hirschi, Travis. 1969. *Causes of Delinquency.* Berkeley and Los Angeles: University of California Press.

Hirschman, Charles. 1983. "America's melting pot reconsidered." *Annual Review of Sociology,* 9, pp. 397–423.

Hochschild, Arlie R. 1989. *The Second Shift.* New York: Viking.

Hodge, Robert W., Paul M. Siegel, and Peter H. Rossi. 1964. "Occupational prestige in the United States: 1925–1963." *American Journal of Sociology,* 70, pp. 286–302.

Hodson, Randy. 1989. "Gender differences in job satisfaction: Why aren't women more dissatisfied?" *Sociological Quarterly,* 30, pp. 385–399.

Hoffer, Eric. 1966. *The True Believer: Thoughts on the Nature of Mass Movements.* New York: Harper & Row.

Hogan, Dennis P., et al. 1990. "Race, kin networks, and assistance to mother-headed families." *Social Forces,* 68, pp. 797–812.

Holt, John. 1968. "Education for the future," in Robert Theobald (ed.), *Social Policies for America in the Seventies.* Garden City, N.Y.: Doubleday.

Hood, John. 1990. "Education: Money isn't everything." *Wall Street Journal,* February 9, p. A10.

Horn, Thelma Sternberg, and Curt Lox. 1993. "The self-fulfilling prophecy theory: When coaches' expectations become reality." Pp. 68–81 in Jean M. Williams (ed.),

Applied Sport Psychology: Personal Growth to Peak Performance. Mountain View, Cal.: Mayfield.

Horner, Matina S. 1969. "Fail: Bright women." *Psychology Today,* November, pp. 36–38.

Hoult, Thomas Ford. 1979. *Sociology for a New Day,* 2nd ed. New York: Random House.

House, James S., et al. 1988. "Social relationships and health." *Science,* 241, pp. 540–545.

Howard, Michael C. 1993. *Contemporary Cultural Anthropology,* 4th ed. New York: HarperCollins.

Howe, Marvine. 1993. "Portugal: A lack of discipline keeps math scores low." *New York Times,* December 9, p. A8.

Hoyt, Homer. 1943. "The structure of American cities in the post-war era." *American Journal of Sociology,* 48, pp. 475–492.

Hoyt, Karen. 1987. *The New Age Rage.* Old Tappan, N.J.: Fleming Revell Co.

Hraba, Joseph. 1979. *American Ethnicity.* Itasca, Ill.: Peacock.

Huber, Joan. 1989. "A theory of gender stratification," in Larel Richardson and Verta Taylor (eds.), *Feminist Frontiers.* New York: Random House, pp. 110–119.

——. 1990. "Macro-micro links in gender stratification." *American Sociological Review,* 55, pp. 1–10.

Humphreys, Laud. 1970. *Tearoom Trade: Impersonal Sex in Public Places.* Chicago: Aldine.

Huntington, Samuel P. 1993. "The clash of civilizations?" *Foreign Affairs,* Summer, pp. 22–49.

Jacobs, Charles, and Mohamed Athie. 1994. "Bought and sold." *New York Times,* July 13, p. A11.

Jacquard, Albert. 1983. "Myths under the microscope." *UNESCO Courier,* 36, November, pp. 25–27.

Janis, Irving L. 1982. *Groupthink: Psychological Studies of Policy Decisions and Fiascos.* Boston: Houghton Mifflin.

Janus, Samuel S., and Cynthia L. Janus. 1993. *The Janus Report on Sexual Behavior.* New York: John Wiley & Sons.

Jaret, Charles. 1983. "Recent neo-Marxist urban analysis." *Annual Review of Sociology,* 9, pp. 499–525.

Jasso, Guillermina. 1985. "Marital coital frequency and the passage of time: Estimating the separate effects of spouses' ages and marital duration, birth and marriage cohorts, and period influences." *American Sociological Review,* 50, pp. 224–241.

Jencks, Christopher. 1994. *The Homeless.* Cambridge, Mass.: Harvard University Press.

Jenness, Valerie. 1993. *Making It Work: The Prostitutes' Rights Movement in Perspective.* Hawthorne, N.Y.: Aldine de Gruyter.

Johnson, Dirk. 1990. "Chastity organization: Starting over in purity." *New York Times,* January 28, p. 12.

Johnson, Julie et al. 1991. "Why do blacks die young?" *Time,* September 16, pp. 50–52.

Johnson, Sterling, Jr. 1987. "This is the wrong message to give." *New York Times,* December 20, p. E20.

Johnson, Susan Moore. 1990. *Teachers at Work: Achieving Success in Our Schools.* New York: Basic Books.

Jones, Charisse. 1994. "Years on integration road: New views of an old goal." *New York Times,* April 10, pp. 1, 15.

Jones, Jacqueline. 1992. *The Dispossessed.* New York: Basic Books.

Jones, Peter et al. 1993. "Premorbid social under-achievement in schizophrenia: Results from the Camberwell collaborative psychosis study." *British Journal of Psychiatry,* 162, pp. 65–71.

Josephson, Wendy L. 1987. "Television violence and children's aggression: Testing the priming, social script, and disinhibition predictions." *Journal of Personality and Social Psychology,* 53, pp. 882–890.

Kalick, S. Michael, and Thomas E. Hamilton III. 1986. "The matching hypothesis reexamined." *Journal of Personality and Social Psychology,* 51, pp. 673–682.

Kalmuss, Debra. 1984. "The intergenerational transmission of marital aggression." *Journal of Marriage and the Family,* 46, pp. 11–19.

Kanin, Eugene J. 1983. "Rape as a function of relative sexual frustration." *Psychological Reports,* 52, pp. 133–134.

Kantrowitz, Barbara. 1991. "Striking a Nerve," *Newsweek,* October 21, pp. 38, 40.

——, and Pat Wingert. 1993. "No longer a sacred cow." *Newsweek,* April 12, p. 57.

Karp, David A., and William C. Yoels. 1993. *Sociology in Everyday Life.* Itasca, Ill.: Peacock.

——, Gregory P. Stone, and William C. Yoels. 1991. *Being Urban: A Sociology of City Life.* New York: Praeger.

Kart, Gary S. 1990. *The Realities of Aging,* 3rd ed. Boston: Allyn and Bacon.

Katchadourian, Herant. 1985. *Fundamentals of Human Sexuality,* 4th ed. New York: Holt, Rinehart and Winston.

——, and John Boli. 1986. *Careerism and Intellectualism Among College Students.* San Francisco: Jossey-Bass.

Katz, Jack. 1988. *Seductions of Crime.* New York: Basic Books.

Kaus, Mickey. 1992. *The End of Equality.* New York: Basic Books.

Keen, David. 1994. *The Benefits of Famine.* Princeton, N.J.: Princeton University Press.

Keller, Helen. 1954. *The Story of My Life.* Garden City, N.Y.: Doubleday.

Kennedy, Paul M. 1988. *The Rise and Fall of the Great Powers.* New York: Random House.

——. 1991. "A declining empire goes to war." *Wall Street Journal,* January 24, p. A10.

Kephart, William M., and Davor Jedlicka. 1988. *The Family, Society, and the Individual,* 6th ed. New York: Harper & Row.

Kerbo, Harold R. 1982. "Movements of 'crisis' and movements of 'affluence': A critique of deprivation and resource mobilization theories." *Journal of Conflict Resolution,* 26, pp. 645–663.

Kerckhoff, Alan C., Richard T. Campbell, and Idee Winfield-Laird. 1985. "Social mobility in Great Britain and the United States." *American Journal of Sociology,* 91, pp. 281–308.

Kessler, Ronald C., Richard H. Price, and Camille B. Wortman. 1985. "Social factors in psychopathology: Stress, social support, and coping processes." *Annual Review of Psychology,* 36, pp. 560–561.

——. 1994. "Lifetime and 12-month prevalence of DSM-III-R psychiatric disorders in the United States." *Archives of General Psychiatry,* 51, pp. 8–19.

Kilker, Ernest Evans. 1993. "Black and white in America: The culture and politics of racial classification." *International Journal of Politics, Culture and Society,* 7, pp. 229–258.

Kilborn, Peter T. 1990a. "Wage gap between sexes is cut in test, but at a price." *New York Times,* May 31, pp. A1, A12.

——. 1990b. "Workers using computers find a supervisor inside." *New York Times,* December 23, pp. 1, 13.

Kim, Paul S. 1983. "Japan's bureaucratic decision-making on the textbook." *Public Administration,* 61, pp. 283–294.

Kimball, Meredith M. 1989. "A new perspective on women's math achievement." *Psychological Bulletin,* 105, pp. 198–214.

Kimmel, Michael S. 1986. "A prejudice against prejudice." *Psychology Today,* December, pp. 47–52.

——. 1992. "Reading men: Men, masculinity, and publishing." *Contemporary Sociology,* 21, March, pp. 162–171.

Kinsey, Alfred C. et al. 1948. *Sexual Behavior in the Human Male.* Philadelphia: Saunders.

Kitahara, Michio. 1982. "Menstrual taboos and the importance of hunting." *American Anthropologist,* 84, pp. 901–903.

Kitano, Harry H. L. 1981. "Asian-Americans: The Chinese, Japanese, Koreans, Filipinos, and Southeast Asians." *Annals,* 454, March, pp. 125–149.

Klag, Michael J., et al. 1991. "The association of skin color with blood pressure in U.S. blacks with low socioeconomic status." *Journal of the American Medical Association,* 265, pp. 599–640.

Klaus, Patsy A., and Michael R. Rand. 1984. "Family violence." *Bureau of Justice Statistics Special Report.* U.S. Department of Justice.

Koenig, Fredrick. 1982a. "Preferences for candidates of college students and their parents in two presidential elections." *Psychological Reports,* 50, pp. 335–336.

——. 1982b. "Today's conditions make U.S. 'ripe for the rumor mill.'" *U.S. News & World Report,* December 6, p. 42.

Kohlberg, Lawrence. 1981. *The Philosophy of Moral Development: Moral Stages and the Idea of Justice.* New York: Harper & Row.

Kohn, Alfie. 1986. *No Contest: The Case Against Competition.* Boston: Houghton Mifflin.

——. 1988. "You know what they say … " *Psychology Today,* April, pp. 36–41.

Kohn, Melvin L. 1977. *Class and Conformity,* 2nd ed. Homewood, Ill. Dorsey.

——. 1980. "Job complexity and adult personality," in Neal Smelser and Erik Erikson (eds.) *Themes of Love and Work in Adulthood.* Cambridge, Mass.: Harvard University Press.

——. 1983. "The benefits of bureaucracy." In Melvin L. Kohn and Schooler (eds.), *Occupational Structure and Personality.* Norwood, N.J.: Ablex.

Kolata, Gina. 1990. "Wariness is replacing trust between physician and patient." *New York Times,* February 20, pp. A1, A10.

——. 1991. "Are U.S. students the worst? Comparisons seen as flawed." *New York Times,* December 24, pp. A1, A6.

Kosters, Marvin H. 1990. "Be cool, stay in school." *The American Enterprise,* March/April, pp. 60–67.

Kotkin, Joel. 1992. *Tribes: How Race, Religion, and Identity Determine Success in the New Global Economy.* New York: Random House.

Kourvetaris, George A., and Betty A. Dobratz. 1982. "Political power and conventional political participation." *Annual Review of Sociology,* 8, pp. 289–317.

Kozol, Jonathan. 1968. *Death at an Early Age.* Boston: Houghton Mifflin.

Kramon, Glenn. 1991. "Medical second-guessing-in advance." *New York Times,* February 24, p. F12.

Krauthammer, Charles. 1990a. "Education: Doing bad and feeling good." *Time,* February 5, p. 78.

——. 1990b. "In praise of low voter turnout." *Time,* May 21, p. 88.

Krenz, Claudia, and Gilbert Sax. 1986. "What quantitative research is and why it doesn't work." *American Behavioral Scientist,* 30, pp. 58–69.

Kristof, Nicholas D. 1990. "More in China willingly rear one child." *New York Times,* May 9, pp. 1, B9.

Krugman, Paul. 1990. *The Age of Diminished Expectations: U.S. Economic Policy in the 1990s.* Cambridge, Mass.: MIT Press.

Kübler-Ross, Elisabeth. 1969. *On Death and Dying.* New York: Macmillan.

Kucherov, Alex. 1981. "Now help is on the way for neglected widowers." *U.S. News & World Report,* June 22, pp. 47, 48.

Kuhn, Thomas S. 1970. *The Structure of Scientific Revolutions,* 2nd ed. Chicago: University of Chicago Press.

Lacayo, Richard. 1987. "Whose trial is it anyway?" *Time,* May 25, p. 62.

——. 1990. "Why no blue blood will flow." *Time,* November 26, p. 34.

——. 1995. "How safe is safe?" *Time,* May 1, pp. 68–72.

Ladd, Everett Carll. 1978. "What the voters really want." *Fortune,* December 18, pp. 40–48.

——. 1983. "Politics in the 80's: An electorate at odds with itself." *Public Opinion,* December/January, pp. 2–5.

Lane, Harlan. 1976. *The Wild Boy of Aveyron.* Cambridge, Mass.: Harvard University Press.

Lapham, Lewis H. 1992. "Fear of freedom." *New York Times,* June 6, p. 15.

Larsen, Otto. 1981. "Need for continuing support for social sciences." *ASA Footnotes,* 9, p. 8.

Lasch, Christopher. 1979. *The Culture of Narcissism: American Life in an Age of Diminishing Expectations.* New York: Norton.

Latané, Bibb, and Steve Nida. 1981. "Ten years of research on group size and helping." *Psychological Bulletin,* 89, pp. 308–324.

Leach, Edmund. 1981. "Biology and social science: Wedding or rape?" *Nature,* 291, p. 268.

Leach, Penelope. 1994. *Children First.* New York: Knopf.

Leakey, Richard E., and Roger Lewin. 1977. *Origins.* New York: Dutton.

Lee, Alfred McClung, and Elizabeth Briant Lee. 1979. *The Fine Art of Propaganda.* San Francisco: International Society for General Semantics.

Lee, Barrett A., and Avery M. Guest. 1983. "Determinants of neighborhood satisfaction: A metropolitan-level analysis." *Sociological Quarterly,* 24, pp. 287–303.

Lee, Richard B. 1979. *The !Kung San: Men, Women and Work in a Foraging Society.* New York: Cambridge University Press.

Lee, Tony. 1990. "Here comes the pink slip." *American Demographics,* March, pp. 46–49.

Lehner, Urban C. 1992. "Is it any surprise the Japanese make excellent loafers?" *Wall Street Journal,* February 28, pp. A1, A10.

Lemarchand, Rene. 1994. "The apocalypse in Rwanda." *Cultural Survival Quarterly,* 18, pp. 29–33.

Lemert, Edwin M. 1951. *Social Pathology.* New York: McGraw-Hill.

Lemon, B. W., K. L. Bengston, and J. A. Peterson. 1972. "An exploration of the activity theory of aging: Activity types and life satisfaction among in-movers to a retirement community." *Journal of Gerontology,* 27, pp. 511–523.

Lemonick, Michael D. 1992. "The ozone vanishes." *Time,* February 17, pp. 60–63.

Lengermann, Patricia Madoo, and Jill Niebrugge-Brantley. 1992. "Contemporary feminist theory." Pp. 447–496 in George Ritzer, *Sociological Theory,* 3rd ed. New York: McGraw-Hill.1995.

Lenski, Gerhard, Jean Lenski, Patrick Nolan. 1995. *Human Societies,* 7th ed. New York: McGraw-Hill.

Leo, John. 1987. "Exploring the traits of twins." *Time,* January 12, p. 63.

Leonard, Eileen B. 1982. *Women, Crime, and Society: A Critique of Criminology Theory.* New York: Longman.

Leslie, Gerald R., and Sheila K. Korman. 1989. *The Family in Social Context,* 7th ed. New York: Oxford University Press.

LeVay, Simon. 1991. "A difference in hypothalamic structure between heterosexual and homosexual men." *Science,* 253, pp. 1034–1037.

Levin, Jack, and William C. Levin. 1980. *Ageism: Prejudice and Discrimination against the Elderly.* Belmont, Calif.: Wadsworth.

Levine, Daniel S. 1993. "Adult students, adult needs." *New York Times,* April 4, Section 4A, pp. 32–33.

Levine, John M., and Richard L. Moreland. 1990. "Progress in small group research." *Annual Review of Psychology,* 14, pp. 585–634.

Levine, Saul V. 1984. *Radical Departures: Desperate Detours to Growing Up.* New York: Harcourt Brace Jovanovich.

Levinson, Marc. 1995. "Hey, you're doing great." *Newsweek,* January 30, pp. 42–44.

Levy, Becca, and Ellen Langer. 1994. "Aging free from negative stereotypes: successful memory in China and among the American deaf." *Journal of Personality and Social Psychology,* 66, pp. 989–997.

Levy, S. G., and W. F. Fenley, Jr. 1979. "Audience size and likelihood and intensity of response during a humorous movie." *Bulletin of Psychonomic Society*, 13, pp. 409–412.

Lewin, Bo. 1982. "Unmarried cohabitation: A marriage form in a changing society." *Journal of Marriage and the Family*, 44, pp. 763–773.

Lewin, Tamar. 1992. "Rise in single parenthood is reshaping U.S." *New York Times*, October 5, pp. A1, A16.

Lewin, Tamar. 1994. "Abortions in U.S. hit 13-year low, a study reports." *New York Times*, June 16, pp. A1, A11.

Lewinsolhn, Peter M. et al. 1993. "Adolescent psychopathology: I. Prevalence and incidence of depression and other DSM-III-R disorders in high school students." *Journal of Abnormal Psychology*, 102, pp. 133–144.

Lewis, Neil A. 1995. "Clinton plan would let FBI infiltrate menacing groups." *New York Times*, April 25, p. A9.

Lewis, Oscar. 1961. *The Children of Sanchez*. New York: Random House.

Liebow, Elliot. 1993. *Tell Them Who I Am: The Lives of Homeless Women*. New York: Free Press.

Lightbourne, Robert, Jr., and Susheela Singh, with Cynthia P. Green. 1982. "The world fertility survey: Charting global child-bearing." *Population Bulletin*, 37, March, pp. 1–54.

Lin, Chien, and William T. Liu. 1993. "Intergenerational relationships among Chinese immigrant families from Taiwan." In Harriette Pipes McAdoo (ed.), *Family Ethnicity: Strength in Diversity*. Newbury Park, Calif.: Sage.

Lin, Nan. 1982. "Social resources and instrumental action." In Peter V. Marsden and Nan Lin (eds.), *Social Structure and Network Analysis*. Beverly Hills, Calif.: Sage, pp. 131–145.

Lincoln, C. Eric, and Lawrence H. Mamiya. 1990. *The Black Church in African American Experience*. Durham, N.C.: Duke University Press.

Lindberg, David C. 1992. *The Beginnings of Western Science: The European Scientific Tradition in Philosophical, Religious, and Institutional Context, 600 B.C. to A.D. 1450*. Chicago: University of Chicago Press.

Linden, Eugene. 1993. "Megacities." *Time*, January 11, pp. 28–38.

Link, Bruce G., Mary Clare Lennon, and Bruce P. Dohrenwend. 1993. "Socioeconomic status and depression: The role of occupations involving direction, control, and planning." *American Journal of Sociology*, 98, pp. 1351–1387.

Linz, Daniel, and Neil Malamuth. 1993. *Pornography*. Newbury Park, Calif.: Sage.

Lipset, Seymour Martin. 1981. *Political Man: the Social Bases of Politics*. Baltimore, Md.: Johns Hopkins University Press.

——. 1987. "Blacks and Jews: How much bias?" *Public Opinion*, July/August, pp. 4–5, 57–58.

——. 1990a. "A unique people in an exceptional country," in S. M. Lipset (ed.), *American Pluralism and the Jewish Community*. New Brunswick, N.J.: Transaction, pp. 3–29.

——. 1990b. "The work ethic—then and now." *Public Interest*, Winter, pp. 61–69.

——, and Earl Raab, 1978. *The Politics of Unreason*, 2nd ed. New York: Harper & Row.

——, and William Schneider. 1983. *The Confidence Gap: Business, Labor, and Government in the Public Mind*. New York: Free Press.

Little, Stratton. 1991. "The 1990 U.S. census." *Encyclopaedia Britannica: 1991 Book of the Year*, pp. 279–280.

Loevinger, Jane, and Elizabeth Knoll. 1982. "Personality: Stages, traits, and the self." *Annual Review of Psychology*, 34, pp. 195–222.

Lord, Lewis J., and Miriam Horn. 1987. "The brain battle." *U.S. News & World Report*, January 19, pp. 58–64.

Lord, Walter. 1981. *A Night to Remember*. New York: Penguin.

Los, Maria. 1990. *The Second Economy in Marxist States*. New York: St. Martin's.

Luttwak, Edward N. 1994. *The Endangered American Dream*. New York: Touchstone/Simon & Schuster.

MacFarquhar, Emily. 1994. "The war against women." *U.S. News & World Report*, March 28, pp. 42–48.

Mack, Raymond W., and Calvin P. Bradford. 1979. *Transforming America*. New York: Random House.

Madsen, Douglas, and Peter G. Snow. 1983. "The dispersion of charisma." *Comparative Political Studies*, 16, pp. 337–362.

Madsen, Jane M. 1982. "Racist images." *USA Today*, 111, p. 14.

Maeroff, Gene I. 1990. "Three missing keys to public-school reform." *Wall Street Journal*, May 21, p. A10.

Malson, Lucien. 1972. *Wolf Children and the Problem of Human Nature*. New York: Monthly Review.

Marcus, Eric. 1993. *Is It a Choice?* New York: HarperSanFrancisco.

Markides, Kyriacos C., and Steven F. Cohn. 1982. "External conflict/internal cohesion: A reevaluation of an old theory." *American Sociological Review*, 47, pp. 88–98.

Markovsky, Barry, and Seymour M. Berger. 1983. "Crowd noise and mimicry." *Personality and Social Psychology Bulletin*, 9, pp. 90–96.

Martin, M. Kay, and Barbara Voorhies. 1975. *Female of the Species*. New York: Columbia University Press.

Marty, Martin E., and R. Scott Appleby (eds.) 1992. *Fundamentalisms Observed*. Chicago: University of Chicago Press.

Martz, Larry. 1991. "The corporate shell game." *Newsweek*, April 15, pp. 48–49.

Marx, Karl. 1859/1970. *A Contribution to the Critique of Political Economy*. New York: International Publishers.

——. 1866/1967. *Capital*, vol. 1. New York: International Publishers.

Masland, Tom. 1992. "Slavery." *Newsweek*, May 4, pp. 30–39.

Massing, Michael. 1993. "The rehabbing of America." *New York Times Book Review*, January 24, p. 10.

Mathews, Tom. 1992. "Secrets of a serial killer." *Newsweek*, February 3, pp. 44–49.

Maybury-Lewis, David. 1994. "What is the future and will it work?" *Cultural Survival Quarterly*, Summer/Fall, p. 1.

Mayo, Elton. 1933. *The Human Problems of Industrial Civilization*. New York: Macmillan.

Mazur, Allan. 1986. "U.S. trends in feminine beauty and over-adaptation." *Journal of Sex Research*, 22, pp. 281–303.

McArdle, Thomas. 1994. "Do kids learn more at home?" *Investor's Business Daily*, March 14, pp. 1, 2.

McCormick, John. 1994. "Why parents kill." *Newsweek*, November 14, pp. 31–34.

——, and Peter McKillop. 1989. "The other suburb." *Newsweek*, June 26, pp. 22–24.

McKenna, Francis R. 1993. *Schooling in America*. Dubuque, IA: Kendall/Hunt.

McKinlay, John B., and Sonja M. McKinlay. 1987. "Medical measures and the decline of mortality," in Howard D. Schwartz (ed.), *Dominant Issues in Medical Sociology*, 2nd ed. New York: Random House.

McLanahan, Sara S. 1983. "Family structure and stress: A longitudinal comparison of two-parent and female-headed families." *Journal of Marriage and the Family*, 45, pp. 347–357.

McNeill, William H. 1963. *The Rise of the West: A History of the Human Community*. Chicago: University of Chicago Press.

McPhail, Clark, and Ronald T. Wohlstein. 1983. "Individual and collective behaviors within gatherings, demonstrations, and riots." *Annual Review of Sociology*, 9, pp. 579–600.

McWilliams, Carey. 1948. *A Mask for Privilege*. Boston: Little, Brown.

Mead, Lawrence M. 1992. *The New Politics of Poverty: The Nonworking Poor in America*. New York: Basic Books.

Mead, Margaret. 1935. *Sex and Temperament in Three Primitive Societies*. Garden City, N.Y.: Mentor.

Meer, Jeff. 1986. "The reason of age." *Psychology Today*, June, pp. 60–64.

Mendez, Juan E. 1990. "U.S. joins Peru's dirty war." *New York Times*, May 7, p. A15.

Mensch, Barbara. 1986. "Age differences between spouses in first marriages." *Social Biology*, 33, pp. 229–240.

Merton, Robert K. 1957. *Social Theory and Social Structure*. New York: Free Press.

——. 1973. *The Sociology of Science: Theoretical and Empirical Investigations*. Edited by Norman Storer. Chicago: University of Chicago Press.

——. 1976. *Sociological Ambivalence and Other Essays*. New York: Free Press.

Michael, Robert T. et al. 1994. *Sex in America: A Definitive Survey*. Boston: Little, Brown.

Michels, Robert. 1915. *Political Parties*. Glencoe, Ill.: Free Press.

Milgram, Stanley. 1967. "The small-world problem." *Psychology Today*, 1, pp. 61–67.

——. 1974. *Obedience to Authority*. New York: Harper & Row.

Miller, JoAnn L. 1991. "Prostitution in contemporary American society." In Elizabeth Grauerholz and Mary A. Koralewski (eds.), *Sexual Coercion*. Lexington, Mass.: Lexington Books.

Miller, Jody. 1995. "Feminist Theory." Pp. 54–62 in Alex Thio and Thomas Calhoun (eds.), *Readings in Deviant Behavior*. New York: HarperCollins.

Mills, C. Wright. 1959a. *The Power Elite*. New York: Oxford University Press.

——. 1959. *The Sociological Imagination*. New York: Grove.

Minkler, Meredith. 1981. "Research on the health effects of retirement: An uncertain legacy." *Journal of Health and Social Behavior*, 22, pp. 117–130.

Mitroff, Ian I. 1974. "Norms and counternorms in a select group of the Apollo moon scientists." *American Sociological Review*, 39, pp. 579–595.

Moberg, David O. 1984. "Review of James Hunter's *American Evangelicalism*." *Contemporary Sociology*, 13, pp. 371, 372.

Molotsky, Irvin. 1988. "Senate votes to compensate Japanese-American internees." *New York Times,* April 21, pp. 1, 9.

Morell, Marie A., et al. 1989. "Would a Type A date another Type A?: Influence of behavior type and personal attributes in the selection of dating partners." *Journal of Applied Social Psychology,* 19, pp. 918–931.

Morelli, Gilda A., and Edward Z. Tronick. 1991. "Parenting and child development in the Efe foragers and Lese farmers of Zaire." Pp. 91–113 in Marc H. Bornstein (ed.), *Cultural Approaches to Parenting.* Hillsdale, N.J.: Lawrence Erlbaum Associates.

Morgan, Gareth. 1989. *Creative Organization Theory: A Resourcebook.* Newbury Park, Calif.: Sage.

Morgan, S. Philip. 1983. "A research note on religion and morality: Are religious people nice people?" *Social Forces,* 61, pp. 683–692.

——. 1984. "Reply to King and Hunt." *Social Forces,* 62, pp. 1089–1090.

Morgen, Sandra. 1994. "Personalizing personnel decisions in feminist organizational theory and practice." *Human Relations,* 47, pp. 665–684.

Morris, Allison. 1987. *Women, Crime, and Criminal Justice.* New York: Basil Blackwell.

Morris, Betsy. 1987. "Shallow roots." *Wall Street Journal,* March 27, pp. 1, 7.

Morris, Martina, Annette D. Bernhardt, and Mark S. Handcock. 1994. "Economic inequality: New methods for new trends." *American Sociological Review,* 59, pp. 205–219.

Morrow, Lance. 1978. "The lure of doomsday." *Time,* December 4, p. 30.

Mortimore, Peter. 1988. *School Matters.* Berkeley: University of California Press.

Mullen, Brian, et al. 1989. "Group size, leadership behavior, and subordinate satisfaction." *Journal of General Psychology,* 116, pp. 155–169.

Mumford, Lewis. 1963. *Technics and Civilization.* New York: Harcourt, Brace and World.

Münch, Richard. 1983. "Modern science and technology: Differentiation or interpretation?" *International Journal of Comparative Sociology,* 24, pp. 157–175.

Murdock, George Peter. 1945. "The common denominator of cultures," in Ralph Linton (ed.), *The Science of Man in World Crisis.* New York: Columbia University Press.

——. 1967. *Ethnographic Atlas.* Pittsburgh: University of Pittsburgh Press.

Myers, David G. 1993. *The Pursuit of Happiness.* New York: Avon Books.

Myers, Jerome K. et al. 1984. "Six-month prevalence of psychiatric disorders in three communities." *Archives of General Psychiatry.* 41, pp. 959 –967.

Naisbitt, John, and Patricia Aburdene. 1990. *Megatrends 2000.* New York: Morrow.

Nanda, Serena. 1994. *Cultural Anthropology,* 5th ed. Belmont, Calif.: Wadsworth.

Nash, Nathaniel C. 1995. "Europe's economies are in an upswing." *New York Times,* January 3, p. C10.

Nazario, Sonia L. 1992. "Medical science seeks a cure for doctors suffering from boorish bedside manner." *Wall Street Journal,* March 17, pp. B1, B8.

Nelson, Mariah Burton. 1994. *The Stronger Women Get, The More Men Love Football: Sexism and the American Culture of Sports.* New York: Harcourt Brace.

Nelson, Mark M. 1990. "Darkness at noon." *Wall Street Journal,* March 1, pp. A1, A13.

Nemy, Enid. 1991. "Numbers are up, status down for the family of one." *New York Times,* February 28, pp. B1, B5.

Neuman, N. Lawrence. 1994. *Social Research Methods: Qualitative and Quantitative Approaches,* 2nd ed. Boston: Allyn and Bacon.

New York Times. 1991. "Private cures for public ills." February 28, p. A18.

New York Times/CBS News. 1994. *New York Times,* December 15, pp. A1, A14.

Newcomb, Theodore. 1958. "Attitude development as a function of reference group: The Bennington study," in Guy E. Swanson et al. (eds.), *Readings in Social Psychology.* New York: Holt, Rinehart and Winston.

Newman, Maria. 1992. "Charismatic movement gains among Catholics." *New York Times,* March 1, p. 17.

——. 1994. "California schools compete for pupils in an open market." *New York Times,* May 25, pp. A1, B8.

Newman, William M. 1973. *American Pluralism: A Study of Minority Groups and Social Theory.* New York: Harper & Row.

Newsweek Poll. 1992. *Newsweek,* September 14, pp. 36–37.

Niebuhr, Gustav. 1992. "The lord's name." *Wall Street Journal,* April 27, pp. A1, A4.

Nielsen, Francois. 1994. "Income inequality and industrial development: Dualism revisited." *American Sociological Review,* 59, pp. 654–677.

Nieuwenhuys, Olga. 1994. *Children's Lifeworlds: Gender, Welfare and Labour in the Developing World.* London: Routledge.

Nisbet, Robert A. 1970. *The Social Bond.* New York: Knopf.

NORC (National Opinion Research Center). 1994. *General Social Surveys, 1972–1994: Cumulative Codebook.* Storrs, Conn.: Roper Center.

Nordheimer, Jon. 1990. "Stepfathers: The shoes rarely fit." *New York Times,* October 18, p. B6.

Nuland, Sherwin B. 1994. *How We Die: Reflections on Life's Final Chapter.* New York: Knopf.

Nye, Joseph, Jr. 1990. *Bound to Lead: The Changing Nature of American Power.* New York: Basic Books.

Oakley, Robert. 1987. "International terrorism." *Foreign Affairs,* 65, pp. 611–629.

Ochse, Rhona, and Cornelis Plug. 1986. "Cross-cultural investigation of the validity of Erikson's theory of personality development." *Journal of Personality and Social Psychology,* 50, pp. 1240–1252.

O'Dea, Thomas F., and Janet O'Dea Aviad. 1983. *The Sociology of Religion,* 2nd ed. Englewood Cliffs, N.J.: Prentice-Hall.

Okraku, Ishmael O. 1987. "Age and attitudes toward multigenerational residence, 1973 to 1983." *Journal of Gerontology,* 42, pp. 280–287.

O'Neill, June Ellenoff. 1994. "The Shrinking Pay Gap." *Wall Street Journal,* October 7, p. A10.

Orwell, George. 1949. *1984.* New York: Signet.

Ostling, George. 1988. "Americans facing toward Mecca." *Time,* May 23, pp. 49–50.

——. 1991. "Superchurches and how they grow." *Time,* August 5, pp. 62–63.

Ostling, Richard N. 1987. "John Paul's feisty flock." *Time,* September 7, pp. 46–51.

Otten, Alan. 1987. "Warning of generational fighting draws critics—led by the elderly." *Wall Street Journal,* January 13, p. 35.

——. 1990. "People patterns." *Wall Street Journal,* February 20, p. B1.

Overall, Christine. 1992. "What's wrong with prostitution? Evaluating sex work." *Signs,* 17, pp. 705–725.

Ozawa, Ichiro. 1994. "Toward a bolder Japan [book excerpts]." *Time,* June 13, pp. 38–47.

Page, Benjamin I. 1983. *Who Gets What from Government.* Berkeley: University of California Press.

Palen, I. John. 1981. *The Urban World,* 2nd ed. New York: McGraw-Hill.

Palisi, Bartolomeo J., and Claire Canning. 1983. "Urbanism and social psychological well-being: A cross-cultural test of three theories." *Sociological Quarterly,* 24, pp. 527–543.

Palmore, Erdman. 1981. *Social Patterns in Normal Aging: Findings from the Duke Longitudinal Study.* Durham, N.C.: Duke University Press.

——, and Daisaku Maeda. 1985. *The Honorable Elders Revisited: A Revised Cross-Cultural Analysis of Aging in Japan.* Durham, N.C.: Duke University Press.

Papousek, Hanus, and Mechthild Papousek. 1991. "Innate and cultural guidance of infants' integrative competencies: China, the United States, and Germany." Pp. 23–44 in Marc H. Bornstein (ed.), *Cultural Approaches to Parenting.* Hillsdale, N.J.: Lawrence Erlbaum Associates.

Pareles, Jon. 1994. "You call that music?" *New York Times Book Review,* August 14, pp.10–11.

Parker, Robert Nash. 1989. "Poverty, subculture of violence, and types of homicide." *Social Forces,* 67, pp. 983–1005.

Parkes, Peter. 1987. "Livestock symbolism and pastoral ideology among the Kafirs of the Hindu Kush." *Man,* 22, pp. 637–660.

Parsons, Talcott, and Robert F. Bales. 1953. *Family, Socialization, and Interaction Process.* Glencoe, Ill. Free Press.

——. 1964/1951. *The Social System.* Glencoe, Ill.: Free Press.

Patterson, Orlando, quoted in Schlesinger, Arthur Jr. 1991. "A new era begins—but history remains." *Wall Street Journal,* December 11, p. A16.

Pearce, Diana M. 1993. "The feminization of poverty: Update. Pp. 290–296 in Alison M. Jaggar and Paula S. Rothenberg (eds.), *Feminist Frameworks,* 3rd ed. New York: McGraw-Hill.

Peek, Charles W., Evans W. Curry, and H. Paul Chalfant. 1985. "Religiosity and delinquency over time: Deviance deterrence and deviance amplification." *Social Science Quarterly,* 66, pp. 120–131.

Peirce, Kate. 1990. "A feminist theoretical perspective on the socialization of teenage girls through *Seventeen* magazine." *Sex Roles,* 23, pp. 491–500.

Peltonen, Anita. 1993. "Finland: A free school system with very few cracks." *New York Times,* December 9, p. A8.

Pennebaker, J. W. 1980. "Perceptual and environmental determinants of coughing." *Basic Applied Social Psychology,* 1, pp. 83–91.

Perlez, Jane. 1992. "For bedouins of Africa, sands are running out." *New York Times,* March 5, p. A4.

——. 1995. "East Europe looks to union with West." *New York Times,* January 3, p. C10.

Perrow, Charles. 1989. "The evolution of organization theory." Pp. 41–48 in Gareth Morgan, *Creative*

Organization Theory: A Resourcebook. Newbury Park, Calif.: Sage.

Pescosolido, Bernice A., and Sharon Georgianna. 1989. "Durkheim, suicide, and religion: Toward a network theory of suicide." *American Sociological Review,* 54, pp. 33–48.

Pillemer, Karl, and David Finkelhor. 1989. "Causes of elder abuse: Caregiver stress versus problem relatives." *American Journal of Orthopsychiatry,* 59, pp. 179–187.

Pines, Maya. 1981. "The civilizing of Genie." *Psychology Today,* September, pp. 28–34.

Pittman, Frank. 1993. "Beyond betrayal: Life after infidelity." *Psychology Today.* May/June, p. 36.

Pizzo, Stephen P., and Paul Muolo. 1993. "Take the money and run." *New York Times Magazine,* May 9, p. 26.

Pollak, Lauren Harte, and Peggy A. Thoits. 1989. "Processes in emotional socialization." *Social Psychology Quarterly,* 52, pp. 22–34.

Pope, Victoria. 1994. "To be young and pretty in Moscow." *U.S. News & World Report,* March 28, p. 56.

Porter, Bruce, and Marvin Dunn. 1984. *The Miami Riot of 1980.* Lexington, Mass.: Lexington Books.

Postman, Neil. 1985. *Amusing Ourselves to Death: Public Discourse in the Age of Show Business.* New York: Viking.

Potterat, John J., et al. 1990. "Estimating the prevalence and career longevity of prostitute women." *Journal of Sex Research,* 27, pp. 233–243.

Power, Thomas G., and Josephine A. Shanks. 1989. "Parents and socializers: Maternal and paternal views." *Journal of Youth and Adolescence,* 18, pp. 203–217.

Prerost, Frank J., and Robert E. Brewer. 1980. "The appreciation of humor by males and females during conditions of crowding experimentally induced." *Psychology,* 17, pp. 15–17.

Prestowitz, Clyde V. 1989. *Trading Places.* New York: Basic Books.

Purvis, Andrew. 1990. "A perilous gap." *Time,* Fall, pp. 66–67.

———. 1992. "A day in the death of Somalia." *Time,* September 21, pp. 32–40.

Quinney, Richard. 1974. *Critique of Legal Order.* Boston: Little, Brown.

Radford, John. 1990. *Child Prodigies and Exceptional Early Achievers.* New York: Free Press.

Ramirez, Francisco O., and John W. Meyer. 1980. "Comparative education: The social construction of the modern world system." *Annual Review of Sociology,* 6,

pp. 369–399.

Ranney, Austin. 1983. "Nonvoting is not a social disease." *Public Opinion,* October/November, pp. 16–19.

Raper, Arthur F. 1970. *The Tragedy of Lynching.* New York: Dover.

Rau, William, and Dennis W. Roncek. 1987. "Industrialization and world inequality: The transformation of the division of labor in 59 nations, 1960–1981." *American Sociological Review,* 52, pp. 359–369.

Regier, Darrel A., et al. 1993. "The de facto US mental and addictive disorders service system: Epidemiologic catchment area prospective 1-year prevalence rates of disorders and services." *Archives of General Psychiatry,* 50, pp. 85–94.

Reich, Robert B. 1994. "The fracturing of the middle class." *New York Times,* August 31, p. A13.

Reinharz, Shulamit. 1992. *Feminist Methods in Social Research.* New York: Oxford University Press.

Reiss, Ira L. 1986. *Journey into Sexuality: An Exploratory Voyage.* Englewood Cliffs, N.J.: Prentice-Hall.

Reitzes, Donald C. 1983. "Urban images: A social psychological approach." *Sociological Inquiry,* 53, pp. 314–332.

Rensberger, Boyce. 1984. "What made humans human." *New York Times Magazine,* April 8, pp. 80–92.

Reskin, Barbara F. 1988. "Bringing the men back in: Sex differentiation and the devaluation of women's work." *Gender & Society,* 2, pp. 58–81.

Restak, Richard M. 1979. *The Brain: The Last Frontier.* Garden City, N.Y.: Doubleday.

Rheem, Donald L. 1986. "Free market system said to be more efficient than state planning." *Christian Science Monitor,* September 22, p. 7.

Rice, Mabel L., et al. 1990. "Words from 'Sesame Street': Learning vocabulary while viewing." *Developmental Psychology,* 26, pp. 421–428.

Richardson, Laurel. 1988. *The Dynamics of Sex and Gender: A Sociological Perspective.* New York: Harper & Row.

Riding, Alan. 1993. "France: A method of teaching that produces readers." *New York Times,* December 9, p. A8.

Riesman, David. 1950. *The Lonely Crowd.* New Haven, Conn.: Yale University Press.

Riley, Matilda White. 1982. "Aging and health in modern communities." *Ekistics,* 296, pp. 381–383.

Rindos, David. 1986. "The evolution of the capacity for culture: Sociobiology, structuralism, and cultural selectionism." *Current Anthropology,* 27, pp. 315–332.

Robbins, William. 1990. "New decade finds new hope on the farm." *New York Times,* May 18, pp. A1, A10.

Roberts, Sam. 1993. *Who We Are: A Portrait of America Based on the Latest U.S. Census.* New York: Times Books.

Roberts, Steven. 1990. "An all-American snapshot: How we count and why." *U.S. News & World Report,* April 2, p. 10.

Robins, Lee N. et al. 1984. "Lifetime prevalence of specific psychiatric disorders in three sites." *Archives of General Psychiatry,* 41, pp. 949–958.

Rockwell, John. 1994. "The new colossus: American culture as power export." *New York Times,* January 30, Section 2, pp. 1, 30.

Rodgers, Bryan, and Susan L. Mann. 1993. "Re-thinking the analysis of intergenerational social mobility: A comment on John W. Fox's "Social class, mental illness, and social mobility." *Journal of Health and Social Behavior,* 34, pp. 165–172.

Rodriguez, Nestor P., and Joe R. Feagin. 1986. "Urban specialization in the world-system: An investigation of historical cases." *Urban Affairs Quarterly,* 22, pp. 187–220.

Roethlisberger, Fritz J., and William J. Dickson. 1939. *Management and the Worker.* Cambridge, Mass.: Harvard University Press.

Rohlen, Thomas P. 1983. *Japan's High Schools.* Berkeley: University of California Press.

Roof, Wade Clark. 1993. *A Generation of Seekers.* New York: HarperCollins.

Rosado, Lourdes. 1991. "Who's caring for grandma?" *Newsweek,* July 29, p. 47.

Rose, Arnold M. 1965. "The subculture of aging," in Arnold M. Rose and Warren A. Peterson (eds.), *Older People and Their Social World.* Philadelphia: F. A. Davis.

——. 1967. *The Power Structure.* New York: Oxford University Press.

Rosecrance, Richard. 1990. "Too many bosses, too few workers." *New York Times,* July 15, p. F11.

Rosenberg, Charles E. 1987. *The Care of Strangers.* New York: Basic Books.

Rosenberg, George S. 1970. *The Worker Grows Old.* San Francisco: Jossey-Bass.

Rosenberg, Morris. 1990. "Reflexivity and emotions." *Social Psychology Quarterly,* 53, pp. 3–12.

Rosenblatt, Roger. 1992. *Life Itself: Abortion in the American Mind.* New York: Random House.

——. 1994. "A killer in the eye." *New York Times Magazine,* June 5, pp. 38–47.

Rosener, Judy B. 1990. "The ways women lead." *Harvard Business Review,* 68, pp. 119–125.

Rosenthal, Robert. 1973. "The Pygmalion effect lives." *Psychology Today,* pp. 56–63.

Rosewicz, Barbara. 1990. "Friends of the earth." *Wall Street Journal,* April 20, pp. A1, A12.

Rosin, Hazel M. 1990. "The effects of dual career participation on men: Some determinants of variation in career and personal satisfaction." *Human Relations,* 43, pp. 169–182.

Ross, Dorothy. 1991. *The Origins of American Social Science.* New York: Cambridge University Press.

Ross, Loretta. 1994. "Why women of color can't talk about population." *The Amicus Journal,* Winter, pp. 27–29.

Ross, Michael W., and Willem A. Arrindell. 1988. "Perceived parental rearing patterns of homosexual and heterosexual men." *Journal of Sex Research,* 24, pp. 275–281.

Rossi, Alice S. 1984. "Gender and parenthood." *American Sociological Review,* 49, pp. 1–19.

Rossi, Peter H. 1989. *Down and Out in America: The Origins of Homelessness.* Chicago: University of Chicago Press.

Rostow, Walt W. 1960. *The Process of Economic Growth.* New York: Norton.

Rothschild, Joyce, and Celia Davies. 1994. "Organizations through the lens of gender: Introduction to the special issue." *Human Relations,* 47, pp. 583–590.

Rothschild, Joyce, and Raymond Russell. 1986. "Alternatives to bureaucracy: Democratic participation in the economy." *Annual Review of Sociology,* 12, pp. 307–328.

Rubenstein, Carin. 1982. "Real men don't earn less than their wives." *Psychology Today,* November, pp. 36–41.

Rubin, Lillian Breslow. 1976. *Worlds of Pain: Life in the Working-Class Family.* New York: Basic Books.

——. 1990. *Erotic Wars: What Happened to the Sexual Revolution?* New York: Farrar, Straus & Giroux.

Russell, George. 1984. "People, people, people." *Time,* August 6, pp. 24–25.

Rutter, Michael. 1983. "School effects on pupil progress: Research findings and policy implications." *Child Development,* 54, pp. 1–29.

Rymer, Russ. 1993. *Genie: An Abused Child's Flight From Silence.* New York: HarperCollins.

Sachs, Andrea. 1993. "9-Zip! I Love It!" *Time,* November 22, pp. 44–45.

Sadker, Myra, and David Sadker. 1994. *Failing at Fairness: How America's Schools Cheat Girls.* New York: Scribners.

Sahlins, Marshall. 1972. *Stone Age Economics.* Chicago: Aldine.

Salins, Peter D. 1991. "In Living Colors," *The New Republic,* January 21, pp. 14–15.

Sapir, Edward. 1929. "The status of linguistics as a science." *Language,* 5, pp. 207–214.

Sawyer, Roger. 1986. *Slavery in the Twentieth Century.* London: Routledge & Kegan Paul.

Sayle, Murray. 1982. "A textbook case of aggression." *Far Eastern Economic Review,* 117, August 20, pp. 36–38.

Schaefer, Richard T. 1988. *Racial and Ethnic Groups,* 3rd ed. Boston: Little, Brown.

Schor, Juliet B. 1991. *The Overworked American: The Unexpected Decline of Leisure.* New York: Basic Books.

Schrof, Joannie M. 1993. "Feminism's daughters." *U.S. News & World Report,* September 27, pp. 68–71.

——. 1994. "Brain power." *U.S. News & World Report,* November 28, pp. 89–97.

Schultz, Duane P. 1964. *Panic Behavior.* New York: Random House.

Schulz, David A. 1982. *The Changing Family,* 3rd ed. Englewood Cliffs, N.J.: Prentice-Hall.

Schur, Edwin M. 1984. *Labeling Women Deviant: Gender, Stigma, and Social Control.* New York: Random House.

Schweinhart, Lawrence J., and David P. Weikart. 1990. "A fresh start for Head Start?" *New York Times,* May 13, p. E19.

Schwochau, Susan. 1987. "Union effects on job attitudes." *Industrial and Labor Relations Review,* 40, pp. 209–224.

Scott, David Clark. 1986. "How 'quality circles' move from the assembly line to the office." *Christian Science Monitor,* August 4, p. 18.

Scully, Diana, and Joseph Marolla. 1984. "Convicted rapists' vocabulary of motive: Excuses and justifications." *Social Problems,* 31, pp. 530–544.

Sears, David O. et al. 1991. *Social Psychology,* 7th ed. Englewood Cliffs, N.J.: Prentice-Hall.

Sebald, Hans. 1986. "Adolescents' shifting orientation toward parents and peers: A curvilinear trend over recent decades." *Journal of Marriage and the Family,* 48, pp. 5–13.

See, Katherine O'Sullivan, and William J. Wilson. 1988. "Race and ethnicity." Pp. 223–242 in Neil J. Smelser (ed.), *Handbook of Sociology.* Newbury Park, CA: Sage.

Seligmann, Jean. 1992. "Variations on a theme." In Arlene S. Skolnick and Jerome H. Skolnick (eds.), *Family in Transition,* 7th ed. New York: HarperCollins.

——. 1993. "Husbands no, babies yes." *Newsweek,* July 26, p. 53.

——. 1994. "The death of a spouse." *Newsweek,* May 9, p. 57.

Sennett, Richard. 1991. *The Conscience of the Eye: The Design and Social Life of Cities.* New York: Alfred A. Knopf.

Seuffert, Virginia. 1990. "Home remedy." *Policy Review,* 52, pp. 70–75.

Shabecoff, Philip. 1990. "Team of scientists sees substantial warming of earth." *New York Times,* April 16, p. A11.

Shanas, Ethel, and George L. Maddox. 1976. "Aging, health, and the organization of health resources," in Robert H. Binstock and Ethel Shanas (eds.), *Handbook of Aging and the Social Sciences.* New York: Van Nostrand Reinhold.

Shapiro, Judith. 1994. "What women can teach men." *New York Times,* November 23, p. A15.

Shapiro, Laura. 1990. "Guns and dolls." *Newsweek,* May 28, pp. 56–65.

Sharpe, Rochelle. 1994. "The waiting game." *Wall Street Journal,* March 29, pp. A1, A8.

Sheets, Kenneth R. 1990. "Labor's agenda for the '90s." *U.S. News & World Report,* March 19, pp. 37–39.

Sheler, Jeffery L. 1994. "Spiritual America." *U.S. News & World Report,* April 4, pp. 48–59.

——. 1990. "Islam in America." *U.S. News & World Report,* October 8, pp. 69–71.

Shellenbarger, Sue. 1991. "Work and family." *Wall Street Journal,* December 11, p. B1.

Shenon, Philip. 1995 "Continued vitality for Southeast Asia." *New York Times,* January 3, p. C10.

Sherif, Muzafer. 1956. "Experiments in group conflict." *Scientific American,* 195, pp. 54–58.

Shibutani, Tamotsu. 1966. *Improvised News.* Indianapolis: Bobbs-Merrill.

Shipman, Pat. 1994. *The Evolution of Racism: Human Differences and the Use and Abuse of Science.* New York: Simon & Schuster.

Shon, Steven P., and Davis Y. Ja. 1992. "Asian Families." In Arlene S. Skolnick and Jerome H. Skolnick (eds.), *Family in Transition,* 7th ed. New York: HarperCollins.

Schor, Juliet B. 1991. *The Overworked American: The Unexpected Decline of Leisure.* New York: Basic Books.

Sidel, Ruth. 1990. *On Her Own: Growing Up in the Shadow of the American Dream.* New York: Viking.

Signorile, Michelangelo. 1995. "H.I.V. positive, and careless." *New York Times,* February 26, p. 15.

Silberner, Joanne. 1990. "Health: Another gender gap." *U.S. News & World Report,* September 24, pp. 54–55.

Simenauer, Jacqueline, and David Carroll. 1982. *Singles: The New Americans.* New York: Simon & Schuster.

Simon, Julian L. 1990. *Population Matters: People, Resources, Environment, and Immigration.* New Brunswick, N.J.: Transaction.

Simpson, Jeffry A., Bruce Campbell, and Ellen Berscheid. 1986. "The association between romantic love and marriage: Kephart (1967) twice revisited."

Personality and Social Psychology Bulletin, 12, pp. 363–372.

Singleton, Royce A. Jr., Bruce C. Straits, and Margaret Miller Straits. 1993. *Approaches to Social Research,* 2nd ed. New York: Oxford University Press.

Sizer, Theodore R. 1984. *Horace's Compromise: The Dilemma of the American High School.* Boston: Houghton Mifflin.

Skinner, B. F. 1983. "Creativity in old age." *Psychology Today,* September, pp. 28, 29.

Skinner, Denise. 1980. "Dual-career family stress and coping: A literature review." *Family Relations,* 29, pp. 473–480.

Small, Albion W. 1916. "Fifty years of sociology in the United States." *American Journal of Sociology,* 1, pp. 721–864.

Smelser, Neil J. 1971/1962. *Theory of Collective Behavior.* New York: Free Press.

Smith, Garry J. 1993. "The noble sports fan." Pp. 3–14 in D. Stanley Eitzen (ed.), *Sport in Contemporary Society: An Anthology,* 4th ed. New York: St. Martin's Press.

Snarey, John. 1987. "A question of morality." *Psychology Today,* June, pp. 6–8.

Snow, David A., and Leon Anderson. 1993. *Down on Their Luck: A Study of Homeless Street People.* Berkeley: University of California Press.

So, Alvin Y. 1990. *Social Change and Development: Modernization, Dependency, and World-System Theories.* Newbury Park, Calif.: Sage.

Solis, Dianna, et al. 1987. "Changing the rules." *Wall Street Journal,* June 5, pp. 1, 12.

Solomon, Jolie, 1989. "Firms grapple with language barriers." *Wall Street Journal,* November 7, pp. B1, B4.

Solorzano, Lucia. 1987. "Beating back the education 'blob'." *U.S. News & World Report,* April 27, p. 74.

Sorrentino, Constance. 1990. "The changing family in international perspective." *Monthly Labor Review,* March, pp. 41–55.

Sowell, Thomas. 1983. *The Economics and Politics of Race: An International Perspective.* New York: Morrow.

——. 1994. *Race and Culture: A World View.* New York: Basic Books.

Spanier, Graham B. 1983. "Married and unmarried cohabitation in the United States: 1980." *Journal of Marriage and the Family,* 45, pp. 277–288.

Spates, James L. 1983. "The sociology of values." *Annual Review of Sociology,* 9, pp. 27–49.

Spitz, René A. 1945. "Hospitalism." *Psychoanalytic Study of the Child,* 1, pp. 53–72.

Starr, Paul. 1983. *The Social Transformation of American Medicine.* New York: Basic Books.

Stearns, Marion S. 1971. *Report on Preschool Programs.* Washington, D.C.: U.S. Government Printing Office.

Steele, Shelby. 1990. *The Content of Our Character: A New Vision of Race in America.* New York: St. Martin's.

Steinberg, Laurence. 1987. "Why Japan's students outdo ours." *New York Times,* April 25, p. 15.

Steinmetz, Suzanne K., et al. 1990. *Marriage and Family Realities: Historical and Contemporary Perspectives.* New York: Harper & Row.

Stevens, Gillian, et al. 1990. "Education and attractiveness in marriage choices." *Social Psychology Quarterly,* 53, pp. 62–72.

Stevens, William K. 1992. "New studies predict profits in heading off warming." *New York Times,* March 17, pp. B5, B9.

Stoll, Clarice Stasz. 1978. *Female & Male.* Dubuque, Iowa: Brown.

Stolzenberg, Ross M. 1990. "Ethnicity, geography, and occupational achievement of Hispanic men in the United States." *American Sociological Review,* 55, pp. 143–154.

Straus, Murray A., et al. 1988. *Behind Closed Doors: Violence in the American Family.* Newbury Park, Calif.: Sage.

Strong, Bryan, and Christine DeVault. 1989. *The Marriage and Family Experience,* 4th ed. St. Paul, Minn.: West.

Strum, Charles. 1993. "School tracking: Efficiency or elitism?" *New York Times,* April 1, p. B5.

Suro, Roberto. 1991. "Where America is growing: The suburban cities." *New York Times,* February 23, pp. 1, 10.

Sutherland, Edwin H. 1939. *Principles of Criminology.* Philadelphia: Lippincott.

Suttles, Gerald. 1970. *The Social Order of the Slum.* Chicago: University of Chicago Press.

Syme, S. Leonard, and Lisa F. Berkman. 1987. "Social class, susceptibility, and sickness," in Howard D. Schwartz (ed.), *Dominant Issues in Medical Sociology,* 2nd ed. New York: Random House.

Szymanski, Albert. 1978. *The Capitalist State and the Politics of Class.* Cambridge, Mass.: Winthrop.

Takaki, Ronald. 1993. *A Different Mirror: A History of Multicultural America.* Boston: Little, Brown.

Tanfer, Koray. 1987. "Patterns of premarital cohabitation among never-married women in the United States." *Journal of Marriage and the Family,* 49, pp. 483–497.

Tannen, Deborah. 1986. *That's Not What I Meant!* New York: William Morrow.

——. 1990. *You Just Don't Understand: Women and Men in Conversation.* New York: Ballantine Books.

———. 1994a. *Gender and Discourse.* New York: Oxford University Press.

———. 1994b. *Talking from 9 to 5.* New York: William Morrow.

Tannenbaum, Frank. 1938. *Crime and the Community.* New York: Columbia University Press.

Taylor, Frederick W. 1911. *Scientific Management.* New York: Harper.

Taylor, Robert Joseph, et al. 1993. "Developments in research on black families: A decade review." In Harriette Pipes McAdoo (ed.), *Family Ethnicity: Strength in Diversity.* Newbury Park, CA: Sage.

Teachman, Jay D. 1987. "Family background, educational resources, and educational attainment." *American Sociological Review,* 52, pp. 548–557.

Tefft, Sheila. 1993. "Rural laborers seek fortunes in burgeoning Chinese cities." *Christian Science Monitor,* May 25, pp. 1, 4.

Terkel, Studs. 1992. *Race: How Blacks and Whites Think and Feel About the American Obsession.* New York: The New Press.

Tharp, Mike. 1987. "Academic debate." *Wall Street Journal,* March 10, p. 1.

Thio, Alex. 1995. *Deviant Behavior,* 4th ed. New York: HarperCollins.

Thomas, Laura. 1990. "Can a new suburb be like a small town?" *U.S. News & World Report,* March 5, p. 32.

Thorne, Barrie. 1993. *Gender Play: Girls and Boys in School.* New Brunswick, N.J.: Rutgers University Press.

Thornton, Arland. 1989. "Changing attitudes toward family issues in the United States." *Journal of Marriage and the Family,* 51, pp. 873–893.

Tilly, Louise A., and Joan W. Scott. 1978. *Women, Work, and the Family.* New York: Holt, Rinehart and Winston.

Tobin, Jonathan N., et al. 1987. "Sex bias in considering coronary bypass surgery." *Annals of Internal Medicine,* 107, pp. 19–25.

Toffler, Alvin. 1990. *Powershift.* New York: Bantam Books.

Toner, Robin. 1992. "Politics of welfare: Focusing on the problem." *New York Times,* July 5, pp. 1, 13.

Toufexis, Anastasia. 1990. "A call for radical surgery." *Time,* May 7, p. 50.

Travers, Jeffrey, and Stanley Milgram. 1969. "An experimental study of the small world problem." *Sociometry,* 32, pp. 425–443.

Treiman, Donald J. 1977. *Occupational Prestige in Comparative Perspective.* New York: Academic Press.

Triandis, Harry C. 1989. "Cross-cultural studies of individualism and collectivism," *Nebraska Symposium on Motivation,* Vol. 37, pp. 41–133.

Trotter, Robert J. 1987. "Mathematics: A male advantage?" *Psychology Today,* January, pp. 66–67.

Trussell, James, and K. Vaninadha Rao. 1989. "Premarital cohabitation and marital stability: A reassessment of the Canadian evidence." *Journal of Marriage and the Family,* 51, pp. 535–540.

Tseelon, Efrat. 1992. "Self presentation through appearance: A manipulative vs. a dramaturgical approach." *Symbolic Interaction,* 15, pp. 501–513.

Tumin, Melvin M. 1953. "Some principles of stratification: A critical analysis." *American Sociological Review,* 18, pp. 387–393.

Turner, Barry A. 1992. "The symbolic understanding of organizations." In Michael Reed and Michael Hughes (eds.), *Rethinking Organization: New Directions in Organization Theory and Analysis.* Newbury Park, Calif.: Sage.

Turner, Ralph H., and Lewis M. Killian. 1987. *Collective Behavior,* 4th ed. Englewood Cliffs, N.J.: Prentice-Hall.

Turner, Ronny E., and Charles Edgley. 1990. "Death as theater: A dramaturgical analysis of the American funeral." Pp. 285–298 in Dennis Brissett and Charles Edgley, eds., *Life as Theater: A Dramaturgical Sourcebook.* New York: Aldine de Gruyter.

Twaddle, Andrew, and Richard Hessler. 1987. *A Sociology of Health,* 2nd ed. New York: Macmillan.

Tyler, Patrick E. 1995. "Daunting challenges for China's leaders." *New York Times,* January 3, p. C10.

Tyree, Andrea et al. 1979. "Gaps and glissandos: Inequality, economic development, and social mobility in 24 countries." *American Sociological Review,* 44, pp. 410–424.

Tyree, Andrea, and Moshe Semyonov. 1983. "Social mobility and immigrants or immigrants and social mobility." *American Sociological Review,* 48, pp. 583–584.

United Nations. 1991. *Contemporary Forms of Slavery.* Geneva: United Nations' Centre for Human Rights.

———. 1994. *Human Development Report 1994.* New York: Oxford University Press.

Useem, Michael. 1979. "Which business leaders help govern?" *Insurgent Sociologist,* 9, Fall, pp. 107–120.

U.S. Commission on Civil Rights. 1992. *Civil Rights Issues Facing Asian Americans in the 1990s.*

Van Leeuwen, Mary Stewart. 1990. "Life after Eden." *Christianity Today,* July 16, pp. 19–21.

Varghese, Raju. 1981. "An empirical analysis of the Eriksonian bipolar theory of personality." *Psychological Reports,* 49, pp. 819–822.

Vealey, Robin S., and Susan M. Walter. 1993. "Imagery training for performance enhancement and personal development." Pp. 200–224 in Jean M. Williams (ed.), *Applied Sport Psychology: Personal Growth to Peak Performance*. Mountain View, Calif.: Mayfield.

Vega, William A. 1992. "Hispanic families in the 1980s: A decade of research." In Arlene S. Skolnick and Jerome H. Skolnick (eds.), *Family in Transition*, 7th ed. New York: HarperCollins.

Verbrugge, Lois M. 1985. "Gender and health: An update on hypotheses and evidence." *Journal of Health and Social Behavior*, 26, pp. 156–182.

Verhovek, Sam Howe. 1990. "Whose law applies when lawlessness rules on Indian land?" *New York Times*, May 6, p. E6.

Vora, Erika. 1981. "Evolution of race: A synthesis of social and biological concepts." *Journal of Black Studies*, 12, pp. 182–192.

Voydanoff, Patricia, and Brenda W. Donnelly. 1989. "Work and family roles and psychological distress." *Journal of Marriage and the Family*, 51, pp. 923–932.

Waitzkin, Howard. 1987. "A Marxian interpretation of the growth and development of coronary care technology," in Howard D. Schwartz (ed.), *Dominant Issues in Medical Sociology*, 2nd ed. New York: Random House.

Wald, Matthew L. 1990. "Guarding environment: A world of challenges." *New York Times*, April 22, pp. 1, 16–17.

Wallerstein, Immanuel. 1987. "World-system analysis." Pp. 309–324 in Anthony Giddens and Jonathan H. Turner (eds.), *Social Theory Today*. Stanford, CA: Stanford University Press.

Wallis, Claudia. 1994. "A class of their own." *Time*, October 31, pp. 53–61.

Walters, Pamela Barnhouse, and Richard Rubinson. 1983. "Educational expansion and economic output in the United States, 1890–1969: A production function analysis." *American Sociological Review*, 48, pp. 480–493.

Walzer, Michael. 1978. "Must democracy be capitalist?" *New York Review of Books*, July 20, p. 41.

Wartzman, Rick. 1992. "Sharing gains." *Wall Street Journal*, May 4, pp. A1, A4.

Watson, James D. 1968. *The Double Helix*. New York: New American Library.

Watson, Roy E. L., and Peter W. DeMeo. 1987. "Premarital cohabitation vs. traditional courtship and subsequent marital adjustment: A replication and follow-up." *Family Relations*, 36, pp. 193–197.

Watson, Russell. 1992. "Ethnic cleansing." *Newsweek*, August 17, pp. 16–20.

———. 1995. "When words are the best weapon." *Newsweek*, February 27, pp. 36–40.

Waxman, Chaim I. 1990. "Is the cup half-full or half-empty?: Perspectives on the future of the American Jewish community," in Seymour Martin Lipset (ed.), *American Pluralism and the Jewish Community*. New Brunswick, N.J.: Transaction, pp. 71–85.

Weaver, Charles N., and Michael D. Matthews. 1990. "Work satisfaction of females with full-time employment and full-time housekeeping: 15 years later." *Psychological Reports*, 66, pp. 1248–1250.

Weber, Max. 1946. *From Max Weber: Essays in Sociology*, translated and edited by H. H. Gerth and C. Wright Mills. New York: Oxford University Press.

———. 1954. *Max Weber on Law and Sociology*. Cambridge, Mass.: Harvard University Press.

———. 1968. *Economy and Society: An Outline of Interpretive Sociology, Volume 1*. Edited by Guenther Roth and Claus Wittich. New York: Bedminster Press.

Weis, Lois (ed.). 1988. *Class, Race, and Gender in American Education*. Albany, N.Y.: State University of New York Press.

Weisheit, Ralph. 1992. "Patterns of female crime," in Robert G. Culbertson and Ralph Weisheit (eds.), *Order Under Law*, 4th ed. Prospect Heights, IL: Waveland.

White, Jack E. 1993. "Growing up in black and white." *Time*, May 17, pp. 48–49.

White, Lynn K., and John N. Edwards. 1990. "Emptying the nest and parental well-being: An analysis of national panel data." *American Sociological Review*, 55, pp. 235–242.

White, Sheldon H. 1977. "The paradox of American education." *National Elementary Principal*, 56, May/June, pp. 9, 10.

Whiteford, Michael B., and John Friedl. 1992. *The Human Portrait*, 3rd ed. Englewood Cliffs, N.J.: Prentice-Hall.

Whorf, Benjamin. 1956. *Language, Thought, and Reality*. New York: Wiley.

Whyte, Martin King. 1992. "Choosing mates—The American way." *Society*, March/April, pp. 71–77.

Wiley, Norbert. 1979. "Notes on self genesis: From me to we to I." *Studies in Symbolic Interaction*, 2, pp. 87–105.

Wilkinson, Doris. 1993. "Family ethnicity in America." In Harriette Pipes McAdoo (ed.), *Family Ethnicity: Strength in Diversity*. Newbury Park, Calif.: Sage.

Williams, Robin M., Jr. 1970. *American Society: A Sociological Interpretation*, 3rd ed. New York: Knopf.

———. 1994. "The sociology of ethnic conflicts: Comparative international perspectives." *Annual Review of Sociology*, 20, pp. 49–79.

Willner, Dorothy. 1983. "Definition and violation: Incest and the incest taboos." *Man*, 18, pp. 134–159.

Wilson, Edward O. 1980. *Sociobiology: The Abridged Edition*. Cambridge, Mass.: Harvard University Press.

Wilson, Warner. 1989. "Brief resolution of the issue of similarity versus complementarity in mate selection using height preferences as a model." *Psychological Reports,* 65, pp. 387–393.

Wilson, William Julius. 1990. "Race-neutral programs and the Democratic coalition." *The American Prospect,* 1, pp. 75–81.

Wimberley, Dale W. 1984. "Socioeconomic deprivation and religious salience: A cognitive behavioral approach." *Sociological Quarterly,* 25, pp. 223–238.

Winch, Robert F. 1971. *The Modern Family.* New York: Holt, Rinehart and Winston.

Wines, Michael. 1993. "Senators approve a bill that eases vote registration." *New York Times,* March 18, pp. A1, 16.

Winslow, Ron. 1989. "Sometimes, talk is the best medicine." *Wall Street Journal,* October 5, p. B1.

Wolf, Naomi. 1993. *Fire with Fire.* New York: Random House.

Wolferen, Karel van. 1990. *The Enigma of Japanese Power.* New York: Vintage Books.

Wood, Julia T. 1994. *Gendered Lives: Communication, Gender, and Culture.* Belmont, Calif.: Wadsworth.

Woodburn, James. 1982. "Egalitarian societies." *Man,* 17, pp. 431–451.

Woodward, Kenneth L. 1987. "Saving souls—or a ministry?" *Newsweek,* July 13, pp. 52–53.

World Bank. 1990. *World Development Report 1990.* New York: Oxford University Press.

——. 1994. *World Development Report 1994.* New York: Oxford University Press.

World Factbook. 1990. Washington, D.C.: U.S. Government Printing Office.

Wright, Stuart A., and Elizabeth S. Piper. 1986. "Families and cults: Familial factors related to youth leaving or remaining in deviant religious groups." *Journal of Marriage and the Family,* 48, pp. 15–25.

Wrong, Dennis H. 1961. "The oversocialized conception of man in modern sociology." *American Sociological Review,* 26, pp. 183–193.

——. 1990. *Population and Society,* 4th ed. New York: Random House.

Wuthnow, Robert. 1994. "Religion and Economic Life." In Neil J. Smelser and Richard Swedberg (eds.), *The Handbook of Economic Sociology.* Princeton, N.J.: Princeton University Press.

Yankelovich, Daniel, and John Immerwahr. 1984. "Putting the work ethic to work. *Society,* 21, January/February, pp. 58–76.

Yoshihashi, Pauline. 1990. "Immigration law's employer sanctions prove to have little impact, study finds." *Wall Street Journal,* April 20, p. A16.

Young, Anne McDougall. 1983. "Recent trends in higher education and labor force activity." *Monthly Labor Review,* 106, February, pp. 39–41.

Young, T.R. 1991. *The Drama of Social Life: Essays in Post-Modern Social Psychology.* Rutgers, N.J.: Transaction Books.

Zagorin, Adam. 1994. "The sins of a sainted bank." *Time,* August 22, pp. 54–55.

Zangwill, Israel. 1909. *The Melting Pot.* New York: Macmillan.

Zenner, Walter P. 1985. "Jewishness in America: Ascription and choice." *Ethnic and Racial Studies,* 8, pp. 117–133.

Zimmerman, Carle C. 1949. *The Family of Tomorrow.* New York: Harper & Brothers.

Zoglin, Richard. 1990. "Is TV ruining our children?" *Time,* October 15, pp. 75–76.

Zur, Offer. 1987. "The psychohistory of warfare: The co-evolution of culture, psyche and enemy." *Journal of Peace Research,* 24, pp. 125–134.

Credits

Unless otherwise acknowledged, all photographs are the property of Scott, Foresman and Company. Page abbreviations are as follow: (T) top, (C) center, (B) bottom, (R) right.

CHAPTER 1

Page 0, Jim Pickerell/The Image Works; p. 4L, M. Kelley/AlaskaStock Images; p. 4R, Sarah Leen; p. 6, Jacob A. Riis Collection/The Museum of the City of New York; p. 7L, Bettmann Archive; p. 7R, Topham/The Image Works; p. 9L, Brown Brothers; p. 9R, Bettmann Archive; p. 10L, Culver Pictures; p. 10R, The University Library/University of Illinois at Chicago/Jane Addams Memorial Collection at Hull House; p. 16L, Focus On Sports; p. 16R, Mark D. Phillips/Photo Researchers; p. 20, Courtesy, Professor Alex Thio; p. 22, First Communications.

CHAPTER 2

Page 30, Matthew Borkoski/Stock Boston; p. 32, Harley Schwadron; p. 33, Bob Kalman/The Image Works; p. 34, R. Stott/The Image Works; p. 37, Copyright 1965 by Stanley Milgram, from the film *Obedience*, distributed by the Pennsylvania State University PCR; p. 45, Deneve Feigh Bunde/Unicorn Stock Photos.

CHAPTER 3

Page 50, Sabine Weiss/Photo Researchers; p. 54, R. Sidney/The Image Works; p. 55, Stone/Sygma; p. 58, PhotoFest; p. 65TL, Lisa Law/The Image Works; p. 65TR, David R. Frazier Photolibrary; p. 65CL, E.E.Kingsley/ Photo Researchers; p. 65CR, Abbey Sea/Unicorn Stock Photos; p. 65B, Sidney Harris; p. 67, Napoleon Chagnon; p. 68, AP/Wide World.

CHAPTER 4

Page 72, David R. Frazier Photolibrary; p. 75, Chris Takagi/Impact Visuals; p. 77, Tony Freeman/PhotoEdit; p. 78, McCurry/Magnum Photos; p. 80, Devore/Anthro-Photo; p. 81, Sidney Harris; p. 82, Holland/Stock Boston; p. 85, N. Warren/Sygma; p. 89, Torin Boyd; p. 92, Pedrick/The Image Works.

CHAPTER 5

Page 96, Dilip Mehta/Contact Press Images; p. 100T, Denny/PhotoEdit; p. 100B, Peter Menzel/Stock Boston; p. 102, Brent Jones; p. 106, J. M. Leroy/Sygma; p. 109, Rick Browne/ Stock Boston; p. 115T, Joseph Nettis/Stock Boston; p. 115B, "Landscape with figures " (detail) by George Tooker, The Marisa Del Re Gallery, New York; p. 116, Milt & Joan Mann/Cameramann International, Ltd.

CHAPTER 6

Page 120, SuperStock, Inc.; p. 123, Bob Daemmrich/ Stock Boston; p. 124, AP/Wide World; p. 125, M. Peterson/JB Pictures Ltd.; p. 128, Azzi/Woodfin Camp & Associates; p. 131, Rick Friedman/Black Star; p. 133, Milt & Joan Mann/Cameramann International, Ltd.; p. 135, Les Stone/Sygma; p. 138, George Hall/ Woodfin Camp & Associates.

CHAPTER 7

Page 142, David C. Phillips; p. 145, Sam Abell; p. 147, AP/Wide World; p. 151, Michael Freeman/PhotoEdit; p. 154, Brent Jones; p. 155, Eiler/Stock Boston; p. 157, Mary Kate Denny/PhotoEdit; p. 163, Oddie/PhotoEdit.

CHAPTER 8

Page 168, Christopher Brown/Stock Boston; p. 172, AP/Wide World; p. 173, Abbas/Magnum Photos; p. 175, Tom & Pat Leeson/Photo Researchers; p. 177L, UPI/ Bettmann; p. 177R, Charles Moore/Black Star; p. 180, Paul Kuroda/*Orange County Register*; p. 184, Martin R. Jones/Unicorn Stock Photos; p. 186, Bob Daemmrich/The Image Works; p. 187, Cartoon Features Syndicate; p. 189, J. P. Loffont/Sygma.

CHAPTER 9

Page 194, Frank Siteman/Stock Boston; p. 197L, Alain Evrard/Gamma-Liaison; p. 197R, Jim Whitmer; p. 199, Will & Deni McIntyre/Photo Researchers; p. 202, Aneal Vohra/Unicorn Stock Photos; p. 207, Robert Brenner/ PhotoEdit; p. 210L, Lerager/Sygma; p. 210R, Rick Browne.

CHAPTER 10

Page 216, Elizabeth Furth/Tony Stone Images; p. 219, Lewis Hine Photo/Library of Congress; p. 221, Neubauer/PhotoEdit; p. 222, G. Bellerose/Stock Boston; p. 223, David Alan Harvey/Woodfin Camp & Associates; p. 225L, Jeff Dunn/The Picture Cube; p. 225R, Timothy R. Murphy/*U.S. News & World Report*; p. 228L, S. Katz/Black Star; p. 228R, Andrew Holbrooke/Black Star; p. 230, Eugen Richards/Magnum Photos; p. 235, Paul Conklin/PhotoEdit; p. 236, Newman/PhotoEdit.

CHAPTER 11

Page 242, Sue Cunningham/Tony Stone Images; p. 246, Dilip Mehta/Contact Press Images; p. 249L, Leonardi/ Gamma-Liaison; p. 249R, Fred Chase/Impact Photos; p. 250, Jean Higgins/Unicorn Stock Photos; p. 252, Mark Peters/SIPA-Press; p. 253, Greg Girard/ Contact Press Images; p. 255, Paul S. Howell/Gamma-Liaison; p. 257, Wolfgang Kaehler; p. 258, Arvind Garg/ Gamma-Liaison; p. 260, Jean Higgins/Unicorn Stock Photos.

CHAPTER 12

Page 262, Brent Jones; p. 265, Jim Whitmer; p. 268, © 1995 S. Kelly-*San Diego Union Tribune*; p. 269, John Running/Black Star; p. 270, Ilene Perlman/Impact Photos; p. 272, N. Russell/Gamma-Liaison; p. 273, Hires/Gamma-Liaison; p. 274, California Institute of Technology; p. 279, J. Bergman/Gamma-Liaison; p. 281, Paul Dagys; p. 282, AP/Wide World; p. 283, Archive Pictures Inc.

CHAPTER 13

Page 288, Gamma-Liaison; p. 291, M. Ruiz; p. 292, Eastfoto/SOVFOTO; p. 294, Bob Daemmrich/Stock Boston; p. 298, Stephanie Maze/Woodfin Camp & Associates; p. 301, David Burnett/Contact Press Images; p. 304, P. Davies/SIPA-Press; p. 305, Jack Kurtz/Impact Photos.

CHAPTER 14

Page 312, Ed Malles/Gamma-Liaison; p. 315, Berliner/ Gamma-Liaison; p. 316, Nancy Coplon; p. 320, Ira Wyman/Sygma; p. 322, Carolina Kroon/Impact Photos; p. 325, Richard Hutchings/PhotoEdit; p. 329, Paul Conklin/PhotoEdit; p. 332, Rob Nelson/Black Star.

CHAPTER 15

Page 334, Karen Kasmauski/Woodfin Camp & Associates; p. 336, Brent Jones; p. 340, Lila Abulughod/ Anthro-Photo; p. 342, Dan Bosler/Tony Stone Images; p. 345, Tom McCarthy/Unicorn Stock Photos; p. 348, Milt & Joan Mann/Cameramann International, Ltd.; p. 349, Culver Pictures; p. 351, M. Ferguson/PhotoEdit; p. 353, M. Ferguson-Cate/PhotoEdit; p. 356, Richard Hutchings/Photo Researchers.

CHAPTER 16

Page 360, David Burnett/Contact Press Images; p. 365, Bob Daemmrich; p. 368, Milt & Joan Mann/ Cameramann International, Ltd.; p. 370, Lawrence Migdale/ Tony Stone Images; p. 372, Larry Barns/Black Star; p. 373, Joseph Nettis/Photo Researchers; p. 377, Jacques Chenet/Woodfin Camp & Associates; p. 378, Jim West/ Impact Photos; p. 380, Will & Deni McIntyre/ Photo Researchers.

CHAPTER 17

Page 384, Alon Reininger/Contact Press Images; p. 388, J. Rodriguez/Black Star; p. 389, David R. Frazier Photo-library; p. 391T, Gabe Kirchheimer/Impact Photos; p. 394L, Sygma; p. 394R, Fritz/Monkmeyer Press Photo Service; p. 402L, Nine Network, Australia/Gamma-Liaison; p. 402R, AP/Wide World; p. 403, Bryson/ Sygma; p. 404, Karen Kuehn/Matrix.

CHAPTER 18

Page 408, Dennis Brack/Black Star; p. 412L, Brain Brake/Photo Researchers; p. 412C, Margaret Bourke-White/Life Magazine/Time Warner Inc.; p. 412R, Henry Grossman; p. 413, G. Schuster/Contact Press Images; p. 417, Jeffrey Markowitz/Sygma; p. 421, Bob Daemmrich; p. 424, R. White/Sygma; p. 426, Nogues/Sygma; p. 429, Jones/Sygma.

CHAPTER 19

Page 432, Don & Pat Valenti/Tony Stone Images; p. 435, Mabel Brady Garven/Collection Copyright Yale University Art Gallery; p. 436, Jonathan Kirn/Gamma-Liaison; p. 440, Torin Boud; p. 442, Jeff Greenberg/ Unicorn Stock Photos; p. 447, Chrysler Corporation; p. 449, AP/Wide World; p. 453L, Olive/Peter Arnold, Inc.; p. 453R, Nichols/Viesti Associates.

CHAPTER 20

Page 456, Chronis Jons/Tony Stone Images; p. 459, Cliché des Musées Nationaux, Paris/Service Photo-graphique de la Reunion des Musées Nationaux; p. 460, Seth Resnick/Gamma-Liaison; p. 461L, AP/Wide World; p. 461R, Philippe Plailly/Science Photo Library/ Photo Researchers; p. 462, Matthew McVay/Tony Stone Images; p. 465, John Troha/Black Star; p. 466, St. Bar-tholomew's Children's Hospital/Science Photo Library/ Photo Researchers; p. 468, R. Maiman/Sygma; p. 471, McCarthy/PhotoEdit; p. 472, Marilyn Humphries/ Impact Photos; p. 473, Chris Brown/Stock Boston; p. 478, Shambroom/Photo Researchers.

CHAPTER 21

Page 482, David Carriere/Tony Stone Images; p. 485, McNeely/SIPA-Press; p. 490, AP/Wide World; p. 492, Unesco; p. 496, H. Bradner/The Image Works; p. 498, Jos'e Azel/Aurora.

CHAPTER 22

Page 504, Kindra Clineff/The Picture Cube; p. 507L, Haun/Stock Boston; p. 507R, National Institute of Anthropology; p. 510, Steven Hansen/Stock Boston; p. 511, Robert Fried/Stock Boston; p. 514, Robert Frerck/ Odyssey Productions, Chicago; p. 517, Calvin Larsen/ Photo Researchers; p. 518, Brad Bower; p. 519, Catherine Karnow/Woodfin Camp & Associates.

CHAPTER 23

Page 526, H. Finkle/Impact Photos; p. 530, James M. Cachero/Sygma; p. 533, UPI/Bettmann; p. 534, Capital Features/The Image Works; p. 537, Michael Hirsch/ Gamma-Liaison; p. 538, Dana Fineman; p. 541, Laski/ SIPA-Press; p. 542, Dilip Mehta/Contact Press Images.

Name Index

Subject Index